FOURTH EDITION

LAW

for

RECREATION AND SPORT MANAGERS

DOYICE J. COTTEN

JOHN T. WOLOHAN

KENDALL/HUNT PUBLISHING COMPANY

4050 Westmark Drive   Dubuque, Iowa 52002

Book Team
Chairman and Chief Executive Officer   Mark C. Falb
Senior Vice President, College Division   Thomas W. Gantz
Director of National Book Program   Paul B. Carty
Editorial Development Manager   Georgia Botsford
Developmental Editor   Lynne Rogers
Vice President, Production and Manufacturing   Alfred C. Grisanti
Assistant Vice President, Production Services   Christine E. O'Brien
Project Coordinator   Angela Puls
Permissions Editor   Renae Horstman
Cover Designer   Suzanne Millius

Cover image © Comstock.

ISBN13: 0-978-0-7575-3045-6
ISBN10: 0-7575-3045-1

Library of Congress Control Number: 2006926992

Printed in the United States of America
10 9 8 7 6 5 4 3 2 1

Contents

8.00 SPORT AND LEGISLATION 529

Dedication

In recognition of her pioneering leadership and accomplishments in the field of law as it pertains to recreation and sport management, we dedicate the 4th edition of *Law for Recreation and Sport Managers* to

Dr. Betty van der Smissen

Dr. van der Smissen has been a leading authority in the fields of law, recreation, and research for over 50 years. She has published countless articles and a number of books, including her 3-volume reference set, *Legal Liability and Risk Management for Public and Private Entities*. She is the author of two chapters in this book and has contributed greatly to its success through her guidance and suggestions regarding the book as a whole.

Dr. van der Smissen played a major role in the founding of the Society for the Study of the Legal Aspects of Sport and Physical Activity (SSLASPA), which has been renamed the Sport and Recreation Law Association (SRLA). In this organization and through personal contact, she has mentored, advised, and encouraged any professional in the field who has sought her help. She has also influenced countless students by her mentoring and teaching while on the faculty at several major universities.

As perhaps the most respected person in the field, Dr. van der Smissen has received numerous awards and honors during her career. By demanding the highest professional standards of herself and her work, she has led other professionals, by her example, to reach for the high bar she has set.

Thanks, Betty, for all your help and for keeping all of us on our toes.

Acknowledgments

I want to take this opportunity to recognize the organization, **Sport and Recreation Law Association (SRLA)**—formerly the Society for the Study of the Legal Aspects of Sport and Physical Activity (SSLASPA). Although the organization in no way sponsors this book, SRLA has always provided inspiration and support and all contributors to the book are members of SRLA. In fact, John and I, as well as ten other contributors, have served as president of the organization. Current and past presidents include, alphabetically:

Cathryn L. Claussen	Rebecca J. Mowrey
Colleen Colles	Andrew T. Pittman
Doyice J. Cotten	Linda L. Schoonmacker
Mary A. Hums	Todd L. Seidler
Lori K. Miller	Linda A. Sharp
Merry Moiseichik	John T. Wolohan

If interested, the reader can learn more about SRLA and possible membership by visiting the Website at http://srlaweb.org/.

Thanks go to our many contributors for making this edition helpful, accurate, and timely—and the best yet! Special thanks to John and my wife, Mary. Thanks also go to Lynne Rogers, Angela Puls, and all the other Kendall/Hunt staff who have contributed to the success of this edition.

Doyice J. Cotten

I would like to express my appreciation to all of the contributing authors for their hard work and dedication to this project, without them this book would not be possible. In addition, I would also like to acknowledge all the administrative support and help I received from Ithaca College. In particular, I would like to give special thanks to Wayne Blann, Jim Gray, Ellen Staurowsky and my administrative assistant Cindy Turo, all of whom are not only great colleagues, but also good friends. I would like to also acknowledge all the students in my sports law classes, who are constantly challenging and amazing me.

I also need to give a special acknowledgement to two people that have worked almost nonstop since the third edition hit the press to get this fourth edition out. They are Doyice Cotten and Lynne Rogers. Doyice, when he is not off visiting some exotic place, is always looking for ways to improve the text and is constantly sending authors current information. Lynne, on the other hand, has the unenviable job of coordinating and keeping both Doyice and me organized and on task, which she does remarkably well.

Finally, special thanks and all my love go to my family, Nicole, J.T and Katie.

John

DOYICE J. COTTEN

Doyice J. Cotten is an emeritus professor of sport management at Georgia Southern University where he taught graduate and undergraduate courses in sport law and risk management. He manages his own writing and risk management consulting business, Sport Risk Consulting.

Dr. Cotten is active in the Sport and Recreation Law Association which he served as president. During his professional career, he has been active in many professional organizations in the areas of sport management and physical education. He served as president of the Georgia Association for Health, Physical Education, and Recreation as well as the editor of the GAHPERD Journal.

Dr. Cotten speaks on legal issues at such conferences as the North American Society for Sport Management (NASSM), the American Alliance for Health, Physical Education, Recreation and Dance (AAHPERD), the Athletic Business Conference; the Sports Business Workshop, the International Conference on Sport Business, the International Health, Racquet & Sportsclub Association (IHRSA), the National Intramural-Recreational Sports Association (NIRSA), the Resort and Commercial Recreation Association (RCRA), the American College of Sports Medicine (ACSM), and the National Equine Law Conference.

Dr. Cotten has published more than 150 articles on legal liability and risk management in such publications as *Journal of Legal Aspects of Sport, Journal of Sport Management, Sports Parks & Recreation Law Reporter, Exercise Standards and Malpractice Law Reporter, Athletic Business,* and *Fitness Management.* He currently writes a bi-monthly column on risk management for *Fitness Management.* His major area of interest is in waivers and releases of liability. He has collected and analyzed about 900 sport- and recreation-related waiver cases and has coauthored two books on the subject. They are *Waivers & Releases of Liability* (5th ed.) and *Legal Aspects of Waivers for Sport, Recreation and Fitness Activities.*

JOHN T. WOLOHAN

John Wolohan is an Associate Professor and Chair of the Sport Management & Media Department at Ithaca College in Ithaca, New York, where he teaches courses in Sports Law and Labor Relations in Sports. Before coming to Ithaca College, Professor Wolohan taught at both Iowa State University, where he was the coordinator of the undergraduate and graduate sports management programs, and Rice University.

Professor Wolohan has published numerous articles in the areas of image rights, intellectual property, athlete's rights, and antitrust issues in sport. Professor Wolohan has published in such leading journals as the *Marquette Sports Law Journal, Seton Hall Journal of Sports Law, Villanova Sports & Entertainment Law Journal, University of Missouri—Kansas City Law Review, Educational Law Reporter, Journal of the Legal Aspects of Sport and the Journal of Sport Management.* In addition, Professor Wolohan also writes the "Sports Law Report" a monthly article that appears in *Athletic Business.*

Professor Wolohan has also made numerous presentations in the area of sports law to such organizations as the American Bar Association, Athletic Business, the International Association of Sports Law, the Sport and Recreation Law Association, the North American Society of Sport Management and the National Organization on Legal Problems of Education (NOLPE).

Professor Wolohan, who is a member of the American and Massachusetts Bar Associations, received his B.A. from the University of Massachusetts—Amherst, and his J.D. from Western New England College.

Contributing Authors

Stacey Altman

Stacey R. Altman is an Assistant Professor in the Department of Exercise and Sport Science at East Carolina University. She currently serves as Program Director for the graduate Sport Management Program and teaches courses in Legal Issues in Sport and in Sport Marketing. She received a B.S. in Political Science from Coastal Carolina University, a M.Ed. in Sport Management from the University of Georgia, and a J.D. from the University of Alabama. Her research interests include the study of antitrust law as it impacts professional sport league creation and operation and constitutional issues as they relate to participation in athletics.

Robin Ammon, Jr.

Robin Ammon, Jr. is a Professor and Chair of the Department of Sport Management at Slippery Rock University, Slippery Rock, PA. He received his B.S. degree from the University of Colorado in Physical Education, his M.S. degree from Louisiana State University in Exercise Science and his doctorate from the University of Northern Colorado in Sport Administration. Dr. Ammon currently teaches classes in Sport Law and in Facility and Event Management at both the undergraduate and graduate levels. He is a co-author of two Sport Facility and Event Management textbooks, plus he has authored chapters in many other edited texts. In addition, Dr. Ammon has over 30 years of practical experience working with crowd and event management as a consultant and manager.

Paul M. Anderson

Paul M. Anderson is the Associate Director of the National Sports Law Institute of Marquette University Law School, where he is also an Adjunct Associate Professor of Law. Professor Anderson teaches courses in amateur sports law, current issues in sports law, selected topics in sports law and advanced legal research-sports law. He is the author of two books, several book chapters and numerous articles. He is the Editor of the Journal of Legal Aspects of Sport and the Faculty Advisor and Supervisor of the Marquette Sports Law Review. He coordinates all events and the student internship program for the Sports Law Program at Marquette University Law School, the nation's most extensive sports law program. He is a practicing attorney most recently associated with The Leib Group, LLC, advisors to the sports and entertainment industry, and is the Chair of the Sports & Entertainment Law Section of the State Bar of Wisconsin. Professor Anderson received his B.A. Phi Beta Kappa from Marquette University and his J.D. from Marquette University Law School.

Thomas A. Baker III

Thomas A. Baker III has a J.D. from Loyola University New Orleans School of Law and a B.A. in Journalism from the University of Southern Mississippi. He is a member of the Louisiana Bar Association and his areas of practice include sport law and commercial litigation. He is currently an instructor at the University of Florida where he teaches Legal Issues in Sport.

Paul J. Batista

Paul J. Batista, Assistant Professor, Texas A & M University; B.S., Trinity University, 1973; J.D., Baylor Law School, 1976. Professor Batista is admitted to practice before the United States Supreme Court, is licensed to appear in all of the courts in Texas, and is a certified Mediator and Arbitrator. He has taught sport law at Texas A&M since 1991, has received the Texas A&M Association of Former Students Distinguished Achievement Award in Teaching, and has been named a Montague Center for Teaching Excellence Scholar. Professor Batista was a NCAA scholarship athlete (baseball) and was a certified Contract Advisor with the National Football League Players Association (NFLPA) from 1986 to 1998. His primary area of research is sport related liability issues in school settings, and he has published articles concerning technology and Internet issues in sport law. He serves on the Editorial Board of the *Journal of Legal Aspects of Sport.*

Matthew T. Brown

Matt Brown is an Associate Professor in the Division of Sport and Entertainment Management at the University of South Carolina. Prior to coming to Columbia, he was an Associate Professor in Sports Administration at Ohio University. He received his B.A. in political science from Truman State University, his M.S. in sport management from Western Illinois University, and his Ed.D. from the University of Northern Colorado in sport administration. At South Carolina, he teaches sport finance and business.

Linda Carpenter

Linda Jean Carpenter, Ph.D., J.D. Professor Emerita of Physical Education and Exercise Science at Brooklyn College of the City University of New York is also a member of the New York State and United States Supreme Court Bars. She has published numerous books and articles as well as speaking at many national and international professional meetings. Her research, including the national longitudinal study on the status of women in sport, coauthored with Vivian Acosta and now it its 29th year, is frequently cited in scholarly writing as well as the lay press and has been used frequently in Senate and Congressional hearings on Title IX and equity in sport. She holds the B.S. and M.S. from Brigham Young University, the Ph.D. from the University of Southern California and the J.D. from Fordham Law School.

Rodney L. Caughron

Rod Caughron, Ph.D., is an Associate Professor in the KNPE/Sport Management department at Northern Illinois University. He received both his B.A. in Political Science and M.S. in Exercise Physiology from Iowa State University and his Ph.D. from The University of Iowa in Athletic Administration. Previous to his current position, Caughron served as Coordinator of Fitness for the Saudi Air Force and worked in the Student Services and ticket office at The University of Iowa. Professor Caughron currently teaches graduate courses in sport law and higher education law, as well as sport management and leadership.

Margaret E. Ciccolella

Margaret E. Ciccolella is a Professor in the Department of Sport Sciences at the University of the Pacific. She received an Ed.D. in exercise physiology from Brigham Young University and a J.D. from Humphreys College. Currently, she teaches graduate and undergraduate course work in sports law and is consulting for Work Well, an organization specializing in research on chronic fatigue syndrome.

Cathryn L. Claussen

Cathryn L. Claussen is an Associate Professor in the Sport Management program at Washington University. She received her Master's Degree in sport sociology/philosophy from the University of Iowa and her Juris Doctorate from Georgetown University Law Center. She played tennis professionally and was an assistant tennis coach while at the University of Iowa. She has published extensively in the area of sports law, with a special focus on civil and constitutional rights in the context of sport.

Colleen Colles

Colleen Colles is an Associate Professor and Chair of the Sport Management Program at Nichols College. She received her bachelor's degree in Health and Fitness Management from Northern Michigan University, her master's degree in Physical Education from Eastern Kentucky University and her doctorate in Sport Administration from the University of Northern Colorado. She has experience as a collegiate volleyball coach, campus recreation director and employee wellness coordinator. She is an active member of SRLA and NASSM and her research interests include gender equity in sport and collegiate athletics.

Daniel P. Connaughton

Dan Connaughton is an Associate Professor in the Department of Tourism, Recreation and Sport Management at the University of Florida. He received a B.S. in Exercise and Sport Sciences and a M.S. in Recreation from the University of Florida, a M.S. in Physical Education (Administration) from Bridgewater State College, and an Ed.D. in Sport Administration from the Florida State University. Dr. Connaughton has held management positions in campus and public recreation departments, aquatic facilities, and health/fitness programs. At the University of Florida, Connaughton teaches classes in the areas of sport law and risk management. He is an author/co-author of a book, several chapters and articles, and is a Fellow with the Research Consortium of the AAHPERD.

Maureen R. Fitzgerald

Maureen Fitzgerald is the Coordinator of the Sport Management Program at the University of Texas at Austin. She received her B.A. in Government from Saint Mary's College in Notre Dame, Indiana and her M.A. and Ph.D. in Sport Management from the Ohio State University. She spent three years as the assistant tennis coach at Ohio State University and was in tennis club management prior to completing her Ph.D. While holding faculty positions at the University of Missouri and the University of Texas she has taught both undergraduate and graduate sport law courses. She is an active member of SSLASPA and NASSM and has served as a member of the NASSM Executive Council. Her research in sports law has centered on gender equity and personnel management issues. Beyond sports law, her two research foci have been managerial mobility and retention and effective marketing of participant focused sports.

Susan Brown Foster

Susan Brown Foster is a Professor and Department Chair for Sport Management in the School of Business at Saint Leo University in Saint Leo, Florida. She received her Bachelor's degree from Florida State University, her Master's degree from Eastern Illinois University, her Doctorate from The Ohio State University, and has additional coursework in legal research. Dr. Foster currently teaches two sport law courses, having previously taught legal issues courses at Ohio State, Western Carolina University, and Flagler College. Her publications include editor positions for two books, seven book chapters, and over 20 articles mostly focusing on legal issues and recreational sport management. She was also profiled in the book *Profiles of Sport Management Professionals: Making the Games Happen.* Prior to moving to Saint Leo in 2003, Dr. Foster taught at Flagler College, was Director of the Sport Management Program at WCU for over ten years, served as Director of Intramurals and Instructional Programs at Saint Louis University. She has also served as Chair of the Sport Management Program Review Council (SMPRC) since 2002 and will continue through 2007.

Gil Fried

Gil Fried is an Associate Professor and Chair of the Management Department at the University of New Haven. Professor Fried received a joint law and sport management degree from the Ohio State University. He is a practicing attorney who represents several national and international sports organizations. His law firm is Sabia & Hartley, LLC in Hartford, CT. He consults on sport facility and finance issues, and has served as the director of risk management for a large facility management company. He has written five books and numerous articles. His primary emphases are sports law, finance and facility administration.

Lynne R. Gaskin

Lynne Gaskin is a Professor of Physical Education and the Associate Dean of the College of Education at the University of West Georgia. She received her B.S. degree from Wesleyan College and her M.S. and Ed.D. degrees from the University of North Carolina at Greensboro. Dr. Gaskin has written and spoken extensively at the national and international levels in the area of sport law. She is a member of 15 professional societies and serves as an officer and as a member of the Board of Directors for a number of professional organizations. She received the Ethel Martus Lawther Award and the Research Excellence Award from the University of North Carolina at Greensboro; the Honor Award from the North Carolina Alliance for Health, Physical Education, Recreation and Dance; the Service Award from Phi Delta Kappa; and the honor award from the Society for the Study of Legal Aspects of Sport and Physical Activity. Dr. Gaskin teaches graduate and undergraduate courses in sport law, marketing, and facility management.

James T. Gray

James T. Gray is a 1986 graduate of Temple University in Philadelphia, and a 1990 graduate of Marquette University Law School in Milwaukee, Wisconsin. He formerly served as assistant director of the National Sports Law Institute at Marquette University Law School. Presently, Gray teaches sports law as an adjunct associate professor to the International Sports Law Centre at Griffith University Law School in Brisbane, Australia, as well as a Visiting Fellow to the T.M.C. Asser Institute in The Hague, The Netherlands and Anglia Polytechnic University in Chelmsford, England. He is co-author of the two volume textbook *Sports Law Practice* and *The Stadium Game*. Further, Gray is a partner at the Milwaukee based law firm, Pierski & Gray, LLP, where he has served as a consultant or has represented professional sports leagues, professional and amateur athletes, and youth sports programs in issues ranging from drug testing, sports based risk management, labor contracts and negotiations, sports television and sports facilities agreements.

Jean Hughes

Jean Hughes is an Assistant Professor in the Recreation Program at the University of Arkansas. She is the managing professor for an interdisciplinary learning/research laboratory that is also a U.S. Forest Service park. She received her undergraduate degree from the University of Central Arkansas and her Masters and Ph.D. degrees are from the University of Arkansas. Her primary teaching and research areas are administration and outdoor recreation.

Mary A. Hums

Mary A. Hums, Ph.D. is a Professor of Sport Administration at the University of Louisville. A Past President of the Society for the Study of Legal Aspects of Sport and Physical Activity (SSLASPA), and recipient of numerous outstanding teaching awards, her extensive national and international research focuses primarily on increasing employment opportunities in sport management for women, racial/ethnic minorities, and people with disabilities. She is a member of the Indiana Softball Hall of Fame.

Lisa Pike Masteralexis

Lisa Pike Masteralexis, Department Head and Associate Professor in the Department of Sport Management in the Isenberg School of Management at the University of Massachusetts-Amherst. She holds a J.D. from Suffolk University School of Law and a B.S. in Sport Management from the University of Massachusetts-Amherst. Professor Masteralexis' teaching and research interests are in legal issues and labor relations in the sport industry. She is the lead editor of *Principles and Practice of Sport Management*, now in its second edition and has also written book chapters for *Sport Law: A Managerial Approach, Sport Marketing, Sport in the Global Village*, and *Management for Athletic/Sport Administration*. She is an Advisory Board member of the Marquette University Law School's National Sports Law Institute and is a partner in a professional athlete management firm.

John D. McMillen

John McMillen is an Associate Professor of sport and recreation law at Bowling Green State University. He received his law degree from Drake University Law School and his B.A., M.Ed. and Ph.D. from the University of Nebraska-Lincoln. His primary research area is the legal aspects of sport art.

Lori K. Miller

Lori Miller completed a three-year administrative assignment as associate dean in College of Education with primary responsibilities in the area of curriculum management, student services, assessment, and accountability. She is a sport management professor and teaches sport law and to both undergraduate and graduate students. She received her B.A. in Business from Emporia State, her M.B.A. from the University of Louisville, a M.Ed. in Physical Education from Texas A&M University, an Ed.D. from Texas A&M University-Commerce, and a J.D. from President's College School of Law. Lori's research focuses on legal issues influencing the business of sport.

Merry Moiseichik

Merry Moiseichik is currently an Associate Professor at the University of Arkansas in Recreation and Sport Management. She received her doctorate from Indiana University in Recreation Administration and Bachelors and Masters from SUNY Cortland in Recreation. Dr. Moiseichik has worked in recreation administration in central New York. Her research interests are in community development and legal aspects both as they affect recreation. She teaches courses in Legal Aspects of Sport and Recreation Services, Sport and Recreation Risk Management as well as other recreation and sport administration courses.

Anita M. Moorman

Anita M. Moorman, J.D. is an Associate Professor in Sport Administration at the University of Louisville where she teaches Sport Law and Legal Aspects of Sport. She joined the faculty at the University of Louisville in 1996. Professor Moorman has a law degree from Southern Methodist University and prior to her academic pursuits, she practiced law in Oklahoma City, Oklahoma in the areas of commercial and corporate litigation for ten years. Professor Moorman also holds an M.S. in Sport Management from the University of Oklahoma, and a B.S. in Political Science from Oklahoma State University. Professor Moorman's research interests include commercial law issues in the sport industry; and legal and ethical issues related to sport marketing practices, brand protection, and intellectual property issues in sport. She has published more than twenty articles in academic journals/proceedings and has given more than forty presentations at national and international conferences.

Rebecca J. Mowrey

Rebecca J. Mowrey is Coordinator for the Graduate Sports Management program and Professor of Sport Management at Millersville University of Pennsylvania. She teaches graduate and undergraduate courses in the areas of sport law, risk management, professional ethics, and additional sport management courses. Dr. Mowrey is President of the Sport and Recreation Law Association and Past President of the Sport Management Council of the National Association for Sport and Physical Education. Her professional contributions include serving as a member of the editorial boards of the Journal of Legal Aspects of Sport, and the Recreational Sports Journal, and as a reviewer for the Sport Management Program Review Council (SMPRC).

R. Gary Ness

R. Gary Ness, Ph.D. has retired from two institutions: University of New Mexico, where, among other things, he served as Director of Intercollegiate Athletics, and Lynchburg College (Virginia) where, as Professor, he initiated the Sports Management Program.

Barbara Osborne

Barbara Osborne, J.D. is currently the Coordinator for the Graduate Program in Sport Administration and an Assistant Professor in the Department of Exercise and Sport Science at the University of North Carolina at Chapel Hill. Prior to her appointment at UNC, she worked for 14 years as an athletics administrator in intercollegiate athletics. Osborne has an undergraduate degree in communications from the University of Wisconsin Parkside, a master's degree in sport administration from Boston University, a law degree from Boston College, and is licensed to practice law in Massachusetts and North Carolina. She has also had experience as a competitive athlete, coach, public relations coordinator, television sports commentator, publisher and sports information director. Osborne's current research focuses on women's leadership in intercollegiate athletics and legal issues in college sport, with emphasis on Title IX and pay equity.

Dennis Phillips

Dennis R. Phillips is an Associate Professor in the School of Human Performance and Recreation at the University of Southern Mississippi. He received his Bachelor's degree from Pacific Lutheran University, Master's degree from Whitworth College and his Doctorate from Springfield College. Dr. Phillips is Associate Director for the School of Human Performance and Recreation, and teaches courses in Sports Law, Policy and Governance, Finance and Economics, Sports Marketing and Management. He coached college basketball for 12 years, played and coached internationally in 17 countries, was assistant college athletic director, and worked for the Volleyball Hall of Fame. Dr. Phillips is active in the Governor's Commission of Physical Fitness and Sport, the National Council for Accreditation of Coaching Education (NCACE), AAHPERD, SRLA and NASSM.

Andy Pittman

Dr. Andy Pittman, Professor and Director of the Sport Management Program at Baylor University, received a B.S. in Physical Education from Baylor University, a M.Ed. from Ohio University in Sports Administration, a Certificate in Accounting and an M.S. in Taxation from the University of Baltimore, and a Ph.D. in Higher Education Administration from Texas A & M University. He has been employed at Baylor since 1981 and prior to that worked for the federal government and the Naval Academy Athletic Association. He is a member of several professional organizations to include AAHPERD, NASSM, the Sports Lawyers Association and SRLA. He has published over 25 abstracts, articles, book chapters and books in the legal area and has over 50 refereed presentations at international, national, regional and state conferences. He is the lead author of *A Casebook Approach to Legal Concepts in Sport: The Most Important Cases of the 20th Century* with J.O. Spengler and Sarah Young and co-author of *Risk Management in Sport and Recreation* with Dan Connaughton and J.O. Spengler.

Gary Rushing

Gary Rushing, Associate Professor, received his Ed.D. from the University of Northern Colorado; B.S. and M.S. from the University of Arizona. Currently, he is coordinator of Sport Management Studies in the Human Performance Department at Minnesota State University, Mankato. His research and teaching areas include a variety of sport management courses such as Legal Aspects of Sport and Physical Activity. He has published in several law reporters and coaching journals and has over twenty years of experience in athletics as a coach and administrator.

Linda L. Schoonmaker

Linda L. Schoonmaker is currently an Associate Professor and Director of Sport Management Programs in the Department of Health and Physical Education at Winthrop University. She received her B.S. and M.S. from SUNY-Brockport and her Ph.D. from The Ohio State University. Prior to assuming her current position, Dr. Schoonmaker taught undergraduate and graduate courses in sport management at Southeast Missouri State University, the University of Missouri-Columbia, and Tulane University. She also has ten years administrative experience in campus recreation, seven of those years as Director of Campus Recreation and facilities at the University of Wisconsin-Whitewater. Dr. Schoonmaker's research focus is in the area of gender equity and interscholastic athletics.

Todd L. Seidler

Todd Seidler is an Associate Professor and coordinator of the graduate program in Sport Administration at the University of New Mexico, one of only a few programs that offer both the Master's and Doctorate in Sport Administration. He received his Bachelor's degree in Physical Education from San Diego State University and taught and coached in high school. He then went to graduate school and earned his Master's and Ph.D. in Sports Administration from the University of New Mexico. Prior to returning to U.N.M., Dr. Seidler spent six years as the coordinator of the graduate Sports Administration program at Wayne State University and then coordinated the undergraduate Sport Management Program at Guilford College. He is a Past President of the Society for the Study of Legal Aspects of Sport and Physical Activity (now the Sport and Recreation Law Association), contributing editor to *From The Gym To The Jury* newsletter, past chair of the Sport Management Council and of the Council on Facilities and Equipment within AAHPERD.

Linda A. Sharp

Linda A. Sharp is an Associate Professor in the Sport Administration program at the University of Northern Colorado. She received her J.D. from Cleveland-Marshall College of Law and practiced corporate law for seven years before entering academe. Her research interests are the legal aspects of education, particularly higher education and sport. She currently teaches sport law, ethics, and issues in collegiate sport to graduate students.

JoAnn Eickhoff-Shemek

JoAnn Eickhoff-Shemek is a Professor and the Coordinator of the Exercise Science program at the University of South Florida in Tampa. Her research in recreation and sport law has focused on standards of practice and legal liability/risk management issues in the health/fitness field. Dr. Eickhoff-Shemek is an associate editor and the legal columnist for *ACSM's Health & Fitness Journal*. She is also the lead author of a new text entitled *Risk Management for Health/Fitness Professionals: Legal Issues and Strategies* to be published by Lippincott Williams and Wilkins in 2007 or 2008. Dr. Eickhoff-Shemek is an ACSM Health/Fitness Director certified and an ACSM Exercise Test Technologist^{SM} certified and a Fellow of ACSM.

David L. Snyder

David Snyder is an Associate Professor of Sport Management at the State University of New York College at Cortland, where he also serves as Interim Chair of the Sport Management Department. He is also a part-time Associate Professor of Sport Management at Tompkins Cortland Community College. Professor Snyder received his J.D. from the University of Tennessee and has been licensed to practice law in New York since 1986. Prior to accepting his current position at Cortland, he served as president of an international sports marketing company headquartered in Tokyo, Japan. He is currently pursuing his doctoral degree in sports management at the Deutsche Sporthochsule Köln in Germany. His doctoral research focuses upon the relationship between Japanese socio-cultural values and the business of professional baseball in Japan.

Ellen J. Staurowsky

Ellen J. Staurowsky is a Professor in the Department of Sport Management & Media at Ithaca College, Ithaca, NY. Dr. Staurowsky received her undergraduate degree in health and physical education from Ursinus College, master's degree in sport psychology from Ithaca College, and doctorate in sport management from Temple University. In addition to publications in scholarly journals such as the American Indian Quarterly, Journal of Sport and Social Issues, Sociology of Sport Journal, Quest, Journal of Sport Management, the International Journal of Sport Sociology, and the International Journal of Sport History, her critiques and analyses on a variety of issues have appeared in *The Chronicle of Higher Education, Street & Smith's Sports Business Journal, The NCAA News, Athletic Business, Athletic Management,* and *News From Indian Country.* In 1998, she co-authored a book along with Allen Sack from the University of New Haven entitled *College Athletes for Hire: The Evolution and Legacy of the NCAA Amateur Myth.*

Stephanie A. Tryce

Stephanie A. Tryce earned a juris doctorate from Temple University School of Law, is a Masters Candidate in Sport Management from the University of Massachusetts-Amherst and earned a B.S. in Business Administration from Drexel University. Ms. Tryce has taught *Introduction to Sport Law, Amateur Sport and the Law* and *Profesional Sport and the Law* for the Sport Management Department of the University of Massachusetts. Currently Ms. Tryce lectures at the Wharton School of the University of Pennsylvania teaching courses in Introduction to Law and the Legal Process and The Sport Industry.

Nita Unruh

Nita Unruh is currently an Associate Professor and Degree Coordinator for the Sport Administration program in the Health, Physical Education, Recreation and Leisure Studies Department at the University of Nebraska-Kearney. She received her Ed.D. in Recreation Administration from the University of Arkansas, M.S. in Leisure Studies from Florida State University and her B.S. from Henderson State University.

Betty van der Smissen

Betty van der Smissen is Professor Emeritus at Michigan State University, where she taught both graduate and undergraduate courses in the legal aspects of sport leisure services. In 2003–2005 she was visiting professor at the University of Northern Iowa and in 2006, she became visiting professor at the University of Arkansas. She is an attorney and member of the Kansas bar. In addition, she holds a doctorate degree in recreation. Dr. van der Smissen is a well known expert in recreation, sport law, and risk management, and has given numerous presentations and workshops on topics related to recreation, sport law, and risk management over the past 30 years. She is perhaps best known for her comprehensive 3-volume sport law reference entitled *Legal Liability and Risk Management for Public and Private Entities.*

Sarah J. Young

Sarah J. Young is an Associate Professor and Undergraduate Curriculum Coordinator with the Department of Recreation, Park & Tourism Studies at Indiana University-Bloomington. She earned her B.S. degree in Recreation and Park Administration from Illinois State University, and earned both her Ph.D. in Leisure Behavior with a minor in Law, and her M.S. in Recreational Sport Administration from Indiana University. Sarah also worked as an Assistant Director of Intramural Sports for nine years with the Division of Recreational Sports at Indiana University. Sandwiched between her IU experiences, Sarah was an Assistant Professor with the Leisure Studies program in the College of Hotel Administration at University of Nevada, Las Vegas for four years. Sarah is an active member of NIRSA, NRPA, and SRLA, and teaches legal aspects of sport and recreation management courses.

Index of Cases

1.00

Introduction to Sport Law

In today's litigious society, it is important that sport and recreation administrators have a sound understanding of the law. The following *Introduction to Sport Law* section consists of three chapters covering a wide range of legal areas intended to provide administrators with a basic introduction to legal principles as they apply to the sport and recreation industry. The first chapter addresses the foundations of the legal system, both federal and state, as well as the process involved in the evolution of a lawsuit. The second chapter introduces the reader to the fundamental techniques and tools of legal research. The third chapter provides an overview of the business structures and legal authority found in the sport and recreation industry.

Gil B. Fried
University of New Haven

If one asked what the term *law* means, one would probably receive a different answer from each person one asked. Black defines law as ". . . a body of rules of action or conduct prescribed by controlling authority, and having binding legal force" (Black, 1990, p. 884). Law implies a multitude of definitions and concepts. Law is abstract, living, constantly changing and evolving. At the same time, laws provide predictability, accountability, justice, protection, and even compassion. Law consists of the entire conglomeration of rules, values, and principles that govern daily conduct that can be enforced by either the government or individual citizens through courts.

Individuals often confuse the law with justice. The law normally provides for one specific interpretation. Justice, however, does not necessarily mean the same thing to all people. Justice varies based on one's education, upbringing, social class, and related factors. Thus, although the law protects one's freedom of speech, many people might not think justice is served by letting a hate group demonstrate on public property. However, our society has determined that laws are often required to protect certain rights or people that the rest of society might not cherish or approve.

The *Significant Case* highlights an injury to a hockey player who used the "law" through the legal system to obtain a remedy for his injury. However, based on the injured player's failure to properly write his complaint, he was prevented from obtaining the justice he thought he deserved.

Fundamental Concepts

Types of Law

Three primary areas of law will be discussed in this chapter—**common law, statutory law, and Constitutional law**. Because laws passed by legislative bodies (statutory laws) can never cover all potential circumstances, conditions, or occasions, common law can be used to provide specific guidance for interpreting the laws.

Common law refers to cases that have been resolved by various courts. The decisions of numerous courts over hundreds of years are combined to form our common law system. For example, numerous principles concerning the liability of an individual who fails to live up to a certain standard of conduct have been developed over the past five centuries. These cases comprise common law and serve as a precedent for future cases involving the same or similar facts. **Precedent** serves to create boundaries by which future cases must be decided. Once a case becomes precedent at a higher court (such as an appellate court [see following]), all future analyses by lower courts in that jurisdiction (of the same or similar facts) must rely on the prior decision. In sport cases, foul ball cases follow precedent, which is why court decisions in foul ball cases often refer to cases from almost 100 years ago to help establish the principle of assumption of risk.

Constitutional law refers to laws embodied in the U.S. Constitution. In addition, each state has its own constitution. An example of Constitutional law in recreation or sport involves prayer in a locker room. Although most athletes are familiar with pregame prayers, the Constitution prohibits states from endorsing any religion. Thus, if a public high school coach required players to pray before a game, the coach would be violating the constitutionally required separation of church and state. Other Constitutional law issues seen in sport include search and seizure issues in athlete lockers and due process rights, such as when the NCAA investigated Jerry Tarkanian and did not have to give him any rights to face his accusers.

Statutory law is law originating from and passed by legislative bodies. All forms of government adopt statutory law including: national, state, municipal, county, and city entities. This body of law is only valid for the area governed by that entity and can cover such topics as zoning, advertising, taxes, or building a recreation or sport facility. Statutory law and Constitutional law are analogous in that both types of law are adopted or changed by a voting system and form the framework of laws that guide our everyday actions. An example of sport-related legislation is the various laws being passed to control the interaction between agents and college athletes. An example of recreation-related legislation is the recreational user statutes that provide immunity protection for landowners who allow recreational users to use the property for free.

There are numerous subcategories of the law including tax, tort, contract, employment, real estate, and sport law, to name a few. One of the broader categories worth mentioning is administrative law. **Administrative law** refers to the body of laws, rules, and regulations that are developed, adopted, and enforced by government units responsible for managing specific government agencies. Although administrative law is not as widely applied as statutory or common law, it still affects a variety of recreation or sport issues. Large portions of the economy are governed by federal administrative agencies. The regulations adopted by national administrative agencies such as the National Labor Relations Board (NLRB) or the Occupational Safety and Health Administration (OSHA) have the force of law. In 1972, Congress passed the law commonly referred to as Title IX. This law requires equal treatment of men and women in programs receiving federal funds. Colleges receiving federal funds are required to provide similar funding to both men's and women's athletic programs. The law is enforced by the Department of Justice, which can help develop and interpret how the law should be enforced and prosecute those schools that do not comply. Administrative law concerns are not relegated to just federal agencies, but can be seen at the state and local level as well. State administrative agencies have jurisdiction over issues such as workers' compensation, facility rentals, and fair employment practices.

How Statutory Laws Are Enacted

Understanding the process by which a bill becomes law is critical for understanding statutory law and how individuals and politicians can identify a problem and then develop an appropriate legal solution. Most state legislatures and the U.S. Congress enact laws using substantially the same procedures. To illustrate this general procedure, the following scenario outlines the revision of the Indiana recreational user statute—from the initial bill to the final adoption.

Indiana had an existing statute that provided liability protection for those landowners who opened their property to individuals for free recreational use. However, it was unclear whether the law applied to hunting and related activities. The primary focus of the bill was the revision of the existing law to clarify the protection afforded to landowners who open their land, including caves, for recreational users involved in hunting, fishing, trapping, or preparing to engage in any of those three activities.

Introducing the Bill

Initially someone approached a state representative and indicated a desire to amend the existing law. Although this bill started in the House of Representatives, it could just as easily have been introduced in the Senate. In this case, the representative authored the revisions and introduced the bill on January 6, 1998. It was read into the record and then referred to the appropriate House committee (Committee on Natural Resources). On January 28, after study and testimony regarding the effects of the act, the committee returned a report to the House analyzing the potential impact that changes in the existing law might have on land use, recreational users, government entities, and other affected parties. The committee could recommend, reject, or be neutral regarding the proposed changes. In this case, the committee recommended adoption of the changes. After being debated in the House, a vote was taken on February 3, with the bill passing 61 to 36. After passing the House, the bill was immediately referred to the Indiana Senate.

Moving from the House to the Senate

Some bills are introduced simultaneously in the House and the Senate; however, in this case, the bill was introduced and passed in one body prior to introduction in the other chamber. After being referred to the Senate, the bill was sponsored by several state senators and referred to the Senate's Committee on Natural Resources. (A sponsor is someone who introduces the bill to the chamber. If a bill passes one chamber, but does not have a sponsor in the second chamber, it dies despite the fact that it has already passed in the other chamber.)

While in the Senate's committee, the bill was amended to address some concerns the senators had. After the changes were made, the revised bill was sent to the Senate floor on February 23, 1998. Although there were 232 senators present, the bill passed by a 49 to 1 vote. Generally, a simple majority of votes is all that is needed to pass a bill. In some cases (e.g., impeachment votes, overriding a governor's veto), a two-thirds majority might be required to pass a bill. Because there were changes in the bill, it had to be referred back to the House of Representatives.

Compromise

If the House accepts the amendments, then they vote to approve the bill, and the appropriate leaders sign it. However, there often is a conflict between the exact languages of the two bills. In this case the House did not accept the revised wording, and on February 25, the House and the Senate leaders appointed a joint committee containing representatives and senators to confer on the two versions and try to reconcile the different versions. In a relatively short time, two days, they were able to work out the differences, and both the Senate and the House unanimously adopted the combined Conference Committee Report. Sometimes the process can take several days or several months.

To the Governor

On March 3, the senate president signed the bill. It was signed two days later by the speaker of the house and sent to the governor for his signature. When the governor receives the bill, he has three choices: (1) he can sign the bill and it becomes law, (2) he can decline to sign the bill and it becomes law in ten days (in most states), or (3) he can veto the bill. If he vetoes the bill, it returns to the originating chamber and requires a two-thirds vote of that body to override. In this case, the governor signed the bill and it became a law on March 16, 1998. Even though it was enacted in March, the law was not to take effect until July 1, 1998.

It should be noted that not all bills are passed this quickly. In fact, numerous bills die each year because the legislature does not have time to act on the bill. Also, even if a bill requiring funding is passed, that bill may be not be implemented if the necessary financial support is not appropriated.

Court System

When a dispute arises involving either the application of a statute or an individual's rights, the dispute is traditionally resolved through an appropriate **court** system. A court is a tribunal established by governments to hear certain cases and administer justice. There are three primary court systems: state, federal, and administrative courts. Legal authority, procedures, and the types of disputes heard are different in each court system.

A **state court** has jurisdiction (authority) to hear a case if the case involves an event or activity that occurred within the state. In addition, the parties to the lawsuit have to reside or conduct significant business activities in the state. Typical cases brought in state court include breach of contract claims, personal injury suits, and suits involving real estate located in the state.

State court systems traditionally consist of general or superior jurisdiction courts, which are referred to by various names in different states. They are commonly called circuit courts, district courts, superior courts, or courts of common pleas. Some states have other special courts such as probate (to handle the estates of deceased persons), juvenile, family law, municipal, city, and small claims courts.

If a party to a suit does not feel the law was properly applied, he or she can appeal the case to an appellate court. An appeal is the process by which a party to a suit can challenge the legal decision rendered by a court. The appeals process is designed to guarantee that the court cannot exercise unchecked or abusive power. If the appellate court's decision is also disputed, the litigant can file another appeal to the state's supreme court. State supreme court decisions are final unless the decision impacts federal laws, treaties, or the Constitution. Appellate courts and the state supreme court can only review issues of law. They cannot review the facts or reanalyze evidence.

A majority of cases are brought in state courts. However, if a dispute involves over $75,000, citizens of different states, or a question involving the Constitution or a federal law question, the case is brought in **federal court**. Federal courts also hear patent, tax, copyright, maritime, and bankruptcy matters. If a party determines that the federal court misapplied the law, the party can petition a federal court of appeals. The United States is divided into twelve judicial districts, each with a federal appellate court. The last resort for any party is to request that the U.S. Supreme Court review a case. The process of applying for review by the Supreme Court involves filing a *writ of certiorari*. A *writ of certiorari* is sent from the Supreme Court to a lower level court when at least four of the nine Supreme Court justices vote to hear the case. The writ requires the lower court to turn the case over to the Supreme Court.

Administrative courts or agencies are created by Congress or state legislatures, and both create and enforce their own rules. All other courts only enforce or interpret rules made by other courts or legislatures. For example, the NLRB is a lawmaker, an executive agency that enforces the law, and a court that interprets and applies the law. If a professional league decided to lock its unionized players out of training camp, the players could file a complaint with the NLRB. The NLRB would investigate and reach a decision concerning the players' complaint. A federal administrator has the power to investigate violations of agency rules and to force individuals to appear before the agency and answer charges against the individuals. Because administrative agencies make, enforce, and judge their own laws, most associations have established separate judicial branches removed from the law-making and enforcing divisions and directed by an administrative law judge. An administrative law judge helps ensure some degree of independence.

A court can only hear a case if it has **jurisdiction** over the people involved or if the issue involved in the case occurred or is located within the court's jurisdiction. Jurisdiction refers to a court's authority to hear and decide a certain case. If a court does not have jurisdiction, then the court cannot hear the case. A court having jurisdiction over a person or company or the subject matter of the dispute can obtain jurisdiction. Thus, federal courts have subject matter jurisdiction over a case if the case involves issues under the federal Constitution, the amount in controversy is over $75,000, or the disputing parties are located in different states. On the other hand, a state court only has jurisdiction if a disputant lives in that state or has significant contacts within the state. Noted track star Butch Reynolds sued the International Amateur Athletic Federation (IAAF) in an Ohio state court. The case centered on IAAF's failure to overturn a competition suspension imposed on Reynolds after an inaccurate drug test. The IAAF did not attend the state court trial, which resulted in a $28.3 million verdict against the IAAF. The case was appealed to a federal court, which overturned the state court's decision. The federal court's decision was based on the fact that the IAAF was not based in Ohio and did not conduct a significant amount of business in Ohio. Therefore, the Ohio court did not have jurisdiction to hear a case involving a non-Ohio-based organization. In a recent case involving two professional hockey players, a Colorado judge dismissed a case brought by former Avalanche forward Steve Moore against Vancouver Canuck's Todd Bertuzzi. Bertuzzi hit Moore in a March 8, 2004, game, fracturing three vertebrae in his neck. The case was dismissed in Colorado because the hit occurred in Canada, and the judge suggested the parties pursue the matter there because Canada was the proper jurisdiction.

Typically courts are distinguished by the types of cases they can hear. **Criminal courts** only resolve criminal matters in which the people, represented by a public prosecutor, bring charges against individual(s) who violate the law through the commission of a misdemeanor or felony. Cases between individuals, corporations, business entities, organizations, and government units involving noncriminal matters are resolved primarily in **civil courts**. The O. J. Simpson murder cases provide an excellent distinction between criminal and civil courts. Simpson was first tried by the State of California for allegedly harming state citizens. The criminal case resulted in a not guilty verdict. The double jeopardy rule prohibits Simpson from ever being tried again on the same charges in a criminal case. However, the victims' families subsequently sued Simpson in civil court. The criminal court decision has no bearing on the civil court case because the two courts require a different burden of proof. In order to convict someone in criminal court, the prosecutors must prove the accused committed the crime beyond a reasonable doubt. On the other hand, a person suing in civil court only has to prove by a preponderance of the evidence that the other side is the guilty party. The criminal standard requires a jury to find the person 100 percent guilty, whereas the civil standard only requires the jury to find the defendant 51 percent guilty.

Legal Process

Detailed rules specify the how, when, and where questions associated with bringing a lawsuit. These rules differ in each court and are often very complex. An example provides the best method of discussing the structure and processes involved in a lawsuit. The following is a fictitious example of such a case.

Sarah Jones was a high school student and interscholastic volleyball star in Houston, Texas. While playing in a sanctioned interscholastic event, Jones attempted to spike a ball, but slipped on a water puddle. Jones tore her knee ligaments. She acquired over $10,000 in medical bills, missed the remainder of the volleyball season, lost $4,000 from not being able to work, and missed her chance to possibly receive a volleyball scholarship from the University of New Haven.

After Jones left the hospital, her father set up an interview with a lawyer to discuss their legal options. The lawyer was Ruth Smith, a young lawyer fresh out of law school. Smith asked numerous questions and discovered from Mr. Jones that he heard one official tell a coach immediately after the accident that the school had failed to sweep the floor prior to the match and the roof had been leaking for over two months. Utilizing her legal prowess, Smith thought she had a great negligence case and accepted the Joneses as clients. Both were clients because Sarah was a minor (under 18) and could not bring the suit herself. Her father had to bring the case on her behalf.

Smith initially performed research and discovered that the likely parties that should be sued included the school, the school district, the volleyball officials, the athletic director, the coach, and the high school athletic association. Jones, who brought the suit to recover her damages, was called the **plaintiff,** while all parties being sued were called **defendants**. Jones and all the defendants lived or operated in Texas. Because there was no federal question, or litigants from different states, Smith's only option was to bring the suit in a Texas state court. Based on the medical expenses and potential future damages, Smith had to bring the case in a specific court with proper jurisdiction.

Smith remembered that special rules applied whenever a governmental entity is sued. Thus, after some initial research, Smith filed a **governmental claim** against the school district. Smith filed the claim specifically to avoid a statute of limitations issue. The **statute of limitations** required the suit to be filed within a certain time period, or Jones would have been forever barred from filing suit. *Each state has its own rules concerning filing a claim against the state. These governmental claim rules are designed to provide the state with notice it might be sued. Some states require the filing of a claim, whereas others allow a party just to name the state in a lawsuit.*

Smith prepared a **complaint** that described key facts available to Jones and provided enough information for the opposing side to know why they were being sued. The complaint specifically identified all known defendants, the reason why jurisdiction was proper, and a statement setting forth what remedies Jones demanded. Smith had a specified amount of time within which she had to serve the defendants with a copy of the complaint that she had already filed with the chosen court. Smith was required to personally serve each defendant with the complaint. *Some states allow a party to mail a complaint or to serve the complaint through a sheriff. A complaint indicates the title of the case, identifies all the parties, designates in which court the case is being filed, and tells the story of the dispute in a specified legal form.*

Within a specified time after receiving the complaint, the defendants filed an **answer** indicating why they were not liable for Jones' injuries. Along with their answer, the defendants served Jones (through her attorney) with several discovery requests. **Discovery** was used as a means to find out what Jones knew about the incident and her damages. The discovery requests included a request to produce all relevant documents in Jones' possession (e.g., medical bills), a request for admissions (e.g., admitting she did not miss any work or she did not receive lower grades as a result of the injury), interrogatories or specific questions (e.g., her age, her address, if she had a driver's license), and a request to take Jones' deposition. Smith responded by serving similar discovery requests on all the defendants. Jones was required to attend a **deposition**, where she had to answer numerous questions, under oath, asked by the defendants' attorneys. Smith had the right to request the same types of discovery from the defendants. *Discovery is the process used to discover information about the opposing parties in a suit. Answers have to be given under oath or the penalty of perjury. Additional discovery tools not specifically addressed earlier could include: a request to inspect the gym, an independent medical examination of Jones, and possibly an independent psychological evaluation if Jones was claiming severe or extreme emotional distress.*

After several months of discovery, the defendants filed a **motion for summary judgment**. Summary judgment motions are brought when a party concludes that, as a matter of law, the undisputed facts are in their favor and they should win without having to go to trial. These motions are solely based on applicable case law and the facts uncovered through the discovery process. The judge determined that there were still issues of facts that were in dispute and as such the judge denied the defendants' summary judgment motion. The parties tried to settle the case, but when they were unable to reach a mutually acceptable settlement, they started preparing for trial. Each side obtained witnesses on its own behalf. The court chose a trial date that was approximately two years after Jones was first injured. *Summary judgment motions are used when there are no disputable facts. Thus in foul ball cases, the stadium/teams typically file a summary judgment motion to dismiss the case based on the fact that there is very well established law concerning assumption of risk. By pursuing summary judgment, a team can reduce the amount of discovery required and save tens of thousands of dollars. If summary judgment fails, then the case will either go to trial or be voluntarily dismissed through settlement.*

Summary judgment is one of several possible pretrial motions. Other such motions include a **demurrer**, **motion to sever**, **motion to strike**, motion to remove for lack of subject matter jurisdiction, and other motions that attack the complaint or require the production of requested discovery material. Such motions are brought when, as a matter of law, one party is or should be required to alter its case. For example, an injured high school athlete might have suffered a great injury, but due to governmental immunity bestowed to the high school principal, the principal could bring a summary judgment motion to be dismissed from the case as a matter of law.

Smith thought the facts favored her client. Her client made a good witness. Thus, Jones demanded a trial by **jury**. The plaintiff in a civil case always has the choice of whether or not he or she wants a jury. The twelve-member jury was required to decide who was telling the truth and ultimately what were the facts. Each side prepared a trial memorandum explaining its case and provided the memorandum to the judge. After resolving some disputes concerning what evidence would be allowed at trial, the judge allowed the parties to pick a jury. Utilizing a process called *voir dire*, each side interviewed prospective jurors and had the right to dismiss all biased jurors or a limited number of jurors that they just did not want. *The size and role of a jury varies in different states. Some juries only examine facts or certain components of a case, whereas other juries are responsible for analyzing all facts and determining damages.*

Smith provided an eloquent **opening statement** that Perry Mason would have envied. The defendants also had a strong opening statement on their own behalf. The trial proceeded with Smith calling Jones as the first witness. After answering all the questions asked by Smith, Jones was **cross-examined** by defendants' attorneys, who were attempting to refute Jones' testimony or highlight any inconsistencies. Jones' father was a **fact witness** because he had specific facts concerning the accident and injuries. Both sides also acquired the services of **expert witnesses** to testify about the standard of care for schools, doctors to testify about Jones' injuries, and several high school volleyball coaches. The trial continued with each side presenting its witnesses and the other side having the opportunity to cross-examine each witness. Each side also introduced documentary evidence. Throughout the trial, each side repeatedly made **objections** to certain questions or the introduction of some evidence. The judge was forced to determine, as a matter of law, which side was correct and which questions or evidence were legally allowable. *The plaintiff always presents his or her case first in civil cases.*

Each side concluded its questioning and then made its final **closing statement**. The closing statements provided a summary of the facts and law espoused by each side during the trial. The jury was given specific instructions by the judge concerning the law and how the jury was to apply the facts to the law. Based on the evidence presented, the jury returned a verdict in Jones' favor. The jury awarded Jones $14,000 for **actual damages** (medical expenses and lost wages) and $40,000 for **pain and suffering**. The lost scholarship was too speculative, thus the jury was barred from awarding damages for that loss.

The defendants were not happy with the jury's conclusion. The defendants' attorneys knew they could not challenge the jury's evidentiary conclusion, but felt the judge gave the jury an incorrect instruction concerning the school's duty to Jones. The judge could have overturned the jury's decision if the judge felt neither the law nor the facts supported it. However, the judge affirmed the jury's decision. Defendants filed a **notice of appeal**, which is the first step in the appeals process. Each side was required to submit a "brief" that outlined its legal analysis and then argue its case in front of the appellate judges. The appellate court, after carefully reviewing the lower court's actions, determined that the lower court made a **procedural mistake** in using an incorrect jury instruction. Therefore, the appellate court **remanded** (sent back) the case to the lower court to retry the case using the correct instruction. *The number of judges hearing an appeal varies in different courts. An appellate court can remand a case, uphold the lower court's decision, or reverse the lower court's decision.*

Before the new trial began, the sides reached a **settlement** in which the school paid Jones $30,000. By the time Jones finally settled the case, she was in college and three years had elapsed since she brought the suit. The appellate court's reasoning was published in the state's official case registry and became precedent for any future cases dealing with the appropriate jury instruction to give concerning a school's duty to its students. However, from reading the published appellate court's decision, a reader would not know that the case was settled once it was remanded to the lower court. The appellate court report only indicated that it was remanding the case to be retried. Rarely does one discover what happens to cases because lower court decisions are not officially published. Furthermore, most cases are settled and the settlement terms are often confidential. Although Jones' fictitious case went to trial, it is estimated that less than 5 percent of all cases filed ever reach a trial. Most cases are dismissed prior to trial, settled, or defeated through summary judgment or other defensive maneuvers. Only state appellate and state supreme court cases are officially published. All federal cases are published. Cases are commonly found in the following reporters: federal district court cases can be found in *Federal Supplement* volumes (cases are cited using the initials F. Supp.), federal appellate cases can be found in the *Federal Reporter* ("F." or "F.2d," the second volume), U.S. Supreme Court cases can be found in three different reporters—*United States Supreme Court Reports* (U.S.), *Supreme Court Reporter* (S. Ct.), and *Supreme Court Reports, Lawyer's Edition* (L. Ed.). Nine different reporters exist for various state courts or regional groupings of courts. These cases are found in the following reporters: *Atlantic Reporter* (A. or A.2d), *Northeastern Reporter* (N.E. or N.E.2d), *Northwestern Reporter* (N.W. or N.W.2d), *Pacific Reporter* (P. or P.2d), *Southeastern Reporter* (S.E. or S.E.2d), *Southern Reporter* (So. or So.2d), *Southwestern Reporter* (S.W. or S.W.2d), *New York Supplement* (N.Y.S.), or *California Reporter* (Cal.Rptr.).

Significant Case

———————— ◇◇◇ ————————

This case involves a legal action taken by a hockey player who was injured by a hockey puck shot by another player. Throughout the case, terms presented in this chapter are shown in bold print. These should help to illustrate the usage of the terms and to clarify their legal meaning.

SAVINO V. ROBERTSON

Appellate Court of Illinois, First District, Second Division
273 Ill. App. 3d 811; 652 N.E.2d 1240; 1995 Ill. App. LEXIS 480; 210 Ill. Dec. 264
June 30, 1995, Decided

Opinion: Justice McCormick

Plaintiff John Savino brought a **negligence action** against **defendant** Scott Robertson after plaintiff was struck and injured in the eye by a hockey puck shot by defendant. The **trial court** granted defendant's subsequent motion for summary judgment, but allowed plaintiff to amend the complaint to allege that defendant's conduct was wilful and wanton. Upon another motion by defendant, the trial court granted summary judgment in favor of defendant on the amended complaint. On appeal from both orders, plaintiff raises the following issues for our consideration: (1) whether a plaintiff must plead and prove wilful and wanton conduct in order to recover for injuries incurred during athletic competition; and (2) whether there was a genuine issue of material fact as to whether defendant's conduct was wilful and wanton in injuring plaintiff. We affirm.

Plaintiff and defendant were teammates in an amateur hockey league sponsored by the Northbrook Park District. Plaintiff and defendant also had met in various "pick-up" games prior to playing in the Northbrook league, but they were neither friends nor enemies. On April 20, 1990, plaintiff and defendant were warming up prior to a game. During warm-up, teams skate around and behind their goal on their half of the ice. Plaintiff was on the ice, "to the right of the face off circle in front of the net." Defendant shot a puck that missed the goal and hit plaintiff near the right eye. Plaintiff lost 80 percent vision in that eye.

On September 11, 1990, plaintiff filed a one-count **complaint** against defendant alleging that defendant was negligent and failed to exercise ordinary care in shooting the puck. Specifically, plaintiff alleged that defendant (a) failed to warn plaintiff that he was going to shoot the puck toward plaintiff; (b) failed to wait until a goalie was present before shooting the puck; (c) failed to warn others that he was shooting the puck; (d) failed to follow the custom and practice of the Northbrook Men's Summer League which required the presence of a goalie at the net before shooting; and (e) failed to keep an adequate lookout.

Defendant filed his **answer to the complaint** and, after **interrogatories** and **discovery depositions** were

taken, defendant moved for summary judgment. (735 ILCS 5/2-1005 (West 1992).) Defendant argued that he was entitled to judgment as a matter of law because plaintiff alleged ordinary negligence. To be entitled to relief for injuries incurred during athletic competition, defendant argued, plaintiff had to plead and prove wilful and wanton conduct or conduct done in reckless disregard for the safety of others. The trial court granted defendant's motion for summary judgment and denied plaintiff leave to amend count I of the complaint. Upon reconsideration, the trial court granted plaintiff leave to file an **amended complaint** to allege a count II based on wilful and wanton conduct.

Defendant filed his **answer to plaintiff's subsequent amended complaint** and the parties engaged in discovery as to count II of that complaint. Defendant later filed another **motion for summary judgment**. Defendant argued that, due to plaintiff's admission that his injury was caused by an accident, plaintiff's case presented no genuine issue of material fact with regard to defendant's alleged wilful and wanton conduct. Defendant further argued that plaintiff could not show that defendant's action was anything more than an ordinary practice shot normally taken during warm-up sessions.

Plaintiff, on the other hand, argued in his **response to defendant's motion** that ordinary negligence should be the standard applied to his case rather than wilful and wanton conduct, because, since the hockey game had not officially begun, he was not a participant at the time of his injury. Plaintiff attached the affidavit of Thomas Czarnik, a hockey coach at Deerfield High School, to his response. According to Czarnik, it was the custom of amateur hockey leagues to wait until the goalie was present in the net before any practice shots were taken.

Czarnik had no knowledge of the rules and usages of the Northbrook Hockey League and had no firsthand knowledge of the incident.

Czarnik also stated that he had seen players in adult hockey leagues take shots at open goals, that is, goals without a goalie present, during the warm-up period and that he had taken shots at open goals. According to Czarnik, the warm-up period was a part of the game of hockey even though the players are not technically playing a game. Czarnik considered plaintiff's injury an accident.

Defendant attached excerpts of Czarnik's deposition in support of his reply to plaintiff's **response to the motion for summary judgment**. Defendant argued that Czarnik's responses demonstrated that plaintiff could not show, as a matter of law, that defendant's conduct was wilful or wanton. Defendant also contended that Czarnik was not a proper **expert** to render an opinion in this case, given his lack of familiarity with adult hockey leagues and lack of knowledge of the rules and usages of the Northbrook Summer Men's Hockey League. The trial court granted defendant's motion for summary judgment. Plaintiff now **appeals** from both orders of the trial court granting summary judgment in favor of defendant.

Our review of the trial court's grant of summary judgment is de novo. (*Superior Investment & Development Corp., Inc. v. Devine* (1993), 244 Ill. App. 3d 759, 767, 614 N.E.2d 302, 185 Ill. Dec. 168.) The granting of summary judgment is proper when the pleadings, depositions and affidavits show that no genuine issue of material fact exists and the moving party is entitled to judgment as a matter of law. (*Estate of Henderson v. W.R. Grace Co.* (1989), 185 Ill. App. 3d 523, 527, 541 N.E.2d 805, 133 Ill. Dec. 594.) In determining whether summary judgment is proper, the court must construe the evidence in a light most favorable to the non-movant and strongly against the movant. (*Schroth v. Norton Co.* (1989), 185 Ill. App. 3d 575, 577, 541 N.E.2d 855, 133 Ill. Dec. 644.)

Plaintiff first argues that he should not have been required to plead wilful and wanton conduct in this case because he was not actually "playing" the game of hockey at the time his injury occurred, but rather was participating in the warm-up practice.

The seminal case on this issue is *Nabozny v. Barnhill* (1975), 31 Ill. App. 3d 212, 334 N.E.2d 258. In *Nabozny*, the plaintiff was the goalkeeper for a teenage soccer league and the defendant was a forward from an opposing team. The game's rules prevented players from making contact with the goalkeeper while he is in possession of the ball in the penalty area. (*Nabozny*, 31 Ill. App. 3d at 214.)

During the game, the ball was passed to the plaintiff while he was in the penalty area. The plaintiff fell onto his knee. The defendant, who had been going for the ball, continued to run towards the plaintiff and kicked the plaintiff in the head, causing severe injuries. (*Nabozny*, 31 Ill. App. 3d at 214.) The trial court directed a verdict in favor of the defendant, holding that as a matter of law the defendant was free from negligence (owed no duty to the plaintiff) and that the plaintiff was contributorily negligent.

In reversing the trial court, the *Nabozny* court held that when athletes engage in organized competition, with a set of rules that guides the conduct and safety of the players, then "a player is charged with a legal duty to every other player on the field to refrain from conduct proscribed by a safety rule. (*Nabozny*, 31 Ill. App. 3d at 215.) The court then announced the following rule:

> *It is our opinion that a player is liable for injury in a tort action if his conduct is such that it is either deliberate, wilful or with a reckless disregard for the safety of the other player so as to cause injury to that player, the same being a question of fact to be decided by a jury. Nabozny, 31 Ill. App. 3d at 215.*

Illinois courts have construed *Nabozny* to hold that a plaintiff-participant injured during a contact sport may recover from another player only if the other's conduct was wilful or wanton. (*Novak v. Virene* (1991), 224 Ill. App. 3d 317, 586 N.E.2d 578, 166 Ill. Dec. 620; *Keller v. Mols* (1987), 156 Ill. App. 3d 235, 509 N.E.2d 584, 108 Ill. Dec. 888; *Oswald v. Township High School District No. 214* (1980), 84 Ill. App. 3d 723, 406 N.E.2d 157, 40 Ill. Dec. 456.) Plaintiff contends, however, that decisions subsequent to *Nabozny* have misconstrued the court's holding in that case. According to plaintiff, *Nabozny* is to be applied only to conduct during a game because *Nabozny* "involved an injury that occurred during a game and therefore, it implicitly recognizes a distinction with pre-game injuries."

In the case at bar, we believe that plaintiff was no less a participant in a team sport merely because he was engaged in "warm-up" activities at the time of his injury. However, assuming arguendo that we were to view plaintiff's action using an ordinary negligence standard, we must find that plaintiff knowingly and voluntarily assumed the risks inherent in playing the game of hockey. Plaintiff's own testimony bears out this fact. Plaintiff was an experienced hockey player, playing from the time he was eight years old. He had played in organized adult leagues for approximately 10 years prior to his accident. Plaintiff testified that while it was "customary" for players to wait for a goalie to be present prior to taking practice shots, in his experience he had seen players take shots at open nets. There was no written rule against taking shots at open nets. Plaintiff was also aware, at the time he stepped onto the ice, that there was a risk of being hit with a puck during "warm-ups." Indeed, according to plaintiff, that risk "always" existed. Nonetheless, plaintiff chose not to wear a protective face mask, since it was not required, even though in his estimation 65–70 percent of his teammates were wearing protective masks during "warm-up" and despite the inherent risk of being hit with a puck, irrespective of the goalie's presence at the net. Based on plaintiff's testimony, we believe that plaintiff voluntarily consented, understood and accepted the dangers inherent in the sport or due to a co-participant's negligence.

We find no reason to abandon the well-established **precedent** of this court, and that of a majority of **jurisdictions**, that a participant in a contact sport may recover for injury only where the other's conduct is wilful or wanton or in reckless disregard to safety.

It is undisputed that plaintiff and defendant were teammates in an organized hockey league. There were rules and usages. Reviewing the evidence in a light most favorable to plaintiff, there appears to be no genuine issue of material fact that practice shots were often taken at an open net and such was the custom of the team.

For the foregoing reasons, we **affirm** both orders of the circuit court granting summary judgment in defendant's favor.

Affirmed.

SCARIANO, P.J., and DiVITO, J., concur.

Recent Trends

One trend that has emerged in recent years is the increased availability of cases and statutes on the Internet. LexisNexis, Westlaw, Legal Information Institute, FindLaw, and others too numerous to name, make legal sources much more readily available than in the past.

References

Publications

Anderson, R., Fox, I., & Twomey, D. (1984). *Business law* (12th ed.). Cincinnati: South-Western Publishing Co.

Black, H. C. (1990). *Black's law dictionary* (6th ed.). St. Paul: West Publishing Co.

Cheeseman, H. (1998). *Business law* (3rd ed.). Upper Saddle River, NJ: Prentice Hall.

Coughlin, G. G. (1983). *Your introduction to law* (4th ed.). New York: Barnes & Noble Books.

Fried, G. (1999). *Safe at first*. Durham, NC: Carolina Academic Press.

Useful Websites

http://caselaw.lp.findlaw.com/cgi-bin/getcase.pl?court=US&navby=case&vol=000&invol=99-62
http://web2.westlaw.com/signon/default.wl
www.archives.state.al.us/legislat/billmap.gif (2000)
www.law.cornell.edu/statutes.html
www.lexis.com

1.20 Legal Research

Anita M. Moorman, J.D.
University of Louisville

It is vital that recreation and sport managers have the ability to perform and analyze legal research for themselves, even though some managers may have access to the advice of an attorney. Sport and recreation managers need a fundamental understanding of legal concepts related to the individual manager's segment of the sport, recreation, or leisure industry. In addition, the ability to conduct legal research will allow the recreation and sport manager to obtain information about current and emerging legal developments. A meaningful understanding of current legal developments is as critical to the recreation and sport manager as is a firm understanding of current developments in communication, marketing, finance, sponsorship, ethics, and many other areas. This chapter will introduce future recreation and sport managers to the variety of legal resources available in the traditional law library as well as from electronic and Internet sources.

Locating legal information is much easier if the searcher has a comfortable understanding of how the legal system works. Thus, it is imperative for the recreation and sport manager to understand that the U.S. judicial system is divided into distinctly separate federal and state systems. Also, what exactly is "the law"? The "law" can mean different things to different people, even though it is intended to be for everyone and is designed to govern whole societies. To govern a society, legislatures (state and federal) enact statutes, which create the need for agencies to write or promulgate rules and regulations to enforce the statutes, which then require the courts to interpret the statutes or rules and fill any gaps left by the legislatures. All these activities are written down, cataloged, stored, indexed, and housed in thousands of volumes. Thus, legal research needs to be well planned to effectively navigate this vast ocean of information.

The purpose of this chapter is to help the reader understand legal research. First, we will look at the legal resources available to the researcher. These include **primary sources** (the actual law), **secondary sources** (explanations/definitions/summaries of the law), and certain **research tools** (digests, electronic databases, computerized legal research). Then we will look at two important techniques to use in conducting legal research. These are **Developing the Research Plan** and **Summarizing Cases**.

Legal Resources

Primary Legal Resources

Primary legal sources include constitutions, statutes, rules and regulations, and court decisions. Primary legal sources represent the actual law, whether it is a decision of the U.S. Supreme Court or a state statute enacted by the State of Oklahoma. *Regardless of the type of legal research being conducted, ultimately only primary legal sources can be relied on in determining what the law requires.*

Constitutions/Statutes/Rules/Regulations

The U.S. Constitution is the supreme law of the land. It both authorizes and restricts conduct of the federal and state governments, as well as conduct of private citizens. Each of the fifty states will similarly have a state constitution governing conduct of the state government and citizens of that state. The U.S. Congress and fifty state legislatures enact laws known as statutes addressing issues ranging from the enforceability of contracts, to ticket scalping, to registration of trademarks. The federal statutes are codified (or published) in a series of volumes known as the *United States Code* (U.S.C.). Each of the fifty states also codifies its state statutes, which are often called civil codes, public laws, session laws, or revised statutes. Both the *United States Code* and the state statutes are bound and published. Many of the bound volumes contain **annotations** that categorize court decisions interpreting the statute in question. These annotations are similar to an index and will assist the researcher in locating specific court decisions and understanding how the statute has been interpreted and applied by the courts. For example, if you were trying to determine whether a federal district court in your state had ruled in a case involving the *Olympic and Amateur Sports Act* (this is the act that created and empowered the U.S. Olympic Committee), you could use the annotations to locate specific cases decided by courts in your state.

Rather than republish the hardback editions of the *U.S. Code* each year, the publishers of these volumes instead print supplements to the hardback volume that contain any amendments or modifications that have been made to statutes. This supplement is called a "**pocket part**," which is a softbound pamphlet that is inserted in a sleeve located inside the back cover of each hardback volume. The publisher will use this process for a number of years before publishing a new series of the hardback volumes. Thus, the most recent amendments or changes to laws will be in the pocket part, so you must always look in the pocket part for any changes passed by Congress or the state legislature since the printing of the original hardback volume. A good example of this is the Sport Agent Responsibility and Trust Act (SPARTA), which is a federal law regulating athlete agents' activities with student athletes and was passed by Congress in September 2004. This law would be cited as the *Sports Agent Responsibility and Trust Act*, 15 U.S.C. § 7801 et seq. (2005). This citation tells us that this act can be found beginning at Section 7801 in Title 15 of the *U.S. Code*. Title 15 of the *U.S. Code* will be published in several volumes as explained earlier. Because the publisher is not going to reprint all of Title 15 every time Congress passes new laws or amends existing laws, you would have to look in the pocket part to find SPARTA.

Congress and the state legislatures also create regulatory bodies such as the Federal Aviation Administration, Environmental Protection Agency, Equal Employment Opportunity Commission, and many others. These regulatory bodies often are required to create rules and regulations to fulfill their assigned purpose. These rules and regulations for federal agencies are codified in the *Code of Federal Regulations* (C.F.R.) and can be a useful resource for research related to a particular agency's activities. A partial list of constitutional and statutory resources is as follows:

U.S. Constitution	State Constitutions
Treaties	Federal Statutes (the *U.S. Code* [U.S.C.])
State Statutes	Municipal Ordinances
Rules of Court	Executive Orders and Promulgations
Rules/Regulations of Federal Administrative Agencies (C.F.R.)	
Rules/Regulations of State Administrative Agencies	
Attorney General Opinions—federal and state	

Court Decisions

A court decision results from a jury verdict or court order that resolves a case or an issue in a case. For example, Tiger Woods may have sued John Brown Company based on the company's unauthorized use of Tiger Woods' name in an advertisement. Tiger Woods' lawsuit or case will probably include several different legal claims such as trademark infringement, violation of the right of publicity, and misappropriation of goodwill. It is possible that John Brown would file a motion for summary judgment (remember this was discussed in the previous chapter) asking the court to dismiss Tiger Woods' trademark infringement claim. When the court either grants or denies the motion for summary judgment, it will enter an order to that effect. This order represents a court decision. Ultimately, if the case goes to trial, another court decision will be entered reflecting the outcome of the trial. Either or both of these court decisions may be published. Thus, if we want to be able to find and read this decision, we must understand when and where these court decisions are published.

Understanding the court system (which was covered in the previous chapter) aids us in locating these decisions. You may recall that court systems are hierarchical in structure, that is, that some courts are superior to others. The highest court is usually a supreme or superior court, followed by an intermediate appellate court, and ending with a district or trial court at the bottom. Most cases will originate at the trial or district court level and work their way *up* through the court system. This process can take years for a case to move through all levels of the court system. Any number of court decisions may be entered in a case as it winds its way through the court system to its ultimate conclusion, so to find court decisions, you need to understand how those decisions are reported. First, we will explore the federal court system and then the state court system.

Federal Courts

In the federal court system, the vast majority of federal cases originate in the U.S. District Court. The U.S. District Court is the federal trial court and the first level within the federal court system. Any appeal from a U.S. District Court decision would be made to the appropriate U.S. Court of Appeals. Any party to the district court action may appeal to the U.S. Court of Appeals. The U.S. Courts of Appeals represent the second level or the intermediate appellate level in the federal court system. As explained in the previous chapter, the court of appeals only exercises appellate jurisdiction. That means cases do not originate in the court of appeals; instead, a case would only reach the court of appeals after a decision has been made in a lower court (such as the district court) and a party appeals from that decision. That appeal requests the appellate court to review a portion of the lower court's decision to determine whether the lower court made a mistake. After the U.S. Court of Appeals renders its decision, a party can still request another appellate review by the U.S. Supreme Court. However, the U.S. Supreme Court is not required to hear these appeals. The appellate jurisdiction of the U.S. Supreme Court is considered discretionary and, as such, requests for appeal (known as petitions for *certiorari*) are rarely granted. The U.S. Supreme Court is the highest court in the land, and its decisions are considered the supreme law of the land, which must be followed by all lower federal and state courts. As the federal courts make these decisions regarding cases, they are published or reported in the reporters listed following.

U.S. District Courts. Federal Supplement and *Federal Supplement Second Series* (cited F. Supp., or F. Supp. 2d). (Note: These reporters are a continuing series of cases reported by the U.S. District Courts from 1932 to the present date. This reporter is in its second series or edition now).

Sample Citation: *Hoopla Sports and Entertainment, Inc. v. Nike, Inc.*, 947 F. Supp. 347 (N.D. Ill. 1996). This citation tells us that this court decision can be located in volume 947 at page 347 in the Federal Supplement. It further tells us that the decision was made by the U.S. District Court for the Northern District of Illinois in 1996.

U.S. Courts of Appeals. Federal Reporter, Federal Reporter Second Series, Federal Reporter Third Series (cited F., F.2d, or F.3d). (Note: These reporters are a continuing series of cases reported by the U.S. Courts of Appeals from 1880 to the present date. This reporter is in its third series or edition now).

Sample Citation: *National Basketball Association v. Motorola, Inc.*, 105 F.3d 841 (2nd Cir. 1997). This citation tells us that this court decision can be found in volume 105 at page 841 in the Federal Reporter Third Series. It further tells us that the decision was made by the U.S. Court of Appeals for the Second Circuit in 1997.

U.S. Supreme Court. U.S. Supreme Court Reports (cited U.S.); Supreme Court Reporter (cited S. Ct.); Lawyer's Edition (cited L.Ed.2d). (Note: These three reporters all report the same Supreme Court cases. *U.S. Supreme Court Reports* is the official Supreme Court reporter, but *Supreme Court Reporter* is most commonly used and user friendly).

Sample Citation: *PGA Tour, Inc. v. Martin*, 532 U.S. 661, 121 S. Ct. 1879, 149 L. Ed. 2d 904 (2001). You will often see all three reporters cited, this is called a string cite. The first part of the string is the citation to the U.S. Supreme Court Reports (532 U.S. 661), followed by the citation to the Supreme Court

Reporter (121 S. Ct. 1879), and ending with the citation to the Lawyer's Edition (149 L. Ed. 2d 904). You may also see a Supreme Court case cited with only one of these three possible citations, such as *PGA Tour, Inc. v. Martin*, 121 S. Ct. 1879 (2001). This citation tells us that this decision can be found at volume 121 at page 1879 in the Supreme Court Reporter. It further tells us that this decision of the U.S. Supreme Court was made in 2001.

State Courts

The state court systems are organized in a similar fashion to the federal courts. Most states will have several trial or district courts located in the various counties in the state. Most cases will originate in the trial or district courts and then follow a similar path as federal cases with appeals going to an intermediate appellate court or directly to the state supreme court. Typically, only decisions made by a state's supreme court are selected for publication in the **state reporters**. These decisions, once published, are organized in a reporter system in two different ways. Each state's decisions can be found in its separate state reporter such as the *California Reporter*. However, many law libraries only carry the individual state reporter for the state in which they are located. For all other states' court decisions, the library will likely have the **regional reporter** that publishes the same state court decisions but grouped together in a specific region. The regional reporters are broken down following.

Atlantic Reporter (cited A. and A.2d)
[Pennsylvania, Vermont, New Hampshire, Maine, Rhode Island, Connecticut, New Jersey, Delaware, and Maryland]
North Eastern Reporter (cited N.E. and N.E.2d)
[New York, Massachusetts, Ohio, Indiana, and Illinois]
North Western Reporter (cited N.W. and N.W.2d)
[North Dakota, South Dakota, Minnesota, Wisconsin, Michigan, Nebraska, and Iowa]
Pacific Reporter (cited P. and P.2d)
[Kansas, Oklahoma, New Mexico, Colorado, Wyoming, Montana, Arizona, Utah, Idaho, Nevada, Washington, Oregon, California, Hawaii, and Alaska]
South Eastern Reporter (cited S.E. and S.E.2d)
[West Virginia, Virginia, North Carolina, South Carolina, and Georgia]
Southern Reporter (cited So. and So.2d)
[Louisiana, Mississippi, Alabama, and Florida]
South Western Reporter (cited S.W. and S.W.2d)
[Kentucky, Tennessee, Missouri, Arkansas, and Texas]

The following sample citations to state reporters follow a similar format to those we examined in the federal courts:

Maisonave v. Newark Bears Professional Baseball Club, 881 A.2d 700 (N.J. 2005). This case can be found in volume 881 at page 700 in the Atlantic Reporter, Second Series. This is a 2005 decision of the New Jersey Supreme Court.

Rowe v. Pinellas Sports Auth., 461 So. 2d 72 (Fla. 1984). This case can be found in volume 461 at page 72 in the Southern Reporter, Second Series and is a 1984 decision of the Florida Supreme Court.

Kelly v. Marylanders for Sports Sanity, Inc. 530 A.2d 245 (Md. Ct. App. 1987). This case can be found in volume 530 at page 245 of the Atlantic Reporter, Second Series; however, notice that it is a 1987 decision of the Maryland Court of Appeals. This is one of those instances where an intermediate appellate court decision was published and the use of the term "App." or "Ct. App." in the parenthesis with the date is how you can distinguish between decisions of the court of appeals and those of the various state supreme courts. If the citation does not contain "App" or "Ct. App," but instead just the state abbreviation as in the first two sample citations, that means the decision was made by the state's highest court (either a supreme court or superior court).

Secondary Resources

Secondary resources include articles, journals, papers, and other written sources that summarize, explain, interpret, or analyze certain issues or topics of the law. In addition to making a scholarly contribution to the understanding of legal issues and topics, they provide the sport and recreation manager with an overview or insight into a particular area. Secondary resources also can be a valuable source for locating additional or related primary sources; however, only primary resources represent the actual law. *Thus, secondary resources should never be solely relied on as legal authority.* Following is a listing of several secondary resources by type and description.

Legal Dictionaries: *Black's Law Dictionary* provides definitions of legal terms. It is a must for studying and researching law. Many paperback, condensed versions are available.

Lawyer Directories: **Martindale-Hubbell** is useful for locating attorneys in any state in the United States.

Annotated Law Reports: **A.L.R.** contains commentary and summary on areas of law. It covers both state and federal courts. The annotation usually includes a case summary together with commentary about the case and how it may or does affect other cases or the current status of the law. **A.L.R.** is very useful if you have a specific case for which you wish to study the impact it has had on the law.

Legal Encyclopedias: *Corpus Juris Secundum* and *American Jurisprudence* (Am. Jur.). A legal encyclopedia functions like a standard encyclopedia and includes topical summaries of numerous legal issues. The summary will also include supporting references to cases, statutes, and other primary and secondary resources. This is a good place to start if you know little or nothing about a topic and want a jumping-off point. These will not provide much analysis and may not contain the latest developments.

Restatement of Law: Torts, contracts, etc. Restatements are comprehensive surveys of a specific and major category of law. For example, the **Restatement of Contracts** summarizes the origin, development, and current application of contract law in the United States noting differences among individual states, majority positions, and the general rule of law for all issues related to contracts. These can be useful to develop a better understanding of the principle and theory of law if the reader has some familiarity with the law already.

Treatises: Textbooks, casebooks, and hornbooks. Treatises are written by scholars and experts on a particular legal issue or topic. These resources are usually very comprehensive and provide an in-depth examination of the issue or topic. Note, however, that a treatise represents the author's interpretation of the law—a treatise is not the actual law. Treatises can provide the reader with substantial references and resources on a specific topic. Most law libraries have extensive collections of treatises. The preeminent publication in the field is the three-volume set by Betty van der Smissen entitled *Legal Liability and Risk Management for Public and Private Entities.* Some sport law treatises include: *Sports Law* by Michael J. Bailiff, Tim Kerr, and Marie Dimitri; *Torts and Sports: Legal Liability in Professional and Amateur Athletics* by Raymond L. Yasser; *Sports Law* by George W. Schubert, Rodney K. Smith, and Jesse C. Trended; *Sports and Law: Contemporary Issues* by Herb Appenzeller; *Fundamentals of Sports Law* by Walter T. Champion, Jr.; *Sports and the Law: Major Legal Cases* by Charles E. Quirk; *The Law of Sports* by John C. Weistart and Cym H. Lowell; *Essentials of Amateur Sports Law, Essentials of Amateur Sports Law*, 2nd ed., and *Essentials of Sports Law*, 3rd ed. by Glenn M. Wong; and *Sports Law* by Michael E. Jones.

Shepard's Citations: **Shepard's Citations** is a publication that allows the researcher to track a court decision or statute through a citation index. The citation index lists court decisions that have cited previous court decisions and court decisions interpreting specific statutory sections. This resource is useful to locate additional cases once the research has located a major or dispositive case. But more importantly, this index tracks any "treatment" of a particular case. Thus, the index identifies if a case the researcher is relying on has been questioned, criticized, followed, reversed, or otherwise interpreted by later court decisions. This is extremely important to ensure that court decisions relied on are indeed still representative of the current legal standard.

Legal Indexes: *Index to Legal Periodicals* (ILP). The ILP allows the researcher to locate law review articles by topic and/or author. Now the **ILP** is available both in the traditional book form and electronically. The researcher can conduct a topical electronic search and will be provided with citation and location information for law review articles on that topic.

Law Review Articles: Published primarily by law schools or professional law associations throughout the United States. To date there are numerous law reviews/journals regularly addressing sport law issues. Some of these include: *Marquette Sports Law Review*; *Villanova Sports & Entertainment Law Journal*; *Univ. Miami Entertainment & Sports Law Review*; *Seton Hall Journal of Sport Law*; *American Bar Association Entertainment & Sports Lawyer*; and *Sports Lawyers Journal*.

Academic Legal Journals: Several academic associations publish journals focused on legal issues. In sport, the Society for the Study of the Legal Aspects of Sport and Physical Activity publishes the *Journal of Legal Aspects of Sport* containing scholarly papers related to legal issues in sport and recreation. Other scholarly publications include *From the Gym to the Jury*; *Sports in the Courts*; *Sports, Parks and Recreation Law Reporter*; and *The Exercise Standards and Malpractice Reporter*.

Business or Academic Journals: Many current legal issues related to sport may be covered in business and academic journals. Many academic business journals also contain special sections for legal developments. For example, the *Sport Marketing Quarterly* has a column entitled Marketing and the Law featured in each issue. *Journal of Marketing & Public Policy* also has a similar feature.

Business Magazines and Newspapers: The sport industry is often the subject of articles in business magazines and daily newspapers. Often current developments in the sport industry have a legal impact. For example, the filing of a case will often be reported in major newspapers both in their print and electronic versions. Street and Smith's *SportsBusiness Journal* often reports on recent legal developments and issues. These articles can help sport managers identify the issues and stay current with legal developments in the sport industry.

Additional Research Tools

The preceding secondary sources are especially helpful in locating topical and/or general information. However, ultimately the researcher must locate primary legal resources. Although the secondary sources will normally identify many useful primary resources, often the primary resources identified are not exhaustive or the most current. At this point several additional research tools are available, including printed digests and a number of electronic databases.

Digests

Digests are particularly useful for locating court decisions on a particular topic. **Digests** are basically subject indexes to the federal and state reporters described earlier. For each state reporter there is a corresponding digest and for federal cases there is a *Federal Practice Digest* as well as several general digests that contain state and federal cases grouped by year. To make it even easier, remember the fifty states are grouped by region, so those court decisions that were published together in a regional state reporter also have a corresponding regional digest (for example, the Atlantic Reporter has a corresponding Atlantic Digest).

For example, if the researcher does not know the citation for a specific case but would like to find cases pertaining to a promoter's liability for an injury to a spectator during a wrestling match in the state of Vermont, the researcher could locate the Vermont or Atlantic Digest and topically search for key words such as "spectator," "wrestling," and "assumption of the risk." The digest will contain a listing of all cases in Vermont or the Atlantic region related to that topic. Now this sounds a bit easier than it actually is, because the law is not always indexed in the manner that an ordinary person may think. Consider the injured spectator example: the actual key word used by the digest to index these cases is "theatres and shows." The digests have **indexes** to help find the appropriate key word, but the researcher will have to explore many variations and be persistent in his or her search. Nevertheless, the digests provide a great wealth of information once the appropriate key word is found.

Electronic and Web-based Research

The availability and efficiency of electronic and Web-based research continues to expand and improve. Now the researcher can accomplish a great deal of his or her research via computer. Although electronic and Web-based sources will never replace a trip to the law library, progress in this area has been tremendous. Many law schools provide students with access to electronic databases known as **WESTLAW** and **LEXIS**, which allow the researcher to search topically or for a specific case or statute. Some law libraries restrict access to these databases to law students. In that case, **LexisNexis Academic Universe**, available through most college and university libraries, is also a wonderful research tool and provides for searching top news; general news topics; company, industry, and market news; legal news; company financial information; law reviews; federal case law; *U.S. Code*; and state legal research. In the event that your library does not have or allow access to any of these resources, there are several additional Web-based research sites.

In addition to using electronic databases, we also have many electronic subscription services available to keep us abreast of current legal developments specific to the sport industry. Many of these services are free, such as the *FindLaw* Website, which offers a free subscription to a weekly e-mail listing current developments in sport law. An excellent paid subscription is available from *Sports Litigation Alerts*. Students are offered reduced subscription rates and will receive a bi-weekly, detailed summary of recent sport law developments. A listing and description of a several other excellent electronic resources is contained at the end of the chapter.

Research Techniques

Developing the Research Plan

Once the researcher is comfortable with the court system and how legal information is codified and reported, it is time to begin the actual research. Having a clearly defined research plan is vital to locating legal information efficiently. Otherwise, the researcher could spend countless hours in the law library with little to show for it. The following six steps represent a good approach to conducting legal research.

Step One: Identify the Problem or Issue

Step One is by far the most important step in the research process. If the issue or problem is not clearly identified, it will be impossible to narrow your search enough to produce meaningful results. A clearly defined issue will also help to discover key words, phrases, and terms that may facilitate the research. However, before you can identify the legal issue involved, you must search current business and professional literature to stay on top of industry activities. For example, when the NCAA sued Coors for an alleged unauthorized ticket promotion, this development may have only initially intrigued sport marketers and appeared to once again raise an issue about combating ambush marketing in the sport industry (Anderson Publications, 2002). However, the actual legal issues in that case may have implications that extend beyond ambush marketing and impact ticket holder rights as well. Thus, from this current development in the business of sport, numerous legal issues may emerge. Several good sources of recent developments in the sport industry are available. The *Chronicle of Higher Education* has sections on college athletics, which report recent educational, administrative, business, and legal developments. Several industry publications such as Street and Smith's *SportsBusiness Journal* also will report emerging business and legal issues. In addition, any current news source will be a good place to locate current trends and issues. Once the general issue has been identified, it then becomes easier to identify the legal issues. However, if instead of a specific recent development, a familiar topic or subject in the sport industry is to be the focus of our research, such as Title IX (Gender Equity), then the *Index to Legal Periodicals* and **LexisNexis Academic Universe** are helpful to track down previous law review articles on the subject. Also, remember electronic sources such as **www.findlaw.com** and **www.law.com** have subject sections available with links to numerous other information sources.

Step Two: Consult an Encyclopedia or Treatise

Once the issue is identified, legal encyclopedias, treatises, and digests will help the researcher gain familiarity with the general area of the law implicated by the current problem or issue. For example, consider the situation where you are interested in researching whether coaches can be terminated from their jobs for violent behavior. Determine what area of law is implicated: labor relations, assault and battery, teacher rights, or some other area. **Encyclopedias** and **treatises** will help to sift through the information to narrow the search to what ultimately may be a simple question of either contract law (Does the coach have a contract, and if so, what does it say about termination?), or employer/employee relations (Is the coach an employee at will, or must the school demonstrate just cause to terminate?). **Digests** will provide references to court decisions related to your issue or subject. If you have discovered that your issue relates to a specific state or federal statute, most statutes contain **Annotations** that identify other related statutes, legislative history, law review articles, and court decisions relating to that specific statutory provision. Step Two will also help to refine the problem or issue defined in Step One as more information becomes available to the researcher.

Step Three: Read and Summarize Cases

Cases identified in Step Two need to be read thoroughly and then summarized according to their importance and relevance to the issue. A sample summary for a key case is provided at the end of this chapter. Any relevant literature such as law review articles, business journal articles, or other literature must be summarized to help frame the importance of the issue to the sport industry.

Step Four: Locate Additional Cases and Shepardize

Once a few key cases are located, locating more recent or relevant cases is fairly simple. For this task the **West's Key Number System** together with the **digests** is critical. Each case published in the West's Reporter System will contain several short summaries indexed by topic and key number throughout the West's Digest System. Basically, once you have found a major case relevant to your problem, finding other similar cases from the same jurisdiction or from other states or federal cases is easy to accomplish using the West's Digest. Shepard's Citations is the most available updating service. *Shepard's Citations* will also help to locate additional cases and verify whether the cases the researcher is relying on are still good law. This process is usually referred to as "Shepardizing." If the cases you are relying on have been reversed, overruled, or somehow disregarded by later courts, your position can be severely weakened. Although the service is a bit cumbersome to use, it is important to make the effort. Most law librarians will demonstrate how to use the service once you have a particular case citation that you would like to update.

Step Five: Determine Any Constitutional or Statutory Connections

Not every problem or issue requires an examination of constitutional and statutory law; however, if a particular article of a constitution or a statute, state or federal, is implicated, it needs to be located and thoroughly read and updated. It is not uncommon for Congress or state legislatures to frequently amend and modify existing statutory laws; thus, the researcher must find the most current version of any statutory provisions. Always be sure to consult the "pocket part" of any statutory volume for the latest amendments or modifications.

Step Six: Organize Your Information

Organizing all the general information, cases, and statutes can be a daunting task, but it is critical to effectively answer your question or problem identified in Step One. It is recommended that if you summarize every case, define and redefine your issue as you gain a better understanding of the issue, search other jurisdictions for similar or dissimilar cases, and then locate any relevant statutory laws, you will be able to integrate all the information together. For example, if your issue deals with gender equity in sports, you will soon learn that not only is there a specific federal statute to consider (Title IX), but numerous court decisions have also been published that help to interpret and understand the statute. Also, you will find that some rules or regulations issued by the Office of Civil Rights help to understand the scope and impact of Title IX. In addition, scholars are frequently writing treatises and law review articles on this subject. A researcher could literally find hundreds of pages of information about Title IX.

So how does a researcher organize hundreds of pages of information? Simple, look back to the original problem or question. Limit or narrow the inquiry to only those bits of information that actually provide an answer to the original problem or question. Once that is completed, it is recommended that you then organize the information as follows:

Statement of Facts: Identify the facts or circumstances that created the need to study the problem.

Statement of the Issue/Problem: State the actual issue, question, or problem that will be answered.

Identification of the Relevant Law: Identify the cases, statutes, or other information needed to understand this issue. This should include a brief summary of relevant cases, relevant statutory language, and other information needed to understand the law.

Application of the Law: This section should include a detailed analysis of the law identified in the *Identification of the Relevant Law* section and how it applies to the *Statement of Facts* section to answer the question identified in the *Statement of the Issue/Problem* section.

Conclusion: Discuss the anticipated effect of your analysis in the *Application of the Law* section. How are recreation and sport managers or the industry affected by this legal issue?

Summarizing Cases

As mentioned earlier, planning and organization are critical to the research plan. Court decisions must be read, summarized, and applied to answer the original research question. Following is an excerpt of a tort case involving an injury received by a fan at a wrestling match.

Significant Case

———————————◇◇◇———————————

This case presents a good opportunity to demonstrate how to condense a case into its most important elements: citation, key facts, issues to be decided, decision of the court, and reasoning of the court. If every important case revealed during your research is summarized in this fashion, you will be able to quickly and efficiently incorporate this information into any report or written findings.

DUSCKIEWICZ V. JACK CARTER, d/b/a/, JACK CARTER ENTERPRISES

Supreme Court of Vermont

52 A.2d 788 (1947)

This is a tort action. The complaint is based upon the alleged negligence of the defendant in conducting a wrestling match, resulting in injury to the plaintiff, a spectator at that contest. The plaintiff had a verdict and judgment below in the sum of $150. . . .

* * *

We first consider the defendant's motion for a directed verdict. Material to this issue the jury could reasonably find the following facts from the evidence, viewed in the light most favorable to the plaintiff.

The defendant does business under the name "Jack Carter Enterprises". As one of his enterprises, Carter put on a show at the armory in Rutland on the evening of June 6, 1945. The principal feature of his show was a wrestling match. Through a booking office in Montreal, Carter engaged as contestants in this match two men skilled in the art of wrestling, one by the name of Savoli and the other's name is Ryan. Ryan had performed for Carter three times previous to this engagement and Savoli, once. At some time before June 6, 1945, Carter went to Rutland and made the necessary arrangements for putting on this show. Compensation for each wrestler, as arranged by Carter through the booking office, was a guaranty that each should receive a certain flat

sum with a percentage option. That is, if the agreed percentage of the gate receipts amounted to more than the sum guaranteed then the wrestler concerned could elect to receive such percentage in lieu of the flat sum named in the guaranty. Compensation paid by Carter did not include payment of hotel bills or other expenses, in addition to payment as above stated.

On the evening of the show Carter saw the wrestlers, made sure that they were ready for the contest but gave them no instructions as to the manner of their behavior during the contest. Savoli then weighed about 230 lbs., and Ryan about 225 lbs. A "ring" was erected in the armory as the arena where the contest was staged. This arena platform was at an elevation of about four feet from the floor and was enclosed by three ropes extending around the outsides of it. Carter inspected this "ring" after it had been set up. Folding chairs fastened together in sets of three or four were provided as seats for spectators. The four or five rows nearest the "ring" were called "ring side seats" and sold for $1.50 each and the others were general admission seats and were cheaper. The chairs were not fastened to the floor.

The plaintiff resides in West Rutland and at the time in question was running a barbershop there. The owner of this shop was in service of the United States armed forces and it was agreed between him and the plaintiff that when the owner returned he was to take over this shop. The owner returned sometime in October or December of 1945 and then took over that business. The plaintiff made about seventy-five dollars per week from his barbering business and he also got about $20 per week as his part of the proceeds of a licensed pin ball machine then in the shop. As stated by the plaintiff in cross examination, he was "a wrestling fan". He invited two of his friends to attend this match with him and at the armory entrance he purchased three tickets for ringside seats. These seats were in the front row nearest the ring. A person in the employ of the defendant ushered them to their seats which were numbered to correspond with numbers on their tickets. The plaintiff paid $1.50 each for the seats. After the match had been going on for some time, one of the wrestlers threw the other through the ropes in the direction where the plaintiff was seated. When the plaintiff saw the wrestler coming he put up his right hand to protect himself from the oncoming wrestler landing on him and as a result he received a sprained hand and wrist. It is for this injury and resulting alleged damages that the plaintiff seeks to recover.

The defendant based his motion for a directed verdict on grounds which may be briefly stated as follows. The plaintiff assumed the risk of the danger which resulted in his alleged injury; the wrestlers were independent contractors and not employees of the defendant and the evidence does not show any negligence on the part of the defendant.

As to the question of assumption of risks, the evidence shows that the plaintiff was a business visitor of the defendant at the time and place in question. He had paid $1.50 for his seat and was occupying it for the purpose as intended by the defendant. * * * An invitee at a place of amusement ordinarily assumes the risk of an obvious danger or of one that is a matter of common knowledge; conversely, such a person does not assume the risk of a hidden or undisclosed danger, not of common knowledge, in the absence of warning or personal knowledge. * * * That the danger which resulted in the plaintiff's injury was not an obvious danger is self-evident. However, the defendant contends that the plaintiff must be taken to have assumed the risks of the danger which resulted in his injury, because he had personal knowledge of it and also because such danger is a matter of common knowledge, and he cites several baseball cases in support of this contention. These cases hold that an invitee, familiar with the game of baseball, buy-

ing a seat in a part of the stands not protected by screens, who is hit by a batted ball during the progress of a ball game proceeding in a normal manner, can not recover, because it is a matter of common knowledge that chance is an important factor in determining the direction a batted ball may take as it leaves the bat. Such spectator assumes the risks of dangers of which he has personal knowledge and also he assumes the risks of those dangers which are matters of common knowledge.

The defendant in his brief makes the following statement. "The intent and purpose of a baseball game is to hit the ball as far as possible, and apparently one of the purposes of a wrestling match is to throw a wrestler as far as possible." It is to be noted that while the defendant makes a positive assertion as to the purpose and object of baseball, he is less positive and more cautious in speaking of the purposes and objects of wrestling. If it is true that one of the objects of wrestling is to throw a wrestler as far as possible from the ring, such purpose can not be said to be a matter of common knowledge, and we so hold. The number of people who know how a wrestling match is conducted and what may reasonably be expected to happen there is small when compared with the great number who know what may reasonably be expected to happen at a baseball game played in the normal manner.

While the record shows that the plaintiff stated in cross examination that he is a "wrestling fan", there is nothing therein showing the rules under which this contest was conducted nor whether such rules permit one wrestler to throw the other from the ring and neither does it appear that the plaintiff had ever seen that done previous to the occasion in question. From what has been hereinbefore stated, it follows that it can not be held as a matter of law that the plaintiff assumed the risks of the danger which resulted in his injury.

Whether the wrestlers were employees of the defendant or were independent contractors is not important in determining the questions before us. The defendant was putting on a show and as a feature of this he engaged these wrestlers to put on this match. It was his business to know the kind and type of performance that he was exhibiting and to use reasonable care as to location of seats and all other matters connected with this enterprise, for the reasonable protection of his invitees. Whether he performed this duty was, under the circumstances, a jury question.

* * *

Judgment reversed. Plaintiff's motion for a new trial on all issues raised by the pleadings is granted, and cause remanded.

Sample Case Summary
Dusckiewicz v. Jack Carter, d/b/a/, Jack Carter Enterprises, 52 A.2d 788 (Vt. 1947).

Key Facts

The Plaintiff, a spectator at a wrestling match, sued Jack Carter *dba* Jack Carter Enterprises for negligence in his presentation of the wrestling match. The Plaintiff purchased ringside seats to watch a professional wrestling match being presented by Carter. Carter selected which wrestlers would be featured and hired two men who were considered skilled in the art of wrestling. Both men had performed for Carter previously. The ring was elevated four feet from the floor and was enclosed by three ropes around the entire ring. During the course of the match one wrestler threw the other through the ropes toward the Plaintiff's seat. The Plaintiff used his right hand to protect himself from the airborne wrestler. The Plaintiff received a sprained hand and wrist.

Issues to Be Decided

1. Whether a spectator at a professional wrestling match has assumed the risk of injury associated with the likelihood that one of the contestants will be thrown from the ring.
2. Whether the risks associated with throwing a wrestler as far as possible from the ring is a matter of common knowledge to ordinary spectators of wrestling events.

Decision of the Court

1. A spectator at a wrestling match does not assume the risk of injury associated with the likelihood that one of the contestants will be thrown from the ring absent evidence of personal knowledge on the part of the spectator of such risks.
2. Risks associated with throwing a wrestler as far as possible from the ring during a wrestling match are not a matter of common knowledge to ordinary spectators.

Reasoning of the Court

The court initially observed that the Plaintiff was a business visitor of the Defendant during the match. As such, an invitee at a place of amusement only assumes the risk of an obvious danger or of dangers that are a matter of common knowledge. Dangers that are hidden or undisclosed are not assumed unless there is evidence of warning or personal knowledge on the part of the injured party.

The Defendant relies on several baseball cases in support of his argument that the risk of a wrestler being thrown as far as possible from the ring is as common to wrestling as the risk of having a baseball being hit as far as possible from the baseball field. The court rejected the Defendant's comparison because the Defendant himself was not persuasive that throwing a wrestler as far as possible from the ring is a purpose associated with wrestling. Further, the court concluded that even if it had been shown that such purpose was associated with wrestling, it was still not reasonable to expect that many spectators would know such purpose. Even though the Plaintiff identified himself as a wrestling fan, there was no evidence that he was aware of any such purpose. The Defendant's other arguments concerning whether the wrestlers were independent contractors were rejected as unimportant to the court's decision.

Electronic and Internet Resources

Electronic and Internet-based resources are now available that make conducting the most basic or advanced legal research much easier. Provided following are a number of Websites, search engines, and electronic resources that should help you rapidly locate current developments in sport law as well as conduct more in-depth research as well.

General Legal Research: Searchable databases that cover a broad range of topics including general federal and state law information, federal and state court decisions:

FindLaw Search Database: www.findlaw.com/

Internet Reference Desk Website:
  www.refdesk.com

Law Library Resource Xchange: www.llrx.com

Law Journal EXTRA! Federal Courts: http://
  lawonline.ljx.com/federal/

Where to Find Court Opinions:
  www.legalonline.com/courts.htm

National Center for State Courts:
  www.ncsc.dni.us/

Law Crawler-Legal Search: www.lawcrawler.com/

The 'Lectric Law Lexicon: www.lectlaw.com//
  ref.html

American Law Source On-Line:
  www.lawsource.com/also/

Government Research Sources: Websites, some searchable, that provide information about government agencies, governmental functions, Congress, and general information.

United States Patent and Trademark Office:
  http://trademarks.uspto.gov/

United States Geological Survey: http://
  mapping.usgs.gov/www.gnis

State and Local Government on the Net:
  www.piperinfo.com/state/states.html

United States Federal Trade Commission:
  www.ftc.gov

United States Department of Labor:
  www.dol.gov.

United States Congress: www.congress.org.

United States Library of Congress: http://
  thomas.loc.gov/

United States Supreme Court: http://
  www.supremecourtus.gov/

University Sponsored Research Sites: Searchable databases and links that include general research of state and federal court decisions, the constitution, and state and federal statutes as well as Websites focused on a single topic, such as Title IX and hazing.

The Legal Information Institute of Cornell Law
  School: www.law.cornell.edu

University of Iowa Gender Equity in Sports
  Project: http://bailiwick.lib.uiowa.edu/ge/

Alfred University Hazing Study: www.alfred.edu/
  news/html/hazing_study.html

The Legal Education Network at the University
  of Pittsburgh: http://jurist.law.pitt.edu/

Indiana State University Sport Law Links: http://
  library.indstate.edu/level1.dir/lio.dir/
  sportslaw.htm#Sports

Law Journals and Associations Sites: Websites with sport law links and general information about sport law studies and research.

Emory Law School: www.law.emory.edu/
  FEDCTS/

Marquette Law School: www.marquette.edu/
  law/sports/links.html

National Sport Law Institute publications: http:/
  /law.marquette.edu/cgi-bin/
  site.pl?2130&pageID=463#YMTC

Sport and Recreation Law Association:
  www.srlaweb.org

Miscellaneous Private Sites: Dozens of individuals and companies offer sport law information and links.

Mark's Sports Law News:
  www.sportslawnews.com/

Insurance Information Website: www.insure.com

Court TV Glossary of Legal Terms:
  www.courttv.com/legalterms/glossary.html

Recent Trends

Legal research is becoming more accessible to lawyers and nonlawyers alike. The availability of electronic and Internet resources regarding sport law topics was presented earlier in this chapter. In addition to being able to search electronically for legal information, legal news and current legal developments are readily available through subscriptions to legal Listserves. Many electronic legal news sources, such as findlaw.com and law.com, now allow the user to register via e-mail to receive daily or weekly updates regarding recent legal developments in the sport industry.

Moreover, many significant court decisions are made available immediately through various Internet sites. Many courts maintain Websites with full-text decisions, and other private Websites will provide links to recent court decisions so that anyone can read and review the full text of the case. This instant access allows recreation or sport managers to access court decisions that could have an immediate impact on their segment of the recreation or sport industry. For example, often a simple Google search will produce links to court opinions or pleadings that are not yet published in any of the traditional sources, but were merely posted to the Internet by a person or an organization with an interest in the topic. This instant access can be very useful in tracking down a rumor or story that you may have heard at a meeting or from a colleague to determine its authenticity and whether to conduct further research as to its impact on your organization.

References

Larsen, S., & Bourdeau, J. (1997). *Legal research for beginners.* Hauppauge, NY: Barron's Educational Series, Inc.

West Publishing Co. (1991). *Sample pages* (3rd ed.). St. Paul, MN: West Publishing Co.

Useful Books on Legal Research

Anderson Publications, Inc. (2002, January). Pending litigation: NCAA. *Legal Issues in College Athletics, 3*(3), 6.

Delaney, S. (2002). *Electronic legal research: An integrated approach.* Albany, NY: West/Thomson Learning.

Elias, S., & Levinkind, S. (2002). *Legal research: How to find and understand the law.* Berkeley, CA: Nolo.

Journal of International Law & Economics. (2002). *Guide to international legal research.* Newark, NJ: LexisNexis/ Matthew Bender.

Manz, W. H. (2002). *Guide to state legislative and administrative materials.* Buffalo, NY: William S. Hein.

Redfield, S. E. (2002). *Thinking like a lawyer: An educator's guide to legal analysis and research.* Durham, NC: Carolina Academic Press.

1.30 Business Structure & Legal Authority

John T. Wolohan
Ithaca College

One of the first, and perhaps most important, decisions a sport or recreation business owner must make is how to organize or structure the new business. For example, should the new sport and recreation organization use one of the traditional common business structures, such as a sole proprietorship, partnership, or corporation, or a newer one, like a limited liability corporation (LLC). Although each business structure has some distinct advantages and disadvantages, such as federal, state, and local taxes, as well as the limited legal liability of the business owners, the type of structure a new sport and recreation organization chooses should depend in large part on the nature of the business. This chapter examines the legal issues surrounding new businesses and identifies some of the advantages and disadvantages of the different business structures used in the sport and recreation industry.

Fundamental Concepts

Three of the most common business structures in sport and recreation include sole proprietorships, partnerships, and corporations. In selecting the business structure or form that is appropriate for your business, sport and recreation administrators should be aware of the following factors: limited legal liability; federal, state, and local tax laws; flexibility; access to capital; cost and ease of formation; and transferability of ownership in the business (Wong, 2002; Hamilton, 2001).

Sole Proprietorships

The most basic business structure, and the easiest one for an individual to start and maintain, is the sole proprietorship. A sole proprietorship is an unincorporated business, owned by one individual, which has no legal existence apart from the owner (Wong, 2002). The courts will automatically view the business as a sole proprietorship, unless the individual starting the business files articles of incorporation with the secretary of state in the state in which the business is located.

The sole proprietorship is one of the most popular business structures in the sport and recreation industry because of the low costs and ease involved in its formation. The cost of formation is low because there are no legal papers to file, thus cutting out legal expenses. In addition, because the income and expenses of the business are attributed to the owner, there are no business or corporate taxes to be paid or additional tax forms to file.

The sole proprietorship does have some disadvantage over other business forms, however. First, because the business has no legal existence apart from the owner, the owner has unlimited personal liability for all the financial and legal risks of the business. Other disadvantages include limited life, the life of the business is limited to the owner, and the business's ability to raise large amounts of capital is limited to the owner's assets or borrowing power (Wong, 2002).

Partnerships

Another common form of business in the sport and recreation industry is the general partnership. A partnership is created when two or more people, each contributing either money, property, labor, or skill, enter into a business with the expectation that each will share in the profits and losses (Wong, 2002). Because a partnership is basically a creation of contract law, no formal written agreement is necessary to create a valid partnership. However, like any good contract, to help avoid future disagreements, it is important that there be a formal written partnership agreement so that all partners understand their rights and obligations and how profits and losses will be shared (Hamilton, 2001). For example, unless otherwise stated in a partnership agreement, the partners will share in the profits and losses of the business equally.

Partnerships enjoy many of the same benefits of the sole proprietorship, such as low costs, ease of formation, and single taxation. Although partnerships have conduit or pass-through taxation, in that income or loss of the partnership is passed on to personal income taxes of the partners, the partnership is required to file an informational tax return. The IRS requires the informational tax return to document the results of the operation, allocating the profit or loss among the partners (Wong, 2002).

The major disadvantage of the partnership over other forms of business is that each partner has a fiduciary duty toward the other partners, through which they are legally bound by each other's actions. As a result of this fiduciary duty, each of the partners has unlimited joint and several liability for the acts of each of the other general partners, regardless of whether the partner consented or had notice of such acts (Miller, 1997). Therefore, it is essential that partners trust each other and are aware of each other's activities. Another disadvantage of the partnership is that because it is created by contract, partners are prohibited from selling or transferring their share in the partnership, even with the consent of the other partners. In order for one to sell or transfer their share in the partnership, the partners must dissolve the first partnership and create a second separate partnership (Miller, 1997).

Limited Partnerships

The only real difference between a limited partnership and a general partnership is that the limited partner(s) enjoys limited legal and financial liability for the debts and legal obligations of the partnership. To receive limited liability, however, the limited partner must not have any involvement in the day-to-day operations of the business (Hamilton, 2001). Once a limited partner becomes involved in the management of the business, he or she becomes a general partner and assumes unlimited joint and several liability for the acts of the partnerships (Wong, 2002).

Corporations

Although there are a number of different types of corporations, all corporations share some basic characteristics. First, to do business as a corporation, the business must file "Articles of Incorporation" with the secretary of state in the state of incorporation. The state of incorporation is usually the state in which the business is located. Once the Articles of Incorporation are filed, the laws of the state of incorporation govern the corporation. Second, all corporations are treated as separate legal entities, with many of the same legal rights as an individual. For example, corporations can sue or be sued, carry on business activities, enter into contracts, and own tangible and intangible assets (Wong, 2002). Third, because a corporation is a separate legal entity, the business can be sold or transferred through the sale of stock, making changes in ownership simple. Fourth, the life of a corporation is unlimited. Because a corporation is a separate legal entity, the life of the business extends beyond the illness or death of the owners, individual officers, managers, or shareholders. Finally, and most importantly, all corporations provide the owner or shareholders with limited liability. In other words, because corporations are treated as individual entities, separate from the owner or shareholders, the only legal and financial liabilities of the owner or shareholder are subject to the money they invested into the company.

In addition to the preceding benefits of corporations, there are a number of disadvantages involved in incorporating; these include the cost, the formal legal requirements, state and federal rules and regulations, and double taxation. First, because to form a corporation, an individual must file articles of incorporation with the secretary of state, a corporation requires more paperwork and record keeping than other business forms. Also, unlike other forms of business, corporations must pay taxes on the income of the business, rather than passing through to the owner's personal income tax (Hamilton, 2001). In addition, individual shareholders must also pay taxes on any dividends the corporation distributes. As a result, the corporation's profits are taxed double, once at the corporate rate and once at the individual shareholder's rate (Wong, 2002). As a result of all these requirements, corporations are more complicated and less flexible than other business structures. Finally, because an attorney is needed to help file all the necessary forms and meet all the requirements and formalities, there is a higher cost associated with the formation of a corporation.

Due to the inherent physical risks associated with most sport and recreation activities, it might seem that the advantages of limited liability are so great that all businesses in the sport and recreation industry should be conducted as corporations (Hamilton, 2001). However, the nature of the business is only one factor that a new business should consider when selecting a business form. For example, you should also consider the tax consequences, cost of formation, the formal requirements, and flexibility and simplicity.

Although all corporations share some of the same characteristics, Congress has created certain tax benefits or other advantages that distinguish different corporations. The following section examines some of the differences between corporate forms.

C Corporations

C corporations are the most common form of corporation. C corporations get their name because the tax rate these corporations use is found in subchapter C of the Internal Revenue Code. C corporations may have an unlimited number of shareholders and may issue more than one class of stock (Hamilton, 2001). In deciding whether to form a new business as a C corporation, it is important to understand that all corporate income that is distributed to shareholders under C corporations is subject to double taxation. For example, as indicated previously, if at the end of the year the business has taxable income, the corporation must pay a corporate income tax. If any income is distributed to the shareholders, each individual shareholder must declare the income on his or her individual taxes and pay a second tax on the same money.

S Corporations

Instead of electing to be taxed under subchapter C of the Internal Revenue Code, a corporation can elect to be taxed under subchapter S; therefore, the choice is more of a tax election. Corporations making this selection are called S corporations. To be eligible for S corporation status, corporations must have fewer than seventy-five shareholders, may not have shareholders who are nonresident aliens, and may only issue one class of stock (Hamilton, 2001). Although S corporations have the same basic features as C corporations, S corporations have the benefit of conduit or pass-through taxation that is typical of partnership or proprietorship (Wong, 2002).

Limited Liability Corporation (LLC)

An extremely popular form of business is the Limited Liability Corporation or Limited Liability Company. The LLC is attractive to businesses because it provides greater flexibility in management of the business and has less-restrictive ownership requirements by combining the best aspects of both the partnership and the corporation forms (Soderquist, 2005). For example, like a partnership, the LLC usually qualifies for pass-through taxation and provides all the members with limited liability protection from business debts. In addition, unlike S corporations, the LLC can have an unlimited number of shareholders, shareholders can be nonresident aliens, and stock ownership is not limited to individuals, estates, and certain trusts but is open to partnerships and other corporations (Wong, 2002). The LLC, because it is designed as a single entity, also provides the business important protection from federal antitrust law. (For more information on single entities and antitrust law see Chapter 8.31). In fact, the LLC is so attractive as a new business form that new professional sports leagues, such as Major League Soccer (MLS), have established themselves as an LLC.

The sport or recreation business may be managed either by its members or by a designated group of managers, who may or may not be members of the company. If the members, as in a partnership, manage the business, each of the members has the same ability as a partnership to bind the entire business through their acts. However, as mentioned earlier, the LLC provides each member limited liability. If a designated group, as in a corporation, manages the business, members do not have the ability to bind the entire business unless they are in the designated group managing the business (Soderquist, 2005).

Publicly Traded Corporations

The main reason for "going public" with your business is financial. For example, in 1998, the Cleveland Indians raised $55 million by selling four million shares of stock in the team. However, besides the financial benefit, there are a number of other issues to consider. First, the organization must comply with all Security and Exchange Commission (SEC) rules and regulations. Second, the corporation must make full financial disclosures concerning profits and losses. Third, because shareholders have certain rights, such as voting on the makeup of the board of directors and attending annual meetings, there are more formalities and less control. Finally, there are the added costs to the organization. The team must have annual board of director meetings, and create and mail annual financial reports, assign staff for investor relations, plus added legal costs (Wong, 2002).

Nonprofit Corporations

Some organizations, due to their special nature or mission, are nonprofit corporations. The major difference between a nonprofit and a regular for-profit corporation is that unlike regular corporations, nonprofit corporations do not have shareholders or owners of any kind (Soderquist, 2005). Instead, nonprofit corporations are run by the members of the organization or people in the community (van der Smissen, 1999). No matter who is running the nonprofit corporation, the members or the people in the community, none of the income or property generated by the nonprofit can be distributed as a dividend (Soderquist, 2005). It should be noted, however, that this does not mean that nonprofit corporations cannot make a profit. It only means that none of the profits can be distributed to the members.

There are generally two types of nonprofit corporations: eleemosynary (or charitable) and mutual benefit. In distinguishing the two types, the courts look at whether the purpose of the corporation is to benefit its members or to benefit some other group (Soderquist, 2005). Private schools and universities are generally classified as eleemosynary, whereas private clubs would generally be considered mutual benefit nonprofit corporations (Soderquist, 2005).

No matter which type of nonprofit corporation (eleemosynary or mutual benefit) the business is classified as, because nonprofit corporations serve a public purpose, they receive a number of benefits or privileges not available to other types of corporations. Some of these benefits include being exempt from most federal and state taxes, special postage rates, and exemption from certain labor law requirements (van der Smissen, 1999). At the federal level, nonprofit corporations are known as having 501 (c)(3) tax status. Even if a corporation is nonprofit, however, it is also important to note that any profits that arise from essentially commercial activities will be taxable in the same manner they would be in a business corporation (Soderquist, 2005).

For a business to be recognized as a nonprofit corporation, it must file the required forms and meet the established legal requirements. Currently every state has legislation establishing nonprofit corporations, and the incorporation process usually follows the same procedure as business corporations.

Public Corporations

Another type of corporation that is involved in providing sport and recreational activities is public corporations. Public corporations are usually municipalities such as cities, towns, and villages (Soderquist, 2005). In addition to municipalities, public corporations are sometimes formed by special legislative acts to perform some special purpose. For example, the National Park Service was formed by Congress and has administrative control over all national parks and forests. In forming a public corporation, like the National Park Service, Congress hopes to take the organization, operation, and finances of the organization from the governmental sphere of influence and place them in a more businesslike structure (Soderquist, 2005).

Significant Case

⟡⟡⟡

The following case examines the decision of Major League Soccer to organize as a limited liability company and whether the league is a single entity for antitrust purposes.

FRASER V. MAJOR LEAGUE SOCCER

United States District Court for the District of Massachusetts
97 F. Supp. 130 (2000)

MEMORANDUM AND ORDER

The individual plaintiffs are the representatives of the certified class of professional soccer players who are or who have been employed by the defendant Major League Soccer, L.L.C. ("MLS"). MLS is a limited liability company ("LLC") organized under Delaware law. The defendant United States Soccer Federation, Inc. ("USSF") is the national governing body for professional and amateur soccer in the United States.

The plaintiffs assert a number of antitrust claims. In Count I, they allege that MLS and several of its investors who operate MLS teams (hereafter "operator-investors" or "operators") have unlawfully combined to restrain trade or commerce in violation to § 1 of the Sherman Anti-Trust Act, 15 U.S.C. § 1, by contracting for player services centrally through MLS, effectively eliminating the competition for those services that would take place if each MLS team were free to bid for and sign players directly. . . . Count III alleges that all defendants have jointly exercised monopoly power in violation of § 2 of the Sherman Act, 15 U.S.C. § 2. In Count IV, the plaintiffs allege that the transaction which brought MLS into existence violated § 7 of the Clayton Act, 15 U.S.C. § 18.

* * *

The plaintiffs have moved for summary judgment as to the defendants' so-called "single entity" defense. The gist of their argument is that although MLS appears to be a single business entity, so that its method of hiring players centrally can be characterized as the act of a single economic actor for antitrust purposes, the organizational form is really just a sham that should be considered ineffective to insulate from condemnation what are in substance illegal horizontal restraints on the hiring of players resulting from the unlawful concerted behavior of the several MLS team operators. . . .

I. RELEVANT FACTS

At the time MLS was formed, no "Division I" or "premiere" professional outdoor soccer league operated in the United States. The last premiere soccer league to operate in this country had been the North American Soccer League ("NASL"), which led a turbulent existence from 1968 until the mid-1980s, when it collapsed. In 1988, Federation Internationale de Football Associa-

tion ("FIFA") awarded to the United States the right to host the 1994 World Cup, soccer's illustrious international competition. In consideration for that award, the organizers of the event promised to resurrect premiere professional soccer in the United States.

In the early 1990s, Alan Rothenberg, the President of USSF and of World Cup USA 1994, with assistance from others began developing plans for a Division I professional outdoor soccer league in the United States. Rothenberg and others at the USSF consulted extensively with potential investors in an effort to understand what type of league structure and business plan they might find attractive. He also consulted antitrust counsel in the hope of avoiding the antitrust problems which other sports leagues such as the National Football League ("NFL") had encountered. Eventually the planners settled on the concept of organizing a limited liability company to run the league, and in 1995 MLS was formed.

The structure and mode of operation of MLS is governed by its Limited Liability Company Agreement ("MLS Agreement" or "Agreement"). The MLS Agreement establishes a Management Committee consisting of representatives of each of the investors. The Management Committee has authority to manage the business and affairs of MLS. Several of the investors have signed Operating Agreements with MLS which, subject to certain conditions and obligations, give them the right to operate specific MLS teams. There are also passive investors in MLS who do not operate teams. None of the passive investors is a defendant here.

Operator-investors do not hire players for their respective teams directly. Rather, players are hired by MLS as employees of the league itself and then are assigned to the various teams. Each player's employment contract is between the player and MLS, not between the player and the operator of the team to which the player is assigned. MLS centrally establishes and administers rules for the acquisition, assignment, and drafting of players, and all player assignments are subject to guidelines set by the Management Committee. Among other things, the guidelines limit the aggregate salaries that the league may pay its players.

Under applicable player assignment policies, MLS centrally allocates the top or "marquee" players among the teams, aiming to prevent talent imbalances and assure a degree of comparability of team strength in order to promote competitive soccer matches. These assignments are effective unless disapproved by a two-thirds vote of a subcommittee of the Management Committee. Most of the rest of the players—the non-"marquee" players—are selected for teams by the individual operator-investors through player drafts and the like. The league allows player trades between teams, but MLS's central league office must approve (and routinely does approve) such trades. Team operators are not permitted to trade players in exchange for cash compensation.

MLS distributes profits (and losses) to its investors in a manner consistent with its charter as a limited liability company, not unlike the distribution of dividends to shareholders in a corporation. Revenues generated by league operations belong directly to MLS. MLS owns and controls all trademarks, copyrights, and other intellectual property rights that relate in any way either to the league or to any of its teams. MLS owns all tickets to MLS games and receives the revenues from ticket sales. There are central league regulations regarding ticket policies, even including limits on the number of complimentary tickets any team may give away. Team operators do retain the ability to negotiate some purely local matters, including local sponsorship agreements with respect to a limited array of products and services and local broadcast agreements, but they do so as agents of MLS.

Under the Operating Agreement, each team operator receives from MLS a management fee. As of the time this action was filed, the management fee consisted of (a) 100% of the first $ 1.24 million, and 30% of the excess over $ 1.24 million, of local television broadcast and sponsorship revenues, the latter percentage subject to some specified annual increase; (b) 50% of ticket revenues from home games, increasing to 55% in year six of the league's operation; and (c) 50% of stadium revenues from concessions and other sources.

Expenses are allocated in a way similar to the allocation of revenues. MLS is responsible for most expenses associated with league operations. For example, MLS pays all player acquisition costs, player salaries, and player benefits. It also pays the salaries of all league personnel (including referees), game-related travel expenses for each team, workers' compensation insurance, fees and expenses of foreign teams playing in exhibition games promoted by MLS within the U.S., league-wide marketing expenses, and 50% of each individual team's stadium rental expense.

The team operators are responsible for the other half of their stadium rents, costs of approved local marketing, licensing, and promotion, and general team administration, including salaries of the team's management and coaching staff.

Passive investors do not pay any team operating expenses or receive any management fee. They share in the general distribution of profits (and losses) resulting from league operations.

Team operators cannot transfer their MLS interests or operational rights without the consent of the Management Committee. That consent may be withheld without cause, but the league is required to repurchase the team operator's interest at its fair market value if approval is withheld. Team operators derive whatever rights they may have exclusively from MLS, and the league may terminate these rights if a team operator violates these provisions or fails to act in the best interest of the league.

* * *

III. THE OPERATION OF MLS

Section 1 of the Sherman Act forbids contracts, combinations, and conspiracies in restraint of trade or commerce. See 15 U.S.C. § 1. Agreements between separate economic actors that have the effect of substantially and unreasonably reducing competition in a particular market violate § 1. The plaintiffs argue that MLS player policies constitute an unlawful agreement among the various team operators to limit or eliminate competition in the market for players' services.

Though the language of § 1 is sweeping, there are some limits to its reach. One critical limitation for the purposes of this case is that the statute does not prohibit single economic entities from acting unilaterally in ways that may, in some manner, decrease competition. . . . Because it is directed against contracts, combinations or conspiracies, § 1 only prohibits collective activity by plural economic actors which unreasonably restrains competition. See *Copperweld Corp. v. Independence Tube Corp.*, 467 U.S. 752 (1984). The MLS defendants contend that MLS is a "single entity" and that even if its policies and practices have the effect of substantially reducing competition for players' salaries, they do not— *cannot* as a matter of law—violate § 1.

MLS is a limited liability company organized under Delaware law. An LLC is a form of statutory business organization that combines some of the advantages of a partnership with some of the advantages of a corporation. Under Delaware law, an LLC is a separate legal entity distinct from its members. Del. Code Ann. tit. 6, § 18-201(b). As in a corporation, investors (shareholders in a corporation, members in an LLC) have limited liability (id., § 18-303), own undivided interests in the company's property (§ 18-701), are bound by the terms of their Agreement (like the corporate Articles), and share in the overall profits and losses ratably according to their investment or as otherwise provided by the organizing Agreement (§ 18-503). The Federal Trade Commission has treated LLCs like corporations. . . . In the present context, there is little reason to treat an LLC such as MLS differently from a corporation.

MLS's operations should therefore be analyzed as the operations of a single corporation would be, with its operator-investors treated essentially as officers and shareholders. There can be no § 1 claim based on concerted action among a corporation and its officers, nor among officers themselves, so long as the officers are not acting to promote an interest, from which they would directly benefit, that is independent from the corporation's success. . . . If an LLC should be considered like a corporation for these purposes, as I conclude it should, then there can be no § 1 violation by reason of concerted action between the LLC as an entity and its members, or between the individual members themselves, unless the members are acting not in the interest of the entity, but rather in their own separate self-interest. The "independent personal stake" exception has not yet been squarely addressed in this Circuit; recognizing the risk that this exception, if left unchecked, might swallow the rule, courts that employ it have done so conservatively.

* * *

The plaintiffs argue that even if MLS is deemed a single entity, the divergent self-interests of the operator-investors provides sufficient cause to invoke the independent personal stake exception. The plaintiffs base this argument largely on their assertion that the operator-investors do not truly share in MLS's profits and losses. Instead of owning undivided interests in the league that are not attached to the operation of any given team, they pay certain operating expenses individually and receive management fees from MLS that are calculated in large part according to their local team-generated revenues. Also, they are able to harvest the value of the particular teams they operate by selling their operational rights or, if the Management Committee vetoes the sale, by requiring the league to pay them the fair market value of their investment.

The management fee arrangement exists in addition to, not in place of, the overall profit and loss sharing specified in the Agreement. Indeed, the fact that there are passive investors in MLS is strong evidence that the payment of management fees and assignment of local expenses do not account for all economic risks and benefits associated with the league's operation.

Furthermore, successful local operation of a team benefits the entire league. The league's net revenues, not just the local operator's management fees, increase when more local revenues are generated.

A similar effect is foreseeable in the market for operator-investor shares. Admittedly, unlike undifferentiated shares of stock, the market value of a team operator's investment will not simply reflect an aliquot share of the whole enterprise, but will also reflect in certain respects the success of the local operation. Nonetheless, unlike competition in most markets, where the value of an enterprise would usually be enhanced if its

competitors grew weaker, the value of the right to operate an MLS team would be diminished, not enhanced, by the weaknesses of other teams, their operators, and the league as a whole. Management fees and operational rights notwithstanding, every operator-investor has a strong incentive to make the league—and the other operator-investors—as robust as possible. Each operator-investor's personal stake is not independent of the success of MLS as a whole enterprise.

The plaintiffs point to other ways in which the operator-investors compete on and off the field. That teams (and, by extension, their operators) compete playing soccer, and that operators directly hire certain staff, such as coaches, to make teams more capable of on-field heroics, does nothing to assist the plaintiffs. Exciting on-field competition between teams is what makes MLS games worth watching. *Chicago Prof'l Sports*, 95 F.3d at 598-99 ("a league with one team would be like one hand clapping"). Game competition, without doubt, is part of the league's entertainment product, not an indicator of divergent economic interests among operators.

On balance, the business organization of MLS is quite centralized. The league owns the teams themselves; disgruntled operators may not simply "take their ball and go home" by withdrawing the teams they operate and forming or joining a rival league. MLS also owns all intellectual property related to the teams. It contracts for local-level services through its operators, who act on its behalf as agents. Operators risk losing their rights to operate their teams if they breach the governing Agreement. The Management Committee exercises supervisory authority over most of the league's activities. It may reject, without cause, any operator's individual attempt to assign the rights to operate a team.

It is true that MLS is run by a Management Committee that can be controlled by the operator-investors, who constitute the majority of the members of the Committee. It is not remarkable that principal investors can collectively control the governing board of an LLC (or of a corporation). That fact hardly proves that the investors are pursuing economic interests separate from the interests of the firm. The notion that the members of the Management Committee of a single firm violate the antitrust laws when they vote together to maximize the price or minimize the cost of the firm's product is easily rejected.

As a factual matter, therefore, there is insufficient basis in the record for concluding that operators have divergent economic interests within MLS's structure. Even if one draws the most favorable inference on the plaintiffs' behalf, there is no reasonable basis for imposing § 1 liability.

MLS's player policies, in particular, do not call for application of the independent personal stake exception. The operator-investors benefit from those policies because centralized contracting for player services results in lower salaries. However, that benefit is, in the MLS structure, a derivative one. No operator has an individual player payroll to worry about; the league pays the salaries. Moreover, the MLS investor gets the lower-cost benefit in exchange for having surrendered the degree of autonomy that team owners in "plural entity" leagues typically enjoy. The reason an individual team owner in one of those other leagues is willing to bid up players' salaries to get the particular players it wants is because by paying high salaries to get desirable players, the owner can achieve other substantial benefits, such as increased sales of tickets and promotional goods, media revenues, and the like. The MLS operator-investors have largely yielded that opportunity to the central league office. Plainly, there are trade-offs in the different approaches. The MLS members have calculated that the surrender of autonomy, together with the attendant benefit of lower and more controlled player payrolls and greater parity in talent among teams, will help MLS to succeed where others, notably NASL, failed. That is a calculation made on behalf of the entity, and it does not serve only the ulterior interests of the individual investors standing on their own. It is not an occasion for application of the independent personal stake exception to the general single-entity rule described in *Copperweld*.

The plaintiffs also argue that the structure of MLS is a sham designed to allow what is actually an illegal combination of plural actors to masquerade as the business conduct of a single entity. The plaintiffs do not argue that the structure of MLS as established by the its organizing Agreement is legally defective so that it should not be recognized as a lawful entity under Delaware law. Rather, they say that even if MLS is a legitimate LLC—a legitimate single entity for state law purposes—a court should disregard that legal form in evaluating under antitrust principles whether the operator—investors are engaged in a horizontal restraint in the market for players' services. To make the argument, the plaintiffs put a reverse spin on the *Copperweld* holding.

Copperweld held that a corporation could not conspire with its wholly owned subsidiary in violation of § 1 because, though the parent and subsidiary were distinct legal entities, the economic reality was that they functioned as a single business enterprise. Cases following *Copperweld* have mainly addressed the question whether to disregard formal distinctions among entities in order to find economic singularity for the purposes of § 1. See, e.g., *Sullivan v. NFL*, 34 F.3d 1091, 1099 (1st Cir. 1994) (NFL, composed of separately owned clubs, not a single entity in the market for ownership of teams); *Chicago Prof'l Sports Ltd. Partnership v. NBA*, 95 F.3d 593, 597-600 (7th Cir. 1996) (characterizing NBA, composed of separately owned clubs, as a single entity for the purpose of league-wide limitations on locally televising games through "superstations," though expressly withholding judgment as to whether NBA was

single entity in other markets, such as player contracting). . . .

The plaintiffs propose that the "economic reality" test should be applied not only to *ignore* formal legal distinctions between separate corporations as the court did in *Copperweld*, but conversely to *envision* distinctions in what is formally a single legal entity when doing so would accurately describe how the business of the entity actually operates. The argument may have some superficial appeal, but on close examination it appears that it rests on a misconception of the scope of the *Copperweld* principle.

It was noted above that the courts have not given the sweeping language of § 1 its broadest possible effect. The "rule of reason" is an obvious example of a limitation on the literal scope of the statutory language. . . .

The *Copperweld* rule similarly limits the reach of the statute's broad language. While concerted action between two separate corporations, one the parent and the other a subsidiary, could literally be described as a "combination" that restrains trade, the Supreme Court concluded that it was not the kind of combination that § 1 was intended to forbid. Like the coordination between a corporation and its unincorporated division, an agreement between a parent and its subsidiary did not represent "a sudden joining of two independent sources of economic power previously pursuing separate interests." *Copperweld*, 467 U.S. at 770. The plaintiffs are correct that the Court was looking to substance, not merely form.

But that does not mean that form is irrelevant. Copperweld does not support the proposition that a business organized as a single legal entity should have its form ignored, or its "veil" pierced, so that courts could examine whether participants in the firm have conducted concerted activity that would violate § 1. Merely posing that proposition suggests how troublesome it would be as a practical matter. It would permit the atomization of firms into their constituent parts, then to have the relationships of those parts examined to see if they produced anticompetitive effects that, had they been brought about by independent economic actors, would have violated § 1. The number of companies that could be vulnerable to examination of internal business decisions under such an approach would be mind-boggling. No case has suggested that it would be appropriate to deconstruct a corporate entity in that way.

Practical objections aside, the theory is also fundamentally incompatible with the axiom the *Copperweld* Court's analysis started with—that coordination of business activities within a single firm is not subject to scrutiny under § 1. *Copperweld* cannot be understood to authorize an "economic reality" analysis that would require rejection of the very premise the holding of the case depended on. Moreover, the plaintiffs' proposition would plainly interfere with the objective of the antitrust laws. "Subjecting a single firm's every action to judicial scrutiny for reasonableness would threaten to discourage the competitive enthusiasm that the antitrust laws seek to promote." *Copperweld*, 467 U.S. at 775.

In sum, the plaintiffs' deconstruction efforts are unavailing. MLS is what it is. As a single entity, it cannot conspire or combine with its investors in violation of § 1, and its investors do not combine or conspire with each other in pursuing the economic interests of the entity. MLS's policy of contracting centrally for player services is unilateral activity of a single firm. Since § 1 does not apply to unilateral activity—even unilateral activity that tends to restrain trade—the claim set forth in Count I cannot succeed as a matter of law.

IV. THE FORMATION OF MLS

In addition to the claim that the player policies of MLS are an unlawful horizontal restraint of trade, the plaintiffs also claim that the very formation of MLS in the first place violated § 7 of the Clayton Act, which prohibits acquisitions or mergers the effect of which "may be substantially to lessen competition, or to tend to create a monopoly" in any line of commerce or activity affecting commerce, 15 U.S.C. § 18, as well as § 1 of the Sherman Act. The two theories are related.

* * *

2. *Existing Market*

. . . There can be no § 7 liability because the formation of MLS did not involve the acquisition or merger of existing business enterprises, but rather the formation of an entirely new entity which itself represented the creation of an entirely new market. The relevant test under § 7 looks to whether competition in *existing* markets has been reduced. . . . Where there is no existing market, there can be no reduction in the level of competition. There are no negative numbers in this math; there is nothing lower than zero. Competition that does not exist cannot be decreased. The creation of MLS did not reduce competition in an existing market because when the company was formed there was no active market for

Division I professional soccer in the United States.

* * *

B. The Sherman Act Claim

In addition to the Clayton Act theory, the plaintiffs urge that the formation of MLS, by which multiple operator-investors combined to create the single entity, also violated the Sherman Act's prohibition of contracts, combinations or conspiracies in restraint of trade.

It is generally held that a coming together that does not violate § 7 of the Clayton Act does not violate § 1 of the Sherman Act either. See *White Consol. Indus. v. Whirlpool Corp.*, 781 F.2d 1224, 1228 (6th Cir. 1986) (failure to show Clayton § 7 violation precluded Sherman § 1 violation for same conduct). A merger of market participants that does not lessen competition and thus does not offend § 7 ordinarily would not constitute a combination in restraint of trade in violation of § 1. Though the statutory provisions present slightly different modes of analysis, when those modes are applied to the same constellation of facts, the answer will ordinarily be the same.

Here, the pertinent facts are that the founding investors of MLS created both a new company and simultaneously a new market, in effect increasing the number of competitors from zero to one. As explained above, that did not represent a lessening of actual or potential competition in an existing market. Similarly, it did not represent a "sudden joining of . . . independent sources of economic power previously pursuing separate interests," see *Copperweld*, 467 U.S. at 770, which is what is forbidden by § 1.

V. CONCLUSION AND ORDER

For all the reasons set forth above, the defendants' motion for summary judgment in their favor under Counts I and IV of the Amended Complaint is GRANTED. It follows that the plaintiffs' motion for summary judgment on the defendants' "single entity" defense is DENIED.

IT IS SO ORDERED.

Recent Trends

Although Major League Soccer (MLS) has survived the past ten years under the LLC structure, some leagues are moving away from the LLC model. For example, after six years of running the WNBA as an LLC, the National Basketball League (NBA) was facing financial woes resulting in the loss of two teams, sagging attendance, labor problems, and teams looking for new owners.

To attract new owners to the WNBA and provide local owners with more incentives, NBA owners in October 2002, voted to allow WNBA teams to have non-NBA owners in non-NBA cities. The first independently owned and operated WNBA team, the Connecticut Sun, started play in 2003 (Bickelhaupt, 2003).

References

Cases

Fraser v. Major League Soccer, 97 F. Supp. 130 (2000).

Publications

Bickelhaupt, S. (2003, Jan. 29). New Sun welcomed by WNBA: Team in Connecticut glad to be given birth in league. *The Boston Globe*, p. F2.

Hamilton, R.W. (2001). *Corporations: Including partnerships and limited partnerships* (7th ed.). St. Paul, MN: West Publishing.

Miller, L. K. (1997). *Sport business management.* Gaithersburg, MD: Aspen Publishers.

Soderquist, L. B. et al. (2005). *Corporations and other business organizations* (6th ed.). Newark, NJ: LexisNexis Publishing Group.

Van der Smissen, B. et al. (1999) *Management of park and recreation agencies.* Ashburn, VA: National Recreation and Park Association.

Wong, G. M. (2002). *Essentials of sports law* (3rd ed.). Westport, CT: Praeger Publishing.

2.00

Negligence Law

Negligence law is law that deals with unintentional torts committed by individuals or organizations. *Negligence* is an unintentional tort that injures an individual in person, property, or reputation. The elements of negligence and which parties are liable are presented in Section 2.10. The first two chapters serve as a foundation for each of the chapters relating to negligence.

It is important that the recreation or sport manager understand that being sued for negligence does not necessarily mean that one will lose that suit. Many defenses are available to the recreation or sport manager and to the entities with which they are associated. Some of these defenses are based in common law, some in contract law, and some in statutory law. Section 2.20, *Defenses*, includes an overview of defenses against liability, followed by chapters that look specifically at immunity, waivers, informed consents, and agreements to participate.

Finally, six chapters are included that deal with recreation and sport management applications. Here one is presented with an in-depth look at some of the liability of the recreation or sport manager. Included in this section is a new chapter on hospitality and tourism law.

* * *

The reader is cautioned, however, regarding a limitation of this or any other text. *Negligence law is primarily state law and, as such, may vary considerably from state to state. It is impossible to cover all the quirks and variations in the various laws and court rulings for each state. It is, therefore, necessary to utilize generalizations or "general rules" when discussing most topics. The reader must understand that these generalizations are not necessarily true in every state and that certain exceptions may exist.*

2.10 NEGLIGENCE THEORY

2.11 Elements of Negligence

Betty van der Smissen
Michigan State University

Although other fields of law are important to the management of sport and recreation programs and services, the greatest number of lawsuits brought against a provider (school, municipality, private enterprise, or non-profit association) is based in negligence liability. Approximately one-third of the colleges and universities in the NCAA have had such legal actions brought against them (Lea & Loughman, 1993). At the high school level, negligence also is the foremost liability issue facing coaches (Wong & Covell, 1995). Hence, it is desirable to understand the elements of negligence and how one might ameliorate such lawsuits.

Negligence is in the tort field. It is an *unintentional tort* that injures an individual in person, property, or reputation. One did not intend to injure an individual, but in fact, an injury did occur. The injury may have occurred because of an act of omission (something one did **not** do) or commission (something one **did** do). Negligence may be ordinary negligence or gross negligence, which are explained later. When one intends to injure another, it is referred to as an *intentional tort*. Intentional torts include willful and wanton, and willful and malicious acts (see also Section 3.00). Then there are those acts that are in between—one certainly did not intend to injure, but by one's actions, intent is inferred because of the disregard for the safety of another, a conscious indifference to consequences. This usually occurs among co-participants and is called *reckless disregard*. The participant who may have disregarded the safety of another participant and thus injured that participant may be liable for the injury (*Dare v. Freefall Adventures*, 2002; Miller, 1996; see also Chapter 2.32, *Supervision*, and Chapter 4.11, *Assault and Battery*).

There are four elements of negligence, *all which must occur or be proven for a person to be held liable for the injury* (*Christensen v. Royal School Dist. No. 160*, 2005).

1. **Duty.** A special relationship exists between the program or service provider (defendant) and the participant (injured individual, plaintiff), which gives rise to an obligation to protect the individual from unreasonable risk of harm.
2. **The act (Breach of duty).** What the provider did (commission) or did not do (omission) to protect the individual was not in accord with the standard of care a prudent professional should provide.
3. **Proximate cause.** The breach of the standard of care was the reason the injury occurred.
4. **Damage or harm.** The individual received physical or emotional injury.

Fundamental Concepts

Fundamental concepts are embodied in each of the four elements of negligence.

Duty

Duty is societal based, that is, the courts and legislatures determine which members of society owe a duty to another. The larger social consequences of imposing a duty are considered (*Bodaness v. Staten Island Aid, Inc.*, 1991). As society changes, so may a duty; for example, some years ago a college stood in loco parentis (in the place of a parent; charged with the parent's rights, duties, and responsibilities) as to its students. Then, the societal attitude changed, and for activities outside the academic/curricular program or officially sponsored cocurricular activities, including recreation and sport (*Kleinknecht v. Gettysburg College*, 1993; *Significant Case in Chapter 2.31, Emergency Care*), colleges no longer were in an in loco parentis relationship. That is, colleges did not owe a duty to protect students or to supervise conduct generally. However, in the 1990s there appeared to be a return to in loco parentis for certain types of activities and student protection (Snow & Thro, 1994).

Duty, as an element of negligence, arises from a special relationship between the service/program provider and the user/participant that requires that the provider protect the individual from exposure to unreasonable risks that may cause injury. This duty should be distinguished from duty meaning function. Often it is said that one owes a duty to supervise, to warn, to instruct, to provide protective equipment, etc. These are functions or responsibilities, not relationships (*Woolsey v. Holiday Health Clubs and Fitness Centers, Inc.*, 1991)

Existence of Special Relationship

Duty has three primary origins. They are (1) from a relationship inherent in the situation; (2) from a voluntary assumption of the duty; and (3) from a duty mandated by statute.

Relationship Inherent. There usually is little question that there is a special relationship, for it exists in most provision of programs and services, that is, it is inherent and obvious—the athlete and coach, the director of a sport camp and its participants, the student and instructor, the athlete and athletic trainer, the user of a facility and the maintenance person, the sponsor of a tournament and the entrants, or the rentor of equipment and the user. When a program or service is provided, usually there also is a concomitant obligation not to expose the participant/user to unreasonable risk of harm (*Dukes v. Bethlehem Cent. Sch. Dist.*, 1995; Rhim, 1996).

Voluntary Assumption. A special relationship also may be established by voluntary assumption when no inherent relationship existed. For example, if a person holding a lifeguarding certificate is on the beach with a friend, but is not employed as a lifeguard, and a person in the water is struggling, there is no legal obligation to endeavor to rescue the person because there is no special relationship. The holding of a certificate for lifesaving or first aid/CPR does not establish a special relationship with whomever might need the skill, and thus does not carry a legal obligation to render aid. *There may be a moral obligation, but not a legal one.* However, if the person decides to rescue, then that person establishes voluntarily a special relationship and therefore a duty with an obligation to perform the rescue with the appropriate standard of care. Or, a special relationship may be established by a person volunteering to be a Little League coach—by such voluntary act a special relationship is established between the coach and young player that requires protection against unreasonable risk to the player (*Blankenship v. Peoria Park Dist.*, 1994; *Roe v. North Adams Community School Corp.*, 1995; see also Chapter 2.22, *Immunity*, relating to immunity for volunteers).

Statutory. A special relationship may be set forth by statutes, such as those established for employment, supervisory requirements, or rendering of first aid in specified situations. Often violation of such statutes is deemed **negligence per se**, that is, negligence "on the face" where one does not have to prove negligence. However, the violation of a statute is not automatically negligence per se, without having to prove negligence. It must still be shown that the violation of the statute was the proximate cause of the injury (*Hinckley v. Krantz*, 1995; *Holbrook v. Executive Conference Center*, 1995; *Jackson v. City of Franklin*, 1991; *Skinner v. Vacaville Unified School Dist.*, 1995).

Foreseeability of Unreasonable Harm

A special relationship may exist, but there may be no duty to be proactive to protect the participant. *There is a duty to be proactive in protecting only when the risk is foreseeable by a prudent professional.* If not foreseeable, how can one protect—thus, no liability. The test of foreseeability is foresight, not hindsight. For example, a student was foreseen as a healthy, 23-year-old, but in fact, suffered in a one-mile timed run extreme exertional rhabdomyolysis (*Turner v. Rush Medical College*, 1989). On the other hand, a basketball player with an injured nose, which had not yet healed, and with eyes swollen and face bruised, was directed by the coach to participate in a scrimmage. It was held predictable or foreseeable that further injury would occur.

The injury need only fall into the general category of risk reasonably anticipated; the specific or exact injury does not need to be foreseen (*Lamorie v. Warner Pacific College*, 1993). It should be made clear that one can have a special relationship and owe a duty to protect, but because there is no foreseeable unreasonable risk, there does not have to be any proactive action. It is not correct to say that there is no duty—the duty is there; there just does not have to be any action (*American Golf Corp. v. Manley*, 1996; *Chudasama v. Metropolitan Gov't of Nashville and Davidon County*, 1995; *Nielson v. Town of Amherst*, 1993). There is another aspect of foreseeability. When an environmental hazard is open and obvious, it is **not** foreseeable that an individual would place oneself in a dangerous position of which they were aware. Thus, although there may be a special relationship, there is no duty to be proactive to protect. (For further discussion of "open and obvious," see Chapter 3.20, *Premises Liability*.)

Foreseeability also may be at issue when there are criminal acts of a third party. See Chapter 4.12, *Criminal Liability for Violence in Sports*; *Locke v. Ozark City Board of Education*, 2005; *Rhinehart v. Boys and Girls Club*, 2005).

Nature of Duty

The nature of the duty to protect is determined by the type of relationship. There are three categories frequently set forth—**invitee, licensee**, and **trespasser**. To these should be added a fourth, **recreational user**. However, although these categories are types of relationships, all are related to premises and the status of the entrant onto the premises (facility or area); therefore, discussion of these may be found in Chapter 3.20, *Premises Liability*. The status affects the nature of the duty in terms of the degree of protection that must be provided to individuals in that type of relationship. The discussion in this chapter focuses only on the invitee and the requirements to protect against unreasonable risk (for protection from risks due to third-party acts, see also Chapters 4.11, *Assault and Battery*, and 4.15, *Sport-Related Crimes*).

The Act (Breach of Duty)

If the duty is to protect against an unreasonable risk of harm, what is that risk to be protected against and what is "unreasonable"? A breach of duty occurs when the act is not in accord with that required by professional standards, which is the duty required.

Types of Risk

There are two types of risk—inherent risks and negligent behaviors.

Inherent Risks. Inherent risks are those integral to the activity. For example, in any of the contact sports, such as football and soccer, it is inherent in the sport that players will collide and may get hurt therefrom. In baseball, the possibility of being hit by a foul ball is an inherent risk taken by spectators. An inherent risk is one that, if removed from the game, would essentially alter the sport, and thereby the sport would lose its integrity. *There is no liability for injury that occurs due to inherent risks of which the injured participant is knowledgeable or should be knowledgeable.* A participant, whether player or spectator, assumes such risks. Although exposure to inherent risks is foreseeable, such risks are **not** "unreasonable" and thus are not something against which one must protect. Of course, as an instructor, leader, or supervisor, one would want to help the participants to better understand the inherent risks of an activity and thus help them to reduce possible injury. *Inherent risks are assumed by the participant under primary assumption of risk; the participant "consents" to those risks* (see also Chapter 2.21, *Defenses Against Negligence*.). Although an injury may occur during a sport activity, inherent risk does not extend to negligent behaviors, such as unsafe facilities and failure to properly supervise (*Wu v. Shattuck-St. Mary's School*, 2005; *Kahn v. East Side Union H.S. Dist.*, 2003).

Negligent Behavior. Negligent behavior is conduct that is not in accord with the standard of care a prudent professional should give, and hence, the participant is subject to "unreasonable risk" of injury. Negligent behavior or conduct may be ordinary negligence or gross negligence. Where **ordinary negligence** is the failure to act with reasonable care and lack of ordinary diligence, **gross negligence** is characterized by a heightened degree of carelessness; an act done with utter unconcern for the safety of others; a conscious indifference to consequences.

The distinction between ordinary and gross negligence is important for many defenses because generally neither waivers nor immunity laws protect one from liability for gross negligence (see Chapter 2.21, *Defenses Against Negligence*; Chapter 2.22, *Immunity*; and Chapter 2.23, *Waivers and Releases*). However, determining when ordinary negligence rises to gross negligence is fact specific and varies by state jurisdiction. What may be gross negligence in one situation may not be in another. There is no **one** definition and no foolproof set of criteria for distinguishing between the two. The difference between ordinary and gross negligence may be one of degree, just short of reckless disregard of the consequences—or it may be a form of reckless and wanton conduct, just short of malice and wanton conduct. Even when a state, by statute, defines negligence, it is still open to wide interpretation. Michigan seems to categorize gross negligence as reckless disregard in its Government Torts Liability Act (MCLS 691: 1407, Sec. 7 [2] [c]). When discussing liability of government agencies, officers, employees, and volunteers, the statute defines gross negligence as "conduct so reckless as to demonstrate a substantial lack of concern for whether an injury results" (see also *Koffman v. Garnett*, 2003).

Four elements seem to be considered in determining if negligence reaches the level of gross, but all four may not be evidenced in a given case:

1. An intentional act or intentional failure to perform a duty, but not a conscious intent to harm
2. An awareness that the conduct will create a risk of harm to another, although the extent may not be appreciated
3. Knowledge of acts that should have given appreciation of the extent of the risk of harm
4. The creation of a risk of harm that is extreme and outrageous, as measured by the *probability* of risk of harm and the *severity* of the harm that might result

Because of the impact of a finding of gross negligence, that is, a waiver or immunity law may not protect one from liability, the determination is of great importance. Unless the facts are so clear as to permit a conclusion as a matter of law, the determination should be made by the "trier of facts," the jury, as to whether a defendant's negligent conduct amounts to gross negligence (Sergent, 2000; *City of Santa Barbara*, Ca. 2nd App., 2006).

Although it is up to the court to determine if an act constitutes ordinary or gross negligence, the following cases help to illustrate the differences between the two. In *Martinez v. Swartzbaugh* (2002), Martinez was a successful bidder for a charity "ride around" in a McLaren race car. Martinez, who was not provided a helmet, seat belt, or other safety devices, was seriously injured when the driver suddenly accelerated to the speed of 140 miles per hour before losing control and crashing the race car. The court agreed with the allegation of gross negligence and reversed the summary judgment of the lower court. In another case (*Hatch v. V.P. Fair Foundation, Inc.*, 1999), a bungee operator arrived late, and in violation of policies in the company safety manual, operated the attraction with five rather than six persons, used an eighteen-year-old controller when the manual specified twenty-five years of age, failed to inspect the equipment as required, failed to conduct a test jump as required, and most importantly, failed to attach the bungee cord to the crane. Hatch was seriously injured. This was deemed reckless conduct because Missouri does not recognize the concept of gross negligence. Also, broken glass is known to be a great hazard in certain locations (e.g., swimming pools, shower rooms, running tracks, sandboxes, beneath a play apparatus on a playground). Not to promptly remove the broken glass after notice may constitute gross negligence. One is given little time to clean up such a great hazard for potential serious injury.

However, recreation and sport managers need to realize that the injury-causing actions in sport and recreation cases seldom reach the level of gross negligence. In each of the following cases, the plaintiff alleged gross negligence on the part of the defendant sport business. In each case, the appellate court felt there was sufficient evidence to remand the case to trial to determine if the defendant's action was ordinary or gross negligence—however, how the jury ultimately ruled in these cases is not reported. In *Eastman v. Yutzy* (2001), an eight-year-old camper was injured while biking with two counselors on a steep, narrow, unevenly paved road. A counselor directed Eastman to shift to a higher gear, to go faster, and then led her by some distance. The plaintiff bumped another camper, lost control, and was injured. In another Massachusetts case (*Zavras v. Capeway Rovers Motorcycle Club*, 1997), the appellate court stated that the minor defendant's actions (e.g., as flagman for a dirt bike race with a series of jumps who failed to signal with his flag that a biker had fallen, thus allowing a number of bikers to crash atop the downed biker) could be found by a jury to be grossly negligent. In another case, after a racetrack collision, the driver was trapped in a burning car. Factors giving rise to the gross negligence claim included only two firefighters were present, they had not trained together, they were unfamiliar with the car design, they had no extrication equipment except prybars, and some of their fire extinguishers were not designed for use in a methanol fire. As a result the driver was trapped for 8 to 10 minutes before other drivers rescued him (*Wolfgang v. Mid-America Motorsports, Inc.*, 1997).

Although gross negligence was alleged in the following cases, each appellate court determined that the action by the defendant did not rise beyond the level of ordinary negligence. A health club patron was injured when the dip station on which he was exercising tipped over, causing him to fall against another piece of equipment. The injured patron alleged gross negligence in failing to properly anchor the dip station to the floor as per manufacturer's instructions, failing to post warning signs, and placing the station too close to other equipment (*Craig v. Lakeshore Athletic Club*, 1997). In *Svacha v. Waldens Creek Saddle Club* (2001), the plaintiff was injured when she fell from a horse because the saddle slipped. In the suit, she alleged gross negligence in not properly supervising, applying, and adjusting the saddle and tack. In *Beaver v. Foamcraft, Inc.* (2002), a go-kart racer was injured when foam padding was torn loose from a course barrier and struck the plaintiff, causing a multikart collision. In a Georgia case, an auto racer was injured in a collision and alleged the operators were grossly negligent in allowing race cars of different classes to compete in the same race (*Barbazza v. International Motor Sports Association*, 2000). In a wrongful death suit resulting from the death of a race sponsor in the pit area, the plaintiff alleged that the design of the track and its barriers constituted gross negligence. The court stated there was no evidence that the operator had consciously disregarded the safety of the participants in the infield area (*United States Auto Club, Inc. v. Smith*, 1999). Plaintiff skydiver sued Freefall Adventures, Inc. alleging reckless operation of the facility on the basis of the actions of another skydiver involved in plaintiff's injury. The court found no evidence of failure to supervise prior to the jump and stated that the operator had no way to control divers during their descent (*Dare v. Freefall Adventures, Inc.*, 2002). In *Waggoner v. Nags Head Water Sports, Inc.* (1998), Waggoner suffered a fractured vertebra when his rented jet ski suddenly accelerated, throwing him off the back.

Standard of Care. The standard of care required is that of a prudent professional. Who determines this standard? The standard may be set forth by statute, ordinance, or regulation; by organizations or agencies; or by the profession. For example, the National Operating Committee on Standards for Athletic Equipment (NOCSAE) sets the standard for football helmets; the Red Cross certification programs in first aid and life-saving have long been the principal requirement for competence where first aid is required and for lifeguards; playground equipment standards are set forth by the Consumer Products Safety Commission (CPSC); the American College of Sports Medicine (ACSM) has established competencies for fitness directors; and the National Athletic Trainers Association (NATA) for athletic trainers. *It behooves every provider to be aware of published standards and guidelines.* A professional will be held thereto. Where there are no published standards, the practices of the profession are the norm. In court, expert witnesses will attest to the accepted, desirable practices. Hence, it is very desirable for professionals to be knowledgeable and keep up-to-date with the latest and best practices through literature and attendance at conferences, workshops, and seminars (see also Chapter 5.21, *Standards of Practice*).

The professional standard of care does not vary based on the qualifications of the person in charge, whether experienced, older, or certified. If one accepts a responsibility for giving leadership to an activity or providing a service, one's performance is measured against the standard of care of a qualified professional **for that situation**. The participant is entitled to the standard of a prudent professional, not a standard dependent on the qualifications of whomever happens to be in charge. Thus, *the professional standard of care is situation-determined*—the nature of the activity, the participants, and the environmental conditions.

Nature of the Activity. The provider must be aware of the skill and abilities that a participant needs to successfully and safely participate in the activity. If the activity is complex (i.e., requires complex skills) the activity leader must understand the skills and abilities needed by the participant. If the activity is simple, the knowledge and proficiency required of the activity leader is less. The activity leader has a duty to identify the inherent risks of the activity and warn the participant of these risks. A leader who is not knowledgeable in and familiar with the activity cannot identify the risks or warn the participant (see also Chapter 2.32, *Supervision*).

Type of Participants. The service provider must not only be aware of the character of the participants (e.g., experienced or novice, highly skilled or lacking motor development, intellectually gifted or developmentally disabled, physically disabled or emotionally distressed), but also understand how to work with them in the specific activity. The provider should know which risks participants may be able to assume and thus better protect them from risks (see Chapter 2.32, *Supervision*).

Environmental Conditions. What is the physical environment related to the activity—layout or condition of the field or the gymnasium and the weather conditions (e.g., is it a hot and humid day, has there been rain resulting in a soggy or muddy field or slippery grass)? What is an "open and obvious" risk, which a participant may assume (see also Chapter 2.21, *Defenses Against Negligence,* and Chapter 3.20, *Premises Liability*)?

Proximate Cause

The act that did not meet the standard of care of a professional must be the cause-in-fact of the injury. *Just because the standard is not met does not mean the defendant is liable.* For example, there may be inadequate supervision, but lack of supervision may not have been the cause of the injury (*Baker v. Eckelkamp,* 1988); or a written organization standard may not have been complied with, but failure to comply may not be the cause of the injury; or instruction in the correct manner of using equipment may not have been given, but improper instruction may not have been the cause of the injury (*Burkart v. Health & Tennis Corp. of America,* 1987).

The act does not have to be the sole cause, but may be a "substantial factor." A minor hurt his wrist playing football and then volleyball. The health-care provider failed to diagnose a fracture from the X-ray, and subsequent surgery was necessary. The court held that there was no evidence of causation between the failure to diagnose the fracture and the subsequent need for surgery; to be proximate cause, negligent conduct must be the substantial factual cause of injury for which damages are sought (*Pascal v. Carter,* 1994). Or there may be a "superseding cause" by the injured. For example, a swimmer drowned in a city-owned pool. He had entered after hours through a hole in the fence or over a brick wall—a trespasser. Negligence was alleged of the city in failing to keep illegal swimmers out of the pool. The court held that even if the city's negligence was a substantial factor, decedent's conduct of being intoxicated (alcohol level .23 percent) was an unforeseeable superseding cause, and the decedent assumed the risk of his own conduct (*Garcia v. City of New York,* 1994; *Sanders v. Kuna Joint Sch. Dist.,* 1994; *Warech v. Trustees of Columbia Univ.,* 1994; *Williams v. Chicago Bd. of Educ.,* 1994).

Damage

The fourth element of negligence is that there must be compensable bodily injury or emotional harm. No damage, no liability. Usually damage is not difficult to prove and is not in question because without it a person would not be suing. Generally, compensable injuries fall into four categories: (1) economic loss (medical expenses, present and future; lost occupational earnings; custodial care; costs incurred by required substitute hired to do work while recovering); (2) physical pain and suffering (usually left to the jury to determine value); (3) emotional distress (e.g., fright and shock, anxiety, loss of peace of mind and happiness, loss of consortium, humiliation and embarrassment, inconveniences); and (4) physical impairment (temporary and permanent, partial or total, e.g., eyesight, hearing, use of an extremity). The plaintiff must submit documentation regarding costs and the jury establishes the amount of an award.

The injured/plaintiff also may seek punitive damages. Punitive damages are seldom awarded for ordinary negligence wherein a person is unintentionally injured, inasmuch as punitive damages are beyond compensatory damages and are to "punish" the tortfeasor or wrongdoer for intentional acts that harm. However, intention is implied as related to reckless disregard for the rights or safety of another, the deliberate indifference to an employee's rights, or child abuse (see also Chapter 4.11, *Assault and Battery*, and Chapter 2.35, *Human Resources Law*).

However, damage, the element, and damages, the result of liability, must be distinguished. What often is at issue is not whether there are compensable injuries, but the amount of damages and who should pay. The allocation of damages, including joint and several liability and under comparative fault, is addressed in Chapter 2.21, *Defenses Against Negligence*.

Significant Case

This is a case that illustrates the necessity that all four elements of negligence be present to show negligence. Each of the three allegations—negligent supervision, negligent instruction, and negligence in failing to inspect the plaintiff's shoes prior to play—fail because the plaintiff did not provide evidence showing that negligence in any of the three areas was a causative factor in producing the injury.

SANDERS V. KUNA JOINT SCHOOL DISTRICT
Court of Appeals of Idaho
125 Idaho 872; 876 P.2d 154; 1994 Ida. App. LEXIS 77
June 16, 1994, Filed

Opinion: Perry, J.

Josh Sanders appeals from a district court order granting summary judgment in favor of the respondents, Kuna Joint School District and Ron Emry. For the reasons stated below, we affirm the judgment.

Facts and Procedure

The underlying facts of this lawsuit are generally agreed upon by all of the parties. On May 15, 1990, Josh Sanders, a student at Kuna High School, attempted to slide into first base during a softball game and broke his ankle. Sanders had been enrolled in a specialized physical education class which provided instruction in weight lifting. On the date of the incident, the instructor, respondent Ron Emry, decided to have the class play softball outside instead of weight lifting. The students were not informed of this decision until after they appeared in the school's weight room. According to Sanders, on that particular day he was wearing a pair of "Saucony Shadows," a shoe designed specifically for running. Once on the softball field, Emry did not give instruction in the game of softball and supervised the game from behind a backstop. During one particular sequence of play, Sanders attempted to slide into first base in order to avoid being tagged out. During the slide, Sanders broke his ankle.

Following proper notice as required by I.C. @@ 6-901 et seq., Sanders filed suit against Emry and the school district as Emry's employer. Sanders claimed that Emry had been negligent by requiring the students to play softball, by failing to adequately supervise the students, including inspecting their footwear, and by failing to properly instruct the students on how to play softball.

After initial discovery was completed, the respondents filed a motion for summary judgment on grounds that, accepting the truth of Sanders' evidence, it did not prove a claim of negligence as a matter of fact. The district court granted the respondents' motion. Sanders now appeals to this Court, claiming that the district court improperly granted the summary judgment.

Analysis

In this case, Sanders would bear the burden of proof at trial to establish the elements of negligence. In Idaho, a cause of action in negligence requires proof of the following: (1) the existence of a duty, recognized by law, requiring the defendant to conform to a certain standard of conduct; (2) a breach of that duty; (3) a causal connection between the defendant's conduct and the resulting injury; and (4) actual loss or damage. Black Canyon Racquetball Club, Inc. v. Idaho First Nat'l Bank, N.A., 119 Idaho 171, 175–76, 804 P.2d 900, 904–05 (1991).

The respondents contended in their summary judgment motion that Sanders had failed to offer sufficient proof of causation. In order to properly analyze the evidence of causation, we must look separately at the negligent instruction and negligent supervision claims.

As to the negligent instruction claim, we agree with the district court that the record reveals a lack of evidence as to causation. Sanders simply claims that Emry failed to instruct the students in the game of softball and that such a failure caused the injury. Sanders does not, however, offer any evidence as to what the instructions should have been, how such instructions would have prevented the injury, or how Sanders improperly slid.

We agree with the conclusion of the district court that a rational jury could not find a causal connection between the failure to instruct and the resulting injury on the evidence presented. Therefore, the district court did not err in granting summary judgment as to Emry's alleged negligent instruction.

With respect to the negligent supervision claim, there are two separate issues we must consider—the actual supervision of the game as it was being played and the failure to inspect the footwear of the students. Again, as with the negligent instruction claim, Sanders' allegation of negligent supervision during the actual game must fail for lack of proof of causation. Sanders alleges that Emry failed to supervise the game and that such a failure caused the injury. Sanders does not offer any evidence, however, as to what the supervision of the game should have entailed, how that supervision was related to sliding or how such supervision would have prevented the injury. The only causal connection offered is the naked inference that if Emry had been standing on the field giving instruction to each student as the class played, this injury would not have occurred. Such an implausible inference does not rise to the level of evidence, however. In short, Sanders has failed to offer sufficient evidence of the causal connection between Emry's alleged negligent supervision and the injury. The district court's conclusion that no reasonable jury, on this evidence, could find a causal connection between the two was correct and, therefore, the summary judgment was properly granted as to this issue.

As to the issue of whether Emry was negligent in failing to inspect Sanders' shoes and should have prevented Sanders from playing in them, there is a mere scintilla of evidence presented. Sanders offered his own deposition testimony that he was playing in shoes that were designed for running. In response to the summary judgment motion, Sanders submitted the affidavit of the owner/manager of an athletic shoe store. The witness states that, "from a safety standpoint I would not recommend the use of the Saucony Shadow Shoe for use as a baseball or softball shoe." No evidence was offered, however, beyond the post hoc inference that because this was a running shoe with a wide sole, it must have caused the injury. Further, there was no evidence how a different shoe would have prevented the injury. Offering the mere coincidence that Sanders was injured and that

he was wearing running shoes at the time is not sufficient to establish a causal connection. There must be some evidence that the shoe caused the injury. The evidence offered, the testimony of Sanders and the owner/manager of the shoe store, is not a sufficient basis upon which a jury could base a verdict for Sanders.

Jurors may draw inferences of causation where such inferences are within the common experience of the average person. In this case, however, we do not believe that the common experience of the average person includes knowledge of the properties of specialized running shoes versus other types of footware. Nor do we think the average person possesses knowledge in the mechanics of sliding or injuries from sliding. Without sufficient evidence on the differences in design, purpose, and function of the shoes worn by Sanders and other shoes, no reasonable jury could infer causation under the facts as presented in this case. Likewise, with no evidence as to the actual mechanics of this injury, a jury should not be left to speculate as what might have been the cause. Sanders has simply failed to offer any competent evidence as to the cause of this injury. Alleging temporally coincidental events is not a sufficient basis upon which a jury could find or infer causation. Therefore, the district court did not err by granting the summary judgment.

As an alternative basis for its summary judgment argument, the respondents asserted that Sanders had failed to offer sufficient evidence as to the existence of a duty. Having decided that the summary judgment was proper on the issue of causation, we need not consider this issue here.

Conclusion

The respondents in this case properly carried their burden on their motion for summary judgment by showing that Sanders was unable to present sufficient evidence on the causal connection between the alleged negligence and the injury. The burden then shifted to Sanders to show that a genuine issue did exist. Sanders failed to meet this burden and therefore the summary judgment was properly granted.

Costs on this appeal are awarded to respondents; no attorney fees are awarded.

WALTERS, C.J., and LANSING, J., concur.

◇◇◇ **OTHER RELEVANT SIGNIFICANT CASES**

Recent Trends

The trends in the early 2000s are not so much related to the fundamental concepts of the elements of negligence as to the responsibilities of the injured participant and the provider (defendant). Most of these trends are discussed in other chapters, so only a brief highlighting of two trends is stated in this section.

Assumption of Risk

There is increased emphasis on the individuals injured taking more responsibility for their own actions in two types of assumption of risk—primary and secondary. Inherent risks of an activity are assumed by the participant under *primary assumption of risk*. The participant has "consented" to these risks by engaging in the activity, and the provider (defendant), thus, is not liable for injuries that occur due to those risks inherent. This places increased responsibility on the participant to know about the activity in which one is participating, understand it in relation to one's own abilities, and appreciate the risks inherent. *Secondary assumption of risk* has to do with the "conduct" of the injured participant. A participant is warned regarding possible injuries that may result in not following instructions, or an environmental condition that exists, or desirable equipment to be used—and then chooses not to heed such warnings by one's "conduct." This is a secondary assumption of risk or a contribution toward causing the injury, which then goes to ameliorating liability under comparative fault statutes. Thus, one of the most important aspects of a defense is that of **warnings**, a responsibility of the provider (defendant) (*Peart v. Ferro*, 2004; *Morgan v. State of Tenn.*, 2004).

Gross Negligence

Another trend is in regard to *gross negligence*. Although there are two types of "protection" for the provider through statutory immunity and valid exculpatory contract clauses in most states, there is increased effort to find the actions of the provider as "gross negligence," rather than ordinary negligence, to void those protections.

References

Cases

American Golf Corp. v. Manley, 473 S.E.2d 161 (1996).

Baker v. Eckelkamp, 760 S.W.2d 178 (Mo. Ct. App. 1988).

Barbazza v. International Motor Sports Association, Inc., 2000 Ga. App. LEXIS 1087.

Beaver v. Foamcraft, Inc., 2002 U.S. Dist. LEXIS 4651.

Blankenship v. Peoria Park Dist., 647 N.E.2d 287 (Ill. App. 1994).

Burkart v. Health & Tennis Corp. of America, 730 S.W.2d 367 (Tex. App. 1987).

Christensen v. Royal School Dist. No. 160, 124 P. 3d 283 (Wash. 2005).

City of Santa Barbara, (Cal 2nd App., 2006).

Chudasama v. Metropolitan Gov't of Nashville and Davidon County, 914 S.W.2d 922 (Tenn. Ct. App. 1995).

Craig v. Lakeshore Athletic Club, Inc., 1997 Wash. App. LEXIS 907.

Dare v. Freefall Adventures, Inc., 793 A.2d 125 (N.J., 2002).

Dukes v. Bethlehem Cent. Sch. Dist., 629 N.Y.S.2d 97 (App. Div. 1995).

Eastman v. Yutzy, 2001 Mass. Super. LEXIS 157.

Garcia v. City of New York, 617 N.Y.S.2d 462 (App. Div. 1994).

Hatch v. V.P. Fair Foundation, Inc., 1999 Mo. App. LEXIS 315.

Hinckley v. Krantz, 658 N.E.2d 797 (1995).

Holbrook v. Executive Conference Center, 464 S.E.2d 398 (Ga. 1995).

Jackson v. City of Franklin, 594 N.E.2d 1018 (1991).

Kahn v. East Side Union H.S. Dist., 75 P. 3d 30 (Cal. 2003).

Kleinknecht v. Gettysburg College, 989 F.2d 1360 (3rd Cir. 1993).

Koffman v. Garnett, 574 SE 2d 258 (Va. 2003).

Lamorie v. Warner Pacific College, 850 P.2d 401 (Or. App. 1993).

Locke v. Ozark City Board of Educ., 910 So.2d 1247 (Ala. 2005).

Martinez v. Swartzbaugh, 2002 Cal. App. Unpub. LEXIS 12192.

Morgan v. State of Tenn., 2004 WL 170352 (Tenn. Ct. App.).

Nielson v. Town of Amherst, 598 N.Y.S.2d 1022 (1993).

Pascal v. Carter, 647 A.2d 231 (Pa. Super. 1994).

Peart v. Ferro, 13 Cal. Rptr. 885 (2004).

Rhinehart v. Boys and Girls Club, 34 Cal. Rptr. 3d 677 (2005).

Roe v. North Adams Community School Corp., 647 N.E.2d 655 (Ind. Ct. App. 1995).

Sanders v. Kuna Joint Sch. Dist., 876 P.2d 154 (Idaho Ct. App. 1994).

Skinner v. Vacaville Unified School Dist., 43 Cal. Rptr. 2d 384 (1995).

Svacha v. Waldens Creek Saddle Club, 2001 Tenn. App. LEXIS 582.

Turner v. Rush Medical College, 1989.

United States Auto Club v. Smith, 1999 Ind. App. LEXIS 1831.

Waggoner v. Nags Head Water Sports, Inc., 1998 U.S. App. LEXIS 6792.

Warech v. Trustees of Columbia Univ., 610 N.Y.S.2d 480 (1994).

Williams v. Chicago Bd. of Educ., 642 N.E.2d 764 (1994).

Wolfgang v. Mid-America Motorsports, Inc., 1997 U.S. App. LEXIS 8817.

Woolsey v. Holiday Health Clubs and Fitness Centers, Inc., 820 P.2d 1201 (Colo. App. 1991).

Wu v. Shattuck-St. Mary's School, 2005.

Wu ex rel Tien v. Shattuck-St. Mary's School, 393 F. Supp. 2d 831 (2005).

Zavras v. Capeway Rovers Motorcycle Club, Inc., 1997 Mass. App. LEXIS 248.

Publications

Lea, M., & Loughman, E. J. (1993). Crew, compliance, touchdowns & torts: A survey exploring the legal needs of the modern athletic department and models for satisfying them. *The Entertainment and Sports Lawyer, 11,* 14–25.

Miller, B. D. (1996). *Hoke v. Cullinan:* Recklessness as the standard for recreational sports injuries [Note]. 23 *N. Ky. L. Rev.,* 409.

Rhim, A. (1996). The special relationship between student-athletes and colleges: An analysis of a heightened duty of care for the injuries of student-athletes [comment]. *Marquette Sports Law Journal, 7,* 329–348.

Sergent, R. S. (2000). Gross, reckless, wanton, and indifferent: Gross negligence in Maryland civil law. 30 *U. Balt. L. Rev., 1.*

Snow, B. A., & Thro, W. (1994). Redefining the contours of university liability: The potential implications of *Nero v. Kansas State University* [commentary]. *Ed. Law Rep., 90,* 989 (July 14, 1994).

van der Smissen, B. (1999). *Legal liability and risk management for public and private entities.* Cincinnati, OH: Anderson Publishing Company.

Wong, G. M., & Covell, D. (1995, March). Duty-bound. *Athletic Business,* 10, 12.

2.12 Which Parties Are Liable?

Doyice J. Cotten
Sport Risk Consulting

Recreation and sport law students often ask, "Why did they sue the school system or the recreation department when it was the teacher or the employee who was negligent?" or "If I am the supervisor, will I be liable if someone in my charge is negligent?" These questions represent just two of the many issues to be considered in answering the question of which parties may be liable when an injury occurs. Where in the past, the party sued was usually the corporate entity or the "deep pocket," today the trend is to sue everyone associated with the incident leading to the injury. For instance, suppose an aerobics instructor at a health club conducts an aerobics class in a room where speakers have been placed very near the participants. A participant loses his or her balance, falls into the speaker, and suffers injury. The participant might well name as individual defendants not only the aerobics instructor, but also the manager of the health club, the program director, the person responsible for room setup and maintenance, the owner of the health club, as well as the health club corporate entity.

The question to be addressed in this chapter is: Who is liable when a negligent act results in an injury? The reader should remember, however, that because the laws regarding liability in such situations differ somewhat from state to state, the discussion will be general in nature. State law in any one state may differ somewhat from these general concepts.

Fundamental Concepts

Three categories of parties may be liable in any given situation. The first category consists of the **employee** or service personnel involved. This is usually the person who committed the negligent act. This category includes persons who generally have actual contact with the participants (e.g., teacher, coach, weight room attendant, referee, aerobics instructor, scoutmaster). Also included in this category are the maintenance personnel or custodians who are often in direct contact with the participant.

The second category is the **administrative or supervisory personnel**. These are generally individuals who have some sort of administrative or supervisory authority over the service personnel. Examples include a director of recreation and intramurals, city recreation director, a principal, a head coach, a school superintendent, a manager of a health club, or a general manager of a professional baseball club. It is important to remember, however, that the classification of this individual can vary with the act being performed. For instance, the department head would be categorized as service personnel when teaching a class, but as administrative when performing scheduling duties.

The third category is the **corporate entity**. This category includes the governing body of the organization. Examples include the county school board, the municipal recreation board, the university board of regents, the corporation board of directors, or the local health club corporation.

Who Is Liable?

The liability of three categories or groups is addressed here—employees or service personnel, administrative/supervisory personnel, and the corporate entity. In general, both employees and administrative/supervisory personnel are liable for their own negligence. In addition, under the doctrine of *respondeat superior*, the employer or corporate entity is liable for injury to a person or property when the injury results from the negligent acts of the employee—so long as the injury occurs while the employee is acting within the scope of his or her authority. Although each can be liable under certain circumstances, state immunity statutes (intended to help protect them from liability in certain situations) affect that liability.

Immunity. Sovereign or governmental immunity, still in effect in some states, generally protects the public corporate entity but not its employees. However, officials of public bodies are generally immune from liability for discretionary acts performed within the scope of their authority (see Chapter 2.21, *Defenses Against Negligence*, and Chapter 2.22, *Immunity*), and a few states do provide the employee with immunity from liability for any act as long as it is in performance of the employee's duties and is not willful and wanton (van der Smissen, 1990). In addition, many states have passed limited liability statutes that provide immunity to certain individuals under selected circumstances. These statutes include recreational use statutes (landowners), Good Samaritan statutes (those who come to the aid of the injured), various sport volunteer statutes (volunteer coaches and officials), and assumption of risk statutes for specific activities, for general activities, and for hazardous recreational activities (providers of recreational activities and sports). Most states also have passed laws that allow either for the indemnification of a public employee or for liability insurance coverage of the employee (see Chapter 2.21, *Defenses Against Negligence*, and Chapter 5.25, *Managing Risk Through Insurance*).

Employees

In the absence of immunity, employees are individually liable for their own negligent conduct. The employee who performed the negligent act is generally the person in close contact with the participant (e.g., a teacher, a lifeguard, a camp counselor, an assistant coach, an athletic trainer, or a maintenance person). If the employee has a duty, breaches that duty by failing to meet the required standard of care, and that breach is the proximate cause of injury to the plaintiff, the employee is negligent and is legally liable. Sometimes employees think they are not liable because they have insurance coverage. Insurance does not prevent or bar liability; however, it may pay the damages in the event of an award.

The aerobics instructor in the example at the beginning of this chapter would fall into the service personnel category. If the instructor breaches a duty to the aerobics class by allowing participation too close to a hazard (the speaker), and that breach is shown to be the proximate cause of the injury, then the instructor is negligent and is legally liable for damages.

Administrative/Supervisory Personnel

Whereas the question regarding liability of service personnel is relatively simple, the question of liability of the administrative or supervisory personnel for the negligence of subordinates is much more complex. *When there is no immunity, the general rule is that administrative/supervisory personnel are individually liable for their own negligent conduct, but are not liable for the negligence of subordinates. The administrator/supervisor is liable, however, if the administrator owes a duty and acts (or omissions) of the administrator enhanced the likelihood of injury* (van der Smissen, 1990).

Administrative duties fall into five categories (van der Smissen, 1990). These duties are

1. to employ competent personnel and discharge those unfit;
2. to provide proper supervision and to have a supervisory plan;
3. to direct the services or program in a proper manner;
4. to establish safety rules and regulations and to comply with policy and statutory requirements; and
5. to remedy dangerous conditions and defective equipment or to warn users of dangers involved.

In the example involving the aerobics instructor, the health club manager would fall into the administrative/supervisory personnel category. Normally the manager is not liable for the negligence of the aerobics instructor unless the manager did something that enhanced the likelihood of injury. In this case, the manager hired a qualified, certified instructor, supervised the program adequately, and the aerobics program was conducted according to standards suggested by a national association. The manager may have breached an administrative/supervisory duty, however, by failing to establish or enforce safety rules regarding hazards on the floor or minimal clear space requirements or by failing to identify and remedy or warn of dangerous conditions. On the other hand, if the presence of the speaker on the floor was a one-time occurrence and the manager had safety rules regarding hazards and space and regularly enforced them, then the manager would not likely be liable because the manager breached no duty and did not increase the likelihood of injury.

The administrative or supervisory personnel are, however, liable for human resources or employment torts committed by their employees. They are liable when the administrator or supervisor is negligent in the employment process (see Chapter 2.35, *Human Resources Law*).

The Corporate Entity

The next question regards the liability of the corporate entity for the negligence of an employee whether that employee is classified as service personnel or administrative/supervisory personnel. The answer to this question is governed by the **doctrine of *respondeat superior***, which states that *the negligence of an employee is imputed to the corporate entity if the employee was acting within the scope of the employee's responsibility and authority and if the act was not grossly negligent, willful/wanton, and did not involve malfeasance* (van der Smissen, 1990). This doctrine is also referred to as **vicarious liability**. So, according to this doctrine, if an employee commits ordinary negligence while engaged in the furtherance of the employer's enterprise, the employer as well as the employee is liable. Refer to *Recent Trends* for a brief discussion of a broader interpretation of this doctrine.

Acts that are beyond the scope of responsibility and authority of the employee are considered ***ultra vires acts***, and generally, such an act relieves the corporate entity of liability via *respondeat superior*. The city in *Myricks v. Lynnwood Unified School District* (1999) was not liable for an accident transporting a team because the trip was not within the scope of the driver's responsibility. Exceptions to this rule occur when the corporate entity benefited from, had notice of, or condoned the act.

In the foregoing example, the aerobics instructor instructing the class was acting within the scope of responsibility and authority and was engaged in the furtherance of the employer's enterprise. If it is shown that allowing activity too near the speakers was ordinary negligence, then not only is the instructor liable, but liability is also imputed to the health club corporate entity.

Respondeat Superior in Human Resources Law. When employment torts are concerned, the corporate entity is liable for the intentional torts and criminal acts of its employees. For more detail, see Chapter 2.35, *Human Resources Law*.

Board Members. *Board members are not individually liable for the actions of the board or for the negligence of employees of the organization.* Board members are, however, individually liable for (1) collective acts of the board or individual acts that are outside the scope of authority; (2) breaches of statutory duty or violation of participant/employee Constitutional rights; and (3) intentional torts (e.g., assault and battery, slander, libel) (Kaiser & Robinson, 1999).

Willful Acts by an Employee. In some cases, the corporate entity can be liable even for **willful torts** committed by the employee (*Glucksman v. Walters*, 1995; *Rogers v. Fred R. Hiller Company of Ga., Inc.*, 1994; *Pelletier v. Bilbiles*, 1967). Each case involved an instance in which an employee who, while on duty, physically assaulted a patron. *Each court stated that a master is liable for the willful torts of his servant if the tort was committed within the scope of the servant's employment and in furtherance of his master's business.* The *Glucksman* court further stated that the fact that the specific method employed to accomplish the master's orders is not authorized nor does it relieve the master of liability.

Volunteers, Trainees, and Interns. The question often arises as to whether the acts of a **volunteer**, a **trainee**, or an **intern** fall under the doctrine of *respondeat superior*. In general, volunteers, trainees, and interns are liable individually for their own negligence. If they were under the control of the corporate entity and were acting within the scope of "employment," authority, and responsibility, the corporate entity is liable under the doctrine of *respondeat superior*. Volunteers of public or nonprofit organizations are immune from liability for their own negligence if they qualify under the federal Volunteer Protection Act of 1997 or a state volunteer immunity statute (see Chapter 2.21, *Defenses Against Negligence*, and Chapter 2.22, *Immunity*). In those instances, the corporate entity is still liable for the negligence of the volunteer (van der Smissen, 1990; Manley, 1995). It is worth noting that the volunteer, trainee, and intern *are held to the same standard of care as that of an experienced, competent professional.*

University Athletes.   An issue that sometimes arises is whether a university is liable under *respondeat superior* for the negligent acts of a university varsity athlete (*Townsend v. The State of California*, 1987; *Hanson v. Kynast*, 1986; *Brown v. Day*, 1990). Courts have ruled the applicability of the doctrine requires an individualized determination of whether a master–servant relationship exists between the tortfeasor and the university (*Townsend v. The State of California*, 1987). The *Townsend* court concluded that whether on scholarship or not, the athlete is not an employee and the university is not vicariously liable for the athlete's negligent acts.

Joint and Several Liability and Uniform Contribution Among Joint Tortfeasors.   The **joint and several liability doctrine** holds that one defendant can be held liable for the total damages even though other defendants were also at fault. If more than one party is found liable, the court does not limit the injured party's recovery against each to a proportionate share of fault. A classic example of this can be found in *Walt Disney World Co. v. Wood* (1987), where Disney was found 1 percent at fault, plaintiff was 14 percent at fault, and other defendants were 85 percent at fault. Under joint and several liability, Disney was ordered to pay the entire 86 percent of damages. However, in the 1980s, most states enacted statutes that provide for **uniform contribution among joint tortfeasors** in equitable portions, but not necessarily equal portions. When one tortfeasor has paid a disproportionate share of damages, that tortfeasor can file suit against the other tortfeasor in a separate action.

In *Universal Gym Equipment, Inc. v. Vic Tanny International, Inc.* (1994), the plaintiff was injured while working on a Universal machine. She had signed a waiver that protected Tanny from litigation, so she sued Universal and obtained a settlement of $225,000. Universal then commenced action against Tanny alleging failure to maintain safe premises and that Tanny had an obligation to indemnify or contribute to any settlement between the injured plaintiff and Universal. Michigan law allowed Tanny to use any defense that would have been valid against liability for the injury to exonerate it from liability for contribution. Thus, the waiver signed by the injured party protected Tanny from liability for contribution to Universal. The court remanded the case to determine if Tanny was grossly negligent—in which case, the waiver would not protect Tanny from liability for the injury nor from liability for the contribution.

Limiting Corporate Liability by Contract

Corporate entities frequently limit their liability through the use of various types of contractual arrangements. The following are four methods in common use.

Leasing Facilities

The use of sport and recreational facilities by another group or organization is a common practice. The details of these transactions can range from free use by oral agreement to a formal lease with a rental charge. In any case, the question is: What is the liability of the owner of the premises when an injury occurs on the premises while being used by another organization? To determine such liability, one must first determine whether the injury was premise related (resulting from unsafe premises) or activity related (resulting from the conduct of the activity) (van der Smissen, 1990). Unless specified in the contract, the owner generally remains liable for premise-related injuries. Second, if the injury is activity related, one must determine if the owner retained *control* over the activity or the use of the premises. Essentially, the liability for activity-related injury generally lies with the party that had control over the activity. Thus, if a university leases an arena to a promoter of an ice skating event and retains no control over how the activity is conducted, the university would not be liable for activity-related injuries, but might be liable if the injury resulted from an unsafe facility.

Facility owners generally require that the leasing party provide a certificate of insurance showing adequate liability insurance for the event. Many require that the owners be named as a co-insured on the policy (see Chapter 2.21, *Defenses Against Negligence*, and Chapter 3.20, *Premises Liability*).

Independent Contractors

An **independent contractor** is an individual or a company that contracts to perform a particular task using his own methods and is subject to the employer's control only as to end product or final result of his work (Black's Law Dictionary, 1990). Examples of persons that are often classified as independent contractors include referees for a contest, an aerobics specialist at a health club, a team physician, or a diving business that teaches scuba diving for a municipal recreation department.

A major reason that employers use independent contractors is to reduce the amount of liability faced by the service provider. *The general rule is that if an injury results from the negligence of the independent contractor, the liability for negligence is shifted from the employer to the independent contractor* (see Table 1 in Chapter 2.21, *Defenses Against Negligence*). Thus, the employer avoids much of the potential liability posed by offering the activity. However, the employer does retain some responsibilities. The employer is responsible (1) for using reasonable care in selecting a competent independent contractor and for inspection after completion; (2) for keeping the premises reasonably safe for invitees and employees; and (3) for "inherently dangerous activities" (e.g., activities presenting substantial harm unless precautions are taken such as fireworks displays, keeping of dangerous animals, ultrahazardous activities).

In *Hatch v. V.P. Fair Foundation, Inc.* (1999), a patron was injured when an independent contractor at a fair failed to attach the bungee cord to the platform prior to the jump. The court ruled that a landowner who hires an independent contractor to perform an "inherently dangerous activity" has a nondelegable duty to take special precautions to prevent injury from the activity. The landowner remains liable for the torts of the contractor even though the landowner was not negligent.

Often, whether one is an employee or an independent contractor is at issue. Courts generally rule that one is an **employee** if one is hired, paid a set wage or salary, is often trained by the employer, works on an ongoing basis, must perform the work as directed by the employer, and is paid by the hour, week, or month. An **independent contractor** is one who is generally engaged for a specific project, usually for a set sum, often paid at the end of the project, may do the job in one's own way, often furnishes one's own equipment, is subject to minimal restrictions, and is responsible only for the satisfactory completion of the job (*Jaeger v. Western Rivers Fly Fisher*, 1994). The distinction is important from a financial standpoint because the classification can affect the amount owed for (1) unemployment contributions; (2) workers' compensation; (3) FICA; and (4) federal and state income withholding. The IRS and other relevant agencies can levy heavy fines for failure to pay sufficient taxes or fees when companies have been improperly classified as independent contractors.

Unfortunately, there is no specific number of these conditions that must be met and no magic formula for weighing these conditions to determine if, indeed, one is an independent contractor. A review board or court may determine that failure, to some degree, to meet any one of the conditions is sufficient to invalidate the claim for independent contractor status. The difficulty in determining whether the person is properly classified as an employee or an independent contractor is illustrated in a recent case dealing with fitness instructors. Fitness Plus provided fitness classes for corporate clients on the premises of the client (*In the Matter of Fitness Plus, Inc.*, 2002). Fitness Plus would assess the needs of the client, contact one of about 30 instructors, negotiate a fee, bill the client, pay the instructor regardless of profit or loss, pay the instructor every two weeks, and report their income on a 1099 form. Most of these procedures fit the conditions for an independent contractor. In selecting the instructors, Fitness Plus conducted interviews; checked background, training, certification, and experience; and usually observed them in a class—seemingly meeting the requirement that they select qualified contractors. Instructors worked generally one to six hours weekly and signed an agreement that their status was that of an independent contractor. The court determined that there was sufficient evidence that Fitness Plus exercised sufficient direction and control over the services of the instructors to support the Unemployment Insurance Appeal Board ruling that they were employees.

Indemnification

An **indemnification agreement** is an agreement by which one party agrees to indemnify, reimburse, or restore a loss of another on the occurrence of an anticipated loss. They are sometimes referred to as **hold harmless agreements** or **save harmless agreements**. Indemnification agreements can be very effective when one business indemnifies another business against loss; however, they are not always enforceable when used as a waiver of liability in which the user of the service must agree to indemnify the service provider for loss resulting from the negligence of the provider (see also Chapter 2.21, *Defenses Against Negligence*).

Waivers

The corporate entity may protect itself and its employees from liability by use of waivers of liability in which the participant or service user contractually releases the business from liability for negligence by the corporate entity or its employees (see also Chapter 2.23, *Waivers and Releases*).

Corporate Liability in Other Situations

Financial Sponsorship

Many organizations provide financial sponsorship for recreational activities or teams. **Financial sponsorship** exists when the sponsoring organization provides financial support but exercises no control over the activity. An example of this type of sponsorship would be civic clubs or private businesses sponsoring recreation department softball teams. Financial sponsorship of this sort generally carries with it no liability. Whether the sponsoring organization is liable for injuries that occur due to negligence depends on several things: (1) was the person in charge an agent of the organization?; (2) did the organization have control over the activity?; and (3) was a duty owed to the participant? (van der Smissen, 1990).

In *Wilson v. United States of America* (1993), the issue was whether an agency relationship existed between the Boy Scouts of America and adult volunteers of a troop so as to provide for vicarious liability for the negligence of the adult troop leaders. The court stated that liability based on *respondeat superior* requires evidence of a master–servant relationship. In this case, there was no liability because the national organization exerts no direct control over the leaders or the activities of individual troops. In an older case, Boy Scouts of America was found liable for the negligence of an adult volunteer at a Scout-o-Rama controlled by the regional council. The key difference was control (*Riker v. Boy Scouts of America*, 1959).

Program Sponsorship and Joint Programming

Program sponsorship exists when an organization or entity organizes an event or maintains control over an event. An example would be when a recreation department organizes and conducts a Fourth of July slate of special activities. **Joint programming** is when more than one entity is involved in program sponsorship. Examples of such sponsorship or programming include an NCAA championship event, an event sponsored and conducted by the University of Georgia and the Southeastern Conference, and a high school game under the auspices of the state high school athletic association.

When leagues or athletic associations exert control over the conduct of the game and the eligibility of the participants, duties are created and liability for negligence emerges. When two organizations are involved in joint programming or joint sponsorship of an activity, each is responsible and liable for injuries resulting from negligence.

Governing Organization Sponsorship

Governing organizations of sports or other activities often sponsor events or lend their name to such events. If the organization has no hand in the actual conduct of the event, it owes no duty to the participants. Of course, there is no liability when there is no duty.

In *Lautieri v. Bai v. USA Triathlon, Inc.* (2003), the liability of a governing organization was at issue. The governing organization was USA Triathlon, Inc. (USAT), and the program sponsor was William Fiske d/b/a Fiske Independent Race Management. Fiske was found to be grossly negligent; however, the court held that for USAT to be liable, it must be established that USAT owed a duty of care to the plaintiff. To accomplish this, the plaintiff would have to show that such a duty has a source (1) existing in social values and customs or that (2) USAT voluntarily, or for consideration, assumed a duty of care to the plaintiff. Evidence indicated that USAT's only involvement was its approval of the application of the organizer of the event. There was no evidence to indicate that USAT was obligated to or was expected to participate in the planning, operation, or supervision of the race.

Joint Ventures

A **joint venture** is "an agreement between two or more persons, ordinarily, but not necessarily limited to a single transaction for the purpose of making a profit" (*Jaeger v. Western Rivers Fly Fisher*, 1994, p. 1224). Some essential elements for a joint venture include combining of property, money, efforts, skill, labor, knowledge, and a sharing of losses and profits. A group of college students who wanted to go white-water rafting, put up notices informing other students of the proposed trip, met, planned the trip, shared resources, and went on the trip, would form a joint venture. It would not be a joint venture if the campus recreation department conceived the idea of the trip, publicized the proposed trip, helped them plan the trip, and supplied equipment for the trip. In the latter case, the university would be a sponsor of the activity and would be liable in the event of negligence. In a true joint venture, there is no group sponsorship and, hence, no liability for the corporation.

Apparent Authority

Apparent authority is a legal doctrine that describes a situation in which the principal (a person or organization) treats a second party in such a way as to lead a third party to think that the second party is an agent of the principal or has the authority to bind the principal. Under agency law, the principal is responsible for or liable for the acts of a second party that the principal allows to appear to have authority. Those in the recreation and tourism industries, in particular, need to take steps to ensure that the relationship between the organization and independent contractors creates no confusion that might cause the client to rely on the appearance of an agency relationship between the principal and the apparent agent.

In a 2004 case (*Cash v. Six Continents Hotels*), two tourists were injured while climbing Dunn's River Falls in Jamaica. Although the tour was provided by Harmony Tours (which had a desk in the hotel lobby), the plaintiffs had booked the tour through their hotel. They claimed the hotel was liable for Harmony Tours' negligence under the doctrine of apparent authority because the hotel allowed it to appear that the company was an agent of the hotel. The court found for the hotel because the hotel did not make representations of an affiliation, had a large sign stating "Harmony Tours" near the desk, and included a statement on the ticket informing that the company was an independent contractor and that the hotel was not responsible.

Significant Case

This significant case was chosen because it addresses the duties and liability of several categories of defendants—vicarious liability of the team sponsor of the player who committed the act resulting in injury, the other financial (or team) sponsor, the softball league hosting the tournament, a national softball association that sponsors the league, the owner of the property, and the insurer of some of the defendants. Also included is a discussion of assumption of risk and participant responsibilities.

ALLEN V. DOVER CO-RECREATIONAL SOFTBALL LEAGUE

THE SUPREME COURT OF NEW HAMPSHIRE
2002 N.H. LEXIS 145
Opinion Issued: September 30, 2002

duggan, J. * * *

The plaintiffs allege the following facts. On September 13, 1998, Carol Allen was injured while participating in a recreational softball game when an errantly thrown softball struck her in the head as she ran to first base. The game was part of an adult, co-recreational, slow-pitch softball tournament.

The defendants are all organizations associated with the softball tournament. The teams playing in the tournament were part of defendant Dover Co-Recreational Softball League (league), which is sponsored by defendant Amateur Softball Association, Inc. (ASA). The ASA promulgates rules that govern the play of its member leagues. The teams playing in this particular game were sponsored by defendant Daniel's Sports Bar and Grill (Daniel's) and defendant Thompson Imports (Thompson). Team sponsors provided t-shirts for the players. The game was played on a field owned by defendant Martel-Roberge American Legion Post #47 (American Legion). Defendant Bollinger Fowler Company (Bollinger) provided liability insurance coverage for the league, ASA, the American Legion, the Daniel's team and the Thompson team.

On the day the plaintiff was injured, she was playing for the Daniel's team in a one-pitch tournament. As set forth in ASA official rules, the softball used when women batted was smaller than the softball used when men batted. This use of different balls is intended to allow the women to hit more competitively with the men. The defendants did not recommend, require or provide helmets for players. Although a slow-pitch game under the ASA official rules is played with five men and five women for each team, the game on September 13 was played with seven men and three women on each team.

When batting for the first time on September 13, Carol Allen hit a ball toward shortstop. A male player for the Thompson team fielded the ball and threw it toward first base. His throw, however, was inaccurate and struck Carol Allen in the head. * * *

The plaintiffs subsequently filed a writ alleging several counts of negligence. First, the plaintiffs allege that the league and Daniel's acted negligently when they conducted the softball game "without utilizing all reasonable safety precautions including but not limited to recommending, requiring, or providing batting helmets for the players, using less dangerous softballs, and maintaining proper male/female player ratios." The plaintiffs further allege that ASA breached its duty to promulgate and enforce rules that required batting helmets to be worn in softball games, use of a less dangerous softball and each team to play with five men and five women, and to otherwise minimize the risk of injury to participants in co-recreational softball games. The plaintiffs also allege that ASA "had a duty to warn, advise, inform and instruct its members regarding the risk of injury to participants in co-recreational softball games and the manner in which such risks could be minimized." As for the American Legion, the plaintiffs claim that as the owner of the softball field, it "had a duty to require that softball games played on its field were played pursuant to rules and in a manner which minimized the risk of injury to participants." The plaintiffs further allege that Thompson "is vicariously liable for the negligence of its shortstop in errantly throwing the softball." Finally, the plaintiffs allege that because Bollinger provided risk management services to its insureds—the league, ASA, the American Legion, the Daniel's team and the Thompson team—"Bollinger had a duty to warn, advise, inform, and instruct its insureds regarding the risk of injury to participants in co-recreational softball games and the manner in which such risks could be minimized." (bold added)

All of the defendants moved to dismiss the case arguing, among other things, that they owed no duty to protect Carol Allen from the inherent risks of injury that arose out of her participation in the softball game. * * *

* * * The court ruled that participants do not owe a duty to other participants to refrain from "injury-causing events which are known, apparent or reasonably foreseeable consequences of the participation" but rather participants "in recreational sporting events owe a duty to other participants to refrain from reckless or intentional conduct [that may injure the other partici-

pants]." Because the plaintiffs alleged that Thompson's shortstop acted negligently, not recklessly or intentionally, when he errantly threw the ball, the court concluded, "Thompson Imports cannot be held vicariously liable under the circumstances of this case."

* * * . The court ruled that the league, ASA, Daniel's, and Thompson, as sponsors, and the American Legion, as owner of the field, owed the plaintiffs "a duty to refrain from reckless[ly] or intentional[ly causing injury to a participant]." Rather than acting recklessly or intentionally to create a risk of injury, the court observed that the defendants' alleged conduct involved the ordinary risks of injury inherent in playing recreational softball. * * * Accordingly, the trial court dismissed all counts of the plaintiffs' writ.

On appeal, the plaintiffs argue that the trial court erred by applying the doctrine of assumption of the risk. Applying the doctrine, the plaintiffs contend, was error because under New Hampshire common law, the doctrine was historically applied only to employer-employee relationships and supplanted altogether when the legislature enacted the comparative fault statute. *See* RSA 507:7-d (1997).

* * *

The comparative fault statute does not apply in this case because the defendants do not claim that Carol Allen acted negligently in causing her own injury; rather, they argue that they owed no duty to protect her against the risk that she would be injured by an errantly thrown softball.

ASSUMPTION OF THE RISK

We next determine the applicability of the doctrine of assumption of the risk. The defendants and the plaintiffs disagree on what the term "assumption of the risk" means and how it should be applied in this case. To resolve this issue, we must examine the history and various uses of the term "assumption of the risk."

The term "assumption of the risk" has been used to express distinct common law theories, derived from different sources, which apply when a plaintiff has knowingly exposed herself to particular risks The three distinct legal concepts encompassed by the term are: (1) a plaintiff's consent in exposing herself to a defendant's negligence; (2) a defendant's negligence together with a plaintiff's negligence which causes the plaintiff injury; and (3) a plaintiff's voluntary participation in a reasonable activity with known risks such that a defendant owes no duty to the plaintiff to protect against harm arising from those risks.

* * *

The third theory, the doctrine of primary implied assumption of the risk, applies when a plaintiff voluntarily and reasonably enters into some relation with a defendant, which the plaintiff reasonably knows involves certain obvious risks such that a defendant has no duty

to protect the plaintiff against injury caused by those risks. * * * This primary implied assumption of risk doctrine, the defendants argue, applies to this case. The plaintiffs, however, contend that this doctrine applies only where there is an employer-employee relationship.

* * *

When, however, a defendant owes no duty to a plaintiff in light of a particular risk, the defendant cannot be held accountable to a plaintiff who is injured upon the plaintiff's voluntary encounter with that risk. * * * In other words, a defendant who has no duty cannot be negligent. Moreover, contrary to the plaintiffs' contention, the comparative fault statute does not supplant this common-law doctrine because a plaintiff's fault is irrelevant in determining whether a defendant has a duty. It is this third theory that is applicable here.

DEFENDANTS' DUTY

Under this theory, we must determine what duty if any the defendants owed to Carol Allen to protect her against the risk that she would be injured when she participated in the softball game. The defendants argue that they owed no duty to protect her against the risk that she might be injured when a softball struck her head because that was an ordinary risk of playing co-recreational softball, a reasonable activity in which she voluntarily participated. We conclude that when Carol Allen voluntarily played softball—a reasonable activity that she knew involved obvious risks—the defendants had no duty to protect her against injury caused by those risks.

However, even if there is no duty to protect a plaintiff against ordinary risks, we must address the standard of care that co-participants, sponsors and organizers owe to participants in recreational sports activities when extraordinary risks are alleged. Generally, "persons owe a duty of care only to those who are foreseeably endangered by their conduct and only with respect to those risks or hazards whose likelihood made the conduct unreasonably dangerous."

* * *

"We believe that the negligence standard, properly understood and applied, is suitable for recreational athletic activities because the conduct of a participant, sponsor or organizer is measured against the conduct that a reasonable participant, sponsor or organizer would engage in under the circumstances. *See Lestina v. West Bend Mut. Ins. Co.*, 501 N.W.2d 28, 33 (Wis. 1993); * * * When one creates an unreasonable risk under the circumstances, however, he has breached the standard of care. *Crawn*, 630 A.2d at 373

To determine the appropriate standard of care to be applied to participants, sponsors and organizers of recreational athletics, we consider: (1) the nature of the sport involved; (2) the type of contest, i.e., amateur, high school, little league, pick-up, etc.; (3) the ages, physical characteristics and skills of the participants; (4)

the type of equipment involved; and (5) the rules, customs and practices of the sport, including the types of contact and the level of violence generally accepted. *See Lestina*, at 33. "A defendant may be held liable to the plaintiff for [unreasonably] creating or countenancing risks other than risks inherent in the sport, or for increasing inherent risks, and in any event will be held liable for reckless] or intentional injurious conduct totally outside the range of ordinary activity involved in the sport, but liability should not place unreasonable burdens on the free and vigorous participation in the sport." A defendant, however, may not be held liable for negligent, or even reckless or intentional injurious conduct that is *not* outside the range of ordinary activity involved in the sport.

In this case, we first consider the nature of the sport of softball. The sport of softball is a reasonable activity, commonly played by men, women and children of varying skill levels. Consistent with this wide variety of players, a wide variety of rules are applied. Whether played by men, women or children, skilled or unskilled, participation in a softball game generally gives rise to the risk that a player may be struck by a ball that has been hit by a batter or thrown by a fielder.

* * *

Under the circumstances of this game, the only duty the defendants had was not to act in an unreasonable manner that would increase or create a risk of injury outside the range of risks that flow from participation in an adult co-recreational softball game. The plaintiffs argue the defendants' duty specifically included taking the following actions: (1) participants had a duty to not make errant throws when fielding the ball; (2) the league, Daniel's and Thompson had a duty to utilize all reasonable safety precautions in their conduct of the games; (3) the American Legion and ASA had a duty to promulgate or enforce rules that would minimize the risk of injury; and (4) ASA and Bollinger had a duty to warn, advise, inform and instruct the league regarding the risk of injury to participants and the manner in which such risks could be minimized. We examine each act the plaintiffs contend was required of the defendants in turn.

The plaintiffs first argue that the shortstop had a duty to not make an errant throw when fielding the ball. Participants in an adult co-recreational slow-pitch softball game have a duty to not create an unreasonable risk of injury. When fielding the ball, therefore, a fielder has a duty to not act unreasonably. In other words, the fielder has a duty to not act in a manner outside the range of the ordinary activity involved in playing softball. A fielder, however, does *not* have a duty to make only accurate throws. Because reasonable fielders commonly make errant throws, being injured by an errant throw is a common risk inherent in and arising out of a softball game. A fielder therefore cannot be held liable

for errant throws that reasonably flow from participation. * * * Accordingly, the plaintiffs' claim based upon the shortstop's errant throw does not constitute a legal basis for relief.

The plaintiffs next argue that the league, Daniel's and Thompson had a duty to utilize all reasonable safety precautions in their conduct of the games. * * * Because we assume the facts as pled by the plaintiffs are true, we will assume that Daniel's and Thompson as team sponsors, in fact, conducted the game. To the extent a team sponsor conducts a game, it has a duty to conduct the game in a manner that does not unreasonably increase the risks that flow from the ordinary play of the game. *See Hacking*, 143 N.H. at 553.

The plaintiffs' complaint alleges that the team sponsors had a duty to conduct this game using certain equipment, specifically batting helmets and "less dangerous softballs." While the plaintiffs allege that batting helmets should have been used when conducting this game, they do not allege that batting helmets are ordinarily worn by players in adult co-recreational slow-pitch softball games. The ASA rules the plaintiffs allege applied to this game do not require batting helmets to be worn. Further, the plaintiffs do not allege that reasonable teams use batting helmets when playing in adult co-recreational softball games. They have thus failed to make an allegation that gives rise to a duty for these team sponsors to recommend, require or provide helmets when conducting an adult co-recreational softball game. Thus, under the circumstances of this game, not recommending, requiring or providing batting helmets did not unreasonably increase or create a new risk outside of the range of ordinary activity.

The plaintiffs further allege that the softball manufactured for use when adult men play softball is less dangerous than the softball manufactured for use when children and women play softball. * * * Because the risk that a player may suffer an injury upon being struck by a ball is an ordinary risk incident to playing softball, using the smaller softball manufactured for use by women to allow the women in a co-ed game to hit more competitively with men did not unreasonably increase the ordinary risks inherent in the game. Therefore, the team sponsors' duty to Carol Allen did not include using the least "dangerous" softball available when conducting an adult co-recreational softball game. * * *

Finally, the plaintiffs allege that the defendants had a duty to adhere to a strict five-male to five-female ratio * * *. Being struck by a ball thrown by a male player is an ordinary risk inherent in co-ed softball. The ratio rule did not unreasonably increase or conceal the risk that Carol Allen would be struck by a ball thrown by a male player. * * *. Thus, by not using a strict five-female to five-male ratio the defendants did not unreasonably increase her risk of injury or create a new risk outside the range of risks that ordinarily flow from participation in an adult co-recreational softball game. Therefore the defendants did not owe a duty to Carol Allen to adhere to the five-male to five-female ratio.

* * *

The plaintiffs' writ also alleges that defendants American Legion, as owner of the softball field, and ASA, as sponsor of the league, had a duty to promulgate or enforce rules that would minimize the risk of injury. * * *. The defendants thus have a duty to promulgate or enforce rules that minimize the risk of injury, if without those rules the game is otherwise unreasonably dangerous. While the plaintiffs allege that promulgating and enforcing rules that required batting helmets, a larger, softer softball, or a certain male-female ratio would make the game safer, they do not allege that failing to promulgate and enforce such rules created risks outside the risks ordinarily involved in softball and made the game unreasonably dangerous. Consequently, the plaintiffs' writ does not allege facts that, if true, would show that the defendants breached the duty they owed to Carol Allen to promulgate and enforce rules that were necessary to minimize injury in an otherwise unreasonably dangerous sport. Therefore, it does not allege a basis for legal relief.

Finally, the plaintiffs allege ASA and Bollinger had a duty to warn, advise, inform and instruct the league regarding the risk of injury to participants and the manner in which such risks could be minimized. As we have previously stated, the defendants may not be held liable to the plaintiffs for creating or countenancing those risks inherent in the sport of softball. * * * Thus, the defendants may be held liable if the plaintiffs allege that a reasonable person would customarily warn, advise, inform and instruct the league regarding the risk of injury to participants and the manner in which such risks could be minimized and their failure to do so caused the plaintiff's injuries. The plaintiffs, however, do not allege that reasonable sponsors and insurers customarily warn or instruct leagues regarding the risk of injury to participants. Therefore the defendants, in this case, had no duty to warn and instruct the league regarding the risk of injury.

In sum, the plaintiffs' writ does not allege any facts from which one could reasonably infer that the standard of care required the defendants to recommend, require or provide helmets, use a less dangerous softball or maintain a ratio of five men and five women on each team, and therefore, the writ does not allege sufficient facts that the defendants unreasonably created a new risk outside the ordinary risks or unreasonably increased the inherent risk that Carol Allen would be injured when struck by a softball while participating in an adult co-recreational softball game. * * * Because the plaintiffs' allegations do not constitute a legal basis for relief, the trial court properly dismissed the case.

Affirmed.

BROCK, C.J., and DALIANIS, J., concurred.

 OTHER RELATED SIGNIFICANT CASES

| Chapter 2.33 *Transportation* | Chapter 5.26 *Workers' Compensation* |

Recent Trends

Broadened Scope of *Respondeat Superior* Doctrine

Traditionally, under the doctrine of *respondeat superior*, an employer is liable for injuries to the person or property of third persons resulting from actions by an employee that were within the scope of employment, but the employer carried no liability for unauthorized acts by employees including willful acts to injure another. In recent years, however, many jurisdictions have extended vicarious immunity to include workplace torts (i.e., the wrongdoing of those in positions of authority), sexual assaults, sexual harassment, and abuse by a party in a position of authority over children (Carter, 1995; van der Smissen, 1996; *Williams v. Butler*, 1991). The concept of "acting within the scope of authority" continues to apply, but is more broadly interpreted to mean any activities that carry out the objectives of the employer (van der Smissen, 1996) and those during which the employer was or could have been exercising control of the activities of the employee (*Longin v. Kelly*, 1995).

Apart from the doctrine of *respondeat superior*, the employer may be held liable for the intentional acts of the employee in cases of employment process negligence (i.e., when the employer in the employment process negligently allows the assignment of an unfit employee or fails to use reasonable care to discover the unfitness of an employee). Liability of the employer can result from negligent hiring, negligent supervision, negligent training, negligent retention, and negligent referral of an employee that is unfit (Carter, 1995; van der Smissen, 1996).

To find a supervisory school official liable for the acts of a subordinate in a case involving physical sexual abuse, the United States Court of Appeals for the Fifth Circuit (*Doe v. Taylor Independent School District*, 1994) established that the supervisor learned of a clear pattern of inappropriate sexual behavior, demonstrated "deliberate indifference" toward the safety of the abused student, and such failure to act resulted in injury to the student. The court in discussing "deliberate indifference," stated that it is sometimes used interchangeably with such terms as "callous disregard," "grossly negligent," and "callous indifference." It explained, however, that "gross negligence" involves a heightened degree of negligence where "deliberate indifference" involves a lesser form of intent. The court held that a supervisory official's liability for the abusive acts of a subordinate arises only when the plaintiff shows that the action or inaction of the official demonstrated "deliberate indifference" to the student's right to personal security and freedom from sexual assault (see Chapter 2.35, *Human Resources Law*).

References

Cases

Cash v. Six Continents Hotels.

Doe v. Taylor Independent School District, 15 F.3d 443 (Texas 1994).

Glucksman v. Walters, 659 A.2d 1217 (Conn. 1995).

Hanson v. Kynast, 494 N.E.2d 1091 (Ohio 1986).

Hatch v. U.P. Fair Foundation, Inc., 1999 MO. App. LEXIS 315.

In the Matter of Fitness Plus, Inc., 2002 N.Y. App. Div. LEXIS 3830.

Jaeger v. Western Rivers Fly Fisher, 855 F. Supp. 1217 (Utah 1994).

Lautieri v. Bai v. USA Triathlon, Inc., 2003 Mass. Super. LEXIS 290.

Brown v. Day, 1990.

Longin v. Kelly, 875 F. Supp. 196 (NY 1995).

Myricks v. Lynnwood Unified School District, 87 Cal. Rptr. 2d 734 (Cal. App. 2 Dist. 1999).

Pelletier v. Bilbiles, 227 A.2d 251 (Conn. 1967).

Riker v. Boy Scouts of America, 183 N.Y.S.2d 484 (1959).

Rogers v. Fred R. Hiller Company of Georgia, Inc., 448 S.E.2d 46 (Ga. 1994).

Townsend v. The State of California, 237 Cal. Rptr. 146 (Cal. 1987).

Universal Gym Equipment, Inc. v. Vic Tanny International, Inc., 526 N.W.2d 5 (Mich. 1994).

Walt Disney World Co. v. Wood, 489 So.2d 61 (1986); 515 So.2d 198 (Fla. 1987).

Williams v. Butler, 577 So.2d 1113 (La. App. 1 Cir. 1991).

Wilson v. United States of America, 989 F.2d 953 (Mo. 1993).

Publications

Carter, P. (1995). Employer's liability for assault, theft, or similar intentional wrong committed by employee at home or business of customer, 13 A.L.R.5th 217.

Kaiser, R., & Robinson, K. (1999). Risk management. In B. van der Smissen, M. Moiseichik, V. Hartenburg, & L. Twardgik (Eds.), *Management of park and recreation agencies* (pp. 713–741). Ashburn, VA: National Recreation and Parks Association.

Manley, A. (1995). Liability of charitable organization under *respondeat superior* doctrine for tort of unpaid volunteer, 82 *A.L.R.* 3d 1213.

van der Smissen, B. (1990). *Legal liability and risk management for public and private entities.* Cincinnati, OH: Anderson Publishing Co.

van der Smissen, B. (1996). *Legal liability and risk management for public and private entities.* Cincinnati, OH: Anderson Publishing Co. (Prepublication supplement)

2.21 Defenses Against Negligence

Doyice J. Cotten

Sport Risk Consulting

In today's litigious society, lawsuits against recreation and sport businesses are common. The fact that a recreation or sport business is sued, however, does not necessarily mean that loss of the suit is inevitable. Many effective defenses may be used by the defendant. Most common defenses are presented in this and the three subsequent chapters (see Chapter 2.22, *Immunity*; Chapter 2.23, *Waivers and Releases*; and Chapter 2.24, *Informed Consents and Agreements to Participate*).

But one should not wait until one is sued to consider defenses! One must plan ahead. Knowing the type of risks one anticipates or that have previously resulted in injury is critical in selecting an appropriate defense. Through effective risk management, potential and existing risks can be identified. Once identified, positioning oneself to ameliorate or transfer liability by allocation of risk can more readily defend against the risks.

There are essentially two types of risk—inherent risks and negligence risks. The **inherent risks** are those that are a normal, integral part of the activity—risks that cannot normally be eliminated without changing the nature of the activity itself. Such injuries as an athlete pulling a hamstring running wind sprints, a person spraining an ankle while hiking over rough terrain, or a football player breaking his collarbone while throwing a block may exemplify the inherent risks of the activity. On the other hand, some injuries result from the **negligence** of the service provider or its employees. The following are some examples where the injury might have been due to negligence: a player injuring a knee when he steps in one of many outfield holes while running for a fly ball, a tumbler injured doing a handspring when no spotter is provided, or a player suffering additional injury when the coach fails to secure proper medical treatment for an injury (see Chapter 2.11, *Elements of Negligence*).

Fundamental Concepts

The allocation of risk to other parties may be accomplished by recreation and sport businesses through the utilization of several defenses. All of these defenses come from one of three sources—common law, contract law, and statutory law. **Common law** is that body of principles and rules of action that derive their authority solely from the prior judgments and decrees of the courts. It is the body of law that develops and derives through judicial decisions—as distinguished from legislative enactments. **Contract law** is that body of law that governs the rules regarding binding agreements between parties. Several means by which risk can be allocated derive from this body of law. **Statutory law** is that body of law that is created by acts of a legislative body. Such laws requiring or prohibiting specific acts or actions may apply to individuals, public recreation and sport entities, or private recreation and sport entities—depending on the intent and wording of the legislation.

Table 1 outlines the allocation of risk in terms of (1) to whom the risk is allocated; (2) who is eligible for the defense; (3) which risks are allocated; (4) the effect on the standard of care required; and (5) the impact on the liability of the service provider. To use the table effectively, one must consider the facts of any given situation. For example, suppose a skateboarder is injured in a skateboard competition. Applying this situation to the table, one of the defenses available to the business conducting the competition would be primary assumption of risk. The risk would be allocated to the player and from the recreation or sport business—assuming the player consented to the activity, participated voluntarily, and understood the risks of the activity. From the table, one can see that this defense could protect the business from liability for the inherent risks of the activity, but does not affect the required standard of care. The business would still be liable for its own ordinary negligence. If the business was negligent, but could show that fault-related conduct by the skateboarder contributed to the injury, then the defense of secondary assumption of risk would apply. Additionally, under comparative-fault statutes, this secondary assumption of risk would ameliorate the financial liability by barring or reducing the negligence award to the skateboarder.

However, suppose the management had required that the skateboarder sign a waiver of liability prior to the event, thus releasing the recreation or sport business from liability for its own negligence. From Table 1, one can see that if the participant is of majority age, the waiver allocates the risk of ordinary negligence from the business to the participant skateboarder.

Defenses Based on Common Law

Elements of Ordinary Negligence Not Proven

Perhaps the best defense against a claim of negligence is that one or more of the elements required for negligence is not present. As discussed in Chapter 2.11, *Elements of Negligence*, to be liable, one must have a legal duty to the plaintiff, must breach that duty, and the breach of duty must be the proximate cause of an injury to the plaintiff. If one of these elements is missing (duty, breach, proximate cause, or injury), then no other defense is necessary—no negligence, no liability.

Primary Assumption of Risk

Primary assumption of risk is a legal theory by which a plaintiff may not recover for an injury received when the plaintiff voluntarily exposed him- or herself to a known and appreciated danger. Primary assumption of risk involves the assumption of well-known risks that are inherent to the activity. In other words, when one knows the inherent dangers involved and voluntarily participates, one assumes those risks inherent in the activity (but not risks of negligence), and the service provider is not liable for injuries resulting from those inherent risks. In *Daigle v. West Mountain* (2001), the court held that although participants assume those risks that are known, apparent or reasonably foreseeable, they do not assume risks that are unique and result in a dangerous condition over and above the usual dangers inherent in the activity.

Primary assumption of risk is presumed when an individual has voluntarily participated in an activity that involves inherent or well-known risks. One is held to have consented, by virtue of one's voluntary participation, to those injury-causing events that are known and reasonably foreseeable (*Truett v. Fell*). Primary assumption of risk acts as a defense in that it relieves the defendant of a duty that might otherwise be owed to the plaintiff. The organizer of an event has a duty to produce a reasonably safe event and is required to use ordinary care not to increase the risk beyond what is inherent in the activity.[1] For example, if a man attends a YMCA, knows and appreciates the risks involved in weight lifting, chooses to lift weights, and injures his back, the YMCA has no duty and bears no responsibility, absent negligence on its part, because of primary assumption of risk (or more specifically, implied assumption of risk [see following]).

The doctrine of primary assumption of risk embodies the legal conclusion that the defendant has "no duty" to protect the plaintiff from a particular risk. In sport-related cases, however, the issue of whether a duty is owed depends on (1) the nature of the activity or sport involved and (2) the relationship of the defendant and the plaintiff to that activity or sport (*Knight v. Jewett*, 1992). The service provider generally has no duty to protect the client against the inherent risks of the sport; however, sometimes the relation-

---

[1] However, a California court (*Saffro v. Elite Racing, Inc.*, 2002) held that the organizer of a marathon has a duty to "take reasonable steps to minimize the risks without altering the nature of the sport, including the provision of sufficient water and electrolyte replacement drinks" at 1.

table ❮ 1 ❯ Allocation of Risk[a,b]

Authority and Defenses	To Whom Risk Is Allocated	Eligibility for Defense	Which Risks Are Allocated	Effect on Standard of Care Owed	Impact on Liability of Provider
COMMON LAW					
Elements of Ordinary Negligence Not Proven	participant	any service provider	injuries not due to provider negligence	none	provider not liable
Primary Assumption of Risk	participant	consent/voluntary; inherent risks; know, understand, & appreciate risks	inherent risks	none	provider not liable for inherent risks
Secondary Assumption of Risk	participant	fault-related conduct; understands dangers; usually age 6 or older	participant fault that enhances chance of injury	none	bars or reduces award
Sovereign & Gov't. Immunity (See Statutory Law following)	participant	public entity only	all risks related to governmental function	reduces duty to willful/wanton	bars provider from liability for ordinary or gross negligence
Ultra Vires Acts	employee	action outside scope of responsibility or authority	ordinary negligence	none	liability shifts from employer to employee alone
CONTRACT LAW					
Waivers	participant	participant of majority age	ordinary negligence	reduces duty to gross negligence	not liable for ordinary negligence
Inherent Risk Agreements					
Informed Consent (ADA, rehab, research, fitness regimen, therapy)	participant or subject	adequately informed of treatment risk; majority age or parental signature	treatment risks	none	stronger primary & secondary assumption of risk defenses
Agreement to Participate (Including Assumption of Risk Agreement)	participant	adequately informed of activity risks and behavioral expectations	inherent risks	none	stronger primary & secondary assumption of risk defenses
Facility Lease Agreements	lessee	authorization for lease by corporate entity; lessee of majority age	activity risks to lessee; facility risks to lessee & lessor	none	not liable for activity risks; lessee & provider share facility risk as per contract
Equipment Rental Agreements	user (renter)	user of majority age	inherent risks; risks from equipment misuse or user misconduct; provider retains risk of equipment failure; may include a waiver	none	not liable for inherent risks or risks from misuse or misconduct
Indemnity Agreements	indemnitor	appropriate relationship	financial loss of indemnitee	none	indemnitee losses pass to indemnitor
Independent Contract for Services	independent contractors	authorization of entity; check contractor credentials	all risks of provider except for "inherently dangerous" activities	none	all liability transfers to indep. contractor (except "inherently dangerous" activities)

[a] Table was adapted with the permission and assistance of Dr. Betty van der Smissen from a chart on allocation of risk in a handout entitled "How to Defend Yourself and Your Program," SSLASPA, 1997.

[b] The reader is cautioned that a table is simply an outline of the subject and that it is impossible to include all elements of the subject or all exceptions. This table is meant as an overview of allocation of risk and the reader is directed to this chapter as well as Chapter 2.22 *Immunity*, Chapter 2.23 *Waivers and Releases*, and Chapter 2.24 *Informed Consents and Agreements to Participate* for more detail regarding the subject.

table ◇1◇ Allocation of Risk[a,b] (continued)

Authority and Defenses	To Whom Risk Is Allocated	Eligibility for Defense	Which Risks Are Allocated	Effect on Standard of Care Owed	Impact on Liability of Provider
STATUTORY LAW **Comparative Fault**	shared with participant based on % fault	fault-related conduct; participant usually age 6 or older; all providers eligible	risk shared for damages; allocation based on % of fault	none	reduces damages by % participant at fault
Legislation-based Immunity Charitable Immunity	participant	charitable, educational, and religious organizations	ordinary negligence	reduces duty to gross negligence	not liable for ordinary negligence
Tort Claims Acts	participant	public entities qualified by specific state statutes	discretionary acts; negligence except dangerous physical conditions usually	reduced to willful/wanton; retain duty for dangerous physical conditions	provider liable for dangerous physical conditions and for willful/wanton acts
Recreational User Immunity	user	owners of natural, undeveloped area; no fee for use of land; specified by state statute	open & obvious premise risks & all activity risks; retain ultrahazardous environmental risks	only duty: to warn of ultrahazardous & of known, hidden hazards	no liability except for ultrahazardous; retains liability for willful/malicious (sometimes gross)
Volunteer Immunity (State)	participant	charitable & educational organization volunteers; safety training in some states	ordinary negligence in most states	volunteer to gross negligence	no effect on liability of provider
Federal Volunteer Protection Act	participant	volunteers of public and non-profit organizations within scope of responsibility who hold appropriate certifications	ordinary negligence	volunteer to gross negligence	no effect on liability of provider
Good Samaritan (First Aid) Immunity	injured party	in good faith; gratuitous	usually ordinary negligence	caregiver to gross negligence	not available to provider
Good Samaritan (AED) Immunity	injured party	in good faith; gratuitous aid; training in some states	usually ordinary negligence	caregiver to gross negligence	immunity in many states
Rec & Sport Provider Immunity Specific Activity Statutes (Equine, skiing, skating, & other specified activities)	inherent to participant, sometimes negligence	usually all providers & participants in specified activities	inherent activity risk to participant; provider retains operational, facility, & premise risks	participant assumes inherent risks; sometimes reduces to gross	not liable for inherent activity-related risks; sometimes not liable for negligence
General Rec & Sport Statutes (Applies to numerous sports & activities in one statute)	inherent to participant	all providers & participants in specified activities	inherent activity risk to participant; provider retains operational, facility, & premise risks	none; participant assumes inherent risks	not liable for inherent activity-related risks; liable for negligence
Hazardous Recreational Activity (Applies to numerous activities in one statute)	participant	public entities & employees w/o fee for activity	inherent activity risks & secondary assumption of risk to participant; provider must warn of dangerous conditions and maintain premises	reduces activity duty to gross; no effect on duty to warn, construct/maintain facility/equipment	not liable for inherent risk or activity-related negligence; liable for operational, facility, & premise risks & failure to warn
Procedural Noncompliance Statute of Limitations	participant	all providers	all risks	none	limits the time during which suit can be filed
Notice of Claim (Tort Claims Act)	participant	only public entities	all risks	none	limits time during which notice of intent to sue must be given

ship between provider and client creates a *duty to not increase the risks* inherent in the activity. For instance, in *El-Halees v. Chauser* (2002), the court found Chauser liable for injury to a six-year-old client due to a fall from a gymnastic apparatus because Chauser left the child unattended on the uneven parallel bars—thereby violating the duty to not increase the risk of injury.

Courts have ruled that three elements must exist for a successful primary assumption of risk defense. They are: *(1) the risk must be inherent to the sport, (2) the participant must voluntarily consent to be exposed to the risk, and (3) the participant must know, understand, and appreciate the inherent risks of the activity.* However, this varies somewhat from state to state (e.g., under Missouri law, a skier assumes the inherent risks of or incidental to skiing, regardless of his or her subjective knowledge of those risks [*Bennett v. Hidden Valley Golf and Ski, Inc.*, 2003]).

It is important that the recreation or sport manager understand that the participant assumes only the risks that are **inherent** to the sport or activity. Examples of inherent risks might include falling while skiing, falling from a horse while horseback riding, or pulling a muscle while putting the shot. The participant does not normally assume risks incurred as a result of the negligence of the service provider. Examples of negligence risks might include being struck by a bat with an untaped handle when it slipped from the batter's hand during a swing, being struck in the face by an elbow in an excessively rough basketball game when the officials failed to control the game, or a football player suffering a facial injury when supplied with a helmet with no face guard.

A person who is playing recreation league softball, a person in a pickup basketball game, or a person on the varsity football team is participating by choice and thus meets the second requirement for primary assumption of risk—**voluntary consent**. Voluntary consent is sometimes at issue in cases regarding injuries in required physical education classes. If the plaintiff is a student in a required class where gymnastics is a required activity and is injured performing a mandatory back handspring, the voluntary consent requirement would be difficult to meet. On the other hand, if the student elected from among several choices to take weight training to meet the physical education requirement, there might be a degree of voluntary participation.

Third, one cannot assume a risk of which one has no **knowledge**, **understanding**, **or appreciation**. Courts have ruled that one must not only know of the facts creating the danger, but also must comprehend and appreciate the nature of the danger to be confronted. Whether one is held to know, understand, and appreciate the risks usually depends on the age of the plaintiff, experience of the plaintiff, and opportunity of the plaintiff to become aware of the risks. Courts have held that it is not necessary that the injured plaintiff foresee the exact manner in which his or her injury occurred (*Tremblay v. West Experience Inc.*, 2002). In some jurisdictions, however, knowledge and appreciation are measured by an objective test and can be determined by law when "any person of normal intelligence in [the plaintiff's] position must have understood the danger" (*Leakas v. Columbia Country Club*, 1993).

One way to strengthen the primary assumption of risk defense is to ensure that participants know, understand, and appreciate the risks of the activity. One effective way to accomplish this is through the use of participant agreements (see Chapter 2.23, *Waivers and Releases*), informed consent agreements, and agreements to participate (see Chapter 2.24, *Informed Consents and Agreements to Participate*). Use of these documents provides documentation that the participant was aware of the risks.

Implied Primary Assumption of Risk and Express Assumption of Risk

There are two types of primary assumption of risk—implied primary assumption of risk and express assumption of risk. **Implied primary assumption of risk** is that form of primary assumption of risk where it is evident by the conduct or actions (i.e., participation) of the individual that the participant has voluntarily taken part in an activity that involves inherent or well-known risks. The participant has signed no document by which he or she assumes the risk.

Express assumption of risk is that form of primary assumption of risk in which the participant sets forth in words (either verbally or in writing) that he or she assumes the *inherent risks* of the activity.[2] Participant agreements (see Chapter 2.23), informed consent agreements, and agreements to participate (see Chapter 2.24) are instruments that can be used to obtain this type of assumption of risk. In these agreements, the participant explicitly agrees to assume the *inherent risks (or the treatment risks)* of the activity. Understanding of the concept of express assumption of risk, however, is complicated by the fact that courts vary as to its definition.

Secondary Assumption of Risk

Secondary assumption of risk (formerly called contributory negligence) involves the voluntary choice or conduct of the participant to encounter a known or obvious risk created by the negligent conduct of the service provider or to fail to follow rules or heed warnings set down by the provider (*Riddle v. Universal Sport Camp*, 1990). The following are three types of situations where secondary assumption of risk may occur. In the first, the participant voluntarily participates when there is a substantial risk that the defendant will act in a negligent manner (e.g., going up in a plane with someone who has a reputation for wild or careless acts). The second is when the service provider has already been negligent and the participant takes part anyway (e.g., playing softball in an outfield that has obvious rocks and holes scattered about). The third is when the participant fails to follow rules or heed warnings. In each case, the conduct of the participant (electing to participate) falls below the standard to which one is required to conform for one's own protection.

Sovereign and Governmental Immunity

Sovereign and governmental immunity are judicial doctrines that prevent one from filing suit against the government and its political subdivisions without their consent (see Chapter 2.22, *Immunity*).

Ultra Vires Act

A defense that can be very helpful to the corporate entity is the defense that the act by the employee was an ultra vires act—one that is not within the authority or scope of responsibility of the employee. Normally under the doctrine of *respondeat superior*, the employer is liable for the negligent acts of the employee (see Chapter 2.12, *Which Parties Are Liable?*). A major exception to this rule, however, is when the employee had no authority or responsibility to perform the act in question. In such a case, only the employee is liable for the negligent act. If a coach injured a youngster while administering corporal punishment when the school had a strict rule prohibiting corporal punishment, the act would be outside the authority of the coach, and the school system would probably escape liability. The coach would still be liable for the act. Note, however, that if the school is aware of the fact that the coach uses corporal punishment and has failed to act on this knowledge, the school will also be liable for the action. In essence, by not taking action in knowing of the coach's behavior, the school is in fact condoning the act.

Defenses Based on Contract Law

Waivers

A **waiver** is a contract in which the participant or user of a service agrees to relinquish the right to pursue legal action against the service provider in the event that *negligence* of the provider results in an injury to the participant (see Chapter 2.23, *Waivers and Releases*).

---

[2] In some jurisdictions, express assumption of risk refers specifically to contractual agreements (i.e., waivers of liability) in which the participant releases the provider from liability for negligence.

Informed Consent

An informed consent agreement is a formal contract or agreement document used to protect the provider from liability for the informed treatment risks of a treatment or program to which the signer is subjected. The agreement is designed to provide full disclosure to the individual regarding both the known risks and the anticipated outcome or benefits of the treatment, thereby enabling the participant to make an informed decision regarding acceptance of the treatment. *By signing the agreement, the signer is agreeing to assume the treatment risks of which he or she is informed. The signer is not agreeing to relieve the entity from liability for injury resulting from negligent acts of the entity or its employees* (see Chapter 2.24, *Informed Consents and Agreements to Participate*).

Agreement to Participate

The **agreement to participate** is a document that helps to inform participants in recreation, sport, or educational activities of (1) the nature of the activity, (2) the risks to be encountered through participation in the activity, and (3) the behaviors expected of the participant. It is designed to help protect the provider from liability for injuries resulting from the inherent risks of the activity, but is informative rather than contractual in nature. The **assumption of risk agreement** is a statement whereby the signer (1) explicitly asserts that the signer knows the nature of the activity, understands the physical and skill demands of the activity, and appreciates the types of injuries that may result from participation; (2) asserts that participation is voluntary; and (3) agrees to assume those risks that are inherent to the activity. *It is essentially the same as the agreement to participate, but in a different format* (see Chapter 2.24 *Informed Consents and Agreements to Participate*).

Facility Leases Agreements

Owners of facilities often permit groups or other businesses to make use of their facilities. A recreational softball team might sign up for a field and conduct a team practice, a facility owner might lease an arena to a promoter for a concert, or a facility owner might lease the entire facility or a part of the facility for a matter of months or years (a university might lease its dressing facilities and practice fields to a professional football team for several months for preseason practice). When an injury occurs at the facility, it is not unlikely that the facility owner will be named as a defendant in a lawsuit regarding the injury. A defense against such litigation may be provided to owners of property/lessors by virtue of their status as lessors or by contractual provisions.

To determine the extent of the liability of the facility owner, one must determine if the injury was **activity related** or **premise related**. Generally, injuries that are activity related are the responsibility of the lessee. When injuries are premise related, liability may rest on both the entity conducting the activity and the facility owner. Generally, the facility owner is responsible for structural type problems, and the entity conducting the activity is often responsible for maintenance type problems. In the instance of the softball team using the field, the facility owner would retain liability. In the case of the football team leasing the facility for preseason practice, the responsibility would probably be shared by lessor and lessee, depending on the nature of the hazard unless the lease contract includes provisions that assign sole responsibility for certain types of hazards to the lessee football team (see Chapter 3.20, *Premises Liability*).

Equipment Rental Agreements

When individuals rent equipment, rental agreements are often used to help protect the rentor. Rental agreements often include a waiver of liability signed by the renter (user) of the equipment as well as an indemnification agreement. In using the waiver in the rental agreement, the provider is passing the liability for a negligence-related injury on to the renter. The indemnification agreement is included to have the renter promise to repay the provider for loss due to litigation resulting from accidents to the renter or to a third party.

Rental agreements also function much like an agreement to participate (see also Chapter 2.24, *Informed Consents and Agreements to Participate*) in that they can inform renters of behavior expected and their responsibility for third-party injuries, and gain affirmation that renters are knowledgeable regarding the use of the equipment. The provider then passes along much of the responsibility for injury to the renter and enhances the position of the provider when comparative negligence is determined. The provider, however, retains liability for injury relating to defective equipment.

Indemnification Agreements

An **indemnification agreement** is an agreement by which one party agrees to indemnify or reimburse another on the occurrence of an anticipated loss. The agreement creates a contractual right under which the loss is generally shifted from a tortfeasor who is passively at fault to one that is actively responsible. Indemnification agreements are commonly included in facility leases to protect the property owner from loss resulting from litigation by the lessee or by a patron naming the owner as a defendant. For instance, a municipality leasing an arena to a wrestling promoter for an event would generally include within the lease a provision by which the promoter agrees to indemnify or reimburse the municipality for any loss resulting from the event. Then if an injury occurs to a spectator and the municipality is named as a codefendant, the promoter is responsible for the municipality's legal fees, any award, and any other related expenses. In *Auburn School District No. 408 v. King County* (1999), the school district agreed to indemnify the county for loss due to the district use of the county swimming pool. A student injured in the pool sued both the county and the school district. The school district was ordered to reimburse the county for its financial loss. This defense is summarized in Table 1.

The law regarding the enforcement of indemnification agreements is more exacting in some states than in others. For instance, in Georgia the public policy is reluctant to cast the burden for negligent actions on one who is not actually at fault. Unless a contract for indemnification explicitly and expressly states that the negligence of the indemnitee is covered, courts will not enforce the contract against the indemnitor. In *Pride Park Atlanta v. City of Atlanta* (2000), the agreement was not enforced because the agreement said ". . . agrees to protect and hold harmless . . . from any and all claims . . ." and did not explicitly refer to negligence by the indemnitee.

Although most indemnity agreements involve two corporate entities, some involve a corporate entity and an individual. Some courts have held that indemnification agreements used with consumers and intended to perform much like a waiver are not enforceable, but indemnification law varies from state to state. A rafting company (*Madsen v. Wyoming River Trips, Inc.*, 1999) required that a father agree to indemnify the company on behalf of himself and his family. When the wife was injured due to negligence of the rafting company, the Wyoming court refused to enforce the agreement stating that such contracts are enforced when the indemnitor is assuming liability for an act that was no fault of the indemnitee. The court ruled that the agreement, which sought to hold an innocent party liable for the negligence of the indemnitee, was void as against public policy.

On the other hand, courts in some states have upheld such agreements (*Beaver v. Foamcraft, Inc.*, 2002). In a 2005 Wisconsin case, a man was injured during a tractor pull contest after signing a waiver and indemnification agreement. The waiver protected against the plaintiff's claims, but did not protect against a loss of consortium claim by the wife. The indemnity language within the document stated clearly and without ambiguity that the plaintiff agreed to indemnify the provider for all claims—thus the indemnity agreement protected the provider from the loss of consortium claim (*Walsh v. Luedtke*, 2005).

In several cases, corporate entities (in an effort to bypass the law in some states that disallows liability waivers signed by parents on behalf of minors) have attempted to gain liability protection by having parents sign indemnity agreements for the child to be able to participate in an activity. Some courts have said that such agreements are enforceable because they involve a contract between two adults (*Eastman v. Yutzy*, 2001). Other courts have ruled such an agreement invalid as against public policy because it is inconsistent with the parent's duty to the child (*Hawkins v. Peart*, 2001; *Cooper v. The Aspen Skiing Company*, 2002).

Independent Contract for Services

An independent contract for services involves an agreement between the corporate entity and an individual or companies that contract to perform a service for the corporate entity (see Chapter 2.12, *Which Parties Are Liable?*). When one contracts with an independent contractor, the corporate entity generally avoids liability for injuries resulting from the negligence of the independent contractor. However, the employer retains the responsibility: (1) to use reasonable care in selecting a competent independent contractor and to inspect after completion of the project; (2) to keep the premises reasonably safe for invitees and employees; and (3) for "inherently dangerous activities" (e.g., fireworks displays, keeping of dangerous animals, and ultrahazardous activities) (see Chapter 2.12, *Which Parties Are Liable?*).

Defenses Based on Statutory Law

Comparative Fault

Comparative fault is not a true defense against liability for negligence. More precisely, it is a method for apportioning damages awarded based on the fault or blame or the relative degree of responsibility for the injury. Comparative fault is based on the fact that both plaintiff and defendant are at fault. The jury compares the fault of each party and generally allocates the fault by percentage.[3] Comparative fault was enacted to ameliorate the harsh effect of contributory negligence where if the plaintiff contributes at all, regardless of the extent, the plaintiff receives no award. **Pure comparative fault** has been adopted by a number of states. In this form, the award to the plaintiff is reduced by the percentage of fault assigned to the plaintiff. For example, suppose the award is $100,000 and the fault is apportioned 75 percent to the plaintiff and 25 percent to the defendant. Because the plaintiff is 75 percent to blame, the plaintiff's award would be reduced by 75 percent, and the plaintiff would receive $25,000. **Modified comparative fault** operates on the theory that the plaintiff is not entitled to recovery if the plaintiff is substantially at fault. State statutes vary—but, in essence, if the fault of the plaintiff is 50 percent or more, the plaintiff is barred from recovery and receives no award. When the fault exceeds these limits, modified comparative fault has the same effect as contributory negligence or fault—acting as a complete bar to recovery.

Legislation-Based Immunity

Several forms of legislation-based immunity affect recreation and sport managers as well as the business entity. **Charitable immunity** is a doctrine that relieves or immunizes charitable organizations from liability for tort. **Federal and state tort claims acts** rescinded sovereign/governmental immunity and enumerated the areas or acts for which immunity was retained. **Recreational user immunity** was passed to protect certain landowners who gratuitously allow others to use their property for recreational purposes. **Volunteer immunity** was enacted to aid in the recruitment of volunteers for public, charitable, and nonprofit entities. **Good Samaritan statutes** protect those rendering aid and utilizing AEDs to victims in cases of emergency. **Shared responsibility and statutory assumption of risk statutes** are intended to help protect providers of recreation and sport activities from liability for injuries resulting from the inherent risks (and negligence in a few statutes) of the activity or sport. These are discussed in detail in Chapter 2.22, *Immunity*.

---

[3] **Contributory fault** (formerly called contributory negligence) exists when the conduct of the plaintiff in any way helps to cause or aggravate the plaintiff's injury. In the past, this was a major defense against negligence claims because in states adhering to the contributory fault doctrine, any contributory fault by the plaintiff, regardless of how slight, served as a complete bar to recovery. Now, however, only four states (Alabama, Maryland, North Carolina, and Virginia) and the District of Columbia hold to this doctrine. In comparative fault states, contributory fault serves to reduce the award to the plaintiff by the proportion of fault allotted to the plaintiff. Even under the comparative fault theory, however, most states bar recovery if the fault of the plaintiff is 50 percent or greater.

Regarding age, the general rule has been that children over the age of fourteen are capable of negligence and children under seven are incapable of negligence. Those between seven and fourteen are judged capable of negligence in certain circumstances. These lines of demarcation seem to be weakening in recent years, as cases in various jurisdictions have begun to allocate contributory fault to children six years of age and under (*Grace v. Kumalaa*, 1963; *Lash v. Cutts*, 1991; *Robertson v. Travis*, 1980).

Procedural Noncompliance

A **statute of limitations** is a restriction on the length of time an injured party has in which to file suit. The law differs from state to state and also with the nature of the claim. In tort claims, states allow one to four years in which to file suit with most allowing two or three years. When minors are involved, the statute of limitations does not begin running until the minor has reached the age of majority. So, if a child is injured at age 11 due to the negligence of an employee at a recreation department, the youngster would have one to four years (the length of the statute of limitations in that state) after reaching the age of 18 in which to file suit.

Notice of claim statutes relate usually to tort claim statutes and provide that the plaintiff must provide the defendant *public entity* with a notice of intent to file suit. This notice must be filed within a period of time (ranging from 90 days to 2 years) following the accident or the right to sue is lost. In essence, the notice of claim is a type of statute of limitations with a similar effect. Not all states have a notice of claim provision in their tort law statutes, and the notice of claim requirements apply only when the defendant is a public entity.

Significant Case

In this case, the defendant claims that the school district is not liable because of recreational user immunity and because of implied primary assumption of risk. The opinion presents an enlightening discussion of each of the defenses.

HOME V. NORTH KITSAP SCHOOL DISTRICT
2 Wn. App. 709; 965 P.2d 1112; 1998 Wash. App. LEXIS 1405
October 2, 1998, Filed

OPINION:

In 1993, Home was a teacher in the Central Kitsap School District, an organization not related to the North Kitsap School District. He taught at Central Kitsap Junior High, where he was also a part-time assistant football coach. Ken Anderson was the head football coach.

On November 3, 1993, Home's Central Kitsap team played an away game on the football field at North Kitsap Junior High. * * * The football field is a permanent facility with football goal posts at each end and a track around the perimeter. It is available for public use when not being used for school events or activities. On November 3, it was being used exclusively for the North Kitsap-Central Kitsap football game, a school-sponsored event to which parents and other spectators were admitted without charge.

When Home and Anderson arrived at the North Kitsap field, they saw a curb "raised several inches above ground level," separating the football area from the track area. The curb ran along the outside of the football field's sideline area, not far from the sideline itself. Home and Anderson thought it was a hazard to any player who might be propelled out of bounds by momentum or by another player. After discussing several courses of action, they decided that Home would station himself in front of the curb, so he could stop any player who might be heading for it. Later, during the game, Home was standing in front of the curb when the Central Kitsap team ran a "sweep" play toward his side of the field. As he testified later: I saw the kid coming to the sideline, I saw the tackler coming and saw imminent collision.

* * * My kid was a full stride out of bounds and starting a second stride when he was impacted. He was going into the cement. And using both hands, I took him to the ground. And the North Kitsap player with most of his weight came across my left thigh. Home was injured, he alleges, as a result of this impact.

In July 1996, Home sued the North Kitsap School District for negligence. North Kitsap moved for summary judgment, contending (1) that it was immune under RCW 4.24.210, the recreational land use statute; (2) that Home was a licensee who could not prove a breach of the duty owed to licensees; and (3) that Home knowingly and voluntarily assumed the risk that culminated in the accident. The trial court granted the motion, and this appeal followed.

I.

North Kitsap argues that RCW 4.24.210 renders it immune from liability to Home. * * * The purpose of RCW 4.24.210(1) is "to encourage owners or others in lawful possession and control of land and water areas or channels to make them available to the public for recreational purposes." RCW 4.24.210(1) provides in pertinent part:

Any public or private landowners or others in lawful possession and control of any lands whether designated resource, rural, or urban, or water areas or channels and lands adjacent to such areas or channels, who allow members of the public to use them for the purposes of outdoor recreation, which term includes, but is not limited to, the cutting, gathering, and removing of firewood by private persons for their personal use without purchasing the firewood from the landowner, hunting, fishing, camping, picnicking, swimming, hiking, bicycling, * * * boating, nature study, winter or water sports, viewing or enjoying historical, archaeological, scenic, or scientific sites, without charging a fee of any kind therefor, shall not be liable for unintentional injuries to such users.

According to Division One, the proper approach when applying this statute is to analyze the purpose for which the landowner was using the land, as opposed to the purpose for which the plaintiff was using the land. We agree, although we observe that a landowner may use the land for different purposes at different times. Here, then, it is necessary to focus on the nature of the landowner's use at the time of the accident being litigated.

* * *

Turning to this case, a North Kitsap school administrator testified that the North Kitsap field, "including the area used for football games, is available for public use when school is not in session and when it is not being used for a scheduled sport, such as a junior high school football game." Thus, it is undisputed that North Kitsap was not holding the football field open for use by members of the public when Home was injured, and North Kitsap is not immune by virtue of RCW 4.24.210.

II.

We next consider whether Home was an invitee or licensee. As we explained in *Thompson v. Katzer*, "An invitee is either a public invitee or a business visitor." "A public invitee is a person who is invited to enter or remain on land as a member of the public for a purpose for which the land is held open to the public." "A business visitor is a person who is invited to enter or remain on land for a purpose directly or indirectly connected with business dealings with the possessor of the land." In contrast, a "licensee" enters the occupier's premises with the occupier's permission or tolerance, either (a) without an invitation or (b) with an invitation but for a purpose unrelated to any business dealings between the two. * * * Here, Home was an assistant football coach invited to North Kitsap's field so that a school-sponsored football game could be played. His presence was related to North Kitsap's business of running its schools, and he was an invitee as a matter of law.

III.

North Kitsap claims that Home assumed the specific risk that culminated in the accident. Home disagrees, arguing primarily that he had no reasonable alternative course of action. Traditionally, the doctrine of assumption of risk has four facets: (1) express assumption of risk; (2) implied primary assumption of risk; (3) implied reasonable assumption of risk; and (4) implied unreasonable assumption of risk. The third and fourth facets, implied reasonable and implied unreasonable assumption of risk, are nothing but alternative names for contributory negligence, and neither is pertinent here. The first and second facets, express assumption of risk and implied primary assumption of risk, raise the same question: Did the plaintiff consent, before the accident or injury, to the negation of a duty that the defendant would otherwise have owed to the plaintiff? If the answer is yes, "the defendant does not have the duty, there can be no breach and hence no negligence." Thus, when either facet applies, it bars any recovery based on the duty that was negated. Although the first and second facets involve the same idea—the plaintiff's consent to negate a duty the defendant would otherwise have owed to the plaintiff—they differ with respect to the way in which the plaintiff manifests consent. With express assumption of risk, the plaintiff states in so many words that he or she consents to relieve the defendant of a duty the defendant would otherwise have. With implied primary assumption of risk, the plaintiff engages in other kinds of conduct, from which consent is then implied. Here, we focus on implied consent, which we alternatively refer to as assumption of risk.

To invoke assumption of risk, a defendant must show that the plaintiff knowingly and voluntarily chose to encounter the risk. Thus, "the evidence must show the plaintiff (1) had full subjective understanding (2) of the presence and nature of the specific risk, and (3) voluntarily chose to encounter the risk." Put another way, the plaintiff "must have knowledge of the risk, appreciate and understand its nature, and voluntarily choose to incur it." Knowledge and voluntariness are questions of fact for the jury, except when reasonable minds could not differ. Whether a plaintiff decides knowingly to encounter a risk turns on whether he or she, at the time of decision, actually and subjectively knew all facts that a reasonable person in the defendant's shoes would know and disclose, or, concomitantly, all facts that a reasonable person in the plaintiff's shoes would want to know and consider. Thus, "The test is a subjective one: Whether the plaintiff in fact understood the risk; not whether the reasonable person of ordinary prudence would comprehend the risk." The plaintiff must "be aware of more than just the generalized risk of [his or her] activities; there must be proof [he or she] knew of and appreciated the specific hazard which caused the injury." And a plaintiff "appreciates the specific hazard" or risk only if he or she actually and subjectively knows all facts that a reasonable person in the defendant's shoes would know and disclose, or, concomitantly, all facts that a reasonable person in the plaintiff's shoes would want to know and consider when making the decision at issue. Whether a plaintiff decides voluntarily to encounter a risk depends on whether he or she elects to encounter it despite knowing of a reasonable alternative course of action. Thus, Division One has said that in order for assumption of risk to bar recovery, the plaintiff "must have had a reasonable opportunity to act differently or proceed on an alternate course that would have avoided the danger." The Restatement comments:

> Since the basis of assumption of risk is the plaintiff's willingness to accept the risk, take his chances, and look out for himself, his choice in doing so must be a voluntary one. If the plaintiff's words or conduct make it clear that he refuses to accept the risk, he does not assume it. The plaintiff's mere protest against the risk and demand for its removal or for protection against it will not necessarily and conclusively prevent his subsequent acceptance of the risk, if he then proceeds vol-

> untarily into a situation which exposes him to it. Such conduct normally indicates that he does not stand on his objection, and has in fact consented, although reluctantly, to accept the danger and look for himself.

* * *

In this case, Home does not seriously dispute that he knew all the facts that a reasonable person would have wanted to know and consider when deciding whether to position himself or herself as Home did. He does contend, however, that a rational trier of fact could find that once he actually and subjectively discovered the hazard that later culminated in the accident, he had no reasonable alternative but to stand in front of it and protect his students. Taking the evidence and inferences in the light most favorable to Home, we think that a rational trier could so find. Accordingly, we conclude that whether Home voluntarily assumed the risk is a question of fact for the jury, and that summary judgment should not have been granted.

Reversed and remanded for further proceedings.

◇◇◇ **OTHER RELATED SIGNIFICANT CASES**

Chapter 2.12 *Which Parties Are Liable?*

Chapter 2.24 *Informed Consents and Agreements to Participate*

Chapter 2.32 *Conduct and Supervision of Activities*

Chapter 2.35 *Products Liability*

Chapter 3.10 *Property Law*

Chapter 4.11 *Assault and Battery*

Recent Trends

The major trend in regard to defenses is the continued movement toward increased immunity for service providers, employees, and volunteers. This is evidenced (1) by the enactment of more statutes protecting service providers from certain aspects of liability (e.g., 46 states now have equine liability statutes); (2) by the ever-broadening definition of what constitutes a discretionary act, thereby expanding the immunity of employees of governmental entities; and (3) by the recent enactment of AED Good Samaritan statutes in every state.

References

Cases

Auburn School District No. 408 v. King County, 1999 Wash. App. LEXIS 1748.

Beaver v. Foamcraft, Inc., 2002 U.S. Dist. LEXIS 4651.

Bennett v. Hidden Valley Golf and Ski, Inc., 2003 U.S. App. LEXIS 1658.

Cooper v. The Aspen Skiing Company, 2002 Colo. LEXIS 528.

Daigle v. West Mountain, (2001 N.Y. App. Div. LEXIS 12326.

Eastman v. Yutzy, 2001 Mass. Super. LEXIS 157.

El-Halees v. Chauser, 2002 Cal. App. Unpub. LEXIS 8124.

Grace v. Kumalaa, 387 P.2d 872 (Hawaii 1963).

Hawkins v. Peart, 2001 Utah LEXIS 177.

Home v. North Kitsap School District, 965 P.2d 1112; 1998 Wash. App. LEXIS 1405.

Knight v. Jewett, 3 Cal.4th 296; 11 Cal. Rptr. 2d, 834 P.2d 696 (1992).

Lash v. Cutts, 943 F.2d 147,152 (1st Cir. 1991).

Leakas v. Columbia Country Club, 831 F. Supp. 1231 (Md. 1993).

Madsen v. Wyoming River Trips, Inc., 1999 U.S. Dist. LEXIS 77.

Pride Park Atlanta v. City of Atlanta, 2000 Ga. App. LEXIS 1330.

Riddle v. Universal Sport Camp, 786 P.2d 641 (Kan. 1990).

Robertson v. Travis, 393 So.2d 304 (La. 1980).

Saffro v. Elite Racing, Inc., 2002 Cal. App. LEXIS 2076 at 1.

Tremblay v. West Experience Inc., 2002 N.Y. App. Div. LEXIS 7591.

Truett v. Fell, 68 N.Y.2d 432.

Walsh v. Luedtke, 2005 Wisc. App. LEXIS 744.

Publications and Presentations

Gregg, C. R. (2000). *Inherent risks.* SSLASPA Conference, Albuquerque, NM.

van der Smissen, B. (1990). *Legal liability and risk management for public and private entities.* Cincinnati, OH: Anderson Publishing Co.

van der Smissen, B. (1997). *How to defend yourself and your program.* Unpublished handout at an SSLASPA Conference.

Volunteer Protection Act of 1997, PL 105-19 (S543) June 18, 1997.

2.22 Immunity

Doyice J. Cotten
Sport Risk Consulting

A major category of defense for individuals and service providers in the fields of recreation and sport management is immunity from liability. Immunity is the state of being exempt from or protected against civil liability under certain circumstances. In this chapter, several types of immunity that apply to recreation and sport managers will be presented—ranging from sovereign immunity to sport-related statutes pertaining to the recreational user, sport volunteers, Good Samaritan acts, statutory assumption of risk, and shared responsibility. Because it is not possible to spell out the law in each state regarding each type of immunity, the reader is encouraged to use Table 1 to research the law in his or her state. Moreover, the reader should consult Table 1 in Chapter 2.21, *Defenses Against Negligence* for a summary of each of these defenses.

Many types of immunity are available to those in the fields of recreation and sport. Each has been designed to provide shelter from liability to one or more protected classes of people or entities. Statutes are aimed at providing protection for public entity service providers (tort claims acts, sovereign immunity, hazardous recreation statutes), private service providers (shared responsibility statutes, statutory assumption of risk statutes), nonprofit and charitable providers (charitable immunity), and property owners (recreational user statutes). Volunteer statutes are available to encourage volunteers (Volunteer Protection Act, state volunteer statutes), sport volunteers (sport volunteer statutes), and medical emergency volunteers (Good Samaritan statutes, AED Good Samaritan statutes). There is also immunity designed to protect public employees (hazardous recreation statutes, tort claims acts, discretionary act immunity) and private employees (AED Good Samaritan statutes).

Fundamental Concepts

Sovereign/Governmental Immunity

Sovereign immunity refers to "the immunity of the state and its agencies, departments, boards, institutions, et al." (van der Smissen, 1990, p. 148). **Governmental immunity**, on the other hand, "is the protection afforded local governing entities, such as municipalities (cities, towns, villages) and schools." (van der Smissen, 1990, p. 148). It is important to understand that although many states distinguish between the two concepts, the terms *sovereign immunity* and *governmental immunity* are often used interchangeably. In this chapter, the term *sovereign/governmental immunity* will be used to refer to both concepts.

There are two major limitations to sovereign/governmental immunity. First, *it applies only to governmental entities*, and second, *it does not extend to the officers, agents, or employees of the governing entity* (except when the statute specifically provides for it). This doctrine of sovereign/governmental immunity was the commanding approach to immunity until the 1950s; however, the last half of the twentieth century has seen most states abolish or significantly weaken and restrict this immunity so that it no longer has the dominant impact that it once did. The rationale for the change was that the immunity was unfair to the innocent victim of negligent actions by the governmental entity or its employees. Common law regarding immunity has been collected and arranged more systematically, or codified, in the tort claims acts. These acts, to be discussed later, extend immunity to government officers, agents, and employees in many states.

Tort Claims Acts

In 1946, Congress passed the **Federal Tort Claims Act** (28 U.S.C. 2671–2680 [1976]) with the intent of waiving sovereign/governmental immunity, thereby allowing liability exposure for the federal government comparable to that of the private sector. The statute removed the power of the federal government to claim immunity from a lawsuit for damages due to negligent or intentional injury by a federal employee in the scope of his/her work for the government. Although the Act allows suit of the government in certain instances, unlike sovereign/governmental immunity, *it provides immunity for federal officials performing discretionary acts within the scope of their responsibilities.*

Individual states began to follow suit, passing their own **state tort claims acts** to enable individuals harmed by torts, including negligence, to file suit under certain conditions. *In essence, what these acts did was to (1) rescind sovereign/governmental immunity at the state level in those states and (2) enumerate those areas or acts for which immunity was retained.*

Discretionary/Ministerial Function

One major change at this time was movement from that of governmental/proprietary function to the discretionary/ministerial doctrine. The **governmental/proprietary doctrine** classified the functions of public entities as either a fundamental **governmental function** (e.g., police, fire, and education), for which immunity was granted, or as a **proprietary function** (e.g., waterworks, electrical power, selling game refreshments, and other for-profit activities), for which no immunity was granted. The **discretionary/ministerial doctrine** grants immunity for discretionary acts, but, for the most part, not for ministerial acts.

Discretionary acts are those that involve deliberation, planning, decision making, policy making, and most often involve managerial-level personnel, such as the athletic director or head of the recreation department. **Ministerial acts** are more likely to involve operational acts, obedience of orders, performance of a duty, implementation of decisions or policies, and lower-echelon employees, such as assistant coaches and aerobics instructors. Under this doctrine, the classification is not based on who performed the act, but on the nature of the act. The rationale behind this immunity is to free the governing body charged with making policy decisions regarding public welfare from suits that might restrain them from performing their duties. Distinction between discretionary and ministerial acts, at best, is difficult and has been growing increasingly so as the courts in some states have persisted in blurring the lines of distinction, often interpreting even trivial decisions as discretionary. Classifying most acts as discretionary, in effect, strengthens the immunity of the employee and the entity.

The governmental/proprietary doctrine provided immunity based on the nature of the function provided by the governmental entity. Immunity was provided if the action was a "public good" function of the entity (an inspection of the recreation facility), but not for proprietary or money-making functions of the entity (operation of a soft-drink machine). The discretionary/ministerial doctrine provides immunity based on the act of the employee—not the function. Thus the same employee might be immune for actions deemed discretionary (policy-related planning for a 5K run) and not immune for actions ruled ministerial (carrying out the policies for a 5K run).

Charitable Immunity

During the first half of the twentieth century, charitable immunity provided substantial liability protection to charitable, educational, and religious organizations. **Charitable immunity** is a doctrine that relieves or immunizes charitable organizations from liability for tort. The doctrine is based on four premises: (1) public policy encourages charitable organizations because they benefit the public; (2) money possessed by such organizations was donated for other purposes and is held in trust; (3) because the recipient of the charity receives benefits, he or she, in turn, accepts the risks of negligence; and (4) there is no *respondeat superior* because the charity does not benefit from the actions of employees.

Charitable immunity, which focused on the protection of the agency or institution, has been repealed in most states. In most of the few states that retain some semblance of charitable immunity, the immunity has been emasculated to the point where its effectiveness is very limited.[1] Today, however, the volunteer protection acts do provide protection for the nonprofit or charitable institution volunteer. In addition, a few states still protect those gratuitously serving such institutions as a member, director, trustee, or board member.

Recreational User Statutes

To encourage private owners of natural, rural areas to allow others to use their property for recreational purposes, state legislatures began passing recreational use statutes in the 1960s. The **recreational user statute** is a law designed to provide protection for the private property owner against lawsuits by parties injured while on the landowner's property for recreational purposes. Originally, the immunity laws applied when four conditions were met: (1) private landowners; (2) no fee charged; (3) unimproved, undeveloped land for recreational use; and (4) owner fulfilled his or her obligation to provide a warning for any known, concealed danger that would not be apparent to the recreational user.

Today, all states have enacted some type of recreational use statute. Although differences exist among the statutes, they were enacted with comparable intent. Statutes generally (1) are intended to encourage landowners to make their property available to the public for recreational use; (2) stipulate that no fee is charged for the use of the land; (3) declare that the owner owes no duty of care to keep the land safe for use for recreational purpose nor to warn of a dangerous condition; (4) state that the landowner extends no assurance that the land is safe for any purpose and does not confer on the user the legal status of invitee or licensee; and (5) say that the landowner does not assume responsibility for or incur liability for any injury, death, or loss to any person or property caused by an act or omission of that person.

Resultant of the immunity provided by most such statutes, the provider's only duty is to warn of ultrahazardous situations and of known hidden hazards. In most states, the provider has no liability except for willful or malicious acts and for ultrahazardous situations. The immunity generally applies to all activity risks and all open and obvious premise risks.

Although enacted with the same purpose in mind, state recreational user statutes differ considerably due to judicial interpretations of the statutes. Courts in some states have broadened the scope of the statutes by interpreting them liberally (e.g., by applying the statute in cases where the injury occurred on a tennis court or when a fee was paid). The reader is encouraged to read an excellent presentation on the subject in Chapter 3.10, *Property Law*. The specific statutes for each state may be found in Table 1 and a summary of recreational user immunity may be found in Table 1 in Chapter 2.21, *Defenses Against Negligence*.

Volunteer Immunity Statutes

Prior to the decade of the 1980s, lawsuits against volunteers in recreation and sport activities were rare. In that decade, insurance coverage became both expensive and difficult to obtain, some coverage was unavailable, more exclusions were included in policies, many agencies discontinued or reduced insurance coverage, volunteer lawsuits began to increase in frequency, and volunteer recruitment became more difficult. This predicament prompted a number of states to pass legislation aimed at protecting certain volunteers in recreational and sport activities (see Table 1).

General Volunteer Immunity Statutes

Additionally, in the late 1980s, state legislatures were encouraged to pass a model act designed to protect volunteers working with certain nonprofit organizations and governmental entities from liability for injuries resulting from the ordinary or gross negligence of the volunteers. The Model State Act called for immunity from civil liability for any act or omission of the volunteer that resulted in damage or injury if the volunteer was acting in good faith and within the scope of duty for a nonprofit organization or governmental entity—so long as the injury was not caused by wanton and willful misconduct and did not involve the

---

[1] Charitable immunity is still strong in New Jersey (*Gilbert v. Seton Hall University*, 2003).

operation of a motor vehicle. The model act, however, intended no protection for the nonprofit or governmental agency for which the volunteer worked.

Subsequently, all states now have either (1) a general volunteer liability statute (often modeled after the Model State Act) designed to provide protection for volunteers, or (2) a statute intended to protect certain volunteers in recreation and sports activities (e.g., coaches, referees), or (3) both types of statutes. The general volunteer statutes vary greatly from state to state. Many of the states protect only directors or officers in the organization, and all have exceptions to immunity. Common exceptions include the motor vehicle exception, action based on federal law, action that constitutes gross negligence, willful and wanton acts, and in a few states, ordinary negligence. Many of these general state statutes are worded such that they should provide immunity for recreation and sport volunteers. Additionally, in 1997 the volunteer was provided with even more protection when Congress enacted the Volunteer Protection Act (discussed in detail later).

Recreation and Sport Volunteer Immunity Statutes

Nineteen states have passed some type of volunteer statute for volunteer sport coaches and officials.[2] In addition, a Hawaii statute protects volunteers at public skateboard parks, and youth sport volunteers are specifically mentioned in the Oklahoma and Texas general volunteer immunity statutes.

Ten points are frequently addressed in recreation and sport volunteer immunity statutes.

1. The volunteer must be **unpaid**. Some statutes specify that officials (e.g., referees, umpires) may receive a small stipend and retain their immunity.
2. The volunteer must act in **good faith**.
3. The volunteer must act within the **scope** of his or her duties.
4. **Protected parties** are usually specified and may include any or all of athletic coach, assistant coach, manager, assistant manager, instructor, official, referee, umpire, leader, league official, athletic trainer, and physician, or other health-care provider. The law in Arkansas, Kansas, and Mississippi restricts eligibility for immunity to sports officials who officiate at any level of competition.
5. Additionally, most statutes define the **type of organization** (e.g., nonprofit, charitable, educational) whose volunteers qualify.
6. Some states stipulate that protected parties must undergo an approved **training program**, usually relating to safety or first aid.
7. Some states specify that immunity does not protect when activities are **unsupervised**.
8. Most, but not all, exclude public and private **school coaches** from immunity.
9. It is the **nature of the act** that is protected. Most include immunity for ordinary negligence, but several include gross negligence, excluding only wanton and willful acts or intentional acts. Pennsylvania and New Mexico statutes specify immunity unless the conduct is substantially below the generally accepted level.
10. Almost all exclude negligence in the operation of a **motor vehicle** from immunity. Volunteer recreation and sport statutes may be found in Table 1.

Volunteer Protection Act (VPA)

The Volunteer Protection Act (VPA) was signed into law in 1997 (Public Law 105-19). This statute preempts state laws (except for those that provide for more volunteer protection than the VPA) and is intended to provide broad protection to volunteers nationwide under the following conditions:

• The volunteer was acting within the scope of the volunteer's responsibilities in the nonprofit organization or governmental entity at the time of the act or omission.
• If appropriate or required, the volunteer was properly licensed, certified or authorized by the appropriate authorities for the activities or practice in the state.

---

[2] Arkansas, Colorado, Delaware, Georgia, Illinois, Indiana, Kansas, Louisiana, Maryland, Massachusetts, Minnesota, Mississippi, Nevada, New Hampshire, New Jersey, New Mexico, North Dakota, Pennsylvania, and Rhode Island.

table **1** State Recreation- and Sport-Related Immunity Legislation

State	Recreational User Statutes	Rec/Sport Volunteer Statutes	Good Samaritan Statutes	AED Good Samaritan Statutes	Equestrian Immunity Statutes	Ski Operator Immunity Statutes	Skating Immunity Statutes	Other Sport & Recreation Statutes	General Sport & Recreation Statutes	Hazardous Recreational Activity Statutes
U.S.	PL. 105-19 42 U.S.C.S. 14,501-14,505	PL. 105-19 42 U.S.C.S. 14,501-14,505		P.L. 107-188 42 U.S.C.S. 238q						
AL	AC 35-15-(1-28)		AC 6-5-332	AC 6-5-332	AC 6-5-337		AC 6-5-342 Skateboard Parks			
AK	AS 09.65.200 AS 34.17.055		AS 09.65.090	AS 09.65.087	AS 09.65.145	AS 05.45.010 to .210				
AZ	ARS 33-1551	ARS 32-1471 ARS 32-1472	ARS 32-1471 ARS 32-1472	ARS 36-2261-64	ARS 12-553	ARS 5-701-707		ARS 12-554 Baseball ARS 12-556 Motor Sports		
AR	ARS 18-11-301 to 307	ARS 16-120-102	ARS 17-95-101	ARS 17-95-605	ARS 16-120-201 to 202					
CA	CCC 846, 846.1		CCHSC 1799.102	ACC 1714.21 HSC 1797.190 SB 911 of 1999	None	5 county ordinances	See Hazardous Rec. Activity Statutes for Skateboard Parks			CGC 831.7
CO	CRS 33-41-101 to 106	CRS 13-21-116	CRS 13-21-15.5	CRS 13-21-108.1	CRS 13-21-119	CRS 33-44-101 to 114		CRS 13-21-111.8(1) Sport Shooting CRS 13-21-120 Baseball CRS 12-15.5 101-111 Outfitters & Guides		
CT	CGSA 52-557f-k			CGSA 52-57b	CGSA 52-557p	CGSA 29-201 to 214				
DE	7 DCA 5901-5907	16 DCA 6835 16 DCA 6836	16 DCA 6801	16 DCA 6801	10 DCA 8140					
FL	FS 375.251		FS 768.13	FS 768.1325	FS 773.01 to .05		FS 316.0085 Skateboard Parks			FS 316.0085
GA	OCGA 51-3-20 to 26; OCGA 27-3-1	OCGA 51-1-20.1	OCGA 51-1-230 OCGA 768.135	OCGA 31-11-53.1 OCGA 51-1-29.3	OCGA 4-12-1 to 5		OCGA 51-1-43	OCGA 27-4-280 to 283 Fishing		
HI	HRS 520-1 to 8	HRS 662D-4	HI 663-1.5	HRS 663-1.5	HRS 663B-1 to 2		HRS 662.19, HRS 46-72.5, HRS 662D-4		HRS 663-1.54	
ID	IC 36-1604		IC 5-330	IC 5-337	IC 6-1801 to 1802	IC 6-1101 to 1109		IC 6-1201 to 1206 Outfitters & Guides		
IL	745 ILCS 65/1 to 7	745 ILCS 80/1	745 ILCS 49/12	410 ILCS 4/30 745 ILCS 49/12	745 ILCS 47/1 to 47/999		745 ILCS 72/1 to 30	745 ILCS 52/1 to 52/99 Hockey Facilities		745 ILCS 10/3 to 109
IN	ICA 14-22-10-2 to 2.5	ICA 34-30-4-2 ICA 34-30-19-3 to 4	ICA 34-30-12-1	ICA 16-31-6.2 ICA 34-30-12-1	ICA 34-31-5-1 to 5		ICA 34-31-6-1 to 4			
IA	ICA 461C.1 to .7		ICA 115.3 ICA 915.3	ICA 147A.10	ICA 673.1 to .4		ICA 670.4 Skateboard Parks			
KS	KSA 58-3201 to 3207	KSA 60-3607	KSA 65-2891	KSA 65-6149a	KSA 60-4001 to 4004					
KY	KRS 150.645 KRS 411.190		KRS 411.148 KRS 411.150	KRS 311.668	KRS 247.401 to 4029					
LA	LRS 9:2791, 2795	LRS 9:2798	LRS 9:2793	LRS 40:1236.11 to .14 LRS 9:2793	LRS 9: 2795.1					

(continued)

table ◇ 1 ◇ State Recreation- and Sport-Related Immunity Legislation (continued)

State	Recreational User Statutes	Rec/Sport Volunteer Statutes	Good Samaritan Statutes	AED Good Samaritan Statutes	Equestrian Immunity Statutes	Ski Operator Immunity Statutes	Skating Immunity Statutes	Other Sport & Recreation Statutes	General Sport & Recreation Statutes	Hazardous Recreational Activity Statutes
ME	14 MRSA 159-A		14 MRSA 164	22 MRSA 2150-C	7 MRSA 4101-4104A	26 MRSA 471-490-G; 32 MRSA 15201 to 15227	8 MRSA 601-608; 8 MRSA 625	8 MRSA 801-806 Amuse Rides; 32 MRSA 15219 Hang Gliding		
MD	MCA 5-1101 to 1109	MCA 5-607; MCA 5-802	MCA 5-603	MCA 13-517	None					
MA	21 MGL 17C	231 MGL 85V	71 ALM 55A; 111C ALM 20	112 ALM 12V1/2	128 MGL 2D	143 MGL 71H to 71S				
MI	MCLA 324.73301		MCLA 691.1501; MCLA 691.1507; MCLA 333.20965	MCLA 333.20965	MCLA 691.1661-.1667	MCLA 408.321 to .344 or MSA 13A.82126	MCLA 445.1721 to .1726	MCLA 681.1541 to .1544; MCLA 691.1544 Sport Shooting; MCLA 342.82126 Snow-mobiling		
MN	MSA 604A.20 to 27	MSA 604A.11	MSA 604A.01	MSA 604A.01	MSA 604A.12					
MS	MCA 89-2-1 to 27	MCA 95-9-3	MCA 63-3-405; MCA 73-25-37	MCA 41-60-33	MCA 95-11-1 to 7					
MO	MAS 537.345 to .348		RSM 537.037	RSM 190.092	MAS 537.325					
MT	MCA 70-16-301 to 302		MCA 27-1-714	MCA 50-6-505	MCA 27-1-725 to 728	MCA 23-2-731-736		MCA 23-2-651 to 656 Snowmobiling; MCA 27-1-733 Rodeos		
NE	NRS 37-729 to 736		NRS 25-21, 186	NRS 71-51, 102	NRS 25-21.249 to .253					
NV	NRS 41.510	NRS 41.630	NRS 41.5000	NRS 41.500	None	NRS 455A.010 to .190	NRS 455B.200 to .300 Skateboard Parks	NRS 455B.010 to 455B.100 Amuse Rides		
NH	NHSA 212:34, NHSA 231-A:1 to 8	NHSA 508.17	RSA 508:12	RSA 153-A:31	NHSA 508:19	NHSA 225-A:1 to :26	NHSA 507-B:11 Skateboard Parks			NHSA 507 B-11
NJ	NJS 13:1B-15.134 to .142; NJS 2A:42A-2 to 10	NJS 2A:62A-6	NJS 2A:62A-1; NJS 26:2K-29	NJS 2A:62A-25	NJ S 5:15-1 to 12	NJS 34:4A-1; NJS 5:13-1 to 11	NJS 5:14-1 to 7	NJS 39:3C-18 to 23		
NM	NMSA 17-4-7	NMSA 41-12-1; NMSA 41-12-2	NMSA 24-10-3	NMSA 34-10B-4	NMSA 42-13-2 to 5	NMSA 24-15-1 to 14				
NY	NY GOL 9-103		NYCLSPH 3000-a	NYCLSPH 3000-a; NYCLSPH 3000-b	None	NY GOL 18-101 to 108; NYLL 865 to 868				
NC	NCGS 38A-1 to 4		NCGS 20-166; NCGS 90-21.14	NCGS 90-21.15	NCGS 99E-1 to 3	NCGS 99C-1 to 5	NCGS 99E-10 to 14			
ND	NDCC 53-08-01 to 06	NDCC 32-3-46	NDCC 32-03.1-02	NDCC 32-03.1-02.3	NDCC 53-10-01 to 11	NDCC 53-09-01 to 11				
OH	ORCA 1533.18; ORCA 1533.181		ORCA 2305.23	ORCA 2305.235	ORCA 2305.321	ORCA 4169.01 to .99	ORCA 4171.01 to .10			

(continued)

table ◆1◆ State Recreation- and Sport-Related Immunity Legislation (continued)

State	Recreational User Statutes	Rec/Sport Volunteer Statutes	Good Samaritan Statutes	AED Good Samaritan Statutes	Equestrian Immunity Statutes	Ski Operator Immunity Statutes	Skating Immunity Statutes	Other Sport & Recreation Statutes	General Sport & Recreation Statutes	Hazardous Recreational Activity Statutes
OK	2 OS 1301-315 76 OS 5, 11 OS 76-10 to 15	76 OS 31	OS 76.5	76 OS 5A	OS 50.1 to .4					
OR	ORS 105.670 to .700		ORS 30.800 ORS 433.830	ORS 30.801	ORS 30.687 to .697	ORS 30.970 to .990				
PA	68 PCSA 477-1 to 7	42 PCSA 8332.1	42 PCSA 8332	42 PCSA 8331.2	2005 SB 618 (Printer's # 1359)	42 PCSA 7102 or 40 PCSA 2051				
RI	RIGL 32-6-1 to 7	RIGL 9-1-48	RIGL 9-1-27.1 RIGL 9-1-34	RIGL 9-1-34	RIGL 4-21-1 to 4	RIGL 41-8-1 to 4		RIGL 9-20-5 Snow-mobiles & ATVs		
SC	SCCA 27-3-10 to 70		SCCA 15-1-310	SCCA 4-76-40	SCCA 47-9-710 to 730		SCCA 52-21-10 to 60			
SD	SDCLA 20-9-12 to 18		SDCLA 32034-3 SDCLA 20-9-3	SDCLA 20-9-4.1	SDCLA 42-11-1 to 5		SDCLA 32-20A-21 to 23	SDCLA 32-20A-21 to 22 Snowmobiling		
TN	TCA 11-10-101 to 105 TCA 70-7-101 to 105		TCA 63-6-218	TCA 63-6-218	TCA 44-20-101 to 105	TCA 68-114-101 -107		TCA 70-7-201-204 White-water rafting		
TX	TCPRC 75.001 to .004	TCPRC 84.0001 to .008	VTCA 74.001 to .003	TCPRC 74.001	TCPRC 87.001 to .005		THSCA 759.001 to .005 THSCA 760.001 to .006			
UT	UCA 57-14-1 to 7		UCA 78-11-22 UCA 26-41-101-106	UCA 28-8-7.5 or 75	UCA 78-27b-101 to 103	UCA 78-27-51 to 54	See Gen Rec & Sport Statutes for Skateboard Parks	UCA 47-3-1 to 3 Sport Shooting; UCA 78-27-61 Amuse Rides; UCA 78-27-62 Hockey Facil	UCA 78-27-63	
VT	12 VSA 5791 to 5795		12 VSA 519	18 VSA 907	12 VSA 1039	12 VSA 1036 to 1038	See Gen Rec & Sport Statutes for Skateboard Parks		12 VSA 1037	
VA	VCA 29.1-.509		VCA 8.00-225	VCA 8.01-225	VCA 3.1-796.130 to .133					
WA	RCW 4.24.200 to .210		RCW 4.24.300	RCW 70.54.310	RCW 4.24.530 to .540	RCW 79A.45.010 to .060				
WV	WVC 19-25-1 to 7		WVC 55-7-15, 16, 19	WVC 16-4D-3 to 4	WVC 20-4-1 to 7	WVC 20-3A-1 to 6		WVC 20-3B-1 to 5 Outfitters & Guides		
WI	WSA 895.52 to .525		WSA 895.48	WSA 895.48	WSA 895.481-1 885.481 3(e)	WSA 895.525	See Gen Rec & Sport Statutes for Skateboard Parks		WSA 895.525	
WY	WYO STAT 34-19-101 to 106		WYO STAT 1-1-120	WYO STAT 35-26-102 to 103	WYO STAT 1-1-121 to 123	WYO STAT 1-1-121 to 123		WYO STAT 1-1-118 Rodeos	WYO STAT 1-1-121 to 123	

- The harm was not caused by willful or criminal misconduct, gross negligence, reckless misconduct, or a conscious, flagrant indifference to the rights or safety of the individual harmed by the volunteer.
- The harm was not caused by the volunteer operating a motor vehicle . . . for which the State requires . . . an operator's license; or . . . insurance.

Of particular interest is the second condition—that the immunity applies only if the volunteer is licensed, certified or authorized when such empowerments are relevant. *It is important to note that the act does not affect the liability of any nonprofit or governmental entity—but rather protects only individuals from liability.* Acts that are not encompassed by the statute include (1) crimes of violence or terrorism, (2) hate crimes, (3) sexual offense convictions, (4) violation of federal or state civil rights law, and (5) those committed while under the influence of drugs or alcohol. Punitive damages can be awarded only if the volunteer's actions constituted willful or criminal misconduct or a conscious flagrant indifference to the rights and safety of the injured party. For losses due to physical or emotional pain, the volunteer will be liable only to the extent of his or her percentage of responsibility.

First Aid Statutes (Good Samaritan)

Every state except one has some form of Good Samaritan statute, which is intended to provide immunity from liability for certain parties who voluntarily and gratuitously come to the aid of injured persons. Good Samaritan laws were developed to encourage both physicians and laypeople to help others in emergency situations.

There is no general legal duty to assist or rescue injured parties in most states. An exception is Vermont, which requires a person who knows that another is exposed to grave physical harm shall give reasonable assistance to the exposed person if he can do so without danger or peril to himself. Penalty for violation, however, is only $100. Mississippi, North Carolina, and South Dakota require that the driver of a vehicle involved in an accident assist injured parties if needed if assisting presents no danger to the one assisting. Most then provide immunity for the driver.

Six elements are common to most Good Samaritan statutes. The first is the stipulation of **who is protected** by the statute. The most common designation is any person who comes to the aid of another in an emergency situation. More than 40 states offer protection for any individual who assists in an emergency situation. Some states, however, restrict the immunity to health-care personnel (physicians, surgeons, nurses, EMS personnel, physical therapists, and/or others) or those with first aid training. Many states exclude health-care personnel from protection if the action is within the scope of the duty.

The second and third elements are that the parties must act in **good faith** and without expectation of **remuneration**. Almost every state specifies one or the other, and most list both. Fourth, almost all of the statutes specify that the action must occur in an **emergency situation** away from a medical facility. Many states also have statutes specific to assisting those choking on food in restaurants. A few statutes limit coverage to more specific situations (e.g., choking, crime victims, cardiopulmonary rescues, life-threatening situations, athletic events), and some apply to volunteer team physicians.

Fifth, the statutes almost always stipulate that the care must be done **at the scene** of the accident. A number also add protection during transport to the hospital.

Finally, virtually all the statutes protect the "Good Samaritan" from liability for injury caused by acts or omissions or **ordinary negligence**. Some statutes specify that the individual must act as a reasonably prudent person would act, and others specify "reasonable aid." Statutes in a few states specify that there is immunity unless there is reckless or willful and wanton conduct.

Thus, although "Good Samaritan" laws differ considerably among states, the typical statute asserts that *any person who, in good faith, gratuitously renders emergency care at the scene of an accident cannot be held liable for injury resulting from acts and omissions unless the conduct constitutes gross negligence or willful/wanton conduct.* Good Samaritan legislation in each state may be found in Table 1. In addition, the concept is summarized in Table 1 in Chapter 2.21, *Defenses Against Negligence.*

AED Statutes

The development of the automated external defibrillator (AED) in the 1990s provided a major technological advance in the fight against sudden cardiac arrest deaths in the United States. The **AED** is a medical device that (1) recognizes the presence or absence of ventricular fibrillation, (2) is capable of determining if defibrillation should be performed, (3) can automatically charge and request delivery of an electrical impulse, and (4) can deliver an appropriate impulse upon action by the operator. Although it has been estimated that more than half of the 250,000 plus deaths annually in the nation could be prevented by timely use of an AED, its widespread use has been hampered by the lack of laws enabling its use by nonmedical personnel.

With the intent of encouraging the extensive use of the AED, some states began passing Good Samaritan legislation specifically aimed at AED usage, whereas others added the AED to existing Good Samaritan statutes. Although all states have now passed some type of AED legislation, that legislation differs significantly from state to state in terms of (1) who is protected, (2) requirements for immunity, and (3) what acts are immunized. AED legislation in each state may be found in Table 1, and the immunity is summarized in Table 1 in Chapter 2.21, *Defenses Against Negligence*.

Parties protected may include any or all of the following: (1) trained users, (2) any user in a perceived emergency, (3) the entity that acquires the device, (4) the prescribing physician, (5) parties who train others to use the AED, or (6) certified health-care professionals. A major difference involves the requirements for immunity. Many states offer immunity for **any user** who acts gratuitously and in good faith in a perceived medical emergency to render emergency care. Many other states provide the same immunity, but only to **trained users**. The definition of trained also differs considerably. Some states require that expected users (or employees) be trained, but that a "Good Samaritan" passerby is immune regardless of training. Legislation in a few states seems to legalize the use of the device, but provides no immunity.

There is also great variance in what acts are immunized by the law. At least one provides immunity only where the user acted as an ordinary reasonably prudent person would have acted—seemingly providing no immunity from negligence. Most specify no immunity protection for grossly negligent actions or willful or wanton misconduct—thereby providing immunity for negligence. Several exclude only willful and wanton actions from immunity—thus apparently creating immunity for grossly negligent acts. Several also seem to provide blanket immunity, specifying no restrictions on the immunity of an AED user.

A number of states (California, New York, Louisiana, Rhode Island, New Jersey, Michigan, and Illinois) have passed statutes requiring AED availability in health clubs. In addition, legislation requiring availability of AEDs at health clubs has been introduced in Kansas.

Cardiac Arrest Survival Act (CASA)

In an effort to further combat sudden cardiac arrest deaths, Congress passed the **Cardiac Arrest Survival Act** (2002) (42 *USCS* 238q[2002]). The legislation, like the state legislation preceding it, is designed to accelerate the widespread use of automated external defibrillators by providing Good Samaritan immunity in those states not having such protection. The legislation was intended to augment existing state "Good Samaritan" laws by providing federal liability protection for both users and purchasers of AEDs.

The law specifies that **"any person who uses** or attempts to use an AED device on a victim of a perceived medical emergency is immune from civil liability for any harm resulting from the use or attempted use of such device," including health-care professionals outside the scope of their license or certification. This immunity to the Good Samaritan user applies regardless of training and protects the user from liability for ordinary negligence. **Any person who acquires the device** is also immune from such liability provided the harm was not due to failure of the acquirer to notify appropriate local entities of the placement of the device, to properly maintain and test the device, or to provide appropriate training to employees using the device.

CASA preempts state law only where state statute does not provide protection for a user or acquirer. Thus, CASA fills in the immunity gaps left by some state legislation because all users and acquirers are covered by state law (if state statute provides immunity) or by federal law (if immunity is not provided for by state law). When state law fails to protect either the user or the acquirer, CASA provides that protection.

Immunity is not provided by CASA (1) for willful or criminal misconduct, gross negligence, reckless misconduct or a conscious, flagrant indifference to the rights or safety of the victim who was harmed; (2) for licensed health professionals operating within the scope of their employment; or (3) for certain health-care providers or leasers of AEDs.

There are also some exclusions that would not normally be relevant to providers of health, fitness, recreation, and sport activities. These are (1) when the person using the device is a licensed or certified health professional acting within the scope of his or her duties; (2) a hospital, clinic, or other entity with the purpose of providing health care; or (3) when the acquirer leased the AED to a health-care entity and an employee caused harm while acting within the scope of the entity.

Shared Responsibility and Statutory Assumption of Risk Statutes

Legislation has been enacted in most states to help protect selected recreation and sport providers from liability for injuries resulting from the inherent risks of particular activities, or in many cases, from certain types of ordinary negligence by the provider. Some of these acts are in the form of shared responsibility statutes, whereas others are more accurately designated as statutory assumption of risk statutes. These acts, originally called **sport safety acts**, usually seek to provide some liability protections for recreation and sport businesses that make certain activities available to the public.

Shared responsibility statutes generally have four distinguishing features. They enumerate the **duties of the recreation or sport provider**. Failure to satisfy these duties constitutes negligence and makes the statute inapplicable. Duties provided in such statutes have been deemed to establish a statutory standard of care. The second earmark of these statutes is that they specify **duties of the participant**. Common duties listed include the responsibility to read and obey signs and to stay within the limits of his or her ability. Failure to perform the required participant duties could constitute secondary assumption of risk. Secondary assumption of risk (formerly called contributory negligence) would serve to decrease situations in which recovery for participants is possible and may, at the same time, increase liability of the participant to other participants. Shared responsibility statutes usually contain certain **provisions that preclude recovery**. Most specify that recovery is not permitted when the injury resulted from inherent risks. Many statutes specifically define the inherent risks of the activity or sport, prompting many courts to grant summary judgment based on the statute. The final feature of these statutes is that **some type of immunity is provided**—or perhaps, more accurately, they reassert that there is *no liability* for injuries resulting from the inherent risks. Some state that there is no liability for injuries resulting from the inherent risks of the activity, whereas others provide that there is no liability unless the provider failed to comply with the specified duties. In some cases, they provide immunity from liability for certain types of negligence.

Some statutes are more accurately classified as **statutory assumption of risk statutes** because the major provision of the statute is to make clear that the participant is assuming the inherent risks of the activity. These statutes usually do not include duties of the participant. Notwithstanding the differences between these two types of statutes, the characteristic they have in common is that they usually are intended to protect the service provider from liability for injury resulting from the inherent risks of the activity and, in many cases, from liability for injuries resulting from ordinary negligence.

These two types of statutes have been grouped into six categories: (1) equine liability statutes, (2) skiing statutes, (3) skating statutes [i.e., roller skating, ice skating, skateboarding, in-line skating, skate parks], (4) statutes pertaining to other activities, (5) general recreation and sport statutes, and (6) hazardous recreational activity statutes.

Equine Liability Statutes

State legislatures have enacted equine liability statutes in forty-four states over the past ten to fifteen years. Equine acts usually include horses, ponies, donkeys, mules, and hinnies. Statutes in some states also include llamas. The laws are designed to protect owners, sponsors, and organizers of named equine activities from liability for equine-related accidents resulting from the inherent risks of the activity and in many cases from ordinary negligence. Most may be closer to statutory assumption of risk statutes than to shared responsibility statutes because they generally do not specify responsibilities or duties of the participant. Although the statutes differ somewhat from state to state, most equine statutes *immunize equine owners from liability for injuries resulting from the inherent risks of equine activities except when the provider*

1. Provided faulty equipment or tack that caused the injury;
2. Failed to make reasonable and prudent efforts to determine the ability of the participant to engage safely in the activity or determine the ability of the participant to safely manage the particular equine;
3. Failed to post warning of known dangerous latent conditions on the facilities; or
4. Commits an act or omission that is below the required level of care. The minimum level described varies by state, but includes ordinary negligence, gross negligence, reckless conduct, and willful and wanton conduct.

In general, these statutes do not provide the same protection as that provided by the immunity statutes in previous sections of this chapter because under most equine statutes, the provider remains liable for injuries resulting from some or all negligent acts.

Statutes generally define the equine activities covered by the law, the categories of providers protected, the immunity provided, the exceptions, signage requirements, and the inherent risks of equine activities. Usually included in the inherent risks are (1) equine behavior propensities, (2) unpredictability of animal reactions, (3) hazards such as surface and subsurface conditions, (4) collisions with other equines and objects, and (5) the potential of a participant to act in a negligent manner that may cause injury. Equine legislation in each state may be found in Table 1.

Ski Operator Immunity Statutes

Ski operator statutes were among the first shared-responsibility statutes—*intended to clarify the duties of the ski operator and the skier and to reduce litigation arising from injuries resulting from the inherent risks of skiing.* At least 27 state legislatures have enacted some type of shared responsibility ski statute. Although these statutes differ considerably, they generally include duties of the ski operator, duties of the skier, a listing of the inherent risks of skiing, and the affirmation that the skier assumes the inherent risks of the activity and that the ski operator is not liable for injuries resulting from the inherent risks. Lists of operator and skier duties are generally extensive. These acts generally include no immunity for ordinary negligence; however, in some states, negligence is limited to the failure to perform specified duties.

States approach inherent risks in various ways. Some states (e.g., Tennessee, New Mexico, and Idaho) express that any injury not caused by a violation of the ski operator duties is an inherent risk of the activity and that subsequent legal action is barred. Colorado, North Carolina, and Alaska statutes specify that a violation of the statute by either operator or skier constitutes negligence. Other states require a jury to determine if the risk was inherent. Ski legislation in each state may be found in Table 1.

Skating Statutes

Eleven states have enacted either roller skating or ice skating shared-responsibility statutes. These statutes generally contain four critical sections: (1) duties of the operator—usually including posting of notices regarding duties of skaters and inherent risks of skating; (2) duties of the skater—usually including skating within the range of one's ability, maintaining control of the skater's speed and course at all times, and heeding safety warnings; (3) some of the inherent dangers of skating; and (4) a declaration that the skater assumes the inherent risks and a statement that a skater or operator who violates duties set forth is liable to an injured person in a civil action. Skating legislation in each state may be found in Table 1. Providers are generally liable only if they breach the operator duties listed in the statute.

Skateboard Parks. Popular types of skating emerging in recent years have included skateboarding, rollerblading, roller skiing, and in-line skating. Several state legislatures have passed legislation protecting providers of facilities for such activities as well as for stunt or freestyle biking.

The Nevada legislature passed a shared-responsibility statute that provides limited protection for an agency or political subdivision of the state that provides skateboard parks for public use. Iowa passed an assumption of risk statute that immunizes municipalities and their employees from liability for injuries result- ing from the inherent risks of skateboarding or in-line skating on public property. The injured person must have known or reasonably should have known that the activity created a substantial risk of injury. Likewise, the Utah and Vermont legislatures established statutory assumption of risk statutes providing protection from liability for inherent risks of skating and skateboard-type activities. The Vermont statute encompassed all providers of all sports, and the Utah statute included counties and municipalities providing facilities for bike riding, biking, skateboarding, roller skating, and in-line skating (see *General Recreation and Sport Immu- nity Statutes*, following). *These statutes have granted protection to governmental providers (except Vermont which included all sport providers) and their employees from liability for injuries resulting from the inherent risks of the activities.*

California, Florida, and New Hampshire have enacted hazardous recreational activity legislation that includes skateboard parks (see *Hazardous Recreational Activity Immunity Statutes*, following). *This legisla- tion grants protection from liability for some types of ordinary negligence to governmental entities (and em- ployees) that provide these activities.*

Statutes Pertaining to Other Activities

Immunity statutes affecting other recreation and sport activities have also been enacted. They include stat- utes dealing with amusement rides (3 states), baseball (2), fishing (1), hang gliding (1), hockey facilities (2), motor sports (1), outfitters and guides (3), rodeos (2), snowmobiling (5), and sport shooting (3). These statutes are as varied as the activities to which they relate. Some are true shared-responsibility statutes, whereas others are more accurately labeled statutory assumption of risk statutes as they simply declare that the participant assumes the inherent risks. However, regardless of the differences among these statutes, *the common link is that they are all intended to protect the provider from liability for injuries resulting from the inherent risks of the activity.* Legislation relating to these activities may be found in Table 1.

Snowmobile statutes usually announce that the operator is not liable for the inherent risks. In some states the immunity is extended to ordinary negligence. They, like the other statutes included in this para- graph, are shared-responsibility statutes as they prescribe duties of participants and operators. Interestingly, in South Dakota, providers renting snowmobiles are liable only if they are grossly negligent. **Outfitter and Guide** statutes, usually true shared-responsibility statutes, designate duties of both operators and participants and limit the liability of the outfitter to those specified duties. They specify that operators are liable only in the event of negligence. **Amusement ride** statutes also fall into this category. They provide for rider and operator duties and specify that the rider assumes the inherent risks. Also of interest, Nevada law states that riders *above age 13* assume the *open and obvious* inherent risks.

Acts relating to many activities are simply statutory assumption of risk statutes. For instance, **sport- shooting** statutes designate that the participant (and spectator in Colorado) assumes the inherent risks of the activity. In Utah, the statute names the risks and specifies that the risks that are obvious and inherent are assumed. Utah and Michigan statutes declare that operators are generally not civilly or criminally liable for noise and limit claims of nuisance. **Rodeo** statutes immunize nonprofit Montana and Wyoming organi- zations sponsoring rodeos from liability for all actions except wanton and willful or intentional acts. The statute is applicable to volunteer participants (including minors with written parental permission) and only in amateur rodeos in Wyoming. New Jersey provides some immunity for persons in the business of **renting bicycles** providing the operator follows statutory requirements. The **hang gliding** statute merely proclaims that participants assume the inherent risks of the activity. The **fishing** statute in Georgia, the **baseball** stat- ute in Colorado, and the **hockey facility** statutes in Utah and Illinois differ in that some spell out risks, some pertain to signage, and most specify duties of the property or facility owner or operator, but not of the par- ticipant (or spectator, in the baseball and hockey statutes). All, however, make it clear that the operator is not liable for injuries resulting from the inherent risks of the activities. Ironically, the baseball statute was named the Colorado Baseball Spectator Safety Act. Legislation relating to these activities may be found in Table 1.

General Recreation and Sport Immunity Statutes

Five states have enacted laws sometimes referred to as **omnibus legislation** (Spengler & Burket, 2001) that is intended to encompass a large number of activities and sports rather than one or two. These laws are designed to give the service provider immunity, in one law, from liability for injuries resulting from the inherent risks of a number of sports. These states are Hawaii, Utah, Vermont, Wisconsin, and Wyoming. The Vermont statute is the most inclusive, including all sports and all providers, and the Utah statute is the least inclusive—protecting only counties and municipalities from liability for rodeos, bike riding, biking, equestrian, skateboarding, roller skating, and in-line skating. Wisconsin and Wyoming protected all providers from more than 20 recreational and sport activities. *In each of these states, providers are immune from liability for inherent risks, but retain liability for the negligence of the entity or its employees.* Most of these statutes prescribe duties of the participant and the provider, and thus, could be classified as shared responsibility statutes.

Hazardous Recreational Activity Immunity Statutes

Legislatures in two states, California and Illinois, have passed statutes similar to the omnibus legislation just mentioned—except for two main differences. First, *the laws protect only public entities and their employees.* Secondly, the statutes protect the service provider and its employees from liability *for at least some types of ordinary negligence.* Protection is not provided (1) for failure to guard or warn of a known dangerous condition; (2) when a fee is charged for participation in the activity (a fee may be charged for entrance into the park); (3) for failure to properly construct or maintain recreational equipment or machinery; (4) when the entity recklessly or with gross negligence promoted the participation; or (5) when the injury resulted from gross negligence or reckless conduct of the entity or its employees. Thus, the entity and its employees are not liable for ordinary negligence except for failure to guard or warn of a dangerous condition and for failure to properly construct or maintain recreational equipment and machinery. In each state, more than thirty sports and activities are included within the protection. California has passed subsequent legislation specifically listing skateboarding as a hazardous recreational activity.

Two other states, Florida and New Hampshire, have passed similar legislation affecting fewer activities. The Florida statute protects governmental entities and their employees from liability for ordinary negligence (except the failure to warn of dangerous conditions of which the participant cannot reasonably expect to have notice) for three hazardous activities—skateboarding, in-line skating, and freestyle bicycling. New Hampshire provides immunity from liability for ordinary negligence for municipalities and school districts that without charge provide facilities for skateboarding, rollerblading, stunt biking, or roller skiing.

◇◇◇ **OTHER RELATED SIGNIFICANT CASES**

The Significant Case for Chapter 2.21, *Defenses Against Negligence* also serves as the Significant Case for this chapter.
Chapter 2.21 *Defenses Against Negligence* (recreational user immunity)
Chapter 2.31 *Emergency Care* (Good Samaritan immunity)
Chapter 3.10 *Property Law* (recreational user immunity)
Chapter 4.16 *Hazing* (discretionary act immunity)
Chapter 5.23 *Crisis Management* (discretionary act immunity)

Recent Trends

Three trends seem to stand out in the area of immunity as it relates to recreation and sport management. First is the growing trend toward having the participant assume responsibility for his or her actions. Participants are increasingly asked to assume the inherent risks of the activity, and liability of the provider may be decreased by the secondary assumption of risk of the participant.

Second, the immunity enjoyed by the provider can be lost by failure of the provider to take action when it has notice of a danger that poses an imminent threat. When aware of such a threat, the provider must take action to warn the participant and/or remove the dangerous condition.

Finally, providers are being granted immunity from liability for injuries resulting from the inherent risks of the activity and, in many cases, from liability for ordinary negligence. This helps to ameliorate the liability fears of the provider and encourages the provider to offer such activities as adventure sports and extreme sports.

References

Case

Gilbert v. Seton Hall University, 2003 U.S. App. LEXIS 11722.

Publications

Brown, J. (1997). Legislators strike out: Volunteer little league coaches should not be immune from tort liability. *Seton Hall J. Sports L., 7*, 559.

Carter-Yamauchi, C. A. (1996). *Volunteerism—A risky business?* Honolulu: Legislative Reference Bureau.

Centner, T. J. (2000). Tort liability for sports and recreational activities: Expanding statutory immunity for protected classes and activities. *J. Legis, 26*, 1.

Centner, T. J. (2001). Simplifying sports liability law through a shared responsibility chapter. *Va. Sports & Ent. L. J., 1*, 54.

Chalat, J. H. (2000). *Survey of ski law in the United States*. Vail, CO: CLE International Ski Liability Conference.

Dawson, R. O. (1999). *Equine activity statutes: Part I—IV*. Retrieved from http://www.law.utexas.edu/dawson/horselaw/update1.htm

Jordan, B. (2001). *What is the Good Samaritan law?* Retrieved from http://pa.essortment.com/goodsamaritanl_redg.htm

Ridolfi, K. M. (2000). Law, ethics, and the Good Samaritan: Should there be a duty to rescue? *Santa Clara L. Rev., 40*, 957.

Runquist, L. A., & Zybach, J. F. (1997). *Volunteer Protection Act of 1997—an imperfect solution*. Retrieved from http://www.runquist.com/article_vol_protect.htm

Slank, N. L. (1999). A symposium on tort and sport: Leveling the playing field. *Washburn L. J., 38*, 847.

Spengler, J. O., & Burket, B. P. (2001). Sport safety statutes and inherent risk: A comparison study of sport specific legislation. *Journal of Legal Aspects of Sport, 11*(2), 135.

van der Smissen, B. (1990). *Legal liability and risk management for public and private entities*. Cincinnati, OH: Anderson Publishing Company.

2.23 Waivers and Releases

Doyice J. Cotten
Sport Risk Consulting

A **waiver** or **release of liability** in the recreation or sport setting is a contract in which the participant or user of a service agrees to relinquish the right to pursue legal action against the service provider in the event that the ordinary negligence of the provider results in an injury to the participant. Injuries in sport and recreation result from one of three causes: (1) inherent risks of the activity (common accidents); (2) negligence by the service provider or its employees; and (3) more extreme acts by the service provider or its employees (i.e., gross negligence, reckless conduct, or willful/wanton conduct). It is important to understand that *the waiver is usually meant to protect the service provider from liability for the ordinary negligence of the service provider or its employees.* It will not generally protect the service provider from liability for extreme forms of negligence.[1] Although providers are not generally liable for injuries resulting from the inherent risks of the activity, the document can include language that will help protect the provider from liability for injuries resulting from inherent risks (see Participant Agreements later in this chapter). The waiver is an important tool in the risk management arsenal of the service provider.

Although waivers are commonly used by more recreation- and sport-related businesses than ever before, many service providers are still under the erroneous impression that waivers are worthless and offer no protection to the service provider. The validity of a waiver, however, is determined by the law in each state, and subsequently, the validity of waivers will vary depending on the state.

Cotten and Cotten (2005) have placed each state into one of four categories depending on the degree of rigor required for a valid waiver by the courts in that state (Figure 1). The first category includes ten states that not only allow waivers, but also have very lenient requirements for their validity. The second category includes sixteen states and Washington, DC, in which waivers are allowed and the requirements for validity are moderate in nature. The third category includes twenty states that allow waivers, but maintain very rigorous requirements for a waiver to be upheld. The final category consists of three states in which waivers will not protect the service provider from liability for negligence. Cases from Rhode Island and Puerto Rico have yielded insufficient information about their waiver law for classification. *Thus, in at least forty-six states and Washington, DC, a well-written, properly administered waiver, voluntarily signed by an adult, can be used to protect the recreation or sport business from liability for ordinary negligence by the business or its employees.*

---

[1] Waivers in four states (Florida, Illinois, Kentucky, and Pennsylvania) can protect the service provider from liability for gross negligence. In three states (Colorado, Texas, and West Virginia), waivers can protect against liability for reckless conduct.

Lenient States		Moderate States			Rigorous States			Not Enforced			Insufficient Information	
AL	GA	CO	DC	FL	AK	AR	AZ	LA	MT	VA	RI	PR
KS	MD	IA	ID	IL	CA	CT	DE					
MA	MI	MN	NC	NM	HI	IN	KY					
NE	ND	OK	OR	SC	ME	MO	MS					
OH	TN	SD	TX	WA	NH	NJ	NV					
		WV	WU		NY	PA	UT					
					VT	WI						

FIGURE 1. Categorization of States Based on Rigor Required for a Valid Waiver

Providers must understand, however, that not all waivers are upheld in lenient states and that many waivers are upheld in rigorous states. The category simply indicates the degree of rigor or specific requirements that must be met in the state for a waiver to be enforceable. Providers should also understand that the law is in a constant state of change so requirements, and the categories into which states are placed, are always subject to change.

Fundamental Concepts

Requirements for a Valid Waiver

A waiver is a legal contract and, as such, must adhere to the basic requirements of contract law. Some contract requirements are presented here, but the reader should refer to Chapter 6.10, *Contract Essentials*, for more information regarding contracts.

Public Policy

A contract or waiver is not valid if it is against **public policy**—sometimes defined as that principle of law under which freedom of contract or private dealings is restricted for the good of the community.[2] A waiver is generally against public policy if (1) it pertains to a service important to the public, (2) the parties are not of equal bargaining power (contracts of adhesion), (3) there is an employer–employee relationship, or (4) it attempts to preclude liability for extreme forms of conduct such as gross negligence, reckless misconduct, or willful and wanton conduct. The general rule in most states is that recreation- or sport-related waivers are not against public policy.

Consideration

A valid contract requires that something of value be exchanged between parties. The courts have held that the opportunity to participate constitutes consideration on the part of the service provider. Waivers usually include language such as, "In consideration for being allowed to participate, I hereby waive. . . ."

Parties to the Contract

Three important points relate to the parties involved in a waiver. They are parties barred from redress, parties protected by the contract, and capacity to contract (see also Chapter 6.10, *Contract Essentials*).

Parties Relinquishing Rights. When signing a waiver, the signer is obviously relinquishing the rights of the signer to hold the service provider liable in the event of injury. However, the spouse or heirs often

---

[2] *Merten v. Nathan*, 321 N.W.2d 173, quoting *Higgins v. McFarland*, 86 S.E.2d 168 at 172 (Va., 1955).

file suit against the service provider when the signer is seriously injured or killed. A phrase in which the signer relinquishes (on behalf of self, spouse, heirs, estate, and assigns) the right to recover for injury or death is usually included in the waiver. Providers should be aware, however, that such a phrase is not enforceable in many states because those states hold that **loss of consortium**[3] and **wrongful death**[4] claims are independent causes of action and are not derivative on whether the signer has or would have had a valid claim.

Parties Protected by the Waiver. The waiver must specify the parties protected by the agreement. Parties for which protection is often sought (e.g., corporation, management, employees, sponsors, volunteers) should be listed. An inclusive phrase such as ". . . and all others who are involved" may be included if desired.

Parties Who Do Not Have Capacity to Contract. The third point of importance regards the capacity of the individual to contract. Contract law specifies that certain classes of individuals do not have the capacity to contract. Among those classes are persons lacking mental capacity, those unduly influenced by drugs or alcohol, and persons who have not reached the age of majority.

Waivers and Minors

It is well-established law that waivers signed only by the minor client are voidable (that is, the minor can void the contract at any time) and therefore unenforceable by the provider. No cases have been found in which a recreation- or sport-related waiver, signed only by the minor, was upheld when challenged in court. As a result, many providers require that a parent sign the waiver on behalf of the minor. Of concern to these service providers is the question of whether waivers are effective when signed by a parent or guardian on behalf of a minor client (**parental waivers**).

The general rule has long been *that a waiver is a contract, and in most states, a minor cannot be bound by a contract whether it is (1) signed by the minor* or *(2) signed by a parent or guardian on behalf of a minor.* So, although the service provider contracting with a minor is bound by the contract, the minor is not. Thus the waiver will not prevent the minor from taking legal action against a negligent service provider. This aspect of this general rule is supported in two cases. In *Dilallo v. Riding Safely Inc.* (1997), a 14-year-old Florida girl signed a waiver absolving a stable of liability. The court held that "a minor child injured because of a defendant's negligence is not bound by her contractual waiver of her right to file a lawsuit." In a Pennsylvania case (*Emerick v. Fox Raceway*, 2004), the court did not enforce a waiver signed by a 16-year-old boy who misrepresented his age to enter a motocross race.

Because waivers signed only by the minor are ineffective, providers have used three strategies in attempting to gain protection. They have (1) required that the parent or guardian sign the waiver on behalf of the minor client (**parental waiver**); (2) required the parent to indemnify the provider (agree to repay the provider for any loss suffered due to the participation of the minor, e.g., monetary award by the court) (**parental indemnity agreement**); and (3) most recently, by requiring the parent to sign a mediation/arbitration agreement by which the parent agrees to submit any claim to mediation and/or arbitration rather than filing a lawsuit (**parental arbitration agreement**). See Chapter 6.24, *Alternate Dispute Resolution*, for more information on mediation and arbitration.

In the past, parental waivers and parental indemnity agreements have not been effective. For example, a 10-year-old girl was injured when another child jumped into a swimming pool on top of her. The girl's mother signed a postinjury release in exchange for a $3275 settlement. Eight years after the accident, on reaching the age of majority, the girl filed suit against the YMCA. The court stated that "It is well settled in Michigan that, as a general rule, a parent has no authority, merely by virtue of being a parent, to waive, release, or compromise claims by or against the parent's child" and ruled that the YMCA was not protected by the release signed by the mother (*Smith v. YMCA of Benton Harbor/St. Joseph*, 1996).

---

[3] **Loss of Consortium** is the loss of material services and intangibles such as companionship and sexual relations. The nonsigning spouse of a participant suffering serious injury often seeks damages for loss of consortium.

[4] The nonsigning spouse or others often seek damages through **wrongful death** actions when the cause of death was a negligent or willful act of another.

In recent years, however, courts in some states have begun to enforce waivers and indemnity agreements signed by parents on behalf of their minor children. California courts were the first to enforce parental waivers. In 1990, *Hohe v. San Diego Unified Sch. Dist.* made it clear that although minors are free to disaffirm contracts signed by the minor, they cannot disaffirm contracts made by the parent or guardian of the minor. Since that time, numerous California courts have ruled similarly. The Supreme Court of Ohio also ruled waivers signed by parents in favor of nonprofit, public service providers are enforceable against the minor child (*Zivich v. Mentor Soccer Club*, 1998). Courts in Connecticut, Florida, Georgia, Massachusetts, North Dakota, and Wisconsin have also enforced parental waivers. In addition, the state legislatures in both Colorado and Alaska have passed statutes providing for the enforcement of parental waivers. In addition, courts in Connecticut and Massachusetts have upheld parental indemnity agreements, and courts in California, Hawaii, Ohio, Louisiana, New Jersey, and Florida have upheld agreements by which parents agreed to submit any claims of the minor to arbitration.

So parental waivers are now enforceable, under certain circumstances, in at least ten states, parental indemnity agreements are enforceable in at least two states, and parental mediation/arbitration agreements are enforceable in at least six states. Consequently, providers in all states might consider the use of such agreements when dealing with minor participants. However, in doing so, the provider should remember two things: (1) always have the parents sign the document and (2) use protection in addition to the waiver.

Format of the Waiver

Waivers are generally found in one of four formats. The first is as a **stand-alone document**—one in which the only function of the document is to provide liability protection for the service provider. The patron is asked to sign a sheet of paper containing only a waiver and related material. The second format is the **waiver within another document**, such as a membership agreement, an entry form, or a rental agreement (see the example in the Significant Case). The third format is a **group waiver**, which generally includes a waiver at the top of a sheet on which several parties sign (e.g., a team roster, sign-in sheet at a health club). Some courts have encouraged providers to use the stand-alone waiver; however, when carefully worded and properly administered, each of these first three formats can be effective. The fourth format is the **disclaimer** of liability, often found on the back of tickets. A disclaimer is a statement asserting that the provider is not responsible for injuries. The disclaimer is not signed, provides no evidence that the participant agreed to it, and with a few exceptions, is ineffective. There is no harm in including such disclaimers on the back of a ticket, but the service provider should operate on the assumption that the statement will not effectively protect the business.

Participant Agreement. Because many courts recommend the use of a stand-alone document, that format will be emphasized in this chapter. In fact, the most comprehensive stand-alone document recommended is called a **participant agreement.** The participant agreement is a relatively new concept in liability protection and is much more than just a waiver. The agreement differs from the basic waiver in that it (1) is designed to improve the rapport and understanding between the provider and the participant; (2) increases the understanding of the rewards and activity risks of the participant, prepares them psychologically for any discomforts, and makes legal action less likely; and (3) allows participants to make more informed decisions as to participation. The mere existence of a waiver or participant agreement can often deter a party from filing a claim. If a claim is filed, either document provides the potential for early dismissal.

Content of the Participant Agreement. The participant agreement is much broader in scope than a simple waiver clause or even a broad stand-alone waiver. The contents of the document are meant to provide protections for the provider and to serve as an exchange of information (providing information about the activity to the participant and collecting information about the participant). Suggested content of the participant agreement is listed following, and a sample agreement is shown in Figure 2.

Lucky Horseshoe Trail Rides Participant Agreement
Assumption of Risk, Waiver of Liability, and Indemnification Agreement

Trail riding is a popular activity enjoyed by young and old alike. It combines wholesome physical activity, adventure, powerful animals, and the natural beauty of the out-of-doors. While the pleasure of such rides is unmistakable, Lucky Horseshoe Trail Rides (hereafter referred to as LHTR) wants to make certain that all riders are fully aware of the various inherent risks involved in such an activity. LHTR feels that it is important that riders know that certain risks cannot be eliminated without destroying the unique character of this activity; that some danger is involved in trail riding; and that on occasion, riders do suffer injury. LHTR does not want to frighten riders or reduce their enthusiasm for a trail ride, but we believe it is important that you be informed of the nature of the activity.

Assumption of Inherent Risks. It is impossible to list all of the inherent risks of horseback trail rides, but some are listed below to give the rider a better idea of the risks involved. Minor injuries such as being scratched by a bush or cactus, muscle soreness, bruises, sunburn, and sprains are frequent occurrences. More serious injuries such as exposure from extreme hot, cold, or wet conditions, altitude sickness, broken bones, concussions, cuts, and bites occasionally occur. Rare catastrophic events such as heart attack, stroke, paralysis, serious internal or head injuries, and death can occur. In addition, these injuries may occur in locations far from emergency medical care.

These injuries may be caused by falls from horses; unpredictable weather changes; the propensity of the horse to behave in ways that may result in injury, harm, or death to those around it; the unpredictability of the animal's reaction to sounds, sudden movement, unfamiliar objects, persons, or other animals; surface or subsurface conditions; collisions with other animals or objects; steep, uneven, or snow-covered terrain; actions of the rider or other riders; failure of tack or other equipment; and errors in judgment of the trail guide or other employees.

I understand that the inherent risks of horseback trail rides are serious and that horseback trail riding is a dangerous activity regardless of the care taken by LHTR and its employees. I have read the previous paragraphs and (1) I know the nature of the activity of horseback trail riding; (2) I understand the demands of this activity relative to my physical condition and riding skill level, and (3) I appreciate the potential impact of the types of injuries that may result from horseback trail riding. I hereby assert that my participation at the LHTR is voluntary and that I knowingly assume all of the inherent risks of the activity.

Waiver of Liability: In consideration of permission to participate in a horseback trail ride, today and on all future dates, I, on behalf of myself, my spouse, my heirs, personal representatives, or assigns, do hereby release, waive, and discharge LHTR (including its officers, employees, and agencies) from liability from any and all claims resulting from the inherent risks of the activity of trail riding or from the ordinary negligence of the LHTR.

This agreement applies to (1) personal injury (including death) from incidents or illnesses arising from horseback trail ride participation at the LHTR (including, but not limited to, in and around the stable and corral, mounting and dismounting, riding, while dismounted during the ride, during any instruction by the staff, and all premises including bleachers, the associated sidewalks and parking lots); and to (2) any and all claims resulting from the damage to, loss of, or theft of property.

Indemnification: I also agree to hold harmless, defend, and indemnify LHTR (that is, defend and pay any judgment and costs, including investigation costs and attorney's fees) from any and all claims of mine, my spouse, family members, or others arising from my injury or loss due to my participation in horseback trail riding (including those arising from the inherent risks of trail riding or the ordinary negligence of LHTR).

I further agree to hold harmless, defend, and indemnify LHTR (that is, defend and pay any judgment and costs, including investigation costs and attorney's fees) against any and all claims of co-participants, rescuers, and others arising from my conduct in the course of my participation in horseback trail riding.

FIGURE 2 Illustrative Participant Agreement

Participant Agreement *(Page 2 of 2)*

Covenant not to Sue, Mediation/Arbitration, Venue, & Severability Clauses: I covenant not to sue LHTR for any present or future claim arising directly or indirectly from my participation in horseback trail riding at LHTR. This includes claims resulting from the inherent risks of trail riding and the ordinary negligence of LHTR.

I agree to engage in good faith efforts to **mediate** any dispute that might arise between me and LHTR. Any agreement reached will be formalized by a written contractual agreement at that time. Should the issue not be resolved by mediation, I agree that the issue will be submitted to **binding arbitration** in _____ County in the State of _____.

Likewise, I understand that if, in spite of this contract, legal action is brought, it must be adjudicated under the laws of the State of ____ and must be brought in the appropriate court housed in _____ County in the State of ____.

I also expressly agree that this Participant Agreement (including Assumption of Risk, Waiver of Liability, Indemnification Agreement, and Covenant not to Sue) is intended to be as broad and inclusive as is permitted by the laws of the State of _____ and that if any portion thereof is held invalid, it is agreed that the balance shall, notwithstanding, continue in full legal force and effect.

Acknowledgements, Assertions, and Agreements:
Health Status—I assert that I:
- Do not have asthma, diabetes, anaphylaxis, epilepsy, heart disease, or high blood pressure.
- Have no other medical problems that would contraindicate participation in horseback trail riding.
- Possesses sufficient physical fitness and skill to enable safe participation in horseback trail riding.

Emergency Care—I authorize or agree:
- LHTR to administer emergency first aid, CPR, and use an AED when deemed necessary by LHTR.
- LHTR to secure emergency medical care or transportation (i.e., EMS) when deemed necessary by LHTR.
- LHTR to share my medical history with emergency medical personnel when deemed necessary by LHTR.
- To assume all costs of emergency medical care and transportation.

Rules & Safety Equipment—I agree:
- To abide by the rules established by LHTR.
- To inform LHTR immediately if I become aware of rider conduct or equipment condition that presents a danger to others or myself.
- That I understand the importance of and agree to wear any required equipment at all times while riding.
- That the LHTR will conduct the activity in good faith and may find it necessary to terminate my participation if the supervisor judges that I am incapable of safely meeting the rigors of the activity. I accept LHTR's right to take such actions for the safety of myself and/or other riders.

Acknowledgment of Understanding: I have read this 2-page Participant Agreement—Assumption of Risk, Waiver of Liability, Indemnification Agreement, and Covenant not to Sue and fully understand its terms. I understand that I am giving up substantial rights, including my right to sue LHTR for injuries resulting from the inherent risks of horseback trail riding or the ordinary negligence of LHTR. I further acknowledge that I am signing this agreement freely and voluntarily, and intend my signature to be a complete and unconditional release of all liability, including that due to ordinary negligence by LHTR, to the greatest extent allowed by the laws of the State of _____.

_____   _____   _____
Printed Name of PARTICIPANT   Signature of PARTICIPANT   Date

Emergency Contact: _____   _____
                    NAME/RELATION   TELEPHONE

FIGURE 2 Illustrative Participant Agreement (continued)

1. Material meant to inform the participant of the **nature of the activity** and to help them understand and appreciate the risks involved
2. An **assumption of inherent risk** to protect against liability for the inherent risks
3. A **waiver** of liability as protection against ordinary negligence
4. An **indemnification agreement** to provide further protection against both the risks of ordinary negligence and the inherent risks
5. Selected clauses for **severability** (provides that if any part of the document is void, the rest remains in effect), for **mediation and/or arbitration** (provides that any claim will be submitted to mediation and binding arbitration, if necessary, rather than entering the court system) [see Chapter 6.24, *Alternative Dispute Resolution*], **venue** (specifies in which state and county any future legal proceedings must take place), and **covenant not to sue** (a contract not to sue to enforce a right of action)
6. Acknowledgments, assertions, and agreements regarding **health status**, **emergency care**, and **rules and safety** (information that allows the provider to better meet the needs of the participant and provide a safer activity environment)
7. A **final acknowledgment of release and assumption of risk** prior to the signatures

The scope of this book does not allow the presentation of further detail. For a complete discussion of waivers and participant agreements, including more than fifty guidelines for writing and preparing waivers and participant agreements, consult Cotten and Cotten, 2005.

Significant Case

◇◇◇

Stokes v. Bally's Pacwest, Inc. provides an excellent, straightforward example of the value of liability waivers in protecting against liability for negligence in the recreation or sport setting. The case illustrates very clearly the need to make sure the waiver is conspicuous and that the document plainly provides for protection against liability for negligence. When read carefully, one can see that Stokes specifically releases Bally's from liability for Bally's negligence. Although the recommended waiver format is the stand-alone waiver, this waiver within another document is very good and provides effective liability protection to Bally. Observe, also, that the fact the appellant did not read the waiver is irrelevant.

STOKES V. BALLY'S PACWEST, INC.
COURT OF APPEALS OF WASHINGTON, DIVISION ONE
113 Wn. App. 442; 54 P.3d 161; 2002 Wash. App. LEXIS 2233
September 16, 2002, Filed

OPINION: COX, A.C.J. –

Persons may expressly agree in advance of an accident that one has no duty of care to the other, and shall not be liable for ordinary negligence (*Chauvlier v. Booth Creek Ski Holdings, Inc.*, 109 Wn. App. 334, 339, 35 P.3d 383 (2001)). Such exculpatory agreements are generally enforceable, subject to three exceptions. Because the "waiver and release" language at issue here was conspicuously stated in the agreement that Michael Stokes signed, we reverse both summary judgment orders and direct entry of summary judgment in favor of Bally's Pacwest Total Fitness Center on remand.

Stokes joined Bally's, a health club. He signed a retail installment contract that evidenced the terms and conditions of membership. The contract contained the waiver and release provisions at issue in this appeal. Several months after signing the agreement, Stokes slipped on a round metallic plate placed in a wooden floor at the club while playing basketball. He injured his knee and shoulder. Stokes sued Bally's, alleging that the health club's negligence caused him serious, painful, and permanent injuries. Bally's moved for summary judgment, which the trial court denied. According to the trial court, there were "material questions of fact whether the 'Waiver and Release' provisions set forth in the Retail Installment Contract [that Stokes signed], were sufficiently conspicuous or knowingly consented to by [him]."

We granted discretionary review of that decision. Pursuant to RAP 7.2, we also granted Bally's permission to renew its summary judgment motion in the trial court in order to allow that court to consider this court's then recent decision in *Chauvlier*. Following Bally's renewed motion, the trial court again denied summary judgment for the same reason that it did before.

* * *

We now focus our attention on the two orders before us. To prevail on his ordinary negligence claim against Bally's, Stokes must establish that the health club owed him a duty. Whether such a duty exists is a question of law. As we recently noted in *Chauvlier*, our Supreme Court has recognized the right of parties, subject to certain exceptions, to expressly agree in advance that one party is under no obligation of care to the other, and shall not be held liable for ordinary negligence

The general rule in Washington is that such exculpatory clauses are enforceable unless (1) they violate public policy; (2) the negligent act falls greatly below the standard established by law for protection of others; or (3) they are inconspicuous (*Scott v. Pacific West Mountain Resort*, 119 Wn.2d 484, 492, 834 P.2d 6 (1992). Neither of the first two of these exceptions is at issue here. The trial court expressly relied on only the third exception in making its rulings, denying summary judgment on the ground that a genuine issue of material fact existed whether the waiver and release clause was inconspicuous.

This court will not uphold an exculpatory agreement if "the releasing language is so inconspicuous that reasonable persons could reach different conclusions as to whether the document was unwittingly signed" (*Chauvlier*, at 341). Conversely, where reasonable persons could only reach the conclusion that the release language is conspicuous, there is no question of the document having been unwittingly signed. Whether Stokes subjectively unwittingly signed the form is not at issue. Rather, the question is whether, objectively, the waiver provision was so inconspicuous that it is unenforceable.

As we stated in *Chauvlier*, a person who signs an agreement without reading it is generally bound by its terms as long as there was ample opportunity to examine the contract and the person failed to do so for personal reasons. Here, Stokes admitted that he did not remember reading the waiver and release provision of the contract. But this admission does not end our review. We must still determine whether the waiver and release language is inconspicuous so as to invalidate Stokes' release of Bally's from any duty to him for its alleged ordinary negligence.

We most recently considered whether a release was inconspicuous and unwittingly signed in *Chauvlier*. The release in that case was printed on a ski pass application. Comparing the release to those considered in *Baker* and *Hewitt v. Miller*, n16 we held that the release was sufficiently conspicuous to be enforceable. We noted that the release was not hidden within part of a larger agreement, and that it was clearly entitled "LIABILITY RELEASE & PROMISE NOT TO SUE. PLEASE READ CAREFULLY!." We also noted that the words "RELEASE" and "HOLD HARMLESS AND INDEMNIFY" were set off in capital letters throughout the agreement, and that the release contained the language, just above the signature line, "Please Read and Sign: I have read, understood, and accepted the conditions of the Liability Release printed above."

At the other end of the spectrum of reported cases is *Baker* (*Baker*, 79 Wn.2d at 202). There, our Supreme Court held that a disclaimer in a golf cart rental agreement, consisting of several lines of release language printed in the middle of a paragraph discussing other information, was so inconspicuous that enforcement of the release would be unconscionable

In *McCorkle*, another division of this court held that a trial court erred in granting summary judgment on McCorkle's negligence claims against a fitness club. The holding was that there were genuine issues of material fact whether a liability statement contained in a membership application McCorkle signed was sufficiently conspicuous.

The provision at issue in that case had as a heading "LIABILITY STATEMENT." In the first few sentences, the provision declared that the member accepted liability for damages that the member or the member's guests caused. The last sentence of the provision stated that the member waived any claim for damages as a result of any act of a Club employee or agent. And nothing in the document alerted the reader to the shift in the liability discussion from liability of the member to waiver of liability for claims against the Club.

The parties now before us cite to other cases, *Hewitt and Conradt v. Four Star Promotions* (*Hewitt*, 11 Wn. App. at 78-80; *Conradt*, 45 Wn. App. at 850). Both are factually distinguishable. In each of those cases, the waiver and release form was in a separate document, not a separate provision in one document

Here, the release is more like that in *Chauvlier* and unlike that in *Baker* or *McCorkle*. In our view, reasonable minds could not differ regarding whether the waiver and release provisions in this retail installment sales contract were so inconspicuous that it was unwittingly signed. The language is conspicuous, as a matter of law, and it was not unwittingly signed.

The release provision in this retail installment contract, which Stokes signed, must be read in context. Several lines above Stokes' signature is a section in bold type, which states:

NOTICE TO BUYER: (a) Do not sign this Contract before you read it or if any of the spaces intended for the agreed terms, except as to unavailable information, are blank. . . .

THIS IS A RETAIL INSTALLMENT CONTRACT, THE RECEIPT OF AN EXECUTED COPY OF WHICH, AS WELL AS A COPY OF THE CLUB RULES AND REGULATIONS AND

A WRITTEN DESCRIPTION OF THE SER-VICES AND EQUIPMENT TO BE PROVIDED, IS HEREBY ACKNOWLEDGED BY THE BUYER.

Immediately following Stokes' signature is a line, starting in bold and capital letters, stating: "WAIVER AND RELEASE: This contract contains a WAIVER AND RELEASE in Paragraph 10 to which you will be bound."

Paragraph 10, which is expressly referenced in the line directly below Stokes' signature, is entitled "WAIVER AND RELEASE." It states as follows:

You (Buyer, each Member and all guests) agree that if you engage in any physical exercise or activity or use any club facility on the premises, you do so at your own risk. This includes, without limitation, your use of the locker room, pool, whirlpool, sauna, steamroom, parking area, sidewalk or any equipment in the health club and your participation in any activity, class, program or instruction. You agree that you are voluntarily participating in these activities and using these facilities and premises and assume all risk of injury to you or the contraction of any illness or medical condition that might result, or any damage, loss or theft of any personal property. You agree on behalf of yourself (and your personal representatives, heirs, executors, administrators, agents and assigns) to release and discharge us (and our affiliates, employees, agents, representatives, successors and assigns) from any and all claims or causes of action (known or unknown) arising out of our negligence. This Waiver and Release of liability includes, without limitation, injuries which may occur as a result of (a) your use of any exercise equipment or facilities which may malfunction or break, (b) our improper maintenance of any exercise equipment or facilities, (c) our negligent instruction or supervision, and (d) you slipping and falling while in the health club or on the premises. You acknowledge that you have carefully read this Waiver and Release and fully understand that it is a release of liability. You are waiving any right that you may have to bring a legal action to assert a claim against us for our negligence.

Unlike the waiver provisions in *Baker* and *McCorkle*, this paragraph discusses only Stokes' agreement to release Bally's from liability for its negligence. Stokes' argument that he believed that the paragraph somehow related to release from liability for his financial obligations under the retail installment sale agreement is wholly unpersuasive. As our Supreme Court stated in *National Bank*, it "would be impossible for a person of ordinary intelligence, much less a person of the intelligence and ability of appellant, to have misunderstood the contents of this instrument upon a casual reading thereof. . ." The same principle applies here. Reasonable persons could not disagree that the content of paragraph 10 is quite clearly a waiver and release of liability for negligence, not financial obligations. Likewise, reasonable persons could not disagree that the waiver and release provisions of the paragraph are conspicuously displayed within the larger document.

Stokes also argues that an exculpatory provision may be placed in a document separate from the retail installment sales agreement, but concedes that this is not required. Bally's counters that RCW 63.14.020 and other laws require that the exculpatory clauses and financial terms and conditions between a health club and its members all must be within one document.

We need not decide in this case whether Bally's' argument is correct. It is sufficient to state that no authority supports the proposition that an exculpatory clause must be contained in a separate document to be enforceable. Rather, what is required is that the release language in a document be conspicuous.

The language at issue in this case is conspicuous and enforceable. Bally's owes no duty to Stokes for his injuries. Summary judgment in favor of Bally's is required.

We reverse both summary judgment orders, and direct entry of summary judgment in favor of Bally's on remand.

WE CONCUR.

◇◇◇ **OTHER RELATED SIGNIFICANT CASES**

Chapter 2.24 *Informed Consents and Agreements to Participate*

Recent Trends

The most significant trend regarding waivers is the continuation of a trend toward the enforcement of agreements signed by parents. Although most states have not addressed the matter, an increasing number seem to be inclined to allow the parent to make such decisions for the minor. A related trend seems to be to enforce arbitration agreements signed by the parent or guardian. An emerging trend is the use of a more comprehensive document, the participant agreement, to encourage an exchange of information as well as provide protection from liability for both inherent and negligence risks.

References

Cases

Bothell v. Two Point Acres, Inc., 1998 Ariz.App. LEXIS 32.

Craig v. Lakeshore Athletic Club, Inc., 1997 Wash. App. LEXIS 907.

Coughlin v. T. M. H. International Attractions, Inc., 1995 U.S. Dist. LEXIS 12499 (Ky).

Davis v. Sun Valley Ski Education Foundation, Inc., 1997 Ida. LEXIS 82.

Dilallo v. Riding Safely Inc., 687 So.2d 353 [Fla. 4th Dist. 1997].

Emerick v. Fox Raceway

Hohe v. San Diego Unified Sch. Dist., 274 Cal.Rptr. 647 (1990).

Huffman v. Monroe County Community School, 564 N.E.2d 961 (Ind., 1991).

Lantz v. Iron Horse Saloon, Inc., 717 So.2d 590 [Fla. 5th Dist. 1998].

Mahoney v. USA Hockey, Inc., 1999 U.S. Dist. LEXIS 19359.

Maurer v. Cerkvenik-Anderson Travel, Inc., 165 Ariz. Adv. Rep. 51 (1994).

Pena v, The Rolladium, 2002 Cal. App. Unpub. LEXIS 1466.

Quinn v. Mississippi State University, 1998 Miss. LEXIS 328 59.

Smith v. YMCA of Benton Harbor/St. Joseph, 550 N.W.2d 262 [Mich. 1996].

Swierkosz v. Starved Rock Stables, 607 N.E. 2d 280 (Ill., 1993).

Zivich v. Mentor Soccer Club, 1998 Ohio App. LEXIS 1577.

Publications

Cotten, D. J., & Cotten, M. B. (1997). *Legal aspects of waivers and releases in sport, recreation and fitness activities.* Canton, OH: PRC Publishing, Inc.

Cotten, D. J., & Cotten, M. B. (2005). *Waivers & releases of liability* (5th ed.). Sport Risk Consulting: www.lulu.com.

van der Smissen, B. (1990). *Legal liability and risk management for public and private entities.* Cincinnati, OH: Anderson Publishing Co.

2.24 Informed Consent Agreements and Agreements to Participate

Doyice J. Cotten
Sport Risk Consulting

This chapter presents two additional documents that can strengthen defenses for the service provider—the informed consent agreement and the agreement to participate.

The **informed consent** is a document used to protect the provider from liability for the informed treatment risks of a treatment, program, or regimen to which the signer is subjected. The factor that makes the informed consent unique is that **something is done to the participant** by another party with the consent of the participant. It may be in the form of medical treatment, rehabilitation, therapy, fitness testing, or a training program (e.g., when one is to be treated for an injury by an athletic trainer, when a participant is to undergo a training program developed by a personal trainer). The document informs the signer of the risks, thereby enabling the signer to make an educated, informed decision. The informed consent is based in contract law, thus the signing parties must be of age. The informed consent offers little or no protection against liability for injuries resulting from negligence.

The **agreement to participate** (not to be confused with the participant agreement in Chapter 2.23) is a document intended to strengthen the defenses against liability for injuries resulting from the inherent risks of the activity. The agreement to participate is an agreement by which the signer is (1) made aware of and acknowledges knowledge of the inherent risks of the activity and (2) is informed of the rules of the activity and behavioral expectations and agrees to abide by them (van der Smissen, 1990). The agreement to participate is often used when persons are about to participate in an activity, sport, or class (e.g., extreme sport participants, physical education class members, participants in intramural or recreational programs). The agreement is based in tort law and does not constitute a formal contract; therefore it is an ideal instrument for dealing with minor participants. Like the informed consent, it provides little protection from liability for negligence. The agreement differs from the informed consent in that it is not a contract, and nothing is *done to* the participant. Rather, the participant is *seeking to* participate.

Two other agreements are addressed in this chapter—the assumption of risk agreement and the parental permission form. The **assumption of risk agreement** is essentially the same as the agreement to participate. It involves different terminology, uses a different format, is usually briefer, and often lacks some of the components found in the agreement to participate, but the function is the same—to help protect the sport or recreation provider from liability from injuries resulting from the inherent risks of an activity. The **parental permission form**, on the other hand, is quite different. This form simply gains parental permission for the minor to participate in the activity. It may have some public relations value in informing the parent about the activity in which the child will be participating, but it has no legal value and provides no protection to the recreation or sport business.

Informed Consent Agreements

The doctrine of informed consent derives from two principles: (1) a person's inherent right to control what happens to his or her body and (2) the physician's fiduciary duty to the patient—to warn the patient of risks and make certain the patient knows enough to make an informed decision regarding his or her care. It is an ethical, moral, and legal concept that is ingrained in American culture.

There are two separate, but related, components of informed consent—**disclosure** and **consent** (Nolan-Haley, 1999). The doctrine requires that those who consent be competent (i.e., of legal age, intellectually capable of consent), sufficiently informed about the treatment to enable an educated decision, and consent voluntarily with no duress (Koeberle & Herbert, 1998).

Medicine

Informed consents originated with and have been primarily used in conjunction with the medical profession. The first cases defining informed consent appeared in the late 1950s and were based on the tort of **battery**—the intentional, unpermitted, unprivileged, and offensive touching (physical contact) of the person of one individual by another. Today most medical cases are based on **negligence** because consent is obtained and the issue is whether the consent was adequately "informed." Informed consent is more than simply getting a patient to sign a written consent form—it is a communication process by which the physician provides relevant information to enable the patient to make an educated, informed decision (American Medical Association, 1998). Although state law regarding informed consent varies from state to state, generally physicians are required to inform regarding the nature of the proposed treatment, foreseeable risk and discomforts, anticipated benefits, alternative procedures, and instructions regarding food, drink, or lifestyles.

Human Subject Research

A major application of the informed consent has been in the area of human subject research. The American College of Sports Medicine (1999) stated that

> By law, any experimental subject or clinical patient who is exposed to possible physical, psychological, or social injury must give informed consent prior to participating in a proposed project. (p. vi)

The Office of Human Subjects Research of the National Institutes of Health outlines requirements for such research. The consent should (1) be obtained in writing, (2) be understandable, (3) be obtained in non-coercive circumstances, and (4) contain no language suggesting a relinquishment of rights.

Some of the elements that should be included in the consent are (1) purpose and duration of the research; (2) description of the procedures, risks, and discomforts involved; (3) benefits and compensation to the subject; (4) alternative procedures; (5) confidentiality policies; (6) compensation and treatment available in the event of injury; (7) whom to contact for questions; and (8) a statement of voluntary participation. They specify that the document should be written at a level below that of a high school graduate—making liberal use of subheads, avoiding multisyllable words when possible, and keeping sentences short and understandable (Office of Human Subjects Research, 2000).

Sport and Fitness

In recent years, informed consents have been used more frequently in sport and fitness. Service providers are becoming more aware of the necessity of utilizing informed consents for participants in certain types of programs. Injury rehabilitation programs, fitness testing, and fitness regimens directed by personal trainers are three examples of situations in which the use of informed consents is standard practice.

Koeberle and Herbert (1998) described the informed consent in the fitness setting as "a voluntary agreement from a client who has been informed of, appreciates, and understands the material and relevant risks associated with participation in the activity or range of activities involved in exercise testing and activity provided through prescription" (p. 52). Because having a client undergo an exercise prescription or fitness test can be construed as either **actual** or **constructive contact**, they stress that an informed consent is necessary to gain the client's permission for contact. Without the informed consent, the fitness professional is risking action for civil or criminal battery. Koeberle and Herbert suggest that informed consents in personal fitness settings do not require consent forms in the same detail as those required of physicians. The trainer is not held to a standard as high as that of the physician because activity programs contain a very low incidence of risk when compared to even the safest medical procedures.

The following guidelines for the content and administration of the informed consent for sport, recreation, and fitness activities are drawn from four sources (Herbert & Herbert, 2002[1]; Independent Review Consulting, Inc., 2000; Koeberle & Herbert, 1998; Olivier & Olivier, 2001).

Content

The content of the informed consent for the recreation, sport, and fitness setting should

- Be in writing on a preprinted form
- Be written in plain, understandable language
- State the purpose of the exercise program, test, or prescribed action
- Include a general description of the exercise program, test, or prescribed action
- List any likely discomforts that might be associated with the program, test, or activity
- List the potential risks and potential benefits of the exercise program, test, or activity
- Be worded to allow all staff members to have physical contact or interact with the participant
- Have participant acknowledge voluntary participation
- Have participant acknowledge that consent was not signed under duress
- Have participant acknowledge an opportunity to ask questions and have them answered to his or her satisfaction
- Have participant acknowledge that the participant read and understood the informed consent document

Administration

The administrative procedures relating to the obtaining and handling of the informed consent can make a difference in the effectiveness of the agreement.

- A separate form should be used for each type of activity (e.g., exercise program, test, rehabilitation, fitness activity).
- The professional should explain the content of the informed consent and give the participant an opportunity to ask and have his or her questions answered satisfactorily.
- The consent form should be signed by the participant and professional and dated.
- A copy of the consent should be provided to the participant.
- The signed and dated consent should be placed in the participant's file.

If the participant is a **minor**,
- It is imperative that one or both parents sign the agreement.
- The provider should use an informed consent form written specifically for parents of minors.
- The consent should contain language directed to the parent by which the parent gives permission for the activity, acknowledges an understanding of the risks, and signs the agreement.

An illustrative informed consent for personal trainers is presented in Figure 1. This form is for illustrative purposes only, and the reader is cautioned to consult a competent attorney for legal advice regarding such a form.

It is important that the recreation or sport manager understand that the informed consent is important in avoiding liability for injuries resulting from the inherent risks of the activity. It is equally important that the recreation or sport manager remember two things about the informed consent: (1) the informed consent is contractual in nature, thus requiring the signature of a parent or guardian when the client is a minor; and 2) the consent provides no protection against liability for injuries resulting from the negligence of the service provider, its employees, or its agents. For such protection, a waiver should be utilized (see Chapter 2.23, *Waivers and Releases*).

---

[1] Consult this publication for an in-depth look at the concept of the informed consent.

Personal Fitness Training Program
Informed Consent

Program Objectives

I understand that my physical fitness program is individually tailored to meet the goals and objectives agreed on by my personal trainer and myself.

Description of the Exercise Program

I understand that my exercise program can involve participation in a number of types of fitness activities. These activities will vary depending on the objectives that my personal trainer and I establish, but can include (1) aerobic activities including, but not limited to, the use of treadmills, stationary bicycles, step machines, rowing machines, and running track; (2) muscular endurance and strength building exercises including, but not limited to, the use of free weights, weight machines, calisthenics, and exercise apparatus; (3) nutrition and weight control activities; and (4) selected physical fitness and body composition tests, including but not limited to strength tests, cardiovascular fitness tests, and body composition tests.

Description of Potential Risks

I understand that my personal trainer cannot guarantee my personal safety because all exercise programs have inherent risks regardless of the care taken by a personal trainer. **I will initial the types of activities (including their risks) that my trainer and I have selected for my program to acknowledge that I understand the potential risks of my training program.**

_____ **Aerobic Activities:** I realize that participation in any cardiovascular activity may involve sustained, vigorous exertion which places stress on the muscles, joints, and cardiovascular system, sometimes resulting in injuries ranging from minor injuries (e.g., muscle soreness, pulled muscles, and musculoskeletal strains and sprains) to the infrequent serious injury (e.g., torn ligaments, heart attack, and stroke) to the rare catastrophic incident (e.g., death, paralysis).

_____ **Muscular Endurance & Strength:** I realize that participation in muscular endurance and strength building activities involves repetitive exertions and maximal exertions, which can result in stress-related injuries ranging from minor injuries (e.g., muscle soreness, muscle strains, and ligament injuries) to the infrequent serious injury (e.g., torn rotator cuffs, herniated disks or other back injuries, crushed fingers, and heart attack) to the rare catastrophic incident (e.g., death, paralysis).

_____ **Nutrition and Weight Control:** I realize that the nutrition and weight control program may involve a dietary change, selected nutritional supplements, and regular exercise. I also understand that no nutrition and weight control program is without risk and that some of the risks range from minor concerns (e.g., failure to achieve my goals, muscle soreness, and strains) to the infrequent serious injury (e.g., physical reaction to food supplements or nutrition products, adverse body reaction to weight loss, or heart attack) to the rare catastrophic incident (e.g., death, paralysis).

_____ **Fitness and Body Composition Tests:** I realize that participation in tests can result in injuries ranging from minor injuries (e.g., muscle soreness, pulled muscles, and sprains) to the infrequent serious injury (e.g., torn ligaments, back injuries, and heart attack) to the rare catastrophic incident (e.g., death, paralysis).

Description of Potential Benefits

I understand that a regular exercise program has been shown to have definite benefits to general health and well-being. **I will initial the types of activities (including their benefits) that my trainer and I have selected for my program to acknowledge that I understand the potential benefits of my training program.**

_____ **Aerobic Activities:** loss of weight, reduction of body fat, improvement of blood lipids, lowering of blood pressure, improvement in cardiovascular function, reduction in risk of heart disease, increased muscular endurance, improved posture, and improved flexibility.

FIGURE 1. Illustrative Informed Consent for Personal Trainers

_____ **Muscular Endurance & Strength:** loss of weight, reduction of body fat, increased muscle mass, improvement of blood lipids, lowering of blood pressure, improved strength and muscular endurance, improved posture.

_____ **Nutrition and Weight Control:** loss of weight, reduction of body fat, improvement of blood lipids, lowering of blood pressure, improvement in cardiovascular function, reduction in risk of heart disease.

_____ **Fitness and Body Composition Tests:** learn current status and gain information regarding areas needing improvement.

Participant Responsibilities

I understand that it is my responsibility to (1) fully disclose any health issues or medications that are relevant to participation in a strenuous exercise program; (2) cease exercise and report promptly any unusual feelings (e.g., chest discomfort, nausea, difficulty breathing, apparent injury) during the exercise program; and (3) clear my participation with my physician.

Participant Acknowledgments

In agreeing to this exercise program:

- I acknowledge that my participation is completely voluntary.
- I understand the potential physical risks and believe that the potential benefits outweigh those risks.
- I give consent to certain physical touching that may be necessary to ensure proper technique and body alignment.
- I understand that the achievement of health or fitness goals cannot be guaranteed.
- I have had a voice in planning and approving the activities selected for my exercise program.
- I have been able to ask questions regarding any concerns, and have had those questions answered to my satisfaction.
- I am in good physical condition, have no disability that might prevent my participation in such activities, and have been advised to consult a physician prior to beginning this program.
- I have been advised to cease exercise immediately if I experience unusual discomfort and feel the need to stop.

I have read and understand the above agreement; I have been able to ask questions regarding any concerns I might have; I have had those questions answered to my satisfaction; and I am freely signing this agreement.

_____   _____   _____   _____   _____
Signature of Participant   Name of Participant (Print)   Date   Signature of Trainer   Date

_____   _____   _____
Signature of Parent/Guardian   Name of Parent/Guardian (Print)   Date
(If Participant is a Minor)

_____   _____   _____
Signature of Parent/Guardian   Name of Parent/Guardian (Print)   Date
(If Participant is a Minor)

FIGURE 1. Illustrative Informed Consent for Personal Trainers (continued)

Documentation

Herbert and Herbert (2002) stressed the importance of documentation and record keeping when working with individuals who have consented to programs. Just as physicians now must keep detailed notes on patient visits (e.g., complaints, treatments, responses to treatment, instructions), personal trainers, therapists, and other providers utilizing informed consents should do the same. Although the extent of documentation required might not be the same, all documentation and notes can serve as evidence and can help the provider recollect the facts if called on to testify in the event of litigation—sometimes years later. Development and use of a standardized form that includes spaces for the date, signature, and notes is suggested.

Agreements to Participate

The agreement to participate, unlike the informed consent, is not a contract. It is simply an agreement by which the participant is informed of the inherent risks and behavioral expectations of participants and affirms his or her assumption of the inherent risks of participation in the activity. However, like the informed consent, the signer (1) must have knowledge of the nature of the activity, (2) must understand the activity in terms of his or her own condition and skill, and (3) must appreciate the type of injuries that may occur. It is important to the provider that the participant understand these inherent risks, and the provider should take steps (e.g., the agreement to participate) to ensure this understanding. Because the agreement is merely informative in nature, it can be used when the participant or client is a minor. The signature of a parent is desirable from a public relations standpoint, but is not mandated.

The agreement has two major purposes. First, it helps to establish the primary assumption of risk defense by establishing that participation was voluntary and that the participant was aware of the inherent risks of the activity. The second purpose is to help establish the secondary assumption of risk defense (sometimes referred to as contributory fault) by showing that the participant knew the expected participant behaviors and agreed to adhere to them. By establishing that the participant was aware of the conduct expected, the secondary assumption of risk defense is strengthened because some of the responsibility for the safety of the participant is transferred to the participant. Whether the state is governed by contributory fault or comparative fault, the participant has a duty to protect himself or herself from unreasonable risk of foreseeable harm. If the participant acted in an irresponsible manner, departing from the expected behaviors, any award the participant might be due is subject to either be reduced or barred completely. It should be noted that *the only effect an agreement to participate has on liability for injury caused by the negligence of the recreation or sport business or its employees is to reduce the award (or in some cases, actually bar recovery) through comparative fault.*

Contents

There are no "magic phrases" that are either legally required or even universally useful in the construction of agreements to participate. There also is no ironclad format that is required. However, certain information should be in any agreement to participate, and the following would serve as a logical order for inclusion (Cotten & Cotten, 2005).

Nature of the Activity

It is important that the activity be described in some detail. The description should be specific to the activity and not generic in nature. It should include a description of what the activity is like, remembering that the less familiar the participant is with the activity, the more detail required in the description. Include negative or unpleasurable aspects that the participant should expect, how much physical stress is involved, and the intensity level of the activity. Each section of the agreement to participate is illustrated in Figure 2.

Possible Consequences of Injury

Two areas should be covered in this section. First, the participant should be made aware of the types of accidents that may occur in the specific sport involved. Here one should list some insignificant accidents that are

Agreement to Participate and Liability Waiver
for Minors Participating in the *Annual 5K Fun Run*

All physical activities involve certain inherent risks. Regardless of the care taken, it is impossible to ensure the safety of all participants. The *5K Fun Run* is a vigorous, cardiovascular activity requiring *sustained running endurance, coordination, and running skill.* Although the *Club* is using care in conducting the event, it is unable to eliminate all risk from the activity.

It is possible for *runners* to suffer common injuries such as *cramps, muscle strains, and sprains.* More serious, but less frequent, injuries such as *broken bones, cuts, concussions, heart attacks, strokes, paralysis, and death* may also occur. These injuries, and others, may result from such incidents as (but not limited to) *slips and falls, tripping, colliding with another runner, imperfections in the street surfaces, heat-related illnesses, and stress placed on the cardiovascular system.*

All *runners* are expected to follow these safety guidelines:

1. *Wear proper footwear.*
2. *Be alert for unanticipated hazards on the course.*
3. *Do not crowd other runners.*
4. *Consume adequate liquids during the run.*
5. *Follow all announced or posted rules.*

I agree to follow the preceding safety rules, all posted safety rules, and all rules common to *running.* Further, I agree to report any unsafe practices, conditions, or equipment to the *race* management.

I certify that (1) I possess a sufficient degree of physical fitness to safely participate in *the 5K Fun Run,* (2) I understand that I am to discontinue *running* at any time I feel undue discomfort or stress, and (3) I will indicate below any health-related conditions that might affect my ability to safely *complete the run* and I will verbally inform activity management immediately.

Circle: Diabetes   Heart Problems   Seizures   Asthma   Other _____

I have read the preceding information and my questions have been answered. **I know, understand, and appreciate the risks associated with *distance runs* and I am voluntarily participating in the activity. In doing so, I am assuming all the inherent risks of the sport.** I further understand that in the event of a medical emergency, *management will call EMS to render assistance and that I will be financially responsible for any expenses involved.*

_____   _____   _____
Signature of Participant   Date   Name of Participant (Please Print)

_____   _____   _____
Signature of Parent   Date   Name of Parent (Please Print)

_____   _____   _____
Signature of Parent   Date   Name of Parent (Please Print)

WAIVER OF LIABILITY: In consideration of being permitted to run in the *5K Fun Run,* on behalf of myself, my family, my heirs, and my assigns, **the undersigned Participant and Parent or Guardian hereby release the *club* from liability for injury, loss, or death** to the minor, while *participating in the run or while in any way associated with participating in the event now or in the future,* **resulting from the ordinary negligence of the *club*, its agents, or employees.**

_____   _____   _____
Signature of Participant   Date   Name of Participant (Please Print)

_____   _____   _____
Signature of Parent   Date   Name of Parent (Please Print)

_____   _____   _____
Signature of Parent   Date   Name of Parent (Please Print)

FIGURE 2. Illustrative Agreement to Participate for Minors

common to the sport (being struck by the ball in racquetball), as well as some serious accidents that occur occasionally (falling and striking one's head on the floor in racquetball). Second, include some of the injuries that can occur in the sport. List some minor injuries that are common to the sport (e.g., bruises, strains, sprains in racquetball), some more serious injuries (e.g., loss of vision, broken bones, concussions), as well as catastrophic injuries (e.g., paralysis and death). Use phrases such as "some of the . . . ," "injuries such as . . . ," and "including, but not limited to . . ." in listing both accidents and injuries.

Behavioral Expectations of the Participant

The major purpose of this section is to transfer some of the responsibility for the participant's safety from the recreation or sport business to the participant. One might list several very important rules to which the participant is expected to adhere. An example in racquetball might be that participants are required to wear eye protection at all times. If there are few rules, they might be listed on the front of the agreement. If there are numerous rules, the participant might be referred to the back of the sheet where they are listed. In either case, giving the participant a copy of these rules would be desirable. Once again, one should not attempt to make the list all-inclusive.

Condition of the Participant

The participant should affirm that he or she possesses the physical condition and required competencies to participate in the activity safely. The required level, which will vary with the activity, should be described in Section I of the agreement. The participant will also affirm that the participant has no physical conditions that would preclude participation in the activity and will identify any conditions of which the recreation or sport business should be aware (e.g., heart problems, seizures, asthma). Particularly for vigorous activities, a statement that the participant should discontinue the activity if undue discomfort or stress occur should be included. Participant affirmation of condition is generally adequate for activities such as 5K runs, health club memberships, and between-inning promotions at baseball games. Other situations might require more confirmation of condition. For example, residential camps usually require health histories, and schools generally demand preparticipatory physical exams prior to varsity competition.

Concluding Statement

This concluding section should contain six items. They are (1) a statement by which the participant affirms knowledge, understanding, and appreciation of the inherent risks of the activity; (2) affirmation that participation is voluntary, if that is the case; (3) an assumption of risk statement; (4) notice of the procedures to be followed in the event of an emergency and the financial responsibility of the participant for emergency actions; (5) insurance requirements; and (6) a space for the signature of the participant (and the parent if the participant is a minor) at the bottom of the agreement. The critical signature is that of the minor; however, the parent's signature is important for public relations purposes.

Optional Sections

Waiver. This is an optional section that may be used with agreements to participate (see Chapter 2.23, *Waivers and Releases*). This section should follow the signature section of the agreement to participate and provide space for a second signature by the participant (and parent, if the participant is a minor) relating specifically to the exculpatory clause (an illustrative agreement to participate including the critical information is given in Figure 2).

Parental Permission Form. This optional section merely gives permission for a minor to participate in the activity—strengthening neither the primary nor secondary assumption of risk defense. Contrary to widespread belief, neither the parent nor child is giving up the right to file suit in the event of injury due to negligence. The form has some public relations value in informing the parent of the activity in which the child will be participating and can be used to gain permission for emergency medical treatment, to assign financial responsibility for such treatment, and to obtain permission for the use of the participant's name and photograph. It may be convenient to include it as a component of the agreement to participate when the participant is a minor.

Using the Agreement to Participate

Some guidelines regarding the use of the agreement to participate can help to ensure the effectiveness of the agreement in strengthening the assumption of risk and the contributory negligence defenses. First, presentation of the agreement should be accompanied by a verbal explanation of the risks participants will encounter through participation and of their responsibility for their own safety. Second, it is important to provide an opportunity for the signer to ask questions and gain clarification. Third, stress the participants' duty to inform you of any dangerous practices, hazardous conditions, or faulty equipment of which they may become aware while participating. This, however, in no way reduces or relieves the recreation or sport business of its duty to inspect the facility, examine the equipment, or supervise the activity. In addition, the language used in both the agreement and the verbal explanation should be appropriate to the age and maturity of the participant.

Finally, keep in mind that the agreement to participate can serve as important evidence in the event of a lawsuit. These records should be safely stored so that they may be retrieved when needed. The time during which a person may file a timely suit varies from one to four years after the injury, depending on the state. However, keep in mind that a minor who is injured can generally file a suit until one to four years after reaching the age of majority. So in the event of an injury, it would be helpful to make and carefully store a file on that individual that would include the agreement to participate along with all other pertinent documentation (e.g., accident report, written statements by witnesses, parental permission slips).

Assumption of Risk Agreement

As stated earlier, the **assumption of risk agreement** is essentially the same as an agreement to participate—though it may be in a different format and briefer. The agreement is a pact by which the participant or client is informed of the inherent risks of the activity and attests that he or she assumes the inherent risk of the activity. The participant or client further confirms that he or she (1) has been informed of the nature of the activity and its inherent risks, (2) understands the activity in terms of its demands on the participant's own physical condition and skill level, and (3) appreciates the type of injuries that may occur and the consequences of such injuries. Finally, the participant or client should verify that his or her participation is voluntary. The agreement can be used prior to participation in recreation and sport activities, prior to internships, or in almost any situation in which the service provider wants documentation that the participant understood and assumed the inherent risks of the activity. The assumption of risk agreement can be a stand-alone document, but is often (and should be) included as part of a liability waiver. *Regardless of its form, the assumption of risk agreement applies to assumption of the inherent risks and offers no protection against liability for provider negligence.*

As with the informed consent and the agreement to participate, the assumption of risk agreement may contain a written characterization of the nature of the activity and a listing of the inherent risks involved. The listing of the risks should not attempt to be all-inclusive, but should include the likely minor injuries, the unlikely major injuries, and the highly unlikely catastrophic injuries or death. One should not shy away from presenting the possibility of serious injuries.

The assumption of risk agreement used in conjunction with a liability waiver helps to provide more protection for the service provider. The waiver protects against liability for negligence, whereas the assumption of risk statement helps to protect against liability for injuries resulting from the inherent risks of the activity. An assumption of risk agreement used with a waiver is presented in Figure 1, Chapter 2.23, *Waivers and Releases,* and an agreement used without a waiver can be seen in the *Fairchild v. Amundson* Significant Case that follows.

The importance of an up-to-date assumption of risk statement was made evident in a recent waiver case (*Niedbala v. SL—Your Partners in Health*, 2002). The Connecticut court failed to uphold a waiver when a health club client was injured while lifting weights because the club had no weight lifting equipment when Niedbala signed the waiver. Waiver language included

> I understand and am aware that strength, flexibility and aerobic exercise, including the use of equipment, is a potentially hazardous activity. I also understand that fitness activities involve a risk of injury and even death and that I am voluntarily participating in these activities and using equipment and machinery with knowledge of the dangers involved. I hereby agree to expressly assume and accept all risks of injury or death.

The plaintiff argued that at the time he signed the waiver, he was not fully aware of the risks he was assuming because the facility did not contain the equipment he was using. The court stated that it was difficult to see how Niedbala could have foreseen the risk of using equipment that was not even on site at the time of signing and noted that he was inexperienced in the use of weights. The court asserted that the procurement of a new agreement when substantially different equipment is added does not create too great a burden for a sports facility.

Significant Case

———————————◇◇———————————

This case illustrates perfectly the value of the assumption of risk agreement. Observe in reading the case four different facts that help to establish that Fairchild was aware of the inherent risks of white-water rafting. It is also important to understand that the assumption of risk document protects Amundson from liability for an injury resulting from the inherent risks of the activity, as contrasted with the waiver case in Chapter 2.23, in which the waiver protects the provider from liability for negligence. Note that in this case, negligence was not at issue before the trial court and was, therefore, not considered by the appellate court.

FAIRCHILD V. AMUNDSON
COURT OF APPEALS OF WASHINGTON, DIVISION ONE
2001 Wash. App. LEXIS 149
January 29, 2001, Filed

Opinion By: Ronald E. Cox

At issue is whether Wild Water River Tours owed a duty to its customer, Thomas Fairchild, for injuries that he suffered during a rafting trip on the Toutle River. Because the doctrine of implied primary assumption of risk bars Fairchild's claim, we affirm the summary dismissal of this action.

In April 1995, Tom Fairchild participated in a whitewater rafting trip on the Toutle River. Rodney Amundson, d/b/a Wild Water River Tours (WWRT), guided the commercial rafting trip. Fairchild had been on whitewater rafting trips before, and knew that one of the dangers inherent in rafting was the possibility that rafters would fall out into the water. He also read brochures of WWRT that described certain dangers of river rafting.

On the day of the rafting trip, Fairchild and his church group assembled near the river under the supervision of WWRT. Fairchild donned a wetsuit, helmet, and life vest issued by WWRT. The rafters all signed an "Acknowledgement of Risk" form. WWRT guides then instructed them on paddling techniques and safety measures. The safety measures included instructions on maneuvering the raft near logs, rocks, and reversals. They also included instructions on swimming in the event rafters are in the water, pulling a swimmer back into the raft, and escaping from underneath a capsized raft.

River rapids are classified on a scale from class I (easiest) to class VI (most difficult). The Toutle River has two class IV rapids, one of which is known as Hollywood Gorge (Gorge). The Gorge also contains a "reversal," a point in the river subject to strong downward pressure that may cause a raft to overturn.

As they approached the Gorge, all the rafts stopped, and Amundson and other WWRT guides got out of the rafts and scouted the Gorge. After everyone returned to their rafts and re-entered the river, Amundson's raft successfully navigated through the Gorge to an eddy just beyond the reversal. Amundson then waited for the other rafts.

As Fairchild's raft entered the Gorge, it was sucked into a reversal, and all the occupants were thrown into the water. Amundson observed this from his raft and immediately paddled out of the eddy and into the river's current to retrieve Fairchild. Amundson and others administered CPR to Fairchild, who had been floating face down in the river, and resuscitated him. Thereafter, Fairchild went to a hospital, where he was treated and released the next day.

Fairchild sued. The trial court granted WWRT's motion for summary judgment.

Fairchild appeals.

Implied Assumption of Risk

Fairchild argues that material factual issues exist as to whether the doctrine of implied primary assumption of risk bars his recovery. We disagree.

We may affirm an order granting summary judgment if there are no genuine issues of material fact and the moving party is entitled to judgment as a matter of law. We consider all facts and reasonable inferences in the light most favorable to the nonmoving party. We review questions of law de novo.

The moving party bears the initial burden of showing the absence of a genuine issue of material fact. Once that burden is met, the burden shifts to the party with the burden of proof at trial to make a showing sufficient to establish the existence of an element essential to that party's case. If the claimant fails to meet that burden, the trial court should grant the motion because there can be no genuine issue of material fact given that a complete failure of proof concerning an essential element of the nonmoving party's case necessarily renders all other facts immaterial.

WWRT asserts that the doctrine of assumption of risk bars recovery. That doctrine has four facets: (1) express assumption of risk, (2) implied primary assumption of risk, (3) implied reasonable assumption of risk, and (4) implied unreasonable assumption of risk. Implied primary assumption of risk is at issue here. It occurs where the plaintiff impliedly has consented to relieve the defendant of an obligation or duty to act. With implied primary assumption of risk, the plaintiff engages in conduct from which consent is then implied. If implied primary assumption of risk is established, it bars any recovery.

At summary judgment, WWRT was required to show that (a) Fairchild had full subjective understanding of the nature and presence of a specific risk, and (b) he voluntarily chose to encounter the risk. Knowledge of and appreciation of the specific risk of danger, and voluntariness are questions of fact for the jury, except when reasonable minds could not differ.

Here, WWRT established both elements of implied primary assumption of risk. First, the evidence shows that Fairchild subjectively knew and understood the specific risk of falling into the water and drowning. Prior to

the rafting trip, Fairchild read WWRT's brochures describing whitewater rafting on the Toutle River. The brochures listed the Toutle River as a class IV river and described rafting on that river as "fast & furious" and "[y]ou'll never know when you're going to hit crushing waves and bottomless holes." Fairchild testified in his deposition that he had been rafting on a slower river before and wanted a more exciting whitewater rafting trip when he signed up with WWRT. Prior to boarding the rafts, WWRT outfitted Fairchild with a wetsuit, helmet, and vest. It also instructed him on swimming techniques. Moreover, Fairchild admitted in his deposition that getting thrown from the raft into a rushing river was a danger inherent to whitewater rafting on the Toutle River. Reasonable minds could not differ in deciding that Fairchild knew of and appreciated the specific risk of falling into the water and possibly drowning. Likewise, reasonable minds could not differ that Fairchild was aware of the above specific risks when he signed the "acknowledgment of risk" form which states that:

> *I am aware that participating in this raft trip arranged by Wildwater River Tours, its agents or associates, that I face certain risks, dangers, and personal property damage. This may include but not be limited to the hazards of traveling down rivers in inflatable rafts, accident or illness in remote places without medical facilities, forces of nature and travel by automobile or other conveyance. In consideration of, and as part payment for the right to participate in this trip and the services and food arranged for me by Wildwater River Tours, and its agents or associates, I do hereby acknowledge all of the above risks. The terms hereof shall serve as my acknowledgment of risk for my heirs, executors and administrators and for all members of my family . . . I have carefully read this agreement and fully understand its contents. (Italics ours)*

The above facts all establish that Fairchild knew of the nature and presence of the specific risk of falling into the river and possibly drowning. It also shows that he voluntarily assumed those risks.

Fairchild attempts to establish that a genuine issue of material fact exists as to his subjective knowledge or understanding of the risk of being thrown into the water. We reject this argument.

"When a party has given clear answers to unambiguous [deposition] questions which negate the existence of any genuine issue of material fact, that party cannot thereafter create such an issue with an affidavit that merely contradicts, without explanation, previously given clear testimony." In his declaration, Fairchild stated that he was not aware of the risk of being thrown into the water at the time he signed the "acknowledgment of risk" form. But this contradicts, without explanation, Fairchild's prior deposition testimony in which he admitted that he knew of that specific risk. Thus, Fairchild has failed to establish a genuine issue of material fact on the issue of whether he subjectively knew the presence and nature of the risk of being thrown into the water.

Fairchild also attempts to show that a genuine issue of material fact exists as to whether he voluntarily chose to encounter the risk of being thrown into the water. He contends that because there were no reasonable alternatives available to him to assuming the inherent risks of river rafting, he did not voluntarily choose to assume those risks. We disagree.

Whether a plaintiff decides voluntarily to encounter a risk depends on whether he or she elects to encounter it despite knowing of a reasonable alternative course of action. In other words, the plaintiff must have had a reasonable opportunity to act differently or proceed on an alternate course that would have avoided the danger in order for assumption of risk to bar recovery.

Here, Fairchild chose to encounter the risk of being thrown into the water despite having numerous reasonable alternatives. He could have chosen to take a slower rafting trip. He could have elected to forego whitewater rafting altogether. He could have chosen not to continue with the trip once he reached the starting point or gotten out when his raft stopped and WRRT guides walked on the bank to scout the Gorge. In sum, Fairchild fails to establish a genuine issue of fact as to whether he voluntarily encountered the risk.

Fairchild also argues that he did not assume the risk of WWRT's alleged negligence in operating the raft because he knew that he might fall out of the raft and into the river. This was not an argument that Fairchild made below. Thus, we need not consider it for the first time on appeal. In any event, there is nothing in this record that establishes that any action or omission of WWRT was outside the scope of the risks that are inherent in the sport of river rafting.

We need not address Fairchild's contention that by signing the "acknowledgment of risk" form, he did not expressly assume the risk of falling into the water. WWRT does not argue that express assumption of risk applies to bar Fairchild's recovery. Rather, the issue is whether implied assumption of risk applies. We hold that it does.

Fairchild also asserts that the trial court improperly placed the burden of proof on him "to show that there was negligence rather than [placing] the burden on [WWRT] to show that no reasonable jury could find negligence from the material facts submitted in the record." There was no improper shifting of burden here. WWRT moved for summary judgment based on implied primary assumption of risk. It was then Fairchild's burden to show whether a genuine issue of material fact exists as to the doctrine. He simply failed to do so.

We affirm the order granting defendants' motion for summary judgment.

Recent Trends

There are two current trends that stand out in this area: (1) the inherent risks of the activity are becoming more the responsibility of the participant than in the past, and (2) the use of informed consents by health clubs and personal trainers is increasing.

References

Cases

Fairchild v. Amundson, 2001 Wash. App. LEXIS 149.
Niedbala v. SL—Your Partners in Health, 2002 Conn. Super. LEXIS 2835.
Stokes v. Bally's Pacwest, Inc., 54 P.3d 161 (2002).

Publications

American College of Sports Medicine. (1999). Policy statement regarding the use of human subjects and informed consent. *Medicine and Science in Sports and Exercise, 31*(7), vi.
American Medical Association. (1998). *Informed consent.* Retrieved from http://www.ama-assn.org/ama/pub/category/4608.html.
Cotten, D. J., & Cotten, M. B. (2005). *Waivers & releases of liability* (5th ed.). Sport Risk Consulting: www.lulu.com.
Herbert, D. L., & Herbert, W. G. (2002). *Legal aspects of preventive, rehabilitative and recreational exercise programs* (4th ed.). Canton, OH: PRC Publishing, Inc.

Independent Review Consulting, Inc. (2000). *Post-approval requirements: informed consent.* Corte Madera, CA: Author.

Koeberle, B. E., & Herbert, D. L. (1998). *Legal aspects of personal fitness training,* (2nd ed.). Canton, OH: PRC Publishing, Inc.

Nolan-Haley, J. M. (1999). Informed consent in mediation: A guiding principle for truly educated decision making. *Notre Dame L. Rev., 74,* 775.

Office of Human Subjects Research (OHSR) National Institutes of Health. (2000). *Guidelines for writing informed-consent documents.* Retrieved from http://ohsr.od.nih.gov/info_6.php3

Olivier, S., & Olivier, A. (2001). Informed consent in sport science. *Sportscience.* Retrieved from http://www.sportsci.org/jour/0101/so.htm

van der Smissen, B. (1990). *Legal liability and risk management for public and private entities.* Cincinnati, OH: Anderson Publishing.

2.31 Emergency Care

James T. Gray

Pierski & Gray, LLP

The term *emergency care* can be defined as those sport-related instances where medical or health care is provided to an ill or injured person on a sudden, immediate, or unexpected basis. Emergency care can include providing medical assistance to those who have suffered from heart attacks, respiratory ailments or diseases, broken limbs, and other conditions when watching or participating in organized sport or recreational activities. Thus, it is imperative for sport and recreation providers to implement an effective emergency care system that promotes health and safety while minimizing the legal liability and insurance premiums of those providing care.

In recognition of the vital role that emergency care plays in recreational and competitive sport as well as within the health club setting, the National Athletic Trainers' Association (NATA) created a sport-related emergency care position paper and provided several recommendations for any organization, institution, or entity that sponsors or hosts sport activities or events. The relevant NATA emergency care recommendations are as follows: (1) each organization that sponsors athletic activities must develop and implement a written emergency plan; (2) the plan should be developed by organizational personnel in consultation with local emergency medical service providers; (3) personnel should be trained in CPR and/or automated external defibrillator (AED), first aid procedures and know how to prevent disease transmission; (4) identify emergency equipment and its location; (5) identify a suitable emergency care communication system and method; (6) have a specific emergency plan for each venue; (7) identify personnel involved with the execution of each emergency plan; (8) identify who will document what happens during the emergency; and (9) rehearse the emergency plan at least annually.

Additional practical considerations for those who provide emergency care include (1) assessing the risk or rate of injury regarding a sport-related endeavor; (2) identifying the number of people participating in the activity; (3) gauging the frequency and duration of each activity; and 4) evaluating the experience and expertise of each participant and supervisor.

Fundamental Concepts

Duty and Liability Related to Emergency Care

To be liable, a service provider must owe a duty to the injured party, the duty to provide care must be breached, the breach must be a proximate cause of the harm sustained, and the injured party must sustain damages. Furthermore, legal issues involving duty and emergency care consider the "existence of a special relationship." In general, courts have found the existence of a special relationship in three instances—(1) from a relationship inherent in the situation, (2) from a voluntary assumption of the duty, and (3) from a duty mandated by statute (see Chapter 2.11, *Elements of Negligence*).

Relationship Inherent in the Situation

The relationship inherent in the situation can give rise to a duty to provide emergency care. Examples of inherent relationships include coach/player, arena manager/spectators, and park director/participants. For instance, a case addressing the duty of facility owners to provide emergency medical care at a concert found that sport or entertainment facilities could expect to experience one medical emergency per hour for every 10,000 to 20,000 patrons in attendance (*Leane v. The Joseph Entertainment Group*, 1994).

Similarly, in *Jarreau v. Orleans Parish School Board* (1992), the court found a school board vicariously liable for the negligence of a high school coach and team trainer in failing to immediately refer an injured player for medical treatment. In this case, a football player fractured his wrist during a game, and the coach continued to play the athlete despite the continued swelling of his wrist and the continued pain associated with this injury. Only at the end of the season did the trainer refer the player for treatment by a physician. The court stated coaches are not expected to diagnose the extent of the injury, but "should recognize their limitations in this regard and seek expert medical advice for their players in the face of continuing complaints involving pain and swelling" (p. 1393). Plaintiffs also alleged, and the trial court found, that the school board was negligent for failing to train the coaches to properly diagnose injuries and for failure to have a physician present.

However, *In re Chicago Flood Litigation* (1997) the Illinois Supreme Court overruled their earlier holding in *Barth by Barth v. Board of Education* (1986) regarding the lack of tort immunity protection for governmental entities engaged in willful and wanton misconduct. In *Barth*, school staff failed to obtain prompt medical treatment for a student injured in a physical education class resulting in permanent physical injury. Thus, in Illinois, there now seems to be government immunity for both negligence and willful and wanton misconduct relative to emergency care.

Voluntary Assumption of Duty

In the emergency care area, the voluntary assumption of duty arises in the context of Good Samaritan laws. Throughout the United States, Good Samaritan statutes have been enacted to protect citizens rendering aid to injured persons at an accident scene or an emergency situation (see Chapter 2.22, *Immunity*). The majority of states apply this statute to all citizens so long as the person giving aid owes no duty to the injured, does not charge a fee, acts in good faith, and is not grossly negligent. One must remember, however, that the one giving aid is not always protected by Good Samaritan statutes and that the duty, once assumed, must be performed in good faith (*Lundy v. Adamar of New Jersey, Inc.* 1994).

As noted in the Significant Case (*Kleinknecht v. Gettysburg College*, 1993), in Pennsylvania, the Good Samaritan law provided immunity to persons rendering emergency care if they were holders of certificates showing that they had completed training in first aid and basic life support. In addition, the court found that "persons" under the Pennsylvania Good Samaritan Law applied only to natural persons, and thus did not provide immunity to employers or other corporate entities (see Chapter 2.21, *Defenses Against Negligence*, and Chapter 2.22, *Immunity*). Similarly, in *Willingham v. Hudson* (2005), the issue was whether the defendant, while under no duty to render aid or assistance to the injured plaintiff, was required to exercise ordinary diligence while providing emergency care or be liable for damages. The court, in ruling in favor of the defendant, concluded that the defendant acted in good faith in an emergency situation, had no duty to render aid to the plaintiff, and did not charge for emergency care services. Therefore, the Good Samaritan statute protected the defendant.

Duty Mandated by Statute

As it pertains to the duty mandated by state statute, states vary greatly in their rules and regulations relative to the emergency care issue (see Chapter 2.22, *Immunity*). For example, some states require sport-related entities and their personnel to possess first aid or CPR certificates, or to maintain certain equipment, such as stretchers and oxygen tanks, or to ensure that medical personnel are present at sports games and practices (van der Smissen, 1990, part C).

Nebraska is one state that mandates, by statute, that coaches must provide emergency care to injured athletes. Nebraska requires that each high school teacher who desires to obtain a coaching endorsement on his or her teaching certificate must successfully complete a course on the prevention and care of athletic injuries. For example, in *Cerny v. Cedar Bluffs Junior/Senior Public School* (2004), a high school football player had sustained an injury. The issue was whether a duty was owed to the injured player by his coaches and how that duty was to be fulfilled pursuant to Nebraska state law. The Nebraska Supreme Court found that the conduct required of "a reasonably prudent person holding a Nebraska teaching certificate with a coaching endorsement in 1995, when a player has sustained a possible head injury was (1) to be familiar with the features of a concussion; (2) to evaluate the player who appeared to have suffered a head injury for the symptoms of a concussion; (3) to repeat the evaluation at intervals before the player would be permitted to reenter the game; and (4) to determine, based upon the evaluation, the seriousness of the injury and whether it was appropriate to let the player reenter the game or to remove the player from all contact pending a medical examination."

In holding in favor of the defendant, the court noted that the coach examined the plaintiff at the prescribed intervals. Further the defendant noted that the plaintiff "appeared to be 100% normal; that his responses were appropriate, that he did not seem confused or disoriented, that his speech was not incoherent or slurred; that his emotions were appropriate; that he did not complain of dizziness, unsteadiness, nausea, or headache; and that he told the coach he felt fine."

Legal Issues Pertaining to Emergency Care

Once a duty has been established to provide emergency care, there is also a duty to deliver emergency care in a reasonable fashion. To avoid or minimize legal liability relative to the delivery of emergency care to injured people, a prudent recreation, sport, or health club entity should (1) plan for emergency care situations, (2) provide a risk assessment of the activity, and (3) ensure that there is adequate and qualified personnel available in the delivery of these services.

Planning for Emergency Care

Although some jurisdictions find that there is no duty for prior preparation for medical emergencies (*Applebaum v. Nemon*, 1984), most jurisdictions have held that there is a duty to prepare for emergency care before emergencies occur (van der Smissen, 1990). An effective emergency plan should be tailored to the nature of the organization, personnel, and recreation or sport involved. A plan need not always be complex. For example, if medically trained people are not available, someone should at least be designated to contact emergency medical personnel via cell phone. Further, the emergency care plan should be reviewed regularly and updated when new activities are offered or withdrawn, personnel are hired or terminated, and financial resources are increased or reduced (see Chapter 5.23, *Crisis Management*).

Assessment

Reasonable planning begins with an assessment of the risk of the activity, the potential dangers, the age, experience, and expertise of those people participating and supervising the activity, as well as the type of injuries to which an emergency care response must be made (see *Wattenbarger v. Cincinnati Reds* [1994] for an injury assessment analysis). For example, an emergency plan that covers downhill skiing would be different from one designed for a golf tournament or a swimming event. Although it may not be possible to anticipate (foresee) all types of accidents that result in injury and that would require an emergency care response, it is important for the recreation or sport manager to be as thorough as possible in identifying the risks of the activity. Further, risk management decisions as to the extent of emergency care should be determined based on the financial resources and qualified personnel available to implement such a plan (see *Estate of Gehling v. St. George's University School of Medicine* [1989] for a discussion of emergency care preparations).

Personnel

All recreation, sport, and health club programs should have personnel who are trained and qualified to administer emergency care. In addition, facility owners and operators and those who organize or sponsor mass gatherings have a duty to provide a reasonable response to life-threatening situations. Further, *this duty may exist regardless of the training of personnel, thus prudent administrators should ensure that their personnel are adequately trained for emergency care procedures* (van der Smissen, 1990; see also Chapter 2.35 *Human Resources Law*).

A good example of an organization that trains people for emergency care services is NATA. Through its certification process, NATA prepares trainers to meet the needs of athletes ranging from high schools through the professional ranks. NATA training helps athletic trainers to provide the highest quality care to athletes when injury occurs. Similarly, some recreation and sport entities (e.g., ski slope operators) have certifications specific to their area (e.g., National Ski Patrol System), and these entities should employ only those with appropriate training and certification. Businesses that do not have certifications specific to their activity or sport should engage personnel with some form of emergency training (e.g., EMT credentials, NATA certification, American Heart Association CPR, American Red Cross first aid certification).

An effective emergency care program should have well-trained individuals filling every position. The ideal approach in providing emergency care for recreation or sport participants and spectators would consist of physicians, certified athletic trainers, coaches, student trainers, health services staff (colleges and universities), and emergency medical technicians (EMTs) provided by the local emergency medical services system working together in a coordinated effort. It should be noted that because of their special skills and training, doctors, trainers, and physical therapists are held to a higher standard of care in the treatment of the sick and injured while administering emergency care than coaches, volunteers, and parents (Schubert, Smith & Trentadue, 1986).

As far as the medical decision-making authority for a member of a sport team is concerned, all final medical decisions regarding participation should rest with the physician. Best-practice emergency care would include a physician conducting preparticipation physical examinations, rendering onsite medical attention to the injured participant as appropriate, providing postinjury treatment, and granting clearance to the injured person regarding return to sport participation or competition.

The best approach to protect the health and safety of sport participants is for the sport organization or entity to provide a physician for all competitions and events as resources permit. For practice or daily sport activities where a physician is not readily available, emergency care decisions should be made by qualified trainers, coaches, or EMTs (see Chapter 2.22, *Immunity*).

Consent for Emergency Care

Consent for emergency care should be obtained prior to recreation or sport participation. If the participants are minors, parental consent for emergency care should be obtained. Further, emergency care consent forms should be maintained using a system that allows for regular review and immediate retrieval of these forms when needed locally or on road trips. Similarly, if the participants are adults, a health-care power of attorney form should be completed in case incapacity should occur. This form should designate who is appointed to make health-care decisions and when health care can be refused when one is determined to be terminally injured with no reasonable chance for recovery.

Record Keeping

It is recommended that recreation and sport managers collect and keep records related to emergency care of injuries. This is important regardless of the type of recreation or sport involved. The need for accurate record keeping is particularly important for those organizations that offer sport participation opportunities to minors.

Emergency care information should be provided on a "need-to-know basis" to abide by **federal** and **state** confidentiality and privacy laws relative to health or medical care records. Emergency care information should include the following: (1) participant medical history; (2) emergency contact card—index cards with the contact number of parents/guardians, preferred hospital, and insurance number for all current team members should be kept in the first aid kit used by the coach for daily practices and games; (3) preparticipation physical examination forms; (4) participant consent for treatment; (5) injury/accident report forms; (6) physician referral information; (7) daily notification procedures or meetings for coaches by trainers regarding the health status of injured or medically based "at-risk" participants; (8) diagnosis and prescribed treatment from physicians for the injured; and (9) daily treatment log maintained by trainer or other health-care professionals.

In the event of an accident or injury, emergency care records should be stored and maintained until the statute of limitations expires (one to four years, depending on the state). When the injured party is a minor, the statute of limitations begins when the minor reaches the age of majority.

Significant Case

The following case is a leading case regarding sport-related emergency care. Two issues—the duty to provide emergency care and the foreseeability of injuries are reviewed. The court found that the College had a "special relationship" with Kleinknecht because (1) he was actively recruited to play intercollegiate lacrosse, (2) he was actively engaged in a college-sponsored practice at the time of his cardiac arrest, and (3) the college's duty of emergency care extended to fall practices. The court's ruling of forseeability raises a warning, reminding emergency care planners that even though a sport may never have experienced a particular injury, the prevalence of that type of injury elsewhere in the same sport makes that injury foreseeable and gives rise to a duty to provide emergency care.

KLEINKNECHT V. GETTYSBURG COLLEGE

United States Court of Appeals, Third Circuit
989 F.2d 1360
Argued Sept. 24, 1992, Decided March 31, 1993

Opinion

II. Factual History

In September 1988, Drew Kleinknecht was a twenty-year old sophomore student at the College, which had recruited him for its Division III intercollegiate lacrosse team. The College is a private, four-year liberal arts school. In 1988, it had an enrollment of about two thousand students and supported twenty-one intercollegiate sports teams involving approximately 525 male and female athletes. . . .

* * *

In September 1988, the College employed two full-time athletic trainers, Joseph Donolli and Garth Biser. Both men were certified by the National Athletic Trainers Association, which requires, inter alia, current certification in both cardio-pulmonary resuscitation ("CPR") and standard first aid. In addition, twelve student trainers participated in the College's sports program. * * *

Because lacrosse is a spring sport, daily practices were held during the spring semester in order to prepare for competition. Student trainers were assigned to cover both spring practices and games. Fall practice was held only for the players to learn "skills and drills," and to become acquainted with the other team members. No student trainers were assigned to the fall practices.

Drew participated in a fall lacrosse practice on the afternoon of September 16, 1988. Coaches Janczyk and Anderson attended and supervised this practice. It was held on the softball fields outside Musselman Stadium. No trainers or student trainers were present. Neither coach had certification in CPR. Neither coach had a radio on the practice field. The nearest telephone was inside the training room at Musselman Stadium, roughly 200-250 yards away. The shortest route to this telephone required scaling an eight-foot high cyclone fence surrounding the stadium. According to Coach Janczyk, he and Coach Anderson had never discussed how they would handle an emergency during fall lacrosse practice.

* * * . Drew was a defenseman and was participating in one of the drills when he suffered a cardiac arrest. According to a teammate observing from the sidelines, Drew simply stepped away from the play and dropped to the ground. . . .

After Drew fell, his teammates and Coach Janczyk ran to his side. Coach Janczyk and some of the players noticed that Drew was lying so that his head appeared to be in an awkward position. No one knew precisely what had happened at that time, and at least some of those present suspected a spinal injury. Team captain Daniel Polizzotti testified that he heard a continuous "funny" "gurgling" noise coming from Drew, and knew from what he observed that something "major" was wrong. Other teammates testified that Drew's skin began quickly to change colors. One team member testified that by the time the coaches had arrived, "[Drew] was really blue."

According to the College, Coach Janczyk acted in accordance with the school's emergency plan by first assessing Drew's condition, then dispatching players to get a trainer and call for an ambulance. Coach Janczyk himself then began to run toward Musselman Stadium to summon help.

The Kleinknechts dispute the College's version of the facts. They note that although Coach Janczyk claims to have told two players to run to Apple Hall, a nearby dormitory, for help, Coach Anderson did not recall Coach Janczyk's sending anyone for help. Even if Coach Janczyk did send the two players to Apple Hall, the Kleinknechts maintain, his action was inappropriate because Apple Hall was not the location of the nearest telephone. It is undisputed that two other team members ran for help, but the Kleinknechts contend that the team members did this on their own accord, without instruction from either coach.

The parties do not dispute that Polizzotti, the team captain, ran toward the stadium, where he knew a training room was located and a student trainer could be found. In doing so, Polizzotti scaled a chain link fence that surrounded the stadium and ran across the field, encountering student trainer Traci Moore outside the door to the training room. He told her that a lacrosse player was down and needed help. She ran toward the football stadium's main gate, and continued on to the practice field by foot until flagging a ride from a passing car. In the meantime, Polizzotti continued into the training room where he told the student trainers there what had happened. One of them phoned Plank Gymnasium and told Head Trainer Donolli about the emergency.

Contemporaneously with Polizzotti's dash to the stadium, Dave Kerney, another team member, ran toward the stadium for assistance. Upon seeing that Polizzotti was going to beat him there, Kerney concluded that it was pointless for both of them to arrive at the same destination and changed his course toward the College Union Building. He told the student at the front desk of the emergency on the practice field. The student called his supervisor on duty in the building, and she immediately telephoned for an ambulance.

Student trainer Moore was first to reach Drew. She saw Drew's breathing was labored, and the color of his complexion changed as she watched. Because Drew was breathing, she did not attempt CPR or any other first aid technique, but only monitored his condition, observing no visible bruises or lacerations.

By this time, Coach Janczyk had entered the stadium training room and learned that Donolli had been notified and an ambulance called. Coach Janczyk returned to the practice field at the same time Donolli ar

rived in a golf cart. Donolli saw that Drew was not breathing, and turned him on his back to begin CPR with the help of a student band member who was certified as an emergency medical technician and had by chance arrived on the scene. The two of them performed CPR until two ambulances arrived at approximately 4:15 p.m. Drew was defibrillated and drugs were administered to strengthen his heart. He was placed in an ambulance and taken to the hospital, but despite repeated resuscitation efforts, Drew could not be revived. He was pronounced dead at 4:58 p.m.

* * *

Prior to his collapse on September 16, 1988, Drew had no medical history of heart problems. * * * In January 1988, a College physician had examined Drew to determine his fitness to participate in sports and found him to be in excellent health. * * *

Medical evidence indicated Drew died of cardiac arrest after a fatal attack of cardiac arrhythmia.

* * *

III. Issues on Appeal

The Kleinknechts present three general issues on appeal. They first argue that the district court erred in determining that the College had no legal duty to implement preventive measures assuring prompt assistance and treatment in the event one of its student athletes suffered cardiac arrest while engaged in school-supervised intercollegiate athletic activity. Second, the Kleinknechts maintain that the district court erred in determining that the actions of school employees following Drew's collapse were reasonable and that the College therefore did not breach any duty of care. Finally, the Kleinknechts urge that the district court erred in determining that both Traci Moore and the College were entitled to immunity under the Pennsylvania Good Samaritan Act.

IV. Analysis

1. The Duty of Care Issue

Whether a defendant owes a duty of care to a plaintiff is a question of law . . . In order to prevail on a cause of action in negligence under Pennsylvania law, a plaintiff must establish: (1) a duty or obligation recognized by the law, requiring the actor to conform to a certain standard of conduct; (2) a failure to conform to the standard required; (3) a causal connection between the conduct and the resulting injury; and (4) actual loss or damage resulting to the interests of another . . .

The Kleinknechts assert three different theories upon which they predicate the College's duty to establish preventive measures capable of providing treatment to student athletes in the event of a medical emergency such as Drew's cardiac arrest: (1) Existence of a special relationship between the College and its student ath letes; (2) foreseeability that a student athlete may suffer cardiac arrest while engaged in athletic activity; and (3) public policy.

* * *

a. Special Relationship

The Kleinknechts argue that the College had a duty of care to Drew by virtue of his status as a member of an intercollegiate athletic team. The Supreme Court of Pennsylvania has stated that "duty, in any given situation, is predicated on the relationship existing between the parties at the relevant time. . ." *Morena, 462 A.2d at 684.* * * *

In support of their argument, the Kleinknechts cite the case of *Hanson v. Kynast*, No. CA-828 (Ohio Ct. App. June 3, 1985), rev'd on other grounds, *494 N.E.2d. 1091 (Ohio 1986)*. In Hanson an intercollegiate, recruited lacrosse player was seriously injured while playing in a lacrosse game against another college. The plaintiff alleged that his university breached its legal duty to have an ambulance present during the lacrosse game. The trial court granted the defendant's motion for summary judgment based on its holding, inter alia, that

> There is no duty as a matter of law for the Defendant College or other sponsor of athletic events to have ambulances, emergency vehicles, trained help or doctors present during the playing of a lacrosse game or other athletic events, and the failure to do so does not constitute negligence as a matter of law.
>
> The court of appeals reversed, . . . By directing the trial court to submit the case to a jury, the court of appeals implicitly held that the university owed a duty of care to the plaintiff.

Although the *Hanson* court did not specify the theory on which it predicated this duty, we think it reached the correct result, and we predict that the Supreme Court of Pennsylvania would conclude that a similar duty exists on the facts of this case. * * * Head Trainer Donolli actively recruited Drew to play lacrosse at the College. At the time he was stricken, Drew was not engaged in his own private affairs as a student at Gettysburg College. Instead, he was participating in a scheduled athletic practice for an intercollegiate team sponsored by the College under the supervision of College employees. On these facts we believe that the Supreme Court of Pennsylvania would hold that a special relationship existed between the College and Drew that was sufficient to impose a duty of reasonable care on the College. * * *

* * *

Here, unlike Sullivan and Bradshaw, Drew was not acting in his capacity as a private student when he collapsed. Indeed, the Kleinknechts concede that if he had been, they would have no recourse against the College. There is a distinction between a student injured while participating as an intercollegiate athlete in a sport for which he was recruited and a student injured at a college while pursuing his private interests, scholastic or otherwise. This distinction serves to limit the class of students to whom a college owes the duty of care that arises here. Had Drew been participating in a fraternity football game, for example, the College might not have owed him the same duty or perhaps any duty at all. There is, however, no need for us to reach or decide the duty question either in that context or in the context of whether a college would owe a duty towards students participating in intramural sports. On the other hand, the fact that Drew's cardiac arrest occurred during an athletic event involving an intercollegiate team of which he was a member does impose a duty of due care on a college that actively sought his participation in that sport.

* * *

In conclusion, we predict that the Supreme Court of Pennsylvania would hold that the College owed Drew a duty of care in his capacity as an intercollegiate athlete engaged in school-sponsored intercollegiate athletic activity for which he had been recruited.

b. Foreseeability

This does not end our inquiry, however. The determination that the College owes a duty of care to its intercollegiate athletes could merely define the class of persons to whom the duty extends, without determining the nature of the duty or demands it makes on the College. Because it is foreseeable that student athletes may sustain severe and even life-threatening injuries while engaged in athletic activity, the Kleinknechts argue that the College's duty of care required it to be ready to respond swiftly and adequately to a medical emergency. . . .

* * *

The type of foreseeability that determines a duty of care, as opposed to proximate cause, is not dependent on the foreseeability of a specific event." Instead, in the context of duty, "the concept of foreseeability means the likelihood of the occurrence of a general type of risk rather than the likelihood of the occurrence of the precise chain of events leading to the injury. . . . Only when even the general likelihood of some broadly definable class of events, of which the particular event that caused the plaintiff's injury is a subclass, is unforeseeable can a court hold as a matter of law that the defendant did not have a duty to the plaintiff to guard against that broad general class of risks within [**28] which the particular harm the plaintiff suffered befell.

* * *

Even this determination that the harm suffered was foreseeable fails to end our analysis. If a duty is to be imposed, the foreseeable risk of harm must be unreasonable. *Griggs, 981 F.2d at 1435.* The classic risk-utility analysis used to determine whether a risk is unreasonable "balances 'the risk, in light of the social value of the interest threatened, and the probability and extent of the harm, against the value of the interest which the actor is seeking to protect, and the expedience of the course pursued.'"

No person can be expected to guard against harm from events which are not reasonably to be anticipated at all, or are so unlikely to occur that the risk, although recognizable, would commonly be disregarded. . . . On the other hand, if the risk is an appreciable one, and the possible consequences are serious, the question is not one of mathematical probability alone. . . . As the gravity of the possible harm increases, the apparent likelihood of its occurrence need be correspondingly less to generate a duty of precaution. . . .

Although the district court correctly determined that the Kleinknechts had presented evidence establishing that the occurrence of severe and life-threatening injuries is not out of the ordinary during contact sports, it held that the College had no duty because the cardiac arrest suffered by Drew, a twenty-year-old athlete with no history of any severe medical problems, was not reasonably foreseeable. Its definition of foreseeability is too narrow. Although it is true that a defendant is not required to guard against every possible risk, he must take reasonable steps to guard against hazards which are generally foreseeable. . . . Though the specific risk that a person like Drew would suffer a cardiac arrest may be unforeseeable, the Kleinknechts produced ample evidence that a life-threatening injury occurring during participation in an athletic event like lacrosse was reasonably foreseeable. In addition to the testimony of numerous medical and athletic experts, Coach Janczyk, Head Trainer Donolli, and student trainer Moore all testified that they were aware of instances in which athletes had died during athletic competitions. The foreseeability of a life-threatening injury to Drew was not hidden from the College's view. Therefore, the College did owe Drew a duty to take reasonable precautions against the risk of death while Drew was taking part in the College's intercollegiate lacrosse program.

Having determined that it is foreseeable that a member of the College's interscholastic lacrosse team could suffer a serious injury during an athletic event, it becomes evident that the College's failure to protect against such a risk is not reasonable. The magnitude of the foreseeable harm—irreparable injury or death to one of its student athletes as a result of inadequate preventive emergency measures—is indisputable. With regard to the offsetting cost of protecting against such risk, the College prophesied that if this Court accepts that the College owed the asserted duty, then it will be required "to have a CPR certified trainer on site at each and every athletic practice whether in-season or off-season, formal or informal, strenuous or light," and to provide similar cardiac protection to "intramural, club sports and gym class." This "slippery slope" prediction reflects an unwarranted extension of the holding in this case.

First, the recognition of a duty here is limited to intercollegiate athletes. No other scenario is presented, so the question whether any of the other broad classes of events and students posited by the College merit similar protection is not subject to resolution. Second, the determination whether the College has breached this duty at all is a question of fact for the jury. . . .This Court recognizes only that under the facts of this case, the College owed a duty to Drew to have measures in place at the lacrosse team's practice on the afternoon of September 16, 1988 in order to provide prompt treatment in the event that he or any other member of the lacrosse team suffered a life-threatening injury.

* * *

In reversing the district court's grant of summary judgment to the College, we predict that the Supreme Court of Pennsylvania would hold that a college also has a duty to be reasonably prepared for handling medical emergencies that foreseeably arise during a student's participation in an intercollegiate contact sport for which a college recruited him. It is clearly foreseeable that a person participating in such an activity will sustain serious injury requiring immediate medical attention.

* * *

It may be that the emergency medical measures the College had in place were sufficient to fulfill this duty. It is also possible that the College could not foresee that its failure to provide emergency medical services other than those which it already had in place would substantially contribute to the death of an apparently healthy student. Nevertheless,

Whether in a particular case the plaintiff has demonstrated, by a preponderance of the evidence, that the defendant's negligent conduct was a substantial factor in bringing about the plaintiff's harm, is normally a question of fact reserved for the jury, and should only be removed from the jury's consideration where it is clear, as a matter of law, that reasonable minds could not differ on the issue.

* * *

Our holding is narrow. It predicts only that a court applying Pennsylvania law would conclude that the College had a duty to provide prompt and adequate emergency medical services to Drew, one of its intercollegiate athletes, while he was engaged in a school-sponsored athletic activity for which he had been recruited. Whether the College breached that duty is a question of fact. . . .

* * *

2. The Reasonableness of the College's Actions

On the duty question, it remains only for us to address the district court's second holding that the conduct of the College's agents in providing Drew with medical assistance and treatment following his cardiac arrest was reasonable. . . .

This is a separate and distinct duty from that which the College had in terms of maintaining prompt and adequate emergency medical attention prior to Drew's collapse. The College does not dispute that a duty of care was imposed on it at the time of Drew's collapse. . . .

* * *

The question of breach must be reconsidered on remand in light of this Court's holding that the College did owe Drew a duty of care to provide prompt and adequate emergency medical assistance to Drew while participating as one of its intercollegiate athletes in a school-sponsored athletic activity.

Moreover, on remand, we think the district court should be careful not to infringe on the province of the factfinder by prematurely deciding whether the College breached its duty.

* * *

3. The Immunity Issue

Finally, we address the College's argument that Pennsylvania's Good Samaritan law provides immunity to both the College and its personnel who rendered emergency care to Drew. This statute provides in pertinent part:

(a) General rule.—Any person who renders emergency care, first aid or rescue at the scene of an emergency . . . shall not be liable to such person for any civil damages as a result of any acts or omissions in rendering the emergency care, first aid or rescue . . . except any acts or omissions intentionally designed to harm or any grossly negligent acts or omissions which result in harm to the person receiving the emergency care, first aid, or rescue . . .

* * *

(b) Exceptions–

* * *

(2) In order for any person to receive the benefit of the exemption from civil liability provided for in subsection (a), he shall be, at the time of rendering the emergency care, first aid or rescue . . . the holder of a current certificate evidencing the successful completion of a course in first aid, advanced life saving or basic life support sponsored by the American National Red Cross or the American Heart Association or an equivalent course

of instruction approved by the Department of Health . . . and must be performing techniques and employing procedures consistent with the nature and level of the training for which the certificate has been issued. 42 Pa. Cons. Stat. Ann. @ 8332(a), (b)(2) (1982)

* * *

The parties do not dispute the district court's determination that neither Coach Janczyk nor Coach Anderson is entitled to immunity. The College, however, argues that it too is entitled to immunity because it is a "person" within the terms of the statute. In general, Pennsylvania statutory law defines the term "person" as including corporations, partnerships, and associations unless the statutory context indicates otherwise. 1 Pa. Cons. Stat. Ann. @ 1991 (Supp. 1992). Section 8332, however, requires a person who seeks immunity to hold certification in an approved first aid, advanced life saving, or basic life support course. We think it is unlikely that the Pennsylvania General Assembly intended that corporations could achieve the requisite certification and receive immunity. Therefore, we reject the College's argument and predict that the Supreme Court of Pennsylvania will not hold that a corporation is entitled to immunity under the Pennsylvania Good Samaritan law.

* * *

Moreover, even if an agent such as Traci Moore is immune, the principal can still be vicariously liable. See *Muntan v. City of Monongahela*, 45 Pa. Commw. 23, 406 A.2d 811, 813-14 (Pa. Commw. Ct. 1979). Thus, the College may not claim immunity either in its own right or derivatively from Moore, regardless of whether she falls within the provisions of the statute.

* * *

V. Conclusion

The district court's holding that the College's duty of care to Drew as an intercollegiate athlete did not include, prior to his collapse, a duty to provide prompt emergency medical service while he was engaged in school-sponsored athletic activity will be reversed. The district court's holding that the College acted reasonably and therefore did not breach any duty owed to Drew following his collapse will likewise be reversed. We will remand this matter to the district court for further proceedings consistent with this opinion. We will reverse the district court's conclusion that the College is entitled to immunity under the Good Samaritan law. . . .

◇◇◇ **ANOTHER RELATED SIGNIFICANT CASE**

Chapter 5.21 *Standards of Practice*

Recent Trends

Emergency Care and Constitutional Rights

Plaintiffs who had alleged negligent emergency care by public sport-related entities and had been barred from filing tort liability claims because of sovereign or government immunity statutes have argued, with limited success, that these sovereign or government immunity statutes are unconstitutional.

For instance, in the *Estate of Barrett v. Unified School District No. 259*, (2001), the Kansas Supreme Court examined the application of the recreational use exception to the Kansas Tort Claim Act ("KTCA"). The plaintiff claimed that the death of a high school football player occurred as a result of the negligent supervision of the football staff. The Kansas Supreme Court held that the recreational use statute applied and the school district was immune from liability for ordinary negligence under the facts. (See *Halper v. Vayo* [1991] for a discussion of sovereign immunity protection for negligent acts as compared to intentional or reckless ones.)

The plaintiff then argued that the recreational use exception as applied in this case violated the Equal Protection Clause of the United States and Kansas Constitutions. The Court in holding against the plaintiff held that "Certainly, the encouragement of the building of recreational facilities for the use of the public is a legitimate purpose. The statute in question seeks to encourage the development of such facilities, and it does so by allowing those facilities immunity for simple negligence."

In a Pennsylvania case, *Burden v. Wilkes-Barre Area School District* (1998), the father of a deceased high school football player alleged that his son's civil rights had been violated when the school district decided not to hire a certified athletic trainer. The District Court held that (1) the district's one-time decision not to hire a certified athletic trainer for high school athletic teams was not official policy of the district, as would support recovery under Section 1983; (2) the district had no affirmative duty under the due process clause to protect the player by providing a trainer; (3) the father failed to sufficiently allege that the board had acted with deliberate indifference to the player's rights; and (4) the father had failed to allege conspiracy actionable under Section 1985.

In a Texas case (*Roventini v. Pasadena Independent School District*, 1997), the parents of a public high school student sued the school district, coaches, trainers, and other school officials under Section 1983 and state law following the student's death due to heat exhaustion during a football practice. Plaintiffs alleged that the Defendant coaches did not attempt to acclimatize the deceased or the other players, did not provide sufficient rest during practice, and did not give players enough water during the four-hour, summer practice. Players were required to perform "gasser" conditioning drills including 200-yard sprints within 45 seconds each. Decedent showed signs of heat stress but was required to continue with the drills. When he collapsed during a "gasser," he received no medical attention and drills continued, followed by a team meeting. Only untrained team managers tried to assist the decedent because the trainer was not on the field. The decedent died within several hours. Plaintiffs alleged that the defendants were liable under 42 U.S.C. section 1983 for violating the decedent's Constitutional rights to life, liberty, health, safety and bodily integrity and to a safe environment protecting him from violations of his rights by state actors. The district, board, superintendent, athletic director, athletic trainer, thirteen football coaches, and principal were sued under Section 1983. All individuals sued only in their official capacities were dismissed; the football trainer and thirteen coaches remained parties to this action. The case was subsequently vacated, 183 F.R.D. 500 (S.D. Tex. 1998) because the plaintiff wrongfully accused defendants of being deliberately indifferent, denying him water despite his pleas, and, thereby, causing his death by dehydration and heat stroke.

Automated External Defibrillators (AED)

Presently, each state has enacted legislation to regulate AED use. In general, state law provides for AED physician oversight, training, and equipment registration requirements. For example, in Alabama, a licensed physician is required to perform AED oversight functions, AED users must receive training from a national recognized course provider, and the entity owning the AED must notify the local emergency care provider of the location and type of AED being used. However, in Pennsylvania, the law does not provide for physical oversight, and there are not any notification requirements. (*See American Heart Association, Compilation of State AED Laws at www.americanheart.org/downloadable/heart*).

Four cases, *Mandel v. Canyon Ranch, Inc.* (1998), *Rutnik v. Colonie Center Court Club, Inc.,* (1998) *Atcovitz v. Gulph Mills Tennis Club, Inc.* (2002) and *Salte v. YMCA* (2004) resulted in verdicts for the defense regarding failure to defibrillate decedents who collapsed during sport activities at fitness/health facilities. Although neither the standards of the American Heart Association (AHA), nor those of the American College of Sports Medicine (ACSM), presently requires the presence and use of AEDs in health and fitness facilities, a number of states, including California, New York, Rhode Island, Michigan, Louisiana, New Jersey, and Illinois have passed legislation requiring AED availability in health (Herbert, 1998, 2000; see Chapter 5.21, *Standards of Practice*).

References

Cases

Applebaum v. Nemon, 678 S.W.2d 533 (Texas 1984).

Atcovitz v. Gulph Mills Tennis Club, Inc. 571 Pa. 580, 812 A. 2d 1218 (2002).

Barth by Barth v. Board of Education, 1986.

Burden v. Wilkes-Barre Area School District, 16 F. Supp. 2d 569 (M.D. Pa. 1998).

Cerny v. Cedar Bluffs Junior/Senior Public School, 267 Neb. 958; 679 N.W. 2d 198 (2004).

Estate of Barrett v. Unified School District No. 259, 272 Kan. 250; 32 P.3d 1156 (2001).

Estate of Gehling v. St. George's University School of Medicine, 705 F. Supp. 761 (1989).

Halper v. Vayo, 210 III. App. 3d 81, 568 NE.2d 914 (1991).

In re Chicago Flood Litigation, 176 Ill. 179, 196; 680 N.E. 2d 265 (Ill. Supreme Ct. 1997).

Jarreau v. Orleans Parish School Board, 600 So.2d 1389 (La. 1992).

Kleinknecht v. Gettysburg College, 786 F. Supp. 449 (M.D. Pa. 1992) rev'd, 989 F.2d 1360 (3rd Cir. 1993).

Leane v. The Joseph Entertainment Group, 642 N.E.2d 852 (Ill. 1994).

Lundy v. Adamar of New Jersey, Inc. 34 F. 3d 1173 (3d Cir. 1994).

Mandel v. Canyon Ranch, Inc., 1998.

Mogabgab v. Orleans Parish School Board, 239 So.2d 456 (La. App. 1970).

Roventini v. Pasadena Independent School District, 981 F. Supp. 1013 (S.D. Tex. 1997).

Rutnik v. Colonie Center Club Inc., 672 N.Y.S.2d 451, 1998.

Salte v. YMCA of Metropolitan Chicago Foundation, 351 Ill. App. 3d 524; 814 N.E. 2d 610 (2004).

Stineman v. Fontbonne College, 664 F. 2d 1082 (E.D. Missouri 1981).

Wattenbarger v. Cincinnati Reds, 28 Cal. App. 4th 746; 33 Cal. Rptr. 2d 732 (1994).

Willingham v. Hudson, 274 Ga. App. 200; 617 S.E. 2d 192 (2005).

Publications

American Heart Association, Compilation of State AED Laws. Retrieved from http://www.americanheart.org/downloadable/heart)

Gallup, E. (1995). *Law and the team physician*. Champaign, IL: Human Kinetics.

Herbert, D. L. (1998).

Herbert, D. L. (2000).

National Athletic Trainers' Association. Emergency Care Position Paper (2002). Retrieved from http://www.nata.org/publications/otherpub/positionstatements.htm.

Schubert, G., Smith, R., & Trentadue, J. (1986). *Sports law*. St. Paul, MN: West Publishing Co.

van der Smissen, B. (1990). *Legal liability and risk management for public and private entities*. Cincinnati, OH: Anderson Publishing Co.

Wong, G. (1994). *Essentials of amateur sports law*. Westport, CT: Praeger.

2.32 Supervision

Lynne P. Gaskin
University of West Georgia

Paul J. Batista
Texas A & M University

When individuals are injured while participating in recreation or sport activities and negligence is alleged, most complaints include allegations regarding supervision. In fact, van der Smissen (1990) estimated that approximately 80 percent of cases involving programmatic situations allege lack of supervision or improper supervision.

Supervision is a broad term denoting responsibility for an area and for the activities that take place in that area (Kaiser, 1986) and includes coordinating, directing, overseeing, implementing, managing, superintending, and regulating (*Longfellow v. Corey*, 1997). The courts have provided direction in defining nonnegligent supervision. In *Toller v. Plainfield School District 202* (1991), for example, the court determined that a teacher used reasonable care by teaching the rules of wrestling; demonstrating wrestling maneuvers; matching students according to height, weight, and size; and closely supervising them. Similarly, when learning an activity, students should receive proper instruction and preparation including basic rules and procedures, suggestions for proper performance, and identification of risks (*Scott v. Rapides Parish School Board*, 1999).

In addition to an instructor's explaining how to use athletic equipment and demonstrating proper techniques, the importance of observing the participant's use of the equipment also has been emphasized (*David v. County of Suffolk*, 2003). The significant case at the end of the chapter (*Kahn v. East Side Union High School District*, 2003) emphasizes the importance of providing consistent, progressive instruction in regard to safe performance of a skill and not coercing participants through threats.

Fundamental Concepts

Duty to Supervise

According to van der Smissen (1990), the **duty to supervise** arises from three sources: (1) a duty inherent in the situation, (2) a voluntary assumption of a duty, or (3) a duty mandated by law (see Chapter 2.11, *Elements of Negligence*). "The basis of the duty is whether or not there is a special relationship between plaintiff and defendant which requires that the defendant take affirmative action to provide a reasonably safe environment" (van der Smissen, 1990, p. 164).

By sponsoring an activity, **inherent in the situation** are relationships that require the defendant organization to exercise reasonable care for the protection of participants under its supervision. Examples of such a relationship include school/students, fitness club/clients, and recreation department/participants. Individual supervisors also have a duty to supervise that arises from the relationships inherent in the situation. These may include teacher/student, coach/player, recreation leader/participant, and supervisor/facility user. Negligence on the part of these individuals may result in both individual liability and liability for the organization.

In certain situations, there is no duty to supervise. The most common of these situations involves the recreational use of undeveloped outdoor land. Other examples include playgrounds at a recreation center, school grounds after hours, public beaches, and a nature trail in a public park. However, the owner of the land, recreation department, school, or other sport or recreation organization can **voluntarily assume** a duty to supervise. If the decision is made to provide supervision (e.g., by having lifeguards supervise a beach and adjacent ocean at an unimproved city beach), such supervision must be nonnegligent or the organization will be liable (*Fleuhr v. City of Cape May*, 1999).

In many cases, state legislatures impose a **statutory duty** to supervise. For example, the Indiana legislature has passed a statute that requires roller skating rink operators to use reasonable care in supervising roller skaters by ensuring that skaters maintain reasonable control of their speed and course at all times, and refrain from acting in a manner that could cause or contribute to an injury to other skaters (Ind. Code § 34-31-6, *et seq.*, 2005). In *St. Margaret Mercy Healthcare Centers, Inc. v. Poland* (2005), the plaintiff was injured while skating when she was knocked to the floor by a skater who was skating very fast and aggressively in violation of the statute. Although the defendant asserted that the plaintiff had assumed the inherent risks of skating, including being knocked down by another skater, the court held the operator liable for not properly supervising according to the requirements imposed by the statute.

When a duty to supervise exists, regardless of its source, the individual in the supervisory role has a duty not to increase the risks inherent in learning, practicing, or participating in the activity or sport (*Rodrigo v. Koryo Martial Arts*, 2002; *West v. Sundown Little League of Stockton, Inc.*, 2002; *Lilley v. Elk Grove Unified School Dist.*, 1998; *Balthazor v. Little League Baseball, Inc.*, 1998; *Bushnell v. Japanese-American Religious & Cultural Center*, 1996).

Forseeability and Causation Factors

When injured plaintiffs allege improper supervision, they must demonstrate that the injury was reasonably foreseeable and that negligent behavior was the proximate cause of the injury. Supervisors are expected to be on site and in reasonable proximity to the activity they are supervising. Failure to be present when an injury occurs, however, does not mean that the supervisor is automatically liable. The plaintiff still must show that the failure to supervise was the **proximate cause** of the injury. No liability exists if the injury would have occurred notwithstanding the supervisor's absence (see also Chapter 2.11, *Elements of Negligence*).

When the plaintiff alleges that the supervisor's absence was the proximate cause of the injury, the plaintiff must prove that the supervisor's presence would have prevented the injury. A number of cases, however, demonstrate that there are situations in which no amount of supervision would have prevented an injury, for example, a roller skater being struck by another skater, basketball players bumping heads while jumping for the ball, a player running head first and colliding with a catcher who was blocking home plate, and a child falling down at a day care center while running in a grassy area of the playground (*Blashka v. South Shore Skating, Inc.*, 1993; *Kaufman v. City of New York*, 1961; *Passantino v. Board of Educ.*, 1976; *Ward v. Mount Calvary Lutheran Church*, 1994).

In contrast, an injured plaintiff prevailed in a case in which he alleged negligent supervision since it was reasonably foreseeable that a catcher chasing a foul ball would trip over spectators who were allowed to congregate close to the base line. The supervisors had stopped the game twice prior to the injury to move the spectators back away from the third-base line and against the fence. The court found the defendants negligent for failing to control the crowd and found that the plaintiff was not guilty of contributory negligence (*Domino v. Mercurio*, 1963).

Nonnegligent supervision entails supervisors taking action to prevent **reasonably foreseeable** injuries to participants. When supervisors leave participants alone, they may be liable for negligent supervision. For example, it was reasonably foreseeable that, when left unattended, boys would throw rocks at girls with the likelihood of serious injury. In this case, one of the girls was blinded (*Sheehan v. St. Peter's Catholic School*, 1971). Similarly, in *Dailey v. Los Angeles Unified School District* (1970), a boy died as a result of a head injury incurred during a slap-boxing incident. The person on duty at the time was in his office eating lunch. Because the injury to the boy was foreseeable and proper supervision would have prevented the injury, the court found that the person on duty was liable for negligent supervision.

In summary, if the potential for injury is foreseeable and the presence of the supervisor would have prevented the injury, the probability of liability is strong. If, however, the injury would have occurred even if the supervisor had been there, there can be no liability. Supervisors cannot ensure the safety of participants and cannot be expected to prevent participants from all injuries that might occur during the course of normal play or sporting activities.

Types of Supervision

Supervision, which may be general, specific, or transitional, should be predicated on the age, skill, experience, judgment, and physical condition of participants and the activity involved. **General supervision** is overseeing individuals or groups involved in an activity and does not require constant, unremitting scrutiny of the activity or facility. General supervision usually is expected for observing participants and activities on the playground, in the gymnasium, in the weight room, on a baseball field, or in the swimming pool when the supervisor is not expected to have every individual under constant supervision (*Fagan v. Summers*, 1972; *Herring v. Bossier Parish School Board*, 1994; *Partin v. Vernon Parish School Board*, 1977; *Stevens v. Chesteen*, 1990). General supervision includes knowing what and how to observe, where to stand and how to move around the area, and when to respond and what action(s) to take if a problem occurs.

Specific supervision is constant and continuous, the type of supervision that is more appropriate for individuals or small groups receiving instruction, involved in high-risk activities, or using areas that have the potential for serious injury. For example, participants who are learning an activity or skill need specific, direct supervision. Similarly, participants who are not able to perform a skill adequately need specific supervision. Specific supervision also is mandated when participants are behaving or are likely to behave in ways that may injure themselves or others. Specific supervision also connotes proximity, that is, how close the supervisor needs to be to the participants or activity to be effective. The more dangerous the activity, the more closely it should be supervised.

According to van der Smissen (1990), supervision cannot be categorized simply as general or specific but frequently is **transitional** in nature, that is, changing from specific, to general, to specific, depending on such factors as the participants' need for instruction, their ability to perform certain activities, their use of equipment, their involvement with others, and their use of the facility. As the potential for harm increases, the degree of supervision should increase proportionally. Specific supervision is appropriate when the supervisor perceives a situation as dangerous. Whether involved in general or specific supervision, or moving from one to the other, supervisors are expected to identify dangerous activities and intervene either to stop the activity or facilitate its continuing safely.

Attributes of Proper Supervision

Qualifications of Supervisors

Supervisors must be competent to adequately supervise the participants involved, activities conducted, and facilities utilized. Whenever possible, supervisors should be regular, full-time employees who have appropriate qualifications and undergo regular staff development to improve their skill and knowledge. Even a qualified supervisor, however, can be remiss if he or she fails to enforce the policies of the organization.

Individuals in supervisory positions should have the **appropriate qualifications**, certification, experience, and training necessary for the job. In 1997, the American College of Sports Medicine delineated six standards to represent the standard of care that must be demonstrated by health and fitness facilities toward users. Notably, one of the six standards explicitly addresses supervision of youth services and programs and another addresses competencies of those responsible for program supervision (American College of Sports Medicine [ACSM], 1997). Although those in supervisory roles in health and fitness facilities may have appropriate certification, advanced training, and specialized qualifications, they also may be held to a higher standard of care, especially if the facility advertises those credentials in attracting members to join the facility (Herbert, 2002). In a joint endeavor with the American Heart Association, ACSM advocated more stringent recommendations for health and fitness facilities for cardiovascular screening, staffing (supervision), and emergency policies and procedures (ACSM & American Heart Association [AHA], 1998). Both of these efforts have been recognized for their importance in assisting health and fitness facilities with standard of care issues (Herbert, 1997, 1998).

Health and fitness facility employees and personal trainers should ensure that all members, especially new members, are instructed in the safe use of the equipment, are observed to ensure that they are using the equipment properly, and are informed of the risks and possible injuries associated with the activity (*Corrigan v. Musclemakers, Inc.*, 1999). In a similar case in which a member was injured on a hack squat machine that he had not properly secured after using, the court in *Thomas v. Sport City, Inc.* (1999) reiterated that the health and fitness facility has a duty to protect members from injury while they are on the premises and that the duty includes making sure that the members know how to use the exercise equipment properly.

Not only must supervisors warn of dangers, they also must see that the warnings are heeded. A teacher warned students to slow down a merry-go-round because it was going too fast. She was liable for negligent supervision when she resolved a dispute over a basketball between other students rather than making sure that the students slowed the merry-go-round (*Rollins v. Concordia Parish School Board*, 1985).

Number of Supervisors

The number of persons required to provide reasonable supervision depends on the participants and the nature of the activity. Moreover, when plaintiffs allege negligence due to an insufficient number of supervisors, they must show that inadequate supervision was the proximate cause of the injury and that additional supervisors would have prevented the injury (*Kaczmarcsyk v. City & County of Honolulu*, 1982). Except for swimming pool and school playground cases, however, the courts generally have not imposed liability when there has been at least one supervisor present (Gaskin, 2003). Instead of focusing on the number of supervisors, the courts generally have examined whether the supervision was reasonable in light of the age, maturity, and experience of the participants and the circumstances that existed at the time of the accident (*Glankler v. Rapides Parish School Board*, 1993).

Established Standards of Conduct

To properly organize and manage an event, a supervisor must be familiar with any standards of conduct or practice that establish criteria for proper handling of the event. *Black's Law Dictionary* (Garner, 2004) defines a **standard** as "a model accepted as correct by custom, consent, or authority" and "a criterion for measuring acceptability, quality, or accuracy." Failure to adhere to recognized standards of practice will leave the supervisor subject to liability. See Chapter 5.21, *Standards of Practice*, for a more detailed discussion of standards of conduct.

Primary Duties of Supervision

Although there are numerous legal duties associated with proper supervision of recreation and sporting activities, authors differ on the number and description of those duties (McCaskey & Biedzynski, 1996; Nygaard & Boone, 1985). These recognized duties can be condensed to six primary general duties, each requiring that the prudent supervisor undertake various specific actions. The six duties are effective planning, proper instruction, warning of risks, providing a safe environment, evaluating the physical and mental condition of participants, and providing emergency care.

Effective Planning

Effective planning is the first, and most important, element of proper supervision. Just as successful coaches prepare game plans for upcoming games, the cautious sport manager will organize every activity or event in advance by taking into account all foreseeable dangers or risks of potential injury to the participants. Recreation and sport managers need to develop, implement, and evaluate a supervisory plan for facilities and individuals on the premises. Although many of the elements of proper supervision overlap, effective planning precedes each of them. Regardless of the situation, a systematic procedure should be developed to document specifically each component to be addressed in supervision: **who**, **what**, **when**, **where**, and **how**. There should be both a master plan (including all the facilities, when they will be used, by whom, for what, and who will be supervising) and a detailed supervisory plan for each area and activity.

Several cases support the necessity of having adequate supervisory plans. In *Dailey v. Los Angeles Unified School Dist.* (1970), negligent supervision was at issue when the supervisory plan did not provide for a formal supervisory schedule and allowed too much discretion on the part of subordinates. In a Florida case (*Broward County School Board v. Ruiz*, 1986), the supervisory plan failed to provide for supervision in an after-school waiting area. Due to inadequate supervisory plans, negligence was found in each of these cases. In *Butler v. D.C.* (1969), no negligence was found because the school was using a supervisory plan. Similarly, in *Glankler v. Rapides Parish School Board* (1993), the court found that the supervisory plan for children on a one-and-one-half-acre playground was reasonable.

Other cases where supervisors have created liability for themselves or their organizations include failure to prepare a plan (*Landers v. School District No. 203*, 1978), deviating from an approved plan (*Keesee v. Board of Education of the City of New York*, 1962), failing to follow an approved plan (*Brahatcek v. Millard School District No. 17*, 1979), and creating a hazardous plan (*DeGooyer v. Harkness*, 1944).

An effective supervisory plan requires detailed planning, development, implementation, evaluation, and revision. Everyone involved in the activity should be involved in developing supervisory plans, evaluating them, and revising them with primary emphasis on maintaining the safety of participants in a safe environment. Although the framework for a supervisory plan may vary, the plan should be in writing, be specific, and be evaluated regularly and periodically to assess its effectiveness.

Proper Instruction

The standard of care imposed on supervisors is the degree of care which persons of ordinary prudence, charged with comparable duties, would exercise under the same circumstances (*Dailey v. Los Angeles Unified School District*, 1970). When a 16-year-old male was permanently paralyzed by injuries sustained while performing a wrestling drill in a required physical education class, the court in *Green v. Orleans Parish School Board* (1978) addressed the issue of whether the teacher's method of conducting the class was so substandard as to create an unreasonable risk of injury to students, thus creating liability for the teacher. In that case, the court described some of the requirements of **proper instruction** to include an explanation of basic rules and procedures, suggestions for proper performance (of wrestling moves), and identification of risks (including the extent of physical conditioning). The court specifically listed the difficulty and inherent dangerousness of the activity, and the age and experience of the students, as factors to be considered in proper instruction. In *Scott v. Rapides Parish School Board* (1999), an 18-year-old student recovered for a knee injury sustained when the track coach gave him a tryout for the long jump without instructions on proper technique.

Proper instruction includes the requirement that participants be trained in the proper use of the premises or equipment involved in the activity. In *Thomas v. Sport City, Inc.* (1999), the court acknowledged that health clubs owe a duty of reasonable care not to injure patrons, which includes the general responsibility to ensure that members know how to properly use the equipment in the gym.

Proper instruction also should be clear, age appropriate, in logical sequence, and repeated as many times as necessary for the participants to understand the activity and should include sufficient time for feedback (including questions and answers) for the instructor to be satisfied that the participants have grasped the directions.

Warnings of Risks

Supervisors of activities have a **duty to warn** of all **inherent risks** associated with the activity. Inherent risks are those that are foreseeable and customary risks of the sport or recreational activity (*Barakat v. Pordash*, 2005). Although most courts have concluded that participants assume the inherent risks of the activities in competitive sporting events, the rule may be different for other activities. When dangerous conditions exist or when there is an elevated risk in conducting the activity, courts have found activity supervisors liable for failure to adequately warn of the risks or dangers involved. In *Corrigan v. Musclemakers, Inc.* (1999), despite the fact that the 49-year-old health club patron had never used a treadmill, her personal trainer placed her on the treadmill, left her unattended, and failed to instruct her how to adjust the speed, stop the belt, or operate the control panel. The court rejected the defendant's argument that plaintiff had assumed the risk, finding that the risks were not obvious to an untrained patron. The prudent supervisor will warn of all risks associated with any activity, assuming that the courts will scrutinize whether or not the participant was aware of all the risks, both inherent and otherwise.

Many states have passed recreational user statutes requiring that written warnings be posted for the proprietor or operator to benefit from limited liability. An example of such statutes is the equine statutes passed in virtually every state. These statutes generally require that the operator post a sign advising participants that taking part in the activity subjects them to assumption of all inherent risks of the activity, and relieves the operator from any liability for injury caused by such risks. (For more on recreational user statutes, see Chapter 2.22, *Immunity* (especially Table 1), Chapter 2.21, *Defenses Against Negligence,* and Chapter 3.10, *Property Law.)*

Providing a Safe Environment

Courts often declare that supervisors are not **guarantors** that participants will not be hurt or injured. Stated another way, supervisors are not charged with a legal duty to protect participants from the inherent risks of the activity or to eliminate all risks of taking part in the activity (*Kahn v. East Side Union High School District,* 2003; *Kelly v. McCarrick,* 2002). However, supervisors have a duty not to increase the risk of harm beyond that which is inherent in the activity (*Kahn,* 2003; *Kelly,* 2002) nor to expose participants to risks that are concealed (*Benitez v. New York City Board of Education,* 1989).

Courts have established different standards for compulsory participation (such as school physical education courses) and purely voluntary activities (such as extracurricular interscholastic school sports). In the latter, courts consistently hold that the participant has assumed the inherent risks of the activity. Hurst and Knight (2003) summarized the difficulty in establishing liability against the coach and school in such cases by indicating that a successful plaintiff must prove "serious misconduct" amounting to "serious inattention, ignorance and indifference." In the compulsory participation circumstance, the defense of assumption of risk may not be a protection from liability when the injured party is compelled to participate by a superior (*Benitez v. New York City Board of Education,* 1989). The court's rationale is that participation and assumption of the risks are no longer voluntarily undertaken by the participant.

Providing a safe environment includes the obligation to provide **safe facilities** for participants by properly maintaining equipment, buildings, playgrounds, and other facilities. Although this duty is charged to the owner or operator, supervisors who work for the owners or operators continually must inspect the facility, repair or eliminate dangerous conditions, and warn users of concealed or hidden hazards. For a more thorough discussion of safe premises, see Chapter 3.20, *Premises Liability.*

Another aspect of a safe environment is the proper use of equipment, particularly **safety equipment**. In *Leahy v. School Board of Hernando County* (1984), the court reversed and remanded a directed verdict for the school when a freshman football player was injured during an agility drill. The player was not provided a helmet because the school did not have a sufficient number of the correct sizes available. The coaches gave no special instructions to the players who did not have helmets or mouthpieces, but had them participate in drills with others who had been issued such equipment. Other cases involving equipment include liability for failing to require that a previously injured football player wear a neck roll according to doctor's instructions (*Harvey v. Ouachita Parish School Board,* 1996), reversal of a summary judgment for the school when a football player was injured after running into a blocking sled that was stored on the sidelines of the practice field (*Cruz v. City of New York,* 2001), reversal and remand of a case in which the school was held not liable for failing to furnish necessary safety equipment (eye goggles) (*Palmer v. Mount Vernon Township High School District 201,* 1995) and furnishing a defective football uniform lacking necessary safety equipment (knee brace) (*Lowe v. Texas Tech University,* 1975). Although the owner or operator has the duty to provide the safety equipment, the supervisor is responsible for its proper usage.

Evaluating the Physical and Mental Condition of Participants

The responsibility to supervise varies with the age and experience of participants, their mental condition, and the nature of the activity in which they are engaged.

Supervisors observing **young children** have a high duty of care (*Ferguson v. DeSoto Parish School Bd.*, 1985). Ordinarily it is necessary to exercise greater caution for the protection and safety of a young child than for an adult who possesses normal physical and mental faculties. A supervisor dealing with children must anticipate the ordinary behavior of children. Children usually cannot and do not exercise the same degree of prudence for their own safety as adults do, and they often are thoughtless and impulsive. This fact imposes a duty to exercise a proportional vigilance and caution on those who deal with children and from whose conduct injury to a child might result (*Calandri v. Ione Unified School Dist.*, 1963).

Children have a known proclivity to act impulsively, without thought of the possibilities of danger. It is precisely this lack of mature judgment that makes supervision so vital. The mere presence of the hand of authority and discipline normally is effective to curb this youthful exuberance and to protect the children against their own folly (*Ohman v. Board of Education*, 1949). In comparison with young children, even **older high school senior athletes** (volleyball players) who are left unsupervised may engage in horseplay and incur debilitating injuries (*Barretto v. City of New York*, 1997). Noteworthy is the fact that at least one court rejected the theory that a lower standard of care is warranted when supervising high school (as opposed to elementary school) students (*Beckett v. Clinton Prairie School Corp.*, 1987).

In comparison with children, **adults** participating in activity generally require less supervision. Just as when dealing with children, however, supervisors must be alert to adults who may be involved in horseplay and be prepared to intervene as necessary.

The reasonableness of supervision also is related to the **abilities of participants**. It is foreseeable that **novice** participants (particularly children) may be injured primarily because they are unfamiliar with, and inexperienced in, the activity. The court found negligent supervision in the *Brahatcek* case, in which one student swung a golf club and hit another student due to inattention on the part of a student teacher (*Brahatcek v. Millard School District*, 1979). Just as inexperienced children need closer supervision, when adults are novices, they also require close supervision because they are not familiar with the activity and its inherent risks.

Generally, greater caution is required for participants with **disabling conditions**, and the courts have provided sound direction for supervising children with disabling conditions, for example, developmentally disabled children on a Special Olympics team walking three blocks away from campus to a gymnasium to practice basketball (*Foster v. Houston General Insurance Co.*, 1982), developmentally disabled children with poor eye–hand coordination running on the playground with other children (*Rodriguez v. Board of Education*, 1984), and an autistic child in a park district summer program walking to a water park (*Downey v. Wood Dale Park Dist.*, 1997).

Mismatching is a situation in which a smaller, younger, less-skillful, and/or less-experienced participant is injured while participating with a larger, older, more skillful, and/or more experienced participant. In *Tepper v. City of New Rochelle School District* (1988), the coach segregated the varsity and junior varsity teams based on the advanced skill level of the varsity players, which he believed was too superior for competition against the junior varsity. Nonetheless, during practice an inexperienced 130-pound member of the school junior varsity lacrosse team was injured when a varsity player twice his weight used an advanced checking technique on him. The trial court's denial of the school district's motion for summary judgment was reversed. Although this case indicates that the supervisor may be liable for mismatching, the courts are divided, with many courts holding that mismatching does not necessarily constitute a breach of duty.

A new twist to mismatching cases involves allegations that the defendant supervisor (teacher, coach, or leader) breached the standard of care by failing to fulfill his or her duties to provide nonnegligent supervision by becoming a participant in the activity. A number of courts have found the defendant supervisor at fault; however, just as many have ruled that participating while supervising did not constitute a breach of duty. Although supervision often includes directing, teaching, and demonstrating techniques, it does not encompass prolonged, active participation that rises to the level of intense one-on-one competition that has a winner and a loser. Under such circumstances, the teacher, coach, or leader may be abandoning the role of supervisor and becoming an equal competitor with the participant(s).

Supervisors who use **coercion** or **threats** to induce participants to perform some activity raise the potential of liability in the event the participant is injured. It is not unusual for participants to make excuses why they should not perform the activity assigned by the supervisor. At that point, the supervisor is placed in the position of both doctor and psychiatrist, trying to determine whether the reluctance is legitimate or not. Caution should be used before coercing participants to continue with the activity. In the significant case in this chapter (*Kahn v. East Side Union High School District*, 2003), the inexperienced swimmer had "a deep-seated fear that she would suffer a traumatic head injury from diving into shallow water" and had so informed her coaches. They ignored her fear and required her to dive, resulting in a broken neck.

Finally, supervisors must use care to determine whether students are physically and mentally prepared to rejoin the activity after suffering an injury. In *Cerny v. Cedar Bluffs Junior/Senior Public School* (2004), a football player suffered a head injury and was further injured at practice the following week. The court made a detailed examination of the evidence, reviewing the standard of care required by a reasonably prudent coach under such circumstances. In another case (*Koch v. Billings School Dist. No. 2*, 1992), a junior high student was encouraged by his teacher to squat-press 360 pounds against the plaintiff's protests. The plaintiff sustained significant injuries when he could not sustain the weight. Although the case was decided on sovereign immunity issues, the court remanded the case to determine whether the teacher was negligent in pushing the student to lift the weight.

Providing Emergency Care

In the event that a participant is injured during the conduct of the activity, a supervisor has a duty to provide proper emergency care. Chapter 2.31, *Emergency Care*, covers this duty in detail.

Factors Requiring Heightened Supervision

Dangerous activities mandate a higher degree of supervision than others. If an activity is dangerous or has the potential to be dangerous, it is essential that supervisors provide participants with instructions, familiarize them with basic rules and procedures necessary for executing skills, and warn them of reasonably foreseeable dangers before they attempt the skill or engage in the activity (*Green v. Orleans Parish School Board*, 1978; *Scott v. Rapides Parish School Board*, 1999). Wrestling, for example, requires continuous and constant supervision (*Carabba v. Anacortes School District No. 103*, 1967).

Adhering to Policies or Standards in Manuals

Knowledge of and adherence to policies in staff manuals have become increasingly important in helping supervisors demonstrate that they know what is expected of them and that they have followed these policies or standards in carrying out their responsibilities. In *Kahn v. East Side Union High School District* (2003), the Red Cross manual for swimming coaches, which the coach indicated that he followed, contained specific recommendations about the progression coaches should use in helping swimmers learn a racing dive, that is, have swimmers begin learning to dive **from the deck and then from the starting blocks in that order in deep water** before progressing to the **deck and then the blocks in shallow water**. The coach's failure to instruct the plaintiff how to perform a shallow water racing dive before she was asked to do so in a competitive swim meet was one of the pivotal factors in the court's decision to reverse and remand the case for further proceedings.

If the defendant fails to follow policies or standards in a manual that has been adopted, developed, and shared by the organization, association, or program, the individual may be accused of negligent supervision. Although having a policy manual demonstrates that there are standards employees are expected to follow, it is equally important that these policies are shared, discussed, and practiced. When policies are clear, well understood, and valued, employees have a sense of confidence in being up-to-date in adhering to standards of practice that reflect strong professional competency.

Significant Case

The California Supreme Court case of Kahn v. East Side Union High School District is a treasure trove of legal principles that includes discussion of many of the subjects covered in this and other chapters. Among the issues discussed in this case are proper supervision, proximate cause, primary assumption of risk, inherent risks, duty not to increase the risks inherent in the activity, coercion to perform by an authority figure (coach), effect of applicable standards or guidelines established by professional associations, and use or nonuse of safety training manuals. The case has been significantly condensed to save space, but the full opinion also includes discussions of premises liability, summary judgment review, proximate cause and intervening acts, and the weight to be given to expert witness testimony.

KAHN V. EAST SIDE UNION HIGH SCHOOL DISTRICT
Supreme Court of California
49 P.3d 349 (2003)

This case presents a question concerning the proper application of the doctrine of primary assumption of risk. At the time of her injury, plaintiff was a 14-year-old novice member of defendant school district's junior varsity [high school] swim team. She was participating in a competitive swim meet when she executed a practice dive into a shallow racing pool that was located on defendant school district's property and broke her neck. She alleged that the injury was caused in part by the failure of her coach, a district employee, to provide her with any instruction in how to safely dive into a shallow racing pool. She also alleged lack of adequate supervision and further that the coach breached the duty of care owed to her by insisting that she dive at the swim meet despite her objections, her lack of expertise, her fear of diving, and the coach's previous promise to exempt her from diving.

* * * In the present case, we recognize that the relationship of a sports instructor or coach to a student or athlete is different from the relationship between coparticipants in a sport. But because a significant part of an instructor's or coach's role is to challenge or "push" a student or athlete to advance in his or her skill level and to undertake more difficult tasks, and because the fulfillment of such a role could be improperly chilled by too stringent a standard of potential legal liability, we conclude that the same general standard should apply in cases in which an instructor's alleged liability rests primarily on a claim that he or she challenged the player to perform beyond his or her capacity or failed to provide adequate instruction or supervision before directing or permitting a student to perform a particular maneuver that has resulted in injury to the student. A sports instructor may be found to have breached a duty of care to a student or athlete only if the instructor intentionally injures the student or engages in conduct that is reckless in the sense that it is "totally outside the range of the ordinary activity" involved in teaching or coaching the sport.

Applying this standard to the present case, we conclude that, on the basis of the declarations and deposition testimony filed in support of and in opposition to defendants' motion for summary judgment, the Court of Appeal majority erred in determining that the doctrine of primary assumption of risk warranted entry of summary judgment in defendants' favor. We conclude that the totality of the circumstances precludes the grant of defendants' motion for summary judgment. Specifically, we refer to evidence of defendant coach's failure to provide plaintiff with training in shallow-water diving, his awareness of plaintiff's intense fear of diving into shallow water, his conduct in lulling plaintiff into a false sense of security by promising that she would not be required to dive at competitions, his last-minute breach of this promise in the heat of a competition, and his threat to remove her from competition or at least from the meet if she refused to dive. Plaintiff's evidence supports the conclusion that the maneuver of diving into a shallow racing pool, if not done correctly, poses a significant risk of extremely serious injury, and that there is a well-established mode of instruction for teaching a student to perform this maneuver safely. The declarations before the trial court raise a disputed issue of fact as to whether defendant coach provided any instruction at all to plaintiff with regard to the safe performance of such a maneuver, as well as to the existence and nature of the coach's promises and threats. Under these circumstances, the question whether the coach's conduct was reckless in that it fell totally outside the range of ordinary activity involved in teaching or coaching this sport cannot properly be resolved on summary judgment. Accordingly, the judgment of the Court of Appeal is reversed.

* * *

Plaintiff did not have prior experience as a competitive swimmer, but she was a competent swimmer and had executed dives into deep water on a recreational basis. She recalled that during a team practice session,

Coach McKay directed other team members to help her practice diving off the deck of the diving pool into deep water. Coach Chiaramonte-Tracy observed her dives, plaintiff asserted, and stated that plaintiff needed more practice. Teammates remarked that plaintiff had gone in too deep. Plaintiff had a deep-seated fear that she would suffer a traumatic head injury from diving into shallow water, and had so informed the two coaches when she joined the team in September. She alleged that during the few weeks between the commencement of the swim season and the accident, the coaches failed to offer her any instruction or training in shallow-water racing diving, nor, prior to the date of her accident, did she receive such instruction from her teammates. McKay assured her that, although three out of the four team members who participate in a relay must dive into the pool, plaintiff would not be required to dive at meets. Rather, she would be the team member who started from inside the pool. At the two or three meets that preceded the occasion on which plaintiff was injured, McKay directed plaintiff to execute the first leg of the relay race, which caused her to start in the water rather than from the deck of the pool.

Plaintiff asserted that McKay informed her, minutes before the meet was to begin * * * that this time he would not permit her to start her relay from inside the pool. She panicked and begged him to change the rotation so she could start in the water. She reiterated that she was afraid to dive into the shallow pool, that she did not know how to perform a racing dive, and that she never had performed one. McKay, she claimed, informed her that unless she dove off the starting block, he would not permit her to participate. (She could not recall whether he said she could not participate in the meet or could not be on the team.) She claimed that he did not give her the option of diving from the deck of the pool. Two teammates offered to show plaintiff how to perform the racing dive, and without any coach's supervision she began to practice diving from the starting block into the shallow racing pool. Plaintiff asserted that the coaches had not directed her to refrain from practicing unless they were present. Plaintiff could see Coach McKay in her peripheral vision. On her third practice dive, she broke her neck.

In support of her opposition to defendants' motion for summary judgment, plaintiff offered a Red Cross safety training manual for swim coaches, a manual whose recommendations McKay stated that he followed. The manual notes that diving into water less than five feet deep is dangerous and that 95 percent of swimming injuries occur in water five feet deep or less. The manual states: "Even an experienced diver can be seriously injured by diving improperly . . . or diving from starting blocks without proper training and supervision." The manual also states that "[i]t is important that swim coaches take all reasonable precautions to prevent acci-

dents in shallow water entries." Coaches should require persons learning the racing dive to perform adequate shallow dives from the deck into the deep pool on a consistent basis, then require students to perform a shallow dive from a starting block into the deep pool. This is important, the manual declares, "because of the increased velocity the swimmer achieves from entering the water from an increased height." Then, "[w]hen the swimmer's skill level has been consistently established from the starting block in deep water and the swimmer is able to maintain his or her racing start depth at two to two and a half feet, the swimmer may proceed to the shallow end. The coach then takes the swimmer through the same steps, beginning with shallow dives from the deck and then moving up to the block."

Plaintiff's expert, Stanley Shulman, had been a certified water safety instructor for 40 years, had coached junior and senior high school swimming for 17 years, and had published a number of studies of swimming injuries. He stated that diving into three and a half feet of water from the deck of a pool or from a starting block is extremely dangerous, and is ultrahazardous if done by a swimmer without adequate training. The sequence of instruction laid out in the Red Cross manual should be strictly followed, he declared, and "[b]efore an inexperienced diver attempts a racing dive into a shallow pool, [he or she] should perfect the same dive off starting blocks in the deep pool. [¶] The dive should be consistently done in the deep pool at a depth not exceeding two to two and a half feet before attempting it in shallow water."

* * *

Although persons generally owe a duty of due care not to cause an unreasonable risk of harm to others (Civ.Code, § 1714, subd. (a)), some activities—and, specifically, many sports—are inherently dangerous. Imposing a duty to mitigate those inherent dangers could alter the nature of the activity or inhibit vigorous participation. In a game of touch football, for example, there is an inherent risk that players will collide; to impose a general duty on coparticipants to avoid the risk of harm arising from a collision would work a basic alteration—or cause abandonment—of the sport.

* * *

But the question of duty depends not only on the nature of the sport, but also on the "role of the defendant whose conduct is at issue in a given case." [*Knight v. Jewett* (1992) 3 Cal.4th 296] Duties with respect to the same risk may vary according to the *role* played by particular defendants involved in the sport.

* * *

We had occasion to comment in passing on an instructor's duty * * * Citing Court of Appeal cases that had been decided subsequent to our decision in *Knight*, we explained that "there are circumstances in which the relationship between defendant and plaintiff gives rise to a duty on the part of the defendant to use due care not to increase the risks inherent in the plaintiff's activity. For example, a purveyor of recreational activities owes a duty to a patron not to increase the risks inherent in the activity in which the patron has paid to engage. [Citations.] Likewise, *a coach or sport instructor owes a duty to a student not to increase the risks inherent in the learning process undertaken by the student.* * * *

The general proposition that a sports instructor or coach owes a duty of due care not to increase the risk of harm inherent in learning an active sport is consistent with a growing line of Court of Appeal opinions that have applied the *Knight* analysis to claims against such defendants. In these cases, the reviewing courts examined the particular circumstances of the sport, its inherent risks, and the relationship of the parties to the sport and to each other. Most also examined the question whether imposing broader liability on coaches and instructors would harm the sport or cause it to be changed or abandoned. In each instance, the Courts of Appeal have agreed that although the coach or athletic instructor did not have a duty to eliminate the risks presented by a sport, he or she did have a duty to the student not to increase the risk inherent in learning, practicing, or performing in the sport. * * *

Subsequent decisions have clarified that the risks associated with *learning* a sport may themselves be inherent risks of the sport, and that an instructor or coach generally does not increase the risk of harm inherent in learning the sport simply by urging the student to strive to excel or to reach a new level of competence. This line of cases analyzes and articulates an important and appropriate limitation on the duty of a sports instructor. The cases point out that instruction in a sport frequently entails challenging or "pushing" a student to attempt new or more difficult feats, and that "liability should not be imposed simply because an instructor asked the student to take action beyond what, with hindsight, is found to have been the student's abilities." * * * As a general matter, although the nature of the sport and the relationship of the parties to it and to each other remain relevant, a student's inability to meet an instructor's legitimate challenge is a risk that is inherent in learning a sport. To impose a duty to mitigate the inherent risks of learning a sport by refraining from challenging a student, as these cases explain, could have a chilling effect on the enterprise of teaching and learning skills that are necessary to the sport. At a competitive level, especially, this chilling effect is undesirable.

* * *

We agree that the object to be served by the doctrine of primary assumption of risk in the sports setting is to avoid recognizing a duty of care when to do so would tend to alter the nature of an active sport or chill vigorous participation in the activity. This concern applies to the process of learning to become competent or competitive in such a sport. Novices and children need instruction if they are to participate and compete, and we agree with the many Court of Appeal decisions that have refused to define a duty of care in terms that would inhibit adequate instruction and learning or eventually alter the nature of the sport. Accordingly, we believe that the standard set forth in *Knight,* * * * as it applies to coparticipants, generally should apply to sports instructors, keeping in mind, of course, that different facts are of significance in each setting. In order to support a cause of action in cases in which it is alleged that a sports instructor has required a student to perform beyond the student's capacity or without providing adequate instruction, it must be alleged and proved that the instructor acted with intent to cause a student's injury or that the instructor acted recklessly in the sense that the instructor's conduct was "totally outside the range of the ordinary activity" (*Knight, supra,* 3 Cal.4th at p. 318,) involved in teaching or coaching the sport.

The Court of Appeal majority in the present case concluded that in light of plaintiff's allegations and supporting evidence, coach McKay merely challenged her to go beyond her current level of competence. We believe that this takes an unduly narrow view of plaintiff's claim and her evidence, which went far beyond a claim that the coach made an ordinary error of judgment in determining that she was ready to perform the shallow-water dive.

As noted above, the Red Cross teaching manual submitted by plaintiff acknowledged that the principal danger faced by persons learning to compete in swimming is the shallow-water dive. The risk presented is not simply that the swimmer might suffer bruises or even break an arm; the risk is that the student may sustain serious head and spinal cord injuries by striking the bottom of the pool. Plaintiff presented evidence, both documentary and expert, that a settled progression of instruction in the dive is considered essential to a student's safety. Her own declaration and deposition testimony was that she had not received any instruction at all from her coaches or teammates on the performance of the shallow-water dive. She also claimed that she had expressed a mortal fear of performing the shallow-water dive and that she had been assured by the coach that she would not be required to perform it. Her evidence was that the coach made a last-minute demand that she take a position in the relay race that would require her to dive, threatening that if she did not comply, either she would be dropped from the team or she would not be permitted to compete that day.

Defendant McKay did not challenge the sequence of instruction prescribed by the Red Cross manual, but said in his declaration and deposition testimony that he generally followed it.

* * *

We agree that the following factors indicated a triable issue with respect to whether the coach's behavior was reckless: the lack of training in the shallow-water dive disclosed by plaintiff's evidence, especially in the face of the sequenced training recommended in the Red Cross manual submitted by plaintiff; the coach's awareness of plaintiff's deep-seated fear of such diving; his conduct in lulling her into a false sense of security through a promise that she would not be required to dive, thereby eliminating any motivation on her part to learn to dive safely; his last-minute breach of that promise under the pressure of a competitive meet; and his threat to remove her from the team or at least the meet if she refused to dive.

Clearly, a disputed issue of fact exists as to whether the coach provided any instruction at all on shallow-water diving, and the nature of the coach's promises and threats to plaintiff also are in dispute. If a jury were to find that defendant coach directed plaintiff (a novice on the swim team) to perform a shallow racing dive in competition without providing any instruction, that he ignored her overwhelming fears and made a last-minute demand that she dive during competition, in breach of a previous promise that she would not be required to dive, we believe the trier of fact properly could determine that such conduct was reckless in that it was totally outside the range of the ordinary activity involved in teaching or coaching the sport of competitive swimming. Accordingly, on this record, we conclude that the trial court erred in granting summary judgment in favor of defendants and that the Court of Appeal erred in affirming that determination.

* * *

Keeping in mind that ultimately it will be plaintiff's obligation to establish the elements of her cause of action before the trier of fact by a preponderance of the evidence, we believe that triable issues of material fact exist regarding the question whether coach McKay breached a duty of care owed to plaintiff, thereby causing her injury, by engaging in conduct that was reckless in that it was totally outside the range of ordinary activity involved in teaching or coaching the sport of competitive swimming.

For the foregoing reasons, the judgment of the Court of Appeal is reversed and the matter is remanded for further proceedings consistent with this opinion.

References

Cases

Andres v. Young Men's Christian Association, 64 Cal. App.4th 85, 74 Cal.Rptr.2d 788 (1998).

Balthazor v. Little League Baseball, Inc., 62 Cal. App.4th 47, 72 Cal. Rptr.2d 337 (1998).

Barakat v. Pordash,—N.E.2d—, 2005 WL 3074729 (Ohio App. 2005).

Barretto v. City of New York, 229 A.D.2d 214; 655 N.Y.S.2d 484 (1997).

Beckett v. Clinton Prairie School. Corp., 504 N.E.2d 552 (Ind. 1987).

Benitez v. New York City Board of Education, 541 N.E.2d 29 (NY 1989).

Blashka v. South Shore Skating, Inc., 598 N.Y.S.2d 74 (App. Div. 2d Dept. 1993).

Brahatcek v. Millard School Dist., 202 Neb. 86, 273 N.W.2d 680 (Neb. 1979).

Broward County School Board v. Ruiz, 493 So.2d 474 (Fla. App. 1986).

Bushnell v. Japanese-American Religious & Cultural Center, 43 Cal. App.4th 525, 50 Cal. Rptr.2d 671 (1996).

Butler v. D.C., 417 F.2d 1150 (1969).

Calandri v. Ione Unified School Dist., 219 Cal. App.2d 542, 33 Cal.Rptr. 333 (1963).

Carabba v. Anacortes School District No. 103, 72 Wash.2d 939, 435 P.2d 936 (Wash. 1967).

Cerny v. Cedar Bluffs Junior/Senior Public School, 679 N.W.2d (Neb. 2004).

Corrigan v. Musclemakers, Inc., 258 A.D.2d 861, 686 N.Y.S.2d 143 (1999).

Cruz v. City of New York, 288 A.D.2d 250 (N. Y. App. Div. 2001).

David v. County of Suffolk, 1 N.Y. 3d 525 (2003).

Dailey v. Los Angeles Unified School District, 470 P.2d 360 (Cal. 1970).

DeGooyer v. Harkness, 13 N.W. 2d 815 (SD, 1944).

Domino v. Mercurio, 17 A.D.2d 342, 234 N.Y.S.2d 1011 (1962), *aff'd*, 13 N.Y.S.2d 922, 193 N.E.2d 893, 244 N.Y.S.2d 69 (1963).

Downey v. Wood Dale Park Dist., 675 N.E.2d 973 (Ill. App. 1997).

Fagan v. Summers, 498 P.2d 1227 (Wyo. 1972).

Ferguson v. DeSoto Parish School Bd., 467 So.2d 1257 (La. 1985).

Fluehr v. City of Cape May, 732 A.2d 1035 (N.J. 1999).

Foster v. Houston General Insurance Co., 407 So.2d 759 (La. Ct. App. 1982).

Glankler v. Rapides Parish School Board, 610 So.2d 1020 (La. App. 1993).

Green v. Orleans Parish School Board, 365 So.2d 834 (La. Ct. App. 1978).

Harvey v. Ouachita Parish School Board, 674 So.2d 372 (La. App. 2 Cir. 1996).

Herring v. Bossier Parish School Board, 632 So.2d 920 (La. Ct. App. 1994).

Kaczmarcsyk v. City & County of Honolulu, 63 Hawaii 612, 656 P.2d 89 (Hawaii 1982).

Kahn v. East Side Union High School District, 75 P. 3d 30 (2003).

Kaufman v. City of New York, 30 Misc.2d 285, 214 N.Y.S.2d 767 (1961).

Keesee v. Board of Education of the City of New York, 235 N.Y.S. 2d 300 (N. Y. Sup. Ct. 1962).

Kelly v. McCarrick, 841 A.2d 869 (Md. Ct. Spec. App. 2002).

Koch v. Billings School Dist. No. 2, 833 P.2d 181 (Mt. 1992)

Landers v. School District No. 203, O'Fallon, 383 N.E.2d 645 (Ill. App. Ct.—5th Dist. 1978).

Leahy v. School Board of Hernando County, 450 So.2d 883 (Fla. Dist. Ct. App. 1984).

Lilley v. Elk Grove Unified School Dist., 68 Cal. App.4th 939, 80 Cal. Rptr.2d 638 (1998).

Longfellow v. Corey, 286 Ill. App.3d 366, 368, 675 N.E.2d 1386 (1997).

Lowe v. Texas Tech University, 540 S.W.2d 297 (Tex. 1976).

Ohman v. Board of Educ., 300 N.Y. 306, 90 N.E.2d 474 (1949).

O. L. v. R. L., 62 S.W.3d 469 (Mo. App. W. D. 2001).

Palmer v. Mount Vernon Township High School District 201, 647 N.E.2d 1043 (Ill. App. Ct. 1995).

Partin v. Vernon Parish School Board, 343 So.2d 417 (La. App. 1977).

Passantino v. Board of Educ., 41 N.Y.S.2d 1022, 363 N.E.2d 1373, 395 N.Y.S.2d 628 (1977), *revg.* 52 A.D.2d 935, 383 N.Y.S.2d 639 (1976).

Rodrigo v. Koryo Martial Arts, 100 Cal. App.4th 946, 122 Cal. Rptr.2d 832 (2002).

Rodriguez v. Board of Educ., 104 A.D.2d 978, 480 N.Y.S.2d 901 (1984).

Rollins v. Concordia Parish School Board, 465 So.2d 213 (La. App. 1985).

Scott v. Rapides Parish School Board, 732 So.2d 749 (La. App. 1999).

Sheehan v. St. Peter's Catholic School, 29 Minn. 1, 188 N.W.2d 868 (1971).

Stevens v. Chesteen, 561 So.2d 1100 (Ala. 1990).

St. Margaret Mercy Healthcare Centers, Inc. v. Poland, 828 N.E.2d 396 (Ind. Ct. App. 2005).

Tepper v. City of New Rochelle School District, 531 N.Y.S.2d 367 (N. Y. Sup. Ct. 1988).

Thomas v. Sport City, Inc., 738 So.2d 1153 (La. App. 2nd Cir. 1999).

Toller v. Plainfield School District 202, 582 N.E.2d 237 (Ill. App. 1991).

Ward v. Mount Calvary Lutheran Church, 178 Ariz. 350, 873 P.2d 688 (Ariz. App. 1994).

West v. Sundown Little League of Stockton, Inc., 96 Cal. App.4th 351, 116 Cal. Rptr.2d 849 (2002).

Publications

American College of Sports Medicine. (1997). *ACSM's health/fitness facility standards & guidelines* (2nd ed.). Champaign, IL: Human Kinetics.

American College of Sports Medicine & American Heart Association. (1998). Recommendations for cardiovascular screening, staffing, and emergency policies at health/fitness facilities. *Medicine & Science in Sports & Exercise, 30*(6), 1009–1018.

Gaskin, L. P. (2003). Supervision of Participants. In D. J. Cotten & J. T. Wolohan (Eds.), *Law for recreation and sport managers* (pp. 138–148). Dubuque, IA: Kendall/Hunt.

Garner, B. A. (Ed.). (2004). *Black's law dictionary* (8th ed.). St. Paul, MN: Thomson/West.

Herbert, D. L. (1997). A review of ACSM's standards & guidelines for health & fitness facilities. *The Sports, Parks & Recreation Law Reporter, 11*(2), 23–24.

Herbert, D. L. (1998). New standards for health and fitness facilities from the American Heart Association (AHA) and the American College of Sports Medicine (ACSM). *The Sports, Parks & Recreation Law Reporter, 12*(2), 30–31.

Herbert, D. L. (2002). Enhanced qualifications of fitness personnel may result in increased liability. *Fitness Management, 18*(2), 36.

Hurst, T. R., & Knight, J. M. (2003). Coaches' liability for athletes' injuries and deaths. *Seton Hall Journal of Sport Law, 13*, 27–51.

Kaiser, R. A. (1986). *Liability and law in recreation, parks, and sports.* Englewood Cliffs, NJ: Prentice Hall.

McCaskey, A. S., & Biedzynski, K. W. (1996). A guide to the legal liability of coaches for a sports participant's injuries. *Seton Hall Journal of Sport Law, 6,* 7–125.

Nygaard, G., & Boone, T. H. (1985). *Coaches guide to sport law.* Champaign, IL: Human Kinetics.

van der Smissen, B. (1990). *Legal liability and risk management for public and private entities.* Cincinnati, OH: Anderson.

Legislation

Limited Liability for Operators of Roller Skating Rinks, Ind. Code § 34-31-6, et seq. (2005).

Volunteer Protection Act of 1997, 42 U.S.C.A. § 14501 *et seq.* (West 2006).

2.33 Transportation

Andy T. Pittman
Baylor University

Paul J. Batista
Texas A&M University

Organizations involved in transporting participants in recreation or sport activities must be concerned about participants' safety and welfare. The potential for liability extends not only to transporting them to and from events, but also to the use of vehicles in completing special tasks associated with the event (such as transporting injured persons to a hospital) and to supervisory concerns before, during, and after transport.

Private agencies, public agencies, and individuals must be aware of the duty of care required by law when transportation is provided. The potential for liability of public colleges and universities, public secondary schools, school boards and districts, or other public agencies such as recreation departments, however, must be considered in light of applicable legislation. Most states have enacted state **tort claims acts** that limit the liability of these institutions with respect to negligence in the operation of motor vehicles. In most states, in instances where no motor vehicle is involved (e.g., the existence of a duty to provide a safe bus stop or the placement of a bus stop), liability will attach only if the action at issue is ministerial in nature as opposed to discretionary. How these terms are defined varies by jurisdiction. Generally speaking, a ministerial act is one in which a particular course of action is required and violation of the act creates a presumption of negligence. In contrast, a discretionary act is one in which several courses of action are available, and the course of action chosen is generally immune from liability. For a more thorough discussion of governmental immunity, see Chapter 2.22, *Immunity*.

Fundamental Concepts

Duty to Provide Transportation

Generally, when recreation or sport activities are sponsored by an organization, there may be a corresponding duty to provide transportation, and such transportation must be provided in a safe manner regardless of the mode of travel. The duty to provide transportation usually begins at the point of departure and continues until those using the transportation have been returned to the original departure point. Liability exists regardless of whether the participants meet at the organization and are then assigned a particular vehicle or they are picked up by the driver at their homes or elsewhere. It may be possible to avoid liability by establishing a policy that no transportation will be provided for anyone for a particular event. In that case, participants are instructed to convene at the site of the event. However, this policy may not be practical if large numbers of people are involved, the distance to travel is far, or participants do not have access to an alternative form of transportation. The organization also needs to establish a policy governing the conditions under which a participant can leave an event by other transportation than that provided by the organization. For minors, parental permission should be required. The supervisor should create a specific policy and ensure that everyone involved in transportation is aware of, and conforms to, the policy. Allowing a parent or participant to avoid the policy requirement will increase the potential for liability.

Duty of Care

When an organization provides transportation, it owes a duty of care with respect to such transportation. Generally, reasonable and ordinary care under the circumstances is the appropriate standard of care. However, there is authority that indicates that the operators of school buses are in the same general position as common carriers and that the highest degree of care consistent with the practical operation of the bus is required. The standard of care required of the drivers will be based on the particular circumstances. Some factors that may be considered in determining the standard of care include the age, knowledge, judgment, and experience of the passengers.

In a situation where a driver or organization has violated a specific statute enacted for the protection of the passengers and such violation is the proximate cause of an injury, the standard of care is deemed irrelevant. In that instance, the organization would be held absolutely liable.

Jurisdictions differ as to the duty required in regard to supervision. In some jurisdictions the duty of care includes a duty to provide a location where participants can wait for the transportation with reasonable safety and a duty to select a discharge point that does not needlessly expose them to any serious safety hazards. The duty to provide a reasonably safe location also may impose a duty on the organization to provide proper supervision. In contrast, courts in other jurisdictions have ruled that the duty of an organization toward participants under its control applies only during the period they are transported to and from the event, commencing when the participant enters the vehicle and continuing until they have been safely discharged. Likewise, absent the existence of a special duty, this duty may not extend to situations where the participant is no longer under the organization's authority or is no longer under its physical custody. To decrease the potential of liability and ensure the safety of participants, the best policy would include providing appropriate supervision from the time the participant arrives at the pickup point at the beginning of the trip until the participant leaves the discharge point at the end of the excursion.

Transportation Options

The transportation of participants to and from recreation or sport events and activities can be accomplished in one of four ways: (1) independent contractor, (2) use of organization-owned vehicles, (3) use of employee vehicles, and (4) use of nonemployee vehicles. The potential for liability varies from situation to situation with the least potential for liability existing where independent contractors are used and the greatest potential where private vehicles are used. The risk of liability is not as high when one independently contracts because most of the risk is transferred. The risk of liability is greatest when nonemployee vehicles are used because the organization has the least control. The keys to the determination of liability are the ownership of the vehicle and the relationship of the driver to the entity responsible for the participants.

Independent Contractor

If an organization can afford it, using an independent contractor for transportation is the best legal option because the contract for service shifts liability to the contractor. The independent contractor may be of two types: common or private carrier. A **common carrier** is in the business of transporting goods or persons for hire. A **private carrier**, on the other hand, only hires out to deliver goods or persons in particular cases. A common carrier may be held to a higher standard of care regarding the qualifications of the driver and the condition of the vehicle than a private carrier or a noncommercial driver.

Authority holds that an organization may delegate its duty of safe transportation to third-party independent contractors. However, whether a third party is an **independent contractor** is determined by who has the right to control the manner in which the work is done, the method of payment, the right to discharge, the skill required, and who furnishes the tools, equipment, or materials needed to accomplish the work. With respect to transportation, if factors such as the use of specific vehicles, the driver, the route, the enroute stops, and the manner of driving are all within the control of the transportation company and its employees, then it is likely the relationship is that of an independent contractor (see Chapter 2.12, *Which Parties Are Liable?*, and Chapter 2.21, *Defenses Against Negligence*).

However, an organization may not be able to avoid liability if the organization is negligent in its selection of an independent contractor. Thus, it is always good administrative practice to investigate independent contractors carefully prior to entering into a contract with them. Several questions and concerns should be addressed in selecting an independent contractor. First, the independent contractor should be required to verify that it has sufficient liability insurance by providing a copy of its **certificate of insurance** regardless of whether it is a common or private carrier (for more information, see Chapter 5.25, *Managing Risk Through Insurance*). Other items to consider when hiring a transportation company include requiring proof of insurance for each vehicle, evidence of an Interstate Commerce Commission license number, age of equipment, company safety record, and availability of information demonstrating preventive maintenance.

Transportation policy became a central theme in the National Transportation Safety Board (NTSB) report regarding the crash of an aircraft transporting members of the Oklahoma State University (OSU) basketball team and other team personnel (www.ntsb.gov). Although it was determined that the pilot's spatial disorientations and failure to maintain positive manual control was the major cause of the accident, the NTSB concluded that OSU did not provide any significant oversight.

OSU policy required charter flights and university airplane flights to be coordinated through the OSU flight department. However, because this specific flight was a donated flight, it was not coordinated through the flight department. Thus no records were on file regarding the pilots or the plane as required by the flight department. OSU has since adapted a comprehensive transportation management system in an attempt to ensure necessary oversight. The policy (#3-0155 April 2000) can be found on the OSU Website at http://home.okstate.edu/policy.nsf/ Click on By Title and then click on Transportation Services Flight Department.

Organization-Owned Vehicles

For some organizations or entities, the use of an independent contractor is not a viable option because of cost. Organization-owned vehicles are the most common means of transporting participants and provide the next best transportation option. Because the organization owns the vehicles, it has the legal responsibility for the safe transportation of the participants. The organization has a duty to see that the vehicles are in safe operating condition and to see that the drivers are properly qualified. In the event of legal action, written policies, checklists, and maintenance records provide documentation that these duties have been addressed.

Driver. Both the driver and the organization can be liable for the negligence of the driver—whether an employee, student, or volunteer. To protect itself, the organization should require that the driver meet established qualifications that may include age, experience, special licenses, training, and verification of driving record.

An employee who acts in the course of and as a means to accomplish the purpose of employment, thereby furthering the master's business, is acting within the scope of employment. Both the driver and the organization can be held liable for the negligent act of the driver. If the driver commits an *ultra vires act* (i.e., an act that is outside the scope of employment), the negligence of the driver is not imputed to the organization. Examples of ultra vires acts include exceeding the speed limit, running a red light or stop sign, and deviating from the designated route. A court held that a baseball coach who, after an away game, drove the school van to purchase some tobacco products and, instead of returning to the hotel, decided to check out the sights of the town, was not acting within the **scope of employment** (*Smith v. Gardner*, 1998). In *Myricks v. Lynwood Unified School District* (1999), the city was not found liable for a driver's negligence because the driver was not acting within the scope of his employment. It is important to emphasize to drivers that they should not deviate from the scheduled route and itinerary without approval.

Vehicle. Being able to establish the road-worthiness of the vehicle is of utmost importance to the organization. With all organization-owned vehicles, the organization is responsible for maintenance, and failure to maintain the vehicle in a safe condition leaves the organization liable. All vehicles need to be maintained by competent maintenance personnel in accordance with the owner's manual and vehicle specifications. Any vehicle with maintenance problems (e.g., defective lights, worn tires) should not be used until the condition is corrected and documented. Complete documentation of all maintenance should be stored in a safe, accessible manner.

Prior to each trip, each vehicle needs to be inspected by a competent authorized maintenance person. After each trip, a similar inspection should be performed and the driver should report any problems encountered on the trip. Pretrip and posttrip vehicle inspection forms need to be developed for this purpose. Emergency equipment (e.g., first aid kit, flares, flashers, and jack) should also be included on these forms and in these inspections.

Policies. Prior to the trip, an administrator or another authorized individual must be informed of and authorize travel plans. A trip request form should be utilized that includes the purpose of the trip, the destination, lodging arrangements, route, contact phone numbers, a list of those traveling, the person in charge, and the driver. Irrespective of the mode of travel (e.g., car, van, bus, plane), policies need to be established that address who can travel, maximum distances, traveling at night, disciplinary action, emergency procedures, driver qualifications, and oversight of the drivers.

Schools. In all states, the right to use a vehicle owned by a school to transport students to activities other than classes is controlled by state law. Some states have no restrictions whereas others restrict the use of school buses to providing transportation to and from classes. Other states restrict use depending on the source of operating funds, which may be a critical factor in the application of governmental immunity. Until the 1970s, cities or schools were often not held liable for injuries resulting from negligence of employees due to immunity laws. Since that time, the doctrine of governmental immunity has been changed in many states by the passage of state tort claims acts (see Chapter 2.22, *Immunity*).

Privately Owned Vehicles

In some cases, organizations may find it necessary to use privately owned vehicles for transportation. Such vehicles may be owned by employees or by nonemployees (e.g., parents, volunteers, and participants). In either case, liability for negligence is generally retained by the organization.

Before the use of private vehicles is permitted, risk management policies should be established to be certain that both vehicles and drivers conform to acceptable safety standards. Such policies might relate to a physical inspection of the vehicle, maintenance records of the vehicle, vehicle insurance, and vehicle registration. Policies should also ensure that the driver is properly licensed, has a good driving reputation, has a violation-free driving record, and has no impairments that would preclude driving.

Employee Vehicles. When an employee, as a part of his or her employment, uses a personal vehicle for transporting students or patrons, a **principal–agent relationship** is established. An organization is **vicariously liable** for employee negligence committed within the course and scope of employment. This will hold true even in the situation of an employee driving another employee's vehicle as in the case of *Murray v. Zarger* (1994). Richard Zarger was a volunteer diving coach for Cory Area (Pennsylvania) High School and was compensated a small salary by the school district. While driving Cherese Murray, a member of the diving team, and three others in the head coach's car, Zarger was involved in an accident that resulted in the death of Murray. The administratrix of Murray's estate brought action for damages allegedly caused by the negligence of the school district, the car owner, and Zarger. The school district argued that Zarger was not an employee of the district on the following grounds: they had no control over the manner in which he performed; Zarger was not responsible for the swim team's performance; there was no agreement between Zarger and the school district; Zarger was used for his special diving skills only; and Zarger was an employee of two other companies. In holding that Zarger was an employee of the school district, the court stated that the definition of "employee" in the applicable state statute did not require that an employee be compensated or possess a formal employment contract with the government unit but that the person act in the government's interests. (For more information on vicarious liability see Chapter 2.12, *Which Parties Are Liable?*)

In another situation, the court held that a student was acting as an employee of the college, thus making the college liable for the acts of the student. Christopher Foster, a senior high school basketball recruit, was visiting Butler County Community College and was injured in a motor vehicle accident. The driver, George Johnson, a student at the college and not an employee, had picked Foster up at the request of the head basketball coach. Johnson did not have liability insurance, his vehicle was unregistered, and he did not have a valid driver's license. The court stated that several facts were relevant in determining the scope of an employment situation: (1) the purpose of the employee's act rather than the method of performance; (2) whether the employee had express or implied authority to do the acts in question; and (3) whether the employee's acts were reasonably foreseeable by the employer. The fact that the act of driving was gratuitous was not fatal to the existence of an employer/employee relationship. The court upheld a judgment in excess of $2 million for the plaintiff (*Foster v. Board of Trustees*, 1991).

Use of privately owned vehicles does increase the risks to the organization; therefore, the establishment and enforcement of **risk management policies** regarding the driver and the vehicle are essential. If the employee uses his or her privately owned vehicle as a service to the organization and in accordance with organization policy, most jurisdictions require that the driver exercise reasonable and ordinary care. The employee will be personally liable for negligent operation of the vehicle, notwithstanding the vicarious liability of the organization.

Nonemployee Vehicles. When an organization has a duty to provide transportation and uses a private vehicle provided by someone who is not an employee, a principal–agent relationship is created. The organization is liable for the negligence of the driver. Because an organization has the least control when nonemployee vehicles are used, this category creates the greatest risk of liability to the organization. It is imperative that the organization institutes and enforces the risk management policies suggested at the beginning of this section.

Other Transportation Issues

State Codes. State legislators enact laws that are related to transportation. However, sometimes it is not clear which part of the code may apply. At issue in *Barnhart v. Cabrillo Community College* (1999) was whether or not an intercollegiate match was a field trip as defined under Title 5, California Code of Regulations, Section 5545. The court of appeals ruled that because school-related athletic activities necessarily include extracurricular sport programs, the trip would be considered a field trip and would fall under the immunity granted in the code.

Many states, in addressing the issue of **limited liability** for volunteer coaches, have included a section on transportation. For example, the New Jersey Code 2A: 62A-6 notes in section d that immunity is not granted to any individual causing damage as a result of negligence while operating a motor vehicle. Although Georgia has a similar statement in the code addressing volunteer coaches, a disparity exists regarding volunteers transporting senior citizens. In this code the volunteer who transports senior citizens is not liable for civil damages for injury if the volunteer was acting in **good faith** and within the scope of duties unless the conduct was **willful and wanton** (Georgia Code Ann. 51-1-42).

The sport and recreation manager should have the organization's attorney review the state codes that are applicable to transportation. Knowledge of the codes is a valuable tool in the policy-making process and can serve to minimize litigation.

Workers' Compensation. If an individual is injured in an automobile accident while within the scope of employment and the business required the employee to be at the place of the accident, workers' compensation may be applicable. While a passenger, Bolton was injured in an automobile accident sometime after midnight while returning from a recruiting trip. In deciding the workers' compensation claim, the court of appeals held that the university, driver, and their insurers enjoyed the protection of the exclusive remedy provision of the workers' compensation scheme (*Bolton v. Tulane University*, 1997).

Significant Case

◇◇◇

Although Clement v. Griffin is not a new case, it was selected for several reasons. First, the court clearly defines the duty of Delgado/State to maintain the vehicle, to select a qualified driver, to properly train the driver, and the vicarious duty to drive the vehicle safely. Second, in terms of transportation risk management, the case can serve as a complete course in How NOT To Do It. About every mistake an organization could make is epitomized. Careful reading reveals a wealth of mistakes and breaches of duty—any one of that could have left the institution liable. Third, this case exemplifies some of the problems encountered when operating vans which have been recently addressed by the National Highway Transportation Safety Administration (NHTSA).

CLEMENT V. GRIFFIN

Court of Appeals of Louisiana, Fourth Circuit
634 So.2d 412 (La. App. 4 Cir. 1994)

Opinion:

I. PROCEDURAL HISTORY

This appeal follows trial court judgments on liability and damages in nine consolidated cases arising from an April 25, 1986 single-vehicle accident caused by the blowout of the right rear tire on a van carrying members of the Delgado Community College baseball team. The plaintiffs filed suit in negligence against Brent S. Griffin, the student coach who was driving the van at the time of the accident, and against Delgado and the State of Louisiana (Delgado/State), as well as various public boards and individuals connected with the school. Additionally, the plaintiff filed suit in strict products liability against both Goodyear Tire and Rubber Company, which manufactured the tire, and Ford Motor Company, which manufactured the van. The claims against the public boards and the individuals were dismissed by agreement of the parties prior to trial. Delgado/State also filed suit in strict products liability against Ford and Goodyear.

* * *

II. FACTS

The accident occurred as the Ford Club Wagoneer van, which was carrying 13 passengers, travelled north on Interstate 59 (I-59) north of Slidell en route to Meridian, Mississippi for an intercollegiate baseball game. When the blowout occurred, Griffin was unable to maintain control; Griffin held a Class A driver's license, but not a Class C chauffeur's license. During the process of the accident, the vehicle rolled over at least three times, finally landing on its wheels in the grassy median of I-59. Several of the passengers were ejected from the vehicle during the accident; two of the passengers were under the van after the accident. The plaintiffs suffered injuries of various degrees, which will be detailed in the "DAMAGES" section of this opinion.

At the time of the accident, the van and the tires were owned by Delgado/State. The tires, including the tire which blew out, were part of the original equipment of the van. The mileage on the van at the time of the accident was 24,013. Ten of the passengers filed suit; two of the passengers and the driver did not file suit.

III. LIABILITY

The general liability issues to be decided in this appeal include the following:

* * *

D. Delgado/State's liability

* * *

The plaintiffs' case against Delgado/State is based purely on negligence. In order to recover from a defendant in negligence, the plaintiff must prove the following elements: (1) that the conduct of which the plaintiff complains was a cause in fact of the harm; (2) that the defendant had a duty to protect against the risk involved; (3) that the defendant breached that duty; and (4) damages. Delgado/State's challenge to the trial court judgment in this case focuses on a combination of the first and third inquiries of this test—that is, whether the plaintiff proved that Delgado/State breached any duty to the plaintiffs and whether that breach caused the accident in question.

* * *

We find specifically that Delgado/State had duties to the plaintiffs to do the following things: (1) properly maintain the vehicle, (2) select a qualified driver for the vehicle, and (3) properly train the driver. Additionally, Delgado/State had a vicarious duty, performed through the driver, to properly operate the vehicle. We will discuss the evidence that those duties were breached and that the breach of those duties caused the accident below.

* * *

1. Improper maintenance

* * *

The most direct evidence concerning the maintenance of the van and the tire was the testimony of Lee Harris Venison, the Delgado mechanic who was responsible for preventive maintenance on all the school's vehicles, including the van. Venison said that it was his duty to maintain the air pressure in the tires of the van, but that he was never instructed about how to service the van or about the proper air pressure for the tires; nor had he ever seen the owner's manual for the van. He stated that he maintained the pressure in the van's tires at 45 p.s.i., as was his custom and practice, and that he saw no damage to the tire when he serviced it. He admitted that he was not sure that he had serviced the van in question on the day of the accident and that he had no personal knowledge of the tire pressure in the van at that time.

Tommy Lee Smith, the athletic director at Delgado, stated that it was not his job to check the tires on the van, that the maintenance department was charged with the duty of checking out the vehicles after each trip. He stated that he assumed that the maintenance department had performed a checkup prior to the trip when the accident occurred. Additionally, Smith claimed that he "looked at the van, not specifically at the tires" prior to the trip, but that he did not notice anything wrong with the tires. If something unusual about the tires had existed, Smith asserted, he would have noticed.

Expert witness Andrew W. McPhate stated that the other Delgado van which he drove while investigating this accident had a p.s.i. of 51 when he took it out for a test, and admitted that driving the van with the tires at that pressure, which was below the recommended 75 p.s.i., could cause tire failure if it occurred over a long period of time. He also stated that driving a tire at 45 p.s.i. during the summertime could result in a great risk of overheating.

* * *

Expert witness Dodson stated that his examination indicated that the tire had been properly inflated most of its life. However, Dodson opined, the tire was run underinflated for a short period of time after it impacted with some foreign object, which resulted in the blowout. * * *

Expert witness Baker said, * * * conflicting evidence on the beads of the tire indicated that the tire did not have enough air for the load it was carrying for much of its life. This conflicting evidence, he said, indicated that the loads carried by the van varied from very heavy loads to very light loads.

* * * Gold also testified that the recommended air pressure for the tires on the Ford van, according to the manual, was 40 p.s.i. in the front tires, and 75 p.s.i. in the rear tires. Additionally, Gold noted that the right rear tire which suffered the blowout had not been rotated, but had always been attached to the rear of the vehicle.

* * *

Thus, the record reveals ample evidence to support the trial court's judgment both that Delgado/State

breached its duty to properly maintain the vehicle and that that breach caused the accident. * * *

2. Selection of driver

Although not specifically addressed in brief by Delgado/State, the plaintiffs attempted at trial to prove that Delgado/State further violated its duties by negligently selecting or allowing Brent Griffin, who was a student coach for the baseball team, to drive the van and that allowing an inexperienced driver to drive the van caused the accident. They claim that Griffin, who possessed only a Class A operator's driver's license, and not a Class C chauffeur's license, was not qualified to drive the van. Further, the plaintiffs claim that Delgado/State made no effort to assure that its own rule that the van be driven only by persons with chauffeur's licenses was followed.

* * *

Griffin testified that he was designated as a driver by Coach Louis Schuerman and that Patrick Prigmore, another team member, was the co-driver. He stated that he had been driving since he was 16, that he held a Class A driver's license, and that no one told him he needed a chauffeur's license to drive the van. No one at Delgado had ever inquired about whether he had previous experience driving a van prior to the accident, Griffin said. Further, Griffin claimed that he was not given any instructions by Delgado to see that the seat belts were used by the passengers. Griffin admitted that he was unable to control the swaying of the van after the blowout occurred.

* * *

Dr. Harry Boyer, president of Delgado College, said that Schuerman, as athletic director and head baseball coach, was charged with the responsibility of determining who would drive the vans and station wagons when the team travelled. * * * Dr. Boyer said that he had told Schuerman that the drivers should be either assistant coaches or specially hired drivers.

* * *

Head coach Schuerman said that he assigned Griffin to be one of the drivers, but he never requested a chauffeur's license. Additionally, Schuerman admitted that he never tried to determine whether Griffin had taken driver's education.

Griffin said that the vans were rarely occupied by adult faculty members when the team made road trips. This testimony was corroborated by the testimony of David Flettrich, who said the vans were not occupied by Delgado staff members, that there was no supervision, and that the vans were not caravanned.* * *

We find that the trial court was not manifestly erroneous in finding, on the basis of the above evidence, that Delgado/State breached its duty to the plaintiffs by selecting or allowing Griffin to drive the van, both because Griffin was not qualified to drive the van since he did not possess a chauffeur's license and because of the internal rule that students not be allowed to drive the vans.

* * * Because Griffin was not qualified to drive the van, he reacted improperly when the blowout occurred. The trial court was thus not manifestly erroneous in finding that the accident would not have occurred had Griffin responded in the correct manner. Thus, the trial court judgment holding Delgado/State liable for the accident in question is not manifestly erroneous.

3. Training of driver

This issue is also not directly addressed by Delgado/State's brief, but is raised by the record evidence. The plaintiffs claim that Delgado/State also breached its duties by failing to train the drivers it selected to operate the van, especially by failing to instruct the drivers on the proper actions to take in the event of the blowout of a tire. Furthermore, the plaintiffs claim that the failure to train the drivers caused the accident.

* * *

Griffin stated that no one at Delgado ever gave him any instructions regarding the speed of the vehicle, or regarding safety issues of any kind.

Assistant coach Smith said that he instructed the students who were driving the vehicles to take their time and to keep the vehicles within 60 mph. Otherwise, he admitted that he did not give them any special instructions. Smith said that he had no knowledge of whether anyone at Delgado had ever instructed Griffin concerning the proper procedures to follow in the event of a blowout.

Head coach Schuerman said that he instructed the drivers of the vans about safety and safety belts, although he admitted that did not remember telling them to wear seat belts. Additionally, he said that he instructed them not to exceed the speed limit, and that they would be responsible for their own tickets if they did.

Several of the witnesses testified to a 1985 blowout on a Ford van owned by Delgado, which was being driven by David Smith at the time. Flettrich said that he was in that van at the time of the blowout, that the driver lost control, and that the van did a 180 degree turn on the interstate, ending up on the shoulder of the road. Flettrich said that no one on the Delgado administrative staff gave instructions on emergency blowouts, even after the 1985 accident. * * *

Thus, we find that the trial judge was not manifestly erroneous in holding Delgado/State liable for the accident since he could reasonably have concluded on the basis of the above evidence that Delgado had failed to properly train Griffin to operate the van and that that failure caused the injuries because of Griffin's improper actions taken after the blowout occurred, as discussed in more detail below.

4. Operation of vehicle

* * *

a. Griffin's actions

Griffin said that he was driving between 55 and 60 mph in a 55 mph zone when the accident occurred. He said that he was in the left lane of traffic at that time and that he did not apply the brakes when he heard the loud noise. Griffin admitted, however, that he did apply his brakes before the vehicle left the roadway, claiming that he "hit the brakes slightly as to gain a little control." He also said that he held the steering wheel straight, but that the vehicle went first into the right lane, then suddenly shot off onto the left side of the highway onto the median.

Maitre, a passenger in the van, estimated the speed of the van at the time of the blowout at 65 to 70 mph, but admitted that he could not see the speedometer immediately prior to the accident. He said 65 to 70 was the customary speed driven by Griffin. When the blowout occurred, Griffin immediately jammed on the brakes, Maitre said; he said that he knew this because he was immediately jerked forward after the blowout. * * *

Reynolds, who was also a passenger in the van on the day of the accident, said he was first aware of a problem about 10 minutes prior to the accident, when he noticed that Griffin was driving recklessly. He said that the van was going 70 mph when the blowout occurred.

Another passenger in the van, Alton Sartin, said that Griffin jammed on the brakes "real hard" and yanked the steering wheel back to the left when the blowout occurred. He said that since he was seated directly behind the driver, he had a better view of Griffin's actions than anyone else in the van. However, Sartin also said that Griffin did not take those actions until after the van started swaying.

* * *

The expert testimony also indicated that Griffin responded negligently when the blowout occurred. Dr. Ehrlich stated that the fact that the driver was speeding was one of the causes of the accident, especially when coupled with the fact that the driver did not know what to do when the blowout occurred. He said that Griffin jammed on his brakes, when he should not have, which resulted in loss of the rearend stability of the vehicle and caused the vehicle to swing sideways, after which there was no control. Speed, Dr. Ehrlich said, was also a factor which made the rollover more violent.

* * *

Additionally, the record contains evidence that Griffin was aware of the fact that the tire was underinflated on the day of the accident, but that he failed to take actions to remedy the situation. Flettrich, who was in another vehicle on that day, testified that he told Griffin that the tire was low earlier that day; that he could see that the tire was low from 10 to 15 feet away. Further,

Reynolds, who was in the van that day, stated that he thought he remembered Griffin telling someone to check the tire before they left. Craig Ledet, a Delgado baseball team member who was not riding in the van at the time of the accident, corroborated this testimony, saying that he noticed that the tire was low the day of the accident and that he was present when Flettrich told Griffin that the tire was low. Griffin testified that he had been told that one of the tires was low before the first trip of the year, and that he had to put air in the tire before he left on that trip; he did not check the tires prior to the trip in question, he said.

Thus, the record evidence is sufficient to support a finding that the trial judge was not manifestly erroneous in finding that Delgado/State breached its vicarious duty, through Griffin's actions, to operate the van in a proper manner under the circumstances. Further, the trial court was not manifestly erroneous in finding that Griffin's improper actions caused the accident. Thus, the trial court was not manifestly erroneous in holding Delgado/State liable for the accident because of the negligent actions of its chosen driver, Griffin.* * *

5. Combination of factors

* * * The evidence was sufficient to prove that Delgado/State breached its duties to the plaintiffs to do the following things: (1) maintain the vehicle, (2) select a qualified driver, and (3) properly train the driver. Furthermore, the evidence is sufficient to prove that Delgado/State breached its duty, performed through Griffin, to operate the vehicle properly under the circumstances.

* * *

Thus, the trial court judgment holding Delgado/State liable for the plaintiffs' injuries caused by the accident is not manifestly erroneous. It is hereby affirmed.

* * *

F. Conclusion on liability issues

* * * The judgment in favor of the plaintiffs and against Delgado/State is affirmed. * * * Delgado/State, as the only party responsible for the accident, is therefore cast for 100 percent of the plaintiffs' damages.

IV. Damages

* * *

V. CONCLUSION

Accordingly, the trial court judgment against Goodyear is reversed, while the judgment against Delgado/State is affirmed. The judgment in favor of Ford Motor Company is also affirmed.

The damage judgments in favor of Mickey Maitre, Alton Sartin, and Mark Abadie are reduced to $1,660,576.75; $150,000; and $234,839.50, respectively. Additionally, the damage judgments in favor of Patrick Prigmore and Kevin Reynolds are increased to $121,673.08 and $54,781.60, respectively. All other damage awards are affirmed. Delgado/State is cast in judgment for 100 percent of all damage awards.

AFFIRMED IN PART;
REVERSED IN PART;
AMENDED.

Recent Trends

Van Accidents

According to the NHTSA (http:nhtsa.gov/cars/problems/studies/15PassVans) between 1990 and 2002, there were 1,576 fifteen-passenger vans involved in fatal crashes that resulted in 1,111 fatalities to occupants of such vans. Of these, 657 vans were in fatal, single-vehicle crashes, of which 349 rolled over. In 2001, 130 occupants of fifteen-passenger vans died in crashes involving these vehicles. Eighty-seven percent of people who died in single-vehicle rollovers of these vehicles were not wearing safety belts.

Although most states require the use of school buses to transport children to and from school and school-related events, some states do not.

- Twenty-nine states have laws or regulations that prohibit the use of vans for transporting public school students to and from school and school-related activities.
- Twelve states have laws and regulations that prohibit the use of vans for transporting public school students to and from school, but allow the use of vans for school activity trips.
- Nine states allow the use of vans for transporting public school students to and from school and school-related activities. In many states, the laws and regulations do not apply to private and church-sponsored schools. (http://nhtsa.gov/cars/problems/studies/15PassVans. Site last visited 2/02/2006).

table ⟨1⟩ Survey of State Laws on 12- and 15-Passenger Vans Used for School Transportation[a,b]

State	To and From School	To and From School-Related Events	Comments
Alabama	No*	No*	*State laws do not apply to private schools
Alaska	No*	Yes*	*State laws do not apply to private schools.
Arizona	No	Yes	
Arkansas	Yes	Yes	
California	No	No	
Colorado	Yes*	Yes*	*Statewide, self-insurance pool for school districts will not insure vans after July 1, 2005.
Connecticut	No	Yes	
Delaware	No	No	
Florida	No*	No*	*Does not apply to private schools or companies that contract directly with parents.
Georgia	No*	Yes*	*State laws do not apply to private schools.
Hawaii	Yes	Yes	
Idaho	No*	Yes	*State statute allows for some exceptions, e.g., students with special needs in remote locations without school buses. *State laws do not apply to private schools.
Illinois	No	Yes	
Indiana	No*	Yes**	*Special education students may be transported in vans. **After June 30, 2006 vans will be prohibited. State laws do not apply to private schools.
Iowa	No	No	
Kansas	No	No	
Kentucky	No	No	
Louisiana	No*	No*	*State laws do not apply to private schools.
Maine	No	No*	*Private schools are exempt from this state regulation.
Maryland	No	No	State law not clear on private schools.
Massachusetts	Yes	Yes	
Michigan	No	No	
Minnesota	No	No	
Mississippi	Yes*	Yes*	*State law does not prohibit the use of vans, but Department of Education will not approve van purchase.
Missouri	No*	Yes*	*State laws do not apply to private schools.
Montana	No*	No*	*State laws do not apply to private schools.
Nebraska	Yes	Yes	
Nevada	No	Yes	
New Hampshire	No	No	
New Jersey	No	No	
New Mexico	No	No	
New York	No	No	
North Carolina	No*	Yes*	*Private schools not covered by state rules.
North Dakota	Yes*	Yes*	*Not allowed after June 1, 2008. Vans can no longer be purchased for these purposes after March 1, 2003. State laws do not apply to private schools.
Ohio	No	No	

table ◇1◇ continued

State	To and From School	To and From School-Related Events	Comments
Oklahoma	No	No	
Oregon	No	No	
Pennsylvania	No*	No*	*Unless the van was registered as a bus in Pennsylvania prior to March 1, 1993, or titled to a public, private, or parochial school prior to March 1, 1993, and was registered as a bus to such school prior to September 15, 1993.
Rhode Island	No*	No**	*Child care organizations are exempt and can use vans for transportation to and from school. **Vans purchased prior to January 1, 2000, can be used until January 1, 2008.
South Carolina	No*	No*	*Vans purchased prior to July 1, 2000, can be used until June 30, 2006.
South Dakota	No	No	
Tennessee	No	Yes	
Texas	No*	Yes	*Private schools not covered by state rules.
Utah	No	No	
Vermont	Yes	Yes	
Virginia	No*	No*	*State laws only apply to public schools.
Washington	No*	No*	*State laws only apply to public schools.
West Virginia	No	Yes	
Wisconsin	Yes	Yes	
Wyoming	No*	No*	*State rules only apply to public schools.

Fifteen-Passenger Vans. Recent research conducted by the National Highway Traffic Safety Administration (NHTSA) found that the risk of a rollover crash is greatly increased when ten or more individuals ride in a fifteen-passenger van (www.nhtsa.dot.gov/hot/15PassVans). The risk of a rollover is increased because the center of gravity of the vehicle is raised when more passengers are transported. Placing any load on the roof also raises the center of gravity and increases the likelihood of a rollover. The result is less resistance to rollover and increased difficulty in steering. The NHTSA identified three major situations that can lead to a rollover in the fifteen-passenger vans: (1) the van goes off a rural road, striking a ditch or soft shoulder, (2) the driver is fatigued or driving too fast, and (3) the driver overcorrects. These conditions were evident in the accidents noted. Review of these accidents revealed the vans were driven by individuals under twenty-two years old (lack of experience) and that in at least three accidents, excessive speed was a factor.

High-profile accidents involving fifteen-passenger vans have led to litigation, usually against the van manufacturer. As a result, vehicle manufacturers have made some modifications to help the stability of the vehicle and have made recommendations for the driver of the vehicle. These adjustments may decrease litigation against the manufacturer, but may result in more legal action against the agency and driver. Sport and recreation managers should know the facts before purchasing or using a fifteen-passenger van. If the entity already owns a van, the manager should contact the manufacturer and the NHTSA to find out how to make the van safer.

On August 10, 2005, Public Law 109-59 Safe, Accountable, Flexible, Efficient Transportation Equity Act: A Legacy For Users (119 STAT. 1144), was passed by the 109th Congress. Section 10309, 15-Passenger Van Safety, addresses new safety standards related to the use of fifteen-passenger vans. The Act defines a fifteen-passenger van as a vehicle that seats ten to fourteen passengers, not including the driver. The Act prohibits a school or school system from purchasing or leasing a new fifteen-passenger van if it will be used significantly by, or on behalf of, the school or school system to transport preprimary, primary, or secondary school students to or from school or an event related to school, unless the fifteen-passenger van complies with the motor vehicle standards prescribed for school buses and multifunction school activity buses under this title. This prohibition does not apply to the purchase or lease of a fifteen-passenger van under a contract executed before the date of enactment of this legislation.

Vans vs. School Buses. The National Highway Traffic Safety Administration (NHTSA) has alerted the public about the danger of substituting passenger vans for school buses. Nine states currently allow vans for school transportation, and twenty-two permit their use to transport students for school-related activities, such as field trips and sporting events. This violates the spirit of the federal law (49 USC 301) that prohibits dealers from selling or leasing a new van for use in transporting children to and from school or a school-related activity. Unfortunately, fifteen-passenger vans are classified as neither passenger cars nor school buses, and as a result they are exempt from many federal motor-vehicle safety standards (Lowe & Mulvihill, 2004). Passing a state law allowing vans to be used for transporting school children does not preempt the federal law—dealers are still subject to penalties (www.schoolbusinfo.org/vans.htm). The law does not apply to college-age students or other adults.

Policy Recommendations. Team travel by van has created a problem that does not have an easy solution. Budget restrictions and squad size are major considerations when choosing to use vans or other modes of transportation. The following policy recommendations have been made that parallel the identified causes of van accidents (Hawes, 2000: LaVetter, 2005: NHTSA, 2005):

- Eliminate fifteen-passenger vans to transport students if possible and travel more frequently by bus.
- Eliminate coaches driving any vehicles and enforce stricter driver qualifications
- Limit the number of passengers in vans to fewer than ten
- Take the rear seats out of fifteen-passenger vans and place passengers and equipment forward of the van's rear axle
- Limit the number of hours or mileage driven per day for each van to 300 miles or five hours and avoid travel between midnight and 6 a.m.
- Check the van's tire pressure frequently—at least once a week
- Consult with your organization's insurance company or risk-management consultants.
- Schedule competition to permit travel by different teams sharing the same bus.
- Set age limits for the driver, hire outside drivers, and give extensive driving training.
- Require seat belts be worn at all times.
- Stress the importance of adhering to speed limits and the possible need to adjust speed due to weather.
- Monitor weather conditions and establish policies that permit coaches to decide when to spend the night in a hotel rather than on the road.
- Review maintenance policies.

References

Cases

Barnhart v. Cabrillo Community College, 90 Cal. Rptr. 2d 709 (Cal. App. 6 Dist. 1999).
Bolton v. Tulane University of Louisiana, 692 So.2d 1113 (La. App. 4 Cir. 1997).
Clement v. Griffin, 634 So.2d 412 (La. App. 4 Cir. 1994).
Foster v. Board of Trustees of Butler County Community College, 771 F. Supp. 1122 (D. Kan. 1991).
Murray v. Zarger, 642 A.2d 575 (Pa. Cmwlth. 1994).
Myricks v. Lynwood Unified School District, 87 Cal. Rptr. 2d 734 (Cal. App. 2 Dist. 1999).
Smith v. Gardner, 998 F. Supp. 708 (S.D. Miss. 1998).

Publications

Hawes (2000).
LaVetter, D. (2005, December 5). Safety must drive decisions in van use. *The NCAA News, 4,* 24.
Lowe, J., & Mulvihill, D. (2004). 15-passenger vans slip through safety gap, *Trial, 40*(3), 26–28, 31–32.
NHTSA. (2005).

Legislation

Ga. Code Ann. 51-1-42.
New Jersey Code 2A: 62A-6.
Pub. Law 109-59 (August 10, 2005). Safe, Accountable, Flexible, Efficient Transportation Equity Act: A Legacy For Users (119 STAT. 1144).
49 U.S.C. §301.

Web Sites

www.nhtsa.dot.gov/hot/15PassVans/
www.ntsb.gov
http://home.okstate.edu/policy.nsf/
www.schoolbusinfo.org/vans.htm/
http://thomas.loc.gov/

2.34 Products Liability

Cathryn L. Claussen
Washington State University

Lori K. Miller
Wichita State University

Products liability significantly influences recreation and sport businesses. Social policy and business ethics mandate the prudent manufacture and distribution of sporting goods products. This chapter traces the fundamental concepts associated with products liability, including the following: (1) the two types of defective products, (2) the three causes of action and available defenses, and (3) potential liability of different types of defendants. Additionally, recent trends in products liability law are addressed.

Fundamental Concepts

Types of Defective Products

Plaintiffs who suffer injury due to the defective nature of a product such as a piece of sport equipment can sue under products liability law. The plaintiff must prove that the product was defective at the time it left the control of the manufacturer and that it was unreasonably dangerous. There are two types of defective products—those afflicted with a manufacturing defect and those with a design defect. **Manufacturing defects** occur as a result of some error in the manufacturing process that causes a flaw in one or more of the otherwise properly designed items. An example of a manufacturing defect is found in *Diversified Products Corp. v. Faxon* (1987). Plaintiff Faxon had purchased a weight machine and assembled it properly according to the manufacturer's instructions. One year later, while he was performing standing curls, a factory-installed eyebolt on the curl bar broke, causing Faxon to fall backward and injure his spine. The court found that the evidence supported an inference that the eyebolt had a manufacturing defect that existed at the time the product was still in the possession of the manufacturer. In contrast, a **defectively designed product** is one that was designed in an unsafe manner to begin with. In *Everett v. Bucky Warren* (1978), the product at issue was an ice hockey helmet that consisted of three protective plates held together by elastic straps that were supposed to allow users to adjust the helmet to fit different sizes of heads. In this case, the plaintiff adjusted the helmet to fit his large head, which caused the gaps between the protective plates to be wide enough that the hockey puck penetrated to his head, resulting in a skull fracture. The court found that this adjustable, three-piece design was defective because it was unreasonably dangerous for the consumer.

Three Causes of Action in Products Liability

There are three potential causes of action in products liability: negligence, strict liability, and breach of warranty. A manufacturer, seller, or supplier can be held liable for **negligence** based on (1) negligent design, manufacture, or distribution of a defective product, or (2) negligent failure to warn about any hidden risks associated with the product that were unreasonably dangerous. A seller or manufacturer can also be subject to **strict liability** for an injury caused by a defective product—this means that they can be held liable regardless of how careful they were in designing or manufacturing it. Both manufacturers and sellers may also be subject to **breach of warranty** claims. Warranties may be express warranties, or they may be implicit in a transaction for a product.

Negligence

Plaintiffs may bring claims for **negligent manufacture** of a defective product, **negligence in designing** a defective product, or **negligent failure to warn** about hidden risks that make a product unreasonably dangerous. Available defenses include (1) no duty of care owed because plaintiff assumed the inherent risks of using that product; (2) the defect or failure to warn was not the proximate cause of the injury; (3) contributory negligence on the part of the plaintiff; (4) secondary assumption of risk where the defect allegedly increased the risk beyond the inherent risks of participating in the sport but the plaintiff assumed the increased risk; and (5) the danger was open and obvious, obviating the need for any warning.

Warnings must include dangers inherent in the normal use of the product as well as dangers resulting from foreseeable misuses (van der Smissen, 1990; *Whitacre v. Halo Optical Products, Inc.*, 1987). In some jurisdictions, failure to warn may constitute a defect even when there is no other design or manufacturing defect (*Garrett v. Nissen*, 1972; *Pavlides v. Galveston Yacht Basin*, 1984). Additionally, warnings must be specific to the risk, but the level of specificity is a judgment call on the part of the courts. In *Dudley Sports Co. v. Schmitt* (1972), a student who was sweeping the floor near a baseball pitching machine stored in a closet suffered severe facial injuries when the throwing arm on the machine snapped through unexpectedly even though the machine was unplugged. The court found that the manufacturer was negligent in designing the machine without a protective guard around the throwing arm mechanism. Additionally, the court ruled that Dudley Sports negligently failed to provide an adequate warning about the specific risks posed by their product. No operating instructions were included with the pitching machine, and the only warning label read as follows:

WARNING! SAFETY FIRST

READ INSTRUCTIONS BEFORE ROTATING MACHINE EITHER ELECTRICALLY OR MANUALLY

STAY CLEAR OF THROWING ARM AT ALL TIMES

DON'T REMOVE THIS PACKING BLOCK UNTIL YOU FULLY UNDERSTAND THE OPERATION OF THE THROWING ARM AND THE DANGER INVOLVED

According to the court, this warning only implied that the machine could be dangerous when in use. In order to be specific enough to be effective, the warning should have mentioned the machine's ability to be triggered even when unplugged. Finally, manufacturers also have a responsibility to warn of defects discovered after a product has been marketed. The court in *Arnold v. Riddell, Inc.* (1995), in deciding for the plaintiffs, recognized the defendant's failure to warn players and coaches although it "knew its [football] helmets did not perform as well as others on crown impacts."

Strict Liability

Strict liability is a concept of "liability regardless of fault." The manufacturer's carefulness is not relevant to a strict liability claim. The rationale for strict liability was summarized by Justice Traynor in *Escola v. Coca-Cola Bottling Co. of Fresno* (1944) as follows.

> Even if there is no negligence, however, public policy demands that responsibility be fixed wherever it will most effectively reduce the hazards to life and health inherent in defective products that reach the market. It is evident that the manufacturer can anticipate some hazards and guard against the recurrence of others, as the public cannot.

Advocates of strict liability argue that it is better to spread losses amongst multiple members of society than to invoke a substantial loss on one individual who is unable to pay. According to this perspective, businesses are in an ideal position to distribute resultant loss via higher prices or insurance. Legal scholars and consumer advocates further argue that a business's cognizance of possible financial loss due to exposure to liability makes the business more safety oriented and thus more willing to upgrade quality-control practices (Garrett, 1972; Nader, 1972; Plant, 1957).

Manufacturers/sellers can be subject to strict liability if (1) they sell an unreasonably dangerous defective product that, during a foreseeable use of the product, causes injury, and (2) the product was unreasonably dangerous at the time it left their control. To be unreasonably dangerous, a product must entail risks that are beyond the contemplation of the ordinary consumer. Many jurisdictions use a risk-utility balancing test (also recommended in the Restatement (third) of Torts (1997)) to determine whether or not a product design is unreasonably dangerous. Under this test, a product is considered unreasonably dangerous if the danger outweighs the social utility of the product as designed. Factors typically considered in risk-utility balancing include (1) the gravity of the danger, (2) the likelihood of injury, (3) the obviousness of the danger, (4) the feasibility and expense of an alternate design, (5) common knowledge of consumers, (6) adequacy of warnings, and (7) the usefulness and desirability of the product as designed (*Byrns v. Riddell, Inc.*, 1976; *Everett v. Bucky Warren*, 1978).

Appropriate defenses to a strict liability claim include secondary assumption of risk, unforeseeable misuse by the consumer, alteration subsequent to leaving the control of the manufacturer, predictable deterioration, waiver, and adequate warning provided. It should be noted that some jurisdictions that use risk-utility balancing treat some of these traditional defenses, including provision of an adequate warning, merely as factors in the balancing of risk versus social utility. Products liability law varies among different jurisdictions, so it is important for sport or recreation managers to know the law in their own particular jurisdiction regarding possible claims and available defenses, as well as how findings of unreasonable danger are typically determined by the courts in that jurisdiction.

Breach of Warranty

Warranties are essentially promises made by the seller, who can then be liable if those promises are broken. Although breach of warranty is a contract-based cause of action, many states no longer require privity of contract (that is, a direct contractual relationship) between the buyer and the consumer for the consumer to be able to sue. Available defenses include unreasonable misuse by the consumer and adequate disclaimer by the manufacturer/seller. Warranties can be either express or implied. As explained by van der Smissen (1990),

> An **express warranty** arises through advertising, sales literature, product labeling, and oral statements and is an assertion of fact or promise by the seller relating to the quality of goods that induces the buyer to purchase the goods. (p. 340)

For example, in *Hauter v. Zogarts* (1975), a golf training device was packaged with the following language, "COMPLETELY SAFE BALL. WILL NOT HIT PLAYER." The language on the package encouraged the player to "drive the ball with full power." The plaintiff was seriously injured when the cord attached to the ball wrapped around his club and the ball hit him in the head. The court found for the plaintiff on the breach of express warranty. According to the court, this statement was "a misrepresentation of material fact upon which plaintiffs justifiably relied" (p. 381). Recreation or sport managers responsible for advertising campaigns or other product or service packaging should use caution when using descriptive terms such as *safe* and *foolproof*. First, very few sport-related products will ever be 100 percent "safe," as recreation or sport in itself invites injury. Second, as explained by the Supreme Court of California in the *Hauter* (1975) decision, "Courts have come to construe unqualified statements . . . liberally in favor of injured consumers."

Implied warranties include both the implied warranty of merchantability and the implied warranty of fitness. The **implied warranty of merchantability** is an implied promise that the product is saleable; that is, it is fit for its ordinary intended use. The implied warranty of merchantability assures one, for example, that a football helmet serves and protects as would any ordinary football helmet on the market. In *Hauter v. Zogarts* (1975), the court found that the defendant also breached the implied warranty of merchantability. The golf training device, intended for use by novices, did not serve as an ordinary training device, as it was foreseeable that the device would injure novice users.

The **implied warranty of fitness** is found when a seller has reason to know the particular purpose of a purchase, and the buyer is relying on the seller's expertise to provide a product fit for that particular purpose. In *Filler v. Rayex Corp.* (1970), a high school baseball coach had purchased sunglasses from the defendant based on the advertisement guaranteeing "instant eye protection." Unlike other sunglasses, advertisements and product packaging specifically identified baseball as a sport where players would be protected by the "scientific lenses." The plaintiff–athlete lost his right eye when a ball hit the lens and it shattered. As explained by the court of appeals "Since they lacked the safety features of plastic or shatterproof glass, the sunglasses were in truth not fit for baseball playing, the particular purpose for which they were sold" (*Filler v. Rayex Corp.*, 1970, p. 338). The implied warranty of fitness extends to the intended product uses as well as foreseeable misuses. There is no liability for the "unforeseeable misuse of a product" (*Back v. Wickes Corp.*, 1978, p. 969).

Potential Liability of Different Types of Defendants

Products liability is intended to provide recourse against parties involved in the chain of production and distribution of products; therefore, manufacturers and sellers are the usual defendants. **Sellers** have a duty to make a cursory inspection of samples of the products they sell to ascertain that they have arrived undamaged from the manufacturer and are fit to sell. **Manufacturers** have an additional duty to inspect and/or test their products for hidden dangers that would pose an unreasonable risk of injury to the ordinary consumer. **Suppliers** of products, such as universities or recreation departments who provide sports equipment to their athletics teams, can of course be liable in negligence for supplying defective products that cause injury when they knew or should have known of the defect. In *Everett v. Bucky Warren* (1978), the court concluded that a jury could find the school negligent when the coach, acting as an agent of the school, negligently selected defectively dangerous hockey helmets. But typically only manufacturers and sellers are subject to strict liability for defective products.

Entities that rent sports equipment can also face liability because the same rationale that supports liability for breach of warranty claims against retail sellers applies to lessors; that is, that consumers place as much reliance on lessors to provide equipment that is fit for its intended use (whether generally or for a particular purpose) as they do on manufacturers and sellers. Additionally, lessors are in the same position as sellers regarding their ability to spread the costs of protecting themselves, as part of the cost of doing business, from losses due to the imposition of damages awards in products liability lawsuits. An example of lessor liability is found in *Perton v. Motel Properties, Inc.* (1998), in which a motel that rented bicycles to its guests was held strictly liable for breaching an implied warranty of fitness when a guest was injured while riding a defective bicycle. The court declared that in renting the bicycles, the motel had made an implied warranty that they were fit for the particular purpose for which they were rented—to be ridden in normal fashion by the renters. In *Hurley v. Larry's Water Ski School* (1985), the court refused to hold the water skiing school strictly liable when a beginner taking lessons was injured by a defective tow bar, on the grounds that the defendant was not a lessor because they never surrendered possession and control of the equipment to the injured user. However, similar to the result in *Perton*, the court in *Hurley* found that an implied warranty of fitness could apply because the plaintiff was relying on Larry's Water Ski School to provide him with proper instruction and equipment fit for a beginner.

In contrast to lessors, entities that are classified as service providers will not usually be subject to strict liability. In *Bhardwaj v. 24 Hour Fitness* (2002), a member of the fitness center was injured while using a defective squat machine. The court compared the defendant fitness center to hotels, YMCAs, and university gymnasiums that install fitness equipment for use by others and asserted that these types of businesses are the final purchasers/consumers of the equipment. Thus, because the fitness center was not engaged in the sale or exchange of its weight machines as products to its members, but was instead simply providing a service (the opportunity to get a fitness workout), it could not be held strictly liable for the plaintiff's injuries. Similarly, businesses that construct sport facilities are not usually subject to strict liability because construction contracts are predominantly contracts for the performance of a service (*Traub v. Cornell University*, 1998). A different result was reached in *Anthony Pools, Inc. v. Sheehan* (1983) when the court separated the provision of a product out of an otherwise predominantly service-oriented contract. Anthony Pools had built a swimming pool and installed a diving board with a defectively designed surface. The court ruled that they could be held liable for breach of the implied warranty of merchantability for an injury caused by the unreasonably dangerous surface of the diving board because the diving board was offered as an optional accessory for the swimming pool. It could thus be considered a sale of goods that was separate from the rest of the pool construction service transaction.

Although not common, strict liability has been imposed on repair service providers. In those cases, the courts reasoned that customers rely on their expertise, they are able to spread the cost of accidents, and imposing strict liability would induce them to invest in safety (see, e.g., *Gentile v. MacGregor Mfg. Co.*, 1985). Consequently, it is important that owners of these businesses be cognizant of the case precedent regarding liability. Recently, however, in *Rodriguez v. Riddell Sports, Inc.* (2001), an equipment reconditioning service was held not to be subject to strict liability for a brain injury caused by a defectively designed football helmet. The court ruled that the company that reconditioned the helmets had no duty to upgrade the design of a product made by another company. According to the court, the manufacturer could not be held strictly liable either because it no longer had control over the product when it was altered by the reconditioning service. Rulings like this one make it risky to use reconditioned equipment because a cause of action in strict liability is eliminated, and a plaintiff would be left with the more difficult task of finding evidence to support a negligence claim against the defendants.

Finally, a manufacturer that is also a sport sponsor may not avoid manufacturer liability by relying on a waiver releasing them from liability in their role as a sponsor. In *Mohney v. USA Hockey, Inc.* (2001), a teenage hockey player became a quadriplegic as a result of the faceguard on his helmet breaking when he crashed into the boards. Bauer and Karhu, the manufacturers of the helmet and faceguard, respectively, were also sponsors of USA Hockey. Plaintiff Mohney had signed a waiver that included language releasing USA Hockey and its sponsors from "any liability" for injuries incurred as a result of the inherent risks of participation. The court ruled that this release's mention of sponsors referred to liability for advertising and sponsorship issues and did not reach the manufacturers in their role as manufacturers. Therefore, although they were also sponsors, manufacturers Bauer and Karhu were potentially liable for the injury caused by the defectively designed helmet. On appeal, the 6th Circuit later found no product liability on the part of the manufacturers (*Mohney*, 2005). However, another court reached a similar outcome on the specific issue of manufacturer liability despite the existence of a sponsorship waiver (*Curtis v. Hoosier Racing Tire Corp.*, 2004).

Significant Case

———————————◇◇◇———————————

This opinion provides a thorough analysis of a design defect case that involves all three products liability causes of action—negligence, strict liability, and breach of warranty. You will notice that the primary assumption of risk doctrine is used to argue that Cornell University owed no duty of care to plaintiff Traub. The issue for the jury is whether or not the rigid rim design of the basketball hoop increased the risk beyond what an ordinary person would assume as inherent risks of playing basketball. Hence, Traub's actual appreciation of the risk (secondary assumption of risk) also becomes relevant. It is also important to note that although it is not mentioned by name, the court endorsed the use of a risk-utility balancing test to determine, for the purpose of strict liability analysis, whether or not the rim was unreasonably dangerous. This is why the court examined whether or not a safer design existed, and why it compared the risks of the rigid rim hoop to the social value and feasibility of using a breakaway hoop. Another important feature of this case is the discussion of the potential liability of different types of defendants, including the manufacturer, retail distributor, and general contractor for the basketball court. Finally, the reason the court mentions whether or not dunking is a foreseeable use of a basketball hoop relates to the manufacturer's duty to design products to withstand foreseeable unintended uses but not unforeseeable misuses.

TRAUB V. CORNELL UNIVERSITY
United States District Court for the Northern District of New York
1998 U.S. Dist. LEXIS 5530

I. Factual Background

A. The Incident

On the date of his accident, Darren—who had been a student at Cornell for approximately ten months—played "pick-up" basketball on the Cornell basketball court. * * * After one or two games, Darren and several other players took turns attempting to dunk a basketball through one of the goals. As Darren descended from his second try, the heel and first joints below the fingertips of his right hand made contact with the rigid rim of the hoop. Darren fell to the macadam surface of the court to the right of the goal. * * * His body landed on top of his wrists. At this point, he was on his right side with his feet angled to the left.

B. Darren's Prior Basketball Experience

Darren began playing basketball approximately ten years prior to his accident. He received training in basketball from camp counselors and basketball coaches and himself coached five to twelve-year-olds. Darren played at the Cornell court approximately fifteen to twenty times prior to his accident. He had tried to dunk a basketball many times but never succeeded. Darren also never jumped high enough to make contact with the rim and never saw anyone else fall backward after making contact with a rigid rim. He claims that he was unaware of the danger posed by dunking a basketball into a goal with a rigid rim.

C. The Basketball Court and the Goals

In the mid-1980s Cornell began plans for a construction project that included the basketball court where Darren fell. Cornell's landscape architect specified a particular Burke model as the basketball equipment for the court. Although Burke's model package included backboard, uprights, supports, and fittings, Gared Sports, Inc. ("Gared"), a third-party defendant, actually manufactured the hoops, rims, and goals. The rims of the goals were rigid, that is, they did not give way on contact.

M & B, the general contractor for Cornell's project, acquired the specified goals from Cushman, a sports equipment retailer. M & B constructed the court as specified in Cornell's specifications and installed the goals in accordance with the instructions accompanying them.

After completing the project in fall 1988, Cornell opened the basketball court for recreational use by "members of the Cornell community." Cornell provided no supervision and imposed no policies or guidelines for use of the court. Cornell also did not post any warnings on the court.

* * *

III. Overview of the Parties' Claims

Central to each of plaintiffs' claims is their contention that rigid rims unreasonably increase the risk to a player of attempting to dunk a basketball. According to plaintiffs' experts, when a player's hands come into contact with a rigid rim, the forward momentum of the player's upper body halts while the player's legs continue to swing under the basket. This pendulum-like effect increases the likelihood of an awkward fall. Plaintiffs' experts suggest that a break-away hoop, which gives way on contact, is less likely to cause a player to have an awkward fall.

Defendants claim that they are entitled to summary judgment for several reasons. First, defendant Cornell argues that the Traubs' negligence claim fails because Darren assumed all risks inherent in playing basketball with a rigid hoop. The remaining defendants—Burke, M & B, and Cushman—argue that the Traubs' strict products liability claims should be dismissed because rigid rims are not unreasonably dangerous or defective. These defendants also argue that the negligence counts should be dismissed because (1) any risks presented by a rigid rim to a player attempting to dunk a ball are obvious; (2) Darren Traub assumed the risk of playing basketball with a rigid rim; and (3) the alleged defect was not the proximate cause of Darren's accident. Burke, M & B, and Cushman also contend that I should (1) dismiss the Traubs' express warranty claims because the defendants made no affirmation on which a purchaser relied and (2) dismiss the Traubs' implied warranty claims because there is no proof that the hoop and backboard were unsafe for the ordinary purpose for which they were intended. M & B also separately argues that it cannot be held liable because (1) it completed the court project in accordance with specifications given to it in Cornell and there were no obvious defects in those specifications and (2) it is not a seller within the meaning of the Uniform Commercial Code or the case law defining strict products liability and negligence.

* * *

DISCUSSION

II. Cornell

The Traubs sued Cornell only on a negligence theory. Cornell urges that it had no duty to Darren because he assumed all ordinary and perceivable risks of playing basketball on a court using a hoop with a rigid rim.

Although assumption of the risk generally is no longer an absolute defense in a negligence action, it sometimes functions like an absolute defense because it eliminates the duty that might otherwise be owed to a plaintiff who assumes the risk of engaging in a particular activity. Participants in an athletic activity consent "to those injury-causing events which are known, apparent or reasonably foreseeable consequences of their participation."

* * *

Cornell contends that Darren clearly assumed the risk of jumping high to dunk a ball because "what goes up must come down." The school argues that in light of Darren's years of basketball experience, his prior experience on the Cornell court, and the clear view he had of the hoop, he cannot credibly argue that he was unaware of the risks of dunking or of the fact that the hoop had a rigid rim. However, Darren does not claim he was unaware of the risk of falling when he attempted to dunk or of the fact that the hoop had a rigid rim, but rather that he was unaware of the enhanced risk presented by a rigid rim. See Traub Aff. PP 2-3. According to Dr. Marc A. Rabinoff, a professor of human performance, sport, and leisure studies and one of plaintiffs' experts, the enhanced risk of which Darren complains results from a phenomenon known as "hanging up," which occurs when a player's fingers, hands, and wrists come into contact with a rigid basketball hoop and "'hang up' momentarily on the rim." As the forward motion of the player's hands stops briefly, the legs and body continue in motion and swing under the basketball goal. Consequently, the player has no effective way to get his legs back under his torso, falls with his back angled toward the ground, and has an increased likelihood of serious injury.

* * *

Rabinoff also states that the danger of hanging-up "is not well known to amateur basketball players" * * * The question, then, is whether Darren's testimony that he lacked an appreciation of the danger presented by dunking with a solid rim is adequate to create an issue of fact on assumption of risk. Darren stated that he had never before jumped high enough to "hang up" on the rim and that he had never seen anyone else fall backward or be injured from "hanging up." Defendants argue that this testimony fails to create an issue of fact because "any person beyond the age of majority who moves in a forward direction and leaps into the air toward a stationary object must be deemed to be aware of the risk that his/her body may make contact with the stationary object which may result in halting the forward momentum of the body." Defendants rely on Section 496D, comment d, of the Restatement (Second) of Torts which indicates that "there are some risks as to which no adult will be believed if he says that he did not know or understand them." This comment does not apply to the phenomenon of hanging up. The examples cited in the comment—the risk of being burned by fire, drowning in water, or falling from a height—are all risks that every adult would indeed understand. In contrast, the risk of having one's fall distorted by hanging up on a rigid object is not necessarily one that would be perceived by every adult.

* * *

Therefore, I must deny Cornell's summary judgment motion on Count I.

III. M & B

Plaintiffs allege claims in negligence, express and implied warranty, and strict products liability against M & B. For varying reasons, each claim fails. M & B offers uncontroverted proof that it followed Cornell's specifications in procuring and installing the hoop and rims. Therefore, in order to hold M & B liable in negligence, the Traubs must show that "the defects [in the design were] so glaring and out of the ordinary as to bring home to the contractor that it was doing something which would be likely to cause injury." * * * Plaintiffs do not identify any defect in the specifications that was so glaring that M & B should have refused to construct the court in accordance with the specifications. Therefore, I grant M & B's motion insofar as it requests dismissal of Count X.

M & B also argues that it is entitled to dismissal of the Traubs' express and implied warranty claims because the transfer of the basketball hoops from M & B to Cornell was not a sale within the meaning of the Uniform Commercial Code warranty provisions.

* * *

The Cornell contract provided for the construction of a recreational area and primarily involved excavation, grading, masonry, paving, concrete, installation, and landscaping. The contract also specified, however, that M & B procure and install a specific model Burke basketball goal. The price of the goal was less than one half of one percent of the total contract price. Long estimates that since M & B's incorporation in 1975, the company has installed no more than twelve to twenty-four basketball goals of any type. M & B has never entered into a contract, the sole or primary purpose of which was to furnish a basketball goal.

* * *

In a "mixed" contract involving both goods and services, the Uniform Commercial Code's warranties do not apply if the service-oriented portions of the transaction predominate over the sales transactions. The uncontroverted facts described above establish that the service aspects of M & B's contract with Cornell predominated over the sales aspects. Therefore, Counts XII and XIII of the complaint must be dismissed.

M & B also argues that the Traubs' strict products liability counts must be dismissed because M & B is no more than a casual or occasional seller of basketball goals. * * * a plaintiff cannot hold a seller liable on a strict products liability theory if the seller "is not engaged in the sale of the product in issue as a regular part of its business." (citing Restatement [Second] of Torts § 402 A, comment f). The policy reasons for the distinction between regular and casual sellers are that (1) regular sellers—unlike casual sellers—can exert pressure on manufacturers for improved safety because of their ongoing relationship with the manufacturer; (2) regular sellers "can recover increased costs within their commercial dealings, or through contribution and or indemnification in litigation; "and (3) by marketing certain products as a regular part of their business, regular sellers assume[] a special responsibility to the public, which has come to expect them to stand behind their goods."

* * *

A contractor who buys only twelve to twenty-four basketball goals in a twenty year period is not in a good position to exert pressure on manufacturers to increase safety standards. This is especially true where the contractor is bound to buy the goal stated in the specifications. In addition, a contractor who buys equipment mandated by the owner cannot be said to be putting its reputation behind the product purchased. Therefore, the Traubs' strict products liability claims against M & B also must be dismissed.

IV. Cushman and Burke

Plaintiffs seek to hold Burke and Cushman liable on theories of express warranty, implied warranty, negligence and strict products liability.

A. Strict Products Liability

The Traubs' strict products liability claims against Burke and Cushman rest on allegations of defective design, defective manufacture, failure to warn, and failure to recall. Because plaintiffs submitted no evidence the rims were improperly manufactured, that claim must be dismissed. Both the failure to warn and the failure to recall claims assume that the design of the rim presented unreasonable dangers. Defendants thus urge that all three claims should be dismissed because plaintiffs can offer no evidence of defective design.

A plaintiff can hold a manufacturer liable in strict products liability for a design defect regardless of the manufacturer's knowledge of the defect. Strict liability may also be imposed on retailers and distributors. To hold a seller or manufacturer liable for a design defect, the plaintiff must establish that the product was "designed so that it was not reasonably safe and . . . the defective design was a substantial factor in causing plaintiff's injury." The plaintiff has the initial burden of showing that the product "was not reasonably safe because there was a substantial likelihood of harm and it was feasible to design the product in a safer manner." "[A] defectively designed product is one which, at the time it leaves the seller's hands, is in a condition not reasonably contemplated by the ultimate consumer and is unreasonably dangerous for its intended use." The product must be safe for its intended use "as well as an unintended yet reasonably foreseeable use." .2d 115, 348 N.E.2d 571 (1976).Plaintiffs urge that a rigid hoop is not reasonably safe because it is more likely to cause injury in the course of dunking than a break-away hoop. Defendants first contend that plaintiffs have not offered any competent proof that the rigid hoop is more likely to cause injury than a break-away hoop.

Plaintiffs' proof on the issue of design defect is contained in the affidavits of their experts. As noted previously, plaintiffs' experts claim that contact with a rigid rim distorts a player's descent from the basket and makes injury more likely. They also claim that breakaway hoops are safer because they soften the direct impact to a player's fingers, hands, and wrists and lessen the possibility of "hanging up" on the rim. * * *

Plaintiffs have also offered competent proof that a safer design existed in the 1980's in the form of a break-away hoop. According to Dr. Roberts, patents on file in the United States Patent and Trademark Office from many years prior to Darren's accident cite improved player safety as a benefit of break-away hoop design. Plaintiffs also offer proof that break-away hoops have been used in indoor competition since the 1960's. Therefore, plaintiffs created issues of fact on both safety and the feasibility of an alternative design that are sufficient to defeat summary judgment on the existence of a defect.

Next, defendants argue that the hoop was in exactly the condition Darren would have anticipated and thus was not defective within the meaning of Robinson, which held that a defective product is one "in a condition not reasonably contemplated by the ultimate consumer." Defendants urge that because Darren was fully aware that the hoop had a rigid rim, he cannot recover in strict products liability. This argument fails because consumer's awareness of the danger of a product is only one factor the jury should consider in determining whether the product is reasonably safe.

Finally, defendants argue—but not with any great spirit—that plaintiffs have not established that dunking is a reasonably foreseeable use of a basketball hoop. Defendants concede "that dunking is a voluntary option attempted by many players of the game." Therefore, I must deny the motion for summary judgment on Counts III and XV.

B. Negligence

Counts II and XIV of the complaint are negligence counts against Burke and Cushman. As to Burke, the Traubs allege (1) failure to exercise reasonable care in designing and constructing the hoop and backboard; (2) failure to keep abreast of developments in the field of recreational equipment and to upgrade its design; (3) failure to warn of the dangers of rigid rims and/or to warn against attempting to dunk a basketball into a basketball goal with a rigid rim; (4) failure to advise of the availability of an alternative safer design; and (5) failure to make reasonable efforts to recall, modify, or replace the hoop. Plaintiffs charge that Cushman was negligent in (1) failing to keep abreast of developments in the field of recreational equipment; (2) selling the backboard and hoop to M & B; (3) failing to advise that a safer hoop design was available; (4) failing to warn; and (5) failing to recall, modify, or replace the hoop after the sale. Defendants seek dismissal of the negligence counts arguing that (1) Darren assumed the risk of using the hoops; (2) they had no duty to warn because any risk the hoops presented was obvious; and (3) plaintiffs presented no proof that any alleged defect was a proximate cause of Darren's injuries. For the reasons discussed under Point II, there are issues of fact concerning assumption of the risk. Similar reasons compel the conclusion that there are issues of fact as to whether the dangers of a rigid hoop are so obvious that defendants had no duty to warn. As previously noted, Darren contends that he did not understand that his fall would be distorted by contact with the rigid rim. The issue of whether an injured party knew of the danger presented by the product that injured him generally is for the jury. Defendants' final argument is that plaintiffs have not offered competent proof that any defect in the product caused Darren's injuries. However, plaintiffs' experts supplied competent proof that the rigid rim design contributed to Darren's injuries. Therefore, I must deny defendants' request for dismissal of Counts II and XIV of the complaint.

C. Express Warranties and Implied Warranties

Counts IV and XVI of the second amended complaint allege that Burke and Cushman breached express warranties. N.Y. U.C.C. § 2-313 provides:

(1) Express warranties by the seller are created as follows:

(a) Any affirmation of fact or promise made by the seller to the buyer which relates to the goods and becomes part of the basis of the bargain creates an express warranty that the goods shall conform to the affirmation or promise.

(b) Any description of the goods which is made part of the basis of the bargain creates an express warranty that the goods shall conform to the description.

(c) Any sample or model which is made part of the basis of the bargain creates an express warranty that

the whole of the goods shall conform to the sample or model.

Plaintiffs contend that the 1988 Burke Catalog, which represents that its goal is of "slam dunk strength," operated as an express warranty that the goal was safe for dunking. Plaintiffs do not allege that they or any of the defendants read or relied on this catalog's representations. In order to show that a seller made an express warranty through a description in an advertisement, plaintiffs must show that a purchaser relied on that representation and that the representation thus became "part of the basis of the bargain." As plaintiffs conceded at oral argument, their express warranty claims must be dismissed because they cannot show that any purchaser relied on the statement in the Burke catalog.

Plaintiffs also claim that Burke and Cushman breached the implied warranty of merchantability. Section 2-314(c) states that in order to be merchantable, goods must be "fit for the ordinary purposes for which such goods are used. . . ." Although a claim for breach of the implied warranty of merchantability is quite similar to a claim of strict product liability/design defect, there are differences. Most importantly, the plaintiff in an implied warranty case need not establish that the social desirability of a safer design outweighs its cost or that an alternative design is feasible. Instead, the plaintiff can prevail by showing that the "product was not minimally safe for its expected purpose." Id. As noted above, plaintiffs created an issue of fact as to whether dunking is part of the expected purpose of a basketball hoop and as to whether the defendants' design was minimally safe for this purpose. Therefore, I must deny summary judgment on the implied warranty claims against Burke and Cushman.

* * *

It is so ordered.

Recent Trends

Seller Can Undermine Its Own Warning

In *Levey v. Yamaha Motor Corp.* (2003), Yamaha Motor Corporation was a distributor of jet boats. As part of its program to demonstrate the boats to prospective buyers, the Yamaha district sales representative conducted a demonstration in rough ocean waters that violated the company's own safety warnings contained in the owner's manual and affixed to the boat. The local dealer's salesperson later emulated the unsafe demonstration for the plaintiff, who was injured as a result. The court found that a product demonstration that violates the seller's warnings can undermine the effectiveness of those warnings and could have been the cause of the salesperson's unsafe demonstration with the plaintiff. Therefore, it reversed a summary judgment for Yamaha and remanded the case to the lower court.

Nutritional Supplements

Nutritional supplements, such as those containing ephedrine, are often used, sold, or distributed by fitness enthusiasts. Users are beginning to sue supplement manufacturers for health problems caused by consumption of those supplements on the grounds that they are unreasonably dangerous. In a recent case, the plaintiff had consumed an average of 125 ephedrine tablets per day when the recommended daily dose was not to exceed six tablets. The plaintiff argued that the supplements were unreasonably dangerous because the manufacturer negligently failed to warn that they were addictive, and also that there was a safer alternate design. The court ruled that the dosage consumed was so outrageous that it was not a foreseeable use of the product. Additionally, the manufacturer's compliance with applicable federal regulations regarding product labeling preempted the state law failure to warn claim (*Green v. BDI Pharmaceuticals*, 2001). Thus, the court found in favor of the manufacturer.

References

Cases

Anthony Pools, Inc. v. Sheehan, 455 A.2d 434 (Md. 1983).

Arnold v. Riddell, Inc., 882 F. Supp. 979 (D. Kan. 1995).

Back v. Wickes Corp., 378 N.E.2d 964 (Mass. 1978).

Bhardwaj v. 24 Hour Fitness, Inc., 2002 Cal. App. Unpub. LEXIS 3288 (Cal. App. 2002).

Byrns v. Riddell, Inc., 550 P.2d 1065 (Ariz. 1976).

Curtis v. Hoosier Racing Tire Corp., 299 F. Supp. 2d 777 (N.D. Ohio 2004).

Diversified Products Corp. v. Faxon, 514 So.2d 1161 (Fla. App. 1987).

Dudley Sports Co. v. Schmitt, 279 N.E.2d 266 (Ind. App. 1972).

Escola v. Coca-Cola Bottling Co. of Fresno, 150 P.2d 436 (1944).

Everett v. Bucky Warren, Inc., 376 Mass. 280, 380 N.E.2d 653 (1978).

Filler v. Rayex Corp., 435 F.2d 336 (1970).

Garrett v. Nissen, 498 P.2d 1359 (N. Mex. 1972).

Gentile v. MacGregor Mfg. Co., 493 A.2d 647 (N.J. Super. L. 1985).

Green v. BDI Pharmaceuticals, 2001 La. App. LEXIS 2390 (La. App. 2001).

Hauter v. Zogarts, 120 Cal. Rptr. 681, 534 P.2d 377 (1975).

Hurley v. Larry's Water Ski School, 762 F.2d 925 (11th Cir. 1985).

Levey v. Yamaha Motor Corp., 825 A.2d 554 (N.J. Super. 2003).

Mohney v. USA Hockey, Inc., 2001 U.S. App. LEXIS 3584 (6th Cir. 2001)

Mohney v. USA Hockey, Inc., 2005 U.S. App. LEXIS 14373 (6th Cir. 2005).

Pavlides v. Galveston Yacht Basin, 727 F.2d 330 (5th Cir. 1984).

Perton v. Motel Properties, Inc., 497 S.E.2d 29 (Ga. App. 1998).

Rodriguez v. Riddell Sports, Inc., 242 F.3d 567 (5th Cir. 2001).

Traub v. Cornell University, 1998 U.S. Dist. LEXIS 5530 (N.D.N.Y. 1998).

Whitacre v. Halo Optical Products, Inc., 501 So.2d 994 (La. App. 2 Cir. 1987).

Publications

Garrett, M. C. (1972). Allowance of punitive damages in products liability claims. *Georgia Law Review, 6*(3), 613–630.

Nader, R. (1972). *Unsafe at any speed: The designed-in dangers of the American automobile.* New York: Grossman.

Plant, M. L. (1957). Strict liability of manufacturers for injuries caused by defects in products: An opposing view. *Tennessee Law Review, 24*(7), 938–951.

van der Smissen, B. (1990). *Legal liability and risk management for public and private entities.* Cincinnati, OH: Anderson Publishing Company.

Legislation

Restatement (Second) of Torts §402A (1965).

Restatement (Third) of Torts §2 and related comments (1997).

2.35 Human Resources Law

Betty van der Smissen
Michigan State University

Whereas most of the chapters in this book focus on the participant/athlete and the conduct of activities and events, the manager should give particular attention to the legal aspects related to employees.

In a study of athletic departments at NCAA schools, more than two-thirds sought legal advice from their institution in-house counsel or a legal firm retained by the institution with regard to employment/personnel law. This was the top-ranked topic for which athletic departments sought legal advice. Execution of contracts (all types, not just employment) was second, 5.6 percent lower. Both were well above all other topics (Lea & Loughman, 1993).

Human resources lawsuits reach smaller organizations as well as the larger ones—disproportionately, 41 percent of all complaints filed with the Equal Employment Opportunity Commission (EEOC) are against organizations that employ 25 to 100 people, although organizations of this size account for only 12 percent of companies in the United States. The average jury award is $842,000, and the average legal fees and court costs are estimated to be $125,000. Even if a case doesn't go to court, one can expect to have $10,000–$20,000 in expenses. Human resources lawsuits are expensive (Caruth & Handlogten, 2000)!

And, in the mid-2000s, the extensiveness of lawsuits and costs has increased, particularly in suits by employees against the organization (their employer), especially as related to what they perceive as their job security, Constitutional rights, and statutory protections. Further, employees are more frequently being included in lawsuits by participants/athletes. Whereas previously many employees thought they were protected if acting within the scope of their employment, this protection has been greatly eroded by the behaviors of the employees as related to their abuse of participants/athletes and their "indifferent disregard" for discriminating and abusive behaviors, which are **not** considered within the scope of employment (see third category on Employee Behaviors).

The field of human resources law, also termed employment or personnel law, is extensive and specialized. Because of the extensiveness of human resources (HR) law and the tremendous financial implications, it is highly desirable to make it an important aspect of risk management (see Chapter 5.10, *Risk Management Theory*), and conduct a human resources (HR) audit annually, just as one takes a financial audit or a legal audit. An HR audit is a systematic assessment of the aspects included in this chapter. Written policies and procedures related to each aspect are essential (see Chapter 5.22, *Audits in Risk Management*; see also Caruth & Handlogten, 2000; McConnell, 2000).

Fundamental Concepts

This section provides only an overview, because HR law reaches into many aspects of the law. Many Constitutional rights, statutory protections, and legal concepts are discussed, particularly as related to the participant/athlete, in other chapters of this book, but the legal concepts are also applicable to employees (see Chapter 7.00, *Constitutional Law;* Chapter 8.10, *Federal Statutes and Discrimination;* Chapter 4.00, *Intentional Torts and Criminal Acts*). The professional athlete, as an employee, is not included in this chapter. (For additional insights, see sources listed in *Publications* at the end of the chapter.)

In this chapter, HR law is presented in three categories: (1) the employment process, (2) the workplace environment, and (3) employee behaviors.

Employment Process

The first basic category of HR law—**employment process**—is concerned with fundamental concepts related to the recruitment, selection, and hiring process; job analyses; the employment contract; benefits, including compensation; grievance and discipline procedures; and termination (see especially Beeler, 2005; Fried & Miller, 1998; Hauge & Herman, 1999).

One of the most critical aspects of the employment process relates to protection of participants from abuse by an employee. Failure to protect is referred to as negligent processing. **Negligent processing** deals with the "fitness" of the employee and includes the aspects of hiring, supervision, training, retention, and referral—but not job competence. Negligent processing is included in the third category, employee behaviors.

The Recruitment, Selection, and Hiring Process

The assurance of equal opportunity for all eligible persons is the essence of this aspect of the process and is based in Constitutional rights and statutory protections (see also Chapter 7.14, *Equal Protection*; Chapter 8.12, *Gender Equity: Coaching and Administration*; Chapter 8.13, *Title VII of the Civil Rights Act of 1964*; Chapter 8.15, *Age Discrimination in Employment Act*; and Chapter 8.16, *Title I of the Americans with Disabilities Act*). The proper procedures and process are critical in avoiding charges of many types of discrimination and unfair treatment, including gender, age, disability, religion, ethnic background, and sexual orientation. One must keep meticulous records and document (see *Kolupa v. Roselle Park District*, 2006),

Background checks are for more than propensity for violence and child abuse. One should also be aware of drug or other felony convictions, especially where one wishes to "give another chance" to a person. (See a federal district court case, *Ott v. Edinburgh Community School Corp.*, 2005.) Ott was convicted of drug charges prior to employment, but was hired anyway. He was then fired when a new superintendent came in and saw his background record. He sued on equal protection rights, due process rights, the Family and MLA, defamation, and inflicting emotional distress.

Another important element of the process is obtaining the best-qualified person. This means competence for the task and appropriate character to work with people. In the early 2000s, there have been an unusual number of inaccurate resumes. One must check for accuracy of **all** information on a resume of finalists for a position. In addition, the references are of great value, not only as related to competence to do the job, but also to validate the character of the applicant. *Volunteers, too, must be checked!*

Job Analyses

Job analyses provide the foundation for many aspects of human resource management as they describe the tasks to be performed and the qualifications to do them. The job analysis determines whether an employee is acting "within the scope of employment." They are essential to performance appraisal and in hiring (e.g., as related to ADA) (see also Beeler, 2005, chap. 15, pp. 444–445)

The Employment Contract

In addition to "regular" contracts of employment, two types of contracts need to be understood—the employment-at-will contract and the contract for an independent contractor. Further, there should be special awareness that the employee manual does not become incorporated as part of the employment contract unless that is the specific intent (see also Chapter 2.12, *Which Parties Are Liable?*)

Benefits, Including Compensation

There should be written policies regarding benefits and compensation. These benefits include such things as a salary scale and criteria for increases, insurance coverage, health-care benefits, payment for time not worked (e.g., holidays, vacation, sick days, family leave), overtime, professional advancement benefits (e.g., paid memberships of professional associations, continuing education assistance or training allocation, conference attendance, access to recreation facilities). State laws govern unemployment insurance and workers' compensation (see Chapter 5.25, *Managing Risk Through Insurance*, and Chapter 5.26, *Workers' Compensation*). The benefits should be distinguished between those mandated by statute (government), such as FMLA, Social Security, and workers' compensation, and those provided by the employing organization, such as retirement plans, health insurance, liability coverage, access to fitness and other facilities, and professional benefits. In *Bender v. Dakota Resorts Management Group* (2005), it was held that a ski lift employee was entitled to benefits for injury sustained while skiing during his work break, based on workers' compensation interpretation, that injury sustained while engaging in recreational activity on employer's premises during break arising out of and in course of "regular incident of employment" is covered.

Grievance and Discipline Procedures

There should be a written grievance procedure, as well as a disciplinary plan. Every employee should know what types of action may be taken. The foundation of such plans rests on a well-drafted standard of conduct and a code of ethics. The standards of conduct should address such areas as job performance, work conduct and attitude, attendance, and punctuality. A code of ethics should encompass such behaviors as acceptance of gifts and bribes, giving preferential treatment, using one's position for personal gain, and engaging in an activity that constitutes conflict of interest (see Beeler, 2005, chap. 14, pp. 427–436). Dispute resolution, a mediation process, should not be overlooked as a grievance strategy.

Termination

Wrongful termination is the principal basis on which lawsuits are brought by discharged employees, alleging discrimination, retaliation, failure to follow procedures, and so on. The EEOC said that federal job-discrimination complaints filed by workers against private employers increased more than 4 percent in 2002, and the number of complaints reached the highest level in seven years. It also was stated that there was a surge in allegations of religious, age, and national-origin discrimination.

To protect against allegations of wrongful termination, it is essential that there be full documentation of both performance appraisals (see subsequent section) and due process. Most wrongful terminations allege lack of due process and infringement of property and liberty interests (see *Campanelli v. Bockrath*, 1996; *Ersek v. Township of Springfield*, 1996; *Barkauskie v. Indian River Sch. Dist.*, 1996; *Fowler v. Smith*, 1995; *Ludwig v. Board of Trustees of Ferris State Univ.*, 1997; see also Fried & Miller, 1998).

Workplace Environment

The workplace environment, as related to the employee, is the focus of the second category of HR law, encompassing fundamental concepts involving (1) the hostile work environment, i.e., harassment and discrimination; (2) performance appraisal; and (3) protective laws and regulations, including the freedoms, child labor laws, and safety.

The workplace environment also includes participant abuse by employees/volunteers, but because this is protection of the participants *from* the employees, it is discussed in the third category, employee behavior. Further, by failure to take appropriate action related to harassment and participant abuse, the organization might be liable, as well as the employee, for the intentional (and sometimes criminal) act of the employee, modifying the doctrine of *respondeat superior* (see *Modifications in the Doctrine of Respondeat Superior* in the third category).

Hostile Work Environment

Although the focus in the mid- to late-1990s was on gender harassment, a hostile workplace also may occur when there is racial, ethnic, age, disability, religious, political affiliation, sexual orientation, or elderly harassment and discrimination. A **hostile work environment** is created when there is unreasonable interference with an individual's work performance or creation of an intimidating, hostile, or offensive working environment. The concept of a hostile work environment is difficult to define, but **five elements** appear essential:

a. That the employee belongs to the protected category
b. That the employee is subject to unwelcome harassment
c. That the harassment was based on gender, age, etc.
d. That the harassment complained of affected the term, condition, or privilege of employment
e. That the employer knew or should have known of the harassment and failed to take prompt, effective remedial action[1]

The last element is critical. What did the employer know and what was done? The *Giordano v. William Paterson College* (1992) case set forth several factors to determine whether an employer's response was sufficiently prompt and adequate to avoid *respondeat superior* liability: (1) whether the employer investigated alleged acts of harassment, (2) type of investigation conducted, (3) postinvestigation remedial steps taken, (4) was a grievance procedure and policy against discrimination in place, and (5) was harassment ended after remedial measures were taken. If the harassment continues, under the doctrine of continuing violation, the statute of limitations does not run (see also *Bell v. Chesapeake & Ohio Ry. Co.*, 1991).

Every school, institution, agency, and organization must have established policies and procedures for dealing with harassment. To whom does an employee make a complaint? A concern in making a complaint to a superior about a supervisor is that of **retaliation**, an actionable claim as exemplified in a case of the coach harassing female gymnasts (*Koop v. Indep. Sch. Dist.*, 1993).

What is harassment? One is familiar with the "reasonable man" concept, but for sexual harassment at the turn of the '90s decade, the "reasonable woman" standard became important in hostile work environment cases. However, in 1993, the Supreme Court did not refer to the "reasonable woman," but rather referred to the gender-neutral "reasonable person." There are two dimensions required for the work environment: (1) that the behavior be severe or pervasive enough to create an objectively hostile or abusive work environment, an environment that a "reasonable person" would find hostile or abusive; and (2) the employee must subjectively perceive that the environment is abusive. Thus, it must be noted that *what constitutes a hostile environment is very much subjective to the person involved and, therefore, there is no objective standard or specific criteria against which to measure an environment for hostility* (see *Harris v. Forklift Systems, Inc.*, 1991; Adler & Pevice, 1993; Childers, 1993; Schimmel, 1994).

Sexual Harassment. Gender discrimination in employment under Title IX (see Chapter 8.12, *Gender Equity: Coaching and Administration*) and Title VII (see Chapter 8.13, *Title VII of the Civil Rights Act of 1964*) usually is thought of as relating to equal opportunity in employment; however, there are two forms of gender discrimination. The other is that which is sexually motivated, referenced as sexual harassment, which gives rise to a hostile workplace. It was almost ten years after Title VII was enacted that the first case was brought on sexual harassment, but the court found no basis under the statute. However, several years later the court overturned this decision and several cases holding similarly and established the two forms of discrimination, making sexual harassment actionable under Title VII.

The EEOC issued guidelines in 1980 defining **sexual harassment** as "unwelcome sexual advances, requests for sexual favors, and other verbal or physical conduct of a sexual nature . . . when submission to such conduct is made either explicitly or implicitly a term or condition of an individual's employment, the basis for employment decisions affecting such individual or has the purpose or effect of unreasonably interfering with an individual's work performance or creating an intimidating, hostile or offensive working environment" (see Chapter 8.14, *Sexual Harassment*).

---

[1] See landmark decision, *Meritor Savings Bank, FSB v. Vinson* (1986); see also Weddle (1995) and *Faragher v. City of Boca Raton* (1994), in which former city life guards sued the city and two supervisors for sexual harassment based on inappropriate touching and lewd remarks (i.e., "hostile environment" claim under Title VII). The city had constructive knowledge of supervisors' sexual harassment proving *respondeat superior*, and judgment was granted for the lifeguards.

Submission to sexual favors that are either a term or condition of an individual's employment or a basis for employment decisions affecting that individual is known as *quid pro quo* sexual harassment. Power by the one seeking the sexual favors serves as its basis, in that the employee is afraid not to accommodate the sexual favor requested because of the "power" that the person holds over the employee's position (e.g., salary, work assignment, promotion, or dismissal). The other type of sexual harassment relates to interference with work performance, creating a hostile workplace.

Performance Appraisals

One of the most critical elements in discrimination in promotion and remuneration (equal pay, merit increase), wrongful discharge, and lack of due process allegations is that of performance appraisal.[2] An appraisal properly documented can support the rationale or basis for the action taken, whether positive or negative toward the employee, and the procedures (due process) used. There are two types of appraisal—**performance-based appraisal**, how well the tasks assigned are being done, and **disciplinary-based appraisal**, the conduct of the employee. Where there is a labor union, the procedures for performance appraisal usually will be specified in the collective bargaining agreement, a process that is very protective of the employees' rights (see, e.g., *Nevels v. Board of Education*, 1991; *Chase v. Pinellas County Sch. Bd.*, 1992; see also Beeler, 2005, chap. 15, pp. 449–453).

Protective Laws and Regulations

Protective laws and regulations include those related to the freedoms, child labor, safety, and participant abuse. The latter because it relates to employee behavior, is discussed in the third category. In addition, one should be familiar with the provisions of the *Fair Labor Standards Act* (FLSA) and its application to the specific setting in which one operates.

Freedoms. The freedoms an employee enjoys extend to both the employment process and the workplace. These include privacy, speech, searches, drug testing, smoking, confidentiality of records, computer privacy, and federal health records privacy act. What is "free speech"? Can one criticize the organization by which one is employed or be politically active and advocate a policy that might not be the best for the organization? What about personal habits, such as smoking, use of drugs, alcohol, language, dress, or hair style? How far can a code of conduct go before infringing unduly on the freedom of the employee?

Child Labor Laws. Sport and recreation are logical activities in which children like to participate in a work capacity. With increased emphasis on school-to-work transition and on-the-job training, in the '90s the Labor Department reviewed child labor laws, particularly for 14- and 15-year-olds. The older teenagers are covered by less restrictive regulations. Child labor laws include not only employment of children but also the use of children around certain maintenance equipment. Impetus was given when it was held a violation to employ a 14-year-old as bat boy with a minor-league team, and also when a 14-year-old student manager for a basketball team was severely injured when washing uniforms (*Byrd v. Bossier Parish School Board*, 1989).

---

[2] A local case illustrates Constitutional rights and performance appraisal. In *Gilder-Lucas v. Elmore County Board of Education* (2005), a nontenured high school teacher became sponsor of the junior varsity cheerleading squad. After tryouts, some parents complained to the principal about the outcome, and the principal asked the adviser to complete a questionnaire regarding tryouts. She reported they were not conducted properly because the adviser of the varsity squad had added some additional requirements in violation of the National Federation of Cheerleaders' guidelines. The principal reported to the parents that there had been no wrongdoing. Shortly after, the principal told the J.V. advisor that he was not renewing her contract. She refused to resign, and the Board of Education fired her. The superintendent was quoted in the newspaper as saying that "several teaching contracts were not renewed because of performance." The adviser sued the Board in federal court alleging Board retaliation after she had exercised her First Amendment rights of free speech and violation of her Fourteenth Amendment rights of due process by firing her. On the First Amendment rights, she failed because she did not prove her speech (response to questionnaire) was a matter of public concern. And, on the Fourteenth Amendment she could not prove that the Board had deprived her of property rights because she did not have tenure or liberty rights because the superintendent's statement was broad and did not name teachers.

Safety. The federal Occupational Safety and Health Administration (OSHA) has primary responsibility for worksite safety; however, about 40 percent of the states also cover workplace safety by legislation. Many aspects of the OSHA regulations affect sport and recreation operations, such as injury/illness records, employee safety posters, posting of signs, blood-borne pathogens, written plans/training, personal protective equipment, safety equipment, electrical safety, toilet facilities, regular inspections, housekeeping, safety conditions, emergency evacuation, machine guarding, hazard communication, and chemicals (free informational booklets can be obtained from www.osha.gov/pls/publications/pubindex.list).

Three aspects of OSHA regulations are of particular importance in recreation and sport. Fairly well known because of its relation to sport injuries and athletic training, is the *Blood-borne Pathogen Standard* (29 C.F.R. 1910.1030), which came out of the fear of contracting AIDS through exposure to blood. The *Hazard Communication (HazCom) Standard* (29 C.F.R. 1910.1200) requires manufacturers to properly label each hazardous substance and employers to write hazard communication plans to train employees about the substances. Substances include cleaning supplies, as well as pesticides for turf. Less known is the *Labeling of Hazardous Art Materials Act,* which focuses on traditional art materials, such as paints, inks, solvents, pastes, crayons, and ceramic glazes. A third aspect addresses the *concern for environmental quality,* especially hidden residues and contaminants, including prior use of asbestos, use of landfills for golf courses and other recreational uses without proper controls, and pesticides and fertilizers on the turf of sport fields. An environmental audit to assess exposure is highly desirable.

Employee Behaviors

Employee behaviors include many types of behavior, such as dishonesty and embezzlement, use of Internet and e-mail for non-work-related purposes, and assault and battery[3]; however, two of the behaviors most involved in lawsuits in the mid-2000s are sexual relationship[4] of employee and participant and participant abuse.

Increasingly there has been concern regarding the physical and sexual abuse of participants, particularly children, but also persons with disabilities and the elderly, by employees and volunteers who provide services, including sport and recreation, to these individuals, whether it be in the public sector of schools and municipalities, the nonprofit sector, or commercial enterprise.

Statutes. Both the federal government and more than three-fourths of the state governments have responded to the concerns about participant abuse by passing legislation.[5] There are three approaches used in legislation—(1) making child abuse a crime[6] and maintaining a registry of child abusers; (2) requiring those working with children to report suspected child abuse to a federal or state agency[7] and giving protection to them for reporting; and (3) requiring criminal background checks for all persons working with children. It is the third approach that applies particularly to employment process negligence (see Nonprofit Risk Management Center publications).

---

[3] In a local case, *Scott v. Neal* (2005), a gym owner was sued for assault and battery when he punched a patron on the treadmill in the face, knocking him unconscious and giving him a broken jaw. Plaintiff was awarded $325,000, of which $175,000 was punitive damages.

[4] In a federal appeals court case, *Flaskamp v. Dearborn Public Schools* (2005), the sexual relationship of the gym teacher with a student was involved. At issue were Fourteenth Amendment due process rights, right to privacy, informational and autonomy-based privacy rights, and fundamental liberty interests.

[5] e.g., National Child Protection Act of 1993, P.L. 103–209, criminal justice agency of each state must report child abuse crime information to National Criminal History Background Check System; Victims of Child Abuse Act of 1990, Subtitle E of Crime Control Act of 1990—Title II, P.L. 101–647, child care worker employee background checks. See your agency or institution personnel office for legislation and regulations specific to your state.

[6] e.g., *State v. Laird* (1989) teacher/coach convicted of molesting a 14-year-old student, 8-year sentence at hard labor with 5 years suspended, not an excessive sentence; *People v. Arnold* (1992) 2 female high school students brought action under sexual battery statute against wrestling coach, convicted of 5 felony counts and 6 misdemeanor counts; *People v. Peters* (1992) 13-year-old student sued gym teacher/swim coach under sexual abuse crime statute.

[7] e.g., C.B. v. Bobo (1995) physical education teacher allegedly sexually abused student, private right of action did not exist under Child Abuse Reporting Act; Doe v. Rains Indep. Sch. Dist. (1995) teacher/coach had sexual relationship with minor student who had been babysitting for him. The court held that it was a violation of a state statute requiring one to report abuse within 48 hours. "State action" was not required to sustain the suit.

Concept of Negligence. The employment process encompasses not only the hiring process, but also retention, supervision, training, and referral. The term *negligent* is placed in front of each of these processes (e.g., negligent hire, negligent supervision). However, there is modification in the meaning of the term. Negligence usually means failure to conduct an activity or provide a service in accord with appropriate professional standards. In this sense, **employment process negligence** would mean employing an incompetent person to conduct the activity or provide the service; however, *when reference is made to* **negligent hire,** *et al., the term means that an employee is hired or a volunteer is assigned who is unfit (i.e., has a propensity for a physically violent or sexually abusive behavior).* The individual may very well be highly competent as related to the activity or service. Further, this "qualification" for a position, consideration of "fitness," also impinges on discrimination in hiring, wherein it is normally stated that only qualifications to do the job or task are pertinent (see 8.16 *Title I of the Americans with Disabilities Act*). But in this situation, "unfitness" is a legal disqualification.

Negligent hire is the most common of the employment processes involved in child abuse and is the subject of the statutes and regulations. The majority of states recognize negligent hiring as an actionable tort. *A key element in the appropriate standard of care is foreseeability* (see Chapter 2.11, *Elements of Negligence*), and for negligent hire, **foreseeability** is characterized by appropriate and adequate background checks. Was the employer diligent in checking background records to eliminate those potential employees who had backgrounds that evidenced foreseeability of possible violent or sexual abuse behaviors? Did the school, organization, or institution do all that was "reasonable" in conducting the background check? If so, then neither the corporate entity nor the administrator is held liable. However, if not, then both are held on "negligent hire."[8] This background checking must be done for volunteers as well as employees, and there are many volunteers in sport, especially youth sport coaches. **All must have their backgrounds checked!**

Not only must there be initial checking of backgrounds for those working with children and youth, but if a person's position is changed from not having contact with children to having contact, then that person must then also have background checked. For example, a person had been hired for a janitorial position and then was promoted to a supervisory position at the city recreation center. The background was not checked when the change in assignment occurred; but, in fact, there was a felony conviction. Action was brought against the city, the city recreation and parks commission, and the gym supervisor for the employee's alleged sexual molestation of several young girls and a young boy. The city also had not complied with its own policies regarding background checking. The personnel department, which usually examined applicants carefully, did not do so in this situation because they were aware that the area supervisor had some knowledge of the applicant-employee (*Williams v. Butler*, 1991). Beware—one may not know acquaintances or even "friends" as well as one might expect. There may be "hidden" backgrounds! Everyone, even long-standing friends, should be subjected to the same checks. *It is essential that an organization, agency, or institution establish well-defined policies and procedures for checking applicant backgrounds* **and have them carried out meticulously** (*U.S. Fidelity & Guaranty Co. v. Open Sesame Child Care Center*, 1993).

Negligent supervision, as negligent hire, is not the supervision of how an activity is conducted, but rather an assessment of the behaviors of the individual employee as related to "fitness," that is, a propensity toward violence or sexual molestation. When such conduct is evidenced, whether observed directly (actual notice) or would have been if proper supervision had been given (constructive notice) or reported by someone else (e.g., participant, parent, other leader), the supervisor/administrator in charge must take immediate action to protect the participants. A principal was found to be *deliberately indifferent* when he received numerous reports about a teacher/coach molesting a 15-year-old student. He regularly dismissed the reports and students' complaints, did not record incidents, and declined to talk with involved students, parents, or the accused teacher/coach. The court distinguished between gross negligence and deliberate indif-

---

[8] e.g., *Doe v. Village of St. Joseph* (1992) action against school for alleged sexual molestation by recreational supervisor of 13-year-old; records check had been conducted prior to hiring and no information suggested any criminal record or propensity; *Doe v. Coffee County Board of Education* (1992) 4 students allegedly sexually abused by basketball coach, background check had been made upon employment. See also Camacho (1993).

ference in that the former is a heightened degree of negligence, whereas the latter is a lesser form of intent. Further, it was stated that the deliberate indifference standard is to be applied in determining an individual supervisor's liability under federal civil rights statute.[9]

A third employment tort is **negligent referral**. Critical elements in checking backgrounds are references and evaluations of past performances; yet, with the litigious society today, individuals may sue for defamation if a "bad" reference is given, particularly as related to "unfit" characterizations. The protection of society (participants) from danger by persons with a propensity for violence or sexual abuse must be balanced with the desire to protect the confidentiality of the individual and the individual's right to a "second chance." It is a very difficult situation for those who are asked to give referrals, and some refuse saying "no comment" or merely providing factual data of dates employed and position description. The courts have tried to help the situation by providing "qualified privilege" to employers giving referrals. Legal action also may be taken against the employer for failure to provide an appropriate referral that included warnings of behaviors that had been evidenced.

Action can be brought for **negligent retention** of an employee or volunteer if one has observed behaviors of "unfitness" or has obtained information evidencing the propensity for violence or sexual abuse, but does not discharge or remove the person from the position that gives contact with participants (children and youth). A 55-year-old park employee worked at the neighborhood playground both in general maintenance and checking out basketballs, games, ropes, and so on. On this day, he told a nine-year-old child to return the jump rope to him at the maintenance shed at 5 PM, where he then for two hours repeatedly raped, assaulted, and sexually abused her, as well as threatened to kill her. He had begun work seven months earlier as part of a work program and had put on his application that he had no arrest or conviction record. Subsequent to employment, a fingerprint check was made, and the personnel department received his record of substantial criminal activity, but took no action. He was considered a utility worker, not involved in working with children. Because this was in a mandated welfare work program, there was no action for negligent hire; however, knowing of the background, this was considered negligent retention. The court held that the doctrine of governmental immunity from tort liability (see Chapter 2.22, *Immunity*) for discretionary function was inapplicable and that the strong public policy favoring rehabilitation of ex-convicts did not excuse the city from compliance with its own procedures requiring informed discretion in the placement of persons with criminal records. Damages in the amount of $2.5 million were awarded (*Haddock v. City of New York*, 1990).

Modifications in the Doctrine of Respondeat Superior

There have been two major modifications in the doctrine of *respondeat superior* (see Chapter 2.12, *Which Parties Are Liable?*). First, under the doctrine, the corporate entity has not been liable for the intentional torts or criminal acts of its employees because such acts are considered outside the scope of authority and responsibility and not for the benefit of the employer. Secondly, the doctrine has deemed that administrative/supervisory personnel are not responsible as individuals for such acts of employees working under them. *However, as related to employment torts, both the corporate entity and the administrative/supervisory personnel, as individuals, are liable.* They can be liable for the injury caused by the intentional tort because they were negligent as related to the employment process that enhanced the likelihood of such intentional tort or crime occurring. This misfeasance most often is an act of omission and referred to as *deliberate indifference*. Deliberate indifference occurs when one is aware of the situation or potential problem, but is indifferent to it by inaction. To be deliberately indifferent implies intent.

---

[9] *Doe v. Taylor Indep. Sch. Dist.* (1994). See also *Hagan v. Houston Indep. Sch. Dist.* (1995) 3 former students brought civil rights action against principal for failing to prevent coach's alleged sexual abuse, principal had taken action on complaints so not deliberately indifferent; *D.T. by M.T. v. Indep. Sch. Dist. No. 16* (1990) alleged acts of sexual molestation against 3 boys' basketball team members engaged in fund-raising activities for summer basketball camp by elementary school teacher/coach, held that school's established procedure in investigating, hiring, and supervising teacher/coach did not amount to deliberate indifference or reckless disregard for civil rights of students.

Significant Case

—◇◇◇—

Doe v. Taylor illustrates several important factors regarding liability for the child abuser, his supervisor, and the organization for which he works. The plaintiff's constitutional right to bodily integrity is discussed, as is the liability of the supervisor for gross negligence or deliberate indifference in the employment process. Note, also, that qualified immunity did not protect the defendants in this case.

DOE V. TAYLOR INDEPENDENT SCHOOL DISTRICT

United States Court of Appeals for the Fifth Circuit
15 F.3d 443; 1994 U.S. App. LEXIS 3846
March 3, 1994, Decided

Opinion: E. Grady Jolly and W. Eugene Davis

Jane Doe was sexually molested by her high school teacher in Taylor, Texas. Defendant Eddy Lankford, principal of Taylor High, and defendant Mike Caplinger, superintendent of the Taylor Independent School District, were sued in their supervisory capacity by Jane Doe for permitting violations of her substantive due process right to bodily integrity. The district court denied their claim of qualified immunity, and they have filed this interlocutory appeal on that issue. We hold, first, that schoolchildren do have a liberty interest in their bodily integrity that is protected by the Due Process Clause of the Fourteenth Amendment and that physical sexual abuse by a school employee violates that right. Second, we hold that school officials can be held liable for supervisory failures that result in the molestation of a schoolchild if those failures manifest a deliberate indifference to the constitutional rights of that child. Next, we conclude that each of these legal principles was clearly established in 1987, when the violations took place. Finally, in analyzing whether Caplinger and Lankford fulfilled the duty that they owed to Jane Doe, we reverse the district court's denial of immunity to defendant Caplinger, but we affirm its denial of immunity to Lankford.

I

Facts

Defendant Jesse Lynn Stroud, a twenty-year veteran of Texas's public education system, was employed by the Taylor Independent School District as a biology teacher and assistant coach from 1981 until 1987. It was no secret within the school community that Coach Stroud behaved inappropriately toward a number of young female students over the course of his employment at Taylor High. He made little effort to conceal his fancy for these female students: he wrote notes to them, he let them drive his truck, he exhibited explicit favoritism toward them in class, and often touched them in an overly familiar, inappropriate way.

Defendant Eddy Lankford became the principal of Taylor High in August 1983. By the fall semester of 1985, complaints about Stroud's behavior had reached his office through various channels. During the previous 1984–1985 school year, Stroud had "befriended" one of his female freshman students. Their friendship far transgressed the boundaries of a normal, appropriate teacher-student relationship.

By the fall of 1985, * * * Stroud had also befriended a new female freshman student, and began a similar inappropriate relationship (note-writing, gift-giving, walking to class, etc.) with her. Principal Lankford approached Stroud outside the fieldhouse during the 1985 football season and spoke to him about being "too friendly" with the freshman student.

Also during the fall of 1985, the school librarian, Mary Jean Livingood, . . . reported the inappropriate behavior she had witnessed to Principal Lankford and also informed him of the two telephone calls she had received from parents.

In May of 1986, Livingood reported to Lankford that she had witnessed an episode of "child molestation" involving Stroud and two freshman female students. . . . Lankford downplayed the incident. . . . Lankford did not warn or discipline Stroud—even mildly—for any incident or conduct. Indeed, Lankford failed to document any of the complaints he received about Stroud.

All of this behavior occurred before defendant Mike Caplinger ever moved to Taylor or worked for the Taylor Independent School District. Caplinger became the superintendent of the Taylor ISD in July 1986; Lankford did not inform Caplinger of any problems— real or potential—with Stroud or with his pattern of conduct.

Plaintiff Jane Doe entered Taylor High as a freshman in August 1986; she was a student in Stroud's biology class. Stroud began his seduction of Doe by writing personal—often suggestive—comments on her homework and test papers.

By late fall, Stroud was touching and kissing Jane Doe. * * * Their physical relationship escalated to heavy petting and undressing in January 1987, when Stroud took Doe and some of her friends, including his own daughter, to a rock concert. There, he bought her alcoholic beverages, took her back to the fieldhouse, and began caressing her in the most intimate of ways. He suggested intercourse, but she refused.

Rumors about Doe and Stroud were rampant among the students and faculty by this time. * * * Sometime in January 1987, Lankford heard that Stroud had taken Doe and other students to the rock concert; that month he also received complaints from four female students in Stroud's biology class about Stroud's favoritism toward certain students. Lankford spoke with Stroud about this complaint, and, for the first time, notified Caplinger about possible problems with Coach Stroud.

In early February 1987, Mickey Miller, the assistant principal of Taylor's middle school, reported to Caplinger that at a basketball game he had witnessed Stroud behaving inappropriately with several freshman girls, including Jane Doe. . . . Caplinger instructed Lankford to speak with Stroud about this incident, which he did; the athletic director, Eddy Spiller, also spoke with Stroud about the report.

On Valentine's Day, Stroud gave Jane Doe a valentine that read: "To my most favorite, prettiest, sweetest, nicest sweetheart in the world! Please don't change cause I need you. I'm in love with you. Forever—for real—I love you." A friend and classmate of Jane Doe's, Brittani B., found the valentine in Doe's purse.

Brittani took the note to Lankford the next day; . . . Lankford did not keep a copy of the note and did not investigate the matter further; he did not tell Superintendent Caplinger about the incident, nor did he speak with Stroud or Doe. His only action was to transfer Brittani out of Stroud's biology class.

In late March or early April 1987, Stroud and Doe had intercourse for the first time. She was fifteen years old. Stroud was her first sexual partner.

Over the next several months, Stroud and Doe had repeated sexual contact. * * * Their romantic relationship—although perhaps not the extent of it—was common knowledge within the Taylor High community, not only among students, but also among the faculty and the parents of many students. Lankford asked a friend whose daughter was a student at the high school to "keep his ears open" for information about Doe and Stroud. On Stroud's performance evaluation by Lankford for the 1986–1987 academic year, however, there was nothing to indicate that Stroud's performance was anything less than fully satisfactory. Indeed, Lankford still had not even informally documented any incident or pattern of conduct relating to Stroud.

In June 1987, Stroud took Doe and some other girls, along with his family, to a local fair, the Corn Festival. . . . Two concerned parents, both prominent members of the community, reported to Caplinger that Stroud was behaving inappropriately with Jane Doe at this festival, that Mrs. Stroud had left the festival because of his behavior, and that there was a possibility that he and Doe had left the festival together. One of the parents also showed Caplinger notes that Stroud had written to his daughter.

In response to the report, Caplinger contacted the parents of the girl who, according to the story, was intoxicated and misbehaving at the festival in the company of Doe and Stroud. When the girl's mother assured him that her daughter had not even been at the festival, that she had been sick and at home, Caplinger dismissed the report as unfounded without investigating further or contacting Jane Doe's parents to discuss the report with them.

In July 1987, Doe's parents discovered photographs of Stroud among Doe's possessions with such handwritten inscriptions by Stroud as: "Please don't ever change and don't ever leave me. I want to be this close always—I love you—Coach Lynn Stroud." Doe's parents immediately scheduled a meeting with Caplinger. . . . He promised to convene a meeting of all the parties involved. After speaking with Doe's parents, Caplinger spoke with Jane Doe privately in his office. He showed her the photographs her parents had just presented to him and inquired about the nature of her relationship with Stroud. Doe suggested that the notes on the photos were just "friendly gestures." She explicitly denied any sexual relations with Stroud.

Caplinger called Lankford after the meeting with the Does, who in turn called Stroud. . . . There, the three men discussed the situation. Caplinger and Lankford warned Stroud to keep his distance from Jane Doe, and that he would be fired "if something was going on." No further action was taken, however; the meeting that Caplinger had promised to schedule never took place, and Stroud did not hear from either Lankford or Caplinger again until October 6, the day he was suspended from employment.

Although Jane Doe was able to stay away from Stroud for the remainder of the summer vacation, when classes resumed in the late summer of 1987, Stroud's sexual advances towards her resumed as well, and soon thereafter they began having intercourse again. Lankford admits that he watched Stroud no more closely than he previously had. The sexual contact continued into the fall of Jane Doe's sophomore year, until October 5, when Doe's mother found more love letters from Stroud among Jane's possessions. The Does then consulted their family lawyer, who agreed to discuss the matter with Jane. Upon meeting with Jane, the attorney learned the truth about her sexual involvement with Stroud. Doe explained that she had kept the matter a secret because she feared the repercussions of disclosure.

The attorney reported the information to Caplinger at once. . . . Caplinger ordered Stroud immediately suspended from employment. Stroud later resigned his position and pled guilty to criminal charges stemming from his molestation of Jane Doe.

II

Procedural History

Jane Doe brought this sec 1983 civil rights lawsuit against Stroud, the school district, Superintendent Caplinger, and Principal Lankford. She charged inter alia that these defendants, while acting under color of state law, deprived her of her constitutional rights guaranteed by the Fourteenth Amendment's Due Process and Equal Protection Clauses, in violation of 42 U.S.C. sec. 1983. Following the denial of their motions for summary judgment on qualified immunity grounds, Caplinger and Lankford filed this appeal. Both contend that they are entitled to qualified immunity because: (1) Jane Doe was not deprived of any constitutional right when she was sexually molested by Coach Stroud; (2) even if Doe was deprived of a constitutional right, they owed her no duty in connection with this constitutional violation; (3) even if Doe was deprived of a constitutional right and they owed her a duty with respect to that right, these issues of law were not "clearly established" in 1987 when the violations took place; and (4) in any event, their response to the situation satisfied any duty that they owed to Doe.

III

Due Process

A

The first step in deciding whether Caplinger and Lankford are entitled to claim qualified immunity from this lawsuit is to determine whether the Constitution, through the Fourteenth Amendment's substantive due process component, protects school-age children attending public schools from sexual abuse inflicted by a school employee. "Section 1983 imposes liability for violations of rights protected by the Constitution, not for violations of duties of care arising out of tort law." . . . To state a cause of action under sec. 1983 for violation of the Due Process Clause, plaintiffs "must show that they have asserted a recognized 'liberty or property' interest within the purview of the Fourteenth Amendment, and that they were intentionally or recklessly deprived of that interest, even temporarily, under color of state law." . . . "The Supreme Court has expanded the definition of 'liberty' beyond the core textual meaning of that term to include [not only] the . . . privileges [expressly] enumerated by the Bill of Rights, [but also] the 'fundamental rights implicit in the concept of ordered liberty' and 'deeply rooted in this Nation's history and tradition' under the Due Process Clause."

Jane Doe's substantive due process claim is grounded upon the premise that schoolchildren have a liberty interest in their bodily integrity that is protected by the Due Process Clause of the Fourteenth Amendment and upon the premise that physical sexual abuse by a school employee violates that right. * * *

If the Constitution protects a schoolchild against being tied to a chair or against arbitrary paddlings, then surely the Constitution protects a schoolchild from physical sexual abuse—here, sexually fondling a 15-year-old school girl and statutory rape—by a public schoolteacher. * * *

B

* * *

This circuit has held that supervisors can be liable for "gross negligence" or "deliberate indifference" to violations of their subordinates.

* * *

The legal elements of an individual's supervisory liability and a political subdivision's liability, however, are similar enough that the same standards of fault and causation should govern. A municipality, with its broad obligation to supervise all of its employees, is liable under sec. 1983 if it supervises its employees in a manner that manifests deliberate indifference to the constitutional rights of citizens. We see no principled reason why an individual to whom the municipality has delegated responsibility to directly supervise the employee should not be held liable under the same standard.

* * *

. . . we adopt the following test, which determines the personal liability of school officials in physical sexual abuse cases. A supervisory school official can be held personally liable for a subordinate's violation of an elementary or secondary school student's constitutional right to bodily integrity in physical sexual abuse cases if the plaintiff establishes that:

1. the defendant learned of facts or a pattern of inappropriate sexual behavior by a subordinate pointing plainly toward the conclusion that the subordinate was sexually abusing the student; and
2. the defendant demonstrated deliberate indifference toward the constitutional rights of the student by failing to take action that was obviously necessary to prevent or stop the abuse; and
3. such failure caused a constitutional injury to the student.

C

We must next consider these legal principles in the context of qualified immunity.

* * *

Although supervisory officials cannot be held liable solely on the basis of their employer-employee relationship with a tortfeasor, they may be liable when their own action or inaction, including a failure to supervise that amounts to gross negligence or deliberate indifference, is a proximate cause of the constitutional violation.

* * *

D

Having established that Jane Doe's constitutional right to bodily integrity and the appellants' duty with respect to that right were clearly established in 1987 when these events occurred, we must determine whether, on the record before us, Lankford and Caplinger have established that they satisfied their duty to Doe, and are thus entitled to summary judgment as a matter of law. The plaintiff in this case has adduced clear summary judgment evidence of deliberate indifference by defendant Lankford toward her constitutional rights.

* * *

Thus, Jane Doe has, in a manner sufficient to withstand a motion for summary judgment, stated a claim under sec. 1983 that defendant Lankford was deliberately indifferent to his subordinate's violation of her constitutional right to bodily integrity.

With respect to whether defendant Caplinger is immune from this lawsuit, however, the evidence presented tells a different story.

* * *

His actions were ineffective, but not deliberately indifferent. Summary judgment should have been granted to defendant Caplinger on the grounds of qualified immunity.

V

* * * we affirm the district court's order denying qualified immunity to defendant Lankford and reverse the district court's order denying qualified immunity to defendant Caplinger. We also remand this case to the district court for further proceedings consistent with this opinion.

AFFIRMED in part, REVERSED in part and REMANDED.

Recent Trends

Essentially this entire area of "employment torts" developed in the decade of the 1990s. In the early 2000s, there are more lawsuits by employees regarding the workplace and employment than ever before, both to retain positions and to increase monetary aspects. However, there is an extensive increase in participants alleging physical and sexual abuse by employees and volunteers. Thus, it behooves all managers to have the various aspects of human resources "in good order," both to prevent lawsuits and, especially, to prevail if sued.

References

Cases

Barkauskie v. Indian River Sch. Dist., 951 F. Supp. 519 (D. Del. 1996).

Bell v. Chesapeake & Ohio Ry. Co., 929 F.2d 220 (6th Cir. 1991)

Bender v. Dakota Resorts Management Group, 700 N.E. 2nd 739 (S.D., 2005).

Byrd v. Bossier Parish School Board, 543 So.2d 35 (La. Ct. App. 1989).

Campanelli v. Bockrath, 100 F.3d 1476 (9th Cir. 1996).

C.B. v. Bobo, 659 So.2d 98 (Ala. 1995).

Chase v. Pinellas Co. Sch. Bd., 597 So.2d 419 (Fla. Dist. Ct. App. 1992).

Doe v. Coffee County Board of Education, 852 S.W.2d 899 (Tenn. Ct. App. 1992).

Doe v. Rains Indep. Sch. Dist., 66 F.3d 1401 (5th Cir. 1995).

Doe v. Taylor Indep. Sch. Dist., 15 F.3d 443 (5th Cir. 1994).

Doe v. Village of St. Joseph, 415 S.E.2d 56 (1992).

D.T. by M.T. v. Indep. Sch. Dist. No. 16, 894 F.2d 1176 (10th Cir. 1990).

Ersek v. Township of Springfield, 822 F. Supp. 218 (E.D. Pa. 1993) aff'd 102 F.3d 79 (3rd Cir. 1996).

Faragher v. City of Boca Raton, 864 F. Supp. 1552 (S.D. Fla. 1994).

Flaskamp v. Dearborn Public Schools, 6th U.S Ct. of Appeals, No. 02-2435 (2005)

Fowler v. Smith, 68 F.3d 124 (5th Cir. 1995).

Gilder-Lucas v. Elmore County Board of Education, U.S. Dist. Ct, Middle Dist. of Ala., Northern Dist., No. 2:04cv825-1 (WO) (2005).

Giordano v. William Paterson College, 804 F. Supp. 637 (D. N.J. 1992).

Haddock v. City of New York, 553 N.E.2d 987 (N.Y. 1990).

Hagan v. Houston Indep. Sch. Dist., 51 F.3d 48 (5th Cir. 1995).

Harris v. Forklift Systems, Inc., 929 F.2d 220 (6th Cir. 1991).

Kolupa v. Roselle Park District, 7th Cir., U.S. Ct of Appeals, No. 05-2925 (2006)

Koop v. Indep. Sch. Dist., 505 N.W.2d 93 (Minn. Ct. App. 1993).

Ludwig v. Board of Trustees of Ferris State Univ., 123 F.3d 404 (6th Cir. 1997).

Meritor Savings Bank, FSB v. Vinson, 477 U.S. 57 (1986).

Nevels v. Board of Education, 822 S.W.2d 898 (Mo. Ct. App. 1991).

Ott v. Edinburgh Community School Corp., U.S. Dist. Ct., Southern Dist. of Indiana, Indianapolis Div., No. 1:03-cv-1413-JDT-WTL (2005)

People v. Arnold, 7 Cal. Rptr. 2d 833 (1992).

People v. Peters, 590 N.Y.S.2d 916 (1992).

Scott v. Neal, Bedford County Circuit Court, No. CLO3010651-00 (2005)

State v. Laird, 547 So.2d 1 (La. Ct. App. 1989).

U.S. Fidelity & Guaranty Co. v. Open Sesame Child Care Center, 819 F. Supp. 756 (N.D. Ill. 1993).

Williams v. Butler, 577 So.2d 1113 (La. Ct. App. 1991).

Publications

Adler, R. S., & Pevice, E. R. (1993). The legal, ethical, and social implications of the "reasonable woman" standard in sexual harassment cases. *Fordham Law Review*, 61, 773–827.

Beeler, C. (2005). Chap. 14 Human resources employment; Chap. 15 Human Resource Management; and Chap. 16 Supervision. In B. van der Smissen, M. Moiseichik, & V. Hartenburg (Eds.), *Management of park and recreation agencies* (2nd ed.). Ashburn, VA: National Recreation and Park Association.

Camacho, R. (1993). How to avoid negligent hiring litigation. *Whittier Law Review*, 14, 787–807.

Caruth, D. L., & Handlogten G. D. (2000, March). Avoid human resource lawsuits. *Fitness Management*, 56–57.

Childers, J. (1993). Notes—Is there a place for a reasonable woman in the law? A discussion of recent developments in hostile environment sexual harassment. *Duke Law Journal*, 42, 854–904.

Fried, G., & Miller, L. (1998). *Employment law—A guide for sport, recreation, and fitness industries*. Durham, NC: Carolina Academic Press.

Hauge, J. C., & Herman, M. L. (1999). Taking the high road—*A guide to effective and legal employment practices for nonprofits*. Washington, DC: Nonprofit Risk Management Center.

Lea, M., & Loughman, E. J. (1993, Fall). Crew, compliance, touchdowns & torts: A survey exploring the legal needs of the modern athletic department and models for satisfying them. *The Entertainment and Sports Lawyer*, 11(3), 14–25.

McConnell, J. H. (2000). *Auditing your human resources department* (2nd ed.). Saronac Lake, NY: Amacon Books (American Management Association).

Herman, M. L. (2004). *No surprises: Harmonizing risk and reward in volunteer management* (3rd ed.). Washington, DC: Nonprofit Risk Management Center.

Mair, D. L., & Herman, M. L. (2003). *Playing to win: A risk management guide for nonprofit sports and recreation*. Washington, DC: Nonprofit Risk Management Center.

Schimmel, D. (1994, May 5). Commentary—Sexual harassment in the workplace: When are hostile comments actionable? *Ed. Law Rep.*, 89, 337.

Shilling, D. (2003). *The complete guide to human resources law*. New York: Aspen Publishers. (annual supplement)

Patterson, J. C. (2004). *Staff screening tool kit* (3rd ed.). Washington, DC: Nonprofit Risk Management Center.

van der Smissen, B. (1990). *Legal liability and risk management for public and private entities*. Cincinnati, OH: Anderson Publishing Company.

Weddle, J. S. (1995, April). Title VII sexual harassment: Recognizing an employer's non-delegable duty to prevent a hostile workplace. *Columbia Law Review*, 95(3), 724–748.

2.36 Hospitality and Tourism Law

Sarah J. Young

Indiana University

Imagine for a moment that you are traveling to an exotic island beach resort in the Caribbean where your travel agent booked reservations for you at a four-star hotel right on the beach. Your departure day finds you waiting for a flight delay that extends into hours causing you to miss your connecting flight and arrive one day late for your vacation. Upon check-in at the hotel, you discover they have overbooked and, because you are a day late, have switched your reservation to a three-star hotel two miles inland. The hotel shuttle is involved in a minor traffic accident en route to your new accommodations, causing you to crack your head on the window. Woozy, you finally get to your hotel, only to find that a family of mice has already taken up residence in your room. You inform the front desk that you must have another room (a clean one!) and go to the restaurant for a bite to eat while the hotel straightens out the room situation. At the restaurant, you eat some bad seafood, which resurrects itself at 3 o'clock in the morning. While you lay curled up on your bed watching the television because your stomach hurts, you learn there is a category-four hurricane headed straight for your location, and authorities are mandating evacuation of the island immediately.

Sound like a tourist's worst nightmare? This might lead one to think about the legal duties and responsibilities of travel agents, airlines, hotels, and restaurants to tourists. Although many of the legal concepts and principles discussed in other chapters of this text apply to tourism settings, there are unique legal aspects that arise because of the very nature of tourism. Barth (2006) recognized the interconnectivity of travel and hospitality as one phenomenon that makes legal issues in tourism unique. For example, vacation packages often include transportation, lodging, meals, and recreation activities. When something goes wrong, and the tourist does not receive what was promised, which service provider should be held liable? It is the reliance of one or more service providers on others for quality performance that makes the area of tourism law more complex. Jurisdiction issues, differences in how travel terms are perceived, identity of the actual service provider, weather, civil unrest, and disease are all factors that can create problems for travelers, tourists, and hotel guests, as well as result in litigation. These factors are phenomena over which hotel and restaurant managers, travel agents, and tour operators may or may not have control. Yet, no one in the travel supply chain is immune from legal action. Therefore, what follows is an overview of legal issues unique to managers in the hospitality and travel industries.

Fundamental Concepts

Hotels and Restaurants

Dating back to English common law, innkeepers and hotel operators had a duty to receive travelers who registered as guests. Today, common law and statutory law identify hotels, motels, and other establishments providing lodging as places of public accommodation and continue to obligate hotel operators to receive all guests. There are circumstances, however, under which the hotel manager may refuse to register an individual as a guest. Typically, if a person is intoxicated, drunk or disorderly, suffers from an obvious contagious disease, brings property into the hotel that could pose a hazard to other guests (e.g., firearms, explosives, animals), or cannot pay for the price of the room, the manager has the right to refuse accommodation (Jeffries, 1995).

For a person visiting a hotel's property to qualify as a guest, the visit must be for the primary purpose for which the hotel operates—the rental of rooms suitable for overnight stay. The duty owed a guest by a hotel is the same as that owed to an invitee. In other words, the hotel owes a guest a reasonably clean and safe accommodation. An example of this duty is provided in *Copeland v. The Lodge Enterprises* (2000), where plaintiff was allegedly bitten by a brown recluse spider while staying at defendant's motel. Plaintiff claimed defendant was grossly negligent in failing to provide a safe premise, free of harmful insects or to warn of their presence. In upholding its duty to provide a reasonably safe accommodation, defendant was able to provide monthly invoices from a pest control service showing they had taken reasonable measures to eliminate such pests.

Overbooking

General contract law is enacted every time a potential guest inquires with the hotel as to the availability of a room for a definite period of time at a specified price. Once agreed upon, either verbally or in writing, a breach of this agreement by either the prospective guest or the hotel can result in liability for damages. The hotel reservation, once made and confirmed, constitutes a contract and binds the hotel to provide accommodations as well as the guest to stay there. Yet, many hotels overbook their rooms because of the persistent problem of no-show guests. History and experience prove that a certain percentage of guests will not use their reservations. As a result, some hotels overbook by the expected attrition rate, and then are not able to accommodate all their reservations when the expected no-show guests do actually appear. *Rainbow Travel Services v. Hilton Hotels, Corp.* (1990) showcases a classic example of the liability that can occur from intentional overbooking. Plaintiff was a tour operator who contracted a block of rooms with the Fontainebleau Hilton in Miami, Florida, for University of Oklahoma football fans. When the fans arrived, there were no rooms available at the Hilton because the hotel overbooked their capacity by 15 percent. Upon further investigation, it was discovered that Hilton had a policy regarding overbooking stating that employees should never admit overbooking, but instead refer to factors beyond the hotel's control. The court ruled in favor of plaintiffs because defendants recklessly accepted more reservations than they were able to accommodate.

Protecting Guest Property

Guests bring a variety of personal property with them during their stays on hotel premises. Typically guests bring money, clothing, jewelry, computers, sports equipment, and perhaps, a vehicle. What is the legal responsibility of the hotel to their guests for this personal property? Historically, this responsibility is based on a rule of absolute liability holding the innkeeper liable for any loss of guest property that was "infra hospitium, or within the inn" (Black, 1990, p. 780). This doctrine emanated from the time when not every innkeeper was honest and often was the culprit of missing guest property. There were exceptions, however, to the absolute liability rule. Loss of property because of an act of God (e.g., tornadoes, floods, earthquakes) and loss of property by a public enemy (e.g., terrorists or acts of war) were two exceptions for which the innkeeper was not held liable. A third exception was the negligence of the guest, such as leaving bags unattended in a hotel lobby, sidewalk, hallway, or public area.

Today most states have enacted statutes limiting liability for guest property loss. If a hotel adheres to the statutes it will be liable for the loss only up to an established maximum amount (e.g., $1,000). This is the case even if a guest's property is worth far more than the maximum amount. Although each state's statutes vary in the details, there are common provisions that hotels must generally follow:

1. The hotel must provide a safe available for guest property.
2. The hotel must post notices communicating the availability of safes.
3. The hotel must communicate to guests that their liability for lost or stolen property is limited.
4. The hotel must communicate the maximum recovery amount allowed.

The availability of limited liability provides an incentive for hotel managers to comply with the strict interpretation of these statutes. Without evidence of compliance, the hotel becomes liable under common law for the full amount of the lost or stolen property.

Within the hospitality industry there are times when a hotel or restaurant manager may be entrusted with a guest's property that is covered under a type of contract law other than the limited liability statute. The theory of bailment is often used by hotels and restaurants for valet parking, coat checks, laundry services, and luggage storage. A **bailment** is defined as the delivery of goods or personal property by one to another with the expectation the property will be returned in the same condition it was received (Black, 1990). *When one hands over possession of his/her personal property for safekeeping by another and the party knowingly has exclusive control over the property, a bailment is established.* The individual who gives his/her property to another is known as the **bailor**, whereas the individual who accepts responsibility for the property is known as the **bailee**. Cournoyer, Marshall, and Morris (2004) identified the essential elements of a bailment as personal property, delivery of possession, acceptance of possession by bailee, and a bailment agreement, either implicit or express. Bailments only involve tangible, personal property like cars, clothing, and sports equipment. Such was the case of *Waterton v. Linden Motor, Inc.* (2006), when plaintiff parked her car in the garage of the hotel where she and her husband had reservations for the night. During the night their car was broken into and several items were stolen. Suing under the theory of bailment, plaintiff claimed the hotel had a duty to replace the lost property and fix the couple's damaged car. The court ruled that even though the car was parked on defendant's premises *no bailment agreement had been established because plaintiff had not given possession of her car to the hotel (i.e., handed over the keys) nor had the hotel specifically accepted responsibility for possession of the car.* Furthermore, because there was a sign posted in defendant's parking garage that purported to limit the inn's responsibility for any loss of or damage to guests' vehicles, the court ruled defendant was not liable for the damages.

Guest Privacy

A registered hotel guest has the right to privacy and peaceful possession of his/her room without disruption from hotel personnel. Cournoyer et al. (2004) identified five exceptions to this right of hotel guests. An innkeeper is authorized to enter a guest's room for normal maintenance, to warn of imminent danger, for nonpayment of the room, when requested to enter by the guest, and upon expiration of the rental period. Unless there is a legal basis for entry, hotel staff and nonguests are not permitted to enter a guest's room at will. However, sometimes guests engage in illegal activity in their hotel rooms. If evidence of illegal activity is discovered by a hotel employee who is legally in the guest's room, the hotel has an obligation to report their findings to the police. This was the case in *United States v. Coles* (2006), when the hotel manager entered a guest's room to see if it was still occupied as well as to discuss with the guest his payment for the room. Upon entering, the manager observed a plastic bag and small vials containing a white substance. Believing he had seen illegal drugs, he contacted the police, which he was obligated to do.

Recreational Facilities

Often hotels will provide additional services and facilities such as spas, swimming pools, workout rooms, trails, putting greens, and other specialized facilities for their guests' enjoyment. In most states, the general standard for hotels is to exercise reasonable care in preventing injury to a guest who uses these activity areas. Whether reasonable care is exercised depends on the facts and circumstances in each case. In *Bradshaw v. ITT Sheraton Corporation* (2005), plaintiff sued after she fell off a carpeted transition incline leading to the dance floor. Summary judgment for the hotel was denied because there were factual questions as to whether defendant failed to exercise reasonable care to protect its guests from harm.

Because they are attractive to guests, especially children, most hotels and motels have aquatics facilities on their property, yet aquatics facilities represent a potential liability to the hotel operator. Attention to detail in maintaining a reasonably safe pool area is emphasized in *Turner v. Holiday Inn Holidome* (1999), where the hotel was found liable, in part, for a young girl's drowning because the hotel manager knew the pool water had a tendency to become cloudy with heavy use. The child, who could not swim, was pulled from the bottom of the pool after another person in her group stepped on her in the cloudy pool water. The court held that defendant had a duty to provide a reasonably safe swimming facility, and that by having actual notice of the cloudy water, had breached that duty.

Because hotels have access to recreational activity areas does not always mean the area is within their **sphere of control.** *Fabend v. Rosewood Hotels and Resorts* (2004) illustrates this concept. Plaintiff sued the Rosewood Hotel and the National Park Service (NPS) after he was injured bodysurfing in the Virgin Islands. He claimed the hotel failed to warn him of a dangerous shorebreak condition on the beach, which created a forceful wave driving him into the sand and leaving him a quadriplegic. Although the hotel advertised the white, sandy beaches in their promotional materials, the NPS maintained physical control over all the beaches. Additionally, NPS provided signs and brochures warning visitors of the dangerous conditions of the park. The court ruled that because the beach was not in the hotel's sphere of control, it did not have a legal duty to warn swimmers of the shorebreak danger.

Administrative Law

Administrative law is defined as the powers, limitations, and procedures of administrative agencies at the federal, state, and local government levels. This area of law affects the hospitality industry through numerous regulatory agencies, administrations, and commissions authorized by different levels of government to enforce compliance with the law.

An example of a **federal administrative agency** is the Occupational Health and Safety Administration (OSHA). OSHA was established to ensure a safe working environment through the setting and enforcement of standards, training, and continual improvements for workplace safety and health. Hospitality managers have a legal obligation under OSHA regulations to meet standards for walking surfaces, stairs, personal protective equipment, laundry equipment, and blood-borne pathogens as well as report, on an annual basis, work-related employee injuries and illnesses. OSHA inspectors are authorized to visit hotel or restaurant properties unannounced during regular work hours to check for compliance with standards. Inspectors are also likely to investigate workplace accidents, as was the case in *Trumps v. Toastmaster* (1997). Plaintiff, a kitchen employee at an upper Manhattan hotel restaurant, was shocked off her feet from an electric current while placing a piece of chicken on an allegedly defective grill. While plaintiff's claim focused on products liability, OSHA inspectors visited the site of the accident to make sure the hotel was not in violation of safety regulations.

Similar to the federal regulatory agencies, there are **state agencies** designed to regulate business and industry. State regulatory agencies are complementary in that they "support and amplify efforts" (Barth, 2006, p. 128) at the federal level, yet are distinct in that they regulate some areas over which states have sole responsibility. For example, an alcoholic beverage commission (ABC) or control board is a state regulatory agency established for the purpose of overseeing applications for alcoholic beverage licenses and controlling the use, manufacture, sale, transport, storage, and advertisement of alcoholic beverages. Food service and lodging operations selling and serving alcohol must be in compliance with ABC regulations or face penalties. In *Thorobred, Inc. v. Louisville/Jefferson County Metro Government* (2005), plaintiff complained of improper and warrantless searches of his establishments by the state's Alcoholic Beverage Control Board (ABCB). Although all plaintiff's properties held licenses to sell alcoholic beverages, he claimed the ABCBs searches were unconstitutional. The court ruled that although the state does have the authority to conduct warrantless inspections of all premises where alcoholic beverages are sold, they must limit the discretion of inspectors in terms of time, place and scope. Although state ABCs do have regulatory power through administrative law, they cannot be unconstitutional in the manner in which inspections are conducted.

Local governmental agencies also regulate hospitality operators. Typical regulatory agencies at the local level include health and sanitation departments, building and zoning commissions, and planning boards. Local fire departments play a crucial role in facility inspections, ensuring emergency lighting and sprinklers are properly installed and maintained, and can even help with fire safety training for hospitality managers and their employees. Failing to provide adequate security and fire protection was plaintiff's claim in *Allen v. Greenville Hotel Partners, Inc.* (2006) after a fire at a Comfort Inn and Suites resulted in the deaths of six guests and severe injuries to 12 additional guests. The cause of the fire was arson, leading to plaintiff's negligence claim for the hotel installing inadequate sprinklers, leaving the back door to the hotel unlocked, and failing to install surveillance cameras. Additionally, plaintiff claimed the hotel had negligently trained their employees to disengage an active fire alarm until confirming the presence of an actual fire. Not only was this alleged training an obvious violation of fire safety codes, but it created an unnecessary delay in warning guests of the fire danger.

Travel and Tourism

Jurisdiction

A resident of New York City was injured while on vacation at a hotel casino in Las Vegas. The injured party sued the hotel for negligence, claiming the hotel's employees left a chair in a common pedestrian area, causing her to fall (*Smith v. Circus Circus Casinos, Inc.*, 2003). In which state, Nevada or New York, should the plaintiff make her claim? Most people expect to file a claim or commence a lawsuit in their local courts, yet when travel is involved, the plaintiff's local court must have jurisdiction (see Chapter 1.10, *The Legal System*). **Jurisdiction** is defined as the authority of the court to "decide a matter of controversy" (Black, 1990, p. 853) as well as maintain control over the subject matter and parties to the dispute. In most states, jurisdiction over corporate defendants is determined by the amount and frequency of business defendants conduct in a given state. Generally, "doing business" depends on factors such as the existence of an office in the state, the solicitation of business, the presence of bank accounts or property in the state, and the presence of employees. The importance of establishing jurisdiction is illustrated in *Heidle v. Prospect Reef Resort* (2005), where plaintiff and her boyfriend vacationed in the British Virgin Islands. Plaintiff was injured when she fell into a cistern after the cover upon which she was standing caved in. As a resident of New York and because she had purchased her vacation package through a travel wholesaler located in her home state, plaintiff brought forth her claim in a New York court. Yet, because defendant did not meet the criteria of doing business in the state of New York, plaintiff was unable to prove that a New York court would have jurisdiction.

Internet Sales. The sale of travel and vacation packages via the Internet has not only increased astronomically over the past decade, but also affects the jurisdiction of legal claims. A number of courts have adopted a sliding scale analysis categorizing Websites as passive, active, or interactive for the purpose of determining whether specific jurisdiction exists (*Zippo Manufacturing, Co. v. Zippo Dot Com*, 1997). A passive Website containing information about the hotel or travel destination available to the general public, but not providing a way to take reservations, is viewed as an insufficient basis for establishing jurisdiction. In *Cervantes v. Ramparts, Inc.* (2003), a California plaintiff filed suit against the Luxor Hotel located in Las Vegas, Nevada, after he slipped and fell in the hotel's restroom. Plaintiff tried to establish that California courts would have jurisdiction over the defendant because defendant maintained a Website accessible in California. The court disagreed, noting the hotel's Website was passive and only provided information about the Luxor. On the other end of the scale, an interactive Website is generally characterized by information, e-mail communication, detailed descriptions of goods and services, and online sales. *Decker v. Circus Circus Hotel* (1999) illustrates this type of web site. Plaintiffs, New Jersey residents, sought relief for personal injury from defendant, a hotel located in Nevada. Defendant provided to the general public a Website on which customers could make reservations. The court ruled that jurisdiction over a defendant could be exercised under two conditions: (1) where the Website is used to actively transact business, and (2) where a consumer can exchange information with the host computer. In *Decker*, a customer could make a reservation on the hotel's Website, resulting in defendants effectively placing their business and its services into the stream of commerce of the state of New Jersey.

Forum Non Conveniens. Related to issues of jurisdiction is **forum non conveniens**, which refers to the discretionary power of the court to decline jurisdiction when "convenience of the parties and justice would be better served if the case was brought forth in another forum" (Black, 1990, p. 655). In determining whether a different venue would be more convenient for the parties involved in a case, the court typically considers three factors provided by an analysis from a 1947 U.S. Supreme Court case (*Gulf Oil Corp. v. Gilbert*). First, the court must determine whether an alternative forum exists. For example, a New Jersey couple was a guest of the Regent Hotel in Hong Kong when the wife fell on a ramp in the hotel and sustained injuries. Plaintiff alleged negligence against the hotel for poor maintenance and failure to install handrails. Hong Kong was deemed an adequate alternative forum because Hong Kong law follows the same basic principles of tort law as does a New Jersey court (*Karlitz v. Regent International Hotels, Ltd.*, 1997)

Secondly, the court must determine the private interest of the litigant including the relative ease of access to sources of proof, availability of compulsory processes to obtain unwilling witnesses' attendance in court, cost of obtaining attendance of witnesses, the possibility of viewing the premises, and any other practical considerations that make the hearing of a case more expedient and less expensive. The third and final consideration balances public interest factors such as court congestion, the burden of jury duty on the people of the community who have no relation to the litigation, and the appropriateness of trying a case in a forum familiar with the governing law of the case. A good illustration of how forum non conveniens works is found in *Becker v. Club Las Velas* (1995). While vacationing in Cancun, Mexico, plaintiff was injured kayaking in a lagoon near Club Las Velas. Plaintiff, a resident of New Jersey, sued defendant for a variety of negligence claims in federal district court because defendants conducted business in New York and maintained an office in that state. Club Las Velas moved to dismiss the case on grounds of forum non conveniens. After determining Mexico was an adequate alternative forum because their laws recognized negligence as a cause of action, the court concluded that private and public interest factors favored the trial taking place in Mexico. This decision was supported by the facts that all defendant's witnesses were located in Mexico and that Mexico had a greater public interest in adjudicating an action concerning a boating accident in a Mexican federal waterway than did New York.

Often tourist destinations and common carriers will include a **forum selection clause** in the agreement between agency and tourist citing any litigation must be brought forth in the court where the agency is headquartered.[1] Dickerson (2004) explained that hospitality and travel providers institute forum selection clauses as a way to discourage guests or travelers from prosecuting their legal claims. For example in the *Decker v. Circus Circus Hotel* (1999) case discussed earlier, although the Website placed the hotel into the stream of commerce, the defendant's Internet site contained a forum selection clause requiring all guests who made their reservations via the Website to agree to have their disputes settled in Nevada courts.

Forum selection clauses are generally enforceable, but must be provided to customers with adequate notice and be reasonable and fair. *Stobaugh v. Norwegian Cruise Line* (1999) provides a good example of when a travel service provider's forum selection clause was deemed fundamentally unfair. Plaintiffs, residents of Texas, had contracted with the cruise line to take a seven-day cruise to Bermuda departing August 31. They received their passenger tickets with all the terms of the agreement, including the forum selection clause, on August 8. A few days before their departure, plaintiffs learned of several tropical storm systems in the Atlantic Ocean. On inquiring with Norwegian about refunds if they decided to cancel on account of the weather, they were told they should proceed with the trip and trust the judgment of the ship's captain. Plaintiffs did as was suggested, and defendant's ship sailed into Hurricane Eduardo, which allegedly resulted in physical and emotional injuries to many passengers on board. Plaintiffs filed a class action lawsuit in Texas court against Norwegian Cruise Lines, who asserted their forum selection clause (based in Florida) as a basis to dismiss the case. The court ruled against the cruise line stating that because their forum selection clause was not clearly communicated to passengers until after they paid in full for the cruise, the clause was not fair nor enforceable.

Liability waivers used to protect cruise lines from liability for injuries aboard ship are not enforceable. Federal statute 46 App. U.S.C.A. sec. 183c reads

> It shall be unlawful for . . . owner of any vessel transporting passengers...to insert any . . . provision or limitation purporting, in the event of loss of life or bodily injury arising from the negligence or fault, . . . to relieve such owner . . . from liability. . . . All such provisions or limitations . . . are declared to be against public policy and shall be null and void and of no effect.

---

[1] Clauses specifying the venue and jurisdiction in which any subsequent legal action may be brought are generally enforced by the courts. Likewise, clauses calling for mandatory arbitration rather than legal action in the courts are also enforced. For more information, see Cotten, D. J., & Cotten, M. B. (2005), chap. 6.

Generally, waivers used by the ship for land tours are enforced. (For more information, see Cotten, D. J., & Cotten, M. B., 2005, chap. 6.)

Transportation

Transportation is another major dimension of the travel and tourism industry with airplanes, cruise ships, buses, tour buses, trains, and taxis serving as common carriers. A **common carrier** is one who takes on the responsibility to transport from place to place any person who chooses to employ it for hire (Black, 1990). A common carrier owes its passengers the highest degree of care with the passenger–carrier relationship continuing until the passenger has had a reasonable opportunity to reach a place of safety. Furthermore, common carriers are vicariously liable for their employees' intentional and negligent torts, even when they are committed outside the scope of employment (*Twardy v. Northwest Airlines, Inc.*, 2001).

Air travel is the method of choice for long-distance travel for many tourists. The contract between an airline and its passengers is known as a **tariff** and outlines the terms to which the passenger agrees when purchasing a ticket. The terms of the tariff affect how passengers are treated and vary among the major carriers. For example, not all airlines have the same policy regarding flight delays and how passengers whose flights are delayed are handled. The terms of handling flight delays are contained in the tariff, or ticket information. On the other hand, federal regulations require all airlines to provide a standard compensation to passengers who are bumped from their flights due to overbooking. Although most passengers accept the airlines' compensation, there are some who choose to claim damages for breach of contract of the tariff. A bumped passenger claiming contract damages may sue for costs of alternate transportation, meals, and compensation for inconvenience caused by the bump. Illustrated in *Stone v. Continental Airlines* (2005), plaintiff and his thirteen-year-old daughter were bumped on Christmas day from their flight from New York City to Telluride, Colorado, for a ski trip. Plaintiff was awarded damages totaling $3,110 for unrecoverable lodging accommodations, lost baggage, and inconvenience of missing the scheduled holiday vacation trip.

For airlines operating international flights, liability for personal injury, damaged or lost baggage, and damages caused by delays is limited by the Warsaw Convention. The **Warsaw Convention** is an international treaty, to which the United States is a party, governing and limiting the liability of air carriers transporting passengers and cargo on international flights. For example, in *Bernardi v. Apple Vacations* (2002) plaintiff originally filed her claim in a Pennsylvania state court for extreme and inhumane conditions suffered by passengers during an international flight. Yet, because the U.S. is a signatory to the convention, not only was defendant's liability limited, but plaintiff's state law claims were preempted by the Warsaw Convention. Applicable only to the actual flight, the Warsaw Convention does not limit the liability of airport security checkpoints for stolen bags, as shown by *Dazo v. Globe Airport Security Services* (2002). The passenger's carry-on bag containing over $100,000 worth of jewelry was stolen as she passed through the metal detector on an international flight connecting in St. Louis, Missouri. The security company attempted to seek shelter from liability through the Warsaw Convention, but the court ruled the limitation on liability did not apply.

Vacations aboard luxury **cruise ships** have increased in popularity with an estimate of more than 11 million people participating in cruises in 2005 (Cruise Industry, 2006). Modern-day cruise ships are essentially floating hotels (Barth, 2006; Dickerson, 2004) with amenities including ice-skating rinks, rock-climbing walls, golf simulators, water slides, private pools, spas, and planetariums. As a result, many of the legal issues of guest safety, security, and liability are similar to those faced by land-based hospitality managers. Furthermore, like all common carriers, those operating cruise ships are subject to a wide array of local, state, federal, and international laws. Yet, in addition to these legal principles, cruise ships and their passengers are subject to **maritime laws**, a system of law relating to navigable waters. In *Mainzer v. Royal Olympic Cruises* (1998) plaintiff claimed damages for defendant's loss of a piece of luggage and for poor service on a South American cruise. The district court found in favor of plaintiff and awarded partial damages. The appellate court dismissed the lower court's ruling, however, because U.S. courts are bound to application of federal maritime law in resolving these types of disputes.

Similar to the limits on liability provided for international air travel, the **Athens Convention** limits liability of cruise ships to passengers aboard cruises not touching a U.S. port. Although the United States is not a signatory to the Athens Convention, many of the cruise lines serving U.S. passengers are owned by companies located in countries that do abide by the terms of the convention. For example, in *Henson v. Seabourn Cruise Line Limited, Inc.* (2005), defendant sought limits on liability from negligence claims by the plaintiff. Defendant cruise line was flagged as a vessel of the Bahamas, which is party to the treaty, and the Athens Convention was included as a term in the ticket contract with the plaintiff. The court ruled, however, that because the cruise was scheduled to make several stops at U.S. ports, U.S. federal law prevailed over the liability limitations of the Athens Convention.

Agency Law

Inherent to understanding legal liability in the travel and tourism industry is agency law, an area of law governed by a combination of contract law and tort law (Cheeseman, 2004). At the heart of agency law is the principal–agent relationship. A party employing another to act on its behalf is known as the **principal**, whereas the **agent** becomes the party agreeing to act on another's behalf. The **principal–agent relationship** is created when both parties agree that the agent has the authority to represent the principal and can enter into contracts on the principal's behalf. This principal–agent relationship is illustrated in *Black v. Delta Airlines, Inc.* (2002), where the defendant airline denied that the travel agency from which plaintiff had purchased tickets was an agent of their company. Plaintiff had purchased two first-class tickets from a travel agency for a trip from Dallas, Texas, to Las Vegas, Nevada. Plaintiff was told by the travel agent that both he and his wife were confirmed for round-trip first-class travel. Yet, on arrival at the terminal gate, only plaintiff's ticket was confirmed for first-class and his wife's ticket was confirmed for coach with a priority wait list for first-class. On further investigation, it was discovered that the travel agency's computer showed confirmed first-class travel for both travelers, but Delta's computer showed confirmed first-class travel for only one ticket. Defendant moved for summary judgment by stating the travel agency was not acting as an agent for their airline. The court denied the motion and ruled that when a travel agent issues a ticket, the travel agent acts on behalf of the carrier.

Formation of the agency relationship can occur through an express agreement, an implied agreement, or an apparent agency. The express agreement involves either an oral or written contract, whereas the implied agreement is inferred by the conduct of both parties. An **apparent agent** is one whom the principal allows others to believe is acting as its agent, regardless of whether or not the principal has actually conferred that authority (Black, 1990, p. 63). This concept is illustrated in *Cash v. Six Continents Hotels* (2004), where a tour operator, Harmony Tours, maintained a desk in the lobby of the Holiday Inn Sunspree Hotel in Montego Bay, Jamaica. Plaintiffs booked a tour with Harmony to Dunn's River Falls, where they were dropped off and left for a long period of time without guidance or assistance. It was during this time that plaintiffs were injured while trying to climb the waterfall. Plaintiffs sued the hotel for negligence, assuming that Harmony was an agent of the hotel. Evidence revealed that Harmony Tours was an independent contractor and that nowhere in the promotional literature of either the hotel or Harmony was it represented that Harmony was an agent of the hotel. Although the hotel allowed Harmony to promote its tours in their lobby, there was no agency relationship between the two service providers.

Travel Agents. Many people making travel plans use the services of a travel agent whose job is to provide customers travel information, organize travel packages, and sell travel services such as airline tickets, cruise vacations, hotel rooms, and excursion trips. Travel agents work on commission from airlines, hotels, tour operators, and other types of travel services, making them legal representatives (agents) of the service provider (principal). Although travel agents are viewed as legal representatives of different travel services, they also have a duty to their customers to act with skill, care, and diligence in rendering the kind of services that can reasonably be expected.

Travel agents are not insurers or guarantors of customers' travel safety including quality issues of lodging accommodations. When a travel agent has knowledge of safety factors or quality issues, he/she has a duty to inform the customer of those facts. For example, in *Shlivko v. Good Luck Travel, Inc.* (2003) plaintiff sought a refund for the price of a vacation trip to London because she was dissatisfied with the unsanitary quality of the hotel accommodations. The court ruled that had defendant known about the quality of the accommodations and withheld that information from the plaintiff, then defendant would be held liable. As it turned out, the court found no evidence that defendant knew or had reason to know of the unsanitary hotel conditions, nor did they have a duty to investigate those conditions without a specific request.

When customers rely on the expertise of travel agents for information about third-party suppliers (such as tour operators), the travel agent has a duty to provide accurate information and take reasonable care in investigating these travel suppliers. The role of the travel agent in terms of third-party suppliers is illustrated in *Adames v. Trans National Travel* (1998). Plaintiff won a trip through a radio station contest that was chartered through defendant, a travel agency that in turn booked the transportation to Cancun, Mexico, and hotel accommodations for seven nights. While on the free trip, plaintiff purchased an excursion tour from an independent tour operator for an island adventure cruise on which plaintiff was injured. Plaintiff sued the travel agency claiming it had a duty to warn of dangers involved with all the activities of the travel package. The court granted summary judgment to the travel agency stating that to find such a duty would necessitate the travel agent to inform travelers of all possible dangers of each third-party excursion and that this would be too large of a burden on the travel industry.

Tour Operators. Tour operators are distinguished from travel agents in that operators are usually in a position to actually provide a travel service, such as excursions, guided tours, and trips. Tour operators are often considered the primary provider of the service, whereas the travel agent is a representative of their services. Tour operators can be held liable for their own negligent actions that result in injuries to tourists. A bicycle tour company could be held liable for selection of a dangerous road for the tour (*Coles v. Jenkins*, 1998). Likewise, a Peruvian tour operator involved in a traffic accident while transporting passengers from the airport could be liable for injuries to the passengers (*Vermeulen v. Worldwide Holidays, Inc.*, 2006). However, like the travel agent, if a tour operator is contracting with another third-party travel supplier, then they are not liable for the negligence of that third-party supplier provided they exercised care in the selection of the supplier.

When a travel agent accepts the additional role of tour operator, the agent assumes the duties and responsibilities of the principal, or the actual service provider. An Arizona travel agency organized, promoted, sold, and operated student vacation tours to Mazatlan, Mexico, which plaintiff's eighteen-year old-daughter, Molly, had purchased. Part of the tour was a train ride called the party train, from which Molly fell when walking from one train car to another (*Maurer v. Cerkvenik-Anderson Travel*, 1994). The travel agency, relying on its role of agent, claimed it had no duty to control the train to make it safe, nor did it have knowledge of the specific condition causing Molly's death. The court disagreed and ruled that because of defendant's dual role as both agent and principal, the travel agency had a duty to warn of dangers of which they were aware, or should have been aware. In another illustration of a travel agent taking on the role of tour operator, a Chicago independent travel agent made arrangements for a private school's eighth-grade graduation trip to Six Flags near St. Louis, Missouri (*Lewis v. Elsin*, 2002). Additionally, the travel agent agreed to serve as the group's tour guide and accompanied them on the trip. Upon check-in at the hotel where the group was staying overnight, defendant left the group and went out for the evening. While absent from the group, one of the students drowned in the hotel's swimming pool. The travel agent/tour guide was sued because he had neglected his role as tour guide and failed to provide for appropriate supervision of the pool area for the group.

Tour operators can gain some protection by using liability waivers and disclaimers. Such agreements are governed by the federal statute, 14 C.F.R. sec. 380.32(x) (1998). The regulation provides that exculpatory agreements in contracts, drawn in accord with the regulation, may expressly provide that the operator is not responsible for personal injuries caused by common direct air carrier, hotel, or other supplier of services unless the tour operator is negligent. (See Cotten, D. J., & Cotten, M. B., 2005, chap. 6, for more detail.)

Significant Case

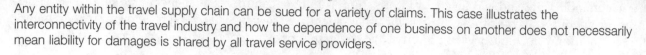

Any entity within the travel supply chain can be sued for a variety of claims. This case illustrates the interconnectivity of the travel industry and how the dependence of one business on another does not necessarily mean liability for damages is shared by all travel service providers.

COLLETTE V. UNIQUE VACATIONS, INC.

State of Massachusetts, Appellate Division, Northern District
2004 Mass. App. Div. 59
2004 Mass. App. Div. LEXIS 19
March 30, 2004, Decided

Opinion By: Judge Greco

The evidence introduced during the trial of this case would have warranted a finding that the plaintiffs' honeymoon at Sandals Resort was ruined by a hurricane. What made this loss the subject of litigation as opposed to merely bad luck was Sandals' Blue Chip Hurricane Guarantee by which Sandals promised a free replacement vacation with round trip airfare if a hurricane interrupted a customer's stay. * * *

After a jury-waived trial, the plaintiffs recovered $3,922.00 on their breach of contract claim against Unique. The trial judge also found that Unique had violated the Consumer Protection Act, G.L.c. 93A, and awarded triple damages to the plaintiffs plus costs and attorney's fees. Unique filed this appeal on the ground *inter alia*, that the evidence was insufficient as a matter of law to warrant the court's findings against it on either the plaintiff's contract claim or their G.L.c. 93A claim* * *

Viewed in the light most favorable to the plaintiffs, the evidence indicated the following: Plaintiffs Heather and Kevin Collette booked their honeymoon trip through the Vacation Outlet at Filene's Basement Store. The accommodation component of that trip was a stay of seven nights to be split between two Sandals resorts in Jamaica at Negril Beach and Montego Bay. One of the main reasons the Collettes picked Sandals was the hurricane guarantee mentioned above, which was set forth in writing in a Sandals' brochure and which they specifically discussed with the Vacation Outlet employee with whom they dealt. The Collettes paid for the accommodations by a check made out to the Vacation Outlet. The Vacation Outlet then, in turn booked the hotel reservations with defendant Unique Vacations, Inc. In so doing, the Vacation Outlet generated a written "Passenger Invoice and Confirmation," which listed Sunburst Holidays as the airline vendor and Unique as the hotel vendor. The Vacation Outlet also forwarded payment to Unique in the amount of the money paid by the Collettes, less Vacation Outlet's commission. The Collettes had no personal dealing with any employee of Unique in planning their honeymoon.

Because of Hurricane Mitch, the Collettes were unable to use many of the facilities at Negril Beach. Three of the four restaurants there were closed, and many resort activities were not available. Moreover, the Collettes were not able to go to the second resort at Montego Bay. During their stay at Sandals, the Collettes had no contact with any employee of Unique to complain about the accommodations or for any other purpose. In fact, the Collettes' only interaction with Unique involved complaints which they made after the trip. After the Vacation Outlet contacted Unique to learn who would be the appropriate person at Sandals to address the Collettes' concerns, the Collettes sent G.L.c. 93A demand letters to Sandals, the Vacation Outlet, and Unique. Sandals and the Vacation Outlet responded, but Unique did not. Sandals' response, however, offered a complimentary stay at its resort but instructed the Collettes to contact Unique to select a date in order to accept its offer.

The Sandals brochure stated that "Sandals Resorts and beaches are represented worldwide by Unique Vacations." Unique is a Florida corporation with its principal place of business in Miami. Its Miami address was listed on the Sandals' brochure. If one were to call the toll free number given in the brochure, one would reach the offices of Unique and would be able to make reservations for any Sandals resort without going through a travel agent such as the Vacation Outlet. There was testimony at trial that Unique provided marketing and reservation services to Sandals and had the exclusive right to use the Sandals name and logo for purposes of taking reservations. No evidence was presented, however, as to who owned the two Sandals Resorts in Jamaica, who owned Unique, who held management positions in the corporations, or who held stock.

In essence, the evidence at trial indicated only that Unique was held out to be the worldwide representative of Sandals and had the exclusive right to use the Sandals name in the booking of reservations. Unique's only connection to the travel arrangements for the Collettes was its acceptance of payment from the Vacation Outlet. There was no evidence of what Unique did with this money. Such evidence would have warranted a finding that Unique was Sandals' agent and, perhaps, that the Collettes knew Unique was Sandals' representative, assuming they read every word in the brochure. However, Unique would not have become a party to any contract made with the Collettes because its principal, Sandals, was disclosed. Moreover, there was no evidence that Unique played any role in formulating or offering the Blue Chip Hurricane Guarantee, that the Collettes dealt directly with Unique in making their decision to go to Sandals, or that they even discussed the Hurricane Guarantee with anyone from Unique.

In these circumstances, the Collettes could have recovered on their breach of contract claim against Unique only if there had been some evidence which indicated that Sandals and Unique were engaged in a joint venture. * * * As noted, there was no evidence in this case that Unique had any role in the control or management of the Sandals resorts, other than to accept bookings. The Collettes' attempt to portray Unique as a Sandals principal is not advanced by their characterization of Unique as a tour operator. First, it is far from clear whether Unique was, in fact, a tour operator, which is defined as a seller of travel services that creates and sells travel packages. In any event, a tour operator is not liable for the negligence of a third part supplier of services which the tour operator does not operate, manage, or control.

* * *

Applying these factors, the evidence in the record before us was insufficient to permit the trial judge to disregard the separate corporate identities of Sandals and Unique. There was no evidence of who owned Sandals and who owned Unique, who ran the two companies, whether Unique did anything other than to take reservations, whether employees of Unique wrote the Sandals brochure or had any say in how the Sandals resorts were run or conversely, whether Sandals actively participated in the day to day operations of Unique. The Collettes could never have been deceived by Unique, never discussed the Guarantee with anyone from Unique, and had no reason to be aware of the mechanics of the reservation process or to be concerned about it. * * *

As the evidence was insufficient to permit a finding of a breach of contract or a G.L.c. 93A violation by Unique, the judgment against the defendant cannot stand. The judgment for the plaintiffs is reversed and vacated. A judgment for the defendant, Unique Vacations, Inc., is to be entered.

Recent Trends

Amusement Park Rides Classified as Common Carriers

In a California Supreme Court decision, amusement park rides can be classified as common carriers requiring a heightened standard of care by park operators. In *Gomez v. Superior Court* (2005), the California court reasoned that because patrons of such rides surrender themselves to the care and custody of the amusement park, the operators owe them the utmost care and diligence for their safe carriage. Defendant, Disney, argued that because the primary purpose of amusement park rides is entertainment that they should not be considered common carriers. The court disagreed by stating the passenger's purpose should not affect the duty of the carrier to exercise the highest degree of care for its passengers. Amusement rides are viewed as common carriers in a number of states besides California. This trend has implications for amusement park owners as well as ride operators, as each should be aware of the interpretation of common carriers in the state of their operation.

ADA Applies to Cruise Ships

Precipitated by a complaint that passengers with disabilities were denied access to various facilities on their cruise ship, the U.S. Supreme Court ruled that Title III of the Americans with Disabilities Act (1990) did apply to cruise ships. In *Spector v. Norwegian Cruise Line, Ltd.* (2005), the Supreme Court ruled that cruise ships fell within Title III's definition of public accommodation and specified public transportation. As long as modifications to allow access would not conflict with a ship's international legal obligations, the Court reasoned the United States has a strong interest in ensuring that its resident cruise passengers enjoy Title III protections on both domestic and foreign-flagged ships. As a result cruise lines must see that all new ships are in compliance with ADA regulations and that reasonable modifications are made in all existing ships.

References

Cases

Adames v. Trans National Travel, 1998 Mass. Super. LEXIS 108 (1998)

Allen v. Greenville Hotel Partners, Inc., 2006 U.S. Dist. LEXIS 1855 (2006)

Becker v. Club Las Velas, 1995 U.S. Dist. LEXIS 6101 (1995)

Bernardi v. Apple Vacations, 236 F. Supp. 2d 465 (2002)

Black v. Delta Airlines, Inc., 160 S.W.3d 68 (2002)

Bradshaw v. ITT Sheraton Corporation, 2005 Mass. Super. LEXIS 331 (2005)

Cash v. Six Continents Hotels, 2004 U.S. Dist. LEXIS 2901 (2004)

Cervantes v. Ramparts, Inc., 2003 Cal. App. Unpub. LEXIS 1283 (2003)

Coles v. Jenkins, 34 F.Supp.2d 381 (1998)

Collette v. Unique Vacations, Inc., 2004 Mass. App. Div. LEXIS 19 (2004)

Copeland v. The Lodge Enterprises, Inc., 4 P.3d 695 (2000)

Dazo v. Globe Airport Security Services, 295 F.3d 934 (2002)

Decker v. Circus Circus Hotel, 49 F.Supp.2d 743 (1999)

Fabend v. Rosewood Hotels and Resorts, L.L.C., 381 F.3d 152 (2004)

Gomez v. Superior Court, 29 Cal. Rptr.3d 352 (2005)

Gulf Oil Co. v. Gilbert, 1947

Heidle v. The Prospect Reef Resort, Ltd., 364 F.Supp.2d 312 (2005)

Henson v. Seabourn Cruise Line Limited, Inc., 2005 U.S. Dist. LEXIS 26221 (2005)

Karlitz v. Regent International Hotels, Ltd., 1997 U.S. Dist. LEXIS 2111 (1997)

Lewis v. Elsin, 2002 Mo. App. LEXIS 435 (2002)

Mainzer v. Royal Olympic Cruises, Ltd., 677 N.Y.S.2d 668 (1998)

Maurer v. Cerkvenik-Anderson Travel, Inc., 890 P.2d 69 (1994)

Rainbow Travel Services v. Hilton Hotels, Corp., 896 F.2d 1233 (10th Cir. 1990)

Shlivko v. Good Luck Travel, Inc., 763 N.Y.S.2d 906 (2003)

Smith v. Circus Circus Casinos, Inc., 304 F.Supp.2d 463 (2003)

Spector v. Norwegian Cruise Line Ltd., 125 S. Ct. 2169 (2005)

Stobaugh v. Norwegian Cruise Line Limited, 5 S.W.3d 232 (1999)

Stone v. Continental Airlines, 804 N.Y.S.2d 652 (2005)

Thorobred, Inc. v. Louisville/Jefferson County Metro Government, 2005 U.S. Dist. LEXIS 22116 (2005)

Trumps v. Toastmaster, Inc., 969 F. Supp. 247 (1997)

Turner v. Holiday Inn Holidome, 721 So.2d 64 (1999)

Twardy v. Northwest Airlines, Inc., 2001 U.S. Dist. LEXIS 2112 (2001)

United States of America v. Coles, 2006 U.S. App. LEXIS 3122 (2006)

Vermeulen v. Worldwide Holidays, Inc., 2006 Fla. App. LEXIS 1551 (2006)

Waterton v. Linden Motor, Inc., 2006 N.Y. Misc. LEXIS 261 (2006)

Zippo Manufacturing Co. v. Zippo Dot Com, 1997

Publications

Barth, S. (2006). *Hospitality law* (2nd ed.). Hoboken, NJ: John Wiley & Sons.

Black, H. C. (1990). *Black's law dictionary* (6th ed.). St. Paul, MN: West Publishing Co.

Cheeseman, H. R. (2004). *Business law* (5th ed.). Upper Saddle River, NJ: Pearson Education.

Cotten, D. J., & Cotten, M. B. (2005). *Waivers & Releases of Liability* (5th ed.). www.lulu.com.

Cournoyer, N. G., Marshall, A. G., & Morris, K. L. (2004). *Hotel, restaurant, and travel law: A preventive approach* (6th ed.). Clifton Park, NY: Delmar Learning.

Cruise industry association predicts a robust 2006. (2006, January 16). *Daily Travel & Tourism Newsletter*. Retrieved February 26, 2006 from http://www.traveldailynews.com

Dickerson, T. A. (2004). Recent development: The cruise passenger's dilemma: Twenty-first-century ships, nineteenth-century rights. *Tulane Maritime Law Journal, 28*, 447–465.

Jeffries, J. P. (1995). *Understanding hospitality law* (3rd ed.). East Lansing, MI: Educational Institute of the American Hotel and Motel Association.

3.00

Property and Environmental Law

The section—*Property and Environmental Law*—consists of three chapters. First is *Property Law*, which introduces the concept of real property and examines recreational user statutes. *Premises Liability*, the second chapter, examines the duty of operators and landowners and their obligation to provide a safe premise. *Environment and Legislation* examines the foundations and issues related to the natural environment.

These three chapters are intended to give the reader a brief overview of some of the most crucial legal concepts relating to property and the environment. Once again, the reader is referred to Section 5.00, *Risk Management*, for some applications relating to this section.

3.10 Property Law

Sarah J. Young
Indiana University

It is important that recreation and sport managers possess a basic understanding of property law because they are responsible for land areas containing sport facilities, parks, and natural attractions, such as lakes, rivers, cliffs, and hiking trails. This chapter will examine property law as it pertains to recreation and sport management with specific focus on real property, recreational use statutes, and nuisance actions.

Fundamental Concepts

Real Property

Real property is land and generally any structure that is affixed to, erected on, or growing on the land. Sport facilities are constructed and maintained on real property. It is essential that the recreation or sport manager possess a sound understanding of the legal aspects of acquisition and control of property.

Rights of Real Property

To gain a basic understanding of property law as it relates to recreation and sport, it is important to first identify the rights an organization has under different modes of acquisition. There are basically two types of rights in real property: fee simple absolute and less than fee simple. **Fee simple absolute** is the term used to describe a landowner who has complete control of the property. Swanson and Arnold (1999) described fee simple absolute as a control that includes "the right to exclude others, to sell or contract away one or more rights, and to make any use of the property not restricted by law" (p. 242). A fee simple title means that the legal holder of the title has the authority to do whatever he desires to the property within the limits of the law.

Less than fee simple describes the use of property that is generally based on a contract. Examples of less than fee simple titles include easements, leases, use permits, and joint use or cooperative agreements (Swanson & Arnold, 1999). The existence of less than fee simple titles is common in recreation, sport, and leisure services. For example, a community sports program conducted by a private association on a school-owned sports complex illustrates a joint use agreement. Additionally, pedestrian access strips across private oceanfront property that enable public access to the beach are an example of a less than fee simple rights in real property.

Modes of Acquisition

A number of modes of property acquisition are available to the recreation or sport manager. The most common one is **purchase** of a parcel of land or a facility. Acquisition of property through purchasing falls under the fee simple absolute category of rights. Typically, when one purchases a piece of property, total control of that land would be assumed. The purchase of property is usually based on a fair market value on which both the buyer and seller agree. However, there are a number of variations that both the buyer and seller may use to make the deal better from each of their perspectives. Buyers may choose to enter into an option to buy with the seller, thereby purchasing the right to buy the property with no other competition until a mutually agreed on date. Sellers may add restrictive covenants into the purchase that dictate how the property may be used. For example, a private off-road club may desire to purchase an open parcel of land from a municipality to be used for dirt bike and ATV trails. However, before purchasing, the buyer notices a noise restriction contained in the purchase agreement. This type of restrictive covenant would be detrimental to the purpose for which the land was to be used by the off-road club. As a result, buyers must be particularly aware of any restrictions in the title.

Gifts are another type of acquisition under the fee simple rights of real property that many recreation, sport, and leisure services agencies can use to their advantage. Property gifts can be made outright by the donor, as part of an annuity plan, or as the result of an individual's will. Although a gift of property is usually considered an asset to an organization, the manager should be aware of possible restrictions or requirements of the gift agreement. This is especially true if the title is not given in fee simple. For example, if a parcel of land is given to an entity, yet the gift is contingent on the performance of some function or service by the recipient, then the entity may want to carefully consider whether the gift is feasible to accept.

Dedication of land is yet another mode of acquisition in real property. This type of acquisition typically corresponds with the fee simple absolute rights. Mandatory or statutory, dedication of land requires land developers to set aside a portion of their development for public use purposes. Because development generally decreases open space, it increases the demand on remaining open spaces or existing park and recreation facilities. This provides the rationale for this type of acquisition (Swanson & Arnold, 1999). Dedication of property can also be a voluntary act whereby a landowner dedicates land for public use. Typically two elements are necessary for a complete dedication: (1) the intention of the owner to dedicate, and (2) acceptance by the public. An example of this nature is found in a Washington case where a private landowner allowed the city to build a road across his property to the beach. The landowner dedicated the right-of-way to the city of Bainbridge Island. In the 100 years since this transaction, the property had been subdivided and developed into lots, with several lot owners challenging the public's use of the right-of-way to gain access to the beach area. In an attempt to prevent public access, several lot owners erected a fence and a locked gate barring passage on the road. The court ruled that although the exact property boundary was not known, the intent of the original landowner had been to dedicate the road on his property to the city, the public had accepted the dedication, and the current lot owners were on notice as to the public nature of the area when they purchased their properties (*City of Bainbridge Island v. Brennan*, 2005).

When the owner of property is unwilling to sell his or her land, another mode of acquisition that can be implemented is known as **eminent domain** or **condemnation**. Under the U.S. Constitution, the taking of private property for public use cannot occur without just and fair compensation to the owner. Eminent domain is the power of the government to take private property, whereas condemnation is the vehicle through which this power is generally exercised. Condemnation of private property is appropriate only when the use of the property will be public, the public interests require it, and the property being condemned is necessary to accomplish a public purpose. This point is illustrated in *Schreiner v. City of Spokane* (1994), where the city condemned the property of a private landowner to construct a multipurpose community center. The community center was to be used for a variety of recreational and sport activities designed to serve the interests of the Spokane community. The court ruled unequivocally that the acquisition of land for the project was undertaken for an undisputed public purpose.

Related to the taking of property is **adverse possession**, or the transfer of property ownership over time in an actual, hostile, open, continuous, and exclusive manner. Dating back to ancient English common law, adverse possession has been used to clarify title to land as well as to discourage property owners from "sleeping on their rights" by neglecting to take the appropriate legal steps to maintain their property. An example of adverse possession is found in *Pascoag Reservoir and Dam, LLC v. Rhode Island* (2002). In this case the state acquired title to a portion of the land under the reservoir on behalf of the public's use of the reservoir for recreational purposes. The state openly took over the property by constructing a boat ramp into the reservoir in opposition to the owners. But because the state acted on behalf of the public and for their continuous access to the reservoir for recreational use, the court allowed the transfer of title under the adverse possession doctrine.

Modes of acquisition falling under the less than fee simple rights of real property include easements, leases, and cooperative agreements. These modes of acquisition most often correspond with less than fee simple rights and refer to acquiring the use of property rather than ownership. An **easement** is defined as extending to certain individuals the right to use the land of another for a specific purpose. Affirmative and negative easements are most commonly recognized. An **affirmative easement** allows the right of use over the property of another such as allowing the public access to a road over the private property of a church camp to gain access to their own private lots (*Lyons v. Baptist School of Christian Training*, 2002). A **negative easement**, on the other hand, restricts use in a particular manner. For example, a scenic easement may restrict the construction of facilities to protect a beautiful vista (Swanson & Arnold, 1999). **Leases** are used extensively in sport and recreation situations and are considered a common method of acquiring the use of land or buildings for a specified length of time. Finally, **cooperative agreements** are frequently used to allow two organizations to share the same facilities.

Land Use Controls

In addition to the acquisition of property, the recreation or sport manager must have a basic knowledge of the legal aspects of controlling the use of land under their supervision. A common law device of controlling land use is the public trust doctrine. **The public trust doctrine** provides that submerged and submersible lands are preserved for public use in navigation, fishing, and recreation. "Historically, the doctrine was applied primarily to water and submerged lands under navigable waters" (van der Smissen, 1990, p. 75); however, the doctrine has evolved to apply to dry lands as well. The main purpose of the public trust doctrine is the idea that certain natural resources belong to the public and should be preserved for the good of society. Further, it is the responsibility of public agencies to control the use of these natural resources and areas so they can be enjoyed by current and future generations. A Michigan case concerning whether the public has a right to walk along the shores of the Great Lakes where a private landowner holds title to the water's edge illustrates the application of the public trust doctrine. Defendant landowners attempted to prevent plaintiff from walking along the shore of Lake Huron, which they maintained was trespassing on their private land. The Supreme Court of Michigan ruled the public trust doctrine preserves the rights of pedestrian use of the shores of the Great Lakes (*Glass v. Goeckel*, 2005).

Another type of land use control commonly implemented in recreation is **zoning**, defined as dividing "a municipality into geographical districts or zones and then regulating the nature and use of land in the various zones" (van der Smissen, 1990, p. 78). The regulation extends not only to the development of the land, but also to the structures on the land and the activities conducted thereon. Further, van der Smissen explained "zoning is primarily a legislative function of the municipality and represents judgment of the elected governing body as to how land should be utilized within its jurisdiction" (p. 79). Determining how property should best be utilized is illustrated in the California case of *Lawler v. City of Redding* (1992). The city authorized construction of a sports complex on municipal property to which some area residents objected. In its review of the complaint against the sports complex, the court ruled that the designated use of a municipal sports facility was consistent with the zoning of the property as well as the long-range plan of the county.

The **control of activities** and the use of property is central to the issue of zoning. Zoning regulations generally correspond with a governmental agency's comprehensive plan to avoid claims of arbitrary or unreasonable zoning ordinances. This also ensures the proper use and development of property for current and future public needs. In New Hampshire, a private landowner challenged the town's zoning ordinance in its requirement of developing a buffer zone around his campground. The plaintiff argued that the buffer zone regulation was onerous and substantially destroyed the value of his campground. The court ruled that the town's zoning ordinance was implemented in a reasonable manner and that the plaintiff had not sought an exemption or amendment for his property. As a result, in an effort to regulate the use of land within the town limits, the zoning ordinances were deemed appropriate (*Quirk v. Town of New Boston*, 1995).

Recreational User Statutes

Recreational user statutes are legislative acts that are established in all states for the purpose of protecting landowners from liability if they permit the public to use their property for recreation at no cost to the user (see Chapter 2.22, *Immunity*). In 1965, the Council of State Governments addressed a growing need in the United States for more recreational land by recommending that states pass an act known as the Model Act encouraging private landowners to open their property to the public for recreational enjoyment and use. Legislation of this type was eventually adopted by all 50 states but with a great deal of variation by state. As a result, one should be familiar with the aspects of the statute for a specific state. Yet, the overall essence of the statute is the provision of a form of immunity for landowners creating a defense for liability for negligence.

General Characteristics

Although each state has its own variation of the recreational user statute and interpretations through case law, there are four general characteristics of the statute common to most states. These common denominators are discussed following.

The first of these characteristics involves the **type of property owners** to which the statute applies. In some states, the immunity protection provided by the statute is targeted toward private landowners, whereas in other states owners of public lands (i.e., local, state, and federal government agencies) are also afforded immunity. The original intent of the Model Act was to encourage private landowners to open their property to the public for recreational use, but a number of states have broadened their interpretation from the private landowner to any property owner, lessees, tenants, occupants, or persons controlling the premises. As a result, many public agencies now look to recreational use statutes as an alternative source of immunity. For example, in Minnesota, a municipality successfully sought immunity under the state's recreational user statute from a plaintiff who was injured in a tennis tournament held at the city's multipurpose facility (*Lundstrom v. City of Apple Valley*, 1998). In another case, a municipality in Georgia was protected by the state's recreational property statute for a near-drowning in a pool under the city's operation (*Baker v. City of Carrollton*, 2001). The broad interpretation of qualified property owners by many states has led to the practice of school districts also seeking protection under recreational user statutes. In *Auman v. School District of Stanley-Boyd* (2001), the Wisconsin court specifically addressed the issue of whether a school district could seek protection under the statute. Although the recreational user statute did not apply in the *Auman* case, the statute shielded the defendant school district from liability for negligence in the Minnesota case of *Fritts v. Clover Park School District* (2003).

A second characteristic of the recreational user statute is that the landowner **cannot charge a fee** for individuals to use the premises. Although most state statutes have provided that immunity will not apply if a fee is charged, there is some variation among the states as to how "fee" is interpreted. Most courts have maintained immunity for landowners except where an actual fee has been charged for entry onto the land. This type of charge is a narrow interpretation of the law, which requires an explicit quid pro quo arrangement of payment in exchange for admission onto the premises. For example, in *Lee v. The Department of Natural Resources of the State of Georgia* (2003), plaintiff claimed his wife dislocated her elbow after tripping over a debris pile near the public restroom of a campground on Ossabaw Island. Although access to the island was free, plaintiff had been required to pay $29 for a wildlife management license to qualify for lottery-selected access to the island. The court ruled that the recreational property act did provide defendant immunity because the hunting license fees did not in any way constitute a fee for admission to the island. Illustrating another perspective of the quid pro quo arrangement, a Washington court ruled that the recreational use statute did not apply to a city owning a moorage dock within a municipal park. Plaintiff slipped and fell on a wet metal ramp leading to the dock. Although the city sought immunity under the recreational use statute and claimed they did not charge fees for use of the park's facilities, they did charge a boat moorage fee. The court ruled that because the city charged a fee of *any* kind, no immunity under the statute was available (*Plano v. City of Renton*, 2000).

Some states hold a narrow interpretation of charging fees, but other states have interpreted the fee more broadly as any type of consideration. In states adhering to the idea that consideration constitutes a charge, almost any form of benefit to the landowner can trigger an exception to immunity. For example, in Nevada, the spouses of the plaintiffs in *Ducey v. United States* (1983) were killed in a flash flood in the Lake Mead National Recreational Area. The users had been boating and camping in the area and had paid rental fees and purchased various supplies from a concessionaire within the recreation area. The terms of the concession agreement obligated the concessionaire to remit less than 2% of its gross annual receipts from boat slip rentals and the general store to the owner of the recreation area. The receipt of this percentage was sufficient to be held as consideration under Nevada's recreational use statute. This was true even though the plaintiffs had not paid a fee to enter the recreational area. It is apparent that one should investigate a specific state's interpretation of charging fees.

A third characteristic of the recreational user statute is that immunity is provided for owners of **unimproved, or undeveloped, rural land retained in its natural condition**. Maloy (1997) defined unimproved lands as "real estate for which there has not been a labor cost or capital improvement intended to enhance its value for another purpose" (p. 59). The Pennsylvania Supreme Court emphasized this characteristic by stating the recreational user statute applied to large, undeveloped tracts of land suitable for outdoor recreation (*Stone v. York Haven Power Co.*, 2000). In another Pennsylvania case, plaintiff was injured while tobogganing in Valley Forge National Historical Park. The claim stated the toboggan hit a mound of snow that had allegedly built up around an old telephone junction box. The plaintiff claimed the junction box fell under the definition of developed or improved lands, but the court ruled the recreational user statute applied because Valley Forge was the type of unimproved property to which the statute was meant to apply (*Blake v. United States of America*, 1998).

The interpretation of this characteristic varies widely from state to state with a number of states applying the statute to developed recreational facilities such as ball fields, playgrounds, and swimming pools. For example, in Kansas, a court ruled that the statute provided defendant immunity after plaintiff slipped and fell in a wet hallway between a swimming pool and a locker room of a building owned by the state (*Robison v. State of Kansas*, 2002). In a recent Michigan case, the very issue of undeveloped lands was debated. Plaintiff in this case had injured her back while riding as a passenger on defendant's ATV and on defendant's 11-acre lot. Although portions of the lot were wooded and undeveloped, plaintiff was injured while riding on the mowed portion of defendant's backyard. The trial court ruled in defendant's favor based on the state's recreational user act. Yet upon appeal, the court reversed the trial court's ruling because the injury occurred while riding on the mowed portion of defendant's property. The appellate court interpreted the recreational user act as only pertaining to large tracts of undeveloped land. The Supreme Court of Michigan accepted the case and after review ruled in favor of defendants by stating there was no indication the legislature intended application of the statute be limited to undeveloped lands (*Neal v. Wilkes*, 2004).

A final general characteristic of the recreational user statute involves **obligations of the landowner**. The owner's only obligation under the statute is to provide a warning for any known concealed danger that would not be apparent to the recreational user. Owners have no duty to warn of open and obvious hazards, nor do they have a duty to warn of conditions that are unknown to them. A Kentucky case involving a skate park illustrates this characteristic. An 11-year-old boy was seriously injured when he inadvertently rode his bike from the beginner's section of a municipal skate park into the advanced section of the park, which contained an 11-foot bowl with nearly vertical walls. Because there had been two similar accidents a couple of months earlier, the city had consulted the park designer, who recommended a soft barrier be situated between the beginners' section and the 11-foot bowl. This barrier had not yet been installed when the accident leading to this case occurred. Although the trial court ruled defendants immune from liability under the recreational user statute, the appellate court was called on to determine whether the city had failed to guard or warn users of the risk. The court found there was evidence to raise a material fact that the city had failed to guard users from concealed hazards and failed to warn users of potential dangers (*Woods v. Louisville/Jefferson County Metro Government*, 2005).

A Two-Pronged Analysis of Applicability

Many states use a two-pronged analysis to determine whether the recreational user statute applies and the defendant is entitled to immunity. The first analysis is whether the activity is a recreational activity. The determination of what constitutes a recreational activity has been the focus of a number of cases. In *Parent v. State of Tennessee* (1999), the Supreme Court of Tennessee ruled that an all-inclusive list explicitly enumerating every single activity that is recreational in nature would be extremely cumbersome. A majority of states use the phrase "included, but not limited to" (van der Smissen, 1990, p. 213) in providing a list of recreational activities. In a Wisconsin case, being a spectator at a freshman football game, for which no admission fee was charged, was considered a recreational activity. The plaintiff, who was injured as she descended the bleachers after the game, could not collect because of the recreational user statute (*Meyer v. School District of Colby*, 1998). Conversely, a Texas court ruled that although a municipality provided recreation activities in an after-school program at a local community center, defendants failed to show that plaintiff had attended the program solely for recreational pursuits, meaning the statute did not apply *(Torres v. City of Waco*, 2001).

The second prong of the analysis is whether the plaintiff is recreating on land suitable for the activity. In *McCarthy v. New York State Canal Corp.* (1998) the court ruled that a concrete seawall on the Mohawk River was an area suitable for the recreational activity of fishing. Once again, there is some variation in the manner in which each state interprets the suitability of the land for recreational activity. In Hawaii, the proper focus is on the landowner's intent (*Howard v. United States of America*, 1999). In other words, if a landowner has opened up lands for recreational use without a fee, then it is not significant that a person coming onto the property may have a nonrecreational or commercial purpose in mind. In Wisconsin, the court must consider a number of different factors, including the nature of the property, the nature of the landowner's activity, and the reason the injured person is on the property (*Rintelman v. Boys and Girls Club of Greater Milwaukee*, 2005). Plaintiff fell while she was walking to move from one building to another at a residential camp. Although the nature of the property was recreational, the reason plaintiff was on the site was not for recreation or leisure purposes. Therefore, the court ruled that defendant was not immune to liability under Wisconsin's recreational use statute.

Nuisance Law

Nuisance is an area of property law dealing with activity or use of one's property that produces material annoyance, inconvenience, and discomfort for those around the property. The law of nuisance is fairly comprehensive and includes that which endangers life and health, gives offense to the senses, violates laws of decency, or obstructs reasonable use of property. Nuisances are typically classified as public or private. **Public nuisances** are acts that obstruct the enjoyment or use of common property or cause inconvenience or damage to the public. For example, plaintiff claimed a nightclub catering to young adults was a public nuisance because of the excessive noise and disorderly behavior that regularly occurred in its parking lot (*Manatee County v. J. Richard Kaiser Enterprises*, 2004). Plaintiffs included residents living within proximity of the club. Because the sounds and vibrations emanating from the club disturbed the peace of the area, the claim was analyzed under a public nuisance doctrine.

Private nuisance is a nontrespassory invasion of another's interest in the use or enjoyment of his or her property. The primary factors to be considered in a private nuisance claim are the gravity of the harm to the plaintiff, the value of the defendant's activity to the community, the burden that will be placed on the defendant if a particular remedy is granted, and whether the defendant's activity was in progress when the plaintiff arrived at the locality. *Cunningham v. City of Grosse Pointe Woods* (2001) provides a good example of a private nuisance. Plaintiffs, homeowners around the Grosse Pointe North High School property, sued defendants alleging the installation of lights at the high school athletic field and occurrence of night games created a nuisance. Plaintiffs sought injunctive relief preventing the conduct of evening sporting events at the school and eventual removal of the athletic field lights. The court acknowledged the lights spilled onto plaintiffs' properties and crowd noise from evening athletic events was loud and disturbing. However, the court ruled the extreme eruptions of sound occurred infrequently and did not constitute an unreasonable burden, especially in light of the benefit that students, parents, faculty, and the community gained from the evening events.

Attractive nuisance is another dimension of nuisance law that is focused on children entering property because they are attracted by a unique, artificial condition such as a swimming pool (*Pagnotti v. Lancaster Township*, 2000) or paintball activity (*Goldhirsch v. Taylor*, 2000). For the doctrine of attractive nuisance to apply, the landowner of the artificial condition should know or have reason to know that children are likely to trespass the premises. Additionally, the landowner should know or have reason to know that the condition will involve an unreasonable risk to trespassing children, and the children, because of their youth and inexperience, will not realize this danger. Finally, the burden of eliminating the condition is minimal to the landowner, yet, he or she fails to protect children from the condition. Attractive nuisance was the claim in *Butler v. Newark Country Club* (2005), when plaintiff's 8-year-old son fell through the ice and drowned in a pond located on a golf course while on his way to the local community center. The boy was accompanied by his 11-year-old sister and 13-year-old cousin, who had tested the ice by stomping on it prior to them playing on the pond. Although the pond was artificial in that it was man-made and contained a large spillway pipe, it was determined that was not the quality that had attracted the children to it. The court ruled that attractive nuisance doctrine did not apply because it was the natural properties (i.e., the frozen pond) that lured the children to venture onto the ice. Generally, park, recreation, and sport facilities are not nuisances, but may become such if not properly planned, located, or managed according to recognized standards.

Significant Case

―――――◇◇◇―――――

A landowner is not protected from liability for actions that are considered willful and wanton. This aspect of the statute is illustrated in the representative case of Sulzen Ex Rel. Holton v. United States of America (1999). Although the Hanging Rock Picnic Area, in this case, fits all the general characteristics needed for immunity under Utah's recreational use statute, the willful or malicious conduct exception was upheld by the court.

SULZEN EX. REL. HOLTON V. UNITED STATES OF AMERICA
U. S. District Court for the District of Utah
54 F. Supp.2d 1212; 1999 U.S. Dist. LEXIS 10283
June 29, 1999 Decided
June 30, 1999 Filed

Opinion By: Judge Tena Campbell

While visiting the Hanging Rock Picnic Area in American Fork Canyon, the plaintiff's daughter, Elizabeth Holton, was struck and killed by a rock which was dislodged by two teenagers climbing on a cliff above. Plaintiffs sued the United States as owner of the picnic area for failure to keep the area safe and for failure to warn Elizabeth Holton of the dangerous conditions in the area. The United States has moved for summary judgment based on the Utah Limitation of Landowner Liability Act. Plaintiffs argue that the Act does not apply to the Hanging Rock Picnic Area, or alternatively, that the United States is not entitled to the protection of the Act because the United States willfully disregarded a life threatening hazard.

* * *

A. Application of the Utah Limitation of Landowner Liability Act

The Federal Tort Claims Act (FTCA) waives the United States' sovereign immunity from tort actions arising from personal injury or death caused by the negligent or wrongful act or omission of any [Federal] employee. Under the FTCA, however, the United States is only liable in the same manner and to the same extent as a private individual under like circumstances. In other words, if a similarly situated private individual would not be liable under the appropriate jurisdiction's laws, then neither is the United States.

Because the accident in this case occurred on federal property in Utah, the tort law of the state of Utah applies. In Utah, the Utah Limitation of Landowner Liability Act (the Act) limits the liability of landowners who have opened their lands to the public free of charge for recreational use. Specifically, a landowner who falls within the scope of the Act owes no duty of care to keep the premises safe or to warn of dangerous conditions. Because the FTCA waives sovereign immunity only to the extent that a private individual would be held liable under like circumstances, the Act applies to immunize the federal government from liability for injuries sustained by a plaintiff engaged in recreational use of federal property.

The United States maintains that the Hanging Rock Picnic Area falls within the protection of the Act and it is therefore entitled to summary judgment as a matter of law. Plaintiff argues that the Act does not apply because the picnic areas was the type of highly developed area that the Act intended to exclude.

* * *

After applying each of these factors to the undisputed facts in this case, the court finds that the Hanging Rock Picnic Area qualifies for limited immunity under the Act because it exhibits most, if not all, of these characteristics.

1. Rural

The Hanging Rock Picnic Area is the type of rural recreation area intended to be covered by the Act. In Utah and other jurisdictions, courts consider the rural nature of the land in determining whether the state's limitation on landowner liability act should apply. To decide if the land is rural, courts look to various characteristics including the remoteness, size and naturalness of the area. Each of these factors support the conclusion that the Hanging Rock Picnic Area is a rural area.

First, the Hanging Rock Picnic Area is a remote area, removed from urban or residential settings. Courts agree that the Act was intended to grant immunity from liability to owners of rural and semi-rural tracts of land, not to owners of land in residential and populated neighborhoods. However, the Hanging Rock Picnic Area is readily distinguishable from the urban or residential areas that other courts have excluded from the protection of the Act. The picnic area, which is located four miles from the mouth of American Fork Canyon in the Uintah National Forest, is certainly not a "stones throw" from a populated residential area. Instead, the Hanging Rock Picnic Area is the type of relatively remote area intended to be covered by the Act.

Second, the Hanging Rock Picnic Area is a part of the Uintah National Forest, a massive expanse of rugged land. Although the grassy picnic area itself is only approximately 200 feet wide by 300 feet long, the grassy area is not a separate and discrete area apart from the rest of the Uintah National Forest. The parties agree that there is not division between the picnic area and the American Fork River, the overhanging cliffs, or the other undeveloped areas of the Uintah National Forest. In fact, Ms. Holton was killed when two teenage boys, who had been visiting the picnic area, dislodged a rock while climbing on the nearby 200 foot cliff. Looking only to the grassy picnic area to determine the size of the land would be an artificial distinction, especially where the accident was caused by activity in an unaltered

and natural area of the forest. When viewed in conjunction with the surrounding Uintah National Forest, the Hanging Rock Picnic Area is part of a large tract of open, vacant land in a relatively natural state within the scope of the Act.

Third, the Hanging Rock Picnic Area is a relatively natural setting in which visitors encounter elements found in the true outdoors, such as cliffs, heavily wooded areas, and rivers. In determining whether the property should be considered rural, some courts have considered whether the injury-causing element is normally found in the true outdoors. In this case, falling rock from an overhead cliff is unquestionably the type of danger only encountered in the true outdoors; such a danger would never be found in someone's backyard. The natural surroundings of the Hanging Rock Picnic Area support the conclusion that the area is the type of rural location intended to be covered by the Act.

2. Undeveloped

The Hanging Rock Picnic Area is relatively natural, undeveloped area of land within the protection of the Act. Plaintiff argues that the picnic area was a developed area because it had public restrooms, a paved parking area, and intentionally planted sod and because the course of the American Fork River had been altered to accommodate the picnic area. Other courts have held, however, that improvements such as shelters, toilet facilities, fireplaces, etc., are merely conveniences incidental to the use of the land for enumerated recreational activities and do not themselves take property out of a rural undeveloped classification. The improvements to the Hanging Rock Picnic Area merely made the area more accessible and enjoyable to the public and did not significantly alter the land's natural state.

The plain language of the Act evinces the legislature's intent to protect owners of relatively undeveloped land regardless of whether the land contains improvements, such as a parking lot or restrooms. The Act expressly includes roads, buildings, and structures within the definition of land covered by the Act. If the legislature intended to exclude all improved land from the scope of the Act, the Act would not expressly cover these artificial conditions.

Although human alterations or additions to the land may so change its character as to render the Act inapplicable, the focus should be on whether the land remains in a relatively natural state or has been developed and changed in a manner incompatible with the intention of the act. Here, the Hanging Rock Picnic Area contains some improvements, but is not developed to the point that it is removed from the type of land covered by the Act.

3. Appropriate for the Type of Activities Listed in the Statute

Application of the Act is limited to owners who have opened their property to the public for recreational purposes. The Act then provides:

Recreational purpose includes, but is not limited to, any of the following or any combination thereof: hunting, fishing, swimming, skiing, snowshoeing, camping, picnicking, hiking, studying nature, waterskiing, engaging in water sports, using boats, using off-highway vehicles or recreational vehicles, and viewing or enjoying historical archeological, scenic, or scientific sites. Utah Code Ann. @ 57-14-2(3) (Supp. 1998)

The undisputed facts show that Hanging Rock Picnic Area is appropriate for many of the activities listed in the statute. The picnic area can be used for fishing, swimming (or at least wading), hiking, picnicking, studying nature or enjoying archeological or scenic sites, most of which cannot be conducted in a small city park like the park at issue in De Baritault. In addition, there is not requirement in the Act that the area be conducive to all of the enumerated activities. Therefore, this factor weighs in favor of finding Hanging Rock Picnic Area within the scope of the Act.

4. Open to the General Public Without Charge

It is undisputed that the picnic area was open to the public free of charge.

5. A Type of Land that Would Have Been Opened in Response to the Statute

The Act was intended to encourage landowners to permit gratuitous recreational use of their land. This policy of encouraging landowners to open land for recreational use applies equally to the federal government as to other landowners. Therefore, federal lands opened to the public are the types of land that would have been opened in response to the statute. It is immaterial that the Hanging Rock Picnic Area was open to the public ten years before the passage of the Act, because the land need not actually be opened in response to the Act, so long as it is the type of land that would have been opened in response to the statute.

Because the Hanging Rock Picnic Area exhibits at least some combination of the characteristics prerequisite to immunity under the recreational use statutes, the government is immune from liability for Ms. Holton's death unless plaintiffs can fall within one of the exceptions in the Utah Code Ann. @ 57-14-3.

B. Willful or Malicious Conduct Exception

The Act provides that an owner of land owes no duty of care to keep the premises safe for entry or use by any person entering or using the premises for any recreational purpose or to give any warning of a dangerous condition, use, structure, or activity on those premises to those persons. However, the Act does not limit liability where the owner charges for use of the land, where the injury is deliberate, willful or malicious, or where the injury results from willful or malicious failure to guard or warn against a dangerous condition, use, structure, or activity.

Plaintiffs argue that the willful or malicious failure to guard or warn exception applies in this case because the United States knew of the falling rock hazard at Hanging Rock Picnic Area and failed to take any action despite such knowledge.

* * *

As evidence that the United States had knowledge of a dangerous condition likely to result in serious injury, plaintiffs rely primarily on the deposition testimony of Robert Eastman, a park ranger. Mr. Eastman testified that before the accident he had observed shale rocks along the river, around the toilet area, and in the parking lot. He also testified that maintenance people had reported finding rocks in the grassy picnic area which would cause indentations in the grass. However, Mr. Eastman stated that he never believed that the rocks were falling from the cliff above. Although the willful and malicious exception requires actual knowledge of a dangerous condition, the question of whether Mr. Eastman knew that the rocks were falling from the overhanging cliff requires a credibility determination not appropriate at the summary judgment stage. Mr. Eastman's knowledge before the accident that shale rocks had left indentations in the grass could support a conclusion that Mr. Eastman knew that rocks were falling from the cliff onto the picnic area and failed to act.

In addition to Mr. Eastman's testimony, plaintiffs point to a Forest Service memoranda and the deposition testimony of Forest Supervisor Peter Karp as evidence that the United States was aware that rocks had been falling from the cliff before the accident. The Forest Service memoranda dated September 7, 1995, indicates that the task force on the Hanging Rock Picnic Area, organized in response to Elizabeth Holton's accident, was concerned that unrecorded near misses have occurred at Hanging Rock. Mr. Karp also stated in his deposition that he was aware that rocks had fallen from the cliff from time to time before the accident. The ambiguity in the Forest Service memoranda and the Karp deposition regarding the time that Forest Service officials learned of the falling rocks raises a question for the trier of fact. Viewing the evidence in the light most favorable to the non-moving party, the fact finder could infer that the Forest Service knew of the falling rocks before Elizabeth Holton's accident.

Because plaintiffs have raised a question of fact as to whether the United States had knowledge of a dangerous condition that was likely to result in serious injury, defendants' motion for summary judgment must be denied. The question of whether the willful or malicious exception applies will be decided at trial.

For the foregoing reasons, defendants' motion for summary judgment is DENIED.

◇◇◇ **ANOTHER RELATED SIGNIFICANT CASE**

Chapter 2.21 *Defenses Against Negligence*

Recent Trends

Legal Issues of Rails to Trails

Railways have traversed both public and private property in the United States for over 150 years under the General Railroad Right-of-Way Act of 1875. The 1875 Act allowed for an easement of up to 200 feet in width for the railway to pass through one's property. With rail traffic diminishing over time, Congress passed the 1983 National Trails Systems Act amendment providing for the preservation of discontinued railway rights-of-way by banking the rights-of-way for possible future reactivation while in the interim using the rights-of-way as recreational trails. The controversy of this issue is not whether the United States may authorize the use of discontinued railways as recreational trails (*Preseault v. Interstate Commerce Commission*, 1990), but whether the landowners should be compensated for the taking of their property for this use. In two states, Idaho (*Hash v. United States*, 2005) and Washington (*Beres v. United States*, 2005), the court has ruled that defendant United States is obligated to compensate landowners for use of their property on conversion of the land to a public trail. The rationale of the court was that the owners' property interests were taken for public use and under the U. S. Constitution, the landowners must be fairly and justly compensated. The dispute places the courts at an interesting juncture between property law and constitutional law. In property law, it is a straightforward proposition that, under certain conditions, title to property may, by operation of law, be transferred to another without compensation. In constitutional law, it is a straightforward proposition that the government cannot take private property without just compensation. It is likely that this issue will become more prevalent, and the courts will have to determine how these two propositions interact with each other.

Constitutionality Challenged

The constitutionality of recreational user statutes has been recently challenged in Washington (*Davis v. State of Washington*, 2000), Kansas (*Barrett v. Unified School District No. 259*, 2001), and North Dakota (*Olson v. Bismarck Parks and Recreation District*, 2002), where plaintiffs argued the statute violated their constitutional guarantee of equal protection. In each of these cases, the courts maintained that recreational user statutes "carried a strong presumption of constitutionality" (*Olson v. Bismarck Parks and Recreation District*, p. 868) and uniformly rejected the claims against them.

Open Only to the Public?

A 2003 decision by the Illinois Supreme Court has altered the way the recreational use act is interpreted and applied to landowners in that state. Precipitated by a negligence claim of a woman injured on a luge-like sled run built in defendant's backyard, the court ruled that defendants were not shielded from liability by the state's recreational use statute because their sled run was not open to the public, but only to invited guests (*Hall v. Henn*, 2003). The interpretation of the law places at odds two sections of the statute. In Section 1, the statute exists "to encourage owners of land to make land and water areas available *to the public* (emphasis added) for recreational or conservation purposes" (§ 745 ILCS 65/1). In Sections 3 and 4, it is stated that landowners are immunized from negligence liability with respect to "any person" who enters their property for recreational purposes (§ 745 ILCS 65/3, 4). The court interpreting the language of the statute concluded the intent of the Act was to immunize landowners from negligence liability with respect to any person who enters their property for recreational purposes, provided that property is open to the public. Further, the court explained that to ignore Section 1's express caveat that property be made available to the public would largely eliminate premises liability in the state of Illinois, and that was clearly not the intent of the legislature when they enacted the statute. Time will tell as to whether or not this interpretation of the law stands as well as its impact on the many rural landowners in that state.

References

Cases

Auman v. School District of Stanley-Boyd, 635 N.W. 2d 762 (2001).

Baker v. City of Carrollton, 547 S.E.2d 689 (2001).

Barrett v. Unified School District No. 259, 32 P.3d 1156 (2001).

Beres v. United States, 64 Fed. Cl. 403 (2005).

Blake v. United States of America, 1998 U. S. Dist. LEXIS 1475 (1998).

Butler v. Newark Country Club, 2005 Del. Super. LEXIS 301 (2005).

City of Bainbridge Island v. Brennan, 2005 Wash. App. LEXIS 1744 (2005).

Cunningham v. City of Grosse Pointe Woods, 2001 Mich. App. LEXIS 1537 (2001).

Davis v. State of Washington, 6 P.3d 1191 (2000).

Ducey v. United States, 713 F.2d 504 (1983).

Fritts v. Clover Park School District No. 400, 119 Wn. App. 1045 (Wash., 2003).

Glass v. Goeckel, 703 N.W.2d 1 (2005).

Goldhirsch v. Taylor, 87 F. Supp.2d 272 (2000).

Hall v. Henn, 802 N.E.2d 797, (2003).

Hash v. United States, 403 F.3d 1308 (2005).

Howard v. United States of America, 181 F.3d 1064 (1999).

Lawler v. City of Redding, 9 Cal. Rptr. 2d 392 (1992).

Lee v. The Department of Natural Resources of the State of Georgia, 588 S.E.2d 260 (2003).

Lundstrom v. City of Apple Valley, 587 N.W.2d 517 (1998).

Lyons v. Baptist School of Christian Training, 804 A.2d 364 (2002).

Manatee County v. J. Richard Kaiser Enterprises, 874 So.2d 38 (2004).

McCarthy v. New York State Canal Corp., 244 A.D.2d 57 (1998).

Meyer v. School District of Colby, 585 N.W.2d 690 (1998).

Neal v. Wilkes, 685 N.W.2d 648 (2004).

Olson v. Bismarck Parks and Recreation District, 642 N.W.2d 864 (2002).

Pagnotti v. Lancaster Township, 751 A.2d 1226 (2000).

Parent v. State of Tennessee, 991 S.W.2d 240 (1999).

Pascoag Reservoir & Dam, LLC v. The State of Rhode Island, 217 F. Supp.2d 206 (2002).

Plano v. City of Renton, 14 P.3d 871 (2000).

Preseault v. Interstate Commerce Commission, 494 U.S. 1 (1990).

Quirk v. Town of New Boston, 663 A.2d 1328 (1995).

Rintelman v. Boys and Girls Club of Greater Milwaukee, 2005 Wisc. App. LEXIS 934 (2005).

Robison v. State of Kansas, 43 P.3d 821 (2002).

Schreiner v. City of Spokane, 874 P.2d 883 (1994).

Stone v. York Haven Power Company, 749 A.2d 452 (2000).

Sulzen Ex Rel. Holton v. United States of America, 54 F. Supp.2d 1212 (D. Utah 1999).

Torres v. City of Waco, 51 S.W.3d 814 (2001).

Woods v. Louisville/Jefferson County Metro Government, 2005 Ky. App. LEXIS 106 (2005).

Publications

Maloy, B. P. (1997). Immunity. In D. J. Cotten & T. J. Wilde (Eds.), *Sport law for sport managers* (pp. 54–62). Dubuque, IA: Kendall/Hunt Publishing Company.

Swanson, T., & Arnold, R. C. (1999). Physical resource planning. In B. van der Smissen, M. Moiseichik, V. J. Hartenburg, & L. F. Twardzik (Eds.), *Management of park and recreation agencies* (pp. 241–293). Ashburn, VA: National Recreation and Park Association.

van der Smissen, B. (1990). *Legal liability and risk management for public and private entities* (Vol. I & II). Cincinnati, OH: Anderson Publishing Company.

Legislation

Illinois Recreational Use of Land and Water Areas Act, § 745 ILCS 65/1 et seq., L.1965, p. 2263.

3.20 Premises Liability

Linda A. Sharp
University of Northern Colorado

Premises liability refers to the body of law that holds a landowner and/or possessor of property liable for injuries sustained by others upon their property (i.e., both land areas and facilities). This chapter examines the legal status of premises users and the legal duties owed each type of user by the landowner and/or possessor of the property.

Fundamental Concepts

Duty of Landowners

Unlike the other applications of negligence law covered earlier in this book, the duty owed by a landowner or operator of a facility in most jurisdictions is dependent on the status (e.g., invitee, licensee, trespasser, recreational user) of the person on the property. That is, *the duty of the landowner may vary depending on the right of the person to be on the property*. These status distinctions are crucial to understanding liability issues in this area. One must be familiar with the law of the state that governs, however, because some states have abolished the "status" distinctions and require the landowner to act with reasonable care under the circumstances, regardless of the status of the person on the property.

Also, to have a duty of care regarding premises liability, a party must truly **control** the premises. There are many instances in which a defendant is sued for a premises liability defect/hazard, and that party, usually a lessee, does not control or have an obligation to maintain the premises under the lease. In such a case, the lessee does not have a duty of care. For example, a student who attended an interscholastic soccer match was injured when he hit a rope that had been strung across a walkway behind the bleachers. The host school was not liable because, under the terms of its lease, the school did not have the necessary control of the premises to impose a duty of care. The school did not have the duty to inspect the premises for defects (*Chaplain v. American Empire Surplus Lines Insurance*, 1999). In *Eisenberg v. East Meadow Union Free School District* (1997), a student manager of a volleyball team was injured at a road game in another district when she tripped and fell as she attempted to retrieve a ball from under the bleachers. Her suit against her own school district was dismissed because her district had no control or obligation to maintain the premises at the school where the game was played. In another case, a mother was injured when she fell into a drainage ditch after she left her son's practice game to walk to her car. Her son's coaches owed her no duty of care because they did not operate or control the property on which she was injured (*Godee v. Illinois Youth Soccer Association*, 2002).

In contrast, if the roof caves in at a sporting event, the facility owner or operator would be the party that owed a duty of care, because the team that rents the facility has no obligation to maintain the roof, and the facility owner (lessor) retained that responsibility.

Status of Premises User

Invitee. A person who is on the property with the consent of the landowner and who brings an economic benefit to the landowner is known as a **business invitee**. *The property owner or operator owes the busi-*

ness invitee the duty of reasonable care. Therefore, a business invitee who sues after suffering personal injury because of a lack of reasonable care by the property owner is the usual negligence case (see Chapter 2.11, *Elements of Negligence*). Examples of business invitees include spectators at a sporting event who have paid an admission charge, paying members of health or fitness clubs, or students attending a school or university. Employees are also considered to be invitees.

There are also public invitees, those who are on land open to the public. The law has a broad definition of **public invitee** that includes any person on land open to the public or to the class of the public of which the entrant is a member. For example, users of public parks are considered to be invitees and thus entitled to ordinary care. Attendees at a free concert in the park or spectators at the city's free fireworks display in the public park are considered to be public invitees.

The duty to invitees is essentially to (1) inspect the premises for hazards, (2) remove or repair dangerous conditions, (3) make the facility reasonably safe, and (4) warn of hidden dangers. The essence of the invitee status is the **invitation** that may be express or it may be implied from custom. An **express invitation** is one in which a party specifically requests a party to come onto the land for a business purpose. This may be illustrated by an advertisement to purchase a ticket and attend a game. An **implied invitation** is one that is based on circumstance (i.e., based on the factual situation, it is reasonable to believe that an invitation has been given). An example of an implied invitation would be the openness of a park to its taxpayers. It may be inferred from the circumstances that citizens are invited to enter the park.

In *McIntosh v. Omaha Public Schools* (1996), an eighth-grader hurt his leg while participating in a two-week spring football camp operated by varsity coaches to familiarize future high school football players with the team. Although the clinics were voluntary, and participants neither paid a fee to attend nor used school equipment, a player had no chance of making the team unless he attended. The Nebraska Supreme Court found that the student was an invitee because he had accepted an invitation to attend the clinic that was being held for the mutual advantage of both parties.

Licensee. A **licensee** is one whose presence on the property is tolerated or is with the permission of the owner, but who does not technically qualify as an invitee. This category includes the social guest who is invited to someone's home but does not bring any economic benefit to the homeowner. Another example of an invitee would be one who enters a ski area as an invitee, but enters a restricted area without permission. That person then becomes a licensee.

When someone is categorized as a licensee, the *property owner owes no duty to inspect the premises or to make the licensee reasonably safe. The landowner is liable for harm created by conditions on the land only if the landowner has knowledge of a dangerous condition and the licensee does not* (Restatement (Second) Torts §342). This means that the landowner does not owe the licensee a duty to seek out hidden dangers.

The status distinctions do make a considerable difference in the outcome of a case. For example, in *Light v. Ohio University* (1986), a woman and her young daughter were using the public university's recreation facilities with no charge. While in the locker room, the daughter pulled a locker over on herself, sustaining injury. The locker came down on the child because it was not properly secured to the wall. The pivotal issue in this suit against the university was whether the plaintiffs were considered to be invitees or licensees. This was critical because if they were invitees, there was a duty of reasonable care owed, which was breached by the university in its failure to properly secure the locker to the wall. However, if the mother and her daughter were licensees, then the university owed only a duty to refrain from willful and wanton misconduct. The final decision in this case was that the plaintiffs were licensees, meaning that the university prevailed because its conduct, although negligent, was not willful and wanton.

Trespasser. **Trespassers** are those who are on the property without permission, either express or implied. If someone is a trespasser, *the property owner or operator owes only a duty not to wantonly inflict injury upon that person* (Restatement (Second) Torts §333). As a property owner, one cannot create a harm that a trespasser could not have anticipated. For example, the owner cannot set a trap so that the trespasser is shot when he opens the door to a cabin in the woods. The property owner's right to protect his or her property from intruders does not extend to setting up a danger that the trespasser could not anticipate.

For the child trespasser who is injured on your property, however, there is another rule of law that may be applicable. The **attractive nuisance doctrine** states that if the trespass by children is reasonably foreseeable and the landowner knows or has reason to know of the danger, and there is reason to believe that the child, because of his or her age, will not be able to protect him- or herself from the danger, the landowner has the duty of ordinary care to protect the child from man-made or artificial dangers on the land that may be expected to attract children. For example, if a homeowner builds a swimming pool in the backyard, there may be liability to the child trespasser drawn to this attractive nuisance, if the homeowner did not use reasonable care in protecting a child trespasser from injury in the pool. *The playground equipment in an open public park cannot be considered an attractive nuisance because the child is not a trespasser in that circumstance.*

In addition, the child must be enticed on the property by the presence of the man-made feature for the attractive nuisance doctrine to apply. In one case, a child was injured by a backstop that fell on him as he and other children played near it. The school district, which was the premises owner, was sued under the attractive nuisance doctrine. The court reasoned that the attractive nuisance doctrine did not apply because the child was brought to the property by his parents to watch an organized baseball game (*Ambrose v. Buhl Joint School District No. 412*, 1994).

Recreational User. The status distinctions of invitee, licensee, and trespasser are common law concepts. All states also have statutes that protect landowners from liability when the public is allowed to use the property for recreational purposes at no charge. When the owner makes the property available for public recreational use without charging admission, the recreational user statutes generally do *not* confer the status of invitee or licensee on the recreational user, thus *the owner owes the* **recreational user** *no duty of care to keep the premises safe or to give warning of dangerous conditions* (see Chapter 2.22, *Immunity*, and Chapter 3.10, *Property Law*). Statutes in most states declare that *the landowner is not liable for injuries suffered by recreational users except when the landowner acts in a willful or malicious manner or fails to warn of hidden ultrahazardous conditions of which the landowner is aware. Examples of ultrahazardous conditions include a firearm range, mad bulls, hidden cliffs, and nonobvious quicksand areas.*

Change in Status of the Property User

Although a person may begin time on the property with one status, the status may change depending on the behavior of the person. Invitee status is usually granted only for a designated area and purpose, known as the **area of invitation**. If the invitee leaves that permissible zone, his or her status may change. For example, in *Tincani v. Inland Empire Zoological Society* (1994), youngsters were taken to the zoo where they paid admission fees. One fourteen-year-old wandered from the public pathways in the zoo and was injured when he fell from a rock outcropping in a part of the zoo not meant for visitor traffic. The duty of care owed to this child became an issue. Although he was an invitee when he entered the zoo and stayed on the permissible walkways, he became a licensee when he left the area of invitation and entered the forbidden area.

Also, in *Howard County Bd. of Educ. v. Cheyne* (1994), a four-year-old child entered an elementary school to attend a sport function sponsored by the county recreation department. She was an invitee when she entered to attend the event. Later, she was injured as she went to retrieve a basketball and struck her face on a piece of physical education apparatus stored in the gym. The court held that it was a jury question as to whether the child exceeded her scope of invitation at the time of her injury.

In a 2002 case (*Spingola v. Whitewater Mountain Resorts of Conn., Inc.*, 2002), the court dealt with whether a person who entered the ski area to engage in snow tubing exceeded the limits of invitation. The plaintiff, who was hurt on a walkway after tubing, stated that he came to the resort in response to an ad. The ski resort argued that the plaintiff should be considered a licensee because he had been given the ticket, did not pay for admission, and did not sign the waiver form. The court held that the transfer of the ticket did not change the plaintiff's status from invitee to licensee.

The Legal Obligations of a Safe Premise

There are certain duties that the facility owner or operator owes an invitee. All these obligations stem from the fundamental obligation to provide a reasonably safe environment. These duties or obligations are (1) to inspect the facility to discover defects or hidden hazards, (2) to remove or repair dangerous conditions, (3) to make the facility reasonably safe, and (4) to warn users of hidden hazards.

The Duty of Inspection

It is clear that the courts expect facility owners to have a regular program of preventive maintenance, including regular inspections. In *Woodring v. Board of Education of Manhasset Union Free School District* (1981), a missing bolt on a track railing resulted in a substantial verdict for the family of a person who fell to his death because a railing on the upper level of a gymnasium became loose. The railing was missing a bolt, but this was not discovered because there was no regular program of inspection of the facility. The appellate court, in affirming the award of $1.4 million, stressed that the school should have liability because it had no preventive maintenance program and failed to regularly inspect the gymnasium.

Landowners are held accountable for dangerous conditions if they have either actual notice or constructive notice of the danger. **Actual notice** means that the facility owner or one of the facility's employees has actually seen the dangerous condition or has been informed of the condition. The *Woodring* case also illustrates that a facility owner may be liable regardless of the fact that there was no actual notice of a defect. In this case, management was not actually aware that the bolt was missing; however, the facility was held liable because facility owners are liable for dangerous conditions of which they have constructive notice. **Constructive notice** means that the facility owner should have been aware of the condition if the facility had acted reasonably in its program of inspection. Under the theory of constructive notice, the school district in the *Woodring* case had constructive notice of the missing bolt because a reasonably prudent facility owner would have done inspections of the facility, thus discovering the missing bolt. *Facility owners are responsible to remedy defects, whether they have actual notice or constructive notice.*

In the case of *Gernat v. State* (2005) a college hockey player sued Buffalo State College when he sustained a career-ending injury. During practice, another player hit him, and he fell through a door that was part of the ice rink. The player alleged that the door latch was defective and that the college had actual or constructive notice. The court disagreed, however, as it found no evidence of actual notice (i.e., that the latch had sprung open before). Also, there was no evidence that the alleged defect was "visible and apparent and existed for a sufficient length of time prior to the accident to permit defendant's employees to discover and remedy it," which would be indicative of constructive notice.

The Duty to Remove or Repair Dangerous Conditions

Once a property owner has actual or constructive notice of a dangerous condition, remedial measures must be taken in a reasonable period of time. What constitutes a reasonable period of time is a question of fact for a jury to decide. In *Van Stry v. State* (1984), a student slipped in a puddle of water in the shower area. The water was in an area away from the showerheads. The school had prior actual knowledge of the problem because the student had informed the instructor about this hazard on prior occasions. The school was liable because it had adequate time to remedy the problem but did not do so. It is important to understand that the school was held to have actual notice of the problem, even though the employee who knew about the problem did not communicate with the proper people in the organization to fix the problem. This means that facility owners need to have sound procedures to make sure that information about facility hazards is conveyed to the people who are responsible for remedying the problem. There should be a reporting procedure with which employees are familiar, and there should be supervisory control of the process to ensure that problems are handled promptly.

In a pole-vaulting case, the university athlete was seriously injured when he fell off the back edge of a landing pit and hit his head. Both coaches knew that vaulters had been injured by second impact injuries of bouncing off the pit mattress and landing outside the pit, and supplemental padding was available but was not used. An appellate court affirmed in favor of the injured athlete because the evidence showed that the accident was reasonably foreseeable (*Moose v. Massachusetts Institute of Technology*, 1997).

There is no general rule about what is a "reasonable period" of time because it is tied to the underlying factual situation. What is a reasonable period of time, based on the circumstances, to first learn of and then remedy a defect? In *Mortiboys v. St. Michael's College* (1973), a student was injured when he fell while skating on an ice rink located on a college campus. The student fell after his skate hit a small lump of ice. The court found for the college because there was no evidence that the small lump of ice had existed for a sufficient period of time to show negligence by the college in failing to discover and eliminate the potential hazard.

Duty to Make the Facility Reasonably Safe

Duty to Control Third Persons. As a part of the owner's duty to keep the facility reasonably safe there may be obligations to protect patrons from the harmful actions of third parties. Under Section 344 of the Restatement (Second) of Torts, *a landowner who opens his property to the public for business purposes, has a duty to exercise reasonable care to protect the public from physical harm caused by the "accidental, negligent, or intentionally harmful acts of third persons."* The liability for the action of the third party is conditioned on its **foreseeability.**

For example, the case of *Bearman v. University of Notre Dame* (1983) illustrates the use of constructive notice to show that injury to the plaintiff should have been foreseeable to the university. The plaintiff was a business invitee attending a football game at the university. The plaintiff left the game early and was injured as she walked through a university parking lot when a person who was drunk fell into her while fighting. The university argued that it should not be liable because it had no actual notice of the fight and could not reasonably be expected to prevent the plaintiff's injury. The court, however, used an analysis based on constructive notice. The university allowed tailgating and knew that alcoholic beverages were consumed. It is common knowledge that the overconsumption of alcohol leads to a variety of bad behaviors, including fighting. Thus, based on this logical chain, the court found that the university did have a duty of care because of the foreseeability of the type of behavior that occurred in this case.

In a more recent case involving Notre Dame football, a spectator was knocked down and injured when other spectators hit her in an attempt to get a football that had gone into the stands. The football entered the stands because the net behind the goalpost failed to catch it. In this case, it was foreseeable that, if the ball was allowed to go into the stands, injury was likely to occur to spectators who would be caught in the melee to get the ball (*Hayden v. University of Notre Dame*, 1999). In a professional football case with similar facts, other fans attacked a spectator in an attempt to gain possession of the ball. The football team was on notice that other fights for balls had occurred and that violence was a persistent problem at the games. The facility had a duty to protect the spectator from violence by other spectators (*Telega v. Security Bureau, Inc.*, 1998).

The question of foreseeability is also the focal point in cases that deal with deliberate attacks by third parties. For example, in *Gragg v. Wichita State University* (1997), a person who attended the Fourth of July fireworks display at the university's stadium was killed by gunfire as she crossed the campus following the display. The person was killed in a case of mistaken identity in a gang-related shooting. Using the totality of circumstances test as a measure of foreseeability, the court held that there was no duty to protect this invitee. In the **totality of circumstances test**, a facility owner may be held liable for a criminal attack even without prior similar incidents of crime. The court will look at prior acts, if they exist, but will also look at the nature, condition, and location of the premises to ascertain if the attack was foreseeable. In this case, the court found that the university had employed reasonable security measures because the shooting was not foreseeable. There had been no other shootings at the event in prior years, and the university had no information that gang members would be present. There was no reason to find liability, even though the crime rate was high in the surrounding neighborhood. In another shooting case, a ricocheting bullet injured a woman as she left the public school where her daughter had competed in a cheerleading event (*Bailey v. District of Columbia*, 1995). The plaintiff alleged that there was insufficient security; however, the court found in favor of the school district. The court noted that although there had been previous shootings in the vicinity of the school, this generic evidence was not sufficient to create a duty to protect against the use of firearms. This court used the prior similar incidents rule to find that the school could not have anticipated the prospect of violent criminal conduct. The **prior similar incidents rule** requires that the similar incidents used to find foreseeability be almost identical in type and geography to the incident in question.

Generally, the totality of the circumstances rule is more helpful to a plaintiff in finding the foreseeability necessary to impose liability on the facility owner for the acts of the third party.

The issue of whether security (see Chapter 5.24, *Crowd Management*) must be provided at all is also a function of the question of foreseeability. For example, in the recent case of *Talasazan v. Northridge Arena Soccer League, Inc.* (2002), opposing players beat an indoor soccer player at the conclusion of the game. The plaintiff alleged that the facility had a duty to provide security guards at the game because it was foreseeable that an altercation of this nature could happen. The court agreed because there were fights in three out of the five contests preceding this game, and the facility had provided guards for four of the five preceding contests.

Duty to Provide for Emergency Response. As a part of the obligation to make the facility reasonably safe, it is expected that facility owners will be able to respond promptly and effectively to emergency situations suffered by those who are using the facility or spectating at the venue. These emergency situations may relate to a variety of circumstances, including weather-related crises, bomb threats, and emergency medical response (see Chapter 5.23, *Crisis Management*).

Emergency medical care *for those who are participating* in an organized activity is not generally the facility owner's obligation; those who are organizing the event are responsible for medical care for the participants (see Chapter 2.31, *Emergency Care*). However, the facility owner is responsible for the emergency care of *facility patrons or spectators*. The owner or operator has a duty to provide personnel who are properly trained to assist in a medical emergency and to have established protocol in place to secure the timely assistance of outside medical personnel.

The facility owner should be aware of local statutes that may require the presence of an ambulance at certain contests or that may mandate the presence of certain medical personnel. Facility association standards may also mandate or recommend certain standards of care regarding emergency medical care, including the provision of automated external defibrillators (AEDs).

Duty to Warn of Hidden Dangers. The duty to warn of hidden dangers means that a warning must be given when a danger would not be obvious to an average user of ordinary intelligence and the user would not have been able to discover the danger and the risk presented on casual inspection.

A landowner does not have to warn of dangers that are open and obvious to the person on the property. For example, in *Robertson v. State of Louisiana* (1999), a university student died from a fall from the natatorium roof that he climbed onto. The student was inebriated when he climbed onto the roof. The court held that there was no building defect because the natatorium roof properly functioned as a roof. Further, there was no need to warn because the dangers of climbing on a roof are well known. The same rationale was applied in a case in which a junior high school student fell through the skylight as he climbed onto the school's roof to retrieve a ball. The skylight was neither defective nor an unobservable dangerous condition (*Kurshals v. Connequot Central School District*, 1996).

Also, there is no duty to warn of a danger if the plaintiff is already aware of the danger. For example, a high school softball player was injured during practice by a ball that took a bad bounce due to "rough" field conditions. Although the court noted that the player was an invitee to whom the school board had a duty to warn, it did not have to advise her about the condition of the field because she was already aware that it was rough (*Daniel v. City of Morganton*, 1997).

Open and Obvious Dangers. According to the Restatement (Second) Torts §343A *"A possessor of land is not liable to invitees for physical harm caused to them by any activity or condition on the land whose danger is known or obvious to them, unless the possessor should anticipate the harm despite such knowledge or obviousness."* In *Paone v. County of Suffolk* (1998), a basketball player was injured when he stepped into a depression on an outside court on school district property. The court had a hole that was about a "foot or two" wide, a "couple of inches" deep, and at least partially covered by grass growing out of the asphalt. The court found for the school district because the player voluntarily chose to play on the court with a faulty surface that was open and obvious. Likewise, in a case dealing with a college baseball player, the player severely injured his knee when he stepped into a hole in the school's baseball field as he attempted to catch a fly ball. The appellate court held that because the player was aware of the depression in the field before the game began and knowingly and voluntarily proceeded to play in the face of an obvious danger, the player assumed the risk (*Zachardy v. Geneva College*, 1999). The same reasoning was used where a high school softball player was injured when she stepped into a hole by home plate (*Gahan v. Mineola Union Free School District*, 1997).

In a case involving a muddy soccer field, the court held that a university soccer player had assumed the risk of playing on the wet, muddy, and slippery field. This was so even though the player had complained about the condition of the field before they began the match. Because the player chose to participate in the game with knowledge of the conditions, she assumed the risk (*Schiffman v. Spring*, 1994).

The **exception to the open and obvious rule** is illustrated by the case of *Menough v. Woodfield Gardens* (1998). In that case, a man playing basketball on an outdoor court at an apartment complex broke his ankle when he came down on a tire filled with concrete used to support the basket. The defendant argued that the tire was an open and obvious danger; however, the plaintiff argued successfully that the facility owner should have anticipated that a person playing basketball could have injured himself falling on the tire because he would be distracted by the game and could not be expected to focus on avoiding the tire. The court held that the **distraction doctrine** was applicable, thus the plaintiff prevailed.

Problem Areas

The following are examples of areas in sport or recreation venues that pose frequent problems for the facility owners or operators.

Bleachers. There are numerous cases dealing with facility liability and bleachers. Many injuries result because bleachers are not properly inspected and maintained. For example, a business invitee was injured when a plank broke in the wooden bleachers at a football game that she was attending. The court held that the issue here was one of proper maintenance, which did not fall under the defendant's immunity (*Ilott v. University of Utah*, 2000). In another case, a spectator at a college baseball game who slipped and fell on a nonuniform step in the bleacher seats was awarded $80,000. The step created an unreasonable risk of harm to the fan (*Rispone v. Louisiana State University*, 1994).

Holes and Playing Surfaces. Holes or other depressions in playing surfaces account for many premises liability cases. If, however, the hole or depression is an open and obvious danger, then the plaintiff will usually have assumed the risk of injury and will not be able to recover (see *Open and Obvious Dangers*, earlier).

Walls and Padding. Often smaller gymnasia are plagued by the problem of players running into the walls behind the baskets. Some courts have found that the player assumed the open and obvious risk of running into the wall by continuing to play in that gym (*Davis v. Savona Central School District*, 1998). However, in another case, a player in a youth league was injured when he ran into the wall behind the basket while trying to block a shot. In that case the court held that there was a factual question as to whether the dimensions of the court and the lack of padding created a dangerous condition beyond the usual dangers inherent in playing basketball (*Greenburg v. Peekskill City School District*, 1998).

Playgrounds. Often critical issues in playground safety cases are the applicability of the Consumer Product Safety Commission's guidelines for playground safety or the American Society for Testing and Materials' standards for playground equipment. Note that a facility owner does not have to explicitly adopt these standards before the standards can be used in a case against the facility. These standards may be used to establish the standard of care that should be applicable in a playground case to allow the jury to assess the proper standard of care (see Chapter 5.21, *Standards of Practice*). These safety codes may be introduced as evidence to illustrate safety practices or rules generally prevailing in the industry (*Elledge v. Richland/Lexington School District Five*, 2000).

Parking Lots and Walkways. Numerous cases are brought based on falls in parking lots or on walkways surrounding the sport or recreational facility. Weather conditions often precipitate falls on icy areas. Generally to win a slip and fall case, the plaintiff needs to show (1) that the facility had actual or constructive notice of the condition, (2) that the condition posed an unreasonable risk of harm, (3) that the defendant did not use reasonable care to reduce or eliminate the risk, and (4) that the failure to use reasonable care proximately caused the injury (*Wal-Mart Stores v. Gonzalez*, 1998).

Safety Glass. On many occasions facilities are sued because participants fall against or through windows or doors with glass. There are local statutes governing the use of safety glass, and a failure to conform to such statutes may subject the facility to liability based on **negligence per se** (automatic negligence when a statute is violated). However, even when statutes do not apply, arguments may be made that a failure to use safety glass in certain locations may be a breach of duty. In a case dealing with a playground situation, a third-grade student, who was racing across a school playground, fell against a glass window in the school building, injuring her hand and arm. The suit alleged the school should have used safety glass in that window. The school was able to prevail because impact-resistant glass was not required for exterior windows that bordered an outdoor play area, and the failure to use safety glass in those windows was not a violation of relevant safety standards (*Ambrosio v. South Huntington Union Free School District*, 1998).

Projectiles in the Stands. Foul balls in baseball or pucks in hockey are examples of projectiles that often go into the stands during a contest. Facility owners or operators have a limited duty of care to spectators regarding projectiles that go into the viewing area as a part of the game. This **limited duty of care** means that the facility operator must screen or otherwise protect the spectators in the areas of greatest risk. The facility must also have a large enough area to protect as many spectators as may reasonably be expected to desire such seating (*Lynch v. Board of Educ. for Oceanside School District*, 1996). When the operator meets the above duty of care, spectators generally assume the risk of being hit with a ball or puck that flies out of the playing area. See the following *Maisonave* case for a discussion of whether the limited duty rule should apply to areas outside the stands.

In *Lowe v. California League of Professional Baseball* (1997), a spectator at a minor league baseball game was hit in the head by a foul ball. The spectator had turned away from the playing field at that moment because the team's dinosaur mascot had hit the spectator with his tail. The appellate court held that because the mascot was not integral to the game, the mascot could increase the danger to fans. The court stated that the mascot was a **distraction** causing the spectator to be unable to get out of the way of the ball. The court left it for the jury to decide whether the mascot's antics during the game were a breach of duty.

Significant Case

————————————◇◇◇————————————

This case addresses whether the limited duty rule (see earlier) should apply areas other than the stands. The plaintiff was injured while he was a patron at a mobile concessions stand on the concourse. The court held that the limited duty rule applies only to the stands, and usual rules of negligence law must apply to other stadium areas in which the plaintiff has a "heightened vulnerability."

MAISONAVE V. NEWARK BEARS PROFESSIONAL BASEBALL CLUB

Supreme Court of New Jersey
881 A. 2d 700 (2005)

———————————————————————————

OPINION: * * *

Here, a foul ball struck plaintiff in the face as he purchased a beverage from a mobile vending cart on the concourse of a minor league stadium. The Appellate Division reversed the trial court's grant of summary judgment in favor of the stadium owners and operators, holding that the trial court erred in finding that defendants had not violated their duty of care as a matter of law.

In this appeal, we survey the law that has evolved concerning owner and operator liability and examine the boundaries of the limited duty rule. In doing so, we must accommodate the interests of both fans and owners. We hold that the limited duty rule, which restricts the tort liability of owners, applies in situations where an injury occurs in the stands. However, public policy and fairness require application of traditional negligence principles in all other areas of the stadium, including, but not limited to, concourses and mezzanine areas.

I.

Plaintiff Louis Maisonave suffered a facial injury when a foul ball struck him in the eye as he stood on the mezzanine at Riverfront Stadium, home field of minor league baseball team, The Newark Bears. The mezzanine is an open walking area exposed on one side to the baseball field. Vendors sell food and beverages on that level, and restrooms are located there. At the time of the incident, the stadium used movable vending carts for the sale of beverages because construction of the stadium had not yet been completed, and the built-in concession stands were not operational. * * * The carts dotted the mezzanine along both the first and third base lines on the field-side of the mezzanine. The vendors * * * stood with their backs to the diamond while the patrons faced it.

Plaintiff, who had watched the action at a railing on the first base side of the field, walked about 100 feet to the closest vending cart. Netting protects the seating area behind home plate and extends for some distance down both base lines. The beverage cart that plaintiff patronized was on the first base line, but beyond the protection of the net.

* * *

[The plaintiff testified in his deposition that he did not see the ball coming]

* * *

Alleging negligence, plaintiff sued The Newark Bears Professional Baseball Club, Inc., which leases Riverfront Stadium from [*76] the Essex County Improvement Authority, and defendant Gourmet Dining Services, which provides food and beverage services to Riverfront Stadium. The trial court granted summary judgment in favor of defendants, finding that they had not breached their duty of care. In reaching that conclusion, the trial court relied on Schneider v. American Hockey & Ice Skating Center, Inc., 342 N.J. Super. 527, 533-34, 777 A.2d 380 (App. Div.), certif. denied, 170 N.J. 387, 788 A.2d 772 (2001), which set forth a two-pronged duty of care for stadium owners and operators:

First, the operator must provide protected seating "sufficient for those spectators who may be reasonably anticipated to desire protected seats on an ordinary occasion," and second, the operator must provide protection for spectators in "the most dangerous section" of the stands. The second component of this limited duty ordinarily may be satisfied by the operator providing screened seats behind home plate in baseball and behind the goals in hockey.

The trial court reasoned that the provision of "at least two vending carts close to home plate and behind the screening, which plaintiff could have utilized," established that defendants had not breached * * * their limited duty to plaintiff and, therefore, were not liable to plaintiff as a matter of law.

The Appellate Division reversed and remanded. Citing Schneider, the panel agreed that "the operators of a commercial sports facility owe a limited duty to spectators." * * * However, focusing on the second part of the Schneider limited duty rule, the Appellate Division stated: When we said that the second component [of Schneider] "may be satisfied by the operator providing screened seats behind home plate in baseball and behind the goals in hockey[,]" our identification of those locations * * * was not intended to be exhaustive nor immutable. Rather, "the measure of that duty is 'due care under all the circumstances.'"

* * *

For the reasons discussed below, we affirm and modify the decision of the Appellate Division.

* * *In our analysis, we consider general principles of tort liability, including the business invitee rule and its application to commercial establishments. Next, we examine the limited duty rule as an exception to the business invitee rule, its origins, its application in New Jersey and other jurisdictions, and concerns about the rule. We then determine whether we should adopt the limited duty rule, and if so, to what extent it should apply to the stands and to other areas of the stadium.

II.

A.

* * *

Although it applied the limited duty rule, our Appellate Division recognized in Schneider that "the operator of a commercial recreational facility, like the operator of any other business, has a general duty to exercise reasonable care for the safety of its patrons." * * *

B.

The limited duty rule is a specialized negligence standard that has protected stadium owners and operators since the early days of modern baseball. * * * Since the early twentieth century, courts have held that "one of the natural risks assumed by spectators attending professional games is that of being struck by batted or thrown balls." * * * Even a brief review of several early baseball cases reveals that many courts that adopted the rule, or a version of it, based their decisions * * *on two facts: that the danger of errant balls was common knowledge and that spectators sitting in unscreened seats assumed the risk of injury. * * * Thus, the rule establishes a fact-specific standard of care for injuries caused by errant balls at baseball stadiums by accounting for the open and obvious nature of the risk that batted balls pose to fans.

In Schneider, supra, our Appellate Division endorsed the limited duty rule, explaining that stadium operators must "provide protected seating sufficient for those spectators who may be reasonably anticipated* * * to desire protected seats on an ordinary occasion." * * * Additionally, stadium operators must "provide protection for spectators in the most dangerous section of the stands." * * *

C.

The scope of the duty that the owners and operators of baseball stadiums owe their patrons is a question of first impression for this Court. However, about one-half of the states have previously addressed this issue. * * * Our research reveals that eleven of those * * * jurisdictions have adopted the limited duty rule. * * * Some states have not applied the rule and instead have adopted baseball-specific statutes. * * * Finally, some courts have applied traditional negligence principles, such as the business invitee rule or comparative negligence.

* * *

III.

With the above case law and commentary as a backdrop, we consider whether * * *the limited duty rule should apply to stadiums, and, more specifically, to the stands. In doing so we are mindful that "recognition of a duty of care, ultimately, rests on considerations of public policy and on notions of fairness." * * *

As the Appellate Division aptly observed, "while watching the game, either seated or standing in an unprotected area, spectators reasonably may be expected to pay attention and to look out for their own safety." * * * It would be unfair to hold owners and operators liable for injuries to spectators in the stands when the potential danger of fly balls is an inherent, expected, and even desired part of the baseball fan's experience. * * *Because the limited duty rule fairly balances the practical and economic interests of owners and operators with the safety and entertainment interests of the fans, we adopt the Appellate Division's opinion in Schneider, to the extent that it holds that owners and operators must offer sufficient protected seating to those who would seek it on an ordinary basis and to provide screening in the most dangerous sections of the stands.

In the interest of clarity, we note that the term "stands" includes the stairs that fans ascend and descend to access their seats in the stands. Similarly, areas immediately adjacent to the stands designated as "standing room only," and dedicated solely to viewing the game, fall within the purview of the limited duty rule. In contrast, multi-purpose areas, such as concourses and playground areas, are outside the scope of the rule, as discussed below.

* * *

IV.

We now must decide whether the limited duty rule should apply to areas other than the stands.

* * *

The validity of the baseball rule diminishes in the context of injuries that occur in stadium areas other than the stands. Fans foreseeably and understandably let down their guard when they are in other areas of the stadium. Once the fan has disengaged him- or herself from the activity on the field and has left the stands, that individual is no longer trying to catch foul balls or even necessarily watching the game. * * * As the Appellate Division noted in addressing this appeal, the defendants are engaged in a commercial venture which by its nature induces spectators to let down their guard. They have a concomitant duty to exercise reasonable care to protect them during such times of heightened vulnerability. The imposition of a duty under these circumstances . . . is not only fair but reasonable.

* * *

C.

Because principles of fairness, and by implication public policy, support the application of traditional tort concepts to areas outside of the stands, we will not expand the scope of the baseball rule past its logical and appropriate borders, that is, the stands. * * *To apply the baseball rule to the entire stadium would convert reasonable protection for owners to immunity by virtually eliminating their liability for foreseeable, preventable injuries to their patrons even when the fans are no longer engaged with the game. * * *

We simply apply traditional tort principles and conclude that the proper standard of care for all other areas of the stadium is the business invitee rule, which provides that a landowner "owes a duty of reasonable care to guard against any dangerous * * * conditions on his or her property that the owner either knows about or should have discovered.

V.

* * *

To recapitulate, the limited duty rule, as set forth above and in Schneider, will apply to injuries occurring in the stands. However, traditional rules of negligence, specifically the business invitee rule, will govern owner and operator liability for injuries that occur in all other areas of the stadium. * * *

We remand this matter to the trial court for application of the standard we have set forth in this opinion to all future proceedings in this matter. The judgment of the Appellate Division is affirmed as modified.

Recent Trends

AED Use

All fifty states have now passed laws or regulations requiring automated external defibrillators (AEDs) in a variety of public buildings, including transportation centers, large office complexes, and other facilities in which there is a likelihood of sudden cardiac arrest. On June 27, 2002, Governor George Pataki of New York signed a law requiring all public elementary and secondary schools to purchase portable AEDs for use on school property during extracurricular activities. (Popke, 2003).

Additionally, other states have passed legislation that mandate the use of AEDs in health clubs but do provide immunity for ordinary negligence while using the equipment. This is an area that is evolving, and the recreation or sport professional must check for applicable state statutes. The Website is http://www.aedriskinsights.com/products.html#aedlc.

References

Cases

Ambrose v. Buhl Joint Sch. Dist. No. 412, 887 P.2d 1088 (Idaho Ct. App. 1994).

Ambrosio v. South Huntington Union Free Sch. Dist., 671 N.Y.S.2d 110 (App. Div. 1998).

Bailey v. District of Columbia, 668 A.2d 817 (D.C. App. 1995).

Bearman v. University of Notre Dame, 453 N.E.2d 1196 (Ind. Ct. App. 1983).

Chaplain v. American Empire Surplus Lines Ins. Co., 731 So.2d 973 (La. Ct. App. 1999).

Daniel v. City of Morganton, 479 S.E.2d 263 (N.C. Ct. App. 1997).

Davis v. Savona Cent. Sch. Dist., 675 N.Y.S. 2d 269 (App. Div. 1998).

Eisenberg v. East Meadow Union Free Sch. Dist., 657 N.Y.S.2d 434 (App. Div. 1997).

Elledge v. Richland/Lexington Sch. Dist. Five, 534 S.E.2d 289 (S.C. Ct. App. 2000).

Gahan v. Mineola Union Free Sch. Dist., 660 N.Y.S.2d 144 (App. Div. 1997).

Gernat v. State, 2005 WL 3017961 (N.Y. App. Div. 2005).

Godee v. Illinois Youth Soccer Ass'n, 764 N.E.2d 591(Ill. App. Ct. 2002).

Gragg v. Wichita State Univ., 934 P.2d 121 (Kan. 1997).

Greenburg v. Peekskill City Sch. Dist., 680 N.Y.S.2d 622 (App. Div. 1998).

Hayden v. University of Notre Dame, 716 N.E.2d 603 (Ind. Ct. App. 1999).

Howard County Bd. Of Educ. v. Cheyne, 636 A.2d 22 (Md. Ct. Spec. App. 1994).

Ilott v. University of Utah, 12 P.3d 1011 (Utah Ct. App. 2000).

Kurshals v. Connequot Cent. Sch. Dist., 643 N.Y.S.2d 622 (App. Div. 1996).

Light v. Ohio University, 502 N.E.2d 611 (Ohio 1986).

Lowe v. California League of Prof. Baseball, 56 Cal. App. 4th 112 (Ct. App. 1997).

Lynch v. Board of Educ. for Oceanside Sch. Dist., 640 N.Y.S.2d 142 (App. Div. 1996).

Maisonave v. Newark Bears Professional Baseball Club, 881 A.2d 700 (N.J. 2005).

McIntosh v. Omaha Public Sch., 544 N.W.2d 502 (Neb. 1996).

Menough v. Woodfield Gardens, 694 N.E.2d 1038 (Ill. App. Ct. 1998).

Moose v. Massachusetts Inst. of Technology, 683 N.E.2d 706 (Mass. App. Ct. 1997).

Mortiboys v. St. Michael's College, 478 F.2d 196 (2d Cir. 1973).

Paone v. County of Suffolk, 674 N.Y.S.2d 761 (App. Div. 1998).

Rispone v. Louisiana State Univ., 637 So.2d 731 (La. Ct. App. 1994).

Robertson v. State of La., 747 So.2d 1276 (La. Ct. App. 1999).

Schiffman v. Spring, 609 N.Y.S.2d 482 (App. Div. 1994).

Spingola v. Whitewater Mountain Resorts of Conn., Inc., 2002 Conn. Super. LEXIS 4024 (Conn. Super. Ct. 2002).

Talasazan v. Northridge Arena Soccer League, Inc., 2002 Cal. App. Unpub. LEXIS 11236 (Cal. App. Ct. 2002).

Telega v. Security Bureau, Inc., 719 A.2d 372 (Pa. Sup. Ct. 1998).

Tincani v. Inland Empire Zoological Society, 875 P.2d 621 (Wash. 1994).

Van Stry v. State, 479 N.Y.S.2d 258 (App. Div. 1984).

Wal-Mart Stores v. Gonzalez, 968 S.W.2d 934 (Tex. Sup. Ct. 1998).

Woodring v. Board of Education of Manhasset Union Free Sch. Dist., 435 N.Y.S.2d 52 (App. Div. 1981).

Zachardy v. Geneva College, 733 A.2d 648 (Pa. Super. Ct. 1999).

Publications

Popke, M. (2003, January). Matters of the heart. *Athletic Business,* 28–31.

Restatement (Second) Torts (1965).

Sharp, L. A. (1990). *Sport law.* Wichita, KS: National Organization on Legal Problems in Education.

van der Smissen, B. (1990). *Legal liability and risk management for public and private entities.* Cincinnati, OH: Anderson Publishing Company.

3.30 The Natural Environment

Jean Hughes
University of Arkansas

Environmental law can be viewed as an emerging field that covers a broad range of issues in diverse legal settings from local ordinances to international treaties. Transboundary agreements are necessary because the scope of many environmental issues is not confined to a given location. In the United States, federal legislation topics include (1) wildlife and endangered species, (2) air, (3) water, (4) solid and hazardous wastes, (5) noise, and (6) forests, parks, and land use. Many federal agencies have been created to write regulations for their specific area of jurisdiction. In addition, under the states rights of the Tenth Amendment, many states have passed environmental statutes that run the gamut from game and fish regulations to recreational land use statutes that encourage opening of private lands to public use. Local municipalities also pass ordinances such as zoning regulations, recycling mandates, and noise statutes impacting both public and private environments. In this chapter special emphasis is placed on environmental legislation affecting outdoor recreation pursuits in the natural environment.

Fundamental Concepts

Foundations of Natural Environment Law

Evidence of environmental legislation can be found in colonial America. Colonial towns frequently set aside common public grounds or village greens owned by the community for harvesting timber, livestock grazing, and recreational activities. As early as 1626, Plymouth colony passed legislation restricting timber cutting on colony land without permission. As early as 1799, Congress began the practice of securing public land for the federal government. By the early 1800s, most of the states had established game preservation laws. It was apparent that with a growing population, natural resources were not limitless (Jensen, 1995).

Many of the early environmental policies were influenced by the philosophies of writers and leaders such as Ralph Waldo Emerson, Henry David Thoreau, John James Audubon, John Muir, Frederick Law Olmstead, Theodore Roosevelt, Gifford Pinchot, Stephen Mather, and Aldo Leopold. Conservation, preservation and even restoration were needed to ensure natural resources for future generations (Ibrahim & Cordes, 2002). In 1872, the U.S. National Park system was created by establishing Yellowstone National Park as a public reserve, and in 1881 the Division of Forestry, a forerunner to the U.S. Forest Service, was inaugurated under the U.S. Department of Agriculture. By 1891, the United States had set aside 13 million acres of forest reserves. This was followed in 1898 by the Park Protection Act to preserve wildlife in the national parks. By the turn of the twentieth century, America's frontier had vanished. It became imperative that laws be enacted to protect, preserve, and wisely manage the nation's natural resources (Dennis, 2001).

Who Owns the Natural Environment?

The natural environment includes the air, water, and land. Ownership is the collection of legal rights to possess, use, enjoy, and convey property. It is the right of a nation or state to assert sovereignty or an individual or group to exert autonomy over an object or property (Garner, 1996). Though an individual or private group may hold title to a piece of land, many treaties, statutes, and regulations are enacted at international, federal, state, and local levels that prohibit unrestricted use of the air, land, and water.

According to the National Wilderness Institute (1995), 39.8% of land in the United States is held communally as federal, state, or tribal land. Of this, 4.7 percent is designated as wilderness under the Wilderness Act of 1964 and thus is "protected and managed so as to preserve its natural conditions and which generally appears to have been affected primarily by the forces of nature, with imprint of man's work substantially unnoticeable." The Bureau of Land Management is the largest landholder with accountability for 38.2% of the federal property.

Definition of Environmental Law

Environmental law, at its broadest, can be defined as the aggregate of all laws affecting use, development, management, and protection of the environment. It encompasses laws, regulations, and executive orders enacted to protect both human health and nonhuman nature. The preponderance of environmental law is derived from two sources: (1) statutory enactments of legislative bodies, and (2) regulations generated by agencies charged by legal authority with protection of the environment. For example, the Transfer Act of 1905 is a statutory enactment that empowered the U.S. Forest Service to manage the National Forest Reserve. In turn, the U.S. Forest Service has the legal authority to generate regulations concerning the use of forest resources.

Environmental legislation can be grouped into four categories—command-and-control laws, environmental assessment mandates, economic incentive policies, and set-aside plans. The preponderance of environmental laws falls into the category of command-and-control legislation that identifies a potentially harmful activity and then prohibits the activity or imposes specific standards on the activity (e.g., Federal Water Pollution Control Act of 1972). Another category of environmental law is environmental assessment mandates that require the identification of an acceptable level of environmental impact and then require an assessment to determine if a proposed activity will breach the acceptable level (e.g., National Environmental Policy Act of 1969). A third category of environmental law is economic incentives for environmentally friendly practices (e.g., Superfund established by the Environmental Protection Agency in 1980). A final method of environmental protection is setting aside of land and water in their natural state (e.g., National Preservation System Act of 1964).

The list of congressional legislation that has been enacted for the protection of the environment is vast. Table 1 summarizes some of the major federal statutes. The environmental movement of the latter part of the twentieth century initiated legislation to address environmental quality related to air, water, and land pollution.

Administrative Agencies

In 1887, Congress began the practice of creating administrative agencies that specialize in specific areas. Because the scope of legislation can become burdensome and time consuming, Congress often passes legislation that creates an agency to oversee a particular area. In turn, this agency writes the regulations (Dennis, 2001). This is particularly evident in the creation of agencies to manage environmental resources. For example, the U.S. Park Service was created to manage national parks, historic places, and monuments. The U.S. Forest Service was established to manage the millions of acres of federal forests and grasslands. This allows Congress to pass broad sweeping legislation that authorizes cabinet secretaries to mandate their personnel to write the specific regulations that carry out the wishes of Congress. Table 2 lists the current departments that impact environmental policies and the regulatory agencies under their authority.

Regulations

Each of the agencies just listed writes regulations that determine how land can be used. The scope of regulations for the management of public lands is daunting. Regulatory agencies frequently address the following areas in their management regulations: recreation use fees; permits; visiting hours; disruptive behavior;

table ❶ Major Federal Environmental Legislation

Acts	Description of Act
Creation Act of 1891	Established the National Forest Reserve.
The Forest Management Act of 1897	(Organic Act) stipulated that management of the forests would ensure long-term survival of the forests and regulated timber harvesting to "dead and mature" trees.
Lacey Act of 1900	Established the Department of the Interior as the federal agency responsible for managing fish and wildlife; also placed controls on interstate shipment of game.
Reclamation Act of 1902	Initiated reclamation projects for constructing water management projects in the western states.
Transfer Act of 1905	Moved responsibility for the national forests from the Department of Interior to the Department of Agriculture.
Antiquities Act of 1905	Gave the President power to establish national monuments on public lands.
National Park Service Act of 1916	Created the National Park Service as the managing agency of the National Park System.
Migratory Bird Treaty Act of 1918	Provides for the protection of migratory birds.
Recreation Act of 1926	Authorizes exchange, sale, or lease of federal lands to states and political subdivisions for recreational purposes.
Migratory Bird Conservation Act of 1929	Enhances the development and management of migratory bird refuges.
Shipstead-Newton-Nolan Act of 1930	Landmark legislation for forest recreation. Set precedent for policy protecting aesthetic qualities of forest lakes; prohibits leasing or timber harvest within 300 feet of the shorelines.
Tennessee Valley Authority Act of 1933	Established TVA as an independent agency for developing and managing Tennessee Valley water projects.
Fish and Wildlife Coordination Act of 1934	Requires wildlife conservation be coordinated with water resource development.
Migratory Bird Hunting Stamp Act of 1934	Requires a fee for all persons over age 16 who hunt waterfowl; proceeds help fund expanding refuges.
Historic Sites Act of 1935	Broadened presidential power for adding historic sites to the National Park System.
Park, Parkway, and Recreational Studies Act of 1936	Directed the National Park Service to do a comprehensive study of public park and recreation areas.
Pittman-Robertson Act of 1937	Established an excise tax on sporting arms and ammunition; proceeds fund state wildlife management.
The Bald Eagle Protection Act of 1940	Prohibited a variety of activities involving the species, including import, export, take, sale, purchase, or barter.
Flood-Control Act of 1944	Expanded the Army Corps of Engineers' responsibility for providing recreational facilities at civil works projects.
Dingell-Johnson Act of 1950	Established a manufacturer's excise tax on fishing equipment; proceeds used by states for fishery management.
Fish and Wildlife Act of 1956	Established the Fish and Wildlife Service for wildlife management.
National Outdoor Recreation Resources Review Commission	1958—established a commission to conduct a nationwide inventory and evaluation of federal, state, and private outdoor recreation resources and make recommendations to accommodate future requirements.
Multiple-Use Sustained Yield Act of 1960	Mandated that national forests are to be administered on multiple-use basis—outdoor recreation, watershed, range, timber, and fish and wildlife.

continued

table 1 Major Federal Environmental Legislation *(continued)*

Acts	Description of Act
Clean Air Act of 1963	Defined clean air standards.
National Preservation System Act of 1964	(The Wilderness Act) established the National Wilderness System, which now contains more than 90 million acres.
Land Water Conservation Fund Act of 1965	Established a fund to subsidize state and federal acquisition of lands and waters for recreational and conservation purposes.
The Endangered Species Conservation Act of 1969	Prohibited the importation into the United States of species "threatened with extinction worldwide."
The Airborne Hunting Act of 1971	Prohibited the use of aircraft to hunt or harass wildlife.
The Water Pollution Control Act of 1972	Decreed that all water be made safe for fishing and swimming.
Florida Keys National Marine Security Protection Act of 1990	Created the largest sanctuary in the U.S. of 26,000 square nautical miles.
The National Parks Air Tour Management Act of 2000	Limits commercial air tour operations to protect natural quiet and aesthetic values of national parks.

operation of vehicles, vessels, and aircraft; activities of swimming, picnicking, camping, hunting, fishing, and trapping; sanitation; fires; control of animals; explosives, firearms, other weapons, and fireworks; abandonment and impoundment of personal property; commercial activities; special events; and unauthorized structures. Other regulations might be written that are specific to a resource area such as those sites that have caves, hot springs, and other unique features.

State and Local Legislation

State governments use a system similar to the federal agencies. They set aside state lands for wildlife refuges, forests, and parks and have regulatory agencies that enact regulations for state public land use. In addition, states regulate hunting and fishing activities on their public lands. To meet the demand for recreational land, many states have enacted recreational land use statutes that limit liability of land and water owners. These statutes create a fourth category of user (recreational user), to whom the landowner owes little duty (See Chapters 2.21, *Defenses Against Negligence*, 2.22, *Immunity*, and 3.10, *Property Law*). This encourages pri-

table 2 Federal Environmental Agencies

Department	Regulatory Agency
Department of Agriculture	U.S. Forest Service
Department of Commerce	National Oceanic and Atmospheric Administration National Marine Fisheries Service
Department of Defense	Army Corps of Engineers
Department of Interior	Bureau of Indian Affairs Bureau of Land Management Bureau of Reclamation National Park Service U.S. Fish and Wildlife Services
Department of Transportation	Federal Highway Administration
Independent Agency	Tennessee Valley Authority

vate owners to open their land to public recreational use. States also enact enabling legislation to allow local governments to provide public services.

At the local level many communities have passed mandatory recycling initiatives, implemented city beautification statutes, established acceptable noise pollution levels, and enacted zoning ordinances that dictate how a piece of land can be used. Furthermore, state enabling laws empower local government to acquire and develop land and facilities for recreational use in local park systems.

Water Laws

Water laws have developed along two paths: riparian rights and prior appropriation doctrine. Riparian refers to the banks of a stream, river, or pond. *Riparian rights* are generally a matter of state law that entitles a landowner whose property borders on a body of water to prevent the diversion or misuse of upstream waters. Owners of property adjacent to a natural body of water usually have the right to make reasonable use of the water. In the arid regions of the country, predominately west of the Mississippi, a *prior appropriation* doctrine emerged as water was diverted from streams and conveyed to remote places. In this instance, whoever used the water first was first in the right to use the water.

As the appropriation doctrine evolved, it was modified such that the water must be diverted for beneficial use. As a result, in times of drought preference is given to domestic and livestock use over factories and mills. Washington is one of the few states that support the dual system of both riparian and prior appropriation for water law (Washington State Department of Ecology, 2006).

Under Oregon law, as in many other states, all water is publicly owned, and water flowing past, through, or under a person's property does not automatically give the landowner the right to use the water (Oregon Water Resources Department, 2006). Furthermore, public access for recreational use is allowed only on officially declared navigable waterways. Yet in Montana, all waters of the state are held in public trust, and public use is allowed on all surface waters capable of recreational use without regard to the ownership of the underlying land (Mon. Code Ann. § 23-2-302 (1997)). Though boaters may be permitted on free-flowing waters of the Pacific Northwest, other recreational users such as hikers, fishermen, and swimmers may not have the same rights in some states (Robertson, 2001).

In North Carolina, on privately owned land, if a body of water is navigable by any craft such as a canoe or a raft, then the public has the right to use the water for recreation and commerce. There is no public use right for man-made ponds on private property, no public use right to travel over private property to obtain access to a body of water, and no public use right to trespass on private property on the banks of streams, rivers, or lakes. When a river or stream is property boundary, the property line is considered to run down the middle of the stream, and the property line will shift as the stream slowly changes course (Andry, 2006).

A new twist to water law is emerging as manmade water parks develop along river and stream channels. In Colorado, the issue is not the diversion of the water, but rather keeping an adequate flow for kayaking runs that are embellished with strategically placed boulders, hydraulic holes, and designer waves. Recreational in-channel diversion (RICD) water rights protect water parks against water flow restrictions during the peak kayaking seasons of the summer months. The statute allows for "the minimum stream flow" that offers "a reasonable recreation experience" (Colo. Rev. Stat.§§ 37-92-103 (10.3)).

Controversy between recreational users and residential users is at the heart of many legal battles. Residents of the mountain resort in Lake Arrowhead, California, have used the lake as a reservoir for drinking water for almost a century. However, a 1914 declaration of water rights designated Lake Arrowhead as recreation use, and water was not to be removed for consumptive purposes. As drought conditions and additional housing developments ensued, the original water rights have been invoked, and residents are now embroiled in a water battle (McCarthy & Watson, 2005).

Admiralty Law or Maritime Law

Admiralty law or maritime law is both substantive and procedural law that governs navigation and shipping. It is not limited to American tidal waters, but also extends to any water navigable for interstate or foreign commerce within the United States.

Though international law seeks uniformity among countries, it is the ship's flag that ultimately determines the source of law. A ship flying the American flag in Norwegian waters is subject to American admiralty law, whereas a ship flying a Norwegian flag in American waters is subject to Norwegian admiralty law (Cornell Law School, 2006). See *Spector v. Norwegian Cruise Line* (2005), in which an American plaintiff brought suit against a Norwegian cruise line pursuant to Title III of the Americans with Disabilities Act. The foreign-flagged ship was operating in U.S. waters and denied the plaintiff, who was a wheelchair user, access to many of the ship accommodations.

Recreational boating comes under admiralty law when on navigable water, and it is enforced by the U.S. Coast Guard. However, the U.S. Army Corps of Engineers under the Rivers and Harbors Appropriation Act of 1899, regulates structures on navigable waterways. In *LeBlanc v. Cleveland* (1999) the court defined navigability for admiralty jurisdiction as a body of water that supports commercial activity. Noncommercial fishing and pleasure boating do not constitute commercial trade or travel. In *Weaver v. Hollywood Casino-Aura* (2001) the court found that admiralty jurisdiction could not be invoked for a personal injury claim on a casino boat because that portion of the river was not navigable.

Admiralty laws are a whole different set of laws. Although almost any crime or tort that happens on land can also happen on board a ship, the laws that control such incidents may be totally different. For example, admiralty law does not allow for collection of workers' compensation for seamen. Instead, the Jones Act of 1920 (46 U.S.C. Sec 688) was passed, which permitted a seaman, inland river worker, or offshore worker to recover for negligence on the part of a vessel's owner, operator, or fellow employees. It also covered issues regarding the seaworthiness of ships. Cruise ships, recreational boats, and diving vessels are under the Jones Act in navigable waters. Admiralty jurisdiction may be recognized in recreational scuba diving cases, but much depends on the role of the dive boat. See *Borden v. Phillips* (2000) and *Sinclair v. Soniform* (1991) to understand admiralty jurisdiction issues in scuba diving. If the accident is solely related to scuba diving and there is no relationship to the operation or maintenance of a vessel, then there is no admiralty jurisdiction.

Natural Environment Issues

The following section will discuss a sampling of environmental legislation issues that relate to outdoor recreation. However, be aware that these are only the "tip of the iceberg," as the scope of legislation associated with environment is far reaching. Some laws are very specific, such as ones that ban cockfighting or prohibit the importation of mongooses. Others are very broad, such as the Water Pollution Control Act of 1972 that was enacted to make all water safe for fishing and swimming.

Preservation

The ever-increasing demand for recreational land dramatically affects environmental quality. There is concern that America's affinity for nature will cause us to "love it to death." This raises the issue of user rights versus environmental protection. In *National Wildlife Federation, et al. v. National Marine Fisheries Service, et al.* (2002) the court granted a temporary injunction. It found that irreparable damage to endangered species of salmon eggs would result if the Corps of Engineers was allowed to dredge a navigable waterway.

Maintaining capacity limitations for the preservation and protection of fragile and scenic areas requires regulation through use permits and use limits. Because of the tremendous resource degradation that can accompany search and rescue operations, proponents of environmental preservation would like to have "rescue free" environments for those who choose to enter pristine wilderness. Some jurisdictions are assessing charges for search and rescue missions when an incident is deemed to be the result of negligence on the part of the recreation participant. Adventure activities with high inherent risks result in moral, ethical, and legal controversy over liability when there is an injury.

Archeological

To protect historical, archaeological and cultural sites, a number of statutes have been passed. The National Historic Preservation Act of 1966 provided for a National Register of Historic Places. Subsequent legislation offered protection to graves, abandoned shipwrecks, and other archaeological resources.

Technology

Technological advances also threaten the environment. In *Voicestream Minneapolis, Inc. v. St. Croix County* (2002), it was argued that a 185-foot wireless tower would obstruct the outstandingly remarkable scenic value of the natural resource and be visually obtrusive and aesthetically unappealing.

Hunting Laws

The Airborne Hunting Act of 1971 prohibits the use of aircraft to hunt or harass wildlife. In *United States of America v. Red Frame Parasail* (2001), the court also found it unlawful to scout wildlife for upcoming hunting expeditions using a parasail. The legislative history showed that the act was intended to discourage unsportsmanlike behavior.

Animals are not the only ones needing protection from harassment. Forty-eight states have laws to protect hunters and anglers from harassment by animal rights advocates. A person may not interfere with someone who is participating in the lawful right of taking game, even if it is merely to try to dissuade the person from hunting. In *State of Connecticut v. Catherine Ball, et al.* (2002), animal-rights activists argued that this bars their First Amendment rights to freedom of speech. The Supreme Court ruling found that activists must use alternative means of protest such as advertising and speaking to groups to convey their antihunting message.

Boating Laws

The U.S. Coast Guard enforces the federal laws for "boating under the influence" (see 33 CFR 95.020). This makes it illegal in every state to operate a boat while under the influence of alcohol or drugs. This law pertains to all boats from canoes and rafts to the largest ships that operate in U.S. waters as well as U.S. vessels on the high seas. The law does not make it illegal to have an open container of alcohol in a boat. However, because most boating fatalities occur from falls overboard, an intoxicated passenger is just as likely to die as an intoxicated operator. Thus, the regulation views everyone with a paddle as an operator.

States have laws regulating the use of boats on waterways. For example, New Hampshire has legislated that no person sixteen years of age or older may operate a powerboat with an engine in excess of 25 horsepower (including electric-powered motors) on public waters without a valid safe boating education certificate. It is a once in a lifetime requirement and does not have to be renewed periodically. States also generally set a minimum age for operating personal watercraft such as jet skis.

Off-Road Vehicles

Off-road vehicles such as motorcycles, four-wheelers, dune buggies, and snowmobiles cause extensive damage to vegetation and wildlife and are a source of disruptive noise pollution to the peaceful habitat of wildlife. The Special Protection of the Public Lands (1977), an executive order signed by the president, stipulates that whenever the director "determines that the use of off-road vehicles will cause or is causing considerable adverse effects on the soil, vegetation, wildlife, wildlife habitat, or cultural or historic resources of particular areas or trails of the public lands," the director should "immediately close such areas or trails to the type of off-road vehicle causing such effects, until such time as he determines that such adverse effects have been eliminated and that measures have been implemented to prevent future recurrence" (Sec. 9 added by Executive Order 11989 of May 24, 1977, 42 FR 26959, 3 CFR, 1977 Comp., p. 120). Horses, pack animals, and mountain bikes have also been blamed for environmental degradation.

Noise Pollution

Local, state, and federal agencies have enacted various noise pollution laws. Efforts have been made to ban or reduce the noise from sources such as leaf blowers, powerboats, jet skis, wave runners, loud car stereos, continual barking of dogs, and overflights by aircraft in national parks. The National Parks Air Tour Management Act, passed in April of 2000, directs the National Park Service and Federal Aviation Agency to develop plans to control commercial air tour noise in parks. Hawaii's two federally designated wilderness areas are especially affected by helicopter tourism. Many outdoor pursuits entail use of motorized equipment, yet the noise is disruptive to the wildlife and impacts the solitude of other park users. Campground regulations often impose quiet hours on campers.

Significant Case

————————◇◇◇————————

The following case illustrates the difficulty in writing clear, concise regulations that cover recreational activities of today and how they will evolve in the future. This case involves the extreme sport of BASE jumping. BASE is an acronym describing the structures—Buildings, Antennae, Spans, and Earth forms—from which participants commonly leap. This activity is similar to hang gliding. It calls for the BASE jumper to leap from a stationary structure and, after enjoying a brief free-fall, to then deploy a parachute enabling the jumper to land safely. It is important to note that the courts have found that technological improvements in the shape, maneuverability, and control of modern parachutes do not cease to make them parachutes. Addressed in the discussion is the issue that a regulation is not unconstitutionally vague if it is capable of a limited interpretation such that ordinary people could understand what conduct is prohibited and those enforcing it are provided with clear standards. This case also addresses the issue of burden of proof in relation to the issuance of a permit.

UNITED STATES OF AMERICA V. OXX, ET AL.

United States District Court for the District of Utah, Central Division
56 F. Supp.2d 1214 (1999)

Opinion By: Bruce S. Jenkins, United States Senior District Judge

Background

On April 18, 1996, the United States filed a petty offense Information charging each of the named defendants in separate counts as to each but joined for convenience with violating 36 C.F.R. § 2.17(a) (3) (1995) by "delivering persons by parachute within the Glen Canyon National Recreation Area without a permit and when not required by an emergency." Investigations by the National Park Service resulted in warrants issued for each defendant. A joint bench trial for all of the defendants was scheduled for September 12, 1996. At the time of pre-trial motion hearings, the Government asserted that during the week of April 28, 1995, through May 3, 1995, each of the named defendants engaged in the activity commonly known as BASE jumping by leaping off the cliffs of Glen Canyon National Recreation Area and then, shortly after leaping, deploying a parachute or similar device to glide to a landing on Lake Powell.

On August 29, 1996, the defendants filed a joint Motion to Dismiss the counts pending against them, asserting, among other things, that the Information was defective. The defendants contended that the Information should be dismissed because section 2.17 (a) (3) of the Park Service regulations does not clearly prohibit BASE jumping, and, as applied to the facts of this case, section 2.17 (a) (3) is ambiguous.

After hearing argument, considering proffered facts and testimony, and reviewing the papers submitted on the motion, the court found that the regulations were not intended to prohibit BASE jumping. The court also concluded that the regulation, as applied to the purported conduct of the defendants, suffered from an incurable ambiguity. The court then dismissed the Information as to each defendant. See United States v. Oxx, 980 F. Supp. 405, 408-09 (D. Utah 1997).

The Government appealed and the Court of Appeals for the Tenth Circuit reversed. See United States v. Oxx, 127 F.3d 1277 (10th Cir. 1997). In doing so, the Tenth Circuit held that the defendants unambiguously used a "parachute" as that term is defined under the regulations. See id. at 1279. The court also concluded that section 2.17 (a) (3) was not ambiguous when applied to the defendants' BASE jumping activities because delivery by "parachute" was clearly prohibited.

Following reversal, this court held extensive pretrial hearings concerning the defendants' motion to suppress and motion to dismiss on pre-emption grounds. Both motions were denied. A bench trial was then held on October 6 and 7, 1999. At the trial's conclusion, and for reasons stated on the record, the court found defendants John M. Henderson and Michael Kvale not guilty of the petty offense charged, respectively, in Counts 8 and 10 of the Information. As to the remaining defendants, the court reserved its decision. Now, for reasons stated below, the court finds defendants William Oxx, Jonathan Oxx, Martin Tilly, Christopher Berke, David Katz and Aaron M. Brennan not guilty of the petty offenses charged in the Information.

Discussion

The defendants have been charged with violating 36 C.F.R. § 2.17 (a) (3), which reads in part:

(a) The following are prohibited:

(1) Operating or using aircraft on lands or waters other than at locations designated pursuant to special regulations.

* * *

(3) Delivering or retrieving a person or object by parachute, helicopter, or other airborne means, except in emergencies involving public safety or serious property loss, or pursuant to the terms and conditions of a permit. 36 C.F.R. § 2.17 (a) (3) (1995). In part, the defendants assert that their alleged conduct does not violate this regulation because BASE jumping cannot be considered as "delivering . . . a person by parachute," within the meaning of section 2.17 (a) (3). Although BASE jumping does involve the use of a parachute, the defendants contend that the types of parachutes used in BASE jumping, and the type of parachutes they allegedly used, permit the jumper to control the parachute and engage in horizontal flight. The defendants argue that this element of flight control makes BASE jumping similar to hang gliding and other forms of powerless flight, and distinguishes the parachutes or "airfoils" allegedly used by the defendants from the parachutes prohibited under the regulations.

The United States, on the other hand, argues that the Tenth Circuit has already answered, in the affirmative, the question of whether BASE jumping parachutes are "parachutes" under section 2.17 (a) (3). Thus, so long as the United States demonstrates, beyond a reasonable doubt, that each defendant, without a permit, used a parachute to deliver himself to a place within the Glen Canyon National Recreation Area, then each defendant is guilty of violating section 2.17 (a) (3).

Analysis

At the outset the court begins its analysis by commenting on the question of whether the devices the defendants used in BASE jumping are "parachutes" as that term is understood under section 2.17 (a) (3). The United States is correct when it argues that the Tenth Circuit's decision in United States v. Oxx resolves this issue. There, the Court of Appeals concluded that because these devices "'retard the fall of a body or object through the air'" they are unambiguously "parachutes" as that term is used in section 2.17 (a) (3). Oxx, 127 F.3d at 1279 (quoting 14 C.F.R. § 1.1). Therefore, despite the uncontroverted evidence now offered by the defendants that the devices they used were capable of extended flight and control—a control that makes these devices more like powered aircraft than simple parachutes—this court is bound to apply the dictates of the Tenth Circuit when it says, in summary, a parachute is a parachute is a parachute.

In all fairness, however, the defendants actual use of these devices suggests that, in this narrow factual circumstance, the Court of Appeals may not have been so far off the mark as alleged by defendants. According to the evidence presented to the court, the more experienced BASE jumpers among the defendants would run to the edge of the cliff and leap off. These jumpers would not immediately deploy their parachutes. Instead, they enjoyed an extended "free-fall" for as long as possible, only deploying their parachute when the prospect of meeting the Earth with the full force of gravity overcame the thrill of free-fall. The less-experienced BASE jumping defendants would also leap off the cliff, but instead of waiting to deploy their parachutes they would immediately deploy their chutes as soon as they began their free-fall. In each instance, it appears that the oft-talked about "rush" one "enjoys" from BASE jumping comes from a combination of the thrill of the free-fall and the danger of the activity. Thus it appears that it is the jump and free-fall, rather than the descent and glide under a parachute, that gives BASE jumping its special appeal.

Moreover, given the limited time it took to complete these BASE jumps, and the relative short heights from which these BASE jumps were made, any flight attributes the parachutes or airfoils may have are, for the most part, secondary to the role the parachutes plays in controlling the jumper's descent and avoiding a gravity-induced re-acquaintance with terra firma. In such a circumstance, the Tenth Circuit's conclusion that the devices used by the defendants are "parachutes," because they were intended to retard the fall of the defendants' bodies through the air, is a fair one.

The conclusion that the devices the defendants allegedly used were parachutes as that term is understood under section 2.17 (a) (3), however, does not alone demonstrate their guilt. As mentioned previously, the defendants are charged with violating 36 C.F.R. § 2.17 (a) (3), which, in relevant part, makes it unlawful to deliver or retrieve a person or object by parachute, "except in emergencies involving public safety or serious property loss, or pursuant to the terms and conditions of a permit." (emphasis added). Counts 1 through 9 of the Information charge the defendants with "delivering persons by parachute within the Glen Canyon National Recreation Area (Utah side) without permit and when not required by emergency." (Petty Offense Information, file dkt. no. 1.) (emphasis added).

A close reading of the regulation and the charge in the Information makes the following clear: in order to violate section 2.17 (a) (3), as charged in this case, a person must deliver him or herself by a parachute without a permit or the existence of an emergency. See 36 C.F.R. § 2.17 (a) (3). The United States apparently agrees with this construction. In its opening statement it emphasized that by the close of evidence "it will prove and establish beyond a reasonable doubt Your Honor that these named defendants . . . delivered themselves by parachute within the Glen Canyon National Recreation area and they did so without a permit and not in an emergency situation all in violation of 36 C.F.R. Section 2.17 Sub. a., Sub 3." (Tr. vol. I, at 5.) (emphasis added). Thus, as understood by the court and the United States, there are three elements to the section 2.17 (a) (3) offense charged in this case: (1) delivery; (2) by parachute; (3) and without a permit or some emergency situation.

Under our Constitution the Fifth Amendment requires, and all parties here would acknowledge, that the United States bears the burden of proving beyond a reasonable doubt that the defendant is guilty of all the elements of a crime. U.S. CONST. amend. V.; In re Winship, 397 U.S. 358, 364, 25 L. Ed. 2d 368, 90 S. Ct. 1068 (1970). It is without dispute that a criminal conviction must rest on a determination that the defendant "is guilty of every element of the crime with which he is charged, beyond a reasonable doubt." United States v. Gaudin, 515 U.S. 506, 510, 132 L. Ed. 2d 444, 115 S. Ct. 2310 (1995). The burden on the United States to prove a defendant's guilt beyond a reasonable doubt cannot be relieved by a defendant's decision not to contest an essential element of the crime. See Estelle v. McGuire, 502 U.S. 62, 69, 116 L. Ed. 2d 385, 112 S. Ct. 475 (1991). Nor may the United States shift the burden to the defendant to try and disprove an essential element. See Mullaney v. Wilbur, 421 U.S. 684, 703-04, 44 L. Ed. 2d 508, 95 S. Ct. 1881 (1975).

After listening to the testimony and carefully reviewing the trial transcript, the court finds that the United States has failed to establish an element of a section 2.17 (a) (3) offense. Nowhere in the exhibits offered and received or in the testimony given has the United States established that the defendants delivered themselves by parachute without a permit. Although three agents for the National Park Service testified at trial, none testified about the absence of a permit. Nor was there any other evidence, direct or circumstantial, that established the nonexistence of a permit.

* * *

The court recognizes that the question of the makeup of the roster of the elements of the alleged offense is a close one. The elements and the burden, as defined in this case by the United States, are reasonable and compatible with the presumption of innocence. That burden, on this record, has not been met. As Sir William Blackstone has noted, ". . . all presumptive evidence of felony should be admitted cautiously: for the law holds, that it is better that ten guilty persons escape, than that one innocent suffer." 4 William Blackstone, Commentaries on the Laws of England *352 (1769). As to whether such a result is fair, Blackstone offers additional sage counsel: "Yet let it be again remembered, that delays, and little inconveniences in the forms of justice, are the price that all free nations must pay for their liberty in more substantial matters."

Conclusion

For the reasons set forth above and for reasons stated by the court on October 7, 1998, the court finds the defendants, William Oxx (Counts 1 and 10), Jonathan Oxx (Count 2), Martin Tilly (Count 3), Christopher Berke (Count 4), David Katz (Count 5), John M. Henderson (Count 8), Aaron M. Brennan (Count 9), and Michael Kvale (Count 10), NOT GUILTY of the offenses charged in the Information. The charges against Steve Mulholland (Count 7) are DISMISSED.

◇◇◇ **OTHER RELATED SIGNIFICANT CASES**

Recent Trends

High-Risk Recreation

There has been a tremendous growth in outdoor adventure activities. High-adventure, high-risk recreation activities, commonly called "extreme sport," "alternative sport," or "action sport," are limited only by one's creativity. They take many forms: bungee jumping, extreme mountain climbing, freestyle motocross, "high air" skateboarding, ice climbing, kitesurfing, mountain boarding, rock climbing, sandboarding, skitching (inline skaters launch themselves from the bumpers of speeding cars), skydiving, sky surfing, skywalking, snowboarding, street luging, wakeboarding, and white-water rafting (rapid riding). The preceding significant case demonstrates one of the many legal issues related to these popular activities. Many states have enacted legislation that shields providers from liability for injuries resulting from the inherent risks of such activities. Additionally, a few have even provided protection from liability for certain types of ordinary negligence by the provider (see Chapter 2.22, *Immunity*, for more information).

Environmental Concerns at Yellowstone

Controversy continues regarding the use of snowmobiles in Yellowstone and other wilderness areas. At the end of the Clinton administration, the Park Service, siding with environmentalist complaints that the vehicles disturb wildlife and cause air pollution, ordered snowmobile use to be phased down by the winter of 2003–2004. In February 2002, air pollution became so great that the Park Service began issuing respirators to employees who wanted to protect themselves from exhaust from some 65,000 snowmobiles entering Yellowstone Park each year (Snowmobilers enjoy last unrestricted winter, 2003). Current restrictions call for limiting the number of vehicles to 720 per day and requiring guides to accompany snowmobilers (Jackson, 2006). A new Environmental Impact Statement on snowmobiling in the region will be released in spring 2006 (National Park Service, 2005).

Illegal Drugs

Many natural areas have become the home for marijuana growing or methamphetamine cooking. Cannabis cultivation on federal lands is especially high in California and Kentucky. Plots vary in size from a few plants to 40,000 plants. Booby traps, explosives and armed guards pose a danger to unsuspecting hikers who happen on the site. Organized Mexican DTOs (Drug Trafficking Organizations) are responsible for much of the activity in California, whereas Kentucky cannabis is generally cultivated by independent locals (National Drug Intelligence Center, 2005)

Methamphetamine cooking is an even more daunting problem because many of the chemicals, which are easily purchased at a local shopping center, are reactive, explosive, flammable, and corrosive. Approximately five pounds of toxic waste is generated for each pound of "meth." The toxic waste is dumped on the land and into streams. Clean-up costs for these "mini-hazardous-waste" sites are extremely expensive, with even the smallest costing between $3,000 and $4,000 and requiring specialized equipment such as hazmat suits. With a four- to six-hour cooking time, clandestine meth labs are mobile and easily transported in the trunk of a car. California, Arizona, and Missouri are the top producers of illegal methamphetamine (Sierra Magazine, 2001).

Environmental Justice

Executive Order 12898, Federal Actions to Address Environmental Justice in Minority Populations and Low-Income Populations issued on February 11, 1994, requires federal agencies to determine the effects of their projects and policies on minority and low income populations. Environmental justice involves the fair treatment of all people regardless of race, ethnicity, or income with respect to the development, adoption, implementation, and enforcement of environmental laws, regulations, and policies. Floyd and Johnson (2002) insisted that environmental justice as a social movement is more than the inequitable placement of hazardous wastes in low-income areas or the disproportionate number of bottom feeder fish taken from inferior quality fisheries by minorities. The larger problem is the unfair representation of minorities and marginalized people in decision making. "The application of environmental justice to natural resource management involves three primary efforts: (a) natural resources ought be allocated through fair procedures (i.e., the interest of the poor as well as the affluent should be considered in resource allocation, (b) benefits and costs of resource management should be distributed fairly, and (c) citizens should have equal access to public resources" (Floyd & Johnson, 2002, p. 69)

References

Cases

Borden v. Phillips, 752 So. 2d 69, 72-73 (Fla , 2000).
Colorado Water Conservation Board v. Upper Gunnison River Water Conservancy District, 109 P. 3d 585 (Colo. 2005).
LeBlanc v. Cleveland, 198 F.3d 353 (U.S. App., 1999).
National Wildlife Federation, et al. v. National Marine Fisheries Service, et al. (U.S. Dist. 2002).
Sinclair v. Soniform, Inc., 935 F. 2d 599 (U.S. App., 1991).

Spector v. Norwegian Cruise Line Ltd., 125 S. Ct. 2169 (2005).

State of Connecticut v. Catherine Ball, et al., 260 Conn. 275; 796 A.2d 542 (Conn. 2002).

Voicestream Minneapolis, Inc. v. St. Croix County, 212 F. Supp.2d 914 (U.S. Dist. 2002).

United States of America v. Oxx, et al., 56 F. Supp.2d 1214 (1999).

United States of America v. Red Frame Parasail, 160 F. Supp.2d 1048 (U.S. Dist. 2001).

Publications

Andry, A. (2006). *Water law in North Carolina*. Applied Resource Economics and Policy Group Department of Agricultural and Resource Economics. http://www.bae.ncsu.edu/programs/extension/publicat/arep/waterlaw.html

Cornell Law School. (2006). *Admiralty*. Retrieved from http://www.law.cornell.edu/wex/index.php/Admiralty

Dennis, S. (2001). *Natural resources and the informed citizen*. Champaign, IL: Sagamore Publishing.

Floyd, M., & Johnson, C. (2002). Coming to terms with environmental justice in outdoor recreation: A conceptual discussion with research implication. *Leisure Sciences, 24*, 59–77.

Garner, B. (Ed.). (1996). *Black's law dictionary* (2nd ed.). St. Paul, MN: West Publishing.

Gordon, D., & Gegax, T. (2002, February 25). Going extreme. *Newsweek, 139*(8), 48, 3p, 3c.

Ibrahim, H., & Cordes, K. (2002). *Outdoor recreation: Enrichment for a lifetime* (2nd ed.). Champaign, IL: Sagamore Publishing.

Jackson, K. (2006, January). Judge upholds Yellowstone snowmobile compromise. *Environment News*. Retrieved from http://www.heartland.org/Article.cfm?artId=18257

Jensen, C. (1995). *Outdoor recreation in America* (5th ed.). Champaign, IL: Human Kinetics.

McCarthy, G., & Watson, G. (2005, August 5). Anger, fear in Arrowhead clarification sought in water decision. *San Bernardino Sun*. Section: News. Retrieved from http://v6.sbsun.com/Stories/0,1413,208%257E12588%257E2996638,00.html

National Drug Intelligence Center. (2005, February). *Marijuana and methamphetamine trafficking on federal lands threat assessment*. Retrieved from http://0225.0145.01.040/ndic/pubs10/10330/index.htm

National Park Service. (2005). *Winter use plan environmental impact statement, Yellowstone and Grand Teton National Parks and the John D. Rockefeller, Jr., Memorial Parkway*. Retrieved from http://www.nps.gov/yell/planvisit/winteruse/

National Wilderness Institute. (1995). *State by state government land ownership*. Retrieved from www.nwi.org/Maps/LandChart.html

Oregon Water Resources Department. (2006). *Oregon water laws*. Retrieved from http://www.wrd.state.or.us/OWRD/PUBS/awuabook_laws.shtml)

Robertson, J. (2001, January 9). Trends in recreational water rights in the pacific northwest. *American Whitewater*. Retrieved from http://www.americanwhitewater.org/content/Articl/display/articleid/131/display/full

Sierra Magazine. (2001). *Welcome to meth country*. Retrieved from http://www.sierraclub.org/sierra/200101/Meth.asp

Snowmobilers enjoy last unrestricted winter. (2003). Retrieved from http://edition.cnn.com/2003/TRAVEL/01/15/snowmobiles.last.ap/

Washington State Department of Ecology. (2006). *Water law, a primer*. Publication number WR-98-152. Retrieved from http://www.ecy.wa.gov/pubs/98152/

Legislation

Airborne Hunting Act of 1971, 16 U.S.C. § 742j-l, as amended 1972.

Antiquities Act of 1906, 16 U.S.C. §§ 431–433 (1906).

Bald Eagle Protection Act of 1940, 16 U.S.C. § 668-668d, 54 Stat. 250 as amended by P.L 86-70 (73 Stat. 143) June 25, 1959; P.L. 87-884 (76 Stat. 1346) October 24, 1962; P.L. 92-535 (86 Stat. 1064) October 23, 1972; and P.L. 95-616 (92 Stat. 3114) November 8, 1978.

Clean Air Act of 1963, P.L. 88-206.

Colo. Rev. Stat.§§ 37-92-103 (10.3).

Dingell-Johnson Act of 1950, 16 U.S.C. §§ 777–777l, as amended 1956, 1959, 1960, 1970, 1976, 1980, 1984, 1986, 1988, 1990, and 1992.

Endangered Species Conservation Act of 1969, 16 U.S.C. §§ 1531–1544, 87 Stat. 884, as amended P.L. 93-205, approved December 28, 1973, repealed the Endangered Species Conservation Act of December 5, 1969 (P.L. 91-135, 83 Stat. 275).

Fish and Wildlife Act of 1956, 16 U.S.C. §§ 742a–754j-2, as amended 1961, 1962, 1964, 1965, 1970–1972, 1974–1976, 1978, 1980, 1982–1984 and 1986.

Fish and Wildlife Coordination Act of 1934, 16 U.S.C. §§ 661–667e, as amended 1946, 1958, 1978 and 1995.

Flood-Control Act of 1944, 16 U.S.C. §§ 460d (and various sections of Titles 33 and 43 U.S.C.); P.L. 78-534, 58 Stat. 887.

Florida Keys National Marine Security Protection Act of 1990, P.L. 101-605 (H.R. 5909).

Forest Management Act of 1897: (Organic Act), 16 U.S.C. §§ 473–478, 479–482 and 551, June 4, 1897, as amended 1905, 1911, 1925, 1962, 1964, 1968 and 1976.

Forest Reserve Act of 1891, (Creation Act of 1891), 26 Stat. 1103.

Historic Sites Act of 1935, 16 U.S.C. §§ 461–467.

Jones Act of 1920, 46 U.S.C. Sec 688.

Lacey Act of 1900, 16 U.S.C. § 701 (1900).

Land and Water Conservation Fund Act of 1965, 16 U.S.C. §§ 460l-4 through 460l-11, (1964), as amended 1965, 1968, 1970, 1972 1974, 1976–1981, 1983, 1986, 1987, 1990, 1991, 1993–1996.

Migratory Bird Treaty Act of 1918, 16 U.S.C. §§ 703–712; Ch. 128; July 13, 1918; 40 Stat. 755 as amended by: Chapter 634; June 20, 1936; 49 Stat. 1556; P.L. 86-732; September 8, 1960; 74 Stat. 866; P.L. 90-578; October 17, 1968; 82 Stat. 1118; P.L. 91-135; December 5, 1969; 83 Stat. 282; P.L. 93-300; June 1, 1974; 88 Stat. 190; P.L. 95-616; November 8, 1978; 92 Stat. 3111; P.L. 99-645; November 10, 1986; 100 Stat. 3590 and P.L. 105-312; October 30, 1998; 112 Stat. 2956.

Migratory Bird Conservation Act of 1929, 16 U.S.C. §§ 715-715r, as amended 1935, 1961, 1962, 1966–1968, 1970, 1973, 1976, 1978, 1983, 1984, 1986, 1988 and 1989.

Migratory Bird Hunting Stamp Act of 1934, 16 U.S.C. §§ 718–718j, as amended 1935, 1949, 1951, 1956, 1958, 1966, 1968, 1971, 1976, 1978, 1982, 1984, 1986, and 1988.

Mon. Code Ann. § 23-2-302 (1997).

Multiple-Use Sustained Yield Act of 1960, 16 U.S.C. §§ 528–531 (1960).

National Environmental Policy Act of 1969, P.L. 91-190, 42 U.S.C. 4321–4347, January 1, 1970, as amended by P.L. 94-52, July 3, 1975, P.L. 94-83, August 9, 1975, and P.L. 97-258, §§ 4 (b), September 13, 1982.

National Historic Preservation Act of 1966, as amended through 2000, 16 U.S.C. §§ 470 et seq.

National Marine Sanctuaries Amendment Act of 2000, P.L. 106-513.

National Outdoor Recreation Resources Review Commission, L. 85-470, June 28, 1958, 72 Stat. 238, as amended by P.L. 86-6, Mar. 25, 1959, 73 Stat. 14; P.L. 87-12, Mar. 29, 1961, 75 Stat. 19.

National Parks Air Tour Management Act of 2000, P.L. 106-181.

National Park Service Act of 1916, 6 U.S.C. §§1–18f-1, as amended 1920, 1921, 1924, 1926, 1928, 1930, 1931, 1933, 1935, 1936, 1939–1941, 1946, 1948–1953, 1955, 1956, 1958, 1960, 1964, 1966, 1967, 1970, 1973, 1975, 1976, 1978, 1980, 1981, 1983, 1984, 1990–1994 and 1996.

National Preservation System Act of 1964, 16 U.S.C. §§ 1131–1136, 78 Stat. 890.

Park, Parkway, and Recreational Studies Act of 1936, 49 Stat. 1894.

Park Protection Act of 1898.

Pittman-Robertson Act of 1937, 16 U.S.C. §§ 669–669i, as amended 1939, 1941, 1946, 1950, 1955, 1956, 1959, 1960, 1970, 1972, 1974, 1976, 1980, 1984, 1986, and 1989.

Reclamation Act of 1902, P.L. 57-161 (1902).

Recreation Act of 1926, 44 Stat. 741.

Shipstead-Newton-Nolan Act of 1930, 16 U.S.C. § 577.

Special Protection of the Public Lands [Sec. 9 added by Executive Order 11989 of May 24, 1977, 42 FR 26959, 3 CFR, 1977 Comp., p. 120].

Tennessee Valley Authority Act of 1933, 48 Stat. 58-59, 16 U.S.C. § 831.

Transfer Act of 1905, 33 Stat. 628.

Water Pollution Control Act of 1972, 33 U.S.C. §§ 1251–1387, as amended 1973–1983, 1987, 1988, 1990–1992, 1994, 1995, and 1996.

4.00

Intentional Torts and Criminal Acts

Some actions go beyond the level of the unintentional tort—negligence. Two such actions included in this section are intentional torts and criminal acts. An **intentional tort** is a tort, or wrong, in which the actor possessed intent or purpose to injure. An intentional tort contains three elements: (1) there must be an injury, (2) the act is the proximate cause of an injury, and (3) there must be intent to bring about the injury. When injury results from an intentional tort, the doctrine of *respondeat superior* does not usually apply. Thus, the tortious party generally stands alone, individually liable. Only the wronged party may bring action against the wrongdoer. Several intentional torts that are of particular interest to the recreation or sport manager are examined in this section. They are assault and battery, defamation, invasion of privacy, breach of fiduciary duty, tortious interference with contract, and hazing. Chapter 4.16, *Hazing* (which addresses both intentional torts and crimes), has been completely rewritten, and the other intentional tort chapters have been revised and updated.

Recreation and sport managers are becoming more concerned with the effects of crimes on their programs. **Criminal law** is that body of law made up of state and federal statutes that define certain offenses of a public nature or wrongs committed against the state and specify corresponding fines and punishment. The punishment for crimes can range from fines to jail terms to long-term prison sentences, depending on the nature of the crime. The state must institute the action, and there is generally no remuneration to the victim. In contrast, in civil suits punishment generally takes the form of a monetary award to the victim.

The reader should look at Section 5.00, *Risk Management*, for approaches to preventing incidents involving intentional torts and criminal acts. Several chapters in the section discuss risk management strategies that can help the recreation or sport manager prevent such acts or be prepared for them when they do occur.

4.11 Assault and Battery

Mary A. Hums
University of Louisville

Recreation or sport managers need to be aware of different contexts in which assault and battery may occur in the recreation or sport setting. This chapter addresses civil assault and battery, including incidents involving participants, fans, and officials. Although the criminal acts we read about (e.g., fans so out of control that they destroy campus and city property after big wins like the 2002 Ohio State–Michigan football game or big losses like Michigan State's 2005 NCAA basketball tourney loss and the highly publicized attacks on tennis star Monica Seles, Houston Astros player Bill Spiers, Kansas City Royals coach Tom Gamboa, and MLB umpire Laz Diaz) gain most of the attention, the civil assault and battery cases sometimes seem tame by comparison. But they are equally important. Any assault or battery, whether addressed as a criminal or a civil matter, is equally repugnant in the world of sport and recreation.

Recreation and sport managers must always remain vigilant regarding security issues surrounding amateur players, fans in the stands, and officials as well as security for highly visible athletes. We see highly visible athletes in scrapes and being arrested frequently (e.g., Ron Artest went into the stands in Detroit after a fan threw a water bottle at him; a University of Nebraska football player punched a University of Missouri fan after a tough loss; and numerous domestic violence incidents), but the recreation or sport manager in a school or recreation setting outside the national spotlight must remember that similar incidents are happening everywhere at an alarming rate.

Recreation and sport managers need to realize that assault and battery may also occur at a high school football game, in a health and fitness club, at an intramural event, at a youth soccer game, on a white-water rafting trip, or in any other recreation or sport setting. Controlling for situations in which assault and battery may occur should be a part of any recreation or sport organization's risk management plan.

Fundamental Concepts

When the terms *assault* and *battery* come to mind, they are most often thought of in terms of criminal law (see Chapter 4.12, *Criminal Liability for Violence in Sports*); however, the recreation or sport manager is more often concerned with civil assault and battery. A distinction must be made between **criminal assault and battery**, which is a crime, and **civil assault and battery**, which is an intentional tort—however, *it is important to understand that, in many cases, the same act can be either or both a crime and an intentional tort*. For instance, suppose an irate parent punches an umpire at a Little League Baseball game. The umpire has the option of filing a civil suit against the parent. If the suit is successful, the umpire may be awarded monetary damages. The umpire also has the option of filing criminal charges against the parent. If the parent is convicted, he or she may serve jail time, be fined, or be punished in some other way by the state. If both civil and criminal remedies are pursued, the outcome of one is independent of the outcome of the other (e.g., the O. J. Simpson case). This chapter focuses on civil assault and battery.

A final point to keep in mind when discussing assault and battery is that although these two terms are often used together, they are, in fact, separate concepts. These intentional torts may occur together or may be independent of each other. In basic terms, **assault** is the threat (noncontact) to use force, whereas **battery** is the actual use (physical contact) of force.

Assault

Assault may be defined as the intentional creation of a reasonable apprehension of imminent and offensive contact without the person's consent. No actual physical contact need occur for an assault to be committed. If a football coach draws back his hand, threatening to strike a youngster, he has committed assault. If he shouts at the boy or threatens to make him run laps, no assault has occurred. To understand the definition of assault, it is helpful to break it down into several parts. Specifically, we should define what is meant by the words *reasonable*, *apprehension*, and *imminent*.

First, what is meant by **reasonable**? The court will look in hindsight at what occurred and ask the question, "Would a reasonable person have believed the contact to be imminent?" If the answer to this question is yes, then it is possible that an assault has occurred. The courts, however, cannot see into the mind of the person committing the assault. For example, it does not matter if the person committing the assault pointed an unloaded gun. There was no way the person being assaulted could have known whether or not the gun was loaded or could have known if the person intended to carry out the assault. The fact is, if someone points a gun at another person, it is reasonable for that person to assume he or she is about to be shot.

Next, one must understand what is meant by **apprehension**. Normally, apprehension is associated with fear or being scared. However, when looking at an assault situation, apprehension is more accurately defined as awareness rather than fear. Here the courts will ask whether the person was aware that some sort of contact was about to occur. If the answer is no, no assault occurred. Because of this, technically one could not assault a person who is asleep or unconscious. A sleeping or unconscious individual is incapable of being aware of imminent contact. Once again the reasonable person standard is applied in determining apprehension on the part of the person who was assaulted.

Finally, **imminent** implies that something is going to happen immediately. The person being threatened believes something is going to happen immediately, not at some unknown time in the future.

Elements of Assault

In order to establish an assault has occurred, the following three elements must be present.

1. The defendant intended to cause harm (or apprehension).
2. The plaintiff felt reasonable apprehension of immediate harm.
3. There was lack of consent by the plaintiff.

Defenses for Assault

A successful defense to assault can be brought by the defendant if he or she can prove that any one of the three elements is missing. For example, at a minor league baseball game, a staff member is throwing a promotional item (a baseball made of soft material) into the stands. However, the staff person is not just tossing the balls; he is throwing them very hard at the fans' heads. If a fan ducks to avoid the ball and then falls, he may claim assault. The thrower will use as a defense the fact that he was not intending to harm anyone, he was just trying to throw the balls up into the stands.

Battery

Battery is defined as the intentional, unpermitted, unprivileged, and offensive touching of the person of one individual by another. In battery, touching means any physical contact. The contact does not have to result in an injury to anyone; the mere contact is enough. The camp counselor who grabs an unruly camper by the arm to remove him from a game may be charged with battery.

The "person" of someone is not confined to his or her physical body, but includes items he or she is carrying. Snatching a purse or stealing a backpack or mobile phone could be considered battery. For battery, as opposed to assault, awareness is not required. It is possible for battery to occur if the person touched is asleep, unconscious, or even if he or she just had his or her back turned to the assailant.

Elements of Battery

Three elements are required for battery. The plaintiff must prove the following.

1. The defendant intended to touch the plaintiff.
2. Actual touching occurred.
3. There was lack of consent by the plaintiff.

Defenses for Battery

There are two fundamental defenses for battery. The first is that the touching was not intentional. The second is that the plaintiff consented to the touching. For example, at a basketball game, a team mascot wants to have a fan dance with him, so he goes up into the stands and grabs a fan by the arm, attempting to pull the fan onto the court. The fan doesn't visibly object, but as the mascot pulls her, he hurts her shoulder. She makes a battery claim against the mascot. The mascot's defense will be that the fan consented to go out onto the court.

Damages

If a defendant is found to have committed civil assault and battery, actual damages may be awarded to the plaintiff. These damages are monetary and can include lost wages, lost earning capacity, medical expenses, and pain and suffering.

Privilege

Some situations in which threatening force or touching without consent occur are not assault and battery because of certain special circumstances. A person may be considered to have what is known as **privilege**, which allows him or her to act in ways normally considered assault and battery. The two most common examples of privilege are acting in self-defense and acting in defense of a third party.

Laws regarding self-defense vary from state to state. In general if a person harms another person and claims self-defense, the circumstances must be examined. First, did the person use reasonable force to get away from the situation? The courts attempt to look into the mind of the person being attacked to determine the answer to this question. Reasonable force can mean different things to different people. If two individuals of the same size are involved in an altercation, striking back with a fist may seem reasonable. If a much larger individual attacks a smaller individual, the smaller person may think it reasonable to pick up an implement and strike back, as opposed to just fighting back with fists. Secondly, did the person who was attacked retreat from the situation when there was opportunity? The duty to retreat once an escape option is available must be considered.

Laws regarding defense of a third party also differ on a state-by-state basis. One issue is the definition of a *third party*. Often this privilege is extended only to people who are defending a family member. The definition of *family member* may also differ from state to state.

Standard of Care Owed Other Participants

Society accepts a certain amount of violence in sport as being part of the game, whereas the same acts would not be considered acceptable outside competition. An ordinary citizen is legally responsible for assaulting or battering another individual, but the expectations are different for the participant in a sporting event. Throwing a 95-mph fastball at a batter's head is sometimes considered strategy in baseball, but throwing a 95-mph fastball at a heckling fan is assault and/or battery.

Traditionally a distinction has been made between the standard of care one participant owes another in contact and noncontact sports. In noncontact sports, participants have generally been held liable for negligent acts that injure fellow participants. For example, if a golfer hits toward the green while another foursome is on the green and strikes another participant, that golfer could be considered negligent and liable for any injury incurred.

In contact sports, reckless misconduct was established as the standard of care in the *Nabozny v. Barnhill* case in 1975. A soccer player recklessly kicked Nabozny in the face and was found liable. The court said that a player was liable for injury if his action was made with a reckless disregard for the safety of the other player.

Blacks' Law Dictionary (1990) describes **reckless misconduct** as when one intentionally does an act or fails to do an act in violation of his duty while knowing or having reason to know of facts that would lead a reasonable man to conclude that such conduct creates an unreasonable risk of harm to another person. The act is characterized by "intent on the part of the defendant to commit the act but no intent to harm the plaintiff by the act" (Wong, 2002, p. 795). This type of action is often called reckless, or willful and wanton, and is accompanied by a knowing disregard of the circumstances. For example, a javelin thrower is practicing on a windy day while his teammates are running on the track. The thrower decides he wants to scare his friends by throwing the javelin so it lands next to the track. He misjudges the distance and the wind and strikes a runner in the leg with the javelin. The thrower intended to throw the javelin near the runners, but did not intend to hit any of them. The javelin thrower knew there was a possibility that if he threw the javelin near people, especially on a windy day, someone could be hit. He disregarded the potential harm and threw the javelin anyway (see also Chapter 2.11, *Elements of Negligence*).

In *Knight v. Jewett*, the California Supreme Court examined the duty of one participant to another. In *Knight*, the parties were playing an informal touch football game. The two collided, prompting Knight to ask Jewett not to play so rough. On the ensuing play, the two collided again and Jewett stepped on Knight's fingers and hand. The injury was so severe that one finger had to be amputated (*Knight v. Jewett*, 1992). The court held: "A participant in an active sport breaches a legal duty of care to other participants—i.e., engages in conduct that properly may subject him or her to financial liability—only if the participant intentionally injures another player or engages in conduct that is so reckless as to be totally outside the range of the ordinary activity involved in the sport" (*Knight v. Jewett*, 1992). Thus, the court held that a participant is not liable for negligent acts. Participants are liable, however, for acts that are grossly negligent or reckless in nature.

Other courts have ruled similarly. In *Crawn v. Campo* (1993), softball catcher Crawn brought action against a runner who violently slid into him at home plate. The trial court used the standard of negligence, but the appellate court remanded the case with a directive to use reckless conduct as the standard of care. Both the *Martin v. Buzan* (1993) and *Pfister v. Shusta* (1995) courts continued to uphold the position that participants owed each other the duty to refrain from reckless, willful and wanton, or intentional misconduct, but were not liable for injuries caused by ordinary negligence. In *Martin*, the plaintiff catcher was injured in a collision at home plate. In *Pfister*, the plaintiff injured his hand and arm when pushed during a spontaneous "kick the can" game in a residence hall. Under the exception to the standard of ordinary care for contact sports created by the appellate court, voluntary participants in contact sports are not liable for **injuries** caused by simple negligent conduct.

In case involving a noncontact sport, *Moser v. Ratinoff* (2003), the plaintiff was injured when two cyclists collided while participating in a recreational ride. The plaintiff claimed the coparticipant defendant was negligent when she swerved and he fell from his bicycle and was injured. Here the court applied the primary assumption of risk doctrine and granted summary judgment for the defendant—thereby, holding that the participant in a noncombat sport was not liable for ordinary negligence. The court cited the *Knight* case in its decision.

In contrast, in *Lestina v. West Bend Mutual Insurance Company* (1993), a soccer player was injured when the defendant slide-tackled him during a recreational league game in which slide-tackling was against the rules. The court held that negligence, rather than recklessness, was the appropriate standard to govern cases involving injuries during recreational team contact sports.

Recent Player Violence Incidents

Player versus player violence seems to be increasing as one reads about the widely publicized violent incidents between players. NHL player Marty McSorley severely slashed Donald Brashear with only seconds left on the clock of a game that was already decided. Although he was fined and suspended, McSorley will play again. Another NHL player, Todd Bertruzzi, was fined a quarter million dollars for an attack on an opponent ("News Tip: Sport Violence . . . ," 2004). The NFL has chosen to begin enforcing penalties and fines for helmet-to-helmet contact on tackles more strictly after a series of such violent incidents (Saunders, 2002). While standing on deck to bat, University of Evansville baseball player Anthony Molina was beaned by Wichita State's Ben Christensen, who was warming up. Christensen threw at Molina because he thought Molina was attempting to time the warm-up pitches. Despite his actions, Christensen was a high draft pick in the amateur draft, signing for over $1 million. He escaped with no criminal charges or civil litigation despite the fact that his victim's baseball career was, for all practical purposes, over.

In a Missouri hockey case, *McKichan v. St. Louis Hockey Club* (1998), a professional hockey goalie was severely injured when struck from behind during a stoppage in play. The lower court found the defendant culpable for the injury on the theory of vicarious liability (Conn, 1999). However, the court of appeals reversed the decision of the lower court. This decision added to the civil court trend of denying professional players access to compensation and punitive damages (Conn, 1999). According to McEvoy and Sharp (1999), not holding participants legally liable for their violent actions may be setting a dangerous precedent.

Violence Involving Officials and Fans

A current issue facing recreation or sport managers in general is the rise not only in violent acts by participants, but also violence against officials and between spectators. The National Association of Sports Officials (NASO) receives two to three reports of assaults on officials every week (National Association of Sports Officials, 2001). As one reads about some of these events, one realizes that sometimes there is no clear delineation between civil and criminal assaults and batteries. Sometimes the key factor is whether the victim seeks redress in a civil court action or prefers criminal charges against the attacker.

In terms of assaults against officials, many people are familiar with the widely publicized incidents where the Baltimore Orioles' Roberto Alomar spit on umpire John Hirschbeck and when Los Angeles Laker guard Nick Van Exel knocked referee Ron Garretson into a scorers' table. Sadly, these incidents represent only the tip of the iceberg. Attacks against officials include such incidents as a thirty-eight-year-old coach punching a sixteen-year-old football referee, a parent coming out of the stands to punch a youth wrestling referee at a match for ten-year-olds, and a fan threatening a high school soccer official with a weapon during a match (Still, 2002).

Although the criminal cases may get national publicity (e.g., as when Thomas Junta attacked and killed Michael Costin at their sons' hockey practice and was found guilty of involuntary manslaughter [Goodman, 2002]), violent acts by parents at local youth sports events are by no means unusual. A report by the National Alliance for Youth Sports reported that 82 percent of people surveyed believed parents behave aggressively at youth sports events. Most notable are parents' assaults on officials (e.g., a parent who bit a coach and shoved an official after the parent's seven-year-old son lost his peewee wrestling match in Pennsylvania; more than 100 people rushed the field, and five adults were charged with assault for attacking a football referee as the crew left the field after a state championship game in Ohio; a "soccer mom" slapped and scratched the face of the fifteen-year-old volunteer referee following a game for nine-year-olds in Virginia; and twenty-six police units responded to a riot that occurred at a youth football game after a parent hit a referee who was marking a ball out of bounds [Still, 2002]).

In addition to attacks on officials, there have been numerous incidents of violence in which fans attacked players or other fans. Members of the Los Angeles Dodgers went into the stands after a fan struck one of them and stole his hat. Tie Domi of the Toronto Maple Leafs fought with a taunting fan, who then fell into the penalty box with Domi. Who can forget the famous "Ice Ball" day at New York Giants Stadium when fans pelted the sidelines with ice balls they made from snow in the stands? That day resulted in 14 arrests, 175 ejections, and 15 injuries (CNNSI, 2002). But the most egregious of all events had to be the night in Detroit when Ron Artest and several Indiana Pacer teammates headed into the stands after Artest had been hit by a water bottle tossed at him by a courtside fan. An unbelievable melee resulted, involving players, fans, and arena security. To combat fan violence, the Philadelphia Eagles have gone so far as to establish a court of law in Veterans Stadium to deal immediately with unruly fans.

Just as with attacks against officials, fan violence has trickled down to other levels as well. For example, in California and Missouri, high school basketball games have been stopped due to fan violence (Toney, 1999). Games have even been scheduled where no fans were allowed in the gymnasium to watch, as happened with the high school basketball game between Ozen and Central High Schools in Beaumont, Texas (Krift, 2006). *Recreation or sport managers need to be aware they may be held accountable for injuries to officials, players, or other fans if they do not provide appropriate security and crowd control measures.*

Significant Case

◇◇◇

This case presents an interesting example of assault and battery involving a player's actions against an official. This is especially relevant given the increased number of violent incidents we are seeing these days. The case also presents a nice synopsis of battery as well as comparative negligence.

BAUGH V. REDMOND

Court of Appeal of Louisiana, Second Circuit
565 So.2d 953; 1990 La. App. LEXIS 1604
June 20, 1990, Rendered

Opinion:

In this action for damages as the result of a battery, defendant, Maurice Redmond, appealed the judgment of the trial court in favor of plaintiff, Jimmie Baugh, and defendant's insurer, Aetna Casualty and Surety Company. Finding the trial court did not err in holding defendant liable for plaintiff's damages and in its apportionment of fault between the parties but erred in holding the insurer was not liable for the intentional tort under the policy provisions, we affirm in part and reverse in part.

Issues Presented

On appeal, defendant presents the following assignments of error:

1. The trial court erred in finding plaintiff had proven by a preponderance of the evidence that defendant intended to commit a battery;
2. The trial court erred in failing to mitigate the general damage award as plaintiff's actions precipitated and provoked the incident;
3. The trial court erred in failing to acknowledge the applicability of comparative fault in an intentional tort case; and,
4. The trial court erred in finding the insurer was not liable based upon a provision excluding liability for bodily injury which was expected or intended from the standpoint of the insured.

Factual Context

On May 20, 1987 plaintiff was umpiring an adult softball game between teams from the Ouachita Parish Sheriff's Department and Ouachita Electric Service, Inc., a Redmond corporation which sponsored the team. During the game plaintiff called a Ouachita Electric Service player out for leaving a base early on a fly ball and defendant became enraged by plaintiff's call. Throughout the remainder of the game, defendant verbally harassed plaintiff and defendant's team eventually lost the game. Following the game, plaintiff and defendant had a confrontation upon exiting the field in which heated words were exchanged and eventually resulted in defendant striking plaintiff in the face. As a result of the blow, plaintiff's eyeglasses were knocked off his face and he incurred a bloody mouth with extensive damage to his teeth.

On August 21, 1987 plaintiff instituted this action for damages naming as defendants Maurice Redmond and Ouachita Electric Service, Inc. Ouachita Electric Service, Inc. was later dismissed from the litigation. In his petition, plaintiff alleged defendant had punched him in the face without provocation, knocking him to the ground, breaking his eyeglasses and causing extensive damage to plaintiff's teeth and bones in his mouth necessitating extensive dental treatment and oral surgery.

Defendant filed a third-party demand naming as third-party defendant his insurer, Aetna Casualty and Surety Company. Defendant alleged the altercation was covered by the liability provisions of the homeowner's policy issued to him by the insurer. Further the insurer was obligated to provide legal representation on the behalf of defendant. However, despite demand, third-party defendant had failed to provide such representation. In its answer, the insurer alleged the incident was not covered by the liability provisions of the policy due to a provision which excluded coverage for any acts which were expected or intended by the insured.

Defendant filed an amending and supplemental answer in which he alleged plaintiff was guilty of contributory negligence which partially contributed to the incident and therefore his recoverable damages should be reduced in proportion to the degree or percentage of fault attributed to him. In the event the court deemed contributory negligence inapplicable, defendant alleged that any damages awarded should be mitigated due to the conduct of plaintiff in escalating the confrontation.

At the trial on the merits the testimony as to the actual battery was conflicting. Plaintiff testified he had served as an umpire for the West Monroe Adult Softball League for approximately ten years. He said defendant began to verbally abuse him after a call, requiring him to warn the team that if defendant did not quiet down he would forfeit the game. Plaintiff allowed the team to play the remaining inning during which defendant continually verbally abused him. After the game ended and he was exiting the Ouachita Electric Service dugout, plaintiff was confronted and threatened by defendant. Plaintiff stated he told defendant he would report the incident to the recreation department and defendant would not be allowed back at the ballpark. Plaintiff turned to walk toward the concession stand with the defendant walking slightly behind him and was struck once unexpectedly by defendant. Plaintiff stated he did not make any threatening gestures and he had placed his face mask underneath his arm. As the result of the blow, plaintiff said he was knocked up against a fence, his glasses were broken and he was bleeding from the mouth. He stated that several officers from the Sheriff's Department had to restrain defendant after the initial blow. Plaintiff was treated at a local hospital and was eventually required to undergo extensive dental treatment and oral surgery, including four root canals and crowns.

* * *

Defendant testified that during the course of the game plaintiff came over to the fence and became angry at him. He was told plaintiff would eject him from the park. After the game ended defendant proceeded to the dugout. When plaintiff walked through the dugout, defendant stated plaintiff's shoulder hit him in the chest and defendant went into the dugout after him. Defendant said they talked as they proceeded through the dugout and plaintiff "hollered" he bet defendant $100 he would be ejected from the ballpark. Plaintiff then turned around with his mask in his hand. Defendant testified he thought at that moment that plaintiff would strike him and he struck plaintiff in the face. He stated he did not intend to hit plaintiff but rather intended to keep plaintiff from striking him. Defendant testified he did not intend that plaintiff be injured or incur damage to his teeth. Defendant stated the testimony of the witnesses as to plaintiff's bleeding surprised him as he did not think he had struck plaintiff that hard.

After the trial on the merits, the trial court found in favor of plaintiff and third-party defendant. In its written opinion, the trial court reviewed the testimony of the parties and witnesses as to the confrontation and found that the evidence established that defendant had allowed himself to become outraged at plaintiff over the call made against his team. * * * The court further awarded plaintiff special damages in the amount of $4812.80 for past medical expenses and lost wages incurred as a result of the battery.

* * *

On defendant's motion for a new trial, the trial court agreed it should have applied the principles of comparative fault to this matter. However, upon reviewing all of the testimony and the factors to be considered in apportioning fault, the trial court found the testimony did not establish by a preponderance of the evidence that plaintiff was at fault in causing or contributing to his injuries. Rather, the evidence established there was unprovoked battery committed by defendant when plaintiff was only trying to exit the playing field. The court further found there was nothing in the record to reverse its previous decision that the insurer's policy of insurance did not provide coverage to defendant for this incident.

Liability for Battery

It is well-settled that a Court of Appeal may not set aside a trial court's finding of fact in the absence of "manifest error" or unless it is "clearly wrong" and, where there is conflict in the testimony, reasonable evaluations of credibility and reasonable inferences of fact should not be disturbed upon review, even though the appellate court may feel its own evaluations and inferences are as reasonable. The trial judge is in a better position to evaluate the credibility of the witnesses and the weight of the evidence than an appellate court who does not see or hear the witnesses. For this reason, a reviewing court should adopt the trial court's findings as its own in the absence of clear error, even if other conclusions from the same evidence are equally reasonable.

* * *

A battery is any intentional and unpermitted contact with the plaintiff's person or anything attached to it or practically identified with it. In order to recover for a battery, plaintiff must prove by a preponderance of the evidence that his damages resulted from an unprovoked attack by defendant. The intention of the defendant need not be malicious nor need it be an intention to inflict actual damage. It is sufficient if the actor intends to inflict either a harmful or physical contact without the other's consent. Liability for a battery depends upon the facts and circumstances of each case. Where the defendant relies upon provocation as justification for a battery, he must prove some conduct or action by the plaintiff sufficient to provoke and arouse defendant to the point of physical retaliation. Louisiana's aggressor doctrine precludes tort recovery by plaintiff if the evidence establishes he was at fault in provoking the difficulty in which he was injured, unless the person retaliating has used excessive force to repel the aggression.

* * *

On appeal, defendant argues the trial court erred in finding plaintiff had proven by a preponderance of the evidence that defendant intended to commit a battery upon the plaintiff. We disagree.

The record shows that defendant had become angry with plaintiff during the game and verbally harassed plaintiff periodically throughout the remainder of the game. After the game concluded defendant proceeded to his team's dugout and confronted plaintiff as he was proceeding through the dugout area, which was his normal practice at the end of each game. Defendant verbally harassed plaintiff about his authority to eject defendant from the park if disruptive during a game. The evidence established that plaintiff continued to walk through the dugout toward the concession stand and was followed closely behind by defendant who was apparently intent upon provoking a confrontation with plaintiff through verbal harassment. There was no evidence that plaintiff pushed or made any threatening moves toward defendant in any manner so as to cause defendant to believe it was necessary to defend himself. Rather, it is clear that the blow to plaintiff was completely unexpected and unprovoked.

Considering all the circumstances surrounding this incident, it appears clear that defendant did intend to strike plaintiff and the trial court was not manifestly erroneous in this determination.

Comparative Negligence

* * *

In assessing comparative fault the trial court must consider the nature of each party's conduct and the extent of the causal relationship between the conduct and the damages claimed. Relevant factors concerning the nature of each party's conduct include: (1) whether the conduct resulted from inadvertence or involved an awareness of the danger, (2) how great a risk was created by the conduct, (3) the significance of what was sought by the conduct, (4) the capacities of the actor, whether superior or inferior, and (5) any extenuating circumstances which might require the actor to proceed in haste, without proper thought.

* * *

It is well-settled that it is within the trial court's discretion to mitigate a general damage award when plaintiff's conduct helps create the circumstances giving rise to the injury. Mere words, even though designed to excite or irritate, cannot excuse a battery. However, words which are calculated to provoke and arouse to the point of physical retaliation may mitigate damages in a civil action. How and when damages are mitigated are determinations which are within the discretion of the trial court.

* * *

Defendant argues the trial court erred in failing to mitigate the general damage award as plaintiff's actions precipitated and provoked the incident and further the trial court erred in failing to acknowledge the applicability of comparative fault in an intentional tort case. This argument is without merit. It is clear from the opinion of the trial court in its denial of defendant's motion for a new trial that the trial court found it should have applied the principles of comparative fault to this matter. However, the court concluded upon a review of the testimony and the factors to be considered in apportioning fault that the testimony did not establish by a preponderance of the evidence that plaintiff was at fault in causing or contributing to his injuries so as to require a reduction of his damages. We agree.

The record shows that when defendant began his attempts to confront plaintiff following the conclusion of the game, plaintiff attempted to avoid such a confrontation by walking ahead of defendant and toward the concession stand. Defendant continued to walk behind plaintiff and to verbally harass him as to his authority to eject defendant from the park. There was no evidence that plaintiff acted verbally or physically to escalate the situation but rather was attempting to avoid any type of confrontation when struck unexpectedly by defendant. Under these circumstances we find plaintiff was not guilty of any comparative fault so as to reduce his recovery for injuries sustained by him.

Insurance Coverage

* * *

In defendant's homeowner's insurance policy which was issued by third-party defendant, Aetna Casualty & Surety Company, the policy provides that personal liability coverage and medical payments to others do not apply to bodily injury or property damage which is expected or intended by the insured.

* * *

A review of the record in light of the above jurisprudence establishes that the trial court erred in holding that the insurer's policy of insurance did not provide coverage to defendant for this incident.

* * *

The circumstances surrounding the conduct of defendant demonstrates his actions were not premeditated and not intended to inflict the serious injury plaintiff sustained. Defendant testified he did not think he had struck plaintiff with enough force to inflict a bloody mouth and he did not intend for plaintiff to be injured. Defendant characterized his blow as a "sharp, quick punch" more in the nature of a provocative gesture rather than a forceful blow intended to inflict serious injury. It is significant to note this incident occurred at a sporting event in which defendant was interested as a sponsor of the team, which circumstance would support the conclusion that the blow was more a gesture of anger and frustration rather than a deliberate effort on the part of the defendant to inflict bodily harm upon plaintiff. As we find the evidence demonstrates defendant did not intend or expect such a serious injury to result from his conduct, we find that coverage under defendant's homeowner policy is not excluded.

Decree

For these reasons, the judgment of the trial court in favor of plaintiff and against defendant is AFFIRMED. The judgment dismissing the third-party demand is REVERSED, and there is judgment in favor of the third-party plaintiff, Maurice Redmond, and against the third-party defendant, Aetna Casualty and Surety Company, for the amount of the judgment on the main demand against defendant, and for attorney fees in the sum of $3000.

 OTHER RELATED SIGNIFICANT CASES

Chapter 1.10 *The Legal System*
Chapter 2.12 *Which Parties Are Liable?*

Chapter 4.16 *Hazing*
Chapter 5.11 *Risk Management Process*

Recent Trends

Third-Party Assaults

Another issue recreation or sport managers, especially facility managers, need to be aware of is third-party assaults that may occur on their premises (see Chapter 3.20, *Premises Liability*, for a complete discussion). Facility managers need to know they may be found negligent if such incidents do occur and if the incidents were foreseeable.

Dealing with Unruly Patrons

Sport managers working in facilities are often faced with unruly patrons. Sometimes fans get loud and boisterous, beyond what is reasonably expected at a game. In addition, this behavior is often fueled by overconsumption of alcohol. When it comes time to remove an unruly patron, what are facility managers allowed to do?

The best strategy for making sure facility employees act properly, particularly security personnel, is training (Fried, 2005). This includes part-time game day staff, such as ushers, as well as full-time employees. Facilities are usually able to hire a limited number of uniformed police officers who are properly trained in handling unruly people, but all members of the staff need to know the proper procedures for defusing a tense situation (Fried, 2005). Employees need to know how much force is allowable if fans or customers become unruly. Most certainly, employees should only use the force necessary to accomplish the task of removing the patron, particularly if the patron has not touched the employee. Remember, battery is touching without consent, and security should not initiate contact with a patron if at all possible. The response will differ if the patron is violent or engaged in an activity that may physically harm the employee or another fan. Again, proper training will be the best deterrent to any improper activity.

Protection for Officials

It is clear that officials are now becoming the target of violent acts by players, coaches, and fans (Cross, 1998). As of 2005, eighteen states have passed specific legislation protecting sports officials (AAU, 2005). According to the late Mel Narol, an expert on assault against officials, in the past an attack on an official was treated as a very minor offense. In some states now, if someone assaults an official, it is either a felony, which requires jail time and a substantial fine, or a high misdemeanor, which requires a substantial fine and maybe some jail time (Robinson, Hums, Crow, & Phillips, 2000). Still (2002) suggested a number of solutions to this problem, including state laws that protect sports officials; punishment in the professional leagues; zero-tolerance rules in college, high school, and recreational leagues; and banning fans who assault officials from attending events.

Some youth sport organizations, such as the American Youth Soccer Association, Massachusetts Hockey, as well as local youth sport organizations on the city or school district level, have written codes of conduct for parents, which include statements about respectful treatment of coaches, officials, and other fans. In the city of El Paso, every parent whose child plays a sport on an El Paso city field must first attend a three-hour parenting class to learn the rules of good sporting conduct. After attending the seminar, each family receives a card. When arriving at their children's games, they must show the card. If they refuse or don't have the card, they can be asked to leave (Deam, 2002). Although initially not a popular move, the number of violent incidents at games has decreased dramatically since the start of the card program. Sport and recreation managers need to be more aware than ever of parental behavior at games.

References

Cases

Baugh v. Redmond, 565 So.2d 953 (La. App. 2 Cir. 1990).

Crawn v. Campo, 630 A.2d. 368 (N.J. Super. A.D. 1993).

Knight v. Jewett, 834 P 2d. 696; 11 (Cal. Rptr. 2d. 2 1992).

Lestina v. West Bend Mutual Insurance Company, 501 N.W.2d 28 (Wis. 1993).

Martin v. Buzan, 857 S.W.2d 366 (Mo. App. E.D. 1993).

McKichan v. St. Louis Hockey Club, 967 S.W.2d 209 (App. Ct. Ed. Mo. 1998).

Moser v. Ratinoff, 1130 (Cal. Rptr. 2d 198 2003).

Nabozny v. Barnhill, 334 N.E.2d 258 (Ill. 1975).

Pfister v. Shusta, 657 N.E.2d. 1013 (Ill. 1995).

Publications and Presentations

AAU. (2005, September 12). *Florida Governor signs bill to protect officials* Florida becomes the 18th state to specifically pass legislation protecting sports officials. Retrieved January 28, 2006 from http://www.aausports.org/default.asp?a=News-Stories/pg_News_officials.htm

Black, H. C. (1990). Black's law dictionary (6th ed.). St. Paul, MN: West Publishing Co.

CNNSI. (2002, September 20). *Previous examples of fan violence*. Retrieved December 31, 2002 from http://sportsillustrated.cnn.com/baseball/news/2002/09/19/fan_violence/

Conn, J. (1999). Professional player on player violence: Another plaintiff failure in redress by the *McKichan* case. *Journal of Legal Aspects of Sport, 9*, 63–74.

Cross, T. (1998). Assaults on sports officials. *Marquette Sports Law Journal, 8*(2), 429–454.

Deam, J. (2002, February 13). Officials work to remind spectators, "It's just a game." *Denver Post*, I1.

Fried, G. (2005). *Managing sport facilities*. Champaign, IL: Human Kinetics.

Goodman, E. (2002, January 18). The case involving "hockey dad" is rife with tragic ironies. *The Desert News*, A10.

Krift, F.A. (2006, January 4). Suspensions, fan lockout follow brawl. *The Beaumont Enterprise*. Retrieved 28 January 2006 from http://www.southeasttexaslive.com/site/news.cfm?newsid=15864327&BRD=2287&PAG=461&dept_id=512588&rfi=6.

McEvoy, C. D., & Sharp, L. A. (1999). A late hit. *Athletic Business*, 22–24.

National Association of Sports Officials. (2001, April 3). *New Mexico governor signs assault protection bill*. Press release. Retrieved December 31, 2002 from www.naso.org/PressReleases/st77.htm

National Association of Sports Officials. (2002, June 3). *Mel Narol suffers fatal heart attack*. Press release. Retrieved December 31, 2002 from www.naso.org/PressReleases/st93.htm

News tip: Sports violence increasingly likely to prompt lawsuits. (2004, March 11). *Duke News*. Retrieved January 28, 2006 from http://www.dukenews.duke.edu/2004/03/sports_0304.html

Robinson, M., Hums, M. A., Crow, B., & Phillips, D. (2000). *Making the games happen: Profiles of sport management professionals*. Gaithersburg, MD: Aspen Publishers.

Rosenthal, E. K. (2004). Inside the lines: Basing negligence liability in sports for safety-based rule violations on the level of play. *Fordham L. Rev., 72*, 2631.

Saunders, P. (2002, October 27). Hit list. *The Denver Post* [Electronic version]. Retrieved December 31, 2002 from www.denverpost.com/Stories/0,1413,36%257E86%257E948329%257E,00.html

Still, B. (2002). *Officials under assault: Update 2002*. Racine, WI: National Association of Sports Officials.

Toney, D. R. (1999). Sporting events, fan violence, and the courts of the future: Make way for a new player, "The Legal Eagle." *The Sports Lawyers Journal, 6*(1), 147–158.

Wong, G. M. (2002). *Essentials of sport law* (3rd ed.). Westport, CT: Praeger.

4.12 Criminal Liability for Violence in Sports

Barbara Osborne
University of North Carolina

Sport violence is not a new phenomenon. As early as 1895, a boxer was acquitted of manslaughter charges in New York for the death of his sparring partner during an exhibition match. In 1906, President Theodore Roosevelt was so distraught after watching the University of Pennsylvania football team attempt to reduce a Swarthmore star lineman to a bloody pulp that he threatened to outlaw football by Executive Order. In 1920, a pitch by New York Yankee Carl Mays killed Cleveland Indian Ray Chapman.

Sport, by its very nature, is a battleground with combatants fighting with every tool available to them to win the contest. Is there violence in sports? Or is it just aggressiveness that is a part of the game? Almost every contact sport carries the risk of violent collisions or hits, and participants are regularly injured by these actions. Fans, coaches, and players all expect a high degree of aggressive play. On the playing fields, acts of aggression are seldom condemned, are usually condoned, and are often praised outright. When aggressiveness on the playing field or in the arena escalates to a violent level during the course of play, should society step in and impose criminal penalties?

Fundamental Concepts

Criminal law is based on society's need to be free from harmful conduct. The law defines criminal conduct and prescribes the punishment to be imposed on a person convicted of engaging in such conduct. Unlike civil law, where the goal is to compensate the wronged party, the broad aim of criminal law is to prevent injury to the public health, safety, morals, and welfare.

Essential Elements of a Crime

Although there may be social justification for prosecuting sports participants for their violent conduct on the field, very few cases have been adjudicated by the criminal courts. A primary reason may be the difficulty in proving that on-field behavior satisfies the essential elements of a crime: an unlawful action and an evil intention. The defendant must commit a voluntary, conscious act, legally known as **actus reus**. The defendant must also possess **mens rea**—a "guilty mind." The four criminal states of mind are intentionally, knowingly, recklessly, and grossly. The standard of proof in criminal cases is "beyond a reasonable doubt"— a higher burden than the "preponderance of the evidence" standard used in civil actions.

Prosecutors struggle to prove the necessary intent of the defendant in sports violence cases—that the player consciously intended to cause bodily injury to the other player. It is assumed that a player operating in a setting in which violence is customary and approved is not acting with criminal intent, but merely following established practices of the sport. In 1978, Oakland Raiders safety Jack Tatum legally tackled New England Patriots wide receiver Darryl Stingley, leaving him paralyzed below the waist. In his 1980 book, *They Call Me Assassin*, Tatum bragged: "I never make a tackle just to bring someone down. I want to punish the man I'm going after. I like to believe my best hits border on felonious assault." These words would seemingly satisfy the requirement of evil intention. However, the words also illustrate standard, acceptable motivation on the playing field.

It is equally difficult to prove that an athlete engaged in unlawful action. A significant number of injuries occur from aggressive acts that are within the rules of the game. Other violent acts, which may border on the illegitimate, are still considered part of the game—baseball pitchers routinely throw warning and revenge pitches, and batters commonly retaliate by charging the mound and starting bench-clearing brawls. Similarly, fighting and use of a stick are customary activities in ice hockey.

There are many other reasons that prosecutors hesitate to file charges against athletes for acts of violence during the course of play. Prosecutors don't view athletes as "real criminals." Similarly, the victim of the athlete's violent actions usually does not want to file criminal charges against a fellow athlete, leaving the prosecution without a complainant. It is difficult to prove the actual elements of criminal conduct and obtain a guilty verdict. Even when prosecutors are successful, the sentences rarely amount to more than a slap on the wrist.

The first criminal case of a professional athlete charged for an act committed during the course of play in the United States, *State v. Forbes* (1975), illustrates the difficulty prosecutors have in convicting athletes. In 1975, Dave Forbes of the Boston Bruins checked Henry Boucha of the Minnesota North Stars against the boards with his elbows up, and Boucha retaliated by punching Forbes. Both players exchanged words from their adjacent penalty boxes. When they returned to the ice, Boucha skated ahead of Forbes who took a swing that struck Boucha in the face with the butt end of his stick. Forbes then jumped on Boucha and continued punching him until a third player separated them. Boucha required 25 stitches to close the cut near his right eye, and subsequent surgeries to repair a small fracture at the base of the eye socket and to correct a double vision problem. Forbes was indicted for aggravated assault with a dangerous weapon. After a highly publicized trial, the jury was split 9–3 in favor of conviction, but was unable to reach a unanimous verdict. The court declared a mistrial and the prosecutors declined to retry the case.

Criminal Assault

The intentional torts of assault and battery (see Chapter 4.11, *Assault and Battery*) should not be confused with criminal assault or battery. Unlike civil law, where the torts of assault and battery are universally defined, each state drafts its own criminal statutes. Although not a source of law, the **Model Penal Code** is a scholarly attempt to compile a comprehensive and coherent body of criminal law. In a majority of jurisdictions, an **assault** is either an attempt to commit a battery or the intentional creation of a reasonable apprehension in the victim's mind of imminent bodily harm. The Model Penal Code divides criminal assault into two categories: simple or aggravated. A person is guilty of **simple assault** if he or she attempts to cause or purposely, knowingly, or recklessly causes bodily injury to another; or negligently causes bodily injury to another with a deadly weapon; or attempts by physical menace to put another in fear of imminent serious bodily injury. A person is guilty of **aggravated assault** if he or she attempts to cause serious bodily injury to another, or causes such injury purposely, knowingly, or recklessly under circumstances manifesting extreme indifference to the value of human life; or attempts to cause or purposely or knowingly causes bodily injury to another with a deadly weapon (Model Penal Code § 2.11.1 [1985]).

Criminal Battery

Criminal battery is defined as the unlawful application of force to the person of another resulting in either bodily injury or an offensive touching. The elements of **simple battery** are a guilty state of mind or extreme disregard of known serious risks; an act; a physical touching or harming of a victim; and causation. Simple battery is a misdemeanor, but aggravated battery is a felony. Most states define acts as **aggravated battery** if a deadly weapon is used or if serious bodily injury is caused. Any ordinary object—hockey stick, baseball, or bat—may become a deadly weapon depending on how it is used. The element that the contact must be unlawful is a determining factor in why most sports violence is treated as noncriminal. Contact in sports is generally considered lawful behavior. The court in *Regina v. Green* (1971) explained the dilemma: "Where do you draw the line? It is very difficult in my opinion for a player who is playing hockey with all the force, vigor and strength at his command, who is engaged in the rough and tumble of the game, very often in a rough situation in the corner of the rink, suddenly to stop and say, 'I must not do that. I must not follow up on this because maybe it is an assault.'"

Homicide

Acts of violence may also occur in a recreational context with criminal repercussions. Nathan Hall worked as a ski lift operator on Vail mountain. After his shift ended and the lifts were closed, he skied down to the base of the mountain. Hall sped straight down the mountain, arms out for balance, bouncing off the moguls, completely out of control. He flew off a knoll and collided with Allen Cobb, crushing Cobb's skull and killing him. The court convicted him of reckless manslaughter.

Involuntary manslaughter is the conscious disregard of a substantial and unjustifiable risk that would cause the death of another. Whether a risk is substantial is determined by assessing both the likelihood that harm will occur and the magnitude of the harm should it occur. Whether a risk is justifiable is determined by weighing the nature and purpose of the conduct against the risk created by that conduct. Involuntary manslaughter may also be categorized as **criminal negligence**. Criminal negligence is categorized by a greater deviation from the *reasonable person* standard than is required for civil liability.

Reckless homicide charges have often been brought against owners and operators of amusement parks. In March 2004, the Rockin' Raceway amusement park manager was found guilty of reckless homicide when a woman riding the Hawk, a pendulum-like ride, fell 60 feet to her death when her safety harness came loose. Two state inspectors and a fair worker were charged with reckless homicide when an eight-year-old boy died from electrical shock while he was standing in line for a bumper car ride.

Defenses

Consent. Consent is not normally a defense to criminal battery because a criminal offense is a wrong against society. Consequently, the person directly harmed cannot consent to the act because the public interest cannot be frustrated by private license—in other words, it is against public policy for an individual to consent to be the victim of a crime. However, the Model Penal Code states that consent may be a defense to criminal charges arising from conduct in a sports event:

> When conduct is charged to constitute an offense because it causes or threatens bodily injury, consent to such conduct or to the infliction of such injury is a defense if . . . the conduct and the injury are reasonably foreseeable hazards of joint participation in a lawful athletic contest or competitive sport. (Model Penal Code § 2.11.2 [1985]).

Some courts have used the **reasonable foreseeability test**, similar to the test commonly used in tort actions (see Chapter 4.11, *Assault and Battery*) to measure consent. It is accepted that players consent to conduct that is within the bounds of the reasonably foreseeable hazards of the game. Conversely, players do not consent to injuries caused by intentional acts that are not part of the game. The complicated issue is determining which acts of violence are reasonably foreseeable. One method is to determine whether the conduct is a customary aspect of the game. In boxing, for example, it is reasonably foreseeable that an opponent would be knocked unconscious, as the objective of boxing is to render an opponent unconscious. Similar conduct, swinging a fist at an opponent's face or head, would not be reasonably foreseeable within the context of the game in sports such as basketball or soccer.

A few courts have applied a **rules of the game test**, where a participant would not consent to acts that were illegal under the rules of the sport. Although this is an easy test to apply, it is an extremely narrow approach to the consent issue. Every foul would be a potential crime—games as we know them would cease to exist as referees would blow the whistle, and the law enforcement officials would rush in to take statements!

William Floyd argued the consent defense unsuccessfully in *State v. Floyd* (1990). Floyd was convicted of two counts of assault without intent to inflict serious injury but causing bodily injury, a serious misdemeanor, for his part in a particularly violent brawl in a four-on-four YMCA recreational basketball game. The championship game was physical—fouls were hard, including considerable hacking and a lot of shoving under the boards. The referee called a foul, words were exchanged, there was some shoving, and one of the players on the court threw a punch. A brawl ensued. The complainant, McHale, was standing on the sidelines when William Floyd, who was also on the sidelines, struck him in the face, knocking him to the floor. McHale suffered a concussion, severe hemorrhaging, and loss of brain tissue. He spent two days in intensive care and permanently lost the sense of smell. William Floyd left McHale unconscious on the floor and proceeded to attack Gregg Barrier and Duane Barrier—Gregg Barrier was also on the sidelines, whereas Duane Barrier had been in the game when play was halted. Duane Barrier suffered a severely deviated septum requiring reconstructive surgery. The defense argued consent, but the court found that there was no nexus between the defendant's actions and playing the game of basketball—particularly when play had ceased and the defendant was not on the court engaged in play at the time of the acts.

Self-defense. Within criminal law, a person who is not the aggressor in an encounter is justified in using a reasonable amount of force against his adversary when he reasonably believes that he is in immediate danger of unlawful bodily harm from his adversary and that the use of such force is necessary to avoid this danger. Applying self-defense is generally problematic for participants in sport for several reasons. First, the **amount of force** used is limited to that which is reasonably necessary. Most unlawful behavior in sports contexts involves contact and then escalating levels of retaliation. Another problem is timing: the participant/defendant must have had an honest belief that the danger of immediate, serious bodily harm was **imminent**. Athletes often retaliate after the danger has passed. The baseball player who charges the mound after being brushed back from the plate is no longer in danger from the pitch. Self-defense is also not a viable defense if the defendant was the initial aggressor in the incident. Additionally, some states allow self-defense only if the defendant had **no reasonable means of retreat**. In most situations, a player can stop the confrontation by retreating.

Significant Case

◇◇◇

The following case is typical of the type of violent act in sports competition that has been prosecuted in the United States and Canada. Note the factors that the court weighs to make their decision: the nature of the game, the nature of the act, the degree of force employed, the degree of risk of injury, and the state of mind of the accused. Consider also the possible defenses. Would Shelley have had a better chance if he had argued self-defense rather than consent?

STATE OF WASHINGTON V. SHELLEY

Court Of Appeals Of Washington, Division One
85 Wn. App. 24, 929 P.2d 489, *1997 Wash. App. LEXIS 51*
January 13, 1997, Filed

OPINION BY: C. Kenneth Grosse

During a rough basketball game, Jason Shelley struck another player and broke his jaw in three places. He was convicted of assault in the second degree after the State successfully argued to the jury that Shelley intentionally punched the other player. On appeal, Shelley claims that he was entitled to argue that the victim consented to the possibility of injury when he decided to play pickup basketball. While we agree that consent may be a defense to assault in athletic competitions, Shelley has failed to establish a factual basis for that defense. Further, while we hold that the consent defense is not

limited to conduct within the rules of the games, rather it is to the conduct and harm that are the reasonably foreseeable hazards of joint participation in an athletic contest, we conclude that Shelley's conduct was not a reasonably foreseeable hazard.

On March 31, 1993, Jason Shelley and Mario Gonzalez played "pickup" basketball on opposing teams at the University of Washington Intramural Activities Building (the IMA). Pickup games are not refereed by an official; rather, the players take responsibility for calling their own fouls. During the course of three games, Gonzalez fouled Shelley several times. Gonzalez had a reputation for playing overly aggressive defense at the IMA. Toward the end of the evening, after trying to hit the ball away from Shelley, he scratched Shelley's face, and drew blood. After getting scratched, Shelley briefly left the game and then returned.

Shelley and Gonzalez have differing versions of what occurred after Shelley returned to the game. According to Gonzalez, while he was waiting for play in the game to return to Gonzalez's side of the court, Shelley suddenly hit him. Gonzalez did not see Shelley punch him. According to Shelley's version of events, when Shelley rejoined the game, he was running down the court and he saw Gonzalez make "a move towards me as if he was maybe going to prevent me from getting the ball." The move was with his hand up "across my vision." Angry, he "just reacted" and swung. He said he hit him because he was afraid of being hurt, like the previous scratch. He testified that Gonzalez continually beat him up during the game by fouling him hard.

A week after the incident, a school police detective interviewed Shelley and prepared a statement for Shelley to sign based on the interview. Shelley reported to the police that Gonzalez had been "continually slapping and scratching him" during the game. Shelley "had been getting mad" at Gonzalez and the scratch on Shelley's face was the "final straw." As the two were running down the court side by side, "I swung my right hand around and hit him with my fist on the right side of his face." Shelley asserted that he also told the detective that Gonzalez waved a hand at him just before throwing the punch and that he told the detective that he was afraid of being injured.

Gonzalez required emergency surgery to repair his jaw. Broken in three places, it was wired shut for six weeks. His treating physician believed that a "significant" blow caused the damage.

During the course of the trial, defense counsel told the court he intended to propose a jury instruction that: "A person legally consents to conduct that causes or threatens bodily harm if the conduct and the harm are reasonably foreseeable hazards of joint participation in a lawful, athletic contest or competitive sport." Although the trial court agreed that there were risks involved in sports, it stated that "the risk of being intentionally punched by another player is one that I don't think we ever do assume." The court noted, "In basketball . . . you consent to a certain amount of rough contact. If they were both going for a rebound and Mr. Shelley's elbow or even his fist hit Mr. Gonzalez as they were both jumping for the rebound and Mr. Gonzalez's jaw was fractured in exactly the same way . . . then you would have an issue." Reasoning that "our laws are intended to uphold the public peace and regulate behavior of individuals," the court ruled "that as a matter of law, consent cannot be a defense to an assault." The

court indicated that Shelley could not claim consent because his conduct "exceeded what is considered within the rules of that particular sport." ***

Later Shelley proposed jury instructions on the subject of consent:

An act is not an assault, if it is done with the consent of the person alleged to be assaulted.

It is a defense to a charge of second degree assault occurring in the course of an athletic contest if the conduct and the harm are reasonably foreseeable hazards of joint participation in a lawful athletic contest or competitive sport.

The trial court rejected these and Shelley excepted. The trial court did instruct the jury about self-defense.

Consent

First, we hold that consent is a defense to an assault occurring during an athletic contest. This is consistent with the law of assault as it has developed in Washington. A person is guilty of second degree assault if he or she "intentionally assaults another and thereby recklessly inflicts substantial bodily harm." One common law definition of assault recognized in Washington is "'an unlawful touching with criminal intent.'" At the common law, a touching is unlawful when the person touched did not give consent to it, and was either harmful or offensive. As our Supreme Court stated in State v. Simmons, "'where there is consent, there is no assault.'" The State argues that because Simmons was a sexual assault case, the defense consent should be limited to that realm. We decline to apply the defense so narrowly. Logically, consent must be an issue in sporting events because a person participates in a game knowing that it will involve potentially offensive contact and with this consent the "touchings" involved are not "unlawful." Our review of the cases and commentary on the issue of consent reveals that although the defense of consent is applied in the realm of sexual assault, it has been sparingly applied by the courts in other areas. The rationale that courts offer in limiting it is that society has an interest in punishing assaults as breaches of the public peace and order, so that an individual cannot consent to a wrong that is committed against the public peace. Urging us to reject the defense of consent because an assault violates the public peace, the State argues that this principle precludes Shelley from being entitled to argue the consent defense on the facts of his case. In making this argument, the State ignores the factual contexts that dictated the results in the cases it cites in support. * * *

If consent cannot be a defense to assault, then most athletic contests would need to be banned because many involve "invasions of one's physical integrity." Because society has chosen to foster sports competitions, players necessarily must be able to consent to physical contact and other players must be able to rely on that consent when playing the game. This is the view adopted by the drafters of the Model Penal Code:

> *There are, however, situations in which consent to bodily injury should be recognized as a defense to crime.... There is ... the obvious case of participation in an athletic contest or competitive sport, where the nature of the enterprise often involves risk of serious injury. Here, the social judgment that permits the contest to flourish necessarily involves the companion judgment that reasonably foreseeable hazards can be consented to by virtue of participation.*

The more difficult question is the proper standard by which to judge whether a person consented to the particular conduct at issue.

The State argues that "when the conduct in question is not within the rules of a given sport, a victim cannot be deemed to have consented to this act." The trial court apparently agreed with this approach. Although we recognize that there is authority supporting this approach, we reject a reliance on the rules of the games as too limiting. Rollin M. Perkins on Criminal Law explains:

> *The test is not necessarily whether the blow exceeds the conduct allowed by the rules of the game. Certain excesses and inconveniences are to be expected beyond the formal rules of the game. It may be ordinary and expected conduct for minor assaults to occur. However, intentional excesses beyond those reasonably contemplated in the sport are not justified. Instead, we adopt the approach of the Model Penal Code which provides that:*
>
> *(2) Consent to Bodily Injury. When conduct is charged to constitute an offense because it causes or threatens bodily injury, consent to such conduct or to the infliction of such injury is a defense if: * * ***
>
> *(b) the conduct and the injury are reasonably foreseeable hazards of joint participation in a lawful athletic contest or competitive sport or other concerted activity not forbidden by law.*

The State argues the law does not allow "the victim to 'consent' to a broken jaw simply by participating in an unrefereed, informal basketball game." This argument presupposes that the harm suffered dictates whether the defense is available or not. This is not the correct inquiry.

The correct inquiry is whether the conduct of defendant constituted foreseeable behavior in the play of the game. Additionally, the injury must have occurred as a by-product of the game itself. In construing a similar statutory defense, the Iowa court required a "nexus between defendant's acts and playing the game of basketball." In State v. Floyd, a fight broke out during a bas-

ketball game and the defendant, who was on the sidelines, punched and severely injured several opposing team members. Because neither defendant nor his victims were voluntarily participating in the game, the defense did not apply because the statute "contemplated a person who commits acts during the course of play, and the exception seeks to protect those whose acts otherwise subject to prosecution are committed in furtherance of the object of the sport." As the court noted in Floyd, there is a "continuum, or sliding scale, grounded in the circumstances under which voluntary participants engage in sport . . . which governs the type of incidents in which an individual volunteers (i.e., consents) to participate." The New York courts provide another example. In a football game, while tackling the defendant, the victim hit the defendant. After the play was over and all of the players got off the defendant, the defendant punched the victim in the eye. The court in People v. Freer held that this act was not consented to:

> *Initially it may be assumed that the very first punch thrown by the complainant in the course of the tackle was consented to by defendant. The act of tackling an opponent in the course of a football game may often involve "contact" that could easily be interpreted to be a "punch". Defendant's response after the pileup to complainant's initial act of "aggression" cannot be mistaken. Clearly, defendant intended to punch complainant. This was not a consented to act.* People v. Freer, 86 Misc. 2d 280, 381 N.Y.S.2d 976, 978 (1976).

As a corollary to the consent defense, the State may argue that the defendant's conduct exceeded behavior foreseeable in the game. Although in "all sports players consent to many risks, hazards and blows," there is "a limit to the magnitude and dangerousness of a blow to which another is deemed to consent." This limit, like the foreseeability of the risks, is determined by presenting evidence to the jury about the nature of the game, the participants' expectations, the location where the game has been played, as well as the rules of the game.

Here, taking Shelley's version of the events as true, the magnitude and dangerousness of Shelley's actions were beyond the limit. There is no question that Shelley lashed out at Gonzalez with sufficient force to land a substantial blow to the jaw, and there is no question but that Shelley intended to hit Gonzalez. There is nothing in the game of basketball, or even rugby or hockey, that would permit consent as a defense to such conduct. Shelley admitted to an assault and was not precluded from arguing that the assault justified self-defense; but justification and consent are not the same inquiry.

Related to his consent argument, Shelley claims that the assault statute is vague when applied to sports altercations because it fails to provide either adequate notice of proscribed conduct, or standards to prevent arbitrary enforcement as to athletes who believe they can be rough because they are accustomed to unprosecuted rough play. A statute is void for vagueness if it either "does not define the criminal offense with sufficient definiteness that ordinary people can understand what conduct is proscribed" or if it fails to "provide ascertainable standards of guilt to protect against arbitrary enforcement." Because his claim does not implicate any First Amendment rights, Shelley cannot claim the statute is facially vague; he may only argue that it is vague as applied to him. Our holding that a defendant is entitled to argue that another player may legally consent to

conduct that causes or threatens bodily harm if the conduct and the harm are reasonably foreseeable hazards of joint participation in a lawful, athletic contest or competitive sport cures any problem with vagueness. With this defense, an ordinary person should understand that intentionally punching a person in an athletic competition may result in criminal prosecution. Accordingly, the crime is defined with sufficient definiteness. Additionally, the statute did not invite arbitrary enforcement by law enforcement on the facts of this case given that breaking another's jaw in three places satisfies the substantial bodily harm element of *RCW 9A.36.021(1)(a)*.

We affirm. * * *

 OTHER RELATED SIGNIFICANT CASES

Chapter 4.11 *Assault and Battery*   Chapter 4.16 *Hazing*

Recent Trends

Juveniles are increasingly being prosecuted for incidents of violence on the playing fields. In San Antonio, an eighteen-year-old was convicted of aggravated assault and sentenced to serve five years in prison as the result of an intentional foul against an opposing player during a high school basketball game. In New Mexico, an eighteen-year-old football player received a six-month sentence for attacking a referee during the course of the game. Criminal charges are pending against a sixteen-year-old for a brutal check and sticking incident in a high school hockey game.

Extending the Scope of Criminal Liability

In 1998, Stephen McKichan, a professional hockey goalie, brought a civil suit against the owner of an opposing team to recover for injuries resulting from a severe body check at the hands of "enforcer" Tony Twist (*McKichan v. St. Louis Hockey Club,* 1998). In this case, the owner was not liable, but a coach or manager could be charged criminally for their bad acts. The crimes of solicitation, conspiracy, and accomplice liability prohibit condoning criminal activity, but they have never been applied to sports.

Solicitation consists of inciting, counseling, advising, inducing, urging, or ordering another to commit an offense with intent that another person commit a crime. A coach or owner who instructs a player to take an opponent out of the game commits solicitation. The actions of Temple University basketball coach John Chaney could be illustrative of solicitation. Chaney ordered player Nehemiah Ingram to cause some damage in a game against St. Joe's. Ingram committed five fouls in four minutes, including a nondisplaced fracture of John Bryant's right arm. The crime of solicitation is complete at the time the instruction is given, even if the player refuses to act on it.

Conspiracy is an agreement between two or more persons to accomplish some criminal or unlawful purpose, or to accomplish a lawful purpose by unlawful means. Under a conspiracy theory, an agreement between coaches and players to physically intimidate an opponent could be prosecuted. In a college baseball game, Wichita State pitcher Ben Christensen threw a ball at Evansville lead-off hitter Anthony Molina while Molina was warming up about 35 feet from home plate. The ball hit Molina in the left eye, fracturing his eye socket in three places, and requiring more than 20 stitches. Christensen explained that he thought Molina was trying to time his warm-up pitches and that he had been coached to brush such hitters back.

Accomplice liability is a common law doctrine that certain persons who aid and abet a crime are liable for the same punishment as the principal. If an athlete were convicted for assault or battery, the coach could be subject to the same punishment as an accomplice. San Antonio High School basketball coach Gary

Durbon was accused of encouraging the violence for which Tony Limon was sentenced. According to witnesses, after the incident, Durbon was overheard telling Tony, "It's about time someone drew some blood." Holding coaches and management responsible for the unnecessarily aggressive acts of their athletes could reduce the encouragement of violence on the playing fields, but it might also change the face of competition as Americans currently know it.

References

Cases

Carroll v. State, 1980 OK CR 89.

Guttenplan v. Boston Professional Hockey Ass'n. Inc., No. 80 Civ. 415 (RLC), 1981 U.S. Dist. LEXIS 10434.

McKichan v. St. Louis Hockey Club, 967, S.W.2d 209 (App. Ct. Ed. Mo. 1998).

People v. Fitzsimmons, 34 N.Y.S. 1102 (N.Y. Sup. Ct. 1895).

People v. Freer, 86 Misc. 2d 280 (1976).

People v. Hall, 999 P.2d 207 (2000).

Re Duchesneau, 7 C.R.3d 70 (Que. Youth Trib. 1978).

Regina v. Ciccarelli, (Ont. Prov. Ct. 1988).

Regina v. Green, 16 D.L.R.3d 137 (Ont. Prov. Civ. 1971).

Regina v. Leyte, 13 C.C.C.2d 458 (Ont. Prov. Civ. 1973).

Regina v. Maki, 14 D.L.R.3d 164 (Ont. Prov. Civ. 1970).

Regina v. Maloney, 28 C.C.C.2d 323 (Ont. Prov. Civ. 1976).

Regina v. Mayer, 41 Man. R.2d 73 (1985).

Regina v. St. Croix, 47 C.C.C.2d 122 (Ont. Co. Ct. 1979).

Regina v. Watson, 26 C.C.C.2d 150 (Prov. Ct. Ont. 1975).

State v. Floyd, 466 N.W.2d 919 (1990).

State v. Forbes, No. 63280 (Hennepin Co. Minn. Dist. Ct. dismissed Aug. 12, 1975).

State v. Holloway, 886 S.W.2d 482 (Tex. Ct. App. 1994).

State v. Limon, No. 1999-CR-2892 (144th Jud. Dist. Ct. Bexar Co. Tex. 2000).

State of Washington v. Shelley, 85 Wn. App. 24, 929 P.2d 489 (1997).

Publications

Barry, M. P., Fox, R. L., & Jones, C. (2005). Judicial opinion on the criminality of sports violence in the United States. *Seton Hall J. Sports L.*, *15*, 1–34.

Berry, R. C., & Wong, G. M. (1993). *Law and business of the sports industries* (Vol. II, 2nd ed.). Westport, CT: Praeger.

Clarke, C. A. (2000). Law and order on the courts: The application of criminal liability for intentional fouls during sporting events. *Ariz. St. L.J.*, *32*, 1149.

Cook, K., & Mravic, M. (1999, May 17). Scorecard: College beanball shocker: A purpose pitch. *Sports Illustrated*, p. 24.

Farber, M. (1997, March 24). The worst job in sports, *Sports Illustrated*, p. 66.

Fritz, K. A. (2002). Going to the bullpen: Using Uncle Sam to strike out professional sports violence. *Cardozo Arts & Ent. L.J.*, *20*, 189.

Harary, C. (2002). Aggressive play or criminal assault? An in depth look at sports violence and criminal liability. *Colum. J.L. & Arts*, *25*, 197–217.

Hockey player pleads guilty to assault. (1998, June 19). *Milwaukee Journal Sentinel*, p. 2.

Jones, M. E. (1999). *Sports law*. Upper Saddle River, NJ: Prentice Hall.

Katz, J. H. (2000). Symposium: Federalism after Alden: Note: From the penalty box to the penitentiary—The people versus Jesse Boulerice. *Rutgers L.J.*, *31*, 833.

MacGregor, J. (1999, March 22). Less than murder. *Sports Illustrated*, p. 112.

Markus, R. M. (1972, July/August). Sports safety: On the offensive. *Trial*, p. 12.

Milloy, R. E. (2000). Basketball player's foul draws a jail term. *N.Y. Times on the Web*, March 9, 2000. Retrieved from www.nytimes.com

Model Penal Code § 2.11.1—2.11.2 (1985).

Restatement (2nd) of Torts § 50 cmt. b (1963).

Shannon, K. (2000). Basketball player jailed for elbow. *Associated Press*, March 10, 2000. Retrieved from http://wire.ap.org

Timmer, J. (2002). Crossing the (blue) line: Is the criminal justice system the best institution to deal with violence in hockey? *V. and. J. Ent. L. & Prac.*, 4, 205.

Weiler, P. C., & Roberts, G. R. (1998). *Sports and the law* (2nd ed.). St. Paul, MN: West Publishing Co.

Weistart, J. C., & Lowell, C. H. (1979). *The law of sports.* Indianapolis, IN: Bobbs-Merrill, 185.

4.13 Defamation

Anita M. Moorman
University of Louisville

Lori K. Miller
Wichita State University

The tort of defamation dates back to early sixteenth-century common law. Defamation law provides recourse for false, insidious, or irresponsible statements that damage an individual's reputation. As defined by *Black's Law Dictionary* (Black, 1990), **defamation** is that which tends to injure reputation; to diminish the esteem, respect, goodwill or confidence in which the plaintiff is held, or to excite adverse, derogatory or unpleasant feelings or opinions against him (p. 417).

Fundamental Concepts

In the sport industry, defamation claims are raised in a variety of settings, such as statements made by an athletic director about reasons for terminating a coach; statements made by a coach about one of his assistant coaches; statements made by a professional athlete about his agent; statements published by a newspaper about an athlete; statements published on an Internet discussion board about an athlete, coach, or owner of a professional sport team; or statements made during a television sports program comparing an athlete to another person convicted of numerous crimes. All these examples, depending on the substance and truthfulness of the statements made, could easily form the basis of a defamation action.

Elements of a Defamation Claim

According to the Restatement (Second) of Torts § 558, the following four elements must exist to establish a defamation claim:

1. A false and defamatory statement of fact
2. Publication[1] to a third party
3. Fault or negligence of the publisher
4. Damage or actual injury

The plaintiff bears the burden of proof in a defamation action (Restatement (Second) of Torts). Under common law defamation, the standard for proving negligence or fault varies depending on whether the person about whom the statement is made is a public or private figure. For example, for a sport celebrity or other public figure, such as Tom Brady of the New England Patriots, to prove negligence or fault (the third element identified earlier), he would have to demonstrate that the person making the statement did so with **actual malice**. To show actual malice, one must show that the speaker knew the statement was false or pub-

---

[1] The "publication" element of the defamation claim is satisfied when defamatory statements are communicated to a third party. You cannot defame someone by speaking to him or her alone or by muttering to yourself. This element of defamation is easily satisfied when claims are made against newspapers and broadcast media.

lished it with a total disregard for whether it was true or false. A private person would only have to prove that the statement was published negligently, which means that the speaker failed to exercise reasonable care to determine whether the statement was true or false. This is a much lower burden of proof for the private individual. The distinction between the burden of proof for public figures as opposed to a private individual, such as spectator or security guard is explained further in the next section. Although private figures are not required to show actual malice to recover for defamation, they must prove actual injury. As defined by the Supreme Court in *Gertz v. Robert Welch, Inc.* (1974), actual injury includes "impairment of reputation and standing in the community, personal humiliation, and mental anguish and suffering" (p. 350).

Franklin and Rabin (1996, p. 880) also observed that "no liability exists if a third person unexpectedly overhears a private conversation between plaintiff and defendant." Further, publications that are merely embarrassing do not qualify as defamatory. Rather, publications must truly reflect "sharp criticism" that damages reputation (Franklin & Rabin, 1996). Regardless, when ascertaining whether a defendant is liable for defamation, the entire publication (e.g., title, punctuation, paragraphing, full article) will be considered versus one particular phrase or statement.

Types of Defamation: Slander and Libel

The tort of defamation includes both slander and libel. Defamatory comments made verbally, such as those heard on television, exemplify **slander**. **Libel** is a broader category of communication. Written comments, photographs, and cartoons, such as those appearing in newspapers and in other written documents, are examples of libel. A verbal comment is **slanderous per se** and a written comment is **libel per se** if it falls into one of the following categories: (1) accuses the plaintiff of criminal conduct, (2) accuses the plaintiff of having a loathsome disease, (3) accuses the female plaintiff of being unchaste, (4) accuses the plaintiff of misconduct in public office, or (5) injures the plaintiff's profession, business, or trade. If a statement falls into one of these categories, it is presumed as a matter of law that the reputation of the individual about whom the false statement was made will be injured. For example, false comments accusing someone of embezzling funds from a community youth sports organization, having sex with an entire football team, or engaging in illegal student athlete recruiting practices could be construed as slanderous per se (Carpenter, 1995). No reasonable person could ever interpret such statements as reflecting positively on the person about whom they were spoken. As explained by the court in *Romaine v. Kallinger* (1988), if a published statement is susceptible of one meaning only, and that meaning is defamatory, the statement is libelous as a matter of law.

Slander and libel were originally recognized as two distinct types of defamation. Libel, written defamatory statements, was thought to be more damaging because, at the time the distinction arose, few persons could read or write. Therefore, anything that was written would carry a louder ring of purported truth (*Matherson v. Marchello*, 1984). In addition, a written defamation could be disseminated more widely and carried a degree of permanence. For example, newspapers and magazines could be retained for weeks, whereas statements made on television vanished within seconds. Technology now secures media statements in a tangible form, and most jurisdictions refer to the two terms (i.e., slander and libel) interchangeably as simply defamation (Pember, 1990).

Defamation and the First Amendment

The tort of defamation, as most tort theories, evolved as a matter of state law. However, unlike other torts, the law of defamation has been influenced significantly by First Amendment considerations since the mid-1960s (Franklin & Rabin, 1996). Allowing one person to sue another person because of what that person said or wrote often collides with the First Amendment freedom of speech and freedom of the press. Thus, the interests of the state in protecting its citizens from defamatory statements is often weighed against the interests preserved in the First Amendment ensuring an open forum for all ideas.

Elaborating on the importance of defamation law to an individual, Justice Stewart said, "The right of a man to the protection of his own reputation from unjustified invasion and wrongful hurt reflects no more than our basic concept of the essential dignity and worth of every human being . . ." (*Rosenblatt v. Baer*, 1966, p. 92). Conversely, critics say defamation law stifles individual commentary, which contributes to the marketplace of ideas. As stated earlier, the judicial system attempts to balance the right to preserve one's reputation with individual Constitutional rights. To promote balance between plaintiff and defendant, Supreme Court decisions have recognized that certain persons enjoy greater protection from damaging statements than do other persons. For example, we have a right to know, ask, and talk about the past financial dealings of our elected officials in a public forum because it may affect their ability to perform and our confidence in them. However, we certainly have no right to know, ask, or talk about the past financial dealings of our next-door neighbor or a coworker in a public forum. Meaning simply that some people, such as a senator, professional athlete, or sports broadcaster, must tolerate more intrusive or hurtful comments made publicly about them based on their position or actions in our society. Thus, three categories have emerged from Supreme Court decisions to help correctly balance individual interests against First Amendment rights. These three categories are public officials, public figures, and private figures.

The Public Official

Defamation law changed drastically in the mid-1960s from earlier sixteenth-century interpretations, which considered attacks on public officials as seditious libels that could be treated as criminal (Franklin & Rabin, 1996). The 1964 Supreme Court decision in *New York Times Co. v. Sullivan* (hereinafter "*New York Times*") revolutionized the way the judiciary interpreted and applied defamation law. As stated by Pember (1990), "This is one of the most important First Amendment cases ever decided . . ." (p. 129). In *New York Times*, the Supreme Court prohibited *public officials* from recovering damages for defamatory comments relating to official conduct unless the plaintiff could prove with convincing clarity that the statement was made with *actual malice*. Communication made with actual malice was defined by the Court as communication made "with knowledge that it was false or with reckless disregard of whether it was false or not" (*New York Times*, 1964, p. 380).

The Supreme Court believed that the public had a right to know and evaluate for themselves how leaders governed. Further, open debate, although at times caustic and unpleasant, ensured the exchange of ideas necessary to bring about political and social change desired by the people (*New York Times*, 1964). Further, the freedom of the people to criticize freely and without actual malice better balances the absolute privilege enjoyed by the public official.

Pember (1990) succinctly defines a **public official** as "someone who works for a government and draws a salary from the public payroll" (p. 133). The Supreme Court also attempted to define the public official. In *Rosenblatt v. Baer* (1966) the Court questioned whether all individuals employed by the state are public officials or just those employed in "high-powered" positions. As stated by Justice Douglas in a concurring opinion, "anyone on the public payroll" qualifies as a public official (p. 89).

It would appear from the preceding decisions that subsequent court decisions would classify all teachers, coaches, and recreation supervisors as public officials. However, the Supreme Court of Kentucky in *Warford v. Lexington Herald* issued a contrary decision in 1990. As decided by this court, an assistant basketball recruiting coach at the University of Pittsburgh was not classified as either a public official or a public or limited-purpose public figure (see the following sections dealing with the public figure and limited-purpose public figure).

The Public Figure

In a subsequent landmark case, *Curtis Publishing Co. v. Butts* (1967), the Supreme Court extended the constitutional protection given to statements about public officials in *New York Times* to public figures as well. Private industry and recognized leaders (i.e., public figures) often have as much societal influence as government officials, hence the similar constitutional protection afforded to those communicating about these individuals. Similar to the standard of proof established in *New York Times*, the *Curtis* court stated that individuals falling into the status of a public figure must prove actual malice to recover for damages. The determination of whether a person is a public figure is a matter of law. Public figure status does not depend on the desires of the individual. A plaintiff may not escape public figure status if he or she voluntarily engages in a course of conduct that invites attention and comment. Indeed, the distinction between public and private figures is based on two considerations: the plaintiff's access to the media and the extent to which the plaintiff, by virtue of a position in the community or involvement in a particular matter of public concern, can be said to invite public comment and attention. As explained by the Supreme Court in *Curtis Publishing Co. v. Butts* (1967), a public figure is an individual who has, because of his or her activities, "commanded sufficient continuing public interest" (p. 155). The Supreme Court recognized the Athletic Director of the University of Georgia (Wally Butts), as a public figure. In *Waldbaum v. Fairchild Publications, Inc.* (1980), the district court observed that many well-known athletes, entertainers, and other personages endorse commercial products. . . . "This phenomenon, regardless of whether it is justified, indicates that famous persons may be able to transfer their recognition and influence from one field to another" (p. 1294). Athletes, like politicians, can sway individual thinking. Consequently, their individual actions are open to public debate and scrutiny.

The *Curtis* court further provided two reasons for its extension of the actual malice standard to public figures as well as public officials. First, the plaintiff–public figure voluntarily "thrusts" himself or herself into the "vortex" of "important public controversies" (*Curtis Publishing Co. v. Butts*, 1967). If society chooses to direct massive public attention to a particular sphere of activity, those who enter that sphere invite such attention and must overcome the *Times* [actual malice] standard (*Chuy v. Philadelphia Eagles Football Club*, 1979, p. 267). Second, like public officials, public figures have "sufficient access to the means of counter argument" via the media. Certainly most, if not all, persons classified as public figures have ready access to the media and public forums in which they can defend themselves or respond to criticism or controversial statements.

The Limited-Purpose Public Person

Persons with instant national recognition and constant national media exposure such as Johnny Carson, Mohammed Ali, Wayne Newton, and William F. Buckley are considered all-purpose public figures (Barron & Dienes, 1979). However, the 1974 Supreme Court decision in *Gertz v. Robert Welch, Inc.* introduced the concept of a limited-purpose public person as ". . . an individual [who] voluntarily injects himself or is drawn into a particular public controversy and thereby becomes a public figure for a limited range of issues" (p. 351). The limited-purpose public figure has instant *local* recognition and constant media coverage on a *local* level. A limited-purpose public figure is a person who becomes a public figure for a specific range of issues by being drawn into or voluntarily injecting him- or herself into a specific public controversy. To determine whether a person is a limited-purpose public figure, we must examine that person's participation in the controversy from which the alleged defamation arose and whether they have attained a general notoriety in the community by reason of that participation (*Daubenmire v. Sommers*, 2004). A three-part test is used to make this determination: The court must determine that (1) there is a public controversy; (2) the plaintiff played a sufficiently central role in that controversy; and (3) the alleged defamation was germane to the plaintiff's involvement in the controversy (*Daubenmire v. Sommers*, 2004). For example, if your community is considering building a multimillion-dollar sports stadium, and a local university professor who is an expert in stadium finance appears on a local radio talk show and actively participates in the public debate on the funding initiative, she may qualify as a limited-purpose public figure, even though in any other context she would have most certainly been a private person. Most sport figures (e.g., coaches, athletes, sport broadcasters) tend to be classified as limited-purpose public figures. Further, many jobs "produce at least limited-purpose public figure status by virtue of the associations it entails" (Franklin & Rabin, 1996, p. 991). To recover in a defamation action, a public figure, including a limited-purpose public figure, must show by clear and convincing evidence that the statements were made with actual malice, that is, with knowledge that the statements were false or with reckless disregard of whether they were false or not. Sufficient evidence must exist to permit the conclusion that the defendant in fact had serious doubt as to the truth of the statements (*Daubenmire v. Sommers*, 2004).

The Private Figure

The "private figure" classification refers to individual citizens who are not involved in public issues or employed as a public official. Distinguishing between a public versus private figure is a critical issue for a plaintiff. Classification as a private person is important, as private figures need only prove that an alleged defamatory statement was negligently made rather than made with actual malice, as discussed earlier. Negligence is the failure to exercise "reasonable care." This is a much lower standard of proof than that required for public officials, public figures, or limited-purpose public figures.

The difficulty comes in ascertaining who qualifies as a "private figure." Defendants allege that private citizens involved in matters of interest to the public constitute limited-purpose public figures, at minimum, and are subject to the actual malice standard of proof required by *New York Times*. According to the Supreme Court's plurality decision in *Rosenbloom v. Metromedia, Inc.* (1971), all publication regarding matters of general interest or public concern should be protected by requiring plaintiffs to prove actual malice. Subsequent courts, concerned about the improper balance between competing interests, repudiated the "public interest" or "subject matter" standard established in the 1971 *Rosenbloom* case.

Two dominant reasons explain why the Court preserved the private person status granting individuals a lower standard of proof. First, it is assumed that private individuals do not have the same ability to access the media as public officials and public figures. Access to the media provides public officials and public figures with an opportunity to refute defamatory statements. The value of media access is illustrated by the Iowa Libel Research Project. According to this research project, almost 75 percent of defamed plaintiffs indicated they would have found adequate recourse if "the news medium would have published or broadcast a correction, retraction or apology" (Pember, 1990). Second, it is said that public figures and public officials relinquish rights when they voluntarily become entangled in an issue of public concern. Private individuals, in comparison, are not attempting to influence society and are not desirous of media attention.

Statements of Fact vs. Expressions of Opinion

Early common law protected statements of opinion from defamatory allegations. The Supreme Court affirmed this sentiment in the *Gertz* case in 1974. As stated by the Supreme Court, "Under the First Amendment there is no such thing as a false idea" (*Gertz v. Robert Welch, Inc.*, 1974, p. 339). However, statements based on false facts, or undisclosed facts, are actionable. In other words, if an opinion is stated, then all the facts that were used in deriving the opinion should be disclosed. This enables an individual to read the facts and then draw his or her own conclusion (i.e., opinion), which may differ from that of the writer or publisher. The decision as to whether a statement constitutes fact or opinion is a question of law for the court to decide.

The Supreme Court in *Milkovich v. Lorain Journal Co.* (1990) further narrowed the protection given to statements of opinion. As explained by the Court, merely prefacing a statement with "In my opinion, . . ." does not insulate an individual from defamation liability. More specifically, the Court stated "Even if the speaker states the facts upon which he bases his opinion, if those facts are either incorrect or incomplete, or if his assessment of them is erroneous, the statement may still imply a false assertion of fact. Simply couching such statements in terms of opinion does not dispel these implications . . ." (p. 2706).

In *Stepien v. Franklin* (1988) the Court of Appeals of Ohio held an assortment of disparaging adjectives to be constitutionally protected opinion. The adjectives included the following: "Stupid," "dumb," "buffoon," "nincompoop," "scum," "a cancer," "an obscenity," "gutless liar," "unmitigated liar," "pathological liar," "egomaniac," "nuts," "crazy," "irrational," "suicidal," "lunatic" (p. 1327). As illustrated earlier, the specific language used by the defendant is overtly injurious. However, the syllabus by the court, justifying its action, stated, "The area of sports is a traditional haven for cajoling, invective, and hyperbole . . ." (p. 1326).

Society commonly accepts rowdy behavior as "part of the game." Even during the 1960s, the era of individual rights, the heckling involved in sport was viewed as commonplace. As explained by the Supreme Court of North Carolina in *Toone v. Adams* (1964), "For present day fans, a goodly part of the sport in a baseball game is goading and denouncing the umpire when they do not concur in his decisions, and most feel that, without one or more rhubarbs, they have not received their money" (p. 136).

The Supreme Court of Ohio (*Scott v. News-Herald*, 1986) concluded that most information conveyed in the sports section of a newspaper is "constitutionally protected." The *Scott* court's decision, although of limited precedential value, is precarious because it suggests that comments about a sport-related figure, regardless of their veracity or the publisher's degree of fault, are constitutionally protected.

Defenses to Defamation Claims

Truth is an **absolute defense** to all claims of defamation. Even if the actual facts turn out to be different than those contained in the statement, a defense of truthfulness may still apply. The statements do not necessarily have to be completely accurate, only substantively correct or truthful for the truth defense to shield them. For example, truth would still serve as a viable defense in the situation where a coach was charged with selling $250,000 worth of steroids to players when in actuality he only sold $125,000.

Privilege, a second defense, refers to "a particular and peculiar benefit or advantage enjoyed by a person, company, or class, beyond the common advantages of other citizens" (Black, 1990, p. 1197). Privileged statements made without malice are immune from defamation liability (*Iacco v. Bohannon*, 1976; *Institute of Athletic Motivation v. Univ. of Ill.*, 1982). Common types of privilege include absolute privilege, qualified privilege, and fair comment.

Absolute privilege is enjoyed by those in (1) a legislative forum (e.g., congressmen, congresswomen, senators, city council members); (2) the judicial forum (e.g., judges, lawyers, plaintiffs, defendants); and (3) administrative and executive branches of government (e.g., presidents, mayors, department heads). Persons occupying these roles have "absolute" privilege, (i.e., there can be no liability for statements, regardless of their falsity or disregard for the truth). This privilege exists to avoid censorship of desired communication that could otherwise possibly benefit society. The media is also protected from liability if during the broadcast or publication of statements during a public debate, defamatory comments are made by individuals who are protected by absolute privilege (Franklin & Rabin, 1996).

Qualified or conditional privilege represents a defense available to other defendants. Similar to absolute privilege, some situations demand the protection of communication to benefit society at large. As explained by Carpenter (1995), qualified statements are those statements made (1) without knowledge of falsity, (2) by a person with reason to communicate the statement, and (3) communicated only to a person with a "justifiable interest in knowing." Individual managers often have qualified privilege, for example, when discussing employee behaviors with superiors and when providing employee references.

Fair comment represents a defense commonly used by media defendants. As explained by Black (1990), fair comment is "A form of qualified privilege applied to news media publications relating to discussion of matters which are of legitimate concern to the community as a whole because they materially affect the interests of all the community" (p. 596). There typically is no liability if the media publishes defamatory information so long as their report represents a fair and accurate summary or restatement of communication available to the public on which they are relying. The fair comment defense is only appropriate when comments are made without malice and statements are based on true facts (Black, 1990; *Cohen v. Cowles Publishing Co.*, 1954; *Conkwright v. Globe News Publishing Company*, 1965).

Neutral reportage represents another defense similar in concept to fair reporting that is available to media defendants in certain circuits. Based on the U.S. Court of Appeals landmark decision in *Edwards v. National Audubon Society* (1977), media defendants can publish statements made by responsible or prominent organizations even though the publisher doubts the veracity of the statements.

Damages

Defamation law encompasses two types of damages (*Matherson v. Marchello*, 1984). First, special damages reflect "actual pecuniary losses that the plaintiff can prove he or she sustained" as a direct result of the defendant's comments (Franklin & Rabin, 1996, p. 895; *Liberman v. Gelstein*, 1992). Lost wages or the loss of identified business customers, for example, are quantifiable and reflect special damages. Second, general damages, on the other hand, reflect nonquantifiable damages such as the presumed damage to one's reputation. Plaintiffs suing for slander must prove special damages unless the cause of action is slander per se. Although an anomaly in tort law, the tort of defamation does not always require proof of damage. For example, in some states, plaintiffs suing for libel are not required to prove special damages (Franklin & Rabin, 1996). Rather, the existence of damage is *presumed* as a result of the publication itself (*Matherson v. Marchello*, 1984).

Significant Case

◇◇◇

The significant case presented following not only outlines the elements of a defamation action very well, but also addresses the defense related to statements of opinion. This case is also particularly helpful for current study because the allegedly offending statements were originally published on a Website. Electronic statements are rapidly becoming the most common subjects of defamation actions, which is a dramatic shift from traditional defamation actions. Historically, many defamation actions involved an individual plaintiff and a print or broadcast publishing company as the defendant. The growth of electronic media has created many more opportunities for actionable statements to be "published" by individuals, Website owners, and publishers.

DIBELLA V. HOPKINS

Southern District of New York

187 F. Supp. 2d 192 (S.D.N.Y. 2002)

[P]laintiff Lou DiBella, a boxing advisor, matchmaker, and television packager formerly employed by the cable network Home Box Office ("HBO"), alleges that he was defamed by defendant Bernard Hopkins, the professional boxer. Hopkins became the undisputed middleweight champion of the world on September 29, 2001, when he beat Felix Trinidad by a final round technical knockout. That fight was the culmination of DiBella's efforts to promote and develop Hopkins's boxing career. Within weeks after the fight, however, Hopkins terminated his relationship with DiBella. Hopkins then publicly accused DiBella of improper conduct. He told several reporters that while DiBella was still employed by HBO, DiBella had asked him for—and he had paid DiBella—$50,000 to arrange for his fights to be televised on HBO. These were, in Hopkins's own words, "some serious, serious allegations." One sports writer observed that Hopkins was alleging that he had paid DiBella "payoffs" that amounted to "bribes." Another wrote that Hopkins had alleged that DiBella had "demanded under-the-table fees to secure dates on HBO."

DiBella contends that Hopkins's accusations were false. He denies that he engaged in any wrongful conduct and he denies that he received any monies from Hopkins while he was still employed at HBO. He alleges that his name and reputation have been tarnished by Hopkins's comments. Consequently, he and his company, DiBella Entertainment, Inc. ("DiBella Inc."), bring this defamation action for damages. . . .

* * *

C. Hopkins's Statements

On or about December 19, 2001, Hopkins made the following statements to Steve Kim, a reporter for Maxboxing.com:

> *Understand, every time I fought, Lou DiBella got paid, even when he was with HBO, which is f**king wrong. What I'm saying is that the bottom line is, the Syd Vanderpool fight, should an HBO employee accept $50,000 while he's still working for HBO . . . Ask HBO why an employee of their company asked me to give him $50,000? And I paid him too. Now, is that ethically right? You think Time Warner wants to hear about that? What I'm telling you right now is some serious, serious allegations, but these guys here try to make it seem like I'm the bad guy and Lou is probably whispering stuff around, too, probably, but he probably isn't saying anything openly. And that influence can hurt me when I get to HBO, being friends with the people over there.*

Kim published the statements in an article on the Internet at Matchbox.com on December 20, 2001. On or about December 21, 2001, in an interview with the Boston Globe, Hopkins claimed that he had paid DiBella $50,000 to get him on HBO:

> *I ain't no snitch but I can back it up. . . . This is a filthy, filthy game and you gotta be filthy to be in it. . . .*
>
> *Nobody in this game does anything for nothing. I'm 36. I got no HBO contract. I can get on a card to make $500,000 if I give him [DiBella] $50,000. Why not? I didn't really see anything wrong with it. It's boxing. . . .*

> *I ain't lying about nothing . . . I got the evidence right here on my coffee table. The wire transfers. The voided check. I know I ain't crazy. To get on that [HBO] card the fee was $50,000. Paying it was a no-brainer.*

The statements were published in the Boston Globe on December 24, 2001. In late December 2001, Hopkins also made the following statements to one or more reporters, as reported in the Las Vegas Review-Journal on December 23, 2001:

> *Lou DiBella . . . lobbied for HBO while he was there and convinced them Bernard would be a good undercard fight with the hopes of [Roy] Jones and Hopkins maybe fighting. In doing that, I paid him. I wired him $50,000.*

* * *

DISCUSSION

A. Defendant's Motion

Hopkins * * * contends first that the defamation claim must be dismissed because his statements were not defamatory because they were "true" and they were "mere statements of opinion that [were] validly held." * * *

The Merits

* * *

b) Defamation

(i) Applicable Law

To state a claim for defamation under New York law, "the claimant must allege facts sufficient to support a finding of a published statement concerning the claimant that is both false and defamatory." Cytyc Corp. v. Neuromedical Sys., Inc., 12 F. Supp. 2d 296, 301 (S.D.N.Y. 1998). Ultimately, New York law requires a libel plaintiff to prove five elements: "(1) a written defamatory statement of fact regarding the plaintiff; (2) published to a third party by the defendant; (3) defendant's fault, varying in degree depending on whether plaintiff is a private or public party; (4) falsity of the defamatory statement; and (5) injury to plaintiff." Meloff v. New York Life Ins. Co., 240 F.3d 138, 145 (2d Cir. 2001) (citation omitted). A plaintiff who is a public figure must establish that the defendant made the statements with actual malice. New York Times v. Sullivan, 376 U.S. 254, 279-80, 11 L. Ed. 2d 686, 84 S. Ct. 710 (1964). "Liability requires clear and convincing evidence of a knowing falsehood or 'subjective awareness of probable falsity.' " *** Under New York law "it is 'fundamental that truth is an absolute, unqualified defense to a civil defamation action,' and 'substantial truth suffices to defeat a charge of libel.' " ***

Statements of subjective opinion are not actionable under New York law. *** "There is no bright line test to aid in determining whether a statement is one of opinion or fact, as 'expressions of 'opinion' may often imply an assertion of objective fact.' " Belly Basics, 95 F. Supp. 2d at 145 (quoting Milkovich v. Lorain Journal

Co., 497 U.S. 1, 18, 111 L. Ed. 2d 1, 110 S. Ct. 2695 (1990)). New York law does, however, prescribe a three-factor test to determine whether a statement is a statement of fact or a statement of opinion: "(1) whether the challenged statements have a precise and readily understood meaning; (2) whether the statements are susceptible of being proven false; and (3) whether the context signals to the reader that the statements are more likely to be expressions of opinion rather than fact." Cytyc Corp., 12 F. Supp. 2d at 301-02. * * *

(ii) Application

Accepting, as I must, the material allegations of the first amended complaint to be true for purposes of this motion, I conclude that plaintiffs have stated a viable defamation claim.

First, the statements that Hopkins made to the reporters in question were statements of fact, not opinion. For example, he said to Maxboxing.com: "Understand, every time I fought, Lou DiBella got paid, even when he was with HBO, which is f**king wrong." He told the Boston Globe: "I got the evidence right here on my coffee table. The wire transfers. The voided check. . . . To get on that [HBO] card the fee was $50,000." He told the Las Vegas Review-Journal: "Lou DiBella . . . lobbied for HBO while he was there. . . . I paid him. I wired him $50,000."

These were statements of fact. They had a precise and readily understood meaning. They could be proven false. They were not made in contexts that would signal to the reader that they were more likely to be expressions of opinion rather than statements of fact; to the contrary, they were made in contexts that clearly suggested they were statements of fact.

Hopkins now argues that he "did not claim that Mr. DiBella was actually paid before he left HBO" and the "gist" of his statements was "that Mr. DiBella rendered services to him with the expectation of payment while an HBO employee and at a time when he had the authority to decide who would participate in its televised boxing tournaments." This argument is incorrect, as the excerpts quoted above demonstrate. Moreover, the fact that at times Hopkins used rhetorical questions in describing his alleged payments to DiBella does not turn his statements into "conjecture, hypothesis, or speculation." Hopkins was clearly stating that (1) he paid DiBella $50,000 to get his fights on HBO (2) while DiBella was still employed by HBO.

The analyses of Hopkins's remarks in the New York Daily News and the Philadelphia Daily News confirm the factual nature of Hopkins's statements. One reporter interpreted Hopkins's statements as alleging that DiBella had paid him "payoffs" and "bribes" and the other interpreted Hopkins's statements as alleging that DiBella had "demanded under-the-table fees to secure dates on HBO." See Belly Basics, 95 F. Supp. 2d at 145-46 (citations omitted). Accordingly, the "mere opinion" defense is rejected.

Second, Hopkins's contention that no defamation lies because his statements were true must be rejected at this point in the proceedings, for the first amended complaint alleges that his statements were false. Indeed, the first amended complaint specifically alleges that DiBella received no monies from Hopkins while he was still employed at HBO. Because I must assume the facts alleged in the first amended complaint to be true for purposes of this motion, Hopkins's truth defense is premature.

The gravamen of a defamation action is injury to reputation, and a defamatory statement is one that exposes an individual to public hatred, shame, and disgrace "in the minds of right-thinking persons." (further citation omitted). Words that affect a person in his profession, business, or trade by imputing to him fraud or dishonesty are defamatory. (citations omitted). Here, Hopkins's statements were defamatory, for he accused DiBella of fraud and dishonesty in his profession, business, and trade. See Shalaby v. Saudi Arabian Airlines, 1998 U.S. Dist. LEXIS 17571, No. 97 Civ. 9393 (DC), 1998 WL 782021 (S.D.N.Y. Nov. 9, 1998) (plaintiff stated defamation claim where complaint alleged defendants had spread false rumors that he accepted bribes and kickbacks from travel agencies while employed by airline). The motion to dismiss is denied as to the defamation claim.

SO ORDERED.

Recent Trends

Recent Cases

Many defamation cases continue to be pursued in the sport industry relating to the termination of coaches, especially college coaches. For example, Mike Price sued Time, Inc. for defamation based on a *Sports Illustrated* article that detailed his actions the night he visited a topless bar in Pensacola, Florida, in April 2003, while he was head coach at Alabama. Alabama fired Price a few days before the article was published. Price sued for $20 million, claiming he was defamed and slandered by the story. He acknowledged being heavily intoxicated, but denied allegations of sex at his hotel. The parties ultimately settled for an undisclosed sum without any admission of wrongdoing on the part of Time (Caldwell, 2005). In another case, Michael McGraw, a former athletic director/men's basketball coach at Green River Community College in the State of Washington, sued GRCC for defamation surrounding his firing. McGraw was fired after an investigation by conference officials revealed he had knowingly used an ineligible player during a game (Highlight case, 2002). College officials stated to others that the ineligible player had played with McGraw's knowledge. McGraw presented substantial evidence at trial demonstrating that these statements were not true and that he had no knowledge of the player's ineligibility. The jury awarded McGraw $1 million on the defamation claim and the award was upheld on appeal.

Defamation cases such as the case involving Evel Knievel highlight an expanding area of concern for sport organizations regarding electronic publications. Statements made or included on Websites, discussion boards, and chat rooms all have the potential to raise questions regarding defamation. For example, Evel Knievel sued ESPN, Inc. based only on a photo caption published on the Website expn.com. The photo showed the aging daredevil motorcyclist with his wife and another woman with a caption that read "Evel Knievel proves that you're never too old to be a pimp" (Anderson Publications, Inc., 2002, October). The district court dismissed Knievel's suit, concluding that the photo was the tenth photo among a seventeen-photo slide show, and that the word *pimp* had meanings other than its literal meaning. The district court noted that calling someone a pimp in the abstract was capable of defamatory meaning, but it lost such meaning in the context used here, and no reasonable person would believe that expn.com was actually accusing Evel Knievel of being a pimp or soliciting prostitution. Although most statements in an Internet chat room would be considered statements of opinion, often statements of opinion are cloaked with statements of fact (such as those statements in *DiBella v. Hopkins*).

Liability Insurance

Liability protection for intentional torts is becoming more common. Employment practices liability insurance, or EPL insurance, covers areas including defamation, invasion of privacy, and sexual harassment (see

Chapter 5.25 *Managing Risk Through Insurance*). Coverage for these types of claims had originally been viewed as against public policy. EPL insurance, although more affordable than before, is still costly. Insurance experts worry that employees with knowledge of an employer's EPL coverage will be more likely to sue. As stated by Jonathan Segal, a labor lawyer, "One question you have to ask yourself is, 'Is (the money) better spent on preventing the problem or on buying insurance to cover it?' " (Schwartz, 1996, p. K18).

References

Cases

Brooks v. Paige, 773 P.2d 1098 (Colo. App. 1988).

Cepeda v. Cowles Magazines and Broadcasting, Inc., 392 F.2d 417 (9th Cir. 1968).

Chuy v. Philadelphia Eagles Football Club, 595 F.2d 1265 (3rd Cir. 1979).

Cohen v. Cowles Publishing Co., 273 P.2d 893.

Conkwright v. Globe News Publishing Company, 398 S.W. 385 (1965).

Curtis Publishing Co. v. Butts, 388 U.S. 130 (1967).

Daubenmire v. Sommers, 805 N.E.2d 571 (Ohio App. 2004).

DiBella v. Hopkins, 187 F. Supp.2d 192 (S.D.N.Y. 2002).

Edwards v. National Audubon Society, 556 F.2d 113 (2nd Cir.), *cert. denied*, 434 U.S. 1002 (1977).

Garrison v. Louisiana, 379 U.S. 64 (1964).

Gertz v. Robert Welch, Inc., 418 U.S. 323 (1974).

Gomez v. Murdoch, 475 A.2d 622 (N.J. Super. A.D. 1984).

Hotchner v. Castillo-Puche, 551 F.2d 910 (2nd Cir. 1977).

Iacco v. Bohannon, 245 N.W.2d 791 (Mich. 1976).

Institute of Athletic Motivation v. Univ. of Ill., 170 Cal. Rptr. 411 (Cal. App. 1982).

Liberman v. Gelstein, 605 N.E.2d 344 (1992).

Masson v. New Yorker Magazine, Inc., 960 F.2d 896 (9th Cir. 1991).

Matherson v. Marchello, 473 N.Y.S.2d 998 (1984).

Milkovich v. Lorain Journal Co., 497 U.S. 1 (1990).

Montefusco v. ESPN, Inc., 2002 U.S. App. LEXIS 19740; 30 Media L. Rep. 2311 (3rd Cir. 2002).

New York Times Co. v. Sullivan, 376 U.S. 254 (1964).

Ollman v. Evans, 750 F.2d 970 (D.C. Cir.), *cert. denied*, 471 U.S. 1127 (1985).

Philadelphia Newspapers, Inc., et al. v. Hepps, et al., 475 U.S. 767 (1986).

Romaine v. Kallinger, 537 A.2d 284 (1988).

Rosenbloom v. Metromedia, Inc., 403 U.S. 29 (1971).

Rosenblatt v. Baer, 383 U.S. 75 (1966).

St. Amant v. Thompson, 390 U.S. 727 (1968).

Scott v. News-Herald, 25 Ohio St. 3d 243, 250 1986.

Stepien v. Franklin, 528 N.E.2d 1324 (Ohio App. 1988).

Toone v. Adams, 137 S.E.2d 132 (1964)

Waldbaum v. Fairchild Publications, Inc., 637 F.2d 1287 (D.C. Cir.), *cert. denied*, 449 U.S. 898 (1980).

Warford v. Lexington Herald, 170 Cal. Rptr. 411 (1990).

Washington v. Smith, 893 F. Supp. 60 (D.D.C. 1995).

Wolston v. Reader's Digest Ass'n, 443 U.S. 157 (1979).

Publications

Anderson, D. (1984). Reputation, compensation, and proof. *William & Mary Law Review, 25*(5), 747.

Anderson, D. A. (1991). Is libel law worth reforming? *University of Pennsylvania Law Review, 140*(2), 487–554.

Anderson Publications, Inc. (2002, August). Focus on: Pending litigation. *Legal Issues in Collegiate Athletics, 3*(10), 4.

Anderson Publications, Inc. (2002, October). Court dismisses Evel Knievel's defamation suit against expn.com. *Computer & Online Industry Litigation Reporter, 20*(8), 5.

Barron, J., & Dienes, C. T. (1979). *Handbook of free speech and free press.* Boston: Little, Brown.

Black, H. C. (1990). *Black's law dictionary* (6th ed.). St. Paul, MN: West Publishing Co.

Caldwell (2005).

Carpenter, L. J. (1995). *Legal concepts in sport: A primer.* Reston, VA: AAHPERD.

Franklin, M. A., & Rabin, R. L. (1996). *Tort law and alternatives: Cases and materials* (6th ed.). Westbury, NY: The Foundation Press.

Highlight case. (2002, February). *Legal Issues in Collegiate Athletics, 3*(4), 3.

Mayer, M. F. (1987). *The libel revolution: A new look at defamation and privacy.* Chelsea, MI: BookCrafters.

Pember, D. R. (1990). *Mass media law* (5th ed.). Dubuque, IA: Wm. C. Brown Publishers.

Ransom, E. (1995). The ex-public figure: A libel plaintiff without a class. *Seton Hall Journal of Sport Law, 5*(2), 389–417.

Restatement (Second) of Torts § 558.

Schwartz, K. (1996, February 18). Liability insurance for employment practices is increasingly common. *The Courier Journal*, p. K18.

Smolla, R. A. (1983). Let the author beware: The rejuvenation of the American law of libel. *University of Pennsylvania Law Review, 132*(1), 1–94.

Soocher, S. (2002, October). Bit parts. *Entertainment Law & Finance, 18*(7), 10.

4.14 Other Intentional Torts:
INVASION OF PRIVACY
BREACH OF FIDUCIARY DUTY
TORTIOUS INTERFERENCE WITH CONTRACT

Gary Rushing
Minnesota State University, Mankato

Intentional torts are deliberate wrongs done to others that cause harm. This type of tort differs from negligence torts in that lack of due care or engaging in abnormally dangerous activity is immaterial. Liability for intentional torts is predicated on the tortfeasor purposely causing harm to another person or engaging in an activity that is substantially certain to harm another (Restatement of Torts, 1965). Recreation or sport-related intentional torts can occur on or off the playing field. This chapter will discuss three common "off-field" intentional torts. They are invasion of privacy, breach of fiduciary duty, and tortious interference with contract.

Invasion of Privacy

Privacy, as defined by the courts, is "the right to be left alone; to live one's life as one chooses free from assault, intrusion or invasion except as they can be justified by the clear needs of the community under a government of law" (*Rosenbloom v. Metromedia, Inc.*, 1971). The legal principles that serve as the bases for privacy protection are found primarily in three sources of the law—the Fourteenth Amendment, the Constitution, and tort law. The Fourteenth Amendment and the Constitution are concerned with the rights claims against any of the various governmental entities. Tort law is devoted to rights claims against a person or persons (Samar, 1991). Further, most states recognize the right of privacy either by means of common law case decisions or by applicable statutes (Carper & Mietus, 1995).

Right of privacy, as found in tort law, involves four distinct theories or ways in which one's privacy can be invaded. Keeton, Dobbs, Keeton, Prosser, and Owen (1984) explained that these ways are not one tort, but a complex of four kinds of invasion. They have little in common except that each represents an interference with the right "to be let alone," which is at the center of all wrongful invasion suits. The four types of invasion are (1) unreasonable intrusion on the seclusion of another, (2) appropriation of another's name or likeness, (3) unreasonable disclosure of private facts, and (4) publicity that unreasonably places the other in a false light before the public. Only one of the torts, not all four, has to be proven for a successful claim of invasion of privacy.

Unreasonable Intrusion on Seclusion

The first form or theory is straightforward and concerned with the invasion of one's home or illegally searching someone's personal belongings or documents. Usually, the intrusion takes the form of window peeking, eavesdropping, excessive surveillance, or constant annoyance (Yasser, McCurdy, Goplerud, & Weston, 2000). However, the courts have extended this tort to include eavesdropping by wiretap, unauthorized examining of a bank account, and compulsory blood testing (Cross & Miller, 1992). Although untested in court, it would seem logical to assume that this notion would also include scanning of cellular phones and computer hacking. In addition to the actual intrusion, any information obtained in these or similar ways that is made public is also invasion of privacy. This is true even if the information obtained is truthful and it serves the public's right to know (Schubert et al., 1986). The requisite question is: Was the intrusion offensive or objectionable to a reasonable person? (Keeton, Smith, & Trentadue, 1984). If so, then it is an illegal invasion of one's privacy.

A court case that illustrates this point is *Bilney v. Evening Star Newspaper Co.* (1979). In this dispute, six members of the University of Maryland basketball team brought action against reporters and newspaper publishers for articles detailing their poor academic standing, thus putting them in danger of being declared ineligible to play. The question was addressed as to how the reporters obtained the academic information that they had published. The court determined that they had obtained the information from an anonymous source and that there was no evidence that the defendant news reporters had learned of the players' academic problems from confidential records or by any acts of invasion or intrusion. However, had the information been obtained through wiretaps, computer hacking, or some other offensive manner, the court may have considered this to be invasion of privacy.

Appropriation

The second form of invasion of privacy involves the **unauthorized use of a person's name or likeness** for commercial purposes such as advertising or trade. The protection provided by this law is especially important to sport figures because it gives them some control over the extent to which their name and likeness can be commercially exploited. Without this control, an athlete would lose a significant source of income from commercial endorsements, trading cards, and other enterprises. It is the most common "privacy" complaint of athletes (Byrd, 1988).

Although sport figures can prohibit most unauthorized use of their names and likenesses, courts have upheld unauthorized uses for editorial purposes as well as when reused by publishers or broadcasters for campaigns to increase circulation or broadcasting audiences. When used in this manner, it is considered to be protected incidental use (Dill, 1986).

In a case that illustrates the salient issues in this area, Joe Namath sued *Sports Illustrated (S.I.)* (*Namath v. Sports Illustrated*, 1975) for the unauthorized use of his photo to promote subscription sales. He contended that this use was commercial and violated his **right to privacy**. Further, because he was in the business of endorsing products and selling the use of his name and likeness, it interfered with his right to profit from such sale. The photograph had originally been used without objection from Namath, in conjunction with a 1969 Super Bowl article. However, because it was reprinted to promote subscription sales, he felt he should be compensated for its use. In siding with *S.I.*, the court noted that the use of the photo was merely "incidental" advertising because it was used to illustrate the quality and content of the periodical in which it originally appeared.

In a similar invasion of privacy case (*Montana v. San Jose Mercury News, Inc.*, 1995), Joe Montana brought action against the *San Jose Mercury News* (SJMN) for misappropriation of his name, photograph, and likeness. At issue was the reproduction of Montana's photograph that originally appeared in conjunction with a 1990 Super Bowl victory for the San Francisco 49ers. His photo had been reproduced in poster form. Some of the posters were sold for five dollars each, and the rest were donated to charity organizations. The court reached a decision similar to that of the *Namath* case and found in favor of SJMN for two reasons. First, the original newspaper account and the subsequent photograph constituted matters in the public interest. Second, the posters were sold to advertise the quality and content of its newspaper. They contained no additional information and they did not convey Montana's endorsement.

In another case, *Palmer v. Schonhorn Enterprises, Inc.* (1967), a toy manufacturing company appropriated the names and career profiles of golfers Arnold Palmer, Gary Player, Doug Sanders, and Jack Nicklaus for use in a game. In this situation, the court sided with the plaintiffs because the commercial use of their names and profiles was done without their permission and without compensation.

The appropriation theory of invasion of privacy generated the right of publicity cause of legal action (Breaux, 2005). **Right of Publicity** was included, for the first time, in the Restatement in 1995 (Restatement (Third) of the Law of Unfair Competition, pp. 46–49). It developed because the "appropriation" form of invasion of privacy was inadequate in protecting the ability of celebrities to control the use of their own name and likeness. The major difference between the two concepts is that redress in a right of privacy dispute is based on the mental duress resulting from "not being left alone," whereas the focus of redress in a right of publicity case is the compensation for the use of one's name and likeness for commercial reasons. Celebrities, including athletes, have had a difficult task in demonstrating to the courts that public exposure caused them mental distress in that "they sought such attention and profited from it" (Stapleton & McMurphy, 1999). For this reason, more and more states are adopting the right of publicity. Currently twenty-five states recognize the right of publicity either by statute or through common law, and it appears that other states will be following the trend (Stapleton & McMurphy, 1999). (For more information, see the *Significant Case* later in this chapter and Chapter 8.23, *Image Rights*.)

Although college athletes cannot individually profit from the use of their pictures, images, or appearances without losing athletic eligibility, they still may want to prohibit the use of their name and likeness. Schools cannot use or authorize the use of an athlete's picture or likeness for commercial purposes without the knowledge or consent of the athlete (NCAA Manual, 2000). A school that does violate this rule would not only be subject to NCAA sanctions but could also be liable for invasion of the affected athlete's privacy.

Unreasonable Disclosure of Private Facts

A third type of invasion of privacy involves public disclosure of private facts about an individual that an ordinary person would find objectionable. Public disclosure suits are sometimes referred to as embarrassment suits because they arise from objections to publicity of embarrassing private information (Dill, 1992). At the center of this type of suit is the balance between the public's right to know and the extent of the intrusion into one's private life. Although secondary issues must be satisfied to prevail in an embarrassment suit (see Keeton et al., 1984, pp. 856–857), where public figures such as sport personalities are concerned, there are two major issues that the courts will address. They are (1) whether the disclosed information was **truly private** or public, and (2) if the disclosed information was **highly offensive** to an ordinary person.

Private v. Public Facts

For a plaintiff to succeed in a public disclosure suit, it must be shown that the disclosed publicity was in an area where there was a legitimate expectancy of privacy. In other words, the disclosure must have involved truly private matters. What constitutes truly private for the average citizen, in terms of publicity, is different from that of a sport figure. Sports personalities, especially the highly paid athletes, have little privacy protection due to their public figure status. A public figure is someone who by "his [or her] accomplishments, fame, or mode of living, or by adopting a profession or calling which gives the public a legitimate interest in his doings, his affairs, and his character, has become a public personage" (Keeton et al., 1984, p. 859). (For an in depth discussion of public-figure status, see Chapter 4.13 *Defamation*.) By way of this notion, the Constitution allows the press to report matters that have become public interest.

The justification for this loss of privacy protection is the result of three considerations about public figures. First, public figures have, to a certain extent, sought publicity and have consented to it. Second, their personalities and affairs have become public and are no longer private business. Third, the press has a right to inform the public about those who have become matters of public interest (Prosser, 1960).

Are college athletes considered public figures? In the previously mentioned case of *Bilney v. Evening Star Newspaper Co.* (1979), because there was no evidence that the defendant news reporters had learned of the players' academic problems through improper methods, the court examined the issue of "public figure" status of the six players. The court reasoned that college basketball is a "big-time" sport and generates a great deal of public interest and excitement throughout the country. The court further stated that the players had "achieved the status of public figures . . . by virtue of their membership on the basketball team (and) . . . having sought . . . the limelight. . . . It's clear at least in this court that college athletes in big time sports are 'public figures'."

In addition to the preceding issues dealing with private information, it should be noted that information that has been previously reported, or that has already been made accessible to the public through public records or other documentation, or that is newsworthy is not considered to be purely private in nature and therefore is discloseable (Berry & Wong, 1993).

Highly Offensive

Even though some facts may be newsworthy and therefore nonprivate, they may not be publishable if they can be viewed as highly offensive to the average person. Because community norms vary from jurisdiction to jurisdiction, courts may have mixed decisions regarding what is permissible disclosure. However, where public figures are concerned, even conservative courts will allow most private truthful facts, although embarrassing, to be disclosed unless they are "unredeemably offensive and not even remotely in the 'public interest' " (Dill, 1992, p. 137).

False Light Intrusion

Under this theory, an invasion of privacy occurs when publicity places the plaintiff in a **false light** in the public eye. For example, in a sport setting, this could occur if someone in the media uses a photograph or makes a statement about a sport figure that gives a false impression to the public. This false impression could emanate from "made-up" details, omitted facts, or misleading context (Dill, 1992).

However, for sport figures to prevail in a false light suit, they must not only show that the published information was false, but also that the disclosure was done by one knowing it was false or who had reckless disregard for the truth. This standard was established in *Time, Inc. v. Hill* (1967), which held that the First Amendment protects reports of newsworthy matters.

False light action is different from libel in that the publicity does not have to be defamatory. The depiction in question could be either complimentary or defamatory. Although most false light cases involve unflattering portrayals, the central issue is "being let alone" from the effects of a false reputation or false publicity (Samar, 1991). Both false light and libel complaints are permitted in some states; however, other states do not recognize false light claims and permit only libel suits.

An example of false light invasion occurred in the case of *Spahn v. Messner, Inc.* (1967). This case centered on an unauthorized biography written about Warren Spahn, a celebrated pitcher for the Milwaukee Braves. The author used "invented dialogue, and imaginary incidents" which he knew to be false and knew to present an untruthful depiction of Spahn. Spahn objected to this portrayal even though parts of the story were complimentary. The court awarded Spahn $10,000 in damages and enjoined further publication of the book.

Breach of Fiduciary Duty

Another intentional tort is breach of fiduciary duty or responsibility. *Black's Law Dictionary* (Black, 1979) defines a **fiduciary** as "[a] person having duty, created by his undertaking, to act primarily for another's benefit in matters connected with this undertaking." As an adjective, it means ". . . relating to or founded upon a trust or confidence" (p. 563). Carper and Mietus (1995) clarified this by adding that a fiduciary relationship is one involving a person in a position of trust who undertakes to act for the benefit of another. Examples of fiduciary relationships include lawyer–client, parent–child, and coach–athlete.

In the sport setting, the fiduciary relationship that is most troublesome is the association between a professional athlete and his or her agent (Ehrhardt & Rodgers, 1988; Powers, 1994). Many professional and college athletes have been hurt by unscrupulous agents. An agent can be responsible for managing many of the athlete's financial concerns. These may include "negotiating the athlete's employment agreement; securing, bartering and reviewing commercial opportunities; providing financial advice and income management; and counseling on legal and tax matters" (Sobel, 1987, p. 705). Because many of these dealings are legally binding to the represented athlete, the law imposes a high obligation of trustworthiness on the agent. If an agent violates this trust and the athlete is harmed as a result, the agent is guilty of tortious conduct and may have to make restitution (Restatement (Second) of Torts #874, 1984, p. 300).

A fiduciary duty requires that the sport agent act with complete honesty in all dealings with athlete–clients. In addition, the agent must avoid any personal **conflicts of interest**. In other words, the interests of the athlete must come before those of the agent. Also, an agent must not represent two adverse parties in the same transaction. For example, representing two or more players vying for the same endorsement contracts or representing a player and the company he is negotiating with for a contract. Finally, an agent must not receive hidden compensation or profits from third parties for transacting the player's business or take advantage of any business opportunity that rightfully belongs to the athlete (Schubert et al., 1986). An agent can avoid liability in this area by fully disclosing any possible conflicts of interest or other potentially improper conduct and obtaining the athlete's prior consent to the action.

Detroit Lions, Inc. v. Jerry Argovitz (1984) offers an instructional example of breach of fiduciary duty. In this case, Billy Sims' agent, Jerry Argovitz, engaged in a series of unethical practices with the intent of inducing Sims to sign a contract with the Houston Gamblers of the United States Football League. After the Gamblers made an offer to Sims, Argovitz failed to give the Detroit Lions an opportunity to match the bid. Sims signed with the Gamblers believing theirs to be the best offer. After it was revealed Argovitz was a substantial owner in the Gamblers' franchise and that he had withheld information that might have swayed Sims' decision, the court allowed Sims to rescind his contract and sign with the Detroit Lions. Sims was unaware of the extent of Argovitz's association with the Gamblers.

Tortious Interference with Contract

This tort involves the intentional inducement of another to breach one's contractual obligations (Schubert et al., 1986). Because contracts play a vital role in sport, this is a significant area of concern. Inducement to break contracts has been alleged in situations such as teams competing for talented players (*Cincinnati Bengals v. William Bergey, et al.*, 1974), boxing promoters arguing over promotion rights (*Don King Productions v. James "Buster" Douglas, et al.*, 1990), and agents interfering with a college player's eligibility (Woods & Mills, 1988).

There are three elements necessary to prove the existence of a wrongful interference tort:

1. A valid, enforceable contract must exist between two parties.
2. The defendant must have known of the contract's existence.
3. The defendant must have, without justification, knowingly induced either of the two parties from full performance of the contract. This interference must have been done for the purpose of advancing the economic interest of the inducer, and it does not matter if the action was done in bad faith or with malice (the intention to harm another), even though in most cases bad faith or malice is usually a factor (Cross & Miller, 1985).

Plaintiff has the burden to prove that the defendant knew of the contract's existence and knowingly induced the breach of the contractual relationship. The defendant can refute the charge if it can be shown that the interference was justified or permissible. For example, aggressive marketing and advertising strategies may entice customers to break contracts with competitors but are not unlawful.

In a significant case involving a tortious interference complaint, the Cincinnati Bengals sued Bill Bergey (*Cincinnati Bengals v. William Bergey, et al.*, 1974), their premier linebacker, the Virginia Ambassadors, and the other eleven teams of the newly formed World Football League (WFL). At the heart of this complaint was the claim that the WFL defendants were inducing a breach of contract by Bergey and, unless enjoined, would do the same with other key players on the Bengals. While under contract with the Bengals, Bergey had negotiated and signed a contract with the Virginia team for his future services. His new contract was to begin when his existing Bengals contract expired. The Bengals felt that his signing of a contract with a different team while under contract with the Bengals would cause him not to perform his current contractual duties with them. The court denied an injunction, primarily because the Bengals failed to show how the negotiations and the subsequent contract signing interfered with the performance of his existing contract.

The more recent case of *Central Sports Army Club v. Arena Association, Inc.* (1997) serves to illustrate another tortious interference cause of action and is instructive in the pertinent elements of a tortious interference situation. The central issue in this case was a contract dispute between the Central Sports Army Club (CSKA), a Russian hockey club, and the Detroit Vipers of the International Hockey League (IHL). A seventeen-year-old Russian hockey player named Sergei Samsonov had originally entered into a one-year contract for the 1996–97 season with CSKA. For several reasons, including not being paid the promised compensation, he decided before the season began to play elsewhere. He retained an agent of Arena Associates, who began to make arrangements for him to play in the United States. This sport agent was working under the assumption that Samsonov did not have a valid contract with CSKA because he was only seventeen when he signed the contract, his father had not signed the contract, and CSKA had failed to fulfill the terms of the contract.

Through his agency (Arena Associates), Samsonov's agent was able to obtain a visa and a 1996–97 player contract with the Detroit Vipers hockey team of the International Hockey League. At the time of his signing the new 1996–97 season contract, the owner of the Vipers believed that Samsonov was under no obligation to play for the Central Sports Army Club. When Samsonov began playing, CSKA filed a lawsuit in the United States claiming among other things that the Detroit Vipers and Samsonov's agents tortiously interfered with their contract with Samsonov.

The first and the most pivotal issue in this tortious interference with contract case was whether or not a valid contract existed. Because Samsonov had signed his first contract when he was a minor and had not obtained his parents' permission, Russian Civil Code as well as New York and Michigan laws allow a minor to void a contract unless he obtained express written consent of parents.

Additionally, even if a valid contract had existed, the plaintiffs failed to show three necessary elements: (1) that the defendants were aware of the contract between the CSKA and Samsonov, (2) that there had been inducement by the defendants, and (3) that the defendants had improper motive (*Central Sports Army Club v. Arena Association, Inc.*, 1997, p. 190).

Significant Case

◇◇◇

The following case provides insight into the relationship between a "right of publicity" claim and a misappropriation privacy claim. It involves former major league baseball players suing to gain complete control of the uses of their names, images, and likenesses. The case concluded that the publication of information concerning professional baseball players' performance statistics, verbal descriptions, and video depictions of their play is in the public interest. It, therefore, is constitutionally protected and cannot lead to liability for violation of the right of privacy or publicity.

GIONFRIDDO V. MAJOR LEAGUE BASEBALL

California Court of Appeal, First District 114 Cal.Rptr.2d 307
Decided, Dec. 10, 2001.

SIMONS, J* * *

The material facts underlying the summary judgment motion are not in dispute. Plaintiffs were four professional baseball players, who played in the major leagues for different periods between 1932 and 1948. Plaintiffs were paid for their performances during each of these seasons.

* * *

It is undisputed that plaintiffs brought great skill to the game of baseball and participated in memorable moments from baseball's past. Coscarart, Camilli and Crosetti appeared in All-Star games, and all four of them appeared in one or more World Series. Plaintiffs' games were played before thousands of spectators and plaintiffs knew their performances were being covered by the media. Their photographs and statistics and accounts of their play were widely disseminated to the public. Plaintiffs understood the important role this media publicity held in promoting interest in professional baseball.

By virtue of their accomplishments and team associations, Baseball has included plaintiffs' names and statistics with other former players in assorted All-Star game and World Series programs, or on its baseball Web sites <http://majorleaguebaseball.com> and <http://www.mlbworldseries.com>. In some instances, plaintiffs' names have appeared within lists of team members or award winners such as the recipients of the "Most Valuable Player" award. In other instances, the references to plaintiffs have occurred in written accounts or video depictions of their play. Some plaintiffs have had still photographs from their playing days and footage of their performances included within video histories of major league baseball produced and/or distributed by defendants Phoenix and MLBP.

* * *

Plaintiffs filed this action, contending that these uses by Baseball were unauthorized and violated their rights of publicity. . . . Their initial complaint was limited to persons who had played part of their major league careers prior to 1947, because that year the standard player contract was revised to add the following language: "[3.] (c) The Player agrees that his picture may be taken for still photographs, motion pictures or television at such times as the Club may designate and agrees that all rights in such pictures shall belong to the Club and may be used by the Club for publicity purposes in any manner it desires."

In due course, Baseball moved for summary judgment or, in the alternative, for summary adjudication. The trial court granted summary judgment, finding that the challenged uses of plaintiffs' names, images and likenesses: (1) were all " 'in connection with [a] news, public affairs, or sports account' " within the meaning of Civil Code section 3344, subdivision (d), and as such did not constitute a "use" for which consent was required under subdivision (a) of that section; (2) constituted publication of matters in the public interest, and as such were protected from civil liability by the First Amendment of the United States Constitution; and (3) were legally permissible under the doctrine of master-servant.

As to Gionfriddo, the court also determined that the uses by Baseball of his name and images were permissible under paragraph 3(c) of the Uniform Players Contract.

* * *

C. Discussion

In California the right of publicity is both a common law right and a statutory right. (Comedy III Productions, Inc. v. Gary Saderup, Inc. (2001) 25 Cal.4th 387, 391, 106 Cal.Rptr.2d 126, 21 P.3d 797 (Comedy III).) The common law right of publicity has been recognized in this state since 1931. (Melvin v. Reid (1931) 112 Cal.App. 285, 297 P. 91; see also Miller, Commercial Appropriation of an Individual's Name, Photograph or Likeness: A New Remedy For Californians (1972) 3 Pacific L.J. 651, 657.) In 1971, the Legislature enacted section 3344, which authorized recovery of damages by any living person whose name, photograph, or likeness was used for commercial purposes without his or her consent. Eight years later, in Lugosi v. Universal Pictures (1979) 25 Cal.3d 813, 160 Cal.Rptr. 323, 603 P.2d

425, our Supreme Court reaffirmed the common law right, which the statute was said to complement. (Id. at p. 819 & fn. 6, 160 Cal.Rptr. 323, 603 P.2d 425.) However the Supreme Court held that, because the common law right of publicity derived from the right of privacy, it did not survive the death of the person whose identity was exploited and was not descendible to heirs or assignees. (Id. at pp. 819-821, 160 Cal.Rptr. 323, 603 P.2d 425.) In 1984, the Legislature enacted a second statutory right of publicity that was "freely transferable" to the assignees or passed to the heirs of deceased persons. (§ 3344.1, subds.(b)-(d).)

1. *Plaintiffs' Common Law Right of Publicity Cause of Action*

The common law right of publicity derives from the fourth category of invasion of privacy identified by Dean Prosser, described as "appropriation" of a plaintiff's name or likeness for the defendant's advantage. (Comedy III, supra, 25 Cal.4th at p. 391 & fn. 2, 106 Cal.Rptr.2d 126, 21 P.3d 797, citing Prosser, Privacy (1960) 48 Cal. L.Rev. 383, 389.) . . . California recognizes the right to profit from the commercial value of one's identity as an aspect of the right of publicity. (Comedy III, supra, 25 Cal.4th at p. 391, 106 Cal.Rptr.2d 126, 21 P.3d 797; Dora v. Frontline Video, Inc. (1993) 15 Cal.App.4th 536, 541-542, 18 Cal.Rptr.2d 790 (Dora).)

Plaintiffs allege that Baseball appropriated their names and likenesses. The elements of this tort, at common law, are: "(1) the defendant's use of the plaintiff's identity; (2) the appropriation of plaintiff's name or likeness to defendant's advantage, commercially or otherwise; (3) lack of consent; and (4) resulting injury." (Eastwood v. Superior Court (1983) 149 Cal.App.3d 409, 417, 198 Cal.Rptr. 342.) Even if each of these elements is established, however, the common law right does not provide relief for every publication of a person's name or likeness. The First Amendment requires that the right to be protected from unauthorized publicity "be balanced against the public interest in the dissemination of news and information consistent with the democratic processes under the constitutional guaranties of freedom of speech and of the press."

We believe this balancing process begins by identifying and weighing the factors properly taken into account. At a minimum, a court must first consider the nature of the precise information conveyed and the context of the communication to determine the public interest in the expression. The public interest must then be weighed against the plaintiffs' economic interests in cases of this sort and the plaintiffs' noneconomic interests if the publicity right relied on is rooted in privacy.

The precise information conveyed by Baseball in this case consists of factual data concerning the players, their performance statistics, and verbal descriptions and video depictions of their play. This information may fairly be characterized as mere bits of baseball's history: names of players included on All-Star and World Series rosters; descriptions of memorable performances from former games included within AllStar and Plaintiffs . . . argue that only "media business[es are] subject to First Amendment free speech/press protections." This argument is meritless. . . . It [is] not the business of the messenger, but the commercial nature of the message that [is the dispositive distinction]. World Series game programs created for the benefit of the media and the enjoyment of the fans; photographs and video clips taken of plaintiffs when they were playing the game themselves, and made available to the public through Web sites, home videos, and other programs presenting historic events from long ago.

In short, they are fragments from baseball's mosaic. It is manifest that as news occurs, or as a baseball season unfolds, the First Amendment will protect mere recitations of the players' accomplishments. "The freedom of the press is constitutionally guaranteed, and the publication of daily news is an acceptable and necessary function in the life of the community. " (Carlisle v. Fawcett Publications, Inc. (1962) 201 Cal.App.2d 733, 746, 20 Cal.Rptr. 405.) "Certainly, the accomplishments ... of those who have achieved a marked reputation or notoriety by appearing before the public such as actors and actresses, professional athletes, public officers, ... may legitimately be mentioned and discussed in print or on radio and television." (Id. at pp. 746-747, 20 Cal.Rptr. 405.) Entertainment features receive the same constitutional protection as factual news reports. Moreover, the public interest is not limited to current events; the public is also entitled to be informed and entertained about our history.

Major league baseball is followed by millions of people across this country on a daily basis. Likewise, baseball fans have an abiding interest in the history of the game. The public has an enduring fascination in the records set by former players and in memorable moments from previous games. Statistics are kept on every aspect of the game imaginable. Those statistics and the records set throughout baseball's history are the standards by which the public measures the performance of today's players. The records and statistics remain of interest to the public because they provide context that allows fans to better appreciate (or deprecate) today's performances. Thus, the history of professional baseball is integral to the full understanding and enjoyment of the current game and its players.

In the uses challenged, Baseball is simply making historical facts available to the public through game programs, Web sites and video clips. The recitation and discussion of factual data concerning the athletic performance of these plaintiffs commands a substantial public interest, and, therefore, is a form of expression due substantial constitutional protection.

Plaintiffs contend that the challenged uses are presented in a commercial context, and thereby constitute "commercial speech," entitled to a reduced level of constitutional protection, without regard to the precise information conveyed. They argue these uses help baseball owners make a profit, and that their "achievements are being exploited to promote the product of baseball with any historical value being a coincidence or merely incidental." Profit, alone, does not render expression "commercial," however. " 'The First Amendment is not limited to those who publish without charge.... [An expressive activity] does not lose its constitutional protection because it is undertaken for profit.' "

Plaintiffs . . . argue that only "media business[es are] subject to First Amendment free speech/press protections." This argument is meritless. . . . It [is] not the business of the messenger, but the commercial nature of the message that [is the dispositive distinction]

The uses challenged in this case are not "commercial speech." The term "commercial speech" has a special meaning in the context of the First Amendment. "[T]he 'core notion of commercial speech' is that it 'does no more than propose a commercial transaction.' " (Hoffman, supra, 255 F.3d at p. 1184, quoting Bolger v. Youngs Drug Products Corp. (1983) 463 U.S. 60, 66, 103 S.Ct. 2875, 77 L.Ed.2d 469.) Here, the disputed uses were included as minor historical references to plaintiffs within game programs and Web sites and in videos documenting baseball's past, rather than in advertisements selling a product. As such, they are readily distinct from uses that do no more than propose a commercial transaction.

* * *

Thus, there is significant public interest in the information conveyed by the challenged uses, and Baseball is not exploiting that interest by inserting the data in an advertisement. Even if Baseball did use the information in such an advertisement, we question whether this would be determinative. A review of the cases finding that commercial speech violates the right of publicity strongly suggests that advertisements are actionable when the plaintiff's identity is used, without consent, to promote an unrelated product.

A celebrity's likeness may be used, however, to advertise a related product. Courts have consistently held that the news media may use celebrity photographs from current or prior publications as advertisements " 'for the periodical itself, illustrating the quality and content of the periodical without the person's written consent.' " If a video documentary contains an unconsented, though protected, use of a person's likeness, there is little question that an advertisement for the documentary, containing a clip of that use would be permissible. Thus, even if Baseball used depictions of players playing the game or recited statistics or historical facts about the game to advertise the game and promote attendance, the commercial speech cases relied on by plaintiffs would be inapposite. The owner of a product is entitled to show that product to entice customers to buy it.

In addition, this is not a situation where Baseball affixed plaintiffs' names or images to merchandise such as T-shirts, lithographic prints, baseball souvenirs or other tangible products in order to market them to the public. Although plaintiffs alleged such activities in their pleadings, they were unable to present any evidence to the trial court of such uses by Baseball.

The uses at issue are entitled to receive the full constitutional protection accorded to noncommercial speech. Given the significant public interest in this sport, plaintiffs can only prevail if they demonstrate a substantial competing interest. They have not.

The right to exploit commercially one's celebrity is primarily an economic right. (Comedy III, supra, 25 Cal.4th at p. 403, 106 Cal.Rptr.2d 126, 21 P.3d 797.) 11 The challenged uses involve statements of historical fact, descriptions of these facts or video depictions of them. Plaintiffs never suggest how Baseball's actions impair their economic interests. It appears equally likely that plaintiffs' marketability is enhanced by Baseball's conduct challenged here. Balancing plaintiffs' negligible economic interests against the public's enduring fascination with baseball's past, we conclude that the public interest favoring the free dissemination of information regarding baseball's history far outweighs any proprietary interests at stake. Therefore, the trial court was correct to grant summary adjudication on this cause of action. (Code Civ. Proc., § 437c, subd. (o)(2).)

2. *Plaintiffs' Statutory Rights Under Section 3344*

Subdivision (a) of section 3344 states in part: "Any person who knowingly uses another's name, voice, signature, photograph, or likeness, in any manner, on or in products, merchandise, or goods, . . . without such person's prior consent, . . . shall be liable for any damages sustained by the person or persons injured as a result thereof." Subdivision (d) of section 3344 states: "For purposes of this section, a use of a name, voice, signature, photograph, or likeness in connection with any news, public affairs, or sports broadcast or account, . . . shall not constitute a use for which consent is required under subdivision (a)."

Here, the trial court found, among other grounds, that the complained of uses of plaintiffs' names, images and likenesses were all " 'in connection with [a] news, public affairs, or sports account' " within the meaning of section 3344, subdivision (d), and as such did not constitute uses for which consent is required under subdivision (a). We agree that these uses come within the "public affairs" exemption to consent provided in subdivision (d).

* * *

The uses challenged by plaintiffs fell within the exemptions set forth in Civil Code section 3344, subdivision (d), and as such do not constitute uses for which consent was required under subdivision (a). The trial court was correct to grant summary adjudication of the statutory right of publicity claim since plaintiffs were unable to establish all of the elements necessary to prove a violation within the ambit of Civil Code section 3344, subdivision (a). (Code Civ. Proc., § 437c, subd. (o)(2).)

* * *

The judgments are affirmed. Defendants shall recover their costs for both appeals.

 ANOTHER RELATED SIGNIFICANT CASE

Chapter 8.23 *Image Rights*

Recent Trends

Right of Privacy

Student Privacy. The Family Education Rights and Privacy Act of 1974 (FERPA) generally prohibits an academic institution from releasing a student's education records without a student's consent, unless the school has been mandated by court order or subpoena. Under FERPA, the school is required by law to inform the student before releasing the information. When records are subpoenaed, the school or the student has an opportunity to go to court to seek to quash the subpoena. However, as a result of the September 11th terrorist attacks, FERPA was amended by the USA PATRIOT Act, which is scheduled to expire in March, 2006. The Patriot Act significantly removes privacy protections from students and allows for the secret release of FERPA information to federal law enforcement agencies. Because the information is obtained via a secret subpoena, students do not have the opportunity to challenge it in court. In addition to FERPA information, information such as test scores, financial aid, and personal finances can also be obtained. This act also provides for a national database that will be made available to federal, state, and local enforcement authorities (Ramsey, 2002). If the Patriot Act is renewed, students will continue to have reduced privacy protection.

References

Cases

Bilney v. Evening Star Newspaper Co., 406 A.2d. 652 (Md. App. 1979).

Central Sports Army Club v. Arena Association, Inc., 952 F. Supp. 181 (S.D.N.Y. 1997).

Cincinnati Bengals v. William Bergey, et al., 453 F. Supp. 129 (1974).

Davis v. Baylor University, 976 S.W.2d 5 (Mo. App. 1998).

Detroit Lions, Inc. v. Jerry Argovitz, 580 F. Supp. 542 (1984).

Don King Productions v. James "Buster" Douglas, et al., 735 F. Supp. 522 (1990).

Holt v. Cox Enterprises, 590 F. Supp. 408 (N.D. Ga. 1984).

Montana v. San Jose Mercury News, Inc., 34 Cal. App.4th 790 (1995).

Namath v. Sports Illustrated, 48 A.D.2d 487; 371 N.Y.S.2d 10 (1975).

Palmer v. Schonhorn Enterprises, Inc., 323 A.2d 458 (1967).

Rosenbloom v. Metromedia, Inc., 403 U.S. 29; 29 L.Ed.2d 296 (1971).

Spahn v. Messner, Inc., 18 N.Y.2d 324; 274 N.Y.S.2d 877; 221 N.E.2d 543; *vacated* 387 U.S. 239; 18 L.Ed.2d 744 (1967).

St. Louis Convention & Visitors Commission v. National Football League, 154 F.3d 851 (8th Cir. 1998).

Time, Inc. v. Hill, 385 U.S. 374 (1967).

Publications

Berry, R. C., & Wong, G. M. (1993). *Law and business of the sports industries* (2nd ed.). Westport, CT: Praeger Publishers.

Black, H. C. (1979). *Black's law dictionary* (5th ed.). St. Paul, MN: West Publishing Co.

Byrd, L. L. (1988). Privacy rights of entertainers and other celebrities: A need for change. *Entertainment and Sports Law Reporter, 5*(95), 95–116.

Breaux, P. (2005). *Introduction to Sports Law and Business.* Reno, NV: Bent Tree Press.

Carper, D. L., & Mietus, N. J. (1995). *Understanding the law* (2nd ed.). St. Paul, MN: West Publishing Co.

Champion, W. T. (1991). *Fundamentals of sport law.* New York: CBC Publishing.

Clarkson, K. W., Miller, R. L., Jentz, G. A., & Cross, F. B. (2004). *West's business law* (9th ed.). Mason, OH: West Legal Studies in Business. Thompson Learning.

Couch, B. (2000). How agent competition and corruption affects sports and the athlete-agent relationship and what can be done to control it. *Seton Hall Journal of Sports, 10*, L 111.

Cross, F. B., & Miller, R. L. (1985). *West's legal environment of business.* St. Paul, MN: West Publishing Co.

Dill, B. (1992). *The journalist's handbook on libel and privacy.* New York: The Free Press.

Ehrhardt, C. W., & Rodgers, J. M. (1988). Tightening the defense against offensive sports agents. *Florida State University Law Review, 16*, 634–674.

Keeton, W. P., Dobbs, D. B., Keeton, R. E., Prosser, W. L., & Owen, D. G. (1984). *Prosser and Keeton on torts* (5th ed.). St. Paul, MN: West Publishing Co.

NCAA Manual. (2000). Rule 12.5.2.1 & 12.5.2.2. NCAA.

Prosser, W. L. (1960). Privacy. *Cal. L. Rev., 48*, 383–398.

Powers, A. (1994). The need to regulate sports agents. *Seton Hall Journal of Sport Law, 4*, 253–274.

Ramsey, K. (September 4, 2002). *Student records open to government.* University Daily Kansan.

Ruxin, R. (1993). *An athlete's guide to agents.* Boston: Jones and Bartlett Publishers.

Samar, V. J. (1991). *The right to privacy.* Philadelphia: Temple University Press.

Schubert, G., Smith, R. K., & Trentadue, J. C. (1986). *Sports law.* St. Paul, MN: West Publishing Co.

Smolla, R. A (1999). Symposium on: Privacy and the Law: The Media's Intrusion on Privacy: Privacy and the First Amendment Right to Gather News. *Geo. Wash. L. Rev., 67*, 1097.

Sobel, S. (1987). The regulation of sports agents: An analytical primer. *Baylor Law Review, 39*, 705–709.

Stapleton, L. L., & McMurphy, M. (1999). The professional athlete's right of publicity. *Marquette Sports Law Journal, 10*, 23–68.

Warren, S., & Brandeis, L. (1890). The right to privacy. *Harvard Law Review, 4,* 193.

Weistart, J. C., & Lowell, C. H. (1979). *Law and sports.* Charlottesville, VA: Michie/Bobbs Co.

Woods, R. P., & Mills, M. R. (1988). Tortious interference with an athletic scholarship: A university remedy for the unscrupulous sports agent. *Alabama Law Review, 40,* 141–180.

Yasser, R., McCurdy, J. R., Goplerud, C. P., & Weston, M. A. (2000). *Sport law.* Cincinnati, OH: Anderson Publishing Co.

Legislation

California Civil Code 1708.8 (1998).

Family Educational Rights and Privacy Act (FERPA) 20 U.S.C. § 1232g.

H.R. 2448, 105th Cong. (1997).

H.R. 3224, 105th Cong. (1998).

H.R. 4425, 105th Cong. (1998).

S. 2103, 105th Cong. (1998).

Restatement (Third) of the Law of Unfair Competition (1995).

Restatement of Torts, Second, Torts 8A (1965).

USA PATRIOT Act H.R. 3162 (2001).

4.15 Sport-Related Crimes:
GAMBLING—TICKET SCALPING—WIRE AND MAIL FRAUD

Andy Pittman
Baylor University

Barbara Osborne
University of North Carolina

Ancient drawings on primitive cave walls indicate that forms of gambling existed thousands of years ago, so it should come as no surprise that gambling has been a problem in the sport industry for many years. Sports betting is the most widespread and popular form of gambling in America, with an estimate of up to $380 billion wagered illegally on sports in 1999. State and federal regulation has done little to slow the growth of sports betting. Like gambling, ticket scalping has long been a problem in the entertainment and sport industries. In an early case in California (*Ex parte Quarg*, 1906), scalpers challenged antiscalping legislation, alleging that it violated their right of free enterprise. At major college and professional sporting events today, it is not unusual to find scalpers fanning their tickets at would-be buyers, selling them for whatever price the market may bear. Unlike gambling and ticket scalping, wire and mail fraud is relatively new to sports. The seminal case in this area is *U.S. v. Walters* (1989) in which two sports agents were accused of using the mail to defraud higher education institutions. Due to improved technology and subsequent expanded use of electronic mail, wire and mail fraud violations in sport and Internet gambling may become more frequent in the twenty-first century.

Gambling

Gambling in some form is now legal in 48 of the 50 states. Only Hawaii and Utah do not have some form of legalized gambling. There are state-sponsored lotteries in 37 states, pari-mutuel betting in 43, bingo in 47 and casinos in 28. Although a majority of Americans view sports gambling as harmless fun, gambling on collegiate and professional sports is a **crime** in all states but Nevada.

Gambling on sports poses special concerns that are uniquely different from legally placing bets on games of chance in casinos or purchasing lottery tickets. The popularity of sports rests on the integrity of sports contests—the honest struggle within the framework of the game to determine who is the superior competitor. Sports gambling leads to game fixing, point shaving, and bribery of athletes and officials. Since the Black Sox scandal of 1919, professional sports figures have been implicated in gambling, point shaving, and game fixing. Baseball players Pete Rose and Denny McLain have been jailed and suspended, and Len Dykstra was placed on probation. Paul Hornung, Alex Karras, and Art Schlicter were suspended from the NFL.

There have also been problems in college sports—Arizona State University, Boston College, University of Kentucky, New York City College, Northwestern University, University of Rhode Island, Seton Hall, and Tulane University basketball teams have been implicated in point shaving scandals. University of Nevada, Las Vegas basketball players have been charged with associating with known gamblers. Football players at Boston College and Northwestern have been implicated for placing bets on sporting events, including several who bet against their own team. In 2004 the University of Michigan was involved in a major infractions investigation involving payments to men's basketball players by a booster from funds generated by an illegal gambling operation.

The ability to regulate gambling was traditionally held by the state under the police power to protect the health, safety, and welfare of the public. Sports gambling, unlike casinos and lotteries, which are regulated and taxed by the state, siphons away revenue, tax dollars, and jobs. Gambling addiction costs the individual, the family, and the community. However, state governments also have a legitimate interest in the ability to raise revenues in any lawful manner they so choose.

The federal government has generally deferred to the states in the regulation of gambling. However, Congress demonstrated the power to regulate sports gambling under the Commerce Clause after congressional investigations in the 1950s uncovered the activities of organized crime in the gambling industry. Evidence indicated that profits from illegal sports wagering helped finance other activities of organized crime, such as funding drug sales and loan sharking. Federal laws related to sports gambling include the following.

- The **Wire Communications Act of 1961** (Wire Act) prohibits the use of wire communications by persons or organizations engaged in the business of wagering, to transmit bets or wagers or information that assists in the placing of bets or wagers. It is important to note that a significant limitation of this legislation is that it does not penalize the individual bettor (18 U.S.C. § 1084). The government has prosecuted more than twenty Internet gambling operators using this legislation.

- The **Interstate and Foreign Travel or Transportation in Aid of Racketeering Enterprising Act of 1961** (Travel Act) prosecutes those who travel in interstate commerce to distribute the proceeds of unlawful activity, commit a crime of violence to further unlawful activity or otherwise promote, manage, establish, or facilitate any unlawful activity (18 U.S.C. § 1952).

- **Racketeer Influenced and Corrupt Organizations Act of 1970** (RICO) prohibits conspiring to engage in criminal enterprise. Although RICO includes sports gambling rings, it is difficult to prove conspiracy and racketeering activity at the level necessary to satisfy the elements of a RICO violation (18 U.S.C. § 1955).

- The **Bribery in Sporting Contests Act of 1979** made it a crime to bribe or attempt to bribe an individual in order to influence the outcome of a sporting contest (18 U.S.C. § 224).

- The **Professional and Amateur Sports Protection Act of 1992** (Bradley Bill) prohibits the expansion of state-sanctioned, authorized, or licensed gambling on amateur and professional sporting events in the United States (28 U.S.C. § 3702).

Internet Gambling

Internet gambling is defined as the placing of real money bets using one's personal computer via the Internet. Internet gambling has exploded to the point now that it is probably the most important issue in sports gambling. In 1996, there were only two Internet sites with sports betting. By 2005, the number of Internet gambling sites was estimated at 1,800. From 2002–2003, revenue from legal Nevada sports betting grew by 11.98 percent, while Internet gambling increased 42 percent. Conservative estimates place the amount of money gambled annually over the Internet at $10 billion. Potential for criminals to use online gambling sites for laundering money, credit card fraud, fraudulent promises to pay bettors, and tax avoidance, as well as prevention of underage gambling, consumer vulnerability, increased bankruptcies, and maintaining the ability of states to decide their own criminal regulatory schemes are all concerns.

The biggest problem with restricting Internet gambling is the issue of **jurisdiction**. First, there are considerable differences in state laws and international laws. The problem then becomes which state law do you enforce, the state in which the gambling site is located or the state in which the bet is placed? What if the Internet site or the bet originates from another country? Australia, Belize, Lichtenstein, Austria, Belgium, Finland, Germany, Honduras, South Africa, Venezuela, Curaçao, Costa Rica, Grenada, Antigua, and the Dominican Republic all have taken steps to legalize Internet gambling to capitalize on the United States' prohibitive legal environment. Some of these countries will refuse to cooperate with those countries that attempt to control or restrict Internet gambling.

State v. Granite Gate Resorts, Inc. (1998) illustrates the jurisdiction problem. Granite Gate was a Nevada corporation that did business as On Ramp, a provider of Internet advertising. One of the sites advertised was WagerNet, an online wagering service that was to be available internationally in the fall of 1995. In the summer of 1995, Jeff Janacek, a consumer investigator for the Minnesota Attorney General's office, contacted WagerNet and was told that the betting service was legal. Subsequently, the state brought action against the nonresident corporation for deceptive trade practices, false advertising, and consumer fraud. The District Court of Ramsey County denied the defendants' motion to dismiss for lack of personal jurisdiction, and the defendants appealed. The Court of Appeals held that the defendants were subject to personal jurisdiction in the state based on their actions of advertising on the Internet a forthcoming online gambling service and developing from the Internet a mailing list that included one or more Minnesota residents.

Minnesota's long-arm statute permits courts to assert jurisdiction over defendants to the extent that federal constitutional requirements of **due process** will allow. To satisfy the Due Process Clause of the Fourteenth Amendment, a plaintiff must show that the defendant has minimum contacts with the forum state such that the maintenance of the suit does not offend traditional notions of fair play and substantial justice. There must be some act by which the defendant purposefully avails itself of the privilege of conducting activities within the forum state, thus invoking the benefits and protections of its laws. A court must consider five factors in determining whether a defendant has established **minimum contacts** with the forum state: (1) the quantity of the defendant's contacts, (2) the nature and quality of the defendant's contacts, (3) the connection between the cause of action and the defendant's contacts, (4) the state's interest in providing a forum, and (5) the convenience of the parties. In close cases, doubts should be resolved in favor of retention of jurisdiction.

Ticket Scalping

Ticket scalping is commonly defined as the reselling of tickets at a price higher than the established value. **Ticket brokers** and **speculators** also engage in this practice; however, courts have recognized this activity as legal when authorized or licensed. Ticket scalping is a large economic enterprise plagued by several problems. Conservative estimates place online ticket scalping sales in 2004 at $2 billion. Although reselling tickets online at face value is legal in all fifty states, seventeen states have restrictions on how much tickets can be marked up by sellers for sale online. From a public policy perspective, there should be equal and fair opportunity for the public to attend sporting events, and all buyers should have equal access to tickets. The public should feel safe and not fear harassment from scalpers. Additionally, the sports enterprise has a legitimate interest in regulating ticket sales and controlling business activity on the grounds.

Recognizing the problems that exist in the sports and entertainment industries, several state legislatures have enacted antiscalping legislation in an attempt to curb the nuisances associated with ticket scalping. Currently forty-five states have some form of regulation. Despite the enactment of antiscalping legislation, ticket scalping continues as an inherent and integral part of the sports and entertainment industries and is practiced by a wide variety of people, both amateur and professional.

Ticket scalping restrictions vary among the states. Pennsylvania holds a person, not possessed of authority, guilty of ticket scalping for selling, bartering, or transferring a ticket to an event for any consideration. Most ticket scalping statutes place restrictions on time, location, price, or the types of events for which tickets may be sold. For instance, in California, Massachusetts, New York, and Pennsylvania, a broker may resell a ticket subject to certain price restrictions. In Massachusetts the maximum markup is $2 plus fees, whereas in Pennsylvania, it is 25 percent of the ticket's original price plus fees. In Arizona, Minnesota, and North Carolina the event owner/promoter has authorization to resell tickets above face value. Arizona and California place restrictions on where tickets may be resold. Georgia, New Mexico, and South Carolina prohibit the resale of tickets for athletic events. Some antiscalping statutes may require licenses for scalpers or ticket brokers to ensure that proper business practices are followed. New Jersey forbids a person to engage in the business of reselling tickets unless that person obtains a license to resell or engage in the business of reselling tickets. Alabama and New York require a person wishing to engage in the act of reselling tickets to procure a license and pay a fee for that license. Illinois permits a ticket broker meeting certain licensing requirements to sell a ticket for more than the price printed on that ticket.

Benefits of Ticket Scalping

Those favoring legalized ticket scalping have supported the practice along four lines: (1) benefits to the buyer, (2) benefits to the scalper, (3) benefits to the event promoter, and (4) benefits to the artist/performer. Benefits to the buyer include the expansion of the buyer's range of available tickets, elimination of the time costs that would be incurred waiting in line, and the occasional purchase of a ticket below face value due to the overstocking of tickets by a scalper. The benefit to the scalper is the potential of enormous profits. The event promoter benefits when the ticket scalper acts as a middleman between the buyer and the promoter. The artist/performer benefits when scalping is a measure of demand that may drive up the bargaining power of the artist for future performances.

Harms of Ticket Scalping

Those opposed to ticket scalping charge that the practice is exploitative and should be regulated or prohibited. They argue that scalping removes the demand for tickets meant for public distribution. Price gouging results when the supply of tickets is reduced. Ticket scalping may also cause crowd control problems, especially if the scalper has sold counterfeit or lost/stolen tickets. Fans often blame the promoter when they perceive the distribution of tickets as being unfair. Sport teams may lose the loyal fans who cannot afford the tickets.

Challenges to Regulation

Scalpers and others argue that regulation of ticket resale is a form of statutory price fixing. Scalpers claim they serve a vital social and economic function by catering to the needs of those who were unable to purchase tickets from the box office directly. When ticket scalpers have challenged antiscalping legislation in the courts, the state has been successful using these four arguments: (1) legitimate interest in protecting the welfare of the public, (2) legitimate interest in ensuring public access to entertainment and sport events, (3) legitimate exercise of a state's police power, and (4) the ticket scalping statute must be rationally related to stated legitimate goals.

Legitimate Interest in Protecting the Welfare of the Public. Generally the courts have recognized that a state has a legitimate interest in protecting the welfare of the public. In *People v. Johnson* (1967), a New York court noted that the purpose and thrust of antiscalping legislation, the preservation of public welfare and advancement of the arts and theater, is to be given effect to accomplish the legislature's intention.

Legitimate Interest in Ensuring Public Access to Entertainment and Sport Events. In *People v. Shepherd* (1978), the California District Court of Appeals held that the unregulated use of the Los Angeles Memorial Coliseum by peddlers of tickets or other property would add congestion, annoyance, and inconvenience in areas where crowds must move rapidly and safely.

Legitimate Exercise of a State's Police Power. If not enacted in a discriminatory or otherwise unconstitutional manner, antiscalping legislation will most likely be upheld as a legitimate exercise of a state's police power. This standard was set forth in *Nebbia v. New York* (1934), where the Supreme Court held that a state, in an effort to promote public welfare and in the absence of other constitutional restrictions, is free to adopt whatever economic policy it deems necessary and enforce that policy by way of legislation adapted to its purpose.

Statute Merely Must be Rationally Related to Stated Legitimate Goals. When pursuing this legislative action, a state is not required to solve the entire problem or provide the best remedy. In *State v. Major* (1979), the Court held that the statute merely has to be rationally related to stated legitimate goals. The three defendants were accused of selling at an illegal price admission tickets to a football game between the Atlanta Falcons and the Minnesota Vikings at the Atlanta-Fulton County Stadium. The tickets were allegedly sold at $5 to $11 above the printed price on the ticket. The defendants challenged the constitutionality of Georgia Code § 96-602, which stated that only authorized ticket agents at established business locations may charge a fee not to exceed $1 in excess of the printed price. The Court reasoned that prohibiting the scalping of tickets is a proper legislative objective and does not violate any due process or property rights that an individual ticket holder may possess.

Although a state may have legitimate goals in protecting the public from ticket scalpers, the state may not violate the constitutional rights of the scalper. Douglas Roberts brought state law tort and civil rights claims against the University of North Carolina police, asserting that he was wrongfully arrested for selling tickets outside the basketball arena, for resisting arrest, and for assaulting an officer. On the evening of January 18, 1995, Roberts was arrested by university police for attempting to sell two tickets to that evening's University of North Carolina basketball game against the University of Virginia. Roberts resisted arrest, was handcuffed, and was taken to the police department where he was questioned. When he continued to resist arrest, Roberts was handcuffed and taken to a magistrate, where arrest warrants were issued.

The trial court held that because under North Carolina law solicitation to sell tickets in and of itself is not a crime under any statute or ordinance, Roberts' Fourth Amendment rights were violated. His attempt to sell tickets did not violate either Ordinance § 13-2, which prohibits door-to-door sales, North Carolina General Statute § 105-53(a) which requires a peddler to obtain a license, or the "scalping statute," North Carolina General Statute § 14-344. Under this statute, a person in North Carolina may place a reasonable service fee, not to exceed three dollars per ticket, to the face value of the tickets sold. Any person who sells or offers to sell a ticket for a price greater than the allowable amount is guilty of a misdemeanor. The Court of Appeals affirmed the decision of the Superior Court, stating that the plaintiff's rights were violated (*Roberts v. Swain*, 1997).

Generally speaking, ticket scalping may constitutionally be regulated or prohibited by a state. Such regulation can be achieved with due process, inasmuch as the prevention of fraud, extortion, exorbitant rates and similar abuses associated with scalping is a legitimate governmental interest. A statute that reasonably addresses those abuses without discrimination or arbitrariness does not deny due process.

Wire and Mail Fraud

Unlike gambling and ticket scalping, which have traditionally been regulated by the states, wire and mail fraud is a federal crime. In 1865, Congress granted the Post Office Department the authority to regulate obscene materials. Additional legislation was passed in 1868 to limit illegal lotteries and monetary schemes. This early legislation met with little success. The first federal mail fraud statute emanates from an 1872 recodification of one of the sections of the Postal Act, making it a federal crime to use the mail system fraudulently.

Federal legislation regarding wire and mail fraud has been criticized by many. Most of the policy concerns with wire and mail fraud legislation are raised in association with overcriminalization: finding a balance between legitimately punishing socially unacceptable behavior and the point where society feels it is not the law's business. This debate focuses on two concerns, discriminatory enforcement and waste of judicial resources. One of the dangers of an expansive interpretation of the mail fraud statute is that it will not be enforced uniformly, but based on prejudices and passions of the day.

To this point, there have been few cases involving wire and mail fraud in a sport setting (*U.S. v. Welch*, 2003; *U.S. v. Gray*, 1996; and *U.S. v. Walters*, 1993). In *U.S. v. Walters* (1989), Norby Walters and Lloyd Bloom were indicted on charges of conspiracy, RICO violations, and mail fraud. Walters had signed fifty-eight college football players to professional football contracts while they were still playing. At the end of their collegiate careers, only two of the original fifty-eight players decided to let Walters represent them. Walters and his partner, Bloom, resorted to threats against the other fifty-six. After a month-long trial and a week of deliberations, the jury convicted Walters and Bloom. However, after a series of appeals, their conviction was overturned. The United States Court of Appeals for the Seventh Circuit in 1993 held that the forms mailed by the colleges to the NCAA verifying the players' eligibility were not sufficiently integral to the defendant's scheme of signing players to contracts prior to the expiration of their eligibility to support a mail fraud conviction. Even if the mailings were sufficient, the defendant did not cause the universities to use the mails. Finally, the conviction could not be sustained on the basis that the defendant deprived the universities of scholarship funds paid to the athletes who were no longer eligible because the defendant did not obtain any property from the universities by fraud.

In *U.S. v. Gray* (1996), Kevin Gray, Gary Thomas, and Troy Drummond were convicted of conspiracy to commit mail and wire fraud, and various counts of mail and wire fraud in violation of 18 U.S.C. §§ 2, 371, 1343 and 1346. The three defendants were assistant men's basketball coaches who executed a fraudulent scheme to establish academic eligibility for five transfer students who were recruited from two-year colleges to play basketball at Baylor University. The coaches provided the recruits with written course work or answers to correspondence exams that were then represented to the various schools as the students' work.

In *U.S. v. Welch* (2003), two members of the Salt Lake City Bid Committee (SLBC) for the 2002 Olympic Winter Games were indicted by a federal grand jury on fifteen bribery-related counts of criminal misconduct in connection with the SLBC's activities in procuring the 2002 Games. According to the indictment, defendants made direct or indirect illegal payments or benefits to International Olympic Committee members totaling approximately $1 million in value. The 10th Circuit Court of Appeals reversed and remanded the District Court's grant of the defendant's motion to dismiss the indictment. The Appellate Court ruled that all the required elements to prove wire and mail fraud were present in this case. However, in the subsequent bench trial, Judge Sam acquitted the defendants on fifteen felony counts of conspiracy, Travel Act violations, and wire and mail fraud relating to the bribery issues.

According to Title 18 U.S.C. §§ 1341–1346 (2002), it is illegal to use the mails or electronic communications for the purpose of executing a scheme to defraud. There are two basic elements to the crime of wire and mail fraud: (1) a scheme and intent to defraud, and (2) use of the mails or wire communications to execute the scheme. Some courts have ruled that the government must also prove a culpable participation in that use by defendant, either by making the use himself or by knowingly causing someone else to make the use.

A **scheme to defraud** is behavior calculated to deceive persons of ordinary prudence and comprehension. This element has two components: fraudulent intent and contemplation to harm or injure. To prove fraudulent intent, the government must show a scheme to defraud by proving that the defendant actually devised or intended to devise such a scheme. The focus is not on conduct but on the state of mind or scheme. A contemplation of harm or injury may be inferred when a scheme has an injurious effect as a necessary result of its execution. It is also necessary that there must be a deprivation of money or property. In *U.S. v. Gray,* the assistant coaches committed fraud by depriving the recruits of scholarships and depriving the university of the right to honest services.

The second element, causing **use of the mails or wire communications to execute the scheme**, has been interpreted to mean that the person acts with the knowledge that use of the mails will follow in the ordinary course of business, or where use of the mails can reasonably be foreseen even though not actually intended. A defendant need not make the mailing personally. It is sufficient that the mailing was a consequence known or reasonably foreseeable to the defendant. There are limitations on the mailing element of the statute: letters mailed before the scheme is conceived or after it is completed are not subject to the mail fraud statute because mailing either before a scheme is conceived or after it has reached fruition does not further the scheme and cannot support a mail fraud conviction. The government must prove that the mailings were related to the alleged fraud. In *U.S. v. Walters,* deceit was an ingredient of Walters' plan, but no evidence existed that he conceived a scheme in which mailings played a role. Conversely, in *U.S. v. Gray,* the assistant coaches deliberately used the mails to transmit the fraudulent course work.

It is not necessary for the government to show that the plan to defraud was complete in all its aspects from its inception to support a conviction for a conspiracy to defraud by the use of the mails. Thus, it is not necessary that any one particular overt act be proven to obtain a conviction for conspiracy to commit mail fraud, and there is no requirement of showing the actual use of the mails.

There are two primary defenses to a mail fraud prosecution: good faith and the statute of limitations. Good faith is a complete defense to a mail fraud prosecution. The good faith defense seeks to demonstrate that there was no intent. The statute of limitations for mail and wire fraud schemes is five years, except those that affect a financial institution, in which case the statute is 10 years. The statute runs from the last overt act in furtherance of the scheme.

Significant Case

◇◇◇

The rapid explosion of Internet sports betting makes this an area ripe for litigation. In 2002, thirty-three virtually identical cases were transferred to the Eastern District of Louisiana through multidistrict litigation. The significant case that follows is actually two cases on appeal that were selected as test cases and consolidated for pretrial purposes (see In re MasterCard Int'l Inc. Internet Gambling Litigation (2002) and Visa Int'l Internet Serv. Ass'n Internet Gambling Litigation, 132 F. Supp. 2d 468, 471). The elements of RICO violations, as well as wire and mail fraud as predicate acts are discussed.

IN RE: MASTERCARD INTERNATIONAL INC. INTERNET GAMBLING LITIGATION

5th Circuit Court of Appeals
313 F.3d 257 (5th Cir. 2002)

DENNIS, Circuit Judge:

In this lawsuit, Larry Thompson and Lawrence Bradley ("Thompson," "Bradley," or collectively "Plaintiffs") attempt to use the Racketeer Influenced and Corrupt Organizations Act ("RICO"), *18 U.S.C. §§ 1961–1968*, to avoid debts they incurred when they used their credit cards to purchase "chips" with which they gambled at on-line casinos and to recover for injuries they allegedly sustained by reason of the RICO violations of MasterCard International, Visa International, and banks that issue MasterCard and Visa credit cards (collectively "Defendants"). The district court granted the Defendants' motions to dismiss pursuant to Rule 12(b) (6) of the Federal Rules of Civil Procedure. We AFFIRM.

I. Thompson and Bradley allege that the Defendants, along with unnamed Internet casinos, created and operate a "worldwide gambling enterprise" that facilitates illegal gambling on the Internet through the use of credit cards. Internet gambling works as follows. A gambler directs his browser to a casino website. There he is informed that he will receive a gambling "credit" for each dollar he deposits and is instructed to enter his billing information. He can use a credit card to purchase the credits. His credit card is subsequently charged for his purchase of the credits. Once he has purchased the credits, he may place wagers. Losses are debited from, and winnings credited to, his account. Any net winnings a gambler might accrue are not credited to his card but are paid by alternate mechanisms, such as wire transfers.

Under this arrangement, Thompson and Bradley contend, "the availability of credit and the ability to gamble are inseparable." The credit card companies facilitate the enterprise, they say, by authorizing the casinos to accept credit cards, by making credit available to gamblers, by encouraging the use of that credit through the placement of their logos on the websites, and by processing the "gambling debts" resulting from the extension of credit. The banks that issued the gamblers' credit cards participate in the enterprise, they say, by collecting those "gambling debts."

Thompson holds a MasterCard credit card issued by Fleet Bank (Rhode Island) NA. He used his credit card to purchase $1510 in gambling credits at two Internet gambling sites. Bradley holds a Visa credit card issued by Travelers Bank USA Corporation. He used his credit card to purchase $16,445 in gambling credits at seven Internet gambling sites. Thompson and Bradley each used his credits to place wagers. Thompson lost everything, and his subsequent credit card billing statements reflected purchases of $1510 at the casinos. Bradley's winning percentage was higher, but he fared worse in the end. He states his monthly credit card billing statements included $7048 in purchases at the casinos.

Thompson and Bradley filed class action complaints against the Defendants on behalf of themselves and others similarly situated. They state that the Defendants participated in and aided and abetted conduct that violated various federal and state criminal laws applicable to Internet gambling. Through their association with the Internet casinos, the Defendants allegedly "directed, guided, conducted, or participated, directly or indirectly, in the conduct of an enterprise through a pattern of racketeering and/or the unlawful collection of unlawful debt," in violation of *18 U.S.C. § 1962 (c)*. They seek damages under RICO's civil remedies provision, claiming that they were injured by the Defendants' RICO violations. They also seek declaratory judgment that their gambling debts are unenforceable because they are illegal.

Upon motions by the Defendants, the district court dismissed the Plaintiffs' complaints. In a thorough and careful opinion, the court determined that the Plaintiffs not only could not satisfy the necessary prerequisites to a RICO claim but also could not establish their standing to bring such a claim. The Plaintiffs now appeal.

II. We review a district court's grant of a Rule 12(b) (6) motion de novo, applying the same standard used below. "In so doing, we accept the facts alleged in the complaint as true and construe the allegations in the light most favorable to the plaintiffs." But "conclusory allegations or legal conclusions masquerading as factual conclusions will not suffice to prevent a motion to dismiss."

III. All RICO violations under *18 U.S.C. § 1962* entail "(1) a person who engages in (2) a pattern of racketeering activity, (3) connected to the acquisition, establishment, conduct, or control of an enterprise." As to the second element, a RICO plaintiff may show that the defendant engaged in the collection of unlawful debt as an alternative to showing the defendant engaged in a pattern or racketeering activity. A RICO claim alleging a violation of § 1962(c), as here, also requires that the defendant "participated in the operation or management of the enterprise itself." Of these required elements, the district court concluded that Thompson and Bradley failed to plead facts showing a pattern of racketeering activity or the collection of unlawful debt; a RICO enterprise; or participation in the operation of management of the enterprise. We agree that the Plaintiffs' allegations do not show a pattern of racketeering activity or the collection of unlawful debt. Because this conclusion, alone, is dispositive, we need not consider whether the Plaintiffs sufficiently alleged the other elements.

"A pattern of racketeering activity requires two or more predicate acts and a demonstration that the racketeering predicates are related and amount to or pose a threat of continued criminal activity." The predicate acts can be either state or federal crimes. Thompson and Bradley allege both types of predicate acts.

On appeal, Thompson alleges that the Defendants' conduct violated a Kansas statute that criminalizes five types of commercial gambling activity. Only two sections of the statute—sections (c) and (e)—are even remotely relevant here. Neither implicates the Defendants' conduct. Because the Defendants completed their transaction with the Plaintiffs before any gambling occurred, that transaction cannot have involved taking custody of something bet or collecting the proceeds of a gambling device. Both of those activities, which constitute commercial gambling under Kansas law, necessarily "can only take place after some form of gambling [has been] completed." Accordingly, we find that Thompson fails to identify a RICO predicate act under Kansas law.

Bradley alleges on appeal that the Defendants' conduct violated a New Hampshire gambling statute aimed at persons who operate or control places where gambling occurs. Bradley did not, however, allege a violation of the statute in his complaint. In any event, this statute is patently inapplicable to the Defendants under the facts alleged. Indeed, Bradley makes no effort in his briefs to explain its applicability. Accordingly, we find that Bradley, too, fails to identify a RICO predicate act under a state criminal law. Thompson and Bradley both identify three substantive federal crimes as predicates—violation of the Wire Act, mail fraud, and wire fraud. The district court concluded that the Wire Act concerns gambling on sporting events or contests and that the Plaintiffs had failed to allege that they had engaged in internet sports gambling. We agree with the district court's statutory interpretation, its reading of the relevant case law, its summary of the relevant legislative history, and its conclusion. The Plaintiffs may not rely on the Wire Act as a predicate offense here.

The district court next articulated several reasons why the Plaintiffs may not rely on federal mail or wire fraud as predicates. Of these reasons, two are particularly compelling. First, Thompson and Bradley cannot show that the Defendants made a false or fraudulent misrepresentation. Because the Wire Act does not prohibit non-sports internet gambling, any debts incurred in connection with such gambling are not illegal. Hence, the Defendants could not have fraudulently represented the Plaintiffs' related debt as legal because it was, in fact, legal. We agree that "the allegations that the issuing banks represented the credit charges as legal debts is not a scheme to defraud." Second, Thompson and Bradley fail to allege that they relied upon the Defendants' representations in deciding to gamble. The district court correctly stated that although reliance is not an element of statutory mail or wire fraud, we have required its showing when mail or wire fraud is alleged as a RICO predicate. Accordingly, we conclude that Thompson and Bradley cannot rely on the federal mail or wire fraud statutes to show RICO predicate acts.

In the alternative, Thompson and Bradley allege that the Defendants engaged in the collection of unlawful debt. Under §1961, a RICO plaintiff may attempt to show that the debt is unlawful because it was incurred or contracted in an illegal gambling activity or in connection with the illegal business of gambling or because it is unenforceable under usury laws or was incurred in connection with the business of lending at usurious rates. Neither Thompson nor Bradley raises the specter of usury. And, as we have already found, the Defendants' conduct did not involve any violation of a state or federal gambling law. Thus, we agree with the district court's conclusion that the Plaintiffs have not sufficiently alleged "the collection of unlawful debt."

Because Thompson and Bradley cannot prove a necessary element of a civil RICO claim, namely that the Defendants engaged in a pattern of racketeering activity or the collection of unlawful debt, we hold that dismissal is proper under Rule 12(b)(6).

Finally, we reiterate the district court's statement that "RICO, no matter how liberally construed, is not intended to provide a remedy to this class of plaintiff." Thompson and Bradley simply are not victims under the facts of these cases. Rather, as the district court wrote, "they are independent actors who made a knowing and voluntary choice to engage in a course of conduct." In engaging in this conduct, they got exactly what they bargained for—gambling "chips" with which they could place wagers. They cannot use RICO to avoid meeting obligations they voluntarily took on.

IV. For the foregoing reasons, we AFFIRM the judgment of the district court.

Recent Trends

Proposed Federal Regulation of Internet Sports Gambling

Several pieces of legislation have been proposed in the twenty-first century. Those in favor of the proposed legislation believe that it will close loopholes in existing legislation, protect the integrity of college and amateur sporting events, and protect student–athletes from pressure from organized crime. Those opposed to the proposals argue that they will be impossible to enforce and infringe on states' rights. Although proposals have received widespread support from educational and sports institutions, none of the proposals have become law.

The **High School and College Sports Gambling Prohibition Act** (S. 718) was proposed in 2000 to prohibit high school, college, and amateur sports gambling in all states, including Nevada. The **National Collegiate and Amateur Athletic Protection Act of 2001** (H.R. 641 and S. 338) was introduced to protect amateur athletics and combat illegal sports gambling through educational and enforcement strategies. The **Student Athlete Protection Act** (2001 H.R. 1100) proposed to amend the Bradley Bill to prohibit high school, college, and amateur sports gambling in all states, including Nevada. Senator John McCain introduced the **Amateur Sports Integrity Act** (S. 718) on May 14, 2001. Title II, § 201 of the bill would prohibit gambling on competitive games involving high school and college athletes and the Olympics. Title III, § 301 would make it unlawful for credit card companies to fund illegal gambling activity. The bill was reintroduced in 2003. A bill to amend Title 18 U.S.C. to expand and modernize the prohibition against interstate gambling and including Internet gambling overseas called the **Combating Illegal Gambling Reform and Modernization Act** was introduced in the House in November 2001, and a report filed by the House Committee on the Judiciary in October 2002. The **Comprehensive Internet Gambling Prohibition Act of 2002** (S. 3006) was proposed on September 25, 2002 to prohibit all Internet gambling. The **Unlawful Internet Gambling Funding Prohibition Act** first proposed in 2001 (H.R. 556) and reintroduced in 2002 (H.R. 21) would have addressed enforcement problems by making it illegal for a gambling business to knowingly accept electronic fund transfers, checks, credit cards, and other forms of payment from a person who participates in Internet gambling.

Although none of these proposals was passed into law, an act that was passed to address terrorism could provide an effective avenue to enforcement of gambling laws. The **USA PATRIOT Act** permits law enforcement officials to gather electronic evidence pertaining to illegal activities, including offshore money laundering regulations. The law does not contain any specific antigambling provisions, but it does regulate banking services and allows the government to seize accounts in offshore banks where there is evidence of illegal activity, which would include gambling. In March 2003, the U.S. Attorney accused PayPal, a subsidiary of eBay, of violating the USA PATRIOT Act. The lawsuit was settled with PayPal paying $10 million of gambling profits from illegal offshore gambling operations.

Sports Gambling and Youth

Much of the proposed legislation stems from a growing concern about the impact of gambling on our youth. Sports pools are among the most popular form of adolescent gambling, with cards run on major sporting events such as the Super Bowl and the NCAA Final Four on high school and college campuses nationwide. Teenagers are three times more likely than adults to become problem gamblers, and one of eight compulsive gamblers in the United States is a teen. Over half of students surveyed in a recent study indicated that gambling had created stress and financial difficulties. It is believed that college athletes are particularly vulnerable to bribery attempts because of financial need, but also because of their competitive nature. Although the NCAA has stiffened penalties for athletes caught participating in gambling activities and significantly increased their educational efforts, sports bribery and tampering with the outcome of sports events is increasing at the college level. There have been as many cases of sports gambling by student–athletes reported to the NCAA in the last ten years as there were in all the years prior to 1995. There is significant concern that sports gambling is likely to continue to escalate at both the college and high school levels.

Cyberscalping

Online ticket sales are becoming increasingly popular with Internet users who are willing to purchase hard-to-get tickets at any price. Consumers need to be aware that online ticket vendors who sell tickets above their face value may be in violation of state antiscalping laws. **Authorized ticket agents**, for example Ticketmaster, are immune from antiscalping legislation due to their statutorily required contractual agreements with event promoters. However, tickets purchased through **online ticket brokers** or **online ticket auctions** may be illegal. Ticket brokers may be reselling tickets within the parameters of the state the broker resides in, but many seemingly ignore out-of-state laws. Similarly, ticket auctions, where a vendor places ticket information online and customers place bids, appear legal. Although no price is set on the ticket, the practice of displaying the current bid may be construed as an offer to sell a ticket above the price allowed by statute. Caveat emptor! Many online ticket vendors place a disclaimer on the Website in an attempt to make the ticket purchaser responsible for following the laws of the state in which the purchaser resides.

Cyberscalping, like all e-commerce, is fraught with jurisdictional issues. Cyberspace is a virtual world located in no particular geographic location and available to anyone, anywhere. Jurisdiction may be the state where the ticket is used to attend the sporting event, the state from which the ticket was sold, the state in which the purchaser resides, or all three. To establish criminal jurisdiction over an individual for acts allegedly committed online, states need to prove by a preponderance of the evidence that a criminal act occurred.

References

Cases

Arlotta v. Bradley Center, 349 F.3d 517 (7th Cir. 2003).

Chaset v. Fleer/Skybox International, 300 F.3d 1083 (9th Cir. 2002).

Ex parte Quarg, 84 P. 766 (Cal. 1906).

In re MasterCard International, Inc., 313 F.3d 257 (5th Cir. 2002).

Nebbia v. New York, 291 U.S. 502 (1934).

People v. Johnson, 278 N.Y.S.2d 80 (1967).

People v. Shepherd, 141 Cal. Rptr. 379 (1977), *cert. denied* 436 U.S. 917 (1978).

Roberts v. Swain, 487 S.E.2d 760 (N.C. App. 1997).

State v. Granite Gate Resorts, Inc., 568 N.W.2d 715 (1997), *aff'd* 576 N.W.2d 747 (1998).

State v. Major, 253 S.E.2d 724 (Ga. 1979).

The Upper Deck Company v. Federal Insurance Co., 358 F.3d 608 (9th Cir. 2004).

U.S. v. Cohen, 260 F.3d 68 (2nd Cir. 2001).

U.S. v. Gray, 96 F.3d 769 (5th Cir. 1996).

U.S. v. Offner, 2004 U.S. App. LEXIS 2088 (2nd Cir. 2004).

U.S. v. Walters, 704 F. Supp. 844 (N.D. Ill. 1989) *motion to dismiss denied*, 711 F. Supp. 1435 (N.D. Ill. 1989), *rev'd on other grounds*, 913 F.2d 388 (7th Cir. 1990), 775 F. Supp. 1173 (N.D. Ill. 1991), 997 F.2d 1219 (7th Cir. 1993).

U.S. v. Welch, 327 F.3d 1081 (10th Cir. 2003).

Publications

Bourdeau, J. (2005). Sending or receiving nonmailable or prohibited matter by post office, *62 Am. Jur. 2d § 130* (August 2005).

Brown, G. T. (2004, December 6). Wagering war on gambling. *The NCAA News*, pp. A1 & A4.

Brown, G. T. (2004, December 6). Task force betting on education as most effective weapon. *The NCAA News*, p. A2.

Claussen, C. L., & Miller, L. K. (2001). The gambling industry and sports gambling: A stake in the game? *Journal of Sport Management, 15*, 350–363.

Cobb, L. Validity of state or local regulation dealing with resale of tickets to theatrical or sporting events, *81 A.L.R.3d* 655.

Copeland, J. (2004, December 6). Sports wagering survey focuses attention on high rates of misbehavior in Divisions II, III. *The NCAA News*, p. A3.

Criscuolo, P. (1995). Reassessing the ticket scalping dispute: The application, effects and criticisms of current anti-scalping legislation. *Seton Hall Journal of Sport Law, 5*(1), 189–221.

Edwards, J. (1971). Annotation: What constitutes "causing" mail to be delivered for purpose of executing scheme prohibited by Mail Fraud Statute (19 USC § 1341). 9 *A.L.R. Fed.* 893 (Supp. 2005).

Elder, J. (1998, Summer). Federal mail-fraud unleashed: Revisiting the criminal catch-all. *Oregon Law Review, 77,* 707–733.

Flavin, K., & Corrigan, K. (1996). Mail and wire fraud. *American Criminal Law Review, 33,* 861–879.

Gibbs, J. M. (2000, Spring). Cyberscalping: On-line ticket sales. *University of Toledo Law Review, 31,* 471–495.

Goldstein, H. (1997, Fall). On-line gambling down to the wire? *Marquette Sports Law Journal, 8,* 1–51.

Goodman, M. (1998). The Federal Mail Fraud Statute: The government's Colt 45 renders Norby Walters and Lloyd Bloom agents of misfortune. *Loyola Entertainment Law Journal, 10,* 315–333.

Green, C., & Hammon, C. (1998). Mail and wire fraud. *American Criminal Law Review, 35,* 943–963.

Kandel, A., & Block, E. (1997). The "de-icing" of ticket prices: A proposal addressing the problem of commercial bribery in the New York ticket industry. *Journal of Law and Policy, VII* (2), 489–508.

Kimpflen, J. Entertainment and Sports Law, *27A Am. Jur.2d §7.*

Lease, S. (2005, June). Criminal Conspiracy, *15A C.J.S. § 230.*

Liddell, P., et al. (2004). Internet gambling: On a roll? *Seton Hall Legislative Journal, 28,* 315–353.

Masoud, S. (2004, Summer). The offshore quandary: The impact of domestic regulation on licensed offshore gambling companies. *Whittier Law Review, 25,* 989–1009.

Montpas, S. (1996, Fall). Gambling on-line: For a hundred dollars, I bet you government regulation will not stop the newest form of gambling. *University of Dayton Law Review, 22,* 163–185.

Norwood, J. M. (2005, Winter). Gambling in the 21st century: Judicial resolution of current issues. *Mississippi Law Journal,* 779–826.

Podgor, E. (1998). Mail fraud: Redefining the boundaries. *St. Thomas Law Review, 10,* 557–577.

Roberts, M. (1997). The national gambling debate: Two defining issues. *Whittier Law Review, 18*(3), 579–609.

Rychlak, R. J. (2003/2004 Winter). A bad bet: Federal criminalization of Nevada's collegiate sports books. *Nevada Law Journal,* 320–336.

Tratos, M. (1997). Gaming on the Internet. *Stanford Journal of Law, Business & Finance, 3*(2), 101–116.

Udovicic, A. (1997, April/May). Sports gambling in the United States. *For The Record,* 2, 4, 6.

Udovicic, A. (1998, Spring). Special report: Sports and gambling a good mix? I wouldn't bet on it. *Marquette Sports Law Journal, 8,* 401–427.

Legislation

Amateur Sports Integrity Act (S. 718; S. 1407; S. 2267).

Combating Illegal Gambling Reform and Modernization Act (HR 3215).

Comprehensive Internet Gambling Prohibition Act (S 3006-IS).

Delaware Code Annotated, Title 29 State Government, Chapter 48 Lotteries, § 4801 (as amended 1994).

Federal Trademark Act of 1946, Lanham Act § 45, 15 U.S.C. §§ 1051–1127 (2005).

Internet Gambling Prohibition Act (HR 3125).

National Collegiate and Amateur Athletic Protection Act of 2001 (S. 338; HR 641).

Nevada Revised Statutes Annotated (Michie), Title 41: Gaming; Horse Racing; Sporting Events (1993).

Oregon Revised Statutes, § 461.213 (1990).

Professional and Amateur Sports Protection, Chapter 178, 28 U.S.C. §§ 3701–3704 (2005).

Prohibition of Illegal Gambling Businesses, 18 U.S.C. § 1955 (2005).

Sentencing Reform Act of 1984, Public Law 98-473, Title II, Chapter II, §§ 211–239, 98 Stat. 1987 (1984) (codified at 18 U.S.C. §§ 3551–3586 (2005)).

Student Athlete Protection Act (HR 1110).

The PATRIOT Act, Publ. L No. 107-56 (Oct. 26, 2001).

Title 18, Crimes and Criminal Procedure, Chapter 19 Conspiracy, U.S.C. §§ 371–373 (2005).

Title 18, Crimes and Criminal Procedure, Chapter 50 Gambling, U.S.C. §§ 1081–1084 (2005).

Title 18, Crimes and Criminal Procedure, Chapter 63 Mail Fraud, U.S.C. §§ 1341–1346 (2005).

Title 18, Crimes and Criminal Procedure, Chapter 119 Wire and Electronic Communications Interception and Interception of Oral Communications, U.S.C. §§ 2510–2522 (2005).

Title 18 U.S.C.A.: Crimes and Criminal Procedure, Part I, Chapter 4: Bribery, Graft, and Conflicts of Interest, § 224 (2005).

Websites

National Gambling Impact Study Commission Final Report (1999), at http://govinfo.library.unt.edu/ngisc/reports/fullrpt.html/

4.16 Hazing

Ellen J. Staurowsky

Ithaca College

On an October day in 1881, seven upperclass students assaulted a Bowdoin College freshman in his dorm room as part of a hazing ritual (*Strout v. Packard*, 1884). The case offers a vivid description of escalating events not unfamiliar to us today. There was an invasion of an unsuspecting student's room, a beating, and general mayhem as more than one assailant threw "missiles" at the student. The issue raised in this case was whether a conspiracy existed among Strout's seven attackers and subsequently, who was liable for the harm done to Strout, who suffered, among other things, a serious eye injury after being hit with a thrown object. In ruling that there was not sufficient evidence to determine that a conspiracy existed, and culpability for the injury could be assigned only to the person from whose hand the object had been thrown, the judges of the Supreme Judicial Court of Maine raised considerations that resonate today about what constitutes hazing and who is responsible. Although the rights of the defendants were upheld in this case, there is a palpable sense in reading the opinion that the judges were aware that justice had not been served by so narrow a reading of the defendants' collective contribution to the events that occurred.

Over 120 years later, there remains much that is not known about the magnitude and degree of hazing as it occurs in school or professional sport and recreational settings, nor is it clear that existing hazing laws address the issues raised by these cases. Attributed in part to the codes of silence that surround hazing and the power of peer pressure that discourages disclosure of incidents, the looming uncertainty of whether hazing can be effectively addressed is also connected to the expansiveness of the term itself and its multiple meanings. For example, in January of 2006, the University of Memphis campus newspaper reported an incident involving female members of the cross country team, who were allegedly taken out for a night of partying by their teammates, appearing in sexually suggestive attire with the words "fresh meat" and "frosh" written on their foreheads. Although editors of *The Daily Helmsman* considered the incident potentially violative of Tennessee antihazing law, team members expressed a belief that the incident was an opportunity to bond (Laurie, 2006).

Recent cases illustrate the range of behaviors that may be identified as hazing. In December of 2005, members of the Argo (IL) Community High School wrestling team allegedly hazed five to seven freshmen during a bus ride home with their coaches present (Phillips, 2005). Rookies were restrained and subjected to one team member shoving his testicles in their faces. At the college level, field hockey players from Frostburg State University pleaded guilty to their role in a hazing incident involving consumption of alcohol, which resulted in an eighteen-year-old teammate being hospitalized with a blood alcohol level four times the legal limit (Associated Press, 2005). The Ontario Hockey League suspended the coach of the Windsor Spitfires, Moe Mantha, for allegedly hazing players by making them strip on the team bus and other management issues (Associated Press, October 18, 2005). In 2004, Marcus Parker, a former member of the Florida A & M marching band, was awarded a $1.8 million court verdict in a civil battery case after suffering kidney failure as the result of being hit with a paddling board ("Marching Band," 2004).

These and other cases show that recreation and sport managers must be proactive in their response to hazing by (1) anticipating that hazing will occur on teams and within student organizations; (2) questioning and monitoring the initiation activities of athletes, students, and employees; (3) working within existing organizational structures to formulate antihazing policies; and (4) developing antihazing education programs. They must also be informed about policies that exist within their organizations and be knowledgeable about the local, state, and national laws that apply to hazing.

Fundamental Concepts

Definition and Scope

Definitions of hazing range from the succinct to the comprehensive. For example, in the state of Ohio, **hazing** "means doing an act or coercing another, including the victim, to do any act of initiation into any student or other organization that causes or creates a substantial risk of causing mental or physical harm to any person" (Ohio Revised Code 2903.31). In contrast, Florida law defines hazing to mean

> any action or situation which recklessly or intentionally endangers the mental or physical health or safety of a student for the purpose of initiation or admission into or affiliation with any organization operating under the sanction of a postsecondary institution. Such term includes, but is not limited to, any brutality of a physical nature, such as whipping, beating, branding, forced calisthenics, exposure to the elements, forced consumption of any food, liquor, drug, or other substance, or other forced physical activity which could adversely affect the physical health or safety of the student, and also includes any activity which would subject the student to extreme mental stress, such as sleep deprivation, forced exclusion from social contact, forced conduct which could result in extreme embarrassment, or other forced activity which could adversely affect the mental health or dignity of the student. (Florida State Code 240.1325)

Whereas the statutory definition of hazing is important, so too is the interpretation of the meaning of the term "student organization." In *Duitch v. Canton City Schools* (2004), a freshmen high school student alleged that on "Freshman Friday," he was beaten in a restroom by eight to ten juniors and seniors. Both the trial and appellate courts found that "the actions of the students did not constitute initiation into any student or other organization" and that "the attack was merely due to the appellant's status as a freshman." Initiation into the entire student body rather than into a specific student organization prevented the appellant from finding relief under the existing hazing law in the state of Ohio.

The vast majority of hazing laws create a link between hazing and student welfare, thus limiting the applicability of the law to manifestations of hazing that may occur in other groups, like professional sport teams or athletic teams sponsored by national sport governing bodies (e.g., U.S. Olympic team). The New York statute reflects consideration for this possibility as seen in the language of the statute, which reads in part, "A person is guilty of hazing in the first degree when, in the course of another person's initiation into or affiliation with any organization . . . " (New York 120.16).

Civil Litigation

This section explores the legal basis on which a hazing victim may establish a cause of action in a civil suit. The question here is whether the offender and/or third party is liable for the injuries sustained by the plaintiff. In a civil case, a hazing victim may be awarded monetary damages.

Negligence. Within the past twenty years, as the number of hazing cases has risen, victims have increasingly sought redress in the courts alleging negligence on the part of athletes who haze as well as coaches, school administrators, and the institutions they represent.

At one time, college officials under the doctrine of in loco parentis could be held liable for hazing because administrators had a duty to care for their students much the same as parents had a duty to care for their children. Changing societal views of college students as young adults rather than dependent children shifted the burden of responsibility for student misbehavior from college officials to students. This does not mean, however, that there is no basis for an institutional or professional duty of care. Under the **landowner-invitee theory**, landlords owe a duty of reasonable care to those who are invited onto their property. Through offers of admission and assessment of fees, a similar relationship exists between institutions of higher education and their students (Crow & Rosner, 2002).

In *Knoll v. Board of Regents of the University of Nebraska* (1999), the Nebraska Supreme Court used this theory to reason that the university had an obligation to take steps to protect a student against reasonably foreseeable acts of hazing, which included abduction from his dorm room on campus, transport to a fraternity house off campus, and harm that accrued as a result of his attempt to escape. The implications of this case point to the necessity for school administrators and employers to acknowledge the history of hazing in athletics and to take proactive measures in the form of antihazing policies and education or risk failing in their duty to protect students and other persons associated with their organization (Crow & Rosner, 2002).

In *Siesto v. Bethpage Union Free School District* (1999), the Nassau County Supreme Court (NY) awarded summary judgment to the plaintiff, a member of the football team, who sustained a serious head wound as a result of a hazing incident that occurred in the locker room just a short distance from the coach's office. In dismissing the affirmative defenses of comparative negligence and assumption of risk asserted by the school district, the trial court determined that athletes who voluntarily participate in athletics do not assume the risk of injury resulting from being hazed.

Another common defense in hazing cases is the *doctrine of immunity*, which frees educational institutions and their employees from liability for negligence (Crow & Rosner, 2002). In *Caldwell v. Griffin Spalding County Board of Education, et al.* (1998), a first-year football player was attacked, beaten, and knocked unconscious in his dorm room during preseason. In a civil suit brought by the player against school officials, the Georgia Court of Appeals upheld a lower court ruling granting summary dismissal on the grounds that the principal, coach, and school board members were immune from civil liability.

However, in *Meeker v. Edmunson* (2005), the U.S. Court of Appeals for the Fourth Circuit determined that a wrestling coach who had authorized physical attacks on rookies by other members of his team was not protected by qualified immunity. The court determined that the action of a school official to cause a student to be beaten is contrary to the constitutional rights of a student under the Fourteenth Amendment.

Following the worldwide distribution of videotaped evidence documenting the violent hazing of girls from Glenbrook (IL) North High School, questions were raised regarding the culpability of adults who had supplied alcohol to the underage participants in the event. Although existing Illinois law does not provide for social host liability, in the wake of this incident Illinois lawmakers are considering the adoption of legislation that would allow victims and their families to recover damages from the adults who willfully give, sell, or deliver alcohol to minors (Vock, 2003).

Signaling what may be increasing attempts to hold parents accountable for the behavior of their children, four former coaches at Mepham High School, who lost their sport-related job assignments following a well-publicized football hazing scandal, sued the parents of three of the students involved in the physical and sexual assaults of younger players, seeking $20 million in damages. The attorney for the coaches reasoned that the parents knew or had reason to know that their sons were prone to violence and did not use care to restrain them ("Ex-coaches sue," 2004).

This section highlights several challenges that exist in establishing who is accountable and can be held liable in hazing cases. First, at the college and university level, negligence hinges on the ability to argue that a special relationship exists between the victim and the institution. In the absence of a **special relationship**, there is no **duty of care**. Second, in determining whether both parties (perpetrator and victim) may bear responsibility for hazing, the mere fact that an athlete agreed to participate on a team, by itself, does not provide a supportable rationale to establish **comparative negligence**. Third, coaches and school administrators may be **immune** from civil liability if their actions fall within the realm of professional discretion. Fourth, parents may be held negligent for not exercising appropriate supervision of their children.

Constitutional Rights. In 1993, a high school football player was accosted by teammates while leaving the showers, forcibly restrained, and bound to a towel rack with athletic tape. His former girlfriend was then led into the locker room to see him hanging there (*Seamons v. Snow*, 2000). Upon Seamon's release from the team because of his refusal to apologize for reporting the incident, he filed suit claiming that his First Amendment rights to free speech had been violated by the coach and the school district (*Seamons v. Snow*, 1994). After the district court granted summary judgment in favor of the defendants in 1998, the appellate court reversed that decision sending the case to trial—asserting for a second time that the coach was not entitled to qualified immunity for suspending Seamons from the team (*Seamons v. Snow*, 2000; see *Significant Case* later in this chapter).

In 2000, the Centennial Area School District (PA) settled a lawsuit brought forward by a former high school wrestler so as to avert a court decision regarding its liability. The wrestler alleged his Fourteenth Amendment right to protection of his own bodily integrity had been violated after the school failed to prevent his hazing, despite knowledge of the activity (*Nice v. Centennial Area School District*, 2000).

In *Perkins, et al. v. Alamo Heights Independent School District* (2002), two high school cheerleaders were stripped of their eligibility to try out for future teams by school authorities because of their involvement in a party where underage drinking and hazing occurred. They sought an injunction claiming their rights under Title IX and the equal protection clause of the U.S. Constitution had been violated because school officials had not provided an adequate hearing prior to taking action and had engaged in disparate treatment of female students. In rejecting their request, the court determined that the "lengthy history of problematic behavior" exhibited by the team and advance warnings about inappropriate behavior served as adequate notice and concluded that the evidence to show disparate treatment was unpersuasive.

These cases highlight two issues pertaining to the protection of student rights for coaches and administrators. In the *Seamons v. Snow* case, Coach Snow potentially violated Brian's First Amendment right to free speech by punishing him for breaking the silence that surrounds hazing. In contrast, the Alamo Heights school officials were successful in defending against allegations of failure to provide due process because they had given appropriate notice and acted preemptively to reduce liability prior to the hazing event occurring.

Other Civil Charges. As a result of *Davis v. Monroe County Board of Education* (1999), school administrators who show deliberate indifference in cases of peer to peer harassment may be subject to liability for the resulting damages. According to attorney David Doty, school administrators should be aware of the implications this holds for their handling of hazing cases ("Hazing is no joke," 2002). The pending case of *Snelling & Snelling v. Fall Mountain Regional School District, et al.* (2001) may well test this theory. Derek and Joel Snelling, members of the basketball team, claimed they were targets of persistent verbal and physical abuse by teammates, and, on occasion, by the coach. Although the district court granted summary judgment to Fall Mountain dismissing Section 1983 claims made by the plaintiffs that the harassment violated their Fourteenth Amendment rights to substantive due process and equal protection, District Judge Joseph DiClerico also found a pattern of harassment that presented a trialworthy issue for action under Title IX and raised an issue as to whether the defendants were deliberately indifferent to the treatment of the brothers (*Snelling & Snelling v. Fall Mountain Regional School District, et al.*, 2001).

Criminal Hazing

In contrast to the civil justice system, where hazing victims personally seek relief for the harms done to them, in the criminal justice system, a state entity, such as a county prosecutor, will bring charges against alleged perpetrators for the purpose of determining whether they are guilty or innocent of a criminal act.

Antihazing Statutes. The number of states that have adopted antihazing statutes has increased dramatically from 25 in 1990 to 44 in 2006. Although the number of athletes charged criminally for their participation in hazing activities has increased as well during that span of time, substantial barriers to the enforcement and prosecution of antihazing laws remain due to the lack of uniformity in the laws from state to state and the modest penalties that go along with them (Crow & Rosner, 2002; Sussberg, 2003). An analysis of current state statutes, which appears in Table 1, reveals

- Thirty-five of the forty-four state codes (80 percent) classify hazing as a misdemeanor, whereas five states expressly provide that hazing resulting in serious bodily harm and/or death is classified as a felony. The classification of hazing as a crime does not supersede or change penalties covered by other criminal statutes (see *Classification of Crime* column). Legislators in Wyoming, one of the states that does not have an antihazing law, are currently considering a bill that would make hazing a misdemeanor or felony if passed (Barron, 2006).
- Eight antihazing statutes (18 percent) specify that it is a crime to fail to report an incident to authorities (see *Is Failure to Notify a Crime?* column).
- Of the existing antihazing statutes, slightly less than a third (12 of 44) require schools to either develop antihazing policies and penalties or devise specific means to educate students, teachers/faculty, and other

table ◆1◆ State Antihazing Laws[1]

State	State Hazing Statute	Classification of Crime	Is Failure To Notify a Crime?	Is Antihazing Policy Required in Schools?	Is Victim's Willingness a Defense?	Public/Private Status of School; Educational Level
Alabama	16-1-23	Class C misdemeanor	Yes	No	Yes	Any school
Alaska	None					
Arizona	15-2301		No	Yes	No	Public
Arkansas	6-5-201	Class B misdemeanor	Yes	No	Yes	Any school
California	32050-1	Misdemeanor	No	No	Yes	Any school
Colorado	18-9-124	Class 3 misdemeanor	No	No	Yes	Any school
Connecticut	53-23(a)		No	No	No	Higher education
Delaware	9301-04	Class B misdemeanor	No	Yes	No	Each institution
Florida	240.326		No	Yes	No	College/university where students receive state financial assistance
Georgia	16-5-61	High and aggravated misdemeanor	No	No	No	Any school
Hawaii	None					
Idaho	18-917	Misdemeanor	No	No	Yes	
Illinois	720 ILCS 120	Class A misdemeanor, Class 4 felony	No	No	Yes	Any school
Indiana	IC 35-4-2-2	Class A or B misdemeanor, Class C or D felony	No	No	No	Not restricted to school settings; any person
Iowa	708.10	Serious or simple misdemeanor	No	No	No	Any school
Kansas	21-3434	Class B misdemeanor	No	No	Yes	Any social or fraternal organization—not limited to schools
Kentucky	164.375		No	Yes	Yes	State colleges & universities
Louisiana	17:1801		No	No	Yes	Only fraternities in any educational institution receiving state funds
Maine	6653		No	Yes	Yes	Public school; postsecondary institution incorporated or chartered by the state
Maryland	27-268H	Misdemeanor	No	No	No	Any school, college, or university
Massachusetts	269-17		Yes	No	No	Any student or other person on public or private property
Michigan	None					
Minnesota	127.465		No	Yes	Yes	Each school board; student or staff hazing

[1] This table was originally put together for this text by Brian Crow and appeared in the 2001 edition. The table was updated and altered for this edition.

table ⟨1⟩ State Antihazing Laws[1] (continued)

State	State Hazing Statute	Classification of Crime	Is Failure To Notify a Crime?	Is Antihazing Policy Required in Schools?	Is Victim's Willingness a Defense?	Public/Private Status of School; Educational Level
Mississippi	97-3-105	Misdemeanor	No	No	Yes	Not specific to schools; any organization
Missouri	578.365	Class A misdemeanor, Class C felony	No	Yes	No	Public or private college or university
Montana	None					
Nebraska	28-311.06	Class II misdemeanor	No	No	Yes	Postsecondary educational institution
Nevada	200.605	Misdemeanor, Gross misdemeanor	No	No	No	High school, college, or university in the state
New Hampshire	631.7	Class B misdemeanor	Yes	No	No	Any school
New Jersey	2c:40-3	4th Degree crime	No	No	No	
New Mexico	None					
New York	120.16	Class A misdemeanor	No	No	Yes	Not specific to schools or students
North Carolina	9:14:35-38	Class 2 misdemeanor	Yes	No	Yes	Any school or college
North Dakota	12.1-17-08	Misdemeanor	No	No	No	Not limited to schools
Ohio	2307.44; 2903.31	Misdemeanor	No	No	No	Any school
Oklahoma	21-1190	Misdemeanor	No	No	No	Any school
Oregon	163.197	Misdemeanor	No	No	Yes	College or university
Pennsylvania	5352	3rd Degree misdemeanor	No	Yes	No	Institution of higher education— associate degree or higher
Rhode Island	11-21-1	Misdemeanor	No	No	Yes	Any school
South Carolina	59-101-200	Misdemeanor	Yes	No	No	Institution of higher learning
South Dakota	None					
Tennessee	49-7-123		No	No	Yes	Higher education institution
Texas	37.152	Misdemeanor	Yes	Yes	No	Any school
Utah	76-5-107.5	Misdemeanor or felony	No	Yes	No (under 21)	High school level
Vermont	76		No	Yes	No	All educational institutions
Virginia	18.2056	Class I misdemeanor	No	No	Yes	Any school
Washington	28B.10.901	Misdemeanor	Yes	No	No	Any school
West Virginia	18-2.33	Misdemeanor	No	Yes	No	Public Schools
Wisconsin	948.51	Class A misdemeanor, Class E felony	No	No	Yes	
Wyoming	None					

Source: www.stophazing.org/law

employees about the state's antihazing laws (see *Is Antihazing Policy Required in School?* column). However, there is considerable variability with regard to the level and type of school to which statutes apply. For example, 44 percent (19 of 43) include any school or other institution, whether private or public, whereas three are restricted solely to public schools. Additionally, 21 percent of the codes (9 of 43) pertain solely to higher education institutions (see *Public/Private Status of School; Educational Level* column).

- Fifty-two percent (23 of 44) of the codes provide that implied or express consent on the part of the victim, or a willingness on the part of the person hazed to participate in their own hazing, is not an available defense (see *Victim's Willingness To Be Initiated Is a Defense* column).

- A further limitation is the lack of conformity across hazing laws regarding the mental harm associated with hazing (Sussberg, 2003). This has implications at several levels. First, there is evidence in existing literature on athlete hazing to show that female athletes are more likely to haze by subjecting victims to circumstances and situations designed to humiliate rather than physically harm. As a consequence, in those instances, an injury perpetrated against a female athlete may not be recognized as hazing. Second, although hazing laws limit the scope to physical harm, the full weight of the harm done to the victim is overlooked because physical attacks have physical and psychological repercussions.

Numerous improvements to existing antihazing laws have been proposed, including the adoption of a federal antihazing statute and the imposition of a duty for school personnel to act on these issues (Edelman, 2004; Sussberg, 2003). Additionally, as Ball (2004) pointed out, the Federal Educational Rights and Privacy Act (FERPA), which prohibits the disclosure of student records, may be in conflict with the Campus Security Act (CSA), which requires colleges and universities to make full reports of crimes committed on their campuses. Given the secretiveness surrounding hazing, the protections afforded students may be contributing to schools maintaining silence around these incidents when they occur.

Whereas the evolution of antihazing law reflects a growing awareness that behavior assumed to be harmless may, in fact, be criminal, the definitional issues that remain to be resolved along with the meager penalties associated with hazing deserve consideration. As Table 2 shows, those convicted of hazing crimes are

table ◇2◇ Penalties for Hazing

State	School Penalty	Minimum Fine	Maximum Fine	Minimum Sentence	Maximum Sentence	Both fine & sentence
Arkansas	Expulsion					
California		$100	$5,000		Not more than one year	Possible
Connecticut	Appropriate penalty					
Florida			$5,000			
Louisiana	Expulsion	$10	$100	10 days	30 days	
Maryland			$500		6 months	Possible
Massachusetts			$3,000		12 months	Possible
Mississippi			$1000–2,000		6 months	Possible
Nebraska			$10,000			
North Carolina	Expulsion		$500		6 months	Possible
Oklahoma			$500		3 months	Possible
Oregon			$1,000			
Pennsylvania	Withhold diploma, other punishment					
Rhode Island			$500	30 days	12 months	Possible
South Carolina	Dismissal, Expulsion					
Texas	$500		$5,000	180 days	12 months	Possible[2]
Washington	forfeit state-funded grants, scholarships, or awards					

[2]According to the Texas statute, "Any other offense under this section which causes the death of another is a misdemeanor punishable by a fine of not less than $5,000 nor more than $10,000, confinement in county jail for not less than one year nor more than two years, or both such fine and confinement." In convictions where the violation did not result in death, the judge may substitute community service for imprisonment.

subject to modest fines that range between $10 and $10,000, imprisonment for as little as ten days to a maximum not to exceed one year, or a combination of both. As the Texas statute reveals, even when death results from hazing, the perpetrator may receive no more than two years in prison.

Significant Case

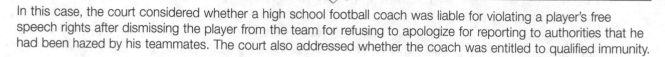

In this case, the court considered whether a high school football coach was liable for violating a player's free speech rights after dismissing the player from the team for refusing to apologize for reporting to authorities that he had been hazed by his teammates. The court also addressed whether the coach was entitled to qualified immunity.

SEAMONS V. SNOW
206 F.3d 1021 (2000)

High school football player who was assaulted by his teammates brought §1983 action against school district, football coach, and school's principal, alleging that player's free speech rights under First Amendment were violated when he was suspended and later dismissed from football team because he refused to apologize for reporting assault to police and school authorities. After summary judgment was granted for all defendants, 864 F.Supp. 1111, that judgment was reversed and remanded, 84 F.3d 1226. Upon remand, the United States District Court for the District of Utah, Dee V. Benson, J., again granted summary judgment for all defendants, 15 F.Supp.2d 1150. Player appealed. The Court of Appeals, Seymour, Chief Judge, held that: (1) if proven, coach's alleged actions could subject him to liability; (2) school district could be liable for coach's alleged conduct; (3) principal's lack of prior knowledge of or involvement in relevant events precluded his liability; and (4) coach was not entitled to qualified immunity.

Affirmed in part, reversed in part, and remanded.

* * *

SEYMOUR, Chief Judge.

This case arises out of the locker-room assault of a high school football player, Brian Seamons, by several of his teammates. Brian filed this action under 42 U.S.C. § 1983 against the school's football coach and principal, as well as the school district. ***

In the fall of 1993, Brian Seamons was a student at Sky View High School in Smithfield, Utah, and a member of the school's football team. On Monday, October 11 of that year, Brian was assaulted in the locker room by a group of his teammates. As Brian emerged from the showers, four teammates grabbed him, forcibly restrained him, and then bound him to a towel rack with highly adhesive athletic tape. Another teammate brought a girl Brian had dated into the locker room so that she could see what had been done to him.

Brian and his parents reported this incident to the police and to school authorities, including Myron Benson, Sky View's principal, and Doug Snow, the football coach. Two days after the assault, Brian and his parents met with Principal Benson and Coach Snow to discuss whether Brian would press criminal charges against the team members who assaulted him and whether Coach Snow would take any disciplinary action against them. Coach Snow stated he did not plan to remove any of the assailants from the team. Brian indicated that, in light of this, he would need to think about whether he wanted to remain on the team.

On Friday, October 15, the football team was scheduled to play an away game at Logan High School. That afternoon Brian informed Coach Snow that he wanted to remain on the team, and the two attended the traditional pre-game team-only spaghetti dinner in the school cafeteria. Coach Snow told Principal Benson that Brian was back on the team and everything had been worked out. In the meantime, Brian went home to get his uniform so he could dress for the game. When he returned to the school, Coach Snow asked Brian to meet with the four team captains, two of whom had participated in the assault. The purpose of this meeting, at which the Coach was present, was to allow the boys to clear up any residual hard feelings prior to the game.

During this meeting, a confrontation occurred between Brian and Dan Ward, a captain who had also been one of the assailants, over whether Brian should have to apologize to the team for reporting the assault to the police and school authorities. Specifically, Dan stated that he thought Brian had "betrayed the team" by reporting the assault and that Brian should not be allowed to play with the team until he apologized. Aplt.App., tab 14 at 376, 379. At this point, Coach Snow intervened and told Brian he needed to "forgive and forget and apologize" to the team captains. *Id.* at 359. When Brian refused, Coach Snow told him to "take the weekend and think about this," because without an apology he couldn't play with the team. *Id.* at 326. This ended the meeting.

Brian did not play in the game that night. He went home and told his parents he wasn't allowed to play because he had refused to apologize to the team. Brian's father, Sherwin Seamons, called the principal and angrily told him what had transpired at the meeting. Principal Benson, surprised to hear that Brian wasn't going to attend the game, drove to Logan High School and discussed the matter with Coach Snow.

The following Tuesday, Brian confronted Coach Snow in school, telling him he wasn't going to apologize to the team and he still wanted to play football. At this point, Coach Snow told Brian that he was "sick of [his] attitude, sick of [his] father's attitude," and that he was off of the team. Aplt.App., tab 15 at 432–33. The following day the remainder of Sky View's football season was canceled.

* * *

A. First Amendment Claim

In ruling on the motion for summary judgment, the district court determined that Coach Snow did not ask Brian to apologize for reporting the assault, and that Brian's ultimate failure to be involved with the football team was unrelated to his speech or refusal to speak. *See Seamons III*, 15 F.Supp.2d at 1155, 1157. Given the conflicting testimony presented at the evidentiary hearing and contained in the depositions, we fail to see how the district court could reach these conclusions without resolving factual disputes—something it cannot do at this stage of the proceedings. *See, e.g., MacLean*, 247 F.Supp. at 190 ("The Court's role in summary judgment proceedings is not to resolve issues of fact, but merely to pinpoint those facts which are not at issue."). We note in particular that the district court devoted a large portion of its opinion to a discussion of the differing accounts of the captains' meeting offered by Brian, Coach Snow, and Dan Ward during the evidentiary hearing. *See Seamons III*, 15 F.Supp.2d at 1156–57.

* * * 1. Whether Coach Snow asked Brian to apologize to the team captains

The district court found that Brian was not asked to apologize for reporting the hazing incident. In his deposition and at the evidentiary hearing, Brian testified to the following: during the captains' meeting Dan Ward told him he had betrayed the team by reporting the assault and demanded an apology; when Brian refused, Coach Snow said he would need to "forgive and forget and apologize" in order to remain playing on the team; Coach Snow further stated, "we would need an apology before we let you back on the team." Coach Snow admits to making statements of this nature, although he denies ever directly telling Brian to apologize. If we credit Brian's version, and we must at this stage, there is clearly a disputed issue of fact as to whether Coach Snow asked Brian to apologize to the team captains.

2. The intended scope of this apology

The district court found that, even if Coach Snow used the word "apologize," he was not asking Brian to apologize for reporting the assault. Instead, the court concluded that "[t]he request for an 'apology' was not a demand, or a request, for Brian to say he was wrong for reporting the hazing incident; it was rather a request for a mutual reconciliation among Brian and his teammates to allow the boys to function together as friends and teammates." *Seamons III*, 15 F.Supp.2d at 1157. Brian testified that Coach Snow's statements regarding the apology came in response to a heated discussion between Brian and Dan Ward, wherein Dan insisted that Brian not be allowed to play unless he apologized for reporting the assault. Coach Snow interrupted the exchange and expressed his desire that Brian apologize in order to remain on the team. Coach Snow further stated that the team would need an apology before Brian could return. When these remarks are taken in context, it is reasonable to infer that Coach Snow was telling Brian he could not return to the team unless he apologized for reporting the assault. In any event, that is how Brian interpreted the statement, and a jury could properly do the same. Thus, the intended scope of the apology is also a matter of dispute.

One difficulty presented here is the fact that the scope of the requested apology is dependent in part on Coach Snow's intent in asking for it. The Coach's purpose in making these statements to Brian is not easily ascertained and requires inferences drawn from the Coach's behavior throughout the meeting and the broader controversy. This is precisely why summary judgment is not appropriate at this stage. * * *

3. Whether Brian's failure to apologize was a significant factor in his dismissal from the team

The district court found that Brian had failed to produce facts showing a "legal causal connection between his speech and his ultimate failure to be involved with the football team." *Seamons III*, 15 F.Supp.2d at 1155. We disagree. There are ample facts in the record to indicate that Brian's suspension and dismissal from the football team were directly related to his failure to apologize for reporting the assault.

Brian testified that when Coach Snow told him to "take the weekend and think about it," he understood he was being told not to participate in that night's game. Aplt.App., tab 14 at 337, 350–52. Coach Snow testified that by making this statement he was telling Brian he couldn't participate in that night's game. *Id.* at 402, 405. Presumably, had Brian offered the apology at the captains' meeting he would have been allowed to suit up for the game. He was at school and ready to play on Friday. There was no indication that he didn't want to play or would be prevented from playing in the Logan game. The only thing that happened to alter this situation was the captains' meeting at which Brian was asked, and refused, to apologize. Thus, there is evidence that Brian's refusal to apologize was directly related to the fact that he couldn't play in the Friday game, which was, in effect, a temporary suspension from the team.

A few days later when Brian told Coach Snow he was not going to apologize, he did not think he needed to apologize, and he still wanted to play football, Coach Snow stated that he was "sick of [his] attitude" and took him off the team for good. Aplt.App., tab 15 at 472. It can clearly be inferred that this final confrontation, which resulted in Brian's dismissal from the team, was a product of Brian's refusal to apologize. * * *

In this case, the record indicates that Coach Snow, and only Coach Snow, was vested by the school district with the authority to make final decisions regarding membership on the Sky View football team. Aplt.App., tab 18 at 434, 436, 492. Because of this delegation of authority, the school district can be held liable for Coach Snow's actions on team membership. *See Pembaur*, 475 U.S. at 483, 106 S.Ct. 1292 ("Authority to make municipal policy . . . may be delegated by an official who possesses such authority . . . ") * * *

B. Qualified Immunity

The district court alternatively found that even if the evidence supported a First Amendment claim, defendant officials were entitled to qualified immunity because "Brian has failed to show *any law* sufficiently well established in 1993 to support the proposition" that under the circumstances of the case he is entitled to relief. *Seamons III*, 15 F.Supp.2d at 1159 (emphasis added). "We review the district court's grant of summary judgment based on qualified immunity de novo, applying the same standard used by the district court." *Roberts v. Kling*, 144 F.3d 710, 711 (10th Cir.1998) (per curiam) (citation omitted).

When the case was last before us, we held that Brian's complaint stated a claim that defendants violated clearly established law and that they therefore were not entitled to qualified immunity. *See Seamons II*, 84 F.3d at 1238–39. We went on to note that defendants could reassert their entitlement to qualified immunity at summary judgment, but only if "Brian's allegations in the complaint prove to be unfounded." *Id.* at 1238. The district court's conclusion that the law was not clear in 1993 is inconsistent with our mandate and relevant case law.

* * *

Coach Snow was the person most directly involved with Brian's suspension and dismissal from the football team. It was his responsibility to determine who played on the team and to make disciplinary decisions. He orchestrated the captains' meeting, instructed Brian not to attend the Logan game when Brian refused to apologize, and arguably dismissed Brian from the team when Brian again expressed an unwillingness to apologize. "[A] reasonably competent public official should know the law governing his conduct." *Chapman v. Nichols*, 989 F.2d 393, 397 (10th Cir. 1993) (quotation omitted). A "precise factual correlation between the then-existing law and the case at-hand is not required." *Patrick v. Miller*, 953 F.2d 1240, 1249 (10th Cir. 1992) (quotation omitted). Coach Snow is not entitled to qualified immunity for his actions with respect to Brian's suspension and removal from the Sky View football team.

In the proceedings below, the district court expressed a belief that this case had gone on for too long, spawned an inordinate amount of controversy, and was not significant enough to warrant time in the federal courts. While this sentiment by a busy judge may be understandable, it cannot justify summary disposition in the face of genuine issues of material fact . . . Brian has asked for his day in court. Because he meets the requirements for stating a claim and alleging material facts in dispute, he is entitled to a trial.

Recent Trends

The cases in this section highlight the growing complexities associated with hazing cases. Trends include greater attention to the obligation of administrators to act once they have been informed of a hazing incident and the degree to which school officials are obligated to protect the rights of all students (victims, perpetrators, observers) when they act; coach accountability; gender and hazing; and the connection between hazing and other violence that happens in school, specifically bullying.

School Official and Perpetrator Accountability—Weymouth v. Pentucket

The issue of the accountability of school officials and those associated with hazing incidents will continue to be further established in the courts in the years ahead. In July of 2004, Matthew Weymouth, a former football player from West Newbury High School, filed a $5 million federal civil rights suit alleging that he had been sexually assaulted by three teammates while at a summer training camp in New Hampshire

(Lawrence, 2004). The suit further accuses officials, including the head football coach and the high school principal, at the Pentucket Regional School District of being deliberately indifferent to hazing and failing to protect him.

Hazing, Sex Crimes, and Coach Accountability

In September of 2003, at a camp in the Pocono Mountains of Pennsylvania, Mepham High School varsity football players lured younger players into a cabin under the pretense that they would be subjected to some form of mild initiation. From that day forward until the end of camp, the new members of the team were sodomized, beaten, subjected to painful and humiliating treatment, and required to haze other players (Wencelblat, 2004). According to accounts, by the end of camp, the entire team knew what had happened but they all remained silent (Wayne County Grand Jury, 2004). There is strong evidence to suggest that if not for the fact that two of the victims required medical treatment for their injuries, the incidents would not have been reported. Ultimately, four identified perpetrators were tried as juveniles rather than adult offenders and charged with involuntary deviate sexual intercourse, aggravated assault, and kidnapping (Wencelblat, 2004). Two pled guilty to felony charges and began serving time in a juvenile facility, a third pled guilty to felony charges and received a sentence of probation, and a fourth pled guilty to a misdemeanor charge.

Once notified that hazing had occurred at the camp, Mepham school officials cancelled the 2003 football season; reassigned the head football coach and one of the assistants, who were tenured teachers to another school in the district; and elected not to reappoint them to their coaching positions the next year. The former coaches alleged they were improperly reassigned without explanation and denied due process to discuss the reasons for their reassignment (*McElroy & Canestero v. Bellmore-Merrick School District*, 2004). Although McElroy and Canestero were unsuccessful in their suit, this case illustrates the difficulties faced in balancing the interests and rights of students and teachers/coaches. The behavior of the coaches had been the subject of a Wayne County (PA) Grand Jury, who considered whether their conduct during the camp constituted crimes of endangering the welfare of children and recklessly endangering another person. The Grand Jury determined that by legal definition the coaches had not acted criminally, although there was "clear evidence that the coaches displayed a lack of common sense accountability." Given a history of previous hazing incidents in the program and in light of this finding, school administrators would have risked allegations of deliberate indifference if they had not acted in the manner they did. At the same time, Mr. McElroy has asserted that the burden of responsibility should have fallen on the players who committed the crimes because they were bound by Mepham High School's student code of conduct (Jones, 2003).

Gender and Hazing—The Glenbrook North Hazing Case

Recent studies reveal that hazing occurs among students in grades 6 through college at rates ranging from just over 17 percent to 79 percent (Campo, Poulos, & Sipple, 2005; Crandall, 2003; Gershel, Katz-Sidlow, Small, & Zandieh, 2003; Hoover, 1999; Hoover & Pollard, 2000). Consistent across these studies is a finding that females are more likely to participate exclusively in acceptable forms of hazing, whereas males are more likely to participate exclusively in unacceptable forms of hazing. Despite this apparent polar finding, there is a tremendous gray area where female athletes and students exhibit tendencies to engage in high-risk behaviors with frequencies that are very close to those of their male counterparts. At the high school level, Hoover and Pollard (2000) reported that girls were consistently involved in all forms of hazing at very high levels: humiliating hazing, 39 percent; substance abuse, 18 percent; and dangerous hazing, 17 percent.

Physical hazing coupled with excessive drinking is not exclusively a male preserve, as seen in the widely publicized Glenbrook North High School case, where a dozen girls and three boys were charged with misdemeanor battery charges. Under the guise of a powder puff football game, girls from the junior class were beaten and covered in mud, paint, feces, and garbage. Five of the victims were hospitalized, with one requiring stitches in her head. In total, the school board suspended thirty-one students for taking part in the incident, and several students were expelled (Fuller, 2003).

Hazing and Bullying

Increasingly, school hazing is being discussed in relationship to and in connection with other forms of violent behavior, including bullying. According to Stuart Green of the New Jersey Coalition for Bullying Awareness and Prevention, hazing is a more severe form of bullying where physical injury is more likely to occur (Cunningham, 2006). As momentum builds for more states to adopt antibullying legislation, there may be an increasing number of hazing victims who seek relief under antibullying laws. According to the watchdog group The Bully Police, twenty-one states currently have antibullying legislation ("The Bully Police," 2006). Federal legislation was also proposed by U.S. Representative John Shimkus (R-IL) in January of 2005 to amend the Safe and Drug-Free Schools and Community Act to include bullying and harassment (H.R. 284).

References

Cases

Caldwell v. Griffin Spalding County Board of Education, et al., 22 Ga. App. 892 (1998).
Davis v. Monroe County Board of Education, 526 U.S. 629; 119 S. Ct. 1661; 143 L. Ed.2d 839 (1999).
Duitch v. Canton City Schools, et al., 157 Ohio App. 3d 80; 2004 Ohio 2173; 809 N.E. 2d 62 (2004).
Knoll v. Board of Regents of the University of Nebraska, 601 N.W.2d 757 (1999).
McElroy and Canestro v. Board of Education of the Bellmore-Merrick Central High School District, 5 Misc. 3d 321; 783 N.S.S.2d 781 (2004).
Meeker v. Edmunson, et al., 415 F. 3d 317 (2005).
Nice v. Centennial Area School District, 98 F. Supp.2d 665 (2000).
Perkins & Phillips v. Alamo Heights Independent School District, et al., 204 F. Supp.2d 991 (2002).
Seamons v. Snow, 864 F. Supp. 1111 (D. Utah 1994).
Seamons v. Snow, 206 F.3d 1021 (2000).
Siesto v. Bethpage Union Free School District, QDS: 72701944 (*New York Law Journal*, December 30, 1999).
Snelling & Snelling v. Fall Mountain Regional School District, et al., 2001 DNH 57 (2001).
Strout v. Packard, 76 Me. 148 (1884).
Weymouth v. Pentucket 52, 82. 112.

Publications

Associated Press. (2005, September 12). Freshman made to sit in own vomit, urine. Retrieved from http://www.espn.go.com/
Associated Press. (2005, October 18). Ex-NHL player Mantha suspended in hazing incident. Retrieved from http://www.espn.go.com/
Barron, J. (2006, January 15). Proposed bills target hazing, bullying on campus. *The Casper Star-Tribune*. Retrieved from http://www.casperstartribune.net/
Campo, S., Poulos, G., & Sipple, J. W. (2005). Prevalence and profiling: Hazing among college students and points of intervention. *American Journal of Health Behavior, 29*(2), 37–149.
Crandall (2003).
Crow, B., & Rosner, S. R. (2002, Winter). Institutional and organizational liability for hazing in intercollegiate and professional team sports. *St. John's Law Review*, 76.
Cunningham, J. H. (2006, January 21). Coaches tackle hazing, bullying. Retrieved from http://www.northjersey.com/
Ex-coaches sue over students' behavior. (2004, August 4). *New York Law Journal, 24*, p. 2.
Fuller, J. (2003, May 21). Judge upholds suspension of 2 Glenbrook North seniors. *Chicago Sun-Times*, p. 12.
Gershel, J. C., Katz-Sidlow, R. J., Small, E., & Zandieh, S. (2003). Hazing of suburban middle school and high school athletes. *Society for Adolescent Medicine, 32*(5), 333–335.
Hazing defined. *Stophazing.org: Educating to eliminate hazing*. Online, Internet.
Hazing is no joke. (2002, January 16). *Your School and the Law, 32*. www.stophazing.org. (accessed January 17, 2002).
Hoover, N. O. (principal investigator). (1999, August 30). National survey: Initiation rites and athletes for NCAA sports teams. Alfred University. Retrieved from www.alfred.edu/news/html/hazing_study.html
Hoover, N. O., & Pollard, N. J. Initiation rites in American high schools: A national survey. Alfred University (2000). Retrieved from www.alfred.edu/news/html/hazing_study.html

Jones, L. (2003, October 14). Hazing in schools: Allegations highlight the challenge of ensuring safety. *New York Law Journal*, p. 16.

Laurie, M. (2006, January 19). Hazing or harmless fun? *The Daily Helmsman*. Retrieved from http:// www.dailyhelmsman.com/

Lawrence, J. M. (2004, July 28). Ex-football player sues school over sex hazing. *The Boston Herald*, p. 13.

Marching band members wins $1.8 M in hazing suit. (2004, November 14). *National Law Journal*, 26(58), 10.

Phillips, K. (2005). High school wrestler accused of playing sexual prank on teammates. *Chicago Sun Times*, p. 20.

Report of the Wayne County Investigative Grand Jury pursuant to 42 Pa. C.S. Section 4552 Investigation #4. No. 26-2003-Criminal Misc. (2004, February 24). Published by *Newsday* on March 10, 2004. Retrieved from http:// www.newsday.com/

Rothstein, K. (2004, February 6). Holy Cross suspends rugby team 5 years for hazing. *The Boston Herald*, p. 15.

Sussberg (2003).

The Bully Police: A watch-dog organization—Advocating for bullied children. (2006). Retrieved from http:// bullypolice.org/national_law.html

Vock, D. (2003, May 20). Lawmakers try again on social host liability measures. *Chicago Daily Law Bulletin*, p. 1.

Legislation

Florida State Code 240.1325

H. R. 284: To Amend The Safe and Drug-Free Schools and Communities Act to Include Bully and Harassment, 109th Congress.

Minnesota State Code 127.465

Ohio Revised Code 2903.31

New York State Code 120.16

Note: These and other state hazing laws may be found at www.stophazing.org

Other Reading

Ball, J. (2004). This will go down on your permanent record (but we'll never tell): How the Federal Education Rights and Privacy Act may help colleges and universities keep hazing a secret. *Southwestern University Law Review*, 477–511.

Edelman, M. (2004, Fall). Addressing the high school hazing problem: Why lawmakers need to impose a duty to act on school personnel. *Pace Law Review*, 15–50.

Wencelblat, P. (2004, Fall). Boys will be boys? An analysis of male-on-male heterosexual sexual violence. *Columbia Journal of Law and Social Problems*, 38–69.

5.00

Risk Management

Many recreation and sport managers erroneously look on risk management as safety or accident prevention. *Risk management* is much more than just safety or preventing accidents—it is an organized plan by which a recreation or sport business can manage or control both the programmatic risks and the financial risks facing the organization. Risk management involves not only *what to do* to control risks, but also involves *why to do it*—thus a sound risk management program is based on the fundamental legal concepts discussed in Sections 2.10, *Negligence Theory*; 2.20, *Defenses*; 2.30, *Recreation and Sport Management Applications*; and 3.00, *Property and Environmental Law*.

Section 5.00 is divided into two major parts. They are Section 5.10, *Risk Management Theory* and 5.20, *Recreation and Sport Management Applications*. *Risk Management Theory* discusses the fundamental concepts comprising risk management. In this edition, the chapter on risk identification and reduction has been blended into the *Risk Management Process* chapter.

In Section 5.20, *Recreation and Sport Management Applications*, several crucial aspects of risk management are addressed. The recreation or sport manager is introduced to the role and importance of standards of practice in the risk management program and to the function of various audits in risk management. Two major problems that must be faced by the recreation or sport manager—crisis management and crowd management—are addressed in newly revised chapters. Finally, *Managing Risk Through Insurance* examines a crucial tool for transferring risks, and *Workers' Compensation* looks at the statute-mandated form of insurance required of recreation and sport businesses.

5.11 Risk Management Process

Robin Ammon, Jr.
Slippery Rock University

Matthew T. Brown
University of South Carolina

Estimates have described sport as one of the ten largest industries in the United States, encompassing over $190 billion (King, 2002). Sport is not just a national phenomenon. When considered on an international basis, sport has reached epic proportions. Recreation constitutes what might be called a growth industry as well. In addition to the parks and recreation field, which is immense, there is the growth in the fitness industry, in traditional participant sports, in adventure sports, in extreme sports, and much more. This surge of recreation and sport activity has created a tremendous potential for injuries and financial losses.

Concern regarding the systematic management of risk in recreation and sport did not begin until the early 1970s. Even though the concept of risk management had been extensively used by private business for some time, the recreation and sport industries' interest in managing risks only came after sovereign governmental immunity began to erode and litigation related to sport and recreation began to rise (van der Smissen, 1990). The focus of risk management in the business industry was financial. When risk management concepts were first applied to the recreation and sport industries, a much broader focus was needed. Sharp (1990) indicated that although financial concerns were important in these industries, the paramount concern was the safety and well-being of both spectators and participants. Therefore, recreation and sport managers must be aware of the potential for injury and loss and must learn to effectively manage the immense risk that exists in their professions. The process of managing and controlling these risks has, over the last two or three decades, resulted in the field of risk management. The purpose of this chapter is to introduce the recreation or sport manager to the basics of the risk management process.

Fundamental Concepts

Risk management has been defined as controlling the financial and personal injury losses from sudden, unforeseen, unusual accidents and intentional torts (Ammon, 1993). van der Smissen (1990) indicated that risk management is the process by which businesses use operational policies and practices to reduce their exposure to risk. Wong and Masteralexis (1998) termed it as "a management strategy to maintain greater control over the legal uncertainty that may wreak havoc on a sport business" (p. 90). In 2002, Corbett described risk management as "managing financial and human resources wisely, governing effectively, making decisions soundly and projecting a positive image towards sponsors, government funders and the community" (¶. 4).

The "loss" resulting from the risk can be physical or financial in nature. For example, risk managers must continually attempt to reduce the risks that injure patrons, thus decreasing the potential for lawsuits. In addition, financial losses may occur due to incidents such as vandalism, poorly written contracts, stolen equipment, and accidents in the facility's parking lot due to poor lighting. Risk management, however, doesn't seek to eliminate *all* risks, but rather creates an environment where the inherent and negligence risks within activities and services provided by an organization are minimized without producing a change in the activity itself.

Function of Risk Management

Recreation and sport managers have been exposed to a new society during the past twenty years—a society that has become enchanted with litigation and a trend to which many professionals in the recreation and sport environment have fallen victim. Society will not tolerate inappropriate behavior or unsafe conditions, and recreation and sport managers must develop an awareness of the hazards for which they will be held accountable. An effective risk management plan will help to control and diminish the risks that confront today's recreation or sport managers.

In recreation and sport, risk management has been used to combine the traditional corporate interest of limiting financial risk with the interest of the recreation or sport industry—providing for increased patron safety. By reducing the injuries to the participants or guests, the business at the same time reduces its financial exposure. When a good risk management plan is implemented, the potential for litigation diminishes. In *Hayden v. Notre Dame* (1999), the net used by Notre Dame in the end zone at football games was not large enough to catch all kicked balls, and no security staff members or student managers were stationed in the crowd to retrieve the balls. If the university had implemented a risk management plan, the court might have ruled that Notre Dame made a reasonable effort to prevent injury from occurring.

The death of thirteen-year-old Brittanie Cecil is a more recent illustration of unfortunate risk. Attending her first hockey game, Cecil was hit in the left temple by a deflected puck at Nationwide Arena in Columbus, Ohio. The force of the puck caused her head to snap backward, tearing her right vertebral artery, which induced a fatal blood clot. In the eighty-five-year history of the National Hockey League (NHL), this was the first spectator death (Steinbach, 2003). In response to this incident, the NHL ordered all its venues to install protective netting prior to the start of the 2002–2003 season. The protective netting was to be a minimum of 118 feet, stretching from the area where the side boards become rounded (the radius point), behind the back of the goal, to the opposite radius point. The net had to be high enough to cover seating in an arena's lower bowl, starting six inches below the top edge of the glass and stretching upward between 20 and 100 feet, depending on arena seating configuration. Further, the NHL mandated that the glass on top of the side boards be a minimum of five feet in height. Glass at the end of the rink was to remain at eight feet in height. (Steinbach, 2003)

Beyond examining risks associated with a specific activity or event, recreation and sport managers must also examine risks related to public liability, excluding negligence, and risks related to their business operations (van der Smissen, 1990). Of increasing concern are financial risks associated with violations of employee rights. Recreation and sport managers now must closely monitor their organization's recruitment, selection, retention, and termination practices (Peterson & Hronek, 1997). van der Smissen (1990) added that recreation and sport managers must also be concerned with risk exposure related to the real and personal property owned by the organization. A comprehensive risk management plan should address all these issues.

The D.I.M. Process

The **D.I.M. process** was developed as a tool to establish an effective risk management program. When used as an anticipatory technique rather than as a reactionary procedure, the D.I.M. process will assist organizations in decreasing the chance of litigation. This simple process involves three basic components: (1) *Developing* the risk management plan, (2) *Implementing* the risk management plan, and (3) *Managing* the risk management plan. Every organization, no matter the size, should have a current risk management plan. Each plan, however, should be specifically developed for that provider. In other words, one organization's plan should not be applied to another (Kaiser & Robinson, 1999). The components used in creating this plan will be similar no matter what type of organization. Thus, managers at golf courses, aquatic centers, ski areas, skateboard parks, or park and recreation departments will utilize the same basic principles.

Developing the Risk Management Plan

Developing a risk management plan consists of three separate stages: (1) identifying the risks, (2) classifying the risks, and (3) selecting methods of treatment for the risks.

Identification Stage

The **identification stage** is one of the key aspects of developing a successful risk management program. If the recreation or sport manager wants to control risks in the program, he or she must first identify those risks. Risks are present in all sport and entertainment facilities and events including privately or municipally owned buildings, professional or intercollegiate entertainment facilities, and outdoor or indoor recreational settings. Each event or activity is different and has its own unique risks or areas of potential loss. Identifying these risks, therefore, needs to be constant and ongoing.

An effective step to identify risk is to create categories of risk and then to list risks within each category. Several approaches can be used to **categorize risk**. Kaiser and Robinson (1999) and van der Smissen (1990) have developed two different approaches.

Kaiser and Robinson (1999) presented an approach in which they listed **five classes of loss**. They are (1) property losses (e.g., natural causes and human causes); (2) financial business losses (e.g., theft, employee injuries, business interruption); (3) contractual losses (e.g., breach of contract); (4) tort liability losses (e.g., negligence, intentional torts, product defects, nuisance claims); and (5) human rights losses (e.g., sexual harassment, employment discrimination, participant discrimination, and physical/sexual abuse). They listed **five types of hazards** common to park and recreation organizations: (1) environmental (e.g., surfaces, holes, weather, water); (2) infrastructure (e.g., structures, areas, roads); (3) programmatic (e.g., failure to: adequately supervise, enforce rules, train personnel, adequately instruct, ascertain participant fitness, or warn); (4) lack of emergency care (e.g., failure to: provide prompt aid, have trained personnel, equip those giving aid, transport appropriately); and (5) transportation hazards (e.g., failure to: use appropriate type vehicle, maintain vehicle, have qualified driver, train and supervise driver, have policy regarding participant drivers).

van der Smissen (1990) has categorized risks as (1) public liability caused by negligence in program services, (2) public liability [excluding negligence], (3) business operations, and (4) property exposures. Figure 1 in Chapter 5.25, *Managing Risk Through Insurance*, was developed using this categorization method. By studying the table, one can see the typical risks included in each category.

Often recreation and sport managers focus on bodily injuries resulting from **public liability caused by negligence.** Injuries may include death, quadriplegia or other paralysis, brain damage, loss of limbs, loss of senses, injury to internal organs, strains, sprains, fractures, ligament damage, cuts, punctures, and abrasions. This type of risk typically relates to the activities or services offered by an organization and often occur when a member of the organization is negligent in performing his or her duties. However, if risk identification is limited to only those bodily injuries that may occur in the services an organization provides, many financial risks to an organization will be overlooked.

Risks grouped under **public liability (excluding negligence)** include such areas as malpractice by personnel, product liability, intentional torts, employment practices, sexual harassment, and civil liberty violations. Recreation and sport managers should note that the management of risk relating to employment law issues is becoming a great concern to many in the recreation and sport industries (Curtis, 2002). A recent study indicated that human resource management was one of the main topics of study that current sport administrators felt should be taught to students earning a master's degree in sports administration (Kreutzer & Brown, 2000). Miller (1998) stated that although 55 percent of sport-related cases in 1995 were negligence cases, 11 percent were employment law cases. These cases involved sexual harassment, discrimination, equal pay disputes, and wrongful termination claims. Curtis (2002) added that the number of discrimination lawsuits in sport and recreation is increasing rapidly. Combining this information with the fact that the number of sexual harassment lawsuits is on the rise in the United States (Equal Employment Opportunity Commission, n.d.), recreation and sport managers need to pay particular attention to the identification of risk in the management of human resources while devising strategies to control this risk.

Property exposures are financial risks related to the ownership of real and personal property. Loss may occur as a result of fire, natural elements like lightning and floods, vandalism, and theft.

Recreation and sport managers can also be exposed to risks via their organization's **business operations**. These risks are financial risks that result from business interruption, embezzlement and theft, the medical condition of employees, the health of key personnel, and employee accidents and injuries. To identify risks associated with business operations, the recreation or sport manager should examine the organization's operational **policies and procedures** to determine if the policies and procedures expose the organization to loss. Also, the manager can **observe** his or her employees at work to identify any activities that may lead to sickness, accidents, or disability.

The methods used to look for potential risks will vary according to the nature of your organization and the extent of your organization's operation. Every organization, though, must establish a systematic procedure to ensure that a complete risk assessment occurs (van der Smissen, 1990). Tools that can be used to identify risks include **questionnaires** and **discussions with employees** relating to employment practices. Recreation and sport managers must interact with their employees to determine if current employment practices may lead to loss. Also, it is helpful to **read the literature** published by professional organizations (e.g., the United States Professional Tennis Association) to learn about risks relating to employment practices of which the manager might not be aware. Finally, the recreation and sport manager can **consult with colleagues** to determine if he or she has overlooked a potential risk in this area. Recreation and sport managers should rely on the help of various **professionals** in identifying potential risks related to property exposures. For example, an insurance agent should be contacted to ensure that the organization will have adequate protection if the property is damaged due to fire or flood. Many agents, based on their experience with previous claims and injury reports, can also help in identifying various risks. For all risks, regular contact with employees and inspections of operations can enhance the previously mentioned methods of risk identification.

Classification Stage

Once the potential risks have been identified the second stage in developing the plan is to **classify the risk**. The purpose of the classification stage is to determine how often (**frequency**) the risk may occur and the degree (**severity**) of the potential loss arising from the risk. Once the various risks have been identified, the risk manager takes each of the identified risks and evaluates them in terms of frequency and severity. The *frequency* of the risk is dependent on the number of times the risk or loss is likely to occur. The risk manager will view each identified risk and assign a frequency of "high," "medium," or "low." The *severity* of the risk is determined by the intensity of the potential injury and/or the degree of the threat to the financial stability of the organization. It is classified as "catastrophic," "critical," "moderate," or "low." The level of severity and the frequency are determined by the risk manager, based on his/her expertise derived from experience and training. It is important to remember that financial loss as well as personal injury losses need to be considered in classifying risks (Kaiser & Robinson, 1999).

A matrix can be created that allows a consistent approach to the classification process. A matrix gives the risk manager a method by which to classify all identified risks on the basis of frequency and extent of potential loss. Table 1 is such a matrix with some of the risks from a municipal basketball tournament placed into their proper categories. *All identified risks should be appropriately placed in the matrix, making clear the classification of each risk.* By placing the identified risks in the matrix, the risk manager will have successfully completed the classification stage. However, it should be noted that risk assessment is an ongoing process, always subject to change.

Treatment of Risk

The final stage in developing the risk management plan is to determine a **treatment** for each identified and classified risk. A treatment is a method used to reduce, control, manage, or eliminate financial risks and bodily injuries. Four basic treatments are available to the risk manager. They are avoidance of the risk, transfer of the risk to another party, retention of the risk by the recreation or sport organization, and reduction of the risk through efforts to reduce the various types of hazards.

The type of treatment a risk manager uses for the identified and classified risks depends on the nature of the risk and the likelihood of the risk occurring. Although it is sometimes difficult to determine the appropriate treatment, a risk matrix can assist in this identification process. This risk treatment matrix gives the recreation and sport manager guidance regarding the treatment needed for any given risk. The manager, having identified and categorized each risk in Table 1, should then refer to Table 2 for the appropriate

table ❶ Risk Category Matrix

	Severity of Injury or Financial Impact			
	Catastrophic Loss	**Critical Loss**	**Moderate Loss**	**Low Loss**
High Frequency	None	None	• Fan suffers hip injury when she trips in poorly lighted area in or about premises • Player injures knee due to uneven playing surface or wet spot on court	• Spectators evade admission fee • Spectator in bleachers suffers gouge from protruding screw
Medium Frequency	None	None	• Vandalism of arena • Player twists ankle on piece of ice thrown from the bleachers	• Incorrect change given to spectators • Fans suffer nausea from poorly prepared food at concession stands
Low Frequency	• Player breaks neck running into unpadded wall • Armed terrorist group takes hostages during tournament	• Spectator suffers facial laceration during altercation in bleachers • Poor crowd management leads to fight between players and fans	• Youth sustains eye injury during on-the-court promotion • Spectator suffers concussion from player diving into crowd after loose ball due to inade-quate buffer zone	• Program seller gives away programs • Players' wallets are stolen from the locker room

treatment. *Note: Although the contents of Table 1 vary from activity to activity, the contents of Table 2, once established by the philosophy and the finances of the organization, remain the same for all activities.*

Avoidance. Avoidance means that these activities should not be included within the content of a program or they should be discontinued if they are presently being offered. Risks should be avoided when they could cause a catastrophic or critical loss with medium or high frequency. In other words, the severity of the incident would be great, and risk management could not control the frequency. Ideally, a risk manager should identify these risks before the accidents occur and avoid them completely. For example, if a high-risk activity (such as "killer ball") has the reputation for causing moderate to severe injuries, the school or recreation program may wish to avoid scheduling the activity if the risks cannot be controlled (*Azzano v. Catholic Bishop of Chicago*, 1999). Decreasing or eliminating the number of activities that recreation and sport organizations offer is not an attractive option. Therefore, avoidance should not be the first choice for a risk manager. It should only be implemented as a last resort when risk is substantial and likelihood of injury is significant. For example, 40 years ago, the use of trampolines was a standard fixture in most physical education programs. Due to the large number (frequency) of students who were injured while jumping on the trampolines as well as the severity of the injuries, the use of trampolines in almost every school district in the United Sates has been eliminated.

Transfer. Transfer is the shifting of the liability or responsibility for loss from the service provider to another party. This type of risk treatment occurs when two conditions exist: (1) the risk of loss is not so substantial as to warrant the avoidance of the activity, and (2) the risk is greater than the organization can assume on its own.

table ◇2◇ Risk Treatment Matrix

	Severity of Injury or Financial Impact			
	Catastrophic Loss	**Critical Loss**	**Moderate Loss**	**Low Loss**
High Frequency	Avoidance	Avoidance	Transfer & Reduction	Transfer/Retain & Reduction
Medium Frequency	Transfer/Avoidance & Reduction	Transfer/Avoidance & Reduction	Transfer & Reduction	Retain & Reduction
Low Frequency	Transfer & Reduction	Transfer & Reduction	Transfer/Retain & Reduction	Retain & Reduction

An important means of transfer is through the purchase of appropriate **insurance** coverage [1] (see also Chapter 5.25, *Managing Risk Through Insurance*, and Chapter 5.26, *Workers' Compensation*). There are many types of insurance policies in existence, and not all apply to the needs of every organization. Property insurance and personal injury liability insurance are often selected to provide protection from potential risks. It is important to understand that the insurance company will only cover the policyholder up to the limits of the coverage. For example, if a defendant has a $1 million liability policy and loses a $3 million judgment, the insurance company will *only* cover the first $1 million (Kaiser & Robinson, 1999).

Another important means of transfer is by **contract**. Examples of these contracts include liability waivers, indemnification clauses, and the use of independent contractors. A **waiver** is a contract by which a person voluntarily gives up the right to sue another party (e.g., the service provider) for its negligence. The signer of the waiver (normally the participant) agrees to accept the risks of harm caused by the negligent actions of the other party. Well-written waivers can protect against ordinary negligence in at least forty-six states (Cotten, 2000). However, a waiver generally does not protect a service provider from liability for gross negligence or reckless misconduct. Also, in most states a waiver signed by, or on behalf of, a minor is unenforceable (see also Chapter 2.23, *Waivers and Releases*).

Indemnification clauses are clauses in a contract that provide for one party to indemnify or reimburse the other for loss. Such clauses are generally included in equipment and facility rental contracts. For instance, an organization leasing a facility generally agrees contractually to indemnify the facility owners against any loss or litigation resulting from the event. These clauses, sometimes called **hold harmless agreements**, require the organization to be compensated by the individuals renting the facility if any damage occurs during the event or if someone is injured and files suit against the facility owner. Thus the risks during the event are *transferred* to the outside organization (see also Chapter 2.12, *Which Parties Are Liable?* and Chapter 2.21, *Defenses Against Negligence*).

An **independent contractor** is a person or business that contracts to perform a specific task for a service provider. Independent contractors provide expertise and are generally free to perform tasks as they see fit. The independent contractor is not an ordinary employee of the organization. Some personnel (e.g., team doctors, referees, personal trainers, and aerobic instructors) may function as independent contractors. These individuals are personally responsible for their unemployment and liability insurance and are generally solely responsible for their negligent actions. Many organizations use independent companies to provide adven-

[1] To reduce expenses, insurance companies often find that it is less expensive to settle lawsuits than litigate the claims. Settlements are often made in cases where the insurance company would have won in court. Many insurance companies have adopted this philosophy, even when they are not liable, because settling is more economical (Kaiser & Robinson, 1999). This strategy may actually backfire by increasing the number of lawsuits because plaintiffs feel that, even with a weak case, they can settle for a substantial sum. As insurance companies gain the reputation of paying off claims, the number of suits will continue to grow. An additional problem that occurs when settling lawsuits involves individual employees defended by the organization. If the insurance company settles the claim, the employee has no opportunity to prove his or her innocence. This stigma can be quite traumatic and remain with the employee for many years.

ture activities (such as white-water rafting, scuba, ropes courses, and rock climbing). In this manner, the organization does not assume liability for the higher risk activity (Kaiser & Robinson, 1999). However, there are exceptions to the rule. One such exclusion is known as the "inherently dangerous activity" exception illustrated in *Hatch v. V.P. Fair Foundation and Northstar Entertainment* (1999). Plaintiff was injured at a multiday fair organized by V. P. Fair Foundation, after the organizer had hired an independent contractor to provide a bungee jumping experience. The contractor violated several of its own safety policies including: number of staff present, age of the controller, and failure to conduct a daily safety inspection. The contractor failed to attach the bungee cord to the crane, resulting in a 170-foot fall and serious injuries to the back, legs, and shoulders of the plaintiff. A jury found that both the fair organization and the contractor were liable and awarded the plaintiff $5 million (see Chapter 2.12, *Which Parties Are Liable?* and Chapter 2.21, *Defenses Against Negligence*).

A combination of these methods of transfer is usually preferable. For example, if the service provider wishes to offer bungee jumping and realizes that the risk involved is too great for the organization, the provider may seek to transfer the risk. In this situation, the risk manager would pay an insurance company a premium to cover any physical or financial damages that may occur (Ammon et al., 2003). In addition, the manager can require that participants sign a liability waiver by which the participant releases the provider from liability for negligence. In doing so the provider has endeavored to transfer the risk to the insurance company and the participant. If the risk is substantial, as in bungee jumping, and cannot be adequately transferred, the activity should be avoided.

Retention. A third treatment of risks, **retention**, means that the organization keeps the risk and assumes financial responsibility for certain injuries or financial losses that may occur. Retention is often preferred for minor or insignificant risks. Retaining these risks is often less expensive than buying insurance to cover them.

Sometimes retention is termed **self-insurance**. In essence, the sport or recreation organization is simply paying a premium to itself. But this is not as easy as it sounds. If utilized, the organization must include retention as a line item in the budget and accumulate a reserve or "pool" of revenue to pay for such injuries (Ammon, Southall, & Blair, 2003). This strategy requires a strong commitment from the organization's upper management not to use the *unspoken-for* capital for other purposes (Kaiser & Robinson, 1999).

Looking at the risk treatment matrix (Table 2), the risks to be retained are those that have a low potential for loss and occur with low to medium frequency. An organization can accept these risks due to the fact that there is very little chance of incurring substantial financial losses. This, of course, is assuming that once the risk manager decides to keep the risk, proper precautions are taken to decrease the occurrence and/or monetary losses associated with the risk.

Reduction. The fourth treatment, and arguably the most important, is the reduction of risks. Risk reduction is a proactive approach to the management of risks. Reduction is designed to reduce the chance loss will occur or reduce the severity of loss if it does occur (Kaiser & Robinson, 1999). The reduction section of the risk management plan establishes operational practices for reducing the likelihood of loss related to the identified risk. All risks cannot be eliminated from an activity, but often the frequency and severity can be minimized by the proper maintenance of property and equipment, establishing emergency procedures, providing better training for personnel, and other risk-reduction techniques. This should be the focus of any risk management program. For example, when efforts are made to reduce the frequency and severity of losses in a Little League baseball program, there is less likelihood that losses will occur over a planned retention level. Requiring batting helmets while on the field, screens in front of dugouts, detachable bases and instruction on how to slide are all specific risk-reduction techniques.

The primary objective of reduction is to be aware of loss potential (from the identification of risk) and to do something to reduce that loss potential. The recreation or sport manager can use four major tools to reduce risk. The first is to **design a regular systematic inspection program**. A system of inspection must be established, a written record of that inspection must be kept, and a system of follow-up on hazards must be implemented. Inspection of facilities and equipment is a key to reducing loss. An organization is liable for the dangerous maintenance situations about which it knows and for those that it should have known if a proper professional job had been done on inspection (*Kubiak v. Wal-Mart Stores*, 1999).

Planned inspection should include machines that have critical parts and maintenance items like chlorine storage for a swimming pool. Persons knowledgeable about the items they are inspecting must complete these inspections. Also, this type of inspection helps locate newly created risks caused by vandalism, abuse or misuse, and theft. If a hazard is found during inspection, a system for addressing the hazard must be implemented. The system should include the following steps: (1) the hazard must be reported to maintenance personnel; (2) the individual overseeing the area where the hazard is located must be notified; (3) the equipment or area must be taken out of service until the repair is made; (4) once the identified hazard is eliminated, maintenance personnel must inform the manager; and (5) there should be established steps to follow in the event the repair has not been made in a reasonable period of time. (See also Chapter 3.20, *Premises Liability*, and Chapter 5.22, *Audits in Risk Management.*)

The second major tool involves **establishing a maintenance program for facilities and equipment**. Almost all park-related personal injury cases are maintenance oriented (Peterson & Hronek, 1997). The maintenance program must be described in an organization's risk management plan and include both preventative and remedial maintenance that occurs on a regular basis.

A third tool involves **training the staff**. Staff should be trained to identify normal wear and tear and general deterioration of equipment, facilities, and other athletic areas that may lead to loss. Employees also need to understand how to conduct activities so that proper care is afforded program participants. The recreation or sport manager should see that his or her staff knows how to make sure participants have the proper skill level and conditioning for activities, understands proper supervision, and understands how to enact the organization's emergency procedures (see also Chapter 2.32, *Conduction and Supervision of Activities*). For most situations, it is important that the staff know certain information about the participant that relates to the individual's ability to participate in the activity safely (van der Smissen, 1990). For example, in a swimming program, the skill level and developmental stage of participants must be known to place them in the proper class. An organization must determine what skill and conditioning level is required for participation in the program for each activity or service.

Finally, the fourth tool recreation and sport managers must use is **a system under which documents related to program participation may be filed.** They also must be able to retrieve these documents when necessary. Forms that should be filed include parental permission forms, agreements to participate, waivers, membership applications, contracts, inspection checklists, accident report forms, health records, records containing operations information, rules and regulations, copies of employee credentials, and any other program-related documents. With the growing threat of litigation, the need to document and to preserve documentation takes on added importance. In a 1995 case (*Nuckley v. Gail M. Woods, Inc.*) a plaintiff was lifting on a "preacher type" curl machine when the chain broke, causing injury. The court ruled for the defendant when the owner of the club was able to provide documentation that the machine had been cleaned the day of the accident and the chain and bolts had been inspected the day before the accident. On the other hand, the court ruled against the defendant in a 1998 health club case (*Leon v. Family Fitness Centers, Inc.*) when it deemed that the waiver used was not worded so as to encompass the risk of injury from simply reclining on a sauna bench. This case demonstrates the need for risk managers to examine their waivers to ensure that documents include the specific language necessary to protect the organization.

When a risk manager develops a risk management plan, the most efficient and effective way to decrease the occurrence of various risks is to use reduction techniques such as the preceding. When a risk manager decides to retain or transfer the risks, he or she must be ready to also incorporate these reduction techniques to ensure that each situation is handled in a manner that will reduce the chance of liability. *A crucial concept to remember is that risk reduction should be a risk management treatment any time an activity is offered— in conjunction with transfer or retention.* If the risks are not managed with the use of reduction techniques, more claims will occur, and greater costs will be incurred. This will create a drain on funds allotted for retained risks and will eventually cause the insurer to raise the organization's premiums to cover the risks in question. By utilizing reduction techniques to reduce the occurrence of risks, the service provider should be able to keep insurance premiums and budgeted expenses at a minimum. In fact, by managing the risks, it is probable that the number of claims will decrease, which may cause the insurance rates to diminish as well (Ammon et al., 2003).

Implementing the Risk Management Plan

The second component in the D.I.M. process consists of implementing the risk management plan. For this, **effective communication** is a key factor. Effective communication is more than telling personnel what to do. It is listening as well. When management is seen to encourage suggestions and consider and act on employee concerns, the employees are more likely to bring their perspectives to management. It is of primary importance to *involve all employees in the risk management process.*

Each individual in an organization must understand the overall risk management plan and risk-reduction strategies and know what his or her role is in implementing the plan. Therefore, it can be said that the effectiveness of the overall plan is in direct proportion to the effectiveness of the communication regarding the plan. If communication about the plan is nonexistent, incomplete, or inadequate, the program will become inoperable, and the risks will not be reduced as they should be. Direct interpersonal communication is required to insure the plan functions properly.

A risk manager can supplement oral communication with printed guidelines outlining risk-reduction techniques. These guidelines can be inserted in the employee manual during the first orientation. Examples of the items covered in the guidelines include the organizational layout and operation, personnel and organizational management, rules and regulations of the business, responsibilities of various employees, correct methods of documenting records and reports, and emergency procedures. The manual is sometimes erroneously termed a "safety manual," but it is really the operating procedures for carrying out the risk management plan (Kaiser & Robinson, 1999).

Some organizations make the mistake of placing the entire risk management plan into every employee manual. The sheer comprehensiveness of the plan will cause many new hires to avoid reading the manual. Only place the pertinent portions of the overall plan into the specific employee's manual. Employee dedication to the process is a key component for a successful risk management plan. It must be clear to each employee that the practices and recommendations mentioned in the manual not only provide a safe environment for the program's participants, but will also protect the employee (Kaiser & Robinson, 1999).

The use of a **sound training program** is another way to ensure communication and the implementation of the risk management plan. An in-service education program can be used to communicate the responsibilities of the staff in relation to the plan and provide an opportunity for individuals to improve their ability to identify various types of risks so that they can fulfill the requirements of the plan more effectively. In-service educational opportunities allow the risk manager to explain the risk management plan to the organization's employees while stressing the importance of implementing the reduction strategies set forth in it. For risk reduction to be effective, three in-service areas need to be addressed on a regular basis: (1) communication of responsibilities—what is each individual's role in implementing the plan; (2) development of professional judgment and decision making—what standard of care is required of each employee; and (3) credential education/training—the provision of expertise or an increased knowledge base that will lead to an increased ability to make sound judgments (van der Smissen, 1990; see also Chapter 2.35, *Human Resources Law*). The risk manager must verify that personnel are qualified for their positions and hold the necessary certifications.

Managing the Plan

The final component of the D.I.M. process is to **manage the plan**. The first step in managing the plan is to **designate a risk manager** and the selection of a risk management committee. Sport and recreation organizations may hire a risk manager or assign one person the role of risk manager as part of his or her other duties. Effective risk managers and risk management committee members share many of the same traits. The risk manager must be a highly motivated individual, must be committed to risk management, and must be able to motivate others to believe in the risk management plan. Whichever system is chosen, the responsible party should monitor the risk management plan, implement changes, assist in fostering a genuine risk management attitude among other employees, conduct inspections, review accidents, and supervise in-service training (van der Smissen, 1990).

The second step in managing the plan is to provide the risk manager and committee with the **authority to lead.** This authority should be described in the policy statement of the organization because it provides a foundation for the plan. The policy statement should clearly delineate the responsibilities of the risk manager. The statement should outline and define the authority of the person responsible for administering the plan.

The management staff and ownership of the organization must also endorse and support the idea of risk management. They must be willing to assist the risk manager or risk management committee with verbal and financial support. The necessary capital to implement the plan along with the resources to purchase insurance policies and to pay the damage claims retained by the organization must be included in the annual budget (Kaiser & Robinson, 1999). Without upper management's support, a risk management plan will not succeed. The risk manager and the risk management committee must be given the freedom to act independently, but within the philosophy of the sport or recreation organization (Ammon et al., 2003).

Just as employee input is vital for the initial risk management policy, the third step in managing the plan is to **provide employees with the opportunity for continual input** into the risk management plan. Including employees on the risk management committee is a possible source for this input. The continual success of a risk management plan mandates that employees, supervisors, and managers on all levels have the ability to interact with each other. Additionally, anyone else whose expertise may improve the quality of the risk management plan should be included in the overall risk management process. The size of the committee depends on the overall goals and size of the organization.

As previously mentioned, risks are constantly changing and shifting due to the activities and programs employed by various organizations. Therefore, risk management plans must also evolve and fluctuate; they are never static. Once a plan is put into place, it should be assessed on an annual basis and sometimes more frequently, depending on the type of risks (Kaiser & Robinson, 1999).

Risk management is a necessity for sport and recreation managers today. Even though many risks can be identified, classified, and treated, some hazards will still exist and accidents will occur. It is impossible and unrealistic to expect a risk manager to eliminate all injuries and financial losses. However, by developing an extensive risk management plan, implementing the plan, and bestowing the authority to manage the plan on a concerned risk manager, recreation and sport managers can diminish a number of dangerous risks.

Significant Case

The Clahassey v. C Ami Inc. case clearly illustrates the value of a sound risk management plan. The defendant obviously held the event in a hazardous location, did not use an adequate number of spotters, and failed to warn of the risks. The case also illustrates the importance of training personnel who will complete incident reports to include essential information and omit potentially harmful editorial comments.

CLAHASSEY V. C AMI INC.

2002 Mich. App. LEXIS 1352
September 24, 2002, Decided

In this negligence action, defendant C Ami Inc. (Traffic Jam Lounge) appeals as of right from a judgment entered in favor of plaintiff following a jury trial in the amount of $77,950.50, including $59,321.50 in attorney fees that defendant was ordered to pay as case evaluation sanctions. We affirm.

This case arises from injuries suffered by plaintiff while participating in a mock sumo wrestling match held at defendant's lounge. The match entailed dressing up in a padded outfit intended to duplicate the exaggerated shape of a sumo wrestler. The outfits apparently impaired the contestants' mobility and prevented them from being able to put their arms out in front of them if they fell forward. The contestants would attempt to push their competitors down and pin them. During the match, plaintiff fell into a bar stool located near the perimeter of the ring, sustaining injuries to her face and mouth.

* * *

Defendant moved for summary disposition under MCR 2.116(C) (8) and (10), arguing that no duty is owed to someone who voluntarily participates in a competition with knowledge of the risks inherent in the activity, and that the risks of the competition at issue here were open and obvious to plaintiff. The trial court denied defendant's motion, concluding that a question of fact regarding whether the risks of the competition were open and obvious existed. We find no error in this decision.

* * *

Generally, a premises owner has a duty to exercise reasonable care to protect his invitees from unreasonable risks of harm posed by dangerous conditions of the land that the possessor knows or should know will not be discovered by invitees. *Bertrand v. Alan Ford, Inc*, 449 Mich. 606, 609; 537 N.W.2d 185 (1995). However, this duty is not absolute and does not extend to conditions which are so open and obvious that an invitee could be expected to discover them herself. Nonetheless, if the risk of harm from a dangerous condition remains unreasonable despite the fact that it is open and obvious, or that the invitee has knowledge of it, the premises owner must still take reasonable care to protect the invitee from that risk.

Here, defendant asserts that no genuine issue of material fact exists that the dangers associated with the sumo event were open and obvious and, therefore, defendant owed no duty to plaintiff. In making this argument below, defendant argued that plaintiff's deposition testimony confirmed that she knew of many of the hazards before she participated in the match. Specifically, defendant pointed out that plaintiff knew that the helmet could cover her eyes, and that she could trip as a result. Defendant also noted that plaintiff knew of the risk of falling out of the ring toward the bar because she had witnessed a previous participant do the same thing.

Plaintiff argued, however, that the suit, which appeared to be soft and padded, allowing a participant to move around easily, was actually stiff and restricted her movements. Thus, plaintiff questioned whether the casual observer would be able to discern the quality of the suit. Plaintiff further pointed out that defendant recognized the need to warn and protect her against the special dangers associated with participation in the match because it required other participants to sign a waiver acknowledging the "inherent and extraordinary risks" involved.

We agree with the trial court that both parties presented plausible arguments, along with supporting evidence, regarding the issue whether the characteristics of the costume and match were open and obvious. We further agree that because reasonable minds could differ on the outcome of this question, summary disposition would have been improper. *Moore v. First Security Casualty Co*, 568 N.W.2d 841 (1997). Although the issue whether a duty exists is generally a question of law for the court, where the determination depends on factual findings, those findings must be made by the jury. *Holland v. Liedel*, 494 N.W.2d 772 (1992). Accordingly, the trial court properly denied defendant's motion for summary disposition.

Defendant next argues that the trial court erred in admitting an "incident report" wherein defendant's disk jockey suggested certain changes in the manner in which the lounge conducted the wrestling matches. Defendant characterizes the report as a subsequent remedial measure inadmissible under MRE 407, while plaintiff argues otherwise. Without deciding that question, we conclude that admission of this evidence would not be error justifying reversal. An error in admitting evidence is harmless unless its admission was "inconsistent with substantial justice." MCR 2.613(A). The gist of defendant's argument here is that admission of this evidence established that defendant had been negligent in failing to provide sufficient spotters for the sumo wrestling event. However, through other evidence properly admitted, the jury had been informed that spotters were required for the event to be conducted safely. Further, the disk jockey himself admitted that as many as six spotters had been used for the event on prior occasions. Plaintiff testified, however, that only two spotters were used on that night she participated in the event and that neither of these individuals was guarding the area near the bar at the time she was injured. In light of the fact that the jury was thus apprised of the insufficiency of spotters being a possible cause of the incident, introduction of the contested evidence, which was merely cumulative on that point, could not be considered "inconsistent with substantial justice."

Defendant next argues that the trial court improperly instructed the jury. First, defendant asserts that the trial court misstated defendant's duty to plaintiff by instructing the jury that defendant would be legally responsible if it knew or should have known the activity was dangerous. Defendant argues that by using the term "dangerous" the trial court lowered the threshold for liability, which it argues can only be imposed where an "unreasonable risk of injury" is involved. In making this argument, however, defendant confuses the general duty owed by a premises owner to an invitee, with that owed in the event the condition is found to be open and obvious.

* * *

Defendant is correct that the law recognizes varying degrees of risk, and imposes varying degrees of responsibility on landowners based on those risks and the nature of the conditions involved. However, the jury instructions accurately reflect these gradations. As our Supreme Court recently stated in *Stitt v. Holland Abundant Life Fellowship*, 462 Mich. 591, 597; 614 N.W.2d 88 (2000), a "landowner has a duty of care, not only to warn the invitee of any known *dangers*, but the additional obligation to also make the premises safe, which requires the landowner to inspect the premises and, depending upon the circumstances, make any necessary repairs or warn of any discovered hazards." [Emphasis added]. However, as explained above, where the danger involved is so open and obvious that a person should be expected to discover the condition themselves; the landowner can be held liable only if the risk of harm from that dangerous condition remains unreasonable despite the fact that it is open and obvious. *Bertrand, supra* at 610–611.

Defendant's argument that only the "unreasonable risk of injury" standard could apply assumes that the jury would have to find that the conditions at issue here were open and obvious. However, as previously discussed, there was a genuine issue of material fact as to whether the conditions were open and obvious. The jury could have found the conditions were not open and obvious, in which case defendant would have a duty to warn of known dangers, *Stitt, supra,* or the jury could have found the condition was open and obvious, in which case defendant would have a duty to protect against unreasonable risks of injury, *Bertrand, supra.* Given that the trial court's instruction accurately reflected defendant's varying duties, we find no error in the trial court's instruction.

Next, defendant argues that the trial court's instructions "completely ignored" application of the open and obvious doctrine. However, while defendant is correct that the trial court never used the phrase "open and obvious," the instructions given nonetheless conveyed the import of that doctrine. In instructing the jury, the trial court stated that to find defendant negligent the jury must find, among other things, that defendant knew or should have appreciated that a patron would not likely discover the risks involved. In so stating, the trial court imparted that if it were likely that plaintiff knew or was likely to discover the risk, then defendant could not be held liable. This was simply another way of stating that the jury could not find defendant liable if the conditions were open and obvious. After all, the test for an open and obvious danger is whether an average user with ordinary intelligence would have been able to discover the danger and the risk presented upon casual inspection. See *Abke v Vandenberg,* 239 Mich. App. 359, 361-362; 608 N.W.2d 73 (2000).

Defendant next argues that the trial court's failure to advise the jury that there was no duty to warn of an open and obvious risk, when coupled with its instruction that a lack of reasonable care could be based upon a failure to warn, created "a legal duty which simply does not exist in Michigan." In doing so, defendant asserts that this situation is analogous to *Riddle v McLouth Steel Products Corp,* 440 Mich. 85; 485 N.W.2d 676 (1992). We disagree.

In *Riddle,* the trial court delivered what formerly was SJI2d 19.03, which instructed that "the possessor must warn the invitee of dangers of which it knows or has created." On appeal, the defendant successfully argued that the instruction was deficient because it incorrectly informed the jurors that a premises owner has an absolute duty to warn an invitee of dangerous conditions, including those that are open and obvious. As a result, SJI2d 19.03 was amended to read that "a possessor must warn an invitee of an open and obvious danger if the possessor should expect that an invitee will not discover the danger or will not protect herself against it." This instruction is essentially the same as that delivered by the trial court in the instant matter. The trial court here instructed the jury that, for a premises owner to be liable, the owner "must have known or should have appreciated that the patron was not likely to discover the risk, or if they discovered the risk, wasn't likely to appreciate the danger involved or for whatever reason wasn't going to be able to protect themselves against it." Defendant fails to show how this instruction significantly departs from the standard instruction, which it sought to have read to the jurors. Accordingly, we reject defendant's assertion that the trial court's instruction, as read, was legally deficient.

* * *

We affirm.

References

Cases

Azzano v. Catholic Bishop of Chicago, 710 N.E.2d 117; 1999 Ill. LEXIS 195.

Clahassey v. C Ami Inc., 2002 Mich. App. LEXIS 1352.

Hatch v. V.P. Fair Foundation and Northstar Entertainment, 990 S.W.2d 126; 1999 Mo. App. LEXIS 315.

Hayden v. Notre Dame, 716 N.E.2d 603; 1999 Ind. App. LEXIS 1697.

James Kubiak v. Wal-Mart Stores, Inc., 132 Ohio App. LEXIS 1774. (1999).

Leon v. Family Fitness Centers, Inc., 71 Cal. Rptr.2d 923 (1998).

Nuckley v. Gail M. Woods, Inc., 654 So.2d 840; 1995 La. App. LEXIS 1051.

Publications

Ammon, R., Jr. (1993). Risk and game management practices in selected municipal football facilities (Doctoral dissertation, University of Northern Colorado, 1993). *Dissertation Abstracts International, 54,* 3366A.

Ammon, R., Jr., & Fried, G. (1998). Assessing stadium crowd management practices and liability issues. *Journal of Convention & Exhibition Management, 1*(2–3), 119–150.

Ammon, R., Jr., Southall, R., & Blair, D. (2003). *Sport facility management: Organizing events and mitigating risks.* Morgantown, WV: Fitness Information Technology, Inc.

Corbett, R. (2002, August). *Risk management for sport organizations and sport facilities.* Presented at the Sports Management: Cutting Edge Strategies for Managing Sports as a Business Symposium, Toronto.

Cotten, D. (2000). *Everything you always wanted to know about waivers but were afraid to ask!* Presented at the 13th Annual Sport, Physical Education, Recreation and Law Conference, Albuquerque, NM.

Curtis, T. (2002, Fall). Still the next big thing: Discrimination lawsuits keep coming in sports as the issue shows no sign of slowing. *SSLASPA Newsletter, 9*(3), 3.

Equal Employment Opportunity Commission. (n.d.). *Sexual harassment charges.* Retrieved January 13, 2003, from www.eeoc.gov/stats/harass.html

Kaiser, R., & Robinson, K. (1999). Risk management. In B. van der Smissen, M. Moiseichik, V. Hartenburg, & L. Twardzik (Eds.), *Management of park and recreation agencies* (pp. 713–741). Ashburn, VA: NRPA.

King, B. (2002, March 11–17). Passion that can't be counted puts billions of dollars in play. *Street & Smith's SportsBusiness Journal, 4*(47), 25–26.

Kreutzer, A. L., & Brown, M. T. (2000, June). *Core business content: Is there a need for inclusion in sport management curriculum.* Paper presented at the meeting of the North American Society of Sport Management, Colorado Springs, CO.

Miller, L. K. (1998). Employment law issues. In H. Appenzeller (Ed.), *Risk Management in Sport* (pp. 403–416). Durham, NC: Carolina Academic Press.

Peterson, J. A., & Hronek, B. B. (1997). *Risk management for park, recreation, and leisure services* (3rd ed.). Champaign, IL: Sagamore.

Sharp, L. A. (1990). *Sport law.* National Organization on Legal Problems of Education (Whole No. 40). USA: PaceSetter Graphics, Inc.

Steinbach, P. (2003, January). Rethinking the rink. *Athletic Business,* pp. 43–48.

van der Smissen, B. (1990). *Legal liability and risk management for public and private entities.* Cincinnati, OH: Anderson Publishing Co.

Wong, G. M., & Masteralexis, L. P. (1998). Legal principles applied to sport management. In L. P. Masteralexis, C. A. Barr, & M. A. Hums (Eds.), *Principles and practice of sport management* (pp. 87–116). Gaithersburg, MD: Aspen Publishers.

5.21 Standards of Practice

JoAnn Eickhoff-Shemek
University of South Florida, Tampa

In a negligence lawsuit, a **standard of care** will be applied to measure the competence of a professional. If the professional's conduct falls below such a standard, he/she may be liable for injuries or damages resulting from such conduct (Black, 1991). The standard of care can be determined in various ways, but one way is from **standards of practice** developed and published by professional organizations. This chapter will focus on the legal implications associated with these types of standards, not those dealing with accreditation, licensure, certification, or statutes.

Standards of practice published by professional organizations are commonly referred to as standards, guidelines, recommendations, or position statements. Many professional organizations have published these documents to provide benchmarks of desirable practices for practitioners and managers. Because these documents can be entered into evidence in a court of law to help determine the standard of care or **duty** that the defendant owes to the plaintiff, it is critical for recreation and sport managers to incorporate these standards of practice into their risk management plans.

Fundamental Concepts

Potential Legal Impact of Published Standards

Published standards of practice can serve as a shield (minimize liability associated with negligence) for the defendant who adheres to them. However, they can also serve a sword (increase liability associated with negligence) for the defendant who does not adhere to them. As demonstrated in Figure 1, *published standards of practice can be introduced as evidence via expert testimony to help determine duty*. If the defendant's conduct is inconsistent with these standards of practice, it can result in a breach of duty that can then lead

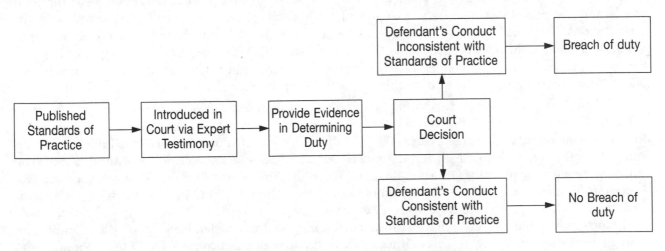

FIGURE 1. Example of the Potential Legal Impact of Published Standards of Practice

to negligence. However, if the defendant's conduct is consistent with the standards of practice, it will be difficult for the plaintiff to prove there was a breach of duty.

For example, in *Mandel v. Canyon Ranch, Inc.* (1998), expert witnesses testified for both parties. An expert witness for the plaintiff claimed the defendant Canyon Ranch breached its duty by failing to utilize a heart defibrillation unit when Mandel had an apparent cardiac arrest while playing walleyball. This expert witness did not introduce into evidence any published standards of practice that required or recommended facilities like Canyon Ranch to have and use a heart defibrillator unit.

An expert witness for the defendant testified that the conduct of the defendant (administering CPR and calling paramedics immediately after Mandel's incident) was consistent with standards of practice published by the American College of Sports Medicine (ACSM). The ACSM publication referred to by this expert witness is entitled *ACSM's Health/Fitness Facility Standards and Guidelines* (Tharrett & Peterson, 1997).

This ACSM book contains six standards and over 500 guidelines (recommendations) for health/fitness facilities. The six standards "represent the standard of care that must be demonstrated by all health/fitness facilities toward their users," whereas the "guidelines are not intended to be standards of practice or give rise to legal duties" (Tharrett & Peterson, 1997, p. ix). Standard #1 in the ACSM book requires health/fitness facilities to have a written emergency plan that can be executed by qualified personnel in a timely fashion; it does not require health/fitness facilities to have or use a heart defibrillation unit. However, the third edition of this book to be published in 2006 may require (via a standard) that health/fitness facilities have an AED.

In *Mandel,* the jury returned a verdict for the defendant Canyon Ranch. It appears in this case that the defendant's expert testimony, at least in part, contributed to the jury's decision for the defendant. This is a good example of how published standards of practice can provide a good defense for defendants, if they are applying them in their daily operations. If Canyon Ranch had not had an appropriate emergency plan and/or had not administered the necessary care after Mr. Mandel's apparent cardiac arrest, as the ACSM standard requires, the outcome of this case could have been quite different.

Standards versus Guidelines: Does It Make a Difference?

Certain professional organizations (e.g., ACSM and the National Strength and Conditioning Association [NSCA]) have distinguished a standard from a guideline (Tharrett & Peterson, 1997; NSCA, 2001). Both ACSM and NSCA have defined standards as requirements that represent the standard of care, whereas guidelines are recommendations that are not intended to be standards of practice or give rise to legal duties. Standards are written as "must" statements, and guidelines are written as "should" statements. Other organizations such as the National Athletic Trainers Association Board of Certification (NATBOC) use the term *standards* in the title of their publication—Standards of Professional Practice, but all the standards are written as "should" or "shall" statements, not "must" statements. To make this issue even more confusing to practitioners, an ACSM position paper titled *Recommendations for Cardiovascular Screening, Staffing, and Emergency Policies at Health/Fitness Facilities* includes requirements (must statements) and recommendations (should statements), though the title specifically states "recommendations."

Though differences clearly exist on how professional organizations define and use the terms *standards* and *guidelines,* does it make a difference to the courts when establishing the standard of care? It probably does not, as demonstrated in *Xu v. Gay* (2003). In *Xu,* Ning Yan died from a severe head injury resulting from a fall off a treadmill that had only 2½ feet clearance behind it at the defendant's fitness facility. The expert witness for the plaintiff, Dr. Marc Rabinoff, stated that the industry's standard of care for the safety distance behind treadmills should be a minimum of five feet. Though he did not specify the industry standards he was referring to, he did state that they were voluntary, not mandatory. Interestingly, the court made no distinction with regard to voluntary or mandatory stating that the "defendant's ignorance of and failure to implement these standards . . . establishes a case of ordinary negligence . . ." (p. 171). It appears from this case that even though the expert witness stated in his testimony that the industry standards were voluntary, the court still considered them as evidence of the standard of care that the defendant owed to Yan.

Therefore, to minimize liability associated with published standards of practice, it is important for recreation and sport managers to implement all of them, regardless of how they are defined and/or stated by their professional organizations.

Standards of Practice and the Law

Published standards of practice often reflect the law. For example, in numerous court decisions recreation and sport programs have been found negligent because they did not have (or administer properly) emergency procedures (van der Smissen, 1990). However, it is important to realize that published standards may not reflect all laws. For example, none of the six ACSM standards specifically require health/fitness facilities to inspect their premises to ensure that they are reasonably safe, yet health/fitness facilities have a legal obligation to do so. This publication does recommend via guidelines that health/fitness facilities inspect their premises and equipment.

Participants that use health/fitness facilities would be classified as **business invitees** to whom the highest duty in law is owed. **Precedence** has been established from case law regarding business invitees, which requires the landowners/occupier to "warn of any known defects upon the premises or of any unknown defects which could be discovered with the application of reasonable care, or he must make the premises safe and free from such defects or dangers" (Herbert & Herbert, 2002, p. 40; see also Chapter 3.20, *Premises Liability*). Therefore, health/fitness facilities should include regular inspections of their equipment and facility as part of their risk management efforts to help ensure their premises are reasonably safe, even though it is not specifically required within the six ACSM standards. *Recreation and sport managers and their risk management advisory committees must carefully consider both applicable laws and published standards of practice when developing their risk management plans.* They should never rely solely on published standards of practice.

Standards of Practice as they Apply to Risk Management

It is essential for recreation and sport managers to incorporate applicable standards of practice into their risk management plan. Managers are ultimately responsible for the development and implementation of the risk management plan. However, all professionals responsible for the program must be involved in various aspects of the risk management process.

Head and Horn (1991) developed a five-step risk management decision-making process: (1) identifying exposure to loss, (2) examining feasibility of alternative techniques, (3) selecting apparently best techniques, (4) implementing the chosen techniques, and (5) monitoring and improving the risk management plan. This five-step approach can be adapted into the following four steps with regard to the application of standards of practice (see also Chapter 5.11, *Risk Management Process*).

Step 1. Identifying and Selecting Applicable Standards of Practice

Because there are so many published standards of practice from a variety of organizations, it is challenging for the recreation or sport manager to be aware of all applicable standards and to determine which ones should be selected and incorporated into the risk management plan. A risk management advisory committee (e.g., experts in the field, a knowledgeable lawyer, and an insurance expert) can provide excellent assistance in this step as well as the remaining steps. Because it is almost impossible to know which standards of practice will be introduced into a court of law, it is best to select those that are the most stringent.

Step 2. Developing Risk Management Strategies That Reflect Standards

This step involves writing procedures that would describe specific responsibilities or duties that staff would carry out given a particular situation. For example, all sponsored programs must have emergency procedures. The written emergency procedures should not only reflect the selected standard of practice, but it should also describe specific tasks that staff must follow when someone is hurt.

Once the written procedures are finalized, they should be included in the staff policy and procedures manual. Policies and procedures from this manual can also be introduced as evidence in determining duty (see *Darling v. Charleston Community Hospital*, 1964, where the defendant's own bylaws along with published standards were entered into evidence to determine duty). It is best for the procedures be written clearly and succinctly without too much detail. Too much detail in the written procedures will not allow for a certain amount of flexibility the staff may need in a particular situation and may make it difficult for the staff to remember everything they are to do.

Step 3. Implementing the Risk Management Plan

Implementation of the risk management plan primarily involves staff training. Staff training will help ensure that the staff's conduct on a daily basis will be consistent with the written policies/procedures and the selected standards of practice. The policy and procedures manual should be used with initial training for new employees as well as regular in-service training throughout the year for all employees. In this regular in-service training, actual practice of a particular procedure (e.g., emergency procedures) should take place. It is also important to explain to staff why it is essential that they carry out their duties appropriately from a legal perspective.

Step 4. Evaluating the Risk Management Plan

Evaluation of the risk management plan should be done throughout the year. For example, the recreation or sport manager should regularly supervise staff to be sure they are carrying out their duties appropriately and if they are not, corrective action should take place, which may involve retraining. Evaluation should also occur after each injury to determine if the staff carried out the emergency procedures correctly and to determine if anything could be done to prevent a similar incident in the future. A formal evaluation of the entire risk management plan should be done at least annually. Like the law, standards of practice are not static and can change and evolve over time. Therefore, written procedures will need to be updated periodically to reflect these changes.

Sources of Published Standards of Practice

Following is a list of some of the professional organizations that have published standards of practice for various types of recreation and sport practitioners/managers. By no means is this a comprehensive list.

Fitness Professionals

1. American College of Sports Medicine: *ACSM's Health/Fitness Facility Standards and Guidelines*
2. American College of Sports Medicine and American Heart Association Joint Position Statements: *Recommendations for Cardiovascular Screening, Staffing, and Emergency Policies at Health/Fitness Facilities* and *Automated External Defibrillators in Health/Fitness Facilities*
3. American College of Sports Medicine: *ACSM's Guidelines for Exercise Testing and Prescription*

Strength and Conditioning Professionals

National Strength & Conditioning Association: *Strength & Conditioning Professional Standards & Guidelines*

Recreation Professionals

1. National Recreation and Park Association: *Code of Ethics and Interpretive Guidelines*
2. American Camp Association: *Foundational Practices for Camp Programs and Services*

Therapeutic Recreational Professionals

American Therapeutic Recreation Association: *ATRA Standards of Practice*

Physical Educators

American Alliance for Health, Physical Education, Recreation and Dance: *Moving into the Future: National Physical Education Standards*

Coaches

American Alliance of Health, Physical Education, Recreation and Dance:
Quality Coaches, Quality Sports: National Standards for Athletic Coaches

Athletic Trainers

National Athletic Trainers Association Board of Certification: *Standards of Professional Practice*

Additional Types of Standards

In addition to standards of practice published by professional organizations that reflect desired **operational practices**, van der Smissen (2000) discussed three additional types of standards involving **technical physical specifications, risk management authorities, and insurance companies**. Technical physical specifications include standards published by independent organizations such as ASTM (American Society for Testing and Materials) and CPSC (Consumer Product Safety Commission). For example, ASTM has published standard specifications for safety signage for fitness equipment/facilities and standard specifications for playground equipment. CPSC has published standard specifications on equipment and facilities such as bicycle helmets, spas, hot tubs, and whirlpools.

Some states and municipalities have risk management authorities that establish standards. Insurance companies also set standards for some recreation and sport activities. It is important for the recreation or sport manager to be aware of these additional types of standards and apply them in their risk management plan as well as those published by professional and independent organizations. As mentioned earlier, a well-qualified risk management advisory committee will be able to assist in this area.

Somewhat different from the preceding standards of practice are accreditation standards. Accreditation applies to institutions and programs that have met certain criteria or standards as established by an accrediting agency. Accreditation helps to ensure quality and assists in the improvement of the institution or program (Understanding Accreditation, n.d.). Examples include (1) Joint Commission on the Accreditation of Healthcare Organizations (JCAHO)—grants accreditation to health-care organizations such as hospitals; (2) North Central Association of Colleges and Schools (NCA)—one of several regional accrediting bodies that grants accreditation to colleges and schools recognized by the Council for Higher Education Accreditation (CHEA); (3) National Council of Accreditation for Teacher Education (NCATE)—grants accreditation to Colleges of Education; and (4) Commission on Accreditation of Allied Health Education Programs (CAAHEP)—grants accreditation to academic programs such as athletic training and exercise science. Once an institution or program achieves accreditation through a formal and lengthy process, it has to be renewed on a periodical basis in order to sustain the accreditation status.

Significant Case

The following case demonstrates that courts do allow expert witnesses to introduce published standards of practice as admissible evidence in determining duty in negligence cases. The trial court in this case excluded evidence provided by expert witnesses involving standards of practice published by ASTM and CPSC. The plaintiffs claimed that the trial court erred in excluding this evidence and appealed. The Court of Appeals of South Carolina (Elledge v. Richland/Lexington School District Five, 2000) found that the trial court did err in refusing to admit relevant evidence of the ASTM and CPCS industry standards. Citing a variety of cases to support its decision, the Court of Appeals stated: "Safety standards promulgated by government or industry organizations in particular are relevant to the standard of care for negligence . . . Courts have become increasingly appreciative of the value of national safety codes and other guidelines issued by governmental and voluntary associations to assist in applying the standard of care in negligence cases. . . . A safety code ordinarily represents a consensus of opinion carrying the approval of a significant segment of an industry, and it is not introduced as substantive law but most often as illustrative evidence of safety practices or rules generally prevailing in the industry that provides support for expert testimony concerning the proper standard of care" (pp. 477–478).

(Emphasis added). The Court of Appeals reversed the trial court's decision, and the Supreme Court of South Carolina affirmed the Court of Appeals decision. This is an excellent case to illustrate that not adhering to published standards of practice can lead to charges of negligence.

ELLEDGE V. RICHLAND/LEXINGTON SCHOOL DISTRICT FIVE

Supreme Court of South Carolina
2002 S.C. LEXIS 235
November 25, 2002, Filed

OPINION: JUSTICE WALLER: We granted a petition for a writ of certiorari to review the Court of Appeals' decision in Elledge v. Richland/Lexington Sch. Dist. Five, 341 S.C. 473, 534 S.E.2d 289 (Ct. App. 2000). We affirm.

FACTS

On December 9, 1994, nine-year-old Ginger Sierra (Ginger) slipped and fell on a piece of playground equipment at Irmo Elementary School where she attended fourth grade. The playground equipment was a metal monkey bar device which the children walked upon; it extended above the ground approximately two feet. As a result of the fall, Ginger broke her right leg. The growth plate in that leg was significantly damaged, and Ginger eventually underwent surgery in both legs to remove the growth plates. * * *

Ginger and her mother, Christine Elledge (collectively respondents), sued petitioner Richland/Lexington School District Five (the District) for negligence. A jury returned a verdict for the District. On appeal, the Court of Appeals reversed and remanded for a new trial. * * *

At trial, James Shirley, the principal at Irmo Elementary since 1990, testified that shortly after he arrived at the school, he had concerns about the school's playground. He was especially concerned by the lack of a fall surface and by the height of some of the playground equipment. As to the monkey bar which Ginger fell on, Shirley stated that children had been walking on it and this was also a concern. In 1991, Shirley contacted Jim Mosteller who redesigned the playground. As part of the playground renovations, the monkey bar which Ginger fell on was modified by Mosteller. Originally, the monkey bar was higher and had a bench underneath it. As part of the modifications performed in 1991, the height was lowered from about four feet to two feet, and the bench was removed. On the modified monkey bar, students would walk or crawl across it, although there were no hand-held supports on the side. Shirley testified that he knew the children were walking across the apparatus after the modification.

Both of respondents' playground safety experts testified that the monkey bar was, in its original form, designed to develop children's upper body strength. Archibald Hardy stated that this piece of equipment was known as a "pull and slide" and the children were supposed to lie back on the bench underneath the bars and pull themselves along the apparatus. According to Hardy, the original design "definitely wasn't for walking" because the metal rungs were small enough for children's hands and were "fairly slick." The modification to the equipment encouraged children to "run up and jump on top of it;" however, Hardy stated that children "shouldn't have been playing on top of it at all." Hardy, who sold to and installed playground equipment for Irmo Elementary, had visited the playground on several occasions since 1992, and had recommended to Shirley that all the older equipment on the playground be "bulldozed."

Steven Bernheim, respondents' other expert, similarly testified about the equipment and stated that it "was not meant as a climber." According to Bernheim, the equipment was safe as originally designed, but in its modified form, it was unsafe because the narrow bars were originally designed for hands, not feet, and no grit had been placed on the metal bars to prevent slipping.

Bernheim stated generally that the playground at Irmo Elementary did not meet the proper safety standards in the industry. Respondents sought, however, to introduce specific evidence regarding the Consumer Product Safety Commission (CPSC) guidelines for playground safety and the American Society for Testing and Materials (ASTM) standards for playground equipment. The trial court granted the District's motion in limine to exclude this evidence. At trial, respondents argued that this evidence was relevant to establishing the District's common law duty of care. The trial court found the evidence inadmissible because the guidelines were not "binding" on the District and the District had not "adopted" them in any way.

Respondents proffered the following evidence. Bernheim would have testified that in 1994, when Ginger fell, the CPSC guidelines and ASTM standards were in effect and would have applied to "any group . . . utilizing the playground equipment for public use," including a school district. He stated that these guidelines are industry standards and are distributed to schools via superintendents' or principals' meetings. Significantly, Bernheim opined that the District should have had policies and procedures in place for retrofitting existing equipment so that it complied with the guidelines. Furthermore, Bernheim believed the modified monkey bar did not comply with the national guidelines because there were no handrails and no grit on the walking surface. According to Bernheim, because Ginger's injury involved getting caught in an entrapment between the ladder areas, it was the type of injury the guidelines are designed to prevent. While Bernheim acknowledged that the industry standards were guidelines only, he stated they are what the playground equipment industry "stands by."

Respondents also proffered testimony from the District's purchasing coordinator, Joe Tommie. According to Tommie, the District would specify in its bids for purchasing new playground equipment that the equipment must meet the CPSC guidelines and ASTM standards. He stated: "That's normally the standard we use to ensure that we purchase safe equipment." * * *

On appeal, respondents argued the exclusion of this evidence was prejudicial error. The Court of Appeals agreed. Stating that "evidence of industry standards, customs, and practices is 'often highly probative when defining a standard of care,' " the Court of Appeals held the trial court erred by excluding evidence of the CPSC guidelines and ASTM standards. Elledge, 341 S.C. at 477, 534 S.E.2d at 290-91. * * * The Court of Appeals found the trial court was under "the mistaken belief that the District must have adopted these national protocols before such evidence was admissible. . . . While such proof might be necessary in attempting to establish negligence *per se*, it is not required when the evidence is offered to demonstrate an applicable standard of care." Id. at 478, 534 S.E.2d at 291. As to the District's argument there was no prejudice from any error, the Court of Appeals stated that the "exclusion of this testimony was clearly prejudicial since such evidence would tend to show the District's compliance with industry standards, which directly conflicts with the District's assertion that such standards were never recognized." Id. at 480, 534 S.E.2d at 292.

ISSUE

Did the Court of Appeals correctly decide that the trial court's exclusion of the CPSC guidelines and ASTM standards evidence was reversible error?

DISCUSSION

The District argues that the trial court correctly excluded the CPSC guidelines and ASTM standards evidence. Specifically, the District maintains respondents failed to establish that these guidelines were accepted and used by school districts in South Carolina to determine the safety of existing playground equipment. In addition, the District contends that even if the trial court erred, the error was not prejudicial. We disagree.

To establish a cause of action in negligence, a plaintiff must prove the following three elements: (1) a duty of care owed by defendant to plaintiff; (2) breach of that duty by a negligent act or omission; and (3) damage proximately resulting from the breach of duty. * * * In

our opinion, respondents' proffered evidence was relevant to, and admissible on, the first required element of negligence—the District's duty of care to respondents. * * * We agree with Chief Judge Hearn's observation that the trial court was under "the mistaken belief that the District must have adopted these national protocols before such evidence was admissible." Elledge, 341 S.C. at 478, 534 S.E.2d at 291.

As recognized by the Court of Appeals, the general rule is that evidence of industry safety standards is relevant to establishing the standard of care in a negligence case. See, e.g., McComish v. DeSoi, 42 N.J. 274, 200 A.2d 116, 120-21 (N.J. 1964) (holding that construction safety manuals and codes were properly admitted as objective standards of safe construction); Walheim v. Kirkpatrick, 305 Pa. Super. 590, 451 A.2d 1033, 1034-35 (Pa. Super. 1982) (holding that safety standards regarding the safe design and use of trampolines, including ASTM standards, were admissible on the issue of the defendants' negligence, even though the defendants were unaware of the standards); Stone v. United Eng'g, 197 W. Va. 347, 475 S.E.2d 439, 453-55 (W.Va. 1996) (no error to admit evidence of safety standards for the design and guarding of conveyors even though the standards had not been imposed by statute and did not have "the force of law"); see generally Daniel E. Feld, Annotation, *Admissibility in Evidence, on Issue of Negligence, of Codes or Standards of Safety Issued or Sponsored by Governmental Body or by Voluntary Association*, 58 A.L.R.3d 148, 154 (1974) (modern trend is to admit safety codes on the issue of negligence). This kind of evidence is admitted not because it has "the force of law," but rather as "illustrative evidence of safety practices or rules generally prevailing in the industry." McComish v. DeSoi, 200 A.2d at 121.

Indeed, the District even acknowledges this is the general rule. Respondents' expert, Bernheim, laid an adequate foundation for the admission of these safety standards when he stated they: (1) were in effect at the time of Ginger's accident, * * * and (2) would have applied to any group using playground equipment for public use, including a school district. Thus, the Court of Appeals correctly held that the trial court erred by excluding evidence of the CPSC guidelines and ASTM standards.

The District, however, argues this evidence was inadmissible because respondents did not show that school districts generally accepted or followed the guidelines with regard to existing playground equipment. * * * We find this argument completely unavailing. Since the evidence showed the District followed the CPSC guidelines when purchasing new playground equipment, and the guidelines are intended for general playground safety which logically includes the maintenance of existing playground equipment, the District's contention that the safety standards somehow did not

apply to it on existing equipment is simply untenable. It is clear to us that a public school is exactly the type of entity to which the public playground safety guidelines should, and do, apply. Simply because the District did not utilize the guidelines in 1994 with regard to existing equipment does not mean that it should not have.
* * *

We find this evidence is highly probative on the issue of defining the District's duty of care. Rules 401, 402, SCRE (evidence is relevant and admissible if it has any tendency to make the existence of any fact of consequence to the action more or less probable than it would be without the evidence); see also Elledge, 341 S.C. at 477, 534 S.E.2d at 290 ("Evidence of industry standards, customs, and practices is 'often highly probative when defining a standard of care.' ") (quoting 57A Am.Jur.2d Negligence § 185 (1999)). Consequently, we hold the trial court abused its discretion by excluding this evidence. * * *

The District further argues that any error made by the trial court did not result in prejudice to respondents. The District contends that the evidence was cumulative to the admitted testimony of respondents' experts and the expert testimony was limited only by excluding specific references to the safety standards. We disagree.

Evidence of objective safety standards is generally offered "in connection with expert testimony which identifies it as illustrative evidence of safety practices or rules generally prevailing in the industry, and as such it provides support for the opinion of the expert concerning the proper standard of care." McComish v. DeSoi, 200 A.2d at 121 (emphasis added); see also Brown v. Clark Equip. Co., 62 Haw. 530, 618 P.2d 267, 276 (Haw. 1980) (evidence of safety codes is "admissible as an alternative to or utilized to buttress expert testimony") (emphasis added).

Respondents sought to introduce evidence of industry standards to identify and establish the duty of care owed by the District to respondents. According to respondents' expert, the modified monkey bar did not comply with the guidelines. According to the District's purchasing coordinator, the District utilized the guidelines to ensure the safety of new equipment purchases. The import of the expert's evidence is clear. Respondents sought to show that the same standards that were used to purchase safe new equipment, should have been used to safely modify and/or maintain the existing equipment.

Furthermore, this type of evidence constitutes an objective standard and as such would have greatly enhanced the opinions offered by respondents' experts. We therefore disagree with the District's argument that the evidence would have been cumulative to the experts' testimony. One of the main purposes of industry standard evidence is to provide support for an expert's opinion on what the applicable standard of care is, and thus, the evidence is not merely cumulative to the expert's testimony. * * *

In addition, we note that the bulk of the experts' testimony went to the element of breach of duty whereas the specific evidence of industry standards was intended to establish the applicable duty of care. In other words, while respondents' experts were allowed to offer their opinions that the equipment did not conform with the industry's guidelines and was not meant to be walked upon, this testimony primarily relates to breach of a duty, not to demonstrating precisely what the objective duty of care was. Since the evidence at issue went to a different element on the negligence cause of action—duty versus breach—clearly the evidence cannot be considered cumulative.

Accordingly, we hold the trial court's error in excluding this evidence prejudiced respondents' case.

CONCLUSION

The general rule is that evidence of industry safety standards is admissible to establish the standard of care in a negligence case. The evidence of CPSC guidelines and ASTM standards which respondents sought to have admitted in the instant case is exactly the type of evidence contemplated by this general rule. The Court of Appeals correctly held the trial court committed reversible error in excluding the evidence. Therefore, the Court of Appeals' opinion is **AFFIRMED.** * * *

Recent Trends

Law and Standards of Practice Will Change

New issues can arise that can potentially change the law and published standards of practice. It is wise for recreation and sport managers (and their risk management advisory committees) to follow these new issues as they arise. For example, it may be required by law or through published standards of practice for all facilities to have and use an AED (Automated External Defibrillator). An AED is a device that can provide an electric shock to restore a normal heart rhythm in a person who has gone into cardiac arrest. If used quickly after a cardiac arrest occurs, it can significantly increase the chances of survival of the victim.

Recently, a number of cases have been filed against health/fitness facilities addressing the issue of whether or not the facilities had a duty to respond with an AED to those participants who were in need of one (Herbert & Herbert, 2002). In addition to the case law that is occurring in this area, some states have passed or are proposing legislation that will require facilities to have at least one AED on the premises (Herbert, 2004; Herbert, 2005).

To date, no professional organizations have published standards of practice that require health/fitness facilities to have an AED, but several organizations have endorsed or encouraged their use. Recreation and sport managers should closely observe this issue as well as other issues as they arise in case and statutory law. These issues often influence changes in future published standards of practice (see also Chapter 2.31, *Emergency Care*, and Chapter 5.23, *Crisis Management*).

Crisis Management

Crisis management is another issue that is receiving a lot of attention. Due to an increased concern of violence in schools and other venues, there has been an increased emphasis in crisis management for recreation and sport managers. Recreation and sport managers may also want to observe what is happening in this area and to monitor any laws and/or standards that result from this concern.

Staying abreast of trends will be an advantage for recreation and sport managers. They can start planning ahead on how they would go about incorporating these trends in their risk management plans if and when they become laws or published standards of practice. Or, in some cases, recreation and sport managers may want to actually apply these trends in their current risk management plan. For example, several health/fitness facilities have already purchased AEDs and have staff trained on their use (see also Chapter 5.23, *Crisis Management*).

References

Cases

Darling v. Charleston Community Hospital, 200 N.E.2d 149 (Ill. App. Ct. 1964).
Elledge v. Richland/Lexington School District Five, 341 S.C. 473 (S.C. Ct. App. 2000).
Elledge v. Richland/Lexington School District Five, LEXIS 235 (S.C. 2002).
Mandel v. Canyon Ranch, Inc., Case no. 31277 (Super. Ct. of Ariz., Pima Co., 1998).
Xu v. Gay, 668 N.W.2d 166 (Mich. App. 2003).

Publications

Black, H. (1991). *Black's law dictionary* (6th ed.). St Paul, MN: West Publishing Company.
Head, G., & Horn, S., II. (1991). *Essentials of risk management* (Vol. I, 2nd ed.) Malvern, PA: Insurance Institute of America.
Herbert, D. (2004). Health clubs and AEDs—new legislation in New York, Rhode Island and Louisiana—bill pending in Illinois. *The Exercise Standards and Malpractice Reporter*, 18(4), 54–59.
Herbert, D. (2005). California passes legislation into law on AEDs and supplements in high school athletics. *The Exercise Standards and Malpractice Reporter*, 19(6), 81, 84–88.
Herbert, D., & Herbert, W. (2002). *Legal aspects of preventive, rehabilitative and recreational exercise programs* (4th ed.). Canton. OH: PRC Publishing, Inc.
NSCA. (2001). *Strength & Conditioning Professional Standards & Guidelines*, available at http://www.nsca-lift.org/Publications/standards.shtml
Tharrett, S., & Peterson, J. (Eds.) (1997). *ACSM's health/fitness facility standards and guidelines* (2nd ed.). Champaign, IL: Human Kinetics.
Understanding Accreditation. (n.d.). Retrieved December 29, 2005 from http://www.collegedegreeguide.com/articles-fr/accredited-college-university.htm
van der Smissen, B. (1990). *Legal liability and risk management for public and private entities*. Cincinnati, OH: Anderson Publishing Company.
van der Smissen, B. (2000). *Standards and how they relate to duty and liability*. Paper presented at the 13th Annual Sport, Physical Education, Recreation and Law Conference, Sponsored by The Society for the Study of the Legal Aspects of Sport and Physical Activity, Albuquerque, NM.

5.22 Audits in Risk Management:
RISK MANAGEMENT PLAN—LEGAL AUDIT—FACILITY AUDIT

Todd L. Seidler
University of New Mexico

College Student Rendered Quadriplegic Receives $9,000,000
Coach Sues for Breach of Contract
Pool Drain Cover Case Settled for $30.9 Million
Programs Eliminated: Title IX Lawsuit Follows
Coach Charged With Sexual Harassment
Soccer Net Cross-bar Crushes Boy to Death
University Loses Age-Discrimination Suit
High School Tennis Player Electrocuted
Overloaded Bleachers Collapse Killing One and Injuring Over 200

These are real headlines of actual incidents. Thousands of people are injured each year as a result of watching, volunteering, working, or participating in sport and physical activities. Many of those injuries result in litigation against the sponsoring organization. Due in part to the expansion of programs, an increase in the number of participants, and the proliferation of personal injury lawsuits, risk management has become one of the most important concerns for today's sport or recreation manager. As covered throughout this text, managers of recreation and sport programs have a number of legal duties they are obligated to perform. A well-run recreation or sport organization will take all reasonable precautions to ensure the provision of safe programs and facilities for all participants, spectators, and staff. As discussed in previous chapters, the establishment of a good, effective, formal risk management program has become the expected standard of practice.

In addition to litigation resulting from physical injury, recreation and sport managers are often faced with a wide variety of other legal actions such as contract disputes, employment issues, Title IX claims, and compliance with OSHA and ADA regulations. As a result of the increase in litigation against recreation and sport agencies, managers of these agencies are increasingly called on to defend themselves and their organizations from legal challenges. The purpose of this chapter is to present three risk management tools for recreation and sport managers—the **risk management plan**, the **legal audit**, and the **facility audit**. Each of these can be of immense value in defending an organization from litigation. Other chapters throughout the text have focused on the risk management process and on many of the legal issues facing today's sport and recreation managers. Throughout this chapter, the reader will be directed to other sections of the text that will expand on the specific topic being discussed.

Risk Management Plan

According to van der Smissen (1996), "There are two types of risks: the risk of financial loss and the risk of personal injury" (p. 173). She goes on to say, "A **risk management plan** is more than safety checklists! It is the systematic analysis of one's operations for potential risks or risk exposures and then setting forth a plan to reduce such exposures" (p. 173). A good risk management plan analyzes all potential risks that an organization faces and selects the optimal method to treat each.

As described in previous chapters, there are four methods of treating risks once they have been identified. They are (1) risk avoidance or elimination, (2) risk reduction, (3) risk retention, and (4) risk transfer (see also Chapter 5.11, *Risk Management Process*).

It is important to recognize that every risk management plan is unique and must be developed specifically for each particular organization. A youth baseball league will be faced with different risks and have different requirements than will a high school athletic department, a college recreation program, or a nonprofit organization sponsoring an event. All components that are appropriate should be included in the risk management plan.

Layers of Protection

In developing a risk management plan, it is important to understand the concept of developing **layers of protection.** This means that whenever an identified risk cannot be completely eliminated, several strategies should be used to treat the risk. Instead of relying on just a waiver to protect against a successful lawsuit, the waiver should be used in conjunction with other methods of treating the risk. In this way, if the waiver is successfully challenged in court, there are several other protections still in place. Examples may include an informed consent, special releases from a physician for a preexisting condition, extra insurance, regular inspections, or special training for personnel. The more layers of protection that are in place, the more likely the organization is to successfully defend itself in court.

The following section is an outline for a risk management plan for a typical recreation or sport organization. This is only an outline, as many of these concerns are discussed in depth in chapters throughout this text. References to the appropriate chapters will be provided when appropriate. It is important to note that this is a generic outline and that each organization must develop a plan that is customized for its particular situation. The reader should also realize there is no one best format or outline for a risk management plan. Most formats are acceptable as long as the appropriate risks are addressed.

Organization Description

It is not always necessary but is often advantageous to begin with an overview and description of the organization along with its purpose and function. The following information may be useful:

- Organization mission statement—statement of philosophy
- A description of the services or programs provided
- An overview of the clientele served
- A description of the facilities and spaces that will be utilized
- The organizational structure of the organization—organizational chart
- Financial resources

Personnel

Review or develop policies and procedures for personnel as might be found in the organization's personnel manual (see also Chapter 2.35, *Human Resources Law*, and Chapter 5.11, *Risk Management Process*). When discussing ways to avoid employment litigation, Schuler and Jackson (1996, p. 608) state, "One excellent avoidance technique is to undertake a comprehensive audit of all employment procedures, policies, and practices to ensure that all are in accord with the rapidly changing state and federal employment laws." The RMP should examine or develop the following personnel-related policies and procedures.

- Develop thorough hiring procedures to ensure that employees are qualified to perform the job they are hired to do. This may include required initial and ongoing training for each position. Background checks should be required for all positions that work with children.
- Develop complete and accurate job descriptions for all personnel, and describe the essential tasks necessary to do each job including individual responsibilities for safety and risk management. (This is also helpful in fully complying with the Americans with Disabilities Act.)

- Provide an evaluation and discipline process that allows for accurate and thoroughly written documentation of employee performance and discipline. This may include termination procedures.
- Develop a procedure to field complaints of sexual harassment in the workplace. Be sure it effectively protects the rights of the accused and the accuser. Ensure compliance with government-mandated training requirements regarding the illegality of sexual harassment.
- Review all policies and procedures for possible due process considerations.
- Provide a location for conducting employment interviews that is fully accessible to those with disabilities, pursuant to the ADA.
- Develop and implement a policy of nondiscrimination in the workplace.
- Ensure the hiring process is not subject to claims of discrimination because of a narrow applicant pool.
- Update the employee handbook, manual, or policy to ensure compliance with recent changes to state and federal employment laws. Check your employment manual for any provisions that are contrary to state or federal law.
- Post all required notices in the workplace (e.g., "Sexual Harassment is Illegal," state and federal wage and hour laws, state and federal OSHA guidelines, state and federal fair employment laws, and the Family and Medical Leave Act).
- Consider if a policy regarding violence in the workplace is appropriate for your situation.
- Ensure compliance with the Immigration and Naturalization Service requirement to complete work authorization (I-9) forms for all employees.

Conduct of Activities

This is a description of the program and the necessary standards for conduct (see also Chapter 2.32, *Conduct and Supervision of Activities*). Issues to consider include the following.

- Proper instruction—Policies ensuring adequate instruction and providing for proper methodology and progression.
- Warnings and participation forms—Review or develop all appropriate preparticipation forms: physical exam, waiver, warning, assumption of risk, parental consent, consent to treat, as well as any other appropriate forms necessary for the activities sponsored by the organization (see also Chapter 2.23, *Waivers and Releases*, and Chapter 2.24, *Informed Consents and Agreements to Participate*).
- Mismatch situations—Review or develop policies to avoid mismatches. (Should prevent mismatches between participants and also between children and staff or other adults) (see also Chapter 2.32, *Conduct and Supervision of Activities*).
- Transportation policy—If transportation is provided for participants, a thorough policy regarding vehicles, inspections, driver qualifications and training, insurance, maintenance, and record keeping is necessary (see also Chapter 2.33, *Transportation*).
- Hazing policy—if applicable, a hazing policy should be developed, communicated and enforced (see also Chapter 4.16, *Hazing*).
- Rules—Develop, communicate, and enforce rules that govern behavior of all participants, spectators, staff, and visitors.

General Supervisory Practices

Supervision is almost always an issue when injuries occur in recreation and sport programs (see also Chapter 2.32, *Conduct and Supervision of Activities*). Some aspects of supervision that need to be addressed are

- A supervisory plan that outlines duties, responsibilities, qualifications, and schedules of supervisors
- Management of behavior of participants, spectators, staff, and visitors; crowd control can be considered an aspect of behavior management (see also Chapter 5.24, *Crowd Management*)
- Rules and regulations for supervisors as well as participants, spectators, staff, and visitors
- Security and access control
- Emergency care of the injured and accident reporting (see also Chapter 2.31, *Emergency Care*)
- Protection of participants, spectators, staff, and visitors from foreseeable criminal acts
- A plan for supervision if the regular supervisor must leave participants for a period of time

Facilities

Recreation and sport managers should attempt to reduce or eliminate the foreseeable hazards related to environmental conditions. A facility audit is a systematic method of identifying the hazards and risks related to a sport or recreation facility and determining the optimal method of treating each. The audit should cover all facilities, equipment, and both indoor and outdoor spaces. A detailed description of the facility risk audit is provided later in this chapter (see also Chapter 3.20, *Premises Liability*). The audit should address

- Hazardous conditions
- Equipment
- Facility layout
- Maintenance
- Security
- Health hazards
- Access control
- ADA
- OSHA
- Signage

Crisis Management and Emergency Action Plans

Identify the crisis and emergency situations that are likely to occur and develop action plans and procedures for each. Include all documentation and forms that are to be used. Regular training of appropriate personnel is necessary. Include first-aid plans, reporting procedures (911), and medical services policies (see also Chapter 2.31, *Emergency Care*, and Chapter 5.23, *Crisis Management*). Examples of emergencies and situations that may be planned for include

- Personal injuries of participants, spectators, staff, visitors
- Staff training (first aid, CPR, AED)
- Emergency communications
- Fire
- Bomb or terrorism threat
- Civil disturbance
- Medical emergencies—care for the injured
- Weather-related emergencies—tornado, hurricane, lightning storm, flood
- Earthquake
- Hazardous material spill
- Evacuation procedures
- Dealing with participants, family members of victims, lawyers, and the media

Insurance Coverage

Make certain the necessary, adequate insurance is in place (see also Chapter 5.25, *Managing Risk Through Insurance*, and Chapter 5.26, *Workers' Compensation*). Every possible situation that can be envisioned should be considered to determine whether all staff, participants, volunteers, administrators, and visitors will be protected. Without adequate coverage, an injured party may even be forced to sue to pay medical bills. Does the insurance plan cover

- Basic medical
- Catastrophic injury
- General liability
- Umbrella liability
- Employment practices liability
- Liability protecting employees

- Property
- Workers' compensation
- Motor vehicle
- Event

Miscellaneous

As mentioned previously, this is a kind of generic risk management outline. The needs of each organization differ depending on its goal, the activities offered, its size, and many other factors. In some organizations other areas should be included in the risk management plan. Some possible topics to add may be identified in the following legal audit section.

The Legal Audit

A **legal audit** is a formal review of policies that attempts to address all pertinent legal aspects of the organization. A legal audit involves a complete legal checkup of the organization in which all aspects of the operation are examined to discover and minimize potential financial threats. Although the line between a risk management plan and a legal audit is often blurred, a legal audit includes more than what is typically thought of as a risk management plan. The legal audit helps ensure the *legal health* of a recreation or sport program and should be done in conjunction with the risk management plan of the organization. The legal audit is typically broken down into a four-step process.

Content of the Legal Audit

A list of the areas that are appropriate to address for the particular organization must be identified. Such a list can sometimes be obtained through legal counsel or from an insurer, but will most likely have to be developed within the organization. The structure of the legal audit covers a number of different categories and will vary somewhat from one organization to another. The legal requirements of a private sport organization may be very different from those of a nonprofit entity. Because some of the categories may not be applicable in certain situations and the number will vary somewhat, it is necessary for the sport or recreation manager to select those that are appropriate for a given situation. Such a comprehensive list of pertinent information helps to create a profile from which one can determine the current and potential *legal health* problems of the entity and to address these problems before they reach crisis proportions. If produced internally, it can be very helpful to develop the audit with the help of legal counsel, financial advisors, insurance specialists, and/or a risk management consultant.

According to Grange and Oliver (1985), some categories that may be included in a legal audit are

- General information regarding the entity
- Governance/authority of the entity
- Function and purposes of the entity
- Policies related to contracts
- Financial information
- Books and records
- Information regarding property/facilities
- Employee and labor relations
- Personnel policies and records
- Operational licenses
- Records supporting tax-exempt status
- Copyright and/or patent records
- Regulatory requirements
- Compliance with government regulations (e.g., Title IX, ADA)

Fried (1999) also provides a list of issues that should be considered for inclusion:

- Partnership agreements
- Corporate formation procedures
- Tax issues
- Advertising liability
- Contract negotiations and compliance
- First aid and OSHA regulations
- Selling food and licensing/permits
- Government relations
- Zoning issues
- Nuisance from noise
- Insurance
- Facility rental agreements
- Sponsorship contracts
- Employment issues
- Employer liability
- Dangerous facilities
- Liability for the acts of volunteers
- Product liability
- Criminal law
- Real estate issues
- Alcohol-related concerns
- Crowd management
- Copyright, trademark, and patent issues
- Property rights
- Spectator violence
- Drug testing

Selecting the Manager and Committee

Once the list has been established, a qualified staff person must be selected and assigned to manage the legal audit process. It is crucial that a person be selected who is sensitive to detail, who has the ability, and has the perceived authority to secure cooperation of other employees. The logical person may be the business manager if one exists in the organization. With smaller organizations, the athletic director or program administrator may be the best one to manage the process. Proper selection is key to a successful audit.

Once the manager has been chosen, a committee can then be selected to help carry out the audit. The members of the committee should represent the various major areas of the business operation. It is important to note that those selected for a legal audit committee are often different from those selected for a risk management committee.

It is also essential to obtain expert evaluation of the audit by legal, financial, and managerial counsel. For example, an attorney can examine the audit from a legal standpoint, a CPA can inspect it from a financial standpoint, and a manager or someone from upper administration can study it from an operational point of view. Large organizations may have the necessary experts available to help, but others may have to hire outside consultants at this point. Specific examples include bringing in a specialist to study an athletic department's compliance with Title IX, hiring an insurance expert to evaluate the organization's current insurance package, or having an attorney review hiring policies and contracts.

Conducting the Audit

When an appropriate committee has been selected, it is time to conduct the audit. Each committee member is selected to study the policies and procedures specific to his or her area of expertise. Often, two or more will share interest areas and should collaborate on their evaluation. The committee should then come together and discuss each part individually with input from all members. As agreement on one area is achieved, the committee addresses the next item in the audit. Eventually, the committee should come to agreement on all aspects of the audit and prepare recommendations to the upper administration.

Implementing the Audit

For the final step, upper administration should receive copies of the completed legal audit. Typically, those overseeing the organization must then decide whether to act on each recommendation. A careful review of the document will help to sensitize them to areas that require immediate attention as well as those requiring long-range consideration. The more support garnered from these administrators, the stronger and more effective the entire process will be. It is important to note that this is an ongoing process. The audit should be reviewed on a regular basis, and it should never be assumed that because it was done before that it is still adequate.

The legal audit is becoming an essential task of sport and recreation managers and has a direct impact on the legal and financial health of their organizations. Sport and recreation managers must become familiar with the details of legal audits and be able to develop and refine them to improve the organization's protection from litigation.

The Facility Audit

A **facility audit** is a systematic method of identifying the hazards and risks related to a sport or recreation facility and determining the optimal method of treating each. A claim of unsafe facilities is one of the most common allegations made in lawsuits alleging negligence in recreation or sport programs. Addressing facility liability, Page (1988) called it one of the largest subcategories within the broad spectrum of tort law. When determining the conduct expected of a facility manager, courts have ruled that they be held to a standard of that of a reasonably prudent and careful facility manager. As specified in Chapter 3.20, *Premises Liability*, a facility operator must take ordinary care to keep the premises in a reasonably safe condition for its users, participants, and spectators. That obligation for ordinary care includes the duties to

- Inspect regularly for hazards or dangers
- Maintain the premises and correct defects
- Warn users, participants, and spectators about hazards or dangers that are not readily apparent
- Warn users, participants, and spectators about the participatory risks of the sport or activity
- Keep users and spectators safe during their use of the premises by having a plan for reasonable supervision and security; using reasonable employee recruiting, selection, hiring, and training practices; and having an emergency action plan (see also Chapter 2.31, *Emergency Care*, and Chapter 5.23, *Crisis Management*)

A facility audit helps to ensure that many of the preceding duties are carried out. If someone is injured in a facility and initiates a lawsuit claiming that the injury was caused by a situation the facility manager should not have allowed to exist, the court will partially base its findings of liability on the concept of foreseeability. Was it foreseeable that the situation in question was likely to cause an injury? If the court determines that a reasonably prudent facility manager would have recognized it as a potential danger and acted to reduce or eliminate the hazard, the chances of being found liable for the injury are greatly enhanced. However, if it is determined that a reasonably prudent facility manager probably would not have identified the situation as likely to cause an injury, the potential for liability is greatly reduced. It is the legal duty of facility managers and program directors to address or treat all foreseeable risks in one way or another to reduce the risk as much as possible.

The best method of performing the preceding duties and ensuring facility safety is through the development of a facility risk audit. This audit consists of a systematic inspection for potential hazards and a system for dealing with the hazards identified. The facility risk audit is broken down into three major parts: (1) initial inspection, (2) risk treatment, and (3) periodic inspections.

Initial Inspection

The **initial inspection** consists of one or more staff members who walk throughout the facility trying to identify as many potential risks or hazards as possible. Typically, the larger the organization or facility, the more people will make up an inspection team. It is often advantageous to include inspectors who have different backgrounds or specialties. A maintenance person will look at the facility from a different point of view than will a coach or a security officer. Each will look at the facility from his/her own unique perspective and possibly identify different hazards. It may also beneficial to have someone from outside the organization come in and inspect. Often, those who work in a facility become used to the environmental conditions they see every day and may not notice a hazard, whereas someone looking at it from a fresh viewpoint may spot it easily. It is often beneficial for two sport or recreation managers to trade off and inspect each other's facility. The more people that are designated to inspect for hazards, the less likely it is that significant hazards will be overlooked. Also, it is often beneficial to hire a professional risk management consultant to come in and assist in conducting the initial inspection and with the development of checklists for daily, periodic, and major inspections.

In addition to identifying hazardous conditions, other facility issues must be addressed as part of the facility audit. Issues that may expose the organization to legal threats other than lawsuits from injury should be identified and dealt with. Among these are access control, security, compliance with ADA and OSHA regulations, and proper signage regarding warnings and rules for facility usage.

The initial inspection should include all areas inside (e.g., gyms, locker rooms, pools, hallways, lobbies) and outside (e.g., playgrounds, fields, sidewalks, parking lots, fences) of the building as well as other areas that may be associated with it. Each inspector should independently tour the entire facility and make a list of potential hazards. The individual lists should then be compiled into one comprehensive list of potential hazards. This comprehensive list must then be prioritized. The priority list will establish the order in which the hazards will be addressed. The more likely a hazard is to cause an injury and the more serious the potential injury, the higher the priority assigned to that hazard. Following completion of the priority list, each hazard must be considered and the best method of treating each determined.

It is important to note that every year or two, the initial inspection should be repeated. And, as noted earlier, involving someone from another facility is recommended.

Risk Treatment

Once the potential hazards in the facility have been identified and prioritized, one or more **risk treatment** methods are utilized to eliminate each risk or at least make it as safe as possible. Chapter 5.11, *Risk Management Process*, provides a good description of treating risks after they have been identified. When treating physical hazards related to facilities or equipment, two methods are typically used.

1. Risk elimination—fix it so that it is no longer a problem
2. Risk reduction—if it cannot be eliminated, make it as safe as possible and identify other methods of treating the remaining hazard

Deciding on the optimal method(s) of risk treatment will rely on the best professional judgment of the facility and risk managers and staff involved. As each hazard is dealt with, the next one on the list can then be addressed. This does not mean that items with a lower priority on the list must wait until the ones before have been treated. If an item cannot be treated immediately, it is important to not wait to go to the next hazard on the list and deal with it. Many situations can be quickly and easily treated and removed from the priority list, whereas others may take some time.

With some hazards it will be obvious how to best remedy the situation. For example, if there is a hole in a soccer field, repair it and determine its source. If it was a one-time incident, the hazard has been eliminated and no more concern is necessary. If, however, the problem is likely to recur, as when the holes are caused by gophers, the cause should be remedied as soon as possible. If it will take some time before it can be fixed permanently, it may be necessary to compensate for it by warning participants of the hazard, using cones to block off the area, posting warning signs, or closing the area until repair is completed.

Another example of risk reduction is illustrated when the sideline of a basketball court is two feet from a concrete block wall, an obvious hazard that must be dealt with. It is probably not possible to completely eliminate the hazard by moving the wall out several more feet. One method to reduce the hazardous situation might be to use floor tape and create a new sideline a few feet inside the current one. It may also be appropriate to warn the participants of the situation and to pad the wall.

Again, for most facility hazards, completely eliminating the dangerous condition is the ideal. When a hazard cannot be completely eliminated, sport and recreation managers must be creative and determine the optimal way to protect everyone involved.

Periodic Inspections

Once the hazards identified through the initial inspection have been treated, a checklist with which to perform periodic facility inspections on a regular, ongoing basis should be developed. This checklist should be designed for each facility and customized for that particular situation. It is all too common that sport and recreation managers will borrow a checklist from another facility, put their name and logo on it, and use it for their facility. This is not a safe or effective practice. Every facility and situation is unique. Therefore, every checklist should be customized for a given situation. It can be very helpful to study checklists from other facilities and borrow ideas from them, but it is essential that each item be suitable for the situation.

It is important to keep the checklist relatively straightforward and simple. If it is so long and complex that it becomes a major operation to perform, it probably won't be performed correctly, if at all. On the other hand, all items of importance must be included.

When developing a facility checklist, the following items should be included in order for it to be as effective as possible.

- Name of the organization
- Inspector's name (printed)
- Date of inspection
- Location of inspection (if needed)
- Inspector's signature
- Problems discovered

Figure 1 is an example of a periodic checklist. When writing the questions for the checklist, it can be very helpful to write them so that if each item is satisfactory, the *Yes* column will be checked (see Figure 1). This way it will be easy to look at each page of the list and see if any checks appear in the *No* column. If none exist, no problems were identified.

Types of Inspections

It is common to develop three different types of inspection checklists. It is always appropriate to develop a brief checklist that can be used for **daily inspections**. Such an inspection should cover safety items that are likely to occur or change quickly such as checking for water or trash on a court or making sure doors are secure.

This should be supplemented by a more in-depth inspection that is carried out less frequently. In most facilities, it is appropriate to conduct a **periodic inspection** on a weekly, biweekly, or monthly basis, whatever is called for by the activities and usage of that particular facility. These inspections might include looking for hazards that are less likely to occur or that take time to develop, such as a frayed cable on a weight machine or loose boards on bleachers. In a spectator facility, however, it is often more appropriate to perform an inspection immediately **prior to each event**.

The third type of inspection should be a **major inspection** of the entire facility, similar to the initial inspection discussed earlier. This should usually be done on an annual basis. The checklist developed in the initial inspection, with modifications made as facility conditions change, can be used for this inspection. It is important to ensure that the checklist is complete and includes any facility changes or additions.

Joe Dailey Recreation Center

Safety Inspection Checklist

Inspector's Name _____Keith Hilsinger_____ Date ___8/22/00___

Location of Inspection _____Weight Room_____

Inspector's Signature _____

Instructions for Inspector: _____

1. Inspect and complete all items.

2. Include comments on all "NO" responses.

3. Fill out and report problems on completion of inspection.

# POTENTIAL HAZARD	YES	NO	COMMENTS
1. Floor and aisles clear of obstacles	✓		
2. Floor clear of standing water and debris	✓		
3. Floor swept, good traction	✓		
4. All loose equipment, mats properly stored	✓		
5. All other equipment properly stored	✓		
6. Weight Room rules clearly posted	✓		
7. Unused weights properly racked	✓		
8. Benches and machines properly positioned	✓		
9. Weight machine cables intact		✓	Cable on chest press frayed
10. All lights undamaged and working	✓		
11. Emergency procedures clearly posted	✓		
12. Emergency telephone accessible	✓		
13. Emergency phone numbers and directions to facility are posted by the phone	✓		
14. Wall pads and mirrors in good shape		✓	Mirror on back wall cracked
15. Access—Ingress and egress points opened or locked as appropriate	✓		
16. Supervisor present	✓		
17. No unsupervised children present	✓		
18. All personal equipment properly stored in hallway	✓		
19. Other		✓	Loose floor tile by bench press
20. Other			

FIGURE 1. Example of a Periodic Checklist

Documentation

If litigation occurs, the court will want to see evidence of what the organization has done to protect others from harm. An organized, thorough, consistent method of documenting all efforts to make a program safe and legally sound is an integral part of any risk management program, legal audit, or facility audit. In each of these, documenting all efforts provides good protection for the organization. Keeping good records is essential if one has to demonstrate in court that everything that could be reasonably expected had been done. The old adage, "If it wasn't written down, it didn't happen" is a great one to apply to such programs. It is important to keep copies of all aspects of the risk management plan as well as the factors addressed in the legal audit. It is essential to document and save everything done that relates to organizational legal issues, safety, and risk management. Finally, all records should be stored in such a way that they are safe, secure, and easily retrievable.

Recent Trends

Along with the increased awareness of the necessity to provide risk management programs and legal audits has come a need for help in developing them. Sport and recreation managers often do not have the background and expertise required to develop a risk management plan that will keep injuries to a minimum and provide maximum protection against litigation. This has created an opportunity for those with such expertise to sell their services and help administrators devise appropriate plans, policies, and procedures. There are currently several risk management consultants that provide such a service in the recreation and sport fields, and the number is increasing. Many risk management consultants have specialized in certain areas and developed great expertise in their area. Examples include playgrounds, aquatics, strength and conditioning, crowd control, and outdoor adventure programs.

Another trend that is making its appearance in the recreation and sport fields is that of the professional risk manager. More and more, large organizations are recognizing the need to have a person who is knowledgeable in risk management on the staff. Large arenas and stadiums, school districts, and city park and recreation departments are examples of entities that are now hiring professionals with these unique skills.

References

Publications

Appenzeller, H. (1993). *Managing sports and risk management strategies*. Durham, NC: Carolina Academic Press.

Appenzeller, H. (2000). *Successful sport management*. Durham, NC: Carolina Academic Press.

Appenzeller, T. (2000) *Youth sport and the law*. Durham, NC: Carolina Academic Press.

Berg, R. (1994). Unsafe. *Athletic Business, 18(4),* 43–46.

Borkowski, R. P. (1997). Checking out checklists. *Athletic Management,* IX(1), 18.

Coalition of Americans to Protect Sports. (1998). *Sports injury risk management & the keys to safety*. North Palm Beach, FL: CAPS.

Cotten, D. J., & Wolohan, J. T. (2003). *Sport law for sport managers*. Dubuque, IA: Kendall/Hunt Publishing Co.

Dougherty, N. J. (1993). *Principles of safety in physical education and sport*. Reston, VA: National Assn. for Sport and Physical Education.

Fried, G. B. (1999). *Safe at first*. Durham, NC: Carolina Academic Press.

Grange, G. R., & Oliver, N. S. (1985). Head off trouble with a legal audit. *Association Management*. Nov. 103 B 104.

Hart, J. E., & Ritson, R. J. (2003). *Liability and safety in physical education and sport*. Reston, VA: National Assn. for Sport and Physical Education.

Jewell, D. (1992). *Public assembly facilities* (2nd ed.). Malabar, FL: Krieger Publishing Co.

Kaiser, R., & Robinson, K. (1999). Risk management. In B. van der Smissen, M. Moiseichik, V. Hartenburg, & L. Twardgik (Eds.), *Management of park and recreation agencies* (pp. 713–741). Ashuba, VA: NRPA.

Maloy, B. P. (1993). Legal obligations related to facilities. *Journal of Physical Education, Recreation, and Dance*, 64(2), 28–30, 68.

Page, J. A. (1988). *The law of premises liability*. Cincinnati, OH: Anderson Publishing Co.

Schuler, R. S. & Jackson, S. E. (1996). *Human resource management: Positioning for 21st century.* St. Paul, MN: West Publishing Co.

Seidler, T. L. (in press). Planning and Designing Safe Facilities. *Journal of Physical Education Recreation and Dance.*

Seidler, T. L. (2005). Conducting a facility risk review. In H. Appenzeller (Ed.), *Risk management in sport: Issues and strategies* (2nd ed., pp. 317–328). Durham, NC: Carolina Academic Press.

Seidler, T. L. (2005). Planning facilities for safety and risk management. In Sawyer, T. (Ed.), *Facility design and management for health, fitness, physical activity, recreation and sports facility development* (11th ed., pp. 129–136). Champaign, IL: Sagamore.

van der Smissen, B. (1990). *Liability and risk management for public and private enterprises.* Cincinnati, OH: Anderson Publishing Co.

van der Smissen, B. (1996). Tort liability and risk management. In B. L. Parkhouse (Ed.), *The management of sport: Its foundations and applications* (pp. 164–183). St. Louis, MO: Mosby.

5.23 Crisis Management

Daniel Connaughton and Thomas A. Baker, III
University of Florida

How important is crisis management to the recreation or sport manager? Contrast two situations in which a crisis was reasonably foreseeable—the 1993 University of Wisconsin/Michigan football game, where it was announced in the school paper that the students would charge the field after a Wisconsin victory, and the June 2000, Atlanta Braves/New York Mets baseball game that was John Rocker's first trip to New York after controversial remarks in a Sports Illustrated *article. In each situation, the potential for a crisis existed with the likelihood of serious injury. In the University of Wisconsin situation, newspapers reported that University management increased uniformed security from about 55 to about 65 officers. The increase proved inadequate, resulting in more than 60 injuries. In contrast, the Mets and New York City increased the number of assigned officers from 60 to 560 (plus an unnamed number of plainclothes officers in the stands), the Mets placed a limit of two on the number of beers that could be purchased at one time, and the Mets constructed a chain-link fence to protect Rocker in the bullpen. As a result of the crisis management measures taken, there were no serious incidents, and consequently, the crisis was averted.*

The potential for many crisis situations regularly confronts the recreation or sport manager. The athletic director learns that one of his athletes just committed suicide. A fire breaks out in the gymnasium. A set of bleachers collapses injuring dozens of spectators. An employee or athlete is arrested and charged with a crime. Each of these situations constitutes a crisis situation. What should staff members do in a crisis situation? A common mistake that many sport or recreation managers make is thinking that they and their staff will know what to do in the event of a crisis. However, in many crisis situations, there is no plan, and the staff does not know how to properly, quickly, and calmly react. According to a recent survey, 93 percent of National Collegiate Athletic Association (NCAA) athletic departments experienced a crisis within the period studied (1999–2000), yet fewer than half of the respondents had written plans in place to deal with the crisis. Furthermore, only 22 percent of the athletic directors reported that they provided any crisis management training to their staffs (Syme, 2005). Having an established crisis philosophy and **Crisis Management Plan (CMP)** will greatly assist an organization in the event of an actual crisis. A comprehensive CMP will address major crisis risks ranging from fires, bleacher collapses, bomb threats, criminal activity, violent acts, litigation against the organization, and major power outages to environmental emergencies such as hurricanes and floods.

On a daily basis, numerous problems, incidents, and issues confront the recreation or sport manager. A serious medical emergency arises when a serious illness or injury occurs involving a participant, spectator, or staff member. Although such situations are important and may involve the utilization of an emergency medical plan, they typically do not constitute a crisis—unless they are improperly handled. Regular incidents require organizational resources to respond, but they are usually readily manageable, and normal business can still take place while the incident is dealt with. Nevertheless, these types of incidents can quickly escalate into crises if they are not brought under control, there is significant media coverage, and/or several resources are required from within, or from outside, the organization. Herman and Oliver (2001) defined a **crisis** as a sudden situation that threatens an organization's ability to survive: an emergency, a disaster, a catastrophe. A crisis may involve a death or injury, lost access to the use of facilities and/or equipment, disrupted or significantly diminished operations, unprecedented information demands, intense media scrutiny, and irreparable damage to an agency's reputation (p. 6). A crisis situation is generally an unforeseen situation that can be extensive in its scope of disruption and damages to the organization. Although a crisis may strike without warning, others may build over time. For example, the sudden accidental death of an athlete or employee may catch everyone in the organization by surprise. In other cases, the actions, or inactions, of key personnel may cause a crisis to come about slowly. In both examples, staff may claim they "never saw it coming." A crisis may result in extensive organizational damage that typically cannot be corrected very easily or quickly. Crises often threaten the organization's mission and reputation and can have an adverse effect on business, fund-raising, and overall public relations. Outside assistance is often necessary. The organization may even need to be closed for a period of time to reestablish services and repair damage.

In summary, crises have common characteristics. First, they are negative. Second, a crisis can create improper or distorted perceptions. Third, crises are almost always disruptive to the organization. Finally, a crisis typically takes the organization by surprise, and the organization is placed in a reactive mode. Therefore, having a crisis management plan is particularly important for smaller organizations because they often have fewer resources to draw from when a crisis erupts. The purpose of this chapter is to assist the recreation or sport manager in becoming more informed about crisis planning and management.

Fundamental Concepts

Crisis management, a subset of risk management, focuses on allowing the organization to achieve its mission under extraordinary circumstances. The top goal of managing a crisis is to prevent it from destroying the organization's ability to achieve its mission and primary goals. Having a crisis management plan in place is critical because it facilitates the establishment of a related, unified organizational philosophy, thereby eliminating the need to decide how to respond and what to do during a crisis situation (Ajango, 2003).

Crisis Management Plan

Every organization is at risk of facing a crisis. How and where a crisis occurs can seldom be controlled. What can be controlled is how an organization prepares, reacts, and responds. A key determinant of how well an organization will cope in the midst of a crisis is how well it addressed its crisis management plan (CMP) before the actual crisis occurs. The steps an organization takes months or even years prior to a crisis occurring may be as important as its immediate response to a crisis.

The primary goal of planning for crises is to develop comprehensive, written contingency plans based on currently existing resources and operational capabilities that will enable the organization to effectively deal with crises. CMPs cannot be copied from a book or from plans developed by other organizations, but rather must be specifically developed for each and every program. Every program has unique factors that must be considered. However, several basic components should form the foundation of CMPs.

A piece that is commonly missing or overlooked when developing CMPs lies in the relationship between the overall CMP and the organization's core values. Whether an organization wants to set, and present, a tone of open communication, care, and concern or one of quiet toughness, the long-term strategy will be a reflection of the organization's values. If employees at all levels do not agree with, or are not aware of, the philosophy behind the CMP, there is a high probability that the plan will not proceed smoothly once it is put into action. Perhaps one of the worst possible things that can happen to an organization undergoing a crisis is for an unexpected lack of agreement on core philosophies to surface. To avoid this pitfall, an organization should prioritize its intent and objectives regarding its CMP. There should be a stated purpose behind the plan, specifically as it relates to the organization's mission and philosophy. Well before a crisis occurs, CMP decision makers should freely discuss how a postaccident investigation would be conducted. Various opinions should be carefully considered. Several other questions should also be carefully considered prior to developing a CMP. Are the needs of a victim(s) a priority? Are employees' opinions secondary? Will legal ramifications drive the plan, or is public reputation more of a concern? It is important to discuss these issues and identify the organization's philosophy and goals prior to the onset of a crisis (Ajango, 2003).

Developing the Plan

The initial step in developing and writing a CMP is to **formulate a planning committee** who will begin the process. Awareness is the initial step to preparedness, and a crucial step in crisis planning is identification. Once the organization's philosophy and goals as they relate to managing a crisis are identified, the committee's primary task is to **identify the significant possible risks and crises** that may arise in their organization. The committee should scrutinize the core functions of the organization to identify and, in many cases, reduce or eliminate risks that could cast the organization into crisis mode. Examples of such crises may include an incident or event that would potentially result in serious injury or death, result in litigation, deter customers or otherwise impair income, impair the organization's ability to meet its core operating expenses, render the organization unable to deliver core services, or garner negative publicity and/or media attention resulting in the death of the organization.

Crisis risks can be categorized into avoidable (preventable) and unavoidable (unpreventable). Avoidable crisis risks may include actual or alleged client/participant maltreatment, service or product failure, severe injuries or death, transportation-related mishaps, and criminal conduct. Unavoidable crisis risks may include natural disasters (hurricanes, tornadoes, floods, wildfires, etc.), bomb threats, hazardous material incidents, terrorist attacks, and utility failures (Herman & Oliver, 2001). Although an organization may not be able to prevent these events from occurring, they can identify which ones are inherent to their area and are more likely to strike and then take steps to be as prepared as practically and reasonably possible to cope with the events if they occur.

Once crisis risks are identified, similar to a risk assessment, a crisis assessment is performed. However, instead of broadly focusing on any potential risk, a crisis assessment highlights the risks that would put the organization into crisis mode. Therefore, situations that could severely jeopardize the organization's credibility and/or resources should be the focus. Similar to classifying risks (see Chapter 5.11), potential crises should be individually assigned frequency and severity ratings. A frequency rating estimates how often this crisis may occur. A severity rating is based on how damaging to the organization the crisis would be if it does occur. Looking at the two ratings, an organization can determine its greatest risks (see Table 1, Risk Category Matrix, in Chapter 5.11, *Risk Management Process*).

The next step is to **develop an action plan** for crisis response for each major crisis risk that may confront the organization. An action plan is a document that details carefully considered courses of action. These alternatives can be selected when a crisis occurs.

When developing such plans, identify all resources that may be needed in each crisis situation. Consider resources in the immediate area. Contact the local/state offices of the Federal Emergency Management Agency (FEMA), American Red Cross, local hospital, police and fire departments, and emergency medical services. Determine how they respond to crisis and how they may be able to assist your organization (Schirick, 2002).

Developing an action plan answers the crucial question: "What will we do if a crisis occurs?" In some cases, aspects of an organization's action plans may be identical, despite the cause, or source, of the crisis. For instance, a uniform step in an action plan may be contacting an insurance broker. In other cases, specific crises may require unique, special responses. A beginning point for formulating action plans is to revisit the major crisis risks initially identified. The following sections present several components that should be considered as general guidelines when developing action plans.

Personnel Issues. There are two phases to personnel preparation. The first involves actions to be taken by the online leader (the person(s) in charge of the activity when the crisis occurs). Personnel should be educated on what immediate steps to follow (e.g., calling 911, activating the CMP). The second phase of personnel preparation involves subsequent actions to take in the crisis situation. The action plan should identify, by job title, those employees who will handle, or actively assist with, the crisis. Specific duties and responsibilities of each responder should be outlined in a simple and very clear format. The action plan should account for personnel educated to render emergency care, communication procedures, an incident reporting system, and a follow-up approach. In addition, personnel should know how to address the ongoing cause of the crisis (e.g., a gunman, terrorist, fire). They should know whom to contact for assistance (see Chapter 2.31, *Emergency Care*).

When developing the action plan and addressing the preceding components, input from various organizational levels and other affected agencies should be solicited. Both managerial and frontline staff should be consulted as well as athletes/participants and outside agencies, including groups such as local EMS, fire and police departments, legal counsel, crisis planning and management consultants, and the organization's insurance company.

Facility Issues. The location of emergency exits and shelters; gas, power, and water shutoff valves; alarm systems; backup power systems; main electrical panels; and fire hoses/extinguishers should be clearly identified. Location(s) for meeting EMS and other authorities (e.g., police, fire, and utility personnel) should be identified. Evacuation procedures should also be developed.

Emergency Equipment Issues. Identify the type of equipment available (e.g., public address and communication equipment, firefighting equipment, first aid kits, automated external defibrillators). Identify where each is stored and who will access it.

Communication Issues. Two major aspects of effective communication are necessary. The first involves the immediate notification of the proper authorities (e.g., police, medical personnel, mental health personnel). Designate who makes such calls and in what order. It is important to identify and get to know outside experts who will work side by side with your organization in a crisis. During a crisis is not the time to meet these key people. Train staff as to where and how to make emergency communications. The location of telephones and other communication devices should be specified, and emergency phone numbers should be identified.

The second aspect of effective communications involves the need to quickly **communicate with constituencies.** For example, an athletic director may need to communicate with EMS, law enforcement, victims and their families, parents of athletes, school officials and other employees, professionals who can provide crisis counseling and other support, news media, and possibly others following a riot incident at a sport event. Before the crisis occurs the following should be considered.

- Who will need to be contacted in the event of a crisis?
- What is the best method to communicate? Consider telephone, broadcast fax, news conference, public address system, intercom, pagers, etc.
- What backup system is available if the primary means of communication is compromised?
- Is the list of personnel that would need to be contacted readily available to more than one staff member?
- Who is responsible for making the communication? One person or a group of people (Herman & Oliver, 2001)?

A crucial factor is communication with the **news media.** It is often the adverse publicity, not the actual damage from the crisis itself, that severely damages the organization. Therefore, a preassigned, trained spokesperson should contact the media at the earliest possible time. When speaking to these parties, the spokesperson should stick to the basic facts (e.g., type of crisis, which medical facility the victim was transported to, number of victims) and never assign or admit fault. The medical staff that are or have provided care should only furnish medical or fatality information. Questions regarding insurance should be answered by the insurance agent/company. Finally, questions regarding liability should be addressed by the organization's risk management department or legal counsel. The staff should also be instructed not to speak to anyone regarding the incident unless approval has been obtained from the designated spokesperson. All requests for information should be immediately directed to the designated spokesperson. (For more on dealing with the media, see the following section.)

Documentation. Determine when and who completes what reports. Assigned personnel should know how to complete them and to whom they should be sent. Establish policies for filing and retaining reports.

Follow-up Procedures. There are several aspects to the follow-up procedures. First, it is necessary for the media spokesperson to follow up with the media. Depending on the crisis and its impact, there may need to be a follow up with the victims, their families, classmates, colleagues, teammates, and/or friends, as well as with employees. Finally, it is important that the CMP be evaluated and modified where necessary.

Developing a Crisis Management Manual

An organization's **crisis management manual** should address the most likely crises it may face and suggest methods for handling those crises. The manual serves as a checklist of what to do when and whom to contact. Herman and Oliver (2001) suggested to keep the format simple and easy to read, use short sentences and bulleted phrases, use flowcharts to indicate responsibilities and actions, include boxes that can be checked when the task is completed, and use tabs for quick access.

Forming a Crisis Response Team

A small team should be formed to coordinate an organization's response to a crisis. This team needs to be formed and trained *before* a crisis occurs. Proper training will allow the team to react more calmly, effectively, and efficiently. The makeup of the crisis response team will vary depending on a number of factors, including the size of the organization, the nature of the services provided by the organization, the likely sources of crisis in the organization, and the organization's prior experience responding to a crisis. The makeup of the team may include the executive director, department heads, senior staff members, physical plant/building superintendent, board members, legal counsel, and outside advisors.

Practicing the Plan

Although responses to certain crises cannot be easily rehearsed, others can be simulated, practiced, or simply discussed to enhance readiness for an actual crisis and to identify any flaws in the action plans. When feasible, the plan should be tested in conditions as close to real life as possible. When flaws are noticed, the plans should be modified accordingly. Every time an organization conducts a CMP drill, key personnel involved should do a brief review of the exercise. Documentation of the review should be maintained by the organization. In between major drills, in-service training and tabletop exercises keep the strategies and process fresh in the minds of staff (Herman & Oliver, 2001).

Surviving a Crisis

The first step in addressing a crisis is to recognize and acknowledge it may be occurring. Oftentimes, individuals in organizations have different perceptions of when a crisis is at hand. It is important to recognize the signs of a crisis so the CMP has the best chance of working effectively.

Activating the plan

Once a crisis has been recognized, the plan should be followed. According to Herman and Oliver (2001), the team leader should contact the crisis response team and attempt to answer the following questions.

- What has occurred?
- Who has been affected by the events thus far? Who are the known victims?
- What steps have been taken to control the crisis? Who has done what?
- Is the media aware of the crisis? Are we prepared to give a statement?

The team should discuss and carefully decide what steps need to be taken to

- Provide and/or arrange care or support for the victims
- Notify key personnel
- Respond to media inquiries
- Brief the staff and key constituents of the organization
- Ensure continued service delivery or coordinate transfer to another provider
- Secure important documents, files, computer backups, etc.
- Ensure that the communication systems are up and operating

Proper Crisis Communication

One of the most important aspects of handling a crisis is communication. How an organization communicates with key constituents, responds to inquiries and criticisms, handles the media, and tells its story may very well determine its survival. A failed communications strategy can be disastrous for any organization. All communication during a crisis should be carefully considered and orchestrated. Whether it is directed to an internal or external audience and whether it is written, visual, or verbal, extra care should be taken when crafting messages. Seymour and Moore (2000) recommended applying the "Five Cs" to crisis communication.

1. Care—The public is often very reluctant to forgive a lack of compassion from an organization whose programs or services caused harm. An effective spokesperson is one who can express empathy and care with conviction and sincerity.
2. Commitment—The organization's message should clearly indicate that it is committed to investigating the incident and preventing future occurrences.
3. Consistency—A clear plan of how the organization will respond and what its spokesperson will say ensures a consistent message.
4. Coherence—It is important to be clear, be concise, and stick to the facts.
5. Clarity—Because the opportunity to convey a message may be slim and come without warning, it is vital to avoid jargon and other language that may confuse the listener.

Dealing with the News Media

Organizations should educate designated spokespersons who will work with the news media during a crisis situation. This aspect of the CMP should address the following details.

- Who decides what information is released?
- Who speaks for the organization/releases materials to media? Typically one spokesperson should be designated. A central spokesperson provides a singular face for the media that the public begins to become familiar with. Centralized information also minimizes miscommunication. Backup spokespeople should be designated in the event that the central spokesperson is unavailable or the subject of the crisis.
- Which members of the news media should be notified in a crisis?
- What are the phone numbers of key media people?
- What are the logistical details including locations where press conferences can be held; phone lines that media can use to call in; backup power supplies; where media can park; and what support staff is available to deal with the media?

At the first sign of a potential crisis involving an organization, whether before or after exposure in the news media, preparations for a timely, accurate, and appropriate response must begin. News media will expect and demand an immediate response. A decision on whether a news conference and/or release would be an appropriate means of conveying information to the news media and public must be made. What means of internal communication will be used if the crisis affects employees and participants should also be determined. At the earliest possible stage, advise staff members of the situation. Give clear instructions regarding handling the media and telephone calls and alert them that they may be called to perform special duties related to the incident. Discuss alternative or additional means of conveying information. This might include such items as letters to parents, clients, or fans, letters to newspaper editors, or consultation with boards.

Information files should be set up to contain all materials related to the incident. Newspapers and television reports should be scanned daily for related stories. If necessary, arrange for videotaping of any TV coverage. Related material, including clippings, statements, memos, and any other documents should be filed in chronological order. Plan to frequently update employees and administrators on the status of the incident. Conduct a follow-up assessment to determine what did and did not work, and what changes might be made in the future for improved media relations during a crisis.

Guidelines for the Media Contact Person

Several strategies exist that will make dealing with the media as positive as possible. In any crisis, try to find out as much information as possible. That way, you avoid inadvertently saying the wrong thing or sending unintended messages.

The following are seventeen guidelines for dealing with the media.

- Always return media calls, even if they call repeatedly and/or are hostile. Ignoring them will not make the problem disappear. The more cooperative you appear, the better.
- Occasionally, a media representative will make a special request. If possible and if it does not violate the CMP, an effort should be made to accommodate reasonable requests.
- Avoid antagonizing media representatives. A sharp tone at a press conference, during a telephone call, or elsewhere may affect your relationship with that individual and with others who may hear the conversation.
- Try to remain levelheaded at all times when speaking to the media. Some of their questions may seem hostile or may seem like a personal attack. It must be remembered that they are trying to get as much information as possible on a crisis-oriented story that may have widespread impact to their audiences.
- Refrain from getting mad or taking it personally when asked tough questions.
- Always try to have an answer for reporters' questions and always tell the truth. However, never be afraid to say, "I don't know, but I'll find out."
- Avoid using "no comment." Doing so often makes it appear that you have something to hide.
- Additionally, stay "on the record" in all interviews. Any comment worth stating should be said "on the record." If you go "off the record," be prepared to hear or read it. Although it is unethical for reporters to report "off the record" comments, anything can, may, and will be done to advance a story.
- Consider how information you release may affect others. If things you say will result in the media calling other organizations or individuals, call them first to warn them of this.
- When speaking to the media, be sure to credit other agencies or individuals assisting with the crisis, including your staff. This enhances relationships and reflects well on you.
- Try to be proactive with new information. If you acquire new information regarding the crisis advise the media.
- Admit when a mistake has been made. This is often the first step to reestablishing confidence and credibility with the public and key constituencies.
- Maintaining a sense of humor is important, but inappropriate humor will work against you.
- Professional dignity is very important, particularly in unpleasant times.
- As the crisis progresses, take notes. They can help you remember things and may be useful for later review.
- If you are on camera, always dress professionally. Casual or mussed clothing may send a signal to viewers that things are out of control.
- Try to give yourself some downtime and stress reduction. Overwork and little sleep can lead to misstatements and irritability.

Debrief Employees and Others Affected

Determine when and who will meet with staff and others affected (teammates, classmates, colleagues, etc.) for debriefing. Have plans for dealing with emotional and mental health needs of staff, classmates, teammates, or friends and family of the victim(s) (Bacon & Anderson, 2003). Have procedures for communicating with the immediate families of all victims. Some organizations may have psychologists or mental health professionals available for the victims and/or their families, whereas others may refer affected individuals to available, trained professionals.

Evaluate the Response

Once the crisis is over, an evaluation should occur in a timely fashion.

- First, consider and review **why the crisis occurred**. What, if anything, could have been done to prevent or limit the crisis?
- Next, **how soon was the crisis noticed and how was it handled** should be evaluated. What was done appropriately or inappropriately should be addressed.
- Were others who were involved or affected timely informed?
- How effective was the crisis response team? Were certain skills or talents missing in the makeup of the team?
- How was the action plan followed? Was it effective and useful? What could have been done better?
- Also, **similar scenarios** should be examined. For example, what would you do in a similar situation in the future?
- Does the plan need to be changed? If so, how? Revising CMPs is an ongoing process.
- Finally, **send notes of appreciation** to those who have been of service, outside and inside the organization, including your own staff.

Significant Case

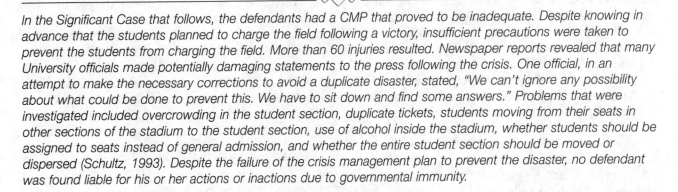

In the Significant Case that follows, the defendants had a CMP that proved to be inadequate. Despite knowing in advance that the students planned to charge the field following a victory, insufficient precautions were taken to prevent the students from charging the field. More than 60 injuries resulted. Newspaper reports revealed that many University officials made potentially damaging statements to the press following the crisis. One official, in an attempt to make the necessary corrections to avoid a duplicate disaster, stated, "We can't ignore any possibility about what could be done to prevent this. We have to sit down and find some answers." Problems that were investigated included overcrowding in the student section, duplicate tickets, students moving from their seats in other sections of the stadium to the student section, use of alcohol inside the stadium, whether students should be assigned to seats instead of general admission, and whether the entire student section should be moved or dispersed (Schultz, 1993). Despite the failure of the crisis management plan to prevent the disaster, no defendant was found liable for his or her actions or inactions due to governmental immunity.

ENEMAN V. RICHTER

COURT OF APPEALS OF WISCONSIN, DISTRICT FOUR
217 Wis. 2d 288; 577 N.W.2d 386
February 5, 1998, Released

OPINION: ROGGENSACK, J. The appellants alleged they suffered personal injuries after a University of Wisconsin football game at Camp Randall Stadium, which injuries they claim resulted from the negligence of David Ward, Patrick Richter, Susan Riseling, Michael Green and David Williams, while the respondents were employed by the State on behalf of the University of Wisconsin. Respondents moved for summary judgment, based on the common law doctrine of public officer immunity. The circuit court concluded there were no material factual disputes and dismissed the appellants' claims. Because we agree that the material facts are not in dispute and that the respondents are entitled to immunity, we affirm.

* * *

BACKGROUND

This is a consolidated appeal of summary judgments dismissing the claims of the appellants, all of whom are alleged to have suffered personal injuries when they were crushed by persons attempting to come onto the playing field at Camp Randall Stadium after the 1993 Wisconsin/Michigan football game. They assert their injuries would not have occurred if certain gates had not been closed by security personnel at the conclusion of the game and that the closing of the gates constituted negligence. David Ward, Chancellor for the University of Wisconsin-Madison; Patrick Richter, Athletic Director for the University of Wisconsin-Madison; Susan Riseling, Chief of Police and Security for the University of Wisconsin-Madison; Michael Green, Camp Randall Facilities and Events Coordinator; and David Williams, a University police officer in Riseling's department, were state governmental employees on the date of the appellants' alleged injuries. They filed an answer denying negligence, and based on their status as state governmental employees, they asserted the affirmative defense of discretionary immunity, on which they moved for summary judgment.

Camp Randall Stadium is the site used for football games and other outdoor events at the University of Wisconsin-Madison. The football field is encircled by a chain link fence with a walkway between the fence and the bottom row of bleachers. Ingress and egress of the bleachers varies, depending on the section of the stadium. Sections O and P are at issue in this lawsuit. The lower rows of sections O and P exit to the walkway and then through the home team tunnel. It was also possible for those rows to exit to the field itself, even though security personnel directed spectators not to do so.

Prior to the 1993 football season, access to the field was limited by hand held ropes, which provided no real barrier to a spectator determined to enter the field. In anticipation of the 1993 football season, the University installed metal gates that could be positioned to close off the walkway at the bottom of the bleachers in order to permit the team to exit the field into the tunnel without interference from the spectators. When the walkway was closed off by the gates, sections O and P spectators' means of egress was restricted, until the team had made its way through the tunnel and the gates were opened again.

On October 30, 1993, after the University of Wisconsin's football team defeated the University of Michigan's team at Camp Randall, many of the students in sections O and P attempted to come onto the playing field. However, a few minutes before the game's end, the gates had been closed and latched by security personal. This provided a significant barrier to the spectators' egress onto the field, and it also created a dead end for tunnel egress from sections O and P, at a time when spectators were moving down the bleachers to exit the stadium or to push onto the field. The appellants were crushed against a metal railing and the gates when security personnel were unable to quickly unlatch the gates to open them.

Ward and Richter had no personal responsibility to manage the crowd at the Camp Randall games. On the other hand, Riseling's, Green's and Williams's activities at Camp Randall were arguably within the scope of the Standard Operating Procedures for Camp Randall relating to crowd control. Additionally, prior to the Michigan game, and subsequent to the installation of the gates, Riseling knew that it was possible that the students might try to rush onto the field at the game's end. In response to this potential for congestion in the student sections, she formulated and issued a directive entitled, "POST GAME CROWD TACTICS," whose goal was "to prevent injury to people—officers, band members and fans." The plan outlined a general strategy to follow which, in her judgment, would have prevented injury. Although her plan was implemented by security personnel, it was not successful.

DISCUSSION

* * *It is well established that this court applies the same summary judgment methodology as the circuit court. Smith v. Dodgeville Mut. Ins. Co., 212 Wis. 2d 226, 232, 568 N.W.2d 31, 34 (Ct. App. 1997). We first examine the complaint to determine whether it states a claim, and then we review the answer to determine whether it presents a material issue of fact or law. Id. If we conclude that the complaint and the answer are sufficient to join issue, we examine the moving party's affidavits to determine whether they establish a prima facie case for summary judgment. Id. If they do, we look to the opposing party's affidavits to determine whether there are any material facts in dispute which entitle the opposing party to a trial. Id. at 233, 568 N.W.2d at 34.

Whether immunity lies because of the common law doctrine of public officer immunity is a question of law which we review de novo. Kimps v. Hill, 200 Wis. 2d 1, 8, 546 N.W.2d 151, 155 (1996) (citing K.L. v. Hinickle, 144 Wis. 2d 102, 109, 423 N.W.2d 528, 531 (1988)). A question of law is also presented when we decide whether the safe place statute applies to this case. Ruppa v. American States Ins. Co., 91 Wis. 2d 628, 639, 284 N.W.2d 318, 322 (1979).

Public Officer Immunity.

* * *

Based on the information before us, we assume, without deciding, that there was a compelling and known danger of injury of sufficient magnitude to create a ministerial duty to act for Riseling, as Chief of Police and Security, due to her knowledge of the possibility of a crowd surge onto the field. However, Riseling did not ignore the potential danger. She, with the assistance of others, formulated a plan, the "POST GAME CROWD TACTICS," the goal of which was "to prevent injury to people—officers, band members and fans."

The plan established no specific tasks that were to be performed at a time certain; rather, it made general statements and set general guidelines such as,

We expect that if Wisconsin wins today, especially if it is a close game, there will be an attempt by fans to come onto the field.

If there is a crowd surge, officers at that point will make the initial decision to move aside and begin pulling back to the goalpost assignment. Lt. Johnson will be observing from the press box and will make decisions on giving the command for all officers to pull back.

There may be times during and after the game when people crowd the fence and put pressure against it. Actively encourage them to move back. If it seems there is danger of the fence breaking (it has in the past) move back to a safe position. * * * Here, the formation of the post-game crowd control plan represented Riseling's judgment about how best to reduce the potential for injury to persons at the game. "A discretionary act is one that involves choice or judgment." Kimps, 200 Wis. 2d at 23, 546 N.W.2d at 161 (citation omitted). Additionally, the implementation of the plan required Riseling, Green and Williams to respond to their assessment of what the crowd's actions required. By its very nature, the way the plan was effected had to change from moment to moment because the plan was responsive to the crowd. Reacting to the crowd also constituted the exercise of discretion. Furthermore, neither the documents nor the testimony contained in any of the portions of the depositions submitted in opposition to respondents' motion for summary judgment established a factual dispute about whether any specific acts were required of any of the respondents. Therefore, we conclude that the decision about what type of a plan to formulate to safely manage the crowd, as well as the implementation of the chosen plan, were discretionary, not ministerial, acts.

4. Non-governmental acts.

* * *

Here, documents provided in support of, and in opposition to, the respondents' motion for summary judgment establish no inconsistency between the actions of those respondents whose job duties took them personally into crowd control management activities, and the University's policy of safe management of the crowd at football games. Rather, they acted in accord with the General Operating Procedures for Camp Randall Stadium. Neither the formulation of the plan nor the implementation of it required highly technical, professional skills, such as a physician's. Therefore, we conclude that the respondents' activities were governmental in nature and we decline to extend the exception to immunity found in Gordon in this context.

* * *

CONCLUSION

Because the appellants have submitted no evidentiary facts from which we could conclude that the respondents had ministerial duties which they failed to perform and because neither the safe place statute nor any other theory of liability put forth by the appellants applies to the respondents, we affirm the summary judgment dismissing appellants' claims against the respondents.

By the Court.—Judgment affirmed.

Recent Trends

Fans getting carried away with out-of-control, rowdy postgame celebrations seem to be a growing trend in college and professional sports. Tragically, on October 22, 2005, a student from the University of Minnesota-Morris died from injuries sustained after football players and fans, exhilarated by a double-overtime homecoming win, pulled down a goalpost. Likewise, November 23, 2002, was somewhat infamous as fans at the Ohio State University (OSU), Clemson University, North Carolina State University, and University of California–Berkeley, swarmed the playing field after football games on that date. Numerous injuries, property damage, clashes with police and security guards, and several arrests occurred. When OSU and the University of Miami played in the 2003 Fiesta Bowl in Arizona, police and OSU officials in Columbus, Ohio, were prepared for postgame troubles. In addition to scheduling extra police and implementing an on-street parking ban for the neighborhoods bordering the OSU campus, Ohio Stadium was locked down and the goalposts were removed for that weekend.

The events of September 11, 2001, changed the way Americans perceive the threat of terrorism in the United States. This new perception is especially true for those who own or operate sport stadiums and arenas. Terrorism is defined as the use of force or violence against persons or property in violation of the criminal laws of the United States for purposes of intimidation, coercion, or ransom. Although high-risk targets include military and government facilities, airports, large cities, and high-profile landmarks, terrorists may also target large public venues such as sport facilities (Federal Emergency Management Agency, 2003). In fact, then Attorney General John Ashcroft classified sport facilities as "soft" targets, meaning that they are at an increased risk for terrorist attack (CNN, 2003).

In response to the risk of terrorism at U.S. sport stadiums and arenas, many governmental and sport organizations have taken proactive, precautionary measures. For example, many sport leagues/associations such as Major League Baseball (MLB, 2002), the NBA (Tolbert, 2003), the NCAA (Pickle, 2003), the NHL (Wallace, 2002), and the NFL (Farley, 2004) have issued wide-ranging security rules and recommendations. Furthermore, a number of industry organizations associated with sport and entertainment venue management have also issued recommendations. For example, the International Association of Assembly Managers (IAAM), in cooperation with the U.S. Department of Homeland Security, offered a free Terrorism Awareness Training Course. This four-hour course focused exclusively on stadiums and arenas to assist security personnel in recognizing and preventing terrorist activity (IAAM, 2004). Representatives from the NFL, NHL, MLB, NBA, and NCAA collaborated with the IAAM and produced the *Best Practices Guide* that provides measures that can be taken by facility managers to protect against terrorism (IAAM, n.d.).

Ultimately, it is up to the owners and operators of sport facilities to determine what needs to be done to deal with a potential terrorism crisis. This chapter has listed several resources that can guide facility managers in developing their CMPs to deal with terrorism. It is imperative that sport facility managers develop their CMPs in accordance with industry standards because failure to do so may result in legal liability. It may seem unfair to impose liability on the owners and operators of sport stadiums and arenas for the actions of third-party terrorists. However, it is likely that victims of terror will not be able to recover from the terrorists to any material degree (Gash, 2003) and will look to the facilities in which they were harmed for recovery.

REFERENCES

Case

Eneman v. Richter, 577 N.W.2d 386; 1998 Wisc. App.

Publications

Ajango, D. (2003). The ultimate goal in crisis response. In *Recreation & Adventure Program Law Conference Proceedings*. Vail, CO. p. C1–6.

Bacon, V. L. & Anderson, M. K. (2003). Crisis interventions for sport related incidents. *The Sport Journal, 6*(4). Retrieved December 15, 2005 from http://www.thesportjournal.org/2003Journal/Vol6-No4/crisis.asp

Cheley, D. (1997, Spring). *Crisis at camp...What do we do now?* Paper presented at American Camping Association Mid-States Conference.

CNN/Sports Illustrated. (2002, November 24). *That kind of Fiesta....Postgame fires, car damage leads to 45 arrests of OSU fans.* Associated Press. Retrieved December 15, 2005 from http://sportsillustrated.cnn.com/football/college/news/2002/11/23/rowdy_fans_ap

CNN. (2003, February 9). Official: Credible threats pushed terror alert higher. *CNN.com.* Retrieved May 28, 2004 from http://www.cnn.com/2003/US/02/07/threat.level/

Farley, G. (2004, January 30). Security blankets Patriots once again. *The Enterprise.* Retrieved May 28, 2004 from http://enterprise.southofboston.com/articles/2004/01/30/news/sports/sports03.txt

Federal Emergency Management Agency. (2003). *Are you ready? A guide to citizen preparedness.* FEMA Publication H-34. Washington, DC: FEMA. Available online at http://www.fema.gov/areyouready/

Gash, J. (2003). At the intersection of proximate cause and terrorism: A contextual analysis of the (proposed) Restatement Third of Torts' approach to intervening and superseding causes. *Kentucky Law Journal, 91*(3), 523–612.

Herman, M. L. & Oliver, B. B. (2001). *Vital signs: Anticipating, preventing and surviving a crisis in a nonprofit.* Washington, DC: Nonprofit Risk Management Center.

IAAM. (n.d.). Center for venue management studies. *Iaam.org.* Retrieved May 28, 2004 from http://www.iaam.org/CVMS/CVMSsafety.htm

IAAM. (2004). Department of Homeland Security presents terrorism awareness training course for stadiums and arenas. Retrieved May 28, 2004 from http://www.iaam.org/2004_meetings/DHS/DHS.htm

Major League Baseball. (2002, April 25). MLB implements new security measures. *MLB.com.* Retrieved May 28, 2004 from http://mlb.mlb.com/NASApp/mlb/mlb/news/mlb_news.jsp?ymd=20020425&content_id=14313&vkey=news_mlb&fext=.jsp

Pickle, D. (2003, January 6). New premium placed on insurance. *The NCAA News.* Retrieved May 28, 2004 from http://www.ncaa.org/news/2003/20030106/active/4001n04.html

Seymour, M. & Moore, S. (2000). *Effective crisis management: Worldwide principles and practice*. New York: Cassell.

Schirick, E. (2002, March). Risk management and crisis response are you prepared? *Camping Magazine*. Retrieved December 15, 2005 from http://www.acacamps.org/campmag/rm023risk.php

Schultz, R. (1993, November 1). Richter looks for solutions. *The Capital Times*, p. B1.

Stoldt, G. C., Miller, L. K., Ayres, T. D., & Comfort, P. G. (2000). Crisis management planning: A necessity for sport managers. *International Journal of Sport Management, 4*, 253–266.

Syme, C. (2005, January 17). Writing about crisis best way to avert one. *The NCAA News Online*. Retrieved December 15, 2005 from http://www2.ncaa.org/media_and_events/association_news/ncaa_news_online/2005/01_17_05/editorial/4202n32.html

Tolbert, B. A. (2003, January 24). Playing it safe: NBA's security chief addresses New York City law alumni. *UB Law Links*. Retrieved May 28, 2004 from http://www.law.buffalo.edu/Alumni_And_Giving/ub_law_links/02-2003/default.asp?ll=5&f=NYCLunch

USA Today. (2003, January 3). *Hello, Columbus*, p. C13. AP Wire.

Wallace, K. (2002, June 3). Stanley Cup finals mean more security for ESA: State, federal officials will be on hand to help with security efforts. *WRAL.com*. Retrieved May 28, 2004 from http://www.wral.com/sports/1489953/detail.html

5.24 Crowd Management

Robin Ammon, Jr.
Slippery Rock University

Nita Unruh
University of Nebraska/Kearney

The number of sport/entertainment facilities constructed in the United States has increased during the past ten to fifteen years. Estimates of total cost are now approaching $9 to 10 billion (US). From 1990–2004 sixty-nine teams in four major leagues (MLB, NBA, NFL, and NHL) built new facilities. In addition, another ten venues opened in 2004–2005. This surge in construction is by no means specific to the United States. In Russia, eight major facilities are being constructed or renovated. This construction includes a new $200 million stadium for the National Team. In addition, the Chinese have spent an estimated $2 billion (US) developing eleven new arenas for the 2008 Summer Olympics (Staff, 2005). This tremendous escalation in sport/entertainment facility construction has provided new, modern venues for a variety of events. The millions of dollars resulting from naming-rights fees, luxury suite rental, as well as television and sponsorship fees at these events have caused owners, managers and administrators to take notice. However, the increased public and media exposure accompanying these events has required sport and recreation managers to have a clear understanding of what it takes to provide a safe environment. A major component in providing a safe, entertaining, and valuable experience for the consumer is effective crowd management.

Fundamental Concepts

A facility or event manager has a duty to provide as safe and secure an environment as possible. van der Smissen (1990) classified **crowd management** as part of the duty facility managers owe their patrons to protect them from unreasonable risk of harm from themselves or other individuals. The International Association of Assembly Managers (1997) defined crowd management as a tool to assist facility or event managers in providing a safe and enjoyable environment for their guests by implementing the facility/event policies and procedures. A crowd manager's responsibilities include managing the movement and activities of the crowd/guests, assisting in emergencies, and assisting guests with specific concerns related to their enjoyment and/or involvement with the event.

Importance of Crowd Management

Maloy (2001) cited five legal obligations of a premises operator to patrons. Of these duties, crowd management is a component of the legal obligation *"to keep safe."* Failure to meet this duty can result in litigation against both the organization and the facility manager. A major concern of the facility manager in relation to any crowd management incident is the foreseeability of the incident.

Foreseeability as defined by Black (1990) is "reasonable anticipation that harm or injury is a likely result from certain acts or omissions" (p. 649). Foreseeability has been discussed as a key element in determining negligence (Ammon, 1993; Ammon & Fried, 1998; Miller, 1993; Sharp, 1990; van der Smissen, 1990). If the facility manager fails to foresee a crowd-related incident that would have been foreseen by a reasonable, prudent facility manager, injuries resulting from the incident leave the organization and manager vulnerable to a lawsuit. **Therefore a** prudent facility manager will **need to** anticipate rather than react (see also Chapter 2.11, *Elements of Negligence*).

Fans rushing onto the athletic field at the end of a game have become a common sight—making such incidents foreseeable. Misinec (2005) discussed how schools differ in their approach to this liability. Some schools, such as Southern Methodist University, take a proactive approach. After one student received a skull fracture from a goalpost incident, SMU spent $90,000 on collapsible goalposts (Deckard, 2005). The University of Florida has implemented extensive crowd management plans to prevent fans from "rushing the field." The University of Florida spends $75,000–$100,000 per game at their 83,000-seat stadium for game staff that includes 210 armed personnel, 2 German shepherds, and 250 peer-group security. Ohio State University takes a different approach. OSU's Chief of Police in 2002 stated, "It's a futile attempt to keep a crowd of 20,000 students off the field. If [an on-field celebration] happens, we let them go out and celebrate" (p. 194). The University of Tulsa head football coach, while trying to motivate students on the night before his team finally snapped a seventeen-game losing streak, told them "he would pay for new goalposts if they became casualties of a victory celebration" (p. 192).

Foreseeability, however, is not as clear as it once was. An example of such a case is the brawl that broke out between players and fans during an Indiana Pacers and Detroit Pistons NBA basketball game in November 2004. Cory Meredith, President of Staff Pro, a national crowd management company, explained, "Security's job has never been to watch the players. It's been to protect the players and keep the fans from getting too close. Security is really just to act as a deterrent" (Gotsch, 2004, p. 3).

Evolution of Crowd Management

An examination of the history of crowd management reveals that some type of security measures were always used at major sport/entertainment events. In the early Roman days lions and other wild animals took care of anyone attempting to "rush the field." Since those early days providing security or bodyguards for events and important persons has become a more structured endeavor.

Two of the early rock-and-roll band promoters, Graham on the West Coast and Fey in the Midwest, are often credited with recognizing the need for an effective crowd management plan. They, along with a few other promoters, realized that uniformed law officers were not the best individuals to use in the protection of the early touring bands. They introduced the concept of **using "peer-group"** security personnel **who are recruited** from the same demographics as the concert fans. Not only were the early "peer group" security better able to relate to the crowds, but the T-shirt security (as they were called) also received specific training in how to deal with rock-and-roll fans.

Many sport and recreation managers contract with outside companies to provide the crowd management service for their venues. This practice of contracting outside agencies is known as **outsourcing**. Some events still use **uniformed** or **off-duty law enforcement** officers, but due to high salaries, improper training, and promoter concerns, using uniformed security for crowd management duties is no longer the industry standard. However, uniformed security is still used to provide security services and to arrest intoxicated or unruly individuals at many events. In addition, because of the heightened concerns since September 11, 2001, more facilities are turning to armed law enforcement officers.

Outsourcing crowd management services has become more prevalent since September 11, 2001, and was especially evident during Super Bowl XXXVI in New Orleans and the 2002 Winter Olympics in Salt Lake City. For the Super Bowl alone, an estimated 3,000 NFL security personnel were on hand (Miller & Pianin, 2002). The police and military presence topped 10,000 at the Winter Games, outnumbering the athletes more than four to one. Most were in uniform, but thousands of undercover agents (men and women of all ages) mingled with fans, shopped for souvenirs, and skied down the slopes while combing the crowd for terrorists (Clarke, 2002).

Contracting or outsourcing crowd management services eliminates the headaches associated with the hiring, firing, training, and scheduling of the crowd management staff. In 1967, Contemporary Services Corporation became the pioneer in peer-group security. It has expanded to provide service to various political, sport, and entertainment venues and events, including the 2004 Summer Olympics and Paralympics in Athens, Greece. At every major sporting event a familiar yellow shirt or jacket emblazed with "Event Staff" helps the spectator know that some measure of security is being provided. Another company that provides security, primarily on the West Coast is Staff Pro. It services over 3,000 concerts, sporting events, conventions, and special events every year (Contemporary Services, n.d.; Staff Pro, n.d.)

Crowd Management Since September 11, 2001

The terrorist actions of September 11 have forever affected the way facilities and events are managed. A recent international survey found that 94 percent of the respondents identified security as the most important component for a stadium event (Geigle, 2002). Thus, for the first time in history, the 2002 NFL Super Bowl and the 2002 Winter Olympics in Salt Lake City were classified as "National Special Security Events." This classification allowed the federal government to take over the control of the security of the event. The Secret Service was put in charge and, along with the Federal Emergency Management Agency (FEMA) and the FBI, a comprehensive security plan was devised.

Operational costs for sport/entertainment events have increased exponentially because insurers now view these types of events as attractive targets for terrorists. Insurance claims from the attacks on September 11 have been estimated to be around $40 billion (Baugus, 2003). The availability of terrorist insurance will remain limited and the premiums astronomical for an indefinite period. It has been estimated that an attack on a major sport/entertainment venue could result in fifteen times the deaths that occurred on 9/11/01 (Abernethy, 2004). Thus it is paramount for sport/entertainment facility operators to recognize their venue's vulnerability and take corrective measures. Guidelines developed and security measures implemented to combat terrorism are effective crowd management techniques under any circumstances.

The Orange Bowl Committee has created a "Security Committee" that looks at issues involving crowd safety and security. This committee discusses a variety of topics, including stadium security, type of search policy, parking concerns, identification of vendors, alcohol policies, transportation of teams, and number of staff necessary for the event. For example, for many years, the bottle and can check was done at the gate. Bags would be opened and guests would show the staff its contents. Security personnel never touched anything. Today, nothing is allowed into the gate except a woman's purse or a diaper bag with baby in tow. All checks are done outside the gates now as well. In addition, during sport events at the Orange Bowl, a reduction in alcohol sales has been implemented. Before the tighter security measures, alcohol was sold up to one minute before the end of the game. Now alcohol sales end at halftime. Credentialing has also changed at the Orange Bowl. In the past paper credentials were issued to almost everyone. Today all event personnel, from the concessionaires to parking attendants, are issued credentials that include signature and photo identification. Finally, when the Orange Bowl hosts "mega" events, such as the BCS National Championship football game, all event staff goes through an FBI background check (M. Morrall, 2005).

Changes in Operational Procedures

Working along with the International Association of Assembly Managers (IAAM) the U.S. Department of Homeland Security has developed a tool that allows venue security managers the opportunity to assess the vulnerabilities of their public assembly facilities. The Vulnerability Self-Assessment Tool (VSAT) is an online program designed for stadium managers to integrate along with their **standard operating procedures.** The VSAT is modeled after programs successfully used by the Transportation Security Administration to identify vulnerability at airports and other transportation facilities. The VSAT was "adapted to incorporate industry safety and security best practices for critical infrastructure to assist in establishing a security baseline for each facility" ("Launch," 2005, p. 1).

Tools such as the VSAT can be implemented and utilized by any type of venue, no matter its size or degree of importance. In addition, the vulnerabilities identified by such tools are not only for threats posed by potential "terrorists." Emotional and violent fans, mentally ill criminals, disgruntled employees and local community members who object to the traffic congestion or noise generated from various events can all also pose a threat to the effective operations of a sport/entertainment facility (Abernethy, 2004). Such a tool should examine such topics as the following.

Physical Security Measures

A small vehicle loaded with explosives parked near a facility can cause tremendous damage and multiple deaths (e.g., the Oklahoma City bombing). Thus the parking and delivery policies of the facility should be examined. Security checks along with biometric verification can be used. Large concrete planters can be situated to keep trucks (or cars) from parking too close to the venue's walls. Filled with flowers and plants, these barriers need not appear ominous. Sensors can be installed to quickly detect the release of chemical and biological agents.

Technological communication networks, such as **closed-circuit television** should be installed around venue access points (e.g., doors, gates, windows). In addition, sensors should also closely monitor access points for the air conditioning, ventilation, and water systems.

Central Monitoring

A control room or command post should be established for the management of facility security and should be located in a position that can survey the overall event. This is crucial for effective communication. Having the command post in a central location will allow the staff to view the entire venue and enable them to utilize binoculars to identify disruptive or intoxicated individuals. In the UK, the command post or control room by statute must have a view of the stadium interior. Unfortunately, although many of the newly constructed sport and entertainment facilities in the United States have enormous resources and the latest in technological advances, many of the command posts are located in the basement or away from the main seating area (Nuttall, 2002). A specific number of staff members should be equipped with multichannel radios, with each channel designated for specific groups (e.g., channel 1—peer group; channel 2—housekeeping; channel 3—law enforcement; channel 4—medical services). Staff members from each group may then be contacted by the command post, via radio, to handle various situations in an expedient and fair manner.

Evacuation

Response time to a terrorist attack becomes critical, especially depending on the type of weapon used. Each facility should have a specific evacuation plan in place for a variety of attack scenarios. Electronic signs and emergency lighting are extremely important. Panic can increase the number of deaths as well as spread any contamination resulting from the attack. Most facilities today have devised an evacuation plan but often leave out important components, such as the evacuation of their disabled guests.

Security Systems

Terrorists conduct a significant amount of surveillance before carrying out an attack. Once they have identified a "soft" target, they begin their plans. An effective security system can discourage them from attempting an attack as well as "harden" the facility. The current system must be examined, threat assessment carried out, and associated probabilities identified. Cost should not be the deciding factor but obviously needs to be taken into consideration. Based on the information collected, a plan can be properly developed to reduce vulnerability to acceptable risk levels (Abernethy, 2004). However, no matter the level of preparedness, the facility manager needs to be able to adapt. For example, Hurricane Katrina taught facility managers that telephone service, water, heating/air conditioning, electricity, and other essential services may be disrupted for extended periods of time. In addition, if the towers used by cell phones are damaged, a sport/entertainment facility (e.g., Louisiana Superdome) can have its communication system rendered totally inoperative. The purchase and use of satellite phones may need to be investigated.

New Technology

The specter of terrorism and interest in increased security has prompted advances in various technologies to combat the threat. These new, cutting-edge measures have come from a variety of industries, including the correctional facility, defense, and law enforcement sectors. New technology has been developed that provides high-powered capabilities for spectator protection to facility managers.

One of these new marvels is an X-ray machine that examines a person's clothing layer by layer to detect weapons. "**Bodysearch**" scans both sides of an individual in less than thirty seconds, and only dense items such as weapons or explosives appear on the image (Nuttall, 2001). **Facial recognition systems**, used in Atlantic City and Las Vegas, have become a controversial piece of technology. One system, FaceTrac™, uses the distance between the eyes, thickness of lips, and angle of cheekbones to compare with database photos of known terrorists. The 2001 Super Bowl received its share of criticism when the Tampa police employed FaceTrac™ (Miller, Stoldt, & Ayres, 2002). **Iris scans** have been introduced, but they are time consuming and only accurate from short distances. Thus, their effectiveness for large crowds remains suspect (Pare, 2001). In March 2002, Virgin Airways began testing JetStream™. Iris patterns of frequent fliers were registered in the United States. Upon landing in London, passengers would look into a camera, and if the iris matched, a barrier was raised allowing access past immigration (Stoller, 2002).

Security Personnel and Authority

Private crowd management and security companies play a large role in managing and controlling the public in office buildings, schools, parks, recreation and sport facilities, and concert venues. Most private security personnel believe their authority comes from various private contract provisions, state and local regulations, tort and criminal law doctrines of assault, as well as trespass and false imprisonment laws (Sklansky, 1999). Many of the claims of illegal searches allege a violation of privacy rights and rely on the Fourth Amendment's guarantee of freedom from unreasonable searches. In determining if a search is legal, the courts look at three issues: (1) if the conduct was considered to be state action, (2) if the conduct could be considered a search, and finally (3) if the search was reasonable. Most legal experts agree that all three criteria are met when photos are taken or a search is required to gain entrance to a recreation or sport facility (Miller et al., 2002).

To illustrate, in *Rhames v. School District of Philadelphia* (2002), a Philadelphia public high school student was suspended after striking another student. Under authority of the dean of students, the security personnel arrested, handcuffed, and removed the student from the building ("Court Finds," 2002). The student sued, stating his federal civil rights were violated under 42 U.S.C. § 1983. The court found the dean to be acting under the authority of state law (i.e., a state actor). Thus, the court decided the security personnel were acting within their authority, and the actions of the student would warrant a prudent man to believe the plaintiff had committed or was committing an offense. The charges were dismissed because the security personnel's probable cause could not be disputed by the plaintiff student.

The courts have placed various limitations on the authority of private crowd management companies. Often, any violation of state law will cause a crowd manager to be held to the same civil and criminal liability as any private individual. In addition, the courts have ruled that a search of a person's belongings without their consent will generally be viewed as trespass. It is a mistake, however, to make too much of these limitations. "In the first place, it is not always true that security guards have only the powers of ordinary citizens. Many private guards, for example, are 'deputized' or otherwise given full or partial police powers by state or local enactment, and most states have codified a *merchant's privilege* that allows store investigators and, in some instances, other categories of private security personnel, to conduct brief investigatory detentions that would be tortuous or criminal if carried out by ordinary citizens" (Sklansky, 1999, Private security law, ¶ 3). Public police have well-defined legal powers, whereas the private security officer's power lies in the ambiguity of his or her predetermined role. The courts, however, have been inconsistent—sometimes treating police and private security similarly and sometimes treating them quite differently (Sklansky, 1999).

Crowd Management Plan

A crowd management plan is an important component of the overall risk management plan of any organization whose activities or events are attended by large numbers of people. The facility manager is either directly or indirectly responsible for both risk management and crowd management. For the facility manager to effectively carry out these responsibilities, an effective crowd management plan addressing such issues as capacity of the venue, geographic location, demographics of guests, and type of event must be designed and implemented. In the event of litigation alleging failure to control crowds, courts will look to see if such a plan existed, if it was in writing, how it was implemented, and how it was disseminated to the involved employees. Each employee needs to be aware of his or her role in the plan, even if it is only a small part (see also Chapter 5.11, *Risk Management Process*).

Trained and Competent Staff

The first component of a good plan is to have properly trained and competent staff to carry out the policies. **Screeners/searchers** are employed as the first group of trained staff to identify and turn away prohibited items. Such items could be bottles, cans, coolers, cameras, weapons, fireworks, umbrellas, or alcoholic beverages. This "search," depending on the event and local statutes, may be a visual screening or a physical "pat down." In light of the terrorist threat emanating from the tragedies on September 11, 2001, this search has become a much more critical element of the crowd management plan. Before September 11, 2001, the biggest concern for event managers stemmed from alcohol problems. Now, crowd managers must make their spectators feel safe while at sport facilities. The NFL implemented a full pat down by security guards before fans were allowed to enter the various stadiums during the 2005 NFL season. This resulted in several lawsuits brought by outraged Tampa and San Francisco fans, **who alleged the policy violated their right to privacy (Estrella, 2005). Ironically enough, the Tampa Bay situation occurred less than a month after a twenty-one-year-old University of Oklahoma student blew himself up outside Oklahoma Memorial Stadium during a football game between Oklahoma and Kansas State (AP, 2005).**

The second group of crowd management personnel is the **ticket takers,** who collect tickets from those entering the facility. The main role of the ticket taker is to ensure that everyone entering the event has a valid ticket for that day's event.

Ushers comprise the third wave of crowd management personnel. They should be well versed in facility layout, knowing directions to and locations of first aid stations, pay phones, restrooms, concession stands, authorized smoking areas, and exits. Ushers should also assist the guests in finding their seats. The usher should observe the patrons and call for assistance when necessary to assist injured patrons, remove food and beverage spills, and defuse potential crowd altercations. The usher is not usually trained to handle disruptive behavior and should refrain from becoming directly involved (Miller, 1993).

The last wave in crowd management is perhaps the most visible—the **peer-group** or **T-shirt** security. Peer-group security is trained to handle crowd disturbances such as unruly, disruptive, or intoxicated patrons. These individuals will also assist in protecting the athletes or performers on the floor or field of the facility. Most recreation, sport, and entertainment facilities also require additional peer-group security personnel to fill various crowd management roles backstage and/or in the press box.

To reduce the risk of a lawsuit due to personnel errors, whether outsourced personnel are used or the facility hires its own security personnel, it is paramount for all staff—ticket takers, screeners, ushers, or T-shirt security—to go through an **orientation program**. This orientation should include an understanding of the facility layout, location of first aid stations, restrooms, telephones, lost and found, emergency exits, and perhaps most important, a clear understanding of their duties and authority (including the legal ramifications of their actions).

Crisis Management and Emergency Action Plan

The second major component in a crowd management plan is to prepare for crises or emergencies. Being prepared for crises and emergencies includes the capacity to respond to two types of situations—a crisis or an individual injury or illness. **Crises** include events such as fire, bleacher collapses, bomb threats, power loss, tornados, and in today's society, terrorist activities. **Emergencies** generally take the form of medical problems (e.g., heart attacks, injuries from falls, heat-related illnesses).

Crisis management plans and emergency action plans are necessary to "ensure that minor incidents don't become major incidents and that major incidents don't become fatal" (ACSM, 1992, p. 29). Such plans must be designed and implemented by crowd managers, practiced, and documented (see also Chapter 2.31, *Emergency Care,* and Chapter 5.23, *Crisis Management*).

Procedure for Handling Disruptive, Unruly, or Intoxicated Patrons

The third component of an effective crowd management plan pertains to dealing with **fan ejections.** Examples of behaviors that could result in an ejection include disruptive or unruly behavior, intoxication, possession of prohibited items that screeners should have removed but overlooked, evasion of admission fees, or field intrusion. Another problem that may necessitate an ejection is third-party assaults. Third-party assaults occur for various reasons, some foreseeable and some not. Unless physical assaults are foreseeable the courts have found that facility or organization managers are not liable for these intentional torts (*Gill v. Chicago Park District*, 1980; *Miller*, 1993). However, if there has been a history of violence or disruptive behavior, the courts have held that actions should be taken to prevent such occurrences (*Bishop v. Fair Lanes Georgia Bowling, Inc.*, 1986; *Cassanello v. Luddy*, 1997; *Leger v. Stockton*, 1988).

Well-written policies should be established that address ways to handle disruptive behavior. The language should be clear and concise, stating what actions will not be tolerated and what measures will result. Ejection policies should be printed on tickets and posted for patrons. Policies may differ among athletic event, recreational activity, or concert depending on the request of the event manager. It is crucial for personnel with ejection authority to be well trained regarding the legal ramifications of their role (e.g., individual liability, understanding of human rights, protection of evidence, excessive force, rules of detention and arrest, and crimes against persons and property). It is also very important that ushers and other staff members who do not have ejection authority receive in-service training regarding their role. Acting appropriately, within the legal boundaries, forestalls lawsuits against both the organization and the staff member (van der Smissen, 1990).

Usually it is best to include a warning before an actual ejection takes place. If an ejection is necessary, it should be carried out swiftly. Handling patrons in this way sends a quick, but firm message to others in the crowd as to what will and will not be tolerated.

Every ejection must be properly documented. This is an extremely crucial step in the ejection process, as it serves to produce a valuable defense for the crowd management employee and facility administration if subsequent litigation ensues (Ammon & Fried, 1998). In addition, photographs or video should be utilized as an additional step in the ejection process. This measure accurately portrays the ejected fan's condition and further protects the employees from unnecessary legal harassment. With today's technology, closed-circuit television is being utilized to scan the crowds, as well as in highly sensitive areas such as entrances, exits, the box office, and concession areas (Fried, 1997)

Effective Communication Network

An effective communication network is the fourth component of an effective crowd management plan. The network allows the crowd management staff to work efficiently and cooperatively to handle situations as they occur. Representatives from each group (facility management, medical, security, and law enforcement) should have input in the organization of the communication network. This communication network should be a part of the employee orientation and training for each event. Crowd management needs more than a *risk avoidance* emphasis. The decisions made in the first two minutes *after* an incident will save lives. Pat downs, limits on bag size, and vehicle barriers are all important, but facility managers have to adopt the philosophy that *incidents will occur*, thus communication is paramount (Nuttall, 2002).

Effective Signage

The fifth component of a crowd management plan is **signage.** Signage is an underutilized tool in risk and crowd management. Signage may be directional or informational in nature, and each has its own specific function. **Directional signs** have a number of important uses. Directional signs provide patrons with directions to important locations such as interstate highway entrances and exits, main roadways, and parking areas. Other directional signs serve to indicate the correct entrance gate or portal, as well as directing the patrons to the ticket office.

Informational signs are signs that inform the public. Prohibited items (e.g., cans, bottles, backpacks, weapons, food, recording devices, and cameras) and rules (including ejection policies) are often communicated through such signs. Spectators appreciate being treated fairly and will normally abide by directives if previously informed. In addition, directional signage helps to provide answers to spectator questions by identifying the location of concession stands, first aid rooms, telephones, restrooms, smoking areas, and exits.

Implementation and Evaluation of the Plan

As with the risk management plan, the last step in a crowd management plan is the **implementation and evaluation** of the plan. A recreation or sport facility will not benefit from a well-written crowd management plan unless it is effectively implemented during an event. Implementation should start with a review of both the risk and crowd management policies before the event. Event-specific activities, such as halftime promotions, VIP guests on the sideline, or band members coming out into the crowd should be discussed. Each staff member should understand how the activity might affect his or her event responsibilities. After an event, all the personnel should come together for a debriefing. They should also look into ways to improve the plan. As stated earlier, a crowd management plan should be flexible and allow for change as needed. Without implementation and evaluation, a well-organized crowd management plan becomes ineffective.

Significant Case

The 1999 Hayden v. Notre Dame case involves a business invitee who was injured by souvenir-seeking fans while attending a football game. The trial court granted summary judgment. The Indiana State Court of Appeals rejected that motion and used elements from premises liability to find in favor of the Haydens. The "totality of the circumstances" as well as "foreseeability" are two concepts germane to this specific case.

HAYDEN VS. NOTRE DAME

Court Of Appeals Of Indiana, Third District
716 N.E.2d 603; 1999 Ind. App. LEXIS 1697
September 28, 1999, Decided

Opinion: Kirsch

On September 16, 1995, William and Letitia Hayden attended a football game on the Notre Dame campus. They were season ticket holders and sat in their assigned seats, which were in the south endzone behind the goalpost. During the second quarter of the game, one of the teams kicked the football toward the goal. The net behind the goalposts did not catch the ball, and it landed in the stands close to Letitia Hayden's seat. Several people from the crowd lunged for the ball in an effort to retrieve it for a souvenir. One of them struck Letitia Hayden from behind, knocking her down and causing an injury to her shoulder.

The Hayden's brought suit against Notre Dame for failing to exercise care to protect Letitia Hayden. Notre Dame moved for summary judgment, arguing that it did not have a legal duty to protect Letitia Hayden from the intentional criminal acts of an unknown third person. The trial court granted Notre Dame's motion. The Hayden's now appeal.

* * *

The Hayden's claim that Notre Dame was negligent in failing to protect Letitia Hayden. In order to prevail on a claim of negligence, a plaintiff must prove: (1) a duty owed to the plaintiff by the defendant; (2) a breach of that duty by the defendant; and (3) injury to the plaintiff proximately caused by that breach. The only element at issue here is whether Notre Dame owed Letitia Hayden a duty under the circumstances. Whether a duty exists is generally a question of law for the court to determine.

The Hayden's argue that this case is governed by premises liability principles and that the relevant standard of care is determined by Letitia Hayden's status as an invitee. The parties do not dispute that Letitia Hayden was a business invitee of Notre Dame. Nonetheless, Notre Dame argues that it owed no duty to protect Letitia Hayden from a third party's criminal act. It contends that the third party's action was unforeseeable, and that it therefore owed no duty to anticipate it and protect Letitia Hayden, a business invitee.

Our Supreme Court recently decided several cases, which articulated the test for determining when a landowner's duty to its invitees extends to protecting them against the criminal actions of third parties that occur on its land. In Delta Tau Delta v. Johnson, 712 N.E.2d 968 (Ind. 1999), the court adopted a "totality of the circumstances" test for determining when such a duty arises. This test "requires landowners to take reasonable precautions to prevent foreseeable criminal actions against invitees." The court explained that, "under the totality of the circumstances test, a court considers all of the circumstances surrounding an event, including the nature, condition, and location of the land, as well as prior similar incidents, to determine whether a criminal act was foreseeable." "A substantial factor in the determination is the number, nature, and location of prior similar incidents, but the lack of prior similar incidents will not preclude a claim where the landowner knew or should have known that the criminal act was foreseeable." Applying the totality of the circumstances test in the case before it, the court held that the defendant-fraternity owed a duty to the plaintiff, a young woman who attended a party at the fraternity house, to take reasonable precautions to protect her from sexual assault by third parties on its premises. The court looked at prior incidents of assault and forced alcohol consumption, as well as the fraternity's awareness of the prevalence of date rape (especially involving fraternity members) and of legal action taken against other fraternities for sexual assault, and concluded that under these circumstances such a duty existed.

In Vernon v. Kroger Co., 712 N.E.2d 976 (Ind. 1999), the court applied the same test to the case of a plaintiff who was beaten on the defendant's store premises by a shoplifter attempting to flee. The plaintiff was attempting to exit the store's parking lot when he inadvertently blocked the vehicle of the fleeing shoplifter. The shoplifter pulled the plaintiff from his vehicle and beat him. The court noted that shoplifting at the store was not an unusual occurrence, that many shoplifters attempted to flee in waiting cars, that some shoplifters used force to escape, that criminal occurrences had happened in the parking lot, and that in the two years prior to this event, the police had made numerous visits to the store for crimes of violence and an increasing number of visits for battery and shoplifting. Based on the totality of the circumstances, the court held that the defendant owed the plaintiff a duty to protect him from the criminal acts of the third party-shoplifter.

* * *

Applying this test to the case before us, we find that the totality of the circumstances establishes that Notre Dame should have foreseen that injury would likely result from the actions of a third party in lunging for the football after it landed in the seating area. As a result, Notre Dame owed a duty to Letitia Hayden to protect her from such injury. The Hayden's were seated in Notre Dame's stadium to watch a football game. Notre Dame well understands and benefits from the enthusiasm of the fans of its football team. It is just such enthusiasm that drives some spectators to attempt to retrieve a football to keep as a souvenir. There was evidence that there were many prior incidents of people being jostled or injured by efforts of fans to retrieve the ball. Letitia Hayden testified that she and her husband had attended Notre Dame football games for many years, and that she witnessed footballs land in the seating area around her many times. On numerous occasions, she saw people jump to get the ball. She testified that she witnessed another woman injured a number of years earlier when people in the crowd attempted to retrieve a football, and that Ms Hayden was knocked off her seat earlier in the game by crowd members attempting to retrieve the ball prior to the incident in which she was injured.

William Hayden testified that the net behind the goalpost caught the ball only about fifty percent of the time that it was kicked. The other half of the time, the ball would fall in the seating area around his seat, and people would try desperately to retrieve the ball. He stated that a few years prior to this incident, he had been knocked off his feet and thrown into the next row by fans eager to retrieve a football, and that he had been jostled a number of times. He stated that Notre Dame ushers witnessed fans being jostled in scrambles for the ball, but did not make aggressive attempts to recover the balls. He testified that in prior years, student managers, who were Notre Dame employees, would aggressively attempt to retrieve balls from fans and were usually successful in returning the balls to the playing field. The managers, however, no longer tried to retrieve the balls and stayed on the playing field.

Based on the totality of the circumstances, we hold that Notre Dame owed Letitia Hayden a duty to take reasonable steps to protect her from injury due to the actions of other fans in attempting to retrieve footballs which land in the seating area. The trial court erred in finding that no duty existed and entering summary judgment in favor of Notre Dame.

Reversed

Recent Trends

Fine the School

As a solution to keep fans off the playing surfaces at athletic events, some conferences have begun to fine the universities that host the events. For example, in February 2005 the Southeastern Conference fined the University of South Carolina $5,000 after fans rushed onto the basketball court to celebrate a Gamecock victory over rival Kentucky. The SEC implemented the policy in December 2004 to "create a safe environment for everyone who participates and attends our athletic events," according to Mike Slive, SEC commissioner. The fine at basketball games is $5,000 for the first offense, $25,000 for the second, and $50,000 for the third ("SEC," 2005).

Crowd Management Legislation

During the summer of 2002 a father and son breached U.S. Cellular Field security, came onto the field, and proceeded to attack the Kansas City Royals first base coach during a baseball game. This confrontation, along with four incidents of field intrusion during the 2004 baseball season at the Great American Ball Park, has prompted state legislators from Ohio to propose legislation pertaining to fans (or terrorists) who enter any restricted area at a place of public amusement. Major League Baseball witnessed thirty-nine field intrusions during the 2004 season, which resulted in thirty-eight arrests. The penalties for this type of action are very light in many states. Ohio state legislators hope that stricter penalties will not only deter these altercations, but also serve as a motivation to prosecute the offenders. The proposed new law would "allow an owner or lessee of a place of public amusement, an agent of the owner or lessee, or a performer or participant at a place of public amusement to use reasonable force to restrain and remove a trespasser from a restricted portion of the place of public amusement" (p. 5). The types of restricted areas covered by the legislation would include playing fields, athletic surfaces, stages, and locker and dressing rooms (Sherborne, 2005).

References

Cases

Bishop v. Fair Lanes Georgia Bowling, Inc., 803 F.2d 1548 (11th Cir. 1986).
Cassanello v. Luddy, 302 N.J. Super. 267; 695 A.2d 325; 1997 N.J. Super. LEXIS 286.
Hayden v. Notre Dame, 716 N.E.2d 603; 1999 Ind. App. LEXIS 1697.
Gill v. Chicago Park District, 407 N.E.2d 671; 1980 Ill. App. LEXIS 3150.
Leger v. Stockton, 249 Cal. Rptr. 688 (July 25, 1988).
Rhames v. School District of Philadelphia, Civil Action No. 01-5647 United States District Court for the Eastern District of Pennsylvania 2002 U.S. Dist. LEXIS 13816.

Publications

Abernethy, B. (2004, November). Worst-case scenarios. *Stadia*. Retrieved November 27, 2004 from http:www.stadia.tv/archive/user/archive_article.tpl?id=20041124173315
American College of Sports Medicine (ACSM). (1992). *ACSM's health/fitness facility standards and guidelines*. Champaign, IL: Human Kinetics.
Ammon, R., Jr. (1993). Risk and game management practices in selected municipal football facilities (Doctoral dissertation, University of Northern Colorado, 1993). *Dissertation Abstracts International, 54*, 3366A–3367A.
Ammon, R., Jr., & Fried, G. (1998). Assessing stadium crowd management practices and liability issues. *Journal of Convention & Exhibition Management, 1*(2–3), 119–150.
Ammon, R., Jr., Southall, R., & Blair, D. (2003). *Sport facility management: Organizing events and mitigating risks*. Morgantown, WV: Fitness Information Technology, Inc.
Associated Press. (2005, October 3). Man blows himself up at University of Oklahoma. *MSNBC.com* Retrieved January 20, 2006 from http://www.msnbc.msn.com/id/9557879
Baugus, R. V. (2003, January/February). Insurance escalates in wake of attacks. *Facility Manager, 19*(1), 28–30.
Black, H. C. (1990). *Black's law dictionary* (6th ed.). St. Paul, MN: West Publishing Co.

Clarke, L. (2002, September 11). Security is measured: Officials struggle with precautions for everyday events security. *The Washington Post*, p. D01.

Contemporary Services Corporation. (n.d.). *About us*. Retrieved January 11, 2006 from http://www.contemporary services.com/pages/about.html

Court finds student's preemptive self-defense argument unconvincing. (2002, November). *Legal Notes for Education, 15*(19), 10.

Deckard, L. (2005, June). Promoting good sportsmanship is an operational issue at most colleges. *VENUEStoday, 4*(18), 6–7.

Estrella, C. (2005, December 16). NFL's pat-down policy challenged 49ers season-ticket holders, ACLU sue to stop searches. *SFGate.com*. Retrieved January 20, 2006 from http://www.sfgate.com/cgi-bin/article.cgi?f=/c/a/2005/12/16/PAT.TMP

Fried, G. (1997, Spring). Risk management for recreation programs in the 1990's. *Texas Entertainment and Sports Law Journal, 6*(1), 6–12.

Geigle, M. (2002, Showcase special). Safe is sound. *Stadia, 19,* 130–133.

Gotsch, N. (2004, November). Basketball brawl prompts reassessment. *VENUEStoday, 3*(37), 3.

International Association of Assembly Managers. (1997, February 15–16). *Duties of a crowd assembly facilitator*. Paper presented at the Crowd Management Curriculum Workshop, Irving, TX.

Launch of online security initiative for international stadia. (2005, January). *Stadia*. Retrieved June 29, 2005 from http:www.stadia.tv/archive/user/archive_article.tpl?id=20050110162214

Maloy, B. P. (2001). Safe environment. In D. Cotton, J. Wolohan, & J. Wilde (Eds.), *Law for recreation and sport managers* (2nd ed., pp. 105–118). Dubuque, IA: Kendall/Hunt.

Miller, L. K. (1993). Crowd control. *Journal of Physical Education, Recreation and Dance, 64*(2), 31–32, 64–65.

Miller, B., & Pianin, E. (2002, February 1). U.S. agencies confront a security triple play; three events pose biggest logistical test since the September 11 attacks. *The Washington Post*, p. A11.

Miller, L. K., Stoldt, G. C., & Ayres, T. D. (2002, January). Search me: Recent events make surveillance efforts even more likely to pass judicial muster. *Athletic Business, 26*(1), 18, 20–21.

Misinec, M. (Spring, 2005). When the game ends the pandemonium begins: University liability for field-rushing injuries. *The Sports Lawyers Journal 12*(1), 181–219.

Nuttall, I. (2001, July). Secure all areas. *Stadia,*(*10,* 83–84.

Nuttall, I. (2002, September/October). Safer stadia—Putting reaction alongside prevention. *Facility Manager, 18*(5), 49.

Pare, D. (2001, October 12). *Biometrics: Keeping an eye on new forms of security*. Retrieved February 10, 2002 from http://www.exn.net/Stories/2001/10/12/53.asp

Perkins, L. B. (2002, November). Safe conduct. *Stadia,*(*19,* 42–46.

SEC fines South Carolina for fans on court. (2005, February 18). *FindLaw*. Retrieved February 19, 2005 from http://news.findlaw.com/scripts/printer_friendly.pl?page=/ap/s/2060/2-18-200502181

Sharp, L. A. (1990). *Sport law*. National Organization on Legal Problems of Education. Topeka, KS: National Organization on Legal Problems in Education.

Sherborne, P. (2005, April). Crowd control legislation considered in Ohio. *VENUEStoday, 4*(14), 4–5

Sklansky, D. A. (1999). The private police. *UCLA Law Review 46,* 1165. Retrieved January 11, 2003 from http://web.lexis-nexis.com/universe/document?_m=01ab7afa12d95de834824d8cc36fbb2b&_docnum=8&wchp=dGLbVlb-lSlAl&_md5=101ffdeb60d9d74d1746007c0d7de8d8

Staff. (2005, November). Stadia's sampling of major news stories. *Stadia, 37,* 4–5.

Staff Pro. (n.d.). *History*. Retrieved January 20, 2006 from http://www.staffpro.com/aboutus/history.asp

Stoller, G. (2002, March 11). Dulles, JFK test iris-recognition systems. *USA Today*, p. B1.

Tierney, R. (2001, September 24). Zumwalt examines the new threat. *Amusement Business, 113*(38), 1, 4.

van der Smissen, B. (1990). *Legal liability and risk management for public and private entities*. Cincinnati, OH: Anderson Publishing Co.

Interview

M. Morrall, personal interview, November 15, 2005.

5.25 Managing Risk through Insurance

Doyice J. Cotten
Sport Risk Consulting[1]

Insurance is a method by which an individual or business pays a defined expenditure (premium) to protect against the possibility of a large, undetermined future loss or expense. Conducting business without insurance is like rock climbing without a safety line—very risky. Insurance spreads the financial risks and costs of an individual or business among a large group of persons or businesses so that the losses of those few who experience them are shared with the many who do not. In so doing, insurance provides protection against financial catastrophe and is an indispensable risk management technique.

Many persons look at the purchase of insurance and risk management as one and the same. This, however, is not true. Risk management involves the identification of risks, determination of the extent of the risks, and the implementation of one or more control approaches. Control approaches include: (1) elimination of the activity; (2) reduction of risks through operational control; (3) retention (through such techniques as self-insurance, current expensing, and deductibles); (4) transfer by contract (through indemnity agreements, exculpatory clauses, and by requiring insurance by the other party); and 5) purchasing insurance from an insurance company.

Obviously, insurance is but one of many techniques available to help manage risks in a recreation or sport business. The recreation or sport manager should purchase insurance to protect against all risks that could have a significant impact on the financial integrity of the business, but should not try to insure against every possible risk and potential loss. In addition to protection against property loss, loss of business income, and monetary judgments in lawsuits, insurance also protects the recreation or sport business from legal expenses resulting from litigation.[2] It is usually less expensive to simply pay for minor losses when they occur. A major danger, however, is that failure to meet claim reporting requirements can jeopardize coverage when a seemingly minor injury (a strained knee) eventually reveals itself as a major injury (an ACL tear). It is obviously important that the recreation or sport manager be knowledgeable enough to determine which risks are of such a magnitude as to allow retention by the business, which can be transferred by contract and which require protection through insurance coverage. The purpose of this chapter is to help the recreation or sport manager become more informed about this aspect of risk management and, subsequently, be able to better protect the business from financial risks.

Fundamental Concepts

Understanding the Policy

To become more knowledgeable about insurance and to be better able to protect the recreation or sport business from financial risks, the recreation or sport manager must learn to read and understand an insurance policy. Most can be long and confusing, particularly if one docs not know exactly what to look for and

---

[1] Special thanks to Denise Brown, Claims Coordinator for **Fitness Pak**, Chico, CA, for making sure this chapter is up-to-date and accurate.

[2] It is estimated that the average legal expense incurred by an insurance company in taking a suit to trial is approximately $35,000. When the business is insured (and the loss is covered), the insurance company absorbs this cost. When there is no insurance, the business incurs this expense (usually, even if the business wins the lawsuit).

does not know the contextual meaning of the terms used. Novick (2000) suggested that the policy should **not** be read like a book or article—from beginning to end. He suggests that the policy be read in the following order for maximum understanding.

Declarations

This is the section that includes the facts and figures regarding your particular policy. This section includes such items as the name of the insured, address, policy period, coverages, amounts of insurance, the applicable deductibles, and the cost of the policy. If parties other than the corporate entity are covered (e.g., employees, directors), those parties should be named in the declarations section. Careful study of this section can help one to better understand the coverage of the policy.

Endorsements

Look for the endorsements at the end of the policy. **Endorsements** are coverage provisions, added by the carrier, which change the terms of coverage in the main body of the policy. These may broaden or extend coverage in certain instances and may limit or reduce coverage in others. This final section of the policy is an identification of the specific endorsements included with your policy.

The reader should turn to the referenced portion in the main body of the policy and note the endorsement number in the margin beside the coverage language the endorsement is to replace. Do this for each endorsement. Then, when the reader begins to read the main body of the policy, the reader can flip to each endorsement at the appropriate time.

Endorsements may be added when the policy is purchased or at a later date as the needs of the recreation or sport business change. Examples of endorsements might include adding insured persons, coverage of fine art, and peak-season coverage (which increases inventory coverage by 25 percent during the peak season when inventory is higher than usual). A separate Difference in Conditions policy or endorsement might be purchased to protect against earthquakes and floods.

Definitions

The key terms of the policy are defined in this section. The reader must understand the terms in this section to understand the coverage that is being purchased. Many key words or phrases used in the document are carefully defined. Examine these carefully because many terms have specific meanings in insurance that may differ from the recreation or sport manager's concept of the term. For instance, one might assume that "personal injury" refers to physical injuries of an individual. However, personal injury refers to injuries caused by such acts as slander, libel, false arrest, false imprisonment, humiliation, and invasion of privacy. The reader should refer back to this section when encountering an unfamiliar term.

Contractual Agreement

This part is the actual contractual agreement between the insurance company and the recreation or sport business. The statement of agreement may be quite short. The section simply states that the insurance company agrees to insure the business to the extent indicated in the declarations in exchange for the agreed-upon premium.

The **coverages section** includes a listing of what is being insured in the policy. Following each coverage is a detailed explanation of what is included in the coverage. For example, the building might be listed including any attached structures. The section might state that rental structures away from the main building are not included. This section will also include the perils that the insurance covers (e.g., fire, theft). Additional benefits coverage includes coverage of newly acquired property.

The **exclusions section** of the policy describes what is not covered by the policy. Items that are often excluded from a standard commercial policy include landscaping, buildings under construction, and cash. Some perils that are usually excluded from the standard policy are earthquake; volcanic eruption; water damage from floods, sewers, or surface groundwater; power interruption; war; and nuclear hazard. When a coverage is needed by the business that is not listed in the inclusions and is excluded by the exclusions, riders or endorsements adding the coverage to the policy may be purchased.

The **conditions section** sets forth the various things the recreation or sport business must do to meet the obligations of the insured. Some of these conditions might include prompt reporting obligations following a loss, giving sworn affirmation of loss, providing an inventory, or provision of receipts.

This section also includes the responsibilities of the insurance company in the event of a claim. Specified here are such things as when cash replacement is mandated, when replacement items may be utilized, procedures to be followed if the insurer and insured fail to agree on the loss, and whether repair is the option of the insurance company.

Determining Necessary Coverage[3]

In reviewing a current insurance policy or when considering the initial purchase of insurance coverage, the recreation or sport business must take four steps to make a wise insurance purchase. First, examine the risks and potential losses that the organization might encounter. Then, establish an effective risk reduction program to reduce the likelihood of the risks occurring. Third, identify the remaining risks and determine which are of a magnitude that can be safely retained by the business and which might be handled by transfer by contract. Finally, the remaining risks that can significantly impact the business should then be covered by an insurance policy that will protect the business from financial loss.

Figure 1 provides a list of financial risks faced by recreation or sport businesses. Of course, the risks faced vary from one type of business to another, so many of the risks listed in the figure will not apply to a particular business, and some businesses may encounter risks that are not listed. Nevertheless, the figure can serve as a guide or checklist in helping the recreation or sport manager make certain the business is properly covered.

Types of Insurance Coverage

There are several types of insurance coverage. Each is designed to offer protection from loss for certain risks. The two types that are most indispensable for a recreation or sport business are property insurance and general liability insurance. Other types of insurance include umbrella liability, liability protection for employees, employment practices liability, motor vehicle, workers' compensation, and event insurance. Each type will be explained following.

Property Insurance

Property insurance is the primary means of protecting the recreation or sport business from loss due to damage or destruction of its facility, the facility contents, and accompanying properties. Three levels of property coverage are offered: basic, broad (or extended coverage), and special form (sometimes referred to as open perils). The **basic coverage** includes protection against a limited number of hazards (e.g., fire, malicious mischief, lightning, explosion, windstorm, aircraft or vehicles, sprinkler leakage, sinkhole collapse, volcanic action, and vandalism). **Broad coverage** includes protection against the exposures listed in basic coverage plus several other exposures (e.g., falling objects, weight of ice, water damage, and smoke). **Special form** coverage includes all losses except those that are specifically excluded (e.g., collapse, burglary, and theft). The recreation or sport manager should examine the policy carefully to determine what risks are included under each type of coverage and should realize that even with special form coverage, some property risks

---

[3] Independent contractors in recreation and sport activities (e.g., aerobics instructors, personal trainers, massage therapists) should remember that their operation constitutes a business entity and needs insurance just as larger recreation and sport businesses do. Independent contractors are not generally covered by the insurance of the club at which they work. By way of example, **Fitness Pak** offers liability plans for ACE-certified professionals with coverage ranging from $1 million to $6 million. The policy covers legal expenses and any financial judgments for covered losses (up to the limits of the policy) against the insured. The policy cost ranges from $155 to $288 annually.

Property Exposures

Fire
Smoke
Natural Elements
  Wind & Tornado Damage
  Flood
  Lightning
  Rain
  Hail
  Earthquake
Debris Removal
Vandalism & Malicious
  Mischief
Riot
Explosion
Boiler & Machinery
Damage to Signs
Glass Coverage
Damage to Parking Lots
  & Fences
Damage by Aircraft

Valuable Papers
Electronic Data Processing
Computer Systems
Money & Property
  Theft, Burglary,
  Disappearance
  Embezzlement & Employee
  Dishonesty
  Off-Premises Coverage
  Counterfeit Losses

Moveable Equipment
  (golf carts, mowers, etc.)
Golf Green Coverage
Damage to Property of Others
  (on your premises)

Company Vehicles
  Damage to Vehicle
  (collision)
  Damage to Vehicle
  (noncollision: theft,
  vandalism, tree limb)
  Damage to Vehicle
  (uninsured motorist)
  Damage to other Vehicles
  or Property

Public Liability (Excluding Negligence)

Malpractice by Personnel
Products Liability
Contractual Liability
  (Including
  Indemnification)
Advertisers Liability
Dram Shop/Host
  Liquor Liability

Intentional Torts
  (Personal Injury)
  Defamation
  False Arrest or
    Imprisonment
  Malicious Prosecution
  Invasion of Privacy
  Wrongful Entry or Eviction
  Assault and Battery
Employment Practices
  Sexual Discrimination
  Racial Discrimination
  Handicap Discrimination
  Age Discrimination
Sexual Harassment
Civil Liberty Violations

Business Operations

Business Interruption
  Loss of Income
  Extra Expenses
Sickness/Accidents/Disability
  of Employees
Health of Key Personnel
Workers' Compensation

Public Liability (Negligence)

Death
Paralysis
Brain Damage
Loss of Limbs
Loss of Senses
Internal Organ Injuries
Infliction of Emotional Stress
Broken Bones
Damaged Ligaments &
  Tendons
Sprains and Strains
Cuts, Punctures, Abrasions,
  & Bruises

Vehicles:
  Injury to Other Persons
  Damage to Property
    of Others
  Damage to Nonowned or
    Leased Vehicles

Directors & Officers Liability
Professional Liability
Independent Contractors
  Liability
Adventure & Tripping Liability
Sponsor Liability
Trip Liability
Event Liability

Watercraft
  Injury to Other Persons
  Damage to Property of
    Others

Injury to Participant
Catastrophic Injury to
  Participant
Pollution Liability
Suits by Employees (for
  Wrongful Termination,
  Breach of Employment
  Contract)

Adapted from van der Smissen, B. (1990). Legal Liability and Risk Management for Public and Private Entities. Cincinnati, OH: Anderson Publishing Company.

FIGURE 1 Typical Financial Risks Faced by Recreation & Sport Businesses

are not covered. If the recreation or sport manager feels more coverage is needed, additional endorsements must be purchased. Some exposures that might not be included and might require additional endorsements include theft by employees, vehicles such as golf carts, and boilers. Property insurance also does not include normal wear and tear, cracking, settling, vermin, earthquakes, or floods.

Two endorsements of special importance to many recreation or sport businesses are **extra expense insurance** and **business income insurance**. Extra expense insurance protects the business against certain indirect losses that may occur. For instance, if a health spa is destroyed by fire, some expenses that may be encountered are rental of another building during rebuilding, leasing equipment, and advertising expense. Business income coverage includes loss of income due to the insured peril and continuing expenses such as the salaries of key personnel while the business is closed.

The recreation or sport manager has other choices when purchasing property insurance. One is whether to purchase **actual cash value** or **replacement cost** insurance. Replacement cost is usually preferred because it pays the entire cost to replace the property rather than an estimate of the actual current value of the property (which might fall far short of what is needed to replace the item). Most policies have a **coinsurance** clause that requires the recreation or sport business to insure the property to at least 80 percent of the replacement cost or actual cash value, depending on the form chosen. Failure to coinsure for the amount specified in the policy will result in a significant decrease in benefits in the event of a loss. The amount of the **deductible** is another decision that must be made. The business pays the deductible when a claim is made. For instance, if a storm does $3,000 damage to the building and the business carries a $500 deductible, the business pays the first $500 and the insurance covers the remaining $2,500. The higher the deductible, the lower the cost of the insurance, so a business can save money by carrying a high deductible and retaining that degree of risk.

The recreation or sport manager should determine what exposures are covered by the property insurance, determine from Figure 1 and a knowledge of the risks of the particular recreation or sport business what property exposures are uncovered, and with the help of the insurance agent, determine the best way to provide the protection needed. Most companies offer packages combining several endorsements at a cost less than purchasing the endorsements individually.

General Liability Insurance

The purchase of **general liability insurance** protects the recreation or sport business from financial loss in the event a person suffers injury or property loss as a result of the negligence of the business or its employees. The policy is called commercial general liability (CGL). If the business is sued and the loss is covered, CGL will cover the legal costs and any award for damages up to the limit of the policy. The insurance company also has the option of paying a settlement to the plaintiff to avoid court expenses and risk of a larger award.

Recreation or sport businesses should and usually do carry general liability insurance with coverage of one million dollars or more. Like property insurance, endorsements may be added to supplement the basic coverage. Some of the common endorsements by businesses include the following. **Errors and omissions** coverage (professional liability or malpractice liability) can protect the business from liability for errors by medical personnel, or, in sport settings, by trainers, therapists, or exercise physiologists. **Cross liability** coverage broadens the policy to protect the business from suits from within the organization. For example, CGL would not protect if an injured volunteer worker sued an employee or if an injured employee sued a director. Cross liability would expand the coverage to include suits other than third-party suits. **Pollution liability** is a coverage often purchased by some recreation or sport businesses (e.g., golf courses). This coverage protects the business if acts by the business result in pollution and damage to neighboring property. For instance, a chemical spill in a stream on a golf course could result in damage to the property of others and subsequent legal action against the business.

There are numerous other exclusions from a CGL policy for which endorsements are available. Some of these are damage to the property of others that is stored on your property (saddle animals, watercraft, golf clubs, etc.), fire damage to adjacent property, advertising, adventure and tripping programs, wrongful dismissal, pollution or contamination of the environment, owned saddle animals, owned watercraft, and human rights violations such as sexual harassment.

Employment Practices Liability

Employment practices liability provides protection for such claims as (1) wrongful termination, (2) sexual harassment, (3) equal pay violations, and (4) discrimination (racial, sex, age, and disability). Some policies cover any violation of certain state and federal statutes, including antidiscrimination laws, Americans with Disabilities Act (ADA), Age Discrimination in Employment Act (ADEA), and the Equal Pay Act. (See also Chapter 2.35 *Human Resources Law*.)

When this type of policy first emerged a few years ago, the costs were prohibitive for most small recreation or sport businesses. The policies also required a very large deductible. As this policy became more popular, both premiums and deductibles decreased, but both are currently increasing.[4]

Umbrella Liability

Umbrella liability is a policy that greatly increases the liability protection at a reasonable cost. The policy might increase liability coverage from $1 million to $5 million or more and would come into effect only after the limit of the CGL has been surpassed. This extension of coverage generally applies to the CGL policy, the vehicle coverage, and the workers' compensation insurance.

Liability Protecting Employees

Some recreation or sport businesses not only purchase liability insurance to protect the business, but also purchase insurance to protect employees in the event of legal action. The most common of these is **directors and officers liability** that generally provides general liability protection of $1 million or more for their "wrongful acts." Wrongful acts include error, misstatement, misleading statement, act, omission, and neglect of duty in the person's insured capacity. Coverage generally excludes actions not within the scope of their duties; breach of contract; fines and penalties; dishonesty, infidelity, or criminal activities; human rights or sexual harassment violations; and failure to maintain adequate insurance.

Some recreation or sport businesses provide **professional** or **malpractice insurance** for some or all employees. The professional insurance is designed to protect the employee from liability for negligence in acts related to giving professional advice or counsel. Suits often name the employee personally because the practice today is to sue all who may be potentially at fault; because the act may be an ultra vires act leaving only the employee as vulnerable, and because with governmental entities, the entity may be immune, leaving only the employee. Malpractice insurance applies primarily to persons in legal or health-related areas. Malpractice insurance protects both the individual and the business.

Professional and malpractice insurance can also be purchased by the individual employee. Policies are often available through a professional organization at very reasonable rates. They may also be purchased from one's insurance company, but the charge will be significantly higher. One should be aware that many exclusions exist on the policies.

Motor Vehicle Insurance

The recreation or sport manager must be certain that all business vehicles are adequately covered. Maintain coverage for damage to the business vehicles (collision, comprehensive, and uninsured motorist); damage to other vehicles, property, or persons (liability); and medical coverage for injured parties. Business vehicles should be covered with a commercial automobile policy. One's personal automobile policy generally is inadequate for use with business vehicles.

In automobile insurance, as in property insurance, the amount of the deductible must be decided for both collision (damages to your automobile from the collision with another object) and comprehensive (damage to your automobile other than from collisions, e.g., vandalism to your auto, tree limb falling on your auto). Once again, the higher the deductible, the smaller the premium.

---

[4] **Fitness Pak** (club insurance specialists located in Chico, CA) have a $1 million policy with a **$10,000** deductible suitable for a large, high-end, single-location club for about **$4,500** per year.

In some recreation or sport businesses, employees occasionally must drive personal automobiles for business purposes. A **nonowned automobile** endorsement may be purchased to insure the business in such cases. Coverage may also be extended to include volunteers who use their own vehicles. If the organization cannot insure the business use of personal vehicles for employees or volunteers, procedures should be instituted to ensure that the owners of all such vehicles have adequate coverage. (Both nonowned automobile and hired vehicle endorsements can be added to the CGL when there is no need for owned auto coverage.)

Many recreation or sport businesses have occasion to rent or lease vehicles for varying periods of time. The business may purchase a stand-alone policy or an endorsement on the firm's automobile policy that covers **hired vehicles**. This policy can provide both liability protection and coverage for the rental vehicle. Be aware, however, that neither the stand-alone policy nor the endorsement (nor for that matter, insurance purchased from the rental company) will cover the loss or theft of personal property or equipment stored in the vehicle.

Other desirable endorsements are **uninsured/underinsured motorist coverage**, **bodily injury coverage**, and **property damage**. This coverage applies in the event that the other party has no insurance or the limits of that party's insurance have been reached. Typically this policy carries a $250 property damage deductible.

Workers' Compensation

Workers' compensation is a no-fault, statutory-based insurance that provides for compensation to employees who suffer injury in the course of their employment. It is mandated in most states (see Chapter 5.26, *Workers' Compensation*). The worker receives compensation for lost income, both temporary and long term, and medical expenses incurred. The law in each state limits the amount of compensatory income allowed. In most states, all recreation or sport businesses with three or more full-time employees are required to carry workers' compensation insurance coverage.[5] The cost of this insurance varies with the amount of risk involved in that type of business and with the claims record of each individual sport business. The premium is based on a certain number of dollars per hundred of payroll for the business. Representative costs per $100 dollars of payroll might range from $15 for a riding club, $6 for a country club, $2 for a health spa, to less than $1 for a business involving all clerical or desk work.

Injured workers simply file a claim to receive compensation for work-related injuries. They neither have to file suit against the employer nor prove negligence or fault on the part of the employer. The employee, however, generally cannot receive compensation for pain and suffering through workers' compensation (see also Chapter 5.26, *Workers' Compensation*).

Event Insurance

Many recreation or sport businesses sponsor or conduct events either on an occasional or a regular basis. For any event, the business should purchase additional liability insurance if the event is not included in the CGL policy of the business. The amount of additional insurance coverage depends on the event and how much investment is involved and/or whether the business is dependent on a profit from the event. Also, many parties (e.g., venue, merchandisers, media, sponsors, concessionaires, and competing teams) may need to be named as additional insureds on your policy.

A common event liability policy would include bodily injury, personal injury, and property damage; an incident policy that would cover payment for medical expense for minor injuries (injured files a claim; no suit necessary); and settlement for uncontested claims in exchange for a release.

An important coverage for many events is that for **nonappearance/cancellation of event**. Bases for cancellation are specified, and the policy generally includes costs, anticipated revenues, and anticipated profits. For some events, **life or accident coverage of participants** is purchased. Other typical endorsements include **automobiles, crime, prize indemnity, fire** (for damages that may not fall under the CGL), and **media coverage** (e.g., loss of signal, failure of transmission, breach of contract by media).

---

[5] In California, the law requires that a business provide workers' compensation coverage even if there is only one employee.

Requiring Insurance of other Parties

There are situations when it is important that a recreation or sport business require that other parties have insurance coverage. Some of these situations include (1) when another party or organization rents your facility for some type of event; (2) when a contractor or his workers are on the premises for remodeling, repair, or other work; and (3) when independent contractors make use of your facility.

Certificate of Insurance. It is good policy to require that such groups provide the recreation or sport business with a certificate of insurance. This proof of insurance is a form (called an ACORD form certificate) from the insurance company verifying that the party is covered by liability insurance. If the presence of the party covers a period of time, it may be necessary to require a certificate of insurance again at a later date to ensure that coverage is still in force.

Additional Insured Endorsement. Many businesses require that the other party (e.g., building contractor doing renovations on the premises) name the recreation or sport business as an additional insured party on their insurance coverage. Additional insured status clearly provides coverage when the additional insured has a claim made against it because of the activities of the named insured. The Additional Insured Endorsement is attached with the ACORD form. The form provides details about the coverage, including the insurance company name, the policy number, the dates and limits of coverage, and the name of the agent.

Event Policy. Recreation and sport businesses that make their facilities available to other groups generally require that the organization or group purchase and show proof of a specified amount of event insurance (see previous section). Health clubs, for instance, often make their club available to groups for a dance, party, or even sleepovers. These provide additional revenue and, at the same time, familiarize a number of potential clients with the club. The club generally requires that the group purchase a 24-hour event policy that can be obtained from a specialty insurance provider. Another example of when a user might be required to purchase event insurance would be when a rock group promoter rents a gymnasium for a rock concert.

Independent Contractors. Most recreation and sport businesses do not provide liability insurance coverage for independent contractors (e.g., physical therapists, massage therapists, and personal trainers in health clubs). It is important that the independent contractor be required to carry liability insurance coverage.

Selecting the Agent and Carrier

Few administrators in recreation or sport management are insurance experts. This fact magnifies the importance of selecting both a good agent and a good carrier.

In selecting the carrier, it is important to select a carrier who specializes in recreation or sport entities similar to yours. Such companies often offer enhancements and riders that nonspecialists cannot provide. They know the unique types of problems faced by your type of business. Also, it is important to make certain the company has an A rating and has been in business for a number of years.

When selecting an agent, try to find one who has at least a few recreation or sport clients similar to your entity. The better the agent understands the recreation or sport business, the more helpful the agent can be in recommending important coverages that might be critical to the business and in eliminating, or reducing, unnecessary coverages. Also, make certain the agent works for a company that specializes in recreation or sport entity protection. Select an agent from your region. The agent should walk through your facility and discuss your exposures with you. Finally, do not select an agent who is inexperienced or will not take the time to explain coverages and help you evaluate your needs.

Recent Trends

There are several significant new trends in insurance coverage that may be particularly relevant to the recreation or sport manager. In general, many types of protection like **coverage enhancement policies** are currently harder to find, are more expensive, and have stricter limitations on their coverage. For instance, where tennis courts in the past were covered like a building, now many companies are insuring them as enhancements and limiting coverage to specified perils—generally excluding wind, which is the major peril.

Employee benefits liability is a type of coverage that is currently very popular, inexpensive, and easy to find. To illustrate the coverage, suppose a club pays for health insurance for its employees, but forgets to add a new employee to the policy. Some time later the person is sick, has a claim, and finds no coverage. Employee benefits liability would cover this oversight. Coverage now is usually on a claims-made basis—meaning claims must be promptly and properly made within the term of the policy. Failure to do so would invalidate coverage.

Employee dishonesty or fidelity coverage is an aspect of property coverage. Fitness Pak no longer includes this coverage in their policy, but does sell it separately as an endorsement.

A popular property protection enhancement is **building ordinance coverage**. This coverage protects the entity in the event fire or some other catastrophe destroys all or part of the building and ordinances require additions that were not in the damaged building. For instance, the addition of an elevator to meet ADA requirement might be required. With this enhancement, the cost to add an elevator would be covered by the policy.

References

Brooks, D. (1985). Property insurance. *Risk management today.* Washington: ICMA.

Castle, G., Cushman, R., & Kensicki, P. (1981). *The business insurance handbook.* Homewood, IL: Dow Jones-Irwin.

Corbett, R. (1995). *Insurance in sport and recreation.* Edmonton, Alberta: Centre for Sport and Law.

Dahlgren, S. (2000, April). Covering your assets. *Athletic Business*, 59.

Kufahl, S. (2002, August). Business without a safety line? *Club Industry*, 18.

Mehr, R., Cammack, E., & Rose, T. (1985). *Principles of insurance.* Homewood, IL: Richard D. Irwin.

Novick, L. B. (2000). *Murky waters: Insurance basics for nonprofits.* Washington, DC: Nonprofit Risk Management Institutes.

Sundheim, F. (1983). *How to insure a business.* Santa Barbara, CA: Venture Publications.

van der Smissen, B. (1990). *Legal liability and risk management for public and private entities.* Cincinnati, OH: Anderson Publishing Co.

Wilkinson, D. G., (Ed.). (1988). *The event planning process.* In M. A. Levine, G. Kirke, D. B. Zitterman, & E. Kert. (Eds.), *Insurance.* Willowdale, Ontario, Canada: The Event Management & Marketing Institute.

5.26 Workers' Compensation

John T. Wolohan
Ithaca College

Under common law, when an employee was injured on the job, there was a good chance the injuries would go uncompensated due to the doctrines of assumption of risk, contributory negligence, and the fellow servant rule (Larson, 1992). Those injured workers who could overcome the preceding defenses usually faced a series of other problems before they received any compensation for their injuries. First, the injured workers, faced with little or no income, were under enormous financial pressure to settle their claim. The injured worker therefore usually received much less than the true value of their claim to support themselves and their families. Second, even if the injured employee was able to withstand the financial pressure and could afford to litigate the claim, the employer was often able to use the court system to his or her advantage and delay paying the employee any compensation. Finally, if the injured worker was lucky enough to recover his or her damages, the award was usually reduced by hefty attorney fees (Prosser & Keeton, 1984).

In an effort to protect injured workers and alleviate the injustice of the common law system, states began to enact workers' compensation legislation modeled after the German and English systems. The first state to enact workers' compensation legislation was New York in 1910. By 1949, every state in the country had enacted some form of workers' compensation law. The workers' compensation legislation, which is different in every state, provides benefits, including lost wages, usually around one-half to two-thirds of the employee's weekly wages, and medical care to an employee who is injured or killed in the course of employment, regardless of fault. The right to compensation benefits is based on one simple test: Was there a work-connected injury? In exchange for this protection, the injured worker agrees to forego any tort claim he or she might have against the employer (Larson, 1992).

Workers' compensation is, therefore, a form of strict liability. It does not matter whether the injury was caused by the employee's negligence or pure accident, *all the employee has to show is that he or she was injured in the course of employment* (Larson, 1992). As a result, the injured worker receives quick financial assistance with minimal interruption in his or her life.

Fundamental Concepts

The basic policy behind the workers' compensation system is that the cost of the product should bear the blood of the worker (Prosser & Keeton, 1984). In other words, the employer is required by the state to compensate the employee through private insurance, state-funded insurance, or self-insurance for any damages suffered by an employee. The employer should treat the cost of workers' compensation insurance as part of the cost of production. These extra costs are then added to the cost of production and passed on to the consumer.

Eligibility Requirement

Although every state has its own workers' compensation laws, there are two requirements that every injured employee must satisfy before he or she can recover workers' compensation benefits. The first requirement is that the person must show that he or she was an employee of the organization. An **employee** is defined as any person in the service of another under any contract of hire. In reviewing the relationship between an individual and a recreation or sport organization to determine if he or she was in fact an employee, the courts use an "economic reality test" (*Coleman v. Western Michigan University*, 1983). Under the economic reality test, the court examines the following factors to determine whether there existed an expressed or implied contract for hire.

1. Does the employer have the right to control or dictate the activities of the proposed employee;
2. Does the employer have the right to discipline or fire the proposed employee;
3. The payment of "wages" and, particularly, the extent to which the proposed employee is dependent upon the payment of wages or other benefits for his daily living expenses; and
4. Whether the task performed by the proposed employee was "an integral part" of the proposed employer's business. (*Coleman v. Western Michigan University*, 1983 at 225)

In *Coleman v. Western Michigan University* (1983), the Michigan Court of Appeals, citing the *Rensing v. Indiana State University Board of Trustees* (1983) decision, concluded that scholarship athletes are not employees within the meaning of the workers' compensation statute. In particular, the court found that Coleman could only satisfy the third factor of the "economic reality test," that his scholarship did constitute wages. As far as the other factors, the court found that the university's right to control and discipline Coleman required by the first two factors was substantially limited. In considering the fourth factor, the court held "that the primary function of the defendant university was to provide academic education rather than conduct a football program." The term *integral*, the court held, suggests that the task performed by the employee is essential for the employer to conduct his business. The "integral part" of the university is not football, the court said, but education and research.

The second requirement every employee must meet before he or she can collect workers' compensation is that **the injury suffered by the employee must have occurred in the course of his or her employment**.

Recreation or sport managers need to be conscious of workers' compensation in the following areas: staff employees, volunteers, and scholarship athletes. With staff employees, it is clear that the recreation or sport manager should follow the local laws governing workers' compensation insurance. How volunteers and scholarship athletes are classified is much more difficult. For example, a number of states, including California, Oregon, Minnesota, and Tennessee, allow "volunteers" to be covered under the employer's workers' compensation plan (Wong & Wolohan, 1996).

Workers Compensation and Small Businesses

As mentioned earlier, workers' compensation is primarily regulated by the individual states, and therefore there is no single cohesive set of rules governing benefits, coverage, or premium computation. There are, however, some things that every business, no matter how big or small, must know. First, no matter how small your business, if you have employees, you need workers' compensation insurance. As a result, workers' compensation insurance can be a significant expense for any small business.

Second, to satisfy the workers' compensation obligations, all an employer has to do is simply purchase an insurance policy. In most states, these policies can be purchased from an insurance company. There are, however, five states and two U.S. territories (North Dakota, Ohio, Puerto Rico, the U.S. Virgin Islands, Washington, West Virginia, and Wyoming), that require employers to get coverage exclusively through state-operated funds (Priz, 2005). Thirteen states also allow employers the option of purchasing their insurance either with the state fund or private insurance. Those states that offer employers this option are Arizona, California, Colorado, Idaho, Maryland, Michigan, Minnesota, Montana, New York, Oklahoma, Oregon, Pennsylvania, and Utah (Priz, 2005).

Third, it is important to remember that if a business fails to carry workers' compensation insurance and an employee is injured, the employer can be required to not only pay the employee's medical expenses, death benefits, lost wages, and vocational rehabilitation out of pocket, but also be liable for any penalties levied by the states (Priz, 2005).

Independent Contractors

Whether an individual is hired as an independent contractor or an employee may impact the obligation an employer has under each state's workers' compensation law. For example, some states require all workers to be covered under its workers' compensation programs, regardless of whether or not they are employees or independent contractors. Some states, on the other hand, only require employees to be covered. As a result, it is important that employers know their state's laws to determine who in fact is covered and what must be required of them to comply (Priz, 2005).

Volunteers

Although covering "volunteers" under your workers' compensation plan may seem like a less-attractive option considering the up-front expense for the organization of paying for workers' compensation insurance, there are a number of important benefits from this option. First, by covering "volunteers" under your workers' compensation plan, if a volunteer is injured, you can save your organization both time and money by avoiding a negligence lawsuit. Second, by covering "volunteers" under your workers' compensation plan, you save your organization from any bad publicity that a lawsuit would generate. Finally, you also protect your volunteers from financial hardship by providing them benefits under workers' compensation (Wong & Wolohan, 1996).

For example, in 1999, a girls' softball umpire in Montana was stepping away from the plate when a player accidentally hit him. When a workers' compensation claim was filed on behalf of the umpire, the investigation revealed that local recreation league umpires and referees had no workers' compensation insurance and possibly no medical coverage at all. Without workers' compensation, recreational league umpires have to rely on their own personal medical insurance. The cost for the league to cover the referees under workers' compensation would have been about $3.08 per referee (Hull, 2000). It is important to note that the decision did not affect officials of school games because they were specifically exempted from the law.

State Legislation Covering Athletes

In affirming the decision of the California Workers' Compensation Appeals Board, the California Court of Appeals in *Graczyk v. Workers' Compensation Appeals Board* (1986) denied workers' compensation benefits to Ricky Graczyk after he sustained head, neck, and spine injuries while playing football for California State University, Fullerton. The Court of Appeals ruled that it was the intent of the state legislature to exclude Graczyk, and all scholarship athletes, from receiving workers' compensation benefits for injuries received on the playing field. The court pointed out that the California State Legislature specifically amended the state's workers' compensation statute to exclude "any person, other than a regular employee, participating in sports or athletics who receives no compensation for such participation other than the use of athletic equipment, uniforms, transportation, travel, meals, lodging, or other expenses incidental thereto" from the definition of employee.

The California State Legislature amended the statute further in 1981 when it specifically excluded "[a]ny student participating as an athlete in amateur sporting events sponsored by any public agency, public or private nonprofit college, university or school, who receives no remuneration for such participation other than the use of athletic equipment, uniforms, transportation, travel, meals, lodging, scholarships, grants in aid, and other expenses" from the definition of employee (*Graczyk v. Workers' Compensation Appeals Board*, 1986; West's Ann. Cal. Labor Code § 3353 (k)). Hawaii, New York, and other states have followed California's example of expressly excluding scholarship athletes from workers' compensation benefits.

Another area where states have amended their workers' compensation statutes is the exclusion of professional athletes. In *Tookes v. Florida State University* (Claim No. 266-39-0855), a basketball player at Florida State University suffered a knee injury during the 1981–82 season, which required him to sit out most of the season. As a result of his injury, Tookes filed a workers' compensation claim for lost wages and medical expenses. Tookes argued that he was an employee of the university, due to his athletic scholarship, and therefore entitled to workers' compensation benefits (Wong, 1994).

The Florida Department of Labor and Employment Security and Industrial Claims judge, however, disagreed. The judge determined that there was no employer–employee relationship between Tookes and the university. Even if there was an employer–employee relationship between Tookes and the university, the judge held that Tookes would still be ineligible for benefits. If Tookes was employed by the university to play basketball, under Florida law he would be considered a professional athlete and therefore a member of a class specifically excluded under the Florida Workers' Compensation Statute (Wong, 1994). Besides Florida, at least five other states—Massachusetts, Missouri, Pennsylvania, Texas and Washington—exclude or limit workers' compensation benefits to professional athletes or have considered amending their state workers' compensation statutes to exclude professional athletes (Wolohan, 1994).

Consequences of Additional Coverage

As illustrated by *Rensing v. Indiana State University Board of Trustees* (1983), the issue of whether or not a scholarship athlete is an employee is a difficult one. For example, in most states, workers' compensation insurance rates are determined by actuarial tables that take into account the number of accidents and claims for that particular group of employees. If athletes were suddenly added into the group of school employees, the number of injuries and claims of the group would rise substantially. This would make it difficult, if not impossible, for colleges and universities to find an insurance company willing to insure them. Even if the school could find an insurance company, the increased exposure would require the insurance company to raise rates. Faced with higher insurance rates and/or the potential liability of self-insuring, many schools would be forced to reevaluate whether the increased cost and exposure is worth having an athletic program.

Other possible consequences follow.

Additional Workers' Compensation Claims

If scholarship athletes are considered employees of their school, there could be an increase in the number of workers' compensation claims filed and benefits paid (Wolohan, 1994).

Tax Effect on School

If scholarship athletes are considered employees of their school, there would be some interesting tax questions for both the colleges or universities and the scholarship athletes. For example, does the scholarship athlete now have to pay taxes on the value of the scholarship? Also, will schools now be required to pay FICA and Medicare tax on the student's income? If so, how are the taxes to be paid (Wolohan, 1994)?

Employee Benefits

If scholarship athletes are considered employees of the school, are scholarship athletes eligible for employee benefits? Besides tuition, room, board, and books, are scholarship athletes now going to be eligible for life, medical, and dental insurance? How about the school's employee retirement plan, would scholarship athletes be eligible (Wolohan, 1994)?

Nonscholarship Athletes

Even if scholarship athletes are considered employees of the school, what about athletes who do not receive athletic scholarships? Because these athletes receive no compensation, they have no contractual relationship with the university to compete in athletics. Therefore, the nonscholarship athlete could never be deemed an employee and would never be covered by workers' compensation (Wolohan, 1994).

NCAA Catastrohpic Insurance Policy

One of the reasons scholarship athletes have sought workers' compensation benefits in the past is to recover out-of-pocket medical expenses. Although most schools will pay the medical expenses of injured athletes, there usually is a limit to their generosity. In fact, it is not uncommon for a school to stop paying an injured athlete's medical and other bills. This is especially true when the injury is permanently disabling, and the injured athlete requires prolonged medical care.

In an effort to alleviate such hardships, and perhaps to prevent future court challenges on the status of scholarship athletes, the NCAA in August 1991 implemented a Catastrophic Insurance Plan covering every student who participates in college athletics. The NCAA's Catastrophic Insurance Plan covers student–athletes, student coaches, student managers, student trainers, and cheerleaders who have been catastrophically injured while participating in a covered intercollegiate athletic activity. The policy has a $50,000 deductible and provides benefits in excess of any other valid and collectible insurance.

The NCAA's Catastrophic Insurance Plan automatically insures every college athlete who participates in NCAA sports against catastrophic injuries. The NCAA's plan is similar to workers' compensation in that it provides medical, dental, and rehabilitation expenses plus lifetime disability payments to students who are catastrophically injured, regardless of fault. The plan also includes $10,000 for burial expenses in case an athlete dies during practice or a game.

The NCAA plan is more attractive than workers' compensation in a number of ways. First, scholarship athletes can collect benefits without litigating the issue of whether or not the athlete is an employee of the college or university. Second, the NCAA's plan provides the athlete with benefits immediately, without time delays, litigation costs, and the uncertainties involved in litigation. Finally, another benefit of the NCAA's plan is that it guarantees that catastrophically injured athletes will receive up to $60,000 toward the cost of completing their undergraduate degree. (For more information on the NCAA's Catastrophic Insurance Plan go to the NCAA Website: http://www.ncaa.org/insurance/catastrophic.html.)

Significant Case

————————————————◊◊◊————————————————

Although maybe not the most recent case, the following case is significant in that it provides the reader with a thorough review of the issues surrounding scholarship athletes who suffer career-ending or life-threatening injuries. In particular, the case analyzes the definitions of "employee" for purposes of the workers' compensation laws.

RENSING V. INDIANA STATE UNIVERSITY BOARD OF TRUSTEES

Supreme Court of Indiana
444 N.E.2d 1170 (1983)

The facts established before the Industrial Board were summarized by the Court of Appeals:

"The undisputed testimony reveals that [Indiana State University Board of Trustees] the Trustees, through their agent Thomas Harp (the University's Head Football Coach), on February 4, 1974 offered Fred W. Rensing a scholarship or 'educational grant' to play football at the University. In essence, the financial aid agreement, which was renewable each year for a total of four years provided that in return for Rensing's active participation in football competition he would receive free tuition, room, board, laboratory fees, a book allowance, tutoring and a limited number of football tickets per game for family and friends. The 'agreement' provided, inter alia, the aid would continue even if Rensing suffered an injury during supervised play which would make it inadvisable, in the opinion of the doctor-director of the student health service, 'to continue to participate,' although in that event the University would require other assistance to the extent of his ability.

The trustees extended this scholarship to Rensing for the 1974–75 academic year in the form of a 'Tender of Financial Assistance.' Rensing accepted the Trustees' first tender and signed it (as did his parents) on April 29, 1974. At the end of Rensing's first academic year the Trustees extended a second 'Tender of Financial Assistance' for the 1975–76 academic year, which tender was substantially the same as the first and provided the same financial assistance to Rensing for his continued participation in the University's football program. Rensing and his father signed this second tender on June 24, 1975. It is not contested the monetary value of this assistance to Rensing for the 1975–76 academic year was $2,374, and that the 'scholarship' was in effect when Rensing's injuries occurred.

* * *

Rensing testified he suffered a knee injury during his first year (1974–75) of competition which prevented him from actively participating in the football program, during which time he continued to receive his scholarship as well as free treatment for his knee injury. The only requirement imposed by the Trustees (through Coach Harp) upon Rensing was attendance at his classes and reporting daily to the football stadium for free whirlpool and ultrasonic treatments for his injured knee.

* * *

As noted above, the financial aid agreement provided that in the event of an injury of such severity that it prevented continued athletic participation, 'Indiana State University will ask you to assist in the conduct of the athletic program within the limits of your physical capabilities' in order to continue receiving aid. The sole assistance actually asked of Rensing was to entertain prospective football recruits when they visited the University's Terre Haute campus.

During the 1975 football season, Rensing participated on the University's football team. In the spring of 1976 he partook in the team's annual three week spring practice when, on April 24, he was injured while he tackled a teammate during a punting drill.

* * *

The specific injury suffered by Rensing was a fractured dislocation of the cervical spine at the level of 4–5 vertebrae. Rensing's initial treatment consisted of traction and eventually a spinal fusion. During this period he developed pneumonia for which he had to have a tracheostomy. Eventually, Rensing was transferred to the Rehabilitation Department of the Barnes Hospital complex in St. Louis. According to Rensing's doctor at Barnes Hospital, one Franz Steinberg, Rensing's paralysis was caused by the April 24, 1976 football injury leaving him 95–100% disabled." Rensing v. Indiana State University Board of Trustees, supra, at pp. 80–82 (footnotes omitted).

Rensing's appeal to the Industrial Board was originally heard by a Hearing Member who found that Rensing had "failed to sustain his burden in establishing the necessary relationship of employer and employee within the meaning of the Indiana Workmen's Compensation Act," and rejected his claim. Id. at p. 83. The Full Industrial Board adopted the Hearing Member's findings and decision; then this decision was reversed by the Court of Appeals.

In this petition to transfer, the Trustees argue that there was no contract of hire in this case and that a student who accepts an athletic "grant-in-aid" from the University does not become an "employee" of the University within the definition of "employee" under the Workmen's Compensation Act, Ind. Code § 22-3-6-1(b), (Burns Supp. 1982). On the other hand, Rensing maintains that his agreement to play football in return for financial assistance did amount to a contract of employment.

Here, the facts concerning the injury are undisputed. The contested issue is whether the requisite employer-employee relationship existed between Rensing and the Trustees so as to bring him under the coverage of our Workmen's Compensation Act. Both the Industrial Board and the Court of Appeals correctly noted that the workmen's compensation laws are to be liberally construed. *Prater v. Indiana Briquetting Corp.*, (1969) 253 Ind. 83, 251 N.E. 2d 810. With this proposition as a starting point, the specific facts of this case must be analyzed to determine whether Rensing and the Trustees come within the definitions of "employee" and "employer" found in the statute, and specifically whether there did exist a contract of employment. Ind. Code § 22-3-6-1, supra, defines the terms "employee" and "employer" as follows:

"(a) 'Employer' includes the state and any political subdivision, any municipal corporation within the state, any individual, firm, association or corporation or the receiver or trustee of the same, or the legal representatives of a deceased person, using the services of another for pay."

"(b) The term 'employee' means every person, including a minor, in the service of another, under any contract of hire or apprenticeship, written or implied, except one whose employment is both casual and not in the usual course of the trade, business, occupation or profession of the employer."

The Court of Appeals found that there was enough evidence in the instant case to support a finding that a contract of employment did exist here. We disagree.

It is clear that while a determination of the existence of an employee-employer relationship is a complex matter involving many factors, the primary consideration is that there was an intent that a contract of employment, either express or implied, did exist. In other words, there must be a mutual belief that an employer-employee relationship did exist. *Fox v. Contract Beverage Packers, Inc.*, (1980) Ind. App., 398 N.E. 2d 709, *Gibbs v. Miller*, (1972) 152 Ind. App. 326, 283 N.E. 2d 592. It is evident from the documents which formed the agreement in this case that there was no intent to enter into an employee-employer relationship at the time the parties entered into the agreement.

In this case, the National Collegiate Athletic Association's (NCAA) constitution and bylaws were incorporated by reference into the agreements. A fundamental policy of the NCAA, which is stated in its constitution, is that intercollegiate sports are viewed as part of the educational system and are clearly distinguished from the professional sports business. The NCAA has strict rules against "taking pay" for sports or sporting activities. Any student who does accept pay is ineligible for further play at an NCAA member school in the sport for which he takes pay. Furthermore, an institution cannot, in any way, condition financial aid on a student's ability as an athlete. NCAA Constitution, Sec. 3-1-(a)-(1); Sec. 3-1-(g)-(2). The fundamental concerns behind the policies of the NCAA are that intercollegiate athletics must be maintained as a part of the educational program and student-athletes are integral parts of the institution's student body. An athlete receiving financial aid is still first and foremost a student. All of these NCAA requirements designed to prohibit student-athletes from receiving pay for participation in their sport were incorporated into the financial aid agreements Rensing and his parents signed.

Furthermore, there is evidence that the financial aid which Rensing received was not considered by the parties involved to be pay or income. Rensing was given free tuition, room, board, laboratory fees and a book allowance. These benefits were not considered to be "pay" by the University or by the NCAA since they did not affect Rensing's or the University's eligibility status under NCAA rules. Rensing did not consider the benefits as income as he did not report them for income tax purposes. The Internal Revenue Service has ruled that scholarship recipients are not taxed on their scholarship proceeds and there is no distinction made between athletic and academic scholarships. Rev. Rul. 77-263, 1977-31 I.R.B. 8.

As far as scholarships are concerned, we find that our Indiana General Assembly clearly has recognized a distinction between the power to award financial aid to students and the power to hire employees since the former power was specifically granted to the Boards of Trustees of state educational institutions with the specific limitation that the award be reasonably related to the educational purposes and objectives of the institution and in the best interests of the institution and the state. Ind. Code § 20-12-1-2(h) (Burns 1975).

Furthermore, we find that Ind. Code § 22-4-6-2 (Burns 1974) is not applicable to scholarship benefits. In that statute, which deals with contributions by employers to unemployment insurance, employers are directed to include "all individuals attending an established school . . . who, in lieu of remuneration for such services, receive either meals, lodging, books, tuition or other education facilities." Here, Rensing was not working at a regular job for the University. The scholarship benefits he received were not given him in lieu of pay for remuneration for his services in playing football any more than academic scholarship benefits were given to other students for their high scores on tests or class assignments. Rather, in both cases, the students received benefits based upon their past demonstrated ability in various areas to enable them to pursue opportunities for higher education as well as to further progress in their own fields of endeavor.

Scholarships are given to students in a wide range of artistic, academic and athletic areas. None of these recipients is covered under Ind. Code § 22-4-6-2, supra, unless the student holds a regular job for the institution in addition to the scholarship. The statute would apply to students who work for the University and perform services not integrally connected with the institution's

educational program and for which, if the student were not available, the University would have to hire outsiders, e.g., workers in the laundry, bookstore, etc. Scholarship recipients are considered to be students seeking advanced educational opportunities and are not considered to be professional athletes, musicians or artists employed by the University for their skills in their respective areas.

In addition to finding that the University, the NCAA, the IRS and Rensing, himself, did not consider the scholarship benefits to be income, we also agree with Judge Young's conclusion that Rensing was not "in the service of" the University. As Judge Young stated:

"Furthermore, I do not believe that Rensing was 'in the service of' the Trustees. Rensing's participation in football may well have benefited the university in a very general way. That does not mean that Rensing was in the service of the Trustees. If a student wins a Rhodes scholarship or if the debate team wins a national award that undoubtedly benefits the school, but does not mean that the student and the team are in the service of the school. Rensing performed no duties that would place him in the service of the university." Rensing v. Indiana State University, supra, at 90.

Courts in other jurisdictions have generally found that such individuals as student athletes, student leaders in student government associations and student resident-hall assistants are not "employees" for purposes of workmen's compensation laws unless they are also employed in a university job in addition to receiving scholarship benefits.

All of the above facts show that in this case, Rensing did not receive "pay" for playing football at the University within the meaning of the Workmen's Compensation Act; therefore, an essential element of the employer-employee relationship was missing in addition to the lack of intent. Furthermore, under the applicable rules of the NCAA, Rensing's benefits could not be reduced or withdrawn because of his athletic ability or his contribution to the team's success. Thus, the ordinary employer's right to discharge on the basis of performance was also missing. While there was an agreement between Rensing and the Trustees which established certain obligations for both parties, the agreement was not a contract of employment. Since at least three important factors indicative of an employee-employer relationship are absent in this case, we find it is not necessary to consider other factors which may or may not be present.

We find that the evidence here shows that Rensing enrolled at Indiana State University as a full-time student seeking advanced educational opportunities. He was not considered to be a professional athlete who was being paid for his athletic ability. In fact, the benefits

Rensing received were subject to strict regulations by the NCAA which were designed to protect his amateur status. Rensing held no other job with the University and therefore cannot be considered an "employee" of the University within the meaning of the Workmen's Compensation Act.

It is our conclusion of law, under the facts here, including all rules and regulations of the University and the NCAA governing student athletes, that the appellant shall be considered only as a student athlete and not as an employee within the meaning of the Workmen's Compensation Act. Accordingly, we find that there is substantial evidence to support the finding of the Industrial Board that there was no employee-employer relationship between Rensing and the Trustees, and their finding must be upheld.

For all of the foregoing reasons, transfer is granted; the opinion of the Court of Appeals is vacated and the Industrial Board is in all things affirmed.

Recent Trends

Fighting Is Integral to Hockey

In 2005, the Virginia Workers' Compensation Commission and the Virginia Court of Appeals ruled that fighting was an integral part of the game of hockey. Ty Jones, who played for the Norfolk Admirals of the American Hockey League, was sent into a game by his coach with instructions to "go get" a particular opponent. Once in the game, Jones started a fight, during the course of which Jones injured his shoulder.

The Admirals argued that Jones's fight was voluntary, or "willful misconduct" under the law, and that because hockey actually has rules prohibiting fighting, the injury should not be covered. In upholding the Virginia Workers' Compensation Commission finding fighting was an integral part of the game of hockey, the Virginia Court of Appeals found that Jones was performing a task that he was employed to perform, fighting. The court also noted that the fight was not a personal undertaking but instead was directed against the other player as part of Jones' employment and in furtherance of the Admirals' business.

Workers' Compensation and the Horse-Racing Industry

An example of the impact workers' compensation insurance premiums can have on an industry is the California racehorse trainers. In the beginning of 2002, many trainers were faced with a dramatic increase in workers' compensation premiums. Rates that were about $24 per $100 of payroll, doubled to $48.40 per $100 of payroll and to $105 per jockey's mount (Stumes, 2002a).

Faced with rising workers' compensation costs, many trainers moved out of state, and those who stayed were forced to buy the expensive policies from the government's State Compensation Fund and pass the costs on to the horse owners.

In December 2002 trainers and owners reached an agreement with another insurance company, American International Group (AIG), to offer lower rates. There had been only one carrier, the government-sponsored State Compensation Insurance Fund. The new rates offered by AIG are $31.28 per $100 of payroll and $73.81, per jockey's mount respectively. One reason AIG's rates are lower is that California Thoroughbred Trainers and Thoroughbred Owners of California were able to get legislation passed to divert money toward the premiums' costs (Stumes, 2002b).

References

Cases

Coleman v. Western Michigan Univ., 125 Mich. App. 35, 336 N.W.2d 224 (1983).

Graczyk v. Workers' Compensation Appeals Board, 184 Cal. App.3d 997, 229 Cal. Rptr. 494, 58 A.L.R. 4th 1245, 34 Ed. Law Rep. 523 (Cal. App. 2 Dist., Aug 8, 1986).

Norfolk Admirals and Federal Insurance Company v. Ty A. Jones, 2005 Va. App. LEXIS 443

Rensing v. Indiana State University Board of Trustees, 437 N.E.2d 78 (1982).

Rensing v. Indiana State University Board of Trustees, 444 N.E.2d 1170 (1983).

State Compensation Fund v. Industrial Commission, 135 Colo. 570, 314 P.2d 288 (1957).

Tookes v. Florida State University, 203.436.0785

University of Denver v. Nemeth, 257 P.2d 423 (1953).

Van Horn v. Industrial Accident Commission, 219 Cal. App. 2d 457, 33 Cal. Rptr. 169 (1963).

Publications

Bacon, J. (1997, Oct. 21) Jury: Injured college athlete ineligible for workers' comp. *USA Today*.

Hull, R. (2000, April 26) Referees and umpires cry foul in workers comp decision. *The Daily Inter Lake*.

Larson, A. (1992). *The law of workers compensation*. New York: Matthew Bender & Co.

NCAA Catastrophic Injury Insurance Policy. http://www.ncaa.org/insurance/catastrophic.html

Priz, E. (2005). *Ultimate guide to workers' compensation insurance*. Irvine, CA: Entrepreneur Press

Prosser, W. L., & Keeton, W. P. (1984). *The law of torts* (5th ed.). St. Paul, MN: West Publishing Co.

Stumes, L. (2002a, Feb. 28) Rising premiums create unstable racing industry. *San Francisco Chronicle*, p. C7

Stumes, L. (2002b, Dec. 22) Trainers, owners get some relief. *San Francisco Chronicle*, p. B15

Wolohan, J. T. (1993, June). Ruling may have Texas-size impact. *Athletic Business, 17,* 22–23.

Wolohan, J. T. (1994). Scholarship athletes: Are they employees or students of the university? The debate continues. *Journal of Legal Aspects of Sport, 4,* 46–58.

Wong, G. M. (1994). *Essentials of amateur sports law* (2nd ed.). Westport, CT: Praeger Publishing.

Wong, G. M., & Wolohan, J. T. (1996, March). Pitching in. Schools have alternatives in determining volunteers' legal status. *Athletic Business, 20,* 10–14.

6.00

Contract Law

Contract law is one of the most fundamental duties performed by sport and recreation administrators. Therefore, it is important for all persons involved in the sport and recreation business to understand the basics of contract law. Further, once a contract is drafted, the recreation or sport manager must implement the terms of the contract and must understand the ramifications of failing to meet the contractual obligations. The following section examines the essentials of contract formation and the elements necessary for a legally valid contract.

The *Contract Law* section is divided into two parts. The first part reviews the fundamental aspects of all contracts, presents some principles of interpretation used by the courts in deciding contract disputes, discusses the concept of breach of contract and the remedies for breach, refers to provisions that are typically found in all contracts, and familiarizes you with the principles relating to signature authority. The first part is also meant as an introduction to subsequent chapters that deal with sport-specific contract law topics in more detail. The second part applies the essential contract elements to employment contracts, college student–athletes' letters of intent, and game, event, and sponsorship contracts.

6.10 Contract Essentials

Linda A. Sharp
University of Northern Colorado

It would be inappropriate to suggest that recreation and sport managers are technically competent to draft their own contracts. Contract law is very complex, and there is a need for legal counsel to draft the provisions of contracts used by recreation and sport enterprises. However, it is important for all persons involved in the sport business to understand the fundamentals of contract law to choose legal counsel wisely and to interact with counsel in the formation of contracts. Further, once a contract is drafted, the recreation or sport manager must implement the terms of the contract and must understand the ramifications of failing to meet the contractual obligations.

As discussed previously, particularly in the risk management chapters contained in Section 5, the principles of risk management are fundamental to any business. Although often the focus of a risk management discussion may be liability issues related to personal injury, it is crucial to understand that risk management must be applied to all contractual undertakings. The economic consequences of failing to take due care in drafting a contract to fully protect the interests of your business may be truly devastating. There is no excuse for failing to take a "preventive" mentality in developing contracts for your business; in most cases the negotiations for any substantial transaction extend for several weeks, if not months.

This "preventive" mentality is exemplified by your attorney's behavior in drafting any contract with the **"worst-case scenario"** in mind. This means that your attorney will draft every contract in a way that will protect your interests even if the worst happens (i.e., the other party terminates or breaches the contract). Any contract is a good one when both parties are behaving amicably; the test of a good contract is whether it protects you when the other party no longer wants to continue its business relationship with you or when you want to terminate your contractual relationship with the other party.

The purpose of this chapter is to acquaint you with the fundamental aspects of all contracts, present some principles of interpretation used by the courts in deciding contract disputes, discuss the concept of breach of contract and the remedies for breach, refer to provisions that are typically found in all contracts, and familiarize you with the principles relating to signature authority. This chapter is also meant as an introduction to subsequent chapters that deal with sport-specific contract law topics in more detail.

Fundamental Concepts

"A contract is a promise, or set of promises, for breach of which the law gives a remedy, or the performance of which the law in some way recognizes a duty" (Restatement (Second) Contracts, Sec.1). This definition of a contract, which is a staple of contract law, is found in the *Restatement (Second) of Contracts*. The *Restatement (Second) of Contracts* was written by a number of legal scholars to give guidance concerning fundamental principles of contract formation, interpretation, remedies and to reflect that contract law is essentially a matter of common law. Some types of business transactions are governed by the Uniform Commercial Code (UCC), variations of which have been added to state statutes, but contract law, for the most part, is governed by common law principles.

Formation of a Contract

For there to be an enforceable agreement, the following elements must be present in every contract.

Offer

An offer is essentially a proposal to form a contract made by the offeror (the party making the offer) to the offeree (the party to whom the offer is made). It is usually a promise, a commitment to do something or to refrain from doing something in the future. It has also been defined as a "manifestation of willingness to enter into a bargain, so made as to justify another person in understanding that his assent to the bargain is invited and will conclude it" (Restatement (Second) Contracts §24).

The offer must be definite as to the "material terms," which are generally: (1) the parties involved; (2) the subject matter; (3) the time and place for the subject matter to be performed; and (4) the consideration, which is usually the price to be paid.

In general, the offeror is free to revoke the offer at any time before acceptance by the offeree. If an offer is terminated, the offeree no longer has the legal ability to accept the offer.

In business transactions, there are usually a number of rounds of negotiation before a contract exists. Often the offeree responds to the initial offer with a counteroffer, this counteroffer concerns the same subject matter as the original offer; it simply proposes different terms than the original offer. When a counteroffer is made, the original offeree becomes the offeror and the original offeror becomes the offeree.

Acceptance

When an offer has been made, no contract can be formed until the offeree accepts the offer. An offer may be accepted only by the person to whom it is made. Further, the offeree cannot reject the offer and then try to accept it. Once the offer is rejected, the offer dies and the offeree cannot then accept the same offer.

A **unilateral contract** means that the offer can only be accepted by performing an act. For example, if A says to B, "If you get me a hot dog from the concession stand, I will pay you $10," B can only accept by performing the act of getting the hot dog. A promise by B to get the hot dog is not an acceptance.

However, a **bilateral contract** implies that B may accept a promise by A with a promise. If A says to B, "If you promise to go get me a hot dog in the seventh inning of the game, I will pay you $10," the offer is accepted when B makes the promise to get the hot dog at the time specified.

An acceptance may not always need to be expressed in words. Sometimes, acceptance may be communicated by conduct or even by silence. For example, in the recent case of *Auburn School District v. King County* (1999), the question of whether a contract could be implied-in-fact from the circumstances arose.

Consideration

Consideration is necessary to the formation of the contract. Even though the parties have mutually agreed to the terms of the contract, there must be an exchange of value to bind the parties. This exchange of value implies that one party gives up or does something in return for the other party's doing the same. The philosophy underlying the necessity of consideration is that courts will not enforce promises that are made unless there is some benefit (i.e., some legal detriment that has been bargained for and exchanged). Thus, if I promise to give you $500 and you do not promise to do anything in return, there is no enforceable contract because there was no legal detriment on your part (i.e., there is a lack of consideration).

However, the question of the adequacy or inadequacy of the consideration is something that generally the courts will not address. For example, I promise to pay you $500 for your used skiing equipment, and you agree to sell me the equipment for that amount. You make no representations to me about the value of the equipment, and I can see that the equipment is quite old and not in good condition. If I regret my decision to buy this equipment and try to get a court to void the contract on the basis that the equipment was not worth $500, I will not succeed. Contract law is premised on the idea that adults should be able to make their own bargains; sometimes a good deal is made and sometimes a bad deal is made, but it is not the prerogative of the courts to intervene and assess whether the consideration was adequate. Therefore, courts will not use their own judgment about consideration; it is up to the parties to ascertain what consideration should be paid. The exception to this principle exists if there is some type of fraud, misrepresentation, duress, or mistake in the contract.

Capacity

Capacity is defined as the legal ability to bind yourself to a contract. The law presumes that certain persons lack the legal capacity to enter into contracts. Therefore, minors (persons under the age of 18) and persons who are mentally incompetent lack the capacity, according to the law, to understand the nature and consequences of the transaction in question.

Legality

Legality means that the underlying transaction must be legal for the contract to be valid and enforceable. For example, a gambling contract will be unenforceable in most jurisdictions because gambling is an illegal activity.

Form of the Contract

Oral Contracts

Most contracts are valid if they are in oral form. The exceptions to this rule are discussed following under the Statute of Frauds section. However, the difficulty with an oral contract is that although the law considers it to be a valid contract, it is often difficult to establish exactly what the terms of the contract are. Because there is no written evidence of the agreement, the ability to enforce the contract has many evidentiary difficulties. Therefore, it is highly recommended that all contracts be put in written form to avoid problems ascertaining just what the agreement entailed.

Statute of Frauds

As discussed earlier, oral contracts are generally enforceable, although not recommended as good business practice. Under the legal principle known as the **Statute of Frauds**, however, there are some situations in which a contract must be put in writing or the contract is not enforceable. Recreation and sport managers should be aware that the following situations fall under the Statute of Frauds, and these contracts must be written to be enforceable: (1) any agreement for the sale of land or an interest in land, (2) a sales contract for goods the value of which exceeds $500, and (3) contracts not to be performed within one year of the date of the agreement (Calamari & Perillo, 1998). An example of the third aspect would be a game contract that is entered into in February 2003 and the game will not be played until September 2005. Because the contract cannot be performed until September 2005, which is more than one year from the date of the agreement, the contract must be in writing.

Form Contracts

All businesses engage in a number of transactions that are repetitive enough to warrant the development of a form contract that may be used whenever that type of transaction occurs. This is important; drafting contracts is time consuming and is often very costly because an attorney must be used for this purpose. It makes operational and economic sense, therefore, to have your routine business operations put into form contracts in which you just insert the details relating to a specific transaction.

However, do not use the contracts to try and cover transactions for which the contract was not developed. You can do your organization a disservice if you try to make your own changes to the document because you may cause it to be interpreted in ways that do not fit with your intent. If the contract terms become ambiguous due to these changes, the document will not be interpreted in your favor. For further information regarding ambiguity, see the following discussion on the principles of contract interpretation.

Principles of Contract Interpretation

When courts are faced with contract disputes, they are guided by a number of interpretive principles in trying to resolve the matter. First, you need to understand that courts are trying to interpret the contract language and, if necessary, to look at the circumstances surrounding the contract to ascertain the parties' intent. It is not the court's role to try to make a new and better contract for the parties. If the language of the contract is clear and not ambiguous, the court refers only to the language of the document. If there is ambiguity, the court may look to evidence outside of the contract (e.g., the course of dealing between the parties) to remedy the ambiguity. If there is no such evidence, the court may use canons or maxims of construction to resolve the dispute.

Any Ambiguity Resolved Against the Drafter of the Contract

One general maxim of construction is that the party that drafts a contract will be the party that is disadvantaged in the resolution of a contract dispute if the contract is ambiguous. This means that if your business is drafting a document, you need to make special efforts to ensure that the agreement is clear and unambiguous. If something in the document is unclear, the court will choose the interpretation that favors the party that did not draft the contract. This is so because the party that drafts the document has every opportunity to make sure the document is clear.

Contract as a Whole

Another maxim of construction is that the court will look at the document as a whole. This means that the court will try to be consistent in the way it interprets a document to try to fulfill the intent of the underlying transaction.

Parol Evidence Rule

This is a rule of construction and a rule of evidence as well. This rule provides that once the parties have agreed to a final and complete written understanding of the matter, no prior oral or written evidence may be introduced to vary the terms of the final or integrated contract.

From a practical viewpoint, this means that when you sign the final version of a contract, you should make certain that all matters that you have previously discussed as being of importance are included in the document. Many drafts of a contract are usually circulated during negotiations. Make sure that the final version has the essential points because the parol evidence rule prevents you from trying to use earlier phone conversations or memos, for example, to alter the terms of the final contract. Of course, both parties may jointly agree to alter or supplement any contract; the parol evidence rule comes into play when a court is asked to interpret the terms of a contract.

Contract Remedies

When one party fails to meet its obligations under contract law, it is known as **breach of contract**. When a contract is breached, it is important to understand that the court is not trying to punish the party for failing to meet its obligations. The court, in providing remedies for contract damages, is only trying "to place the aggrieved party in the same economic position he would have had if the contract had been performed" (Calamari & Perillo, 1998). This means that punitive damages are not recoverable in a contract case, except in rare circumstances where there is fraud or some other type of misconduct involved.

Damages must be shown with **substantial certainty** because courts will not award damages based on mere speculation (Restatement (Second) Contracts, §352). Damages may generally be recovered for those amounts that arise naturally from the breach as well as damages that are in the contemplation of the parties at the time the contract is made (Calamari & Perillo, 1998, § 14.5). These losses that are not direct but are foreseen or reasonably foreseeable by the breaching party are known as **consequential damages**.

Monetary Remedies

The usual remedy in a breach of contract case is **monetary damages**, which, in most cases, will put the other party in the same economic position as if the contract had been performed. In a contract for the sale of goods, damages are usually calculated based on the difference between contract price and market price. For example, let's assume a park district wished to purchase new playground equipment from Vendor X. Vendor X quoted a price of $5,000, and the park district entered into a contract to buy the equipment at that price. Vendor X, however, then refused to sell the equipment, thus breaching the sales contract. The park district is entitled to monetary damages, which would put the district into the same position as if the contract were performed. Therefore, the park district may procure the equipment from another vendor, and the damage award will be the difference between the contract price and the market price. If the park district were able to buy the equipment from Vendor Y for $5,500, the monetary damages would be $500.

Another legal principle may come into play, however. Because the underlying philosophy of contract damages is not to punish the breaching party, the nonbreaching party must take reasonable efforts to lessen the consequences of the breach. This is known as the **duty to mitigate**, and it means that the nonbreaching party must try, in a reasonable manner, to lessen the amount of damages that must be paid. In the preceding sales contract, it would not be appropriate for the park district to accept a bid of $6,000 for the same equipment from Vendor Z to make the damages $1,000 instead of $500. The park district, as the nonbreaching party, has the duty to mitigate or lessen the damages if reasonably possible.

There is also the concept of **liquidated damages**, which means that parties may jointly agree as to the amount of damages to be paid by a breaching party. When the contract is entered into, the parties negotiate a damage payment, which will reasonably approximate the amount of the breach, and this becomes the amount designated as liquidated damages. This amount cannot be designated as a penalty or the court will not enforce it. This is a common provision in coaches' contracts. For further discussion of this concept, see Chapter 6.21, *Employment Contracts*.

Specific Performance

In rare cases, it may not be possible to remedy the breach with only monetary damages. In such a case, **specific performance** may be used, which means that the breaching party must perform the terms of the contract because money will not suffice to compensate the nonbreaching party. This remedy, however, may only be used when there is a unique item involved. For example, you are a collector of sports memorabilia and you contract to purchase the jersey worn by Joe Namath when the New York Jets won the Super Bowl. This is a unique item because there is only one jersey in existence, which was worn on the date in question. If the other party breaches the contract and refuses to sell you the jersey you purchased, the court may order the seller to give you the jersey for the purchase price. Because the item is one-of-a-kind, you could not purchase it elsewhere for any amount of money.

You could not use this "uniqueness" claim, however, to force someone to perform the contract with you for personal services. For example, let's assume that you are the owner of the Colorado Avalanche NHL team and one of your star players, goalie Patrick Roy, does not want to play for you any more, even though he is under contract to do so. Even though he is a "unique" performer, a court will not force him to continue to play for you, using the remedy of specific performance. There are two reasons for this. First, courts will not force people to engage in behavior that may be interpreted as involuntary servitude. Second, if a court forced Patrick Roy to play, who would determine if his efforts were competent? It would be impossible to have a judge oversee his performance on a nightly basis to see whether his performance met his team's superstar expectations.

Rescission and Restitution

In some cases, particularly when fraud, mistake, or duress exists, the court may **rescind** the contract. This means that the court "undoes" the contract and puts the parties back into the positions they occupied before the contract was agreed upon. Both parties then make **restitution** to each other by returning whatever goods, property, and so on were transferred under the contract or an equivalent amount of money.

Promissory Estoppel

There are some situations in which a disadvantaged party may find a remedy although all the elements of a formal contract may not exist. **Promissory estoppel** is a doctrine in which the court substitutes detrimental reliance for the element of consideration (Restatement (Second) Contracts, § 90). Although the court cannot proceed based on normal contract principles, it seeks to remedy an injustice when a party relies on another party's promises. The elements of promissory estoppel are (1) a promise is made that should reasonably be expected to induce reliance, (2) there is reliance on that promise, and (3) an injustice occurs to the party who relies on the promise.

In Chapter 6.22, you will learn about athletic grants-in-aid, which, according to NCAA rules, may only be offered as one-year contracts. Let's assume that a university basketball coach does not want to renew the grant-in-aid for one player, who is now a senior. The player, who cannot afford to pay for his final year of school, does not have any remedy using normal contract law principles. The grant-in-aid has not been awarded to him for his final year, so he has no recourse under the contract. However, he may be able to meet the elements of promissory estoppel if he can show the following: (1) when he was being recruited, the coach promised him that he would be given athletic aid for his four years at the school, assuming he retained academic eligibility; (2) in reliance on that promise, the student came to this school; and (3) an injustice has been done in refusing to award the student–athlete financial aid for his final year. In this situation, the case for the student–athlete is particularly favorable because the reliance is even stronger due to the **disparity in bargaining power** between the parties. In this case, the coach, as a representative of a powerful educational institution, is "doing business" with a relatively naïve young man who has very little understanding of contract law. The student–athlete's reliance on promises made in this type of situation would be considerable.

Typical Provisions found in All Types of Contracts

Designation of the Parties—This section identifies who the parties to the contract are and what their "role" is within the contract, e.g., seller or buyer, lessor or lessee.

Duties and Obligations—This section sets forth the duties and obligations that each party has agreed to assume under the contract and when these actions are to be performed. For example, in a sales contract for sporting equipment, the seller agrees to provide the equipment by a certain date, and the buyer agrees to pay for the equipment by a certain date.

Representations and Warranties—A warranty is a legal promise that certain facts are true. For example, if there is a sales contract for a unique item of sports memorabilia, the seller will warrant that he has legal ownership of the item in order to sell it. The seller will also represent that, to the best of his knowledge, the item is a genuine item. For contracts involving the sale of goods, certain warranties may be implied under state law.

Termination Clauses—The termination clauses set forth each party's right to terminate the contract under certain circumstances. Generally, these clauses define the breach of contract events that trigger a right to end the contract. For example, if a professional athlete refuses to show up at the contests in which he is to play, he has breached his contract with the employing team, and the team has the right to terminate the contract. These clauses also discuss the way in which parties must give notice to terminate the contract and describe ways in which a party may "cure" or remedy a breach before the other party may terminate the contract.

Remedies—These clauses set forth the types and amounts of damages that may be recovered in the event of breach.

Arbitration—An arbitration clause provides that the parties must use some method of alternative dispute resolution such as arbitration or mediation to resolve their differences. Some clauses provide that the dispute cannot be resolved in a court of law but only by arbitration or mediation. Other clauses provide that the parties may bring the dispute to court, but only after they have tried to resolve the dispute through alternative methods.

Merger Clause—As discussed earlier under the Parol Evidence rule, it is important that both parties understand that they are signing the final version of a contract. This clause indicates that this contract is the final and integrated understanding of the parties and that all prior discussions and negotiations are merged into the document at this time.

Signature Authority

To conduct business, organizations must empower their employees to carry out transactions for the organizations. There are limits to the authority each employee possesses, however, and this is the degree of **actual authority** conveyed to the employee.

What happens if an employee exceeds his/her actual authority in contracting with a third party? May the third party hold the organization to the contract in such a case?

For example, let's assume that the manager of a retail sporting goods store has the actual authority to enter into contracts up to a $10,000 limit. An equipment provider has done business with this store and the manager on many previous occasions and the contracts have always been honored. On this occasion, however, the manager signed a contract for goods in the amount of $15,000, and the corporation that owns this franchise argues that it should not be bound to this contract because its manager exceeded his actual authority in signing the contract.

Can the equipment provider enforce this contract? Most likely, because the equipment provider can use the principle of **apparent authority** to bind the organization. To use this principle, a third party must reasonably rely on the employee's apparent ability to enter into such a transaction (Cross & Miller, 2001). In this case, the equipment provider could show such reasonable reliance based on past dealings with the manager and the usual custom in the industry. There would not be reasonable reliance if we changed the facts to suggest that the manager was entering into a million dollar transaction; a store manager would never have the authority to enter into a transaction of such magnitude.

If you wish to protect against the principle of apparent authority being used against your organization, you need to either convey the actual limits of authority to the third party or you may wish to use documents that make it clear to a third party that a transaction in excess of $X may not be entered into by only one employee. You may wish to use a countersignature line to indicate this.

Significant Case

—◇◇◇—

In this case season ticket holders who had purchased stadium builder licenses (SBLs) brought a class action against a professional football team for breach of contract. The Pennsylvania Supreme Court held that the parol evidence rule barred the admission of an SBL brochure, which the plaintiffs argued set forth different seating arrangements. The brochure, however, was inadmissible because it was information not included within the purchase contract for the SBLs.

YOCCA V. PITTSBURGH STEELERS SPORTS INC.

Supreme Court of Pennsylvania
854 A. 2d 425 (2004)

OPINION:

Appellants, the Pittsburgh Steelers Sports, Inc., t/d/b/a the Steelers Pittsburgh Football Club, and the Sports & Exhibition Authority of Pittsburgh and Allegheny County (collectively, the "Steelers"), appeal from the order of the Commonwealth Court which reversed the order of the Court of Common Pleas of Allegheny County granting the Steelers' preliminary objections to the class action complaint filed by Appellees, Ronald A. Yocca, Paul and Patty Serwonski, and Ronald P. Carmassi, individually and on behalf of all similarly situated persons who purchased "stadium builder licenses" ("SBLs") from the Steelers. For the reasons that follow, we reverse the Commonwealth Court's order.

This dispute involves the sale of SBLs, which are essentially "licenses" that grant the licensee the right to buy annual season tickets to Pittsburgh Steelers football games. According to Appellees, sometime in October 1998, they received a brochure from the Steelers (the "SBL Brochure" or the "Brochure"), which advertised a new football stadium that the Steelers planned to construct for the Pittsburgh Steelers football team and advised them of the opportunity to purchase SBLs for football games in that stadium. The SBL Brochure explained that the new stadium would be both bigger and better than the existing stadium, Three Rivers Stadium, and would have more seats closer to the field.

* * *

The SBL Brochure then stated that any person could purchase an SBL for $ 250 to $ 2,700, depending on the section in which the SBL purchaser's seat would be located. * * * According to the SBL Brochure, each SBL purchaser would be assigned a particular seat in the new stadium and have the right and obligation to buy season tickets for that seat as long as the Steelers football team continues to play in the new stadium. * * * However, the Brochure also stated that all SBL purchasers would be free to either transfer their rights to purchase season tickets or terminate their SBLs if at some point in the future they determined that they no longer wanted to purchase season tickets for the seats assigned to them.

The Brochure further provided that any person interested in purchasing an SBL was required to fill out the application that was included in the SBL Brochure and submit it along with a non-refundable deposit equaling one-third of the price of the desired SBL seat (or seats) by November 30, 1998. * * * The application further asked the SBL applicant to specify the section of the stadium where he would most like to sit (and calculate the amount due for a seat in that section), as well as list those sections of the stadium that were his second and third preferences. . Notably, the SBL Brochure included two small diagrams of the planned stadium. * * * The first diagram depicted the general locations of the sections in the lower level of the stadium while the second diagram showed the general locations of the sections in the upper level of the stadium. Neither diagram was sufficiently detailed so as to show the number of rows or seats in the sections. However, based on the lower level diagram, one of the sections in the lower level, the Club I Section, only appeared to include seats between the twenty-yard lines of the football field. . Similarly, the depictions of certain sections in the upper level diagram, namely, Sections D, E, and F, appeared to show each section as having the same number of rows.

The SBL Brochure indicated that first priority for seats would be given to those SBL applicants who already had season tickets in Three Rivers Stadium and who applied for seats in a section of the new stadium that corresponded with their current seating sections. With regard to those applicants, the SBL Brochure stated: "We will try to assign seats as close to your current seat location as the new stadium seating configuration will allow." According to the Brochure, after seats were assigned to those applicants with first priority, seats would be assigned to all other applicants based on a "random computerized priority number" placed on every application received by the November 30th deadline. Significantly, the SBL Brochure not only made clear that an SBL applicant's first seating preference was "not guaranteed," * * * but also that no SBL applicant was assured the right to purchase an SBL.

* * *

The SBL Brochure further notified SBL applicants: "You will be mailed a contract by the end of March 1999, notifying you of your Section assignment. The contract must be signed and returned within 15 days. If the completed contract is not returned as required, your season ticket holder discount seating priority and deposit will be forfeited." * * * According to the SBL Brochure, SBL applicants would be given their actual seat assignments "in the Spring of 2001 after the seats have been physically installed in the new stadium."

* * *

Appellees allege that after reviewing the SBL Brochure, they decided to purchase SBLs. Accordingly, each Appellee completed his application in the SBL Brochure, indicating his seating preferences, and mailed the application and the required deposit to the Steelers by November 30, 1998. In August 1999, the Steelers sent each Appellee a letter (the "August 1999 Letter"), advising them that they had been assigned SBL seats and notifying them of the stadium sections in which their seats were located. The letter also reminded Appellees that they would soon be mailed a contract that they would have to sign to purchase SBLs to the seats assigned to them. A document containing two diagrams (the "August 1999 Diagrams") was attached to the August 1999 Letter to show "the location of all sections." Like the earlier diagrams included in the SBL Brochure, the August 1999 Diagrams only offered a general description of the location of each section, and did not indicate how many rows or how many seats were in any given section. However, in spite of the lack of specificity in both sets of diagrams, it was apparent that the parameters of the sections in the August 1999 Diagrams varied from those in the earlier diagrams. Specifically, in the August 1999 Diagrams, the Club I Section appeared larger than it had in the earlier diagrams, apparently including seats between the ten-yard lines, instead of only those seats between the twenty-yard lines. In addition, the depictions of Sections D, E, and F in the August 1999 Diagrams no longer appeared to be equal in size, but rather, Sections D and E appeared larger than Section F.

* * *

Two months after Appellees received the August 1999 Letter, the Steelers mailed them three documents: (1) a "Stadium Builder License and Club Seat Agreement" or a "Stadium Builder License Agreement" (collectively, the "SBL Agreement" or "Agreement"); (2) a document entitled "Additional Terms and Conditions of Stadium Builder License and Club Seat Agreement" or "Additional Terms and Conditions of Stadium Builder License" (collectively, the "Additional Terms document"); and (3) another copy of the document containing the August 1999 Diagrams. The SBL Agreement was a two-page document requiring the signatures of the named person, partnership, or corporation purchasing an SBL, i.e., the "Licensee," as well as the Public Auditorium Authority of Pittsburgh and Allegheny County, i.e., the "Authority" or the "Licensor." The Agreement specified the number of SBLs the Licensee would be purchasing, the section (or sections) in which the SBL seats would be located, and the total fee for the SBLs. Moreover, to assist the Licensee in identifying the location of his seats, the Agreement directed the Licensee to Exhibit A, which it described as representing the "Stadium Seating Area." While the document containing the August 1999 Diagrams was not specifically labeled as "Exhibit A," it was clearly meant to be Exhibit A as it was the only document attached to the contract documents, i.e., the SBL Agreement and the Additional Terms document, and as it clearly described the "Stadium Seating Area."

The SBL Agreement also stated that the Licensee and the Licensor agreed to the terms and conditions in the Additional Terms document, which it expressly incorporated by reference as part of the Agreement. The Additional Terms document was a four-page document outlining the use of SBLs (including the fact that the Licensee would be notified of his seats prior to the first season of play in the stadium), the SBL fee, the term of an SBL, a Licensee's duty to continually purchase season tickets to maintain his SBL, the terms and conditions associated with transferring an SBL, and the conduct expected of Licensees and their guests. The Additional Terms document also contained a clause stating that the Licensee "has read and understands the terms of this Agreement," * * * and an integration clause, which stated as follows:

Entire Agreement; Modification. This Agreement contains the entire agreement of the parties with respect to the matters provided for herein and shall supersede any representations or agreements previously made or entered into by the parties hereto. No modification hereto shall be enforceable unless in writing, signed by both parties.

* * *

Appellees signed the SBL Agreement and paid the remaining installments due for the SBLs assigned to them. Moreover, in accordance with the provisions in the SBL Agreement, Appellees purchased season tickets for the 2001 Steelers' football season for the SBL seats awarded to them. In the spring of 2001, after all of the seats in Heinz Field were installed, the Steelers informed Appellees of the specific locations of their SBL seats. Appellees subsequently used their seats, and according to Appellees, they immediately discovered that the seats were not located where they expected them to be based on the diagrams in the SBL Brochure. Appellees contend that several of the seating sections surrounding the football field were expanded to include a greater area of seats than shown in the SBL Brochure diagrams. Thus, although Appellees acknowledge that the names of the sections associated with each of their seats are the ones that they had requested to sit in, they assert that their seats are actually in other less desirable and less expensive sections according to the SBL Brochure diagrams.

Specifically, Appellee Ronald A. Yocca alleges that he applied for and was awarded two SBL seats in the Club I Section. Mr. Yocca contends that based on the lower level diagram in the SBL Brochure, he reasonably believed that his Club I seats would be located between the twenty-yard lines of the football field. However, Mr. Yocca's seats ended up on the eighteen-yard line, two yards outside of the twenty-yard line. Similarly, Appellees Paul and Patty Serwonski and Ronald P. Carmassi were granted SBL seats in Section D in the upper level. Mr. and Mrs. Serwonski and Mr. Carmassi allege, much like Mr. Yocca, that based on the upper level SBL Brochure diagram, they reasonably believed that their seats would be within the first twelve rows of the upper deck. Their seats, however, are in the sixteenth row of the upper deck.

As a result of their dissatisfaction with their seats, Appellees commenced the instant class action against the Steelers in early August 2001. In their complaint, Appellees initially assert that the Steelers breached their contract with Appellees. According to Appellees, the terms in the SBL Brochure constitute the terms of the parties' contract and the Steelers breached those terms by failing to: (1) provide them with seats in the sections depicted in the two diagrams included in the SBL Brochure; (2) issue seats to them in accordance with the priority promised in the SBL Brochure; and (3) refund their deposits or reduce their future payments, as promised by the SBL Brochure, once the Steelers learned that they could not give Appellees seats in the higher priced sections they had requested.

* * *

In its opinion, the trial court initially pointed out that because the SBL Agreement was a fully integrated agreement that represented all of the terms of the parties' agreement, it superseded all of the parties' previous negotiations and agreements, including the terms in the SBL Brochure. The court then explained that Appellees' breach of contract claims failed as a matter of law because they were solely based on the terms in the SBL Brochure and the parol evidence rule prohibited evidence of those terms from being used to alter the plain terms of the SBL Agreement.

* * *

Appellees appealed from the trial court's decision to the Commonwealth Court. On August 28, 2002, the Commonwealth Court entered an order * * * reversing the trial court's dismissal of Appellees' claims for breach of contract * * * . With respect to Appellees' breach of contract claim, the Commonwealth Court found that the terms in the SBL Brochure constituted the terms of the parties' contract. Therefore, the court determined that the parol evidence rule did not preclude review of Appellees' claims concerning the SBL Brochure terms, and the trial court improperly granted a demurrer on Appellees' breach of contract claim.

* * *

The Steelers subsequently filed a petition for allowance of appeal with this Court, arguing that the Commonwealth Court erroneously reversed the trial court's order dismissing Appellees' claims for breach of contract * * *

The Steelers initially argue that the Commonwealth Court improperly reversed the trial court's order dismissing Appellees' breach of contract claims because the parol evidence rule bars any consideration of Appellees' claims, which are wholly based on the terms in the SBL Brochure. We agree.

* * *

This Court has explained the parol evidence rule as follows:

Where the parties, without any fraud or mistake, have deliberately put their engagements in writing, the law declares the writing to be not only the best, but the only, evidence of their agreement. All preliminary negotiations, conversations and verbal agreements are merged in and superseded by the subsequent written contract . . . and unless fraud, accident or mistake be averred, the writing constitutes the agreement between the parties, and its terms and agreements cannot be added to nor subtracted from by parol evidence.

* * *

Therefore, for the parol evidence rule to apply, there must be a writing that represents the "entire contract between the parties." To determine whether or not a writing is the parties' entire contract, the writing must be looked at and "if it appears to be a contract complete within itself, couched in such terms as import a complete legal obligation without any uncertainty as to the object or extent of the [parties'] engagement, it is conclusively presumed that [the writing represents] the whole engagement of the parties . . . ." An integration clause which states that a writing is meant to represent the parties' entire agreement is also a clear sign that the writing is meant to be just that and thereby expresses all

of the parties' negotiations, conversations, and agreements made prior to its execution.

* * *

Once a writing is determined to be the parties' entire contract, the parol evidence rule applies and evidence of any previous oral or written negotiations or agreements involving the same subject matter as the contract is almost always inadmissible to explain or vary the terms of the contract.

* * *

In the instant case, we cannot agree with the Commonwealth Court that the SBL Brochure represented the terms of the parties' contract concerning the sale of SBLs. Contrary to the Commonwealth Court's understanding, the SBL Brochure did not represent a promise by the Steelers to sell SBLs to Appellees. Rather, the Brochure was merely an offer by the Steelers to sell Appellees the right to be assigned an unspecified seat in an unspecified section of the new stadium and the right to receive a contract to buy an SBL for that later-assigned seat. *** Moreover, by sending in their applications with the initial non-refundable payment, Appellees simply secured their right to be considered for assigned seats and the opportunity to receive a subsequent offer to purchase SBLs for those seats. In this respect, the SBL Brochure was similar to an option contract in that it merely gave Appellees the option to possibly accept an offer for SBLs at some later date.

* * *

On the other hand, the SBL Agreement clearly represented the parties' contract concerning the sale of SBLs. Unlike the SBL Brochure, the SBL Agreement reflected a promise by the Steelers to actually sell Appellees a specific number of SBL seats in a specified section. Furthermore, the SBL Agreement detailed all of the terms and conditions of that sale, i.e., the precise number of seats to be sold to the named Licensee, the exact section in which those seats were located (including a visual depiction of that location), the total amounts due for each SBL, the dates those amounts were due, and all of the rights and duties associated with owning an SBL, including the Licensee's right to transfer the SBL. Most importantly, the SBL Agreement explicitly stated that it represented the parties' entire contract regarding the sale of SBLs. *** Accordingly, we find that the SBL Agreement represented the parties' entire contract with respect to the sale of SBLs and that the parol evidence rule bars the admission of any evidence of previous oral or written negotiations or agreements entered into between the parties concerning the sale of the SBLs, such as the SBL Brochure, to explain or vary those terms expressed in the SBL Agreement.

* * *

Having determined that the SBL Agreement was the parties' whole contract and cannot be supplemented by the parties' previous negotiations or agreements, including the SBL Brochure, we agree with the trial court's conclusion that Appellees' breach of contract claims must be dismissed.

Accordingly, we reverse the Commonwealth Court's order reversing the trial court's order dismissing Appellees' claims for breach of contract.

* * *

References

Cases

Auburn Sch. Dist. v. King County, 1999 Wash. App. LEXIS 1748 (1999).
Yocca v. Pittsburgh Steelers Sports, Inc., 854 A.2d 425 (Pa. 2004).

Publications

American Law Institute. (1981). *Restatement (second) of the law of contracts.* St. Paul, MN: American Law Institute.
Calamari, J. D., & Perillo, J. M. (1998). *The law of contracts* (4th ed.). St. Paul, MN: West Publishing.
Cross, F. B., & Miller, R. L. (2001). *West's legal environment of business.* St. Paul, MN: West Publishing.
Sharp, L. A. (2001). Contract law and sport applications. In B. L. Parkhouse (Ed.), *The management of sport* (3rd ed., pp. 199–212). New York: McGraw-Hill.

6.21 Employment Contracts

Rodney L. Caughron
Northern Illinois University

Historically, employment contracts in sport and recreation were a matter of a handshake or a simple letter of agreement. With the increased level of compensation—both in contractual salary and outside income—and the tenuous nature of a coach or administrator's position, employment contracts have evolved into complex legal documents, often involving complicated negotiations. No matter how complicated the contracts have become, employment contracts are essentially the same as other contracts in the "real" world. The only difference is that they have the propensity to be broken on a much more frequent basis—often with the assent of both parties. That is why the more complicated and specific a contract can be crafted, the more both parties will benefit because the contracts reduce ambiguity and specifically define the terms of the contractual association (Yasser, McCurdy, Goplerud, & Weston, 2000).

Fundamental Concepts

As competition and winning have become more vital to the economic interests of the sport organization, both intercollegiate and professional, the tenure of coaches and administrators at a particular institution have become more tenuous (Greenberg & Thomas, 2005, p. 9). If the coach doesn't win, the organization will try to "unload" them (as demonstrated in *Cole v. Valley Ice Garden*, 2005), in many cases by buying the coach or administrator's contract out to secure a new person for the position. It is necessary, therefore, that both parties be protected by an employment contract that is meticulously drafted to satisfy the needs of both the coach/administrator and the institution (Greenberg, 2001).

Elements of a Common Contract

Although it is important to note that no two contracts will be alike, Greenberg (2001) has identified a number of elements that are commonly found in every intercollegiate coaching contract. These elements can also serve as a model for other employment contracts. These contracts often involve perquisites and other common employment benefits as well as salary. It is important to note that although all contracts have most of the same elements, each contact should be tailored for the particular job. Following are some of the most common elements of a sport-related contract.

Duties and Responsibilities

- The contract should state that the employee agrees to devote his/her best effort to full-time performance as the position requires.
- There should be a specific list of responsibilities required to be performed by the employee.
- The contract should also include a general phrase that the employee agrees to perform other duties assigned to him or her, and mutually agreed upon.

Term of Employment

- The length of the contract should be explicit. For example in *Lindsey v. University of Arizona* (1987) the terms of employment were unclear. Due to breach of an oral commitment by the university to extend his contract for three additional years, Lindsey won a substantial judgment. In another case, *Small v. Juniata College* (1997), the court found that Small's employment contract was for a one-year term and that the college personnel manual termination procedures did not affect the status of these one-year appointments.

Rollover Provisions

- Rollover provisions allow the organization to extend an employee's contract for an extra year, usually after a successful season, with the mutual agreement of the employee and organization. Even NCAA President Myles Brand was able to exercise a two-year rollover extension to his current contract, renewing the contract through 2009 ("NCAA president," 2005).
- Rollover provisions tend to be one-sided in favor of the employee, exemplified in the statement by *Atlanta Journal-Constitution* reporter Jeff Schultz, who stated, "Now a coach can have an iron-clad, no-escape contract signed in vampire blood . . . then weasel out of rollover contracts and jump across the street for a raise" (Schultz, 2006, p. 1H). This is especially true when the contract's rollover agreement requires specific terms of notice for terminating the employee, allowing the employee to collect more monetary damages if the contract is terminated by the organization. For example, in *Cherry v. A-P-A Sports, Inc.* (1983), Cherry's contract provided that if his contract was not renewed for an additional two years, he would automatically receive $35,000 in compensation.

Reassignment Clause

- A reassignment clause allows for the removal of the employee from the originally contracted position and reassignment to another position that is consistent with the employee's education and experience. For example, in *Monson v. State of Oregon* (1995), the University of Oregon had included a provision for reassignment, which they exercised, changing his assignment from men's basketball coach to golf coach. The court upheld the reassignment because it was part of the contractual language.
- The issue of reassignment and "future" loss of income due to the reassignment was addressed in *Smith v. Alanis & Zapata County Independent School District* (2002). Smith was hired as the head high school football coach and athletic coordinator, but was reassigned midyear in accordance with his contract. Smith claimed that his removal as head coach, although not reducing his current salary per the contract, would have an effect on future income as a head coach. The court concluded that contract law in Texas did not allow compensation for future earning capacity, and therefore, the actions of the school district were within the scope of the employment contract.
- A reassignment clause should be coupled with the avoidance of any language in the contract that gives the employee the right to be in any specific titled position (e.g., head coach).
- A reassignment clause places the burden of terminating the contract on the employee if he/she chooses not to take the reassignment.
- A reassignment clause should specify the compensation the employee will receive in the new assignment.

Compensation Clause

- A compensation clause should include the guaranteed base salary, terms of pay increases over the time of the contract, fringe benefits, moving and relocation expenses, bonuses, additional retirement benefits, and other compensation that the organization itself provides the employee.
- All compensations should be specifically delineated and agreed upon.

Fringe Benefits

- This area can include myriad benefits that organizations are offering employees and administrators. They may include complementary cars, travel, loans, moving and housing expenses, and tickets. Many of the benefits are offered to the normal employee, but in many situations the benefits for the coach or administrator are inflated or outside the normal employees benefits.
- The type, amount, date the benefit is available, and penalties for termination of contract should be explicitly written out within the contract.

Bonuses and Incentives

- Bonuses and incentives are becoming more important to all employees. They may include signing bonuses, incentives based on team success, and in the case of college and university coaches and administrators, graduation rates of student–athletes.

Provisions for Outside and/or Supplemental Income

- These sources of income may include radio and television contracts; endorsements; shoe, apparel and equipment contracts; income from speeches and written materials, as well as camps and other various sources of supplemental income.
- The organization should include in the contract that it is not legally liable for claims arising from these outside income sources.
- A provision in the contract should stipulate that the organization retains the right of final approval for all agreements for outside income sources made by the employee.

Termination Clause

- A termination clause should state that termination may be caused by the death or disability of the employee. For example, in *Maddox v. University of Tennessee* (1995), the court upheld the dismissal of Maddox, an alcoholic, due to his arrest for drunk driving. Maddox contended that his dismissal was due to his alcoholism, which violated the Americans with Disabilities Act of 1990 (ADA) and the Rehabilitation Act of 1973. The court did not agree, commenting that the termination was for his criminal act and the subsequent negative publicity. In a similar case, ABC TV terminated an employee after he was arrested for selling cocaine. The plaintiff claimed he was covered under ADA, but the court ruled that his termination was based on the plaintiff's breach of the morals clause in his contract because he lied about the situation (*Nader v. ABC Television*, 2005).
- The contract should also contain a termination for "just cause" clause so that if the employee violates either the organization's rules, its affiliation rules, civil or criminal laws, moral turpitude, refusal to perform duties, etc., the employee can be fired. These may be explicitly expressed or implied in the contract or in the "customs and mores" of the organization or society. For example, in *Deli v. University of Minnesota* (1994), the head women's gymnastics coach and her husband, the assistant coach, were terminated when the gymnasts viewed a videotape of the coach and her husband having sex. The court upheld the dismissal of both of the coaches, based on the indiscretions with the videotape and for other "just cause" reasons. Other examples are *Hamm v. Poplar Bluff R-1 School District* (1997), *McKenzie v. Wright State University* (1996), and *Farner v. Idaho Falls School District* (2000). In *Hamm*, the court upheld the termination of a junior high coach for having a fourteen-year-old female student at his residence; whereas in *McKenzie v. Wright State University* (1996); the court upheld the dismissal of McKenzie for NCAA rules violations, which were specifically mentioned in her employment contract as cause for termination. The *Farner* case demonstrated how the master contract for high school teachers, when incorporating coaching and extra duties, requires the same "just cause" for termination as does the teaching aspect of the contract. To terminate without just cause violates the individual's due process rights.

- The contractual clause concerning termination for just cause should also include the rights of due process that the employee may or may not retain. This could include a formal hearing within the organization or the use of an arbitrator. For example, in *Stamps Public Schools v. Colvert* (1996), Colvert was able to prove that the school district had violated its own procedures and had not given him his contractually guaranteed due process. This was also the case with Rick Neuheisel, former head football coach at the University of Washington. Neuheisel was fired six months before the end of his original contract with Washington based on a questionable investigation by the NCAA concerning Neuheisel's involvement in an NCAA men's basketball betting pool. Washington fired Neuheisel because he originally denied involvement and then admitted to it. Neuheisel filed a lawsuit against Washington based in part on the university's denial of contractually guaranteed due process and the subsequent hearing. Neuheisel and Washington later settled for a cash payment of $2.5 million (from the NCAA for defamation) and $500,000 in cash and $1.5 million in a forgiven loan from the university (Greenberg & Thomas, 2005, p. 8).

- Termination without cause allows the organization to fire the employee for any reason. This will usually come with a price, in that the organization will usually have to negotiate a settlement with the employee if a termination occurs. This was not the case in *Frazier v. University of the District of Columbia* (1990), however, where the court found that Frazier was an at-will employee and could be terminated at any time.

Buyout Provisions

- A buyout provision allows the employee or institution to terminate the contract on the payment of a specified amount of money. For example in *Tolis v. Board of Supervisors of Louisiana State University* (1992), the court upheld an oral agreement to buy out Tolis's contract, which the defendants later violated. The court held that the Board of Supervisors must abide by their oral buyout agreement.
- A buyout provision may include a liquidated damages clause (see *Vanderbilt University v. DiNardo*, 1999).
- An interesting situation that caught both the coach and owner in a tight predicament was the $7 million buyout provision that was not exercised against George Karl, former head coach with the Milwaukee Bucks, whose contract was not extended, yet the owner at the time, Herb Kohl—who was trying to sell the team—refused to exercise the buyout to save money and make the team more marketable. This essentially left Karl a lame duck coach, but without any remedy except to quit and forfeit his contract (Hunt, 2003).

Arbitration Agreement

- An arbitration agreement is a clause in the contract that stipulates that if any dispute arises from the interpretation of the contract or other factors concerning the contract, the issues will be dealt with through arbitration (see *Miami Dolphins Ltd. v. Williams*, 2005).
- The areas to be arbitrated should be specifically delineated within this section of the contract.
- The benefit of arbitration is that it reduces the cost of litigation for both parties. A good example of this is when Bill Parcells broke his contract with the New England Patriots and signed a contract to coach with the New York Jets. Instead of taking the issue to court, both sides allowed National Football League Commissioner Paul Tagliabue to arbitrate the dispute.
- An interesting case challenging the ability of NFL Commissioner Tagliabue to serve as the arbitrator in contract disputes within the NFL involved coaches with the Minnesota Vikings, who after they were fired claimed they were entitled to incentive pay under their contract. The appellants filed suit to remove Tagliabue as the arbitrator in their dispute, but the court stated that nowhere in the Federal Arbitration Act is there an allowance to challenge an arbitrator—biased or not—prior to a decision by the arbitrator (*Alexander, et al. v. Minnesota Vikings Football Club LLC & National Football League*, 2002).

Although these elements may not be exhaustive, they set a framework from which sport and recreation managers involved in contract development can operate.

Discussion of Contract Issues

Typically in sports the employee has the advantage in any contractual situation in which the employee unilaterally decides to terminate the contract. If an employee unilaterally terminates his or her contract, thus breaching the conditions of the contract, the sport organization has essentially no remedy to "force" the employee to perform their duties. The reason the courts are reluctant to enforce such contracts is that to compel performance of a contractual duty would constitute a violation of the Thirteenth Amendment's prohibition against involuntary servitude. In addition, the court has stated that it would be unable to monitor the level of coaching performance and enforce proper coaching skills in a coaching contract (Cozzillio & Levinstein, 1997).

Although unable to compel the employee to perform his or her duties, the sport organization may acquire injunctive relief, which prohibits the employee from acquiring similar employment at another sport organization. This was evident in the case of Chuck Fairbanks and the New England Patriots. Fairbanks, who was head coach of the New England Patriots, breached his contract with New England to take the head coaching position with the University of Colorado. To prevent Fairbanks from leaving, the Patriots obtained injunctive relief, prohibiting the University of Colorado from entering into a coaching contract with Fairbanks (*New England Patriots Football Club Inc. v. University of Colorado*, 1979).

In some instances, problems arise between parties of an employment contract based on their personal relationships and friendship. One typical situation is when there is a verbal understanding that in the future a specific employment relationship will be consummated contractually by the two parties, and the agent of the organization does not have the authority to make such an agreement, or due to the fact that it is only an agreement and not yet a contract, the relationship does not transpire. This was the case in *Barnett v. Board of Trustees for State Colleges and Universities A/K/A University of Louisiana System* (2001). Barnett was originally hired as basketball coach at Northwestern State University in 1994. A plan was formulated by Barnett and the then–university president, which would elevate Barnett to athletic director in 1996. A letter from the president was sent to Barnett confirming this agreement in 1995, pending approval by the university Board of Trustees. Louisiana state law required personnel appointments at the university to be approved by the Board of Trustees. Before Barnett could be appointed to the athletic director's position, a new president took office at the institution, and someone else was hired as athletic director. Barnett filed suit against the university for breach of contract. The court ruled that no contract existed because all contracts had to be submitted to the board, and Barnett was aware of this prerequisite from the beginning of the agreement. This case demonstrates the importance of employees knowing the exact procedural requirements for contracts with a particular institution or organization to become valid and actionable. *Meinders v. Dunkerton Community School District* (2002) is an example of a similar situation at the high school level.

It is interesting to note that even when an employee breaches his or her contract and jumps from one organization to another, in most cases the parties involved eventually agree on a settlement, either financial or, in the case of professional teams, financial and possible trade of draft picks. For example, the New York Jets settled with the New England Patriots to obtain Bill Parcells for a reported $300,000 charitable donation and the Jets' third- and fourth-round draft picks in 1997, their second-round choice in 1998, and their first-round pick in 1999 (Rosenthal, 1997).

In most cases the coach or administrator is offered a contract that includes a base salary and perquisites to which all other organizational employees are entitled. In addition, the contract will often also specifically list other perquisites that the coach or administrator may be entitled to, although not always explicitly delineating each item. For example, in *Rodgers v. Georgia Tech Athletic Association* (1983), Rodgers, the head football coach at Georgia Tech, asked the court to award him the value of the perquisites for the remainder of his terminated contract. In reaching its decision, the court eliminated those perquisites directly related to the function of Rodgers' job as head coach (i.e., a secretary), but awarded Rodgers the value of those items that were regularly provided to him either through the Association or from outside sources (i.e., television and radio revenues). The court also eliminated items that were gifts, and those items that the Association did not have knowledge of or contemplate as part of the contract. Therefore, the *Rodgers* case set a precedent that allows coaches or administrators to recover items that are specifically or tacitly provided for by the sport organization and those items that the coach or administrator and the organization would normally expect to be perquisites under the contract (*Rodgers v. Georgia Tech Athletic Association*, 1983).

Independent Contractor vs. Employee

A growing issue in the sport, fitness, and recreational industries is the hiring of independent contractors to perform duties that were typically performed by employees. Although the use of independent contractors is a good way to reduce costs and an organization's legal liability, not every individual will actually meet the standards of an "independent contractor." The classification of workers has significant implications for the employer in terms of taxes, tort liability, and other forms of employee compensation (Caughron & Fargher, 2004).

Darryll Halcomb Lewis brought to light the importance of this issue when dealing with sports officials. Halcomb Lewis states that if a sports official hurt on the job is considered an independent contractor, two consequences result: (1) the referee is barred from filing a worker's compensation claim, and (2) that absent legislated immunity, the organization hiring the official may be held liable for those injuries (Halcomb Lewis, 1998, p. 253). This was echoed in *Wadler v. Eastern College Athletic Conference* (2003), in which a claim of Title VII discrimination based on race was dismissed against an athletic conference, et al., due to a lack of an employer–employee relationship—essentially recognizing a college baseball umpire as an independent contractor due to the employment relationship he had with the defendants in the case.

Although no specific test has been adopted universally by all jurisdictions, the Internal Revenue Service has developed a checklist that includes twenty criteria for determining whether someone is an independent contractor or an employee. The status of the individual is dependent on the following (the more reliant the individual is on the employer, the greater likelihood they are an employee).

1. Instructions—level of instruction to accomplish the work, and the level of supervision
2. Training—initial and ongoing training
3. Integration—independence of individual within the workplace
4. Services rendered personally—ability of individual to subcontract
5. Hiring, supervising, and paying assistants—ability to hire and treat others as employees by the worker
6. Continuing relationship—the relationship is based on a specific period of time or completion of a specific task
7. Set hours of work—role of the employer in setting the schedule of the individual
8. Full-time required—role of the employer in setting minimum or full-time work requirement
9. Doing work on employer's premises—the level of on-site supervision and reliance on employer's facilities and equipment
10. Order or sequence set—level the employer sets the pattern of work by individual
11. Oral or written reports—the amount of paperwork the individual must file with the employer
12. Payment by the hour, week, or month—method of payment and the inclusion of sick and vacation days
13. Payment of business and/or traveling expenses—level of compensation employer provides individual to perform work
14. Furnishing of tools and materials—level of use by individual of employer's equipment
15. Significant investment—records are kept to identify individual's contribution (e.g., purchase of equipment) to the employer's facilities
16. Realization of profit or loss—level the individual is responsible for their own business accounting and insurance
17. Working for more than one firm—do the customers pay the individual directly, and can the individual contract with other employers in the same business
18. Making services available to the public—level of independence the individual has in marketing, advertising, and working independent of employer
19. Right to discharge—level of ability of employer to discipline and fire individual
20. Right to terminate—can the individual end relationship with employer or are they bound contractually (Internal Revenue Service, pp. 298–299) (see Caughron & Fargher, 2004, for a full explanation of the classification process)

Significant Case

―――――◇◇◇―――――

This case covers a multitude of contractual issues that are important to individuals involved in contract development and negotiations. The most important issue this case brings forward is that when developing a contract, each side must specifically state their expectations concerning elements of the agreement and write them out explicitly. This is illustrated in the reasons given in the contract for a lengthy contract, program stability, as well as the acceptance of liquidated damages, and the inclusion of the extension into the entire scope of the original contract. Lastly, this case shows that the court will recognize conditional acceptance of contracts, even verbal, which determine the enforcement of the contract.

VANDERBILT UNIVERSITY V. DINARDO

United States Court of Appeals for the Sixth Circuit
174 F.3d 751 (6th Cir. 1999)

Opinion: J. Gibson

On December 3, 1990, Vanderbilt University and Gerry DiNardo executed an employment contract hiring DiNardo to be Vanderbilt's head football coach. Section one of the contract provided:

The University hereby agrees to hire Mr. DiNardo for a period of five (5) years from the date hereof with Mr. DiNardo's assurance that he will serve the entire term of this Contract, a long-term commitment by Mr. DiNardo being important to the University's desire for a stable intercollegiate football program. . . .

The contract also contained reciprocal liquidated damage provisions. Vanderbilt agreed to pay DiNardo his remaining salary should Vanderbilt replace him as football coach, and DiNardo agreed to reimburse Vanderbilt should he leave before his contract expired. Section eight of the contract stated:

Mr. DiNardo recognizes that his promise to work for the University for the entire term of this 5-year Contract is of the essence of this Contract to the University. Mr. DiNardo also recognizes that the University is making a highly valuable investment in his continued employment by entering into this Contract and its investment would be lost were he to resign or otherwise terminate his employment. . . . Accordingly, Mr. DiNardo agrees that in the event he resigns or otherwise terminates his employment as Head Football Coach, prior to the expiration of this Contract, and is employed or performing services for a person or institution other than the University, he will pay to the University as liquidated damages an amount equal to his Base Salary (later negotiated as his net salary), . . . multiplied by the number of years (or portion(s) thereof) remaining on the Contract.

* * *

Vanderbilt initially set DiNardo's salary at $100,000 per year. DiNardo received salary increases in 1992, 1993, and 1994.

On August 14, 1994, Paul Hoolahan, Vanderbilt's Athletic Director . . . talk(ed) to DiNardo about a contract extension. (DiNardo's original contract would ex-

pire on January 5, 1996). Hoolahan offered DiNardo a two-year contract extension. DiNardo told Hoolahan that he wanted to extend his contract, but that he also wanted to discuss the extension with Larry DiNardo, his brother and attorney.

Hoolahan telephoned John Callison, Deputy General Counsel for Vanderbilt, and asked him to prepare a contract extension. Callison drafted an addendum to the original employment contract which provided for a two-year extension of the original contract, specifying a termination date of January 5, 1998. Vanderbilt's Chancellor, Joe B. Wyatt, and Hoolahan signed the Addendum.

On August 17, Hoolahan returned to Bell Buckle with the Addendum. He took it to DiNardo at the practice field where they met in Hoolahan's car. DiNardo stated that Hoolahan did not present him with the complete two-page addendum, but only the second page, which was the signature page. DiNardo asked, "what am I signing?" Hoolahan explained to DiNardo, "it means that your contract as it presently exists will be extended for two years with everything else remaining exactly the same as it existed in the present contract." Before DiNardo signed the Addendum, he told Hoolahan, "Larry needs to see a copy before this thing is finalized." Hoolahan agreed, and DiNardo signed the document. . . .

On August 16, Larry DiNardo had a telephone conversation with Callison. They briefly talked about the contract extension, discussing a salary increase. Larry DiNardo testified that as of that date he did not know that Gerry DiNardo had signed the Addendum, or even that one yet existed.

DiNardo stated publicly that he was "excited" about the extension of his contract. . . .

On August 25, Callison faxed Larry DiNardo "a copy of the draft Addendum to Gerry's contract." Callison wrote on the fax: "let me know if you have any questions." The copy sent was unsigned. Callison and Larry DiNardo had several telephone conversations in late August and September, primarily discussing the television and radio contract. . . .

In November 1994, Louisiana State University contacted Vanderbilt in hopes of speaking with DiNardo about becoming the head football coach for L.S.U. Hoolahan gave DiNardo permission to speak to L.S.U. On December 12, 1994, DiNardo announced that he was accepting the L.S.U. position.

Vanderbilt sent a demand letter to DiNardo seeking payment of liquidated damages under section eight of the contract. Vanderbilt believed that DiNardo was liable for three years of his net salary: one year under the original contract and two years under the Addendum. DiNardo did not respond to Vanderbilt's demand for payment.

Vanderbilt brought this action against DiNardo for breach of contract. DiNardo removed the action to federal court, and both parties filed motions for summary judgement. The district court held that section eight was an enforceable liquidated damages provision, not an unlawful penalty, and that the damages provided under section eight were reasonable. *Vanderbilt University v. DiNardo*, 974 F. Supp. 638, 643 (M.D. Tenn. 1997). The court held that Vanderbilt did not waive its contractual rights under section eight when it granted DiNardo permission to talk to L.S.U. and that the Addendum was enforceable and extended the contract for two years. *Id*. at 643-45. The court entered judgement against DiNardo for $281,886.43. *Id*. at 645. DiNardo appeals.

I.

DiNardo first claims that section eight of the contract is an unenforceable penalty under Tennessee law. DiNardo argues that the provision is not a liquidated damage provision but a "thinly disguised, overly broad non-compete provision," unenforceable under Tennessee law.

* * *

Contracting parties may agree to the payment of liquidated damages in the event of a breach. *See Beasley v. Horrel*, 864 S.W.2d 45, 48 (Tenn. Ct. App. 1993). The term "liquidated damages" refers to an amount by the parties to be just compensation for damages should a breach occur. *See id*. Court will not enforce such a provision, however, if the stipulated amount constitutes a penalty. *See id*. A penalty is designed to coerce performance by punishing default. *See id*. In Tennessee, a provision will be considered one for liquidated damages, rather than a penalty, if it is reasonable in relation to the anticipated damages for breach, measured prospectively at the time the contract was entered into, and not grossly disproportionate to the actual damages. *See Beasley*, 864 S.W.2d at 48; *Kimbrough & Co. v. Schmitt*, 939 S.W.2d 105, 108 (Tenn. Ct. App. 1996). When these conditions are met, particularly the first, the parties probably intended the provision to be for liquidated damages. However, any doubt as to the character of the contract provision will be resolved in favor of finding it a penalty.

* * *

DiNardo contends that there is no evidence that the parties contemplated that the potential damage from DiNardo's resignation would go beyond the cost of hiring a replacement coach. . . .

DiNardo's theory of the parties' intent, however, does not square with the record. The contract language establishes that Vanderbilt wanted the five-year contract because "a long-term commitment" by DiNardo was "important to the University's desire for a stable intercollegiate football program," and that this commitment was of "essence" to the contract. Vanderbilt offered the two-year contract extension to DiNardo well over a year before his original contract expired. Both parties understood that the extension was to provide stability to the program, which helped in recruiting players and retaining assistant coaches. Thus, undisputed evidence, and reasonable inferences therefrom, establish that both parties understood and agreed that DiNardo's resignation would result in Vanderbilt suffering damage beyond the cost of hiring a replacement coach.

* * *

The stipulated damages clause is reasonable under the circumstances, and we affirm the district court's conclusion that the liquidated damages clause is enforceable under Tennessee law.

* * *

II.

DiNardo next argues that Vanderbilt waived its right to liquidated damages when it granted DiNardo permission to discuss the coaching position with L.S.U. Under Tennessee law, a party may not recover liquidated damages when it is responsible for or has contributed to the delay or nonperformance alleged as the breach. *See V.L. Nicholson Co. v. Transcom Inv. And Fin. Ltd., Inc.*, 595 S.W.2d 474, 484 (Tenn. 1980).

Vanderbilt did not waive its rights under section eight of the contract by giving DiNardo permission to pursue the L.S.U. position. *See Chattem, Inc. v. Provident Life & Accident Ins. Co.*, 676 S.W.2d 953, 955 (Tenn. 1984) (waiver is the intentional, voluntary relinquishment of a known right). First, Hoolahan's permission was quite circumscribed. Hoolahan gave DiNardo permission to talk to L.S.U. about their coaching position; he did not authorize DiNardo to terminate his contract with Vanderbilt. Second, the employment contract required DiNardo to ask Vanderbilt's athletic director for permission to speak with another school about a coaching position, and Hoolahan testified that granting a coach permission to talk to another school about a position was a "professional courtesy." Thus, the parties certainly contemplated that DiNardo could explore other coaching positions, and indeed even leave Vanderbilt, subject to the terms of the liquidated damages provision. *See Park Place Ctr. Enterprises, Inc. v. Park Place Mall Assoc.*, 836 S.W.2d 113, 116 (Tenn. Ct.

App. 1992) ("all provisions of a contract should be construed as in harmony with each other, if such construction can be reasonably made . . ."). Allowing DiNardo to talk to another school did not relinquish Vanderbilt's right to liquidated damages.

* * *

III.

DiNardo claims that the Addendum did not become a binding contract, and therefore, he is only liable for the one year remaining on the original contract, not the three years held by the district court.

A.

DiNardo argues that the Addendum did not extend section eight, or that there is at least a question of fact as to whether the Addendum extended section eight.

. . . When the agreement is unambiguous, the meaning is a question of law, and we should enforce the agreement according to its plain terms. *Richland Country Club, Inc. v. CRC Equities, Inc.*, 832 S.W.2d 554, 557 (Tenn. Ct. App. 1991).

DiNardo argues that the original employment contract explicitly provides that section eight is limited to "the entire term of this five-year contract," and the plain, unambiguous language of the Addendum did not extend section eight. He points out that the Addendum did not change the effective date in section eight, unlike other sections in the contract.

The plain and unambiguous language of the Addendum read in its entirety, however, provides for the wholesale extension of the entire contract. Certain sections were expressly amended to change the original contract expiration date of January 5, 1996, to January 5, 1998, because those sections of the original contract contained the precise expiration date of January 5, 1996. The district court did not err in concluding that the contract language extended all terms of the original contract.

B.

DiNardo also claims that the Addendum never became a binding contract because Larry DiNardo never expressly approved its terms. DiNardo contends that, at the very least, a question of fact exists as to whether the two-year Addendum is an enforceable contract.

* * *

Under Tennessee law, parties may accept terms of a contract and make the contract conditional upon some other event or occurrence. *See Disney v. Henry*, 656 S.W.2d 859, 861 (Tenn. Ct. App. 1983). DiNardo argues that the Addendum is not enforceable because it was contingent on Larry DiNardo's approval.

There is evidence from which a jury could find that Larry DiNardo's failure to object did not amount to acceptance of the Addendum. The parties were primarily negotiating the radio and television contract during the fall of 1994. We cannot say that Larry DiNardo's failure to object by December 12, 1994, constituted an acceptance of the Addendum as a matter of law.

* * *

Accordingly, we affirm the district court's judgement that the contract contained an enforceable liquidated damage provision, and we affirm the portion of the judgement reflecting damages calculated under the original five-year contract. We reverse the district court's judgement concluding that the Addendum was enforceable as a matter of law. We remand for a resolution of the factual issues as to whether Larry DiNardo's approval was a condition precedent to the enforceability of the Addendum and, if so, whether the condition was satisfied by Larry DiNardo's failure to object.

We affirm in part, reverse in part, and remand the case to the district court for further proceedings consistent with this opinion.

 OTHER RELEVANT SIGNIFICANT CASES

Recent Trends

Arbitration

In two cases that include the requirement for dispute resolution through arbitration, the courts upheld the use of arbitration as a method to settle such disputes. In *McGrann v. First Albany Corporation* (2005)—which has some elements akin to big-time college and professional coaching contracts—McGrann claimed that First Albany Corp. (FAC) breached his contract by terminating him after the company had made extensive commitments to him. The dispute went to an arbitrator, and a judgment was handed down in McGrann's favor. The case was then taken to federal court to confirm the arbitrator's judgment, with FAC disputing the validity of the arbitrator's decision. The court sided with McGrann, stating that the contract was ambiguous, and that the arbitrator had not exceeded his authority (*McGrann v. First Albany Corporation*, 2005, pp. 23–24). Another court went on to clarify the justification of an arbitrator's judgment by stating that there are only three cases where the court will overturn an arbitrator's decision: (1) corruption, fraud, or other undue means involved; (2) partiality or corruption on the part of the arbitrator; and (3) the arbitrators exceeded their powers (*Prescott v. Northlake Christian School*, 2005, p. 19).

Disclosure of Coaches Contracts

As coaches' salaries get larger and larger and more complicated with university incentives and outside non-university-related income, one might begin to see a greater call for full disclosure of these coaches' true employment packages. In the case of *University System of Maryland v. The Baltimore Sun Company* (2004), the court was asked to allow full disclosure of the University of Maryland's head football coach Ralph Friedgen's full contract including "any separate letters of understanding, side letters or similar documents specifying incentives, bonuses, broadcast agreements, athletic footwear contracts, and other matters. . . ." (p. 81). The *Baltimore Sun* based its request under the Maryland Public Information Act (MPIA), which required state agencies to disclose public employees' "salaries" when requested. The issue in this case—and discussed earlier when speaking of the complexity of current sport contracts— was whether or not non-university-related income that the university is required to approve (e.g., TV, radio, endorsements) was covered under the act. The court in this case took an interesting tack in determining what was and was not covered under the MPIA. The court stated that each item must be viewed in camera by the court, depending on the nexus between the coach's position as a coach for a particular institution and his or her connection with the outside income specifically as that particular coach (essentially, are they being paid because they are coach of the University of Maryland or as a college coach who happens to work for a particular institution) (pp. 105–106).

Covenant Not to Compete

Covenants not to compete are also commonly used in coaching contracts. For example, in the new football coach's contract, the school could include a clause prohibiting the coach from accepting another head coaching position at any school in the same conference for five years after leaving his current school. The purpose of the clause is to protect the competitive advantage of the school, while at the same time not overly restricting the coach's future earning possibilities. If the clause is too restrictive in scope or time (*MacGinnitie v. Hobbs Group*, 2005), courts will refuse to enforce it against the coach. This concept was supported in two recent cases in which the courts stated the restriction must be based on a geographical limitation, which it seems an athletic conference would apply (*Farm Credit Services v. Wysocki*, 2001; *Advance Technology Consultants, Inc. v. Roadtrac, L.L.C.*, 2001).

Federal Statutes

In several cases, coaches have used statutory laws, such as Title VII of the Civil Rights Act of 1964 and Title XI, to challenge the termination of their contracts. For example, in *Lamb-Bowman v. Delaware State University* (2002), a women's basketball coach claimed she was discriminated against based on gender and was being retaliated against due to her complaint that there were disparities between the men's and women's programs at the school. The court found no Title VII gender discrimination and retaliation issues, and that her dismissal was based on her coaching record. In a more recent and more publicized case, involving Arkansas Head Basketball Coach Nolan Richardson, Richardson claimed that he was fired based on his race and his willingness to speak publicly about the subject. The court, however, failed to find any evidence of racial bias in the firing and dismissed the case (*Richardson v. Sugg*, 2004).

The preceding cases provide a lesson for all sport managers to continually document all personnel situations that may reasonably lead to an employee's termination for cause.

An interesting situation in the NBA between player Vin Baker and the Boston Celtics involved claims of discrimination based on the American's With Disabilities Act (ADA), breach of the uniform player contract, and breach or misrepresentation of precontractual physical conditions. Baker was an alcoholic, which led to his termination by the Celtics and the subsequent charges and countercharges by the two sides. In the end, an undisclosed settlement was reached by Baker and the Celtics (a common result in disputes in sport, as discussed earlier). The situation did demonstrate that although collective bargaining agreements (CBA) between players and owners of professional teams are often easily analyzed, in the area of alcoholism in the National Basketball Association's CBA, there still remains ambiguity as to the rights to terminate a player's contract by the team (Marshall, 2005).

At-Will Employees

In an interesting non-sport-related development concerning at-will employees vs. contractual employees, the court in *McClease v. R.R. Donnelley & Sons Inc.* (2002) ruled that at-will employment constitutes a contract within the meaning of 42 U.S.C. Section 1981. This sentiment was shared by Alex Long, who stated that "tortuous interference claims have the potential to undercut the employment at-will rule" (Long, 2001). The impact of this issue could place sport organizations at risk for discriminatory-based dismissals of at-will employees under greater legal scrutiny and potentially cause organizations to suffer financially from such suits. This concept was discussed at great length by Russell Joki (2005). Joki argued that coaches' contracts, supplemental to their teaching contracts, are still contractually based employees. Therefore, coaching positions should not be considered at-will employment situations, allowing for full contractual protection of the coach in case of termination.

References

Cases

Advance Technology Consultants, Inc. v. Roadtrac, L.L.C., 250 Ga. App. 317; 551 S.E.2d 735; 2001 Ga. App. (2001).

Alexander, et al. v. Minnesota Vikings Football Club LLC & National Football League, 649 N.W.2d 464 (2002).

Barnett v. Board of Trustees for State Colleges and Universities A/K/A University of Louisiana System, 806 So. 2d 184; 2001 La. App. LEXIS 1676 (La.App. 1 Cir, 2001).

Cherry v. A-P-A Sports, Inc., 662 P.2d 200 (Colo. App. 1983).

Cole v. Valley Ice Garden, 113 P. 3d 275 (Mont. 2005).

Deli v. University of Minnesota, 511 N.W.2d 46 (Minn. Ct. App. 1994).

Farm Credit Services v. Wysocki, 2001 WI 51; 243 Wis. 2d 305; 627 N.W.2d 444 (2001).

Farner v. Idaho Falls School District, 135 Idaho 337; 17 P.3d 281 (2000).

Frazier v. University of the District of Columbia, 742 F. Supp. 28 (D.D.C. 1990).

Hamm v. Poplar Bluff R-1 School District, 21584 (Mo. Ct. App. 1997).

Lamb-Bowman v. Delaware State University, 39 Fed. Appx. 748; 2002 U.S. app. LEXIS 13140 (2002).

Lindsey v. University of Arizona, 157 Ariz. 48, 754 P.2d 1152 (Ariz. Ct. App. 1987).

MacGinnitie v. Hobbs Group, LLC, 2005 U.S. App. LEXIS 16853; 18 Fla. L. Weekly Fed. C 832 (11th Cir. 2005).

Maddox v. University of Tennessee, 62 F.3d 843 (6th Cir. 1995).

McClease v. R.R. Donnelley & Sons Inc., 226 F.Supp. 2d 695 (2002).

McGrann v. First Albany Corp., 2005 U.S. App. LEXIS 19762 (8th Cir. 2005).

McKenzie v. Wright State University, 683 N.E.2d 381 (Ohio App. 1996).

Meinders v. Dunkerton Community School District, 645 N.W.2d 632 (IA Sup. 2002).

Miami Dolphins Ltd. v. Williams, 356 F. Supp. 2d 1301 (S.D. Fla. 2005).

Monson v. State of Oregon, 901 P.2d 904 (Or. App. 1995).

Nader v. ABC Television, 2005 U.S. App. LEXIS 19536 (2nd Cir. 2005).

New England Patriots Football Club Inc. v. University of Colorado, 592 F.2d 1196 (1st Cir. 1979).

Prescott v. Northlake Christian School, 2005 U.S. App. LEXIS 13684 (5th Cir. 2005).

Richardson v. Sugg, 325 F. Supp. 2d 919 (E.D. Ark. 2004).

Rodgers v. Georgia Tech Athletic Association, 303 S.E.2d 467 (Ga. Ct. App. 1983).

Small v. Juniata College, 547 Pa. 731; 689 A.2d 235 (1997).

Smith v. Alanis & Zapata Independent School District, 2002 Tex. App. Lexis 5437 (TX App, 3rd 2002).

Stamps Public Schools v. Colvert, No. CA95-318 (Ark. Ct. App. 1996).

Tolis v. Board of Supervisors of Louisiana State University, 602 S.2d 99 (La. App. 1992).

University System of Maryland v. The Baltimore Sun Company, 381 Md. 79; 847 A.2d 427 (MD App. 2004).
Vanderbilt University v. DiNardo, 174 F.3d 751 (6th Cir. 1999).
Wadler v. Eastern College Athletic Conference, 2003 U.S. Dist. LEXIS 14212 (S. Dist, N.Y. 2003).

Publications

Caughron, R., & Fargher, J. (2004). Independent contractor and employee status: What every employer in sport and recreation should know. *Journal of Legal Aspects of Sport, 14*(1), 47–61.

Cozzillio, M., & Levinstein, M. (1997). *Sport law: Cases and materials.* Durham, NC: Carolina Academic Press.

Greenberg, M. (2001, Fall). College coaching contracts revisited: A practical perspective. *Marq. Sports L.Rev., 12*, 153–226.

Greenberg, M., & Thomas, R. (2005, April–June). The Rick Neuheisel case—lessons learned from the "washout" in Washington. *For the Record: The Official Newsletter of the National Sports Law Institute, 16*(2), 6–11.

Halcomb Lewis, D. (1998, Winter). After further review, are sports officials independent contractors? *American Business Law Journal, 35*, 249.

Hunt, M. (2003, June 3). Limbo tune doesn't get coaches dancing. *Milwaukee Journal Sentinel*, p. 01C.

Internal Revenue Service. (n.d.). *Internal Revenue Manual, 4600 Employment tax procedures*, Exhibit 4640-1. Washington, DC: Department of the Treasury, Internal Revenue Service.

Joki, R. (2005). The history and application of supplemental contracts for coaches—does due process exist in their game plan? *Idaho Law Review, 41*, 293–328.

Long, A. (2001, Summer). The disconnect between at-will employment and tortuous interference with business relationships: Rethinking tortuous interference claims in the employment context. *Arizona State Law Journal, 33*, 526.

Marshall, J. (2005, Spring). Fired in the NBA! Terminating Vin Baker's contract: A case study in collective bargaining, guaranteed contracts, arbitration, and disability claims in the NBA. *Sports Lawyers Journal, 12*(1), 2–42.

NCAA president receives 2-year extension. (2005, August 5). *The Associated Press*, Sports News.

Rosenthal, J. (1997, March 7). Parcells case a journey through contract law precedent. *New York Law Journal.*

Schultz, J. (2006, January 13). AD exit strips Hewitt of ally. *The Atlanta Journal-Constitution*, p. 1H.

Yasser, R., McCurdy, J., Goplerud, C., & Weston, M. (2000). *Sports law: Cases and materials* (4th ed). Cincinnati, OH: Anderson Publishing Co.

6.22 Letters of Intent and Scholarships

Dennis R. Phillips
University of Southern Mississippi

A *"letter of intent"* is a legal term for "the intention to enter into a formal agreement (as a contract) or to take some specified action as stated" (FindLaw Legal Dictionary). **The National Letter of Intent** (NLI) is a binding agreement signed by a prospective student–athlete and an institution of higher learning or conference. The document, which outlines the grant-in-aid provisions and penalties for the student–athlete if he or she reneges on that commitment, binds both the student–athlete and the institution to the terms of the scholarship agreement for one academic year. The student–athlete commits to an institution and receives a guaranteed amount of scholarship aid stipulated in the agreement. The agreement is valid for one academic year and not predicated on extenuating circumstances such as "making the team," staying healthy, or stability in the coaching staff. According to the National Letter of Intent Website (www.national-letter.org/overview/), the two main goals of the program are to (1) reduce and limit recruiting pressure on student–athletes; and (2) promote and preserve the amateur nature of collegiate athletics. Signing the NLI also effectively ends the recruiting process and allows the student–athlete the security to enjoy his or her senior year without the undue pressures of recruiting.

The collegiate institution also receives benefits from the NLI. The letter of intent has the basic purposes of reducing recruiting time and expense for the institution, allowing the school to accurately determine the number of incoming athletes, avoid worries of "losing" athletes to other schools who refuse to honor verbal commitments, and foster a sense of responsibility by student–athletes and their parents to the obligations they have made.

The NLI was developed in 1964 and is currently administered by the Collegiate Commissioners Association (CCA) and *not* the NCAA. The NLI program is a voluntary program that is national in scope. There are currently 55 conferences and over 500 collegiate institution members, including virtually all NCAA Division I schools, except the service academies and the Ivy League. A large number of NCAA Division II institutions participate; however, no NCAA Division III, National Association of Intercollegiate Athletics (NAIA), junior colleges, or preparatory schools are members of the NLI (www.national-letter.org).

The NLI has evolved from an original one-page document to the present four-page agreement that includes official interpretations and rules governing the commitment. Despite the relatively straightforward appearance and intent of the document, legal and ethical questions remain. Does this document constitute a "contractual" relationship that is binding under the legal principles of contract law? Due to the fact that the NLI is not required by the NCAA (although they have established rules governing its procedures), is this simply a "gentleman's agreement" with little legally enforceable powers? Because the student–athlete is frequently under the age of majority when he or she signs the documents, should the student have the right to void the agreement due to a lack of legal competency? Are the benefits of the NLI tilted so much to the side of the university over the prospective student–athlete that the agreement becomes unfair or lacks "mutuality"? Is the success of the program based solely on the integrity of the individuals and institutions involved? Is there an adequate appeals process when procedures are not accurately followed in the administration of the NLI program? This chapter examines the rules and contractual validity of the letter of intent and resulting scholarship.

Fundamental Concepts

The NLI contains a thorough explanation of the policies and guidelines of the agreement. In addition to the stipulations contained within the NLI itself, the Collegiate Commissioners Association has developed a National Letter of Intent Internet Website, www.national-letter.org/, which contains further interpretations concerning the document. The Website includes a full text copy of the NLI, History, Frequently Asked Questions (FAQs) concerning its application, and password-secured official forms for membership use, such as the Administrative Guidelines and Interpretations, Penalty Provisions and Appeals Process, Qualified Release Agreement, and Appeals Form.

Standard Provisions

Some of the key provisions of the NLI follow.

*   **The NLI has strict signing and filing deadlines, and only applies to prospective student–athletes entering four-year institutions as full-time students for the first time.** The NLI can only be signed during one of the "official" signing dates for each sport in the NCAA. The student–athlete must sign the agreement within 14 days following issuance. The institution listed in the NLI has 21 days to file the signed document with their conference office. The conference office then will contact all other member conferences, and a recruiting ban on that student–athlete will commence. This procedure constitutes one of the main reasons for existence of the program. The statute of limitations of the program is four years. Institutions and prospective student–athletes are subject to penalties for signing at nonauthorized times.
*   A **financial aid award statement is required** in writing at the time the NLI is signed. The NLI is rendered null and void if the award is not present.
*   The **failure to attend** the institution committed to in the NLI, and subsequent attendance by the student–athlete in another institution, results in a one-year ban on competition in athletics. The student–athlete also loses one season of athletic eligibility in all sports. In October 2004 this rule was changed from the previously harsher penalty of loss of **two** seasons of eligibility and a **two**-year ban on competition (personal communication, January 30, 2006).
*   A **Qualified Release Agreement (QRA)** allows the student–athlete and institution to mutually agree to release each other of any obligations contained in the signed NLI. The QRA must be signed by all the original signees and will allow the student–athlete to transfer to another institution. If the latter college is a member of the NLI, the student–athlete will not be allowed to compete in his or her first year of residence and will lose one season of competition.
*   The **NLI is rendered null and void** if (1) the student–athlete is denied admission into the college; (2) the student–athlete is a "nonqualifier" for financial aid (NCAA Bylaw 14.3); (3) the student–athlete does not attend any NLI member institution for one academic year following signing the NLI; (4) the student–athlete serves active duty in a branch of the armed forces of the United States; (5) the student–athlete participates in an official church mission for at least eighteen months; (6) the institution decides to discontinue the sport involved in the NLI agreement; or (7) the institution named in the NLI is guilty of a conference or NCAA recruiting violation.
*   **No additions or deletions are allowed** in the agreement.
*   **The NLI agreement is made with the institution and not the coach.** This is an important stipulation because of the importance of the coach in the recruiting process and the frequency of terminations and resignations of intercollegiate coaches.

NCAA Involvement

Although the NCAA denies any involvement in the management of the National Letter of Intent Program, they do provide rules and regulations affecting those who sign and administer it. The *2005–06 NCAA Division I Manual (Bylaw Article 13—Recruiting)* lists specific regulations concerning the document's delivery, signing, publicity, and follow-up. Early, late, regular, and midyear "official" signing dates are listed in order to assist both the student–athletes and institutions in the decision-making process. Early signing dates effectively "lock in" commitments one year in advance of college enrollment. Although there are many "pros" and "cons" of signing early, the phrase "caveat emptor" (buyer beware) becomes appropriate when a prized recruit is injured, has disciplinary problems, or develops academic deficiencies. In turn, questions arise from the student–athletes concerning the validity of the NLI when a coach resigns to take another job or is terminated from his or her position.

The NCAA is also an integral part of the process in terms of their investigative and enforcement process. Because the NLI is null and void when the institution named in the NLI is guilty of a conference or NCAA recruiting violation, many prospective athletes have the option to attend another college or university. This fact is especially significant in the Southeastern Conference, the home of the administration of the NLI, where there have been nine major violations in football committed since 1990 (Barnhart, 2002).

The Appeals Process

According to Karl Hicks, former NLI administrator, 250 to 300 NLI appeals take place every year, with about 50 of them difficult enough to require interpretation and judgment by committees involved in the appeals process. In the thirty-year history of the NLI, the CCA has never been in court; however, it is frequently threatened, and the NLI is often discussed in lawsuits involving other areas of eligibility, discipline, worker's compensation, or scholarship issues (K. Hicks, personal communication, November 20, 2000). One reason for the lack of lawsuits, according to former Southeastern Conference Assistant Commissioner and NLI Administrator Eugene Byrd, is that a strong attempt to settle the matter in an equitable fashion agreeable to both parties usually settles the matter before it reaches trial (E. Byrd, personal communication, January 30, 2003). Another reason for the lack of time spent arguing the merits of the NLI in court may be the organization of the appeals process. A student who wishes to appeal any penalty associated with the NLI agreement must attempt to secure an NLI Qualified Release Agreement (QRA) and present it with the application for appeal form. The appeals application form requests documentation of any extenuating circumstances that the student–athlete feels would justify special consideration and exemption from the normal penalties accrued through failure to comply with NLI obligations. The application is sent to the NLI Director for review. The Director then presents all information to the *NLI Steering Committee* for review and decision. A decision of the NLI Steering Committee may be appealed to the *NLI Appeals Committee* within thirty days of the decision. Conference commissioners or representatives from member conferences comprise the membership of both of the appeals committees. The NLI Appeals Committee's decision is final and binding. All appeals decisions must be made within one month of the application. It is interesting to note that *institutions* cannot appeal a decision made by a committee in the appeals process and are precluded, as a condition of membership in the NLI program, from bringing legal action against the national letter of Intent Program or the Collegiate Commissioners Association.

Legal and Ethical Issues

There are a number of legal issues concerning the NLI. The contractual nature of the agreement and supporting scholarship, the "capacity" of parties signing the agreement, "remedies" for breach of contract, the application of "good faith" standards, "performance criteria," and legal jurisdiction are some of the legal "gray" areas involved in the implementation of the NLI.

Contractual Nature of the NLI and Scholarship

There are usually three signatures on every NLI: the prospective student–athlete, his/her parent or guardian if they are not of the age of majority, and the college institution's athletic director. The NLI states that the signature of the student–athlete invalidates any previous oral promises that might contradict its terms and is a variation of the "parol evidence" rule in traditional contract law doctrine that emphasizes that the written document is paramount. This is an interesting concept in light of the fact that most of the time the student is a minor and must have the agreements cosigned by an adult. In the event of a charge of breach of contract involving a minor, the involved adult cosigner is usually deemed liable. However, for all practical means, if the student–athlete backs out on their commitment, remedies are limited. After all, it is not the adult that receives the scholarship or loses seasons of competition or eligibility, and it is difficult to put a monetary amount for "damages" incurred in the breach of contract.

The issue of whether the NLI and the associated scholarship offer constitutes a legal and binding contract has been well settled by the courts. For example, in *Taylor v. Wake Forest University* (1972), the courts reasoned that the scholarship contract was bilateral in nature requiring obligations from **both** the institution and the student–athlete. If either failed to live up to their commitment (in this case participation on the team) then the contract would be breached. In *Ross v. Creighton University* (1992), the courts held that a college who recruited a student–athlete had an "identifiable contractual promise" to help the student obtain the educational benefits promised to him during the recruiting process.

Still other courts (*Begley v. Corporation of Mercer University*, 1973; *Gulf South Conference v. Boyd*, 1979) have held that the elements of a binding contract—offer and acceptance, consideration, capacity, and legality—are contained in the NLI and scholarship documents. An athletic grant-in-aid is offered for a period of one academic year. The prospective student–athlete's signature is perceived as acceptance of the offer, with binding provisions and penalties on both parties attached to the agreement. The "capacity" of the minor is presumed as a part of the requirement of the parent or guardian's signature as contract guarantor.

The issue of the NLI and accompanying financial aid agreement as contract arose in *Shepherd v. Loyola Marymount University,* when Kisha Shepherd, a basketball player, was dismissed from the team and lost her athletic scholarship. She claimed the racially discriminatory and hostile environment at practice was a violation of the California Fair Employment and Housing Act. She filed suit in April 2000 for breach of oral contract involving renewal of her annual scholarship and sought monetary damages equal to the cost of tuition, books, and room and board. Both the trial court and subsequent appeals court ruled that the Fair Employment and Housing Act only applied to those who were employees of the university and that none of the documents she signed (NLI or scholarship agreement) indicated an employer/employee contractual agreement among the parties.

Several other courts have found however, that the scholarship agreement does create an employee/employer relationship that is contractual in nature and provides benefits such as workers' compensation and health insurance.

Consideration

The scholarship agreement is binding on the institution for one academic year. The "consideration" is the financial aid amount required by the NLI and accompanied scholarship forms. The *NCAA Manual* (Bylaw Article 15—Financial Aid) details the terms of the grant-in-aid offered to the student–athlete. Elements such as tuition, room and board, books, and required fees are listed as "permissible" financial aid as a part of the "consideration" of the agreement. The commitment is for a period of one year and must be renewed on an annual basis thereafter. The NCAA prohibits a scholarship offer contingent on the physical fitness or condition level of the student–athlete. If the student–athlete is accepted for admission and is deemed a "qualifier" or "partial qualifier" by the NCAA Clearinghouse for eligibility, they must be awarded the agreed-upon grant-in-aid monetary amount, even if their physical condition prevents them from participating in athletic events in college during that academic year. NCAA Bylaw Article 15 further acknowledges that a grant-in-aid **may not be** cancelled or reduced during the course of the term of the "contract" on the basis of skill, or on-the-field, or court performance criteria. However, cancellation or reduction of the grant-in-aid **is allowed** for the following reasons: (1) the student–athlete becomes academically ineligible for intercollegiate competition, (2) the student–athlete has fraudulently represented themselves in the NLI or scholarship agreement, (3) serious misconduct takes place requiring disciplinary action by the institution, or (4) the student–athlete voluntarily withdraws from the sport. In all cases, due process requires the opportunity for a hearing and appeals process for the involved student–athlete. Notification of renewal or nonrenewal of any grant-in-aid must take place by July 1 of the subsequent academic year.

Performance

Performance is usually an integral part of a contractual agreement. Contract law requires that both sides be obligated to perform their listed duties to avoid a breach of duty. The obligations of the student–athlete require satisfactory academic progress, acceptable campus behavior, compliance with NCAA and conference regulations, and participation in team activities. Whether the athlete has a "good game," or "bad game," however, is not a part of the contractual criteria and cannot affect the terms of the previously signed agreement. Despite the fact that athletes have occasionally been "awarded" with the "$100 handshake" by over-zealous boosters following an outstanding performance, additional funds, awards, or benefits defined by the NCAA as "pay" violates the "amateur status" of college athletes and renders them ineligible. However, rules of appearance, conformity, dress, or behavior (written or unwritten) are often allowed by the courts as conditions of voluntary team participation, as long as they do not violate constitutional rights of the individual. For example, a junior college athletic department was able to establish appearance standards of hair length and no facial hair as conditions of team participation despite that fact that it was not a written element of the scholarship agreement.

The bilateral nature of most contractual agreements requires certain duties on behalf of both parties. In the case of the NLI, however, little is required in terms of performance level by the institution or coaching staff. Beyond the obvious duty of providing the agreed-upon level of financial aid and staying within the boundaries of NCAA rules and regulations, there are no demands made on the coach for methods of conditioning, amount of playing time, practice conditions, philosophy or strategies used, or type of discipline used in the coaching of his or her team. The student–athlete has no recourse to disengage from their obligations in the event they disagree with their coach in the areas of his/her domain and purview, without voiding the scholarship agreement. In *Knapp v. Northwestern University* (1996), Nicholas Knapp, a high school basketball player, suffered from ventricular fibrillation, and doctors implanted a Medtronic defibrillator to prevent cardiac arrest. He continued to play high school basketball and signed an NLI with Northwestern University. Prior to the season starting his freshman year, the team physician determined that he was medically ineligible to play. He continued to receive his athletic scholarship for the remainder of the year, but sued Northwestern for violation of the Rehabilitation Act of 1973 and breach of the duty of fundamental fairness. Knapp claimed that he suffered a de facto expulsion from the NCAA and the Big Ten Conference by being forced to transfer to another school to play. The court ruled that he failed to prove an economic interest by stating that he would not be able to secure a college education without the scholarship. It also indicated that any future in professional basketball was too speculative. He also failed to prove the claims of breach of contract by clearly showing the contractual duties of both parties in the NLI. The fact that a student–athlete must participate to fulfill the obligations indicated in the NLI and scholarship agreement should be as apparent as the duty the college has to provide the equipment, facilities, and coaching that allows him to play. Knapp alleged that he desired to live up to his commitment, but the school prevented him from doing so and thereby breached their duty. The court granted Northwestern's motion to dismiss the charges.

Good Faith and Fundamental Fairness

Although there are no professional player unions, collective bargaining agreements (CBA), or standard player contracts (SPK) in college athletics, negotiation is arguably involved in the scholarship process. General contract law principles mandate that the parties involved in the contract exhibit "good faith" during the negotiation (*U.C.C. sec. 1–203; Restatement (2d) of Contracts, sec. 205*). Certainly a good bit of negotiation is involved in the competitive recruiting environment of major college athletics. However, there is no room for modification (addendum or deletion) in the NLI. Indeed the admission of negotiation in the scholarship agreements would violate the very nature of amateurism espoused by the NCAA. The specific elements of allowable financial aid and rules and regulations of the NLI are binding and nonnegotiable. In contract law, if one side has an undue advantage of bargaining power so as to make the agreement unfair or inequitable, the courts may view the agreement as one of "adhesion," "lack of mutuality," or "unconscionability" (Walker, 1980). Many lawyers and agents believe that the NLI is an example of the powerful side (university) taking advantage of a much weaker side (high school athlete). Michael Lee, labor lawyer in Michigan, stated, "A contract is usually, 'I give you something, you give me something.' If there is not mutual consideration, it cannot be a contract. In this case, the individual student doesn't get anything. This is essentially a one-sided pledge" (Wetzel, 2003). Arn Tellem, sport agent and CEO of SFX Basketball, which represents such notables as Kobe Bryant and Tracy McGrady, added, "It requires a one-way commitment from the player and not a mutual commitment from the school. There is no commitment to even admit the player to the school" (Wetzel, 2003). However, the NLI is voluntary, and the heavily recruited student–athlete retains a tremendous amount of freedom in the college decision-making process, despite the fact that he or she cannot negotiate any scholarship collateral agreements.

Although most courts have found that there is no proprietary interest or "right" to participate in athletic competition, students and parents continue to file what have come to be known as "disappointment lawsuits." Disappointment lawsuits arise when students and parents perceive that the athlete is not receiving the proper amount of playing time, is not in the "starting lineup," or the coach is misusing his or her abilities. These kinds of lawsuits are often structured around federal constitutional protections such as the violation of due process or equal protection provisions. Richard Lapchick, the Director of the Institute for Diversity and Ethics in Sport at the University of Central Florida, regards most of the disappointment lawsuits as "frivolous." One Southern District Texas judge commented on a case involving a baseball player whose family sued the coach over not making their son the starting pitcher in a key playoff game, "The courts should not get involved in second guessing a coach's decision to play one person over another. Federal judges issue opinions and orders, not starting line-ups" (Epstein, 2005).

When verbal promises made during the recruitment of the prospective student–athlete (e.g., "starting," amount of playing time, position played, future earnings potential, individual marketing opportunities, or professional sport contracts) do not become reality, is there a breach of duty? A legal term called **promissory estoppel** may enter the picture in such events. It "prevents a promisor from denying the existence of a promise when the promisee reasonably and foreseeably relies on the promise and to his or her loss acts or fails to act and suffers an injustice that can only be avoided by enforcement of the promise" (FindLaw Legal Dictionary). The *Brian Fortay v. University of Miami* case is an example of how broken promises and broken dreams can happen if the prospective student–athlete does not read and understand the NLI completely. Brian Fortay was one of the most highly recruiting high school quarterbacks in the country in 1988. He made a verbal commitment to head coach Jimmy Johnson to accept a scholarship to attend the University of Miami (Florida). In exchange, he was told that the school through its coaches and officials would provide guidance both on and off the field. Through numerous conversations with coaches and university officials, Fortay claimed that he was promised the starting quarterback position for at least three years, and that he would follow the footsteps of former Miami greats Jim Kelly, Bernie Kosar, and Vinny Testaverde as a future NFL quarterback. He signed the NLI on February 8, 1989, and by the end of the month, Miami coach Jimmy Johnson accepted the head coaching position with the NFL Dallas Cowboys. Fortay and his father inquired about a release from his NLI commitment; however, according to Fortay, new coach Dennis Erickson promised him that he would be the starting quarterback for at least his last two years at Miami. Following two unproductive years as a redshirt player and backup, Fortay was told he would not be the starting quarterback his third season.

After transferring to Rutgers University and finished his last two seasons sharing the quarterback position in a part-time starting quarterback role, Fortay brought the first of its kind of lawsuit against Miami for breach of contract based on the promises of coaches during the recruiting process. Bylaw Article 10—Ethical Conduct of the *NCAA Manual* implores athletes, coaches, and administrators to conduct themselves with *Honesty* and *Sportsmanship*. Was the Fortay case simply a misunderstanding of the NLI that clearly states that the agreement is with the *institution* and *not* the *coach*? Did he forget that the NLI also states that any previous written or oral agreements made prior to the signing of the NLI are null and void? Was this a case of unethical conduct and dishonesty, or was it a legal breach of contract based on commitments made but not delivered?

"Oral commitments" have increased greatly in recent years and have become a source of difficulty for college administrators and coaches. Increased recruiting pressures have encouraged prospective student–athletes to make promises they may not really mean. One current recommendation by some NCAA Division I football coaches is to add an early NLI signing date similar to the one that basketball has. Tales of athletes retracting on previous oral commitments (often called decommitting and recommitting) seem to be commonplace. Georgia assistant football coach Rodney Garner stated, "We're in an era, now, where so many kids are committing and then changing their minds that it seems like that's the protocol" (Read, 2001, p. 3). The statement, "It has often been said that oral commitments aren't worth the paper they're not written on" (Read, 2001, p. 1), may have been relevant in two more recent cases of alleged "reneged" scholarship offers. Peter Coates filed suit against Northwestern University on behalf of his son Andrew, a high school basketball player in Washington. The Coateses claimed that Andrew was courted via e-mail for several years by then–Northwestern Basketball coach, Kevin O'Neill, following an outstanding high school career in the greater Seattle area. The Coateses claimed they received an e-mail scholarship offer in May, which was confirmed orally during an on-campus visit in June 1998. After verbally accepting the offer in June, Coach O'Neill allegedly rescinded the offer after seeing an ill and injured Andrew play poorly during a summer basketball camp. The Coateses sued Northwestern University for unspecified damages for tuition at the University of Pennsylvania, where Andrew eventually attended. The case was settled out of court by an undisclosed settlement.

A change of coaches often tenders previous oral recruiting promises invalid, but usually it is the student–athlete who asks for an NLI release to pursue a grant-in-aid from another school. In two recent cases, however, it was the coaches that allegedly asked signed basketball players to release the schools from their financial promises. Tony Jones was one of five players who had signed an early period letter of intent to play basketball at Baylor University. However, coach Scott Drew later asked him to release the school from their commitment so that Tony could pursue basketball playing opportunities at another institution. Tony's father believed that the coach had asked his son to leave to make room for another player he wanted more. The coach denied the allegations, but it does bring up the ethical issues in recruitment and early signing commitments (Miller, 2006). Similarly, Amanda Brown, an all-district selection and player of the year in high school, signed an NLI with Oklahoma State University. The OSU coach at the time of her signing was Julie Goodenough. Following her third consecutive twenty-loss season, Coach Goodenough resigned the following March and was replaced by Kurt Budke. According to Amanda's father, coach Budke sent her a release form and told that family that she would never play for him, and that he would honor the financial commitment, but would not allow her to practice, dress, or travel with the team. Big 12 Conference commissioner Kevin Weiberg said, "It [NLI] is essentially in many respects a tender of financial aid, and I think it could raise a number of questions, some legal. From my perspective, institutions have to be very careful that they're dealing always in an ethical way" (Miller, 2006, p. 2).

Significant Case

◇◇◇

The following case is an illustration of the difficulties involved with contract issues surrounding the National Letter of Intent and athletic scholarships. The questions that arise in a case like this concern the role of the university and the responsibility of the student–athlete in the educational process. What promises are made by coaches that could be interpreted as "consideration"? What penalties for both student–athlete and university are inherent in the process? Is there unequal bargaining power in the system that often becomes visible with a coaching change following the NLI commitments?

ROSS V. CREIGHTON UNIVERSITY
United States Court of Appeals for the Seventh Circuit
957 F.2d 410; 1992 U.S. App. LEXIS 3038

Disposition: AFFIRMED in part, REVERSED in part and REMANDED

Kevin Ross filed suit against Creighton University for negligence and breach of contract arising from Creighton's alleged failure to educate him. The district court dismissed Mr. Ross' complaint for failure to state a claim. For the following reasons we affirm in part and reverse in part the judgment of the district court

Kevin Ross was a 6'9" high school basketball star in the Kansas City area. He signed a scholarship offer from Creighton University, a university with high academic reputation located in Omaha Nebraska. Ross was admitted to the university despite coming from an academically disadvantaged background with ACT scores measuring in the bottom 5th percentile of college-bound seniors. Creighton realized Mr. Ross' academic limitations, however in order to induce him to play basketball * * 3 assured him that he would receive sufficient tutoring so that he "would receive a meaningful education." Mr. Ross attended Creighton from 1978 to 1982, acquiring 96 of the required 128 credits for graduation. He achieved a "D" average in several courses such as Marksmanship and Theory of Basketball, that did not count toward degree completion. A secretary was employed to read his assignments and prepare and type his papers. He left Creighton with the overall language skills of a fourth grader and the reading skills of a seventh grader. Mr. Ross then enrolled, at Creighton's expense, for a year of remedial education at the Westside Preparatory School in Chicago. He attended classes with elementary children, and later enrolled in Roosevelt University in Chicago, but was forced to withdraw (* * 4) because of financial difficulties. In 1987, Mr. Ross suffered what he termed a "major depressive episode," during which he barricaded himself in a Chicago motel room and threw furniture out the window.

Mr. Ross filed suit against Creighton on the basis of three complaints of negligence. 1. He argued that Creighton committed "educational malpractice" by not providing him with a meaningful education and preparing him for employment after college. 2. Mr. Ross also claimed that Creighton negligently inflicted emotional distress upon him by enrolling him in a stressful environment in which he was unprepared, and then failed to give him adequate remedial help to enable him to succeed. 3. The third complaint argued "negligent admission" for admission of unprepared students, while contracting to promise to deliver a meaningful college education and degree. . . without providing the necessary tutoring, "red-shirt" opportunity, study skills, and pay for a college education. For those reasons, Ross charged Creighton with breach of promise and breach of contract.

Creighton moved to dismiss the complaint, and the Federal District Court granted the motion. The court held that the charge of "Educational Malpractice would not be allowed in the Illinois Supreme Court and characterized the theory as "beloved of commentators, but not of courts." A realization of the collaborative nature of education and the potential deluge of similar suits caused the court to reject this cause of action. The claim of negligent infliction of emotional distress exists in Illinois only if the Plaintiff was physically harmed by the negligent act. The charge of negligent admission was rejected due to the unreasonable burden that could place upon college admission departments admitting marginal students, and the potential high cost of tort damages resulting from such admissions.

In the analysis of the arguments of educational malpractice the courts noted that such arguments had been rejected by an overwhelming number of states. The realization that the attainment of an educational degree requires a collaboration between teacher and student, with the ultimate responsibility of success remaining always with the student. The courts also noted that if every student who felt deprived of an education would sue the school for damages, the courts would be overwhelmed and schools would have to close.

On the charge of "infliction of emotional distress" courts have usually used the stand of proof of physical harm in order to assure that the emotional distress was genuine. Since Ross could not prove that he was physically injured, this claim was rejected.

In response to Ross' claim of "breach of contract" the court ruled that the "relationship between university and student is at least in part contractual. . . . but how far the duties under a contract of education can be enforced in the courts is another matter. The court reasoned that the University had a duty to admit only students who are "reasonably qualified" and able to perform academically. While Ross had argued that he was not made aware of his woeful inadequacies in academic preparation, nor did Creighton do enough to remedy those inadequacies, the court noted that the decision of who was "reasonably qualified" was largely subjective and better left to the admitting institution and the intelligence and educability of the plaintiff.

The argument that Creighton violated the written and oral contractual agreement with Mr. Ross centered around the exchange of the Mr. Ross' promise to play basketball in exchange for participation in the academic program despite his deficient academic background. The court reasoned that the basic relationship between a student and a private college is contractual in nature. However, the courts refused to delve into the qualifications of students, or the measurement of achieve of those students as they matriculate toward graduation. The court argued that it was not enough for the plaintiff to charge that the education was not good enough. They had to focus on a specific promise that the university made that was not honored. The courts clearly placed the onus of responsibility of attainment of an education clearly in the hands of the student.

Recent Developments

NLI Initial and Continued Academic Eligibility

Several cases have indirectly attacked NCAA rules on initial eligibility and the Clearinghouse interpretations on acceptable core classes. The NLI is declared null and void in the event a prospective student–athlete does not meet school admission standards or fails to meet eligibility qualifications. In *Bowers v. NCAA*, Michael Bowers sued the NCAA and three universities who recruited him to play football under the assumption that he would be a "qualifier." The NCAA Clearinghouse ruled that he was well short of the required thirteen core classes because he had enrolled in several special-education classes due to a diagnosed learning disability. The special-education classes fell below the standard of "regular instructional level" classes and therefore did not count toward the required core classes. He therefore would not qualify to receive an athletic scholarship.

In *Pryor v. NCAA*, a soccer player named Kelly Pryor and Warren Spivey, a football player, brought suit claiming that their NLI and adjoining scholarship agreements were ruled invalid because of failure to meet Proposition 16 standards and become full qualifiers. Pryor eventually was upgraded to "partial qualifier" status due to a learning disability and received her scholarship, but was unable to compete her first year. They argued "intentional" discrimination under Title VI, violation of Title III of the ADA and Section 504 of the Rehabilitation Act, and that Proposition 16 denied black student–athletes the opportunity to make and perform contracts because it harmed their ability to get athletic scholarships. The NCAA won judgment in the case.

In *Williams v. University of Cincinnati*, Charles Williams brought suit for breach of contract after being declared academically ineligible and subsequently having his scholarship revoked. Williams attempted to complete his degree from Chaffee Junior College to compete at Cincinnati by passing several summer courses at the junior college and other colleges in the Los Angeles area. Following intense, high pressure and unethical efforts by his former junior college coach and assistant coaches from Cincinnati, he obtained eligibility to play. However, the NCAA investigated the circumstances of his initial eligibility and declared him ineligible during the course of the season. In his written opinion, Judge Shoemaker ruled for the university and stated, "Quite frankly, it was [Williams] who breached the terms of the NLI by his poor academic performance."

Grayshirting

When the NCAA decided to limit the number of football scholarships awarded in the early 1990s, coaches sought ways to deal with this hardship. The plan is called grayshirting, and it began as a way to accommodate student–athletes who needed additional physical development or more concentrated study time to score well on SAT or ACT tests. Grayshirting also provides more opportunities to comply with the maximum number of 25 scholarships a year and 85 overall in Division IA football. The major difference between grayshirting and redshirting is that grayshirt student–athletes cannot attend their chosen school full-time (twelve credit hours or more). However, they still can redshirt once they have enrolled full-time, which usually is deferred until the spring semester of the following year.

Antonio Lewis, defensive back for West Virginia University was a beneficiary of the grayshirt rule. The *Washington Post* metro player of the year in 2003, he was left in limbo by the NCAA Clearinghouse until nearly the start of school. He decided to sit out a semester before beginning his career with the Mountaineers and gained strength and insight into a new position for spring practice. Another example is quarterback Brent Schaeffer, who did not enroll at the University of Tennessee until the second semester, participated in spring practice, then became the starting quarterback for the Volunteers the following fall, his first at the school (Antonik, 2004).

Future Developments

College recruiting continues to evolve and become more dependent on technology as well as a promotion tool and media "event." Phone calls are now considered "old school," as the Internet, high-tech cell phones, text and instant messaging, e-mails, hand-held BlackBerrys, Treos, and Sidekicks have connected with a generation that thrives on instant communication with anyone, anywhere. Since the NCAA only regulates the amount and timing of telephone calls, these technological communication devices have revolutionized the recruiting process leading up to the signing of the NLI. Instant communication is not without perils and frustration, however, as some student–athletes have reported receiving text messages constantly from 6:30 AM till 11:30 PM, including during class. Parents have reported huge cell phone bills stemming from the avalanche of text messaging from recruiters (Sondheimer, 2005).

Thousands of prospects have their own profile Web pages with personal information and performance measuring standards. Players and coaches alike frequently refer to two of the largest Internet recruiting sites, Rivals.com and Scout.com, for up-to-date signing information. Both services boast a paying membership of over 350,000 members with over a million page visits per day (Freeman, 2006).

NLI Reform Recommendations

Stacey Meyer (2004) advocated several NLI changes that would make the process more equitable for the student–athlete and reduce the unequal bargaining power inherent in the current system. The first recommendation was to have the NCAA take over the administration of the NLI from the Collegiate Commissioner's Association. Doing so would allow the NCAA more power to set and enforce rules and procedures that directly affect the players and coaches involved in NCAA competitions. Recruiting is covered in the *NCAA Manual Bylaws*, as well as extensive sections under eligibility, financial aid, ethical conduct, awards and benefits, enforcement, and several other topicss. The NCAA governs all the other procedures of recruiting and publishes a *Guide for Prospective Student–Athletes*. This would give the student–athlete and parents one location for all information concerning recruitment. Revision of the NLI contract is the second recommendation. The inclusion of such bargaining and negotiation subjects as playing time, positions of play, and starting assignments would allow the player to have in writing what coaches are verbally promising now without legal ramification. The last recommendation would allow the student–athlete to be released to sign another NLI with a different institution within 30 days following the exit of the head coach who recruited them and left to accept another job.

References

Cases

Begley v. Corporation of Mercer University, 367 F. Supp. 908 (E.D. Tenn. 1973).
Bowers v. NCAA, 118 F. Supp. 2d 494 (DNJ 2000).
Fortay v. University of Miami (Civil Action No. 93-3443), 1994 U.S. Dist. LEXIS 1865.
Gulf South Conference v. Boyd, 365 So. 553 (Sup. Ct. Ala. 1993).
Knapp v. Northwestern University: No. 95 C6454, 1996 WL 495559 (N.D. Ill. Aug. 18, 1996).
Pryor v. NCAA, 288 F.3d 548 (3rd Cir. 2002).
Ross v. Creighton University, 957 F. 2d 410 (7th Cir. 1992).
Shepherd v. Loyola Marymount University, 2002 Daily Journal DAR 11545 (Cal.App.2nd District).
Taylor v. Wake Forest University, 191 S.E. 2d 379, cert. den. 192 S.E. 2d 196 (N.C. 1972).
Williams v. University of Cincinnati, 752 N.E. 2d 367, 2001 OhioMisc.LEXIS 10 (OhioCt. 2001).

Publications

Antonik, J. (2004, September 9). *No Fear.* Retrieved from http://www.msnsportsnet.com/page.cfm?story=6709
Barnhart, T. (2002, June 17). These days, there's no excuse for not knowing rules. *The Atlanta Journal Constitution online edition. Retrieved from* www. Accessatlanta.com/ajc/sports/0802/0818secrules.html
Epstein, T. (2005, Spring). Splinters from the bench: Feasibility of lawsuits by athletes against coaches and schools for lack of playing time. *Virginia Sports & Entertainment Law Journal.* Retrieved from http://web.lexisnexis.com/universe/document?_m=13864d89ac1023ce4489ce6422735
Freeman, J. (2006, January 30). Internet services feed the frenzy of college recruiting. *OregonLive.com* . Retrieved from http://www.oregonlive.com/printer.ssf?/bse/sports/1138595122323760.xml&coll

NCAA. (2005). *2005–2006 NCAA Division I Manual*. Indianapolis, IN. Author.

Miller, J. (2006, January 6). Letters of intent: There's a catch. *DallasNews.com*. Retrieved from http://www.dallasnews .com/cgi-bin/bi/gold_print.cgi

Read, D. (2001, January, April/May). In a word. *Athletic Management, 13*(3). Retrieved from http:// www.momentummedia.com/articles/am/am1303/word.htm

Sondheimer, E. (2005, October 28). Phone calls are so old school: Recruits get the message in many high-tech ways. *Los Angeles Times Home Edition*, Part D, p. 1. Retrieved from http://web.lexisnexis.com/universe/ document?_m=61f5940613ef2d2e1906f6

Walker, D. M. (1980). *The Oxford companion to law*. New York: Oxford University Press.

Wetzel, D. (2003, January 20). Bad letter of intent: Letter of intent benefits schools not student–athletes. *Sportsline.com*. Retrieved from http://www.hsbaseballweb.com/letter_of_intent.htm

Legislation

Vocational rehabilitation and other Rehabilitation Services Act, 42 U.S.C.S. § 794, 42 U.S.C.S. § 1981.

U.C.C. Section I-203; Restatement (2d) of Contracts, sec. 205.

Website

www.national-letter.org

6.23 Game, Event, and Sponsorship Contracts

John D. McMillen
Bowling Green State University

Planning, implementing, and managing a sport or recreation game/event is a complex task. Today's sport and recreation manager may be required to arrange everything from hiring an event management firm, to leasing the facility, to securing corporate sponsorships. The instruments that bind all these arrangements together are game, event, and sponsorship contracts.

Understanding the essential components of game, event, and sponsorship contracts is important because these agreements often involve large sums of money as well as legally obligate the sport and recreation manager and host organization to the terms of the agreement. This chapter, therefore, is designed to provide a general overview of the primary contractual issues sport and recreation managers should be familiar with when working with these kinds of agreements. With foresight and planning, game, event, and sponsorship agreements can help ensure that the game/event runs as planned.

Fundamental Concepts

Depending on the game/event, a variety of parties will enter into contracts with the host organization. These include corporate sponsors, vendors, concessionaires, officials, insurance brokers, mascots, personnel, and television or radio networks, just to name a few. The legal principles associated with these agreements parallel the requirements of performance or service contracts discussed in Chapter 6.10, *Contract Essentials*. These contracts, for example, identify the parties; specify the time, place, and manner of performance; list the obligations of the parties; and set forth provisions in case one party cannot carry out its obligation. The primary difference between game, event, and sponsorship contracts and other types of contracts is the bargained-for subject matter. The type of arrangement desired, therefore, will dictate the specific terms and content of the agreement.

Sponsorship Contracts

A sponsorship contract, whether it is between a company and an athlete or a company and a sport or recreation event, is a legal document that binds two or more parties to agreed-upon obligations. Sponsorship deals have grown dramatically in the past decade, from $11.1 billion in 1997 to an estimated $26.5 billion in 2005 (SponsorClick, 2002).

Logistically, sponsorship contracts are an agreement whereby corporate sponsors provide financial packages or some in-kind product (e.g., uniforms, equipment, soft drinks) to the game/event in exchange for advertising space or a promise to use the product by the host organization in a manner that is beneficial to the sponsor. The exact terms of these agreements are then drafted into a **sponsorship contract**. These contracts vary in their construction from a relatively simple $1,500 signage arrangement found in many minor league baseball leagues and some college football bowl games (Heller & Hechtman, 2000) to a sophisticated Olympic sponsorship agreement valued well into the millions of dollars.

Fundamental clauses of a sponsorship agreement include the length of the agreement, the rights granted to the host organization and sponsor, form of payment, use of any marks or products, and termination of the agreement. Although sport and recreation managers likely will not draft sponsorship contracts, it often is the manager's duty to secure whatever agreements are necessary to make the game/event run as planned. The following are additional clauses that sport and recreation managers should be familiar with when working with sponsorship contracts.

Exclusive and Nonexclusive Rights

One of the most important components of sponsorship agreements is the "exclusivity" clause. Many sponsors demand exclusive sponsorship rights within their product or service category. Nike, for example, would not likely sponsor a sport or recreation event if the event already has a sponsorship agreement with Adidas or Reebok. An exclusive sponsorship contract does not mean, however, that competitors will not attempt to advertise their product at or near the event. *Ambush marketing,* sometimes referred to as *parasite marketing,* is a marketing strategy that attempts to dilute an official sponsor's association with a game/event. In other words, a nonpaying sponsor attempts to affiliate its organization with the event even though it has not paid for the rights to do so.

Ambush marketing occurs in a variety of ways. One common instance is when a nonsponsory company purchases advertising time before or during an official event, allowing the company to associate itself with a sport or recreation event without having to pay any sponsorship fees. In other instances, a nonsponsory company might use a logo, symbol, or words that are similar to the logo of the official game/event sponsor (e.g., Buy our pizza while you are watching the "Big Game"). If these images create a "likelihood of confusion," this could violate the Lanham Act (see Chapter 8.22, *Principles of Trademark Law*). There have also been instances where companies bought advertising rights directly outside the venue sponsored by a competitor company (e.g., if Northwest Airlines advertised on a billboard just outside the United Center in Chicago).

Many nonsponsory companies are creative in their ambush marketing strategies and technically may not violate the law. For example, in *National Hockey League, et al. v. Pepsi-Cola Canada Ltd.,* the National Hockey League alleged that although Pepsi did not have any rights to NHL trademarks, it used "confusingly similar" marks in a contest called the "Diet Pepsi $4,000,000 Pro Hockey Playoff Pool," whereby fans matched information under bottle caps with actual NHL playoff results to become eligible for prizes. The Supreme Court of British Columbia ruled that Pepsi used a sufficient disclaimer stating that it was not an official sponsor of the NHL. In essence, the judge stated that because Pepsi sells soft drinks and the NHL's product is hockey, there can be no confusion in the consumers' minds as to which product belongs to which company (Wong, 2002). Cases such as this stress the importance of an airtight sponsorship agreement.

Legal issues may also arise between two official sponsors of the same event. During the 1994 World Cup, for example, both Sprint and MasterCard were official corporate sponsors. MasterCard secured exclusive rights to all debit and credit cards, whereas Sprint negotiated exclusive local and long-distance telephone rights. As a promotion, however, Sprint created phone cards, and MasterCard sued, alleging that Sprint's cards infringed on its exclusive debit card rights. This case was arbitrated and settled by allowing Sprint to give away, not sell, its existing phone cards (see *MasterCard International v. Sprint Communications Co.,* 1994).

Another aspect to consider in sponsorship agreements is what efforts the host organization will take to preserve and protect the sponsor's rights should ambush marketing occur. No sponsorship agreement can prevent ambush marketing from occurring, but the contract can help the host organization and its official sponsors to better understand what steps are going to be taken to minimize its affects (Moorman & Greenwell, 2005).

Venue Concerns

Security, concessions, personnel, and facility leases are the primary provisions covered in the venue portion of the sponsorship agreement. If the venue already has permanent corporate signage, this may pose special legal concerns. For example, it is not unusual for a new event to be sponsored by a competitor of the venue's current sponsor (e.g., Visa versus MasterCard). Some organizations, therefore, may even request that no signs be present at or around the local vicinity of the venue, a common requirement of the NCAA at its Final Four basketball tournament. In these instances, the signage must either be covered up or the existing sponsorship contracts renegotiated. It also may be helpful for the host organization to seek a "variance of contract," meaning the original agreement is amended to temporarily suspend the agreement for a specific period of time while the new sport or recreation tenant occupies the venue. Managers, therefore, will need to examine all current venue agreements to determine whether there are a certain number of days or events before a competing company legally can have a presence in the venue. Otherwise, the new venue agreement could violate an existing contract. In other words, venue rights could greatly impact which corporations managers can solicit to sponsor an upcoming sport or recreation game/event.

Option to Renew and Right of First Refusal

Options to renew and the right of first refusal are also important clauses in a sponsorship agreement. The **option to extend or renew** gives sponsors the choice to lengthen the current agreement when the contract expires. The **right of first refusal** allows sponsors to make an offer to retain sponsorship rights for future games/events. In practical terms, the right of refusal also allows sponsors to walk away from negotiations with the option to match any competitor's offer. Depending on the length of the original contract, sport and recreation managers can protect themselves from these clauses by a provision that mandates that a specific time frame be designated by which the sponsor must declare its intention to either continue or dissolve the relationship. Eight months to a year should be sufficient time for sport and recreation managers to secure another sponsor should the corporate sponsor discontinue its involvement.

Intellectual Property Rights

Many athletic associations and professional sport leagues, such as the NFL and NBA, have a small number of "primary" sponsors that guarantee the association or league a set amount of money or product and services in exchange for certain sponsorship rights (Wong, 2002). In other words, the company has the right to use the association's or league's logo while promoting its product. These rights are often seen on television commercials with a phrase similar to, "Southwest Airlines, the official airline of the NFL."

In addition, consumers spend millions of dollars on licensed sport and recreation products each year. From these sales corporations generate a portion of their revenue from the use of team/corporate sponsor logos, known as trademarks (see Chapter 8.22, *Principles of Trademark Law*). Sport and recreation managers, therefore, must be careful to properly secure and protect the trademarks associated with the game/event (see *Marvel Entertainment Group, Inc. v. The Hawaiian Triathlon Corp.*, 1990).

The agreements that legally allow managers to use corporate logos during the game/event are referred to as **licenses**, or a clause might be written directly into the sponsorship agreement: "Sponsor grants a non-exclusive license to use any trademark or other intellectual property rights in connection with providing the management provisions stated herein" (Heller & Hechtman, 2000). All "works for hire" (see Chapter 8.22, *Principles of Trademark Law*) also should be included into the agreement: "As part of the services provided, all original logos, concepts, designs, mechanicals, and layouts for the event shall be deemed 'works made for hire' and the Sponsor shall be considered the 'author' of such works" (Heller & Hechtman, 2000).

Sport and recreation managers should also recognize that all promotional materials must be examined to determine whether it abides by the appropriate intellectually property laws. Signage, T-shirts, pamphlets, logos, Websites, and other game/event promotional materials cannot infringe on the rights of the trademark, copyright, or patent owner. To avoid excessive delays in the approval process, sport and recreation managers should specify an appropriate turnaround time to view these materials. It is also important to negotiate how long the materials or logos can be used after the game/event has concluded. It may be both a contract and trademark violation to display logos after the time period specified in the contract. For example, if the Orange Bowl requires that FedEx terminate all uses of its Orange Bowl logos on its trucks within 30 days after the bowl game, failure to do so would not only breach the contract but would also violate the Orange Bowl's intellectual property rights.

Finally, managers must be cognizant of potential geographic rights. International sponsors, for example, may seek authority to use trademarks in some or all countries participating in the event, whereas national sponsors in all likelihood will only be interested in using the marks in the host country. These kinds of clauses are popular in larger venues like World Cup Soccer and the Olympic Games. However, the Internet has added a new twist on geographic rights. Because the Internet has no boundaries, all games or events potentially could have national or international appeal. Therefore, the host organization may want to incorporate specific language to protect these territorial rights. One possible solution is to limit the trademark's use to a certain language on the Web page (e.g., English or Spanish) or per event/sport.

Fees and Expenses

Equally important as the actual services to be performed in the sponsorship agreement is the payment of fees and expenses. Management fees for sport and recreation events can run into the hundreds of thousands of dollars depending on the nature and length of the event. Understandably, event management firms seek fair compensation and timely reimbursement for expenses in the agreement, whereas the corporate sponsor is most concerned that the fees correspond to the nature of the services provided. In general, sponsorship agreements must state the specific amount of money or in-kind goods or services and reimbursement of expenses that are to be performed by all parties. Payment schedules and delivery of services should also be expressly defined to avoid any confusion.

In addition, many events now require sponsors to guarantee a certain amount of services and money to market the event. Other possible areas to negotiate include privileges associated with the sponsorship of the game/event, such as tickets, signage, hospitality, and travel. For smaller events, these items often are included as a benefit, but any of these stipulations should be incorporated into the sponsorship agreement to avoid any future misunderstandings.

Media Issues

Depending on the size and commercial draw of the game/event, sport and recreation managers may have to deal with a variety of media contracts, such as cable, satellite, television, radio, and the Internet. Most television contracts include exclusivity and territorial stipulations that then can be licensed to smaller markets or different stations. NBC, for example, obtained the exclusive rights for the 2002 Winter Olympic Games, but then licensed these rights for limited use to the cable network TNT, allowing it to broadcast Olympic coverage that was limited to specific days and certain hours. Whatever the median of technology used, these types of clauses are certain to become even more common with the increasing international demand for U.S. sporting events.

Other Considerations

It is important that host organization clarify in the agreement all the services it will perform. At the same time, managers should seek an agreement whereby the sponsor acknowledges that the nature of the event may make it impossible to list all the services to be rendered. In other words, managers need authority to go beyond the scope of services outlined within the agreement when necessary to successfully perform the duties associated with the event. To protect managers who are required to perform duties or services outside the written agreement, a provision should be included that allows an adjustment in management fees.

Managers also should keep in mind that some sponsors may demand an **approval clause** for other co-sponsors. For example, Pepsi may not want to sponsor an event with McDonalds because of its affiliation with Coca-Cola.

Term and **cancellation** clauses are important in case the game/event is cancelled. These clauses not only allow corporate sponsors and sport and recreation managers the ability to commit to the event, but also ensure flexibility if the event is cancelled. The recent assault of hurricanes along the Gulf and Florida coasts are prime examples of why these clauses are necessary. Overall terms of the agreement can be as short as a few weeks or as long as several years, and cancellation provision may be "at-will," which requires no prior notice, or it can require that certain conditions be met before cancellation.

State law governs the **jurisdiction** of the sponsorship contract. Consequently, a contract's effect may vary depending on the laws of a particular state. Therefore, to avoid possible jurisdiction problems, the agreement should specify the state law to be applied should a dispute arise. For example, if the host organization is in Ohio and the corporate sponsor principally is located in California, the contract might state that "Ohio law will govern this agreement."

Confidentiality may be an important component of sponsorship agreements, particularly if one party provides the other with access to proprietary information such as marketing plans, financial information, client lists, and sales information (Heller & Hechtman, 2000). Also, like all other contracts, sponsorship contracts should define any specific conditions that will be considered a breach of contract as well as specify the amount of **damages**, known as "liquidated damages," should a breach occur. All liquidated damages, however, must be reasonable and based on the actual damage or loss incurred by the nonbreaching party. Otherwise, a court may refuse to enforce excessive liquidated damages. Finally, parties may wish to consider **indemnification** provisions. For example, "Sponsor will indemnify and hold harmless Event Management Firm and its shareholders, affiliates, officers, directors, and employees from and against all claims, expenses, suits, and judgments arising from or connected with a breach of this agreement by the Sponsor, any negligent or intentional acts of the Sponsor in connection with the event, or any violation of the intellectual property rights of a third party associated with the use of the Sponsor's trademarks" (Heller & Hechtman, 2000).

Due to increased work stoppages in professional sports, a growing trend is to include a "force majeure" or **work stoppage provision** into the sponsorship contract (Wong, 2002). Although typically associated with facility or event contracts, these clauses are becoming more common in sponsorship agreements and protect against unforeseeable natural or human events that are beyond the control of the parties of the contract and render the contract impossible (Wong, 2002). This provision may protect one or both parties in the event of a work stoppage from things such as a strike or a lockout, such as the 2004/05 National Hockey League work stoppage.

Another trend is to designate **alternative dispute resolution** provisions within contracts to protect the organization in case of a disagreement regarding the terms of the agreement. Because litigation is expensive, arbitration is the preferred method of resolution, as it provides a speedy and relatively inexpensive means to resolve disputes. If possible, the chosen law should be that of the organization's home state because of convenience and knowledge of the applicable law (see Chapter 6.30, *Alternative Dispute Resolution*).

Game and Event Contracts

Game contracts are agreements designed to facilitate a game/contest between two organizations. Because of these agreements' potential impact on present and future game schedules, these contracts should be prepared with care and under the advisement of legal counsel. In general, both game and event contracts will contain many of the same provisions as sponsorship agreements. For example, sport and recreation managers will need to consider intellectual property rights, as well as the location, date, and time of the game, provisions for officials, governing rules, potential television and radio rights, lease agreements, complimentary or paid tickets, travel expenses and other related costs, and any potential termination and breach procedures.

Event contracts are similar to game contracts in design and concept. The term *event*, however, has a dual meaning. It can signify a single sport/recreation event (e.g., the Super Bowl) or a combination of events (e.g., the NCAA basketball tournament). Event contracts are also synonymous with pre- and postevent activities. In other words, event contracts may not only refer to a game contract, but also to individual or combined agreements for the entire operation of an event from the facility lease, concessions, marketing, and corporate sponsorships, to potential radio or television rights. Like game contracts, event contracts should be prepared with care and include the essential components of game contracts, as well as any other clauses specific to the event's operations.

Lease Agreements

To increase revenues, many organizations now lease facilities to third parties for rental fees. The facility lease may directly influence the success and ease in which a game/event operates (see *Houston Oilers v. Harris County Texas, et al.*, 1997). Whereas a facility lease agreement may be as simple or complex as the parties desire, under the Statute of Frauds (see Chapter 6.10, *Contract Essentials*), all leases must be in writing. In addition to routine elements of time, keys, and opening and closing schedules (Clement, 1998), sport and recreation managers should consider using escape clauses, options to renew, assignment rights, maintenance, restrictive covenants, exit clauses, parking, concessions, merchandise revenue, insurance, and indemnification clauses, as well as sponsorship and signage stipulations in the lease portion of the agreement (Miller, 1997).

Personnel

A variety of employees are needed to run a sport or recreation game/event. Hiring and retaining quality professional employees, therefore, is central to all sport and recreation venues. Sport and recreation managers must be cognizant of how to limit liability regarding personnel issues. Managers, for example, often hire officials, police and/or crowd-control personnel, concessionaires, and emergency personnel. Each of these arrangements can be negotiated for a single game/event or an entire season. Because of the potential liability associated with the type of employment relationship between the host organization and the event personnel (e.g., volunteers, interns, at-will employees, and independent contractors), sport and recreation managers should carefully construct the written agreement to clarify the employment relationship (see Chapter 6.21, *Employment Contracts*). For example, an at-will employment relationship easily can be defined by the event contract: "The parties shall be and act as independent contractors and under no circumstances will this agreement or the relationship between the parties be construed to be an agency, partnership, joint venture, or employment agreement" (Heller & Hechtman, 2000). Furthermore, managers should be aware that some personnel may ask to be a "secured" party, meaning that they will be paid first should the event become bankrupt. Typically, secured employees seek 25 percent up front, 50 percent with satisfactory progress, and the remaining 25 percent on the completion of the work (Irwin, Sutton, & McCarthy, 2002).

Significant Case

◇◇◇◇

The following case is a breach of contract claim brought by Ford Motor Company against professional stock car driver Kasey Kahne. This case illustrates how even the smallest conflict quickly can turn into a lawsuit. This case is just another example of why a qualified attorney should draft contracts to ensure that all parties and their rights are protected.

FORD MOTOR COMPANY V. KASEY KAHNE

United States District Court for the Eastern District of Michigan, Southern Division
379 F. Supp. 2d 857 (2005)

I. BACKGROUND

Dan Davis, the Director of Ford Racing Technology first met Kasey Kahne in May 2000 while attending a USCA Midget race where Kahne was participating. During his deposition, Davis explained that Kahne came highly recommended, had "raw talent," and possessed strong potential for future development as a race car driver. Accordingly, Ford sought to enter "into a business arrangement with [Kasey Kahne] whereby [Ford] would help develop him into a driver of a Ford product in the future," giving Kahne "some compensation to get started."

Davis's efforts resulted in a September 2000 agreement between Ford and Kahne for the young driver to race with Ford or a Ford supported racing team. This 2000 Kahne-Ford agreement was effective through August 29, 2002 "with an option to renew [the] agreement for an additional two years with similar terms, to be negotiated in 2002." The agreement also gave Ford some protection for bringing its racing resources to the table through a right of first refusal. In essence, the contract provided Ford the opportunity to match any racing-related or driving-related employment offer that Kahne might receive during the term of the agreement.

The Kahne-Robert Yates Racing Contract

On February 4, 2002, Kahne and RYR executed a "Contract for Services" for Kahne to drive exclusively for RYR in NASCAR sanctioned racing series. The Kahne-Yates agreement applied to the 2002, 2003, and 2004 NASCAR racing seasons, with an option for RYR to extend the agreement for the 2005 and 2006 seasons. The agreement also provided to RYR the sole right to determine whether Kahne would race in the NASCAR Busch or Winston (Nextel) Cup Series.

The Kahne-Ford 2002 Agreement

While Kahne was working out his contract with RYR, he and Ford were negotiating the contract at issue in this case (as the 2000 Kahne-Ford agreement would expire on August 29, 2002). After lengthy negotiations between the parties, Ford and Kahne executed their second agreement, a "Personal Services Agreement" signed in May 2002. The parties agreed that their 2002 contract would not include a right of first refusal.

Kahne's Contract With Evernham Motorsports

On October 2, 2003, Kahne, through Kasey Kahne Incorporated, executed an agreement with Evernham Motorsports, LLC (a Dodge team) where Kahne would drive full-time on the NASCAR Nextel Cup Series.

Kahne maintains that his agreement with RYR that covered the 2004 season was voided by RYR because it could not provide him a race team in either the NASCAR Nextel Cup or the Busch series. During the 2003 season, Kahne received from Evernham Motorsports an inquiry regarding his availability to drive full-time in the Busch and Nextel Cup Series, and claims that RYR had no plans to race Kahne in the 2004 Busch or Nextel Cup Series. William Seaborn, Vice-President of Marketing for RYR, testified that RYR communicated these facts to Kahne during an August 13, 2003 lunch meeting with Robert Yates, Kahne, Rod Moskowitz (Kahne's agent), and himself. Kahne cites the deposition testimony of Robert Yates, claiming that this testimony establishes that RYR had handed Kahne off to Ford (under the impression that Ford was placing Kahne with a good Busch team) and that because Yates could not offer Kahne a "good seat" in a stock car in either the Busch or Nextel Cup Series, RYR's contract "rights were over" and RYR had "no deal" without sponsorship to support a NASCAR Busch or Cup team for Kahne under their agreement. After realizing that RYR would not have a team for which Kahne could drive and that Ford was "going to take [Kahne]," Robert Yates stated that he had "no contract."

Kahne also avers that, without a deal to race for RYR, he wrote a letter to Dan Davis on August 29, 2003, informing Davis that he was "ready to go to Nextel Cup in 2004." Kahne's position is that because no open full-time rides in the Nextel Cup Series existed with any Ford team and that Ford declined to arrange or offer him a full-time opportunity to race in NASCAR's premier stock car racing series for 2004, the parties (when assuming an enforceable agreement exists) simply failed to negotiate a mutually acceptable series and team.

Conversely, Ford characterizes Kahne's actions leading to his agreement to sign with Evernham Motorsports as a "nefarious plan" driven by a more lucrative deal from another racing organization. According to Ford, rumors of Kahne's potential departure from Ford Racing began circulating in the spring of 2003. Bill Seaborn of RYR specifically asked Kahne about the rumors in April 2003, but Kahne indicated that he had no plans to leave Ford. Despite Kahne's assurances to Seaborn, Ford notes that a faxed copy of the Kahne-Ford 2002 agreement was sent to Kahne's agent with the phrase "mutually acceptable . . ." underscored.

Ray Evernham testified that Kahne phoned him and set up an appointment to meet at Evernham's office sometime around Memorial Day 2003. Kahne met with Evernham and they discussed Kahne's potential interest in driving for Evernham Motorsports. Evernham inquired about Kahne's contractual status with Ford and stated that he "was very clear that - - that [he] didn't want to be in the middle of that." According to Evernham's testimony, Kahne told him that he did not have "a contractual, binding status with Ford" or that "he had fulfilled all his contractual obligations." Kahne told Evernham that RYR did not have any racing opportunities for Kahne.

Following this meeting with Kahne at Evernham's office, Evernham was approached by Kahne's agent, on or about June 15, 2003, regarding Kahne's interest in driving for Evernham Motorsports. According to Evernham, he was not interested in Kahne if he had "any contractual obligations" and Kahne's agent informed him that "all [Kahne] had was an agreement to agree and if [Evernham] felt like [he] had something for them, [he] needed to get it on paper and send it to him."

Evernham Motorsports ("EMS") responded to the request for "something in writing" by sending a July 11, 2003 "Informal Summary of Evernham Motorsports'[s] offer to Kasey Kahne." This informal summary provided that EMS and Dodge would partner with a current Busch team or start a new Busch team with Kahne as the driver and that EMS would enter a third car for Kahne to drive in at least five Nextel Cup races during 2004. Ford maintains that the "current Busch team" referred to by EMS was in fact Akins Motorsports, which at the time was under contract with Ford.

Kahne executed a "Driver Contract" with Akins Motorsports. Under this agreement, Kahne was to drive the "# 38 Great Clips Sponsored car in the 2004 NASCAR Busch Series;" this was the same car he had driven for Ford during the 2003 Busch Series.

On October 7, 2003, after he had executed agreements with EMS and Akins Motorsports, Kahne sent a letter to Dan Davis noting that he had not received Davis's September 24, 2004 letter until October 6, 2003 (after he had executed his new contracts) and advising Ford Racing as follows: "As Ford is unable to place me with a full-time Nextel Cup Series team in 2004, which you have once again confirmed in your letter to me of September 24, 2003, I am most sorry to inform you that our Ford contract must be terminated immediately." Kahne also sent a letter to Robert Yates on October 7, 2003. In this letter, Kahne informed RYR of his understanding that the 2002 Kahne-Yates agreement had been terminated based on RYR's representations made during their August 13, 2003 meeting.

Following Kahne's decision to sign contracts with EMS and Akins Motorsports for the 2004 NASCAR season (and for several seasons thereafter), RYR and EMS executed a November 21, 2003 agreement where RYR agreed to release Kahne from his contractual obligations under the Kahne-Yates agreement "conditioned upon the signing of a Kahne/Ford Motor Company agreement which releases Kahne from his contractual duties to Ford." RYR, however, has not joined this action nor, to the court's knowledge, has RYR asserted any claim against Kahne under the Kahne-Yates agreement. Indeed, the issue of whether the 2002 Kahne-Yates contract was "voided" or whether RYR could maintain a breach of contract action against Kahne is simply not before the court.

Ford is alleging that Kahne is in breach of the 2002 Kahne-Ford agreement. Ford has not asserted claims under the Kahne-Yates agreement, nor argued that it is a party to the Kahne-Yates agreement. Ford claims its 2002 contract for personal services with Kahne is not an unenforceable "agreement to agree," that Kahne and Ford had reached agreement on all material terms, and that Kahne failed to fulfill his obligations under the contract.

* * *

III. DEFENDANT'S SUMMARY JUDGMENT MOTION

Defendant makes two arguments in his motion for summary judgment. First, Defendant argues that the 2002 Kahne-Ford Racing personal service agreement is unenforceable under Michigan law because the parties left material terms open and subject to future negotiation and mutual agreement. The 2002 agreement expressly provides that Ford would offer Kahne opportunities to drive in "one or more mutually acceptable racing series with a reasonably competitive team," and that "the specific series and team will be determined jointly," subject to five enumerated "considerations." Defendant argues that this express language and the testimony of Ford Racing executives Dan Davis and Greg Specht (who negotiated the contract with Kahne) required subsequent negotiations between the parties on the material terms of the actual racing "series" and the specific "team" that Kahne would work with each year. As such, Defendant maintains that the entire agreement is unenforceable under Michigan law.

Second, Defendant argues that, even assuming the agreement is enforceable, he has fully satisfied his obligation to negotiate a mutually acceptable racing opportunity for the 2004 racing season. Specifically, after driving for Ford Racing teams in the NASCAR Busch Series in 2002 and 2003, Kahne requested a full-time driving position with a team that would compete in NASCAR's top series, the Nextel Cup Series. Kahne argues that Ford refused to provide such an opportunity, precluding a mutual agreement on the "series" and the "team" as contemplated by the 2002 contract.

Plaintiff Ford counters by arguing that the parties' 2002 personal services agreement reflects their agreement on all material and essential terms and that there exists, at least, a triable issue of fact as to whether the parties reached agreement on all material and essential terms. Ford claims that a reasonable jury could conclude that the parties did not view the "series" or "team" as an open essential term (i.e. that they had agreed on the essential term that Kahne would race in an agreeable series and for a reasonably competitive Ford team).

Ford argues that the contract required Kahne to race for a "team" utilizing "Ford vehicles and/or engines" having sponsors compatible with the business interests of Ford. It also maintains that the "series" term describes the different racing circuits and cars used in those series. For instance, Ford lists the following as "series," NASCAR, CART, IRL, or open-wheel" versus "closed-wheel" racing circuits. It claims that the use of the term "series" by the parties' was not intended to cover the different racing circuits or levels of stock car racing sanctioned by NASCAR (e.g. Nextel Cup versus Busch Grand National versus the Craftsman Truck circuit). In short, Ford argues that these limitations on any discretion that Kahne had in mutually agreeing on the racing "series" or jointly selecting the Ford "team" for each racing season show that the parties had reached agreement on all material and essential terms and, therefore, the entire agreement is not rendered unenforceable.

In response to Defendant's second argument in the motion for summary judgment, Ford maintains that Kahne breached his express promise to drive for a Ford team in an agreed upon series and at least violated an implied covenant of good faith and fair dealing in the performance of his contract with Ford that included discretion in reaching agreement on particular non-essential terms. See *Stephenson v. Allstate Ins. Co.*, 328 F.3d

822, 826 (6th Cir. 2003). Ford claims that Kahne hindered its ability to provide a mutually acceptable racing opportunity by his involvement and negotiation of an agreement with Evernham Motorsports.

The court agrees with Defendant that the 2002 Kahne-Ford personal services agreement is not enforceable under Michigan law. No reasonable jury could conclude, based on the record evidence presented, that the parties had reached agreement on all material or essential terms. First, the clear and unambiguous language of the contract shows that the parties intentionally left the material terms of the racing "series" and "team" for future negotiation and mutual agreement or joint determination.

This language makes the selection of Kahne's racing "series" and his racing "team" subject to mutual agreement or joint determination, even if this mutual agreement was also limited by the enumerated "considerations" as Ford maintains. Because the unambiguous language requires future agreement on these terms, the contract fails if they are essential or material terms.

Second, the sworn testimony of Ford's own representative establishes that these contract terms were intentionally left open for future joint agreement by the parties and that these terms were "very important."

Specht also testified that these open contract terms, selecting an appropriate "series" and Ford "team" were "very important" to both Ford and to the driver. (*Id.* at 127.) Likewise, Davis testified that Ford spends a lot of time matching the driver with the right car owned by the right racing team and that this decision is very important, even acknowledging that it "can be an essential thing to a driver." Davis explained that the parties intended the term "series" to mean different types of racing (e.g. open-wheel racing circuits versus stock car racing circuits) and not the various series or levels within NASCAR sanctioned stock car racing (e.g. Nextel Cup versus Busch Series versus Craftsman Truck Series). (Davis Dep. at 226-28.) Davis explained that Kahne and Ford had already mutually agreed on NASCAR stock car racing as the racing "series." But he also stated that leaving open (and subject to mutual agreement) the "series" and "team" for which Kahne would drive permitted Kahne to "move around" or "change his mind." (*Id.* at 227.)

In addition, no reasonable jury could conclude that the selection of the "series" or Kahne's racing "team" was non-essential term in the parties' agreement. There is nothing in the record to suggest that selection of the racing team for Kahne as a professional race car driver was a non-essential term of contract for driving services. Indeed, Dan Davis's September 24, 2003 letter to Kahne recognizes that it takes time and planning to ensure a driver is "compatible" with "the team, crew chief, team members, and team management." The selection of a team includes a crew chief with whom the driver

works to improve the car before and during each race at multiple tracks. Race teams also vary in terms of their relative financial resources, technical and engineering support and resources, testing data on various tracks where races will be run, and (as demonstrated by Yates testimony) in which circuits that they run. For example, there are several racing organizations participating in NASCAR sanctioned racing series with multiple cars that share information between their race teams (so-called "multiple car teams") such as Roush Racing, Inc., Hendrick Motorsports, Joe Gibbs Racing, EMS, and RYR. Roush Racing, Inc. and RYR, both organizations using Ford vehicles, are prime examples. *See, e.g. http://www.roushracing.com/sponsorship/default.asp*

Most importantly, Ford has failed to identify sufficient evidence from which a reasonable jury could conclude that it and Kahne did not view which "series" or racing "team" he would drive for as a material or essential term of the contract. Even if, as Ford argues, the contract limited Kahne to Ford or Ford-approved "reasonably competitive" race "teams," the selection of such a Ford race team was still an open and essential term of the contract that was to be determined jointly, and there is insufficient evidence for a reasonable jury to conclude otherwise.

As explained above, no reasonable jury could conclude that the race team employing Kahne was a settled or non-essential term of the parties' agreement. That Yates had the contractual right to determine the NASCAR series in which Kahne would participate while racing for RYR is of no consequence to whether Ford left this material term open for future negotiation. The Kahne-Yates agreement is a separate contract not being sued on in the present action. In fact, the language attributing the contractual right for Yates to determine which NASCAR series to run shows that RYR and Kahne believed that the particular series within NASCAR sanctioned stock car racing was material in their agreement.

The terms left open for future agreement in this case are closer to those left open in *Hansen v. Catsman*, 371 Mich. 79, 123 N.W.2d 265 (Mich. 1963). In *Catsman*, the plaintiff alleged that he and defendants entered into a contract whereby a realty company, in exchange for rental payments, would erect a drug store. *Id.* at 266. The agreement provided that the Defendant contemplated erecting the drug store and that the plaintiff contemplated leasing the store. *Id.* When the defendant backed out of the plan, the plaintiff sued and the trial court determined that the parties' agreement was not an enforceable contract. *Id.* The Michigan Supreme Court affirmed, ruling that the parties agreement was unenforceable because it left several essential terms for future negotiations, explaining:

Regarding the agreement in the present case, several essential terms were left for future negotiations, such as, for example, the requirement that plans, etc., be acceptable to both parties. It was stated in the agreement, that plans were not, as of the time of signing, formalized. This left, perhaps, the most significant feature of the venture open for further discussion and negotiations. In a like manner, the instrument additionally supports this construction in its provision for forfeiture 'if for any reasonable reason the plans, specifications and design are unacceptable to either party.' What may constitute a 'reasonable reason' is left to conjecture. At the very least, it is a matter for future negotiations, within the proscriptions of the Socony-Vacuum Case, supra. *Id.* at 267. The Court also found that the use of the word "contemplates" provided another reason to find that the agreement not enforceable, as this demonstrated that the agreement was simply a memorandum of intentions. *Id.*

Ford's argument that the parties agreed for Kahne to race with a "reasonably competitive" Ford team is also without merit. The contract stated that Ford would provide Kahne "with opportunities to participate in one or more mutually acceptable racing series with a reasonably competitive team." When reading this language in isolation, one could argue that "mutually acceptable" modifies only the "series" and not the reasonably competitive team. However, the very next line in the contract states that "the specific series *and team* will be determined jointly and will be subject to the following considerations." (*Id.* (emphasis added).) This unambiguous statement requiring joint selection of the team, coupled with the testimony of Davis and Specht cited above, permits but one conclusion: the selection of the team was subject to mutual agreement (even if limited by the objection component of being a "reasonably competitive team").

For the reasons explained above, the court will grant Defendant's motion for summary judgment.

* * *

Recent Trends

Stadium naming rights first appeared in 1987 when the Los Angeles Forum was renamed "the Great Western Forum" (Mayer, 2005). Since then, naming rights have become a lucrative revenue generating tool (Mayer, 2005). The NFL Houston Texans currently have the largest naming deal of $300 million with Reliant Energy Inc. (Mayer, 2005). Modern naming right agreements go beyond the name of the stadium itself and include the naming rights to entryways, the field, or even breezeways (Mayer, 2005). These agreements may be a separate agreement or part of a larger corporate sponsorship agreement (Mayer, 2005).

If an athlete endorses a sport or recreation event, the contract should incorporate many of the clauses discussed within the chapter. In addition, the contract should take into consideration any possible league rules and policies surrounding the marketing of its athletes. The NHL, for example, does not permit its players to be involved in any endorsement of alcoholic or tobacco products.

References

Cases

Ford Motor Company v. Kasey Kahne, 379 F. Supp. 857 (ED Mich., 2005).
Houston Oilers v. Harris County Texas, et al., 960 F. Supp 1202 (S.D. Texas 1997).
Marvel Entertainment Group, Inc. v. The Hawaiian Triathlon Corp., 132 F.R.D. 143 (S.D. N.Y 1990).
MasterCard International v. Sprint Communications Co., 23 F.3d 397 (2d. Cir. 1994).
National Football League Properties v. Dallas Cowboys Football Club, 922 F. Supp. 849 (S.D.N.Y. 1996).
National Hockey League, et al. v. Pepsi-Cola Canada Ltd., 42 C.P.R.3d 390 (B.C. 1992).

Publications

Clement, A. (1998). *Law in sport and physical activity* (2nd ed.). Aurora, OH: Sport and Law Press, Inc.
Graham, S., Goldblatt, J., & Delpy, L. (1995). *The ultimate guide to sport event management and marketing*. Chicago: Richard D. Irwin.
Heller, J. G., & Hechtman, J. A. (2000). Corporate sponsorships of sports and entertainment events: Considerations in drafting a sponsorship management agreement. *Marq. Sports L. Rev., 11*, 23.
Irwin, R. L., Sutton W. A., & McCarthy, L. M. (2002). *Sport promotion and sales management*. Champaign, IL: Human Kinetics.

Masteralexis, L. P., Barr, C. A., & Hums, M. A. (1998). *Principles and practice of sport management.* Gaithersburg, MD: Aspen Publishing.

Mayer, F. A. (2005). Stadium financing: Where we are, how we got here, and where we are going. *Vill. Sports & Ent. L. Forum, 12,* 195.

Miller, L. K. (1997). *Sport business management.* Gaithersburg, MD: Aspen Publishing.

Moorman, A. M., & Greenwell, T. C. (2005). Consumer attitudes of deception and the legality of ambush marketing practices. *J. Legal Aspects of Sport, 15,* 183.

Wong, G. M. (2002). *Essentials of amateur sports law* (3rd. ed.). Westport, CT: Greenwood Publishing Group.

6.24 Alternative Dispute Resolution:
ARBITRATION, NEGOTIATION, AND MEDIATION

Rebecca J. Mowrey
Millersville University of Pennsylvania

The focus of the legal system on trials and the popularity of televised courtroom dramas from *Law and Order* to *The People's Court* might lead you to think of litigation as the only road to resolving legal disputes. In reality, litigation is just one, albeit the most popular, of several avenues that individuals or groups can pursue for legal remedy. **Alternative dispute resolution** (ADR) is a blanket term that includes negotiation, mediation, and arbitration as alternatives to courtroom adjudication of disputes, with mediation and arbitration being the most commonly used of the three (**www.law.cornell.edu/adr.html**). The use of ADR can be voluntarily pursued by the disputing parties or mandated by a contract or waiver (see also Chapter 2.23, *Waivers and Releases*). Recreation and sport managers interested in personnel-related cases and disputes would be well served to develop a working knowledge of all ADR procedures, language, and the benefits of each specific process. It is important to recognize issues and situations where ADR approaches will be more appropriate than the traditional litigation process.

Fundamental Concepts

Court adjudication can be a costly and lengthy process. In recognition of this fact, the federal government established the **Administrative Dispute Resolution Act of 1990**, 5 U.S.C.A. 581, which requires all federal agencies to establish policies for the voluntary use of ADR as a "prompt, expert and inexpensive means of resolving disputes as an alternative to litigation in federal courts." The **Federal Arbitration Act of 1925**, 9 U.S.C. Section 1 (FAA) established federal law supporting arbitration as an alternative to litigation. And the American Bar Association approved the **Uniform Arbitration Act of 1955** (UAA) to establish procedure and policy standards for arbitration. Thirty-five states have adopted the UAA, making it possible for arbitrator decisions to be potentially enforceable under federal and state law (**www.adr.org**).

ADR Basics

Generally Assumed ADR Benefits v. Litigation

- Reduced costs (i.e., no attorney fees, limited discovery)
- Usually significantly faster/less time in dispute (i.e., limited pretrial discovery, overscheduled courts)
- "Expert's" decision instead of a nonexpert jury or judge
- Greater flexibility and creative solutions instead of win/lose
- Proceedings and outcome can be kept confidential
- Considered best option when there is a desire to maintain or reestablish the relationships in conflict
- Increased satisfaction with the outcome and process

Generally Assumed ADR Limitations v. Litigation

- Legal precedent, if desired, is not established through ADR
- Absence of procedural safeguards if an arbitrator makes an error of law or fact

- Limited opportunity for appeal (in most cases only granted for arbitrator bias, fraud, decision rendered exceeded arbitrator's authority)
- Enforcement of decision is voluntary unless bound by contract (CBA)

Negotiation

Negotiation refers to a consensual bargaining process used primarily to resolve disputes and complete transactions such as labor contracts. The intent of the negotiation process is to arrive at an agreement that is acceptable to all involved parties. The negotiators in these situations are attempting to obtain their client's goals and directives, so some concessions or compromises might be made to obtain the client's desired outcomes. You have likely engaged in hundreds of informal negotiations in your lifetime as you agree to trade resources with your friends, such as the use of your car, computer, phone, video games, or your proofreading skills, for something of theirs that you value. There are four basic steps to negotiation: (1) planning how you will approach the other parties, (2) exchanging information and requests, (3) offering and counteroffering concessions and compromises, and (4) reaching an agreement that is mutually acceptable to all parties (www.adr.org). Negotiations are typically confidential, so you will rarely have the opportunity to follow the progress of a negotiation unless you are one of the principal parties involved. However, information concerning many agreements in professional sports, including the standard player contracts for selected professional teams, can frequently be accessed electronically through Websites.

Mediation

Mediation is a process in which a **neutral mediator** works collaboratively with the opposing parties to identify the areas of conflict and to assist them in reaching a settlement or agreement that is mutually satisfactory (www.mediate.com). Mediation is a consensual, nonbinding process, as the **mediators** have no power to impose or force a solution on the parties. The neutrality of the mediator is critical to ensure a sense of fairness while maintaining the integrity of the process. In some cases, the ability of the mediator to offer a different perspective will help resolve the conflict (www.campus-adr.org). You may have served unofficially as a mediator while keeping the peace between friends or classmates. If so, you have discovered one of the unique aspects of mediation versus negotiation or arbitration—the goal is to preserve the relationships and to reach an amicable resolution. As a result, mediation is a good choice for disputants who have strategic alliances or common interests that need to be maintained, such as teammates and coworkers (www.mediate.com). Another distinction of mediation is the potential to invoke the use of this process as a conflict intervention or conciliation as part of a larger conflict management program. In other words, as a conflict is developing and escalating, disputants might seek the involvement of a mediator before their conflict reaches a point of stalemate. The role of mediation in this manner is particularly effective when dealing with repetitive conflicts between individuals who need or wish to continue their working relationship (www.adr.org).

Arbitration

Arbitration is the most formal of the ADR approaches discussed in this chapter, yet it is much less rigid than traditional litigation. It might help you to think of the arbitration process as a simplified trial with limited discovery and relaxed rules regarding evidence (www.adr.org). Although organizations may attach unique elements to their **arbitration clause**, most proceedings contain the following five elements.

1. Demand for arbitration—a written demand for arbitration identifying the parties, the dispute, and the relief or remedy sought must be submitted to the opposing party. The arbitration request is less formal than writing a complaint in a civil action, but the issues to be arbitrated must be clear.
2. Response—the opposing party typically responds in writing, stating whether they agree that the issue is subject to arbitration under the existing contract or other relevant documents.
3. Selection of arbitration panel—a single arbitrator or panel with sufficient knowledge of the subject matter is selected. This process might be described in the arbitration clause of a contract or a permanent arbitrator might be designated.

4. Arbitration hearing—although similar to a trial in some respects, namely, the presentation of witnesses, documents, briefs, memoranda, and closing arguments, the process differs from a trial in that written transcripts are only provided if the parties order them, the evidentiary rules are relaxed, and the extent of discovery and cross-examination are often limited (UAA of 1955).

5. Decision—after hearing from all parties the arbitrator renders a decision (**www.adr.org**).

The decision of an arbitrator may be disputed and, under the Federal Arbitration Act, be vacated if: (1) the award was procured by corruption, fraud, or undue means; (2) there was evident partiality or corruption in the arbitrators, or either of them; (3) the arbitrators were guilty of misconduct in refusing to postpone the hearing, on sufficient cause shown, or in refusing to hear evidence pertinent and material to the controversy; or of any other misbehavior by which the rights of any party have been prejudiced; or (4) the arbitrators exceeded their powers, or so imperfectly executed them that a mutual, final, and definite award on the subject matter submitted was not made (9 U.S.C. § 11).

Arbitration differs from negotiation and mediation significantly, as the arbitrator is not concerned with reaching a decision that is agreeable to the disputing parties. In this process a dispute is submitted to a neutral third party or **arbitrator**, who listens to the disputants and considers the submitted evidence and then makes a decision or award. The use of arbitration may be mandated in some contracts but be completely voluntary in others. In **voluntary arbitration** situations, the arbitration is mutually agreeable to both parties and may be **binding** or **nonbinding**, as determined in advance by the involved parties or the arbitration agreement. In **mandatory arbitration** situations, the disputing parties are often required to utilize arbitration as their sole method of addressing unresolved grievances according to the arbitration clause of their employment contracts (see Chapter 6.21, *Employment Contracts*), and in these cases the decision is typically binding (**www.adr.org**). Arbitration decisions are not typically subject to any further judicial review or appeal unless there is evidence that the arbitrator committed fraud or some other form of professional misconduct during the proceeding. If this is the case, the Federal Arbitration Act of 1925 provides for an appeal, and for review of the decision by a judge or court. There are two common approaches to determining the number of arbitrators; either the disputing parties agree on one arbitrator or they are each represented by their own arbitrators and a third impartial arbitrator joins them to form an **arbitration panel**. Disputing parties can seek assignment of an arbitrator from several nongovernment organizations, such as the **American Arbitration Association** (AAA), which maintains a registry of qualified arbitrators or "neutrals."

Arbitration agreements have recently begun to appear in waivers and service contracts, requiring signers to pursue arbitration, not litigation. In *Cronin v. California Fitness* (2005), it was revealed that the two-page contract gym members sign includes an arbitration agreement capping damages for either party at an amount equal to the annual membership fee. Furthermore, the party making the claim must pay the arbitration cost, discovery is restricted, and the arbitration results must be kept confidential.

Collective Bargaining, Labor Disputes, and ADR

Many employee groups, including professional athletic players associations, have a **collective bargaining agreement** (CBA) with their employers. A CBA refers to an agreement between the employer and the labor union or organization that regulates the terms and conditions of employment for all the employees of a single employer. In some labor matters, the CBA may mandate that certain disputes (e.g., differences in interpretation of the CBA, grievances, salary issues) must be resolved through mandatory arbitration or that mediation may be sought by either party (**www.campus-adr.com**). The collective bargaining agreements of the professional sport leagues in the United States provide for grievances to be addressed through an arbitration process. However, every CBA contains specific clauses and procedures regarding how and when arbitration will be used that are unique to that CBA and the related parties (Cozzillio & Levinstein, 1997). The right to pursue arbitration may be negated if a party fails to respond in the stated time frame or expressly waives the right to arbitration. You can locate the CBAs of various professional leagues through sport law–related Internet sites or by contacting the leagues directly. (See also Chapter 8.33, *Labor Relations in Professional Sports*, for additional information regarding labor disputes in sport.)

When the parties of a CBA agree to enter into arbitration, the issues the arbitrator(s) is to address are clearly communicated. For example, in the *Matter of the Arbitration Between Terrell Owens and the National Football League (NFL) Players Association v. the Philadelphia Eagles and the NFL Management Council* (2005), an arbitrator was asked by the grievants, Terrell Owens and the NFL Players Association, to examine the decision of the Philadelphia Eagles' management to suspend Owens. Specifically, the arbitrator was asked to reach a decision on the following two issues: (1) Was the four-week disciplinary suspension for just cause; if not, what should the remedy be? (2) Was it a violation of the CBA for the Club to exclude the Player from games and practices, following the four-week suspension? The arbitrator's conclusions and decision follow:

In summary, there is ample room to find that the Club could respond to this Player's actions, suspending him without pay to the limits permitted by the collective bargaining agreement for his behavior in this matter. Thereafter, the Coach properly exercised his inherent discretion to conclude that, on balance, the team would be better protected and better off by practicing and fielding a team that did not include Mr. Owens. The problem—a continuing one—was almost entirely off-field, and the response properly dealt with that reality. Both responses, the disciplinary and the discretionary, were specifically understood by these parties and fully countenanced as part of this collective bargaining relationship. The disciplinary side of the equation is expressly established in Article VIII. The non-disciplinary response is part of the core and character of a coaches discretion; significantly, but predictably, it is nowhere constrained by the CBA. The finding, therefore, is that the Club has shouldered its burden of providing clear and convincing evidence of the Player's misconduct and, moreover, that the four-week suspension was for just cause. Additionally, there was no violation of the labor agreement inherent in the Club's decision to pay Mr. Owens, but not to permit him to play or practice, due to the nature of his conduct and its destructive and continuing threat to the team.

AWARD
The grievance is denied.
Richard I. Bloch, Esq.
November 23, 2005

ADR Applications in Sport and Recreation

In professional sports almost all disputes between the players and teams are resolved through an arbitration process. For example, in *Sprewell v. Golden State Warriors* (2001), NBA player Latrell Sprewell brought suit against the Warriors for civil rights violations and sought to set aside the arbitrator's decision following sanctions he received as a result of physically attacking the head coach during and after a practice session in 1997. The court upheld the arbitrator's decision that the suspension of ten games by the Warriors and the NBA suspension for the remainder of the 1997–98 season were permissible under the terms of the NBA and National Basketball Players' Association Collective Bargaining Agreement (*Sprewell v. Golden State Warriors*, 2001).

In the context of intercollegiate sports, the NCAA has utilized ADR approaches to resolve disputes in limited cases. In 1991, the NCAA enacted a legislative policy that capped or restricted the earnings or salaries of some coaching staff personnel at NCAA universities and colleges. These restricted-earnings coaches could not be compensated more than $12,000 during the traditional academic year and no more than $4,000 for summer employment (*Law v. NCAA*, 1998). The NCAA's restricted-earnings policy was found to be in violation of federal antitrust law (see Chapter 8.32, *Antitrust Law: Amateur Sport Applications*). The NCAA appealed the decision of the district court and also entered into mediation with the plaintiffs. As a result of the mediation process, a $54.5 million settlement was announced in 1999 (**www.ncaa.org**).

ADR and International Sport Disputes

Disputes in international sport settings raise several unique dilemmas, such as when to follow the legal system of the host country versus that of the athlete's country of residence. Also, most legal systems do not accommodate the need for nearly immediate decisions to remove athletes from further competition or to approve them for continued competition. The arbitration format is ideal for addressing international disputes that are bound by different judicial systems.

Members of the International Olympic Committee (IOC) realized the need for effective and efficient conflict resolution and established the Court of Arbitration for Sport (CAS) to address disputes submitted by international athletes, governing bodies, national Olympic committees, and sport federations (**www.tas-cas.org**). Since establishing the CAS, arbitration has been used to bridge the gap between differing legal systems and to reach a speedy decision that is imperative during the multiday events of the Olympics and world championships. The CAS consists of three divisions: the Appeals Arbitration Division, the Ad Hoc Division, and the Ordinary Arbitration Division. Athletes who disagree with the decisions of their sport federation or sport regulation body during non-Olympic times would seek arbitration through the CAS Appeals Arbitration Division. The Ad Hoc Division is charged with resolving disputes that occur during the Olympic Games, whereas the CAS Ordinary Arbitration Division addresses commercial contract disputes (i.e., official vendors and media). The CAS has courts in Lausanne, Switzerland; New York City, New York, USA; and Sydney, Australia. Unless all parties agree to follow another country's form of law, the CAS court will use Swiss law or the law of the country where the involved sport federation is located (**www.tas-cas.org**). The International Council of Arbitration for Sport (ICAS) was established in 1994 to administer the CAS and to provide a process for arbitration that is neutral and independent of the IOC. The primary responsibilities of the ICAS are to select neutral arbitrators and to protect the rights of all parties (Oschutz, 2002).

To better appreciate the specific need for and use of arbitration in international sports, consider the case of Canadian snowboarder Ross Rebagliati and the IOC. During the 1998 Nagano, Japan, Olympic Games, Rebagliati was awarded the gold medal in the snowboard giant slalom on February 8, 1998. On February 11, 1998, the IOC Executive Board notified Rebagliati that his gold medal was rescinded based on the finding of marijuana in his postcompetition drug test by the IOC Medical Commission. Rebagliati agreed to binding arbitration and appealed the decision through the CAS. After hearing the facts and reviewing the documentation, the CAS reversed the IOC decision and reinstated Rebagliati as the gold medal recipient on February 12, 1998. Additional CAS awards can be found at their Website **www.tas-cas.org**.

Another growing area of international litigation is concerned with the protection of intellectual property, including Internet and electronic commerce. With the expansion of the Internet, an increasing number of **cybersquatters** have purchased domain names (.org, .com, .net) that potentially infringe on established trademarks (see Chapter 8.22, *Principles of Trademark Law*). This issue is especially important to professional and university athletic teams, sport merchandisers, and sport media, who stand to lose millions of dollars as a result of domestic and global trademark violations (**www.wipo.org**). As mentioned previously, international disputes are troublesome for those seeking traditional litigation as a remedy. Established in 1994, the **World Intellectual Property Organization (WIPO)** resolves intellectual property disputes through arbitration and mediation (**www.wipo.org**).

Significant Case

The following case illustrates the differences between an arbitration proceeding and traditional litigation. Look for which CAS Division is involved in this case and why. Compare and contrast the procedures used in this case to others in this text and determine the benefits and disadvantages for the involved parties. This arbitration panel was able to convene 16 hours after the athlete's complaint was received, and they rendered a decision within 24 hours. The CAS arbitrators' immediate availability to convene, coupled with their expertise regarding the subject matter, and the reduced amount of background discovery required by arbitration, led to a timely and informed decision.

COURT OF ARBITRATION FOR SPORT (CAS)/AD HOC DIVISION— OLYMPIC WINTER GAMES IN SALT LAKE CITY

FINAL AWARD in the arbitration between
Gaia Bassani-Antivari (the "Applicant") and
The International Olympic Committee (IOC) (the "Respondent")
CAS arbitration No. CAS OG 02/003, (www.tas-cas.org) Salt Lake City, 12 February 2002

* * *

1 Fact

1.1 The Applicant is a 23-year-old Grenada national who has represented Grenada in international ski competition since 1998. She has competed under the auspices of the Grenada International Sports Foundation ("GISF"), which had applied in 1997 for affiliation with the Grenada Olympic Association ("GOA"), the Grenada National Olympic Committee ("NOC"). The GISF was accepted by the Fédération Internationale de Ski ("FIS") as a FIS member during its 41st Congress on 22 May 1998.

1.2. Though an Italian native and also an Italian national, the Applicant has never represented another country in the Olympic Games and is ranked 474 on the 2001 FIS Point List in the Slalom and fulfilled the FIS qualification criteria for participation in the XIX Olympic Winter Games in Salt Lake City ("the Games"). The Applicant has never been sanctioned for any rule violation.

1.3. In August 2001, the President of the GISF submitted to the GOA the documentation necessary for the GOA to enter the Applicant to compete in the Games. The GOA did not send an entry form for the Applicant to the Salt Lake Organizing Committee ("SLOC").

1.4. On 18 December 2001, the President of GOA advised SLOC that Grenada would not be participating in the Games.

1.5. On 25 January 2002, the GOA informed the GISF that it was unable to sanction the participation of the Applicant because the GISF was not an affiliate of the GOA. To date, the GOA has not accepted the GISF application for affiliation.

1.6. In an effort to resolve any outstanding issues regarding her eligibility to compete in the Games, the Applicant procured from a friend and submitted both her and her coach's entry forms dated 1 February 2002 directly to the SLOC on the SLOC form used by NOCs for this purpose (the "Entry Form").

1.7. On 4 February 2002, the Applicant flew to Salt Lake City, Utah, expecting to represent Grenada in the Games and also to march in the Opening Ceremonies of the Games under the Grenada flag. However, upon arriving in Salt Lake City, the Applicant was told by Mr. Toulson of the International Olympic Committee ("IOC") that the GOA never filed an Entry Form on her behalf to SLOC. The Applicant immediately attempted to contact the GOA in order to find out why she was unable to participate in the Games.

1.8. On 7 February 2002, the Applicant spoke with Ms. Veda Bruno-Victor, Secretary General for the GOA, who stated that the GOA would not change its decision and would not submit an Entry Form to SLOC for the Applicant.

1.9. On 7 February 2002, the Applicant filed an appeal to the IOC, requesting that the IOC overturn the GOA's decision not to enter the Applicant in the Games

and declare the Applicant eligible to participate in the Games.

1.10. On 10 February 2002, the IOC rendered its decision denying the Applicant's request to compete in the Games citing Rule 49(1) of the Olympic Charter (the "Charter") which requires the NOCs to enter competitors into the Games and Rule 41(2) of the Charter which assigns responsibility to the Chef de Mission of an NOC to supervise its delegation. The decision further states that it is undesirable for individual competitors to be allowed to participate in the Olympic Games in the absence of an NOC to take responsibility for them and that GOA is not obligated to send competitors to the Olympic Winter Games.

2 Legal aspects

2.1 Procedure

2.1.1. At 06:05pm on 11 February, the Applicant filed an application before the CAS Ad Hoc Division of the Olympic Winter Games in Salt Lake City. The application included a legal brief and some documentary evidence. The Applicant requested that CAS allow the Applicant's entry to the Games and declare her eligible to compete therein.

2.1.2. On 11 February 2002, the President of the CAS Ad Hoc Division appointed as arbitrators Mr. Yves Fortier (Canada), President of the Panel, Mr. Dirk-Reiner Martens (Germany) and Mrs. Maidie Oliveau (USA).

2.1.3. The parties were summoned to appear for a hearing at 10:30am on 12 February 2002 at which the Applicant, her counsel and the representatives of the IOC were present. The IOC did not file any written pleadings but submitted some documentary evidence during the hearing.

2.2 Legal framework

2.2.1. These proceedings are governed by the CAS Arbitration Rules for the Games (the "CAS Ad Hoc Rules") enacted by the International Council of Arbitration for Sport ("ICAS") on 5 November 2001. They are further governed by Chapter 12 of the Swiss Private International Law Act of 18 December 1987 ("PIL Act"). The PIL Act applies to this arbitration as a result of the express choice of law contained in art. 17 of the CAS Ad Hoc Rules and as the result of the choice of Lausanne, Switzerland as the seat of the Ad Hoc Division and of its panels of Arbitrators, pursuant to art. 7 of the CAS Ad Hoc Rules.

2.2.2. The jurisdiction of the CAS Ad Hoc Division arises out of art. 1 of the CAS Ad Hoc Rules read in conjunction with Rule 74 of the Charter.

2.2.3. Under art. 17 of the CAS Ad Hoc Rules, the Panel must decide the dispute "pursuant to the Olympic Charter, the applicable regulations, general principles of law and the rules of law, the application of which it deems appropriate."

2.2.4. According to art. 16 of the CAS Ad Hoc Rules, the Panel has "full power to establish the facts on which the application is based."

3 Discussion

3.1. The Applicant contends that the Panel does have jurisdiction to decide the merits of her application on the basis of either Rule 74 of the Charter or the Entry Form signed by the Applicant and delivered to the SLOC, even though this Entry Form was not submitted by her NOC.

3.2. The Applicant argues that if the Panel were to require a valid Entry Form to be submitted on behalf of a competitor seeking entry to the Games, the CAS Ad Hoc Division would not have jurisdiction to hear the appeal of any eligibility decisions.

3.3. The Applicant contends that she was improperly denied entry to the Games by virtue of the GOA's determination not to enter the Applicant as a representative of Grenada for the following reasons:

3.3.1. Pursuant to its Constitution, the GOA has the obligation to accept the application for affiliation by GISF and upon the completion of the paperwork for such application, which is merely a bureaucratic technicality, the Applicant should be eligible to compete in the Games for Grenada.

3.3.2. She should be granted the right to compete in the Games since it is no fault of hers that she is caught up in the bureaucratic misunderstanding between GISF and GOA, she is eligible by virtue of the FIS standards and has paid her own way to be available to compete on behalf of Grenada in the Games.

3.3.3. Pursuant to Rule 49(1) of the Charter, the IOC has the discretion to enter a competitor into the Games regardless of the NOC's decision not to enter him/her.

3.4. The Applicant requests that the Panel take into account the special circumstances under which she proceeded in good faith believing she would be entered in the Games. She asks that the Panel find that she is the representative of the GOA in the Games.

3.5. The Respondent argues that the Panel does not have jurisdiction to decide the Applicant's request on the basis of art. 1 of the CAS Ad Hoc Rules which provides that the Ad Hoc Division resolve by arbitration any disputes covered by Rule 74 of the Olympic Charter and by the arbitration clause in the Entry Form. Since there is no accepted Entry Form in this instance, the Respondent argues that the Panel does not have jurisdiction to grant the relief requested.

3.6. The Respondent however did not wish to prevent the Applicant from submitting to the Panel the merits of her case.

3.7. In addition, the Respondent argues that the GOA is not entering a delegation to these Games, and that even if it were to do so at this time, the application would be submitted after the deadline.

3.8. The Respondent also argues that the Olympic Charter sets forth the responsibilities of the NOC with respect to the entry and supervision of its delegation at the Olympic Games pursuant to Rules 31 and 32 of the Charter but does not allow for the direct entry by competitors.

3.9. In addition, *avers* the Respondent, on the basis of the GOA Constitution, the NOC has the right to conclude that it is not required to affiliate the GISF as a competent national association since the GISF is not within Grenada.

3.10. The Respondent also argues that the IOC does not have the right to enter competitors in the Olympic Games pursuant to the provisions of Rule 49(1) of the Charter, but rather that the IOC can review an entry form only after it has been submitted by the NOC.

4 Decision

4.1. Initially, the Panel must determine whether it has jurisdiction to hear the present application. It is well established that CAS panels have the power to determine the scope of their jurisdiction.

4.2. Rule 74 of the Charter provides as follows: *"Any dispute arising on the occasion of, or in connection with, the Olympic Games shall be submitted exclusively to the Court of Arbitration for Sport, in accordance with the Code of Sports–related Arbitration."*

4.3. The CAS Ad Hoc Rules were adopted by the ICAS on 5 November 2001. They form an integral part of the Code of Sports–related Arbitration. Art. 1 of the CAS Ad Hoc Rules stipulates that: "The purpose of the present Rules is to provide, in the interests of the athletes and of sport, for the resolution by arbitration of any disputes covered by Rule 74 of the Olympic Charter and by the arbitration clause inserted in the entry form for the Olympic Games (the "OG"), insofar as they arise in the host country of the OG between 1 February 2002, and 24 February 2002."

4.4. The Panel must find the legal basis for its jurisdiction within the parameters of these two provisions.

4.5. The debate before the Panel on this issue of jurisdiction centers on the word "and" in art. 1 of the CAS Ad Hoc Rules. Is the word used in a disjunctive or conjunctive sense? If the word is used in a disjunctive sense, it is not necessary for the Panel even to consider the necessity of a valid entry form since, argues the Applicant, Rule 74 by itself confers jurisdiction on the Ad Hoc Division of CAS. If, on the other hand, the word is used in a conjunctive sense, the jurisdiction of the Panel is founded both on the provisions of Rule 74 and on the arbitration clause contained in a validly submitted entry form.

4.6. The Panel has no difficulty, in the context of the Olympic Games, in finding that the word "and" is used in the conjunctive sense. The Panel finds support for its conclusion in the use of words "ainsi que" in the French text of the Article. It would be illogical to confer jurisdiction for a competitor on the CAS Ad Hoc Division (as opposed to the regular CAS procedure) to resolve any dispute arising on the occasion of, or in connection with, the Olympic Games only on the basis of Rule 74 without a link to these Games, such as the arbitration clause contained in a validly endorsed entry form. Consequently, the Applicant's first argument in respect of this issue must fail.

4.7. However, this finding by the Panel does not put an end to the jurisdictional question. Subsidiary, the Applicant argues that the Panel has jurisdiction to hear her application even if art. 1 was read to require both Rule 74 and the arbitration clause contained in the entry form since the Applicant's Entry Form was, in all respects, valid.

4.8. The Panel recalls that the Applicant had attempted to submit directly to SLOC an Entry Form to the Games unendorsed by her NOC. The Panel heard evidence from Ms. Vida Bruno-Victor, the Secretary General of the GOA, that the GOA had positively refused to endorse the Applicant's Entry Form. In fact, it is abundantly clear that the GOA, in the exercise of its authority, declined to send any delegation to the Games.

4.9. In the opinion of the Panel, the Entry Form at issue in the present case is, in the words of counsel for Respondent, an "inchoate document." An Entry Form which is not endorsed by the competitor's NOC is a unilateral document which has no binding legal effect. In particular, it cannot trigger the applicability of the arbitration clause found therein.

4.10. Therefore, the Applicant has no standing to assert before this Panel that she has a dispute covered by Rule 74 of the Charter and by the arbitration clause in the Entry Form. Without this standing, this Panel has no jurisdiction to entertain the present application and the Panel so finds.

4.11. Furthermore, even if the Panel has so concluded, in the event that the CAS Ad Hoc Division had jurisdiction, it would still reject the Applicant's request for the following reason.

4.12. The 10 February 2002 IOC Executive Board decision relies on Rule 49(1) of the Charter which provides: *1. Only NOCs recognized by the IOC may enter competitors in the Olympic Games. The right of final acceptance of entries rests with the IOC Executive Board. 2. An NOC shall only exercise such attributions upon the recommendations for entries given by national federations. If the NOC approves thereof, it shall transmit such entries to the OCOG. The OCOG must acknowledge their receipt. NOCs must investigate the validity of the entries proposed by the national federations and ensure that no one has been excluded for racial, religious or political reasons or by reason of other forms of discrimination. 3. The NOCs shall send to the Olympic Games only those competitors adequately prepared for high level international competition.*

Through its IF, a national federation may appeal to the IOC Executive Board against a decision by a NOC on the matter of entries.

4.13. The Applicant has submitted both in her brief and in her oral arguments that the second sentence of Rule 49(1) gave the IOC "the right of final acceptance" and that this Rule included a right for the IOC, and hence this Panel, to accept a competitor in the Games even if he/she was not entered by his/her NOC.

4.14. The Panel rejects this argument. The text of the first sentence of Rule 49(1) of the Charter is unambiguous: it is within the NOCs' exclusive authority to enter competitors in the Olympic Games. This principle is confirmed *inter alia* in Rule 31(3) of the Charter ("The NOCs have the exclusive power for the representation of their respective countries at the Olympic Games and . . .") and in Bylaw 8.1 to Rules 31 and 32 of the Charter (". . . They [the NOCs] decide upon the entry of competitors proposed by their respective national federations").

4.15. Therefore, the Panel has to interpret the second sentence of Rule 49(1). More particularly, the Panel must address the question whether this provision gives the IOC Executive Board, and thus this Panel, the right to enter a competitor in the Games even though there is no Entry Form submitted by an NOC for this competitor either because the competitor's nomination by the national federation was not accepted by the NOC or because—as is the case here—the NOC decided not to send any delegation to the Games.

4.16. The Panel is of the opinion that neither the IOC Executive Board nor this Panel has this right. The provision in question clearly gives the IOC Executive Board "the right of final acceptance of entries"; this presupposes that there is an "entry" before the IOC Executive Board. Pursuant to the first sentence of Rule 49(1), the NOCs have exclusive authority to enter competitors in the Games. In the Panel's view, there is no room for any other interpretation. According to its own rules, the IOC does not have the discretion which the Applicant wants to confer upon it, i.e., to overrule the NOC and to enter a competitor on an individual basis. By the same reasoning, this Panel does not have this authority.

4.17. It has been suggested that this reading of Rule 49 leaves the competitors without an effective remedy against NOC selection decisions which may run counter to the Charter to which the NOCs are bound (see Bylaw 2, Rules 31 and 32 of the Charter: "The statutes of each NOC shall, at all times, be in accordance with the Olympic Charter and refer expressly to the latter").

4.18. The Panel is not prepared to adopt this argument. As is well known, there is ample case law in the jurisdiction of many countries with respect to whether or not a competitor has an enforceable right to have his/her NOC enter him/her in the Olympic Games. The national courts of a given country or other designated competent authority constitute the appropriate forum to rule on this question. There has been a significant number of cases where competitors have in fact succeeded in their national forum with such requests. *** On the basis of the foregoing facts and legal aspects, the Ad Hoc Division of the Court of Arbitration for Sport renders the following decision: The application filed by Ms. Gaia Bassani-Antivari on 11 February 2002 is denied. THE AD HOC DIVISION OF THE COURT OF ARBITRATION FOR SPORT, Yves Fortier, President of the Panel; Dirk-Reiner Martens, Arbitrator; Maidie Oliveau, Arbitrator

Reprinted with permission from the Court of Arbitration for Sport.

Recent Trends

ADR Online or ODR

Although many ADR professionals profess that the most enduring and satisfying resolutions emerge from disputants facing each other across a table, others envision a Website as a virtual mediation, negotiation, or arbitration table. The busy schedules of sport and recreation personnel might make face-to-face ADR impractical, whereas online ADR, or ODR, holds new possibilities. Primary stakeholders could be actively involved in mediation and negotiation through the use of ubiquitous conversations and agreements reached in discussion boards. As sport and recreation managers enter the field with increasing comfort and access to advanced technology, it is only logical that the Internet will be used for more purposes, perhaps including ODR. In their book, *Online Dispute Resolution*, Katsh and Rifkin (2001) argue that ODR software can be developed to actually assist mediators, and that disputants are prone to accept ODR if the three critical factors of convenience, trust, and expertise are adequately satisfied.

ADR Hybrids

As you have been reading this chapter, you may have considered that some disputes would be best resolved through the use of a combination of ADR approaches. Consider a situation in which the parties agree to mediation and are making good progress until they encounter an issue to which they are unable to find a mutually agreeable resolve. The parties might decide to continue the mediation process while submitting to arbitration the issues they cannot resolve through mediation (Haslip, 2001). This blended approach is referred to as mediation-arbitration (med-arb), and the reverse, arb-med, is also being used by parties in dispute (Haslip, 2001).

ADR, Sport Specialists, and Violence

The ICAS, AAA, and the professional player associations have already increased the demand for arbitration and negotiation specialists who are knowledgeable about sport. It is likely that the value of mediation will continue to be appreciated in these situations as well (Galton, 1998). Historically, it is common for the professional sport model to influence the intercollegiate, interscholastic, and club sport programs. Jeffrey Schalley (2001) argued that arbitration can be used to eliminate violence in sports. He proposed that language could be added to the CBA arbitration clauses to address "injury compensation resulting from reckless or intentional torts." Would this work as a deterrent? Without a CBA available in amateur sport settings, perhaps an arbitration clause regarding violence will begin to appear in athlete codes of conduct and/ or in waivers (see Chapter 2.23, *Waivers and Releases*) and in participation agreements (see Chapter 2.24, *Informed Consents and Agreements to Participate*). As schools, universities, and communities address the growing concerns regarding "bullying," hazing, and conflict among their student athlete populations, the position of ADR sport specialist might become as commonplace as that of team physician.

The Globalization of Sport and the Role of Arbitration

The efforts to establish international and global sport leagues, coupled with the expansion of annual international competition, will result in increased disputes between participants, management, spectators, and other related constituents. U.S. professional sport programs continue to expand the number of contests that are scheduled outside the United States. As we have seen with Olympic situations, the arbitration model for addressing disputes between parties representing more than one country is preferable to litigation. The globalization of sport will continue to raise numerous challenges for the sport law community, and ADR procedures provide more flexibility and responsiveness than a common law system. We will likely see arbitration as the model for dispute resolution in the emerging international leagues, as sport federations have already seen the benefits of the Olympic Court of Arbitration. A parallel organization may be created to address non-Olympic international sport disputes.

References

Cases

Cronin v. California Fitness, 2005 Ohio App.LEXIS 3056.
Law v. NCAA, 134 F.3d 1010 (10th Cir. 1998).
Sprewell v. Golden State Warriors, 266 F.3d 979 (9th Cir. 2001).

Arbitration Proceedings

Mr. Ross Rebagliati and International Olympic Committee (IOC). (CAS, Ad Hoc Div., Ref: Arb., NAG 2, Final Award; www.tas-cas.org).

Publications

Cozzillio, M., & Levinstein, M. S. (1997). *Sports law cases and materials.* Durham, NC: Carolina Academic Press.
Donegan, F. (1994). Examining the role of arbitration in professional baseball. *Sports Lawyer Journal, 1,* 183.
Galton, E. (1998). Mediation programs for collegiate sports teams. *Dispute Resolution Journal, 53,* 37–39.
Haslip, S. (2001). A consideration of the need for a national dispute resolution system for national sports organizations in Canada. *Marquette Sports Law Review, 11*(2), 245–270.
Katsh, E., & Rifkin, J. (2001). *Online dispute resolution: Resolving conflicts in cyberspace.* San Francisco: Jossey-Bass.
Oschutz, F. (2002). Harmonization of anti-doping code through arbitration: The case law of the court of arbitration for sport. *Marquette Sports Law Review, 12*(2), 675–702.
Schalley, J. (2001). Eliminate violence from sports through arbitration, not the civil courts. *The Sports Lawyers Journal, 8*(1), 181–206.

Legislation

Administrative Dispute Resolution Act of 1990, 5 U.S.C.A. 581.
Federal Arbitration Act of 1925, 9 U.S.C.
Uniform Arbitration Act of 1955.

Websites

www.adr.org
www4.law.cornell.edu/cgi-bi...re.law.cornell.edu/topics/adr.html
www.campus-adr.org
www.mediate.com
www.ncaa.org
www.sportslaw.org
www.tas-cas.org
www.mediate.com
www.wipo.org

7.00

Constitutional Law

The United States Constitution provides everyone certain rights and protections. Before the courts can apply constitutional protections, however, certain threshold questions must be asked. The following section examines the constitutional safeguards of the First, Fourth, Fifth, and Fourteenth Amendments as they apply to due process, equal protection, and the right to privacy and how they relate to the sport and recreation industries.

The *Constitutional Law* section is divided into two parts. The first part examines some of the fundamental principles of Constitutional law, including state action, due process, equal protection, and search and seizure. This part also serves as an introduction to the principles of Constitutional law. The second part examines how the issues of due process, equal protection, and search and seizure apply specifically to the sport, health and fitness, and recreation industries.

7.11 Judicial Review, Standing, and Injunctions

Lisa Pike Masteralexis
University of Massachusetts Amherst

Sport and recreation managers make decisions regarding athletic rules and regulations daily. When making these decisions, sport managers do not possess complete control over rules and regulations. Although courts generally take a "hands-off" approach to reviewing decisions of private athletic organizations, in a limited number of situations courts will review the actions of private athletic organizations. A court may grant a review of an athletic organization's action provided the plaintiff has standing. A plaintiff seeking judicial review of an athletic organization's decision will ask the court to grant an order (injunctive relief) to bar the athletic organization from going forward with its decision.

Fundamental Concepts

Judicial Review

Scope of Review

As a general rule, courts decline to intervene in the internal affairs of private, voluntary organizations that govern professional and amateur sports. The reasoning behind this policy is that membership in the organizations is voluntary and the organizations are self-regulating. The court will, however, review the decisions where one of the following conditions is met:

1. The rule or regulation challenged by the plaintiff exceeds the scope of the athletic association's authority.
2. The rule or regulation challenged by the plaintiff violates an individual's constitutional rights.
3. The rule or regulation challenged by the plaintiff violates an existing law, such as the Sherman Antitrust Act or the Americans with Disabilities Act.
4. The rule or regulation challenged by the plaintiff is applied in an arbitrary and/or capricious manner.
5. The rule or regulation challenged by the plaintiff violates public policy because it is considered fraudulent or unreasonable.
6. The athletic association breaks one of its own rules.

The harshness of a rule is not by itself grounds for judicial review. Relief is granted only where the plaintiff can prove to the court that one of the preceding conditions has been met. Even where a rule is subject to review, the court's role is limited. A court will not review the merits of the rule, but simply decide whether the application of the rule is invalid on the basis of meeting one of the five conditions listed.

Application

Despite the standards listed earlier, decisions to grant injunctions in cases that appear factually similar may vary. This is due to variations in precedent across jurisdictions or differences in regional standards, such as when a community is given the right to determine standards. An example would be in the distinction between free speech and obscenity. The U.S. Supreme Court has deferred to communities to define obscenity, so what may be considered obscene in Dallas might not be considered obscene in New York City. It may also be due to the application of state laws or state constitutional rights that grant greater protections than federal laws. One area in which this is common is where states have stronger privacy protections than the Fourth Amendment.

Married Students.   One area where there has been some variation is when an amateur athletic association has imposed rules barring married students from participation in high school athletics. In one case, *Estay v. La Fourche Parish School Board* (1969), a married high school student challenged his exclusion from all extracurricular activities. The Louisiana Court of Appeals held that the school board had the authority to adopt the regulation. The regulation survived equal protection scrutiny because the court found there was a rational relationship between the rule and its stated objective of promoting completion of high school before marriage. Finally, the court held that the rule was not arbitrary and capricious, for it was applied uniformly and impartially against anyone who sought to participate in extracurricular activities, not simply athletics. Eight years later and in another jurisdiction, the Colorado Court of Appeals ruled for the student–athlete, stating that he possessed a fundamental right to marry and the reasons proffered by the school board did not establish a compelling state interest to justify the violation of the plaintiff's equal protection rights (*Beeson v. Kiowa County School District*, 1977).

Alcohol and Drugs.   Similarly, jurisdictions vary when enforcing rules that prohibit the use of alcohol and drugs, often called good conduct rules. If the rules address a legitimate sport-related purpose, courts will often find that they are within the scope of the association's authority. But where the rule is intrusive and broadly attempts to regulate the conduct of a student–athlete during the off-season or conduct unrelated to athletic participation, a court will likely strike it down. In *Braesch v. De Pasquale* (1978), the Supreme Court of Nebraska ruled that a rule prohibiting drinking served a legitimate rational interest by directly affecting the discipline of a student–athlete. The court also ruled that the rule was not arbitrary nor an unreasonable means to attain the legitimate end of deterring alcohol use among student–athletes. On the other hand, in *Bunger v. Iowa High School Athletic Association* (1972), another court struck down a good conduct rule prohibiting the use of alcoholic beverages. During the summer, the plaintiff was riding in a car containing a case of beer. The car was pulled over by the police, and the four minors in the car were issued citations. The plaintiff reported the incident to his athletic program and was suspended in accordance with the state athletic association rule. The Iowa Supreme Court held the rule was invalid on the grounds that it exceeded the scope of the athletic association's authority. The Court based its decision on the fact that the incident was outside the football season, beyond the school year, and did not involve the illegal use of alcohol.

Cases involving athletic association rules that infringe on the constitutional right to freedom of expression have also exhibited variation. In *Williams v. Eaton* (1972), a group of fourteen African-American football players for the University of Wyoming sought permission from their coach to wear black armbands in their game against Brigham Young University to protest the beliefs of the Mormon Church. The coach dismissed them from the team for violating team rules prohibiting protests. In a court action challenging the rule, the court held that the First Amendment rights of the players to freedom of speech could not be paramount to the rights of others to practice their religion free from a state-supported (University of Wyoming) protest. On the other hand, *Tinker v. Des Moines Independent School District* (1969) held that student–athletes wearing politically motivated black armbands protesting the Vietnam War in a public high school were found to have a constitutionally protected right to freedom of expression.

Standing

Standing is a plaintiff's right to bring a complaint in court. To establish standing the plaintiff must meet three criteria:

1. The plaintiff bringing the action must have sustained an injury in fact.
2. The interest that the plaintiff seeks to be protected is one for which the court possesses the power to grant a remedy.
3. The plaintiff must have an interest in the outcome of the case.

The question of standing is generally raised by the defense seeking to dismiss a case and not one the court will raise on its own. In other words, as an initial matter, the plaintiff does not possess a burden of proof with regard to standing, but may be forced to show standing when the defendant in a case raises the issue.

Injunctive Relief

Types of Injunctive Relief

There are four types of injunctive relief available: the temporary restraining order, the preliminary injunction, the permanent injunction, and specific performance.

The **temporary restraining order** is generally issued to a plaintiff in an emergency situation, without notice (appearance at hearing) to the defendant, and is usually effective for a maximum of ten days. Before a court will grant the temporary restraining order, a plaintiff must prove that he/she will face irreparable harm and that money damages would be an inadequate remedy. The **preliminary injunction** is granted to a plaintiff prior to a trial on the merits of a legal action and lasts throughout the trial process of the case. The defendant is given notice to appear at the hearing for the injunction and may argue against the granting of the preliminary injunction. To be awarded a preliminary injunction, the plaintiff must prove:

1. The plaintiff will face a substantial threat of irreparable harm without the preliminary injunction. (Often where money damages would be an inadequate remedy, granting the injunction would provide the only remedy.)
2. The balance of the hardships favors the plaintiff.
3. The plaintiff possesses a likelihood of success on the merits of the pending case.
4. Granting the injunction will serve the public interest.

A **permanent injunction** requires the plaintiff to prove the same four elements but is awarded as a remedy following a full hearing on the merits of the case. Finally, **specific performance** is a court order that may be available to the victim of a breach of contract. Specific performance requires that a defendant comply with (honor) the contract. Because money is generally an adequate remedy for a contract breach, specific performance is rarely used. The court will grant this remedy in situations where the subject matter is extremely rare. An example in sport where a court may be willing to grant specific performance is with a breach of a contract for the sale of sports memorabilia. There may be only one Honus Wagner baseball card in the world, and money may be an inadequate remedy to replace the card if the seller were to break the contract. In such a case the nonbreaching party might seek an injunction for specific performance because the card is priceless and rare.

Specific performance will not be granted to enforce a contract of a professional athlete. Although there may be only one Michael Jordan, if he were to break his contract with the Washington Wizards, the court would not grant the Wizards a specific performance injunction to force Jordan to honor his contract with the club. The reason is that by granting such an injunction, the court would be forcing Jordan to work and would find its order in conflict with the U.S. Constitutional prohibition against slavery. In such cases, however, there is a remedy for professional teams. Courts are willing to grant negative injunctions against athletes who breach their contracts. A negative injunction is actually a preliminary or permanent injunction (depending on the time it is sought by the team—prior to trial or as part of a breach of contract award at the end of trial). The effect of the negative injunction is to prohibit the player from playing his or her sport for any other team or event than the plaintiff's. In this way the court is not ordering the athlete to work, but simply prohibiting him/her from playing his/her sport anywhere except for the team possessing the valid and enforceable contract.

Scope

When a plaintiff seeks judicial review of a decision, the plaintiff will also request a temporary restraining order and/or a preliminary injunction to bar the rule from being applied. Injunctive relief is designed to prevent future wrongs, rather than to punish past actions. It is only used to prevent an irreparable injury that is suffered when monetary damages will be inadequate to compensate the injured party. An injury is considered irreparable when it involves the risk of physical harm or death; the loss of a special opportunity; or the deprivation of unique, irreplaceable property. For example, a high school senior student–athlete may be granted an injunction to compete in a championship game because he/she may never again have that opportunity.

Significant Case

◇◇◇

The Indiana High School Athletic Association case that follows provides an excellent example of an appellate court's review of the grounds for granting a preliminary injunction against conduct that is arbitrary and capricious and conduct that violates an organization's own rules. The case also discusses in detail the concept of public interest in the granting of injunctive relief. The case involves an appeal by Indiana High School Athletic Association (IHSAA) of the trial court's issuance of a permanent injunction against the IHSAA's denial of full eligibility and a hardship exception for a student–athlete. The trial court found that the IHSAA's decision was arbitrary and capricious. Upon appeal, the IHSAA asserts that the trial court's findings are clearly erroneous, given the broad discretion afforded to its eligibility decisions.

THE INDIANA HIGH SCHOOL ATHLETIC ASSOCIATION, INC. V. DURHAM

Court of Appeals of Indiana, Fifth District
748 N.E.2d 404 (2001)

FACTS

In the summer of 1999, Bernard Durham (B.J.) transferred from Park Tudor High School (Park) to North Central High School (North Central). B.J. participated in varsity cross-country and track during his freshman and sophomore years at Park. B.J. had attended private school, either at Park or at St. Richard's School since second grade. B.J. has three brothers who also attended private schools.

During 1998, B.J.'s mother, Joan Durham, and her husband, Tim Durham, separated and initiated divorce proceedings. Tim is not B.J.'s biological father. B.J.'s biological father lives in France and does not contribute to B.J.'s support. * * * [T]he time came to sign 1999-2000 re-enrollment contracts for B.J. and his three brothers in their private schools. At that time, Joan and Tim's divorce was not yet final. Joan decided not to sign the contracts because she could no longer afford the tuition to send her children to private schools. She instead enrolled her sons in the public school system where they resided. B.J. enrolled in North Central. In the fall of 1999, an IHSAA transfer form was completed on behalf of B.J. so that he could continue participating in sports at North Central. Joan indicated on the form that the recent divorce created such a financial burden on her that she could not afford to keep B.J. enrolled at a private school. Joan also provided the IHSAA with financial information and court filings to support the listed reason for B.J.'s transfer. * * *

Park, as the sending school, also had to offer the reason for B.J.'s transfer. Initially, Park had included in the transfer form that B.J. told coaches, administrators, and other students that "he wanted to go to a better track/c.c. [cross-country] program and that is why he is leaving." B.J. denied making such statements. However, Park changed its position after speaking with its athletic director who had subsequently learned that B.J.'s family situation prompted the transfer. Park recommended that B.J. be awarded full eligibility to compete in sports at North Central. On August 25, 1999, IHSAA Assistant Commissioner Sandy Searcy granted B.J. only limited eligibility, which prohibited B.J. from competing at the varsity level, and denied B.J. a hardship exception.

The Durhams, through North Central's athletic director, appealed that decision to the IHSAA Executive Committee. The Durhams were led to believe that the question of whether B.J. transferred for athletically motivated reasons would not be an issue discussed at the hearing scheduled before the Executive Committee. A hearing was held, at which B.J., Joan, and the athletic directors from both schools testified. Evidence was presented that B.J. had been running with the junior varsity cross-country team at North Central, and that if he enjoyed full eligibility, B.J. would be one of the school's top runners. Joan testified that B.J. had suffered a great deal as a result of the IHSAA's decision. She relayed that he had problems with anxiety in the past, and that his running had helped him through this difficult time for his family. B.J. testified that he did not want to leave Park, and that he refused to explain why he was leaving when asked about the move at Park. Assistant Commissioner Searcy also testified that she was convinced that the change in the Durham's financial circumstances was permanent and substantial although not beyond their control. Park's athletic director, referring to Park's initial comment on B.J.'s transfer form, stated that the reference was the result of bantering between athletes and coaches due to the rivalry with North Central.

The Executive Committee agreed with Assistant Commissioner Searcy's decision, denying B.J. full eligibility and issuing findings. The Executive Committee concluded that B.J. transferred schools without a change in residence and failed to fit within any of the criteria of the Transfer Rule to gain full eligibility. Further, the Committee determined that B.J. did not meet the necessary conditions to gain full eligibility through the hardship exception to the Transfer Rule. Even though Searcy had testified that there had been a permanent and substantial change in financial circumstances, the IHSAA Executive Committee reasoned that B.J. failed to produce sufficient proof that the reason for transfer was beyond the control of him and his family. The IHSAA also noted that some evidence existed that the transfer may have been motivated by athletic reasons, even though the Durhams did not know that this was an issue before the Executive Committee.

District Court's Order

The Durhams sought a temporary restraining order in court. On September 17, 1999, the trial court granted the temporary restraining order. On September 20, 1999, B.J. filed the complaint asking that the IHSAA's decision be overturned and that a permanent injunction be issued. * * *On October 22, 1999, the court granted the permanent injunction and found that the IHSAA's findings were arbitrary and capricious. * * * The IHSAA appealed.

DISCUSSION

Upon appeal, the IHSAA asserts that the trial court applied the standard of review over its decisions improperly. The IHSAA contends that its rulings are entitled to great deference and should be reversed only if they are willful and unreasonable without consideration of the facts and circumstances in the case. In this case, the IHSAA argues that the trial court merely reweighed the evidence and substituted its own decision. The Durhams insist that this case is moot because the time for the injunction has expired * * *. Alternatively, the Durhams counter that the IHSAA's conduct is not free from judicial review, and the IHSAA violated its own rules in denying B.J. a hardship exception.

I. IHSAA—Background and Rules

The IHSAA is a voluntary association designed to regulate interschool athletic competition. It establishes standards for eligibility, competition, and sportsmanship. For each school year, the IHSAA publishes a manual containing * * * specific rules regarding eligibility. The rule in question in this case is Rule 19, known as the Transfer Rule. The Transfer Rule guides athletic eligibility when a student moves to a new school district. Rule

19-4 provides that a student will be ineligible for 365 days if he or she transfers schools for "primarily athletic reasons." Further, Rule 19-6.2 gives the IHSAA the authority to grant limited eligibility to a student who transfers to another school without a corresponding change of residence by his or her parent(s)/guardian(s). However, if one or more of the criteria under Rule 19-6.1 are met, then a student may enjoy full and immediate eligibility, even without a change of residence by his or her parent(s)/guardian(s).

If none of the criteria in Rule 19-6.1 are met, then a student must fall within the hardship exception to the Transfer Rule to gain full and immediate eligibility. Rule 17.8, entitled "Hardship" grants the authority to set aside any rule, including the Transfer Rule, if certain conditions are met. In particular, Rule 17-8.1 lists these three conditions:

a. Strict enforcement of the Rule in the particular case will not serve to accomplish the purpose of the Rule;

c. The spirit of the Rule has not been violated; and

d. There exists in the particular case circumstances showing an undue hardship that would result from enforcement of the Rule.

Further, among those situations to receive general consideration for a hardship exception is: "a change in financial condition of the student's family may be considered a hardship, however, such conditions or changes in conditions must be permanent, substantial and significantly beyond the control of the student or the student's family." IHSAA Manual, Rule 17-8.4.

When a student moves to a new school district, an investigation and a transfer report must be completed if athletic eligibility at the new school is desired. Included in this report are forms filled out by the sending school, the receiving school, and the student and/or the student's parent(s)/guardian(s). The report must include the relevant circumstances and documents and recommendations regarding immediate eligibility from both schools.

II. Mootness

Initially, the Durhams assert that the IHSAA's appeal should be denied because the case is moot. The Durhams contend that there are no outstanding issues between the parties because the injunction has been lifted, the issue of attorney fees has been decided, and North Central did not win any State titles with B.J.'s participation. However, the IHSAA replies that the problem with the majority of litigation surrounding eligibility decisions is that the injunction granted by the trial court expires before the matter has been fully litigated and appealed. The IHSAA also contends that the case is not moot because its Restitution Rule, below, allows the IHSAA to make the school forfeit victories, team awards, and funds received from a tournament if it has been determined that an ineligible student athlete has competed for that school.

The Restitution Rule, Rule 17-6 of the IHSAA By-laws, reads:

If a student is ineligible according to Association Rules but is permitted to participate in interschool competition contrary to Association Rules but in accordance with the terms of a court restraining order or injunction against the student's school and/or the Association and the injunction is subsequently voluntarily vacated, stayed, or reversed or it is finally determined by the court that injunctive relief is not or was not justified, any one or more of the following action(s) against such school in the interest of restitution and fairness to competing schools shall be taken:

a. Require individual or team records and performances achieved during participation by such ineligible student be vacated or stricken;

b. Require team victories be forfeited to opponents;

c. Require team or individual awards earned be returned to the Association; and/or

d. If the school has received or would receive any funds from an Association tournament series in which the ineligible individual has participated, require that the school forfeit its share of net receipts from such competition, and if said receipts have not been distributed, authorize the withholding of such receipts by the Association.

Alternatively, the IHSAA argues that even if the issues have been decided in this case, this court should hear the case because it involves questions of public interest.

An issue becomes moot when it is no longer live and the parties lack a legally cognizable interest in the outcome or when no effective relief can be rendered to the parties. * * * When the principal questions in issue have ceased to be matters of real controversy between the parties, the errors assigned become moot questions and the court will not retain jurisdiction to decide them. * * * An actual controversy must exist at all stages of the appellate review, and if a case becomes moot at any stage, then the case is remanded with instructions to dismiss. The Durhams insist that the IHSAA failed to assert evidence that there is a live controversy. The evidence about how the Restitution Rule may create a live controversy was introduced only through the Appendix to the IHSAA's Reply Brief.

* * *

Regardless of whether we consider the affidavit, an exception to the mootness doctrine applies. The IHSAA relies upon the exception that an otherwise moot case may be decided on the merits if the case involves a question of great public interest. Indiana courts recognize that a moot case can be reviewed under a public inter-

est exception when it involves questions of great public importance. *** The IHSAA argues that this exception applies to the instant case because the issue involves children and education, matters that are considered of great public concern, and our court has previously held that a challenge to an IHSAA eligibility rule is an issue of substantial public interest. * * * We agree.

While at first glance high school athletics may not seem to be of great public importance, according to the IHSAA, over 160,000 students statewide participate in sports under the IHSAA eligibility rules. Thus, this issue touches many in our state. Further, the issue of eligibility when a student transfers schools has arisen several times and has been the subject of much litigation* * * Also, the specific issue of a student transferring schools after his or her parents' divorce is likely to recur. * * * The public interest exception to the mootness doctrine applies to this case, allowing us to decide the merits.

III. Were the Trial Court's Findings Clearly Erroneous?
A. Our Standard of Review

The IHSAA asserts that the trial court's findings were clearly erroneous. In this case, the trial court issued an injunction to prevent the IHSAA from enforcing its ruling against B.J. When we review an injunction, we apply a deferential standard of review. * ** The grant or denial of an injunction is discretionary, and we will not reverse unless the trial court's action was arbitrary or constituted a clear abuse of discretion.* * *An abuse of discretion occurs when the trial court's decision is clearly against the logic and effect of the facts and circumstances or if the trial court misinterprets the law. *Id.*

* * *

B. Did the Trial Court Fail to Apply the Correct Standard of Review Governing IHSAA Decisions?

The IHSAA argues that the trial court failed to apply the deferential standard of review afforded to its administrative rulings in granting the Durham's request for a permanent injunction. In *Carlberg*, 694 N.E.2d 222, our supreme court delineated how a trial court should review an administrative ruling made by the IHSAA. Although the IHSAA is a voluntary association, the court held that student challenges to IHSAA decisions are subject to judicial review. *Id.* at 230. The court reasoned that student athletes in public schools do not voluntarily subject themselves to IHSAA rules, and students have no voice in rules and leadership of the IHSAA. *Id.* The court then determined that IHSAA decisions are analogous to government agency decisions and, hence, adopted the "arbitrary and capricious" standard of review used when courts review government agency action. *Id.* at 231. The arbitrary and capricious standard of review is narrow, and a court may not substitute its judgment for the judgment of the IHSAA. *Carlberg*, 694 N.E.2d at 233. "The rule or decision will be found to be arbitrary and capricious 'only where it is willful and unreasonable, without consideration and in disregard of the facts or circumstances in the case, or without some basis which would lead a reasonable and honest person to the same conclusion.' " *Id.* (quoting *Dep't of Natural Res. v. Ind. Coal Council, Inc.*, 542 N.E.2d 1000, 1007 (Ind. 1989), *cert. denied*, 493 U.S. 1078 (1990)).

In particular, the IHSAA takes issue with the trial court's holding that because B.J. met all of the criteria for the hardship exception, the IHSAA erred in denying him one. The IHSAA contends that even if B.J. would have met all of the criteria listed in the Hardship Rule, Rule 17-8.1, he is not entitled to mandatory relief. Rather, the IHSAA maintains that relief under the Hardship Rule is a matter of grace. In other words, the IHSAA has the discretion of whether to grant a hardship exception even if the Durhams proved that 1) strict enforcement of the Transfer Rule will not serve to accomplish the purpose of the Rule, 2) the spirit of the Transfer Rule has not been violated, and 3) an undue hardship would result if the Transfer Rule was enforced

* * *

However, the IHSAA's position leaves its administrative decisions denying a hardship exception free from judicial review of any sort. While the text of the Hardship Rule states that the IHSAA "shall have the authority to set aside the effect of any Rule," the IHSAA's stance that it can deny a hardship exception even when the student meets the listed criteria implies both that it may have no ascertainable standards for granting or denying a hardship and that its hardship determinations are free from judicial review. IHSAA Manual, Rule 17-8.1. If the IHSAA is truly analogous to a governmental agency, then it must also establish standards on which to base its decisions.

Our supreme court in *Carlberg*, established the appropriate standard of review for IHSAA decisions in no uncertain terms. To reiterate, the *Carlberg* court stated that an IHSAA decision is arbitrary and capricious if it is "willful and unreasonable, without consideration and in disregard of the facts or circumstances in the case, or without some basis which would lead a reasonable and honest person to the same conclusion." 694 N.E.2d at 233 (citation omitted). The IHSAA's suggestion that the Hardship Rule is entitled to an increasingly narrow standard of judicial review flies in the face of the *Carlberg* decision. In *Carlberg*, the supreme court upheld the IHSAA's Transfer Rule in part because there are provisions in place to lessen the severity of the rule. *Carlberg*, 694 N.E.2d at 233. The court reasoned that granting immediate and full eligibility either under the listed exceptions to the Transfer Rule or under the Hardship Rule and granting limited eligibility at the junior varsity or freshman level serves to balance the possible harsh effects of the Transfer Rule. *Id.* If we accepted the IHSAA's assertion that its decisions to deny a hardship exception fall under a more stringent standard of review than the arbitrary and capricious standard enunciated in *Carlberg*, then we would be taking away one of the underpinnings of that case.

Thus, we hold that trial courts may determine whether the denial of a hardship exception in a particular case was the result of arbitrary and capricious action by the IHSAA. In this case, the trial court did not fail to give weight to the IHSAA's broad discretion, as the IHSAA alleges. Rather, in rendering its decision that the IHSAA acted arbitrarily and capriciously, the trial court looked at the IHSAA's particular decision with respect to B.J., applied the appropriate standard, and concluded that the IHSAA's conduct rose to the level of willful and unreasonable decisionmaking that was in disregard of the facts and circumstances before it. For this, the trial court was well within its discretion.

C. Were the IHSAA's Findings Clearly Erroneous?

Finally, the IHSAA asserts that even if the trial court used the appropriate standard of review governing its decisions, the trial court's findings were clearly erroneous. The IHSAA asserts that the evidence, as adduced in its written findings, supports its denial of full eligibility and a hardship exception. In particular, the IHSAA asserts that some evidence existed that B.J. transferred for athletically motivated reasons. It points to the bantering about North Central having a better cross-country and track program. The trial court concluded that this was "hearsay within hearsay" and was not substantial evidence. The IHSAA counters that hearsay is admissible during administrative proceedings, and can be found to be substantial evidence of probative value. * * * The IHSAA also contends that the Durhams failed to establish that the purpose of the Transfer Rule would not be served by denying B.J. a hardship exception due to this evidence of "school jumping."

Here, the trial court did not abuse its discretion in holding that the IHSAA's conclusion that there was some evidence supporting that B.J. transferred for athletic reasons was arbitrary and capricious. Although hearsay may be admissible in administrative proceedings, this evidence of bantering was based upon Park Tudor's mistaken assumption that B.J. was transferring for athletic reasons. As soon as Park Tudor officials learned of the Durhams' circumstances, the transfer report was corrected to reflect that they recommended that B.J. be given full eligibility under a hardship exception. Thus, any evidence of athletic motivation was recanted by Park Tudor. Further, Park Tudor's retraction is against their own interest, as it would seem that Park Tudor would be interested in not having B.J. compete against it due to its rivalry with North Central. Despite this, Park Tudor supported B.J.'s pursuit of a hardship exception.

Additionally, the Durhams were led to believe that athletic motivation would not be an issue in B.J.'s case. It is unfortunate that the IHSAA listed athletic motivation as a reason for transfer even though little or no evidence supports it. This practice was denounced in *Martin*, 731 N.E.2d at 11, which noted that the IHSAA uses the possibility of an athletically-motivated transfer, although admittedly not primarily athletically motivated, as a "poison pill" to keep students from receiving a hardship exception even if there is no substantial evidence to that effect. In the instant case, the trial court recognized this practice and found no evidence in the record to support the IHSAA's conclusion that athletic motivation played a role in B.J.'s transfer. Thus, the trial court's findings with respect to athletic motivation were not clearly erroneous.

Further, the IHSAA argues that B.J. did not establish undue hardship because he failed to show that his family's circumstances were beyond his or his family's control and that he could not afford to attend private school. The IHSAA contends that the trial court merely reweighed the evidence of the family's finances, and that the Durhams still enjoyed a high standard of living. The IHSAA concluded that the decision to send B.J. to North Central was a choice.

Rule 17-8.1, the general section of the Hardship Rule, states that the IHSAA may grant a hardship exception if 1) strict enforcement of the rule in the particular case will not serve to accomplish the purpose of the rule; 2) the spirit of the rule has not been violated; and 3) there exists in the particular case circumstances showing an undue hardship that would result from enforcement of the rule. Thereafter, specific circumstances are listed as candidates for hardship exceptions. One such circumstance that may be considered a hardship is a change in financial condition of the student or a student's family if the change is permanent, substantial, and significantly beyond the control of the athlete or the athlete's family.

The Seventh Circuit Court of Appeals considered this issue in *Crane*, 975 F.2d 1315, and held that the IHSAA's denial of full eligibility was arbitrary and capricious where a student whose parents were divorced had transferred schools after a change in custody. *Crane*, 975 F.2d at 1322. The IHSAA has concluded that the student failed to prove that the move was beyond his control, as the change in custody occurred after Crane had some discipline problems and trouble with his grades in school. The Seventh Circuit, finding that this decision was arbitrary and capricious, reasoned that the IHSAA had ignored the plain language of its rules and instead used "rambling rationalizations" to come to a "pre-ordained result." *Id.* at 1323, 1325. The court noted that the IHSAA changes its interpretation of its rules depending upon the situation before it. *Id.* at 1325. We also addressed this issue in *Avant*, 650 N.E.2d 1164 (Ind. Ct. App. 1995). In *Avant*, we held that the IHSAA's denial of a hardship exception was supported by the evidence. *Id.* at 1169. Avant transferred from a private to a public school, and Avant's

enrollment at a private school created a financial hardship on the family. However, the family's financial situation had not changed, and there was also evidence that Avant had disagreements with his basketball coach. Further, the family's financial situation was never listed on the transfer report. Thus, we concluded that the IHSAA's decision to deny Avant a hardship exception was not arbitrary and capricious. *Id.*

Unlike *Avant*, in this case there was a change in the Durhams' family finances due to the divorce, and this change was documented in the transfer report submitted to the IHSAA. This change was caused by something beyond their control, Joan's recent divorce. Included in the specific list of situations receiving consideration for a hardship exception is a substantial and permanent change in financial condition of the student or the student's family significantly beyond the control of the student or the student's family. With the evidence submitted by Joan in the IHSAA administrative proceedings regarding her recent divorce and family's change in finances, no reasonable and honest person could conclude that the Durhams have not met this specific consideration listed within the Hardship Rule.

The trial court in the case before us found that the IHSAA ignored its own rules and instead interjected a condition of undue hardship not found in its rules that the Durhams prove their poverty before B.J. be given a hardship exception. We agree.

Contrary to IHSAA's assertion, the Hardship Rule does not read that an athlete's family must prove that it is a hardship case. In fact, financial hardship or poverty is not contained within the change in financial condition provision or the Hardship Rule generally. Instead, the "hardship" referred to in the Hardship Rule focuses on the hardship faced by the student athlete if the rule is strictly enforced. In this case, B.J. would face a hardship if he had to run at the junior varsity level because through no fault of his own and without any athletic motivation, B.J. was forced to transfer schools because of a substantial and permanent change in his family's financial condition. Just as in *Crane*, the IHSAA is attempting to adjust its interpretation of the Hardship Rule to meet the particulars of this case.

Even if we were to read a financial hardship requirement into the Hardship Rule, the Durhams would meet such a condition. The evidence in the record is undisputed that Joan had a significant amount of debt and her income had decreased by sixty-seven percent as a result of the divorce. At first glance, Joan's taxable income of $134,620 may not appear to suggest a family in financial hardship. However, a closer look reveals that Joan's monthly expenses are about equal to her monthly income. Joan's mortgage and utilities total $96,000 yearly, and she has many other regular expenses including health care, insurance, and various household expenses. Joan also has no assets that she could access to alleviate her financial burdens. Although Joan may be able to sell her house, she would net very little in proceeds after her mortgage debt was satisfied. Further, Joan would like to keep her children in the family home to avoid more disruption in their lives, in light of the divorce. The IHSAA should not be in the business of second-guessing personal financial decisions, but should accept the circumstances as they are.

Given the evidence in this case, the trial court did not abuse its discretion in overturning the IHSAA's denial of full eligibility and refusal to grant a hardship exception. While it may be true that in other cases, *see IHSAA v. Vasario*, 726 N.E.2d 325, 333 (Ind. Ct. App. 2000) and *Avant*, 650 N.E.2d at 1169, we have recognized the IHSAA's broad discretion in refusing to grant a student a hardship exception, this discretion is not unreviewable and is subject to the arbitrary and capricious standard upon review. The evidence in this case overwhelmingly leads to the conclusion that the reasons the IHSAA created the Transfer Rule, deterrence of athletic recruiting and equality in competition, would not be served by denying B.J. a hardship exception. The trial court did not simply reweigh the evidence and substitute its opinion, but instead found that the IHSAA ignored the facts and circumstances before it in rendering its decision. No reasonable and honest person would have concluded that B.J. should be denied a hardship exception in this case. This case embodies the reason the Hardship Rule was created. Although the IHSAA contends that its decisions are virtually unreviewable, a court does have the discretion to identify arbitrary and capricious conduct. The trial court in this case properly identified arbitrary and capricious action by the IHSAA.

Judgment affirmed.

Recent Trends

There is a growing use of courts by athletes seeking injunctions to overturn athletic organization decisions. As a result, in elite-level amateur athletics, the athletic associations as well as professional sport organizations are turning to arbitration as the forum for decisions on rules and eligibility to be made. For national governing bodies, international federations, and Olympic Committees, the Court for Arbitration in Sport (CAS), as well as organizations such as the American Arbitration Association (AAA), are the forums used as mandated by rules and regulations in these governing bodies. In professional sport, labor grievance arbitration is also the model used to resolve disputes, and AAA provides the arbitrators for the cases. The policies setting forth this procedure are negotiated through the collective bargaining process. For more information, see Chapters 6.24, *Alternative Dispute Resolution*, and 8.33, *Labor Law*.

References

Cases

Beeson v. Kiowa County School District, 567 P.2d 801 (Colo. Ct. App. 1977).
Braesch v. De Pasquale, 265 N.W.2d 842 (Neb. Sup. Ct. 1978).
Bunger v. Iowa High School Athletic Association, 197 N.W.2d 555 (Sup. Ct. 1972).
Estay v. La Fourche Parish School Board, 230 So.2d 443 (La. Ct. App. 1969).
Indiana High School Athletic Association, Inc. v. Durham, 748 N.E.2d 404 (2001).
Tinker v. Des Moines Independent School District, 383 F.2d 988, rev'd 393 U.S. 503 (1969).
Williams v. Eaton, 468 F.2d 1079 (10th Cir. 1972).

Publication

Wong, G. M., & Masteralexis, L. P. (2005). Sport Law. In L. P. Masteralexis, C. A. Barr, & M. A. Hums (Eds.), *Principles and practice of sport management*. Sudbury, MA: Jones and Bartlett Publishers.

7.12 State Action

Stacey Altman
East Carolina University

In litigation in which an individual claims that he or she has been deprived of rights guaranteed by the United States Constitution, the courts will first consider whether the deprivation was caused by conduct "fairly attributable" to a governmental entity (*Lugar v. Edmondson Oil*, 1982). The only exceptions to this general rule of requiring a finding of state action before applying the analysis appropriate to constitutional claim involved have been made in situations involving the Thirteenth Amendment. The Thirteenth Amendment protects individual rights against interference from public and private action. All other provisions of the Constitution that protect individual rights apply, either by their express language or implicit meaning, only to the conduct of state (governmental) actors (Emanuel, 1998).

In some cases, determining whether conduct is attributable to a governmental entity, and thus subject to constitutional challenge, is fairly easy. For instance, if the claim is that a federal statute itself violates the Constitution (e.g., by inappropriately categorizing based on gender or race), the existence of state action is apparent because the statute had to have been enacted by a legislative unit of government. However, if the claim is that an eligibility rule enforced by a state high school athletic association or college conference violates a constitutionally protected right, determining the existence of the requisite state action to sustain the claim is more complex.

Fundamental Concepts

State Action Analysis

The U.S. Supreme Court's first articulation of the state action requirement occurred in the *Civil Rights Cases* (1883). The Court held that the guarantees of equal protection and due process, given by the Fourteenth Amendment, apply by their own terms exclusively to state action (Emanuel, 1998). Historically, courts have used two theories to determine whether seemingly private conduct is fairly attributable to the state for the purpose constitutional analysis: (1) the **public function theory** and (2) the **nexus or entanglement theory** (Wong, 1988). Some Supreme Court watchers and courts maintain that there is a third theory, the **mutual contacts or symbiotic relationship theory**, that serves as a catchall category for the various ways the Supreme Court has used the measure the relationship between private actors and the state (Rotunda & Nowak, 1999).

Although courts have been deciding cases requiring a determination regarding state action for more than a century, "state action is a variable concept that vexes the interests of bright line-drawing" (Lively, Haddox, Roberts & Weaver, 1996). As the Court put it, "The doctrines are too generally phrased to be self-executing; the cases are sensitive to fact situations and lack neat consistency, thus the analysis should include attention to the "ad-hoc cases that have not yet congealed into formal categories" (*Logiodice v. Trustees of Maine Central Institute*, 2002, pp. 26–29). The following paragraphs address these theories and what further guidance courts and commentators have provided for making a state action determination.

Public Function Theory

Under the public function theory, the courts consider whether a private actor is performing functions that have been traditionally reserved to government or that are governmental in nature (Rotunda & Nowak, 1999). This theory emerged in what have been called the "*White Primary Cases.*" In *Smith v. Allwright* (1944), the Court held that because the election process is a public function, private political parties are agents of the state when controlling the nominating process. In *Terry v. Adams* (1953), the rationale in *Smith* was extended to "preprimaries" (Emanuel, 1998). The public function theory has also been used to ascribe state actor status to a private company when it owns and operates a town that provides the services and contains the residential and commercial areas that any other municipality would (*Marsh v. Alabama*, 1946). In *Marsh*, the Court held that for the purpose of exercising First Amendment rights, the conduct of the Gulf Shipbuilding Corporation, which owned the town, was subject to constitutional scrutiny. In another case involving First Amendment guarantees, the Court held that the operation of shopping centers could also be considered a public function, thus making certain activities occurring at the center constitutionally protected (*Amalgamated Food Employees v. Logan Valley Plaza*, 1968). In *Lloyd Corp., Ltd. v. Tanner* (1972), the Court, suggested that the holdings in *Marsh* and *Logan Valley* should be narrowly construed and noted that the holding in *Logan Valley* was "carefully phrased" to apply only to picketing "directly related in its purpose to the use to which the shopping center property was being put," (*Lloyd Corp,* 1972). Then, in *Hudgens v. NLRB* (1976), the Court overruled *Logan Valley* completely by denying relief to picketers who claimed a right to advertise their strike in a shopping center. *Hudgens* marked the beginning of the Court's unwillingness to continue to broadly construe what activity is considered a public function. Today, it is likely that public function theory will be applied only if two conditions are met: (1) the function is one that is traditionally the exclusive domain of the state, and (2) a statute or constitutional provision actually requires the state to perform the function (Emanuel, 1998; see also *Jackson v. Metropolitan Edison Co.,* 1974; *Flagg Bros. v. Brooks,* 1978). Using those conditions, the Court rejected claims that contained contentions that the operation of a nursing home (*Blum v. Yaretsky,* 1982) and the provision of education (*Rendell-Baker v. Kohn,* 1981) were public functions.

Nexus/Entanglement Theory

The nexus theory involves a determination regarding the extent of government's involvement with private activity rather than an analysis of the type of conduct the private actor is engaged in. When applying the nexus theory, courts have held that private activity may be deemed state action when government is heavily involved in it, commands or encourages it, or is benefited by it (Emanuel, 1998). *Shelley v. Kraemer* (1948) illustrated how government might command private activity (Drew, 2001). At issue in *Shelley* was the judicial enforcement of covenants that restricted property from being owned by anyone other than Caucasians. The Court held that judicial enforcement of the covenants would be, in essence, actively commanding private actors to engage in conduct subject to challenge under the Constitution (Drew, 2001). At issue in *Burton v. Wilmington Parking Authority* (1961) was whether a relationship between a public parking facility and a private restaurant (located within the public parking facility) could lead to a finding of state action that would, in turn, enable the restaurant's discriminatory policies to be disputed. The Court found that because the public parking facility's financial success was so heavily dependent on the lease with the restaurant, the state's involvement was sufficient to attribute the restaurant's actions to the state. By contrast, in *Blum*, the Court refused to find such a symbiotic relationship between government and a nursing home despite the fact that the state heavily subsidized the operation of nursing home and paid for 90 percent of the patients' medical expenses (Blum, 1982). *Blum* and the two state action cases that immediately followed, *Rendell-Baker* and *Lugar*, limit the scope of the nexus theory such that state regulation or subsidization alone will not be enough to warrant a finding of state action. It is the *Blum* trilogy that appears to be most relevant for understanding subsequent state action cases (Pierguidi, 2000).

Application to Sport and Recreation Organizations

Courts have held that the action of any public school, state college, or any of their officials is state action, thus deprivations of constitutionally protected rights by such entities are actionable (Wong, 1988). When private organizations govern or administer sport and recreation, state action is not so readily apparent.

Recreational Clubs and Facilities

In *Evans v. Newton* (1966), the Supreme Court held that the operation of a park owned by private trustees constituted state action. Justice Douglas, writing for the Court, seemed to be invoking the public function theory when he stated that, "the service rendered even by a private park of this character is municipal in nature" (*Evans*, 1966). Yet, he also noted that the city's entwinement in the management and control of the park (cleaning, watering, and patrolling) and the park's tax-exempt status had a significant impact on the decision to subject the policy of allowing only whites to use the park to judicial review. Operation of other recreational facilities, such as country clubs or amusement parks, has not been, nor it is likely to be, construed as governmental in nature because subsequent cases have held that only those functions traditionally exclusively carried out by government will be deemed public functions (Emanuel, 1998). A notable exception is the interesting case of *Pitt v. Pine Valley Golf Club* (1988), where the plaintiff claimed that a membership rule that restricted home ownership in the Borough of Pine Valley to members of the Pine Valley Golf Club violated the Fifth and Fourteenth Amendments of the Constitution. When making the requisite state action inquiry, the court noted that the club was in essence issuing a zoning ordinance. Because the power to make zoning ordinances is traditionally reserved to the state, the court found state action to be involved.

In *Perkins v. Londonderry Basketball Club* (1999), the court held that a voluntary, nonprofit organization that enjoyed tax-exempt status was not a state actor, even though it availed itself of public facilities free of charge and its board members were also members of the town's Recreation Commission. In *Hippopress v. SMG* (2003), the plaintiff was unable to demonstrate that there was a sufficiently close relationship between SMG, a facility management group, and the City of Manchester, which had contracted with SMG to manage its multipurpose sports and entertainment venue to establish SMG's conduct as state action. Without meeting this threshold, *Hippopress* was unable to proceed with its state and federal constitutional claims.

Cases where state action was found to exist in circumstances similar to those describe earlier include *Fortin v. Darlington Little League* (1975), where the extent of public facility use has been important, and *Stevens v. New York Racing Association* (1987), where the plaintiff was able to show the existence of state action under the "symbiotic relationship" theory. The court noted that state action existed because of the extent state funding. (See also Chapter 7.26, *Private Clubs in Sport and Recreation*.)

High School Athletic Associations

Historically, most courts have found state high school interscholastic athletic associations to be state actors. (See, e.g., *Oklahoma High School Ass'n v. Bray*, 1963; *Louisiana High School Athletic Ass'n v. St. Augustine High School*, 1968; *Moreland v. West Pennsylvania Interscholastic Athletic League*, 1978; *Griffin High School v. Illinois High School Ass'n*, 1987; and *Indiana High School Ass'n v. Carlberg*, 1997.) Some courts found the requisite state action for sustaining constitutional claims under the nexus theory. When using the nexus theory, courts typically note the following factors in support of finding a nexus between the association and the state: (1) public (tax-supported) schools make up the majority of the association's membership; (2) the association's officials are public school employees; (3) the association and its members use public facilities that have been built and are maintained by public funds; (4) association members are eligible for state retirement programs; and (5) the association is subsidized by the state by either direct funding or tax concessions (Lehr & Altman, 2001). In *Barnhorst v. Missouri State High School Association* (1980), the court found that the functions served by the state high school athletic association were similar enough to the functions of the state in providing education to find state action under the public function theory (Wong, 1988).

Unlike most courts, the Sixth Circuit consistently declined to declare state high school athletic associations to be state actors. In *Burrows v. Ohio High School Athletic Ass'n* (1989), the court concluded that OHSAA was "clearly" an analogous organization to the NCAA and with that being the case, they were bound by *Graham v. NCAA* (1986). In *Graham*, the court held that the NCAA's function, the governance of athletics, was not a function traditionally reserved to the state. Thus, the court could not find that the OHSAA was a state actor when it had not found the NCAA to be such. In *Brentwood*, the court held that because the TSSAA was founded as a voluntary association, received no direct state funding, scheduled only state tournaments (not the majority of the state's athletic contests), paid for the use of public facilities when used, and was not empowered by the state code to conduct interscholastic events, there was nothing to suggest state involvement. What confusion the court may have caused by this line of cases was eliminated when the Supreme Court reversed the Sixth Circuit in *Brentwood*. The edited text of the Court's decision is included later in the chapter. In brief, by a 5-4 majority, the Court held that the association's regulatory activity should be treated as state action owing to the pervasive entwinement of state school officials in the structure of the association.

Since *Brentwood*, the Sixth Circuit Court of Appeals has found high school athletic associations to be state actors (*Cmtys. for Equity v. Mich. High School Athletic Ass'n*, 2004, *vacated and remanded on other grounds*, 125 S.Ct. 1973, 2005). Other jurisdictions continue to find high school athletic associations state actors. (See, e.g., *Rottman v. Pennsylvania Athletic Ass'n*, 2004, and *Jones v. W. Va. State Bd. of Educ.*, 2005.)

National Organizations Governing College Athletics

Over 1,250 public and private institutions of higher education are members of the National Collegiate Athletic Association (NCAA). Membership is available to any accredited four-year school that meets its standards. Junior and community colleges are not eligible for NCAA membership, but are often members of the National Junior College Athletic Association (NJCAA). Some schools, despite being eligible for NCAA membership, have chosen to join the National Association of Intercollegiate Athletics (NAIA) (Jones, 1999). All these associations are private organizations, and membership is voluntary.

Prior to the mid-1980s, these organizations were usually considered state actors and thus were subject to the requirements of the Constitution. The most widely discussed cases addressing this issue involve the NCAA. In *Regents of the University of Minnesota v. NCAA* (1976), the court acknowledged that the action taken by the NCAA had generally been accepted as the equivalent of state action (Wong, 1988). For other examples, see *Buckton v. NCAA* (1973), (holding that in supervising and policing most intercollegiate athletics nationally, the NCAA performed a public function, sovereign in nature, which subjected it to constitutional scrutiny) and *Howard University v. NCAA* (1975), (holding that pervasive influence of state-supported universities in the NCAA required a finding of state action).

The tendency of courts to find that the NCAA was a state actor came to a halt in the mid-1980s. In 1984, the Fourth Circuit ruled, in *Arlosoroff v. NCAA*, that the NCAA's regulation of intercollegiate athletics was not a function traditionally reserved to the state and that even if the NCAA's regulatory function may be of some public service, it is not enough to convert it to state action. Moreover, unless the eligibility rule was adopted as a result of governmental compulsion, there could be no state action (*Arlosoroff*, 1984). In 1988, the Supreme Court decided *NCAA v. Tarkanian*. In *Tarkanian*, the NCAA Committee on Infractions found the University of Nevada, Las Vegas (UNLV) had committed several violations of NCAA rules, ten of which had been committed by Coach Tarkanian. Though it was obvious throughout the investigative process that UNLV wanted to keep its winning coach, ultimately the university suspended him when faced with the order to show cause for avoiding further penalty (Kitchen, 1996). The lack of a cooperative relationship between UNLV and the NCAA was not lost on the majority of the Court. In reaching the conclusion that the NCAA's involvement in the events that led to the suspension of the coach did not constitute state action, the Court relied the following factors: (1) the NCAA was not a joint participant with UNLV when the NCAA represented the interests of its entire membership in the investigation of a member institution, (2) the NCAA never had power to directly discipline university employees, (3) UNLV voluntarily complied with NCAA rules, and (4) neither the university, nor any arm of the state, had delegated to the NCAA any governmental powers for the purposes of its investigation (e.g., to subpoena witnesses).

College Conferences

In those cases that have determined intercollegiate athletic conferences to be state actors, the following factors were important: (1) the public nature of the of the members of the college athletic conference, (2) that the conference received direct funds or tax breaks from the state, and (3) that the contests sponsored by the conference were held in public facilities (Wilde, 2000). In *Stanley v. Big Eight Conference* (1978), the fact that the conference was composed solely of state-supported public universities, which delegated to the Big Eight certain functions such as supervision over intercollegiate athletics, was enough to establish the requisite state action to proceed with the procedural due process claim involved. However, judicial dicta in *Weiss v. Eastern College Athletic Conference* (1983) and the holding in *Hairston v. Pac-10 Conference* (1994) suggest that conferring state actor status on college conferences, at least for the purpose of constitutional claims, may be more difficult after the late 1970s. In *Weiss*, where the ECAC and NCAA were codefendants, it was not necessary to consider the state action requirement to dispose of the case. Still, Judge Green commented that nothing of record merited "a conclusion that the rulemaking functions of defendants were state functions, that a symbiotic relationship existed between defendants and a state, or that the state was involved in defendants' conduct" (*Weiss*, 1983). In *Hairston*, plaintiffs were unsuccessful in their claim, because they had failed to distinguish *Tarkanian*, which was "dispositive" on the issue of whether state action was involved (*Hairston*, 1994).

Organizations Created by Governments

Like the American Legion, Big Brothers/Big Sisters of America, and the National Ski Patrol System, Inc., the United States Olympic Committee (USOC) is a federally created private organization. In a close decision in *San Francisco Arts & Athletics, Inc. v. USOC* (1987), the Court concluded that the USOC's federal charter and the rights granted to it by the Amateur Sports Act of 1978 (e.g., exclusive control over the word "Olympic" and certain symbols) did not entwine the USOC and federal government to the extent that would warrant a finding of state action. In support of their conclusion, the Court cited a case in which U.S. athletes challenged the USOC's decision to boycott the 1980 Olympics. When presented with the issue of determining whether the USOC's decision amounted to state action in *DeFrantz v. USOC*, 1980, Judge Pratt, writing for the court, stated:

> The USOC is an independent body, and nothing in its chartering statute gives the federal government the right to control that body or its officers. Furthermore, the facts here do not indicate that the federal government was able to exercise any type of "de facto" control over the USOC. . . . All it had was the power of persuasion. We cannot equate this with control. To do so in cases of this type would be to open the door and usher the courts into what we believe is a largely nonjusticiable realm, where they would find themselves in the untenable position of determining whether a certain level, intensity, or type of "Presidential" or "Administrative" or "political" pressure amounts to sufficient control over a private entity so as to invoke federal jurisdiction. (1181, 1194)

Professional Sports Leagues

Rarely have the activities of professional sport leagues or teams been deemed state action. Professional sport leagues, whether described as joint ventures of independent clubs or as a single entity, are most often characterized as private businesses (Wilde, 2000). They do not perform a function that has been traditionally reserved to the state, and historically entwinement with government has been limited. In *Ludtke v. Kuhn* (1978), the Court did recognize that the New York Yankees' entwinement with government was sufficient to consider the team's enforcement of Commissioner Kuhn's policy of excluding female reporters from the clubhouse state action. The aspects of the situation that the Court noted as important included (1) the city had exercised its power of eminent domain to acquire Yankee Stadium; (2) the city was authorized by statute to lease the stadium to the Yankees (not the highest bidder); and (3) the stadium was renovated at a cost of $50 million to the city. Conversely, in *Long v. NFL* (1994), the fact that a city collected an amusement tax on tickets or that it constructed a stadium for a team were not enough to find the state involvement necessary to sustain a constitutional challenge to the NFL's drug testing policy (Wilde, 2000 citing Cruz, 1995).

Legal commentators have increasingly addressed the notion that the activities of professional sport leagues could be deemed state action. For example, Guggenheim (1998) argued that a challenge to the Cleveland Indians "Chief Wahoo" mark might viably claim that the Indians' use of the mark constitutes discriminatory state action based on the team's relationship with the city and Jacobs Field. Fielder (2002), in arguing that the Pickens clause unconstitutionally restrained the free speech rights of NFL players, reasoned that the relationship between Cincinnati Bengals, Inc. and Hamilton County could serve as state involvement required to subject the clause to review. In a time when professional sport franchises usually receive, among other things, the use of modern public facilities (including stadiums and parking areas) without the burden of maintenance, tax incentives, and the use of the city's name that arguably enhances the team's ability to attract fans and sponsors, entwinement may be more readily apparent (Guggenheim, 1998).

Significant Case

———————————◇◇◇———————————

The following case illustrates what factors are considered when making a determination as to whether a state high school athletic association is a state actor. Note that the Court did not use the public function theory, but instead found the requisite state action under the nexus theory. The fact that the member schools were all within one state, that there was "bottom-up" and "top-down" entwinement, and the need for harmony among the circuits all appeared to be important in the Court's determination.

BRENTWOOD ACADEMY V. TENNESSEE SECONDARY ATHLETIC ASSOCIATION
United States Supreme Court
531 U.S. 288 (2001)

Opinion: Justice Souter delivered the opinion of the Court.

The action before us responds to a 1997 regulatory enforcement proceeding brought against petitioner, Brentwood Academy, a private parochial high school member of the [Tennessee Secondary School Athletic] Association. The Association's board of control found that Brentwood violated a rule prohibiting "undue influence" in recruiting athletes, when it wrote to incoming students and their parents about spring football practice. The Association accordingly placed Brentwood's athletic program on probation for four years, declared its football and boys' basketball teams ineligible to compete in playoffs for two years, and imposed a $3,000 fine. When these penalties were imposed, all the voting members of the board of control and legislative council were public school administrators.

* * *

Our cases try to plot a line between state action subject to Fourteenth Amendment scrutiny and private conduct (however exceptionable) that is not, *Tarkanian*; *Jackson* v. *Metropolitan Edison Co.*, 419 U.S. 345 (1974). The judicial obligation is not only to " 'preserve an area of individual freedom by limiting the reach of federal law' and avoid the imposition of responsibility on a State for conduct it could not control," *Tarkanian*, *supra*, at 191 (quoting *Lugar*), but also to assure that constitutional standards are invoked "when it can be said that the State is *responsible* for the specific conduct of which the plaintiff complains," *Blum*. If the Fourteenth Amendment is not to be displaced, therefore, its ambit cannot be a simple line between States and people operating outside formally governmental organizations, and the deed of an ostensibly private organization or individual is to be treated sometimes as if a State had caused it to be performed. Thus, we say that state action may be found if, though only if, there is such a "close nexus between the State and the challenged action" that seemingly private behavior "may be fairly treated as that of the State itself." *Jackson*, *supra*, at 351.

* * *

Our cases have identified a host of facts that can bear on the fairness of such an attribution. We have, for example, held that a challenged activity may be state action when it results from the State's exercise of "coercive power," *Blum*, 457 U.S. at 1004, when the State provides "significant encouragement, either overt or covert," *ibid.* or when a private actor operates as a "willful participant in joint activity with the State or its agents," *Lugar*, *supra*, at 941. We have treated a nominally private entity as a state actor when it is controlled by an "agency of the State," *Pennsylvania* v. *Board of Directors of City Trusts of Philadelphia*, 353 U.S. 230, 231 (1957) (*per curiam*), when it has been delegated a public function by the State, cf., *e.g.*, *West* v. *Atkins*, *supra*, at 56; *Edmonson* v. *Leesville Concrete Co.*, 500 U.S. 614, 627-628 (1991), when it is "entwined with governmental policies" or when government is "entwined in [its] management or control," *Evans* v. *Newton*, 382 U.S. 296 (1966). * * *

To be sure, it is not the strict holding in *Tarkanian* that points to our view of this case, for we found no state action on the part of the NCAA. We could see, on the one hand, that the university had some part in setting the NCAA's rules, and the Supreme Court of Nevada had gone so far as to hold that the NCAA had been delegated the university's traditionally exclusive public authority over personnel. Id. at 190. But on the other side, the NCAA's policies were shaped not by the University of Nevada alone, but by several hundred member institutions, most of them having no connection with Nevada, and exhibiting no color of Nevada law. Id. at 193. Since it was difficult to see the NCAA, not as a collective membership, but as surrogate for the one State, we held the organization's connection with Nevada too insubstantial to ground a state action claim. Id. at 193, 196.

But dictum in *Tarkanian* pointed to a contrary result on facts like ours, with an organization whose member public schools are all within a single State. "The situation would, of course, be different if the [Association's] membership consisted entirely of institutions located within the same State, many of them public institutions created by the same sovereign." Id. at 193. To support our surmise, we approvingly cited two cases: *Clark* v. *Arizona Interscholastic Ass'n.*, 695 F.2d 1126 (CA9 1982), cert. denied, 464 U.S. 818 (1983), a challenge to a state high school athletic association that kept boys from playing on girls' interscholastic volleyball teams in Arizona; and *Louisiana High School Athletic Assn.* v. *St. Augustine High School*, 396 F.2d 224 (CA5 1968), a parochial school's attack on the racially segregated system of interscholastic high school athletics maintained by the athletic association. In each instance, the Court of Appeals treated the athletic association as a state actor.

Just as we foresaw in *Tarkanian*, the "necessarily fact-bound inquiry," *Lugar*, 457 U.S. at 939, leads to the conclusion of state action here. The nominally private character of the Association is overborne by the pervasive entwinement of public institutions and public officials in its composition and workings, and there is no substantial reason to claim unfairness in applying constitutional standards to it.

The Association is not an organization of natural persons acting on their own, but of schools, and of public schools to the extent of 84% of the total. Under the Association's bylaws, each member school is represented by its principal or a faculty member, who has a vote in selecting members of the governing legislative council and board of control from eligible principals, assistant principals and superintendents.

Although the findings and prior opinions in this case include no express conclusion of law that public school officials act within the scope of their duties when they represent their institutions, no other view would be rational, the official nature of their involvement being shown in any number of ways. Interscholastic athletics obviously play an integral part in the public education of Tennessee, where nearly every public high school spends money on competitions among schools. Since a pickup system of interscholastic games would not do, these public teams need some mechanism to produce rules and regulate competition. The mechanism is an organization overwhelmingly composed of public school officials who select representatives (all of them public officials at the time in question here), who in turn adopt and enforce the rules that make the system work. Thus, by giving these jobs to the Association, the 290 public schools of Tennessee belonging to it can sensibly be seen as exercising their own authority to meet their own responsibilities. Unsurprisingly, then, the record indicates that half the council or board meetings documented here were held during official school hours, and that public schools have largely provided for the Association's financial support. A small portion of the Association's revenue comes from membership dues paid by the schools, and the principal part from gate receipts at tournaments among the member schools. Unlike mere public buyers of contract services, whose payments for services rendered do not convert the service providers into public actors, see *Rendell-Baker*, 457 U.S. at 839-843, the schools here obtain membership in the service organization and give up sources of their own income to their collective association. The Association thus exercises the authority of the predominantly public schools to charge for admission to their games; the Association does not receive this money from the schools, but enjoys the schools' moneymaking capacity as its own.

In sum, to the extent of 84% of its membership, the Association is an organization of public schools represented by their officials acting in their official capacity to provide an integral element of secondary public schooling. There would be no recognizable Association, legal or tangible, without the public school officials, who do not merely control but overwhelmingly perform all but the purely ministerial acts by which the Association exists and functions in practical terms. Only the 16% minority of private school memberships prevents this entwinement of the Association and the public school system from being total and their identities totally indistinguishable. To complement the entwinement of public school officials with the Association from the bottom up, the State of Tennessee has provided for entwinement from top down. State Board members are assigned ex officio to serve as members of the board of control and legislative council, and the Association's ministerial employees are treated as state employees to the extent of being eligible for membership in the state retirement system.

As mentioned, the terms of the State Board's Rule expressly designating the Association as regulator of interscholastic athletics in public schools was deleted in 1996, the year after a Federal District Court held that the Association was a state actor because its rules were "caused, directed and controlled by the Tennessee

Board of Education," *Graham* v. *TSSAA*, No. 1:95-CV-044, 1995 WL 115890, (ED Tenn., Feb. 20, 1995).

But the removal of the designation language from Rule 0520-1-2-.08 affected nothing but words. Today the State Board's member-designees continue to sit on the Association's committees as nonvoting members, and the State continues to welcome Association employees in its retirement scheme. The close relationship is confirmed by the Association's enforcement of the same preamendment rules and regulations reviewed and approved by the State Board (including the recruiting Rule challenged by Brentwood), and by the State Board's continued willingness to allow students to satisfy its physical education requirement by taking part in interscholastic athletics sponsored by the Association. The most one can say on the evidence is that the State Board once freely acknowledged the Association's official character but now does it by winks and nods.

* * *

The entwinement down from the State Board is therefore unmistakable, just as the entwinement up from the member public schools is overwhelming. Entwinement will support a conclusion that an ostensibly private organization ought to be charged with a public character and judged by constitutional standards; entwinement to the degree shown here requires it.

Entwinement is also the answer to the Association's several arguments offered to persuade us that the facts would not support a finding of state action under various criteria applied in other cases. These arguments are beside the point, simply because the facts justify a conclusion of state action under the criterion of entwinement, a conclusion in no sense unsettled merely because other criteria of state action may not be satisfied by the same facts.

The Association places great stress, for example, on the application of a public function test, as exemplified in *Rendell-Baker* v. *Kohn*, 457 U.S. 830 (1982). There, an apparently private school provided education for students whose special needs made it difficult for them to finish high school. The record, however, failed to show any tradition of providing public special education to students unable to cope with a regular school, who had historically been cared for (or ignored) according to private choice. It was true that various public school districts had adopted the practice of referring students to the school and paying their tuition, and no one disputed that providing the instruction aimed at a proper public objective and conferred a public benefit. But we held that the performance of such a public function did not permit a finding of state action on the part of the school unless the function performed was exclusively and traditionally public, as it was not in that case. The Association argues that application of the public function criterion would produce the same result here, and we will

assume, *arguendo,* that it would. But this case does not turn on a public function test, any more than *Rendell-Baker* had anything to do with entwinement of public officials in the special school.

For the same reason, it avails the Association nothing to stress that the State neither coerced nor encouraged the actions complained of. "Coercion" and "encouragement" are like "entwinement" in referring to kinds of facts that can justify characterizing an ostensibly private action as public instead. Facts that address any of these criteria are significant, but no one criterion must necessarily be applied. When, therefore, the relevant facts show pervasive entwinement to the point of largely overlapping identity, the implication of state action is not affected by pointing out that the facts might not loom large under a different test.

* * *

The assertion of such a countervailing value is the nub of each of the Association's two remaining arguments, neither of which, however, persuades us. The Association suggests, first, that reversing the judgment here will somehow trigger an epidemic of unprecedented federal litigation. Even if that might be counted as a good reason for a *Polk County* decision to call the Association's action private, the record raises no reason for alarm here. Save for the Sixth Circuit, every Court of Appeals to consider a statewide athletic association like the one here has found it a state actor. This majority view began taking shape even before *Tarkanian*, which cited two such decisions approvingly, see *supra*, at 9, (and this was six years after *Blum, Rendell-Baker*, and *Lugar*, on which the Sixth Circuit relied here). No one, however, has pointed to any explosion of § 1983 cases against interscholastic athletic associations in the affected jurisdictions. Not to put too fine a point on it, two District Courts in Tennessee have previously held the Association itself to be a state actor, see *Graham*, 1995 WL 115890; *Crocker* v. *Tennessee Secondary School Athletic Assn.*, 735 F. Supp. 753 (MD Tenn. 1990), affirmance order, 908 F.2d 972, 973 (CA6 1990), but there is no evident wave of litigation working its way across the State. A reversal of the judgment here portends nothing more than the harmony of an outlying Circuit with precedent otherwise uniform.

Nor do we think there is anything to be said for the Association's contention that there is no need to treat it as a state actor since any public school applying the Association's rules is itself subject to suit under § 1983 or Title IX of the Education Amendments of 1972, 86 Stat. 373, 20 U.S.C. §§ 1681-1688. If Brentwood's claim were pushing at the edge of the class of possible defendant state actors, an argument about the social utility of expanding that class would at least be on point, but because we are nowhere near the margin in this case, the Association is really asking for nothing less than a dispensation for itself. Its position boils down to saying that the Association should not be dressed in state clothes because other, concededly public actors are; that Brentwood should be kept out of court because a different plaintiff raising a different claim in a different case may find the courthouse open. Pleas for special treatment are hard to sell, although saying that does not, of course, imply anything about the merits of Brentwood's complaint; the issue here is merely whether Brentwood properly names the Association as a § 1983 defendant, not whether it should win on its claim.

The judgment of the Court of Appeals for the Sixth Circuit is reversed, and the case is remanded for further proceedings consistent with this opinion.

When the merits of the case were considered on remand, the recruiting rule at issue in Brentwood was found to be an unconstitutional violation of the First and Fourteenth Amendments (Brentwood Academy v. Tennessee Secondary School Athletic Ass'n, 2003).

Recent Trends

The courts have also used the threshold state action analysis when considering nonconstitutional claims. For example, in *Breighner v. Mich. High Sch. Ath. Ass'n*, (2004), the Supreme Court of Michigan found that the Michigan High School Athletic Association was not subject to Michigan's Freedom of Information Act (FOIA), as it was not a public body by terms set out by that particular statute. However, the court did acknowledge that the association may be a state actor for the purpose of the additional claim of a due process violation involved in the controversy. The *Breighner* opinion is consistent with what has occurred on the collegiate level. (See, e.g., *Kneeland v. NCAA and Southwest Athletic Conference* (1988), reversing the lower court's designation of the NCAA and the Southwest Athletic Conference as "governmental bodies" for the purpose of applying the Texas Open Records Act.)

References

Cases

Amalgamated Food Employees v. Logan Valley Plaza, 391 U.S. 308 (1968).

Arlosoroff v. NCAA, 746 F.2d 1019 (4th Cir. 1984).

Barnhorst v. Missouri State High Sch. Ath. Ass'n, 504 F.Supp. 449 (W.D. Mo. 1980).

Blum v. Yaretsky, 457 U.S. 991 (1982).

Breighner v. Mich. High Sch. Ath. Ass'n, 683 N.W.2d 639 (Mich. 2004).

Brentwood v. Tennessee Secondary Sch. Ath. Ass'n, 531 U.S. 288 (2001).

Brentwood v. Tennessee Secondary Sch. Ath. Ass'n, 304 F. Supp.2d 981 (M.D. Tn 2003).

Buckton v. NCAA, 366 F.Supp. 1152 (D. Mass. 1973).

Burrows v. Ohio High Sch. Ath. Ass'n, 891 F.2d 122 (6th Cir. 1989).

Burton v. Wilmington Parking Authority, 365 U.S. 715 (1961).

Civil Rights Cases, 109 U.S. 3 (1883).

Cmtys. for Equity v. Mich. High Sch. Ath. Ass'n, (6th Cir. 2004).

DeFrantz v. USOC, 492 F.Supp. 1181 (D.D.C. 1980).

Evans v. Newton, 382 U.S. 296 (1966).

Flagg Bros. v. Brooks, 436 U.S. 149 (1978).

Fortin v. Darlington Little League, 514 F.2d 344 (1st Cir. 1975).

Graham v. NCAA, 804 F.2d 953 (6th Cir.1986).

Griffin High Sch. v. Illinois High Sch. Ass'n (7th Cir. 1987).

Hairston v. PAC-10 Conference, 893 F.Supp 1485 (W.D. Wash. 1994) aff'd., 101 F.3d 1315 (9th Cir. 1996).

Hippopress, LLC v. SMG, 837 A.2d 347 (N.H. 2003).

Howard Univ. v. NCAA, 510 F.2d 21 (D.C. Cir. 1975).

Hudgens v. NLRB, 424 U.S. 507 (1976).

Indiana High School Association v. Carlberg, No. 79S02-9605-CV-361 (Ind. December 19, 1997).

Jackson v. Metropolitan Edison Co., 419 U.S. 345 (1974).

Jones v. West Virginia State Bd. of Educ., 622 S.E.2d 289 (W.Va. 2005).

Kneeland v. NCAA and Southwest Athletic Conference, 850 F.2d 224 (1988).

Lloyd Corp. Ltd. v. Tanner, 407 U.S. 551 (1972).

Logiodice v. Trustees of Maine Central Institute, 296 F.3d 22 (1st Cir. 2002).

Louisiana High Sch. Ath. Ass'n v. St. Augustine High School, 396 F.2d 224 (5th Cir. 1968).

Long v. NFL, 870 F.Supp 101 (N.D. Pa. 1994).

Ludtke v. Kuhn, 461 F.Supp. 86 (S.D. N.Y. 1978).

Lugar v. Edmondson Oil Co., 457 U.S. 922 (1982).

Marsh v. Alabama, 326 U.S. 501 (1946).

Moreland v. West Pennsylvania Interscholastic Ath. League, 572 F.2d 121 (3rd Cir. 1978).

NCAA v. Tarkanian, 488 U.S. 179 (1988).

Oklahoma High Sch. Ass'n v. Bray, 321 F.2d 269 (10th Cir. 1963).

Perkins v. Londonderry Basketball Club, 196 F.3d 13 (1st Cir. 1999).

Pitt v. Pine Valley Golf Club, 695 F.Supp.778 (D. NJ, 1988).

Regents of the Univ. of Minnesota v. NCAA, 560 F.2d 352 (8th Cir. 1976).

Rendell-Baker v. Kohn, 457 U.S. 830 (1982).

Rottman v. Pennsylvania Ath. Ass'n, 349 F.Supp.2d 922 (W.D. Pa 2004)

San Francisco Arts & Athletics, Inc. v. USOC, 483 U.S. 522 (1987).

Shelley v. Kraemer, 334 U.S. 1 (1948).

Smith v. Allwright, 321 U.S. 649 (1944).

Stanley v. Big Eight Conference, 463 F.Supp. 920 (W.D. Mo. 1978).

Stevens v. New York Racing Ass'n, 665 F.Supp 164 (E.D.N.Y. 1987).

Terry v. Adams, 344 U.S. 883 (1953).

Weiss v. Eastern College Ath. Conference, 563 F.Supp. 192 (E.D. Pa. 1983).

Publications

Drew, J. N. (2001). The Sixth Circuit dropped the ball: An analysis of *Brentwood Academy v. Tennessee Secondary School Athletic Association* in light of the Supreme Court's recent trends in state action jurisprudence. *Brigham Young University Law Review*, 1313–1347.

Emanuel, S. (1998). *Constitutional law* (17th ed.). Frederick, MD: Aspen Publishers.

Fielder, T. E. (2002, Spring/Summer). Keep your mouth shut and listen: The NFL player's right to free expression. *University of Miami Business Law Review, 10,* 548–583.

Guggenheim, J. A. (1998). The Indian's chief problem: Chief Wahoo as state sponsored discrimination and disparaging mark. *Cleveland State University Law Review, 46,* 217–237.

Jones, M. E. (1999). *Sports law.* Upper Saddle River, NJ: Prentice Hall.

Kitchen, J. (1996). The NCAA and Due Process. *Kansas Journal of Law and Public Policy,* 5, 71–78.

Lehr, C., & Altman, S. (2001, July). Finally a resolution: High school athletic associations are state actors! *The Sports Medicine Standards and Malpractice Reporter, 13,* 39–41.

Lively, D. E., Haddon, P. A., Roberts, D. E., & Weaver, R. L. (1996). *Constitutional law: Cases, history and dialogues.* Cincinnati, OH: Anderson Publishing Co.

Pierguidi, D. J. (2000). Absent strong connections to a state government, a high school athletic association cannot be construed as a state actor. *Brentwood Academy v. Tennessee Secondary School Athletic Ass'n. Seton Hall Journal of Sport Law, 10,* 435–493.

Rotunda R., & Nowak, J. (1999). Treatise on constitutional law: Substance and procedure (3rd ed.). St. Paul, MN: West Wadsworth.

Wilde, T. Jesse. (2000). State Action. In D.J. Cotten, J.T. Wolohan and T.J. Wilde (Eds.), *Law for Recreation and Sports Managers* (2nd Ed.). Dubuque, IA: Kendall/Hunt Publishing Co.

Wong, G. M. (1988). *Essentials of amateur sports law.* Dover, MA: Auburn House Publishing Company.

7.13 Due Process

Linda L. Schoonmaker
Winthrop University

Although the framers of the U.S. Constitution did not have sport and recreation in mind when they drafted it, the guarantees and rights granted to citizens that are contained in the document have had, and will continue to have, an impact on the sport and recreation industries. As a result, sport and recreation managers must have an understanding of our constitutionally protected rights and how they impact sport and recreation programs.

Fundamental Concepts

One of the rights contained in the U.S. Constitution is that of due process. Due process, which is defined as "a course of legal proceedings according to those rules and principles which have been established by our jurisprudence for the protection and enforcement of private rights" (*Pennoyer v. Neff*, 1877), is protected by the constitutional guarantees found in both the Fifth and Fourteenth Amendments to the U.S. Constitution. Enacted in 1791, the Fifth Amendment applies to the federal government. It states, "No person shall . . . be deprived of life, liberty, or property without due process of law." The Fourteenth Amendment was enacted in 1868 and extends the applicability of the due process guarantee to the states. The Fourteenth Amendment reads " . . . nor shall any state deprive any person of life, liberty, or property without due process of law." Many state constitutions also prohibit the denial of due process. The due process guarantee applies to governmental action and not to those of private entities.

Before proceeding with a deprivation of due process claim, a plaintiff must clear two hurdles. First, the plaintiff must establish that there is state action. Second, the deprivation must infringe on a life, liberty, or property interest.

State Action

As discussed earlier, the due process guarantees found in the Fifth and Fourteenth Amendments to the U.S. Constitution apply to governmental action and not to those of private entities. Therefore, to establish any constitutional claim, including due process, the plaintiff must demonstrate that the constitutional violation is the result of action taken by a federal or state government or a representative of the government. For a more detailed review of state action, see Chapter 7.12.

Life, Liberty, or Property Interest

Because a deprivation of a life interest is never raised in the sport industry, the rest of this section examines liberty and property interests. The U.S. Supreme Court has defined **liberty interest** as follows: "without doubt, it denotes not merely freedom from bodily restraint but also . . . generally to enjoy those privileges long recognized . . . as essential to the orderly pursuit of happiness by free men" (*Meyer v. Nebraska*, 1923). With regard to due process and deprivation of a liberty interest, the Court in *Wisconsin v. Constantineau* (1971) stated, "Where a person's good name, reputation, honor, or integrity is at stake because of what the government is doing to him, notice and an opportunity to be heard are essential" (p. 437). In a later case, the Court extended the requirements that are necessary to invoke a liberty interest. In that case, the Court concluded that: ". . . this line of cases does not establish the proposition that reputation alone, apart from some more tangible interests such as employment, is either "liberty" or "property" by itself sufficient to invoke the . . . protections of the Due Process Clause" (*Paul v. Davis*, 1976). This "more tangible interests" requirement has become known as the **"stigma plus"** test.

An example of the application of this "stigma plus" test in the sport industry is found in *Stanley v. Big Eight Conference* (1978). In this case, Stanley was relieved as head football coach at Oklahoma State University because of an NCAA investigation that implicated him in NCAA rules violations. Stanley brought a due process suit claiming that the action taken would have a stigmatizing effect on his ability to pursue his livelihood as a coach. The ruling of the Court states that: ". . . the 'more tangible interest' is Stanley's employment with OSU which has recently been terminated due at least in part to the allegations contained in the report, and his professional reputation which will determine his future employment opportunities" (*Stanley v. Big Eight Conference*, 1978, p. 928).

The U.S. Supreme Court has defined a **property interest** as follows: "To have a property interest in a benefit, a person clearly must have more than an abstract need or desire for it. He must have more than a unilateral expectation of it. He must, instead, have a legitimate claim of entitlement" (*Board of Regents v. Roth*, 1972, p. 577).

In the collegiate setting, plaintiffs have asserted that they either have a property right because he/she has a scholarship or has a property right in a future professional career. In *Hall v. University of Minnesota* (1982), the court ruled that Hall did have a protected property right based on his future opportunity to play professional basketball. In another example, *Gulf South Conference v. Boyd* (1979), the court found that there was a property right of present economic value in a college athletic scholarship.

Although the athlete who possesses a scholarship and/or a legitimate professional career opportunity may have a protected property interest, the same cannot be said for an athlete who has neither, for the courts generally have not recognized a right to participate in intercollegiate athletics (*Colorado Seminary v. NCAA*, 1978).

In the interscholastic setting, the "entitlement" most often asserted in the sport setting is that of the right to participate in athletics. This right to participate arises from the threshold issue of whether there is a right to an education. The Supreme Court has specifically stated that education is not among the rights afforded explicit or implicit protection in the Constitution (*San Antonio Independent School District v. Rodriguez*, 1972). Even though the right to an education is not grounded in the U.S. Constitution, a state may grant a right to an education either explicitly and implicitly by requiring school attendance (*Goss v. Lopez*, 1975). After determining that the plaintiff has a right to an education based on mandatory attendance, the determination must be made of whether or not that right includes the right to participate in interscholastic athletics.

Usually the courts have not found a right to participate in interscholastic athletics, but rather find that participation is a privilege. Over time, the courts, both at the federal and state levels, have generally been consistent in this view (*Morrison, et al. v. Roberts*, 1938; *State of Indiana v. Lawrence Circuit Court*, 1959; *Taylor v. Alabama High School Athletic Ass'n*, 1972; *Niles v. University Interscholastic League*, 1983; *Zehner v. Central Berkshire Regional School District*, 1996; *Wooten v. Pleasant Hope R-VI School District and Stout*, 2000.)

Although the overwhelming majority of courts have not found a right to participate in interscholastic athletics, interestingly at least two courts have found a right to participate in interscholastic athletics (*Moran v. School District #7, Yellowstone County*, 1972; *Duffley v. New Hampshire Interscholastic Athletic Association*, 1982). And at least one court has ruled that although there is no right to participate in interscholastic athletics, a student's interest in participating is not entirely unprotected (*Stone v. Kansas State High School Activities Association*, 1988). The court's rationale was that participation is part of the total educational experience provided by schools.

Due Process Analysis

After a plaintiff has cleared the previously discussed hurdles, he/she can then proceed with demonstrating to the court how their due process rights have been violated. Due process of law is composed of two areas of inquiry. The first is **substantive due process**, which requires the regulation or rule to be fair and reasonable in content as well as application. The essence of substantive due process is protection from arbitrary and capricious actions. The inquiry in substantive due process asks two questions: (1) Does the regulation or rule have a proper purpose? if so, (2) Does the regulation or rule clearly relate to the accomplishment of that purpose?

Over time, the courts have adopted general principles that serve to guide them in their decisions regarding rules and regulations of voluntary associations. As a general rule, courts will not interfere with the internal affairs of voluntary associations. In the absence of mistake, fraud, collusion, or arbitrariness, the decisions of the governing body of an association will be accepted as conclusive. Voluntary associations may adopt reasonable bylaws and rules that will be deemed valid and binding on the members of the association unless the bylaw or rule violates some law or public policy. It is not the responsibility of the courts to inquire into the expediency, practicability, or wisdom of the bylaws and regulations of voluntary associations. These general principles are equally applicable to cases involving athletic governing bodies (*Kentucky High School Athletic Association v. Hopkins County Board of Education*, 1977).

The rationale that athletic governing bodies state for their rules and regulations is that it is their responsibility to create and administer rules and regulations that maintain a level playing field for all participants. Examples of courts upholding the rules and regulations of athletic governing bodies include *Berschback v. Grosse Pointe Public School District and Ternan v. Michigan High School Athletic Association, Inc.*, 1986; *Palmer v. Merluzzi*, 1989; and *Spring Branch Independent School District, et al. v. Stamos*, 1985. In each of these cases, the court deemed the rule or regulation that was at issue to be rationally related to its stated purpose. In the following cases, the courts found that the actions of the athletic governing body were unreasonable, capricious, and arbitrary: *Diaz v. Board of Education of the City of New York*, 1994; *Manico v. South Colonie Central School District*, 1992; and *Tiffany v. Arizona Interscholastic Association, Inc.*, 1986.

The second area in the due process inquiry involves **procedural due process**, which addresses the methods used to enforce the regulation or rule. Procedural due process examines the decision-making process that is followed to determine whether the regulation or rule has been violated and what sanction, if any, will be imposed. The goal of procedural due process is to ensure fair treatment.

After it has been determined that procedural due process is due to the plaintiff, the question becomes, What procedures should be followed to ensure fair treatment? Over time, the U.S. Supreme Court has provided guidance in answering that question. "Due process is flexible and calls for such procedural protections as the particular situation demands" (*Morrissey v. Brewer*, 1972, p. 481). "Parties whose rights are to be affected are entitled to be heard; and in order that they may enjoy that right they must be notified" (*Baldwin v. Hale*, 1863, 223, 233). The greater the deprivation, the greater procedural due process owed to the plaintiff (*Goldberg v. Kelly*, 1970). Finally, the Court developed a balancing test to be used to determine the extent to procedural due process (*Mathews v. Eldridge*, 1976). In that case the Court stated, "First, the private interest that will be affected by the official action; second, the risk of an erroneous deprivation of such interest through the procedures used, and the probable value, if any, of additional or substitute procedural safeguards; and finally, the Government's interest, including the function involved and the fiscal and administrative burdens that the additional or substitute procedural requirement would entail" (*Mathews v. Eldridge*, 1976, p. 335).

As these procedural due process requirements apply to an educational setting, we look to the opinion of the U.S. Supreme Court in *Goss v. Lopez*, (1975). In *Goss*, a number of students in schools in the Columbus, Ohio, school district were suspended from school for ten days for disruptive behavior. The students brought suit claiming their due process rights had been violated. The Court ruled that for suspensions of ten days or less the students "must be given *some* kind of notice and afforded *some* kind of hearing" (*Goss v. Lopez*, 1975, p. 579). The Court further outlined the procedures that needed to be followed to meet the standard they had established. Specifically, the student must be given oral and written notice of the charges against him and, if he denies them, an explanation of the evidence the authorities have and an opportunity to present his side of the story. Also, there be no delay between the time of the notice and the time of the hearing (*Goss v. Lopez*, 1975, pp. 581–582).

We can see the application of the standards established in *Goss* in two sport cases, *Pegram v. Nelson* (1979) and *Palmer v. Merluzzi* (1989). In both the cases, student–athletes were suspended from school for ten days and from athletics for four months and sixty days, respectively. In both cases, the student–athletes were given notice and a hearing that afforded them the opportunity to refute the allegations against them. The courts in both cases ruled that the procedures that were followed afforded the student–athletes all the procedural due process they were owed (*Pegram v. Nelson*, 1979, pp. 1139–1141; *Palmer v. Merluzzi*, 1989, pp. 95–96).

Four other sport cases provide the sport and recreation manager with further guidance in the development of due process procedures. In the first case, *Kelley v. Metropolitan County Board of Education of Nashville* (1968), the plaintiff high school student–athlete was suspended from athletic competition by the Board of Education without being formally charged with a rule violation. The court held that due process requires published standards, formal charges, notice, and a hearing and granted an injunction that prevented the enforcement of the suspension (*Kelley v. Metropolitan County Board of Education of Nashville*, 1968, pp. 492, 498–499).

In the second case, *Behagen v. Intercollegiate Conference of Faculty Representatives* (1972), two student–athletes were suspended for fighting with their opponents during a collegiate basketball game. They brought suit claiming they were denied due process. The court held that their due process rights had been violated. In its opinion, the court outlined the procedures that needed to be followed to meet rudimentary requirements of due process. The procedures are as follows: (1) written notice of the time and place of the hearing at least two days in advance; (2) notice of the specific charges; (3) a hearing in which the athletic director hears both sides of the story; the hearing should include the presentation of direct testimony in the form of statements by each of those directly involved in relating their versions of the incident; (4) a list of witnesses to the plaintiff prior to the hearing; (5) a written report of the findings of fact and the basis for punishment; (6) tape recordings of the proceedings; and (7) an appeals procedure (*Behagen v. Intercollegiate Conference of Faculty Representatives*, 1972, p. 608).

The third case is *Butler v. Oak Creek-Franklin School District* (2001). In this case, the plaintiff was given a twelve-month suspension for violation of the Athletic Code. The court detailed the due process that was owed to the plaintiff, specifically, (1) predeprivation process, (2) notice, (3) need for a hearing, and (4) the right to an impartial decision maker (*Butler v. Oak Creek-Franklin School District*, 2001, pp. 1111–1116).

The fourth case, *Stanley*, was discussed earlier. Stanley was relieved as head football coach at Oklahoma State University because of an NCAA investigation that implicated him in NCAA rules violation, and Stanley filed suit claiming his due process rights had been violated. In its opinion, the Court provided guidance as to steps that could be followed to meet the demands of due process. Those steps are (1) notice of the infractions with which plaintiff is charged; (2) a list of witnesses the defendants will utilize to support each charge could be provided to the plaintiff; (3) plaintiff could report in writing each charge he specifically denies; (4) a list of witnesses the plaintiff wishes to have produced for confrontation and cross-examination could be provided to the defendant; and (5) the plaintiff could furnish the names of the witnesses he will rely on in his defense of each charge (*Stanley v. Big Eight Conference*, 1978).

The guarantee of due process protections for athletes who participate in international competitions are contained in the constitutions and bylaws of the International Olympic Committee (IOC), its member National Olympic Committees (NOCs), International Sport Federations (IFs), and National Sport Federations (NFs). In 1983, the IOC established the Court of Sport Arbitration (CAS; Netzle, 1992). The CAS operated as an arm of the IOC until 1994, when it was restructured as an independent agency and renamed the International Court for the Arbitration of Sport (ICAS). The restructuring was deemed necessary following criticism that the CAS was too closely tied to the IOC. Beginning with the 1996 Summer Olympics in Atlanta, the IOC and its member NOCs, IFs, and NFs all agreed to submit disputes to mandatory and binding arbitration conducted by the ICAS. In addition, there is a mandatory and binding arbitration clause in the Olympic entry form that all athletes, coaches, and officials must sign as a condition of their Olympic participation (Bitting, 1998; Raber, 1998; Rueben, 1996). The number of cases brought before the ICAS has increased since the Atlanta Games as athletes and sport governing bodies become more aware of the process of arbitration (Grenig, 2001; McLaren, 2001a, 2001b; Nafziger, 2001).

Significant Case

◇◇◇

In this case, the plaintiff tried to demonstrate to the court that her reputation as an athlete was a constitutionally protected right and that as a result she should be accorded due process rights. In addressing this question, the court examined the plaintiff's potential financial opportunities and the due process she might be owed.

NATIONAL COLLEGIATE ATHLETIC ASSOCIATION V. YEO
Supreme Court of Texas
171 S.W.3d 863 (2005)

When Coach Michael Walker recruited Joscelin Yeo, a high school student in the Republic of Singapore, to enroll at the University of California at Berkeley, she had already achieved fame in her country as a swimmer. At Berkeley, she won numerous All-American awards and was a member of a world-record-setting relay team in 1999.

Before the 200-2001 school year, Walker left Berkeley for the University of Texas at Austin. He was helping coach the Singapore Olympic team, of which Yeo was a member, and she went with him to UT-Austin. Berkeley and UT-Austin are both members of the National Collegiate Athletic Association ("NCAA"), which prescribes rules for determining the eligibility of student athletes to engage in competition. A member that violates these rules is subject to sanctions. NCAA rules generally prohibit a student who transfer from one four-year member institution to another from participating in intercollegiate athletic competitions for one full academic year, but this restriction may be waived under certain circumstances if the former institution does not object. Berkeley refused to waive the restriction, and thus Yeo was ineligible to compete at UT-Austin for an academic year.

As permitted by NCAA rules, Yeo did not enroll in classes for the fall semester of 2000 in order to compete in the Olympics. In compliance with the one-year restriction, she did not participate in intercollegiate events during the semester or the spring semester, when she was enrolled in classes. UT-Austin mistakenly believed that Yeo's first semester had counted toward satisfying the restriction and that she was free to engage in competition beginning the fall semester of 2001. After Yeo competed in four events, Berkeley complained to the NCAA, UT-Austin confessed its error and agreed that Yeo would sit out the reminder of the semester, but the NCAA required that she not participate in the first four events the following spring, to match the four events in which she had been disqualified. Yeo did not know of

UT-Austin's discussions with the NCAA and simply did as UT-Austin told her.

UT-Austin then added three swimming events at the beginning of its spring semester schedule. After Yeo had sat out those events and a fourth one, UT-Austin allowed her to rejoin the swim team, but Berkeley again complained, arguing that the added events could not be used to satisfy the one-year restriction. NCAA staff agreed and on March 6 issued a decision that Yeo not participate in the next three regularly scheduled events, including the 2002 NCAA women's swimming and diving championship on March 22. UT-Austin immediately appealed the staff decision to the NCAA Student-Athlete Reinstatement Committee ("the SARC"), and a telephonic hearing was scheduled for the next day. For the first time, UT-Austin told Yeo of the problem and advised her simply to plea for sympathy. She did, but at the conclusion of the hearing, the SARC upheld the staff decision.

At UT-Austin's suggestion, Yeo then obtained legal counsel, who persuaded Berkeley on March 15 to waive Yeo's one-year restriction, something it had refused to do before. Counsel mover SARC to reconsider, especially in light of this development, but it refused.

On March 20, Yeo sued UT-Austin and its vice president for institutional relations and legal affairs, Patricia Ohlendorf, to enjoin them from disqualifying her from competing in the championship meet two days later and for a declaration that UT-Austin had denied her procedural due process as guaranteed by the Texas Constitution. That same day, the trial court issued a temporary restraining order granting Yeo the injunctive relief requested. On March 21, the NCAA intervened in the action, but Yeo moved to strike the intervention, and after a hearing later that day, the trial court granted Yeo's motion. The next morning, the NCAA sought mandamus relief from the court of appeals, and UT-Austin appealed from the temporary restraining order. That afternoon, the court of appeals denied the petition for mandamus and dismissed the interlocutory appeal for want of jurisdiction. Yeo competed in the championship meet.

In November 2002, after a trial to the bench, the trial court rendered judgment for Yeo, declaring that UT-Austin had denied Yeo procedural due process guaranteed by the Texas Constitution, thereby depriving her of protected liberty and property interests. The court permanently enjoined UT-Austin from declaring Yeo ineligible in the future without affording her due process and from punishing her for participating in past competitions, including the 2002 women's championship. The trial court also awarded Yeo $164,755.50 in attorney fees through an appeal to this Court.

The NCAA appealed from the order striking its intervention, and UT-Austin appealed from the judgment. The court of appeals affirmed. We granted the NCAA's and UT-Austin's petition's for review.

Since the championship meet in March, 2002, Yeo has, of course, moved on. When the briefs were filed in this case, we were told that Yeo had graduated from UT-Austin, received a Rhodes Scholarship, and ended her college swimming career. But none of the parties argues that the case has become moot, because the injunction prevents the NCAA from imposing retroactive sanctions under its "Restitution Rule". We agree that the case is not moot.

We first consider whether Yeo has an interest protected by due process of law under article I, section 19 of the Texas Constitution. In doing so, we look as usual to cases construing the federal constitutional guarantee of due process as persuasive authority. The parties have not identified any difference between the state and federal guarantees material to the issues in this case.

Yeo does not challenge our holding in *Stamos* that a student has no interest in participating in extracurricular activities that is protected by the Texas Constitution's guarantee of due process of law. Nor does she dispute that under NCAA rules, she was ineligible to participate in the 2002 women's swimming and diving championship. Yeo argues that she was entitled to notice and a meaningful hearing before NCAA rules were applied to her because of her unique reputation and earning potential. Had she been disqualified from competing in the championship meet, she contends, people would have suspected that it was her own misconduct and not for UT-Austin's mistakes in attempting to comply with NCAA rules. Yeo acknowledges that the United States Supreme Court has held that reputation alone is not a protected liberty or property interest. But it is the degree of her interests, Yeo contends, and not merely their character, that bring them within constitutional protection. A student-athlete with a lesser reputation or less certain of her earning potential, she contends, would not have the same rights. The court of appeals agreed:

In connection with the permanent injunction, the trial court made several material findings of material fact that are essentially unchallenged: (1) Yeo had already established a world-class reputation and her "good name, outstanding reputation, high standing in her community, her unblemished integrity and honor are particularly important in the Republic of Singapore and in light of her cultural background"; (2) if NCAA rules did not prohibit athletes from accepting professional compensation while competing in NCAA sanctioned events, Yeo "would be immediately eligible to capitalize on her public persona by entering into lucrative endorsement and marketing opportunities as well as being eligible for prize winnings due to her performance as a member of Singapore's national team"; and (3) "UT-Austin represented to [Yeo] at the time she transferred from [Cal-Berkeley] to become a student-athlete at UT-Austin that UT-Austin would not jeopardize or compromise [Yeo's] eligibility to compete on behalf of UT-Austin in NCAA competition."

These findings of fact support Yeo's theory that her athletic reputation, which was established even *before* she began attending Cal-Berkley and competing under NCAA regulations, constitutes a protected interest for purposes of due course of law. Yeo had competed in two Olympic games before attending college and had been named sportswoman of the year and Olympic flag-bearer for her native country, Singapore. At both the temporary restraining order and permanent injunction hearings, Yeo represented that it was this continuing interest in her athletic and professional reputation that UT-Austin had damaged by its actions.

Here, Yeo presented testimony from multiple witnesses indicating that she had established a reputation as a world-class athlete in her home country of Singapore *separate and apart from her intercollegiate swimming career*. As a result, much of her reputation had been build outside of the United States and the structure of NCAA intercollegiate athletics. We cannot say that the trial court erred in holding that Yeo had a protected interest under these facts.

UT-Austin, joined by various *amici curiae*, contends that an affirmance in this case will create a protected interest in every intercollegiate student-athlete to participate in athletic events. We reject this argument and note that we reach this decision because of the unique fact pattern with which we are presented. Based upon the largely undisputed findings of fact, Yeo had already established a protected interest in her reputation as an athlete long before she came to this country to swim competitively as a student-athlete under NCAA rules. Our holding that Yeo, under these facts, has a protected interest should not be read as extending that same protection to every other intercollegiate athlete. The determination of whether a student-athlete has a protected interest is necessarily fact-specific, depending on that athlete's specific situation and reputation. Each such case must be decided on its own merits, in light of the financial realities of contemporary athletic competition. We hold that Yeo's established liberty interest in her reputation as an athlete is entitled to due course of law protection and we affirm the trial court's decision in that regard.

We reject Yeo's argument and the court of appeals' holding. The United States Supreme Court has stated, and we agree, that whether an interest is protected by due process depends on its *weight* but on its *nature*. Yeo does not take issue with this principle but argues in effect that the weight of an interest can determine its nature. A stellar reputation like hers, Yeo contends and the court of appeals concluded, is categorically different from a more modest reputation. We disagree. The loss of either may be, to its owner, substantial. The court of appeals held that whether a reputation is constitutionally protected must be decided case by case, but it did not suggest a measure for distinguishing one case from another, and neither does Yeo. We see none, which convinces us that the *nature* of one's interest in a good reputation is the same no matter how good the reputation is.

Yeo's claimed interest in future financial opportunities is too speculative for due process protection. There must be an actual legal entitlement. While student-athletes remain amateurs, their future financial opportunities remain expectations.

Yeo argues that her reputation and future financial interests are entitled to constitutional protection under our decision in *University of Texas Medical School v. Than*. There we held that a medical student charged with academic dishonesty had a protected liberty interest in a graduate education. But since *Than* we have refused to accord a student's interest in athletics in the same protection. We decline to equate an interest in intercollegiate athletics with an interest in graduate education.

Accordingly, we hold that Yeo has asserted no interests protected by article I, section 19 of the Texas Constitution. The case must therefore be dismissed. While we need not reach the NCAA's arguments that it should have been permitted to intervene, we expressly disapprove the court of appeals' conclusions that the NCAA's interests were not sufficiently implicated to warrant intervention, and that intervention would have unduly complicated the case.

We have twice reminded the lower courts that "judicial intervention in [student athletic disputes] often does more harm than good." As the Fifth Circuit has said, judges are not "super referees". Along the same vein, the United States Supreme Court has observed: "Courts do not and cannot intervene in the resolution of conflicts which arise in the daily operation of school systems and which do not directly and sharply implicate basic constitutional values." We reiterate this counsel to the trial courts and courts of appeals.

The judgment of the court of appeals is reversed, and judgment is rendered that Yeo take nothing.

◇◇◇ **OTHER RELEVANT SIGNIFICANT CASES**

Chapter 7.12 *State Action*

Chapter 7.21 *Voluntary Associations and Eligibility Issues*

Recent Trends

Two of the most debated issues in athletics involve the NCAA and what due process protections are afforded to student–athletes. For example, because the student–athletes are not members of the NCAA, if a student is found in violation of NCAA rules, the student does not have the right to address the issue directly with the NCAA; the member school must act on his or her behalf. Another issue of concern is the impact of NCAA sanctions on the institution's athletics program and the punishment of current student–athletes who had no part in the wrongdoing. In both cases it has been argued that the NCAA does not afford student–athletes the due process they are owed (Keegan, 2005; Maskevich, 2005).

References

Cases

Baldwin v. Hale, 68 U.S. 223 (1863).

Behagen v. Intercollegiate Conference of Faculty Representatives, 346 F. Supp. 602 (D. Minn. 1972).

Berschback v. Grosse Pointe Public School District and Ternan v. Michigan High School Athletic Association, Inc., 397 N.W.2d 234 (Mich. App. 1986).

Board of Regents v. Roth, 408 U.S. 564 (1972).

Butler v. Oak Creek-Franklin School District, 172 F. Supp. 2d 1102 (E.D. Wis. 2001).

Colorado Seminary v. NCAA, 417 F. Supp. 885 (D. Colo. 1976), *aff'd*, 570 F.2d 320 (10th Cir. 1978).

Diaz v. Board of Education of the City of New York, 618 N.Y.S.2d 984 (Sup. 1994).

Duffley v. New Hampshire Interscholastic Athletic Association, 446 A.2d 462 (Sup. Ct. N.H. 1982).

Goldberg v. Kelly, 397 U.S. 266 (1970).

Goss v. Lopez, 419 U.S. 565 (1975).

Gulf South Conference v. Boyd, 369 So. 553 (Sup. Ct. Ala. 1979).

Hall v. University of Minnesota, 530 F. Supp. 104 (D. Minn. 1982).

Kelley v. Metropolitan County Board of Education of Nashville, 293 F. Supp. 485 (M.D. Tenn. 1968).

Kentucky High School Athletic Association v. Hopkins County Board of Education, 552 S.W.2d 685 (Ky. App. 1977).

Manico v. South Colonie Central School District, 584 N.Y.S.2d 519 (Sup. 1992).

Mathews v. Eldridge, 424 U.S. 319 (1976).

Meyer v. Nebraska, 262 U.S. 390 (1923).

Moran v. School District #7, Yellowstone County, 350 F. Supp. 1180 (D. Mont. 1972).

Morrison, et al. v. Roberts, 183 Okl. 359, 82 P.2d 1023 (Sup. Ct. Okl. 1938).

Morrissey v. Brewer, 408 U.S. 471 (1972).

National Collegiate Athletic Association v. Yeo, 114 S.W. 3d 584, rev'd 171 S.W. 3d 863 (Tex. 2003).

Niles v. University Interscholastic League, 715 F.2d 1027 (5th Cir. 1983).

Palmer v. Merluzzi, 868 F.2d 90 (3rd Cir. 1989).

Paul v. Davis, 424 U.S. 693 (1976).

Pegram v. Nelson, 469 F. Supp. 1134 (M.D. N.C. 1979).

Pennoyer v. Neff, 95 U.S. 714 (1877).

San Antonio Independent School District v. Rodriguez, 411 U.S. 1 (1972).

Spring Branch Independent School District, et al. v. Stamos, 695 S.W.2d 556 (Tex. 1985).

Stanley v. Big Eight Conference, 463 F. Supp. 920 (W.D. MO. 1978).

State of Indiana v. Lawrence Circuit Court, 162 N.E.2d 250 (Sup.Ct. Ind. 1959).

Stone v. Kansas State High School Activities Association, 761 P.2d 1255 (Kan. App. 1988).

Taylor v. Alabama High School Athletic Association, 336 F. Supp. 54 (M.D. Ala. 1972).

Tiffany v. Arizona Interscholastic Association, Inc., 726 P.2d 231 (Ariz. App. 1986).

Wisconsin v. Constantineau, 400 U.S. 433 (1971).

Wooten v. Pleasant Hope R-VI School District and Stout, 139 F.Supp. 835 (W.D. Mo. 2000).

Zehner v. Central Berkshire Regional School District, 921 F. Supp. 850 (D. Mass. 1996).

Publications

Bitting, M. R. (1998). Comments: Mandatory, binding arbitration for Olympics athletes: Is the process better or worse for "job security?" *Florida State University Law Review, 25*, 655.

Due process law in Florida struck down. (1994, November 21). *NCAA News*, pp. 1, 20.

Grenig, J. E. (2001). Symposium: Arbitration of Olympic eligibility disputes: Fair play and the right to be heard. *Marquette Sports Law Review, 12*, 261.

Keegan, M. M. (2005). Due Process and the NCAA: Are innocent student-athletes afforded adequate protection from improper sanctions? A call for change in the NCAA enforcement procedures. *Northern Illinois Law Review, 25*, 297.

Maskevich, K. E. (2005). Getting due process into the game: A look at the NCAA's failure to provide member institutions with due process and the effect on student-athletes. *Seton Hall Journal of Sports Law, 15*, 299.

McLaren, R. H. (2001a). Article and Speech: The Court of Arbitration for Sport: An independent arena for the world's sports disputes. *Valparaiso University Law Review, 35*, 379.

McLaren, R. H. (2201b). International sports law perspective: Introducing the Court of Arbitration for Sport: The Ad Hoc Division at the Olympic Games. *Marquette Sports Law Review, 12*, 515.

Nafziger, J. A. R. (2001). Article and Speech: Arbitration of rights and obligations in the international sports arena. *Valparaiso University Law Review, 35*, 357.

Netzle, S. (1992). The Court of Arbitration for Sport: An alternative for dispute resolution in U.S. sports. *The Entertainment and Sports Lawyer, 10*, 1–4, 25–28.

Raber, N. K. (1998). Article: Dispute resolution in Olympic sport: The Court of Arbitration for Sport. *Seton Hall J. Sports L., 8*, 75.

Rueben, R. (1996). And the winner is . . . Arbitrations to resolve disputes as they arise at Olympics. *ABA Journal*, 20.

7.14 Equal Protection

Cathryn L. Claussen
Washington State University

"No state shall . . . deny to any person within its jurisdiction the equal protection of the laws." With this language, the Equal Protection Clause of the Fourteenth Amendment to the United States Constitution provides a guarantee that laws, rules, and regulations will be applied in a fair and nondiscriminatory fashion. Although this clause is aimed at the states, its content is considered applicable to the federal government as well under the Due Process Clause of the Fifth Amendment. Therefore, the Equal Protection Clause serves to place a limit on the government at all levels. The essence of equal protection is that, absent a constitutionally permissible reason for different treatment, similarly situated people should receive similar treatment by the law. Thus, the Equal Protection Clause provides individuals with a means of challenging the constitutionality of a rule or law that has deprived them of a fundamental right or has singled them out for different treatment based on their membership in a prescribed category of people.

Originally, the Fourteenth Amendment, along with the Thirteenth and Fifteenth Amendments, was aimed at eliminating the vestiges of African-American slavery in the aftermath of the Civil War. Over the intervening years, numerous court decisions have applied the Equal Protection Clause to laws and rules that have classified people based on characteristics other than race. In the context of sport, this means that public institutions may not, without good reason, discriminate in the provision of services, participation opportunities, or employment.

Fundamental Concepts

State Action

To find a violation of the Equal Protection Clause requires a finding of state action. The concept of state action is discussed in more detail in Chapter 7.12, *State Action*. It is enough to reiterate here that the government must have been sufficiently involved with the deprivation of an individual's rights to warrant invoking the protection of the Constitution. Public schools and universities, as well as state or local departments of recreation, are considered branches of the government; hence, they are state actors for purposes of equal protection analysis. Courts have also, upon occasion, declared that private entities sufficiently intertwined with publicly owned facilities have engaged in state action.

Purposeful Discrimination

Equal Protection Clause analysis requires a finding that the government engaged in purposeful, rather than unintentional, discrimination. By itself, an unintended discriminatory effect is insufficient grounds for an equal protection violation.

Standards of Review

Deprivation of Fundamental Right—Strict Scrutiny

There are two possible bases on which to challenge a law on equal protection grounds. The first is to allege selective deprivation of a right that is considered to be fundamental in our society, such as the right to vote or the right to travel freely among the different states. A law that deprived people of such a fundamental right would receive heightened scrutiny by the courts because of the serious nature of the deprivation. Because sport participation has commonly been ruled to be a privilege rather than a right, this basis for a lawsuit has limited relevance in the sport management context.

Classification into Group to Receive Different Treatment

The second basis for an equal protection challenge is to claim that the particular law unfairly discriminates by classifying people into a group singled out for different treatment. The Supreme Court has, over the years, established a three-tiered standard of review for this type of equal protection claim. The Court has ruled that certain classifications are more suspicious than others and therefore trigger different levels of judicial review. Thus, this hierarchically arranged set of tests is based on the type of classification found in the law at issue. Laws containing suspect classifications (race, ethnicity, national origin, alienage) will be subjected to strict scrutiny, the highest level of review. Classifications based on gender or legitimacy of birth are considered quasi-suspect classifications, and laws containing these will receive intermediate level scrutiny. The lowest level of scrutiny, called rational basis review, is used to judge all group classifications other than those established by the Court as suspect or quasi-suspect.

Strict Scrutiny. Laws that include classifications based on race, ethnicity, national origin, or alienage are considered suspect classifications because there is virtually never any constitutionally permissible justification for segregating people on such bases. Suspect classifications are considered unjustifiable for three primary reasons. The first is that people have historically been subjected to discrimination on the basis of race or national origin, so to continue to classify people on such bases would tend to make one suspect the perpetuation of prejudice. The second reason is that groups defined by race or national origin have suffered from political powerlessness because they are discrete and insular minority groups. In other words, they have not traditionally been part of the mainstream culture, have tended to remain to themselves, and so have not been able to fend for themselves politically and effect change for their benefit. Finally, the third reason race and national origin are considered suspect classifications is that they are based on immutable characteristics, that is, traits that are unchangeable. It is deemed fundamentally unfair to discriminate against individuals based on these characteristics that cannot be altered.

The courts will be suspicious of any law that makes such a suspect classification and will give it strict, or highest level, scrutiny. The test for a law under strict scrutiny is whether that law is *necessary* to achieve a *compelling* governmental interest. In other words, the government must have an essential objective in mind, and the law it passed must be the only way to accomplish that objective. If there is a less discriminatory means to achieve a worthy end, it must be used instead of the challenged law. Almost every law containing a suspect classification fails the test of strict scrutiny and is ruled unconstitutional.

In *St. Augustine High School v. Louisiana High School Athletic Association* (1968), the state high school athletic association had a membership admission rule that allowed the existing members to vote to deny membership to an all-black high school that otherwise met all the conditions for membership. The court was suspicious of this voting requirement because it had been first instituted at the annual meeting in which for the first time in the history of the association an all-black school was to be considered for membership. The court believed that the purpose of this voting provision was to enable the association to deny membership without having to justify its action. Based on this conclusion, the court found sufficient evidence that membership was denied on the basis of race and concluded that because there was no compelling reason to distinguish between white and black schools, the rule violated the Equal Protection Clause.

Intermediate Scrutiny. In *Craig v. Boren* (1976), decided one year after *Indiana High School Athletic Association v. Raike,* the Supreme Court refined the middle tier of equal protection review and has since applied it to the quasi-suspect classifications of gender and legitimacy of birth. These are considered somewhat suspect because of their similarity to suspect classifications like race in that they are based on immutable characteristics that have often in the past been used as reasons for discrimination. Yet, they are only quasi-suspect because, in the estimation of the Court, it is justifiable to differentiate on the basis of sex more frequently than on the basis of race, for example. In other words, sex differences may make a difference in ability to perform certain tasks, whereas racial differences rarely make a legitimate difference.

Nevertheless, such instances are uncommon, and the courts will be fairly suspicious of laws that include quasi-suspect classifications and will subject them to intermediate scrutiny. The test under intermediate scrutiny is whether the challenged law is *substantially related* to an *important* governmental interest. Although this language appears synonymous with the strict scrutiny test, it is meant to be a slightly less rigorous examination of the law at issue. Still, most laws containing quasi-suspect classifications are also struck down as unconstitutional violations of equal protection.

In *Ludtke v. Kuhn* (1978), a female sports reporter was denied access to the locker room of the New York Yankees solely because of her sex. State action existed because the stadium was owned by the city and supported by public funds, and the profitability of the city's lease depended in part on publicity about the team. The defendants argued that there were three important interests at stake in excluding female reporters: (1) protecting the privacy of the players, (2) preserving baseball's status as a family sport, and (3) adhering to traditional standards of decency and propriety. The court found only the first to be an important interest meriting consideration under intermediate scrutiny. However, totally excluding female reporters from the locker room was not substantially related to achieving that important interest, because the court was able to identify less discriminatory means to accomplishing the goal of protecting player privacy (such as the use of backdrops or the wearing of towels). Therefore, the court held that the exclusion policy violated the Equal Protection Clause.

In *Haffer v. Temple University* (1987), Temple was spending far less money in support of its women's athletics programs than its men's programs. The university argued that it was justified in spending more on men's sports because of their greater potential for garnering publicity and generating revenue. The court agreed that the university had important interests in using intercollegiate athletics to secure favorable publicity and revenue, but questioned whether the disparity in expenditures was substantially related to accomplishing those goals. The plaintiffs had produced evidence that certain women's teams might generate interest and revenue if they received greater expenditures for marketing and promotion, so spending less on the women's programs was not a well-tailored attempt to accomplish the university's goals.

Rational Basis Review. The lowest level of equal protection scrutiny is applied to all group classifications other than those established by the Supreme Court as suspect or quasi-suspect. These are classifications that have not historically been sufficiently associated with invidious discrimination so as to raise the suspicion of the Court. The test for a law under rational basis review is whether that law is *reasonably related* to a *legitimate* governmental interest. As long as the government can articulate an arguably legitimate goal and appears to have a rational basis for enacting the law at issue in an attempt to realize that goal, the law will be upheld. Nearly all classifications receiving rational basis review are found to be constitutional under the Equal Protection Clause. In *Schaill by Kross v. Tippecanoe County School Corp.* (1988), the school district had a rule that singled out student–athletes from the rest of the student body for drug testing. Because the category of student–athletes is not a suspect or quasi-suspect classification, the drug-testing policy received rational basis review. In the view of the court, the school district had a legitimate interest in maintaining a drug-free environment for athletics based on concern for the health and safety of student–athletes. The court concluded that the drug-testing program was a reasonable means of attaining that goal, given the heightened health and safety concerns associated with the physical and mental intensity of athletics participation compared to other school activities. Thus, the court held that the drug-testing rule did not violate equal protection.

Under- and Overinclusiveness

Sometimes courts will invalidate a law because, in its application, it is either underinclusive or overinclusive, or both at the same time. If the law is not well tailored to accomplishing its purpose, it may sweep with too wide a net and affect too broad a spectrum of people, with the result that it is overinclusive. Or, it may not sweep wide enough to accomplish its purpose and affect the lives of too narrow a range of people, with the result that it is underinclusive. Or, finally, it may do both at the same time. Affecting too many people unnecessarily or affecting too few exclusively are both unfair applications of a law that result in unequal protection. This is because either similarly situated people are being treated dissimilarly, or dissimilarly situated people are being treated alike.

In *Indiana High School Athletic Association v. Raike* (1975), the state association had a rule prohibiting married high school students from participating in interscholastic athletics. Prior to the mid-1970s, the usual reason that high-school-age students got married was because they had engaged in premarital sex and the girl had become pregnant. The association's purpose for having the rule was to encourage students to avoid such problems by depriving them of the opportunity to participate in athletics if they did have to get married. The rule was held to violate equal protection because it was both overinclusive and underinclusive. The court, using intermediate scrutiny because the rule burdened the near-fundamental right of marriage, found that the rule was not narrowly tailored to achieve the association's important purpose of preserving a wholesome atmosphere in athletics. It was overinclusive because it excluded all married students, even those who might have been of high moral character. It was simultaneously underinclusive because it only excluded married students and overlooked those unmarried students who might have engaged in premarital sex. Over- or underinclusiveness, and especially both together, were evidence of the lack of precision required for the rule to be substantially related to the government's important purpose of preserving wholesomeness. Hence, the court decided that the rule violated equal protection.

Significant Case

—◇◇—

Although the following case refers to the legality of an outdated conduct rule (prohibiting married high school students from participating in athletics), it includes one of the clearest available discussions of the three-tiered standard of review used in deciding Equal Protection Clause cases. Additionally, it provides a good illustration of a rule that was held to be simultaneously under- and overinclusive.

INDIANA HIGH SCHOOL ATHLETIC ASSOCIATION V. RAIKE

Court of Appeals of Indiana
329 N.E.2d 66 (1975)

Opinion:

Facts

The essential facts most favorable to the trial court's judgment are:

On November 27, 1971, Raike was a senior in good standing enrolled in the Rushville High School in Rushville, Indiana. On that date, Raike, being seventeen years of age, married a sixteen-year-old Rush County female and approximately two weeks later, a child was born to Mrs. Raike. The trial court specifically found that this marriage "conformed exactly to the statutory mandate of Burns Ind. Stat. Ann. @ 44-101 (IC 1971, 31-1-1-1)" [now 31-1-1-1, et seq.].

Prior to this marital union Raike actively participated in Rushville's athletic program, including football, wrestling and baseball.

Being aware of certain rules adopted by IHSAA and Rushville prohibiting married students from participating in athletics, Raike sought unsuccessfully prior to his marriage to avoid operation of these rules.

He then filed, on December 16, 1971, a complaint against Rushville and IHSAA seeking a Declaratory Judgment and a Temporary Restraining Order (with Affidavits). The Temporary Restraining Order was granted the same day (ex parte) and on September 21, 1972, the Superior Court of Marion County, Room No. 6, made findings of fact and conclusions of law and entered a Declaratory Judgment and Permanent Injunction against IHSAA and Rushville enjoining them from enforcing their restrictive rules prohibiting married high school students from engaging in athletic competition and extra-curricular activities. In granting injunctive relief the trial court specifically found that the rules in question violated equal protection of the laws guaranteed Raike under the Fourteenth Amendment to the Constitution of the United States and that the same rules were also violative of due process of law as guaranteed Raike by the Fourteenth Amendment of the Constitution of the United States.

The parties have stipulated that enforcement of the rules in question constitutes State action.

* * *

Issue

Do the Rules of Rushville and IHSAA prohibiting married high school students from participating in athletics and extra-curricular activities deny Raike equal protection of the laws as guaranteed by the Fourteenth Amendment of the U. S. Constitution?

Additional Facts

Raike attacks these rules as being discriminatory:

The Rushville Rule:
Married students, or those who have been married, are in school chiefly to meet academic needs and they will be disqualified from participating in extra-curricular activities and Senior activities except Commencement and Baccalaureate.

The IHSAA Rule:
Students who are or have been at any time married are not eligible for participating in intraschool athletic competition. (Rule 14 of its By-laws) (Collectively referred to as the Rules)

The trial court found that Rushville was subject to the rules and regulations of IHSAA and evidence was introduced showing IHSAA's avowed purpose to be:

The purpose of this Association shall be to encourage and direct wholesome amateur athletics in the schools of Indiana. In keeping with this purpose the Association shall regulate, supervise, and administer interscholastic athletic activities among its member schools. All such activities shall remain an integral factor in the total secondary educational program. (As emphasized in Haas v. South Bend Community School Corp., infra. Article Two of the Constitution of IHSAA)

Also, there was evidence that IHSAA was originally organized in 1903 in an attempt to establish and maintain uniformity of rules and regulations in athletic events.

High school principals, teachers, coaches and consultants testified to the reasons justifying the existence of the Rules. Their testimony may be summarized as follows:

1. Married students need time to discharge economic and family responsibilities, and participating in athletics and extra-curricular activities would interfere with these responsibilities.
2. Teenage marriages should be discouraged so as to reduce the high percentage of divorce and school dropout rates among married students.
3. Athletes serve as models or heroes to other students and teenage marriages are usually the result of pregnancy so that immorality is encouraged if married students participate without sanction in athletics.
4. If married students participate in athletics, a double standard must be applied, thereby causing discipline, training and administrative problems.
5. Unwholesome interaction between married and nonmarried students is prevented by avoidance of undesirable "locker room talk."

After Raike was permitted to participate in athletics as a married person, his athletic and academic career showed marked improvement. He won the sectional wrestling championship and was elected captain of the wrestling team. Similarly, in baseball Raike's batting average improved by almost 100 points from the prior year and the baseball team's record improved from the prior year.

Raike was able to maintain a B average, hold down a part-time job, engage in athletics and at the same time discharge his family responsibilities.

* * *

Conclusion

It is our opinion that the Rules prohibiting a married high school student from participating in athletics and extra-curricular activities do not bear a fair and substantial relation to the objective sought, and therefore deny Raike equal protection of the laws contrary to the Fourteenth Amendment of the U. S. Constitution.

* * *

In reviewing a classification for equal protection impurity, classic constitutional methodology requires us to determine the appropriate standard of review to be used. That choice determines how closely the justification for the classification will be scrutinized.

A. Standards of Review
A two-tier approach has been developed by the United States Supreme Court in evaluating and reviewing equal protection cases. . . . The "low" tier or low scrutiny test presumes constitutionality of the classification and will not disturb the state action unless the classification bears no "rational relationship" to a legitimate governmental interest . . . a minimal test. If it bears some rational relationship to a legitimate government purpose, the classification can withstand equal protection scrutiny, even though there be significant deviation from an ideal classification.

At the other end of the scale of judicial review of challenged classifications is the second tier approach or high scrutiny test. If the classifying criteria are grounded upon certain "suspect traits," such as race, alienage or national origin, or if that classification impinges upon rights deemed "fundamental," e.g., the right to vote, interstate travel, the right to appeal a criminal conviction, freedom of association, then "strict" judicial scrutiny will be brought to bear on the classification and it will not stand unless justified by a compelling governmental interest.

The rigidity of the two-tier test inevitably led to a blurring of this somewhat artificial dualism. In recent years various courts and commentators have sensed modification of the two-tier approach. They point to a "new" or hybrid approach to equal protection which is more flexible. By its terms, the classification must be justified by something more than any "reasonably conceivable" set of facts. Rather it:

> must rest upon ground of difference having a fair and substantial relation to the object of the legislation, so that all persons similarly circumstanced shall be treated alike. (Village of Belle Terre v. Boraas (1974), 416 U.S. 1)

* * *

In summary, then, under the traditional two-tier approach of the United States Supreme Court, the classification was initially examined to determine if it was "suspect" or if a "fundamental right" was violated by the statutory or regulatory scheme; if not, the low scrutiny, rational basis test for review was used. Judicial review of classifications will be more flexible if the "new" or intermediate approach is followed by the reviewing court. The general principle seems to be that the more important and closer the individual's interest comes to a specific constitutional guarantee, the greater the degree of judicial scrutiny. The importance of the standard of review adopted is that the result reached is in large part a product of that initial decision.

* * *

With this background as to the standards of judicial review available for examination of classifications questioned as violative of the equal protection clause, it is meet that we now inspect the classification before us.

* * *

B. Intermediate or Sliding Scale Scrutiny

While it is true high school students do not have a fundamental or absolute right to participate in interscholastic athletics, it is, nevertheless, a right that "should be encouraged as it provides students the opportunity to cultivate good habits and to develop their mental and physical abilities." *Haas v. South Bend Community School Corp.*, supra, 259 Ind. at 524, 289 N.E.2d at 499–500.

High school students, with some limitations, also enjoy "the vital personal right(s)" of marriage (loving), which is considered by some to rise to the level of a fundamental right.

A classification which prohibits participation in athletic competition solely because of the marital status of the high school student shackles two important rights, and thereby prompts us to adopt as a standard of review the intermediate scrutiny test. Our specific authority for this constitutional methodology is Haas, a case holding IHSAA's rule prohibiting females from engaging in interscholastic golf competition to be violative of the equal protection clause. Justice Hunter, speaking for the majority, cited and relied on *Reed v. Reed*, supra. To withstand constitutional challenge, then, the classification:

> must be reasonable . . . and must rest upon some ground of difference having a fair and substantial relation to the object of the legislation, so that all persons similarly circumstanced shall be treated alike. (Reed v. Reed, (1971), 404 U.S. 71, 76, 92 S.Ct. 251, 254, 30 L.Ed.2d 225, 229; Royster Guano Co. v. Virginia (1920), 253 U.S. 412, 415, 40 S.Ct. 560, 64 L.Ed. 989. Haas, 259 Ind. at 522, 289 N.E.2d at 498)

So our next task is to ascertain the objective of the Rules. If the classification created bears a fair and substantial relation to the objective treating all persons similarly situated alike, then the classification is not violative of equal protection.

Article Two of the Constitution of IHSAA declares that:

> The purpose of this Association shall be to encourage and direct wholesome amateur athletics in the schools of Indiana. In keeping with this purpose the Association shall regulate, supervise and administer interscholastic athletic activities among its member schools.

So the avowed purpose of IHSAA in promulgating its rules and regulations, including those in question, is to regulate and supervise interscholastic high school athletics so as to create a wholesome atmosphere . . . an atmosphere free of corrupting influences. To this stated purpose must be added the testimony of IHSAA's experts and various high school officials. Throughout their testimony runs the same thread . . . the elimination of immoral or corrupting influences, and married students inject an immoral and corrupting influence into an otherwise wholesome atmosphere.

Other reasons are given in justification of the Rules, such as the desirability of eliminating premarital sex and teenage marriages with or without resulting pregnancies, and the reduction of high dropout rates and high divorce rates among married high school students. But such justification appears to be more an effect of the Rules than their ultimate objective.

Thus we arrive at the conclusion that the objective of the Rules is to preserve the integrity and wholesome atmosphere of amateur high school athletics by prohibiting married students from participating therein because they are bad examples and their participation interjects an unwholesome influence. The unwholesome influence is said to result from discussion of marital intimacies and other corrupting "locker room talk," and further, from hero worship of married students (who may or may not have engaged in premarital sex with resultant pregnancy and forced marriage).

It is obvious that the classification used to attain the desired objective is one prohibiting all married high school students from participating in athletics solely on the basis of their present or previous married status; i.e., dissimilar treatment is afforded married and unmarried students . . . all in the name of preventing married students from exerting an unwholesome effect on high school athletics.

While the Rules as drawn may reasonably contribute in some measure to the realization of that goal, they are unreasonable in that the classification is not narrowly drawn—it is both over- and under-inclusive.

The classification is over-inclusive in that it includes some married students of good moral character who would not corrupt the morality of their fellow students or contribute to an unwholesome atmosphere.

It is under-inclusive in that it includes neither unmarried high school students who participate in athletics as team members, student managers or trainers, and yet may engage in premarital sex nor unmarried high school students who may be of a depraved nature, all of whom are as likely to be a corrupting influence as married high school students.

The classification simultaneously catches too many fish in the same net and allows others to escape.

In effect, those similarly situated are not similarly treated, and therefore there is no fair and substantial relation between the classification and the objective sought.

In the succinct words of Reed, "all persons similarly circumstanced shall be treated alike". . . and they were not.

Insofar as the classification discourages teenage marriages resulting from pregnancies, it is also defective in that it contravenes established public policy allowing teenage high school students of Raike's age to legitimate offspring resulting from premarital sex.

* * *

C. "Low" Tier (Low Scrutiny)

It is possible to apply the low scrutiny test to the Rules and conclude that there is no rational basis whatsoever to support such a classification. Judge Eschbach, in *Wellsand v. Valparaiso Community School Corp.*, supra, No. 71 H 122 (N.D. Ind. 1971)(2) (Unpublished opinion), after examining each of IHSAA's six reasons justifying the same "marriage rule" now before us, concluded that it was constitutionally defective as a violation of equal protection because there was no "rational basis for the classification of students into different groups and a different treatment accorded each group."

* * *

We prefer to rest our decision on the reasoning of Haas, Sturrup, and Reed, recognizing that such reliance does not necessarily eliminate the possibility that there may be some rational basis or rational connection between a classification and the object sought to be obtained.

◇◇◇ **OTHER RELEVANT SIGNIFICANT CASES**

Chapter 8.11 *Gender Equity: Opportunities to Participate*
Chapter 8.12 *Gender Equity: Coaching and Administration*
Chapter 8.13 *Title VII of the Civil Rights Act of 1964*

Recent Trends

Scheduling Male and Female Sports Seasons Differently

The central issue in *Communities for Equity v. Michigan High School Athletic Association* (2001) was whether or not scheduling high school girls' sports in nontraditional seasons (compared to boys' sports) was inequitable in violation of Title IX and the Equal Protection Clause. Plaintiffs claimed that the seasons allocated to girls' sports were disadvantageous to the athletes in that they were required to (1) compete on school nights to avoid conflicts with other male sports, (2) compete in unfavorable weather conditions, and (3) compete in seasons that did not match well with typical college recruitment periods. The court found that the MHSAA intentionally treated males and females differently by scheduling their sports seasons at different times of the year and by scheduling the girls' seasons at nontraditional times. The MHSAA argued that there were important reasons for the scheduling differences, including maximizing participation opportunities by optimizing use of available facilities, officials, and coaches. The court applied intermediate scrutiny in holding that although this was an important governmental objective, there was no evidence that the discriminatory scheduling was substantially related to achieving that goal. According to the court, even if there were logistical difficulties with the availability of facilities, officials, and coaching personnel, the girls' teams should not have been the only teams burdened with the most disadvantageous seasons. Thus, the MHSAA scheduling rule was struck down as unconstitutional.

Reverse Discrimination

At issue in *Kelley v. Board of Trustees, University of Illinois* (1994) was whether the university's decision to eliminate the men's swimming program as part of its effort to better comply with Title IX constituted reverse discrimination on the basis of sex. The plaintiffs, who had been members of the men's swimming team, sued under Title IX and the Equal Protection Clause, claiming that the university's decision discriminated against them because they were males. The court held that neither law was violated by targeting a men's sport for elimination because the university's action was an attempt to comply with federal law. Furthermore, the court concluded that Title IX itself does not violate the Equal Protection Clause because Congress had articulated an important goal of prohibiting sex discrimination in educational institutions; moreover, the statute is substantially related to achieving that goal because as a remedial measure it directly protects the disproportionately burdened sex. The same conclusion was reached in *Miami University Wrestling Club v. Miami University* (2002), a case in which members of the men's wrestling, soccer, and tennis teams sued arguing that their teams were eliminated on the basis of sex in violation of Title IX and the Equal Protection Clause. The court utilized the same rationale as the *Kelley* court in reaching its decision.

Discrimination Against Coaches on the Basis of Race or Sex

One issue in *Blalock v. Dale County Board of Education* (1999) was whether or not the female plaintiff, a high school teacher and girls' volleyball, softball, and basketball coach, had received discriminatory treatment compared to the male coaches. Among other allegations, Blalock claimed that the athletic director had required her, but not the male coaches, to attend all meetings of the school athletic club. This requirement made it necessary for Blalock to quit a part-time job that she held. The court denied the defendant athletic director's motion for summary judgment, allowing this claim to go forward to trial. In doing so, the court identified intermediate scrutiny as the appropriate standard of review for sex discrimination claims under the Equal Protection Clause.

In *Cameli v. O'Neal* (1997), a white male high school basketball coach was fired by the principal, ostensibly for three reasons: "(1) lack of continuity in the overall basketball program; (2) Cameli's unfair treatment of some of his basketball players; and (3) the overall performance of the varsity basketball team" during his last season. Cameli claimed he was fired on the basis of his race, alleging that Principal O'Neal had made several comments asserting that Cameli was unable to work well with a black assistant coach, that he exhibited a pattern of unfair treatment of black athletes, and that their school should and would soon have a black head men's basketball coach. The Court rejected O'Neal's qualified immunity defense because there is no immunity for an employee serving in a discretionary function when termination of employment on the basis of race was a clear Constitutional violation at the time of his action. In the Court's view, a question for the jury existed as to whether or not the facts of this case amounted to a racially discriminatory termination of employment, and therefore denied O'Neal's motion for summary judgment.

High School Athletic Association Transfer Rule

In *Parker v. Arizona Interscholastic Association* (2002), plaintiff Parker challenged the constitutionality of a transfer rule. The new open enrollment statute in Arizona had made it possible for any student to transfer to any school within the school district. Parker argued that, in light of that law, the transfer rule imposing one year of ineligibility for athletics competition treated athletes differently from other students in violation of the Equal Protection Clause. The court applied the rational basis test because the issue did not involve a suspect class or a fundamental right (following the majority of jurisdictions in the view that there is no fundamental right to participate in athletics). Upon applying rational basis review, the court concluded that the purpose of the transfer rule—to deter recruitment and athletically motivated transfers—was a legitimate governmental purpose and that the rule was a reasonable means of attaining that goal. This holding further solidified the position of the majority of jurisdictions that athletics transfer rules do not violate the Equal Protection Clause.

Eligibility of Homeschooled Students

A majority of courts have ruled that homeschooled students do not have a constitutional right under the Equal Protection Clause to participate in interscholastic athletics in the public schools (Batista & Hatfield, 2005).

References

Cases

Blalock v. Dale County Board of Education, 84 F. Supp.2d 1291 (M.D. Ala. 1999).

Cameli v. O'Neal, 1997 U.S. Dist. LEXIS 9034 (N.D. Ill. 1997).

Communities for Equity v. Michigan High School Athletic Association, 178 F. Supp.2d 805 (W.D. Mich. 2001), *aff'd*, 2004 U.S. App. LEXIS 15437 (6th Cir. 2004), *vacated and remanded*, 2005 U.S. LEXIS 3714 (2005).

Craig v. Boren, 429 U.S. 190 (1976).

Haffer v. Temple University, 678 F. Supp. 517 (E.D. Pa. 1987).

Indiana High School Athletic Association v. Raike, 329 N.E.2d 66 (Ind. App. 1975).

Kelley v. Board of Trustees, University of Illinois, 35 F.3d 265 (7th Cir. 1994).

Ludtke v. Kuhn, 461 F. Supp. 86 (S.D. N.Y. 1978).

Miami University Wrestling Club v. Miami University, 302 F.3d 608 (6th Cir. 2002).

Parker v. Arizona Interscholastic Association, 2002 Ariz. App. LEXIS 185.

Schaill by Kross v. Tippecanoe County School Corp., 679 F. Supp. 833 (N.D. Ind. 1988).

St. Augustine High School v. Louisiana High School Athletic Association, 270 F. Supp. 767 (E.D. La. 1967), *aff'd*, 396 F.2d 224 (5th Cir. 1968).

Publications

Batista, P. J., & Hatfield, L. C. (2005). Learn at home, play at school: A state-by-state examination of legislation, litigation and athletic association rules governing public school athletic participation by homeschool students. *Journal of Legal Aspects of Sport, 15*, 213–255.

Council to sponsor learning disability legislation. (1996, April 29). *NCAA News*, pp. 1, 24.

National Collegiate Athletic Association. (1999). Author. No. 98-47: Eligibility—Students with Learning Disabilities. Retrieved May 24, 2000 from http://www.ncaa.org/databases/legislation/1998/98-047.html

Legislation

United States Constitution, Amendment XIV.

7.15 Search and Seizure/Right to Privacy

Margaret E. Ciccolella
University of the Pacific

The right of privacy is fundamental to American heritage and to rights guaranteed by the U.S. Constitution. It should be noted that the word *privacy* is not found in the U.S. Constitution. However, privacy interests are found in the "penumbra" of rights guaranteed throughout the Constitution (e.g., the First, Fourth, Fifth, and Fourteenth Amendments safeguard privacy interests relevant to freedom of expression, substantive due process, equal protection, and search and seizure of one's person and/or personal effects).

The heart of search and seizure privacy protections is found in the Fourth Amendment of the U.S. Constitution. The primary purpose of this chapter is to focus on privacy interests of student athletes as they relate specifically to the Fourth Amendment of the U.S. Constitution. Perhaps no issue illustrates this better than case law on urinalysis drug testing of high school and intercollegiate athletes. The significant case for this chapter, *University of Colorado v. Derdeyn* (1993), considered random, suspicionless drug testing of college athletes by using a Fourth Amendment analysis. It may be helpful to refer to Chapter 7.23, *Drug Testing*, for a review of its significant case, *Vernonia v. Acton* (1995). These two cases came to different conclusions regarding the constitutionality of drug testing of athletes and offer an opportunity for legal and factual comparisons.

Fundamental Concepts

The Fourth Amendment

The Fourth Amendment to the U.S. Constitution states: "The right of the people to be secure in their persons, houses, papers, and effects against unreasonable searches and seizures, shall not be violated, and no Warrant shall issue, but upon probable cause, supported by Oath or affirmation, and particularly describing the place to be searched, and the persons or things to be seized" (U.S. Constitution, Amendment IV).

The Fourth Amendment, made applicable to the states by virtue of the Fourteenth Amendment, guarantees that individuals are protected against *"arbitrary invasions by governmental officials"* (*O'Connor v. Ortega*, 1987). Note that only unreasonable searches and seizures are prohibited. Also, in the context of conduct by law enforcement, warrants based on probable cause are required.

Once a search or seizure is characterized as "unreasonable," it is unconstitutional and therefore is prohibited. In the context of athletics, searches of lockers, personal items, or a person become potentially serious invasions of privacy by the language of the Fourth Amendment. Valid warrants based on probable cause are rarely the situation in athletics because school searches are not typically under the authority of law enforcement. More commonly, in the context of public-school-aged and college-aged athletes, searches and seizures occur under the authority of school officials.

In trying to distinguish constitutionally permissible from constitutionally prohibited conduct under the Fourth Amendment, the courts must consider three basic issues. First, does the conduct represent state (governmental) action? Second, is the conduct a search? Third, is the search reasonable?

Is There State Action?

The Fourth Amendment protects individuals from invasions of privacy by the government. It does not protect against the conduct of private individuals or organizations. Therefore, the first question the courts must answer is, Was there state action? The NCAA is not subject to Fourth Amendment scrutiny because the regulatory functions of the NCAA are considered to represent private and not state action (*Arlosoroff v. NCAA*, 1984). Action or conduct by state, local, or federal officials is state or governmental action for purposes of the Fourth Amendment. For example, public but not private schools are subject to Fourth Amendment standards of review.

Is the Conduct a Search?

Under the Fourth Amendment, a search occurs when an expectation of privacy that society is prepared to consider reasonable is infringed (*Schaill v. Tippecanoe County School Corp.*, 1989). The U.S. Supreme Court has held that the collection and testing of urine constitute a search under the Fourth Amendment (*Skinner v. Railway Labor Executives' Assn.*, 1989). This is especially relevant to athletes subject to mandatory urine testing. In *Skinner*, the Court stated:

> It is not disputed, however, that chemical analysis of urine, like that of blood, can reveal a host of private medical facts about an employee, including whether he or she is epileptic, pregnant, or diabetic. Nor can it be disputed that the process of collecting the sample to be tested, which may in some cases involve visual or aural monitoring of the act of urination, itself implicates privacy interests. (pp. 1413–14)

There remains a legitimate expectation of privacy for both the college and public school student that a student's urine is not subject to public scrutiny. The courts continue to hold that the mandatory urine testing of student–athletes constitutes a search and seizure (*University of Colorado v. Derdeyn*, 1993; *O'Halloran v. University of Washington*, 1988; *Vernonia v. Acton*, 1995).

This does not mean that mandatory urine testing of students will result in a violation of the Fourth Amendment. In *O'Halloran v. University of Washington* (1988), the constitutionality of drug testing college athletes was upheld even though it was concluded that "the NCAA's urine testing program is a search for Fourth Amendment analysis." In 1995, the Supreme Court held that mandatory, random urinalysis testing of public school athletes represented a reasonable search under a Fourth Amendment analysis (*Vernonia v. Acton*, 1995). Most recently, the Supreme Court extended this holding to public school students who participate in all extramural activities (*Board of Education v. Earls*, 2002).

Is the Conduct a Reasonable Search?

Because the courts have determined that the testing of urine represents a search, the crucial question is whether the search is reasonable. Only unreasonable searches are prohibited by the Fourth Amendment. However, the test of reasonableness under the Fourth Amendment is not capable of precise definition or mechanical application. The Supreme Court consistently asserts that what is "reasonable" depends on the context within which a search takes place (*National Treasury Employees Union v. Von Raab*, 1989; *O'Connor v. Ortega*, 1987; *Skinner v. Railway Labor Executives' Assn.*, 1989). In *New Jersey v. T.L.O.* (1985), the proper standard for assessing the legality of a school search by school officials was determined. In this case, school officials searched a student's purse for drugs. *The Supreme Court held that reasonableness of a search involved a twofold inquiry.* First, *was the search justified at its inception* (e.g., Was there reasonable suspicion for the search?)? Second, *was the search reasonable in its scope* (e.g., Were the measures adopted reasonably related to the objectives of the search and not excessively intrusive in light of the age and sex of the student and the nature of the infraction?)?

In light of the *T.L.O.* holding and in the context of warrantless school searches, it is common for a court to determine reasonableness by (1) considering the existence of reasonable suspicion for the search, and (2) balancing the degree of intrusion on individual privacy interests against governmental interests in conducting the search.

Reasonable Suspicion. Reasonable suspicion has been defined as "the existence of reasonable circumstances, reports, information, or reasonable direct observation" leading to the belief that illegal drugs have been used (*Horsemen's Benevolent & Protective Assn. v. State Racing Commission*, 1989). The University of Colorado (CU) amended its suspicionless urine testing program by including a rapid eye examination (REE). REE became the basis for a subsequent mandatory urinalysis on the basis that a positive REE test provided reasonable suspicion of drug use. Other physical and behavioral characteristics were also used as a basis for reasonable suspicion, including excessive aggressiveness and poor health habits (*University of Colorado v. Derdeyn*, 1993).

In *Vernonia v. Acton* (1995), however, the U.S. Supreme Court rejected the individualized suspicion requirement in the case of high school athletes and ruled that random, suspicionless urinalysis testing of public school athletes was permissible under the Fourth Amendment. In support of its decision, the court pointed to the students' lack of privacy in the locker room and the voluntary nature of school sports.

Balancing Test. In addition to considering the existence of reasonable suspicion, the courts typically balance the degree of the intrusion on an individual's privacy interests against the government's interests in testing.

Privacy Interests of the Student–Athlete

Privacy interests of athletes have included the following arguments (*Hill v. NCAA*, 1994):

1. There are few activities in our society more personal or private than the passing of urine. Therefore, the visual or aural monitoring of urination implicates privacy interests.
2. Monitored urine collection is embarrassing and degrading, thereby violating privacy and dignitary interests protected by the Fourth Amendment.
3. Chemical analysis of urine violates medical confidentiality because it can reveal a host of private medical facts (e.g., epilepsy, pregnancy, diabetes).
4. Urinalysis testing interferes with privacy rights associated with the right to control one's own medical treatment, including the right to choose among legal medications.
5. Urinalysis testing attempts to regulate "off-the-field" personal conduct thereby violating the right to engage in constitutional protections for enormously diverse personal actions and beliefs.

Alternatively, it has been argued that athletes subject to drug testing have diminished expectations of privacy rendering a Fourth Amendment analysis an insufficient basis on which to declare a Constitutional violation. For example, "communal undress" inherent in athletic participation suggests a reduced expectation of privacy. Also, health examinations are fairly routine to participants in vigorous activities. In the context of such examinations, viewing is tolerated among relative strangers that would be firmly rejected in other contexts (*O'Halloran v. University of Washington*, 1988). Also, as the Supreme Court of the United States noted in *Vernonia v. Acton*, "legitimate privacy expectations are even less with regard to student athletes. School sports are not for the bashful. They require 'suiting up' before each practice or event, and showering and changing afterwards. Public school locker rooms, the usual sites for these activities, are not notable for the privacy they afford" (pp. 2392–2393).

Governmental Interests Served by Urine Testing

The other side of the balancing test considers the governmental interests served by urine testing. In the context of urine testing of student–athletes, the government must show a special need because the testing exceeds the normal need for law enforcement and occurs in the absence of a warrant or probable cause. A search unsupported by probable cause can be constitutional, we have said, "when special needs, beyond the normal need for law enforcement, make the warrant and probable-cause requirement impracticable" (*Vernonia v. Acton*, 1995, p. 2391).

Examples of special needs that have been successfully asserted to justify warrantless, mandatory urine testing of the intercollegiate athlete include (1) providing fair and equitable competition, (2) guarding the health and safety of student–athletes, and (3) deterring drug use by testing (*Hill v. NCAA*, 1994; *O'Halloran v. University of Washington*, 1988). With regard to public school athletes, these needs as well as the role of the school standing in loco parentis to the children entrusted to it have recently and successfully been argued to support mandatory, random urinalysis testing of public school athletes (*Vernonia v. Acton*, 1995). The doctrine of in loco parentis has no role in higher education. The role of guardian may help distinguish disparate holdings of cases dealing with random, suspicionless drug testing of college as opposed to public school athletes:

[A] proper educational environment requires close supervision of schoolchildren, as well as the enforcement of rules against conduct that would be perfectly permissible if undertaken by an adult (*New Jersey v. T.L.O.*, 1985, p. 741).

Fourth Amendment rights . . . are different in public schools than elsewhere; the "reasonableness" inquiry cannot disregard the schools' custodial and tutelary responsibility for children. . . . So also when the government acts as guardian and tutor the relevant question is whether the search is one that a reasonable guardian and tutor might undertake (*Vernonia v. Acton*, 1995, pp. 2392, 2397).

We therefore find of only marginal relevance holdings by other courts that high school student–athletes have a diminished expectation of privacy under the Fourth Amendment (*University of Colorado v. Derdeyn*, 1993, p. 939 [in reference to drug testing of college athletes by the University of Colorado]).

Significant Case

◇◇◇

This case considers whether a policy of random, suspicionless urine testing of college athletes violates the Fourth Amendment to the U.S. Constitution. Specifically, this case illustrates the competing privacy interests of the students balanced against the government's interests in testing. It is important to note that college-aged athletes were the focus of the policy as opposed to younger public-school-aged athletes. Recent case law suggests that the age of the student may be a crucial factor in the legal analysis of such a policy.

UNIVERSITY OF COLORADO V. DERDEYN
Supreme Court of Colorado
863 P.2d 929 (1993)

Opinion:

We granted certiorari in order to determine whether random, suspicionless urinalysis-drug-testing of intercollegiate student athletes by the University of Colorado, Boulder (CU), violates the Fourth Amendment to the United States Constitution or Article II, Section 7, of the Colorado Constitution. Following a bench trial conducted in August of 1989 in which a class of current and prospective CU athletes challenged the constitutionality of CU's drug-testing program, the Boulder County District Court permanently enjoined CU from continuing its program. The trial court found that CU had not obtained voluntary consent from its athletes for such testing, and it declared such testing unconstitutional under both the federal and state constitutions. The Colorado Court of Appeals generally affirmed. See Derdeyn v. University of Colorado, 832 P.2d 1031 (Colo. App. 1991). We agree with the court of appeals, that in the absence of voluntary consents, CU's random, suspicion-

less urinalysis-drug-testing of student athletes violates the Fourth Amendment to the United States Constitution and Article II, Section 7, of the Colorado Constitution. We further agree, that the record supports the finding of the trial court that CU failed to show that consents to such testing given by CU's athletes are voluntary for the purposes of those same constitutional provisions. Accordingly, we affirm the judgment of the court of appeals.

I.

CU began a drug-testing program in the fall of 1984 for its intercollegiate student athletes. CU has since amended its program in various ways, but throughout the existence of the program participation was mandatory in the sense that if an athlete did not sign a form consenting to random testing pursuant to the program, the student was prohibited from participating in intercollegiate athletics at CU.

* * *

CU's third amended program, which became effective August 14, 1988, contained numerous changes. First, it added alcohol, "over-the-counter drugs," and "performance-enhancing substances such as anabolic steroids" to the list of drugs for which students could be tested. Second, the term "athlete" was defined to include "all student participants in recognized intercollegiate sports, including but not limited to student athletes, cheerleaders, student trainers and student managers." Third, random "rapid eye examination (REE)" testing was substituted for random urinalysis, and a urinalysis was performed only after a "finding of reasonable suspicion that an athlete has used drugs," and at the athlete's annual physical examination. Failure to perform adequately on an REE was considered "prima facie reasonable suspicion of drug use [except with regard to steroids]," and the student was required to provide a urine specimen for testing purposes if the student did not perform adequately on the REE. In addition, if a student exhibited "physical or behavioral characteristics indicating drug use including, but not limited to: tardiness, absenteeism, poor heath [sic] habits, emotional swings, unexplained performance changes, and/or excessive aggressiveness," this was also considered reasonable suspicion of drug use, and the student was required to take a urine test. Fourth, urine samples were to be collected "within the Athletic Department facilities," and athletes were "directed to provide a urine specimen in a private and enclosed area" while a monitor remained outside. The monitor would then receive "the sample from the athlete and check the sample for appropriate color, temperature, specific gravity and other properties to determine that no substitution or tampering has occurred." Fifth, the athletes were required to give their consent to releasing test results to the Head Athletic Trainer at [CU]; my parent(s) or legal guardian(s), if I am under the age of 21; the head coach of any intercollegiate sport in which I am a team member; the Athletic Director of [CU]; my work supervisor (if applicable) and the Drug Counseling Program at the Wardenburg Student Health Center.

* * *

Following a bench trial conducted in August of 1989, the trial court entered its written findings of fact, conclusions of law, and order and judgment. The trial court found that "obtaining a monitored urine sample is a substantial invasion of privacy." It found that the REE does not function, in any sense, as "reasonable suspicion" of drug use. Because of its disastrous ability to predict drug use, it functions more as an avenue to inject arbitrary judgments into an otherwise random selection of students for testing. Similarly, it found that "like the REE, the [other] reasonable suspicion criteria [as set forth by CU] are incapable of indicating drug use to any degree" (emphasis in original). The trial court also found that while the University labels the program as a "Drug Education Program", there is little education. . . . There is no ongoing educational component of the program. Testing is clearly its major focus. Finally, the trial court found that there is no evidence that the University instituted its program in response to any actual drug abuse problem among its student athletes. There is no evidence that any person has ever been injured in any way because of the use of drugs by a student athlete while practicing or playing a sport.

* * *

The fact that CU's athletes signed forms consenting to random drug testing did not alter the trial court's conclusion. Rather, the trial court found that CU failed to demonstrate that the consents given by the athletes were voluntary, and also held that "no consent can be voluntary where the failure to consent results in a denial of the governmental benefit."

On these bases, the trial court declared that CU's drug-testing program was unconstitutional. It permanently enjoined CU from "requiring any urine samples from student athletes for the purposes of drug testing, whether those tests occur on a random basis or as a result of the 'reasonable suspicion' criteria stated," and it permanently enjoined CU from "requiring student athletes participation in the Rapid Eye Exam procedure." In addition, the trial court held that "reasonable suspicion" is not the appropriate standard to warrant urinalysis-drug-testing of athletes by CU, and that such testing is impermissible absent probable cause under either the Fourth Amendment or Article II, Section 7, of the Colorado Constitution.

The Colorado Court of Appeals generally affirmed.

* * *

We granted CU's petition for writ of certiorari on the following issues:

In the context of the University's drug-testing program, is suspicionless drug testing constitutionally reasonable?

Can student athletes give valid consent to the University's drug-testing program if their consent is a condition of participation in intercollegiate athletics at the University?

* * *

II.

The Fourth Amendment to the United States Constitution protects individuals from unreasonable searches conducted by the government, Von Raab, 489 U.S. at 665, even when the government acts as the administrator of an athletic program in a state school or university. See *Schaill ex rel. Kross v. Tippecanoe County Sch. Corp.*, 864 F.2d 1309 (7th Cir. 1989*); Brooks v. East Chambers Consol. Indep. Sch. Dist.*, 730 F. Supp. 759 (S.D. Tex. 1989); cf. *New Jersey v. T.L.O.*, 469 U.S. 325, 333-37, 83 L. Ed. 2d 720, 105 S. Ct. 733 (1985) (holding that the Fourth Amendment prohibits unreasonable searches and seizures conducted by public school officials acting as civil authorities). Furthermore, because it is clear that the collection and testing of urine intrudes upon expectations of privacy that society has long recognized as reasonable, . . . these intrusions must be deemed searches under the Fourth Amendment Skinner, 489 U.S. at 617. It follows that CU's urinalysis-drug-testing program must meet the reasonableness requirement of the Fourth Amendment.

* * *

A search must usually be supported by a warrant issued upon probable cause. Von Raab, 489 U.S. at 665. However, neither a warrant, nor probable cause, nor any measure of individualized suspicion is an indispensable component of reasonableness in every circumstance. Id.; Skinner, 489 U.S. at 618-24. Rather, where a Fourth Amendment intrusion serves special governmental needs, beyond the normal need for law enforcement, it is necessary to balance the individual's privacy expectations against the Government's interests to determine whether it is impractical to require a warrant or some level of individualized suspicion in the particular context.

* * *

CU advances alternative theories to support its claim that its drug-testing program is reasonable under the Fourth Amendment. First, CU argues that its drug-testing program is reasonable under the Fourth Amendment because of the student athletes' diminished expectations of privacy and the compelling governmental interests served by the program. Second, CU argues that even if its drug-testing program is not otherwise constitutionally reasonable, there is no constitutional violation because its student athletes voluntarily consent to testing. We address these arguments in turn.

A.

CU argues that its drug-testing program is reasonable under the Fourth Amendment because of the student athletes' diminished expectations of privacy and the compelling governmental interests served by the program. We therefore consider in turn (1) the degree to which CU's drug-testing program intrudes on the reasonable expectations of privacy of student athletes and (2) the magnitude of the governmental interests served by the program. We then balance these factors in order to determine whether CU's drug-testing program is reasonable under the Fourth Amendment.

* * *

[W]e now consider CU's arguments that the magnitude of the intrusion of its drug-testing program on the reasonable expectations of privacy of its student athletes was minimal.

(a) CU argues that collection of the urine sample in a closed stall with aural monitoring minimizes any intrusion. We agree that aural monitoring is less intrusive than visual monitoring, but as we have already noted, the trial court found that CU and the other defendants have refused to agree that they will not return to the policy which was initially challenged in this class action [i.e., the policy according to which students were visually monitored while providing a urine sample]. In fact, defendants have indicated that there are circumstances under which they would return to that policy.

* * *

(b) CU argues that student athletes' expectations of privacy with regard to urinalysis are diminished because they routinely give urine samples as part of an annual, general medical examination, and because they regularly undergo close physical contact with trainers. In this regard, it is true that the United States Supreme Court has recognized that urine tests are less intrusive when the "sample is . . . collected in a medical environment, by personnel unrelated to the [employee's] employer, and is thus not unlike similar procedures encountered often in the context of a regular physical examination." Skinner, 489 U.S. at 626-27. Similarly, the Seventh Circuit Court of Appeals has stated that if an individual is required by his job to undergo frequent medical examinations, then that individual will perceive random urinalysis for drug-testing purposes as being less intrusive. Dimeo, 943 F.2d at 682. In this case, however, the trial court heard testimony that samples for random urinalysis-drug-testing were not collected in a medical environment by persons unrelated to the athletic program.

* * *

(c) CU argues that student athletes' expectations of privacy with regard to urinalysis are diminished because they submit to extensive regulation of their on- and off-campus behavior, including maintenance of required levels of academic performance, monitoring of course selection, training rules, mandatory practice sessions, diet restrictions, attendance at study halls, curfews, and prohibitions on alcohol and drug use.

* * *

Although it is obviously not amenable to precise calculation, it is at least doubtful that the testimony relied upon by CU fully supports CU's assertion that its student athletes are "extensively regulated in their on and off-campus behavior," especially with regard to all of the particulars that CU asserts. More importantly, none of the types of regulation relied on by CU entails an intrusion on privacy interests of the nature or extent involved in monitored collection of urine samples.

(d) CU argues that student athletes' expectations of privacy with regard to urinalysis are diminished because they must submit to the NCAA's random urinalysis-drug-testing program as a condition of participating in NCAA competition. In this regard, CU's athletic director testified that at NCAA championship events, the NCAA conducts random drug testing of athletes as well as testing of the top three finishers and certain starting players, and evidence in the record suggests that NCAA athletes are required to sign consent forms to such testing.

* * *

Despite the fact that students might dislike the NCAA drug-testing program, it seems that they must consent to it in order to be NCAA athletes, and submission to one such program could reduce the intrusiveness of having to submit to another. On the other hand, the trial court heard testimony suggesting that part of what is intrusive about the CU program is that it transformed what might otherwise be friendly, trusting, and caring relations between trainers and athletes into untrusting and confrontational relations.

(e) CU argues that student athletes' expectations of privacy with regard to urinalysis are diminished because the consequences of refusing to provide a urine sample are not severe. We appreciate that in comparison to losing one's job, as would be the consequence in some government employee/drug-testing cases, e.g., Bostic, 650 F.Supp. at 249, not being able to participate in intercollegiate athletics can be regarded as less of a burden. It is, to be sure, only a very small percentage of college athletes whose college "careers" are essential as stepping stones to lucrative contracts—or to any contract—as professional athletes. On the other hand, however, we must also recognize that many intercollegiate athletes who otherwise could not afford a college education receive athletic scholarships that enable them to obtain a college degree and thereby increase their earning potential.

* * *

(f) Finally, CU argues that student athletes expectations of privacy with regard to urinalysis are diminished because positive test results are confidential and are not used for the purposes of criminal law enforcement. It is true that an intrusion by the government outside the context of criminal law enforcement is generally less of an intrusion than one for the purposes of law enforcement. However, as a matter of law, we already take this fact into account when we analyze this case according to the standards of cases like Skinner and Von Raab, rather than according to the standards of typical cases in the area of criminal procedure where there are very few and well defined exceptions to the requirement of a warrant based on probable cause. In other words, were we to attribute less weight to the students' privacy interests because this is not a criminal case, and also start with the premise that Skinner and Von Raab control, we would be, in effect, giving double weight in our analysis to the fact that we are not dealing with an issue in criminal procedure.

* * *

(g) Having reviewed the record in light of each of CU's assertions, it is clear that in some places CU seems its case, while in others, it has a valid point. On balance, however, we are in full agreement with the conclusion of the trial court that CU's random, suspicionless urinalysis-drug-testing of athletes is an "intrusion [that] is clearly significant."

* * *

CU asserts several interests in maintaining its drug-testing program. These interests are preparing its athletes for drug testing in NCAA championship events, promoting the integrity of its athletic program, preventing drug use by other students who look to athletes as role models, ensuring fair competition, and protecting the health and safety of intercollegiate athletes.

We begin our consideration of these interests by observing that suspicionless urinalysis-drug-testing by the government has been upheld in numerous cases, and in many of those cases, courts have characterized the relevant government interests as "compelling." Skinner, 489 U.S. at 628 (government has "compelling" interest in testing railroad employees whose "duties [are] fraught with such risks of injury to others that even a momentary lapse of attention can have disastrous consequences"); Von Raab, 489 U.S. at 670 (government has "compelling interest in ensuring that front-line [drug] interdiction personnel [in the United States Customs Service] are physically fit, and have unimpeachable integrity and judgment"); id. at 677 (government has a compelling interest in protecting truly sensitive information from those who might compromise such information); id. at 679 (government has "compelling interests in preventing the promotion of drug users to positions where they might endanger the integrity of our Nation's borders or the life of the citizenry"); Cheney, 884 F.2d at 610 (government has a "compelling safety interest in ensuring that the approximately 2,800 civilians who fly and service its airplanes and helicopters are not impaired by drugs"). However, the Supreme Court has not held that only a "compelling" interest will suffice, see Skinner, 489 U.S. at 624; cf. Von Raab, 489 U.S. at 666, and some courts have upheld suspicionless urinalysis-drug-testing by the government without finding a compelling interest. Dimeo, 943 F.2d at 681, 683, 685 (explaining that decreasing levels of intrusiveness require decreasing levels of government justification, declining to characterize as compelling the government's interest in protecting professional jockeys, starters, and outriders from injuring one another at the race track, characterizing the state's financial interest as "substantial," and holding that these two interests outweigh "the very limited privacy interest[s]" of professional jockeys, starters, and outriders); International Bhd. of Elec. Workers, Local 1245 v. Skinner, 913 F.2d 1454, 1462, 1463, 1464 (9th Cir. 1990) (finding that the government has a "great" interest in the safety of the natural gas and hazardous liquid pipeline industry, and holding that this "strong" interest is sufficient to justify random urinalysis testing of pipeline workers). Hence, rather than trying to characterize CU's interests as "compelling," "strong," "substantial," or of some lesser degree of importance, we think it is more instructive simply to compare them with other types of commonly asserted interests that have been held sufficient or insufficient to justify similar intrusions.

* * *

CU asserts no significant public safety or national security interests. This is not by itself dispositive, but absent a showing by CU that its athletes have a greatly diminished expectation of privacy or that its program is not significantly intrusive, the great majority of cases following Skinner and Von Raab clearly militate against the conclusion that CU's program is a reasonable exercise of state power under the Fourth Amendment. This is so despite the fact that CU's interest in protecting the health and safety of its intercollegiate athletes, like its interest in protecting all of its students, is unquestionably significant.

We have not been persuaded that CU's athletes have a greatly diminished expectation of privacy, nor are we persuaded that CU's program is not significantly intrusive. In addition, we question whether some of the interests asserted by CU are even significant for Fourth Amendment purposes. For example, although the integrity of its athletic program is, like all the other interests asserted by CU, a valid and commendable one, it does not seem to be very significant for Fourth Amendment purposes. See Local 1245 v. NRC, 966 F.2d at 525 (In evaluating a program for random drug testing of employees absent individualized suspicion, the court said, "The NRC wisely decided to refrain from pursuing its integrity of the workforce rationale on appeal. This rationale has almost uniformly been rejected by the courts as insufficient to justify drug testing of employees."); O'Grady, 888 F.2d at 1196. Similarly, although the promotion of fair competition builds character in athletes and enhances the entertainment value of athletic events, CU does not explain why the promotion of fair competition is itself an important governmental interest, just as it does not explain why preventing the disqualification of its athletes at sporting events is an important governmental interest.

We therefore hold, based on a balancing of the privacy interests of the student athletes and the governmental interests of CU, that CU's drug-testing program is unconstitutional under the Fourth Amendment. More specifically, we hold that random, suspicionless urinalysis-drug-testing by CU of student athletes is unconstitutional under the Fourth Amendment if that testing is conducted according to the procedures utilized in any of CU's drug-testing programs to the date of trial, or if that testing is conducted in a manner substantially similar to any of the procedures utilized in any of CU's drug-testing programs to the date of trial. Furthermore, because the Colorado Constitution provides at least as

much protection from unreasonable searches and seizures as does the Fourth Amendment, CU's drug-testing program is also unconstitutional under Article II, Section 7, of the Colorado Constitution.

B.

CU asserts, however, that even if its drug-testing program is not otherwise constitutionally reasonable, there is no constitutional violation because its student athletes voluntarily consent to testing. We next address that argument.

A warrantless search of an individual is generally reasonable under the Fourth Amendment if the individual has voluntarily consented to it. Schneckloth v. Bustamonte, 412 U.S. 218, 219, 222, 36 L. Ed. 2d 854, 93 S. Ct. 2041 (1973). A voluntary consent to a search is "a consent intelligently and freely given, without any duress, coercion or subtle promises or threats calculated to flaw the free and unconstrained nature of the decision." People v. Carlson, 677 P.2d 310, 318 (Colo. 1984) (citing Bustamonte, 412 U.S. 218, 36 L. Ed. 2d 854, 93 S. Ct. 2041, and People v. Helm, 633 P.2d 1071 (Colo. 1981)). Whether consent to a search was voluntary "is a question of fact to be determined from all the circumstances. . . ." Bustamonte, 412 U.S. at 248-49. * * *

The trial court heard specific direct testimony from several intercollegiate student athletes who described how and when they were presented with consent forms to sign, and why they signed them. CU had the opportunity to cross-examine these students, and to present direct testimony of its own. The intercollegiate student athlete who testified on behalf of CU was not asked about how or when she was told of the drug-testing program, how or when she was presented with a consent form to sign, or why she signed the form. The Athletic Director for CU and CU's Head Athletic Trainer testified in general about how and when intercollegiate student athletes are notified about the drug-testing program, although neither testified about how and when the students are actually presented with consent forms to sign.

* * *

The evidence produced during this trial failed to establish that the consents given by the University's student-athletes are voluntary. It is quite clear that they are "coerced" for constitutional purposes by the fact that there can be no participation in athletics without a signed consent.

* * *

The trial court permanently enjoined CU "from requiring any urine samples from student athletes for the purposes of drug testing. . . ." In view of our conclusion that it was unnecessary to address the unconstitutional conditions issue, we recognize the possibility that in the future CU might be able to devise a program involving truly voluntary consents to drug testing. In such event, CU is free to apply for modification or dissolution of the injunction.

III.

For the foregoing reasons, we affirm the judgment of the court of appeals.

 OTHER RELEVANT SIGNIFICANT CASES

Chapter 7.12 *State Action*

Chapter 7.23 *Drug Testing*

Recent Trends

Comparison of Derdeyn to Vernonia

In *Vernonia v. Acton* (1995), the Supreme Court of the United States held that random urinalysis drug testing of students who participate in public school athletics did not violate students' federal or state constitutional rights to be free from unreasonable searches. As in *University of Colorado v. Derdeyn* (1993), the Fourth Amendment to the U.S. Constitution was the heart of the analysis. In contrast to *Derdeyn*, the *Vernonia* court held that the governmental interests in drug testing outweighed a student–athlete's Fourth Amendment privacy interests.

In reconciling these two cases, it may be helpful to consider that *Vernonia* involved public-school-aged athletes. The circumstance of children entrusted to the schools via "loco parentis" was likely the most crucial factor distinguishing the holdings of the two cases. Additionally, in *Derdeyn*, visual and aural monitoring of urine for both males and females was at issue, whereas in *Vernonia*, visual monitoring of males was limited and only aural monitoring occurred with females. Finally, in *Derdeyn*, the intent of the program included safeguarding health, safety, integrity, and fairness in the athletic program and deterring drug use by other students who see athletes as role models. In *Vernonia*, these arguments were also used. However, an emphatic argument included the disciplinary problems faced by schools dealing with a sharp increase in drug use by students.

Other Privacy Issues

Privacy protections are seen beyond Fourth Amendment protections. As with the Fourth Amendment, interpretation of the nature and extent of privacy protections have been contested within the context of athletics. First Amendment protections dealing with personal conduct and expression have been challenged by considering the authority of the schools to regulate hair length (*Menora v. Illinois High School Assn.*, 1982; *Tinker v. Des Moines Indep. Comm. School District*, 1969), dress (*Dunham v. Pulsifer*, 1970; *Zeller v. Donegal School District*, 1975), on- and off-court/field behavior (*Bunger v. Iowa H.S. Athletic Assn.*, 1972), marriage/parenthood of student–athletes (*Davis v. Meek*, 1972; *Estay v. LaFourche Parish School Board*, 1969; *Indiana High School Athletic Assn. v. Raike*, 1975; *Perry v. Granada Municipal School District*, 1969) and free speech interests regarding the university mascot (*Crue v. Aiken*, 2002). Confidentiality of educational records protected by the Family Educational Rights and Privacy Act, also known as the "Buckley Amendment," has been challenged (*Marmo v. NYC Board of Education*, 1968). The Freedom of Information Act, often used as a basis on which to challenge confidentiality, has been challenged itself (*Arkansas Gazette Co. v. Southern State College*, 1981). Clearly, privacy exceeds Fourth Amendment protections and is addressed throughout the Constitution and in federal statutory law.

Concluding Remarks

Our continued legal determination of fundamental educational questions will ultimately dictate the policies that shape the future of privacy interests of student–athletes in this country. More importantly, our decisions regarding constitutional protections may have repercussions on our most basic rights. As the trial court in *University of Colorado v. Derdeyn* emphasized:

> We must remember that, after all, it is only athletic games we are concerned with here. . . . The integrity of athletic contests cannot be purchased at the costs of privacy interests protected by the Fourth Amendment. . . . A government that invades the privacy of its citizens without compelling reason, no longer abides by the constitutional provisions essential to a free society. (*University of Colorado v. Derdeyn*, 1993)

Do we sacrifice Constitutional principles to dictate either conduct of or information about athletes? Perhaps, we should be mindful of the Supreme Court's admonition that students "do not shed their constitutional rights . . . at the schoolhouse gate" (*Tinker v. Des Moines Indep. Comm. School District*, 1969, p. 736). Perhaps there is no real disagreement that all students have constitutional rights, "in" or "out" of the schoolhouse gate. It may well be that what we must continue to resolve is the nature of those rights based on such factors as age and circumstance.

References

Cases

Arlosoroff v. NCAA, 746 F.2d 1019 (1984).
Arkansas Gazette Co. v. Southern State College, 620 S.W.2d 258 (1981).
Board of Education v. Earls, 122 S.Ct. 2559 (2002).
Bunger v. Iowa H. S. Athletic Assn., 197 N.W.2d 555 (1972).
Crue v. Aiken, 204 F. Supp. 2d 1130 (2002).
Davis v. Meek, 344 F. Supp. 298 (1972).
Dunham v. Pulsifer, 312 F. Supp. 41 (1970).
Estay v. LaFourche Parish School Board, 230 So.2d 443 (1969).
Hill v. NCAA, 7 Cal.4th 1 (1994).
Horsemen's Benevolent & Protective Assn. v. State Racing Commission, 532 N.E.2d 644 (1989).
Indiana High School Athletic Assn. v. Raike, 329 N.E.2d 66 (1975).
Marmo v. NYC Board of Education, 289 N.Y.S.2d 51 (1968).
Menora v. Illinois High School Assn., 683 F.2d 1030 (1982).
National Treasury Employees Union v. Von Raab, 109 S.Ct. 1384 (1989).
New Jersey v. T.L.O., 105 S.Ct. 733 (1985).
O'Connor v. Ortega, 107 S.Ct. 1492 (1987).
O'Halloran v. University of Washington, 679 F. Supp. 997 (1988).
Perry v. Granada Municipal School District, 300 F. Supp. 748 (1969).
Schaill v. Tippecanoe County School Corporation, 864 F.2d. 1309 (1989).
Skinner v. Railway Labor Executives' Assn., 109 S.Ct. 1402 (1989).
Tinker v. Des Moines Indep. Comm. School District, 89 S.St. 733 (1969).
University of Colorado v. Derdeyn, 863 P.2d 929 (1993).
Vernonia v. Acton, 115 S.Ct. 2386 (1995).
Zeller v. Donegal School District, 517 F.2d 600 (1975).

Legislation

U.S. Constitution, First, Fourth, and Fourteenth Amendments.

7.21 Voluntary Associations and Eligibility Issues

R. Gary Ness
University of New Mexico, Lynchburg College (retired)

Colleen Colles
Nichols College

By definition, a voluntary association is "a group of individuals joined together on the basis of mutual interest or common objectives, especially a business group that is not organized or constituted as a legal entity" (Random House, 1997). Accordingly, state high school athletic associations, the National Federation of High Schools (NFHS), the National Collegiate Athletics Association (NCAA), the National Parks and Recreation Association (NPRA), and the Boy and Girl Scouts of America are all examples of voluntary sport and recreation associations (see also Chapter 7.26, *Private Clubs in Sport and Recreation*).

In reviewing the rules these voluntary associations establish for eligibility or the right to participate in the organization, the courts have historically been reluctant to overturn the bylaws, rules, and regulations of these voluntary associations unless they violate constitutional law or public policy or were enforced in an arbitrary or capricious manner (Conn, 2003). By joining these groups, the courts believe that participants agree to follow the rules and regulations of such organizations (*Indiana High School Athletic Association, Inc. v. Reyes*, 1997).

The jurisdiction of courts with regard to voluntary associations and some of the specific eligibility requirements enacted by such organizations are the focus of this chapter. In particular, this chapter will examine the eligibility requirements of both state high school athletic associations and the NCAA.

Fundamental Concepts

Voluntary associations get their authority to govern through a combination of federal, state, and local legislation and, in some cases, litigation (Conn, 2003). States often grant school boards the authority to join governing associations, thereby relieving themselves of the oversight, decision making, and enforcement. Local schools have significant independence in determining the rules and regulations regarding their participation in interscholastic sports; however, state athletic associations play a significant role by providing statewide governance for interscholastic athletics (Mitten, Davis, Smith, & Berry, 2005). The purposes and objectives of these organizations vary slightly from state to state, but in essence their main objective is "to create, establish and provide for, supervise and conduct interscholastic athletic programs throughout the state consistent with the educational values of the high school curriculums . . . " (http://www.ag.state.mi.us/opinion/datafiles/1970s/op05348.htm).

Judicial Review

Generally, the courts will not interfere with the internal affairs of a voluntary association. For example, in *Rottmann v. Penn Interscholastic Athletics Association* (2004), the court held that

> In the absence of mistake, fraud, collusion or arbitrariness, the decisions of such associations will be accepted by the courts as conclusive. Such associations may adopt reasonable rules which will be deemed

valid and binding upon the members of the association unless the rule violates some law or public policy. It is not the responsibility of the federal courts to inquire into the expediency, practicability, or wisdom of those regulations. (p. 933)

As noted in *NCAA v. Yeo* (2005), "Judicial intervention in [student athletic disputes] often does more harm than good . . ." and "judges are not 'super referees' "(p. 870). This notion of judicial deference to the associations was highlighted by the court in *NCAA v. Lasege* (2001) when it stated that members of voluntary associations should be free from unwarranted interference from the courts and members should be allowed to "paddle their own canoe."

However, there are limited exceptions to this noninterference tenet. For example, in *Florida High School Athletic Association v. Marazzito,* (2005) the court affirmed that courts may intervene in the internal affairs of a voluntary association under *exceptional circumstances.* Specifically, a court should only intervene under the following two conditions: (1) a substantial property, contract, or economic rights will be adversely affected by the association's action and the internal procedures of the association were unfair or inadequate, or (2) the association acted maliciously or in bad faith.

The courts have also consistently ruled that the regulations and/or decisions of associations cannot be unreasonable, arbitrary, or capricious (*Robinson v. Illinois High School Athletics Association,* 1963; *Indiana High School Athletic Association v. Durham,* 2001). When allegations of "unreasonableness" arise, courts will decide if the rule has a rational relationship to a reasonable goal of the association (Mitten et al., 2005).

It is important to note that the member schools are considered "voluntary" members of the governing associations, so judicial review is very limited; however, students are not deemed "voluntary" members and are therefore afforded the stricter arbitrary and capricious standard of review. The focus of many lawsuits involving voluntary sport and recreation associations is on the arbitrary and capricious standard and violations of constitutional rights.

Arbitrary and Capricious Standard

In *Indiana High School Athletic Association v. Carlberg* (1997), the Supreme Court of Indiana found that the transfer rule advanced a legitimate goal of the IHSAA and as enforced against Carlberg was not arbitrary and capricious and therefore did not violate the student's federal right of equal protection. In reaching this decision, two important points were noted by the Court. First, the arbitrary and capricious standard of review is narrow, and the Court cannot substitute its judgment for the judgment of the IHSAA. Second, the Court stated, "The rule or decision will be found to be arbitrary and capricious 'only where it is willful and unreasonable, without consideration and in disregard of the facts or circumstances in the case, or without some basis which would lead a reasonable and honest person to the same conclusion' " (p. 233).

In another case involving a transfer student's request for a hardship exception, the IHSAA's decision to deny the student–athlete eligibility was deemed arbitrary and capricious because the IHSAA did not take into account that a substantial change to the family's financial condition had occurred and that the change was out of the student's control. Thus, the court determined that the student should have met the requirements for a hardship waiver (*IHAA v. Durham,* 2001).

State or Federal Constitutional Rights

Because high school athletic associations are widely accepted as state actors, the decisions of these associations are subject to constitutional review (*Brentwood Academy v. Tennessee Secondary School Athletic Association,* 2001; *NCAA v. Tarkanian,* 1988; *Communities for Equity v. Michigan High School Athletic Association,* 2000; see also Chapter 7.12, *State Action*). As state actors, these voluntary associations cannot deny citizens equal protection and/or due process guaranteed by the federal Constitution (see Chapter 7.14, *Equal Protection*). The Equal Protection Clause of the Fourteenth Amendment provides a constitutional method for checking the fairness of the application of the law. If an association cannot demonstrate a connection between the rule and its purpose, then an equal protection violation may have occurred.

In *Crane v. IHSAA* (1992), the trial court found that Crane's equal protection and due process rights were violated by the IHSAA transfer eligibility rules. The court of appeals affirmed the trial court's decision; however, the higher court based its decision on the arbitrary and capricious application of the rule. Because state law is addressed prior to constitutional issues, when the court of appeals found the rule to be arbitrary and capricious, it did not address the question of whether there was also a violation of the Equal Protection Clause.

In the 2004 case of *Rottmann v. PIAA*, the court found the antirecruiting rule being challenged by the coach was not unconstitutional and that it did not violate the plaintiff's right to free speech, nor was it vague or overbroad. Also, in *Babi v. Colorado High School Activities Association* (2003), a coach claimed he was denied both a property right to his job and due process when he was suspended from his coaching position because one of his athletes violated CHSAA participation rules. In addressing the property right, the Court stated that a person "must have more than an abstract need or desire for it. The person must have a legitimate claim of entitlement to it." The court found the plaintiff did have a property right to his employment with the school district, but no property interest with the CHSAA. The court also found no delay in the CHSAA hearing process, thus no lack of due process.

It should be noted, however, that although high school athletic associations have been deemed state actors for constitutional purposes, the NCAA has not. Therefore, although the actions of state high school associations are subject to review, the courts will not review those of the NCAA.

High School Privilege

High school eligibility rules are essentially the products of state high school activities/athletics associations. Such associations are usually privately chartered and may or may not have direct advisory functions to a state board of education. Typically, local school districts' representatives to the association decide in parliamentary fashion the rules for conducting the athletic events throughout the state. Such agreement is necessary to ensure that fairness reigns in athletics competition across the state. Because each state association is unique, rule variance exists between states. However, despite their distinctions, consistency is readily apparent.

These associations are created to deal with the management of *extracurricular activities*, which by definition are all those activities for students that are sponsored or sanctioned by an educational institution that supplement or complement, but are not a part of, the institution's required academic program or regular curriculum. Participation is voluntary and, more important, a *privilege* in the reasoning of courts, which may be extended at the discretion of the school board. The board, therefore, may decide, usually through its participation in the state high school athletics association, the terms under which students may exercise the privilege. When eligibility standards are challenged in the courts, they must in most circumstances withstand only rational basis scrutiny (see Chapter 7.14, *Equal Protection*). This means that if the requirements are rationally related to the purpose of activity and not arbitrary, capricious, or unjustly discriminatory, they will be upheld by the courts (Wong, 1994).

Academic Standards

Alternative means of demonstrating academic eligibility for athletic participation in high schools include grade point average (GPA), courses passed in previous and/or current semesters, courses passed in previous year, percent daily attendance, enrollment in minimum number of classes, enrollment in minimum full-credit courses, GPA or passing grades in current or previous grading periods, and maintaining a grade of 70 in each class during six-week grading period to stay eligible for the next six-week grading period (Texas). Thus, a variety of standards are used by different states to demonstrate academic qualification for athletic participation in high schools.

The Texas standard is the notorious "no pass, no play rule" passed by the legislature in 1985 and challenged all the way to the U.S. Supreme Court in 1986. The Supreme Court refused to hear the Texas law citing the lack of federal question. In so doing, it allowed a Texas court decision affirming the law to stand. In 1995 the Texas legislature modified the law to make it more permissive. For instance, failing students could rejoin the team if they are passing after three weeks; plus, failing students can practice or rehearse during the suspension period.

Transfer Rules

High school associations create transfer rules to preclude student–athletes from "jumping" (enrolling in different school) for reasons pertaining to athletics. There are many legitimate reasons for transfers involving such things as family relocations, employment, and divorce and as such constitute a basis for exceptions within the rules. Oregon has passed a statute preventing implementation of the transfer rule if the student moved with his or her parent as opposed to moving in with friends just to play for another school.

Transfer rules appear to be popular targets for legal challenges based on claims of violations of equal protection, freedom of religion, right to travel, and due process (see *Beck v. Missouri State High School Activities Association*, 1993). Yet courts have generally upheld transfer rules under rational judicial scrutiny. Because no fundamental right is being violated, nor any suspect class being established, the transfer rule need only be rationally related to a legitimate state interest to be upheld by the court. If, however, the student–athlete can establish fraud, collusion, or arbitrariness, the possibility exists for a successful challenge.

Redshirting

The practice of delaying or postponing an athlete's competition to extend the athlete's career is known as "redshirting." For purposes of maximizing athletic success, redshirting is an effective strategy to take advantage of an extra year's growth and maturity and, of course, skill development. Moreover, parents of team sport athletes have demonstrated a willingness to "hold back" students a year in school to create an aggregate of student–athletes more likely to win championships. High school athletics association rules do not permit the practice of redshirting because it is contrary to the educational mission. Furthermore, redshirting creates unfair competition advantages, possible dangerous mismatches, and unwarranted exclusion of peer student–athletes.

On the other hand, high school athletics associations recognize illness or injury and purely academic determinations of grade level as legitimate reasons for exceptions to rules precluding redshirting and make appropriate allowances. To handle the problem of redshirting, however, ***rules of longevity*** must be invoked. Longevity rules determine the limits for participation in terms of (1) semesters/years allowed to complete competition, and (2) a maximum age beyond which interscholastic competition may not continue. For example, most high school association rules limit a student athlete to eight consecutive semesters in which to complete interscholastic competition. Similarly, most associations do not permit competition among student–athletes who have reached their nineteenth birthday before beginning his/her senior year.

In general, courts have agreed with the rational argument that longevity and redshirting regulations preserve the privilege of interscholastic sports competition, consistent with their educational mission.

Intercollegiate Regulations

Individual eligibility rules for intercollegiate competition begin at the specific institution where the student is enrolled. Depending on the institution's characteristics and mission, specific eligibility standards for representing that institution in intercollegiate athletic competition may be imposed. Such standards must reflect at a minimum the requirements of the conference in which it competes and, further, the association of conferences and institutions in which it holds membership. The largest such association of four-year institutions is the National Collegiate Athletics Association (NCAA). This discussion will focus on the eligibility rules and bylaws of the NCAA and various legal challenges of those rules.

Article 1.3.1 of the *NCAA Manual* (2000–01) declares its basic purpose:

The competitive athletics programs of member institutions are designed to be a vital part of the educational system. A basic purpose of this Association is to maintain intercollegiate athletics as an integral part of the educational program and the athlete as an integral part of the student body and, by so doing, retain a clear line of demarcation between intercollegiate athletics and professional sports. (p. 1)

Thus, the NCAA is a private, voluntary association of four-year institutions that share a common interest in preserving amateur intercollegiate athletics as part of the educational mission.

Academic Regulations

To maintain the educational mission, the NCAA has legislated at the annual conventions of its members explicit rules for qualifying individuals academically for competition on two dimensions: initial and continuing. To meet *initial* qualifications (i.e., to be academically eligible to compete on matriculation), the student–athlete must currently demonstrate the following (Bylaw 14.02.9.1):

a. Graduation from high school
b. Successful completion of a required core curriculum of a minimum number of courses in specified subjects
c. Specified minimum GPA in the core curriculum, and
d. Specified minimum SAT or ACT score

Determination of initial eligibility is currently made at a centralized clearinghouse by a consulting service under direction of the NCAA staff. If the student satisfactorily meets the standards, the student is deemed a "qualifier" and is academically eligible to participate and receive athletically related financial aid. If the standards are not met, the applicant is restricted from competing (but may practice), may not receive athletically related financial aid, and surrenders one of his or her four years of competition eligibility.

To satisfy *continuing eligibility* requirements, the student–athlete must demonstrate a consistent record of progress toward a degree. To register "satisfactory progress" the student–athlete's academic record at the beginning of the fall semester or quarter of each year in residence must indicate completion of a requisite percent of course requirements in the student–athlete's particular academic program at a requisite percent of the GPA required for graduation at the particular institution.

In addition, the student–athlete must be enrolled full time (minimum twelve semester credit hours) to maintain current athletic eligibility. Dropping below full-time enrollment immediately disqualifies the student for athletic competition.

Transfer Rules

NCAA rules governing eligibility following transfer from one institution to another are rather complex because of the great mobility of the age group. The purposes of transfer rules are to preclude recruitment of athletes from one institution to another and to discourage interruptions of academic progress due to transfers because of reasons pertaining to athletics. The general principle stated in Bylaw 14.5.1 requires a student who transfers to a member institution from any other collegiate institution to complete one full academic year of residence at the certifying institution before being eligible to compete. There are multiple exceptions to this requirement, the most notable being those involving transfers from two-year colleges.

Longevity

The NCAA, too, is concerned with the problems presented by interminable eligibility and older-than-expected participants. With regard to the former, the NCAA decided four years of intercollegiate competition is the maximum allowable, regardless of where or at how many institutions the competition takes place. Further, the individual student–athlete is permitted five consecutive calendar years from original matriculation to complete four years of eligibility. Thus, an accommodation is possible following a transfer or even a redshirt year for maturation or injury.

With regard to age, the membership became alarmed at the infusion of older athletes, particularly foreign athletes with the advantage of seasoning and experience, supplanting the scholarships of younger athletes. So, in 1980 the membership passed "the age rule," Bylaw 14.2.4.5, which credits any organized sports competition in a particular sport in each 12-month period following the athlete's twentieth birthday as a year of NCAA competition eligibility.

Challenges/Defenses

The annual edition of *The NCAA Manual*, once voluminous and complex, is now published in separate "federated" versions, one for each of the three divisions of membership. Time will tell if the trifurcation of the manual along with specialized alterations of legislative procedures to meet specific needs of each division effectively deal with objections to controversial bylaws. Thus it is likely that affected parties will continue to seek relief in the courts.

The constitutionality of specific bylaws is the most frequent complaint. For example, many feel that the inclusion of standardized test scores as a factor in determining initial eligibility favors wealthier, better prepared students and discriminates against economically disadvantaged students. Thus, many feel that "Proposition 48," the informal name for the initial proposal passed in the 1986 NCAA convention, violates the Fourteenth Amendment guaranteeing equal protection under the law (see Chapter 7.14, *Equal Protection*). However, the Fourteenth Amendment protects only against actions taken by *state actors* and does not protect against the actions or conduct of a private organization (see Chapter 7.12 for an explanation of state action). A successful challenge of Proposition 48, therefore, must be based on a finding that the NCAA is a state actor.

Although court decisions rendered in the 1970s found the NCAA a state actor, particularly involving the NCAA's enforcement activities, more recent cases have contradicted that view. Two notable challenges, *Parish v. NCAA* (1975) and *Howard University v. NCAA* (1975), failed in their arguments that the 1.600 Rule, precursor to Proposition 48, violated constitutional rights, even though federal courts deemed the NCAA a state actor in both cases. In *Parish*, the Fifth Circuit Court of Appeals held that the rule did not violate constitutional rights because participating in athletics fell outside the protection of the law. In *Howard University*, the 1.600 Rule was upheld as being narrowly and reasonably related to the private goals of the NCAA and not an infringement on constitutional rights.

The first test of the NCAA as a state actor to reach the U.S. Supreme Court was *NCAA v. Tarkanian*. In a 1988 decision the court agreed with the NCAA, holding that the NCAA in no way acted with state authority. Tarkanian had argued that the NCAA's Infractions Committee, which had found his involvement in thirty-eight recruiting violations, forced UNLV, his employer, to suspend him. Tarkanian's argument that the threat of NCAA sanctions forced his suspension was countered by the court's judgment that UNLV could, at any time, withdraw its NCAA membership. Furthermore, the court confirmed the NCAA is a private organization with no actual ties to the state or state authority so that any actions taken by the NCAA were private and not within the umbrella of protection of the Fourteenth Amendment.

More recently, in 1999 the NCAA won an appeal for summary judgment from the Third Circuit of the U.S. Court of Appeals overturning the Eastern District Court of Pennsylvania's permanent injunction against the use of Proposition 16 to establish initial eligibility for prospective student–athletes. In *Cureton v. NCAA* (1999), the plaintiffs, a group of African-American student–athletes, were denied initial eligibility because they failed to meet required scores on standardized tests. At the district court level, the plaintiffs were able to establish that the NCAA's Proposition 16, requiring standardized test scores among other factors, had a disparate impact on African-American student–athletes in violation of Title VI of the Civil Rights Act of 1964. Title VI prohibits discrimination by race, color, or national origin by any program receiving federal financial assistance. In overturning the district court, the Third Circuit Court acknowledged that although the NCAA receives financial support from the U.S. Department of Health and Human Services for its annual summer National Youth Sports Program, such funding does not preclude discrimination with respect to the NCAA's primary function—organizing for intercollegiate athletic competition—for which it receives no federal subsidization. Furthermore, the Third Circuit Court refused the argument that the NCAA is a recipient of federal funds for accepting membership dues from public institutions. Thus, relying on the Supreme Court in *Tarkanian*, the circuit rejected the controlling function of the NCAA while recognizing member institutions' freedom to reorganize.

Significant Case

◇◇◇

Although the following case involves a challenge to a rule that limits a student's athletic eligibility to the first eight semesters following the student's commencement of the ninth grade ("the eight semester rule"), the Court's review of the issue is typical of how it would review any eligibility challenge.

WASHINGTON V. INDIANA HIGH SCHOOL ATHLETIC ASSOCIATION (IHSAA)

United States Court of Appeals for the Seventh Circuit
181 F.3d 840 (7th Cir. 1999)

BACKGROUND

Mr. Washington is a learning disabled student at Central Catholic High School ("Central Catholic") in Lafayette, Indiana. Throughout elementary school, he had been allowed to advance to the next grade despite academic insufficiency. He was held back, however, in the eighth grade. During the first semester of the 1994-95 academic year, while he was repeating the eighth grade, he continued to receive failing grades. School officials then decided that he might do better if he stayed with his class, and they therefore advanced him to the ninth grade at Lafayette Jefferson High School at the beginning of the second semester during the 1994-95 academic year. In this new environment, Mr. Washington continued to fail during that semester and throughout the following academic year. Early in the 1996-97 academic year, a school counselor suggested that Mr. Washington drop out of high school. Mr. Washington took that advice.

In the summer of 1997, Mr. Washington participated in a three-on-three basketball tournament sponsored by Central Catholic. At the tournament, Mr. Washington met the coach of the Central Catholic basketball team, Chad Dunwoody. Mr. Dunwoody was also a teacher at the school. After conversations with Dunwoody, Mr. Washington decided to attend Central Catholic. Mr. Washington entered school and began playing basketball.

The IHSAA has a rule that limits a student's athletic eligibility to the first eight semesters following the student's commencement of the ninth grade ("the eight semester rule"). The purposes of that rule, according to the IHSAA, include discouraging redshirting, promoting competitive equality, protecting students' safety, creating opportunities for younger students and promoting the idea that academics are more important than athletics. Under the rule in question, because Mr. Washington entered the ninth grade during the second semester of the 1994–95 academic year, he would no longer be eligible to play basketball in the second semester of the 1998–99 year (nine semesters after he began the ninth grade).

Central Catholic applied for a waiver of the eight-semester rule for Mr. Washington.

* * *

Even though it had granted waivers for physical injuries in the past, the IHSAA denied Mr. Washington's application. Mr. Washington appealed the denial to the IHSAA Executive Committee, which denied the appeal.

* * *

B.

1. Applicable Standards

In deciding whether to grant a preliminary injunction, a district court must first determine whether the moving party has demonstrated some likelihood of succeeding on the merits and an inadequate remedy at law if preliminary relief is not granted. If the movant has demonstrated both of these factors, the court must then consider the irreparable harm that the nonmovant will suffer if the preliminary relief is granted, balanced against the harm to the movant. Finally, the court must weigh the public interest by considering the effect of granting or denying relief on nonparties.

* * *

2. Likelihood of Success on the Merits

We turn first to whether the district court was correct in its determination that the plaintiffs have demonstrated a "likelihood of success on the merits." In the preliminary injunction context, a "likelihood of success" exists if the party seeking the injunctive relief shows that it has a "better than negligible" chance of succeeding on the merits.

a. Whether the IHSAA excluded Mr. Washington from playing basketball "by reason of" his disability.

To receive protection under Title II of the ADA, the plaintiffs must establish that the IHSAA rendered Mr. Washington ineligible to play "by reason of" his disability. The IHSAA contends that Mr. Washington has not presented any evidence that the IHSAA discriminated intentionally on the basis of disability. It further submits that Mr. Washington's ineligibility stems not from his disability but from the application of a facially neutral eight-semester rule and the passage of time. In reply, the plaintiffs contend that they need not prove intentional discrimination. They further submit that they must show only that, but for Mr. Washington's disability, he would be eligible.

(i)

We cannot accept the suggestion that liability under Title II of the Discrimination Act must be premised on an intent to discriminate on the basis of disability. This court previously has recognized that a plaintiff making a claim under the Rehabilitation Act need not prove an impermissible intent. *See McWright v. Alexander*, 982 F.2d 222, 228-29 (7th Cir. 1992) (holding that disparate impact claims are cognizable under the Rehabilitation Act). As we have noted, this and other circuits interpret § 504 of the Rehabilitation Act and Title II of the ADA as coextensive, except for differences not relevant here. Although the Supreme Court has not held squarely that a plaintiff need not prove discriminatory intent, it has implied that requiring such proof would be contrary to the intent of Congress. *See Alexander v. Choate*, 469 U.S. 287, 295-97, 83 L. Ed. 2d 661, 105 S. Ct. 712 (1985). In *Choate*, the Court indicated that there is strong support in the legislative history for the proposition that the Rehabilitation Act was not intended to prohibit solely intentional discrimination.

In our view, the Sixth Circuit outlined correctly in McPherson the various methods of proof in § 504 Rehabilitation Act or Title II ADA claims: discrimination under both acts may be established by evidence that (1) the defendant intentionally acted on the basis of the disability, (2) the defendant refused to provide a reasonable modification, or (3) the defendant's rule disproportionally impacts disabled people. Here we deal with the second approach.

* * *

We simply hold that it is possible to demonstrate discrimination on the basis of disability by a defendant's refusal to make a reasonable accommodation. Therefore, we conclude that the plaintiffs need not prove that the IHSAA intended to discriminate on the basis of disability. The statute simply requires that the plaintiffs establish that the defendant's refusal to grant Mr. Washington a waiver was a failure to make a reasonable accommodation.

(ii)

The IHSAA's argument that Mr. Washington has not been excluded from playing basketball by reason of his disability, but rather by reason of the passage of time, could be interpreted as an argument based on causation rather than an argument based on intent. Such an argument, however, must also fail.

There must be a causal connection between the disability and Mr. Washington's ineligibility. The IHSAA submits that no such causality exists and that it is the mere passage of time, and not the disability, that caused Mr. Washington's ineligibility in this case.

* * *

We believe, moreover, that Mr. Washington has met the causation requirement for his claims. The "by reason of" language merely indicates that he must establish that, but for his learning disability, he would have been eligible to play sports in his junior year. *See Dennin v. Connecticut Interscholastic Athletic Conference, Inc.*, 913 F. Supp. 663, 669 (D. Conn.), *dismissed as moot*, 94 F.3d 96 (2d Cir. 1996). Simply stated, Mr. Washington claims that his disability caused him to drop out of school; otherwise he would have been able to play high school basketball. In the absence of his disability, the passage of time would not have made him ineligible. There is ample record evidence to support Mr. Washington's claim. Mark Zello, a school psychologist, testified at the preliminary injunction hearing. He stated that Mr. Washington's learning disability caused him to fail at school, and that students with learning disabilities like Mr. Washington's have a high drop-out rate. Moreover, Zello testified that Mr. Washington has above average intelligence and, without the learning disability, would be fully capable of performing in high school. Under these circumstances, the district court was justified in concluding that, but for Mr. Washington's learning disability, he would not have dropped out of school.

b. Whether Mr. Washington is a "qualified individual" under Title II of the ADA

(i)

To receive protection under Title II of the ADA, Mr. Washington must be a "qualified individual." *See* 42 U.S.C. § 12132. Under Title II, a qualified individual is "an individual with a disability, *who with or without reasonable modifications to rules*, . . . meets the essential eligibility requirements for the . . . participation in programs or activities provided by a public entity." 42 U.S.C. § 12131(2) (emphasis added). Similarly, under the analogous section of the Rehabilitation Act, "'an otherwise qualified person is one who is able to meet all of a program's requirements in spite of his handicap' . . . with *reasonable accommodation*." *Knapp v. Northwestern Univ.*, 101 F.3d 473, 482 (7th Cir. 1996) (*quoting Southeastern Community College v. Davis*, 442 U.S. 397, 406, 60 L. Ed. 2d 980, 99 S. Ct. 2361 (1979)).

The parties disagree whether waiver of the eight semester rule in Mr. Washington's case constitutes a "reasonable modification." Resolution of this issue turns on whether waiver of the rule would generally be a fundamental alteration to the purpose of the IHSAA rule or would create undue financial and administrative burdens. *See School Bd. of Nassau County v. Arline*, 480 U.S. 273, 288 n.17, 94 L. Ed. 2d 307, 107 S. Ct. 1123 (1987); *Davis*, 442 U.S. at 412; *McPherson v. Michigan High Sch. Athletic Ass'n*, 119 F.3d 453, 461 (6th Cir. 1997) (en banc).

In determining whether a person is a "qualified individual" and whether the modification is reasonable, a divided panel of one circuit has held that, before the court addresses whether modification of the rule would be a reasonable modification in the specific case at hand, it must determine "whether an individual meets all of the essential eligibility requirements." *Pottgen v. Missouri State High Sch. Activities Ass'n*, 40 F.3d 926, 929 (8th Cir. 1994). Under this approach, even if waiver of a rule would be reasonable under the circumstances of the particular case, the waiver would not be required if the rule itself is generally an essential or necessary eligibility requirement. *See id.* We think, however, that the better view is to ask whether waiver of the rule in the particular case at hand would be so at odds with the purposes behind the rule that it would be a fundamental and unreasonable change.

In short, we believe that the analysis of Chief Judge Richard Arnold in dissent in the Pottgen case and of the en banc majority of the Sixth Circuit in McPherson is more compatible with the congressional intent. In analyzing an employment discrimination claim under § 504 of the Rehabilitation Act, the Supreme Court has stated:

The remaining question is whether [the plaintiff] is otherwise qualified for the job . . . . To answer this question in most cases, the district court will need to conduct an *individualized inquiry* and make appropriate findings of fact. Such an inquiry is essential if § 504 is to achieve its goal of protecting handicapped individuals from deprivations based on prejudice, stereotypes, or unfounded fear, while giving appropriate weight to such legitimate concerns of grantees as avoiding exposing others to significant health and safety risks. *School Bd. of Nassau County v. Arline*, 480 U.S. 273, 287, 94 L. Ed. 2d 307, 107 S. Ct. 1123 (1987) (emphasis added). The ADA regulations similarly indicate that Arline requires an individualized analysis. Moreover, commentators overwhelmingly agree that an individualized inquiry is necessary.

We think that the individualized approach is consistent with the protections intended by the ADA. The entire point of Arline's statement that a person is otherwise qualified if he is able to participate with the aid of reasonable accommodations is that some exceptions ought to be made to general requirements to allow opportunities to individuals with disabilities. To require a focus on the general purposes behind a rule without considering the effect an exception for a disabled individual would have on those purposes would negate the reason for requiring reasonable exceptions.

(ii)

We now turn to an examination of the particular situation before us in this case.

At the outset, it must be noted that the eight semester rule that the Sixth Circuit refused to waive in McPherson and the eight semester rule in this case are distinct in a very material respect. The Michigan rule restricts eligibility to eight semesters of enrollment, while the Indiana rule creates ineligibility automatically eight semesters from the first day of enrollment, even if the student was not enrolled for the full eight semesters. Under the Indiana rule, the eligibility "clock" therefore continues to "tick" when a student drops out of school; the clock does not tick for the Michigan student who drops out of school. Notably, Mr. Washington requested only that the semesters that he was absent from school because of his disability not count toward his eight semesters of eligibility; he did not ask that the IHSAA be prohibited from allowing the eligibility clock to run while he was enrolled. Indeed, he is merely asking that the IHSAA apply a rule identical to the rule the MHSAA applies to its students.

We believe that the district court was on solid ground in determining that waiver of the eight semester rule in Mr. Washington's case would not create a fundamental alteration of the eight semester rule. Such a minimal request for a rule modification is much more reasonable and less fundamental than the waiver requested in McPherson. The IHSAA's argument to the contrary is particularly unpersuasive because it has granted waivers of the eight semester rule in the past, thereby establishing that waivers do not always work fundamental alterations of the rule. Moreover, none of the dangers that motivated adoption of the rule is present in this case. The primary goals of the rule are to control redshirting, to prevent the preeminence of athletics over academics, and to keep larger, more advanced players from dominating competition. Mr. Washington was clearly not redshirted—nobody was interested in his basketball abilities until he had already left school. Moreover, waiver of the rule in Mr. Washington's case does not indicate that athletics is valued over education. Indeed, waiver of the rule in Mr. Washington's case has promoted his education. Mr. Washington has re-entered school because of basketball, has improved his grades in part due to the influence of basketball and his coach, and is even considering going to college. Application of the eight semester rule to Mr. Washington does not appear to add anything to the protections provided by the IHSAA's age limit rule, which generally limits the size, strength and athletic maturity of student athletes.

Nor will the record support the argument that a waiver of the rule in Mr. Washington's case would place an undue administrative or financial burden on the IHSAA. The record indicates that Mr. Washington is the only student athlete to seek a waiver because of a learning disability in more than a decade. The few case-by-case analyses that the IHSAA would need to conduct hardly can be described as an excessive burden. The IHSAA already conducts individualized inquiries into whether student athletes with physical impairments should receive a waiver; requiring such an analysis in disability cases will not be a significant additional burden.

In the end, then, McPherson is based upon a case-specific individualized assessment that entertaining a waiver argument under a rule that counted only enrolled semesters, in some of which the student was academically ineligible, would give a green light to redshirting. By contrast, and as conceded by the IHSAA, there was no risk of redshirting in this case. The granting of a waiver to Mr. Washington frustrates no purpose of the rule.

C. Balancing the Interests

The IHSAA also asks that we review the district court's conclusion that the irreparable harm to the plaintiffs outweighed any threatened harm to the IHSAA and the public. This court reviews the district court's balancing of the equities under an abuse of discretion standard and the findings of fact for clear error. *See TMT North America, Inc. v. Magic Touch GmbH,* 124 F.3d 876, 881 (7th Cir. 1997).

The district court found that Mr. Washington would be irreparably harmed if he did not obtain an injunction, because if he were not allowed to play, he would lose out on the chance to obtain a college scholarship and he would have a diminished academic motivation. The IHSAA's first argument is that the loss of a potential college scholarship is too speculative to constitute irreparable harm. However, Purdue University basketball coach Gene Keady testified at the preliminary injunction hearing that Mr. Washington would be harmed by an inability to play basketball in his high school games because basketball scouts would not have an opportunity to view him playing. Dunwoody, Mr. Washington's coach and academic mentor, testified to the same effect. The district court's finding is therefore not clear error.

The IHSAA also argues that the district court erred in determining that irreparable harm would stem from Mr. Washington's loss of academic motivation if he were declared ineligible. The IHSAA notes that Mr. Washington would not be prohibited from continuing to attend Central Catholic, or any other school, if he had been ineligible to play basketball. The district court did not commit clear error in finding that Mr. Washington would suffer irreparable harm from a lost academic desire. Zello, the school psychologist, testified that basketball is an important part of Mr. Washington's academic success at Central Catholic. Before he started at Central Catholic, Mr. Washington had experienced a career of academic failure due to his learning disability. His lack of self confidence prevented him from performing well academically. By giving him something at which he could excel, basketball improved his confidence in other areas of life, including education.

On the other side of the balance, the IHSAA argues that it would face financial and administrative burdens in determining who is eligible for waiver, that another student-athlete would be displaced by Mr. Washington and that Mr. Washington would change the level of competition. However, the district court's finding that the administrative burden would not be significant is supported by the record; Mr. Washington was the first student with a learning disability to bring such a request within more than a decade. The court also determined that the displacement of another student by Mr. Washington's presence on the basketball team did "not over-balance the scale against the well-documented harm to Eric if his eligibility is terminated." Moreover, the court noted that the public's interest in maintaining a level field of competition would not be overly affected. The district court's balancing the IHSAA's interests against Mr. Washington's interests was not an abuse of discretion.

Conclusion

For the foregoing reasons, we affirm the judgment of the district court.

◇◇◇ **OTHER RELEVANT SIGNIFICANT CASES**

Chapter 7.13 *Due Process*

Recent Trends

Separating Public and Private Schools

Proposals to separate private and public high schools for postseason competitions have been addressed by several state athletic associations. Proponents of the measures believe that separating the schools will address the competitive inequities created by the private schools' ability to "recruit" students regardless of geographic boundaries. Opponents argue that the separation will dilute the competition and cause major restructuring for the governing associations (Evans, 2005).

Homeschooled Student Eligibility

Should students schooled at home be permitted to participate for local school athletic teams? In *McNatt v. Frazier School District* (1995), a student schooled at home sued the local school board for denying him eligibility to play for the district's junior high basketball team, thereby denying his rights under the Equal Protection Clause of the Fourteenth Amendment and the Civil Rights Act. The District Court upheld the decision of the school board. Similarly, in *Angstadt v. Midd-West School District* (2003), the parents of a homeschooled girl alleged violations of her First and Fourteenth Amendment rights when, as an enrolled ninth grade student at a local charter school, she was denied participation in the local public school district's athletic programs. She alleged she was deprived of a liberty or property interest without due process of law because of unreasonable, arbitrary, and capricious requirements. Again, the courts found no statutory right to participate in extracurricular activities.

As homeschooling becomes more prevalent and more acceptable, expect state legislatures to consider statutes providing accommodations for such students. In the meantime, expect homeschoolers to organize for athletic competition purposes in a manner similar to the public schools, particularly for individual and dual-sport competition.

References

Cases

Angstadt v. Midd-West School District, 377 F.3d 338. (U.S. App. 2004).

Babi v. Colorado High School Athletics Association, 77 P. 3d 916 (Colo. App. 2003).

Beck v. Missouri State High School Activities Association, 837 F. Supp. 998 (E.D. Mo. 1993).

Brentwood Academy v. Tennessee Secondary School Athletic Association, 531 U.S. 288 (2001).

Communities for Equity v. Michigan High School Athletic Association, 80 F. Supp. 2d. 729 (W.D. Mich. 2000).

Crane v. Indiana High School Athletic Association, 975 F. 2d 1315 (7th Cir. 1992).

Cureton v. NCAA, 198 F.3d 107 (3rd Cir. 1999).

Florida High School Athletic Association v. Marazzito, 891 So. 2d 653 (Fl. App. 2005).

Howard University v. National Collegiate Athletic Association, 510 F.2d 213 (D.C. Cir. 1975).

Indiana High School Athletic Association v. Avant, 650 N.E. 2d 1164 (Ind. App. 1995).

Indiana High School Athletic Association v. Carlberg, 694 N.E.2d 222 (Supr. Ct. Ind. 1997).

Indiana High School Athletic Association v. Durham, 748 N.E.2d 404 (Ind. App. 2001).

Indiana High School Athletic Association v. Reyes, 694 N.E.2d 249 (Ind. App. 1997).

McNatt v. Frazier School District, 1995 WL 568380 (W.D. Pa.).

NCAA v. Tarkanian, 488 U.S. 179 (1988).

NCAA v. Lasege, 53 S.W. 3d (Supr. Ct. KY, 2001).

NCAA v. Yeo, 171 S.W. 3d 863 (Supr. Ct. Texas 2005).

Parish v. National Collegiate Athletic Association, 506 F.2d 1028 (5th Cir. 1975).

Robinson v. Illinois High School Athletics Association, 195 N.E. 2d 277 (Ill. App.1963).

Rottmann v. Pennsylvania High School Athletic Association, 349 F. Supp.2d 922 (W.D. Penn. 2004).

Washington v. Indiana High School Athletic Association, 181 F.3rd 840 (7th Cir. 1999).

Publications

Conn, J. (2003) Voluntary Sport and Recreation Associations. In D. J. Cotton & J. T. Wolohan (Eds.), *Law for recreation and sport managers* (3rd ed., pp. 476–482). Dubuque, IA: Kendall/Hunt Publishing Co.

Evans, M. (2005). Thursday vote could separate state's public, private high schools. (2005, October 19). *The Associated Press State & Local Wire*. Retrieved November 16, 2005, from Lexis Nexis Academic database

Mitten, M. J., Davis, T., Smith, R. K., & Berry, R. C. (2005). *Sport law and regulation: Cases, materials, and problems*. New York: Aspen Publishers.

NCAA. (2000–01). *NCAA manual*. Indianapolis, IN: Author.

Random House. (1997). *Webster's college dictionary*. New York: Author.

Wong, G. M. (1994). *Essentials of amateur sports law* (2d ed.). Westport, CT: Praeger Publishing.

Legislation

United States Constitution, Amendment XIV

7.22 Conduct Issues

Cathryn L. Claussen
Washington State University

Grooming and dress codes, rules against the use of alcohol and drugs, rules against unsportsmanlike conduct, and rules requiring generally worthy conduct are all examples of good conduct rules used in amateur athletics. The source of such rules may be an athletic association, school, or coach. Conduct rules are important because they affect student eligibility to participate in athletics.

Fundamental Concepts

Authority to Regulate Conduct

In most states, the state legislature has the authority to regulate education. Typically, the legislature delegates that authority, including the authority to make rules governing extracurricular activities like athletics, to school boards or similar supervisory bodies. Often, a state statute will grant further authorization for school boards to join state high school athletics associations, which are the bodies responsible for most of the rule making concerning athletics participation.

Standards for Valid Conduct Rules

Nonconstitutional Standard of Reasonableness

The school districts, individual schools, and coaches as agents of the schools are vested with broad discretionary authority to create and enforce rules that are reasonably related to carrying out the functions of the institution. There are two criteria for determining the validity of a rule under an administrative law standard, which is used when no constitutional challenge is brought against the relevant rule. These criteria are (1) the rule must govern conduct that directly affects the effective operation of the school, and (2) the rule must not be arbitrary or unreasonable. In *Bunger v. Iowa High School Athletic Association* (1972), the leading case illustrating the application of this nonconstitutional standard, the conduct rule in question prohibited "possession, consumption or transportation of alcoholic beverages or dangerous drugs." In addition, a student would lose eligibility if caught "in a vehicle stopped by a law officer and alcoholic beverages and/ or dangerous drugs are found in the vehicle," and it was determined that the athlete had knowledge that such beverages or drugs were in the vehicle. The Iowa Supreme Court acknowledged that ineligibility could be enforced if a student consumes, "possesses, acquires, delivers, or transports beer," whether during an athletics season or during any part of the school year. The court even indicated its probable support of a rule making an athlete ineligible for violating a beer law during summer vacation. These situations were thought to have a direct bearing on the operation of the school. However, the student in *Bunger* was simply riding in a car, outside the school year, with knowledge of the presence of beer but having committed no improper or illegal use of the substance. In this instance, the court felt that the part of the beer rule prohibiting such conduct did not directly affect the effective operation of the school. Further, although asserting that rules applying to extracurricular activities may reasonably be broader in scope than other school rules because athletes represent the school and are role models, the court concluded that the beer rule at issue went beyond the bounds of reasonableness. In the words of the court:

> School authorities may make reasonable beer rules, but we think this rule is too extreme. Some closer relationship between the student and the beer is required than mere knowledge that the beer is there. The rule as written would even prohibit a student from accepting a ride home in a car by an adult neighbor who had a visible package of beer among his purchases (*Bunger* at 565).

Constitutional Standard—Due Process Clause

In *Palmer v. Merluzzi* (1988), a high school student who had smoked marijuana and drunk beer on campus was suspended from the football team for sixty days in addition to the usual ten-day suspension from school. At issue was whether the penalty of suspension from football violated the Due Process Clause by depriving the student–athlete of a property interest in athletic participation when the student had not been afforded notice of the potential for such a penalty nor a hearing before it was imposed. The court reviewed decisions in New Jersey as well as several other jurisdictions, the vast majority of which had concluded that the state had created no legitimate claim of entitlement to participate. In contrast to the entitlement to a public education, participation in athletics is considered a privilege rather than a right. It should be noted that a small minority of jurisdictions have found a protectable property interest in participation in school athletics programs based on the idea that such participation may serve as a training ground for later opportunities to receive college athletics scholarships or professional sport contracts. The majority position, however, is that the potential for such future opportunities is too speculative in any given case to be considered an existing, and hence protectable, property interest. The court in *Palmer* sided with the majority position in holding that the student–athlete had no right to due process and upheld the suspension.

Equal Protection Clause

In *Dunham v. Pulsifer* (1970), a high school tennis player challenged a grooming code specifying acceptable hair length, a rule that did not apply to any group of students except athletes. The court ruled that choice of hairstyle was a fundamental right that could not be regulated unless the rule passed the test of strict scrutiny. The school board's justifications for the grooming rule were reviewed to determine whether the rule was necessary to accomplish a compelling governmental interest. The school board asserted four interests it claimed were compelling: (1) maximizing performance by eliminating the potential detrimental effects of long hair, (2) preventing dissension on the team, (3) maintaining team discipline, and 4) enforcing conformity to social norms and providing uniformity in hair length rules between the various sports teams. The court found that (1) long hair did not hinder performing well in tennis, (2) there was no evidence of dissension on the team, (3) discipline may be a compelling interest, but demanding obedience to a rule unrelated to the objectives of participation was unreasonable, and (4) requiring conformity and uniformity for their own sakes and unrelated to any performance objective was unreasonable. In light of these findings, the court held that the grooming code violated the Equal Protection Clause. (It should be noted that federal courts across the country are divided on the issue of whether dress and grooming codes are constitutional. Some courts have ruled that students' choices regarding dress and grooming are merely personal preferences that do not implicate any fundamental rights, whereas others have ruled that such choices involve a fundamental right to freedom of expression or a due process liberty interest in self-expression.)

In *Palmer v. Merluzzi* (1988), the student's suspension from football for drug and alcohol use was issued under a school policy prohibiting athletics participation by students who had "not demonstrated good citizenship and responsibility." The court, finding that there is no fundamental right to participate in athletics and finding no suspect classification to be involved, applied rational basis review to the rule singling out athletes to be held to a good citizenship standard. The school's use of suspension from an extracurricular activity to accomplish its objective of enforcing compliance with its drug policy was held to be a reasonable means of achieving a legitimate end, and the court dismissed the equal protection claim.

Freedom of Speech and Religion

Conduct issues can include expressive conduct (e.g., student protest activities) and conduct involved in the practice of one's religious beliefs. Rules governing these types of conduct may be challenged on First Amendment grounds.

Freedom of Speech

In the public school context, expressive conduct that would elsewhere be protected by the First Amendment Freedom of Speech is protected unless it constitutes a substantial disruption of the educational environment. In *Tinker v. Des Moines Independent School District* (1969), students wearing black armbands and planning a demonstration to protest United States involvement in the Vietnam War were suspended for violating their school's policy against such protests. They claimed their freedom of speech was violated, and the Supreme Court agreed, ruling that the school's policy was unconstitutional because there was no evidence that the protest activity had substantially interfered with the learning environment.

Freedom of Religion

Grooming and dress codes can sometimes conflict with traditional religious practices. In *Menora v. Illinois High School Association* (1982), a Jewish athlete wished to wear his yarmulke during basketball competition to practice his religious belief that males must keep their heads covered at all times. The defendant association argued in support of its "no headgear rule," claiming that loose head coverings could create dangerous playing conditions. The court ruled against the student, reasoning that the safety concerns were a valid basis for the rule, and thus the rule did not impermissibly infringe on his right to freely exercise his religion. The court did, however, state that the schools should consider adopting a rule that permitted secure forms of head coverings for such athletes because this would constitute a means of accomplishing their safety objective that would be less restrictive to individuals than the total ban on headgear.

In a similar case, but one in which there were no safety considerations, the decision went in favor of the students. In *Moody v. Cronin* (1980), two students refused to attend required physical education classes because they would have had to wear shorts and shirts in a coeducational setting, which would have violated their religion's views on propriety and modesty. Despite the school's arguments that physical education classes were a required part of the curriculum and that Title IX had been interpreted to require such classes to be offered in a coeducational setting, the court found for the plaintiffs. It ruled that the school could not force the students to violate their religious beliefs by requiring their participation in such a setting.

Significant Case

—————————————————◇◇◇—————————————————

The following case illustrates the application of both the Due Process Clause and the Equal Protection Clause to a conduct rule challenged on constitutional grounds. It is important to note the explanation of the majority position that athletics participation is a privilege and not a protectable right (property interest). It is also important to note that this case discusses only two levels of review for Equal Protection Clause analysis. That is because this case was decided before the intermediate scrutiny test had become widely accepted as a third level of review.

PALMER V. MERLUZZI

United States District Court for the District of New Jersey
689 F. Supp. 400 (1988)

This litigation involves . . . plaintiff Daniel Palmer's (Palmer) claim that defendants, Peter L. Merluzzi (Merluzzi) and the Hunterdon Central Board of Education (The Board of Education) violated plaintiff's Fourteenth Amendment right to due process when they suspended him from participating in extracurricular events for sixty days. In the instant motion, defendants have moved for summary judgment.

Background

At all relevant times, Palmer was a senior at Hunterdon Central High School (the High School) located in Raritan Township. Merluzzi was the Superintendent of Schools for the Hunterdon Central Regional School District. The Board of Education is the duly elected governing body for the Hunterdon Central Regional School District.

Daniel Palmer was a starting wide receiver on the high school football team. He also was enrolled in a high school course known as "Careers in Broadcasting." On the evening of September 28, 1986, in conjunction with this course, Palmer and three other students had been assigned to the high school radio station. The next morning, school administrators questioned the students, including Palmer, about the discovery of beer stains and a marijuana pipe at the radio station. At this meeting, Palmer admitted to Dr. Paul Grimm, the school disciplinarian, that he had smoked marijuana and drank beer the previous night at the radio station.

Palmer was then suspended by Dr. Grimm for ten days pursuant to Policy 5380 of the High School and the Student Handbook. This suspension applied to both curricular and extracurricular activities of the school. Dr. Grimm telephoned Palmer's father, James Palmer, later that morning to inform him about the incident and the resulting suspension. Written confirmation of the ten day suspension dated September 30, 1986 was mailed to Palmer's parents and received on or about October 2, 1986. In that letter, Dr. Grimm specified the dates of suspension as being September 30 through October 13, 1986. This letter made no mention that any additional penalties were being considered.

On or about October 3, 1986, Dr. Grimm, Merluzzi, and several other administrators met to consider whether additional punishment should be imposed upon Palmer and the other students. Specifically, the possibility of suspending the students from extracurricular activities was discussed. Apparently, the majority of the administrators present agreed that suspension from extracurricular activities was warranted. However, a definitive decision to impose an additional penalty was not made at this juncture.

Thereafter, Merluzzi contacted two local drug and alcohol rehabilitation centers for a recommendation as to how to handle the situation. Specifically, Merluzzi sought information concerning "what would [be] . . . a reasonable period of time to accomplish some change in attitude amongst those individuals." Merluzzi did not inform the representatives he questioned that he was considering suspending the students from extracurricular activities. Merluzzi was told that sixty days was a reasonable period of time "to undergo some change." Id. Besides the incident in question, there was no evidence before Merluzzi that Palmer was a drug/alcohol abuser or that he had even previously used drugs or alcohol; Merluzzi did not even review Palmer's file before contacting the rehabilitation centers.

On or about October 9, 1986, Palmer's father heard rumors that additional penalties might be imposed on his son. Mr. Palmer telephoned Dr. George Collier, President of the Board of Education, to discuss his concerns. During that conversation, Mr. Palmer was advised by Dr. Collier to address the matter in writing to the Superintendent of Schools, and further, that the matter might be discussed in more detail at a Board of Education meeting scheduled for October 13, 1986. Neither Mr. Palmer or his son ever received formal notice that further disciplinary action against Dan Palmer was being considered or that they should attend the upcoming Board meeting.

Sometime before the October 13th Board of Education meeting, Merluzzi decided to recommend to the Board that Palmer and the other students be suspended from extracurricular activities for sixty days. In reaching this decision, Merluzzi primarily relied on Policy 138 which states in pertinent part:

No student may participate in a scheduled event if he was not in attendance on the day of the athletic event, or the day preceding a weekend event. No student may participate who has not demonstrated good citizenship and responsibility. No student who has not returned all equipment may participate in a succeeding season.

* * *

Discussion

1. Property Interest—Due Process

Palmer alleges in Count I of his complaint that the defendants violated his right to due process under the Fourteenth Amendment when they suspended him from participating in extracurricular activities for sixty days without notice and a hearing. Palmer claims that participation by students in extracurricular activities rises to the level of a property interest and, therefore, he had the right to procedural due process before defendants imposed the suspension on him. Defendants have moved for summary judgment on the ground that New Jersey and the majority of jurisdictions do not recognize a student's property interest in extracurricular activities, and, there being no property interest, Palmer was not entitled to due process protection before the suspension was imposed.

* * *

The Fourteenth Amendment to the United States Constitution prohibits state action which deprives "any person of life, liberty or property without due process of law." The threshold question in this case is whether Daniel Palmer's interest in participating in extracurricular activities rises to the level of a property interest protected by procedural due process. If Palmer has a property interest in participating in extracurricular activities then the inquiry shifts to what process he is due before his "right" to participate is denied. If Palmer has no protectible liberty or property interest then the constitutional guarantee of due process is not applicable to defendants' interference with his participation in extracurricular activities.

First, I will consider Palmer's claimed property interest. Property interests are not created by the constitution but rather "are created and their dimensions defined by existing rules or understandings that stem from an independent source such as state law." Property interests must reflect a person's "legitimate claim of entitlement to a specific government benefit" and not an "abstract need or desire" or a "unilateral expectation." On the basis of state law, Palmer undeniably had a legitimate claim of entitlement to a public education. New Jersey law requires that local authorities are to provide a free education to all residents over five and under twenty years of age, and compulsory attendance in schools is required of all students between the ages of six and sixteen. '

* * *

New Jersey is not alone in recognizing that students do not have a federally protected property interest in extracurricular activities. The great majority of state and federal courts which have considered this issue have reached a similar conclusion.

* * *

A minority of decisions, however, have held that students have a property interest in extracurricular activities. These cases rest on the premise that extracurricular activities, specifically interscholastic athletics, serve as a springboard to college scholarships and professional opportunities. For example, in Duffley v. N.H. Interscholastic Athletic Assoc., 122 N.H. 484, 446 A.2d 462 (N.H. 1982), the New Hampshire Supreme Court, finding a due process right under the State Constitution, held that:

It is apparent that interscholastic athletics are considered an integral and important element of the educational process in New Hampshire. It follows that the right to participate in them at least rises above that of a mere privilege. Recognizing this, and the stark fact that a student's ability to attend college and further his education may, in many instances, hinge upon his athletic ability and athletic scholarships we hold that the right of a student to participate in interscholastic athletics is one that is entitled to the protections of procedural due process under Part I, Article 15 of our State Constitution. See also, Boyd v. Board of Education of McGehee School District No. 17, 612 F. Supp. 86, 93 (D.Ark. 1985) (a student's participation in interscholastic athletics is important to a student's education and economic development. Thus, the "privilege of participating in interscholastic athletics must be deemed a property interest protected by the due process of the Fourteenth Amendment.") Behagen v. Intercollegiate Conference of Faculty Representatives, 346 F. Supp. 602, 604 (D.Minn. 1972) (participation in athletics has "the potential to bring students great economic rewards").

Another view advanced by one court is to analyze the degree of exclusion from extracurricular activities in determining whether procedural due process is implicated. Pegram v. Nelson, 469 F. Supp. 1134, 1140 (M.D.N.C. 1979). For example, in Pegram the court found that the denial of a student's opportunity to participate in one or several extracurricular activities would not give rise to a right to due process. Id. "However, total exclusion from participation in that part of the educational process designated as extracurricular activities for a lengthy period of time could, depending upon the particular circumstances, be a sufficient deprivation to implicate due process." In Pegram, a four month extracurricular suspension did not constitute a lengthy amount of time.

* * *

Notwithstanding these few cases which hold that a property interest exists because of the potential for future education or professional opportunities or which implicate the due process clause because of the nature and length of the extracurricular suspension, it is clear that this Court must look to New Jersey law in determining whether Daniel Palmer had a property interest in participating in extracurricular activities.

Here, New Jersey case law, consistent with the majority of state and federal courts, specifically rejects the notion that participation in extracurricular activities is anything but a privilege. Therefore, Palmer has no property interest in playing varsity football and his suspension from that activity as well as other extracurricular activities, did not have to comport with due process. Thus, it is recommended that summary judgment be entered in favor of defendants on these claims.

Equal Protection

Palmer claims that his suspension from extracurricular activities violated his right to equal protection. Essentially, Palmer argues that no other student has ever received a penalty of this magnitude and the penalty is not rationally related to a legitimate governmental objective. The Fourteenth Amendment to the United States Constitution provides in pertinent part:

No state shall . . . deny to any person within its jurisdiction the equal protection of the laws.

In analyzing an equal protection claim a court must first determine what standard of review to employ. The first standard, strict scrutiny, should be used in cases involving 1) a government act classifying people in terms of their ability to exercise a fundamental right or 2) a governmental classification that distinguishes between persons in terms of any right, upon some suspect basis. The second standard, the rational relationship test, mandates that "classifications that neither regulate suspect classes nor burden fundamental rights be sustained if they are rationally related to a legitimate governmental interest." It is well settled law that a right to a public education is not a fundamental right under the federal constitution. . . . Because neither a fundamental right nor a suspect class is involved here the defendants' conduct must be analyzed under the rational relationship test.

Under this test, I must determine whether the extracurricular suspension of Daniel Palmer was "rationally related to a legitimate governmental interest." The defendants' articulated interest in suspending Palmer was to ensure that only students who display "good citizenship and responsibility" may participate in interscholastic sports and to see "a change in attitude from an individual involved with drugs or alcohol."

* * *

Keeping in mind the Supreme Court's reluctance to have federal courts "second guess" policy decisions, I find that Palmer's suspension was rationally related to enforcing the legitimate goal of ensuring compliance with school drug policy. Superintendent Merluzzi con-

sulted with faculty members, drug rehabilitation programs and school policies regarding drug/alcohol abuse before imposing the suspension. While the penalty was severe, it reflected an approach to deal with a complex social program that I cannot find irrational.""Palmer's argument that defendant's conduct was arbitrary and capricious because his punishment was more severe than other students violating school policy is similarly without merit. . . . All students involved in the incident at the radio station, including Palmer, received the same punishment. To go back and view the penalties meted out to others for similar offenses would constitute an unnecessary foray into second guessing the judgment of the Board in many different situations. That is simply unwarranted.

In conclusion, because Palmer has not demonstrated an equal protection violation, nor could he do so even with further discovery, I recommend that his equal protection claim be dismissed with prejudice.

 OTHER RELEVANT SIGNIFICANT CASES

Chapter 7.13 *Due Process*

Chapter 7.21 *Voluntary Associations and Eligibility Issues*

Recent Trends

Misconduct Due to Disability

Attention deficit hyperactivity disorder (ADHD) has been identified as a disability that can cause disruptive behavior. In *Bercovitch v. Baldwin School, Inc.* (1998), the school suspended the plaintiff for misconduct stemming from his ADHD condition. The court concluded that this suspension violated the school's duty to reasonably accommodate the plaintiff's disability. However, in *Long v. Board of Education District 128, et al.* (2001), the court decided in favor of the school. A high school athlete with manic depression had been arrested for behavior that violated the school's code of conduct, and so the school suspended him from all extracurricular activities. Extracurricular activities were written into his Individualized Education Plan (IEP), however, so the student requested that the suspension be waived so he could play lacrosse and football as an accommodation for his disability. The school denied this request, so the student sued under the disability laws. In balancing the interest of the school in consistent enforcement of its conduct rules against the student's interest in following his IEP, the court concluded that the school's interest was the stronger. It found that the harm caused to the plaintiff by the suspension was minimized by the opportunity to participate in summer athletics programs not sponsored by the school.

Tattoos

Many student–athletes are wearing tattoos, but some grooming codes forbid them or require them to be invisible when the athlete is dressed for competition. In *Stephenson v. Davenport Community School District* (1997), a non-sport-related case, a student was forced to undergo medical treatment to remove a tattoo of a cross. Failure to remove it would result in suspension and possible expulsion from high school under a regulation forbidding the display on school grounds of symbols of gang activity. The student alleged that this violated her constitutional rights. The court found that the First Amendment freedom of speech was not implicated because, by the student's own admission, her tattoo was not intended to convey any meaningful message, but was simply self-expression. However, the court cited precedent holding that there is a Due Process Clause liberty interest in determining one's hair length and found this applicable to the analogous situation of determining personal appearance by choosing to wear a tattoo. Under a Due Process Clause analysis, the court found the regulation void for vagueness because it failed to provide adequate notice of proscribed conduct. This conclusion was based on the fact that the term *gang* was not well defined and because the regulation gave school administrators too much discretion in determining what constituted a gang symbol. Gang symbols around the country include such things as cross symbols, basic colors like red and blue, baseball caps, bandannas, earrings, and untied shoelaces. According to the court, the grooming code in this case could potentially have been violated in four ways by a non-gang-member male student wearing a Duke University baseball cap, a cross earring, and shoes with untied laces. Thus, the regulation was held unconstitutional because it was too vague.

Similar conclusions were reached in two cases where fairgoers were ejected from the fairgrounds under dress code policies aimed at gang symbols, one for wearing his baseball cap backwards and one for wearing a Hell's Angels vest (*Hodge v. Lynd*, 2000; *Gatto v. County of Sonoma*, 2002).

A recent decision that went the other way was the unpublished case of *Stotts v. Community Unit School District No. 1* (2000). Stotts had a dragon tattooed on his back in violation of a team's grooming code rule and was suspended. He sued under the First Amendment and the Equal Protection Clause, seeking an injunction against enforcement of the suspension. The court denied his request for an injunction, finding that he did not have a strong likelihood of success if the case were to be fully tried. The 7th Circuit later dismissed the case as moot because Stotts had graduated by the time the appeal reached the court.

References

Cases

Bercovitch v. Baldwin School, Inc., 133 F.3d 141 (1st Cir. 1998).
Bunger v. Iowa High School Athletic Association, 197 N.W.2d 555 (Iowa 1972).
Dunham v. Pulsifer, 312 F. Supp. 411 (D. Vermont 1970).
Gatto v. County of Sonoma, 120 Cal. Rptr. 2d 550 (Cal. App. 2002).
Hodge v. Lynd, 88 F. Supp. 2d 1234 (D.N.M. 2000).
Long v. Board of Educ. Dist. 128, et al., 167 F. Supp. 2d 988 (N.D. Ill. 2001).
Menora v. Illinois High School Association, 683 F.2d 1030 (7th Cir. 1982).
Moody v. Cronin, 484 F. Supp. 270 (C.D. Ill. 1980).
Palmer v. Merluzzi, 689 F. Supp. 400 (D. N.J. 1988).
Stephenson v. Davenport Community School District, 110 F.3d 1303 (8th Cir. 1997).
Stotts v. Community Unit School District No. 1, 230 F.3d 989 (7th Cir. 2000).
Tinker v. Des Moines Independent School District, 393 U.S. 503 (1969).

Legislation

United States Constitution, Amendment I.
United States Constitution, Amendment XIV.

7.23 Drug Testing

John T. Wolohan

Ithaca College

Perhaps the greatest threat facing the integrity of sports, as well as the health and safety of today's athletes, is the continued use performance-enhancing drugs. In an attempt to protect their sports and athletes from this threat, athletic administrators and organizations from the interscholastic, intercollegiate, Olympic, and professional levels have implementing drug-testing programs. However, as the Bay Area Laboratory Co-Operative (BALCO) scandal, which erupted in June 2003, when a syringe containing the designer steroid THG (tetrahydrogestrinone) was anonymously sent to the United States Anti-Doping Agency (USADA) and eventually involved some of the biggest names in professional sports and international track and field, demonstrated, athletic administrators and organizations seem to be fighting a losing battle.

In their haste to rid sports of performance-enhancing drugs, however, some people have voiced concern that spots and recreational organizations may be violating the privacy rights of the very athletes they are trying to protect. This chapter examines the various legal principles raised when an institution or organization implements a drug-testing program for athletes.

Fundamental Concepts

The main legal areas governing drug testing of athletes are constitutional law and labor law. The law that will govern a particular complaint depends on the individual. For example, drug testing high school or college athletes raises a number of constitutional issues concerning the athlete's right to due process and privacy, as well as protection against illegal search and seizure and self-incrimination. The drug testing of professional athletes will usually be resolved through internal grievance and arbitration systems set up within the league's collective bargaining agreement (CBA).

Constitutional Law

The first question to ask whenever a constitutional law issue arises is, "Is there *state action*?" The safeguards of the U.S. Constitution apply only when state action is present. State action is defined as any action taken directly or indirectly by a state, municipal, or federal government. Therefore, before an athlete can claim that a drug-testing program violated his or her constitutional rights, the entity being challenged must be shown to be part of the federal, state, or municipal government. (For more information on state action, see Chapter 7.12.)

As discussed in Chapter 7.12, public high schools and colleges are state actors, and students attending these institutions benefit from the protections afforded under the constitution. Private entities, such as the NCAA and professional sports teams, on the other hand, are not subject to constitutional challenges. For example, in *Long v. National Football League* (1994), a former football player sued the NFL after he tested positive for anabolic steroids and was suspended pursuant to the league's drug-testing policy. In dismissing his claim, the District Court held that Long failed to show a sufficiently close nexus between the actions of the city and city officials and the decision of the NFL to establish an actionable constitutional claim based on his suspension for anabolic steroids. The court concluded that Long was suspended based on independent medical conclusions and NFL policy objectives over which the state had no influence.

Even when the state is involved in the drug testing of professional athletes, the courts have afforded wide latitude to such programs. For example, in *Shoemaker v. Handell* (1986), five jockeys challenged the New Jersey Racing Commission's regulations requiring drug testing of jockeys. The jockeys claimed that this constituted an illegal search and seizure and was a violation of their Fourth Amendment rights. The Court of Appeals, in upholding the regulations, held that the commission's concern for racing integrity warranted the tests and that as long as the commission kept the results confidential, there was no violation of the jockeys' rights.

The Fourth Amendment

Once state action has been established, an organization must meet the requirements of the Fourth Amendment to the U.S. Constitution before it can implement a drug-testing program. The Fourth Amendment provides that

> [T]he right of the people to be secure in their persons, houses, papers and effects, against unreasonable searches and seizures, shall not be violated, and no Warrants shall issue, but upon probable cause, supported by Oath or affirmation, and particularly describing the place to be searched and the persons or things to be seized.

For any drug test to be constitutional under the Fourth Amendment, the "search" or test must be reasonable. To determine whether a drug test satisfies the reasonableness requirement, the court must balance the intrusion of the test on an individual's Fourth Amendment interests against its promotion of legitimate governmental interests. In conducting this balancing test, the court examines the following three factors.

The first factor to be considered is whether the individual has a *legitimate privacy expectation* on which the search intrudes. The Fourth Amendment only protects those expectations of privacy that society recognizes as legitimate. What expectations are legitimate varies, of course, depending on whether the individual asserting the privacy interest is at home, at work, in a car, or in a public park. In addition, the legitimacy of certain privacy expectations may depend on the individual's legal relationship with the state. For example, the expectation of privacy by high school students would be less than individuals in college or members of the general population. The reason high school athletes would have lower privacy expectations is due to the fact that schools have a custodial and tutelary responsibility for the students. Also affecting the privacy expectations of athletes is the fact that athletes shower and change together before and after each practice or game; therefore, their expectation of privacy is small. As the Supreme Court noted in *Vernonia School District v. Acton* (1995), "high school sports are not for the bashful."

The second factor to be considered is the *character of the intrusion*. In determining the character of the intrusion, the court examines both how the drug test collects samples and the type of information being collected. For example, is the individual required to give a blood test, which courts would find invasive, or a urine sample, which is far less invasive? As for the type of information that is obtained by the test, the test should only look for illegal drug and performance-enhancing drugs. Another issue that impacts the character of the intrusion is who receives the test results and how the information is used. The test information should only be disclosed to those limited individuals who have a need to know.

The final factor to be considered is the *nature and immediacy of the governmental concern* and the efficacy of the drug test in meeting those concerns. In other words, the court must determine whether the state's interest in conducting the drug test is important enough to justify intruding on an individual's genuine expectation of privacy.

The Fourth Amendment also requires that before any search can be conducted there must be *probable cause*. The Supreme Court, however, has recognized that a search unsupported by probable cause can be constitutional when the state has special needs. As the Supreme Court noted in *Vernonia School District v. Acton* (1995), because of the student's age, the state has "special needs" in the public school context. Those same "special needs," however, do not exist at the college, Olympic, or professional levels.

Consent Forms

An individual can voluntarily waive his or her Fourth Amendment rights and submit to a drug-testing program. However, even when an individual consents to a drug test, there can be constitutional problems. For example, in *University of Colorado v. Derdeyn* (1993), a group of student–athletes who had signed consent forms challenged the university's mandatory drug testing program. In upholding the student's challenge, the Colorado Supreme Court held that the university failed to show that the students' consent to such testing was voluntary. Absent such voluntary consent, the court concluded that the university's random, suspicionless urinalysis drug-testing program violated the students' constitutional rights.

State Constitutions

It is also important to note that individual state constitutions may afford more liberal protections to citizens with respect to search and seizure when compared to the U.S. Constitution. For example, in *Hill v. NCAA* (1994), Jennifer Hill, a member of the swimming team at Stanford University, challenged the NCAA's drug-testing program by arguing that it violated her privacy rights under the California State Constitution. In particular, Hill pointed to the NCAA's procedure for collecting urine samples and the consent form, which asked students to disclose medical and sexual information.

In ruling against Hill, the California Supreme Court held that the NCAA's drug-testing policy involving monitoring of urination, testing of urine samples, and inquiry concerning medication did not violate the students' constitutional right to privacy. In holding that the program was consistent with the privacy provisions of the state constitution, the California Supreme Court held that the NCAA's interest in protecting both the health and safety of the athletes and the integrity of the programs outweighed Hill's privacy interests.

Another case involving a state constitutional challenge is *Bally v. Northeastern University* (1989). David Bally alleged that Northeastern's policy requiring student–athletes to consent to drug testing as a condition of participating in intercollegiate sports violated his civil rights and right to privacy. The Massachusetts Supreme Judicial Court, however, rejected both of these arguments.

Due Process

Another theory used by athletes to challenge the constitutionality of drug-testing programs is due process. As discussed in Chapter 7.13, to establish a violation of due process, an individual must establish that he or she has some type of property or liberty interest that has been adversely affected. Unfortunately, for the student–athletes, it is clear from past court decisions that participation in athletics is not a property right, but is a privilege not protected by Constitutional due process safeguards. For example, in *Brennan v. Board of Trustees* (1997), John Brennan, a student–athlete at the University of Southwestern Louisiana, challenged a positive drug test for anabolic steroids on due process grounds. In the case, Brennan requested and received two administrative appeals in which he contended that the positive test results were "false" due to a combination of factors, including heavy drinking and sexual activity the night before the test and his use of nutritional supplements. Following the unsuccessful appeals, USL complied with the NCAA regulations and suspended Brennan from intercollegiate athletic competition for one year. In rejecting his claim, the court held that Brennan had no liberty or property interest in participating in intercollegiate athletics.

Labor Law

Another legal area governing drug testing is labor law. In professional sports, the conduct of the players is governed by a contract that is negotiated between the league, representing the owners, and the players' association, representing the players. This contract or collective bargaining agreement addresses the conditions of the athletes' employment. Because drug-testing programs affect an athlete's condition of employment (if they test positive they cannot play), it is a mandatory subject of bargaining and must be part of the CBA.

Significant Case

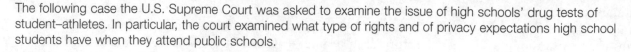

The following case the U.S. Supreme Court was asked to examine the issue of high schools' drug tests of student–athletes. In particular, the court examined what type of rights and of privacy expectations high school students have when they attend public schools.

VERNONIA SCHOOL DISTRICT 47J V. ACTON
United States Supreme Court
515 U.S. 646, 115 S.Ct. 2386 (1995)

According to the District Court: "[T]he administration was at its wits end and . . . a large segment of the student body, particularly those involved in interscholastic athletics, was in a state of rebellion. Disciplinary actions had reached 'epidemic proportions.' The coincidence of an almost three-fold increase in classroom disruptions and disciplinary reports along with the staff's direct observations of students using drugs or glamorizing drug and alcohol use led the administration to the inescapable conclusion that the rebellion was being fueled by alcohol and drug abuse as well as the student's misperceptions about the drug culture." At that point, District officials began considering a drug-testing program. They held a parent "input night" to discuss the proposed Student Athlete Drug Policy (Policy) and the parents in attendance gave their unanimous approval. The school board approved the Policy for implementation in the fall of 1989. Its expressed purpose is to prevent student athletes from using drugs, to protect their health and safety, and to provide drug users with assistance programs.

The Policy applies to all students participating in interscholastic athletics. Students wishing to play sports must sign a form consenting to the testing and must obtain the written consent of their parents. Athletes are tested at the beginning of the season for their sport. In addition, once each week of the season the names of the athletes are placed in a "pool" from which a student, with the supervision of two adults, blindly draws the names of 10% of the athletes for random testing. Those selected are notified and tested that same day, if possible. The student to be tested completes a specimen control form which bears an assigned number. Prescription medications that the student is taking must be identified by providing a copy of the prescription or a doctor's authorization. The student then enters an empty locker room accompanied by an adult monitor of the same sex. Each boy selected produces a sample at a urinal, remaining fully clothed with his back to the monitor, who stands approximately 12 to 15 feet behind the student. Monitors may (though do not always) watch the student while he produces the sample, and they listen for normal sounds of urination. Girls produce samples in an enclosed bathroom stall, so that they can be heard but not observed. After the sample is produced, it is given to the monitor, who checks it for temperature and tampering and then transfers it to a vial. The samples are sent to an independent laboratory, which routinely tests them for amphetamines, cocaine, and marijuana. Other drugs, such as LSD, may be screened at the request of the District, but the identity of a particular student does not determine which drugs will be tested. The laboratory's procedures are 99.94% accurate. The District follows strict procedures regarding the chain of custody and access to test results. The laboratory does not know the identity of the students whose samples it tests. It is authorized to mail written test reports only to the superintendent and to provide test results to District personnel by telephone only after the requesting official recites a code confirming his authority. Only the superintendent, principals, vice-principals, and athletic directors have access to test results, and the results are not kept for more than one year. If a sample tests positive, a second test is administered as soon as possible to confirm the result. If the second test is negative, no further action is taken. If the second test is positive, the athlete's parents are notified, and the school principal convenes a meeting with the student and his parents, at which the student is given the option of (1) participating for six weeks in an assistance program that includes weekly urinalysis, or (2) suffering suspension from athletics for the remainder of the current season and the next athletic season. The student is then retested prior to the start of the next athletic season for which he or she is eligible. The Policy states that a second offense results in automatic imposition of option (2); a third offense in suspension for the remainder of the current season and the next two athletic seasons.

In the fall of 1991, James Acton, then a seventh grader, signed up to play football at one of the District's grade schools. He was denied participation, however, because he and his parents refused to sign the testing consent forms. The Actons filed suit, seeking declaratory and injunctive relief from enforcement of the Policy on the grounds that it violated the Fourth and Fourteenth Amendments to the United States Constitution and Article I, § 9, of the Oregon Constitution. After a bench trial, the District Court entered an order denying the claims on the merits and dismissing the action. 796 F.Supp., at 1355. The United States Court of Appeals for the Ninth Circuit reversed, holding that the Policy violated both the Fourth and Fourteenth Amendments and Article I, § 9, of the Oregon Constitution. 23 F.3d 1514 (1994). We granted certiorari.

II

The Fourth Amendment to the United States Constitution provides that the Federal Government shall not violate "[t]he right of the people to be secure in their persons, houses, papers, and effects, against unreasonable searches and seizures . . ." We have held that the Fourteenth Amendment extends this constitutional guarantee to searches and seizures by state officers, Elkins v. United States, 364 U.S. 206, 213 (1960), including public school officials, New Jersey v. T.L.O., 469 U.S. 325, 336–337 (1985). In Skinner v. Railway Labor Executives' Assn., 489 U.S. 602, 617 (1989), we held that state-compelled collection and testing of urine, such as that required by the Policy, constitutes a "search" subject to the demands of the Fourth Amendment.

As the text of the Fourth Amendment indicates, the ultimate measure of the constitutionality of a governmental search is "reasonableness." At least in a case such as this, where there was no clear practice, either approving or disapproving the type of search at issue, at the time the constitutional provision was enacted, whether a particular search meets the reasonableness standard "'is judged by balancing its intrusion on the individual's Fourth Amendment interests against its promotion of legitimate governmental interests.'" Skinner, supra, at 619. Where a search is undertaken by law enforcement officials to discover evidence of criminal wrongdoing, this Court has said that reasonableness generally requires the obtaining of a judicial warrant. . . . But a warrant is not required to establish the reasonableness of all government searches; and when a warrant is not required (and the Warrant Clause therefore not applicable), probable cause is not invariably required either. A search unsupported by probable cause can be constitutional, we have said, "when special needs, beyond the normal need for law enforcement, make the warrant and probable-cause requirement impracticable." Griffin v. Wisconsin, 483 U.S. 868, 873 (1987).

We have found such "special needs" to exist in the public school context. There, the warrant requirement "would unduly interfere with the maintenance of the swift and informal disciplinary procedures [that are] needed," and "strict adherence to the requirement that searches be based upon probable cause" would undercut "the substantial need of teachers and administrators for freedom to maintain order in the schools." T.L.O., 469 U.S., at 340, 341. The school search we approved in T.L.O., while not based on probable cause, was based on individualized suspicion of wrongdoing. As we explicitly acknowledged, however, " 'the Fourth Amendment imposes no irreducible requirement of such suspicion,' " id., at 342, n. 8. We have upheld suspicionless searches and seizures to conduct drug testing of railroad personnel involved in train accidents, see Skinner, supra; to conduct random drug testing of federal customs officers who carry arms or are involved in drug interdiction, and to maintain automobile checkpoints looking for illegal immigrants and contraband, . . . and drunk drivers. . . .

III

The first factor to be considered is the nature of the privacy interest upon which the search here at issue intrudes. The Fourth Amendment does not protect all subjective expectations of privacy, but only those that society recognizes as "legitimate." What expectations are legitimate varies, of course, with context, depending, for example, upon whether the individual asserting the privacy interest is at home, at work, in a car, or in a public park. In addition, the legitimacy of certain privacy expectations vis-a-vis the State may depend upon the individual's legal relationship with the State. For example, in Griffin, we held that, although a "probationer's home, like anyone else's, is protected by the Fourth Amendmen[t]," the supervisory relationship between probationer and State justifies "a degree of impingement upon [a probationer's] privacy that would not be constitutional if applied to the public at large." 483 U.S., at 873, 875. Central, in our view, to the present case is the fact that the subjects of the Policy are (1) children, who (2) have been committed to the temporary custody of the State as schoolmaster. Traditionally at common law, and still today, unemancipated minors lack some of the most fundamental rights of self-determination—including even the right of liberty in its narrow sense, i.e., the right to come and go at will. They are subject, even as to their physical freedom, to the control of their parents or guardians. . . . When parents place minor children in private schools for their education, the teachers and administrators of those schools stand in loco parentis over the children entrusted to them. In fact, the tutor or schoolmaster is the very prototype of that status. . . . In T.L.O. we rejected the notion that public schools, like private schools, exercise only parental power over their students, which of course is not subject to constitutional constraints. 469 U.S., at 336. Such a view of things, we said, "is not entirely 'consonant with compulsory education laws,' " and is inconsistent with our prior decisions treating school officials as state actors for purposes of the Due Process and Free Speech Clauses, T.L.O., at 336. But while denying that the State's power over schoolchildren is formally no more than the delegated power of their parents, T.L.O. did not deny, but indeed emphasized, that the nature of that power is custodial and tutelary, permitting a degree of supervision and control that could not be exercised over free adults.

"[A] proper educational environment requires close supervision of schoolchildren, as well as the enforcement of rules against conduct that would be perfectly permissible if undertaken by an adult." 469 U.S., at 339. While we do not, of course, suggest that public schools as a general matter have such a degree of control over children as to give rise to a constitutional "duty to protect" . . . we have acknowledged that for many purposes "school authorities ac[t] in loco parentis," . . . with the power and indeed the duty to "inculcate the habits and manners of civility." id., at 681. Thus, while children assuredly do not "shed their constitutional rights . . . at the schoolhouse gate," Tinker v. Des Moines Independent Community School Dist., 393 U.S. 503, 506 (1969), the nature of those rights is what is appropriate for children in school. . . .

Fourth Amendment rights, no less than First and Fourteenth Amendment rights, are different in public schools than elsewhere; the "reasonableness" inquiry cannot disregard the schools' custodial and tutelary responsibility for children. For their own good and that of their classmates, public school children are routinely required to submit to various physical examinations, and to be vaccinated against various diseases. Particularly with regard to medical examinations and procedures, therefore, "students within the school environment have a lesser expectation of privacy than members of the population generally."

Legitimate privacy expectations are even less with regard to student athletes. School sports are not for the bashful. They require "suiting up" before each practice or event, and showering and changing afterwards. Public school locker rooms, the usual sites for these activities, are not notable for the privacy they afford. The locker rooms in Vernonia are typical: No individual dressing rooms are provided; shower heads are lined up along a wall, unseparated by any sort of partition or curtain; not even all the toilet stalls have doors. As the United States Court of Appeals for the Seventh Circuit has noted, there is "an element of 'communal undress' inherent in athletic participation," Schaill by Kross v. Tippecanoe County School Corp., 864 F.2d 1309, 1318 (1988). There is an additional respect in which school athletes have a reduced expectation of privacy. By choosing to "go out for the team," they voluntarily subject themselves to a degree of regulation even higher than that imposed on students generally. In Vernonia's public schools, they must submit to a preseason physical exam (James testified that his included the giving of a urine sample, App. 17), they must acquire adequate insurance coverage or sign an insurance waiver, maintain a minimum grade point average, and comply with any "rules of conduct, dress, training hours and related matters as may be established for each sport by the head coach and athletic director with the principal's approval." Record, Exh. 2, p. 30, P 8. Somewhat like

adults who choose to participate in a "closely regulated industry," students who voluntarily participate in school athletics have reason to expect intrusions upon normal rights and privileges, including privacy. See Skinner, 489 U.S., at 627.

IV

Having considered the scope of the legitimate expectation of privacy at issue here, we turn next to the character of the intrusion that is complained of. We recognized in Skinner that collecting the samples for urinalysis intrudes upon "an excretory function traditionally shielded by great privacy." 489 U.S., at 626. We noted, however, that the degree of intrusion depends upon the manner in which production of the urine sample is monitored. Under the District's Policy, male students produce samples at a urinal along a wall. They remain fully clothed and are only observed from behind, if at all. Female students produce samples in an enclosed stall, with a female monitor standing outside listening only for sounds of tampering. These conditions are nearly identical to those typically encountered in public restrooms, which men, women, and especially schoolchildren use daily. Under such conditions, the privacy interests compromised by the process of obtaining the urine sample are in our view negligible. The other privacy-invasive aspect of urinalysis is, of course, the information it discloses concerning the state of the subject's body, and the materials he has ingested. In this regard it is significant that the tests at issue here look only for drugs, and not for whether the student is, for example, epileptic, pregnant, or diabetic. See id., at 617. Moreover, the drugs for which the samples are screened are standard, and do not vary according to the identity of the student. And finally, the results of the tests are disclosed only to a limited class of school personnel who have a need to know; and they are not turned over to law enforcement authorities or used for any internal disciplinary function. . . .

Respondents argue, however, that the District's Policy is in fact more intrusive than this suggests, because it requires the students, if they are to avoid sanctions for a falsely positive test, to identify in advance prescription medications they are taking. We agree that this raises some cause for concern. In Von Raab, we flagged as one of the salutary features of the Customs Service drug-testing program the fact that employees were not required to disclose medical information unless they tested positive, and, even then, the information was supplied to a licensed physician rather than to the Government employer. See Von Raab, 489 U.S., at 672-673, n. 2. On the other hand, we have never indicated that requiring advance disclosure of medications is per se unreasonable. Indeed, in Skinner we held that it was not "a significant invasion of privacy." 489 U.S., at 626, n. 7. It can be argued that, in Skinner, the disclosure went only to the medical personnel taking the sample, and the Government personnel analyzing it, . . . and that disclosure to teachers and coaches—to persons who personally know the student—is a greater invasion of privacy. Assuming for the sake of argument that both those propositions are true, we do not believe they establish a difference that respondents are entitled to rely on here. The General Authorization Form that respondents refused to sign, which refusal was the basis for James's exclusion from the sports program, said only (in relevant part): "I . . . authorize the Vernonia School District to conduct a test on a urine specimen which I provide to test for drugs and/or alcohol use. I also authorize the release of information concerning the results of such a test to the Vernonia School District and to the parents and/or guardians of the student." App. 10-11. While the practice of the District seems to have been to have a school official take medication information from the student at the time of the test, that practice is not set forth in, or required by, the Policy, which says simply: "Student athletes who . . . are or have been taking prescription medication must provide verification (either by a copy of the prescription or by doctor's authorization) prior to being tested." Id., at 8. It may well be that, if and when James was selected for random testing at a time that he was taking medication, the School District would have permitted him to provide the requested information in a confidential manner—for example, in a sealed envelope delivered to the testing lab. Nothing in the Policy contradicts that, and when respondents choose, in effect, to challenge the Policy on its face, we will not assume the worst. Accordingly, we reach the same conclusion as in Skinner: that the invasion of privacy was not significant.

V

Finally, we turn to consider the nature and immediacy of the governmental concern at issue here, and the efficacy of this means for meeting it. In both Skinner and Von Raab, we characterized the government interest motivating the search as "compelling." Skinner, supra, 489 U.S., at 628, (interest in preventing railway accidents); Von Raab, supra, 489 U.S., at 670 (interest in insuring fitness of customs officials to interdict drugs and handle firearms). Relying on these cases, the District Court held that because the District's program also called for drug testing in the absence of individualized suspicion, the District "must demonstrate a 'compelling need' for the program." 796 F.Supp., at 1363. The Court of Appeals appears to have agreed with this view. See 23 F.3d, at 1526. It is a mistake, however, to think that the phrase "compelling state interest," in the Fourth Amendment context, describes a fixed, minimum quantum of governmental concern, so that one can dispose of a case by answering in isolation the question: Is there a compelling state interest here? Rather, the phrase describes an interest that appears important enough to justify the particular search at hand, in light of other factors that show the search to be relatively intrusive upon a genuine expectation of privacy. Whether that relatively high degree of government concern is necessary in this case or not, we think it is met. That the nature of the concern is important—indeed, perhaps compelling—can hardly be doubted. Deterring drug use by our Nation's schoolchildren is at least as important as enhancing efficient enforcement of the Nation's laws against the importation of drugs, which was the governmental concern in Von Raab, or deterring drug use by engineers and trainmen, which was the governmental concern in Skinner. School years are the time when the physical, psychological, and addictive effects of drugs are most severe. "Maturing nervous systems are more critically impaired by intoxicants than mature ones are; childhood losses in learning are lifelong and profound"; "children grow chemically dependent more quickly than adults, and their record of recovery is depressingly poor." . . . And of course the effects of a drug-infested school are visited not just upon the users, but upon the entire student body and faculty, as the educational process is disrupted. In the present case, moreover, the necessity for the State to act is magnified by the fact that this evil is being visited not just upon individuals at large, but upon children for whom it has undertaken a special responsibility of care and direction. Finally, it must not be lost sight of that this program is directed more narrowly to drug use by school athletes, where the risk of immediate physical harm to the drug user or those with whom he is playing his sport is particularly high. Apart from psychological effects, which include impairment of judgment, slow reaction time, and a lessening of the perception of pain, the particular drugs screened by the District's Policy have been demonstrated to pose substantial physical risks to athletes. . . .

As for the immediacy of the District's concerns: We are not inclined to question—indeed, we could not possibly find clearly erroneous—the District Court's conclusion that "a large segment of the student body, particularly those involved in interscholastic athletics, was in a state of rebellion," that "[d]isciplinary actions had reached 'epidemic proportions,'" and that "the rebellion was being fueled by alcohol and drug abuse as well as by the student's misperceptions about the drug culture." 796 F.Supp., at 1357. That is an immediate crisis of greater proportions than existed in Skinner, where we upheld the Government's drug-testing program based on findings of drug use by railroad employees nationwide, without proof that a problem existed on the particular railroads whose employees were subject to the test. . . . As to the efficacy of this means for addressing the problem: It seems to us self-evident that a drug problem largely fueled by the "role model" effect of athletes' drug use, and of particular danger to athletes, is effectively addressed by making sure that athletes do not use drugs. Respondents argue that a "less intrusive means to the same end" was available, namely, "drug testing on suspicion of drug use." Brief for Respondents 45-46. We have repeatedly refused to declare that only the "least intrusive" search practicable can be reasonable under the Fourth Amendment. Skinner, supra, at 629, n. 9 (collecting cases). Respondents' alternative entails substantial difficulties—if it is indeed practicable at all. It may be impracticable, for one thing, simply because the parents who are willing to accept random drug testing for athletes are not willing to accept accusatory drug testing for all students, which transforms the process into a badge of shame.

Respondents' proposal brings the risk that teachers will impose testing arbitrarily upon troublesome but not drug-likely students. It generates the expense of defending lawsuits that charge such arbitrary imposition, or that simply demand greater process before accusatory drug testing is imposed. And not least of all, it adds to the ever-expanding diversionary duties of schoolteachers the new function of spotting and bringing to account drug abuse, a task for which they are ill prepared, and which is not readily compatible with their vocation. . . . In many respects, we think, testing based on "suspicion" of drug use would not be better, but worse.

VI

Taking into account all the factors we have considered above—the decreased expectation of privacy, the relative unobtrusiveness of the search, and the severity of the need met by the search—we conclude Vernonia's Policy is reasonable and hence constitutional. We caution against the assumption that suspicionless drug testing will readily pass constitutional muster in other contexts. The most significant element in this case is the first we discussed: that the Policy was undertaken in furtherance of the government's responsibilities, under a public school system, as guardian and tutor of children entrusted to its care. Just as when the government conducts a search in its capacity as employer (a warrantless search of an absent employee's desk to obtain an urgently needed file, for example), the relevant question is whether that intrusion upon privacy is one that a reasonable employer might engage in, see O'Connor v. Ortega, 480 U.S. 709; so also when the government acts as guardian and tutor the relevant question is whether the search is one that a reasonable guardian and tutor might undertake. Given the findings of need made by the District Court, we conclude that in the present case it is.

We may note that the primary guardians of Vernonia's schoolchildren appear to agree. The record shows no objection to this districtwide program by any parents other than the couple before us here—even though, as we have described, a public meeting was held to obtain parents' views. We find insufficient basis to contradict the judgment of Vernonia's parents, its school board, and the District Court, as to what was reasonably in the interest of these children under the circumstances. The Ninth Circuit held that Vernonia's Policy not only violated the Fourth Amendment, but also, by reason of that violation, contravened Article I, § 9, of the Oregon Constitution. Our conclusion that the former holding was in error means that the latter holding rested on a flawed premise. We therefore vacate the judgment, and remand the case to the Court of Appeals for further proceedings consistent with this opinion.

It is so ordered.

 OTHER RELEVANT SIGNIFICANT CASES

Chapter 7.12 *State Action*

Chapter 7.15 *Search and Seizure/Right to Privacy*

Recent Trends

Extension of Vernonia

In 2002, the U.S. Supreme Court extended the scope of *Vernonia* to include all extracurricular activities. In *Board of Education v. Earls* (2002), the school district instituted a policy that required all students who participated in any competitive extracurricular activities, including band members, choir members, academic team members, and athletic team members, to submit to drug testing.

In upholding the policy, the U.S. Supreme Court held that the drug-testing policy reasonably served the school district's important interest in detecting and preventing drug use, and the policy did not violate the Fourth Amendment's prohibition against unreasonable searches and seizures.

DNA Testing

In 2005, the Chicago Bulls attempted to have one of their players, Eddy Curry, submit to a DNA test. Curry had missed the last thirteen games of the previous season after he was diagnosed with an irregular heartbeat. The Bulls, worried that Curry might have hypertrophic cardiomyopathy, an abnormal heart condition that combines a thickening or enlarging of the heart muscle and weak pumping power, insisted that Curry take a DNA test to determine whether he was susceptible to the same ailment that killed former Boston Celtics guard Reggie Lewis and Loyola Marymount star Hank Gathers. Curry refused the request, saying it violated his privacy, and the Bulls traded him to New York (Brennan, 2005).

With the amount of money involved in professional sports contracts, it seems likely that more and more teams will request players take DNA tests before signing them to long-term contracts.

World Anti-Doping Agency

In March 2003 the World Anti-Doping Agency announced a consolidated drug-control program for all international sports that creates a single list of banned drugs, a system for testing for them, and penalties for violators. The comprehensive antidrug code, which was signed by sixty-five sports federations and over fifty nations, including the United States, Britain, Russia, France, Germany, and Australia, covers all Olympic sports, the federations that govern them, and all their athletes. Up until the agreement, each Olympic sport had its own drug program.

Although the code does not apply to America's professional sports leagues, athletes from the NBA and the NHL who take part in the Olympics and certain other international competitions are subject to the code. That means they will face random drug testing, unannounced and out of competition.

Any sport that fails to follow the rules can be barred from the Olympics, and any nation that refuses to comply with the code may be barred from playing host to the Games. In addition, athletes will be held responsible for all positive findings, no matter how the drug got into their bodies. The penalties, which will result in a two-year suspensions the first time an athlete tests positive and a lifetime ban the next time, can be waived if athletes are able to show they were not at fault (Litsky, 2003).

The Drug Free Sports Act

Introduced by Representative Cliff Stearns (R-FL) in the wake of allegations of widespread steroid use in baseball, the Drug Free Sports Act is intended to establish a common drug-testing policy, using the standards set by the WADA for the NFL, NBA, NHL, Major League Baseball, Major League Soccer, and Arena Football League. The legislation would require a two-year ban for a first offense and a lifetime ban for a second; it would mandate two tests per athlete each year (H.R. 3084).

New Jersey Plans Broad Steroid Testing for School Sports

In December 2005 New Jersey became the first state to require random steroid testing for athletes on high school teams that qualify for postseason play. The program, which will test only for performance-enhancing drugs in championship tournaments, is scheduled to begin with the 2006–07 school year and will be overseen by the state's interscholastic athletic association. The group is now weighing possible penalties for students who test positive. One proposal would exclude them from competition but would allow their teams to play.

In issuing the order, the governor said that he felt compelled to issue the order after reviewing the findings of the task force he appointed earlier this year to study the use of steroids by student–athletes. The study, by the state's Division of Health Services, found that steroid use among New Jersey high school students had increased from 3 percent in 1995 to about 5 percent in 2001 (Jones, 2005).

Some people, however, have express concern over the cost of the program. Currently, New Jersey offers championships in thirty-one sports, typically involving about 10,000 students. Under the testing plan, about 5 percent of the participants, or 500 students, will be tested at random, which would bring the cost of the testing program to about $50,000 in the first year.

Several other states, including Illinois, Minnesota, and Rhode Island, had considered antisteroid legislation during 2005, but no programs were enacted. Officials in New Mexico have started random testing of student–athletes in four school districts as part of a pilot program that the state hopes to eventually expand statewide (Jones, 2005).

References

Cases

Bally v. Northeastern University, 403 Mass. 713, 532 N.E.2d 49 (1989).
Board of Education of Independent School District No. 92 of Pottawatomie County v. Earls, 536 U.S. 822 (2002).
Brennan v. Board of Trustees, 691 So.2d 324 (1997).
Foschi v. United States Swimming, Inc., 916 F. Supp. 232 (1996).
Hill v. National Collegiate Athletic Association, 865 P.2d 633, 26 Cal. Rptr.2d 834 (1994).
Long v. National Football League, 870 F. Supp. 101 (1994).
Shoemaker v. Handell, 795 F.2d 1136 (1986).
Trinidad School District v. Lopez, 963 P.2d 1095 (1998).
University of Colorado v. Derdeyn, 863 P.2d 929 (Colo. 1993).
Vernonia School District v. Acton, 515 U.S. 646 (1995).

Publications

Brennan, C. (2005, Oct. 13). Curry's case foreshadows DNA-tests-in-sports fight. *USA TODAY*, p. 7C.
Curtis, T. (1997). *Drug testing*. In D. J. Cotten & T. J. Wilde (Eds.), *Sport law for sport managers* (pp. 328–338). Dubuque, IA.: Kendall/Hunt Publishing.
Litsky, F. (2003, March 6). International drug code adopted for Olympic sports. *New York Times*, Sec. D, p. 5.
Jones, R. (2005, December 21). In first, New Jersey plans broad steroid testing for school sports. *The New York Times*, p. 1A.
Schmuck, P. (2003, March 7). Fehr still playing for time in addressing ephedrine issue; Union director to meet with O's players today. *The Baltimore Sun*, p. 1C.
Wong, G. M. (1994). *Essentials of amateur sports law* (2nd ed.). Westport, CT: Praeger Publishing.

Legislation

United States Constitution, Fourth Amendment

7.24 Participants with Disabilities

John T. Wolohan
Ithaca College

In the sport and recreation field, the line between lawful refusal to extend eligibility requirements and illegal discrimination against individuals with disabilities is getting cloudier all the time. This is especially true since 1990, when the Americans with Disabilities Act (ADA) was signed into law. Yet even with the enactment of the ADA, individuals with disabilities still face a number of obstacles in their struggle to participate in athletics. This chapter examines some of the many problems of individuals with disabilities in their fight to participate in sport and recreation activities.

Fundamental Concepts

As recently as 1970, children with learning disabilities were denied access into a number of state public school systems because it was thought that their presence would interfere with the learning environment of students without any disabilities (Clement, 1988). To remedy this situation, Congress, in the early 1970s, began enacting federal legislation designed to increase the opportunities available to individuals with disabilities (Clement, 1988). The first law passed by Congress was the Rehabilitation Act of 1973.

The Rehabilitation Act of 1973

Section 504 of the Rehabilitation Act states that

> No otherwise qualified handicapped individual in the United States, . . . shall solely by reason of his handicap, be excluded from participation in, be denied the benefits of, or be subjected to discrimination under any program or activity receiving Federal financial assistance. . . . (29 U.S.C. 794 (Supp. V 1993))

One of the stated intents of the Rehabilitation Act was to provide individuals with disabilities the opportunity to participate in physical education and athletic programs or activities without being discriminated against due to their disability.

For an individual to successfully pursue a claim under § 504, he or she must establish four elements: (1) that he or she is an *individual with a disability*; (2) that he or she is *otherwise qualified* for the athletic activity; (3) that he or she is being excluded from athletic participation *solely by reason of* their disabilities; and (4) that the *school, or institution is receiving federal financial assistance* (29 U.S.C. 794).

Because most challenges under § 504 hinge on the determination of the "otherwise qualified" element or the "solely by reason of" element, an examination of the meaning of those two elements is important. The U.S. Supreme Court, in *Southeastern Community College v. Davis* (1979), interpreted the phrase "otherwise qualified" to mean someone who is able to meet all of a program's requirements in spite of his or her handicap (*Southeastern Community College v. Davis*, 422 U.S. 397, at 406, 1979). Davis, who suffered from a serious hearing disability, sought entry into Southeastern Community College's school of nursing. The Supreme Court, in finding that Davis's hearing disability made it impossible for her to safely complete the nursing program, stated that § 504 of the Rehabilitation Act does not compel an institution to disregard an individual's disability or to make substantial modifications in their programs to accommodate individuals with disabilities.

In *Alexander v. Choate* (1985), the Supreme Court addressed what types of modifications would be required under § 504 when it held that although an organization need not be required to make fundamental or substantial modifications to accommodate an individual's disability, *it may be required to make reasonable ones*. Reasonable accommodation may include (1) making facilities used by employees readily accessible to and usable by individuals with disabilities, and (2) job restructuring, part-time or modified work schedules, acquisition or modification of equipment or devices, the provision of readers or interpreters, and similar actions (34 C.F.R. § 104.12. (b)).

The requirement that an individual be excluded *solely by reason of* the disability is met if the individual is being excluded due to their disability. For example, in *Poole v. South Plainfield Board of Education* (1980), the South Plainfield Board of Education denied Richard Poole the right to participate in South Plainfield's interscholastic wrestling program due to the fact that he was born with one kidney. Therefore, the court concluded that Poole was being excluded from participation in athletics "solely by reason of" the fact he had one kidney.

The issue of whether someone is being excluded "solely by reason of" their disability is more difficult when an individual, due to an illness or learning disability, is over the athletic association's maximum age requirement by the time he or she reaches their senior year in high school. *University Interscholastic League (UIL) and Bailey Marshall v. Buchanan* (1993) is a perfect illustration of the problem presented in these cases. In *UIL v. Buchanan* two nineteen-year-old students who were diagnosed with learning disabilities sought a permanent injunction against the enforcement of UIL's rule requiring all athletes to be under nineteen years old. In support of the age requirement, the UIL argued that the age requirement was necessary to ensure the safety of the participating student–athletes and to ensure the equality of competitors. The UIL also argued that the age rule did not discriminate against the plaintiffs because of their handicaps, but was applied equally against all students. Therefore, the plaintiffs were ineligible due to their ages, not their handicaps.

The Court of Appeals in affirming the trial court's injunction, enjoined UIL from enforcing the age rule against the plaintiffs, held that except for their handicaps the students would have turned nineteen after September 1 of their senior year and would have been age-eligible to participate in interscholastic athletics. In determining whether UIL had made reasonable accommodations for the plaintiffs' disabilities, the Court of Appeals examined the waiver mechanism UIL had in place for other eligibility rules. The waiver of the age rule, the Court of Appeals found, would be a reasonable accommodation by UIL to ensure that individuals with disabilities achieve meaningful access. The UIL's "no exception" policy to the age requirement, therefore, had to yield to the reasonable accommodation requirement of § 504 of the Rehabilitation Act.

For other cases challenging high school athletic association eligibility rules, see *Dennin v. Connecticut Interscholastic Athletic Conference* (1996); *Johnson v. Florida High School Activities Association* (1995); *Pottgen v. Missouri State High School Athletic Association* (1994); and *Sandison v. Michigan High School Athletic Association* (1995).

Individuals with Disabilities Education Act (IDEA)

On the heels of the Rehabilitation Act of 1973, Congress enacted the Education for All Handicapped Children Act of 1975. The purpose of the Education for All Handicapped Children Act was to increase the educational opportunity available to children with disabilities by providing the children a free appropriate public education that emphasizes special education and related services designed to meet their unique needs (20 U.S.C. 1400 (c)). In 1990, the Education for All Handicapped Children Act was amended and renamed the **Individuals with Disabilities Education Act (IDEA)**.

To satisfy the goal of the IDEA, local educational agencies, together with the student's teacher and parents, are required to develop a written statement or individualized education program (IEP) outlining achievable educational objectives for the student. Although less specific with regard to athletics than those pursuant to § 504 of the Rehabilitation Act, the regulations adopted under the IDEA do require each public agency to ensure that a variety of educational programs and services, including physical education, available to children without disabilities are available to those covered under the act. Besides providing educational programs and services, each public agency is also required to provide nonacademic and extracurricular activities and services in such manner as is necessary to afford children with disabilities an equal opportunity for participation in those services and activities (34 C.F.R. § 300.306(a)). For example, in *Lambert v. West Virginia State Board of Education* (1994), a high school basketball player, who has been deaf since birth, won the right to require her school to provide her with a sign language interpreter so that she could compete on the girl's basketball team. In holding that the Board of Education was required to provide a signer for the plaintiff, the court found that the assistance of a signer was a reasonable accommodation that provided the plaintiff with equal access to extracurricular activities.

Another example of a student–athlete successfully using the IDEA to gain participation rights is *Crocker v. Tennessee Secondary School Athletic Association* (1992). In *Crocker* the plaintiff transferred from a private school into his local public high school so that he could receive the special education he needed, which was not available in the private school. When the plaintiff attempted to participate in interscholastic athletics at his new school, the TSSAA ruled that he was ineligible. According to TSSAA rules, any student who transfers from one TSSAA member school to another is ineligible to participate in interscholastic sports for 12 months. The plaintiff argued that the TSSAA, by enforcing its transfer rule, was depriving him of his rights guaranteed under the IDEA. In ruling for Crocker, the Court held that because the plaintiff's transfer was motivated by his handicap, TSSAA's refusal to waive its transfer rule violated the IDEA.

Another important issue under IDEA is whether the student's participation in interscholastic athletics is a related service that should have been incorporated into his or her individualized education program (IEP). The importance of including participation in interscholastic athletics in a student's IEP can be seen in *T.H. v. Montana High School Association* (1992). In *T.H. v. MHSA*, the plaintiff, after being diagnosed as having a learning disability, was provided with an IEP in accordance with the IDEA. One component of the IEP was for the plaintiff to participate in interscholastic athletics as a motivational tool. Before his senior year, the Montana High School Association ruled T.H. ineligible to compete in interscholastic athletics due to his age. The court, in finding for the plaintiff, held that when participation in interscholastic sports is included as a component of the IEP, the privilege of competing in interscholastic sports is transformed into a federally protected right.

Ted Stevens Olympic and Amateur Sports Act

Another piece of legislation impacting the rights of individuals with disabilities is the **Ted Stevens Olympic and Amateur Sports Act** (36 U.S.C. § 220501). Originally passed in 1978 and called the Amateur Sports Act (36 U.S.C. §371), the law grants the U.S. Olympic Committee (USOC) exclusive jurisdiction over amateur athletics in the United States, including all matters pertaining to U.S. participation in the Olympic Games, the Paralympic Games, and the Pan-American Games.

In particular, the Amateur Sports Act required the USOC to "encourage and provide assistance to amateur athletic programs and competition for handicapped individuals, including, where feasible, the expansion of opportunities for meaningful participation by handicapped individuals in programs of athletic competition for able-bodied individuals" (36 U.S.C. § 374 (13)).

The USOC attempted to accomplish this goal by establishing the Committee on Sport for the Disabled and by financially supporting various other sports organizations, such as Disabled Sports USA and the Wheelchair Sports USA, to name a couple.

In 1998, the Amateur Sports Act was amended and renamed Ted Stevens Olympic and Amateur Sports Act, after the law's sponsor, Senator Ted Stevens of Alaska. The Ted Stevens Olympic and Amateur Sports Act places a greater responsibility on the USOC and its constituent organizations to serve elite athletes with a disability, in particular Paralympic athletes. As a result of the 1998 amendments, the USOC has sought to expand the opportunities available to athletes with disabilities by establishing a Paralympic Division within the USOC, providing increased funding and logistical support for athletes and sporting bodies, and recognizing Paralympic athletes as members of the USOC Athletes Advisory Committee and providing other avenues for input from Paralympic athletes.

Not everyone, however, has been happy with the amount of money and other support the USOC provides to Paralympic athletes. For example, in 2003, a lawsuit was filed by Scot Hollonbeck, a wheelchair racer who had won multiple medals at three Paralympics, seeking equitable access to programs and services that the USOC provided to U.S. Olympic athletes (Michaelis, 2003).

The Americans with Disabilities Act (ADA)

Perhaps the most powerful weapon individuals with disabilities have in their fight to participate in interscholastic athletics is **The Americans with Disabilities Act (ADA)**. Signed into law July 26, 1990, the purpose of the ADA is "to provide a clear and comprehensive national mandate for the elimination of discrimination against individuals with disabilities." The ADA focuses on eradicating barriers by requiring public entities to consider whether reasonable accommodations could be made to remove any barrier created by a person's disability (Wolohan, 1997). The ADA defines a "qualified individual with a disability" as any individual with a disability, either physically or mentally, "who, with or without reasonable modifications to rules, policies, or practices, the removal of architectural, communication . . . barriers, or the provision or auxiliary aids and services, meets the essential eligibility requirements for the receipt of services or the participation in programs or activities provided by a public entity" (42 U.S.C. 12115). The ADA is divided into five sections covering the rights of the disabled in the areas of employment, public services, transportation, and telecommunications. The three sections athletic administrators should be aware of are Title I, which covers employment; Title II, which covers public services; and Title III, which covers public accommodations and services operated by private entities.

Even if an individual is able to meet all the requirements of the ADA, the law does not require an organization to accommodate a person *"when that individual poses a direct threat to the health or safety of others"* (28 C.F.R. § 36.208). For example, in *Anderson v. Little League Baseball, Inc.* (1992), a youth baseball coach, who was confined to a wheelchair and had coached Little League Baseball for the previous three years as an on-field coach, sued the league after it adopted a policy prohibiting coaches in wheelchairs from on-field coaching. In support of the policy, the league claimed that the coach posed a direct threat to the health or safety of the athletes and that the policy was intended to protect the players from collisions with the wheelchair. In ruling for the coach, the Court said that the league's policy fell markedly short of the requirements of the ADA. The court found no evidence indicating that the plaintiff posed a direct threat to the health or safety of others.

Title I—Employment

Title I provides that "no covered entity shall discriminate against a qualified individual with a disability because of the disability of such individual in regard to job application procedures, the hiring, advancement, or discharge of employees, employee compensation, job training, and other terms, conditions, and privileges of employment" (42 U.S.C. § 12112). Title I of the ADA is covered in more detail in Chapter 8.16, *Title I of the Americans with Disabilities Act.*

Title II—Public Services

The section that covers the activities of high school athletic associations is Title II—Public Services. Title II, which is based on § 504 of the Rehabilitation Act, provides that "no qualified individual with a disability shall, by reason of such disability, be excluded from participation in or be denied the benefits of the services, programs, or activities of a public entity, or be subjected to discrimination by any such entity" (42 U.S.C. § 12132).

In interpreting the meaning of Title II, the Courts used the case history of § 504 of the Rehabilitation Act. To establish a violation of Title II of the ADA, therefore, an individual must establish the following elements: (1) that he or she is a "qualified individual with a disability"; (2) that he or she is "otherwise qualified" for the activity; (3) that he or she is being excluded from athletic participation "solely by reason of" their disabilities; and (4) that he or she is being discriminated against by a public entity.

Title III—Public Accommodations and Services Operated by Private Entities

The provisions of Title III provide that "no individual shall be discriminated against on the basis of disability in the full and equal enjoyment of the goods, services, facilities, privileges, advantages, or accommodations of any place of public accommodation by any person who owns, leases, or operates a place of public accommodation" (42 U.S.C. § 12182).

Significant Case

---◇◇---

The following case raises two interesting questions concerning the application of the Americans with Disabilities Act: first, whether the Act protects access to professional golf tournaments by a qualified entrant with a disability; and second, whether a disabled contestant may be denied the use of a golf cart because it would "fundamentally alter the nature" of the tournaments to allow him to ride when all other contestants must walk.

PGA TOUR, INC. V. CASEY MARTIN
United States Supreme Court
532 U.S. 661 (2001)

JUSTICE STEVENS delivered the opinion of the Court.

This case raises two questions concerning the application of the Americans with Disabilities Act . . . to a gifted athlete: first, whether the Act protects access to professional golf tournaments by a qualified entrant with a disability; and second, whether a disabled contestant may be denied the use of a golf cart because it would "fundamentally alter the nature" of the tournament, to allow him to ride when all other contestants must walk.

I

Petitioner PGA TOUR, Inc., a nonprofit entity formed in 1968, sponsors and cosponsors professional golf tournaments conducted on three annual tours. About 200 golfers participate in the PGA TOUR; about 170 in the NIKE TOUR; and about 100 in the SENIOR PGA TOUR. PGA TOUR and NIKE TOUR tournaments typically are 4-day events, played on courses leased and operated by petitioner. The entire field usually competes in two 18-hole rounds played on Thursday and Friday; those who survive the "cut" play on Saturday and Sunday and receive prize money in amounts determined by their aggregate scores for all four rounds. The revenues generated by television, admissions, concessions, and contributions from cosponsors amount to about $ 300 million a year, much of which is distributed in prize money.

There are various ways of gaining entry into particular tours. For example, a player who wins three NIKE TOUR events in the same year, or is among the top-15 money winners on that tour, earns the right to play in the PGA TOUR. Additionally, a golfer may obtain a spot in an official tournament through successfully competing in "open" qualifying rounds, which are conducted the week before each tournament. Most participants, however, earn playing privileges in the PGA TOUR or NIKE TOUR by way of a three-stage qualifying tournament known as the "Q-School."

Any member of the public may enter the Q-School by paying a $ 3,000 entry fee and submitting two letters of reference from, among others, PGA TOUR or NIKE TOUR members. The $ 3,000 entry fee covers the players' greens fees and the cost of golf carts, which are permitted during the first two stages, but which have been prohibited during the third stage since 1997. Each year, over a thousand contestants compete in the first stage, which consists of four 18-hole rounds at different locations. Approximately half of them make it to the second stage, which also includes 72 holes. Around 168 players survive the second stage and advance to the final one, where they compete over 108 holes. Of those finalists, about a fourth qualify for membership in the PGA TOUR, and the rest gain membership in the NIKE TOUR.

Three sets of rules govern competition in tour events. First, the "Rules of Golf," jointly written by the United States Golf Association (USGA) and the Royal and Ancient Golf Club of Scotland, apply to the game as it is played, not only by millions of amateurs on public courses and in private country clubs throughout the United States and worldwide, but also by the professionals in the tournaments conducted by petitioner, the USGA, the Ladies' Professional Golf Association, and the Senior Women's Golf Association. Those rules do not prohibit the use of golf carts at any time.

Second, the "Conditions of Competition and Local Rules," often described as the "hard card," apply specifically to petitioner's professional tours. The hard cards for the PGA TOUR and NIKE TOUR require players to walk the golf course during tournaments, but not during open qualifying rounds. On the SENIOR PGA TOUR, which is limited to golfers age 50 and older, the contestants may use golf carts. Most seniors, however, prefer to walk.

Third, "Notices to Competitors" are issued for particular tournaments and cover conditions for that specific event. Such a notice may, for example, explain how the Rules of Golf should be applied to a particular water hazard or man-made obstruction. It might also authorize the use of carts to speed up play when there is an unusual distance between one green and the next tee.

The basic Rules of Golf, the hard cards, and the weekly notices apply equally to all players in tour competitions. As one of petitioner's witnesses explained with reference to "the Masters Tournament, which is golf at its very highest level . . . the key is to have everyone tee off on the first hole under exactly the same conditions and all of them be tested over that 72-hole event under the conditions that exist during those four days of the event."

II

Casey Martin is a talented golfer. As an amateur, he won 17 Oregon Golf Association junior events before he was 15, and won the state championship as a high school senior. He played on the Stanford University golf team that won the 1994 National Collegiate Athletic Association (NCAA) championship. As a professional, Martin qualified for the NIKE TOUR in 1998 and 1999, and based on his 1999 performance, qualified for the PGA TOUR in 2000. In the 1999 season, he entered 24 events, made the cut 13 times, and had 6 top-10 finishes, coming in second twice and third once.

Martin is also an individual with a disability as defined in the Americans with Disabilities Act. Since birth he has been afflicted with Klippel-Trenaunay-Weber Syndrome, a degenerative circulatory disorder that obstructs the flow of blood from his right leg back to his heart. The disease is progressive; it causes severe pain and has atrophied his right leg. During the latter part of his college career, because of the progress of the disease, Martin could no longer walk an 18-hole golf course. Walking not only caused him pain, fatigue, and anxiety, but also created a significant risk of hemorrhaging, developing blood clots, and fracturing his tibia so badly that an amputation might be required. For these reasons, Stanford made written requests to the Pacific 10 Conference and the NCAA to waive for Martin their rules requiring players to walk and carry their own clubs. The requests were granted.

When Martin turned pro and entered petitioner's Q-School, the hard card permitted him to use a cart during his successful progress through the first two stages. He made a request, supported by detailed medical records, for permission to use a golf cart during the third stage. Petitioner refused to review those records or to waive its walking rule for the third stage. Martin therefore filed this action. A preliminary injunction entered by the District Court made it possible for him to use a cart in the final stage of the Q-School and as a competitor in the NIKE TOUR and PGA TOUR. Although not bound by the injunction, and despite its support for petitioner's position in this litigation, the USGA voluntarily granted Martin a similar waiver in events that it sponsors, including the U.S. Open.

IV

Congress enacted the ADA in 1990 to remedy widespread discrimination against disabled individuals. In studying the need for such legislation, Congress found that "historically, society has tended to isolate and segregate individuals with disabilities, and, despite some improvements, such forms of discrimination against individuals with disabilities continue to be a serious and pervasive social problem." . . .

To effectuate its sweeping purpose, the ADA forbids discrimination against disabled individuals in major areas of public life, among them employment (Title I of the Act), public services (Title II), and public accommodations (Title III). At issue now, as a threshold matter, is the applicability of Title III to petitioner's golf tours and qualifying rounds, in particular to petitioner's treatment of a qualified disabled golfer wishing to compete in those events.

Title III of the ADA prescribes, as a "general rule":

"No individual shall be discriminated against on the basis of disability in the full and equal enjoyment of the goods, services, facilities, privileges, advantages, or accommodations of any place of public accommodation by any person who owns, leases (or leases to), or operates a place of public accommodation." 42 U.S.C. § 12182(a).

The phrase "public accommodation" is defined in terms of 12 extensive categories, which the legislative history indicates "should be construed liberally" to afford people with disabilities "equal access" to the wide variety of establishments available to the nondisabled.

It seems apparent, from both the general rule and the comprehensive definition of "public accommodation," that petitioner's golf tours and their qualifying rounds fit comfortably within the coverage of Title III, and Martin within its protection. The events occur on "golf courses," a type of place specifically identified by the Act as a public accommodation. § 12181(7)(L). In addition, at all relevant times, petitioner "leases" and "operates" golf courses to conduct its Q-School and tours. § 12182(a). As a lessor and operator of golf courses, then, petitioner must not discriminate against any "individual" in the "full and equal enjoyment of the goods, services, facilities, privileges, advantages, or accommodations" of those courses. *Ibid.* Certainly, among the "privileges" offered by petitioner on the courses are those of competing in the Q-School and playing in the tours; indeed, the former is a privilege for which thousands of individuals from the general public pay, and the latter is one for which they vie. Martin, of course, is one of those individuals. It would therefore appear that Title III of the ADA, by its plain terms, prohibits petitioner from denying Martin equal access to its tours on the basis of his disability. . . .

Petitioner argues otherwise. To be clear about its position, it does not assert (as it did in the District Court) that it is a private club altogether exempt from Title III's coverage. In fact, petitioner admits that its tournaments are conducted at places of public accommodation. Nor does petitioner contend (as it did in both the District Court and the Court of Appeals) that the competitors' area "behind the ropes" is not a public accommodation, notwithstanding the status of the rest of the golf course. Rather, petitioner reframes the coverage issue by arguing that the competing golfers are not members of the class protected by Title III of the ADA.

According to petitioner, Title III is concerned with discrimination against "clients and customers" seeking to obtain "goods and services" at places of public accommodation, whereas it is Title I that protects persons who work at such places. As the argument goes, petitioner operates not a "golf course" during its tournaments but a "place of exhibition or entertainment," . . . and a professional golfer such as Martin, like an actor in a theater production, is a provider rather than a consumer of the entertainment that petitioner sells to the public. Martin therefore cannot bring a claim under Title III because he is not one of the " '*clients or customers*' of the covered public accommodation.' " Rather, Martin's claim of discrimination is "job-related" and could only be brought under Title I—but that Title does not apply because he is an independent contractor (as the District Court found) rather than an employee.

* * *

We need not decide whether petitioner's construction of the statute is correct, because petitioner's argument falters even on its own terms. If Title III's protected class were limited to "clients or customers," it would be entirely appropriate to classify the golfers who pay petitioner $ 3,000 for the chance to compete in the Q-School and, if successful, in the subsequent tour events, as petitioner's clients or customers. In our view, petitioner's tournaments (whether situated at a "golf course" or at a "place of exhibition or entertainment") simultaneously offer at least two "privileges" to the public—that of watching the golf competition and that of competing in it. Although the latter is more difficult and more expensive to obtain than the former, it is nonetheless a privilege that petitioner makes available to members of the general public. In consideration of the entry fee, any golfer with the requisite letters of recommendation acquires the opportunity to qualify for and compete in petitioner's tours. Additionally, any golfer who succeeds in the open qualifying rounds for a tournament may play in the event. That petitioner identifies one set of clients or customers that it serves (spectators at tournaments) does not preclude it from having another set (players in tournaments) against whom it may not discriminate. It would be inconsistent with the literal text of the statute as well as its expansive purpose to read Title III's coverage, even given petitioner's suggested limitation, any less broadly.

* * *

V

As we have noted, 42 U.S.C. § 12182(a) sets forth Title III's general rule prohibiting public accommodations from discriminating against individuals because of their disabilities. The question whether petitioner has violated that rule depends on a proper construction of the term "discrimination," which is defined by Title III to include:

"a failure to make reasonable modifications in policies, practices, or procedures, when such modifications are necessary to afford such goods, services, facilities, privileges, advantages, or accommodations to individuals with disabilities, *unless the entity can demonstrate that making such modifications would fundamentally alter the nature* of such goods, services, facilities, privileges, advantages, or accommodations." § 12182(b)(2)(A)(ii) (emphasis added).

Petitioner does not contest that a golf cart is a reasonable modification that is necessary if Martin is to play in its tournaments. Martin's claim thus differs from one that might be asserted by players with less serious afflictions that make walking the course uncomfortable or difficult, but not beyond their capacity. In such cases, an accommodation might be reasonable but not necessary. In this case, however, the narrow dispute is whether allowing Martin to use a golf cart, despite the walking requirement that applies to the PGA TOUR, the NIKE TOUR, and the third stage of the Q-School, is a modification that would "fundamentally alter the nature" of those events.

In theory, a modification of petitioner's golf tournaments might constitute a fundamental alteration in two different ways. It might alter such an essential aspect of the game of golf that it would be unacceptable even if it affected all competitors equally; changing the diameter of the hole from three to six inches might be such a modification. Alternatively, a less significant change that has only a peripheral impact on the game itself might nevertheless give a disabled player, in addition to access to the competition as required by Title III, an advantage over others and, for that reason, fundamentally alter the character of the competition. We are not persuaded that a waiver of the walking rule for Martin would work a fundamental alteration in either sense.

As an initial matter, we observe that the use of carts is not itself inconsistent with the fundamental character of the game of golf. From early on, the essence of the game has been shot-making—using clubs to cause a ball to progress from the teeing ground to a hole some distance away with as few strokes as possible. That essential aspect of the game is still reflected in the very first of the Rules of Golf, which declares: "The Game of Golf consists in playing a ball from the *teeing ground* into the hole by a *stroke* or successive strokes in accordance with the rules." . . . Over the years, there have been many changes in the players' equipment, in golf course design, in the Rules of Golf, and in the method of transporting clubs from hole to hole. Originally, so few clubs were used that each player could carry them without a bag. Then came golf bags, caddies, carts that were pulled by hand, and eventually motorized carts that carried players as well as clubs. "Golf carts started appearing with increasing regularity on American golf courses in the 1950's. Today they are everywhere. And they are encouraged. For one thing, they often speed up play, and for another, they are great revenue producers." There is nothing in the Rules of Golf that either forbids the use of carts, or penalizes a player for using a cart. That set of rules, as we have observed, is widely accepted in both the amateur and professional golf world as the rules of the game. The walking rule that is contained in petitioner's hard cards, based on an optional condition buried in an appendix to the Rules of Golf, is not an essential attribute of the game itself.

Indeed, the walking rule is not an indispensable feature of tournament golf either. As already mentioned, petitioner permits golf carts to be used in the SENIOR PGA TOUR, the open qualifying events for petitioner's tournaments, the first two stages of the Q-School, and, until 1997, the third stage of the Q-School as well. Moreover, petitioner allows the use of carts during certain tournament rounds in both the PGA TOUR and the NIKE TOUR. . . .

Petitioner, however, distinguishes the game of golf as it is generally played from the game that it sponsors in the PGA TOUR, NIKE TOUR, and (at least recently) the last stage of the Q-School—golf at the "highest level." According to petitioner, "the goal of the highest-level competitive athletics is to assess and compare the performance of different competitors, a task that is meaningful only if the competitors are subject to identical substantive rules." The waiver of any possibly "outcome-affecting" rule for a contestant would violate this principle and therefore, in petitioner's view, fundamentally alter the nature of the highest level athletic event. The walking rule is one such rule, petitioner submits, because its purpose is "to inject the element of fa-

tigue into the skill of shot-making," and thus its effect may be the critical loss of a stroke. As a consequence, the reasonable modification Martin seeks would fundamentally alter the nature of petitioner's highest level tournaments even if he were the only person in the world who has both the talent to compete in those elite events and a disability sufficiently serious that he cannot do so without using a cart.

The force of petitioner's argument is, first of all, mitigated by the fact that golf is a game in which it is impossible to guarantee that all competitors will play under exactly the same conditions or that an individual's ability will be the sole determinant of the outcome. For example, changes in the weather may produce harder greens and more head winds for the tournament leader than for his closest pursuers. ... Whether such happenstance events are more or less probable than the likelihood that a golfer afflicted with Klippel-Trenaunay-Weber Syndrome would one day qualify for the NIKE TOUR and PGA TOUR, they at least demonstrate that pure chance may have a greater impact on the outcome of elite golf tournaments than the fatigue resulting from the enforcement of the walking rule.

Further, the factual basis of petitioner's argument is undermined by the District Court's finding that the fatigue from walking during one of petitioner's 4-day tournaments cannot be deemed significant. The District Court credited the testimony of a professor in physiology and expert on fatigue, who calculated the calories expended in walking a golf course (about five miles) to be approximately 500 calories—"nutritionally . . . less than a Big Mac." 994 F. Supp. at 1250. What is more, that energy is expended over a 5-hour period, during which golfers have numerous intervals for rest and refreshment. In fact, the expert concluded, because golf is a low intensity activity, fatigue from the game is primarily a psychological phenomenon in which stress and motivation are the key ingredients. . . .

Moreover, when given the option of using a cart, the majority of golfers in petitioner's tournaments have chosen to walk, often to relieve stress or for other strategic reasons. . . .

Even if we accept the factual predicate for petitioner's argument—that the walking rule is "outcome affecting" because fatigue may adversely affect performance—its legal position is fatally flawed. Petitioner's refusal to consider Martin's personal circumstances in deciding whether to accommodate his disability runs counter to the clear language and purpose of the ADA. As previously stated, the ADA was enacted to eliminate discrimination against "individuals" with disabilities, and to that end Title III of the Act requires without exception that any "policies, practices, or procedures" of a public accommodation be reasonably modified for disabled "individuals" as necessary to afford access unless doing so would fundamentally alter what is offered, § 12182(b)(2)(A)(ii). To comply with this command, an individualized inquiry must be made to determine whether a specific modification for a particular person's disability would be reasonable under the circumstances as well as necessary for that person, and yet at the same time not work a fundamental alteration. . . .

To be sure, the waiver of an essential rule of competition for anyone would fundamentally alter the nature of petitioner's tournaments. As we have demonstrated, however, the walking rule is at best peripheral to the nature of petitioner's athletic events, and thus it might be waived in individual cases without working a fundamental alteration. Therefore, petitioner's claim that all the substantive rules for its "highest-level" competitions are sacrosanct and cannot be modified under any circumstances is effectively a contention that it is exempt from Title III's reasonable modification requirement. But that provision carves out no exemption for elite athletics, and given Title III's coverage not only of places

of "exhibition or entertainment" but also of "golf courses," . . . its application to petitioner's tournaments cannot be said to be unintended or unexpected. . . .

Under the ADA's basic requirement that the need of a disabled person be evaluated on an individual basis, we have no doubt that allowing Martin to use a golf cart would not fundamentally alter the nature of petitioner's tournaments. As we have discussed, the purpose of the walking rule is to subject players to fatigue, which in turn may influence the outcome of tournaments. Even if the rule does serve that purpose, it is an uncontested finding of the District Court that Martin "easily endures greater fatigue even with a cart than his able-bodied competitors do by walking." The purpose of the walking rule is therefore not compromised in the slightest by allowing Martin to use a cart. . . . As a result, Martin's request for a waiver of the walking rule should have been granted.

* * *

The judgment of the Court of Appeals is affirmed.

 OTHER RELEVANT SIGNIFICANT CASES

Chapter 8.16 *Title I of the Americans with Disabilities Act*

Recent Trends

Eligibility Rights of the Disabled

Several states' high school athletic associations are amending bylaws to address the special needs of learning disabled students, and many more are expected to follow. As special-needs students have been increasingly mainstreamed into public and private schools, athletic associations are being forced to investigate the adequacy of their rules, regulations, and exemptions. Recently, a decision by the OSHAA declaring a football player academically ineligible was overturned by the district court. The player, who had documented learning disabilities, made up work over the summer with the assistance of a tutor. The district court found that the student–athlete's school had not implemented the player's Individual Educational Plan (IEP) properly, thus making it beyond the student's control. The court ruled that OSHAA's exceptions to the "no makeup rule" were unreasonable because they did not include a situation that addressed the aforementioned circumstances (*Ingram v. Toledo City School District Board of Education*, 2004).

Recreational Activities

Ever since the U.S. Supreme Court's ruling in Martin, sport and recreation administrators around the country have been forced to ask themselves what rules are essential to the nature of sport. In *Kuketz v. Petronelli*, 821 N.E.2d 473 (MA. 2005), Stephen Kuketz, a nationally ranked wheelchair racquetball player, wanted to join the Brockton Athletic Club men's "A" league so that he could compete against the best able-bodied players available to help prepare for upcoming international wheelchair competitions. Because of his physical limitations, however, Kuketz requested that the club allow him the wheelchair-racquetball-standard two bounces during "A" league play, instead of the one bounce allowable under standard racquetball rules.

Citing safety reasons, the club rejected Kuketz's request. Disappointed with the decision, Kuketz sued the club claiming the decision violated both federal and state antidiscrimination laws, and that the ADA required the club to conduct an individualized assessment both of his abilities and of the reasonableness of the requested modification.

In evaluating whether the club unlawfully discriminated against Kuketz when it refused to modify its policies and practices, the Supreme Judicial Court of Massachusetts held that unlike the use of carts in golf, the allowance for more than one bounce in racquetball was inconsistent with the fundamental character of the game. As expressly articulated in the rules of racquetball, the court found that the essence of the game of racquetball is the hitting of a moving ball with a racquet before the second bounce. Giving a player in a wheelchair two bounces and a player on foot one bounce in head-to-head competition would alter such an essential aspect of the game that it would be unacceptable, even if it affected all competitors equally. In addition, the court found that unlike golf, the speed at which racquetball is played is important and is one of the factors distinguishing players in different levels. Therefore, if one player were allowed to play the game with two bounces, it would require a change in the strategy, positioning, and movement of the players during the game and would essentially create a new game, with new strategies and new rules.

As for Kuketz's argument that the club should do an individual assessment of his particular circumstances before rejecting his specific modification requests, the court found that this argument was based on a misreading of the ADA and *Martin*. In particular, the court held that although an individualized inquiry was required by the ADA, no assessment was necessary if waiving the one-bounce rule would cause a fundamental alteration to the nature of the event. Therefore, because Kuketz's requested modification would in fact require the waiver of an essential rule of competition, the club did not need to make an individualized inquiry to determine the reasonableness of those modifications (Wolohan, 2005).

References

Cases

Alexander v. Choate, 469 U.S. 287 (1985).

Anderson v. Little League Baseball, 794 F. Supp. 342 (1992).

Booth v. El Paso Independent School District, Civil No. A-90-CA-764 (Tex. Dist. Ct. 1990).

Crocker v. Tennessee Secondary School Athletic Association, 980 F.2d 382 (6th Cir. 1992).

Dennin v. Connecticut Interscholastic Athletic Conference, 913 F. Supp. 663 (1996).

Ingram v. Toledo City School District Board of Education, 2004.

Johnson v. Florida High School Activities Association Inc., 899 F. Supp. 579 (M.D. Fla. 1995).

Knapp v. Northwestern University, 101 F.3d 473 (7th Cir. 1996).

Kuketz v. Petronelli, 821 N.E.2d 473 (MA. 2005).

Lambert v. West Virginia State Board of Education and the West Virginia Secondary School Activities Commission, 447 S.E.2d 901 (W.Va. 1994).

PGA Tour v. Casey Martin, 532 U.S. 661 (2001).

Poole v. South Plainfield Board of Education, 490 F. Supp. 948 (D. N.J. 1980).

Pottgen v. Missouri State High School Athletic Association, 40 F.3d 926 (8th Cir. 1994).

Sandison v. Michigan High School Athletic Association, 64 F.3d 1026 (6th Cir. 1995).

School Board of Nassau County, Fla. v. Arline, 480 U.S. 273 (1987).

Southeastern Community College v. Davis, 422 U.S. 397 (1979).

T.H. v. Montana High School Association, CV 92-150-BLG-JFB (1992).

University Interscholastic League and Bailey Marshall v. Buchanan, 848 S.W. 2d. 298 (1993).

Williams v. Wakefield Basketball Association (CA-01-10434-DPW) (2003).

Publications

Clement, A. (1988). *Law in sport and physical activity*. Dubuque, IA: Brown & Benchmark.

A win for a boy who just wants to play. (1999, November 18). *The Santa Fe New Mexican*, D-1.

Michaelis, V. (2003, July 29). Citing inequities, Paralympians sue USOC. *USA TODAY*, Sec. C, p. 3.

Wolohan, J. (1997a). An ethical and legal dilemma: Participation in sports by HIV infected athletes. *Marq. Sports L.J.*, 7, 345.

Wolohan, J. (1997b). Are age restrictions a necessary requirement for participating in interscholastic athletic programs? *UMKC. L. Rev.*, 66, 345.

Wolohan, J. (2003, March). The big dance: Administrators must tread carefully when deciding whether to accommodate individuals with disabilities. *Athletic Business,* pp. 20–24.

Wolohan, J. (2005, June). Bounce check: A club is not required to change its racquetball league rules for a wheelchair athlete. *Athletic Business,* pp. 18–22.

Legislation

The Rehabilitation Act of 1973, 29 U.S.C. § 701 *et seq.*

The Individuals with Disabilities Education Act, 20 U.S.C. § 1400 *et seq.*

The Americans with Disabilities Act, 42 U.S.C. § 12101 *et seq.*

The Amateur Sports Act, 36 U.S.C. § 371–396.

Ted Stevens Olympic and Amateur Sports Act, 36 U.S.C. § 220501-220529.

7.25 Religious Issues

Susan Brown Foster
Saint Leo University

Although the courts have been faced with myriad religious issue cases, one of the central themes running through all the challenges is the inherent conflict between the Establishment Clause and Free Exercise Clause. Both clauses can be found in the First Amendment to the U.S. Constitution, which states: "Congress shall make no law respecting an establishment of religion, or prohibiting the free exercise thereof; or abridging the freedom of speech, or of the press; or the right of the people peaceably to assemble, and to petition the Government for a redress of grievances."

The courts have interpreted these words under the **Establishment Clause** to mean the government or any of its entities may not promote a specific religion. At the same time, under the **Free Exercise Clause**, the courts have ruled that the government may not stand in the way of any individual who wishes to practice his/her religion. As a result, public institutions find it difficult to apply either of the two clauses too vigorously without violating the other clause.

Fundamental Concepts

The Dichotomies

The Establishment Clause v. Freedom of Speech

The trigger point for the numerous cases regarding the First Amendment is: What is middle ground between the establishment of religion and allowance for freedom of speech? As stated in *Board of Education of the Westside Community Schools v. Mergens* (1990), there is a "crucial difference between government speech endorsing religion which the Establishment Clause forbids, and private speech that may contain a prayerful message, which the Free Speech and Free Exercise Clauses protect." In attempting to assist governmental bodies in determining a safe haven approach for student prayer, the courts have established several general concepts.

Student-Initiated Prayer

In *Santa Fe Independent School District v. Doe* (2000), students voted on whether or not to have an "invocation" and then voted on the person to deliver it. The U.S. Supreme Court ruled against the School District because it felt

- There was substantial control over content by the principal.
- An invocation had historically been delivered before football games.
- The message was labeled an invocation.
- There was perceived intent to continue the practice of delivering a religious message.

In *Adler v. Duval County School Board* (2001), it was the students who decided whether or not to have an opening or closing message at graduation. If the students decided to have such a message, the senior class selected a student volunteer(s) to give the message. The content of the message was left up to the individual student. No one was allowed to review content. The Eleventh Circuit Court clearly felt that this process exonerated the school board from establishing any religion while still allowing a prayer to be said if the volunteer so chose, thus supporting Freedom of Speech.

Administrative Control and Influence

In 1992, on remand from the Supreme Court following their *Lee v. Weisman* (1992) decision in which the court ruled that providing for nonsectarian prayer by a school-selected clergyman violated the Establishment Clause, the Fifth Circuit rendered its "Clear Creek Prayer Policy" in *Jones v. Clear Creek Independent School District* (1992). This policy allowed a student-selected, student-given, nonsectarian, nonproselytizing invocation and benediction at high school graduation.

Similar to *Adler, Santa Fe,* and *Jones* is *Appenheimer v. School Board of Washington Community High School District 308* (2001), where the school indicated they allowed elected senior class officers to make a decision regarding the inclusion of an invocation at commencement. The officers solicited volunteers for all speeches, including the invocation. The U.S. Central District Court for Illinois disallowed the practice because the Chair of the English Department had the final say over content and prohibited a student from speaking if it was felt the prayer was inappropriate.

Although *Adler, Jones,* and *Appenheimer* are not Supreme Court decisions, these decisions enforce the common theme in *Santa Fe* that administrative control will render any prayer policy invalid. The Courts have indicated an invocation is possible if true student control can be proven. The Freedom of Speech and Free Exercise Clauses in the First Amendment do not permit suppression of student-initiated prayer. To do so would display hostility toward religion, a violation of the Free Exercise Clause. Some courts have implied and stated that teaching students that prayer itself is forbidden is a demonstration of hostility and leads into the next dichotomy.

Religion v. Prayer

This second dichotomy is a little more subtle. The courts have stated that the offering of a prayer, especially when there is no reference to deity, is not necessarily religious entanglement. The rationale lies behind the fact that one prayer, any prayer, does not necessarily endorse any specific religion. In *Chaudhuri v. State of Tennessee* (1997), the Tennessee State University administration, after repeated challenges to its prayer allowance at university functions, authorized a moment of silence. At the graduation ceremony following the initiation of this policy, a university-selected local pastor and prominent educator asked the audience to stand in a moment of silence. The audience proceeded to recite "The Lord's Prayer." The Sixth Circuit Court implied that many religions cite this prayer, and it was not an endorsement of any particular religion even if a local pastor was invited by the administration to ask the audience to stand.

Other courts have expressed the opinion that religion is not irrelevant to education. Religious thought is part of education and many curricula. However, teaching of a particular religion or advancing particular religious views by educators is forbidden under the entanglement theory.

Graduation Ceremonies v. Extracurricular Activities

Courts have ruled that graduation is, and has always been, a rather solemn occasion, which has historically been marked with prayer. However, as the Supreme Court noted in *Santa Fe*, "regardless of whether one considers a sporting event an appropriate occasion for solemnity, the use of an invocation to foster such solemnity is impermissible when it constitutes prayer sponsored by the school." Additionally, the court felt that because school officials were present and had authority to stop the prayer, it implied the school district's endorsement.

Another case dealing with prayer at a sporting event is *Doe v. Duncanville Independent School District* (1995). The Fifth Circuit Court allowed the singing of a religious-themed song before each game for secular reasons, but disallowed prayer before a game due largely to entanglement, while still stating there was no solemnity in a basketball game.

Several parties have attempted to assert a **limited open forum theory** as a rationale for providing free speech. To establish a limited open forum, an individual must first show that there is governmental intent to open the event to the public. A graduation ceremony is generally not a public event. Individuals are invited to attend by virtue of their relationship with one of the graduates. Second, a public forum may be limited to specific speakers to discuss specific subjects, thus the term "limited open forum." The graduation ceremony itself is not open to general assembly or for debate of a number of different issues. If a public forum is to be created, the government must allow general access.

The limited public forum has been used extensively in cases for one main reason: if graduation is designated as a limited public forum, the government cannot discriminate against speech even if the message is religious. In general, a gathering is a public forum if general access or random use is allowed. The Eleventh Circuit Court in *Santa Fe*, citing *Perry Education Association v. Perry Local Educators' Association* (1983), discussed three classifications.

1. *Traditional public*—A venue that is generally acceptable of assembly and debate (e.g., parks and streets)
2. *Public created by government designation*—A place or channel of communication for use by the public at large for assembly and speech or for discussion
3. *Nonpublic*—Government-owned property to which the First Amendment does not guarantee access

In *American Civil Liberties Union of New Jersey v. Black Horse Pike Regional Board of Education* (1996), a principal denied an ACLU member the right to speak at graduation on the topic of safe sex and condom use after the senior class voted to have some form of prayer at graduation. The court highlighted this as an example of the control administrators have over the speech topics at graduation, thus establishing a nonpublic use of public property. In *Adler*, the plaintiffs claimed the school board provided a platform and opportunity for prayer, thus creating the situation where a student graduation speaker converted a private speech into a "public, state-sponsored speech." In rejecting this argument, the court held that by simply "providing the platform, the speech becomes public." The Eleventh Circuit Court, citing the 1984 Equal Access Act, stated that the northern Florida county school board policy of allowing student-elected speakers to deliver a message of any content did not violate the Establishment Clause. The graduation venue is equally available for religious or secular expression as would be allowed under the Equal Access Act, but support for designating graduation ceremonies as public forums, limited or otherwise, is not there.

The Maturity of the Audience

In several cases, the courts have indicated that the age of an audience can be a determining factor too. College graduation ceremonies, where religious exercise was permitted, is one example. *Chaudhuri* involved a college professor who practiced Hinduism and the college custom of allowing prayers or moments of silence at university-related events. *Tanford v. Brand* (1996) involved a law professor, two law students, and a senior who protested the practice of allowing a 150-year-old tradition of invocations and benedictions at Indiana University graduations. Both courts indicated that one purpose of higher education is to advance and foster appreciation of diverse viewpoints. Merely asking a mature adult audience to stand and listen to a nonsectarian, nonproselytizing message did not coerce individuals into endorsing or accepting another religion. In both cases, the university selected the clergyman to deliver the message. This practice was identical to the situation in *Lee v. Weisman* (1992), where a middle school administration selected a rabbi. However, the *Lee* court felt the age of the audience led to coercion because the students would not have as much freedom, nor feel as comfortable, to state an objection due to peer pressure.

Prayer in postsecondary education has largely gone untested by the Supreme Court, as acknowledged by the Fourth Circuit in *Mellen v. Bunting* (2003). Even so, this Circuit went on to rule that a supper prayer at Virginia Military Institute (VMI) violated the Establishment Clause citing coercion as the main constitutional issue. Recently, the courts have been active, and more is being written about the maturity of the audience (Elliott, 2005; Pihos, 2005; *Newdow v. Congress of the United States of America*, 2005; *Simpson v. Chesterfield County Board of Supervisors*, 2005).

The Three Tests

The Supreme Court has established three complementary and occasionally overlapping tests to examine religious practices challenged under the First Amendment. These tests include the three-part *Lemon* Test, the Coercion Test, and the Endorsement Test.

The Lemon Test

The three-part **Lemon test** is the one with the longest pedigree. Under the *Lemon* test, a government practice is unconstitutional if (1) it lacks a secular purpose, (2) its primary effect either advances or inhibits religion, or (3) it excessively entangles government with religion (*Lemon v. Kurtzman*, 1971).

The Coercion Test

In the **coercion test**, which the Court announced in *Lee v. Weisman* (1992), school-sponsored religious activity is analyzed to determine the extent, if any, to which it has a coercive effect on students. "Unconstitutional coercion [occurs] when: 1) the government directs 2) a formal religious exercise 3) in such a way as to oblige the participation of objectors" (*Jones v. Clear Creek Independent School District*, 1992). For example, in *Santa Fe*, the Supreme Court stated that band members and cheerleaders who are required to attend a football game because of their membership in those groups in effect are coerced into listening to any prayer or message delivered. This was part of their rationale in striking down prayer before football games.

The Endorsement Test

The **endorsement test**, created by Justice Sandra Day O'Connor in a concurring opinion in *Lynch v. Donnelly* (1984), seeks to determine whether the government endorses religion by means of the challenged action. In deciding that a city's inclusion of a nativity scene in its Christmas display was constitutional, Justice O'Connor felt the clarifying test for the Establishment Clause was that governmental intent or a governmental practice not convey or communicate a message of endorsement or disapproval of religion.

For example, in *Ingebretsen on Behalf of Ingebretsen v. Jackson Public School District* (1996), Mississippi had passed a "School Prayer Statute" allowing students to initiate nonsectarian, nonproselytizing prayer at compulsory and noncompulsory events including sporting events. The Fifth Circuit Court, while ruling the practice constitutional for graduation, held the statute was unconstitutional under all the tests for other events. The Fifth Circuit Court stated that allowing school officials in their capacity to lead students in prayer, it does not set aside for anything else not only constituted coercion but clearly endorsed religion.

Significant Case

The following case involves student-initiated prayer before a high school football game. Although it is clear that a public school cannot promote a specific religion, it is not clear what happens when the school allows student-initiated prayer. In examining the case, it is important to look at how much, if any, control school administrators have over the content or the student selected to give the prayer.

SANTA FE HIGH INDEPENDENT SCHOOL DISTRICT V. DOE

United States Supreme Court
530 U.S. 290 (2000)

Prior to 1995, the Santa Fe High School student who occupied the school's elective office of student council chaplain delivered a prayer over the public address system before each varsity football game for the entire season. This practice, along with others, was challenged in District Court as a violation of the Establishment Clause of the First Amendment. While these proceedings were pending in the District Court, the school district adopted a different policy that permits, but does not require, prayer initiated and led by a student at all home games. The District Court entered an order modifying that policy to permit only nonsectarian, nonproselytizing prayer. The Court of Appeals held that, even as modified by the District Court, the football prayer policy was invalid.

* * *

We granted the District's petition for certiorari, limited to the following question: "Whether petitioner's policy permitting student-led, student-initiated prayer at football games violates the Establishment Clause." We conclude, as did the Court of Appeals, that it does.

II

The first Clause in the First Amendment to the Federal Constitution provides that "Congress shall make no law respecting an establishment of religion, or prohibiting the free exercise thereof." The Fourteenth Amendment imposes those substantive limitations on the legislative power of the States and their political subdivisions. . . . In Lee v. Weisman, we held that a prayer delivered by a rabbi at a middle school graduation ceremony violated that Clause. Although this case involves student prayer at a different type of school function, our analysis is properly guided by the principles that we endorsed in Lee.

As we held in that case:

> *"The principle that government may accommodate the free exercise of religion does not supersede the fundamental limitations imposed by the Establishment Clause. It is beyond dispute that, at a minimum, the Constitution guarantees that government may not coerce anyone to support or participate in religion or its exercise, or otherwise act in a way which 'establishes a [state] religion or religious faith, or tends to do so.'* " Id. at 587.

In this case the District first argues that this principle is inapplicable to its October policy because the messages are private student speech, not public speech. It reminds us that "there is a crucial difference between government speech endorsing religion, which the Establishment Clause forbids, and private speech endorsing religion, which the Free Speech and Free Exercise Clauses protect." . . . We certainly agree with that distinction, but we are not persuaded that the pre-game invocations should be regarded as "private speech."

These invocations are authorized by a government policy and take place on government property at government-sponsored school-related events. Not every message delivered under such circumstances is the government's own. We have held, for example, that an individual's contribution to a government-created forum was not government speech. . . . Although the District relies heavily on Rosenberger and similar cases involving such forums, it is clear that the pre-game ceremony is not the type of forum discussed in those cases. The Santa Fe school officials simply do not

"evince either 'by policy or by practice,' any intent to open the [pre-game ceremony] to 'indiscriminate use,' . . . by the student body generally." . . . Rather, the school allows only one student, the same student for the entire season, to give the invocation. The statement or invocation is subject to particular regulations that confine the content and topic of the student's message. By comparison, in Perry we rejected a claim that the school had created a limited public forum in its school mail system despite the fact that it had allowed far more speakers to address a much broader range of topics than the policy at issue here. As we concluded in Perry, "selective access does not transform government property into a public forum." 460 U.S. at 47.

Granting only one student access to the stage at a time does not, of course, necessarily preclude a finding that a school has created a limited public forum. Here, however, Santa Fe's student election system ensures that only those messages deemed "appropriate" under the District's policy may be delivered. That is, the majoritarian process implemented by the District guarantees, by definition, that minority candidates will never prevail and that their views will be effectively silenced.

Recently, in Board of Regents of Univ. of Wis. System v. Southworth, 529 U.S. 217 (2000), we explained why student elections that determine, by majority vote, which expressive activities shall receive or not receive school benefits are constitutionally problematic:

"To the extent the referendum substitutes majority determinations for viewpoint neutrality it would undermine the constitutional protection the program requires. The whole theory of viewpoint neutrality is that minority views are treated with the same respect as are majority views. Access to a public forum, for instance, does not depend upon majoritarian consent. That principle is controlling here."

Like the student referendum for funding in Southworth, this student election does nothing to protect minority views but rather places the students who hold such views at the mercy of the majority. Because "fundamental rights may not be submitted to vote; they depend on the outcome of no elections," . . . the District's elections are insufficient safeguards of diverse student speech.

In Lee, the school district made the related argument that its policy of endorsing only "civic or nonsectarian" prayer was acceptable because it minimized the intrusion on the audience as a whole. We rejected that claim by explaining that such a majoritarian policy "does not lessen the offense or isolation to the objectors. At best it narrows their number, at worst increases their sense of isolation and affront." 505 U.S. at 594. Similarly, while Santa Fe's majoritarian election might ensure that most of the students are represented, it does nothing to protect the minority; indeed, it likely serves to intensify their offense.

Moreover, the District has failed to divorce itself from the religious content in the invocations. It has not succeeded in doing so, either by claiming that its policy is " 'one of neutrality rather than endorsement' " or by characterizing the individual student as the "circuit-breaker" in the process. Contrary to the District's repeated assertions that it has adopted a "hands-off" approach to the pre-game invocation, the realities of the situation plainly reveal that its policy involves both perceived and actual endorsement of religion. In this case, as we found in Lee, the "degree of school involvement" makes it clear that the pre-game prayers bear "the imprint of the State and thus put school-age children who objected in an untenable position." 505 U.S. at 590.

The District has attempted to disentangle itself from the religious messages by developing the two-step student election process. The text of the October policy, however, exposes the extent of the school's entanglement. The elections take place at all only because the school "board has chosen to permit students to deliver a brief invocation and/or message." The elections thus "shall" be conducted "by the high school student council" and "upon advice and direction of the high school principal." The decision whether to deliver a message is first made by majority vote of the entire student body, followed by a choice of the speaker in a separate, similar majority election. Even though the particular words used by the speaker are not determined by those votes, the policy mandates that the "statement or invocation" be "consistent with the goals and purposes of this policy," which are "to solemnize the event, to promote good sportsmanship and student safety, and to establish the appropriate environment for the competition."

In addition to involving the school in the selection of the speaker, the policy, by its terms, invites and encourages religious messages. The policy itself states that the purpose of the message is "to solemnize the event." A religious message is the most obvious method of solemnizing an event. Moreover, the requirements that the message "promote good citizenship" and "establish the appropriate environment for competition" further narrow the types of message deemed appropriate, suggesting that a solemn, yet nonreligious, message, such as commentary on United States foreign policy, would be prohibited. Indeed, the only type of message that is expressly endorsed in the text is an "invocation"—a term that primarily describes an appeal for divine assistance. In fact, as used in the past at Santa Fe High School, an "invocation" has always entailed a focused religious message. Thus, the expressed purposes of the policy encourage the selection of a religious message, and that is precisely how the students understand the policy. . . . We recognize the important role that public worship plays in many communities, as well as the sincere desire to include public prayer as a part of various occasions so as to mark those occasions' significance. But such religious activity in public schools, as elsewhere, must comport with the First Amendment.

The actual or perceived endorsement of the message, moreover, is established by factors beyond just the text of the policy. Once the student speaker is selected and the message composed, the invocation is then delivered to a large audience assembled as part of a regularly scheduled, school-sponsored function conducted on school property. The message is broadcast over the school's public address system, which remains subject to the control of school officials. It is fair to assume that the pre-game ceremony is clothed in the traditional indicia of school sporting events, which generally include not just the team, but also cheerleaders and band members dressed in uniforms sporting the school name and mascot. The school's name is likely written in large print across the field and on banners and flags. The crowd will certainly include many who display the school colors and insignia on their school T-shirts, and jackets. It is in a setting such as this that "the board has chosen to permit" the elected student to rise and give the "statement or invocation."

In this context the members of the listening audience must perceive the pre-game message as a public expression of the views of the majority of the student body delivered with the approval of the school administration. In cases involving state participation in a religious activity, one of the relevant questions is "whether an objective observer, acquainted with the text, legislative history, and implementation of the statute, would perceive it as a state endorsement of prayer in public schools." . . . Regardless of the listener's support for, or objection to, the message, an objective Santa Fe High School student will unquestionably perceive the inevitable pre-game prayer as stamped with her school's seal of approval.

The text and history of this policy, moreover, reinforce our objective student's perception that the prayer is encouraged by the school. When a governmental entity professes a secular purpose for an arguably religious policy, the government's characterization is, of course, entitled to some deference. But it is nonetheless the duty of the courts to "distinguish a sham secular purpose from a sincere one." . . .

According to the District, the secular purposes of the policy are to "foster free expression of private persons . . . as well [as to] solemnize sporting events, promote good sportsmanship and student safety, and establish an appropriate environment for competition." We note that the District's approval of only one specific kind of message, an "invocation," is not necessary to further any of these purposes. Additionally, the fact that only one student is permitted to give a content-limited message suggests that this policy does little to "foster free expression." Furthermore, regardless of whether one considers a sporting event an appropriate occasion for solemnity, the use of an invocation to foster such solemnity is impermissible when, in actuality, it constitutes prayer sponsored by the school. And it is unclear what type of message would be both appropriately "solemnizing" under the District's policy and yet non-religious.

Most striking to us is the evolution of the current policy from the long-sanctioned office of "Student Chaplain" to the candidly titled "Prayer at Football Games" regulation. This history indicates that the District intended to preserve the practice of prayer before football games. The conclusion that the District viewed the October policy simply as a continuation of the previous policies is dramatically illustrated by the fact that the school did not conduct a new election, pursuant to the current policy, to replace the results of the previous election, which occurred under the former policy. Given these observations, and in light of the school's history of regular delivery of a student-led prayer at athletic events, it is reasonable to infer that the specific purpose of the policy was to preserve a popular "state-sponsored religious practice."

School sponsorship of a religious message is impermissible because it sends the ancillary message to members of the audience who are non-adherents "that they are outsiders, not full members of the political community, and an accompanying message to adherents that they are insiders, favored members of the political community." . . . The delivery of such a message over the school's public address system, by a speaker representing the student body, under the supervision of school faculty, and pursuant to a school policy that explicitly and implicitly encourages public prayer is not properly characterized as "private" speech.

III

The District next argues that its football policy is distinguishable from the graduation prayer in Lee because it does not coerce students to participate in religious observances. Its argument has two parts: first, that there is no impermissible government coercion because the pre-game messages are the product of student choices; and second, that there is really no coercion at all because attendance at an extracurricular event, unlike a graduation ceremony, is voluntary.

The reasons just discussed explaining why the alleged "circuit-breaker" mechanism of the dual elections and student speaker do not turn public speech into private speech also demonstrate why these mechanisms do not insulate the school from the coercive element of the final message. In fact, this aspect of the District's argument exposes anew the concerns that are created by the majoritarian election system. The parties' stipulation clearly states that the issue resolved in the first election was "whether a student would deliver prayer at varsity football games," and the controversy in this case demonstrates that the views of the students are not unanimous on that issue.

One of the purposes served by the Establishment Clause is to remove debate over this kind of issue from governmental supervision or control. We explained in Lee that the "preservation and transmission of religious beliefs and worship is a responsibility and a choice committed to the private sphere." 505 U.S. at 589. The two student elections authorized by the policy, coupled with the debates that presumably must precede each, impermissibly invade that private sphere. The election mechanism, when considered in light of the history in which the policy in question evolved, reflects a device the District put in place that determines whether religious messages will be delivered at home football games. The mechanism encourages divisiveness along religious lines in a public school setting, a result at odds with the Establishment Clause. Although it is true that the ultimate choice of student speaker is "attributable to the students," the District's decision to hold the constitutionally problematic election is clearly "a choice attributable to the State."

The District further argues that attendance at the commencement ceremonies at issue in Lee "differs dramatically" from attendance at high school football games, which it contends "are of no more than passing interest to many students" and are "decidedly extracurricular," thus dissipating any coercion. Attendance at a high school football game, unlike showing up for class, is certainly not required in order to receive a diploma. Moreover, we may assume that the District is correct in arguing that the informal pressure to attend an athletic event is not as strong as a senior's desire to attend her own graduation ceremony.

There are some students, however, such as cheerleaders, members of the band, and, of course, the team members themselves, for whom seasonal commitments mandate their attendance, sometimes for class credit. The District also minimizes the importance to many students of attending and participating in extracurricular activities as part of a complete educational experience. As we noted in Lee, "law reaches past formalism." 505 U.S. at 595. To assert that high school students do not feel immense social pressure, or have a truly genuine desire, to be involved in the extracurricular event that is American high school football is "formalistic in the extreme." We stressed in Lee the obvious observation that "adolescents are often susceptible to pressure from their peers towards conformity, and that the influence is strongest in matters of social convention." Id. at 593. High school home football games are traditional gatherings of a school community; they bring together students and faculty as well as friends and family from years present and past to root for a common cause. Undoubtedly, the games are not important to some students, and they voluntarily choose not to attend. For many others, however, the choice between whether to attend these games or to risk facing a personally offensive religious ritual is in no practical sense an easy one. The Constitution, moreover, demands that the school may not force this difficult choice upon these students for "it is a tenet of the First Amendment that the State cannot require one of its citizens to forfeit his or her rights and benefits as the price of resisting conformance to state-sponsored religious practice."

Even if we regard every high school student's decision to attend a home football game as purely voluntary, we are nevertheless persuaded that the delivery of a pregame prayer has the improper effect of coercing those present to participate in an act of religious worship. For "the government may no more use social pressure to enforce orthodoxy than it may use more direct means." As in Lee, "what to most believers may seem nothing more than a reasonable request that the nonbeliever respect their religious practices, in a school context may appear to the nonbeliever or dissenter to be an attempt to employ the machinery of the State to enforce a religious orthodoxy." The constitutional command will not permit the District "to exact religious conformity from a student as the price" of joining her classmates at a varsity football game.

The Religion Clauses of the First Amendment prevent the government from making any law respecting the establishment of religion or prohibiting the free exercise thereof. By no means do these commands impose a prohibition on all religious activity in our public schools. . . . Indeed, the common purpose of the Religion Clauses "is to secure religious liberty." . . . Thus, nothing in the Constitution as interpreted by this Court prohibits any public school student from voluntarily praying at any time before, during, or after the school day. But the religious liberty protected by the Constitution is abridged when the State affirmatively sponsors the particular religious practice of prayer.

IV

Finally, the District argues repeatedly that the Does have made a premature facial challenge to the October policy that necessarily must fail. The District emphasizes, quite correctly, that until a student actually delivers a solemnizing message under the latest version of the policy, there can be no certainty that any of the statements or invocations will be religious. Thus, it concludes, the October policy necessarily survives a facial challenge.

This argument, however, assumes that we are concerned only with the serious constitutional injury that occurs when a student is forced to participate in an act of religious worship because she chooses to attend a school event. But the Constitution also requires that we keep in mind "the myriad, subtle ways in which Estab-

lishment Clause values can be eroded," . . . and that we guard against other different, yet equally important, constitutional injuries. One is the mere passage by the District of a policy that has the purpose and perception of government establishment of religion. Another is the implementation of a governmental electoral process that subjects the issue of prayer to a majoritarian vote.

The District argues that the facial challenge must fail because "Santa Fe's Football Policy cannot be invalidated on the basis of some 'possibility or even likelihood' of an unconstitutional application." . . . Our Establishment Clause cases involving facial challenges, however, have not focused solely on the possible applications of the statute, but rather have considered whether the statute has an unconstitutional purpose. Writing for the Court in Bowen, THE CHIEF JUSTICE concluded that "as in previous cases involving facial challenges on Establishment Clause grounds, . . . we assess the constitutionality of an enactment by reference to the three factors first articulated in Lemon v. Kurtzman, 403 U.S. 602, 612 (1971) . . . which guides 'the general nature of our inquiry in this area' . . . Under the Lemon standard, a court must invalidate a statute if it lacks "a secular legislative purpose." . . . It is therefore proper for us to examine the purpose of the October policy.

As discussed, the text of the October policy alone reveals that it has an unconstitutional purpose. The plain language of the policy clearly spells out the extent of school involvement in both the election of the speaker and the content of the message. Additionally, the text of the October policy specifies only one, clearly preferred message—that of Santa Fe's traditional religious "invocation." Finally, the extremely selective access of the policy and other content restrictions confirm that it is not a content-neutral regulation that creates a limited public forum for the expression of student speech. Our examination, however, need not stop at an analysis of the text of the policy.

This case comes to us as the latest step in developing litigation brought as a challenge to institutional practices that unquestionably violated the Establishment Clause. One of those practices was the District's long-established tradition of sanctioning student-led prayer at varsity football games. The narrow question before us is whether implementation of the October policy insulates the continuation of such prayers from constitutional scrutiny. It does not. Our inquiry into this question not only can, but must, include an examination of the circumstances surrounding its enactment. Whether a government activity violates the Establishment Clause is "in large part a legal question to be answered on the basis of judicial interpretation of social facts. . . . Every government practice must be judged in its unique circumstances. . . ." Our discussion in the previous sections demonstrates that in this case the District's direct involvement with school prayer exceeds constitutional limits.

The District, nevertheless, asks us to pretend that we do not recognize what every Santa Fe High School student understands clearly—that this policy is about prayer. The District further asks us to accept what is obviously untrue: that these messages are necessary to "solemnize" a football game and that this single-student, year-long position is essential to the protection of student speech. We refuse to turn a blind eye to the context in which this policy arose, and that context quells any doubt that this policy was implemented with the purpose of endorsing school prayer.

Therefore, the simple enactment of this policy, with the purpose and perception of school endorsement of student prayer, was a constitutional violation. We need not wait for the inevitable to confirm and magnify the constitutional injury. . . . Therefore, even if no Santa Fe High School student ever offered a religious message, the October policy fails a facial challenge because the attempt by the District to encourage prayer is also at issue. Government efforts to endorse religion cannot evade constitutional reproach based solely on the remote possibility that those attempts may fail.

This policy likewise does not survive a facial challenge because it impermissibly imposes upon the student body a majoritarian election on the issue of prayer. Through its election scheme, the District has established a governmental electoral mechanism that turns the school into a forum for religious debate. It further empowers the student body majority with the authority to subject students of minority views to constitutionally improper messages. The award of that power alone, regardless of the students' ultimate use of it, is not acceptable. . . . Such a system encourages divisiveness along religious lines and threatens the imposition of coercion upon those students not desiring to participate in a religious exercise. Simply by establishing this school-related procedure, which entrusts the inherently nongovernmental subject of religion to a majoritarian vote, a constitutional violation has occurred.

Our examination of those circumstances above leads to the conclusion that this policy does not provide the District with the constitutional safe harbor it sought. The policy is invalid on its face because it establishes an improper majoritarian election on religion, and unquestionably has the purpose and creates the perception of encouraging the delivery of prayer at a series of important school events.

The judgment of the Court of Appeals is, accordingly, affirmed.

◇◇◇ **OTHER RELEVANT SIGNIFICANT CASES**

Chapter 7.11 *Judicial Review, Standing, and Injunctions*   Chapter 7.12 *State Action*

Recent Trends

The Legislative Exception Test or Marsh Analysis

Recent cases and journal articles are utilizing the Legislative Exception Test and the *Marsh* Analysis more vigorously when analyzing establishment clause cases involving prayer at the opening of government meetings. The two tests are essentially intertwined.

The Legislative Exception Test, also known as the History and Traditions or Historical Intent tests (Mullin, 2003), is being used when the practice being adjudicated is aligned with the intent of Establishment Clause by the framers. This is most notably used when a historical tradition of prayer has existed (Elliott, 2005) and is also referred as the *Marsh* Analysis. It is a result of *Marsh v. Chambers* (1983) in which the Supreme Court ruled that the long-established practice of prayer to open Nebraska legislative sessions was constitutional. In 2005, the Supreme Court even acknowledged their *Marsh* decision by stating they approved government-led prayer to God in *McCreary County, KY v. American Civil Liberties Union of Kentucky*. Although *Marsh* is not new, recently the courts have been busy hearing cases where the *Marsh* analysis has been applied (*Simpson v. Chesterfield County Board of Supervisors*, 2005; *Doe v. Tangipahoa Parish School Board*, 2005; *Hinrichs v. Bosma*, 2005; *Dobrich v. Walls*, 2005; *Van Orden v. Perry*, 2005; *Doe v. The School District of the City of Norfolk*, 2003; *Wynne v. Town of Great Falls, South Carolina*, 2004; *Newdow v. Eagen*, 2004; *Freethought Soc. of Greater Philadelphia v. Chester County*, 2003).

Diverse Issues, Clearer Direction

There is still a diversity of issues at all federal court levels regarding religion and the First Amendment. Moments of silence (*Brown v. Gilmore*, 2001), funding for students in private religious schools under school voucher programs (*Zelman v. Simmons-Harris*, 2002), displays of the Ten Commandments on government property (*American Civil Liberties Union of Ohio Foundation, Inc. v. Ashbrook, 2004; Van Orden v. Perry*, 2005), and the apparent conflict of leasing of public park land to the Boy Scouts and their requirements that a scout leader must swear a belief to a deity (*Barnes-Wallace v. The Boy Scouts of America*, 2003) are examples of recent cases involving the Establishment and Free Exercise clauses.

In deciding these religious cases, no court is using one single test to validate their rulings. In fact, former Chief Justice William Rehnquist acknowledged in his dissenting opinion in *Santa Fe* that the Court has been unwilling to use any single test in rendering decisions regarding the Establishment Clause.

Since the *Santa Fe* (Supreme Court) and *Adler* (Supreme Court denied certiorari) decisions, however, the decisions of the courts are becoming more predictable. With the exception of *Mellen*, it is becoming clearer that a more mature audience (adults, legislative prayer, higher education) is not necessarily coerced when a prayer is cited. The establishment and free exercise of religion in relation to historical observance will not necessarily render a decision of neutrality or removal of the perceived religious practice. However, administrative control in public schools will almost always render any "voluntary" prayer a violation of the First Amendment.

References

Cases

Adler v. Duval County School Board, 250 F.3d 1330 (11th Cir. 2001), *cert. denied*, 534 U.S. 1065 (2001).
American Civil Liberties Union of New Jersey v. Black Horse Pike Regional Board of Education, 84 F.3d 1471 (1996).
American Civil Liberties Union of Ohio Foundation, Inc. v. Ashbrook, 375 F. 3d 484 (6th Cir. 2004).
Appenheimer v. School Board of Washington Community High School District 308, 2001 WL 1885834 (C.D. Ill.).
Barnes-Wallace v. The Boy Scouts of America, 275 F. Supp. 2d. 1259 (S.D. Cal. 2003).
Board of Education of Westside Community Schools v. Mergens by and through Mergens, 496 U.S. 226 (1990).
Brown v. Gilmore, 258 F.3d 265 (2001).
Chaudhuri v. State of Tenn., 130 F.3d 232 (1997).
Dobrich v. Walls, 380 F. Supp. 2d 366 (2005).
Doe v. Duncanville Independent School Dist., 70 F.3d 405 (1995).
Doe v. Tangipahoa Parish School Board, 2005, 2005 WL 517341 (E.D.La.).
Doe v. The School District of the City of Norfolk, 340 F. 3d 605. (8th Cir. 2003).
Freethought Soc. of Greater Philadelphia v. Chester County, 334 F. 3d 247 (3rd Cir. 2003).
Hinrichs v. Bosma, 2005 WL 3263883 (S.D. Ind.).
Ingebretsen on Behalf of Ingebretsen v. Jackson Public School Dist., 88 F.3d 274 (C.A. 5, 1996).
Jones v. Clear Creek Independent School Dist., 977 F.2d 963 (C.A. 5, 1992).
Lee v. Weisman, 505 U.S. 577 (1992).
Lemon v. Kurtzman, 403 U.S. 602 (1971).
Lynch v. Donnelly, 465 U.S. 668 (1984).
Marsh v. Chambers, 463 U.S. 783 (1983).
McCreary County, KY v. American Civil Liberties Union of Kentucky, 125 S.Ct. 2722 (2005).
Mellen v. Bunting, 327 F. 3d 355 (C.A. 4, 2003).
Newdow v. Congress of the United States of America, 383 F. Supp.2d 1229 (E.D. CA, 2005).
Newdow v. Eagen, 309 F. Supp. 2d 29 (D.C. 2004).
Perry Education Association v. Perry Local Educators' Association, 460 U.S. 37 (1983).
Santa Fe High Independent School District v. Doe, 530 U.S. 290 (2000).
Simpson v. Chesterfield County Board of Supervisors, 404 F. 3d 276 (4th Cir. 2005).
Tanford v. Brand, 932 F. Supp. 1139 (S.D. Ind., 1996).
Van Orden v. Perry, 125 S. Ct 2854 (2005).
Wynne v. Town of Great Falls, South Carolina, 376 F. 3d 292 (C.A. 4, 2004).
Zelman v. Simmons-Harris, 536 U.S. 639 (2002).

Publications

Elliott, D. E. (2005). Finalist of the Second Annual DCBA Writing Contest: Collegiate team prayer and the First Amendment. *DuPage County Bar Association Brief, 17,* 22.

Mullin, S. A. (2003). The place for prayer in public policy: A reevaluation of the principles underlying the decision in *Santa Fe Independent School District v. Doe. S. Tex. L. Rev., 44,* 555–644.

Pihos, D. N. (2005). Assuming maturity matters: The limited reach of the Establishment Clause at public universities. *Cornell Law Review, 90,* 1349–1376.

7.26 Private Clubs in Sport and Recreation

Anita M. Moorman
University of Louisville

Sport, recreation, and leisure activities have often joined together persons with similar interests and ideas. Historically, private clubs have existed in the United States for more than 100 years allowing the association of persons with mutual interests in activities including yachting, hunting, golf, swimming, tennis, and billiards. The first country clubs were created by wealthy, white, Anglo-Saxon Protestants as early as 1880 (Jolly-Ryan, 1997). Still today the most recognizable private clubs, and the focus of this chapter, are golf and country clubs. Even though this chapter will focus on golf and country clubs, the legal principles discussed apply equally to any private club. In 1950 nearly two of three golf courses were private. Today, however, that ratio has reversed itself, and public courses account for more than 70 percent of all golf facilities in the United States (National Golf Foundation, 2006a). Despite the decline in the number of private golf courses, many legal issues still surround the operation and management of private clubs.

The primary legal issues affecting private clubs involve the constitutional guarantees of freedom of association, discrimination claims, and fair employment practices. Historically, private country clubs have used race, national origin, religion, and gender as a basis for discrimination. Such discrimination by public clubs or resorts would run afoul of the U.S. Constitution, as well as any number of federal and state antidiscrimination statutes. The purpose of this chapter is to identify issues affecting sport and recreation managers of private clubs, examine constitutional rights associated with private club membership, examine both state and federal legislation impacting private clubs, and discuss relevant court decisions related to private clubs.

Fundamental Concepts

Constitutional Considerations

Freedom of Association and Equal Protection Issues

The Bill of Rights protects individual liberty and property interests from interference by the federal government. The most important expansion of civil rights in the United States was the enactment of the Thirteenth and Fourteenth Amendments. The Thirteenth Amendment abolished slavery throughout the United States. Following enactment of the Thirteenth Amendment, many states enacted what were known as "black codes," which were intended to limit the civil rights of the newly freed slave. The Fourteenth Amendment was passed to counter the "black codes" and ensure that no state "shall make or enforce any law which shall abridge the privileges or immunities of the citizens of the United States" (U.S. Const. Amend XIV; see *Equal Protection* discussion in Chapter 7.14). However, the U.S. Constitution does not restrict private conduct including discriminatory actions. As discussed in Chapter 7.12 (*State Action*), the constitution restricts governmental and state actors, not private citizens. So although public recreation organizations and resorts must not discriminate or deny equal opportunities to persons, private clubs may, and often do, deny membership or restrict benefits of membership to certain classes of people. The private golf and country club defends its practices as guaranteed under the First Amendment.

The First Amendment to the U.S. Constitution, although it does not expressly guarantee freedom to associate, has been interpreted to permit free and exclusive association of individuals. The freedom of association is deemed to be implicit in the expressive and religious freedoms guaranteed by the First Amendment (Overbeck, 1984). The Supreme Court first recognized the right of association as a separate, constitutionally protected right in *NAACP v. Alabama ex rel. Patterson*, 1958. The Supreme Court has stated that "an individual's freedom to speak, to worship, and to petition the government for the redress of grievances could not be vigorously protected from interference by the State unless a correlative freedom to engage in group effort toward those ends were not also guaranteed" (*Roberts v. U.S. Jaycees*, 1984). Thus, private persons are free to associate with whomever they desire and exclude those with whom they do not wish to associate.

The Supreme Court further divided the right to association into two categories: intimate association and expressive association. *Intimate association* is defined as deep attachments and commitments between a selectively small number of individuals with whom one shares distinctively personal aspects of one's life. This definition comes very close to describing the right to privacy embodied in the Fourth, Ninth, and Fourteenth Amendments. Intimate association must involve a very small number of individuals. Many courts have required fewer than 20 members to claim intimate association. Clearly, most golf and country clubs would have 200 to 300 members if not more; thus, intimate association is not the aspect of free association most private clubs would assert in defense of exclusionary practices. *Expressive association*, however, is often asserted by private clubs defending their discriminatory practices. Expressive association is the right to associate with others in pursuit of political, social, economic, educational, religious, and cultural ends (*Roberts v. U.S. Jaycees*, 1984). However, even expressive association has limits. For example, the Supreme Court has held that "the forced inclusion of an unwanted person in a group infringes the group's freedom of expressive association if the presence of that person affects in a significant way the group's ability to advocate public or private viewpoints" (*Boy Scouts of America v. Dale*, 2003).

Indeed, there is an inherent conflict between governmental interests and efforts to eliminate discrimination against citizens and the First Amendment association rights of members of private clubs. The constitutional right of association is not absolute, but must be balanced against compelling governmental interests. Thus, for the government to restrict or limit the extent to which a private club can exclusively associate and discriminate, the government must demonstrate that the restriction is *necessary* to achieve a *compelling* governmental interest. Both the federal government and many state legislatures have identified the elimination of discriminatory practices as a compelling governmental interest and have enacted remedial civil rights and human rights legislation to curb discrimination.

Federal Civil Rights Act

The Civil Rights Act of 1964 (Civil Rights Act) is a comprehensive legislative plan to prohibit discrimination. The goal of the Civil Rights Act of 1964 was to eliminate discrimination and to create disincentives to discriminate (42 U.S.C. §§ 1981, 1983, 1985 & 2000). The Civil Rights Act prohibits discrimination in employment practices (§ 2000e), discrimination in places of public accommodation (§ 2000a), and discrimination by persons acting under color of state law (§ 1983). In addition, the Civil Rights Act of 1866, which ended slavery, also bars racially motivated and intentionally discriminatory acts in the making and enforcement of private contracts (42 U.S.C. § 1981). Many sections in the Civil Rights Act contain exemptions or exceptions for private clubs. These exemptions or exceptions are designed to strike a balance between the government's interest in eliminating discrimination and the constitutional protections of freedom of association we discussed in the previous section. This balance will be explored more fully this section.

Title VII—Nondiscrimination in Employment

Section 2000e (Title VII of the Civil Rights Act of 1964) applies to employers with fifteen or more employees who work at least twenty weeks per year, and whose business impacts interstate commerce. Title VII makes it unlawful for an employer to discriminate against an employee on the basis on race, color, religion, sex, or national origin (42 U.S.C. § 2000e-2(a)). Title VII expressly excludes private clubs from its scope and provides that the term *employer* does not include *a bona fide private membership club* (other than a labor organization) that is exempt from taxation under section 501(c) of the Internal Revenue Code of 1954 (42 U.S.C. § 2000e(b)). Thus, private golf and country clubs would not be considered "employers" under Title VII if they are indeed a bona fide private membership club. The EEOC has promulgated a three-part inquiry for assessing whether an organization qualifies as a private club pursuant to § 2000e(b). According to the EEOC policy statement, an organization is a bona fide private club if: "(1) it is a club in the ordinary and common meaning of that word; (2) it is private; and (3) it requires meaningful conditions of limited membership" (*EEOC v. The Chicago Club*, 1996). To determine whether a club is truly private, the EEOC recommends and the courts have applied three factors:

- The extent to which it limits its facilities and services to club members and their guests
- The extent to which and/or the manner in which it is controlled or owned by its membership
- Whether and, if so, to what extent and in what manner, it publicly advertises to solicit members or to promote the use of its facilities or services by the general public (*EEOC v. The Chicago Club*, 1996).

Courts deciding issues pertaining to Title VII and the private club exclusion have been less concerned with the associational rights of the private club members. "A private club's employment decisions are not constitutionally relevant to the individual members' abilities to define their own identities by choosing with whom they wish to associate" (*EEOC v. The Chicago Club*, 1996, p. 1432). The court of appeals in *Chicago Club* leveled harsh criticism against the EEOC for challenging The Chicago Club's private club exclusion where The Chicago Club restricted memberships, did not advertise, and controlled the membership process. Access provided to guest members and the size of the club was not considered relevant to the court determination of whether the club was "private" for purposes of Title VII.

Title II—Nondiscrimination in Places of Public Accommodation

Section 2000a (Title II of the Civil Rights Act of 1964) prohibits discrimination based on race, color, religion, or national origin in *places of public accommodation* affecting interstate commerce. It is important to note that discrimination on the basis of gender is not prohibited under Title II. An establishment is a place of public accommodation under Title II if its operations affect commerce and it is one of four categories of establishments that serve the public. The categories provided in Title II are as follows:

1. Any inn, hotel, motel, or other establishment which provides lodging to transient guests, other than an establishment located within a building which contains not more than five rooms for rent or hire and which is actually occupied by the proprietor of such establishment as his residence;
2. Any restaurant, cafeteria, lunchroom, lunch counter, soda fountain, or other facility principally engaged in selling food for consumption on the premises, including, but not limited to, any such facility located on the premises of any retail establishment; or any gasoline station;
3. Any motion picture house, theater, concert hall, sports arena, stadium or other place of exhibition or entertainment; and
4. Any establishment (A)(i) which is physically located within the premises of any establishment otherwise covered by this subsection, or (ii) within the premises of which is physically located any such covered establishment, and (B) which holds itself out as serving patrons of such covered establishment (Title II of ADA).

Private golf and country clubs are considered places of exhibition or entertainment because most private clubs provide sports activities either in the form of direct participation or through viewing sports activities as spectators (*Brown v. Loudoun Golf & Country Club, Inc.*, 1983; Jolly-Ryan, 1997). Once an organization is covered by one of the four categories in Section 2000a, the next question is whether the activities affect interstate commerce. The commerce requirement has been easily satisfied with regard to golf and country clubs due to golf outings with out-of-state professionals and guests, guest memberships, snack bars open to the general public, out-of-state golf teams playing on the course, and service contracts fulfilled by out-of-state contractors (see *Brown v. Loudoun Golf & Country Club, Inc.*, 1983; *Evans v. Laurel Links, Inc.*, 1966; *U.S. v. Lansdowne Swim Club*, 1989). Thus, because private golf and country clubs are places of public accommodation and affect interstate commerce, they are subject to the act unless they qualify for an exemption.

Similar to Title VII, Title II also addresses private membership clubs. Where Title VII excludes private membership clubs from the scope of the act, Title II exempts private membership clubs from complying with the statutory mandate. Section 2000a(e) provides:

Private establishments. The provisions of this title [42 USCS §§ 2000a–2000a-6] shall not apply to a private club or other establishment not in fact open to the public, except to the extent that the facilities of such establishment are made available to the customers or patrons of an establishment within the scope of subsection (b).

The organization claiming an exemption has the burden to prove that it is in fact not an establishment open to the public. The private club exemption must also be considered in light of the legislative intent to only protect the genuine privacy of private clubs whose membership is genuinely selective (*U.S. v. Lansdowne Swim Club*, 1989). Courts interpreting the private club exemption have developed a factor analysis to weigh in reaching a determination. The following factors are considered:

- The genuine selectivity of the group in the admission of its members
- The membership's control over the operations of the establishment
- The history of the organization
- The use of the facilities by nonmembers
- The purpose of the club's existence
- Whether the club advertises for members
- Whether the club is profit or nonprofit
- The formalities observed by the club such as bylaws, meetings, etc. (*U.S. v. Lansdowne Swim Club*, 1989)

Application of these factors is done on a case-by-case basis, and no single factor is dispositive of the private club issue (Jolly-Ryan, 1997). Courts have reached varying conclusions as to whether a private club was "truly private" in the association sense. A club's membership policies must truly indicate a plan or purpose of exclusiveness and be genuinely selective. Selection by recommendation has been an indictor of genuine selectivity; however, if the applicant is not subject to any background investigation and the club cannot demonstrate some established criteria for acceptance, it is likely that the club will be concluded not to be selective (*Nesmith v. YMCA*, 1968; *U.S. v. Lansdowne Swim Club*, 1989; and *Wright v. Cork Club*, 1970).

The amount of control exercised by the members over club operations is also relevant. If a club is truly private, it is only natural that its members will possess the authority to determine how it is organized, operated, and maintained. In cases where members did not actually own the club facilities, control the day-to-day operations of the club, or retain profits from club operations, the private club exemption has been denied (see *Daniel v. Paul*, 1969; *Durham v. Red Lake Fishing & Hunting Club, Inc.*, 1987; *U.S. v. Richberg*, 1968; and *Wright v. Cork Club*, 1970). Additionally, if clubs advertise and allow the public to use any of their facilities such as banquet rooms, meeting/conference rooms, or snack bars, the entire club will become subject to the statute (*Cornelius v. BPOE*, 1974; *New York v. Ocean Club*, 1984; *U.S. v. Jack Sabin's Private Club*, 1967; and *U.S. v. Lansdowne Swim Club*, 1989). One club was held to be not private due to a telephone directory listing under "Bathing Beaches—Public" rather than "Clubs" (*Castle Hill Beach Club v. Arbury*, 1955).

Section 1981—Nondiscrimination in Private Contracts

Section 1981 prohibits certain racially motivated acts that are intentionally discriminatory, including the making and enforcement of private contracts (42 U.S.C. § 1981). This prohibition applies to both private and state actors. Thus, a private golf and country club is subject to the statutory mandate. A person aggrieved by a violation of this statute must demonstrate (1) that he/she is a member of a racial minority, (2) the defendant's intent to discriminate on the basis of race, and (3) the discrimination concerned the making or enforcement of a contract (*Gibbs-Alfano v. The Ossining Boat & Canoe Club, Inc.*, 1999). In *Gibbs-Alfano*, the plaintiffs were members of the Ossining Boat & Canoe Club. Gibbs-Alfano was expelled from the club for allegedly using foul language. She contended that other members of the club who were white also used foul language but were not expelled. She and her husband further contended that her expulsion interfered with their contractual rights.

It is well settled that Section 1981 forbids racial discrimination in club privileges and memberships (*Tillman v. Wheaton-Haven Recreation Ass'n., Inc.*, 1973). This applies to private clubs as well as public organizations. Unlike Section 2000, Section 1981 does not contain an exemption or exclusion for private clubs. Private clubs have argued that such an exemption should be implied in Section 1981, but this argument has been generally unsuccessful in the courts (see *Crawford v. Willow Oaks Country Club*, 1999; *Gibbs-Alfano v. Ossining Boat & Canoe Club*, 1999; *Guesby v. Kennedy*, 1984). In addition, in the situation where the city, county, or state either licenses or leases property to a private club, both the club and the governmental entity may be subject to a Section 1981 claim if the club discriminates on the basis of race (*Gibbs-Alfano v. Ossining Boat & Canoe Club*, 1999). Furthermore, a Virginia district court observed that the freedom to associate with persons and groups cannot reasonably be construed as the freedom to discriminate in the context of an employment relationship. Once an employment relationship exists, the choice has already been made to associate with that employee. Private clubs are free to associate with whomever they choose when hiring a new employee, but once a private club hires an employee, that employee must be treated in a nondiscriminatory manner (*Crawford v. Willow Oaks Country Club*, 1999).

Section 1983—Nondiscrimination by Government Employees/Entities

Section 1983 prohibits any person acting under color of law from depriving any citizen of the United States of any rights, privileges, or immunities secured by the Constitution and law of the United States. It is clear that Section 1983 only applies to persons acting on behalf of a governmental entity. Thus, all public recreation clubs, resorts, or areas would be covered by the statute; however, private clubs do not come under the statute's mandate. Public recreation clubs, resorts, or areas affected could include public golf courses, parks, lakes, camping areas, college and university facilities, or any other area owned, operated or maintained by a governmental entity. Although a private club would have no direct responsibility for a violation of Section 1983, it could expose a city, county, or state to liability if the governmental entity is involved in a close relationship with the private club. For example, where a city grants licenses or leases for a private club to operate, the private club can be deemed to be acting under color of state law if it deprives someone of membership privileges. Typically, the courts will examine the relationship to determine whether there is a mutually beneficial relationship between the private club and the city and whether the private club appears to be performing a public function such as operating a public recreation area or promoting public safety in recreation (*Gibbs-Alfano v. Ossining Boat & Canoe Club*, 1999).

State and City Civil Rights and Human Rights Acts

As discussed earlier, the U.S. Constitution provides no protection from private discrimination. Similarly, federal civil rights statutes only provide protection to a limited class of persons in a limited number of situations. Thus, many states and municipalities have adopted much broader antidiscrimination laws. The scope of *state antidiscrimination statutes* generally exceeds the scope of federal statutes as to both the classes of individuals they protect and the type of organizations governed (Goodman, 1999). For example, many state public accommodation statutes not only prohibit discrimination on the basis of race, religion, and national origin, but also prohibit discrimination on the basis of gender, sexual orientation, age, disability, personal appearance, marital status, and familial status (see, e.g., California Civil Code, 1982/1999; District of Columbia Civil Code, 1992; Massachusetts General Law, 1998; Minnesota Statutes Annotated, 1966/1984; New Jersey Statute Annotated, 1993; New York Executive Law, 1998; and Rhode Island General Laws, 1994).

Discrimination Against Women

Of particular concern with regard to private golf and country clubs is the continued discrimination against women. Probably one of the more notable private golf clubs that continues to openly discriminate against women is Augusta National Golf Club. Augusta independently administers the prestigious Masters professional golf tournament, but despite this very open and public use of its course for this tournament, the country club has maintained its "private" status by meeting the factors laid out in *Lansdowne*. Although some commentators question whether Augusta could actually meet the "truly private" test (Tofilon, 2005), there may be other ways in which discriminatory practices can be challenged.

For example, a similar controversy erupted in 1990 related to Shoal Creek, an Alabama country club, which was slated to host the 1990 PGA Championship (Rhode, 2002). Shoal Creek discriminated against blacks. After civil rights groups threatened to picket and boycott sponsors, several sponsors withdrew their support. Within a few weeks, Shoal accepted its first black member. In addition, the four major golf organizations (PGA, USGA, PGA Tour, and LPGA) adopted antidiscrimination policies prohibiting them from holding a tournament at a course that excludes individuals based on race, sex, or national origin. At Augusta similar threats of boycotts also were made.

Martha Burk is the Chair of the National Council of Women's Organizations (NCWO) and has led a public battle against Augusta to open its membership to women. Since 2003, the NCWO has aggressively pursued the corporations whose CEOs are members of Augusta and also pursed those corporations who continued to sponsor the Master's Tournament. In addition, members of Congress have introduced legislation known as the Maloney-Sherman-Slaughter bill, which would eliminate tax write-offs for corporations that use the twenty-four all-male golf clubs ("Ending tax deductions," 2003). California has had a similar statute since 1987 that denies the business entertainment deduction to any clubs practicing discrimination. Thus, a business lunch at a discriminatory club could not be written off as a tax deduction. The proposed federal legislation was not passed by Congress, but the battle against Augusta will certainly continue.

Martha Burk's battle has eroded the sponsorship of the Master's Tournament, but has not deterred the President of Augusta, Hootie Johnson, from steadfastly maintaining the club's right to exclude women. Following Burk's efforts in 2004, Augusta National Golf Club announced that it would forgo television sponsors so the tournament would be broadcast commercial free. Three sponsors returned in 2005: IBM, SBC, and ExxonMobil. For 2006, IBM, AT&T, and ExxonMobil have all signed on as sponsors of the tournament.

Public reaction is often mixed in that many men and women are not persuaded of the importance of this issue. In response, Martha Burk stated, "Far from being a place where friends gather for golf, Augusta National is a gathering of corporate power players like no other. Deals are made, careers are changed, and even national policy is affected through relationships such as those of the 19 members of Augusta National who sit on the Council on Foreign Relations. All of this while shutting women out. It is no surprise that women are not advancing in business and in the boardrooms. And there is no question that women farther down the ladder are affected in pay, promotion, and a hostile corporate culture" (Burk, 2005). As sport managers, our personal views on this issue may certainly vary, but we must also critically examine whether exclusionary practices, even if constitutional, are good business.

Even though there are only twenty-four men's-only golf clubs in the United States that still exclude women as members, several still discriminate regarding tee times and access to certain club benefits (e.g., men's-only grill) (Tofilon, 2005). Women are subject to discrimination in many ways, ranging from absolute exclusion or ineligibility for membership to more subtle forms of discrimination such as limited tee times, limited voting rights, and limited access to club tournaments. Women have long recognized the advantages and benefits that club memberships could offer them in the development of business contacts to advance their careers (Sawyer, 1993). Moreover, the National Golf Foundation's 20/20 Vision for the Future consistently identifies women as the primary focus for targeting new players to the game of golf. In its industry report for 2003, the NGF identified four priorities, one of which provided: "In targeting new players, the focus should be where the opportunity is greatest, and we believe that begins with women. We should . . . determine the most effective way to bring women into the game" (National Golf Foundation, 2004). Thus, although excluding women from some private clubs may be constitutionally permissible, for the vast majority of private clubs, women are an important target market, and exclusionary or discriminatory practices ultimately may prove to be unwise from a business perspective.

In addition, women are beginning to successfully avail themselves of state and city civil rights acts in response to discrimination by private clubs. For example, nine female members of the Haverhill Golf and Country Club in Haverhill, Massachusetts, received a jury award of $1.9 million for the club's discriminatory practices and violations of the Massachusetts antidiscrimination statute (Tebo, 2000). Massachusetts' antidiscrimination statute prohibits sex discrimination in places of public accommodation. Haverhill, an ostensibly private club, was found to be a place of public accommodation because its facilities were open to nonmembers at various times for banquets, meetings, and golf outings (*Borne v. The Haverhill Golf and Country Club*, 1999). Additionally, female members of the Bear Hill Golf Club in Massachusetts were also successful in a case against the club for excluding them from the all-male golf tournaments held on weekends at the club (*Wanders v. Bear Hill Golf Club, Inc.*, 1998). The *Wanders* court concluded that Bear Hill did not follow any discernible selection pattern, nonmember groups were allowed to use club facilities, banquet services/facilities were advertised to the general public, and nonmember income accounted for more than 5 percent of club revenue. Thus, the court concluded that Bear Hill was not covered by the private club exemption and had violated the antidiscrimination statute.

Wanders and *Haverhill* are strong examples that discrimination on the basis of gender by private clubs is becoming more and more suspect. Even though federal antidiscrimination statutes provide little protection from gender discrimination, it appears as though state and city antidiscrimination statutes may well finally afford women equal access and privileges in the private golf and country club.

Discrimination Involving Domestic Partners

A number of state and city civil or human rights acts prohibit discrimination on the basis of sexual orientation as well as race, gender, and religion. In addition, a few states have also enacted laws that enable same-sex couples to marry, form a civil union, or formally register as a domestic partnership. In those states legal challenges have been raised against golf and country clubs that do not allow persons in a domestic partnership to enjoy the same benefits of married members (Lambda Legal, 2005). Typically, this arises when a club offers membership benefits where both the member and the spouse enjoy full membership benefits such as unlimited tee times and unlimited access to the restaurant and other services of the club. However, for the gay or lesbian member, his or her domestic partner is not accorded equal benefits and instead is treated as a guest. Typically, a member may only be able to have a domestic partner accompany him or her as a guest five or six times per year and then is also required to pay guest fees for those visits.

Two types of legal challenges have been raised to these discriminatory practices. The first challenge is based on alleged violations of local nondiscrimination or human rights laws. For example, a golf club's refusal of membership to a gay person may violate a state or local law that prohibits discrimination on the basis of sexual orientation. The second challenge is based on state equal rights statutes, domestic partner recognition statutes, or the equal protection provisions of the state constitutions. For example, if a gay couple has legally married or entered into a legally recognized civil union or registered domestic partnership, the state equal rights act and/or the state constitution may prohibit discriminating against that couple by excluding them from benefits or services available to nongay married couples. Both of these challenges have been raised recently by gay or lesbian couples for alleged discrimination by golf and country clubs.

In *Koebke v. Bernardo Heights Country Club* (2005), the California Supreme Court held that the club's refusal to provide the same membership benefits to a lesbian couple who were in a registered domestic partnership as was provided to heterosexual married couples was in violation of the Unruh Civil Rights Act. In another case, the Atlanta Human Relations Committee ruled that a local country club was in violation of the city's nondiscrimination ordinance by refusing to allow domestic partners the same rights as member spouses (Rostow, 2004).

Significant Case

The following case illustrates the eight-factor test for determining if a club is "truly private." Examining the specific circumstances considered by the court of appeals and relied on by the district court helps to understand some of the protections granted to private organizations and clubs as well as the legal issues involved when an individual challenges the organization or club's rules and practices.

UNITED STATES OF AMERICA V. LANSDOWNE SWIM CLUB

United States Court of Appeals for the Third Circuit
894 F.2d 83 (1990)

This appeal is taken from the judgment of the district court, after a non-jury trial, that the Lansdowne Swim Club (LSC) discriminated against blacks on the basis of race or color in violation of Title II of the Civil Rights Act of 1964, 42 U.S.C. §§ 2000a-2000a-6 (1982). LSC challenges the findings of the district court on three grounds: that it is an exempted private club, that it is not a place of public accommodation, and that the United States failed to prove a pattern or practice of racial discrimination. We will affirm the judgment of the district court.

I. Because the district court opinion thoroughly sets forth the facts, United States v. Lansdowne Swim Club, 713 F. Supp. 785 (E.D. Pa. 1989), we shall only summarize them here. LSC, a nonprofit corporation organized under the laws of Pennsylvania, is the only group swimming facility in the Borough of Lansdowne, Pennsylvania. Since its founding in 1957, LSC has granted 1400 full family memberships. Every white applicant has been admitted, although two as limited members only. In that time, however, LSC has had only one non-white member.

The uncontroverted experiences of the following Lansdowne residents are significant. In 1976, the Allisons wrote to LSC requesting an application but LSC did not respond. Dr. Allison is black; his three children are part-black. In 1977, the Allisons twice again wrote for an application but LSC did not respond. The following year, the Allisons repeated the procedure with similar results. In 1983, the Allisons filed a timely application and otherwise qualified for membership but were rejected. The following year, the Ryans filed a timely application and otherwise qualified for membership. Nonetheless, they were rejected. Two of the Ryans' adopted children are black. The Ryans then complained to the media and picketed LSC, joined by the Allisons. In 1986, the Iverys, who are black, filed a timely application and otherwise qualified for membership. Nonetheless, they were rejected (as were the Ryans and Allisons who had again applied). * * *

II. LSC's first argument is that it is a private club. Under Title II, "a private club or other establishment not in fact open to the public" is exempt from the stat-

ute. 42 U.S.C. § 2000a(e). LSC has the burden of proving it is a private club. See Anderson v. Pass Christian Isles Golf Club, Inc., 488 F.2d 855, 857 (5th Cir. 1974). Although the statute does not define "private club", cases construing the provision do offer some guidance. The district court distilled eight factors from the case law as relevant to this determination, three of which it found dispositive of LSC's public nature: the genuine selectivity of its membership process, e.g., Tillman v. Wheaton-Haven Recreation Ass'n, 410 U.S. 431, 438, 35 L. Ed. 2d 403, 93 S. Ct. 1090 (1973), its history, e.g., Cornelius v. Benevolent Protective Order of Elks, 382 F. Supp. 1182, 1203 (D. Conn. 1974), and use of its facilities by nonmembers, id. Appellant disputes these findings.

First, the court concluded that LSC's membership process was not genuinely selective. Essential to this conclusion was the court's finding that "LSC possesses no objective criteria or standards for admission." The court identified four "criteria" for admission to LSC: being interviewed, completing an application, submitting two letters of recommendation and tendering payment of fees. We agree, and LSC apparently concedes, that these criteria were not genuinely selective. Nonetheless, LSC challenges the court's failure to consider membership approval a criterion for admission. We agree with the district court, however, that a formal procedure requiring nothing more than membership approval is insufficient to show genuine selectivity. See Tillman, 410 U.S. at 438–39. In addition, LSC stipulated that the only information given to the members prior to the membership vote is the applicants' names, addresses, their children's names and ages, and the recommenders' identities. In such a situation, the court was correct to conclude that LSC "provides no information to voting members that is useful in making an informed decision as to whether the applicant and his or her family would be compatible with the existing members." Therefore, even if membership approval were considered a fifth criterion, it would not make the process any more genuinely selective in this case.

The district court also found the yields of the membership process indicative of lack of selectivity. Since

1958, LSC has granted full memberships to at least 1400 families while denying them to only two non-black families. LSC contends that emphasizing the few instances of non-black applicant rejection "misconstrues the significance of selectivity. The crucial question should be whether the members exercised their right to be selective rather than the statistical results of the exercise of that right." As the Court of Appeals for the Fourth Circuit noted a decade ago, formal membership requirements "have little meaning when in fact the club does not follow a selective membership policy." Wright v. Salisbury Club, Ltd., 632 F.2d 309, 312 (4th Cir. 1980) (citing Tillman, 410 U.S. at 438-39). We find the evidence of lack of selectivity convincing.

Second, the court concluded that "the origins of LSC suggest that it was intended to serve as a 'community pool' for families in the area and not as a private club." We believe there was ample evidence to support this finding. A founder of LSC testified that LSC was created as a community pool for the neighborhood children. LSC's stipulations confirm the public nature of the facility: organizers solicited Lansdowne-area residents, conducted public recruitment meetings and accepted every family that applied for membership before opening.

Third, the court concluded that use of the facility by non-members "undercut LSC's claim that it is a private club." Among other reasons, the court cited the following factors. LSC hosts several swim meets and diving meets each year but does not prohibit the general public from attending. LSC also sponsors two to four pool parties each year, for which members and associates may sell an unlimited number of tickets to persons who are not members. In addition, LSC's basketball and volleyball courts, located on its parking lot, are open to the public. Finally, LSC permits the local Boys' Club to use its parking lot for an annual Christmas tree sale that is open to the public. Although LSC contends such use is de minimus, we are persuaded otherwise.

III. LSC also contends that it is not a "place of public accommodation" as defined in Title II. Under the statute, a place of public accommodation has two elements: first, it must be one of the statutorily enumerated categories of establishments that serve the public, 42 U.S.C. § 2000a(b); second, its operations must affect commerce, id.

A. The district court concluded that the whole complex, both the recreational areas and the snack bar, was an establishment which served the public. The court began by identifying LSC as a "place of . . . entertainment ", one of the categories of covered establishments. "LSC concedes that its swimming and other recreational areas make it an 'establishment'", but maintains that the snack bar is not a covered establishment. The district court held that "bifurcation has no support in the plain language of the Act or the case law interpreting it." Under the facts in this case, we agree. Nonetheless, the court also found the snack bar to be a "facility principally engaged in selling food for consumption on the premises", another category of covered establishments. LSC stipulated that "food for consumption on the premises of the Club is sold" at the snack bar. We believe these findings were sufficient to render the entire facility a covered establishment which serves the public.

B. The district court also concluded that the "affecting commerce" requirement was met. Initially, the court discussed the recreational areas, which it correctly deemed a place of entertainment under § 2000a(b)(3). Under Title II, the operations of a place of entertainment affect commerce if "it customarily presents . . . sources of entertainment which move in commerce". Id. § 2000a(c)(3). The court found the sliding board, manufactured in Texas, and guests from out of state to be sources of entertainment which moved in commerce. See Scott v. Young, 421 F.2d 143, 144-45 (4th Cir.) (both recreational apparatus originating out of state and patrons from out of state who entertain other patrons by their activity constitute "sources of entertainment which move in commerce") (relying on Daniel v. Paul, 395 U.S. 298, 307-08, 23 L. Ed. 2d 318, 89 S. Ct. 1697 (1969)), cert. denied, 398 U.S. 929, 90 S. Ct. 1820, 26 L. Ed. 2d 91 (1970). Implicitly conceding this, LSC argues that they do not satisfy "the requisite degree of interstate involvement." Nonetheless, the court found both to be "customarily presented", the sliding board because it is permanently installed, and the out of state guests because they attend regularly and constitute a significant percentage of the guests (13% in 1986, 8% in 1987). We believe these findings, and the court's consequent finding that operation of the recreational areas affects commerce, are supported by the evidence.

The court then considered the snack bar, which it correctly deemed a facility principally engaged in selling food for consumption on the premises under § 2000a(b)(2). Under Title II, the operations of this category of covered establishments affect commerce if " it serves or offers to serve interstate travelers or a substantial portion of the food which it serves . . . has moved in commerce". Id. § 2000a(c)(2). The court found the "affecting commerce" requirement satisfied in three ways. First, it was stipulated that the snack bar serves interstate travelers. Although LSC contends that the statute is meant to cover tourists lured from other states by advertising, the plain language of the statute provides no support for this view. Second, the court found that the snack bar offers to serve all users of the facility, including guests. Third, the court found that a substantial portion of the food served by the snack bar has moved in interstate commerce. The parties stipulated that the syrup used in the "Coca-Cola" beverages was produced in Maryland. The court found that many of the purchases at the snack bar were for cold drinks, of which "Coca-Cola" beverages were the most popular. Nonetheless, appellant claims the substantiality test has not been met, citing Daniel v. Paul, 395 U.S. 298, 23 L. Ed. 2d 318, 89 S. Ct. 1697 (1969), in which the Supreme Court found the test met when three of the four foods sold had moved in interstate commerce. Id. at 305. In light of the broad remedial purpose of Title II, we refuse to read the requirement or Daniel so narrowly. These findings are not clearly erroneous.

* * *

 OTHER RELEVANT SIGNIFICANT CASES

Recent Trends

European Commission

The European Union is facing similar challenges as those raised against Augusta and other private clubs for discriminatory practices toward women. The European Commission's directive on equal treatment between men and women in goods and services may limit private clubs' ability to discriminate against women (BBC News, 2006). This directive will take effect in 2007 and should eliminate discriminatory practices such as restricted tee times and limited access to the bar or restaurants. The directive may not ban truly private single-sex clubs as long as they are legitimate on the grounds on freedom of association. However, Ireland's exclusive Portmarnock Golf Club, which has a men-only membership policy, is being challenged in the courts by Ireland's Equality Authority. It is not certain what impact, if any, this EU directive will have on that case.

State Tax and Liqour Licensing Laws

It is clear from cases decided in Massachusetts, California, and Minnesota that state antidiscrimination laws are being used successfully to defeat discriminatory practices by private clubs. In addition, state licensing and regulatory schemes may also be used to combat discrimination. For example, many private clubs seek state liquor licenses, use permits, leases, zoning permits, and tax exemptions to operate. Some states have conditioned the awarding of such licenses, permits, and exemptions on the promise of the recipient that it will not engage in discriminatory practices (Ewing, 2000). Elimination of discrimination at the local and state level appears to be much more effective than it has been at the federal level. Discrimination on the basis of gender has been challenged most frequently. For example, three female members of the Coatesville Country Club in Pennsylvania filed a gender discrimination complaint with the Pennsylvania Human Relations Commission to gain equal access to the golf course, governance opportunities, and amenities at the course (Batchelor, 2002). If a married couple joined the Coatesville Country Club with a family membership, the husband was designated as the member, and the wife had a restricted membership excluding her from the course until 10:30 AM. In addition, only the husband, as the "member," held voting rights.

Strategic Planning

The National Golf Foundation has identified women and racial minorities as the two fastest growing markets in the golf industry. The Golf 20/20 Research Initiative undertaken by the National Golf Foundation and The World Golf Foundation has identified as one of its primary player development strategies to be more focused on women and on golf's emerging fan base (National Golf Foundation, 2004). Women account for 24 percent of the golfing population and almost 40 percent of new golfers, but less than 2.5 percent of "core" golfers (those who golf at least eight times per year) (National Golf Foundation, 2004). Thus, the National Golf Foundation has identified women as their primary target for expanding their consumer base. In addition, although women do not play as frequently as men, when they do play they spend as much as men spend (National Golf Foundation, 2004). Of particular interest to the future of golf is that women influence 87 percent of all sales in the golf shop (National Golf Foundation, 1998). The success of Tiger Woods has also drawn tremendous interest in golf from African Americans. Since, 1996, the African-American golfer population has increased 30 percent (National Golf Foundation, 2006b).

References

Cases

Borne v. The Haverhill Golf and Country Club, Lexis 523 (Mass. Super. 1999).

Boy Scouts of America v. Dale, 530 US 640 (2003).

Brown v. Loudoun Golf & Country Club, Inc., 573 F. Supp. 399 (E.D. Va. 1983).

Castle Hill Beach Club v. Arbury, 144 N.Y.S.2d 747 (Sup. Ct. 1955).

Citizen's Council on Human Relations v. Buffalo Yacht Club, 438 F. Supp. 316 (W.D. N.Y. 1977).

Cornelius v. BPOE, 382 F. Supp. 1182 (D. Conn. 1974).

Crawford v. Willow Oaks Country Club, 66 F. Supp.2d 767 (E.D. Va. 1999).

Daniel v. Paul, 395 U.S. 298, 89 S. Ct. 1697 (1969).

Durham v. Red Lake Fishing & Hunting Club, Inc., 666 F. Supp. 954 (W.D. Tex. 1987).

EEOC v. The Chicago Club, 86 F.3d 1423 (7th Cir. 1996).

Evans v. Laurel Links, Inc., 261 F. Supp. 474 (E.D. Va. 1966).

Gibbs-Alfano v. The Ossining Boat & Canoe Club, Inc., 47 F. Supp.2d 506 (S.D. N.Y. 1999).

Guesby v. Kennedy, 580 F. Supp. 1280 (D. Kan. 1984).

Koebke v. Bernardo Heights Country Club, S124179, Supreme Court of California (2005, August 1).

NAACP v. Alabama ex rel. Patterson, 357 U.S. 449 (1958).

Nesmith v. YMCA, 397 F.2d 96 (4th Cir. 1968).

New York v. Ocean Club, 602 F. Supp. 489 (E.D. N.Y. 1984).

Roberts v. United States Jaycees, 104 S. Ct. 3244 (1984).

Tillman v. Wheaton-Haven Recreation Ass'n., 410 U.S. 431 (1973).

United States v. Jack Sabin's Private Club, 265 F. Supp. 90 (E.D. La. 1967).

United States v. Lansdowne Swim Club, 713 F. Supp. 785 (E.D. Pa. 1989).

United States v. Richberg, 398 F.2d 523 (5th Cir. 1968).

Wanders v. Bear Hill Golf Club, Inc., Lexis 650 (Mass. Super. 1998).

Wright v. Cork Club, 315 F. Supp. 1143 (D.C. Tex. 1970).

Publications

Batchelor, J. (2002, October 16). Country club accused of discrimination. *The Legal Intelligencer, 227*(75), 3.

Burk (2005).

BBC News. (2005, January 5). EU challenge to golf club sexism. *BBC News*. Retrieved January 30, 2006 from http://newsvote.bbc.co.uk/

Ending tax deductions for discrimination. (2003, June 11). Press release of Congresswoman Carolyn B. Maloney. Retrieved January 30, 2006 from http://www.house.gov/maloney

Ewing, S. (2000). Open space tax benefits threatened for golf course owners. Retrieved January 30, 2006 from http://www.library.findlawcom/2000/Oct/1/130529.html

Goodman, M. L. (1999). Note: A Scout is morally straight, brave, clean, trustworthy—and heterosexual? Gays in the Boy Scouts of America. *Hofstra Law Review, 27*, 825.

Jolly-Ryan, J. (1997). Chipping away at discrimination at the country club. *Pepperdine Law Review, 25*, 495.

Lambda Legal. (2005). *Koebke v. Bernardo Heights Country Club*: Victory!. Retrieved January 30, 2006 from http://www.lambdalegal/org

National Golf Foundation. (1998). *A strategic perspective on the future of golf*. Retrieved from http://www.ngf.org/opportunities/

National Golf Foundation. (2004). *Golf 20/20 Industry Report for 2003. National Golf Foundation Website*. Retrieved February 10, 2006 from www.ngf.org

National Golf Foundation. (2006a). *Frequently asked questions about the game and business of golf*. Retrieved February 10, 2006 from http://www.ngf.org/cgi/whofaq.asp#2

National Golf Foundation. (2006b, February 1). *News Releases: Rounds finished year flat.* Retrieved February 10, 2006 from http://www.ngf.org

Overbeck, A. M. (1984). Case note: Constitutional law—Freedom of association—Sex discrimination—Associations and societies—Enforcement of the Minnesota Human Rights Act to require the United States Jaycees to accept women as regular members does not violate its male members' freedom of association, and the Act is neither unconstitutionally vague nor overbroad. *University of Cincinnati Law Review, 53,* 1173.

Rhode, D. (2002, October 7). Tee time for equality. *National Law Journal, 24*(55), A13.

Rostow, A. (2004, January 13). Gays win bias complaint against golf club. Retrieved January 30, 2006 from http://www.gay.com

Sawyer, T. H. (1993). Private golf clubs: Freedom of expression and the right to privacy. *Marquette Sports Law Journal, 3,* 187.

Tebo, M. G. (2000, February). Teed off. *American Bar Association Journal, 86,* 26.

Tofilon, J. L. (2005, Fall). Masters of discrimination: Augusta National Golf Club, freedom of association, and gender equality in golf. *The Journal of Gender, Race & Justice, 9,* 189–210.

Legislation

United States Constitution, Amendments I, IX, & XIV.

42 U.S.C. § 1981 (2000).

42 U.S.C. § 1983 (2000).

42 U.S.C. § 1985 (2000).

42 U.S.C. § 2000a (2000).

42 U.S.C. § 2000e (2000).

Cal. Civ. Code § 51 (West 1982 & Supp. 1999).

D.C. Code Ann. § 1–2501 (1992).

Mass. Gen. Law § 151 (1998).

Minn. Stat. Ann. § 363.01-.14 (West 1966 & Supp. 1984).

N.J. Stat. Ann. § 10:5-4 (West 1993).

N.Y. Exec. Law § 296(2)(a) (McKinney 1998).

R.I. Gen. Laws § 1-24-2 (1994).

8.00

Sport and Legislation

In addition to the federal Constitution, Congress has also enacted a number of laws that affect the sport and recreation industry. The *Sport and Legislation* section examines those laws and the impact they have on the industry. The section is divided into four parts. The first part reviews federal laws as they apply to discrimination in the sport and recreation industry. The section examines such areas as gender equity and race, age, sex, and disability discrimination. The second part examines intellectual property law. In particular, the chapters review how important copyright, trademark, and patent law are to the sport and recreation industries. The third part examines federal antitrust and labor laws and how they are applied to professional and amateur sports. The final part of the *Sport and Legislation* section examines sport agent legislation. In particular, the chapter reviews sport agent legislation and the impact of the Uniform Athlete Agent Act of sport agents.

8.11 Gender Equity:
OPPORTUNITIES TO PARTICIPATE

Linda Jean Carpenter, Emerita
Brooklyn College

Sport is the laboratory experience through which students gain skills such as decision making, risk evaluation, teamwork, leadership, self-appraisal and personal esteem. These skills are the same skills that allow graduates to successfully use their other academic skills in their adult lives and employment circumstances.

Sport's place on campus in the form of intramurals, recreation, athletics, and physical education is defensible, not because of any possible revenue generation or because of fan support, but because of the valuable skills it provides, which are not easily obtained elsewhere in the educational setting.

The skills obtainable through sport have value to both female and male participants. The legal imperatives for equity found in the Fourteenth Amendment of the U.S. Constitution and Title IX of the Education Amendments of 1972 (and a variety of similarly worded state legislation) are the two most frequently used tools to judicially increase gender equitable participation in sport.

Between the Fourteenth Amendment and Title IX, most circumstances within education are covered. The Fourteenth Amendment requires a state actor; Title IX doesn't. Title IX requires the presence of federal financial assistance, the Fourteenth Amendment doesn't. Both cover gender discrimination. Both cover employees and students.

Fundamental Concepts

Constitutional Issues

The Equal Protection Clause of the Fourteenth Amendment is the generic protector of equal rights. It guarantees that no *state actor* such as a federal, state, or local governmental agency, or, for example, public school and recreation program, can gratuitously classify people and treat them differently based on those classifications without having a defensible reason.

Levels of Scrutiny

Strict/High: Necessary to Accomplish a Compelling State Interest

The defensible reason required to constitutionally treat people differently varies depending on the classification scheme employed. If, for example, a public school (*state actor*) classified its students by race and then treated its African-American students differently, the reason used to defend the constitutionality of such an action would have to withstand the Court's highest level of scrutiny. The school would need to show that its racially based discrimination was *necessary to accomplish a compelling state interest*. It is difficult to imagine a reason for racial discrimination that would meet such a test.

Mild/Low: Rationally Related to a Legitimate State Interest

As an alternative example, consider the scenario where a public school's (*state actor*) physical education program classified its students by skill level and, as a result, restricted its beginning-level students to a beginning-level course while allowing the more highly skilled students to have access to a variety of advanced electives. The Court would use a lower level of scrutiny to determine if discrimination based on skill level was constitutional. The school would only have to show that its discrimination was *rationally related to a legitimate state interest*. Protecting beginners from the injuries likely to occur if they participated with highly skilled athletes or performed advanced movements for which they were either untrained or unconditioned would appear to be rationally related to the legitimate state interest of protecting the health and safety of the community's schoolchildren.

Intermediate/Midlevel: An Evolving Middle Ground

Most classification schemes are reviewed by the courts using either the strict/high or mild/low levels of scrutiny. Typically only those classifications based on race, alienage, or nationality face strict/high scrutiny. Almost all other classification schemes face only the mild/low level.

In the last few decades, however, we have seen the judicial review of classification schemes based on age, gender, and disability elevated from the mild/low level of scrutiny to a reasonably amorphous midlevel of scrutiny.

In its June 1996 decision involving coeducation at Virginia Military Institute (116 S.Ct. 2264) the Supreme Court elevated the scrutiny applied to *gender* discrimination even higher within this middle ground to a level requiring an exceedingly persuasive justification. Thus if a state actor discriminates on the basis of gender, it will need to show that doing so was considerably more than rationally related to a legitimate state interest, but it will not need to show that it was necessary to accomplish a compelling state interest.

Why is discrimination based on age, disability, and particularly gender becoming more difficult to justify constitutionally? The change probably reflects the changing attitudes of society to this type of discrimination as reflected in various civil rights legislation such as Titles VI, VII, and IX.

Cases involving gender discrimination in sport have used the Fourteenth Amendment, but the more prevalently used tool is Title IX. For this reason, and because of the presence of a fuller discussion of constitutional issues elsewhere in this text, the remaining portion of this chapter dealing with participation issues will focus on Title IX.

Title IX

A Brief History

Title IX was enacted by Congress on June 23, 1972, to prohibit gender discrimination in the nation's education programs. Three basic elements must all exist for Title IX's jurisdiction to be triggered. The elements are

- *Gender discrimination.* Title IX does not protect against discrimination based on race or age; it protects solely against gender discrimination.
- *Federal funding.* The receipt of federal funding is required so that the enforcement of Title IX has administrative teeth. If an institution is found to be violating Title IX, its federal funding may be terminated. However, no federal money has ever been removed from a campus due to a Title IX violation. Thus the administrative enforcement teeth have never yet been used.
- *Education program.* The definition of this element brought early controversy to the implementation of Title IX. The U.S. Supreme Court's 1984 *Grove City v. Bell* decision resulted in the word *program* being defined as a "subunit" of an institution. As a result of *Grove City*, any subunit that did not receive federal funding would not be obligated to refrain from gender discrimination. Thus college-level athletics and physical education programs, which typically receive no federal funding, were no longer obligated by Title IX to refrain from gender discrimination. In 1988, however, Congress passed the Civil Rights Restoration Act of 1987 over presidential veto saying, in effect, that the Court had misunderstood Congress' intent to have Title IX apply on an institutionwide basis. So, as of 1988, Title IX once again applies to college-level athletics and physical education programs, as well as to all education programs in institutions that receive federal funding.

Title IX Enforcement

There are three main pathways to enforce Title IX. The complainant or plaintiff may select any of the three and need not exhaust in-house remedies first.

Each institution under the jurisdiction of Title IX must have a designated Title IX officer. The Title IX officer's job is to educate the faculty, staff, and students about the rights and responsibilities imposed by Title IX and to deal with any Title IX complaints filed in-house.

The second method of enforcement is through the Office for Civil Rights of the U.S. Department of Education. Once an administrative complaint is filed with the OCR (legal standing is NOT required in order to file), the OCR investigates and, if violations are found, negotiates a "letter of resolution" with the institution in which the institution agrees to a time frame and a list of changes to be made.

The third method involves the filing of a federal lawsuit by someone with legal standing. This method has found increasing favor among plaintiffs since the Supreme Court's unanimous 1992 *Franklin v. Gwinnett County Public Schools* decision, which made it clear that compensatory and even punitive damages are available to victims of intentional gender discrimination under Title IX.

Title IX Requirements

When Title IX was enacted in 1972, there was only the one-sentence law saying:

> No person in the United States shall, on the basis of sex, be excluded from participation in, be denied the benefits of, or be subjected to discrimination under any education program or activity receiving Federal financial assistance.

In addition to the one-sentence law, formal regulations were promulgated and ultimately gained the force of law. Even though most Title IX cases and controversies have related to its application to sport, Title IX applies to all of education. However, because of continuing controversy about the details of Title IX's implementation in the area of sport, policy interpretations were adopted in 1979. Policy interpretations do not have the force of law but courts are required to give them significant deference. Another, yet much weaker, source of information about the requirements of Title IX is found in the 1990 *OCR Investigator's Manual*, which provides insight into how the OCR views its own requirements.

Recreation Program Application

Recreation programs are also often under the jurisdiction of Title IX. As long as all three elements (federal money, allegations of sex discrimination, and education program) are met, recreation programs are included in the jurisdiction of Title IX. It would be difficult to conceive of a campus-based recreation program that would not be under Title IX jurisdiction.

Nonscholastic, community-based recreation programs need not be operated by the state or federal government to be under the jurisdiction of Title IX. The recreation program's primary activity need not be conducting educational programs; it only needs to include an educational component in its programs to be under the jurisdiction of Title IX. If a recreation program is found to be under the jurisdiction of Title IX, offering more activities or more participation opportunities for its male clients, offering those activities in better facilities, or providing a higher quality officiating staff for its male clients, would be examples of potential Title IX violations.

Athletics Application

There are many specific requirements of Title IX relating to coaching, facilities, equipment, travel, and so on. However, if a female is not provided an opportunity to participate, it matters very little if she would have had equal access to coaching, facilities, equipment, travel, and so on. Therefore, let's focus on participation opportunities. In short, if you are not on the team, you don't need a uniform. So, we will focus on the legal requirements for participation rather than on the treatment of athletes once they are participating.

Title IX's regulations require that "the selection of sports and levels of competition effectively accommodate the interests and abilities of members of both sexes." According to the policy interpretations (U.S. Department of Education Athletic Guidelines, 1979), an institution has effectively accommodated the interests of its students if it satisfies any ONE of the following three benchmarks:

1. Participation opportunities for male and female students are provided in numbers substantially proportionate to their respective enrollments; or
2. The institution can show a history and continuing practice of program expansion demonstrably responsive to the developing interest and abilities of the members of the underrepresented sex; or
3. The institution can show that it is fully and effectively meeting the interests and abilities of the underrepresented sex.

Institutions that have maintained their commitment to the legal requirements of gender equity over the years have had no difficulty in meeting either Benchmark 2 or 3 and thus don't even need to address the issue of proportionality found in Benchmark 1.

However, institutions that have ignored the requirements of Title IX or that have failed to implement plans to provide equitable athletic participation opportunities for their female students, more than three decades after the passage of Title IX, are now facing a quandary. They have not satisfied Benchmark 2 because they have not expanded their program for their female students. Similarly, if a group of female athletes demonstrates interest and ability sufficient to support the creation of a team in a particular sport in which it would be reasonable to find suitable competition in the school's traditional competitive region, the institution cannot claim that it has satisfied Benchmark 3. That leaves Benchmark 1: proportionality. For many reasons, including past discrimination and social influences, very few schools meet Benchmark 1. Typically, the Courts have found such institutions to be violating Title IX's requirement to effectively accommodate the interests and abilities of its female (historically underrepresented sex) student–athletes. Such institutions are therefore at risk of losing their federal funding in addition to being liable for possible compensatory and punitive damages.

Consternation and controversy surrounding the measurement of equitable participation has been unabated by the fact that the status of the law and the application of the three-prong test (as found in the 1979 Policy Interpretations and as reiterated unchanged in the form of a 1996 clarification letter from the Office for Civil Rights) has been very straightforward.

One of the three tests of participation, the proportionality prong (Benchmark 1) was created to provide a "safe harbor". In this context "safe harbor" means that a school that can show it has met the proportionality prong will be exempt from creating additional participation opportunities for females, even if there are significant numbers of females who are denied participation. The school would be granted the "safe harbor" exemption because it is assumed that if its ratio of female athletes mirrors the ratio of females in the student body, gender equity in participation has been met.

Reality has demonstrated that schools that have not gradually moved toward compliance over the years or that have left favored teams' budgets and inflated participation numbers unrestrained find that they can meet none of the three prongs in any reasonable way. They can't rewrite history to meet prong 2, and they can't claim that they have met the interests and abilities of the underrepresented sex (prong 3) as long as there are sufficient able and interested females wanting to participate. The only prong over which such an institution has retained any degree of control is the proportionality prong.

Some institutions have manipulated compliance within the proportionality prong in ways that, in effect, reduce participation for males and sometimes even the historically underrepresented females. By canceling men's minor sport teams, the absolute number of male participants is reduced, and the male/female athlete ratio moves closer to the ratio in the student body without having to increase participation opportunities for women. This manipulation is contrary to the spirit of Title IX. Even so, administrators have often defended their decision to cut men's minor sport teams, rather than restrain favored teams, by placing the blame for the cancellation of men's teams on Title IX. The popularity of various sports waxes and wanes even in the absence of Title IX, but those whose sports are cut are understandably frustrated.

Frustration born of the manipulation of the proportionality prong resulted in the creation of the Commission on Opportunity in Sport during the summer of 2002 under the direction of the then-Secretary for the Department of Education. The Commission was created to "strengthen enforcement" and "expand. . . opportunities to ensure fairness for all athletes." The Commission members were asked to respond to eight questions, some of which might be reflective of preconceived notions of the answers and some of which seem far afield of the requirements of Title IX. The eight questions are

1. Are Title IX standards for assessing equal opportunity in athletics working to promote opportunities for male and female athletes?
2. Is there adequate Title IX guidance that enables colleges and school districts to know what is expected of them and to plan for an athletic program that effectively meets the needs and interest of their students?"
3. Is further guidance or other steps needed at the junior- and senior-high-school levels, where the availability or absence of opportunities will critically affect the prospective interests and abilities of student athletes when they reach college age?
4. How should activities such as cheerleading or bowling factor into the analysis of equitable opportunities?
5. The [Education] Department has heard from some parties that whereas some men athletes will "walk on" to intercollegiate teams—without athletic financial aid and without having been recruited—women rarely do this. Is this accurate and, if so, what are its implications for Title IX analysis?
6. How do revenue-producing and large-roster teams affect the provision of equal athletic opportunities?
7. In what ways do opportunities in other sports venues, such as the Olympic, professional leagues, and community recreation programs, interact with the obligations of colleges and school districts to provide equal athletic opportunity? What are the implications for Title IX?
8. Apart from Title IX enforcements, are there other efforts to promote athletic opportunities for male and female students that the department might support, such as public–private partnerships to support the efforts of schools and colleges in this area?

The Commission's hearings were robust with strong rhetoric on all sides. The Commission's report, which was vague in direction, did little to calm any partisan fears. A minority report was issued and all interested in the issue of Title IX awaited some further action from the OCR. When further action finally came, it came in the form of a "Letter of Further Guidance." The Letter of Further Guidance reaffirmed OCR's support of the existing requirements of Title IX and promised more diligent enforcement. The Letter also renewed the appropriateness of the three-part test, including the proportionality option.

How would you respond to each of the Commission's questions after seeking out data and a variety of points of view? For one organization's response, check the following Website:

http://www.aahperd.org/nagws/template.cfm?template=titleix_papers.html

For a time, it seemed that finally, Title IX and its requirements were settled in both practice and in the law. Then, on January 11, 2005, OCR issued another letter, this time known as the "Additional Clarification of Intercollegiate Athletics Policy: Three-Part Test—Part Three." (See the following Website for a copy of the letter and also for the accompanying technical manual: http://www.ed.gov/about/offices/list/ocr/docs/title9guidanceadditional.html.)

The 2005 Additional Clarification Letter was much more than a clarification. It provided for the use of an OCR-created survey instrument to assess interest and ability among students. The survey contains no standard for measuring sufficient interest, and thus regardless of the results, no finding of sufficient interest would be mandated. If a school elects to use the OCR survey instrument, even via an e-mail survey sent to student accounts, the school gains a presumption of having met the interests and abilities of its historically underrepresented students, regardless of the results of the survey (due to the lack of standards to measure sufficient interest). To make clear: the simple use of the survey, regardless of its outcome, conveys the presumption. According to the 2005 Additional Clarification of Letter, the presumption of compliance is only rebuttable "if the OCR finds direct and very persuasive evidence of unmet interest sufficient to sustain a varsity team, such as the recent elimination of a viable team for the underrepresented sex or a recent, broad-based petition from an existing club team for elevation to varsity status." The hurdle to be overcome to rebut the presumption is very high indeed.

In part because of the difficult-to-overcome presumption, the use of an e-mail survey format, which is unlikely to produce high response rates (a nonresponse is interpreted as disinterest), and the format of the questions within the OCR survey instrument, the NCAA swiftly called on the OCR to withdraw the 2005 Additional Letter. Furthermore, the NCAA strongly urged its member institutions to refrain from using the OCR survey.

As of this writing OCR has not withdrawn its letter, and only few, if any, NCAA members have elected to use the survey instrument offered in the letter.

Opportunities to Participate Free from Harassment

Having the opportunity to participate but facing sexual harassment while participating is not much of an opportunity at all. Sexual harassment invades many areas of human interaction, and the Fourteenth Amendment to a small degree and Titles VII and IX to a larger degree are useful tools with which to combat sexual harassment.

Title IX is specifically applicable to sexual harassment of both students and their teachers and coaches. Title VII applies only in the workplace, and thus does not protect students, but Title VII has been the fountain from which much of Title IX's strength in the area of sexual harassment has flowed. See Chapter 8.14 for a full discussion of harassment.

Significant Case

Although a relatively old case, the following case is used to illustrate the Title IX guidelines published by the office for civil rights and those requirements needed to come into compliance with the law.

ROBERTS V. COLORADO STATE UNIVERSITY

United States Tenth Circuit Court of Appeals
998 F.2d 824 (10th Cir. 1993)

Current and former members of the Colorado State University's fast pitch softball team sued the university after it announced the discontinuation of the fast pitch softball program. The students, suing as individuals, claimed Title IX violations.

The district court found Title IX violations existed and issued a permanent injunction reinstating the softball program. When, somewhat later, the court held a status conference, the court found the institution had been apparently dragging its feet. Therefore, the court amplified its earlier orders to require defendant to hire a coach promptly, recruit new members for the team, and organize a fall season. . . . [*Italics* indicate text summarized by author.]

A.

This controversy concerns one subject of the regulations implementing Title IX. 34 C.F.R. § 106.41(c) provides:

A recipient which operated or sponsors interscholastic, intercollegiate, club or intramural athletes shall provide equal athletic opportunity for members of both sexes. In determining whether equal opportunities are available the Director [of the Office for Civil Rights] will consider, among other factors:

(1) Whether the selection of sports and levels of competition effectively accommodate the interests and abilities of members of both sexes[.]

Although § 106.41(c) goes on to list nine other factors that enter into discrimination of equal opportunity in athletics, an institution may violate Title IX simply by failing to accommodate effectively the interests and abilities of student athletes of both sexes.

In 1979, the Department of Health, Education, and Welfare issued a policy interpretation explaining the ways in which institutions may effectively accommodate the interests and abilities of their student athletes.

The Policy Interpretation delineates three general areas in which the OCR will assess compliance with the effective accommodation section of the regulation, as follows:

1. The determination of athletic interests and abilities of students;

2. The selection of sports offered; and
3. The levels of competition available including the opportunity for team competition.

The OCR assesses effective accommodation with respect to opportunities for intercollegiate competition by determining:

(1) Whether intercollegiate level participation opportunities for male and female students are provided in numbers substantially proportionate to their respective enrollments; or

(2) Where the members of one sex have been and are under represented among intercollegiate athletes, whether the institution can show a history and continuing practice of program expansion which is demonstrably responsive to the developing interest and abilities of the members of that sex; or

(3) Where the members of one sex are under represented among intercollegiate athletes, and the institution cannot show a continuing practice of program expansion such as that cited above, whether it can be demonstrated that the interests and abilities of the members of that sex have been fully and effectively accommodated by the present program.

In effect, "substantial proportionality" between athletic participation and undergraduate enrollment provides a safe harbor for recipients under Title IX. In the absence of such gender balance, the institution must show that it has expanded and is continuing to expand opportunities for athletic participation by the under represented gender, or else it must fully and effectively accommodate the interests and abilities among members of the under represented gender.

In addition to assessing whether individuals of both sexes have the opportunity to compete in intercollegiate athletics, the OCR also examines whether the quality of competition provided to male and female athletes equally reflects their abilities. This will depend on whether, program wide, the competitive schedules of men's and women's teams "afford proportionally similar numbers of male and female athletes equivalently advanced competitive opportunities," id., or "[w]hether the institution can demonstrate a history and continuing practice of upgrading the competitive opportunities available to the historically disadvantaged sex as warranted by developing abilities among the athletes of that sex." However, "[i]nstitutions are not required to upgrade teams to intercollegiate status or otherwise develop intercollegiate sports absent a reasonable expectation that intercollegiate competition in that sport will be available within the institution's normal competitive regions."

B.

The district court found that plaintiffs met their burden of showing that defendant could not take shelter in the safe harbor of substantial proportionality. The district court reviewed a substantial quantity of statistical data, and made the undisputed finding that following the termination of the varsity softball program, the disparity between enrollment and athletic participation for women at CSU is 10.5 percent. Defendant maintains that, as a matter of law, a 10.5 percent disparity is substantially proportionate.

The OCR has instructed its Title IX compliance investigators that "[t]here is no set ratio that constitutes 'substantially proportionate' or that, when not met, results in a disparity or a violation." Investigator's Manual at 24. However, in the example immediately preceding this statement, the Manual suggests that substantial proportionality entails a fairly close relationship between athletic participation and undergraduate enrollment. Furthermore, in a Title IX compliance review completed in 1983, the OCR found that CSU's athletic participation opportunities for men and women were not substantially proportionate to their respective enrollments. During the three years that were the subject of that review, the differences between women enrolled and women athletes were 7.5 percent, 12.5 percent, and 12.7 percent. The district court relied on these sources, as well as expert testimony that a 10.5 percent disparity is statistically significant, in concluding that CSU could not meet this first benchmark. *See also Cohen v. Brown University*, 809 F. Supp. 978,991 (D.R.I. 1992) (11.6 percent disparity not substantially proportionate) *aff'd*, 991 F.2d 888 (1st Cir. 1993). Without demarcating further the line between substantial proportionality and disproportionality, we agree with the district court that a 10.5 percent disparity between female athletic participation and female undergraduate enrollment is not substantially proportionate. The fact that many or even most other educational institutions have a greater imbalance than CSU does not require a different holding.

C.

The district court also found that defendant could not prove a history and continuing practice of expansion in women's athletics at CSU. Defendant argues that the district court should have given greater weight to its dramatic expansion of women's athletic opportunities during the 1970s. In essence, defendant suggests reading the words "continuing practice" out of this prong of the test. In support of this position, defendant offers anecdotal evidence of enforcement at other institutions, and the OCR's 1983 finding of compliance for CSU, which was contingent upon CSU's fulfilling the provisions of a plan that CSU never met.

Although CSU created a woman's sports program out of nothing in the 1970s, adding eleven sports for women during that decade, the district court found that women's participation opportunities declined steadily during the 1980s. Furthermore, although budget cuts in the last twelve years have affected both men and women athletes at CSU, the district court found that women's participation opportunities declined by 34 percent, whereas men's opportunities declined by only 20 percent. The facts as found by the district court (and largely undisputed by defendant) can logically support no other conclusion than that, since adding women's golf in 1977, CSU has not maintained a practice of program expansion in women's athletics, and indeed has since dropped three women's sports.

We recognize that in times of economic hardship, few schools will be able to satisfy Title IX's effective accommodation requirement by continuing to expand their women's athletics programs. Nonetheless, the ordinary meaning of the word "expansion" may not be twisted to find compliance under their prong when schools have increased the relative percentages of women participating in athletics by making cuts in both men's and women's sports programs. Financially strapped institutions may still comply with Title IX by cutting athletic programs such that men's and women's athletic participation rates become substantially proportionate to their representation in the undergraduate population.

The heart of the controversy is the meaning of the phrase "full and effective accommodation of interests and abilities." Defendant maintains that even if there is interest and ability on the part of women athletes at CSU, the university is obliged to accommodate them only to the extent it accommodates men. Thus, the argument goes, plaintiffs cannot be heard to complain because both women's softball and men's baseball were eliminated in the last round of cuts and there are more disappointed male than female athletes at CSU. The First Circuit rejected this position in *Cohen*, and so do we. "[T]his benchmark sets a high standard; it demands not merely some accommodation, but full and effective accommodation. If there is sufficient interest and ability among members of the statistically under represented gender, not slaked by existing programs, an institution necessarily fails this prong of the test." Id. at 898.

Based on the district court's subsidiary findings of fact, we conclude that plaintiffs met the burden of showing that CSU has not accommodated their interest and abilities fully and effectively. Questions of fact under this third prong will be less vexing when plaintiffs seek the reinstatement of an established team rather than the creation of a new one. Here, plaintiffs were members of a successful varsity softball team that played a competitive schedule as recently as the spring of 1992. Although apparently four plaintiffs have transferred and one has been dismissed, seven or eight plaintiffs remain at CSU for at least part of the 1993–94 school year and would be eligible to play on a reinstated team. We agree with the district court that CSU fails the third prong of effective accommodation test.

 OTHER RELEVANT SIGNIFICANT CASES

Chapter 8.12 *Gender Equity: Coaching and Administration*

Recent Trends

Does Title IX protect members of discontinued men's teams?

No. Title IX protects the participation rights of the historically underrepresented sex. In the athletics programs of most schools the historically underrepresented sex would be female. In a 1994 Illinois case (*Kelly v. University of Illinois*) the men's swimming team was cut but the women's team was not. The U.S. Court of Appeals, Seventh Circuit held that even after the cut, men's participation in athletics was more than substantially proportionate to their enrollment and indeed, if the women's team had been cut, the university would have increased the lack of proportionality sufficiently to be vulnerable to a Title IX claim by the women.

Is the lack of money a defense to Title IX?

No. Budgetary constraints that either force teams to be cut or prohibit their addition are not a defense to the requirements of Title IX. Cases demonstrating this principle include *Cook v. Colgate University* (1993) and *Favia v. Indiana University of Pennsylvania* (1993).

Should failure of Benchmark 1 (proportionality) solely create an irrefutable presumption of either compliance with or violation of Title IX's accommodation/opportunity requirement?

No. According to the discussion found in a 1996 Louisiana case (*Pederson v. Louisiana State University*), Benchmark 1 should not be used as the solitary indicia of compliance or failure concerning participation opportunities. In the absence of information concerning the interests and abilities of female athletes, reliance solely on Benchmark 1 is inappropriate, according to the U.S. District Court for the Middle District of Louisiana, as well as lower level cases in other jurisdictions. Discussion concerning Benchmark 1's role in determining if sufficient participation opportunities exist has been heated in the past few years. Some voices have accused the OCR of focusing solely on Benchmark 1 as determinative indicia. OCR has, in turn, restated its commitment to the Policy Interpretation's three-part test. In effect, the *LSU* decision supports OCR's restatement that where Benchmark 1 is not satisfied, proceed to determine if either Benchmark 2 or 3 is appropriate. The First Circuit's decision in *Cohen v. Brown University* (1995) (*cert. denied* by the U.S. Supreme Court) supports this view. OCR has repeatedly indicated that meeting any of the three benchmarks is acceptable, and it places no priority on Benchmark 1. Benchmark 1's critics have typically been those schools that have failed to meet or even approach either of the other two benchmarks.

References

Cases

Cohen v. Brown University, 991 F.2d 888 (1st Cir. 1993), 8879 F. Supp. 185 (D. R.I. 1995), *cert. denied.*

Cook v. Colgate University, 802 F. Supp. 737 (1992) vacated as moot 992 F.2d 17 (2nd Cir. 1993).

Davis v. Monroe County Board of Education, 526 U.S. 629 (1999).

Favia v. Indiana University of Pennsylvania, 7 F.3d 332 (3rd Cir. 1993).

Franklin v. Gwinnett County Public Schools, 503 U.S. 60 (1992).

Grove City v. Bell, 465 U.S. 555 (1984).

Kelley v. University of Illinois, 35 F.3d 265 (7th Cir. 1994).

Mercer v. Duke University, No. 01-1512, 4th Circuit, November 15, 2002.

Oncale v. Sundowner Offshore Services, 523 U.S. 75 (1998).

Pederson v. Louisiana State University, 912 F. Supp. 892 (La. 1996).

Roberts v. Colorado State University, 814 F. Supp. 1507 (D. Colo.) *aff'd in relevant part sub nom. Roberts v. Colorado State Bd. of Agric.*, 998 F.2d 824 (10th Cir.), *cert. denied*, 114 S. Ct. 580 (1993).

Publications

U.S. Department of Education. (1979). Athletic Guidelines.

Legislation

Title VII: 42 USC sections 2000e-17, plus additions made by the Civil Rights Act of 1991, Pub.L. No. 102–166, 105 Stat 1071 (1991).

Title IX: Education Amendments of 1972, §§ 901–909 as amended, 20 U.S.C.A. §§ 11681–11688. 40 Fed. Reg. 24, 128 (1975) current appearing at 34 C.F.R. §§ 106 (1992).

U.S. Department of Education Athletic Guidelines; Title IX of the Education Amendments of 1972; A Policy Interpretation; Title IX and Intercollegiate Athletics, 44 Fed. Reg. 71, 413, 71, 423 (1979).

8.12 Gender Equity:
COACHING AND ADMINISTRATION

Maureen P. Fitzgerald
University of Texas at Austin

When people in scholastic and intercollegiate athletics hear the term *gender equity*, most think of what it means relative to participation opportunities for student–athletes (see Chapter 8.11). Certainly, the accommodation of students' interests and abilities relative to participating in athletics is a key gender equity issue; however, the term also encompasses other important legal concerns such as the equitable selection and/or treatment of the coaches and athletics administrators.

Decisions regarding the selection, hiring, and compensation of coaches or administrators should not be based on gender. Yet, at a time when the participation opportunities for female athletes have been increasing, there has been a dramatic decline in the number of females coaching and administering female teams (Acosta & Carpenter, 2006). Females that coach at the college level earn ". . . only sixty-two percent of what men make" (Osborne & Yarborough, 2001, p. 233). Clearly there is a gender gap in salaries.

A heightened sense of urgency and pressure to provide equitable opportunities was placed on academic institutions when the Supreme Court, in *Franklin v. Gwinnett County Public Schools* (1992), ruled that compensatory damages were available for plaintiffs under Title IX as a cause of action. Since *Franklin*, several plaintiffs have filed employment discrimination claims using Title IX, the Equal Pay Act (EPA), and Title VII. Even though no pay equity case has made it to the Supreme Court, the lower court decisions are instructive relative to pay equity issues in coaching and administration and can assist in shaping the selection, hiring, and compensation decisions of managers in sport. In addition, the Equal Employment Opportunity Commission (EEOC) in October, 1997 issued guidelines to clarify the Commission's position on sex-based compensation issues for coaches in educational institutions (i.e., regarding the application of the EPA and Title VII). These guidelines, in conjunction with recent trial court decisions, serve to directly address some of the most common arguments put forth by the plaintiff institutions when they are faced with a pay equity claim from one of their coaches.

Fundamental Concepts

The legal areas most relevant to employment discrimination in athletics are the Equal Pay Act of 1963, Title VII of the Civil Rights Act of 1963 (see Chapter 8.13), Title IX (See Chapter 8.11), and the Equal Protection Clause of the Fourteenth Amendment (using Section 183 of the Civil Rights Act of 1871) of the U.S. Constitution.

The Equal Pay Act of 1963

The Equal Pay Act (EPA) of 1963 prohibits an employer from discriminating between employees on the basis of sex:

> . . . by paying wages to employees in such establishment at a rate less than the rate at which he pays wages to employees of the opposite sex in such establishment for equal work on jobs the performance of which requires equal skill, effort and responsibility, and which are performed under similar working conditions,

except where such payment is made pursuant to (i) a seniority system; (ii) a merit system; (iii) a system which measures earnings by quantity or quality of production; or (iv) a differential based on any other factor other than sex . . .

To succeed under the EPA, the plaintiff must prove that the employer paid different wages to an employee of the opposite sex for equal or "substantially equal" work (*Laffey v. Northwest Airlines, Inc.*, 1976). The courts have established that the equality of work does not have to be identical but must be "substantially equal" (*Schultz v. Wheaton Glass Company*, 1970). The Department of Labor regulations require job content, not job title, be the basis for establishing equality (29 C.F.R. § 800.121 (1980)). As per the Department of Labor regulations, equal skill is "based upon the experience, training, education and ability required in performing the job; effort is defined as the amount or degree of physical or mental exertion required to perform the job successfully; and responsibility is judged on the degree of accountability required with emphasis on the importance of the job obligation" (Luna, 1990).

The EPA established and courts have affirmed (*Corning Glass Works v. Brennan*, 1974) that job content is measured as equal based on four statutory factors: skill, effort, responsibility, and the working conditions required to perform the job. A defendant can utilize one of four affirmative defenses: seniority system, merit system, system that measures earnings by quantity or quality of production, or pay differential that is based on any factor other than the sex of the employee (29 U.S.C. § 206 (d) (l) (1982)). In sex-based pay discrimination cases, the fourth affirmative defense (i.e., any factor other than sex) has been a "catchall defense" that has been utilized by and provided the most success for defendant employers (Luna, 1990).

The *Stanley v. USC* (1994) decision recognizing the differences in the areas of responsibilities, skills, efforts, and working conditions (for coaches of men's and women's teams) potentially hinders the EPA from being a truly effective cause of action. In *Stanley I* (1994), the Ninth Circuit held that the areas of public relations, promotional activities, and years spent as a coach illustrated how different wages for the coaches of two similar teams were justified. "Employers may reward professional experience and education without violating the EPA . . ." (*Soto v. Adams Elevator Equipment Company*, 1991). In addition, the *Stanley* Court concluded that the marketplace value of skills (e.g., coaches of men's teams receive higher salaries than coaches of women's teams—nationally) and the duty to generate revenue are important factors in justifying greater pay for coaches of male teams.

In 1999, the Ninth Circuit Court in Stanley II decided ". . . that no genuine issue of material fact existed regarding whether USC had violated the Equal Pay Act" (Giampetro-Meyer, 2000, p. 368). The Court (1999) held that even though Stanley had established that both she and Raveling had the same basic job tasks/responsibilities, Raveling's experience and qualifications were superior to those of Stanley.

The court however, failed to decide whether the differences in any additional tasks they had were due to the revenue generation responsibilities that Raveling had (i.e., the university's argument) or to the historical/ingrained difference in treatment of male and female teams at the university (i.e., *Stanley*'s argument) (Giampetro-Meyer, 2000). *Stanley*'s argument was supported by *Hudon v. West Valley School District No. 208* (2004) when the court sided with the plaintiff's position that an overreliance on the market forces argument could perpetuate historical discrimination against traditionally female-dominated job classifications. The court further commented that underpaying women because the market would bear it was not allowed.

In addition to the cases discussed thus far in the area of pay equity claims, other trial court decisions provide insight into this specific area of gender equity. For example, there are several cases involving female coaches who were paid less than their male counterparts, where the EPA, Title VII, and Title IX claims were dismissed or a summary judgment was granted to the defendant institutions (*Bartges v. University of North Carolina at Charlotte*, 1995; *Harker v. Utica College of Syracuse University*, 1995; *Morris v. Fordham University*, 2004; *Rallins v. The Ohio State University*, 2002; *Weaver v. The Ohio State University*, 1998; *Williams v. Eau Claire Public Schools*, 2005). *Harker* raised several issues (e.g., about extra benefits given exclusively to coaches of male teams) but I, like the Court, was persuaded that the university relied on factors other than sex (including revenue generation) when deciding to pay the male coaches more (Fenton & Fitzgerald,

1998). Both *Harker* and *Bartges* might have benefited from providing a more detailed/coherent picture of the inequities to establish a prima facie case. Though a settlement was reached in *Lowrey v. Texas A & M University* (1998), the court initially decided that "material questions of fact existed on Lowrey's claims under the 3 statutes" (i.e., Title IX, Title VII, & EPA) (Giampetro-Meyer, 2000, p. 369) and decided to deny Tarleton State's (part of the Texas A & M System) motion for summary judgment.

The courts found sex discrimination in two 1998 cases. In *Dugan v. Oregon State University* (1998) former softball coach Vicki Dugan was awarded $1.28 million under the Equal Pay Act after she alleged the university paid her less than male coaches and retaliated against her after she raised concerns about equity. The institution claimed she was dismissed because her team record was 0–24. She presented a coherent picture of the inequities and was able to substantiate her retaliation claim. It is also interesting to note that the jury decided that the athletics director should pay $60,000 in compensatory damages and $125,000 in punitive damages (Snow, 1999). In *Perdue v. City University* (1998), Molly Perdue received over $200,000 in damages. She was the women's basketball coach and women's sports administrator, yet was paid almost $67,000 less than the combined salaries of her male comparators. The jury agreed that Brooklyn College had engaged in intentional discrimination and in turn awarded almost $135,000 in liquidated damages and $85,000 in compensatory damages (because Brooklyn College's behavior was willful/intentional).

The willingness of the court in *Stanley I & II* to accept the arguments of the defendants suggests that perhaps the EPA is not the most effective cause of action. Yet, Perdue (1998) and Dugan (1998) successfully brought EPA claims due to their effectiveness in establishing that their job was substantially equal to her comparators. Because wage discrimination cases in higher education and athletic administration are relatively scarce in comparison to private industry, as more claims are brought forward the courts will have the opportunity to further clarify the potency of the EPA and the weight they are willing to give the EEOC guidelines in these types of cases.

Title VII of the Civil Rights Act of 1964

Another legal weapon available to plaintiffs in sex-based wage discrimination lawsuits is Title VII of the Civil Rights Act of 1964. In its current form, Title VII provides

It shall be an unlawful employment practice for an employer:

1. to fail or refuse to hire or to discharge any individual, or otherwise to discriminate against any individual with respect to his compensation, terms, conditions, or privileges of employment, because of such individual's race, color, religion, sex, or national origin; or
2. to limit, segregate, or classify his employees or applicants for employment in any way, which would deprive or tend to deprive any individual of employment opportunities or otherwise adversely affect his status as an employee, because of such individual's race, color, religion, sex, or national origin.

To establish a prima facie Title VII case of discrimination, a plaintiff must establish (1) the defendant was subject to the provisions of the statute, (2) the plaintiff is entitled to protection of the statute, and (3) the plaintiff has not been provided the benefits of the statute. If the plaintiff is able to establish these three conditions, the burden then shifts to the defendant, who must advance evidence of legitimate nondiscriminatory reasons for its conduct. In this context, it is important to note that *County of Washington v. Gunther* (1981) established that Title VII incorporated only the four affirmative defenses against wage discrimination claims (e.g., seniority system, merit system, system that measures quantity or quality of work, or differential is based on "factor other than sex") and not the "equal work standard." (For more information on Title VII, see Chapter 8.13.)

Title IX of the Education Amendments of 1972

The third key piece of legislation for sex-based wage discrimination cases in athletics is Title IX of the Education Amendments of 1972. It is beyond the scope of this chapter to address the multiple events, cases, and pieces of legislation that helped to shape how Title IX is interpreted and enforced today. However, relative to Title IX's effectiveness in sex discrimination in athletic employment cases, it is appropriate to provide cursory analysis of the legal ramifications of key cases and the impact the Civil Rights Amendment of 1987 can have on employment discrimination cases.

The Civil Rights Restoration Act of 1987 "clarified that entire institutions and agencies are covered by Title IX . . . if any program or activity within the organization receives federal aid" (Pub. L. No. 100–259, 102. 28 (1988)). The reestablishment of the "institution-wide" interpretation of Title IX, in conjunction with the Supreme Court's decision in *North Haven Board of Education v. Bell* (1982), set the stage for the filing of employment discrimination cases in athletic employment. *North Haven Board of Education v. Bell* (1982) established that Title IX is a viable cause of action for employees in education, while in 1979, the Supreme Court ruled in *Cannon v. University of Chicago* that Title IX provided a private right of action. The combination of these two cases and the institutionwide interpretation afforded by the Civil Rights Restoration Act of 1987 means that Title IX provides another viable cause of action for employment discrimination cases in educational institutions.

Of the multiple Title IX regulations, Subparts D and E address employment discrimination in educational institutions. It has been suggested that Subpart E, in particular, was intended to provide equity for all employees (including those in athletics) at federally funded institutions. Therefore, these specific Title IX regulations might provide "a basis on which coaches can sue for sex-based employment discrimination without regard to the effect discrimination has on their athletes, and without having to prove program noncompliance with Title IX" (Claussen, 1996).

Perhaps the greatest potential for successfully litigating a pay discrimination case in athletics lies in the utilization of Title IX as a cause of action. The acceptance by the Ninth Circuit in *Stanley v. USC* of USC's argument that factors other than sex (e.g., skills, responsibilities) and market forces are the basis for the different wages paid to coaches of males and female teams suggests that both the EPA and Title VII may not be the most effective causes of action. However, it is not yet clear the level of deference the courts are willing to pay to the EEOC guidelines (Weiss, 2002).

It is important to note that the Ninth Circuit's analysis in *Stanley v. USC* (1994) was limited to a review of a denial of a preliminary injunction. In fact, the Ninth Circuit stated that it could not "evaluate the persuasive impact of the evidence that the parties may bring forth at trial" (p. 1024). By contrast, *Tyler v. Howard University* (1993), a similar suit brought by the women's basketball coach contending the university had violated the Equal Pay Act, Title IX, and the District of Columbia Human Rights Act by paying her less than the men's basketball and football coaches, was decided by a jury trial based on the evidence after the full discovery phase of the trial. In *Tyler*, the jury awarded (after the judge merged remedies that factually and legally overlapped) $1,060,000 to the plaintiff.

In *Pitts v. Oklahoma* (1994), the head women's golf coach successfully utilized Title VII and Title IX to win a decision against Oklahoma State University. Ann Pitts, the women's coach, was paid $28,000 less than the men's coach. In the end, the university was found to have violated Title VII and Title IX, but not the Equal Pay Act. Similarly, Pam Bowers sued Baylor University for back pay and benefits (compensatory damages of $1 million, and punitive damages in excess of $3 million) utilizing only Title IX as a cause of action (*Bowers v. Baylor University*, 1994). She claimed that as the head women's basketball coach at Baylor she was not paid equitably relative to the men's coach and that the university had retaliated against her for reporting discriminatory practices. An out-of-court settlement was reached between Bowers and Baylor University prior to the scheduled trial date of September 5, 1995. In *Kemether v. Pennsylvania Interscholastic Athletic Association* (1998) a female basketball referee prevailed when she alleged sex discrimination because she was excluded from working boys' games. The jury awarded her $314,000 in compensatory damages (Heckman, 2003).

Section 1983 of the Civil Rights Act

In addition to the legal theories already addressed, it has been suggested that a constitutional challenge using the Equal Protection Clause of the Fourteenth Amendment might be the most effective legal theory to utilize in an effort to provide pay equity for male and female coaches of same-sport teams (Dessem, 1980). Section 1983 of the Civil Rights Act "provides a vehicle for obtaining a remedy for violations of other federally protected rights." Section 1983 is most frequently used to enforce rights governed under the Equal Protection Clause of the Fourteenth Amendment to the U.S. Constitution, which prohibits discrimination based on gender. Thus sex discrimination involving state action violates the Equal Protection Clause, and Section 1983 provides a remedy for such violations. Under the Equal Protection Clause, discriminatory state action based on gender is allowed only if it is necessary to achieve "important governmental objectives" and the discriminatory action is substantially related to the achievement of those objectives (Henson, 1992).

EEOC Enforcement Guidance on Sex Discrimination in the Compensation of Sports Coaches in Educational Institutions

In 1997 the Equal Employment Opportunity Commission (EEOC) issued *Enforcement Guidance on Sex Discrimination in the Compensation of Sports Coaches in Educational Institutions* (EEOC Notice Number 915.002) in an effort to clarify the commission's position on the application of the Equal Pay Act and Title VII to sex discrimination claims. The notice contains a brief background on pay discrimination in educational institutions and an in-depth legal analysis section. This section of the guidelines specifically addresses the key EPA issues that have been at the heart of the most prominent pay equity cases in sport thus far—selecting a comparator or comparators, what makes coaching jobs substantially equal, and the relevancy of affirmative defenses utilized by institutions (EEOC Notice, 1997). Title VII is briefly reviewed, and the commission's position on how Title VII applies to issues not covered by the EPA (i.e., when the "equal work" requirement of the EPA is not met) is succinctly addressed. The most significant part of the document is the one that details how the EEOC interprets how the EPA applies to claims brought by coaches (Giampetro-Meyer, 2000; Narol & Martin, 1998).

Relative to a plaintiff identifying a comparator or comparators, the guidelines pointed out that positions must be examined in detail on a case-by-case basis due to differences that can exist from school to school. Once the comparator(s) have been established, analyzing if the jobs are "substantially equal" must be examined utilizing the four elements in the statute (i.e., skill, effort, responsibility, and working conditions), yet the guidelines caution that the focus is to remain on overall job content. If one coach possesses skills, education, or abilities that are above and beyond those on their comparator, that cannot be taken into consideration for determining if the jobs are substantially equal, if the skills, education, or abilities are not required to perform the specific job in question.

To determine if the two coaching positions require equal effort, the analysis is not to be limited to coaches of like sports due to the similar duties that all coaches perform: (1) teaching and coaching, (2) counseling and advising of student–athletes, (3) general program management, (4) budget management, (5) fund-raising, (6) public relations, and (7) at the college level, recruiting (EEOC Notice, 1997, at II.A.2.b). A closely related concern, for plaintiffs and defendant institutions is establishing if any differences in responsibilities justify unequal pay. The guidelines point out that the "jobs need not be identical." The commission's interpretation of "equal responsibility" highlighted the point that "the Commission will examine whether the institution has afforded male and female coaches the opportunity to take on responsibilities in a nondiscriminatory fashion" (EEOC Notice, 1997, at II.A.2.c). Two examples were utilized in the guidelines to emphasize that it is the responsibilities, *not* the job title, that matter. In other words, merely having one or two more assistant coaches to supervise does not necessarily mean the jobs are not substantially equal. The commission went on to clarify that "if an educational institution has discriminated against a female head coach by failing to provide her with comparable assistant coaching support compared to what is provided to a male head coach, it cannot justify paying her a lower salary based on the claim that she has a less responsible position" (EEOC Notice, 1997, at II.A.2.c). Finally, the guidelines make the assumption that working conditions for most coaches are similar for the purposes of the EPA.

The largest part of the EEOC Notice focused on the affirmative defenses typically utilized by defendant institutions. Once the plaintiff has identified a comparator(s) and established that the jobs are substantially equal, the burden shifts to the employer to demonstrate that one of the four exceptions to the EPA (i.e., affirmative defenses) applies to the position/situation in question. The Commission stated that the EEOC is

> aware of the following justifications that have been advanced as factors other than sex in order to justify pay differentials in coaching: (a) the male coach produces more revenue for the school than the female coach; (b) the male coach must be paid higher wages in order to compete for him; (c) salary is based on prior salary; (d) salary is linked to the sex of the student-athletes rather than the sex of the coach; (e) the male coach has superior experience, education, and ability; and (f) the male coach has more duties. (EEOC Notice, 1997, at II.A.3)

Descriptive examples and clarification of the commission's position are presented in the guidelines for each of the aforementioned justifications. An overview of the commission's key clarifying points are listed following.

(a) *Revenue as a factor other than sex*—the commission will carefully analyze this defense to determine "whether the institution has provided discriminatorily reduced support to a female coach to produce revenue for her team" (EEOC Notice at II.A.3.a). In other words, if comparable resources necessary to attract spectators and generate revenue were made available to the male and female coaches of similar sports, then revenue could be a factor other than sex.

(b) *Marketplace as a factor other than sex*—the EEOC distinguished between *"marketplace value"* and *"market rate value"* as a defense. The market rate defense, which is based on the assumption that women are available for positions for lower salaries due to "market factors," has been rejected by the EEOC and the courts. In contrast, the marketplace value defense is not sex-based, and salary decisions are founded on the employer's consideration of an individual's value (specifically job-related characteristics that are relevant to the position) (EEOC Notice at II A.3.b).

(c) *Reliance on employee's prior salary as a factor other than sex*—the guidelines cautioned that "using prior salary alone may perpetuate lower salaries traditionally paid to women that are based on sex discrimination." The guidelines outline several steps employers can take to avoid using prior salary in a way that would *not* qualify it as a "factor other than sex" defense (EEOC Notice at II A.3.c).

(d) *Sex of athletes as a factor other than sex*—the virtual exclusion of women coaching men's teams illustrates that the sex of the athlete is not an acceptable factor other than sex in the opinion of the Commission (EEOC Notice at II A.3.d).

(e) *Experience, education, and ability as a factor other than sex*—judgment needs to be made on a case-by-case basis relative to determining if superior experience, education, or abilities can justify pay differences (EEOC Notice at II A.3.e).

(f) *More duties*—if additional duties are used as a defense for paying one sex higher wages, then the pay must be related to those extra duties. Additionally, the institution cannot provide the opportunity to take on extra duties in a discriminatory way and then use that unfair distribution to justify the pay inequity (EEOC Guidelines, 1997, at II.A.3.f).

Though the guidelines very specifically address many of the common issues that have surfaced in pay equity cases involving sports coaches or administrators, they have yet to be utilized in an appellate court decision. In *Stanley v. University of Southern California* (1999) (i.e., Stanley II) the court referred to these key issues but stopped short of articulating their opinion on the application of the guidelines to those issues. Weiss (2002) went so far as to suggest that the EEOC guidelines are one of the best weapons available to a plaintiff because it places ". . . greater burdens on the institutions to prove these defenses are not motivated by institutional or societal discrimination" (p. 169).

Significant Case

◇◇◇

The following case illustrates the difficulty that plaintiffs have had in convincing a court that male and female coaches (who are comparators) should be paid the same. In discussing the plaintiff's failure to show a probability of success on the merits, the court in this case articulated a rationale for why the work performed by similarly situated male and female coaches is viewed as substantially different.

STANLEY V. UNIVERSITY OF SOUTHERN CALIFORNIA
United States Court of Appeals for the Ninth Circuit
13 F.3d 1313 (1994)

Opinion:

Marianne Stanley, former head coach of the women's basketball team at the University of Southern California (USC), appeals from an order denying her motion for a preliminary injunction against USC and Michael Garrett, the athletic director for USC (collectively USC).

Coach Stanley contends that the district court abused its discretion in denying a preliminary injunction on the ground that she failed to present sufficient evidence of sex discrimination or retaliation to carry her burden of establishing a clear likelihood of success on the merits. Coach Stanley also claims that the court misapprehended the nature of the preliminary injunction relief she sought. In addition, she argues that the district court clearly erred in finding that USC would suffer significant hardship if the preliminary injunction issued. Coach Stanley further asserts that she was denied a full and fair opportunity to present testimonial evidence at the preliminary injunction hearing and to demonstrate that USC's purported justification for paying a higher salary to George Raveling, head coach of the men's basketball team at USC, was a pretext for sex discrimination and retaliation. We affirm because we conclude that the district court did not abuse its discretion in denying the motion for a preliminary injunction. We also hold that the district court did not deny Coach Stanley a full and fair opportunity to present evidence of sex discrimination, retaliation, and pretext.

I. Pertinent Facts

Coach Stanley signed a four-year contract with USC on July 30, 1989, to serve as the head coach of the women's basketball team. The expiration date of Coach Stanley's employment contract was June 30, 1993. Coach Stanley's employment contract provided for an annual base salary of $60,000 with a $6,000 housing allowance.

Sometime in April of 1993, Coach Stanley and Michael Garrett began negotiations on a new contract. The evidence is in dispute as to the statements made by the parties. Coach Stanley alleges in her declarations that she told Garrett that she "was entitled to be paid equally with the Head Men's Basketball Coach, George Raveling[,] and that [she] was seeking a contract equal to the one that USC had paid the Head Men's Basketball Coach" based on her outstanding record and the success of the women's basketball program at USC. She also requested a higher salary for the assistant coaches of the women's basketball team. According to Coach Stanley, Garrett verbally agreed that she should be paid what Coach Raveling was earning, but he asserted that USC did not have the money at that time. He indicated that "he would get back [to her] with an offer of a multi-year contract . . . that would be satisfactory." Garrett alleges in his affidavit, filed in opposition to the issuance of the preliminary injunction, that Coach Stanley told him that "she wanted a contract that was identical to that between USC and Coach Raveling."

On April 27, 1993, Garrett sent a memorandum which set forth an offer of a three-year contract with the following terms:

1993–94 Raising your salary to $80,000 with a $6,000 housing allowance.

1994–95 Salary of $90,000 with a $6,000 housing allowance.

1995–96 Salary of $100,000 with a $6,000 housing allowance.

Presently, Barbara Thaxton's base salary is $37,000 which I intend to increase to $50,000. It is not my policy to pay associate or assistant coaches housing allowances. Therefore that consideration is not addressed in this offer.

The memorandum concluded with the following words: "I believe this offer is fair, and I need you to respond within the next couple of days so we can conclude this matter. Thank you." According to Garrett, Coach Stanley said the offer was "an insult."

Coach Stanley alleged that, after receiving this offer, she informed Garrett that she "wanted a multi-year contract but his salary figures were too low." Coach Stanley also alleged that she told Garrett she "was to make the same salary as was paid to the Head Men's Basketball Coach at USC." Garrett asserted that Coach Stanley demanded a "three-year contract which would pay her a total compensation at the annual rate of $96,000 for the first 18 months and then increase her total compensation to the same level as Raveling for the last 18 months." He rejected her counter offer.

* * *

II. Procedural Background

On August 5, 1993, Coach Stanley filed this action in the Superior Court for the County of Los Angeles. She also applied ex parte for a temporary restraining order (TRO) to require USC to install her as head coach of the women's basketball team.

* * *

On August 6, 1993, the Los Angeles Superior Court issued an oral order granting Coach Stanley's ex parte application for a TRO, pending a hearing on her motion for a preliminary injunction. . . . On the same day that the TRO was issued, USC removed the action to the District Court for the Central District of California. On August 11, 1993, the district court ordered that the hearing on Coach Stanley's motion for a preliminary injunction be held on August 26, 1993, and that the TRO issued by the state court be extended and remain in effect until that date.

Pursuant to Coach Stanley's request, the district court reviewed Coach Raveling's employment contract in camera. Later that day, the district court denied the motion for a preliminary injunction.

III. Discussion

The gravamen of Coach Stanley's multiple claims against USC is her contention that she is entitled to pay equal to that provided to Coach Raveling for his services as head coach of the men's basketball team because the position of head coach of the women's team "requires equal skill, effort, and responsibility, and [is performed] under similar working conditions." She asserts that USC discriminated against her because of her sex by rejecting her request. She also maintains that USC retaliated against her because of her request for equal pay for herself and her assistant coaches. According to Coach Stanley, USC retaliated by withdrawing the offer of a three-year contract and instead presenting her with a new offer of a one-year contract at less pay than that received by Coach Raveling.

We begin our analysis mindful of the fact that we are reviewing the denial of a preliminary injunction. There has been no trial in this matter. Because the hearing on the preliminary injunction occurred 21 days after the action was filed in state court, discovery had not been completed. Our prediction of the probability of success on the merits is based on the limited offer of proof that was possible under the circumstances. We obviously cannot now evaluate the persuasive impact of the evidence that the parties may bring forth at trial.

A. Standard of Review.

We review the denial of a motion for preliminary injunction for abuse of discretion. . . . An order is reversible for legal error if the court did not apply the correct preliminary injunction standard, or if the court misapprehended the law with respect to the underlying issues in litigation. An abuse of discretion may also occur if the district court rests its conclusions on clearly erroneous findings of fact.

Coach Stanley argues that she did not seek a mandatory preliminary injunction. She asserts that she was "not seeking to be instated by USC, she was seeking to continue her employment with USC." Appellant's Opening Brief at 28. Coach Stanley maintains that she requested a prohibitory preliminary injunction and that the district court erred in applying the test for a mandatory preliminary injunction.

* * *

Coach Stanley's four-year contract terminated on June 30, 1993. She was informed by Garrett on July 15, 1993, that her employment contract had expired and that she should not perform any services for the university until both parties entered into a new contract. On August 6, 1993, the date this action was filed in state court, Coach Stanley was no longer a USC employee.

Accordingly an injunction compelling USC to install Coach Stanley as the head coach of the women's basketball team and to pay her $28,000 a year more than she received when her employment contract expired would not have maintained the status quo. Instead, it would have forced USC to hire a person at a substantially higher rate of pay than she had received prior to the expiration of her employment contract on June 30, 1993. The district court did not err in concluding that Coach Stanley was seeking a mandatory injunction, and that her request was subject to a higher degree of scrutiny because such relief is particularly disfavored under the law of this circuit. Anderson, 612 F.2d at 1114.

B. There Has Been No Clear Showing of a Probability of Success on the Merits of Coach Stanley's Claim for Injunctive Relief.

In light of our determination that Coach Stanley requested a mandatory preliminary injunction, we must consider whether the law and the facts clearly favor granting such relief. To obtain a preliminary injunction, Coach Stanley was required to demonstrate that her remedy at law was inadequate.

* * *

1. Merits of Coach Stanley's Claim of Denial of Equal Pay for Equal Work.

The district court concluded that Coach Stanley had failed to demonstrate that there is a likelihood that she would prevail on the merits of her claim of a denial of equal pay for equal work because she failed to present facts clearly showing that USC was guilty of sex discrimination in its negotiations for a new employment contract. The thrust of Coach Stanley's argument in this appeal is that she is entitled, as a matter of law, "to make the same salary as was paid to the Head Men's Basketball Coach at USC." Appellant's Opening Brief at 9. None of the authorities she has cited supports this theory.

* * *

Coach Stanley has not offered proof to contradict the evidence proffered by USC that demonstrates the differences in the responsibilities of the persons who serve as head coaches of the women's and men's basketball teams. Coach Raveling's responsibilities as head coach of the men's basketball team require substantial public relations and promotional activities to generate revenue for USC. These efforts resulted in revenue that is 90 times greater than the revenue generated by the women's basketball team. Coach Raveling was required to conduct twelve outside speaking engagements per year, to be accessible to the media for interviews, and to participate in certain activities designed to produce donations and endorsements for the USC Athletic Department in general. Coach Stanley's position as head coach did not require her to engage in the same intense level of promotional and revenue-raising activities. This quantitative dissimilarity in responsibilities justifies a different level of pay for the head coach of the women's basketball team.

* * *

The evidence presented by USC also showed that Coach Raveling had substantially different qualifications and experience related to his public relations and revenue-generation skills than Coach Stanley. Coach Raveling received educational training in marketing, and worked in that field for nine years. Coach Raveling has been employed by USC three years longer than Coach Stanley. He has been a college basketball coach for 31 years, while Coach Stanley has had 17 years experience as a basketball coach. Coach Raveling had served as a member of the NCAA Subcommittee on Recruiting. Coach Raveling also is the respected author of two best-selling novels. He has performed as an actor in a feature movie, and has appeared on national television to discuss recruiting of student athletes. Coach Stanley does not have the same degree of experience in these varied activities. Employers may reward professional experience and education without violating the EPA. Soto v. Adams Elevator Equip. Co., 941 F.2d 543, 548 & n.7 (7th Cir. 1991).

Coach Raveling's national television appearances and motion picture presence, as well as his reputation as an author, make him a desirable public relations representative for USC. An employer may consider the marketplace value of the skills of a particular individual when determining his or her salary. Horner, 613 F.2d at 714. Unequal wages that reflect market conditions of supply and demand are not prohibited by the EPA. EEOC v. Madison Community Unit Sch. Dist. No. 12, 818 F.2d 577, 580 (7th Cir. 1987).

The record also demonstrates that the USC men's basketball team generated greater attendance, more media interest, larger donations, and produced substantially more revenue than the women's basketball team. As a result, USC placed greater pressure on Coach Raveling to promote his team and to win. The responsibility to produce a large amount of revenue is evidence of a substantial difference in responsibility. See Jacobs v. College of William and Mary, 517 F. Supp. 791, 797 (E.D. Va. 1980) (duty to produce revenue demonstrates that coaching jobs are not substantially equal).

Coach Stanley did not offer evidence to rebut USC's justification for paying Coach Raveling a higher salary. Instead, she alleged that the women's team generates revenue, and that she is under a great deal of pressure to win. Coach Stanley argues that Jacobs is distinguishable because, in that matter, the head basketball coach of the women's team was not required to produce any revenue. Jacobs, 517 F. Supp. at 798. Coach Stanley appears to suggest that a difference in the amount of revenue generated by the men's and women's teams should be ignored by the court in comparing the respective coaching positions. We disagree.

At this preliminary stage of these proceedings, the record does not support a finding that gender was the reason that USC paid a higher salary to Coach Raveling as head coach of the men's basketball team than it offered Coach Stanley as head coach of the women's basketball team. Garrett's affidavit supports the district court's conclusion that the head coach position of the men's team was not substantially equal to the head coach position of the women's team. The record shows that there were significant differences between Coach Stanley's and Coach Raveling's public relations skills, credentials, experience, and qualifications; there also were substantial differences between their responsibilities and working conditions. The district court's finding that the head coach positions were not substantially equal is not a "clear error of judgment." Martin v. International Olympic Comm., 740 F.2d 670, 679 (9th Cir. 1984).

2. Merits of Coach Stanley's Claim of Retaliation

The district court also rejected Coach Stanley's claim that USC terminated her contract or failed to renew her contract in retaliation for her involvement in protected activities. Rather, the court found that her contract had expired and she refused to accept any of the renewal options that USC offered.

* * *

IV. Conclusion

The district court did not abuse its discretion in denying a mandatory preliminary injunction. Coach

Stanley did not meet her burden of demonstrating the irreducible minimum for obtaining a preliminary injunction: "that there is a fair chance of success on the merits." Martin v. International Olympic Comm., 740 F.2d at 675.

* * *

The evidence offered at the hearing on the motion for a preliminary injunction demonstrated that Coach Stanley sought pay from USC equal to Coach Raveling's income from that university, notwithstanding significant differences in job pressure, the level of

responsibility, and in marketing and revenue-producing qualifications and performance. A difference in pay that takes such factors into consideration does not prove gender bias or violate the Equal Pay Act. The unfortunate impasse that occurred during the negotiations for the renewal of the employment contract of an outstanding basketball coach followed the offer of a very substantial increase in salary—not sex discrimination or retaliation. Because Coach Stanley failed to demonstrate that the law and the facts clearly favor her position, the judgment is AFFIRMED.

 OTHER RELEVANT SIGNIFICANT CASES

Chapter 8.11 *Gender Equity: Opportunities to Participate*   Chapter 8.13 *Title VII of the Civil Rights Act of 1964*

Recent Trends

178 F.3d 1080 [9th Cir. 1999]).Though there has been a steady flow of sex discrimination lawsuits initiated by coaches of women's teams and/or administrators of those athletic programs, two key questions regarding the applicability of Title IX for these claims have lingered. Did Title IX provide an appropriate cause of action for retaliation claims? Did Title IX offer protection for both male and female coaches of female teams?

In 2005 the U.S. Supreme Court answered both of those questions in *Jackson v. Birmingham Board of Education* (2005). Roderick Jackson, a girls" basketball coach at a public high school, complained of inequitable funding and access to athletic equipment and facilities for his team. He was subsequently removed from his position as basketball coach. Jackson filed suit against the board claiming they (1) retaliated against him for complaining about the inequities and (2) such retaliation violated Title IX. The Supreme Court ruled in Jackson's favor stating that Title IX ". . . encompasses claims of retaliation for complaints about sex discrimination" (p. 371). The Court clarified that Jackson was protected from discrimination retaliation even though the unfair treatment was due to him bringing a Title IX complaint on behalf of others (i.e., females on his girls' basketball team). This recent development is important because it delineates that Title IX does protect both male and female coaches and administrators who might advocate for female athletes by using Title IX to bring discrimination claims forward on behalf of the participants.

The only other development of note has been the use of state sovereign immunity, as derived from the Eleventh Amendment of the Constitution, as a legal strategy for shielding state educational institutions from Title VII and EPA claims. In *Lewis v. Smith* (2003) and *Mehus v. Emporia State University* (2004) the court failed to be swayed by that argument and decided states are not immune.

There is clearly a limited amount of case law on employment discrimination in intercollegiate athletics. Court decisions in each new case further define this area of law and, in turn, necessarily affect how administrators must approach gender equity and discrimination in employment. If courts in the future share the same view as the Ninth Circuit in *Stanley* (1994 & 1999), it is likely that the existence and the content of job descriptions and performance appraisals will become more important. These management tools could aid a plaintiff or a defendant in their respective efforts to clearly establish the responsibilities and duties required of a particular position. If the head men's and women's coaching positions are indeed not substantially the same, then these differences should be quite evident and easily discernible within the job descriptions and performance appraisals.

Due to the lack of clear legal precedent, it is up to individual administrators and their institutions to eliminate pay discrimination and work toward gender equity in employment. Athletics administrators must examine the salaries of employees relative to their specific duties and responsibilities, and the job opportunities/responsibilities provided to the individual in that position (e.g., only offering alumni speaking engagements to coaches of male teams) rather than basing salary decisions on the sex of the individual or the students they teach/coach. As they begin to do this, it will provide an important step toward achieving gender equity for male and female coaches and administrators by proactively battling sex discrimination in employment. If they fail to equitably compensate the coaches of female teams the EEOC guidelines, in conjunction with detailed job responsibility/duty evidence, have the potential to increase the success rate for that plaintiff who brings a Title VII or EPA claim.

References

Cases

Bartges v. University of North Carolina at Charlotte, 908 F. Supp. 1312 (W.D. N.C. 1995).

Bowers v. Baylor University, 862 F. Supp. 142 (W.D. Tex. 1994).

Cannon v. University of Chicago, 441 U.S. 677 (1979).

Corning Glass Works v. Brennan, 417 U.S. 188 (1974).

County of Washington v. Gunther, 452 U.S. 161 (1981).

Dugan v. Oregon State University, No. 95-6250-HO (D. Or. 1998).

Franklin v. Gwinnett County Public Schools, 503 U.S. 60 (1992).

Grove City College v. Bell, 464 U.S. 555 (1984).

Harker v. Utica College of Syracuse University, 885 F. Supp. 378 (N.D. N.Y. 1995).

Horn v. University of Minnesota, 91 Fair Empl. Prac. Cas. (BNA) 1147 (D.Minn (2003) aff'd Horn v. Univ. of Minn., 2004 U.S.App.Lexis 6466) (8th Cir. Minn. Apr. 6, 2004).

Hudon v. West Valley School District No. 208, 97 P.3d 39 (2004)(Wash. Ct. App. 2004).

Jackson v. Birmingham Board of Education, 544 U.S. 167 (2005)

Kemether v. Pennsylvania Interscholastic Athletic Association, 15 F.Supp 2d 740 (E.D. Pa. 1998).

Laffey v. Northwest Airlines, Inc., 567 F.2d 429 (D.C. Cir. 1976), *cert. denied*, 434 U.S. 1906 (1978).

Lewis v. Smith, 255 F.Supp 2d 1054 (D.Ariz 2003).

Lowrey v. Texas A & M University, 11 F. Supp.2d 895 (S.D. Tex. 1998).

Mehus v. Emporia State University, 295 F.Supp. 2d 1258 (D.Kan. 2004).

Morris v. Fordham University, 93 Fair Empl. Prac. Cas. (BNA) 1364 (S.D.N.Y. 2004).

North Haven Board of Education v. Bell, 456 U.S. 512 (1982).

Perdue v. City University, 13 F. Supp.2d 326 (E.D. N.Y. 1998).

Pitts v. Oklahoma, No. CIV-93-1341-A (W.D. Okla. 1994).

Rallins v. The Ohio State University, 191 F.Supp. 2d 920 (S.D.Ohio 2002).

Schultz v. Wheaton Glass Company, 421 F.2d 259 (3rd Cir.), *cert. denied*, 398 U.S. 905 (1970).

Soto v. Adams Elevator Equipment Company, 914 F.2d 543 (7th Cir. 1991).

Stanley v. University of Southern California, 13 F.3d 1313 (9th Cir. 1994).

Stanley v. University of Southern California, 178 F.3d 1069 (9th Cir. 1999).

Tyler v. Howard University, No. 91-CA11239 (D.C. June 28, 1993).

Williams v. Eau Claire Public Schools, 397 F.3d 441 (6th Cir. 2005), *cert. denied*, 2005 U.S. LEXIS 6251 (U.S., Oct. 3, 2005).

Weaver v. The Ohio State University, 71 F. Supp.2d 789 (S.D. Ohio 1998).

Publications

Acosta, V., & Carpenter, L. Women in intercollegiate sport—A longitudinal, National study—twenty nine year update 1977–2006. Retrieved from http://webpages.charter.net/womeninsport/

Claussen, C. L. (1994/1995). Title IX and employment discrimination in coaching intercollegiate athletics. University of Miami *Entertainment & Sports Law Review, 1*, 1–20.

Dessem, R. L. (1980). Sex discrimination in coaching. *Harvard Women's Law Journal, 3,* 97–117.

Fenton, A., & Fitzgerald, M. P. (1998). Compensation issues in coaching of women's amateur sports: A study of the legal precedents and an evaluation of three methods of relief. *Journal of Legal Aspects of Sport, 8,* 124–140.

Giampetro-Meyer, A. M. (2000). Recognizing and remedying individual and institutional gender-based wage discrimination in sport. *American Business Law Journal, 37,* 343–387.

Heckman, D. (2003, Winter). The glass sneaker: Thirty years of victories and defeats involving Title IX and sex discrimination in athletics. *Fordham Intellectual Property, Media, & Entertainment Law Journal, 13,* 551–616.

Henson, D. (1992, March 8). *Gender equity in sport: What is she entitled to?* Presented at The University of Texas Gender Equity in Sport Conference, Austin, TX.

Luna, G. (1990). Understanding gender-based wage discrimination: Legal interpretation and trends of pay equity in higher education. *Journal of Law and Education, 3,* 371–384.

Narol, M., & Martin, J. A. (1998). A new defense to the old defenses? The EEOC Equal Pay Act Guidelines, *Marquette Sports Law Journal, 9,* 175–196.

Osborne, B., & Yarborough, M. V. (2001, Winter). Pay equity for coaches and athletic administrators: An element of Title IX. *University of Michigan Journal of Legal Reform,* 231–251.

Snow, B. A. (1999). Broadening the demand for gender-equity in athletics: Financial aid and coaches' compensation. *Educational Law Reporter, 130,* 965–984.

Weiss, M. (2002, Fall). Pay equity for intercollegiate coaches: Exploring the EEOC enforcement guidelines. *Marquette Sports Law Review, 13,* 149–168.

Legislation

Civil Rights Act of 1987 (Pub. L. No. 100–259, 102 Stat. 28).

District of Columbia Human Rights Law, D.C. Code §1-2501 et seq.

EEOC Notice Number 915.002, *Enforcement Guidance on Sex Discrimination in the Compensation of Sports Coaches in Educational Institutions* (Oct. 29, 1997) Online. Internet. http://www.eeoc.gov/policy/docs/coaches.html

Equal Pay Act of 1963 (29 U.S.C. § 206(d)(1) (1982)).

Fair Labor Standards Act of 1938, 52 Stat. 1060.

Title VII of Civil Rights Act of 1964 (42 U.S.C. § 2000 2(a)(1)(2) (1982)).

Title IX of the Educational Amendments of 1972, 86. Stat. 235 (codified at 20 U.S.C. § 1681–1688 (1990)).

8.13 Title VII of the Civil Rights Act of 1964

Lisa Pike Masteralexis
Stephanie A. Tryce
University of Massachusetts-Amherst

The Civil Rights Act of 1964 is a comprehensive federal law prohibiting discrimination in many settings, including elections, housing, federally funded programs, education, employment, and public facilities and accommodations. Title VII of the Civil Rights Act addresses employment discrimination and is the focal point of the act. It became the first comprehensive federal law prohibiting employment discrimination. An employer may distinguish between applicants or employees provided the employer's criteria are within Title VII's limits. Generally, a distinction that is made on the basis of an employee's characteristics (race, gender, religion, national origin), it will be discriminatory under Title VII.

Fundamental Concepts

Scope

Title VII broadly prohibits discrimination in employment. Section 703 (a) states:

> It shall be an unlawful employment practice for an employer—(1) to fail or refuse to hire or to discharge any individual, or otherwise discriminate against any individual with respect to his compensation, terms, conditions, or privileges of employment, because of such individual's race, color, religion, sex, or national origin; or (2) to limit, segregate, or classify his employees or applicants for employment in any way which would deprive or tend to deprive any individual of employment opportunities or otherwise adversely affect his status as an employee, because of such individual's race, color, religion, sex, or national origin. (42 U.S.C. §§ 2000e-2(a))

Title VII applies to employers with fifteen or more employees working at least twenty calendar weeks whose organizations affect interstate commerce. Employers can be individuals, partnerships, joint ventures, corporations, unincorporated associations, and government entities. The definition also includes employment agencies and labor organizations (unions or players associations). Title VII, however, excludes from its definition of employer the U.S. government and some departments of the District of Columbia, Native American tribes, and bona fide membership clubs, such as country clubs. To be considered a bona fide membership club under Title VII, the club must qualify for tax-exempt status under the charitable exemption provision of the Internal Revenue Code and must be established for defined social or recreational purposes or for a common literary, scientific, or political objective.

Graves v. Women's Professional Rodeo Association, Inc. (1990) makes clear that professional associations that sanction events will not be considered employers unless they clearly fit the definition of employer. In *Graves*, a male rodeo barrel racer charged that the defendant nonprofit association that organized female rodeo contestants and sanctioned events had discriminated against him on the basis of gender when it denied him membership. The court found that the WPRA was not an "employer" under Title VII because its members were not employees. The court relied on the two key factors to determine the WPRA was not an employer. First, the WPRA did not pay wages, withhold taxes, or pay insurance for members. Second, although the WPRA did exercise a degree of control over members through its rules, those rules only permitted an opportunity for members to compete for prize money raised by rodeo sponsors, not by the WPRA.

Administration of Title VII.

The Equal Employment Opportunity Commission (EEOC) is a five-member, presidential-appointed administrative agency charged with the administration of Title VII. As a governmental agency the EEOC carries out a number of functions. The EEOC investigates charges of employment discrimination and attempts to conciliate alleged violations. Where the EEOC does not find reasonable cause to go forward with conciliation or where conciliation is not fruitful, the complaining party may proceed with a private Title VII lawsuit. The EEOC may also file suit in federal district court to enforce Title VII, or it may intervene in any private employment discrimination lawsuit. For example, in *EEOC v. National Broadcasting Co., Inc.*, the EEOC brought suit on behalf of a female applicant for the position of television sports director alleging sex discrimination in violation of Title VII. Additionally, the EEOC creates guidelines and regulations for the interpretation of Title VII. Although the guidelines and regulations do not possess the full force and effect of law, they are subject to great judicial deference. For example, in *Meritor Savings Bank, FSB v. Vinson* (1986), the U.S. Supreme Court relied on EEOC guidelines to define hostile environment sexual harassment.

Civil Rights Act of 1991

The Civil Rights Act of 1991 was introduced into Congress with the stated goal of negating five U.S. Supreme Court decisions that severely limited important protections granted by employment discrimination laws. The Act also established a Glass Ceiling Commission and a Glass Ceiling Initiative through the Department of Labor to examine whether a glass ceiling existed to keep women and minorities underrepresented in management and decision-making positions in business.

This Act amended the Civil Rights Act of 1964 to permit jury trials and compensatory and punitive damages in addition to back pay for *all* claims of intentional discrimination under Title VII, not just racial and ethnic discrimination. Defendants will be liable for declaratory or injunctive relief and attorney's fees where a plaintiff proves that discrimination based on protected class status was a motivating factor for any employment practice, even if other factors also motivated the decision (called *mixed motive cases*). A plaintiff is not, however, entitled to back pay, reinstatement, or compensatory or punitive damages in mixed motive cases.

The Civil Rights Act of 1991 prohibits the practice of "race norming," a practice whereby test scores are adjusted on the basis of race or other Title VII classification. It also adopted the defenses of "business necessity" and "job related" as bases for which an employer can justify an employment practice challenged as discriminatory. In disparate impact cases the employer must demonstrate that the challenged practice is job related for the position in question and is consistent with a business necessity.

Finally, the 1991 Act eliminated challenges to affirmative action consent decrees from individuals who had notice and an opportunity to object when the decree was entered or whose interests were adequately represented by another individual or organization.

Classes Protected Under Title VII

Title VII prohibits employment discrimination on the basis of race, color, religion, gender, or national origin in hiring, firing, training, compensating, designating work assignments, promoting, demoting, or any other employment activity. Thus, any employment decision, practice, or policy that segregates individuals and treats them differently on the basis of the preceding classifications violates Title VII.

Race

Although much of the U.S. Civil Rights Movement focused on the treatment of African Americans, Title VII's definition of race is much broader. It is not limited to ethnological races, but protects all classes of people from dissimilar treatment, including, but not limited to Hispanics, Native Americans, and Asian

Americans. As Player (1988) elaborated, "Ethnologists may not classify Hispanics as a 'race,' yet discrimination against American Hispanics is said to be 'racial' because of their mixed race heritage" (p. 299). The same can be said of those from the Middle East, where discrimination against Semitic people would be racial (Id.). For instance, Zimmer, Sullivan, and Richards (1988) raised as an example the discrimination of the Holocaust in which no distinction was made between religious and nonreligious Jews or Jews from various national origins, but rather the discrimination was made on racial lines. These two examples are also indicative of discrimination on the basis of national origin.

Racial discrimination cases involving coaches and athletic directors arose from decisions made in the course of public school desegregation. For example, in *Cross v. Board of Education of Dollarway, Arkansas School District* (1975), the plaintiff, a black high school football coach in an all-black elementary and high school in a segregated school district, was demoted to assistant coach when his school became the junior high and the black high school students were moved into the white high school. Cross was passed over for the position twice, whereas white coaches with fewer qualifications were hired. On the second instance, the school superintendent suggested the defendant school board deviate from its policy to promote within to search outside the district for a white coach. The superintendent was of the opinion that the white players would not play for a black coach and the community was not ready for a black head coach and athletic director. The school board then never even considered Cross's application for the position. The court found the school board's refusal to even consider Cross's application was clear evidence of individual disparate treatment on the basis of Cross's race. As a result Cross was entitled to back pay equal to the difference in the amount he would have received and that which he did receive as assistant coach. In addition, the defendant was ordered to promote Cross to head football coach and athletic director or to compensate him at a salary comparable to the positions.

In *Johnson v. NFL* (1999), J. Edwards Johnson V, an African American, played football for the University of Miami Hurricanes from 1992–1998. While at Miami, Johnson converted to Islam. Johnson authored an article on the subject of race and religion, which appeared in the school newspaper. A public controversy ensued as a result. Prior to the start of the 1997–1998 football season, Johnson was listed among potential draft selections for offensive lineman for the NFL. Several teams indicated an interest in Johnson; one NFL team invited him to a "tryout" a week prior to the draft. On the day of the draft, a media outlet announced that an NFL team had drafted Johnson; however, it was later reported that the team had in fact not drafted him.

After not being drafted by any NFL team, Johnson filed a charge of racial and religious discrimination with the EEOC, who issued a right-to-sue letter, though they did not address the charge on the merits. Johnson filed a complaint against the NFL Commissioner, the Atlanta Falcons, NFL Europe, and other related individuals. The district court judge in rejecting the defendant's motion to dismiss stated that the plaintiff specifically alleges the he was denied an "equal opportunity" for employment in the NFL and NFL Europe "based on his race, religion and expression of rights as they relate to both race and religion." Although the suit was allowed to proceed against the NFL, the district court judge did not allow Johnson to pursue discrimination claims under Title VII against the NFL Commissioner and the president of an NFL team, stating that individual officers or supervisors are not "employers" for the purposes of Title VII.

In April 2005 a California jury awarded Mike Terpstra, former California State University Stanislaus men's basketball coach, $540,000 in damages in a reverse race discrimination case. Terpstra, a white male, claimed his race was a factor in the university's decision to allow his contract to expire after the 2002–2003 season, because they were interested in replacing him with a black coach. Although Terpstra was ultimately replaced with another white male coach, the jury found that race was a factor when the university allowed his contract to expire.

Color

An employer's distinction on the basis of skin pigment or the physical characteristics of an applicant or employee's race are discriminatory. For instance, if an employer favors light-skinned African Americans over dark-skinned African Americans, it is treating African Americans differently as a race on the basis of color. Thus, color discrimination often intersects with racial discrimination.

National Origin

In national origin discrimination cases, the focus is on one's ancestry. This does not include territories of the United States such as Puerto Rico or the Virgin Islands. Title VII does not prohibit employment discrimination solely on the basis of citizenship. For example, in *Dowling v. United States* (1979), the plaintiff argued that the National Hockey League and the World Hockey Association only hired Canadian referees, and thus discriminated against him on the basis of his national origin. The court dismissed the claim as it stated that Title VII does not bar employment discrimination on the basis of alienage or citizenship. However, the lack of U.S. citizenship may not be used as a method of disguising discrimination that is actually based on race or national origin. An employer may follow a policy of employing only U.S. citizens, but may not give unequal treatment to different noncitizens based on their country of origin. Rules that require communication in "English only" are allowed only where the employer can prove that such a rule is a business necessity.

Sex

Title VII's sex discrimination cases have primarily involved women, but it also applies to men. For example, in *Medcalf v. University of Pennsylvania* (1998), an EEOC investigation found that University of Pennsylvania had discriminated against male applicants when hiring the new women's crew coach. The EEOC found that Penn took extraordinary measures to recruit only female candidates and that the university failed to interview Andrew Medcalf, its assistant men's rowing coach, even though he was highly recommended by both his immediate supervisor and several current male and female rowers. More recently, in *Babyak v. Smith College* (2001), a jury awarded James Babyak $1.65 million in an age and gender bias and retaliation case. Babyak, a former coach for the basketball and soccer teams at Smith, a women's college, was fired from his position in 1997 due to poor performance. Babyak, 56, however, maintained that the college wanted a younger woman for the position. He also established that his performance was satisfactory by pointing to the facts that, in the 1995–1996 season, the basketball team, under his direction, won more games than any other basketball team in the history of Smith College and the soccer team had won six conference championships.

The gender of the employee discriminated against, not the gender of the athletes an employee coaches, is the basis for Title VII discrimination. The plaintiffs in *Jackson v. Armstrong School District* (1977) lost their Title VII claim due to the fact that they were paid less money because they were coaching girls' basketball, rather than due to the fact that they were women. The defendant avoided liability by establishing that men coaching girls' basketball were paid the same amount as the women.

Title VII's protection against sex-based discrimination includes sexual harassment, but does not include discrimination on the basis of sexual orientation. In 1978 Congress amended Title VII's language "on the basis of sex" to include protection against discrimination on the basis of pregnancy, childbirth, or other related medical conditions (including abortion). An employer cannot refuse to hire or cannot fire a qualified woman because she is pregnant, has had a child, or has had an abortion. Likewise, an employer cannot leave coverage for pregnancy or childbirth related conditions out of an insurance or disability plan offered to all employees. An employer may, however, refuse to include coverage for abortion, except where the life of the mother is endangered.

The theory of sexual harassment comes from this section of the Act. Liability for sexual harassment was introduced as a legal theory in the late 1970s and continues to evolve, with the most recent decisions focusing on same-sex harassment and employer liability (both are discussed in Chapter 8.14, *Sexual Harassment*).

Religion

All well-recognized faiths and even those considered unorthodox (provided the court is convinced that the purported belief is sincere and genuinely held, and not simply adopted for an ulterior motive) are protected under Title VII. An employer must make **a reasonable accommodation** to an employee's religious practices and observances, unless it would place an **undue hardship** on the employer. An employer's obligation is simply to make a reasonable accommodation to an employee. For example, in *Simmons v. Sports Training Institute* (1990), the plaintiff, a Seventh Day Adventist whose religion prohibited him from working on the Sabbath, from sundown Friday until sundown Saturday, sued his employer for religious discrimination. After his conversion to the religion, the plaintiff only informed the employer that he could not work on Saturdays, so the employer accommodated his religious practices by changing his schedule to Monday through Friday 6:00 AM to 2:00 PM. Thereafter the defendant hired the plaintiff's brother to work the graveyard shift, as well as the Saturday shift, which had previously been covered by his brother prior to his conversion to the Seventh Day Adventist religion. This required the brother to work a double shift. Eventually, the brother fell asleep on the job, and in an effort to keep his brother employed, the plaintiff swapped shifts with his brother. The plaintiff, however, against his employer's wishes, had his brother work double shifts for three weeks in a row. The plaintiff had requested the time off and was granted two of the three weeks. The plaintiff took the third week against his employer's wishes and was fired for insubordination. The plaintiff charged discrimination on the basis of his religious needs. The court refused to find religious discrimination, as the employer had reasonably accommodated the employee and the employee was fired for an unauthorized vacation.

Theories of Liability

Courts applying Title VII have established four theories of liability: individual disparate treatment, systemic disparate treatment, disparate impact, and retaliation.

Individual Disparate Treatment

There are two ways to prove intentional discrimination. The first is where direct evidence of intent exists through the defendant's statements. In *Morris v. Bianchini, et al.* (1987), the plaintiff and another woman were passed over for promotion to athletic director of the health and fitness club in favor of less qualified males. The reason they were given was that the club sought "a macho, male image" for its athletic director. This statement was used as evidence of intent by the club's management to discriminate against two qualified women in favor of a less qualified candidate on the basis of gender. A second example is *Biver v. Saginaw Township Community Schools, et al.* (1986), in which the plaintiff alleged discrimination in failing to hire her for a boys' or girls' basketball team coaching position. The court accepted as evidence of the school superintendent's discriminatory intent his statement that "hell would freeze over before he would hire a woman for a boys' coaching position." The superintendent claimed it was not discriminatory, as his policy was to hire men to coach boys and women to coach girls. The plaintiff challenged the credibility of his explanation by showing many instances in which men were hired to coach girls.

A second method by which one can prove discrimination is through the use of an *inference*. A plaintiff can establish an inference for the court by comparing how an employer treats similarly situated employees of different protected classes. The model for reliance on an inference to prove discriminatory intent was established by *McDonnell Douglas Corp. v. Green* (1973). According to *Texas Department of Community Affairs v. Burdine* (1981), the McDonnell Douglas model is as follows: "[f]irst, the plaintiff has the burden of proving by the preponderance of the evidence a prima facie case of discrimination. Second, if the plaintiff succeeds in proving the prima facie case the burden shifts to the defendant 'to articulate some legitimate nondiscriminatory reason for the employee's rejection.' Third, should the defendant carry this burden, the plaintiff must then have an opportunity to prove by a preponderance of the evidence that the legitimate reasons offered by the defendant were not its true reasons, but were a pretext for discrimination." Thus, "[t]he ultimate burden of persuading the trier of fact that the defendant intentionally discriminated against the plaintiff remains at all times with the plaintiff" (*Texas Department of Community Affairs v. Burdine*, 1981). Under this widely relied upon standard, a *prima facie case* is established by the plaintiff showing:

(if applicant)
1. Applicant is a member of a protected class.
2. Applicant applied for a job for which the employer was seeking applicants.
3. Applicant was qualified to perform the job.
4. Applicant was not hired.
5. Employer filled the position with a non-minority or continued to search.

(if employee)
1. Employee is within the protected class.
2. Employee was performing the task satisfactorily.
3. Employee was discharged or adversely affected by change in working conditions.
4. Employee's work was assigned to one in a nonminority category.

The burden then shifts to the defendant to rebut the plaintiff's presumption by producing evidence that the plaintiff was rejected and someone else preferred for a ***legitimate, nondiscriminatory reason*** (*Texas Department of Community Affairs v. Burdine*, 1981). The defendant's burden is one of production, not persuasion. For the reason to be legitimate it must be lawful, clear, and reasonably specific. In other words, when comparing the chosen applicant or employee with the plaintiff, the defendant should elaborate on the criteria necessary for hiring or promotion, the basis for the comparison of the candidates, and that the person hired or promoted, rather than the plaintiff, possessed the qualities the defendant was seeking (*Herman v. National Broadcasting Co., Inc.*, 1984). The defendant need not prove that the chosen employee was a superior candidate, but simply that there were legitimate, nondiscriminatory reasons to justify the employer's decision. It is difficult for a defendant to raise this defense without clear qualification criteria for hiring. For instance, in *Jackson v. World League of American Football* (1994), the court refused to grant summary judgment in a racial discrimination case where the World League of American Football had not set clear qualifications for the position of head football coach. Once the employer provides a legitimate, nondiscriminatory reason for the alleged discrimination, the burden then shifts back to the employee to prove that the legitimate reason is in fact a ***pretext*** for intentional discrimination. There are a number of ways a plaintiff may establish evidence of pretext, including

1. providing direct evidence of prejudice toward the plaintiff or members of the protected class;
2. presenting statistical evidence of an unbalanced work force;
3. presenting evidence of a rejection of a high number of protected class members; and
4. proving that the articulated reason for rejection has not been consistently applied to members of the majority as it has to protected class members. (Player, 1988)

An example of the last point occurred in *Davis v. McCormick* (1995), where the plaintiff female coach was subject to a more stringent disciplinary policy and her discipline was arguably more severe than any male coach's discipline. The court found that this raised a reasonable inference that the plaintiff's discipline was a pretext for intentional discrimination.

A plaintiff may also present the fact that the legitimate, nondiscriminatory reason was not given to the plaintiff at the time the employment decision was made as evidence that it was an afterthought and, thus, a pretext. For example, in *Baylor v. Jefferson County Board of Education* (1984), a black teacher-coach proved the defendant school board's transfer of him to a teaching-only position was racially motivated. Baylor successfully proved that the defendant's legitimate, nondiscriminatory reason for the job transfer was developed after his hearing and decision to transfer him out of coaching were made.

Finally, failing to comply with the usual hiring procedures may indicate that discriminatory actions were involved. For instance, as noted earlier in *Cross* (1975), the school superintendent suggested that the school board deviate from its policy of promoting from within to search outside the district for a white coach. Thus, the school board never even considered Cross's application and hired a white coach from outside the school district. In *Peirick, v. Indiana University-Purdue* (2005) the Court refused to grant summary judgment in a sex discrimination case where the plaintiff offered sufficient evidence that demonstrated "either that a discriminatory reason more likely motivated the employer or that the employer's proffered explanation is unworthy of credence."

Harassment. The Supreme Court in *Meritor Savings Bank, FSB v. Vinson* (1986) stated that the EEOC "has held and continues to hold that an employer has a duty to maintain a working environment free of harassment based on race, color, religion, sex, [or] national origin . . . and that the duty requires positive action where necessary to eliminate such practices or remedy their effects." Courts have applied this theory to harassment on the basis of race (*Johnson v. NFL*), religion (*Compston v. Borden, Inc.*, 1976), national origin (*Cariddi v. Kansas City Chiefs Football Club*, 1977), and gender (*Meritor Savings Bank, FSB v. Vinson*, 1986). By far, the application of the harassment theory is most developed for discrimination on the basis of sex. Sexual harassment is a type of disparate treatment employment discrimination. A thorough discussion of sexual harassment is found in Chapter 8.14. The hostile environment theory of liability can also be applied to harassment on the basis of race, color, religion, or national origin.

Systemic Disparate Treatment

Under the theory of systemic disparate treatment, plaintiffs challenge broad sweeping employment policies that are discriminatory, such as an employer's policy not to hire women or to segregate employees by race. A plaintiff's initial burden is to "establish by preponderance of the evidence that discrimination is an employer's standard operating procedure—the regular, rather than the unusual practice" (*Lowery v. Circuit City*, 1998,) *quoting Teamsters v. United States*, 1977). This creates an inference that hiring or promotion practices were made in furtherance of this discriminatory policy.

When challenging systemwide patterns or practices, plaintiffs often rely on statistical evidence bolstered with evidence of individual discriminatory treatment. The statistics will compare the racial, ethnic, or gender balance of the qualified labor population with the population of a workforce that draws employees from that population. In *Teamsters* (1977), the court stated that statistics showing an imbalance are probative because such imbalance is often a telltale sign of purposeful discrimination. Absent discrimination, it is assumed that over time nondiscriminatory workplace practices will result in a workforce that is representative of a region's general population.

Once a plaintiff establishes a presumption of a discriminatory pattern or practice, the burden then shifts to the employer to demonstrate why an inference of discriminatory animus could not be drawn from the plaintiff's evidence. Here the defendant has two options. First, the defendant can attack the plaintiff's statistical evidence as inaccurate or insignificant. Second, the employer may seek to provide a nondiscriminatory explanation for the apparently discriminatory result. As with individual disparate treatment, once a defendant produces this explanation, the burden will shift to the plaintiff to persuade the court that the defendant's stated explanation is in fact a pretext for discrimination.

Disparate Impact

Disparate impact discrimination exists where a plaintiff is challenging a neutral employment practice, regardless of intent, that has a discriminatory effect on a protected group. According to the court in *Wynn v. Columbus Municipal Separate School District* (1988), the disparate impact model is often misunderstood and misapplied. This model only applies where the employer has instituted a specific procedure, usually a criterion for employment, which the plaintiff can show has a causal connection with a protected class's imbalance in the workforce (*Pouncy v. Prudential Insurance Co. of America*, 1982).

The prima facie case requires that the employee or the EEOC prove that the employment practice or policy has an adverse impact on the protected group to which the employee belongs. This is usually established through statistical evidence documenting the impact of the practice on the protected class. The use of statistical evidence is difficult and the plaintiff's methodology may be attacked as flawed. For instance, in *Wynn v. Columbus Municipal Separate School District* (1988), a plaintiff female coach used the disparate impact model to challenge her employer's practice of having the head football coach also serve as the athletic director. She argued that the practice had a disparate impact on females, because it was extremely rare that a female would be qualified to be a head football coach. The plaintiff presented as evidence an examination of her state, Mississippi. Of the 192 high school athletic directors in the state only 62 were not head football coaches, no women were head football coaches, and just two athletic directors were women. The court found her theory flawed on two grounds. First, the fact that very few women in Mississippi were selected to serve as athletic director had very little relationship to the issue of whether the defendant, Columbus School District, discriminates against women as athletic director. Second, the plaintiff's statistical evidence is drawn from a pool that includes not only females from the protected class, but a number of nonmembers of that class, namely males who are not qualified as football coach and thus, are denied the athletic director position as well. The court stated the better approach would be to consider the discriminatory treatment of qualified female coaches in the Columbus schools who had been denied the position of athletic director. Thus, the plaintiff lost on her disparate impact claim, but was successful under her disparate treatment theory.

Employers may also rebut the plaintiff's argument by attacking the statistical analysis or producing evidence that the practice is job related. This requires proof that the challenged employment practice is necessary to achieve some legitimate business objective, the practice actually achieves that objective, and there is no reasonable method of accomplishing the objective without a discriminatory. Once the employer establishes the barrier is job related, the burden shifts back to the plaintiff to prove that the barrier is a pretext for discrimination, by showing there are other adequate devices that do not discriminate against a protected class.

Retaliation

Title VII provides a cause of action for retaliation in response to a plaintiff's filing of a claim of employment discrimination. Section 704 (a) of Title VII provides that

> it shall be an unlawful employment practice for an employer to discriminate against any of his employees . . . because [that employee] has opposed any practice made an unlawful employment practice by this subchapter, or because he has made charge, testified, assisted or participated in any manner in an investigation proceeding, or hearing under this title. (42 U.S.C. § 2000e-3(a))

The plaintiff's burden of proof in retaliation claims mirrors that in other Title VII suits. The plaintiff bears the initial burden of establishing a prima facie case of retaliation. To establish the prima facie retaliation case, the plaintiff must show by a preponderance of the evidence that (1) the plaintiff engaged in a statutorily protected activity, (2) adverse action was taken against the plaintiff by the employer subsequent to and contemporaneously with such activity, and (3) a causal link exists between the protected activity and the adverse action (*Jalil v. Advel Corp.*, 1989). Once the plaintiff has established a prima facie case, the defendant may introduce evidence providing legitimate, nonretaliatory reasons for its conduct. If the defendant properly introduces such evidence, the burden shifts back to the plaintiff to show that the defendant's justification is merely pretext for unlawful retaliation.

An example of a retaliation case is *Lowrey v. Texas A&M University d/b/a Tarleton State University* (1998) wherein Lowrey, former women's basketball coach, alleged that defendants were liable under Title VII, Title IX, and 42 U.S.C. § 1983 and the Constitution's First and Fourteenth Amendments for retaliating against her by removing her as Women's Athletics Coordinator in response to comments she made criticizing the university and its officials on gender equity issues.

Additional Defenses

Bona Fide Occupational Qualification

It is not illegal to discriminate on the basis of religion, gender, or national origin if an employer can show the classification is a bona fide occupational qualification. Race and color are never bona fide occupational qualifications. The bona fide occupational qualification defense requires the employer to prove that members of the excluded class could not safely and effectively perform essential job duties and the employer must have a factual basis for believing that persons in the excluded class could not perform the job. The bona fide occupational qualification must also be reasonably necessary to the normal operation of the business. An example might be a situation where a boys' overnight recreational program hires only male floor counselors. If the counselors will live in dorms with the boys, the recreation program may prefer males for the comfort of the boy campers and for role modeling. Finally, customer preference cannot be the basis for a bona fide occupational qualification.

Business Necessity

Business necessity serves as a defense to a disparate impact discrimination claim, where a particular practice causes a protected class to face discrimination. The employer may prove that a particular practice is job related and thus a business necessity despite the discriminatory impact of the practice (*Griggs v. Duke Power Co.*, 1971).

Affirmative Action

Affirmative action involves giving preference to those underrepresented in the workplace. These policies often possess goals/timetables for increasing the percentage of the underrepresented to rectify past discrimination. The affirmative action policy may be voluntary or court ordered as a result of a Title VII or IX lawsuit. Affirmative action policies often result in discrimination against the overrepresented classes, termed reverse discrimination. It is legal provided

- The discrimination results from a formal, systematic program.
- The program is temporary, operating only until its goals are reached.
- The program does not completely bar the hiring/promotion of non-minorities.
- The program does not result in the firing of non-minority workers.
- The program does not force the employer to hire/promote unqualified workers.

Where the program is court ordered, it must be based on actual evidence of discrimination. Where the program is voluntary, it must be based actual evidence of discrimination or evidence that those in underrepresented groups had been underutilized in the past.

Remedies.

Section 706(g) provides the following power to remedy employment discrimination under Title VII:

> If the court finds that the respondent has intentionally engaged in or is intentionally engaging in an unlawful employment practice . . . the court may enjoin the respondent from engaging in such unlawful employment practice, and order such affirmative action as may be appropriate, which may include, but is not limited to, reinstatement or hiring of employees with or without back pay . . . or any other equitable relief as the court deems appropriate. . . .

A successful plaintiff most often is awarded back pay. A back pay order requires the defendant to pay all lost wages and benefits that would have been earned were it not for the illegal discrimination. The trial court may grant interest on these wages.

Significant Case

———————————◇◇◇———————————

The following case is an example of a Title VII lawsuit involving a retaliation claim. The employees argued that they were dismissed because of their opposition to the NFL's discriminatory employment practices.

THOMAS, ET. AL. V. NATIONAL FOOTBALL LEAGUE PLAYERS ASSOCIATION

U.S. Court of Appeals for the District of Columbia Circuit
131 F.3d 198 (1997)

EDWARDS, *Chief Judge*:

A principal claim in this case is that the defendant, acting pursuant to "mixed motives," unlawfully retaliated against the plaintiffs in violation of Title VII, 42 U.S.C. § 2000e *et seq.* (1994). The issues on appeal require us to delimit the requirements of *McDonnell Douglas Corp. v. Green,* 411 U.S. 792, (1973), *Texas Dep't of Community Affairs v. Burdine,* 450 U.S. 248 (1981), and *Price Waterhouse v. Hopkins,* 490 U.S. 228 (1989), with respect to a plaintiff's *prima facie* case, a defendant's burden of production, and the ultimate burdens of persuasion, in a retaliation/mixed-motives case.

The actions giving rise to this lawsuit occurred when Eugene Upshaw, Executive Director of the National Football League Players Association ("NFLPA"), first laid off, then terminated employees Valerie Thomas and Rita Raymond on the stated grounds that they had been disloyal in criticizing NFLPA staff and policies in an anonymously distributed document and in several legally taped telephone calls. Julie Taylor-Bland (Bland at the time of the events) resigned in the aftermath of the firing of the other two. Before leaving the employ of the NFLPA, Thomas and Bland had suggested, in conversations with management that NFLPA promotion policy discriminated against African-American women. The three women subsequently sued the NFLPA, charging that the lay-off and discharge of Thomas and Raymond, and the alleged constructive discharge of Bland, came in retaliation to their opposition to discriminatory employment practices, and hence violated Title VII.

After trial, the District Court granted judgment as a matter of law to the NFLPA on the plaintiffs' claim that there existed a pattern and practice of discrimination at the NFLPA. * * * It then found that Thomas had been unlawfully fired, that Raymond had not made out a *prima facie* case of retaliation, and that Bland had not been fired at all. The trial court granted Thomas back pay and prejudgment interest, but declined to reinstate her. *Thomas, et al., v. National Football League Players Ass'n*, 941 F. Supp. 156 (D.D.C. 1996), *reprinted in* J.A. 279. * * *Thomas, et al., v. National Football League Players Ass'n*, No. 91-3332 (D.D.C. Nov. 26, 1996). The NFLPA now appeals the decisions adverse to it; Thomas, Raymond, and Bland cross-appeal the decisions adverse to them.

We affirm the District Court's judgment on the merits as to Thomas, Raymond, and Bland's claims.

* * *

I. BACKGROUND

In 1988, Thomas, Raymond, and Bland worked for the NFLPA and belonged to Office and Professional Employees International Union, Local 2 ("Local 2"). After the NFLPA's unsuccessful strike against the owners during the 1987 season, the NFLPA's finances suffered, and NFLPA Executive Director Upshaw devised a new budget for the NFLPA which sought to reduce personnel costs through attrition. The board of directors of the NFLPA met during the first week of March 1988, and elected George Martin president and Mike Davis vice president. The board declined to adopt Upshaw's proposed budget, instead demanding a ten percent reduction in personnel costs by lay-off.

After a banquet held in conjunction with the board meeting, Martin convened an informal gathering in his hotel room that included Thomas and Bland. Thomas and others complained about promotional opportunities for African-Americans and women in the Local 2 bargaining unit. Some time after March 10, 1988, Martin organized a second meeting, which Thomas and Bland also attended. Similar concerns were raised, and someone present accused Upshaw of racism.

In the weeks that followed, Martin and Davis conducted personal and telephone interviews with staff on a range of employment-related subjects. Interviewees were assured of confidentiality. In their interviews, Thomas and Bland expressed views on race and sex discrimination at the NFLPA. Davis also interviewed Raymond. Around the same time, Upshaw implemented the NFLPA board's directive to lay off some employees to cut costs. Prior to the lay-offs, Upshaw heard from Davis that Thomas and Raymond had criticized various employees in telephone conversations with Davis, and were suspected of producing and circulating a document harshly critical of the NFLPA. The document was headed and referred to as "What every player should know about the NFLPA." It included, among other allegations, a variety of claims about unfair promotion practices at the NFLPA. It did not include allegations of racial discrimination.

On March 18, 1988, Upshaw laid off six employees, including Thomas and Raymond. When Thomas returned to her office after learning of the lay-offs, she discovered workers changing the locks on her door and shutting down her computer. At a time proximate to the lay-offs, Martin undertook to investigate the employees' allegations of misconduct at the NFLPA, and asked Upshaw about minority issues at the NFLPA. Martin told Upshaw that Thomas had called him a racist and had complained about promotion of African-Americans and women. Martin and Davis each gave copies of the "What every player should know" memorandum to Upshaw. Davis told Upshaw about his telephone conversations with Thomas and Raymond and that Raymond had mailed him a copy of the memorandum.

On March 23, 1988, Davis gave Upshaw tapes of his telephone conversations with Thomas and Raymond. According to Upshaw's uncontradicted testimony, the conversations included ad hominem attacks on various NFLPA employees, including Upshaw. On the tapes, Raymond promised to send a copy of the "What every player should know" memorandum to Davis. Upshaw concluded that Thomas and Raymond had written the memo.

On April 12, 1988, five of the six employees laid off on March 18 were fired for cause. Upshaw sent each employee an identical letter explaining the firing on the grounds that the employees had libeled and slandered NFLPA personnel; had violated confidentiality; and had shown disloyalty towards and intentionally embarrassed the NFLPA. Upshaw later testified that he fired Thomas and Raymond for what he believed they had said and written about the NFLPA employees. Some weeks later, Bland asked Upshaw about a newly open paralegal/secretary position, and Upshaw told her that he "did not see her in the job"; on May 20, 1988, Bland resigned.

Local 2 pursued grievances against the NFLPA on behalf of Thomas and Raymond. The grievances were appealed to arbitration and an arbitrator ruled that the two had been dismissed without just cause. The arbitrator's award ordered reinstatement, but the NFLPA failed to comply. Thomas, Raymond, and Bland also filed timely charges with the Equal Employment Opportunity Commission ("EEOC"), which, after some delay, issued "no cause" determinations on all their claims. At trial, the District Court dismissed as a matter of law plaintiffs' claim of a pattern and practice of discrimination. It found for Thomas and awarded her back pay, without reinstatement, with prejudgment interest for twenty-one months after her firing, based on expert testimony that estimated the time it should have taken Thomas to find new employment. The District Court found against Raymond, who did not appear at trial. Finally, the District Court found that Bland had not been constructively discharged.

II. ANALYSIS

Burdens of Pleading, Production, and Persuasion Under Title VII

Title VII makes it unlawful to retaliate against an employee who "has opposed any practice made an unlawful practice" by the statute. 42 U.S.C. § 2000e-3(a). The legal framework for analyzing retaliation claims under Title VII is as follows.

As in all Title VII cases, the plaintiff must first make out a *prima facie* case of unlawful employment action. *McDonnell Douglas Corp. v. Green*, 411 U.S. 792 (1973). Where retaliation is alleged, a *prima facie* case requires a showing that (1) plaintiff engaged in protected activity, (2) plaintiff was subjected to adverse action by the employer, and (3) there existed a causal link between the adverse action and the protected activity. *Mitchell v. Baldrige*, 759 F.2d 80, 86 (D.C. Cir. 1985). A rebuttable presumption of unlawful discrimination arises when a plaintiff makes out a *prima facie* case. *Texas Dep't of Community Affairs v. Burdine*, 450 U.S. 248, 254 (1981). The defendant may rebut the presumption by asserting a legitimate, non-discriminatory reason for its actions. The defendant's responsibility at this stage has been characterized as a "burden of production," because the ultimate burden of persuasion remains with the plaintiff.

When a defendant satisfies the burden of production, the presumption of discrimination dissolves; however, the plaintiff still has the opportunity to persuade the trier of fact that the defendant's proffered reason was not the actual or sole basis for the disputed action. The plaintiff may aim to prove that a discriminatory motive was the only basis for the employer's action, or the plaintiff may seek to show that the employer was motivated by both permissible and impermissible motives. The plaintiff often will—quite reasonably—argue both alternatives. *See Price Waterhouse v. Hopkins*, 490 U.S. 228, 247 n.12 (Brennan, J.) * * * Where a plaintiff argues that discriminatory motivation constituted the only basis for the employer's action, the plaintiff may persuade the trier of fact of the pretextual nature of the defendant's asserted reason "either directly by persuading the court that a discriminatory reason more likely motivated the employer or indirectly by showing that the employer's proffered explanation is unworthy of credence." *Burdine*, 450 U.S. at 256.

Where, on the other hand, the plaintiff argues that the action resulted from mixed motives, a slightly different model operates. A plaintiff asserting mixed motives must persuade the trier of fact by a preponderance of the evidence that unlawful retaliation constituted a substantial factor in the defendant's action. *Price Waterhouse*,

490 U.S. at 276 (O'Connor, J., concurring); *id.* at 259 (White, J., concurring). When the plaintiff successfully shows that an unlawful motive was a substantial factor in the employer's action, the defendant may seek to prove in response that it would have taken the contested action even absent the discriminatory motive. If the defendant fails to persuade the trier of fact by a preponderance of the evidence that it would have taken the action even absent the discriminatory motive, the plaintiff will prevail.

This burden on a defendant in a mixed-motives case has been characterized both as an affirmative defense, and as a shifting burden of persuasion. The question of characterization is "semantic," and need not be definitively resolved. What is noteworthy, however, is that under *Price Waterhouse* a defendant who is guilty of acting pursuant to an unlawful motive may nonetheless escape liability by proving that it would have made the same decision in the absence of the unlawful motivation. In short, the ultimate burden of persuasion as to the facts constituting the defense properly falls on the defendant in a mixed-motives case, because the plaintiff has proven that unlawful motivation constituted a substantial factor in the defendant's action. "Where a plaintiff has made this type of strong showing of illicit motivation, the factfinder is entitled to presume that the employer's discriminatory animus made a difference to the outcome, absent proof to the contrary from the employer." *Price Waterhouse*, 490 U.S. at 276 (O'Connor, J., concurring).

Appellant's Claims

1. *Meaning and Requirement of Direct Evidence* Appellant NFLPA, the defendant below, argues that, under *Price Waterhouse*, the burden of persuasion shifts to the defendant only where the plaintiff has provided "direct" rather than "inferential" evidence of discriminatory animus. We reject this contention. Under *Price Waterhouse*, the burden of persuasion shifts to the defendant when the plaintiff has shown by a preponderance of "any sufficiently probative direct or indirect evidence" that unlawful discrimination was a substantial factor in the employment decision. *White v. Federal Express Corp.*, 939 F.2d 157, 160 (4th Cir. 1991).

* * *

As this court recently noted, "the distinction between direct and circumstantial evidence has no direct correlation with the strength of [a] plaintiff's case." *Crawford-El v. Britton*, 93 F.3d 813, 818 (D.C. Cir. 1996) (*en banc*), *cert. granted*, 117 S. Ct. 2451 (U.S. 1997). The purported distinction between "circumstantial" or "inferential" and "direct" evidence urged here does not make logical sense, because the decision to shift the burden of persuasion properly rests upon the strength of the plaintiff's evidence of discrimination, not the contingent methods by which that evidence is adduced. Such a distinction is incompatible with both the facts and the logic of *Price Waterhouse*. Burden-shifting under Price Waterhouse requires "evidence of conduct or statements that both reflect directly the alleged discriminatory attitude and that bear directly on the contested employment decision." *Fuller v. Phipps,* 67 F.3d 1137, 1142 (4th Cir. 1995). This formulation should be read carefully; evidence may "bear directly" on a decision without referring to it specifically. Nonetheless the quotation from *Fuller* correctly clarifies that "direct" describes a relationship between proof and incidents and not a characterization of the proof itself.

A number of other circuits have concluded, correctly in our view, that there is no bar on using circumstantial or inferential evidence to shift the burden of persuasion under *Price Waterhouse*. [Citations omitted]

* * *

Defendants Notice of the Shifting Burden of Persuasion

The NFLPA next argues that a defendant must somehow receive "notice" before the District Court that the burden of persuasion has shifted to it under the mixed-motives model of the case. Appellant's claim depends on a mistakenly formalistic conception of the order and allocation of proof in Title VII cases. It is true that a written synthesis of the case law describing tests and burdens for assessing a Title VII retaliation claim gives the appearance of an algorithm. The law has developed in this way for good reason: when a district court articulates its reasoning in a Title VII case, it benefits from conscientiously completing the analytic steps required by the Supreme Court. The steps of the analysis aim to assure compliance with the law and uniformity in its application. This is not to say, however, that the case law aims to stifle the parties in the course of litigation. It is quite the contrary.

Pleadings in the alternative, vagaries of evidence, and the general disorderliness of testimonial narrative all ensure that various elements of proof do not present themselves to the trial court in a regimented fashion. For this reason, the Title VII algorithm need only govern the trial court's assessment of the evidence, not the precise order in which that evidence is presented. What the Supreme Court has said of the *prima facie* case approach of *McDonnell Douglas* applies as forcefully to the entire Title VII framework: it was "never intended to be rigid, mechanized, or ritualistic. Rather, it is merely a sensible, orderly way to evaluate the evidence in light of common experience as it bears on the critical question of discrimination." *Furnco Constr. Corp. v. Waters,* 438 U.S. 567, 577, (1978). The Title VII algorithm was designed to clarify the question of whether discrimination occurred, not "to make [courts'] inquiry even more difficult." *United States Postal Serv. Bd. of Governors v. Aikens,* 460 U.S. 711, 716 (1983). Thus, it is ridiculous to suggest, as the NFLPA does here, that a trial court must give some kind of "notice" to a defendant during the course

of a trial as soon as it appears that the burden of persuasion has shifted. Professional football games may be played in clearly defined "quarters," but we do not litigate Title VII claims in this way.

Furthermore, the argument that a defendant might somehow suffer prejudice absent notice of burden-shifting makes little sense in light of the normal progress of Title VII litigation. If a defendant has evidence tending to show that it would have discharged the plaintiff notwithstanding any discriminatory motive, it would be foolish not to introduce this evidence under its *Burdine* burden of production to rebut the *prima facie* case of discrimination. The defendant would introduce this evidence regardless of whether the case fell under the *Burdine* rubric of single reason or the *Price Waterhouse* rubric of mixed motives. Where the factfinder concludes that the employer's decision resulted from mixed motives, it will consider the self-same exculpatory evidence as a proffered refutation of the argument that discrimination constituted a substantial factor in the employment decision. * * * Accordingly, we conclude that no formal notice of burden-shifting is required under *Price Waterhouse*

District Court Decision on the Merits

The District Court * * * found that Thomas engaged in protected activity by participating in two conversations with Martin in which she raised the issue of discrimination against women and African-Americans in promotion at the NFLPA, and by distributing the memo to Martin. The District Court found that the NFLPA fired Thomas "immediately following" the protected activity, and permissibly concluded that Thomas had made out a *prima facie* case. Because it did not find evidence that Raymond engaged in protected conduct, the District Court correctly found that Raymond had not made out a *prima facie* case. The District Court further found that Bland was not constructively discharged, because she had not presented evidence of aggravating factors making her work intolerable Neither of these conclusions was clearly erroneous; the legal framework for both was correct.

The District Court then assessed the evidence that served to refute the NFLPA's claim that it had non-discriminatory reasons sufficient to fire Thomas. It found that the way in which the firing followed Upshaw's learning of Thomas's taped comments; the unusual security measures surrounding the firing; and Upshaw's possession of the memorandum which he believed Thomas had co-authored sufficed to prove that Thomas's firing was motivated "in substantial measure" by her protected activity. This constituted an acceptable finding of mixed motives, and was not clearly erroneous. Although the District Court did not cite *Price Waterhouse*, it correctly concluded that the burden of persuasion had shifted, and that as a result "it was NFLPA's burden to demonstrate that Thomas would have been discharged regardless of her protected activity." In the District Court's view, "the NFLPA failed to sustain that burden" in that it did not successfully separate permissible from impermissible motives in its decision. This conclusion was not clearly erroneous, either, but reflected the factfinder's assessment of the evidence surrounding the firing.

Appellant urges that even if the burden did shift to it, it established adequately that it would have fired Thomas regardless of her protected actions, because it fired other employees who did not engage in protected activity. This argument, which the NFLPA calls a "syllogism," is thoroughly defective. It is a *non sequitur* to argue that if an employer fires several employees with legal motivation, all other firings that occur simultaneously also acquire the color of legality. The NFLPA could have retaliated against Thomas for protected activity, and then fired other employees at the same time either to mask its retaliation or in a corporate fit of pique.

Rejection of Statistical Evidence

The District Court correctly ruled as a matter of law that plaintiffs did not make out a *prima facie* statistical case of a pattern and practice of discrimination on the part of the NFLPA. The crucial basis for this ruling was that plaintiffs' expert did not consider the relevant qualifications of those passed over or approved for promotion. A *prima facie* case of statistical disparity must include the minimum objective qualifications of the applicants. Here, the expert did not account for minimum qualifications. Indeed, he could not have done so, because Appellees never specifically requested qualification standards from Appellant in discovery. We need not reach the District Court's other reasons for dismissal, because even if the trial court had found adequate sample size and statistical significance (which it did not), a non-discriminatory, qualifications-based reason for the disparate impact could have existed. * * *

The Relief

The District Court awarded Thomas back pay from the date of her firing to December 1989, by which time, it found, she should have secured employment. The District Court did not abuse its discretion in weighing expert testimony regarding job availability to arrive at this time period.

* * *

The District Court did not abuse its discretion in declining to reinstate Thomas. Although the acrimony of litigation alone probably would not suffice to rule out reinstatement, *see Dickerson v. Deluxe Check Printers, Inc.*, 703 F.2d 276, 281 (8th Cir. 1983), the District Court's denial of reinstatement reflected its own observation that some of Thomas's actions "might well have warranted discharge [as it] reasonably concluded that reinstatement would not serve the interests of justice where the employee engaged in behavior that could conceivably have given rise to a legitimate discharge under other circumstances.

The District Court awarded Thomas prejudgment interest on the back pay. The presumption strongly favors prejudgment interest, but the trial court may disallow interest where attributable to substantial, unexplained delay by the plaintiff. Although Thomas reasonably awaited the EEOC's disposition of her request for a right to sue letter, which was delayed through no fault of her own, the same cannot be said of the three-year period during which Thomas and her co-plaintiffs repeatedly amended their complaint. The District Court must reconsider this issue on remand.

* * *

III. CONCLUSION

For the foregoing reasons, the judgment of the District Court is affirmed regarding Thomas, Raymond, and Bland.
So ordered.

◇◇◇ **OTHER RELEVANT SIGNIFICANT CASES**

Chapter 7.14 *Equal Protection*
Chapter 8.12 *Gender Equity: Coaching and Administration*
Chapter 8.14 *Sexual Harassment*

Recent Trends

Same-Race Racial Harassment

In *Ross v. Douglas County* (2001), the Eighth Circuit Court of Appeals held that an African-American employee could assert a claim of racial harassment directed toward him by his African-American supervisor. The court found that the African-American supervisor's behavior was discriminatory "whatever the motive." Furthermore, the Court determined that "the only reason Ross was called a 'nigger' was because he was black" and that the supervisor's race "did not alter this." The case, however, does not serve to make clear the distinction between the content of the improper behavior at issue and the motivation for the behavior in the first instance. Juries are likely to have difficulty separating the obvert racial nature of the conduct from whether racial bias was the reason for the harassment in the first place. We will have to wait to see if the U.S. Supreme Court will bring clarity to the issue in the future.

Sexual Orientation Discrimination

Although Title VII does not protect against sexual orientation discrimination in the workplace, thirteen states have added protection against discrimination on the basis of sexual orientation in their employment discrimination laws. At the same time, and possibly in response to this movement, a number of jurisdictions have sought to prohibit homosexuality in their state and/or local governments.

In *Price Waterhouse v. Hopkins* (1989) the U.S. Supreme Court stated that where the employer bases employment decisions on gender stereotyping, a Title VII claim may be sustained. The key in the determination is whether the harassment occurred because of the victim's sex. In *Bibby v. Philadelphia Coca Cola Bottling Co.*, (2001) the Third Circuit of Appeals in rejecting plaintiff's claim of unlawful harassment, enumerated three ways to prove same-sex harassment occurred on account of the victim's sex: "(1) proof that the harasser sexually desires the victim; (2) proof that the harasser displays hostility to the presence of a particular sex in the workplace; and (3) proof that the harasser's conduct was motivated by a belief that the victim failed to conform to the stereotypes of his or her gender."

Transsexual Discrimination

The scope of sex discrimination claims under Title VII has broadened to include transsexuals. In *Smith v. City of Salem* (2004), the U.S. Court of Appeals for the Sixth Circuit held that a transsexual has a viable cause of action under Title VII if he is discriminated against because of his failure to conform to sex stereotypes by exhibiting less masculine and more feminine mannerisms and appearance. The Sixth Circuit, relying on *Price Waterhouse*, found that "sex" encompasses both the biological differences between men and women and gender discrimination, which is based on the failure to conform to stereotypical gender norms. Although Title VII does not protect against sexual orientation discrimination, per se, it is possible that the decision in *Salem* could be used by homosexuals and lesbians to bring claims under Title VII by asserting that they have been discriminated against for failure to conform to stereotypical gender norms.

References

Cases

Babyak v. Smith College, No. 99-204 (Hampden Co., Mass., Dist. Ct. 2001).

Baylor v. Jefferson County Board of Education, 733 F.2d 1527 (11th Cir. 1984).

Bianchi v. City of Philadelphia, No. 99-CV-2409, 2002 WL 23942 (E.D. Pa. Jan 2, 2002)

Bibby v. Philadelphia Coca Cola Bottling Co.,No. 00-1261 (3d Cir. August 1, 2001.

Biver v. Saginaw Township Community Schools, et al., 805 F.2d 1033 (6th Cir. 1986).

Cariddi v. Kansas City Chiefs Football Club, 568 F. Supp. 87 (8th Cir. 1977).

Compston v. Borden, Inc., 424 F. Supp. 157 (S.D. Ohio 1976).

Cross v. Board of Education of Dollarway, Arkansas School District, 395 F. Supp. 531 (E.D. Ark. 1975).

Davis v. McCormick, 898 F. Supp. 1275 (C.D. Ill. 1995).

Dowling v. United States, 476 F. Supp. 1018 (D. Mass. 1979).

EEOC v. National Broadcasting Co., Inc., 753 F. Supp. 452 (S.D. N.Y. 1990).

Graves v. Women's Professional Rodeo Association, Inc., 907 F.2d 71 (8th Cir. 1990).

Griggs v. Duke Power Co., 401 U.S. 424 (1971).

Herman v. National Broadcasting Co., Inc., 774 F.2d 604 (7th Cir. 1984).

Jackson v. Armstrong School District, 430 F. Supp. 1050 (W.D. Penn. 1977).

Jackson v. World League of American Football, 65 Fair Emp. Prac. Cas. 358 (S.D. N.Y. 1994).

Jalil v. Advel Corp., 873 F. 2d 701 (3rd Cir. 1989).

Johnson v. NFL, No. 99 Civ. 8582 (DC) (SD NY, 1999).

Lowery v. Circuit City, 158 F.3d 742 (1998).

Lowery v. Texas A&M University d/b/a Tarleton State University, 11 F.Supp.2d 895 (1998).

McDonnell Douglas Corp. v. Green, 411 U.S. 792 (1973).

Medcalf v. University of Pennsylvania, 2001 U.S. Dist. Lexis 10155.

Meritor Savings Bank, FSB v. Vinson, 477 U.S. 57 (1986).

Morris v. Bianchini, et al., 43 Fair Emp. Prac. Cases 647 (E.D. Va. 1987).

Peirick, v. Indiana University-Purdue, 2005 U.S. Dist. LEXIS 32479.

Pouncy v. Prudential Insurance Co. of America, 668 F.2d 795 (5th Cir. 1982).

Price Waterhouse v. Hopkins, 490 U.S. 228, 250-51 (1989).

Ross v. Douglas County, 244 F.3d 620 (2001).

Simmons v. Sports Training Institute, 52 Fair Emp. Prac. Cas. 1322 (S.D. N.Y. 1990).

Smith v. City of Salem, 378 R.3d 566 (6th Cir. 2004).

Teamsters v. United States, 431 U.S. 324 (1977).

Texas Department of Community Affairs v. Burdine, 450 U.S. 248 (1981).

Wynn v. Columbus Municipal Separate School District, 692 F. Supp. 672 (N.D. Miss. 1988).

Publications

Player, M. A. (1988). *Employment discrimination law*. St. Paul, MN: West Publishing Co.

Zimmer, M. J., Sullivan, C. A., & Richards, R. F. (1988). *Cases and materials on employment discrimination*. Boston: Little, Brown, and Co.

Legislation

Title VII of the Civil Rights Act of 1964, 42 U.S.C. § 2000e et seq. (1990).

8.14 Sexual Harassment

Barbara Osborne
University of North Carolina at Chapel Hill

One of the most important issues facing sports and recreation administrators today is sexual harassment. Whether it is a health club owner promising to promote an aerobics instructor in exchange for sexual favors, baseball players waiting to take batting practice making comments about track athletes' bodies while they are completing their workouts, or a coach initiating inappropriate conversations, touching, or engaging in sexual relationships with athletes at the club, middle school, high school, and collegiate levels, sexual harassment is a major problem in the sports and recreation industry and in society as a whole.

Fundamental Concepts

Sexual Harassment in the Workplace

Title VII

Although the Civil Rights Act of 1964 was enacted to prevent discrimination on the basis of race, color, religion, sex, or national origin, the Court did not recognize sexual harassment as sex discrimination until *Williams v. Saxbe* in 1976. In that case, the Supreme Court ruled that sexual harassment is a form of sex discrimination actionable under Title VII if the harassment places an artificial barrier on employment. Other early cases, *Barnes v. Costle* (1977) and *Miller v. Bank of America* (1979) narrowly recognized sexual harassment only in situations when the subordinate's employment opportunities were conditioned on entering into a sexual relationship with a superior, commonly described as quid pro quo sexual harassment.

The Equal Employment Opportunity Commission (EEOC) is the administrative agency charged with enforcing Title VII. It was not until 1980 that the EEOC Guidelines first acknowledged sexual harassment as "discrimination because of sex". The Guidelines took a broader approach than the courts and defined sexual harassment as

Unwelcome sexual advances, requests for sexual favors, and other verbal or physical conduct of a sexual nature constitute sexual harassment when

1) submission to such conduct is made either explicitly or implicitly a term or condition of an individual's employment
2) submission to or rejection of such conduct by an individual is used as the basis for employment decisions affecting such individual, or
3) such conduct has the purpose or effect of unreasonably interfering with an individual's work performance or creating an intimidating, hostile or offensive working environment.

It is important to note "unwelcome" as a key to the definition of sexual harassment. Conduct is unwelcome if the employee did not solicit or incite it and when the employee regards the conducts as undesirable or offensive. A charging party's claim will fail if the allegedly offensive conduct was "welcome."

Quid Pro Quo Harassment

The first two conditions listed in the EEOC definition of sexual harassment describe the traditional exchange of sexual favors referred to as **quid pro quo** sexual harassment. Typically, these cases involve the employer's granting or denying an employment benefit based on the employee's response to the employer's sexual advances. In these cases, the courts uniformly apply strict liability in the same manner that they apply it in racial or religiously motivated cases under Title VII.

Hostile Environment

The third condition listed in the EEOC definition of sexual harassment is commonly known as **hostile environment**. The first case recognizing hostile environment sexual harassment was *Meritor Savings Bank, FSB v. Vinson* (1986). The Supreme Court referred to the EEOC guidelines in recognizing that the repeated actions of a supervisor could so contaminate the work environment that it altered the conditions of employment. The Court also expanded the scope of Title VII to include situations that did not result in direct or tangible economic loss. However, the Supreme Court did not define what behavior would constitute a hostile environment, only stating that the harassment must be so severe that it creates an abusive working environment.

Determining whether or not there is a hostile environment is a three-step approach:

1. Totality of the circumstances
2. Whether a reasonable person in the same or similar circumstance would find the conduct sufficiently severe or pervasive to create an intimidating, hostile or abusive work environment (objective test)
3. Whether the plaintiff perceived the environment to be hostile or abusive (subjective test)

Totality of the Circumstances. Because sexual attraction may play a role in the day-to-day social exchange between employees, the distinction between invited, uninvited-but-welcome, offensive-but-tolerated, and flatly rejected sexual advances may be difficult to discern. An examination of the totality of the circumstances—the nature of the conduct, the context in which the incidents occurred, the frequency of the conduct, its severity and pervasiveness, whether it was physically threatening or humiliating, whether it was unwelcome, and whether it unreasonably interfered with an employee's work performance—is necessary. A list of sexually harassing behaviors is provided in Table 1. Whether there is a repeated pattern of relatively

table ⟨**1**⟩ Sexually Harassing Behaviors

Behavioral
Ogling, leering, staring, gestures, mooning, flashing

Verbal
Request for dates, asking personal questions, lewd comments, dirty or sexual jokes, whistling, catcalling, obscene calls, sexual comments or rumors

Written/Visual
Love letters, poems, obscene letters, cards, notes, posters, pictures, cartoons, graphics, sexual graffiti

Touching
Violation of personal space, patting, rubbing, pinching, bra-snapping, caressing, blocking movement, kissing, groping, grabbing, tackling, hazing

Power
Retaliation, using position to request dates or suggest sexual favors, gender-directed favoritism, disparate treatment, hazing rituals, bullying, intimidation, condescending or patronizing behavior

Threats
Quid pro quo demands, conditioning evaluations or references on sexual favors, retaliation for refusal to comply with requests

Force
Attempted rape or assault, rape, assault, pantsing, stripping, extreme forms of hazing, stalking, sexual abuse, physical abuse, vandalism

benign behavior or a single incident of gross behavior is not conclusive. The most important analysis is whether the conduct negatively altered the work environment.

Reviewing all the circumstances in determining whether an environment is hostile or abusive also requires both a subjective and an objective test. The *reasonable person (objective test)* requires the plaintiff to prove that the conduct is severe or pervasive enough that a reasonable person would objectively find it hostile or abusive. The *employee's perception (subjective test)* requires that the plaintiff subjectively perceive the environment to be so hostile and abusive that it altered the employment climate. However, in *Harris*, the Supreme Court established that the plaintiff does not have to prove psychological injury to prove that she was sexually harassed.

Agency Principles. If the three steps of the hostile environment test are satisfied, the Supreme Court in *Meritor* indicated that agency principles should guide the determination of liability. Under agency principles, it is clear that a master is liable for the torts of his servants while acting within the scope of their employments. It is also generally accepted that a supervisor's sexual harassment of a subordinate would not be conduct within the scope of employment. However, the employer may be liable if the employer intended the conduct or the consequences of the conduct, or if the employer was negligent or reckless.

Under the EEOC guidelines issued in 1999, an employer is always liable for the actions of a supervisor that result in a tangible effect of employment status of the victim. A **tangible employment action** is defined as requiring a significant change in employment status, such as hiring, firing, failing to promote, reassignment with significantly different responsibilities or a decision causing a significant change in benefits. The employer is liable for harassment by coworkers if the employer knew or should have known of the misconduct, unless it can show that it took immediate and appropriate corrective action. Harassment by nonemployees—for example customers, vendors, or club members—are the employer's responsibility under a similar negligence standard, which also takes into account the extent of the employer's control over the harasser.

The Supreme Court and the 1999 Guidance allow for an employer to avoid liability with a two-part **affirmative defense**. The employer bears the burden of proving by a preponderance of the evidence both of these elements:

1. The employer exercised reasonable care to prevent and promptly correct harassment.
2. The employee unreasonably failed to take advantage of any preventive or corrective opportunities provided by the employer or to avoid harm otherwise.

To show reasonable care to prevent and correct harassment, the employer must have established, publicized, and enforced antiharassment policies and grievance procedures prior to the complaint of harassment. This includes handing out a copy of the policy and complaint procedure to every employee, posting them in central locations, and including them in employee handbooks. The policy and procedures should include a clear explanation of prohibited conduct, an assurance of protection from retaliation for the complainant, a clearly described complaint process, and a promise of confidentiality. The complaint procedure should also provide accessible contact people to receive complaints (although some courts have ruled that reporting to any employee in a supervisory role is sufficient). A prompt, thorough, and impartial investigation should be conducted as soon as the employer learns of a complaint. The employee should be assured that immediate and appropriate corrective measures will be taken, and the employer should initiate intermediate protective measures against further harassment. If it is determined that harassment has occurred, the employer must take immediate corrective/disciplinary action to effectively end the harassment.

The Guidance also established that the employer must show that the employee did not exercise reasonable care by taking advantage of preventive opportunities, complaint procedures, or other ways to avoid harm. A failure to complain in a timely manner about persistent harassment could eliminate the employer's liability. If some, but not all, of the harm could have been avoided by an earlier compliant, damages awarded would likely be reduced.

Once the employer has established both parts of the affirmative defense, the employee has the opportunity to rebut the employer's assertion that the employee unreasonably failed to complain or otherwise avoid harm. The 1999 Guidance lists three explanations that may be reasonable: (1) risk of retaliation, (2) employer-created obstacles in the complaint process or procedures, and (3) belief that the complaint mechanism is not effective.

Although it is illegal to retaliate against an individual for opposing employment practices that discriminate based on sex or for filing a discrimination charge, testifying, or participating in any way in an investigation, proceeding, or litigation under Title VII, research indicates that most employees who fail to report harassment fear retaliation. It is the employer's burden to prove that this fear is unwarranted. One of the easiest ways to satisfy this burden is to have and promote a complaint process that maintains confidentiality and does not punish employees who complain. The typical harassment scenarios and the likely consequences are presented in Table 2.

Title IX of the Education Act of 1972

The other major act of legislation related to sexual harassment is Title IX of the Education Act of 1972. Although it is most often referenced in relation to girls' participation in sport, Title IX prohibits discrimination on the basis of sex by any educational institution receiving federal funds. Although almost all school sports programs fall within the Title IX regulation, only recreation programs within educational settings that receive federal funds would be required to comply with the legislation.

The Office of Civil Rights (OCR) in the U.S. Department of Education is responsible for enforcing Title IX. In the 2001 OCR guidance, sexual harassment is defined as it applies to educational institutions as "unwelcome conduct of a sexual nature . . . in each case, the issue is whether the harassment rises to a level that it denies or limits a student's ability to participate in or benefit from the school's programs based on sex."

Because the case law under Title VII is more developed, the courts have often referred to Title VII to guide them in Title IX cases. However, the Supreme Court takes a very different approach to institutional liability under Title IX compared to employer liability under Title VII. *Gebser v. Lago Vista Independent School District*, 118 S. Ct. 1989 (1998)—decided just 4 days before the *Burlington* and *Faragher* cases—indicates that damages under Title IX are only available when the institution has actual knowledge of the offensive behavior. The Court explicitly rejected the application of agency principles that it applies in Title VII sexual harassment cases. Relying on the "contractual nature" of Title IX, the Court reasoned that Title IX as a Spending Clause statute requires that the institution have actual notice and be deliberately indifferent to the reported behavior before it would be held liable.

table **2** Employer Liability for Hostile Environment Sexual Harassment

	Employer knew of harassment but did not respond	Employer knew of harassment, took immediate and appropriate corrective action	Employer had no knowledge of harassment
Harasser is supervisor	Strict liability if there is a tangible employment action; if no tangible employment action may avoid liability by establishing affirmative defense	No negligence/no liability because affirmative defense is established	Vicarious liability unless affirmative defense is established
Harasser is coworker	Liability based on negligence	No negligence/no liability	No liability because there is no agency relationship
Harasser is nonemployee, customer, member, vendor, etc.	Liability based on negligence, will consider extent of the employer's control	No negligence/no liability	No liability because there is no agency relationship

Adapted from B. Glenn George. (1999). Employer liability for sexual harassment: The buck stops where? *Wake Forest Law Review, 34*(1), 20.

For example, in *Davis v. Monroe County Board of Education* (1999), a fifth grader suffered sexual harassment by one of her classmates over several months. Although the victim and her mother repeatedly informed her teachers of the harassment, no one at the school made any effort to separate the two students (who sat next to each other in class) or to discipline the harasser. The Supreme Court concluded that student–student sexual harassment claims under Title IX should be analyzed in the same way as teacher–student sexual harassment. The Court found that schools are responsible for both preventing peer sexual harassment and for handling claims of peer sexual harassment in a prompt and effective manner on actual notice.

The OCR Revised Sexual Harassment Guidance explains the liability of the educational institution under Title IX. If the employee engages in sexual harassment while carrying out responsibilities to provide benefits and services to students, the institution is responsible for the discriminatory conduct, remedying its effects, and preventing future occurrences whether or not it has notice of the harassment. If the employee is acting outside the scope of his or her assigned duties (and sexually harassing behavior is almost always considered outside the scope of the employee's duties), the institution must take prompt and effective action to stop the harassment and prevent its recurrence on notice of the harassment. The institution is considered to have engaged in its own discrimination if it fails to act and allows the student to be subjected to a hostile environment that denies or limits the student's ability to participate in or benefit from the school's program. The institution is responsible for peer or third-party harassment if the institution knew or reasonably should have known of the harassment and failed to take prompt and effective action. This liability is based on the contractual nature of Title IX, which promises an educational environment free from discrimination.

Whether the harasser is an employee or a peer, the victim of sexual harassment bears the burden of proving the following elements:

1. That she is a member of a protected group based on her sex
2. That she was subjected to unwelcome conduct of a sexual nature, either quid pro quo or hostile environment sexual harassment
3. That the conduct was so severe, pervasive, and objectively offensive that it denied equal access to the school's educational opportunities or benefits
4. That a school official with authority to take corrective action had actual knowledge or notice of the behavior
5. That the school official was deliberately indifferent to the conduct and failed to reasonably respond

The Supreme Court in *Gebser* and *Davis* did not address the issue of whether a school could raise an affirmative defense by having an effective sexual harassment policy. Schools are required by Title IX to adopt and publish grievance procedures to address sexual discrimination. The procedures do not have to be specific to harassment, but should provide an effective manner for preventing and addressing sexual harassment. The OCR recently reissued the following criteria for evaluating a school's grievance procedure:

1. Notice of policies and procedures must be sent to students, parents (for elementary and secondary students), and employees, including where complaints may be filed.
2. The procedure must actually be applied to complaints alleging harassment.
3. An adequate, reliable, and impartial investigation of the complaints must be conducted, including the opportunities to present witnesses and other evidence.
4. A designated, prompt time frame should be established for the complaint and investigative process.
5. Notice of the outcome of the complaint must be given to the parties involved.
6. An assurance must be made that the school will take corrective measures to eliminate current harassment and similar instances of harassment in the future.

If an educational institution implements these guidelines when developing its sexual harassment policies and procedures, it should function to reduce instances of harassment and provide protection for its students. It may also mitigate liability if a complaint is made to the OCR or a civil suit is filed.

Coach/Athlete Sexual Harassment

Although the liability of the institution is the same when the harasser is a coach and the victim is an athlete as that for teacher/student harassment, there are unique circumstances in the athletics context that merit closer attention. First, although Title IX has increased the number of female athletes, the number of female coaches has decreased. This increases the number of men coaching female athletes and also increases the opportunity and possibility of sexual harassment. Male coach/female athlete is not the only context in which sexual harassment occurs, but it is significantly greater than any other combination.

Touching, keeping track of the athlete's life outside athletics, and nicknames are routinely accepted as part of being an athlete and could be harmless. However, this conduct should be measured by the unwelcomeness standard used by Title VII: conduct is unwelcome if the athlete did not request or invite it and it is offensive to the victim. The power dynamic in coach–athlete relationships (factors such as power, trust, and control) may affect the ability of a female athlete to freely consent or decline sexual contact, so administrators and coaches must measure whether the conduct is harassing by its impact on the athlete, and not just by the intent of the coach.

Peer Sexual Harassment in Athletics

Complaints of peer harassment are increasing dramatically. A female swimmer from the University of Pittsburgh filed a civil suit seeking reinstatement to the university swim team claiming she was released as a result of her complaints of harassment against a swimmer on the men's team. A former placekicker on the University of Colorado football team publicly alleged that she was sexually harassed by her teammates, which led to her transfer to the University of New Mexico. She stated that she was "treated like a piece of meat" during her season with the team in 1999 and repeatedly called "names that are unrepeatable." The student–athlete indicated she approached the coach several times during the season, but the harassment persisted.

Athletic departments, coaches, and admissions offices should think long and hard before recruiting or accepting students with histories of sexual misconduct or assault. In August 2003, a former student at the University of Georgia filed a lawsuit for $25 million against the university naming the president, the athletic director, and the former basketball coach as defendants. The suit claimed that these individuals were aware that the student–athlete who allegedly raped the plaintiff had a history of sexual assaults before he was recruited and admitted to the university. The student–athlete had been accused of sexual harassment and assault at the community college he was recruited from and was facing a federal lawsuit stemming from the accusations. Given the past history of the recruited student–athlete, it is arguable that the institution had "notice" and should have made efforts to prevent future harassment from occurring.

Significant Case

—◇◇◇—

This is the leading case of sexual harassment in the recreation industry. The Supreme Court addressed the conflict of opinions issued by the lower courts and thoroughly explains the new standards for establishing employer liability under Title VII.

BETH ANN FARAGHER V. CITY OF BOCA RATON

United States Supreme Court
524 U.S. 775 (1998)

Between 1985 and 1990, while attending college, petitioner Beth Ann Faragher worked part time and during the summers as an ocean lifeguard for the Marine Safety Section of the Parks and Recreation Department of respondent, the City of Boca Raton, Florida (City). During this period, Faragher's immediate supervisors were Bill Terry, David Silverman, and Robert Gordon. In June 1990, Faragher resigned.

In 1992, Faragher brought an action against Terry, Silverman, and the City, asserting claims under Title VII, *42 U.S.C. § 1983,* and Florida law. So far as it concerns the Title VII claim, the complaint alleged that

Terry and Silverman created a "sexually hostile atmosphere" at the beach by repeatedly subjecting Faragher and other female lifeguards to "uninvited and offensive touching," by making lewd remarks, and by speaking of women in offensive terms. The complaint contained specific allegations that Terry once said that he would never promote a woman to the rank of lieutenant, and that Silverman had said to Faragher, "Date me or clean the toilets for a year." Asserting that Terry and Silverman were agents of the City, and that their conduct amounted to discrimination in the "terms, conditions, and privileges" of her employment, Faragher sought a judgment against the City for nominal damages, costs, and attorney's fees.

Following a bench trial, the United States District Court for the Southern District of Florida found that throughout Faragher's employment with the City, Terry served as Chief of the Marine Safety Division, with authority to hire new lifeguards (subject to the approval of higher management), to supervise all aspects of the lifeguards' work assignments, to engage in counseling, to deliver oral reprimands, and to make a record of any such discipline. Silverman was a Marine Safety lieutenant from 1985 until June 1989, when he became a captain. Gordon began the employment period as a lieutenant and at some point was promoted to the position of training captain. In these positions, Silverman and Gordon were responsible for making the lifeguards' daily assignments, and for supervising their work and fitness training.

The lifeguards and supervisors were stationed at the city beach and worked out of the Marine Safety Headquarters, a small one-story building containing an office, a meeting room, and a single, unisex locker room with a shower. Their work routine was structured in a "paramilitary configuration," with a clear chain of command. Lifeguards reported to lieutenants and captains, who reported to Terry. He was supervised by the Recreation Superintendent, who in turn reported to a Director of Parks and Recreation, answerable to the City Manager. The lifeguards had no significant contact with higher city officials like the Recreation Superintendent.

In February 1986, the City adopted a sexual harassment policy, which it stated in a memorandum from the City Manager addressed to all employees. In May 1990, the City revised the policy and reissued a statement of it. Although the City may actually have circulated the memos and statements to some employees, it completely failed to disseminate its policy among employees of the Marine Safety Section, with the result that Terry, Silverman, Gordon, and many lifeguards were unaware of it.

From time to time over the course of Faragher's tenure at the Marine Safety Section, between 4 and 6 of the 40 to 50 lifeguards were women. During that 5-year period, Terry repeatedly touched the bodies of female employees without invitation, would put his arm around Faragher, with his hand on her buttocks, and once made contact with another female lifeguard in a motion of sexual simulation. He made crudely demeaning references to women generally, and once commented disparagingly on Faragher's shape. During a job interview with a woman he hired as a lifeguard, Terry said that the female lifeguards had sex with their male counterparts and asked whether she would do the same.

Silverman behaved in similar ways. He once tackled Faragher and remarked that, but for a physical characteristic he found unattractive, he would readily have had sexual relations with her. Another time, he pantomimed an act of oral sex. Within earshot of the female lifeguards, Silverman made frequent, vulgar references to women and sexual matters, commented on the bodies of female lifeguards and beachgoers, and at least twice told female lifeguards that he would like to engage in sex with them. Faragher did not complain to higher management about Terry or Silverman. Although she spoke of their behavior to Gordon, she did not regard these discussions as formal complaints to a supervisor but as conversations with a person she held in high esteem. Other female lifeguards had similarly informal talks with Gordon, but because Gordon did not feel that it was his place to do so, he did not report these complaints to Terry, his own supervisor, or to any other city official. Gordon responded to the complaints of one lifeguard by saying that "the City just [doesn't] care."

In April 1990, however, two months before Faragher's resignation, Nancy Ewanchew, a former lifeguard, wrote to Richard Bender, the City's Personnel Director, complaining that Terry and Silverman had harassed her and other female lifeguards. Following investigation of this complaint, the City found that Terry and Silverman had behaved improperly, reprimanded them, and required them to choose between a suspension without pay or the forfeiture of annual leave.

On the basis of these findings, the District Court concluded that the conduct of Terry and Silverman was discriminatory harassment sufficiently serious to alter the conditions of Faragher's employment and constitute an abusive working environment. The District Court then ruled that there were three justifications for holding the City liable for the harassment of its supervisory employees. First, the court noted that the harassment was pervasive enough to support an inference that the City had "knowledge, or constructive knowledge" of it. Next, it ruled that the City was liable under traditional agency principles because Terry and Silverman were acting as its agents when they committed the harassing acts. Finally, the court observed that Gordon's knowledge of the harassment, combined with his inaction, "provides a further basis for imputing liability on [sic] the City." The District Court then awarded Faragher one dollar in nominal damages on her *Title VII claim*.

A panel of the Court of Appeals for the Eleventh Circuit reversed the judgment against the *City*. Although the panel had "no trouble concluding that Terry's and Silverman's conduct . . . was severe and pervasive enough to create an objectively abusive work environment," it overturned the District Court's conclusion that the City was liable. The panel ruled that Terry and Silverman were not acting within the scope of their employment when they engaged in the harassment, that they were not aided in their actions by the agency relationship, and that the City had no constructive knowledge of the harassment by virtue of its pervasiveness or Gordon's actual knowledge. * * *

Since our decision in *Meritor*, Courts of Appeals have struggled to derive manageable standards to govern employer liability for hostile environment harassment perpetrated by supervisory employees. While following our admonition to find guidance in the common law of agency, as embodied in the Restatement, the Courts of Appeals have adopted different approaches. We granted certiorari to address the divergence, and now reverse the judgment of the Eleventh Circuit and remand for entry of judgment in Faragher's favor.

II

A

Under Title VII of the Civil Rights Act of 1964, "it shall be an unlawful employment practice for an employer to fail or refuse to hire or to discharge any individual, or otherwise to discriminate against any individual with respect to his compensation, terms, conditions, or privileges of employment, because of such individual's race, color, religion, sex, or national origin." *42 U.S.C. § 2000e-2*(a)(1). We have repeatedly made clear that although the statute mentions specific employment decisions with immediate consequences, the scope of the prohibition " 'is not limited to "economic" or "tangible" discrimination,' " and that it covers more than " 'terms' and 'conditions' in the narrow contractual sense." Thus, in *Meritor* we held that sexual harassment so "severe or pervasive" as to " 'alter the conditions of [the victim's] employment and create an abusive working environment' " violates *Title VII*.

So, in *Harris*, we explained that in order to be actionable under the statute, a sexually objectionable environment must be both objectively and subjectively offensive, one that a reasonable person would find hostile or abusive, and one that the victim in fact did perceive to be so. We directed courts to determine whether an environment is sufficiently hostile or abusive by "looking at all the circumstances," including the "frequency of the discriminatory conduct; its severity; whether it is physically threatening or humiliating, or a mere offensive utterance; and whether it unreasonably interferes with an employee's work performance." Most recently, we explained that Title VII does not prohibit "genuine but innocuous differences in the ways men and women routinely interact with members of the same sex and of the opposite sex." A recurring point in these opinions is that "simple teasing," offhand comments, and isolated incidents (unless extremely serious) will not amount to discriminatory changes in the "terms and conditions of employment."

These standards for judging hostility are sufficiently demanding to ensure that Title VII does not become a "general civility code." Properly applied, they will filter out complaints attacking "the ordinary tribulations of the workplace, such as the sporadic use of abusive language, gender-related jokes, and occasional teasing." We have made it clear that conduct must be extreme to amount to a change in the terms and conditions of employment, and the Courts of Appeals have heeded this view.

While indicating the substantive contours of the hostile environments forbidden by Title VII, our cases have established few definite rules for determining when an employer will be liable for a discriminatory environment that is otherwise actionably abusive. Given the circumstances of many of the litigated cases, including some that have come to us, it is not surprising that in many of them, the issue has been joined over the sufficiency of the abusive conditions, not the standards for determining an employer's liability for them. There have, for example, been myriad cases in which District Courts and Courts of Appeals have held employers liable on account of actual knowledge by the employer, or high-echelon officials of an employer organization, of sufficiently harassing action by subordinates, which the employer or its informed officers have done nothing to stop. In such instances, the combined knowledge and inaction may be seen as demonstrable negligence, or as the employer's adoption of the offending conduct and its results, quite as if they had been authorized affirmatively as the employer's policy. * * *

Finally, there is nothing remarkable in the fact that claims against employers for discriminatory employment actions with tangible results, like hiring, firing, promotion, compensation, and work assignment, have resulted in employer liability once the discrimination was shown.

A variety of reasons have been invoked for this apparently unanimous rule. Some courts explain . . . that when a supervisor makes such decisions, he "merges" with the employer, and his act becomes that of the employer. Other courts have suggested that vicarious liability is proper because the supervisor acts within the scope of his authority when he makes discriminatory decisions in hiring, firing, promotion, and the like. Others have suggested that vicarious liability is appropriate because the supervisor who discriminates in this manner is aided by the agency relation. Finally, still other courts have endorsed both of the latter two theories.

The soundness of the results in these cases (and their continuing vitality), in light of basic agency principles, was confirmed by this Court's only discussion to date of standards of employer liability, in *Meritor,* which involved a claim of discrimination by a supervisor's sexual harassment of a subordinate over an extended period. In affirming the Court of Appeals's holding that a hostile atmosphere resulting from sex discrimination is actionable under Title VII, we also anticipated proceedings on remand by holding agency principles relevant in assigning employer liability and by rejecting three *per se* rules of liability or immunity. We observed that the very definition of employer in Title VII, as including an "agent," expressed Congress's intent that courts look to traditional principles of the law of agency in devising standards of employer liability in those instances where liability for the actions of a supervisory employee was not otherwise obvious, and although we cautioned that "common-law principles may not be transferable in all their particulars to Title VII," we cited the Restatement § 219-237, with general approval.

We then proceeded to reject two limitations on employer liability, while establishing the rule that some limitation was intended. We held that neither the existence of a company grievance procedure nor the absence of actual notice of the harassment on the part of upper management would be dispositive of such a claim; while either might be relevant to the liability, neither would result automatically in employer immunity. Conversely, we held that Title VII placed some limit on employer responsibility for the creation of a discriminatory environment by a supervisor, and we held that Title VII does not make employers "always automatically liable for sexual harassment by their supervisors," contrary to the view of the Court of Appeals, which had held that "an employer is strictly liable for a hostile environment created by a supervisor's sexual advances, even though the employer neither knew nor reasonably could have known of the alleged misconduct," *477 U.S. at 69-70.*

Meritor's statement of the law is the foundation on which we build today. * * *

B

The Court of Appeals identified, and rejected, three possible grounds drawn from agency law for holding the City vicariously liable for the hostile environment created by the supervisors. It considered whether the two supervisors were acting within the scope of their employment when they engaged in the harassing conduct. The court then enquired whether they were significantly aided by the agency relationship in committing the harassment, and also considered the possibility of imputing Gordon's knowledge of the harassment to the City. Finally, the Court of Appeals ruled out liability for negligence in failing to prevent the harassment. Faragher relies principally on the latter three theories of liability.

I

A "master is subject to liability for the torts of his servants committed while acting in the scope of their

employment." Restatement § 219(1). This doctrine has traditionally defined the "scope of employment" as including conduct "of the kind [a servant] is employed to perform," occurring "substantially within the authorized time and space limits," and "actuated, at least in part, by a purpose to serve the master," but as excluding an intentional use of force "unexpectable by the master."

Courts of Appeals have typically held, or assumed, that conduct similar to the subject of this complaint falls outside the scope of employment. In so doing, the courts have emphasized that harassment consisting of unwelcome remarks and touching is motivated solely by individual desires and serves no purpose of the employer. For this reason, courts have likened hostile environment sexual harassment to the classic "frolic and detour" for which an employer has no vicarious liability.

These cases ostensibly stand in some tension with others arising outside Title VII, where the scope of employment has been defined broadly enough to hold employers vicariously liable for intentional torts that were in no sense inspired by any purpose to serve the employer . . .

The proper analysis here, then, calls not for a mechanical application of indefinite and malleable factors set forth in the Restatement, but rather an enquiry into the reasons that would support a conclusion that harassing behavior ought to be held within the scope of a supervisor's employment, and the reasons for the opposite view. The Restatement itself points to such an approach, as in the commentary that the "ultimate question" in determining the scope of employment is "whether or not it is just that the loss resulting from the servant's acts should be considered as one of the normal risks to be borne by the business in which the servant is employed."

In the case before us, a justification for holding the offensive behavior within the scope of Terry's and Silverman's employment was well put in Judge Barkett's dissent: "[A] pervasively hostile work environment of sexual harassment is never (one would hope) authorized, but the supervisor is clearly charged with maintaining a productive, safe work environment. The supervisor directs and controls the conduct of the employees, and the manner of doing so may inure to the employer's benefit or detriment, including subjecting the employer to Title VII liability." It is by now well recognized that hostile environment sexual harassment by supervisors (and, for that matter, co-employees) is a persistent problem in the workplace. An employer can, in a general sense, reasonably anticipate the possibility of such conduct occurring in its workplace, and one might justify the assignment of the burden of the untoward behavior to the employer as one of the costs of doing business, to be charged to the enterprise rather than the victim.

Two things counsel us to draw the contrary conclusion. First, there is no reason to suppose that Congress wished courts to ignore the traditional distinction between acts falling within the scope and acts amounting to what the older law called frolics or detours from the course of employment. Such a distinction can readily be applied to the spectrum of possible harassing conduct by supervisors, as the following examples show. First, a supervisor might discriminate racially in job assignments in order to placate the prejudice pervasive in the labor force. Instances of this variety of the heckler's veto would be consciously intended to further the employer's interests by preserving peace in the workplace. Next, supervisors might reprimand male employees for workplace failings with banter, but respond to women's shortcomings in harsh or vulgar terms. A third example might be the supervisor who, as here, expresses his sexual interests in ways having no apparent object whatever of serving an interest of the employer. If a line is to be drawn between scope and frolic, it would lie between the first two examples and the third, and it thus makes sense in terms of traditional agency law to analyze the scope issue, in cases like the third example, just as most federal courts addressing that issue have done, classifying the harassment as beyond the scope of employment.

The second reason goes to an even broader unanimity of views among the holdings of District Courts and Courts of Appeals thus far. Those courts have held not only that the sort of harassment at issue here was outside the scope of supervisors' authority, but, by uniformly judging employer liability for co-worker harassment under a negligence standard, they have also implicitly treated such harassment as outside the scope of common employees' duties as well. If, indeed, the cases did not rest, at least implicitly, on the notion that such harassment falls outside the scope of employment, their liability issues would have turned simply on the application of the scope-of-employment rule.

It is quite unlikely that these cases would escape efforts to render them obsolete if we were to hold that supervisors who engage in discriminatory harassment are necessarily acting within the scope of their employment. The rationale for placing harassment within the scope of supervisory authority would be the fairness of requiring the employer to bear the burden of foreseeable social behavior, and the same rationale would apply when the behavior was that of co-employees. The employer generally benefits just as obviously from the work of common employees as from the work of supervisors; they simply have different jobs to do, all aimed at the success of the enterprise. As between an innocent employer and an innocent employee, if we use scope of employment reasoning to require the employer to bear the cost of an actionably hostile workplace created by one class of employees (*i.e.*, supervisors), it could appear just as appropriate to do the same when the environment was created by another class (*i.e.*, co-workers).

The answer to this argument might well be to point out that the scope of supervisory employment may be treated separately by recognizing that supervisors have special authority enhancing their capacity to harass, and that the employer can guard against their misbehavior more easily because their numbers are by definition fewer than the numbers of regular employees. But this answer happens to implicate an entirely separate category of agency law (to be considered in the next section), which imposes vicarious liability on employers for tortious acts committed by use of particular authority conferred as an element of an employee's agency relationship with the employer. Since the virtue of categorical clarity is obvious, it is better to reject reliance on misuse of supervisory authority (without more) as irrelevant to scope-of-employment analysis.

2

The Court of Appeals also rejected vicarious liability on the part of the City insofar as it might rest on the concluding principle set forth in § 219(2)(d) of the Restatement, that an employer "is not subject to liability for the torts of his servants acting outside the scope of their employment unless . . . the servant purported to act or speak on behalf of the principal and there was reliance on apparent authority, or he was aided in accomplishing the tort by the existence of the agency relation." Faragher points to several ways in which the agency relationship aided Terry and Silverman in carrying out their harassment. She argues that in general offending supervisors can abuse their authority to keep subordinates in their presence while they make offensive statements, and that they implicitly threaten to misuse their supervisory powers to deter any resistance or complaint. Thus, she maintains that power conferred on Terry and Silverman by the City enabled them to act for so long without provoking defiance or complaint.

The City, however, contends that § 219(2)(d) has no application here. It argues that the second qualification of the subsection, referring to a servant "aided in accomplishing the tort by the existence of the agency relation," merely "refines" the one preceding it, which holds the employer vicariously liable for its servant's abuse of apparent authority. But this narrow reading is untenable; it would render the second qualification of § 219(2)(d) almost entirely superfluous (and would seem to ask us to shut our eyes to the potential effects of supervisory authority, even when not explicitly invoked). The illustrations accompanying this subsection make clear that it covers not only cases involving the abuse of apparent authority, but also to cases in which tortious conduct is made possible or facilitated by the existence of the actual agency relationship.

We therefore agree with Faragher that in implementing Title VII it makes sense to hold an employer vicariously liable for some tortious conduct of a supervisor made possible by abuse of his supervisory authority, and that the aided-by-agency-relation principle embodied in § 219(2)(d) of the Restatement provides an appropriate starting point for determining liability for the kind of harassment presented here. Several courts, indeed, have noted what Faragher has argued, that there is a sense in which a harassing supervisor is always assisted in his misconduct by the supervisory relationship. The agency relationship affords contact with an employee subjected to a supervisor's sexual harassment, and the victim may well be reluctant to accept the risks of blowing the whistle on a superior. When a person with supervisory authority discriminates in the terms and conditions of subordinates' employment, his actions necessarily draw upon his superior position over the people who report to him, or those under them, whereas an employee generally cannot check a supervisor's abusive conduct the same way that she might deal with abuse from a co-worker. When a fellow employee harasses, the victim can walk away or tell the offender where to go, but it may be difficult to offer such responses to a supervisor, whose "power to supervise—[which may be] to hire and fire, and to set work schedules and pay rates—does not disappear . . . when he chooses to harass through insults and offensive gestures rather than directly with threats of firing or promises of promotion." Recognition of employer liability when discriminatory misuse of supervisory authority alters the terms and conditions of a victim's employment is underscored by the fact that the employer has a greater opportunity to guard against misconduct by supervisors than by common workers; employers have greater opportunity and incentive to screen them, train them, and monitor their performance.

In sum, there are good reasons for vicarious liability for misuse of supervisory authority. That rationale must, however, satisfy one more condition. We are not entitled to recognize this theory under Title VII unless we can square it with *Meritor's* holding that an employer is not "automatically" liable for harassment by a supervisor who creates the requisite degree of discrimination, and there is obviously some tension between that holding and the position that a supervisor's misconduct aided by supervisory authority subjects the employer to liability vicariously; if the "aid" may be the unspoken suggestion of retaliation by misuse of supervisory authority, the risk of automatic liability is high. To counter it, we think there are two basic alternatives, one being to require proof of some affirmative invocation of that authority by the harassing supervisor, the other to recognize an affirmative defense to liability in some circumstances, even when a supervisor has created the actionable environment.

There is certainly some authority for requiring active or affirmative, as distinct from passive or implicit, misuse of supervisory authority before liability may be imputed. That is the way some courts have viewed the familiar cases holding the employer liable for discriminatory employment action with tangible consequences, like firing and demotion. And we have already noted some examples of liability provided by the Restatement itself, which suggests that an affirmative misuse of power might be required.

But neat examples illustrating the line between the affirmative and merely implicit uses of power are not easy to come by in considering management behavior. Supervisors do not make speeches threatening sanctions whenever they make requests in the legitimate exercise of managerial authority, and yet every subordinate employee knows the sanctions exist; this is the reason that courts have consistently held that acts of supervisors have greater power to alter the environment than acts of co-employees generally. How far from the course of ostensible supervisory behavior would a company officer have to step before his orders would not reasonably be seen as actively using authority? Judgment calls would often be close, the results would often seem disparate even if not demonstrably contradictory, and the temptation to litigate would be hard to resist. We think plaintiffs and defendants alike would be poorly served by an active-use rule.

The other basic alternative to automatic liability would avoid this particular temptation to litigate, but allow an employer to show as an affirmative defense to liability that the employer had exercised reasonable care to avoid harassment and to eliminate it when it might occur, and that the complaining employee had failed to act with like reasonable care to take advantage of the employer's safeguards and otherwise to prevent harm that could have been avoided. This composite defense would, we think, implement the statute sensibly, for reasons that are not hard to fathom.

Although Title VII seeks "to make persons whole for injuries suffered on account of unlawful employment discrimination," its "primary objective," like that of any statute meant to influence primary conduct, is not to provide redress but to avoid harm. As long ago as 1980, the Equal Employment Opportunity Commission (EEOC), charged with the enforcement of Title VII, *42 U.S.C. § 2000e-4*, adopted regulations advising employers to "take all steps necessary to prevent sexual harassment from occurring, such as . . . informing employees of their right to raise and how to raise the issue of harassment." and in 1990 the Commission issued a policy statement enjoining employers to establish a complaint procedure "designed to encourage victims of harassment to come forward [without requiring] a victim to complain first to the offending supervisor." It would therefore implement clear statutory policy and complement the Government's Title VII enforcement efforts to recognize the employer's affirmative obligation to prevent violations and give credit here to employers who make reasonable efforts to discharge their duty. Indeed, a theory of vicarious liability for misuse of supervisory power would be at odds with the statutory policy if it failed to provide employers with some such incentive.

The requirement to show that the employee has failed in a coordinate duty to avoid or mitigate harm reflects an equally obvious policy imported from the general theory of damages, that a victim has a duty "to use such means as are reasonable under the circumstances to avoid or minimize the damages" that result from violations of the statute. An employer may, for example, have provided a proven, effective mechanism for reporting and resolving complaints of sexual harassment, available to the employee without undue risk or expense. If the plaintiff unreasonably failed to avail herself of the employer's preventive or remedial apparatus, she should not recover damages that could have been avoided if she had done so. If the victim could have avoided harm, no liability should be found against the employer who had taken reasonable care, and if damages could reasonably have been mitigated no award against a liable employer should reward a plaintiff for what her own efforts could have avoided.

In order to accommodate the principle of vicarious liability for harm caused by misuse of supervisory authority, as well as Title VII's equally basic policies of encouraging forethought by employers and saving action by objecting employees, we adopt the following holding in this case and in *Burlington Industries, Inc.* v. *Ellerth*, also decided today. An employer is subject to vicarious liability to a victimized employee for an actionable hostile environment created by a supervisor with immediate (or successively higher) authority over the employee. When no tangible employment action is taken, a defending employer may raise an affirmative defense to liability or damages, subject to proof by a preponderance of the evidence, see *Fed. Rule. Civ. Proc. 8(c)*. The defense comprises two necessary elements: (a) that the employer exercised reasonable care to prevent and correct promptly any sexually harassing behavior, and (b) that the plaintiff employee unreasonably failed to take advantage of any preventive or corrective opportunities provided by the employer or to avoid harm otherwise. While proof that an employer had promulgated an antiharassment policy with complaint procedure is not necessary in every instance as a matter of law, the need for a stated policy suitable to the employment circumstances may appropriately be addressed in any case when litigating the first element of the defense. And while proof that an employee failed to fulfill the corresponding obligation of reasonable care to avoid harm is not limited to showing an unreasonable failure to use any complaint procedure provided by the employer, a demonstration of such failure will normally suffice to satisfy the employer's burden under the second element of the defense. No affirmative defense is available, however, when the supervisor's harassment culminates in a tangible employment action, such as discharge, demotion, or undesirable reassignment.

Applying these rules here, we believe that the judgment of the Court of Appeals must be reversed. The District Court found that the degree of hostility in the work environment rose to the actionable level and was attributable to Silverman and Terry. It is undisputed that these supervisors "were granted virtually unchecked authority" over their subordinates, "directly controlling and supervising all aspects of [Faragher's] day-to-day activities." It is also clear that Faragher and her colleagues were "completely isolated from the City's higher management." The City did not seek review of these findings.

While the City would have an opportunity to raise an affirmative defense if there were any serious prospect of its presenting one, it appears from the record that any such avenue is closed. The District Court found that the City had entirely failed to disseminate its policy against sexual harassment among the beach employees and that its officials made no attempt to keep track of the conduct of supervisors like Terry and Silverman. The record also makes clear that the City's policy did not include any assurance that the harassing supervisors could be bypassed in registering complaints. Under such circumstances, we hold as a matter of law that the City could not be found to have exercised reasonable care to prevent the supervisors' harassing conduct. Unlike the employer of a small workforce, who might expect that sufficient care to prevent tortious behavior could be exercised informally, those responsible for city operations could not reasonably have thought that precautions against hostile environments in any one of many departments in far-flung locations could be effective without communicating some formal policy against harassment, with a sensible complaint procedure. . . .

III

The judgment of the Court of Appeals for the Eleventh Circuit is reversed, and the case is remanded for reinstatement of the judgment of the District Court.

It is so ordered.

Recent Trends

State Legislative Protection. State legislation can greatly enhance protection against sexual harassment, In *Morehouse v. Berkshire Gas Co.*, obscenely defaced photos of plaintiff Sheryl Morehouse were posted at the Berkshire Gas Company Fall Classic Golf Tournament (one was hung at the first tee, another was affixed to a garbage barrel at the fifth tee and was urinated on, another was attached to the flag at the ninth hole, and at least five more defaced photos were recovered from various other spots). Under

Mass. Gen. Laws ch. 151B, s 4(5) individuals may be held liable for aiding or abetting discriminatory conduct that is prohibited under state law. Under Title VII, only the employer is liable for the acts of employees under the guidelines previously discussed and outlined in Table 2. Massachusetts legislation broadens the application of sexual harassment protection by holding individuals liable for their behavior, as well as others as aiders or abettors. This state legislation also extends the scope of responsibility of the employer, even when the supervisory employees are not acting within the scope of their employment (such as socially golfing at an outing).

References

Cases

Barnes v. Costle, 561 F.2d 983 (D.C. 1977).
Burlington Industries, Inc. v. Ellerth, 524 U.S. 742 (1998).
Davis v. Monroe County Board of Education, 119 S.Ct. 1161 (1999).
Faragher v. City of Boca Raton, 524 U.S. 775 (1998).
Gebser v. Lago Vista Independent School District, 524 U.S. 274 (1998).
Harris v. Forklift Systems, Inc., 510 U.S. 17 (1993).
Meritor Savings Bank, FSB v. Vinson, 477 U.S. 57 (1986).
Miller v. Bank of America, 600 F.2d 211 (9th Cir. 1979).
Morehouse v. Berkshire Gas Co. 989 F. Supp. 54, 61 (D. Mass. 1997).
Williams v. Saxbe, 1976 413 F.Supp. 654 (DDC 1976).

Publications

George, B. G. (1999). Employer liability for sexual harassment: The buck stops where? *Wake Forest Law Review, 34*(1), 1–25.

Legislation

Title VII of the Civil Rights Act, 42 U.S.C. 2000e et seq. (2006).
Title VII Guidelines on Discrimination Because of Sex, 29 C.F.R. 1604.11
EEOC Notice 915.002 (6/18/1999) Enforcement Guidance: Vicarious Employer Liability for Unlawful Harassment by Supervisors.
Title IX of the Education Act of 1974, 20 U.S.C. 1681 (2005).
OCR Notice: Revised Sexual Harassment Guidance: Harassment of Students by School Employees, Other Students, or Third Parties (11/02/2000) 65 Fed. Reg. 213. pp. 66091-66114.

8.15 Age Discrimination in Employment Act

David Snyder

State University of New York College at Cortland

The Equal Employment Opportunity Commission (EEOC) reported that $69 million in damages were awarded in 2004 under the Age Discrimination in Employment Act (ADEA). The $69 million figure, which excludes monetary awards from litigation, represents the highest amount recovered from ADEA-related cases in a single year from 1992 to 2004. For 2004, that breaks down to approximately $130,930 awarded for each claim that was deemed to have "reasonable cause." The total damages derived from ADEA complaints in 2004 rose 141 percent from $48.9 million in 2003 (EEOC Website, http://www.eeoc.gov/stats/adea.html). This data does not include age discrimination actions based on other federal and state laws.

Although not all age discrimination claims involve sport or recreation, there have been a number of age discrimination lawsuits initiated by coaches, and these cases appear to be on the rise. For example, in 2005, Ferne Labati, the former coach of the University of Miami's women's basketball team, filed a lawsuit against her former employer alleging age- and gender-based discrimination. Labati, who was sixty years old when she was fired, was replaced by a thirty-seven-year-old. She was inducted into the university's Sports Hall of Fame just eleven months before she was terminated. Another example is Don Moreau, the former baseball coach at Loyola University, New Orleans, who filed an age discrimination lawsuit against the university in 2003. Loyola claimed that Moreau, who had coached baseball at Loyola for twelve years, needed a college degree to be a full-time coach at Loyola. Moreau, who was sixty-five years old at the time he was fired, was replaced by a thirty-three-year-old as head baseball coach.

In addition, the stakes in age discrimination cases are often high. In 2000, two former golf coaches at California State University at San Bernardino were initially awarded $1.2 million from a jury as part of an age discrimination case against their former employer. This amount was reduced to $750,000 on appeal. Two years after being fired as a sportscaster by ABC Sports in 1998, former Olympian Donna De Varona filed a $50 million unlawful termination lawsuit against her former employer alleging she was discriminated based on her age and gender. The case was later settled out of court. These examples, coupled with the legal costs to defend such cases, reflect the financial risk involved with age discrimination litigation.

With people living longer, healthier lives, our workforce is steadily growing older. This demographic shift has often come into direct conflict with the economic reality of reductions in the labor force and other cost-cutting measures. The tension between an aging society and these dynamic market forces, and the growing risk of liability in these cases make it vital for sport and recreation managers to have a clear understanding age discrimination laws.

Fundamental Concepts

Federal Legislation

The Age Discrimination in Employment Act of 1967 (ADEA)

The Age Discrimination in Employment Act protects employees and job applicants who are forty years of age or older from employment discrimination based on age. The ADEA, which applies to employers with 20 or more employees, pertains to various terms and conditions of employment, including but not limited to the hiring process, compensation schemes, promotion decisions, job assignments, training opportunities, temporary layoffs, and termination of employment.

Although the ADEA was modeled after Title VII, there are some noteworthy differences between the two statutes. One such distinction is that the definition of what constitutes an "employer" under the ADEA is broader than Title VII. Unlike Title VII, the ADEA does not exclude groups such as religious organizations or Native American tribes, among others, from being characterized as "employer" under the statute. The ADEA specifically defines an "employer" as "a person engaged in an industry affecting commerce who has twenty or more employees for each working day in each of twenty or more calendar weeks in the current or preceding calendar year" (29 U.S.C.A. §630(b)).

There are some limitations to the scope of the ADEA. For example, certain employees that are vital to public safety and welfare, such as police officers, cannot seek protection under the ADEA. Employees under forty years of age cannot seek relief under the ADEA, even if they are subject to discrimination in the workplace based on age.

Enforcement of the ADEA falls under the purview of the Equal Employment Opportunity Commission (EEOC). A party alleging age discrimination under the ADEA is generally required to file a claim with the EEOC within 180 days from the date of the challenged conduct. However, that deadline may be extended if the claimant also has a claim under state law (see following).

Until recently, the only way to establish a claim under the ADEA was for the plaintiff to prove that age was the motivating factor for the challenged conduct. One theory of liability under the ADEA is for the plaintiff to prove **disparate treatment** by a direct showing that the employer intentionally discriminated or displayed discriminatory animus against the plaintiff solely because of the plaintiff's age. Another theory is that the defendant engaged in **systemic disparate treatment** by instituting widespread employment practices that displayed a pattern of discrimination based on age. In 2005, the U.S. Supreme Court substantially expanded the ADEA by also allowing claims based on **disparate impact** (see *Smith v. City of Jackson*, 2005 later in this chapter under Recent Trends for details). In *City of Jackson*, the Court held that an employment practice that discriminates based on age could be considered unlawful under the ADEA, regardless of the discriminatory intent of the employer.

To establish a prima facie case under the ADEA, the plaintiff must establish the following elements by a preponderance of the evidence:

1. The plaintiff is an employee or applicant for employment with the employer.
2. The employee is a member of the protected class (i.e., forty years old or above).
3. The employer has twenty or more employees.
4. The plaintiff was qualified for the job (if an applicant for employment) or was performing the duties and responsibilities of the job satisfactorily. (if an employee).
5. The plaintiff suffered some adverse condition with respect to their employment (e.g., was not hired, was fired).
6. The employer hired someone outside the protected class (for job applicants) or replaced the plaintiff with someone outside the protected class (for employees).

In addition to these theories of liability, it is unlawful to retaliate against someone for filing an age discrimination charge, participating in an investigation, or testifying in a proceeding or lawsuit filed under the ADEA. The ADEA states, "It shall be unlawful for an employer to discriminate against any of his employees or applicants for employment, for an employment agency to discriminate against any individual, or for a labor organization to discriminate against any member thereof or applicant for membership, because such individual, member or applicant for membership has opposed any practice made unlawful by this section, or because such individual, member or applicant for membership has made a charge, testified, assisted, or participated in any manner in an investigation, proceeding, or litigation under this chapter" (29 U.S.C.A. §623(d)). The elements for a retaliation claim under the ADEA are identical to the filing of such a claim under Title VII.

It is also a violation of the ADEA to harass older workers or subject them to a hostile work environment (*Eggleston v. South Bend Community School Corporation*, 1994). Once again, the criteria for a harassment claim under the ADEA and Title VII are the same.

Once the plaintiff establishes a prima facie case under the ADEA, the burden shifts to the defendant to establish a defense by a preponderance of the evidence. One affirmative defense that can be asserted in ADEA cases is that *other reasonable factors besides age* prompted the employer's conduct. Another defense to a claim under the ADEA is to prove that a **bona fide occupational qualification (BFOQ)** exists by demonstrating that age is a legitimate factor to consider for the performance of that particular job (e.g., airline pilots, firefighters, police officers) Certain seniority systems may be free from ADEA attack, provided the scheme does not discriminate against older workers. (For a discussion of reduction of benefit plans to older workers, see the OWPA following.)

Assuming the defendant is able to provide a legitimate, nondiscriminatory reason for the alleged discrimination, the burden then shifts back to the plaintiff to refute the defendant's purported rationale by showing that the justification offered is merely a **pretext** for actual discrimination. Plaintiffs typically attempt to establish pretext by offering evidence of pervasive bias against members of the protected class (older workers in this case) or by introducing into evidence data reflecting inequity or favoritism among certain classes of employees.

If the plaintiff prevails in age discrimination claim under the ADEA, the plaintiff is entitled to back pay for lost wages. The plaintiff may also receive liquidated damages if the defendant's conduct is found to be willful. In addition, the court may, in its discretion, order that the plaintiff be reinstated or promoted or award the plaintiff front pay for loss of future wages (*Moore v. The University of Notre Dame*, 1998).

Older Workers Benefit Protection Act (OWBPA)

In 1990, Congress amended the ADEA with the enactment of The Older Workers Benefit Protection Act (OWBPA), which specifically prohibits employers from denying benefits to older workers. However, under the OWBPA, an employer may reduce the benefit plans for older workers provided that the cost of such plans is the same as the cost of providing benefits to younger employees.

The OWBPA is also significant in that it imposes extremely stringent standards for settling a claim under the ADEA. There is no counterpart to these provisions in Title VII, and as a result, it is more difficult to settle an ADEA case.

In addition, the OWBPA contains very specific criteria that must be met for an employee to waive rights secured under the ADEA. To be valid, such a waiver must

1. Be in writing.
2. Be clear and unambiguous.
3. Clearly make reference to ADEA rights or claims.
4. Only apply to current rights and claims. It cannot waive future rights or claims that might arise in the future.
5. Be in exchange for valuable consideration.
6. Contain a clause advising the employee to consult an attorney before signing the waiver.
7. Allow the employee twenty-one days to consider the waiver before it becomes effective.
8. Give the employee at least seven days to revoke the waiver after signing it.

State Legislation

In addition to federal law, most states have some type of law prohibiting age discrimination. Some state statutes provide different or greater protection than the ADEA, and therefore they may provide relief in circumstances where the ADEA does not apply. For example, some states allow age discrimination cases for workers younger than forty years of age. Other states statues extend age discrimination protection to workplaces with fewer than twenty employees. In a few states, age discrimination can be a criminal offense.

In addition, states typically have their own administrative agencies that handle age discrimination claims based on state law, as well as their own deadlines for filing such claims. EEOC refers to such state agencies as **Fair Employment Practices Agencies (FEPAs).** The EEOC and the FEPAs have agreements that are designed to enable the state and federal agencies to work together efficiently and that allow for "dual filing" when a party has a claim based on both state and federal law. The general 180-day deadline for filing an ADEA claim with the EEOC is extended to 300 days if the charge also is covered by a state law.

For these reasons, it is important for the sport and recreation manager to be aware of the applicable state laws concerning age discrimination in addition to the pertinent federal legislation.

Alternative Legal Grounds for Relief

In addition to state and federal age discrimination laws, other areas of law may provide the basis for a claim in situations where an individual is discriminated against based on age. However, these are not considered true "age discrimination" cases because the cause of action is not based on a law that prohibits discrimination based on age. For example, Maurice Clarett's lawsuit against the NFL challenged the league rule making players ineligible for the draft until they were three seasons removed from their high school graduations. Although the impact of the league rule was to discriminate against Clarett based on his age, his suit was based on the claim that the league unreasonably restrained free trade in violation of antitrust law.

Significant Case

─────────────◇◇◇─────────────

One of the more publicized sport-related age discrimination cases involved the termination of Joe Moore as assistant football coach at Notre Dame University. Moore prevailed against Notre Dame on his age discrimination claim at trial and was awarded back pay and liquidated damages by the jury. After the trial, Moore moved to either be reinstated to his former position or awarded front pay in addition to the damages already awarded him by the jury. The portion of the decision dealing with Moore's request for attorney's fees and costs has been omitted.

JOSEPH R. MOORE V. UNIVERSITY OF NOTRE DAME
UNITED STATES DISTRICT COURT FOR THE NORTHERN DISTRICT OF INDIANA
22 F. Supp. 2d 896 (1998)

This cause is before this Court on Plaintiff's Motion for Award of Reinstatement/Front Pay and Plaintiff's Bill of Costs. Plaintiff, Joseph R. Moore (Moore) filed a claim in this Court against The University of Notre Dame (Notre Dame) alleging age discrimination, retaliation, and defamation. Only the age discrimination claim survived summary judgment. The case went to trial in Lafayette on July 9, 1998. On July 15, 1998, after four and one-half hours of deliberation, the Jury found that Notre Dame had violated the Age Discrimination in Employment Act (ADEA) and awarded Moore back pay in the amount of $42,935.28. Additionally, because the jury determined that Notre Dame's violation of ADEA was willful, Plaintiff also was awarded liquidated damages in the additional amount of $42,935.28. Judgment must and now does enter in favor of the plaintiff, Joseph E. Moore and against the defendant, Notre Dame in the amount of $85,870.56. Accordingly, the Court now considers Moore's post-trial motions.

* * *

I. RELIEF UNDER THE ADEA

The remedial scheme for a discriminatory discharge is designed to make a plaintiff who has been the victim of discrimination whole through the use of equitable remedies. *See Albemarle Paper Co. v. Moody*, 422 U.S. 405, 95 S. Ct. 2362, 45 L. Ed. 2d 280 (1975) (discussing equitable remedies for Title VII); *Straka v. Francis*, 867 F. Supp. 767 (N.D. Ill. 1994) (stating that ADEA and Title VII are treated similarly regarding available remedies). When confronted with a violation of the ADEA, a district court is authorized to afford relief by means of reinstatement, back pay, injunctive relief, declaratory judgment, and attorney's fees. 29 U.S.C. § 626(b); *McKennon v. Nashville Banner Pub'g Co.*, 513 U.S. 352, 357-58, 115 S. Ct. 879, 884, 130 L. Ed. 2d 852 (1995); *see also Lorillard v. Pons*, 434 U.S. 575, 584, 98 S. Ct. 866, 872, 55 L. Ed. 2d 40 (1978). Additionally, in the case of a willful violation of the Act, the

ADEA authorizes an award of liquidated damages equal to the back pay award. 29 U.S.C. § 626(b).

* * *

Moore now asks the Court to reinstate him in his former coaching position, or to award five year's front pay in lieu of reinstatement. Notre Dame contends that Moore has received all relief to which he was entitled and therefore asks this Court to deny Moore's Motion for Reinstatement/Front Pay.

A. Reinstatement

Although reinstatement is the preferred remedy in a discrimination case, it is not always appropriate. The factors which should be considered when determining its propriety include, hostility in the past employment relationship and the absence of an available position for the plaintiff. Civil Rights Act of 1964, § 701 *et seq.*, as amended, 42 U.S.C.A. § 2000e *et seq.*; *McKnight v. General Motors Corp.*, 973 F.2d 1366, 1370 (7th Cir. 1992); *Ward v. Tipton County Sheriff Dept.*, 937 F. Supp. 791 (S.D. Ind.1996). Additionally, under ADEA, when a period for reinstatement is relatively short, such that plaintiff is close to retirement, the strong preference in favor of reinstatement is neutralized by the increased certainty of potential loss of pay permitting consideration of a front pay award. *See McNeil v. Economics Laboratory, Inc.*, 800 F.2d 111, 118 (7th Cir. 1986), *cert. denied*, 481 U.S. 1041, 107 S. Ct. 1983, 95 L. Ed. 2d 823 (1987), overruled on other grounds by *Coston v. Plitt Theatres, Inc.*, 860 F.2d 834 (7th Cir. 1988). *See also, Chace v. Champion Spark Plug Co.*, 732 F. Supp. 605 (D. Md. 1990).

1. Hostility

The decision to reinstate a discriminatorily terminated employee is consigned to the sound discretion of the district court which should not grant reinstatement "where the result would be undue friction and controversy." *McKnight v. General Motors Corp.*, 908 F.2d 104, 115 (7th Cir. 1990); *Wilson v. AM General Corp.*, 979 F. Supp. 800 (N.D. Ind. 1997) (may consider friction that exists between employer and employee unrelated to discrimination). Evidence that hostility developed between the employer and employee during litigation may also be considered, but is not dispositive. *U.S. E.E.O.C. v. Century Broadcasting Corp.*, 957 F.2d 1446 (7th Cir. 1992); *Cassino v. Reichhold Chemicals, Inc.*, 817 F.2d 1338 (9th Cir. 1987).

In the present case, Moore's reinstatement would cause significant friction as well as disruption of the current football program. Moore and Davie, his direct supervisor, are no longer on speaking terms. During trial, sufficient evidence was presented to infer that Moore and Davie would be unable to engage in a workable relationship. Reinstatement in this instance is impracticable. Moreover, even if hostility and undue friction were not a problem, reinstatement is not appropriate in this case.

2. Available Position

The Seventh Circuit has also held that reinstatement can reasonably be denied when "someone else currently occupies the employee's former position." *Century Broadcasting*, 957 F.2d 1446 (*quoting Graefenhain v. Pabst Brewing Co.* 870 F.2d 1198, 1208 (7th Cir. 1989). Other Circuits hold similarly. *See e.g., Ray v. Iuka Special Mun. Separate School Dist.*, 51 F.3d 1246, 1254 (5th Cir. 1995); *Shore v. Federal Express Corp.*, 777 F.2d 1155, 1157-59 (6th Cir. 1985); *Spagnuolo v. Whirlpool Corp.*, 717 F.2d 114, 119-122 (4th Cir. 1983) (holding that reinstatement is not appropriate if it requires bumping or displacing innocent employee in favor of plaintiff). The law is clear. Even if this Court determined that reinstatement is warranted, it is not an appropriate remedy in this case as there is no available position to which Moore could return. Therefore, the Court turns to the more difficult issue of whether front-pay is warranted.

B. Front Pay

Plaintiff is incorrect in stating that "if the Court rejects Moore's request for reinstatement, it *must* award him front pay." (Pl.'s Mem. at 7) (emphasis added). Front pay is an available remedy under ADEA, however, such an award remains discretionary with court. *Williams v. Pharmacia Opthalmics, Inc.*, 926 F. Supp. 791 (N.D. Ind. 1996), *aff'd*, 137 F.3d 944 (7th Cir. 1997); *Downes v. Volkswagen of America, Inc.*, 41 F.3d 1132, 1141 (7th Cir. 1993); *Tennes v. Commonwealth of Massachusetts Dept. of Revenue*, 944 F.2d 372, 381 (7th Cir. 1991); *Drago v. Aetna Plywood, Inc.*, 1998 U.S. Dist. LEXIS 12249, No.96C2398, 1998 WL 474100 (N.D. Ill. Aug. 3, 1998). The Seventh Circuit has defined front pay as "a lump sum . . . representing the discounted present value of the difference between the earnings (an employee) would have received in his old employment and the earnings he can be expected to receive in his present and future, and by hypothesis, inferior, employment. *Century Broadcasting*, 957 F.2d 1446, 1463 n.18 (quoting *McKnight*, 908 F.2d 104, 116). *See also, Downes*, 41 F.3d 1132, 1141, n. 8. Such a remedy may especially be indicated when the plaintiff has no reasonable prospect of obtaining comparable employment or when the time period for which front pay is to be awarded is relatively short. *Inks v. Healthcare Distributors of Indiana, Inc.*, 901 F. Supp. 1403 (N.D. Ind. 1995). *See e.g., Nelson v. Boatmen's Bancshares, Inc.*, 26 F.3d 796 (8th Cir. 1994) (front pay appropriate when employee is nearing retirement age); *Duke v. Uniroyal, Inc.*, 928 F.2d 1413 (4th Cir. 1991); *Linn v. Andover Newton Theological School, Inc.*, 874 F.2d 1 (1st Cir. 1989); *Stratton v. Department for the Aging for the City of New York*, 922 F. Supp. 857 (S.D. N.Y. 1996) (all holding similarly). The court determines the amount of front pay to award depending on whether:

1. the plaintiff has a reasonable prospect of obtaining comparable employment;
2. the time period for the award is relatively short;
3. the plaintiff intends to work or is physically capable of working; and
4. liquidated damages have been awarded.

Williams, 926 F. Supp. 791, 796 (finding an award of front pay in Title VII context proper and consistent with the 1991 amendments). Front pay is awarded for a reasonable period of time, until a date by which the plaintiff, using reasonable diligence, should have found comparable employment. *Hutchison v. Amateur Electronics Supply, Inc.*, 840 F. Supp. 612 (E.D. Wisc. 1993), *aff'd. in part, rev'd in part*, 42 F.3d 1037 at 1045 (7th Cir. 1994). Moreover, an award must be grounded in available facts, acceptable to a reasonable person and not highly speculative. *Downes*, 41 F.3d at 1142. It cannot be based simply on a plaintiff's own stated intentions with regard to how long he or she would have worked. *Pierce v. Atchison, Topeka & Santa Fe Ry. Co.*, 65 F.3d 562, 574 (7th Cir.1995).

Notre Dame contends that Moore is not entitled to front pay because 1) evidence acquired by Notre Dame after Moore's discharge would have led to his discharge based on legitimate, non-discriminatory reasons, 2) Moore's award of liquidated damages has already made him whole, and 3) Moore has failed to make reasonable efforts to mitigate his damages.

1. Award of Liquidated Damages

The fact that Moore is entitled to damages based on the jury's finding of a wilful violation does not conclusively preclude front pay. Front pay *may be* less appropriate when liquidated damages are awarded. *Id.* (emphasis added); *Hybert v. Hearst Corp.*, 900 F.2d 1050, 1056 (7th Cir. 1990) (liquidated damages are a relevant consideration in determining *whether and how much* front pay to award). Authority clearly states that liquidated damages is *one* factor to be considered in awarding front pay and does not stand for the proposition that front pay and liquidated damages may never be awarded to the same plaintiff. *Century Broadcasting*, 957 F.2d 1446, 1450; *McNeil*, 800 F.2d 111, 118; *Graefenhain*, 870 F.2d 1198, 1,205. Furthermore, an award of front pay, constituting an estimate of what the employee might have earned had he been reinstated at the conclusion of trial is necessarily speculative, this speculative aspect should not deter courts from fashioning awards that accomplish ADEA's goal of making a wronged employee whole. *Selgas v. American Airlines, Inc.*, 104 F.3d 9 (1st Cir. 1997), on remand 977 F. Supp. 100 (D. P.R 1997).

In the present case, Notre Dame argues that Moore's jury award of $42,935.28 and liquidated damages award of $42,935.28 makes him whole and that further compensation would "be a total award greater than the statute contemplates." *Avitia v. Metropolitan Club of Chicago, Inc.*, 49 F.3d 1219, 1232 (7th Cir. 1995). The Court disagrees. Moore's 1996–97 annual salary was $79,552.08. Assuming an annual increase of 4%, his 1997–98 salary would have been $82,734.16 and his 1998–99 salary $86,043.53. In addition to loss of salary, Moore also lost several benefits. It is unlikely he will be able to duplicate the benefits and prestige the Notre Dame position provided him. Moreover, as Moore is at or near retirement age, it is unlikely he will find comparable employment at the salary level he enjoyed while at Notre Dame. *Compare, Stratton*, 922 F. Supp. 857 (S.D. N.Y. 1996) (finding front pay appropriate in ADEA action, where it was clear from evidence presented at trial that employee, who was now 66 years of age, had no reasonable prospect of obtaining positions similar to that she previously held). The evidence showed that Moore had coached at Notre Dame for nine years and intended to continue in that position until retirement. Moore has been unable to replace his Notre Dame position with a comparable one. He is currently earning $46,600 and working three jobs. In this Court's opinion, the jury award has not "made him whole" and front pay may be appropriate.

2. After-Acquired Evidence

Notre Dame also asserts that Moore is not entitled to front pay because Notre Dame Administrators made it clear that had they known of Moore's alleged physical and verbal abuse of players, they would have terminated him immediately. Notre Dame argues that evidence of the alleged abuse was "after acquired" and therefore precludes both front pay and reinstatement.

What sets an after-acquired evidence case apart * * * is that the articulated "legitimate" reason for terminating the employee was non-existent at the time of the adverse decision and could not possibly have motivated the employer to the slightest degree. *Delli Santi v. CNA Ins. Companies*, 88 F.3d 192 (3d Cir. 1996). Furthermore, "Where an employer seeks to rely upon after-acquired evidence of wrongdoing, it must first establish that the wrongdoing was of such severity that the employee in fact would have been terminated on those grounds alone if the employer had known of it at the time of discharge." ADEA, 29 U.S.C. § 621 *et seq.*; *McKennon*, 513 U.S. 352, 115 S. Ct. 879, 130 L. Ed. 2d 852; *Moos v. Square D Co.*, 72 F.3d 39 (6th Cir. 1995); *Coleman v. Keebler Co.*, 997 F. Supp. 1102 (N.D. Ind. 1998); *Vandeventer v. Wabash Nat. Corp.*, 887 F. Supp. 1178 (N.D. Ind. 1995). It is this Court's opinion that Notre Dames argument fails on both points.

* * *

First, the after-acquired evidence doctrine does not bar front pay to a discharged employee whose alleged wrongdoing was known to the employer at the time of the discharge and was asserted as being a reason for the discharge. *Delli Santi*, 88 F.3d 192, 205. It is this Court's opinion that Defendant's knowledge of Moore's coaching behavior does not fall within the ambit of after-acquired evidence as set forth in *McKennon*. Moore coached football at Notre Dame for nine years. Davie knew of, and in fact argued that Moore's behavior was one of the reasons for his termination. The record is replete with such evidence. (Trial Tr. July 10, 1998 p. 18, 19, 30-38). The jury apparently rejected this argument. Based on its defense at trial, Notre Dame cannot now claim that this "legitimate" reason was non-existent at the time of the adverse decision and could not possibly have motivated it to the slightest degree. *Delli Santi*, 88 F.3d 192, 205-06.

Notre Dame has also failed to establish that Moore's alleged wrongdoing was of such severity that he in fact would have been terminated on those grounds alone. Football is an aggressive sport. Coaching a winning team requires a degree of "killer instinct." Notre Dame's blanket assertion that if certain administrators had known of Moore's alleged abuse of players, Moore would have been immediately fired is insufficient to prove that such would have actually occurred. This assertion is nothing more than an excuse made after the fact. Additionally, this Court will not speculate, like defendant does, as to the reason the jury did not award a large amount of back pay. (Def.'s Mem. at 4). An award of back pay less than requested does not necessarily mean the jury concluded Moore would have been terminated for nondiscriminatory reasons and it does not therefore preclude front pay. *See Curtis v. Electronics & Space Corp.*, 113 F.3d 1498, 1504 (8th Cir. 1997); *Downes*, 41 F.3d 1132, 1143-44 (7th Cir. 1994). Accordingly, this Court finds Defendant's after-acquired evidence argument without merit.

3. Failure to Mitigate

Notre Dame finally argues that Moore is not entitled to front pay because he failed to undertake reasonable efforts to mitigate his damages. This Court disagrees. Generally, an ADEA plaintiff satisfies the mitigation of damages requirement that he use "reasonable diligence in attempting to secure employment" by demonstrating his commitment to seeking active employment and by remaining ready, willing and able to work. However, a plaintiff's duty to mitigate his damages is not met by using reasonable diligence to obtain any employment, rather the employment must be comparable employment. *Finch v. Hercules Inc.*, 941 F. Supp. 1395 (D. Del. 1996). The Seventh Circuit has defined "comparable work" as a position that affords "virtually identical promotional opportunities, compensation, job responsibilities, working conditions and status" as the previous position. *Best v. Shell Oil Co.*, 4 F. Supp. 2d 770 (N.D. Ill. 1998) (quoting *Hutchinson*, 42 F.3d 1037 at 1044). The goal of mitigation is to prevent the plaintiff from

remaining idle and doing nothing. Furthermore, an employee is not required to go to heroic lengths in attempting to mitigate his damages, but only to take reasonable steps to do so. *Suggs v. ServiceMaster Educ. Food Management*, 72 F.3d 1228 (6th Cir. 1996); *Ford v. Nicks*, 866 F.2d 865 (6th Cir. 1989). Furthermore, a claimant has no obligation to accept lesser employment . . . or relocate to a new community. *See, e.g., Ford Motor Co. v. E.E.O.C.*, 458 U.S. 219, 231-32, 102 S. Ct. 3057, 3065-66, 73 L. Ed. 2d 721 (1982); *Coleman v. City of Omaha*, 714 F.2d 804, 808 (8th Cir. 1983); *Glass v. IDS Financial Services, Inc.*, 778 F. Supp. 1029 (D. Minn. 1991); *Raimondo v. AMAX, Inc.*, 843 F. Supp. 806 (D. Conn. 1984).

When evaluating the reasonableness and duration of a job search a court may consider the plaintiff's background and individual characteristics. *Rasimas v. Michigan Dep't of Mental Health*, 714 F.2d 614, 624 (6th Cir.1983) (for example, older claimants need not exert same effort as younger claimants); *Sellers v. Delgado College*, 902 F.2d 1189, 1193 (5th Cir. 1990). Moreover, it is the defendant's burden to prove that a plaintiff has failed to discharge his duty. *Smith v. Great American Restaurants, Inc.*, 969 F.2d 430 (7th Cir. 1992); *Padilla v. Metro-North Commuter R.R.*, 92 F.3d 117, 125 (2d Cir. 1996). In the present case, Notre Dame has not met this burden. Moore sought and obtained employment shortly after his discharge. He currently works at three different jobs. The fact that he did not accept a position at Cornell does not indicate a failure to mitigate. That position offered a $40,000 salary, significantly less than Moore's former salary, and involved a tenuous situation where the head coach was seeking other employment. Nor does the fact that Moore did not apply for certain positions mentioned by defendant indicate a failure to mitigate. *Compare Buchholz v. Symons Mfg. Co.*, 445 F. Supp. 706 (E.D. Wis. 1978) (62-year-old salesman, who was discharged in violation of ADEA was not required to relocate for three years of employment until planned retirement as a reasonable effort to mitigate damages). Moore is presently sixty-six years old. The options available to him are not as great as those available to someone younger. Moore has demonstrated his willingness to work, but, the chances of finding "comparable work" as defined by the Seventh Circuit, *supra*, are slim. It is this Court's opinion that Moore used reasonable diligence in attempting to obtain employment.

* * *

3. Summary

The purpose of front pay under the Age Discrimination in Employment Act is to ensure that a person who has been discriminated against on the basis of age is made whole, not to guarantee every claimant who cannot mitigate damages by finding comparable work an annuity to age 70. *Anastasio v. Schering Corp.*, 838 F.2d

701 (3d Cir. 1988). Furthermore, the risk of non-continuity of future employment in a "volatile" must be considered in determining an award of front pay, *Price v. Marshall Erdman & Assoc., Inc.*, 966 F.2d 320, 327 (7th Cir. 1992); 901 F. Supp. 1403, 1408, and the Court has considered this fact.

Defendant's argument that front pay is too speculative when the plaintiff's profession has a high turnover rate (Def.'s Mem. at 12) does not preclude a front-pay award. *See Century Broadcasting*, 957 F.2d 1446 (front pay improperly denied on grounds employment in industry was tenuous). In this case, such an award is not "highly speculative." The Court has solid evidence concerning Moore's annual salary and the number of years he hoped to continue his employment. While Moore asserts that five years front pay is warranted, this Court disagrees. The evidence presented at trial establishes that Moore expressed a desire to work two more years and then retire. There was no guarantee that Davie would remain at Notre Dame longer than his current contract or that Moore would indefinitely remain in Davie's employ. The evidence also suggests that Moore and Davie had philosophical differences which may have lead to a parting of the ways. With all evidence considered, the Court finds an award of two years front pay sufficient. The front pay is calculated as follows:

Had Moore remained at Notre Dame his total 1998 salary would have been $84,388.84. Subtracted from this amount is Moore's annual salary from his present employment. Moore testified that he currently earns $1,600 for his services as assistant football coach at Cathedral Preparatory School, $15,000 for his work with the Baltimore Ravens, and $30,000 from his work with Tollgrade Communications. His total current yearly earning amount is therefore $46,600. The difference between Moore's Notre Dame salary and his current salary is $37,788.84 per year. This amount is multiplied by a period of two years and yields a total of $75,577.68. Because the Court is not including an additional amount for lost benefits and is not factoring in any increase for the second year, no discounting of the front pay award is warranted. *See Stratton v. Dep't for the Aging for City of New* York, 132 F.3d 869, 882 (2d Cir. 1997); *see e.g. Gusman v. Unisys corp.*, 986 F.2d 1146, 1147-48 (7th Cir. 1993). Thus, the total front pay award equals $75,577.68 plus post judgment interest.

* * *

CONCLUSION

For the preceding reasons it is hereby ordered that Plaintiff's Motion for Reinstatement is DENIED. Plaintiff's Motion for Award of Front Pay is GRANTED "in part as modified herein". Plaintiff is awarded front pay in the amount of $75,577.68 plus post-judgment interest.

It is further ordered that Plaintiff's Motion for Costs and Fees is GRANTED. Plaintiff is awarded costs in the total amount of $9,672.45. Plaintiff is also awarded attorney fees and expenses in the total amount of $394,865.74.

Finally, pursuant to jury verdict, the Plaintiff is awarded $42,935.28 in back pay and an additional $42,935.28 in liquidated damages.

IT IS SO ORDERED.

Recent Trends

In 2005, the U.S. Supreme Court issued a decision that had a major impact on age discrimination law. In *Smith v. City of Jackson, Mississippi*, 125 S. Ct. 1536 (2005), the Supreme Court held that age discrimination cases under ADEA could be brought based on a disparate impact theory. Prior to the decision in *City of Jackson*, most federal courts had ruled that such claims were not permitted. Now, under the authority of *City of Jackson*, seemingly "neutral" employer practices can be held to violate the ADEA if they result in a disparate impact on older workers. The plaintiff no longer has to establish that the employer intended to discriminate to prevail under the ADEA.

Although this represents a significant change in the law, it remains to be seen what impact, if any, this ruling will have on ADEA cases in the future. Although both the ADEA and Title VII now permit claims based on a disparate impact theory, the Supreme Court noted in *City of Jackson* that the scope of the disparate impact theory under the ADEA is narrower than Title VII because under the ADEA, employer conduct is permitted as long as it is based on "reasonable factors" other than age. Title VII does not contain an analogous provision. So although this case represents a clear expansion of the ADEA to now include disparate impact cases, it is clear the applicability of the disparate impact theory is not as broad under the ADEA as under Title VII. Future interpretations and applications of the holding in *City of Jackson* by both state and federal courts will help lend clarity to the impact of this ruling to future age discrimination cases.

References

Cases

Eggleston v. South Bend Community School Corp., 858 F. Supp. 841 (N.D. Ind 1994).
Lane v. Colorado High School Activities Association, No. 96-Z-2143 (Colorado 1996).
Moore v. The University of Notre Dame, 22 F. Supp. 896 (1998).
Smith v. City of Jackson, Mississippi, 125 S. Ct. 1536 (2005).

Legislation

Age Discrimination in Employment Act, 29 U.S.C.A. §§ 621-634.
Age Discrimination Act of 1975, 29 U.S.C.A. §§ 6101-6107.

Websites

Equal Employment Opportunity Commission (EEOC): www.eeoc.gov
U.S. Department of Labor: www.dol.gov

8.16 Title I of the Americans with Disabilities Act

Mary A. Hums
University of Louisville

What do the following athletes have in common: Magic Johnson (basketball), Tamika Catchings, (basketball), Neil Parry (college football), Kyle Maynard (college wrestling), Marla Runyan (track and field), and Casey Martin (golf)? Each has some type of disability. Johnson is HIV-positive. Catchings is hearing impaired. Parry is a below-the-knee amputee. Maynard is a congenital amputee, born with incomplete arms and legs. Runyan is visually impaired. Martin has a circulatory disorder. Yet each has had a successful athletic career. Events such as the Paralympic Games and the athletes with disabilities who compete in them are becoming more visible every day. But what about other people with disabilities who wish to work as sport and recreation managers in some segment of the sport and recreation industry? What barriers do they face and what kind of legal protections do they have against employment discrimination? In addition to addressing facility issues, the Americans with Disabilities Act (ADA) provides guidelines for employers when dealing with employees with disabilities. These guidelines help ensure equal opportunity for people with disabilities by opening up the definition of who is a "qualified individual" to people of all abilities.

Fundamental Concepts

The Americans with Disabilities Act of 1990 (ADA) is not limited to facility accessibility issues, but addresses employment issues as well. It is important to remember that the ADA covers the entire scope of the employment process. Title I of the ADA states "[N]o covered entity shall discriminate against a qualified individual with a disability because of the disability of such individual in regard to job application procedures, the hiring, advancement or discharge of employees, employee compensation, job training, and other terms, conditions, and privileges of employment" (42 U.S.C. 12112(a)). According to Miller, Fielding, and Pitts (1993), sport managers must be aware of ADA requirements as they relate to selection criteria, application accessibility, job application and interview inquiries, medical exams and inquiries, reasonable accommodations, and essential job functions. This chapter focuses primarily on the question of reasonable accommodation. Before examining the ADA's application to sport organizations, some basic definitions must be established.

Employer

According to Title I, § 12111 [sec. 101] (5)(a) of the ADA, the term *employer* means "a person engaged in an industry affecting commerce who has 15 or more employees for each working day in each of 20 or more calendar weeks in the current or preceding calendar year, and any agent of such person." In *Jones v. Southeast Alabama Baseball Umpires Association* (1994), an umpire who wore a prosthetic leg had his request to work an increased number of varsity high school baseball games denied and proceeded to file an ADA claim. The Umpires' Association filed for summary judgment, claiming it did not fall under ADA coverage because it did not employ umpires for more than twenty weeks. Jones was able to show that because the Association assigned umpires during both the school year and for summer youth games, it actually employed umpires for approximately six months, and therefore the Association's request for summary judgment was denied.

Disability

Under the ADA, the term *disability* means (a) a physical or mental impairment that substantially limits one or more of the major life activities of such individual; (b) a record of such impairment; or (c) being regarded as having such an impairment § 12103 [Sec. 3] (2). Although the ADA does not specifically define "major life activities," the Department of Health and Human Services defines it as "functions such as caring for one's self, performing manual tasks, walking, seeing, hearing, speaking, breathing, learning, and working" (45 C.F.R. 84.3(j)(2)(i)(1985)).

Qualified Individual with a Disability

According to Title I, § 12111 [Sec. 101] (8) of the ADA, a "qualified individual with a disability" means: "an individual who, with or without reasonable accommodation, can perform the essential functions of the employment position that such an individual holds or desires." In order to be qualified, a person must still meet certain prerequisites for the position. For example, a teacher who could not pass the required national teachers' examination could be considered not qualified for a teaching position (*Pandazides v. Virginia Board of Education*, 1992). In *Sawhill v. Medical College of Pennsylvania* (1996), the plaintiff, a licensed clinical pathologist, was told his termination was because he did not fit into his department's future plans, but later discovered his termination was related to his disability (clinical depression). The plaintiff alleged termination based on his disability violated the ADA. The defendant's motion to dismiss was denied. The term "qualified individual with a disability" does "not include any employee or applicant who is currently engaging in illegal use of drugs, when the covered entity acts on the basis of such use" (42 U.S.C. 12112(a)). In *Collings v. Longview Fibre Company* (1995), Collings and seven other employees alleged Longview Fibre wrongfully terminated them for their drug addiction disability in violation of the Americans with Disabilities Act. The employees were discharged because of their drug-related misconduct at work and not because of their alleged substance abuse disability. The regulations accompanying the ADA indicate that employers may discharge or deny employment to people illegally using drugs, and the courts have recognized a distinction between termination of employment because of misconduct and termination because of a disability.

Reasonable Accommodation/Undue Hardship

According to the Job Accommodation Network (2002):

> The duty to provide reasonable accommodation is a fundamental statutory requirement because of the nature of discrimination faced by individuals with disabilities. Although many individuals with disabilities can apply for and perform jobs without any reasonable accommodations, there are workplace barriers that keep others from performing jobs which they could do with some form of accommodation. These barriers may be physical obstacles (such as inaccessible facilities or equipment), or they may be procedures or rules (such as rules concerning when work is performed, when breaks are taken, or how essential or marginal functions are performed). Reasonable accommodation removes workplace barriers for individuals with disabilities.

A reasonable accommodation means making some modifications in the work environment that allows a person with a disability an equal employment opportunity. These accommodations take place in three aspects of employment (Colker & Milani, 2005):

- to ensure equal opportunity in the employment process
- to enable a qualified individual with a disability to perform the essential functions of a job
- to enable an employee with a disability to enjoy equal benefits and privileges of employment. (p. 20)

To comply with the ADA, employers must make reasonable accommodations for their workers with disabilities. However, employers only need to do so if providing the reasonable accommodation does not result in undue hardship. According to Title I, § 12111 [sec. 101] (9) of the ADA, a *"reasonable accommodation"* may include

(a) making existing facilities used by employees reasonably accessible to and usable by individuals with disabilities; and
(b) job restructuring, part-time or modified work schedules, reassignment to a vacant position, acquisition or modification of equipment or devices, appropriate adjustment or modifications of examinations, training materials or policies, the provision of qualified readers or interpreters, and other similar accommodations for individuals with disabilities.

When making reasonable accommodations, employers should consider using the following process (U.S. Department of Labor, 2003):

Step 1: Decide if the employee with a disability is qualified to perform the essential functions of the job with or without an accommodation.
Step 2: Identify the employee's workplace accommodation needs.
Step 3: Select and provide the accommodation that is most appropriate for the employee and employer.
Step 4: Check results by monitoring and evaluating the effectiveness of the accommodation
Step 5: Provide follow-up, if needed.

According to Title I, § 12111 [sec. 101] (10)(a) of the ADA, an **undue hardship** is "an action requiring significant difficulty or expense, when considered in light of the factors set forth in subparagraph (b)":

(b) In determining whether an accommodation would impose an undue hardship on a covered entity, factors to be considered include:
(i) the nature and cost of the accommodation needed under this Act;
(ii) the overall financial resources of the facility or facilities involved in the provision of reasonable accommodation; the number of persons employed at such a facility; the effect on expenses and resources, or the impact otherwise of such accommodation upon the operation of the facility;
(iii) the overall financial resources of the covered entity; the overall size of the business of the covered entity with respect to the number of its employees; the number, type and location of its facilities; and
(iv) the type of operation or operations of the covered entity, including the composition, structure, and functions of the workforce of such entity; the geographic separateness, administrative, or fiscal relationship of the facility or facilities in question to the covered entity.

The courts have interpreted the meaning of reasonable accommodation and undue hardship differently in different cases (Churchill, 1995). Some reasonable accommodations include working at home for an employee who experiences pain while commuting (*Sargent v. Litton Systems*, 1994); taking a leave of absence for alcoholism treatment (*Schmidt v. Safeway*, 1994); eliminating heavy lifting and strenuous work (*Henchey v. Town of North Greenbush*, 1993); allowing a police officer to carry food, glucose, and an insulin injection kit (*Bombrys v. City of Toledo*, 1993); and transferring an employee to a city where better medical care was available (*Buckingham v. United States*, 1993). There are instances, however, when the courts have indicated that the requested accommodations were unreasonable or would have resulted in undue hardship. Reasonable accommodation did not require allowing an employee who has unpredictable violent outbursts to remain in the workplace (*Mazzarella v. U.S. Postal Service*, 1993), accommodating frequent or unpredictable absences (*Jackson v. Veteran's Administration*, 1994), or assigning limited tasks that substantially reduce an employee's contribution to the company (*Russell v. Southeastern Pennsylvania Transportation Authority*, 1993). Accommodations do not have to be expensive according to the Job Accommodation Network, a service of the Office of Disability Employment Policy of the U.S. Labor Department. When examining the average cost of workplace accommodations made between October 1992 and August 1999, 20 percent were cost-free, 51 percent cost $500 or less, 11 percent cost between $501 and $1000, 6 percent cost between $1001 and $2000, 8 percent cost between $2001 and $5000, and 4 percent cost more than $5000 (Job Accommodation Network, 1999). Some examples of accommodations and their cost are

A timer with an indicator light allowed a medical technician who was deaf to perform laboratory tests. Cost $27.00;

A groundskeeper who had limited use of one arm was provided a detachable extension arm for a rake. This enabled him to grasp the handle on the extension with the impaired hand and control the rake with the functional arm. Cost $20.00;

A desk layout was changed from the right to left side to enable a data entry operator who is visually impaired to perform her job. Cost $0;

A blind receptionist was provided a light probe which allowed her to determine which lines on the switchboard were ringing, on hold, or in use. (A light-probe gives an audible signal when held over an illuminated source.) Cost $50.00 to $100.00;

A person who had use of only one hand, working in a food service position could perform all tasks except opening cans. She was provided with a one-handed can opener. Cost $35.00 (Job Accommodations Network, 2006, Acquisition or Modification section, ¶ 12)

Providing reasonable accommodations for employees need not be excessively expensive or complicated. According to the Job Accommodation Network (2000), a variety of reasonable accommodations can be made for employees with disabilities. A carpentry supervisor who had no functional hearing was required (as part of his job) to order supplies from various vendors. A text telephone used in conjunction with the local relay service allowed the supervisor to make the necessary orders. A maintenance technician restricted from working in extreme temperatures was accommodated with a modified schedule not requiring her to work outside in these conditions. People with low vision who must access information from a computer screen have a variety of accommodation options available. Those who benefit from larger type might find screen magnification software helpful. The creative use of scheduling may be helpful in maximizing an employee's productivity while accommodating potential problems with fatigue related to an illness such as cancer or HIV. The use of flexible scheduling, longer rest breaks, frequent short breaks, part-time work, or self-pacing may be helpful. Allowing an employee to work from home may be another alternative to consider.

Significant Case

This case offers a good example of the ADA in action. It also involves an illness we do not always think of as being a disability, alcoholism. We usually think of disability in terms of a mobility disability or perhaps a hearing or visual impairment.

MADDOX V. UNIVERSITY OF TENNESSEE

United States Court of Appeals for the Sixth Circuit
62 F.3d 843 (1995)

Opinion: Bailey Brown, Circuit Judge.

The plaintiff-appellant, Robert Maddox, a former assistant football coach at the University of Tennessee, brought suit against the school, its Board of Trustees, and its athletic director, Doug Dickey (collectively "UT"), under § 504 of the Rehabilitation Act of 1973, as amended, 29 U.S.C. § 701, et seq., and the Americans with Disabilities Act of 1990 ("ADA"), 42 U.S.C. § 12101, et seq., alleging discriminatory discharge on the basis of his disability, alcoholism. The district court granted UT's motion for summary judgment, concluding that Maddox was not terminated solely by reason of, or because of, his handicap, but rather, because of a well-publicized incident in which Maddox was arrested for driving under the influence of alcohol. Maddox appealed. We AFFIRM.

I. Facts

On February 17, 1992, Doug Dickey, acting as UT's athletic director, extended to Maddox an offer of employment as an assistant football coach. The position did not carry tenure and was terminable at will in accordance with the policies of the Personnel Manual. As part of the hiring process, Maddox completed an application. On the line after "Describe any health problems or physical limitations, which . . . would limit your ability to perform the duties of the position for which you are applying," Maddox wrote "None." In response to the question "have you ever been arrested for a criminal offense of any kind?" Maddox replied "No." These responses were not accurate. According to what Maddox alleges in this lawsuit, he suffers from the disability of alcoholism. Also, Maddox was arrested three times before 1992, once for possession of a controlled substance, and twice for driving a motor vehicle under the influence of alcohol. As to the first answer, Maddox claims that it is in fact correct because "it has never affected my coaching ability . . . I never drank on the job." As to the second question, Maddox claims that another university employee, Bill Higdon, advised him not to include the information concerning his prior arrests on the application.

On May 26, 1992, after Maddox began working at UT, a Knoxville police officer arrested Maddox and charged him with driving under the influence of alcohol and public intoxication. According to newspaper reports, the accuracy of which is not contested, Maddox backed his car across a major public road at a high rate of speed, almost striking another vehicle. When stopped by the officer, Maddox was combative, his pants were unzipped, and he refused to take a breathalyzer. He also lied to the arresting officer, stating that he was unemployed. This incident was highly publicized, and UT was obviously embarrassed by the public exposure surrounding the event.

Maddox entered an alcohol rehabilitation program at a UT hospital after his arrest. UT first placed Maddox on paid administrative leave. In June 1992, however, Dickey and then Head Coach Johnny Majors determined that the allegations were accurate and jointly issued a letter notifying Maddox that his employment was being terminated. They testified that termination was necessary because of: 1) the criminal acts and misconduct of Maddox; 2) the bad publicity surrounding the arrest; and 3) the fact that Maddox was no longer qualified, in their minds, for the responsibilities associated with being an assistant coach. Both Dickey and Majors deny that they were aware that Maddox was an alcoholic or that Maddox's alcoholism played any part in the decision to discharge him. Nevertheless, Maddox brought this action alleging that the termination was discriminatory on the basis of his alcoholism in violation of his rights under the Rehabilitation Act and the ADA. UT responded by filing a motion for summary judgment which the district court granted. The court recognized that, under both statutes, a plaintiff must show that he was fired by reason of his disability. In the court's view, summary judgment was appropriate because Maddox could not establish the existence of a genuine issue of material fact with respect to whether he had been fired by reason of his status as an alcoholic rather than by reason of his criminal misconduct. Maddox now appeals.

II. Analysis

1. Standard of Review

Review of a grant of summary judgment is de novo, utilizing the same test used by the district court to determine whether summary judgment is appropriate. A court shall render summary judgment when there is no genuine issue as to any material fact, the moving party is entitled to judgment as a matter of law, and reasonable minds could come to but one conclusion, and that conclusion is adverse to the party against whom the motion is made.

2. Maddox Was Not Terminated Because of His Disability

Maddox raises a number of issues on appeal which he contends show that the district court erred in granting summary judgment to the defendants. Maddox first alleges that the district court erred in analyzing his claim under the Rehabilitation Act. Section 504 of the Act provides, "no otherwise qualified individual with a disability . . . shall, solely by reason of her or his disability, be excluded from the participation in, be denied the benefits of, or be subject to discrimination under any program or activity receiving Federal financial assistance." 29 U.S.C. § 794(a). Thus, in order to establish a violation of the Rehabilitation Act, a plaintiff must show:

(1) The plaintiff is a "handicapped person" under the Act; (2) The plaintiff is "otherwise qualified" for participation in the program; (3) The plaintiff is being excluded from participation in, being denied the benefits of, or being subjected to discrimination under the program solely by reason of his handicap; and (4) The relevant program or activity is receiving Federal financial assistance.

It is not disputed in this case that UT constitutes a program receiving Federal financial assistance under the Act. Likewise, we assume, without deciding, that alcoholics may be "individuals with a disability" for purposes of the Act. . . . Thus, our analysis focuses on whether Maddox is "otherwise qualified" under the Act and whether he was discharged "solely by reason of" his disability. The burden of making these showings rests with Maddox.

In support of its motion for summary judgment, UT contended that both factors weighed in its favor. First, Dickey and Majors contended that they did not even know that Maddox was considered an alcoholic in making both the decision to hire and fire him. Moreover, they contended that Maddox was discharged, not because he was an alcoholic, but because of his criminal conduct and behavior and the significant amount of bad publicity surrounding him and the school. UT alternatively contended that Maddox is nevertheless not "otherwise qualified" to continue in the position of assistant football coach.

The district court granted UT's motion for summary judgment, specifically holding that UT did not discharge Maddox solely by reason of his disability. The court found it beyond dispute that Maddox's discharge resulted from his misconduct rather than his disability of alcoholism. The court noted,

It cannot be denied in this case, Mr. Maddox was charged with . . . [driving while under the influence and public intoxication] which would not be considered socially acceptable by any objective standard. The affidavit testimony of Mr. Dickey and Mr. Majors is clear on the point that it was this specific conduct, not any condition to which it might be related, which provoked the termination of Mr. Maddox's employment.

As a result, the court found it unnecessary to decide the alternative ground of whether Maddox was "otherwise qualified."

Maddox contends that the district court erred in distinguishing between discharge for misconduct and discharge solely by reason of his disability of alcoholism. Maddox claims that he has difficulty operating a motor vehicle while under the influence of alcohol and therefore he characterizes drunk driving as a causally connected manifestation of the disability of alcoholism. Thus, Maddox contends that because alcoholism caused the incident upon which UT claims to have based its decision to discharge him, UT in essence discharged him because of his disability of alcoholism. In support, Maddox relies on Teahan v. Metro-North Commuter R.R. Co., 951 F.2d 511, 516-17 (2d Cir. 1991), cert. denied, 121 L. Ed. 2d 24, 113 S. Ct. 54 (1992), in which the Second Circuit held that a Rehabilitation Act plaintiff can show that he was fired "solely by reason of" his disability, or at least create a genuine issue of material fact, if he can show that he was fired for conduct that is "causally related" to his disability. In Teahan, the defendant company discharged the plaintiff because of his excessive absenteeism. The plaintiff responded by claiming that his absenteeism was caused by his alcoholism and therefore protected under the Rehabilitation Act. The district court disagreed and granted summary judgment for the employer because, the court found, Teahan was fired for his absenteeism and not because of his alcoholism. The Second Circuit reversed the district court's grant of summary judgment on appeal, however, rejecting the court's distinction between misconduct (absenteeism), and the disabling condition of alcoholism. The court presumed that Teahan's absenteeism resulted from his alcoholism and held that one's disability should not be distinguished from its consequences in determining whether he was fired "solely by reason" of his disability. Id. Thus, Maddox argues that, in the instant case, when UT acted on the basis of the conduct allegedly caused by the alcoholism, it was the same as if UT acted on the basis of alcoholism itself.

We disagree and hold that the district court correctly focused on the distinction between discharging someone for unacceptable misconduct and discharging someone because of the disability. As the district court noted, to hold otherwise, an employer would be forced to accommodate all behavior of an alcoholic which could in any way be related to the alcoholic's use of intoxicating beverages; behavior that would be intolerable if engaged in by a sober employee or, for that matter, an intoxicated but nonalcoholic employee.

Despite Teahan, a number of cases have considered the issue of misconduct as distinct from the status of the disability. In Taub v. Frank, 957 F.2d 8 (1st Cir. 1992), the plaintiff Taub, a heroin addict, brought suit against his former employer, the United States Postal Service, alleging discriminatory discharge under the Rehabilitation Act. The Post Office discharged Taub after he was arrested for possession of heroin for distribution. The district court granted the Post Office's motion for summary judgment and Taub appealed. The First Circuit affirmed and held that Taub could not prevail on his Rehabilitation Act claim because his discharge resulted from his misconduct, possession of heroin for distribution, rather than his disability of heroin addiction. The court reasoned that addiction-related criminal conduct is simply too attenuated to extend the Act's protection to Taub.

The conduct/disability distinction was also recognized by the Fourth Circuit in Little v. F.B.I., 1 F.3d 255 (4th Cir. 1993). In Little, the F.B.I. discharged the plaintiff, known by his supervisors to be an alcoholic, after an incident in which he was intoxicated on duty. The district court granted summary judgment in favor of the F.B.I. on the basis that the plaintiff was no longer "otherwise qualified" to serve as an F.B.I. agent. The Fourth Circuit affirmed, noting as an additional basis that the plaintiff's employment was not terminated because of his handicap. The court noted, "based on no less authority than common sense, it is clear that an employer subject to the . . . [Rehabilitation] Act must be permitted to terminate its employees on account of egregious misconduct, irrespective of whether the employee is handicapped." Id.; see also Landefeld v. Marion Gen. Hosp., Inc., 994 F.2d 1178, 1183 (6th Cir. 1993) (Nelson, J., concurring) ("The plaintiff was clearly suspended because of his intolerable conduct, and not solely because of his mental condition.")

Moreover, language within the respective statutes makes clear that such a distinction is warranted. Section 706(8)(c) of the Rehabilitation Act states:

"Individuals with a disability" does not include any individual who is an alcoholic whose current use of alcohol prevents such individual from performing the duties of the job in question or whose employment, by reason of such current alcohol abuse, would constitute a direct threat to property or the safety of others.

Likewise, the ADA specifically provides that an employer may hold an alcoholic employee to the same performance and behavior standards to which the employer holds other employees "even if any unsatisfactory performance is related to the alcoholism of such employee." 42 U.S.C. § 12114(c)(4). These provisions clearly contemplate distinguishing the issue of misconduct from one's status as an alcoholic.

At bottom, we conclude that the analysis of the district court is more in keeping with the purposes and limitations of the respective Acts, and therefore, we decline to adopt the Second Circuit's reasoning in Teahan. Employers subject to the Rehabilitation Act and ADA must be permitted to take appropriate action with respect to an employee on account of egregious or criminal conduct, regardless of whether the employee is disabled. In the instant case, for example, while alcoholism might compel Maddox to drink, it did not compel him to operate a motor vehicle or engage in the other inappropriate conduct reported. Likewise, suppose an alcoholic becomes intoxicated and sexually assaults a coworker? We believe that it strains logic to conclude that such action could be protected under the Rehabilitation Act or the ADA merely because the actor has been diagnosed as an alcoholic and claims that such action was caused by his disability.

3. Pretext

Maddox alternatively contends that even if UT has successfully disclaimed reliance on his disability in making the employment decision, the district court nevertheless erred in determining that Maddox had produced no evidence that the reasons articulated by UT were a pretext for discrimination. A Rehabilitation Act plaintiff may demonstrate pretext by showing that the asserted reasons had no basis in fact, the reasons did not in fact motivate the discharge, or, if they were factors in the decision, they were jointly insufficient to motivate the discharge.

Maddox first alleges that Dickey and Majors knew that Maddox was an alcoholic. Setting aside for a moment the legal significance of this statement, it is not supported factually in the record.

Maddox also claims that he knew of other coaches in the football program who drank alcohol in public and who were arrested for DUI but who were not discharged. This point is also irrelevant. Whether Maddox had such knowledge is immaterial. There is no evidence in the record establishing that Majors or Dickey had knowledge of the public intoxication of any other coach, or failed to reprimand or terminate any coach who they knew to have engaged in such behavior.

Maddox finally contends that UT's conclusion that he is no longer qualified to be an assistant coach at UT is without merit. Maddox claims that his misconduct did not affect his "coaching" responsibilities because an assistant coach's duties are limited to the practice and playing fields, and do not comprise of serving as a counselor or mentor to the players or serving as a representative of the school. Maddox relies on the fact that none of these functions were explained to him in his formal job description.

We first note that this allegation seems more appropriate for determining whether he was "otherwise qualified" rather than whether he was discharged because of his disability. Nevertheless, Maddox's position is simply unrealistic. It is obvious that as a member of the football coaching staff, Maddox would be representing not only the team but also the university. As in the instant case, UT received full media coverage because of this "embarrassing" incident. The school falls out of favor with the public, and the reputation of the football program suffers. Likewise, to argue that football coaches today, with all the emphasis on the misuse of drugs and alcohol by athletes, are not "role models" and "mentors" simply ignores reality.

The district court's grant of summary judgment in favor of the defendants is AFFIRMED.

 OTHER RELEVANT SIGNIFICANT CASES

Chapter 7.24 *Participants with Disabilities*

Chapter 8.11 *Gender Equity: Opportunities to Participate*

Recent Trends

HIV/AIDS

A question facing sport managers, particularly in professional sports, is the issue of HIV-positive athletes and their ability to participate in sport as employees who are covered by the ADA. If an HIV-positive professional athlete retains the physical skills to compete at his or her professional level, then he or she is a "qualified individual with a disability" within his or her specific sport organization. The next, and more difficult, issue is whether or not the athlete poses a significant threat to other athletes, such that accommodating the participation of such an athlete creates an undue hardship on an employer. Currently, there have been no confirmed cases of HIV transmission involving contact between professional sport participants. Boxing commissions in a number of states, however, have already implemented policies barring HIV-positive boxers from fighting. Boxers and other individual sport athletes, however, may not fall under ADA coverage as employees, whereas team sport athletes would. Sport managers must keep current with medical findings regarding HIV transmission and must also keep in mind that any HIV-positive athletes they employ may be protected by the ADA, as well as the Rehabilitation Act and any applicable state laws.

What most sport organizations have done, rather than restricting participation by HIV-positive individuals, is to enact rules designed to lessen the potential transmission (Hearn, 2000). All athletes, coaches, and other sport and recreation mangers need to keep up-to-date on the latest scientific information concerning HIV and its transmission, as well as any legal developments. In addition, these managers must always keep in mind the dignity of the infected individuals in terms of confidentiality and ethical treatment (Hums, 1994; Wolohan, 1997). According to Stone (2005), "The challenge for the athlete with HIV/AIDS probably arises from the lack of information and understanding about persons with HIV and AIDS generally. Our society continues to be uninformed and thereby confused and uncertain about transmission issues for persons with HIV and AIDS. Prejudice, stigma, and discrimination can be overcome by providing information and education to the public at large. The views of athletic directors in regard to individuals with HIV and AIDS most likely indicate a broader and deeper misunderstanding throughout society when it comes to HIV and AIDS."

Recent ADA Legislation

In the case *University of Alabama v. Garrett* (2001), the Supreme Court ruled that state governments could not be sued under the ADA for discriminating against workers with disabilities. In particular, the Supreme Court ruled that Congress lacked the power to make states liable for monetary damages under the ADA.

In this particular case, Garrett was a nurse working in the university medical center. She was diagnosed with breast cancer and took time off work while recovering from surgery. When she was ready to return to work, she was informed that she was demoted, as her supervisors believed that she would be unable to perform the functions of her job due to her disability. Advocates for people with disabilities interpret this decision as a major setback (Williams, 2001). In terms of its application to sport, sport and recreation mangers who work for colleges and universities should be aware of the potential ramifications for them. For example, a campus recreation department administrator who suffers an injury resulting in having to use a wheelchair may be in jeopardy of losing his or her position, and a coach who suffers a severe neck injury in an automobile accident may not be allowed to return as a head coach if university officials deem him or her incapable of satisfactorily performing the duties of being a head coach. Although the Garrett case did not occur in the sport setting, its application in a sport setting is feasible.

The most notable ADA case involving sport was the *PGA Tour v. Martin* (2001) Supreme Court case. In this case, Martin, a professional golfer who suffered from a painful circulatory condition known as Klippel-Trenaunay-Weber Syndrome, was allowed to use a cart to compete. The majority of the *Martin* case decision revolved around Title III of the ADA, which deals with discrimination in places of public accommodation, which is covered in a different chapter. Martin initially claimed employment discrimination under Title I, but the District Court found him to be an independent contractor rather than an employee (*PGA Tour v. Martin*, 2001). After the Martin case, some questions were raised about whether the case would "open the flood gates" for athletes with disabilities to challenge sport organizations to provide modifications. Although this has not happened, Stone (2005) suggested sport organizations on lower competitive levels, such as recreational sport or high schools, be more lenient in their approach to athletes with disabilities, whereas professional sport could be more stringent. In general, athletes with disabilities have been included more often on lower levels of competition (Hums & Wolff, 2006). What is most important is that situations be evaluated on a case by case basis.

References

Cases

Bombrys v. City of Toledo, 849 F. Supp. 1210 (N.D. Ohio 1993).

Buckingham v. United States, 998 F.2d 735 (9th Cir. 1993).

Collings v. Longview Fibre Company, 63 F.3d 828 (1995).

Henchey v. Town of North Greenbush, 831 F. Supp. 960 (N.D. N.Y. 1993).

Jackson v. Veterans' Administration, 22 F.3d 277 (11th Cir. 1994).

Jones v. Southeast Alabama Baseball Umpires Association, 864 F. Supp. 1135 (M.D. Ala. 1994).

Mazzarella v. U.S. Postal Service, 849 F. Supp. 89 (D. Mass. 1993).

Pandazides v. Virginia Board of Education, 804 F. Supp. 794 (1992).

PGA Tour v. Martin, 532 U.S. 661 (2001).

Russell v. Southeastern Pennsylvania Transportation Authority, 2 A.D. Cas. [BNA] 1419 (E.D. Pa. 1993).

Sargent v. Litton Systems, 841 F. Supp. 956 (N.D. Cal. 1994).

Sawhill v. Medical College of Pennsylvania, 1996 U.S. Dist. LEXIS 4097.

Schmidt v. Safeway, 864 F. Supp. 991 (D. Ore. 1994).

University of Alabama v. Garrett, 531 U.S. 356 (2001).

Publications

Ahearn, K. (2000). HIV positive athletes. *Sport Lawyers Journal, 7*, 279.

Churchill, S. S. (1995, June). Reasonable accommodations in the workplace: A shared responsibility. *Massachusetts Law Review*, 73–83.

Colker, R., & Milani, A. A. (2005). *The law of disability discrimination handbook*. Newark, NJ: Lexis Nexis.

Hums, M. A. (1994). AIDS in the sport arena: After Magic Johnson, where do we go from here? *Journal of Legal Aspects of Sport, 4*(1), 59–65.

Hums, M. A., & Wolff, E. A. (2006, January). *Inclusion of athletes with disabilities: Connections and collaborations.* Presented at the Annual NAKPEHE Conference, San Diego, CA.

Job Accommodation Network. (1999). *Accommodation benefit/cost analysis.* Retrieved January 3, 2003 from http://www.jan.wvu.edu/media/Stats/BenCosts0799.html

Job Accommodation Network. (2000). *Home page.* Retrieved from http://www.jan.wvu.edu/

Job Accommodation Network. (2002). *Enforcement guidance: Reasonable accommodation and undue hardship under the Americans with Disabilities Act.* Retrieved January 2, 2003 from http://www.eeoc.gov/docs/accommodation.html#general

Job Accommodation Network. (2006). Technical assistance manual: Title I of the ADA. Retrieved February 2, 2006 from http://www.jan.wvu.edu/links/ADAtam1.html#III

Miller, L. K., Fielding, L. W., & Pitts, B. G. (1993). Hiring concerns impacting the sport practitioner. *Journal of Legal Aspects of Sport, 3*, 3–15.

Stone, D. (2005). The game of pleasant diversion: Can we level the playing field for the disabled athlete and maintain the national pastime, in the aftermath of *PGA Tour, Inc. v. Martin*: An empirical study of the disabled athlete. *St. John's L. Rev., 79*, 377.

U.S. Department of Labor. (2003). *Workplace accommodation process.* [Electronic version]. Retrieved January 2, 2003 from http://www.dol.gov/odep/pubs/ek97/process.htm

Williams, J. (2001, March 7). The high court's low blow to the disabled. *Business Week Online.* Retrieved January 2, 2003 from http://web.lexis-nexis.com/universe/document?_m=326f6a671ab89549a3610379003e0f32&_docnum=55&wchp=dGLbVtb-lSlAl&_md5=4a436db3eb8b2672605bc8618f84cda9

Wolohan, J. (1997). An ethical and legal dilemma: Participation in sports by HIV infected athletes. *Marquette Sports Law Journal, 7*, 373.

Legislation

Americans with Disabilities Act of 1990, 42 U.S.C.A. § 12101 et seq. (West, 1993).

8.21 Copyright and Patent Law

Merry Moiseichik
University of Arkansas

Copyright and patent are both forms of intellectual property. The U.S. Constitution grants Congress the power to enact laws governing patents and copyrights. Article 1, Section 8 of the Constitution states: "Congress shall have the power . . . to promote the Progress of Science and useful Arts, by securing for limited Times to Authors and Inventors the exclusive Right to their respective Writings and Discoveries. . . ."

Copyright law protects artistic endeavors, whereas patent law safeguards inventions, designs, and ideas. The use and protection of intellectual property is becoming more important to the sport and recreation industry. For example copyright becomes an issue in designs of logos and stadiums, ownership of television and video game rights, and use of music in recreational settings.

Fundamental Concepts

Copyright

Congress enacted the United States Copyright Act of 1909 to protect the work of authors and other creative persons from the unauthorized use of their copyrighted materials and to provide a financial incentive for artists to produce, thereby increasing the number of creative works available in society. This legislation was completely revised in 1976 to take into account changing technology and to become more inclusive of the types of medium technology produced. In 1989 the United States became a member of the Berne Convention, where an international copyright treaty was created. This brought about the new revision of the Copyright Act in 1990. The act was revised still again in 1994 because of the United States' entrance into the North American Free Trade Agreement and the passing of the Visual Artists Rights Act of 1990, and again in 1999 and 2002 to reflect changing technology and the Internet. This is a complicated law, and although many know of its existence, most are not aware of its specific contents.

The purpose of copyright is to protect those who have put much time and energy into some creative project. These creators deserve to reap the financial benefits of their work. The law is economically motivated, designed to protect the rights of those who provide the many creative endeavors we hear and see daily.

A copyright gives the owner of the work the exclusive right to copy, reproduce, distribute, publish, perform, or display the work. There are two fundamental criteria for copyright protection: (1) the work must be original, and (2) it must be in some tangible form that can be reproduced (17 U.S.C. § 102). Registration of a copyright is not required for protection, although no action for infringement can be instituted until the copyright has been registered (17 U.S.C. § 401). The protection exists as soon as the work is fixed in some tangible form, such as on paper, a videotape, a cassette tape, on canvas, and so forth. Copyright protection lasts seventy years beyond the death of the author or for ninety-five years for anonymous works or works made for hire (17 U.S.C. § 301). The federal government grants registration of a copyright, which provides procedural advantages in enforcing rights under law.

There are eight broad categories of copyright protection, including (1) literary works; (2) musical works; (3) dramatic works; (4) pantomime and choreographic works; (5) pictorial, graphic, and sculptural works; (6) motion pictures and other audiovisual works; (7) sound recordings; and (8) architectural works (17 U.S.C. § 102).

To appreciate what can be copyrighted, it is instructive to consider what cannot be. "In no case does copyright protection for an original work of authorship extend to any idea, procedure, process, system, method of operation, concept, principle, or discovery, regardless of the form in which it is described, explained, illustrated, or embodied in such work" (17 U.S.C. § 102). Government documents and works in the public domain do not have copyright protection either. Works in the public domain include those with expired copyrights and works where copyright has not been requested (17 U.S.C. § 105).

Works that do not hold originality cannot be considered for copyright (17 U.S.C. § 104). This would include standard works such as calendars, height and weight charts, tape measures, and lists of tables (Talab, 1986). This allows freedom to make use of these articles. The outline of a calendar cannot be copyrighted, but the format and the pictures that go with the calendar can be. This allows recreation or sport programs, for example, to use a common calendar and add their own dimensions including pictures, special events, and any additional information specific to their programs. Similarly, no copyright can be held for blank forms that are used to obtain information (17 U.S.C. § 201). Therefore, agencies can use anyone's accident report form or registration form as long as the forms do not include creative authorship and just request information. They are designed to gather information and not to convey it.

Competitions do not hold a copyright as they do not fall within "Original works of authorship." (*National Basketball Association v. Motorola, Inc.* (US Court of Appeals, 2nd Circuit, 1997)) You can copyright the broadcasts, but the underlying games cannot be copyrighted.

Works where authorship is small cannot hold a copyright (17 U.S.C. § 102). This includes slogans, titles, names, variations, typographic ornamentation, lettering, or coloring. If slogans, titles, names, etc., were copyrighted, there would be a loss of freedom to speak. Such words like "uh huh" would then belong to certain companies like Pepsi, and with those words, Pepsi's right to control how they are used. These short sayings are protected by the trademark laws (see Chapter 8.22, *Principles of Trademark Law*).

Facts also cannot be copyrighted. Research data are facts. Any raw data collected can be used by anyone. In *Feist Publications v. Rural Telephone Service Co.* (1991), Feist Publications published a telephone book. They had done all the research to put it together. Rural Telephone Service used the Feist book and reorganized it using addresses as the listing. The court found that Feist had published facts. Rural Telephone used the facts, just in a different way. It was not infringement.

Rights of the Copyright Owner

A copyright gives its owner certain rights to the works, including (1) the right to reproduction; (2) the right to preparation of derivative works including translation from language to language and from one form to another (i.e., from book to movie, from movie to play); (3) the right to public distribution; (4) the public performing rights, which include live renditions that are face to face, on recordings, broadcasts, and retransmissions by cable; (5) the right to the public display, specifically written or art work; and (6) to perform the copyrighted work publicly by means of a digital audio transmission (17 U.S.C. § 106). This section has been strengthened with the Visual Artists Rights Act of 1990 (VARA), which has become section 106A of the Copyright Act (17 U.S.C. § 106A). Among the rights afforded artists by this law is the right to prevent any intentional distortion, mutilation, or other modification of that work. This allows the artist to control the visual art work until his or her death. In *Phillips v. Pembroke Real Estate* (2003) a renowned sculptor brought suit against a manager of a public sculpture park on Boston Harbor. He was seeking preliminary injunction to prevent the manager from modifying the park and from altering sculptures that he created specifically for the park. Pembroke wanted to build an office building and a convention center in the park and move the sculpture to a different location. In the suit, the artist stated that his design was created with the environment in mind and it would negatively effect the art if it were moved. An expert testified that if Phillips' sculpture was moved, it would impact his reputation as an artist because he would no longer have an important piece in an important location: his art will be "in exile." The court granted preliminary injunction even though delay on the project would cost $120,000.

Section 113 provides the rights of the owner of a building in which works of art are a part of a building. If the owner wants to remove the work, she must notify the artist. The artist may reject removal. The artist should keep their name and address registered with the copyright office for this purpose. For this reason, managers who wish to include artwork and murals in their buildings and parks should maintain copyright ownership as part of their contract.

Who is the owner of the copyright? It vests initially in the author or creator of the work. However, in the case of a "work made for hire," the employer or person for whom the work was prepared is the owner of the copyright. Section 201(b) of the Copyright Act provides that "the employer or other person for whom the work was prepared is considered the author for the purpose of this title, and, unless the parties have expressly agreed otherwise in a written instrument signed by them, owns all of the rights comprised in the copyright." In *Baltimore Orioles v. Major League Baseball Players* (1986), the players claimed part ownership of the copyright to televised games because they were the ones being filmed and retained ownership in their own likenesses. The Seventh Circuit, however, found for the Orioles, based on the fact that the players were working for the club at the time of the game and the filming, and therefore, the Orioles owned the copyright, not the players. This was likened to actors and actresses who do not own the copyright of the films in which they appear unless specifically stated in the contract. Even if the contract gives an actor a percentage of the film's profit, it does not mean that he or she owns a percentage of the copyright unless it is specifically stated.

Fair Use

An important section of the law for those who are not creators, but are users of copyrighted works, is the fair use section (17 U.S.C. §107). This section was passed to strike a balance between the copyright monopoly and the greater interest of society (Hohensee, 1988). There are four factors to ascertain fair use: (1) the purpose and the character of use, whether it is for commercial or for nonprofit educational purposes; (2) the nature of the copyrighted work; (3) the amount and substantiality of the material used in comparison with the whole; and (4) the effect of the use on the potential market or value of the work (17 U.S.C. § 107).

Fair use allows for "criticism, comment, news reporting, teaching, scholarship, or research." For example, Ted Giannoulas, the creator of the sports mascot "the Chicken," was sued by the owners of Barney, a purple dinosaur in a children's TV show. The Chicken, as part of a pregame show, beat up on Barney. The court ruled it was a parody and thus fair use (*Lyons Partnership, L.P. v. Giannoulas*, 1999).

A primary motivator for the passage of the fair use section was the use of copyrighted works for educational purposes. The educational fair use test is based on three rules: (1) brevity (using small parts of the whole); (2) spontaneity (if there is time to request permission, it should be requested); and, (3) cumulative effect (how will it affect the creator?). The copying is not allowed when it replaces a book that would be purchased. Consumables are not allowed to be copied under any circumstances. Therefore coloring books, consumable material, cannot be copied for use in afterschool or day care programs.

In *Basic Books, Inc. v. Kinkos Graphics* (1991), the court considered whether the production of professors' course packets, which were a compilation of articles directly relating to one course, were a violation of copyright or educational fair use. The court found that Kinkos had violated the copyright laws in creating the packets. Kinkos' motivation was not educational, but to make a profit from the works of others, and, therefore, the educational fair use exemption did not apply. Kinkos advertised and did its best to get the business of professors. According to Martin (1992), the case was not decided using the fair use test. If that was the case, in his opinion, there should have been joint infringement against the professors as well, because the professors provided the material to be copied for use in their courses. No professors were named in the case. Instead, the court looked at the profit motive and the amount of commercialism used by a national corporation selling copyrighted works.

Music and Performance

Musical scores that are performed by band and chorus should be purchased. However, there are guidelines in § 110 of the Copyright Act, similar to the educational fair use guidelines, to allow for music and dramatic performances by nonprofit agencies, religious institutions, or for educational uses. Performance of music is legal without paying royalties if it is not for profit and all money goes to charity. Music and dramatic works can be performed in classrooms, for religious assembly, and for transmission to the public, without any purpose of direct or indirect commercial advantage and without payment of any fee or other compensation for the performance to its performers, promoters, or organizers. There can be no direct or indirect admission charged unless the proceeds, after deducting the reasonable costs of producing the performance, are used exclusively for educational, religious, or charitable purposes and not for private financial gain (17 U.S.C. § 110). The 2002 amendments specifically discuss the transmission of these performances. It is not legal to make digital displays of these works unless they are specifically and only for registered students. They also cannot be transmitted or stored where public has access to them for any length of time other that what is absolutely necessary.

Section 110 does not include colleges and universities playing their pep music at games or for fraternities and sororities using music at parties. Licenses must be secured from performance rights agencies. This exemption also does not include music played at conferences, even though one may define that as an educational setting (Dickson, 1990). For conferences, conventions, or workshops, special licenses must be purchased to allow the playing of background music, music at socials, or live performances. This license is purchased by the convention center or the conference directors and is negotiated based on the size of the conference, the use of the music, and the number of conferees.

Public Performance Restrictions

According to the Copyright Act (17 U.S.C. § 101), a performance or display is public if it is open to the public or at any place where a substantial number of persons outside a normal circle of a family and its social acquaintances are gathered. This includes any place where people are not specifically invited and there is use of music or video displays. For public performances, a license must be obtained. This even includes dormitory public areas. Both in 1987 and in 1990 there was an attempt to seek an exemption for nursing homes and long-term care medical facilities so that these facilities could show movies without a license in their general living areas. The lobbying by the motion picture industry was so strong, however, that this exemption did not pass. Nursing homes, who often use videos as a leisure activity for their residents, must obtain a license to show them in their public areas, even though they do not charge a fee for viewing and the people who would be watching live in the facility. Thus the same would be true for college dormitories, camps, day cares, and so forth. To show a video in a public setting, one must have a license.

Music is also affected by public performance restrictions. Playing cassette tapes in a public place, for example, is prohibited without a license. If a manager of a fitness center, for example, wants to play background music in the center and people have paid to be members, the manager must obtain a license. If that same center has aerobic instructors who play tapes during exercises, the center must have a license, especially if there is profit (Bath, 1992). It is not the responsibility of the aerobics instructor to get the license; it is the responsibility of the center in which the class is being given. It is not particularly expensive, and the amount is decided by the size of the facility, the amount of use, and the number of participants in the program. Cases involving copyright infringement for public performances of music include *Tallyrand Music, Inc. v. Frank Stenko* (1990), involving background music played in a skating rink; *Broadcast Music, Inc. v. Melody Fair Enterprises, Inc.* (1990), involving a club where musical compositions were performed by live artists; *Tallyrand Music Inc. v. Charlie Club Inc.* (1990), where the health club's license covered music played in their restaurant and bar, but not for aerobics classes; and *Broadcast Music Inc. v. Blueberry Hill Family Restaurants, Inc.* (1995), where a restaurant chain operated jukeboxes that patrons played for free.

Television and Radio Broadcasting

The Copyright Act protects any original works of authorship fixed in any tangible medium, including motion pictures and other audiovisual works. The broadcast, by radio or television, of a live sporting event is eligible for protection. The Act has become a significant source of protection for the major professional sport leagues to combat the unauthorized interception of commercial-free feeds of broadcast signals. The issue has focused on sport bars where sport fans gather to watch satellite transmission of games that could only be seen through the use of satellite dish antenna systems (Sutphen, 1992). The professional sport leagues contend that the piracy of distant network satellite signals of games both devalues advertising revenues when patrons at sport bars watch contests commercial free and affects local ticket sales when a blacked-out game is broadcast in a local sport bar.

In 1976, Congress enacted 17 U.S.C. § 110(5), the "home-use" exemption, to limit the exclusive rights granted copyright owners under 17 U.S.C. § 106(4) to perform and publicly display their copyrighted work. Section 110(5) bars a finding of infringement when the transmission is received by equipment similar to the type "commonly used in private homes." In 1998, the "Fairness in Music Licensing Act of 1998" (17 U.S.C. § 110-5B) was incorporated into the Copyright Act to provide business establishments with the right to use radio, television, and cable transmission on a limited basis without infringement. The business establishments cannot charge for the programming and cannot provide retransmissions. Thus, the clause exempts commercial businesses that use standard radio or television equipment in their establishments to provide entertainment as long as they are not transmitting cable or some other pay-per-view transmission. Sport bars have attempted to use the "home-use" exemption to exempt their interception of satellite feeds by contending that satellite dish equipment is commonly used in private homes. Such arguments have, at least to date, been unsuccessful. Thus, sport bars or other public establishments desiring to transmit cable or pay-per-view broadcasts must have a license (*Cablevision Systems Corp. v. 45 Midland Enterprises, Inc.*, 1994; *National Football League v. McBee & Bruno's, Inc.*, 1986; *National Football League v. Play by Play Sports Bar, et al.*, 1995).

This "home-use" exemption clause does not include rebroadcasting. It is a copyright infringement to tape a copyrighted program and exhibit it at another time in a public setting without explicit permission from the producers. The broadcasting rights of time and place are reserved for the broadcasters. On the other hand, it is legal to tape a show for later viewing if it is done in the confines of a home with friends and family. This is considered time shifting and has been held legal in nonpublic settings (*Sony Corp. v. Universal Studios*, 1984). In *Sony Corp.*, Universal Studios attempted to enjoin the production of home-use videotape recorders, under the theory that the machines could be used for the unauthorized copying of movies owned by Universal Studios, to be viewed at a later time. In finding for Sony, the court found that in-home time shifting would not cause any actual harm to Universal Studios. The result in *Sony*, however, did not affect the right to time-shift in public places, which remains a copyright violation. A sport bar, for example, cannot tape a game for later viewing in their establishment without infringing on copyright.

Internet

The Internet is a major issue in copyright infringement, as it has made pirating music easily available to the general public. Starting with Napster, which was a Website that allowed the downloading of music from the Internet without charge, there is an ongoing battle with copyright protection. Although Napster was eventually shut down by the court (*A & M Records, Inc. v. Napster, Inc.* 2002), file sharing did not stop, as more sophisticated software was developed. Direct file-to-file sharing occurs regularly. However, Digital Millennium Copyright Act of 1998 17 U.S.C. § 512a protects the Internet service providers as long as they do not get directly involved in the file sharing.

The House of Representatives held hearings on "Digital Music Interoperability and Availability" to discuss the ways to curb file sharing that violates copyright (Digital Music, 2005). The purpose is to provide a mechanism that would make sure that copyrighted music was protected and that musicians and artists reaped their just benefits for their creations. As of this writing, it had not passed.

Patent

Patent is a second type of intellectual property. Whereas copyright's purpose is to advance creativity and the arts, patent law is designed to advance science and invention. To that end, a person can obtain a patent for "any new and useful process, machine, manufacture, or composition of matter, or any new and useful improvement" (35 U.S.C. § 101). A patent is not allowed for laws of nature, natural phenomena, and abstract ideas.

Patents, therefore, can be obtained for new sports equipment that would allow the user to hit harder or further or jump higher. Patents can also be obtained for designs. In sport, the shoe companies patent their new designs for shoes.

The invention must be newly created by the filer and useful for the patent to be granted. The purpose of the patent is to allow the holder of the patent to have a monopoly on the way the invention is used for a period of 20 years. That includes the right to "exclude others from making, using, offering for sale, or selling" the patented invention. This permits the holder to gain benefits encouraging further advancement.

Originally it was thought that patents were for inventions. As the courts have been more lenient in their interpretation of what could be patented, there is lots of controversy. As the courts began allowing patents for business methods and mathematical formulas, doors have opened to a wide variety of patents, and sport entrepreneurs have taken advantage of the climate. Dale Miller, for example, patented his grip on the golf club for his putt (Kukkonen, 1998). Nolan Ryan has patented a pitch (Smith, 1999). This trend creates questions as to what else will be patented in the near future. For example, if someone created a new football formation or a new method for moving a soccer ball, this process could be patented. With a patent, the creator would have complete control over who could use it and when. Imagine if the Fosbury Flop in high jump had been patented (Wilson, 1997).

The problem with patenting sport moves is that it would be extremely difficult to enforce. Mr. Miller's grip can only be used by him and others who pay for the right. But, unless he is right there, how will he know a recreation golfer is using it? Such enforcement is more difficult than other, more tangible objects (Kukkonen, 1998). The second problem with such patents is that they will affect competition. When a player invents a new move that obviously creates advantage, the playing field no longer starts level (Smith, 1999). Loren Weber (2000) sees this to be especially inviting to those in extreme sports. Because the competitors are individuals using specially named moves, the moves would be easy to patent. Weber says they should be copyrighted and put on video to put it into tangible form. However, in light of *NBA v. Motorola*, it would be the video that was copyrighted and not the move. The move could be patented though and video used for submission to the patent board.

The patent act is in the process of being revised. It will be interesting to see if they tighten the list of what should receive a patent. One of the issues is the quality of the patents being awarded, which has given rise to increased legislation and backlog in the patent system. There are 800,000 applications awaiting awards (Proposal to Reform the Patent Office, 2005).

Significant Case

---◇◇◇---

The following case examines the issues surrounding the golf video game used in bars. The question before the court was whether a look-alike game was an infringement of copyright.

INCREDIBLE TECHNOLOGIES INC. V. VIRTUAL TECHNOLOGIES INC.

United States Court of Appeals, Seventh Circuit
400 F.3d 1007 (2005)

OPINION:

* * *

As anyone who plays it knows, golf can be a very addicting game. And when real golfers want to tee-it-up, they head for their favorite course, which might be a gem like Brown Deer in Milwaukee, a public course that nev-ertheless plays host to an annual PGA Tour event every July. What most golfers do not do when they want to play 18 is head for a tavern. Also, most people are quite familiar with Tiger Woods. But who knows Jeff Harlow of Florissant, Missouri? This case is about "golfers" who prefer taverns to fairways and aspire to be more like Harlow than Tiger. Our case concerns video golf.

Golden Tee, made by Incredible Technologies, Inc. (IT), is an incredibly successful video golf game, one of the most successful coin-operated games of all time, beating all kinds of classic games like PAC-MAN and Space Invaders. Forty thousand Golden Tee games (in a dedicated cabinet) were sold between 1995 and August 2003. The game can be found in taverns all over America and in other countries as well. IT spends millions on advertising, and the game generates huge profits in return. The version we will be discussing is Golden Tee Fore!, which IT started selling in February 2000.

* * * With money galore tied into the Golden Tee game, the people at IT, understandably, were not happy when PGA Tour® Golf, made by Virtual Technologies, Inc. (d/b/a Global VR), appeared on the tavern scene with a competing game. That's why we have before us IT's appeal from the denial of a preliminary injunction in its copyright/trade dress case against Global VR.

IT has been manufacturing the Golden Tee game since 1989 and has several copyrights on various versions of the game. Involved in this appeal are copyrights on the video game imagery presented on the video display screen and the instructional guide presented on the control panel. * * *

Golden Tee employs a software program which projects images and sounds through a video screen and speakers in a kiosk-like display cabinet. The images are of players and golf courses. In front of the screen is a control panel with a "trackball" in the center, which operates the game. The "trackball" is a plastic white ball embedded on the game board. Approximately 1/4 of the ball is visible to the player. The rest of the ball is underneath the game board.

To play the game the trackball is rolled back for the golfer-player's back swing and pushed forward to complete the swing. As in real golf, the virtual golfer must choose the club to be used and, for an accurate shot, consider things like wind and hazards (indicated on the display screen) on the course.

Aware of Golden Tee's popularity, Global VR determined to create a game that was similar enough to Golden Tee so that players of that game could switch to its new game with little difficulty. It obtained a Golden Tee game and delivered it to NuvoStudios (Nuvo), the firm hired to develop the new game. NuvoStudios was instructed to design a game that dropped into a Golden Tee box to work with its controls, which should correspond as closely as possible to Golden Tee, so that a Golden Tee player could play the new game with no appreciable learning curve.

Nuvo worked from the existing software of a computer golf game—Tiger Woods Golf—and made modifications to convert from a game, played on personal computers and operated with a mouse, to an arcade game, operated as is Golden Tee, with a trackball and buttons. Nuvo essentially copied, with some stylistic changes, the layout of buttons and instructions found on the Golden Tee control panel. Global VR terminated Nuvo's services before the work on the new game was completed, but it hired key Nuvo personnel to finish the job. The goal of making it easy for Golden Tee players to play the new game remained.

The completed new game, PGA Tour Golf, is very similar to the Golden Tee game. The size and shape of PGA Tour Golf's control panel, and the placement of its trackball and buttons, are nearly identical to those of Golden Tee. The "shot shaping" choices are depicted in a similar way and in the same sequence. Although the software on the two games is dissimilar, both allow a player to simulate a straight shot, a fade, a slice, a draw, a hook, etc. by the direction in which the trackball is rolled back and pushed forward. Although other games, such as Birdie King and Sega's Virtua Golf have used trackballs, Golden Tee claims to be the first to use both a backward and forward movement.

There are also significant differences between the two games. Golden Tee is played on make-believe courses and the player is given a generic title, like "Golfer 1." The PGA game, on the other hand, uses depictions of real courses, such as Pebble Beach and TPC at Sawgrass, and it permits a player to adopt the identity of certain professional golfers—Colin Montgomerie and Vijay Singh, to name a few. The cabinets are somewhat different, within the realm of what is possible in arcade game cabinets, and the games use different color schemes.

IT filed this lawsuit in February 2003. Its request for a temporary restraining order was denied, and * * * hearing was held on its request for a preliminary injunction. In denying the injunction, the district court found that Global VR had access to and copied IT's original instruction guide and the video display expressions from Golden Tee. But the court said that IT had not shown a likelihood of success on the merits of this lawsuit, in part because (1) IT's expressions on its control panel are not dictated by creativity, but rather are simple explanations of the trackball system; at best, they are entitled to protection only from virtually identical copying; (2) the video displays contain many common aspects of the game of golf; and (3) IT's trade dress is functional because something similar is essential to the use and play of the video game.

To establish copyright infringement, a plaintiff must prove "(1) ownership of a valid copyright, and (2) copying of constituent elements of the work that are original." *Feist Publ'ns, Inc. v. Rural Tel. Serv. Co.*, 499 U.S. 340, 361, 111 S.Ct. 1282, 113 L.Ed.2d 358 (1991). Copying may be inferred where the "defendant had access to the copyrighted work and the accused work is substantially similar to the copyrighted work." *Atari, Inc. v. North American Philips Consumer Elecs. Corp.*, 672 F.2d 607, 614 (7th Cir.1982); *Warner Bros., Inc. v. American Broad. Cos.*, 654 F.2d 204 (2nd Cir.1981). The test for substantial similarity may itself be expressed in two parts: whether the defendant copied from the plaintiff's work and whether the "copying, if proven, went so far as to constitute an improper appropriation." *Atari*, 672 F.2d at 614. Because it is pretty clear here that Global VR set out to copy the Golden Tee game, the second question comes closer to the issue we must face, and it leads us to the "ordinary observer" test: "whether the accused work is so similar to the plaintiff's work that an ordinary reasonable person would conclude that the defendant unlawfully appropriated the plaintiff's protectible expression by taking material of substance and value." *Atari*, 672 F.2d at 614. It seems somehow fitting that the *Atari* case, involving the insatiable little yellow circle PAC-MAN, is a leading case guiding us through the maze of copyright law as applied to video games.

In these games, an ordinary observer, seeing a golf game on the video display and a trackball to operate the game, might easily conclude that the games are so similar that the Global VR game must infringe the Golden Tee game. But because ideas—as opposed to their expression—are not eligible for copyright protection, *see Mazer v. Stein*, 347 U.S. 201, 74 S.Ct. 460, 98 L.Ed. 630 (1954), protection does not extend to the game itself. *Atari*, 672 F.2d at 615; *Chamberlin v. Uris Sales Corp.*, 150 F.2d 512 (2nd Cir.1945). For other reasons, which we will soon discuss, protection does not extend to the trackball. It is clear, then, that the concept of the ordinary observer must be viewed with caution in this case, and we must heed the principle that, despite what the ordinary observer might see, the copyright laws preclude appropriation of only those elements of the work that are protected by the copyright. *Atari*, 672 F.2d at 614.

In fact, there are several specific limitations to copyright protection with some relevance to this case. One is the *scènes à faire* doctrine. The doctrine refers to "incidents, characters or settings which are as a practical matter indispensable, or at least standard, in the treatment of a given topic." These devices are not protectible by copyright. *Atari*, 672 F.2d at 616. For instance, the mazes, tunnels, and scoring tables in Atari's PAC-MAN were *scènes à faire*.

In addition, the Copyright Act provides that copyright protection does not extend to any "method of operation · · · regardless of the form in which it is described, explained, illustrated, or embodied in such work." 17 U.S.C. § 102(b). The Court of Appeals for the First Circuit has declined to extend copyright protection to a set of commands for a computer program. Even if there are multiple methods by which an operation can be performed, a plaintiff's choice of a particular method of operation is not eligible for protection. *Lotus Dev. Corp. v. Borland Int'l, Inc.*, 49 F.3d 807 (1st Cir.1995).

Useful articles and functional elements are also excluded from copyright protection. *American Dental*

Ass'n v. Delta Dental Plans Ass'n, 126 F.3d 977 (7th Cir.1997). A useful article is defined in the copyright act as "an article having an intrinsic utilitarian function that is not merely to portray the appearance of the article or to convey information." The design of a useful article is considered a "pictorial, graphic, or sculptural work only if, and only to the extent that, such design incorporates pictorial, graphic, or sculptural features that can be identified separately from, and are capable of existing independently of, the utilitarian aspects of the article." 17 U.S.C. § 101. The separability issue has caused considerable consternation. See our recent discussion in *Pivot Point International, Inc. v. Charlene Products, Inc.*, 372 F.3d 913 (7th Cir.2004).

The exclusion of functional features from copyright protection grows out of the tension between copyright and patent laws. Functional features are generally within the domain of the patent laws. As we said in *American Dental*, an item may be entirely original, but if the novel elements are functional, the item cannot be copyrighted: although it might be eligible for patent protection,

[a]n article with intertwined artistic and utilitarian ingredients may be eligible for a design patent, or the artistic elements may be trade dress protected by the Lanham Act or state law.126 F.3d at 980.

That means that the elements of our two games, which are most significant and most clearly similar, are not before us. The trackball system of operating the game is not subject to copyright protection. Functional features, such as the trackball system, might, at least potentially might, be eligible for patent protection. *See American Dental Ass'n*, 126 F.3d 977. But that protection would be for a significantly shorter period of time than copyright protection. So the anomaly is that a party can conceivably obtain more significant protection for the relatively less significant aspects of its product. For instance, in this case we are concerned, not with the trackball system but with things such as whether arrows pointing to the direction a golf ball will fly are sufficiently original to merit protection under the copyright laws.

However, as IT acknowledges, Golden Tee was not the first video golf game to use the trackball format, making a patent somewhat unlikely.

With this discussion out of the way, we move to the issues which are before us, as framed by IT. Those issues are whether the district court erred as a matter of law in creating a new "best explanation exception" to copyright protection; whether the district court erred as a matter of law in finding that the *scènes à faire* doctrine eliminated copyright protection for its video game expressions; and whether the district court erred as a matter of law in concluding that IT's trade dress in the control panel is functional. * * *

IT first contends that the district court misunderstood how the trackball system works, which led it to commit a legal error in evaluating the control panel and instructions. As we said, to operate both games, the trackball is rolled back toward the player to effectuate the back swing of the golfer on the video screen and pushed forward to complete the down swing. Directions on the control panel show how to make various shots, such as a draw, a fade, etc., by changing the angle at which the trackball is rolled back and forward. Nine specific shots are shown on the video display. The district court referred to "the" 9 different shot examples shown on the control panel. This, IT contends, shows that the district court thought that the 9 shots were the only possible shots when, in fact, subtle variations exist so that many more than 9 shots are available.

This fundamental misunderstanding, IT says, led the district court to a legal error. As IT puts it in a heading in its brief, the "district court erred as a matter of law in creating a revolutionary new 'best explanation' exception to copyright protection." The result of the new exception would be that the " 'best' physics textbook would have no copyright protection and could be freely copied, simply because it is the 'best.' "That argument certainly grabs one's attention: * * * The district judge here, Matthew F. Kennelly, concluded that the instructions on the control panel were not creative expressions and that there was "no evidence in the record to suggest that IT considered anything other than how best to explain its trackball system when it designed the text and instructional graphics featured on Golden Tee." It is from this rather innocuous statement that IT says the judge created a wholly new exception. We disagree with that interpretation. In context, it seems clear that what the judge was saying is that while there arguably are more ways than one to explain how the trackball system works, the expressions on the control panel of Golden Tee are utilitarian explanations of that system and are not sufficiently original or creative to merit copyright protection. Furthermore, the judge said, to the extent they might be subject to a copyright, they would merit protection only against virtually identical copying.

What IT is talking about on the control panel are the following: a horizontal graphic which shows the trackball motions used to control the flight path of the ball and small indicating arrows above the graphic; three white buttons of the left side of the trackball and two buttons, one red, one white, on the right of the trackball; and the textual instructions in the bottom right corner. Undoubtedly, there is similarity between the two games in the instructions on the control panel as well as in the layout of the controls themselves.

As to the instructions, we cannot say that the district judge abused his discretion in finding that the element of creativity is slight and can be protected only against identical copying, which does not exist. The element of creativity in the instructions is less than minimal. Both games use arrows to indicate the direction in which to

roll the trackball in order to obtain certain results. While it is possible that something other than an arrow could have been used to indicate direction, use of an arrow is hardly imaginative or creative in this situation. Also, the designs of the arrow surrounding the trackball differ significantly in the two games as do the graphics showing shot-shaping possibilities.

To a large degree, the layout of the controls seems to have been dictated by functional considerations. The trackball almost necessarily must be in the center of the control panel so that right- and left-handed players can use it equally well. It must not be so close to the upright video display that a player would smash her hand into the screen too forcefully after making a shot. Global VR claims that the buttons must be aligned across the center of the control panel for ease of manufacturing. We do not find an abuse of discretion in the district court's conclusions that the buttons appear to have been placed where they are for purposes of convenience and cannot be said to be expressive. We also note that on Golden Tee, the white button to the right of the trackball is labeled "backspin" and provides for just that; on the Global VR game, the corresponding button is labeled "shot type" and provides for backspin and topspin.

IT also contends that the district court erred as a matter of law in finding that the *scènes à faire* doctrine applied to eliminate copyright protection for the video imagery. Global VR, of course, disagrees, although it acknowledges that, in an appropriate case, the imagery of a video arcade game may be protected by a copyright. However, Global VR argues that in this case the elements over which IT claims protection are inherent either in the idea of video golf or are common to the creation of coin-operated video games in general. The district court agreed and determined that many elements of the video display were common to the game of golf. For instance, the wind meter and club selection features were found to account for variables in real golf and so were indispensable to an accurate video representation of the game. Furthermore, the court said that the game selection features, such as the menu screens which indicate the number of players and other variables of the game, are common to the video-game format.

As we said, *scènes à faire* refers to incidents, characters, or settings which are as a practical matter indispensable, or at least standard in the treatment of a given topic. Looking again at *Atari*, we see that the court found that the game was primarily unprotectable:

PAC-MAN is a maze-chase game in which the player scores points by guiding a central figure through various passageways of a maze and at the same time avoiding collision with certain opponents or pursuit figures which move independently about the maze. *Atari*, 672 F.2d at 617. Certain expressive matter in the game was treated as *scènes à faire* and would therefore receive protection only from virtually identical copying. The court said that the "maze and scoring table are standard game devices, and the tunnel exits are nothing more than the commonly used 'wrap around' concept adapted to a maze-chase game." *Atari*, 672 F.2d at 617. The use of dots to award points was also *scènes à faire*. The allegedly infringing game, K.C. Munchkin, had slight but sufficiently different versions of these items to preclude a finding of infringement. The court went on to find, however, that the concepts of the central figure as a "gobbler" and the pursuing figures as "ghost monsters" were wholly fanciful and thus subject to more protection. K.C. Munchkin had "blatantly similar features," giving Atari a likelihood of success of showing infringement.

In contrast, we see no error of law in Judge Kennelly's finding that the Global VR video display is subject to the *scènes à faire* doctrine. Like karate, *see Data East USA, Inc. v. Epyx, Inc.*, 862 F.2d 204, 209 (9th Cir.1988), golf is not a game subject to totally "fanciful presentation." In presenting a realistic video golf game, one would, by definition, need golf courses, clubs, a selection menu, a golfer, a wind meter, etc. Sand traps and water hazards are a fact of life for golfers, real and virtual. The menu screens are standard to the video arcade game format, as are prompts showing the distance remaining to the hole. As such, the video display is afforded protection only from virtually identical copying.

Given that certain items are necessary to making the game realistic, the differences in the presentation are sufficient to make IT's chances of success on the merits unlikely. Global VR has "real" courses and "real" golfers; Golden Tee's courses are imaginary and its golfers generic. In the Global VR game, a golf bag appears on the screen as the player chooses a club for the shot he intends to play. Global VR offers a "grid" mapping the green as a guide for putting. Golden Tee has no such device. Also, the Global VR game has a helicopter that whirls overhead from time to time. Both games mimic condescending real television golf announcers, but the announcers use different phrases: "the fairway would be over there" and "I don't think that's going to help a whole lot" in Global VR versus "That can only hurt," "You've got to be kidding," and "You can lead a ball to water but · · ·" from the Golden Tee announcers. Judge Kennelly did not abuse his discretion on this point.

* * *

The decision of the district court denying IT's request for preliminary injunction relief is AFFIRMED substance of the Gaste opinion.

 OTHER RELEVANT SIGNIFICANT CASES

Chapter 8.22 *Principles of Trademark Law*

Recent Trends

The Internet will continue to be in the forefront of copyright issues. The copyright owners are fighting issues on five fronts. Lobbying for new legislation, educating the public so they understand the reasons behind blocking infringement, litigating more individual infringers to set examples, increasing the methods for making it difficult to copy, and licensing. The United States has the longest copyright protection, and this has created a problem overseas, where the copyrights have run out and copyrighted information is public domain. Treaties are being reconsidered to see if agreements on this can be obtained (Yu, 2004). Finally, in the area of patent, there is reconsideration of what should receive a patent. Business methods and natural processes are being reconsidered by Congress. All these areas will affect the sports industry in the future.

References

Cases

A & M Records, Inc. v. Napster, Inc., 284 F.3d. 1091 (C.A. 9, 2002).
Baltimore Orioles v. Major League Baseball Players, 805 F.2d 663 (7th Cir. 1986).
Basic Books, Inc. v. Kinkos Graphics Corp., 758 F. Supp. 1522 (S.D. N.Y. 1991).
Broadcast Music, Inc. v. Blueberry Hill Family Restaurants, Inc., 899 F. Supp. 474 (N.D. Nev, 1995).
Broadcast Music, Inc. v. Melody Fair Enterprises, Inc., 1990 WL 284743 (W.D. N.Y. 1990).
Cablevision Systems Corp. v. 45 Midland Enterprises, Inc., 858 F. Supp. 42 (S.D. N.Y. 1994).
Diamond v. Chakrabarty, et al., 447 U.S. 303 (1980).
Feist Publications v. Rural Telephone Service Co., 111 S.Ct. 1282 (1991).
In re Aimster Copyright Litigation, N.D. Ill. 2000 (Slip copy) 1-19.

Lyons Partnership, L.P. v. Giannoulas, 179 F.3d 384 (5th Cir. 1999).

National Basketball Association and NBA Properties, Inc. v. Motorola, Inc. DBA SportsTrax, 105 F.3d 841 (2nd Cir., 1997).

National Football League v. McBee & Bruno's, Inc., 792 F.2d 726 (8th Cir. 1986).

National Football League v. Play by Play Sports Bar, et al., 1995 WL 753840 (S.D. Tex. 1995).

Phillips v. Pembroke Real Estate, Inc., 288 F. Supp 2d 89 (D. Mass. 2003).

Sony Corp. v. Universal Studios, 104 S. Ct. 774 (1984).

Tallyrand Music Inc. v. Charlie Club Inc., 1990 WL 114561 (N.D. Ill. 1990).

Tallyrand Music Inc. v. Frank Stenko, 1990 WL 169163 (M.D. Pa. 1990).

Publications

Bath, M. (1992, February). Permission to use music: It's the law. *Aquatics International,* 6.

Dickson, J. F. (1990, March). Copyright laws change meeting tunes. *Successful Meetings,* 31–33.

Digital Music Interoperability and availability. (2005). Hearing before Subcommittee on Courts, The Internet, and Intellectual Property of the Committee of the Judiciary, House of Representatives, 109th Cong., 1.

Hohensee, J. M. (1988). The fair use doctrine in copyright: A growing concern for judge advocates. *Military Law Review, 19,* 155–197.

Kukkonen, C. A. (1998). Be a good sport and refrain from using my patented putt: Intellectual property protection for sports related movements. *Journal of the Patent and Trademark Office Society, 80,* 808.

Martin, S. M. (1992). Photocopying and the doctrine of fair use: Duplication of error. *Journal of Copyright Society of the U.S.A., 345,* 429–525.

Patent Office Reform. (2005). Hearing before the Courts, The Internet, and Intellectual Property of the Committee of the Judiciary, House of Representatives, 109th Cong., 1.

Smith, J. A. (1999). It's your move—No it's not! The application of patent law to sports moves. *University of Colorado Law Review, 70,* 1051.

Sutphen, L. S. (1992). Sports Bars' interception of the National Football League's satellite signals: Controversy or compromise. *Seton Hall Journal of Sport Law, 2,* 203–231.

Talab (1986).

Weber, L. (2000) Something in the way she moves: The case for applying copyright protection to sports moves. *Columbia–VLA Journal of Law and the Arts, 23,* 317.

Wilson, D. C. (1997). The legal ramifications of saving face: An integrated analysis of intellectual property and sport. *Villanova Sports and Entertainment Law Journal, 4,* 227.

Yu, P. K. (2004) The escalating copyright wars. *Hofstra Law Review,* 907–957.

Legislation

Copyright Remedy Clarification Act, 104 U.S.C. 2749 (1990).

The 1976 Copyright Act 17 U.S.C. § 101 et seq. (2000).

Patents 35 U.S.C. § 101 et seq. (2000).

Visual Artists Rights Act of 1990, 104 U.S.C. 5128 (1990).

8.22 Principles of Trademark Law

Paul M. Anderson
National Sports Law Institute of Marquette University Law School

One of the most valuable assets that a recreation or sport management organization possesses is its name, logo, or some other defining characteristic that the public will recognize when viewing its products or services. These characteristics help promote and sell the products and services of the organization. Because such identifying marks are so valuable, competitors will often engage in counterfeiting or other behavior that harms the value or association of these characteristics with the original organization. It has been estimated that U.S. companies lose at least $250 billion a year to counterfeiting behavior, whereas the worldwide impact has been estimated to be 5 to 7 percent of global merchandise trade, or the equivalent of $512 billion in lost sales (McCarthy, 2005). One of the strongest ways for an organization to protect itself is by seeking trademark protection for the organization's name, logo, or other defining symbols.

Fundamental Concepts

The purpose of trademark law is to protect the owner of a mark and to prevent others from using the mark in a way that will cause consumer confusion. The Federal Trademark Act of 1946, known as the Lanham Act, governs the law of trademarks and their registration and provides causes of action that protect trademark rights from infringement.

According to the Act, a **trademark** is any word, name, symbol, or device, or any combination thereof, adopted or used by some entity to identify their goods and distinguish them from those manufactured or sold by others. A trademark serves several important functions: (1) it identifies a seller's goods and distinguishes them from those sold by others; (2) it signifies that goods come from one particular source; (3) it indicates that products are of a certain quality; and (4) it advertises, promotes and assists in selling the particular goods (McCarthy, 1991).

Trademarks can also be categorized by strength. The strongest marks are **arbitrary or fanciful marks** that bear no direct relationship to the product itself, such as "Adidas" for sports apparel, and "Ping" for golf clubs. These marks are inherently distinctive because they serve as an indicator of the source of the goods rather than describing the goods themselves.

Next are **suggestive marks** that hint at the characteristics of the goods or services, but require some consumer imagination to be understood as descriptive. For instance, although some consumers would understand a "Hot Pocket" to be a warm food item, it takes a bit of imagination to understand that the name stands for a meal wrapped in a flaky crust.

Descriptive marks identify a characteristic or quality of a good or service. For example, if a golf ball that produces a loud screeching sound when hit were named the "Screech Golf Ball," this name could be a descriptive trademark. These marks only receive trademark protection after they obtain "**secondary meaning**." Secondary meaning is obtained through widespread use and public recognition so that the mark primarily indicates the source of the good or service instead of the good or service itself. For example, collegiate team logos and color schemes, although not in themselves inherently distinctive, obtain secondary meaning once they have been associated with the respective team or university by use in the marketplace.

Generic marks receive no trademark protection because they refer to the name or class of the good or service and are so common or descriptive that they are not indicative of the source or sponsorship of the good or service. Some companies who originally adopt distinctive names or logos eventually lose their trademark rights in these same names or logos because they become so well known, such as *Kleenex* for facial tissue and *Jell-O* for gelatin.

The Lanham Act also protects service marks and collective marks. A **service mark** is a mark used in the sale of advertising or services to identify and distinguish the services of one entity from the services of others. Whereas a trademark identifies the source and quality of a product, a service mark identifies the source and quality of an intangible service. The mark "NCAA," as it stands for events and services related to the National Collegiate Athletic Association, is a service mark. A **collective mark** is a trademark or service mark used by the members of a cooperative, association, or other collective organization to indicate membership in that organization. Examples of collective marks in sports include "NBA," "NFL" and "Big East."

Use and Registration

To create ownership rights in a trademark, the trademark owner must be the first to use the mark in trade and make continuous, uninterrupted use thereafter. Once the trademark is used, consumers can rely on it to identify and distinguish the owner's particular goods or services from those of others. With registration, a trademark right extends to the use of the mark across the United States. Federal registration also provides constructive notice to others that the registrant owns the trademark and can exclusively use the mark. Every ten years the trademark can be reregistered to provide continuous protection.

An example follows that is of an actual trademark—the mark for *Marquette Sports Law Review*.

Reg. No. 2,620,764

United States Patent and Trademark Office

Registered Sep. 17, 2002

TRADEMARK
PRINCIPLE REGISTER

MARQUETTE SPORTS LAW REVIEW

MARQUETTE UNIVERSITY (WISCONSIN CORPORATION)
615 N. 11TH STREET ROOM 015
MILWAUKEE, WI 53233

FOR: LAW REVIEW JOURNALS, IN CLASS 16
(U.S. CLS. 2, 5, 22, 23, 29, 37, 38 AND 50).

FIRST USE 12-1-2000; IN COMMERCE 12-1-2000.

OWNER OF U.S. REG. NO. 1,800,716. NO CLAIM IS MADE TO THE EXCLUSIVE RIGHT TO USE "SPORTS LAW REVIEW," APART FROM THE MARK AS SHOWN.

SER. NO. 76-280,685, FILED 7-6-2001

NAME OF EXAMINING ATTORNEY

Infringement

Even if a recreation or sport management organization registers its trademarks, legal disputes may still arise when another organization develops a product that includes similar marks. The first organization can then sue the offending organization for trademark infringement.

To sustain a claim for trademark infringement under Section 1114(a) of the Lanham Act, the owner of the trademark must establish the following.

- First, the trademark owner must establish that she has a protectable property right in the trademark. Use and registration can establish a valid protectable right in a particular trademark.
- Second, the trademark owner must show that the other party's use of a similar mark is likely to cause confusion, mistake, or deceive consumers as to who is the true source of the mark. Courts will focus on any number of the following factors when evaluating whether an ordinary consumer will be confused:

  (1) Strength of the mark
  (2) Similarity between the marks
  (3) Similarity between the products and marketing channels used to sell them
  (4) Likelihood that the trademark owner will expand their use of the mark on future products
  (5) Evidence of actual confusion
  (6) Defendant's "good faith" intent in adopting the mark
  (7) Quality of the defendant's product
  (8) Sophistication of the consumers

The *Dream Team Collectibles, Inc. v. NBA Properties, Inc.* (1997) case involved a challenge to the NBA's use of the mark "Dream Team," which had been used to refer to the USA basketball teams that played in the 1992 and 1996 Olympic Games and the 1994 World Championships. Dream Team Collectibles (DTC) began using the mark in 1986 on collages of sports trading cards and on sport-related merchandise. In 1990 DTC filed for trademark registration of the "Dream Team" moniker. In 1991 and 1993 NBA Properties applied for trademark registration but was denied due to DTC's registration. In analyzing whether the NBA's use of the mark created a likelihood of confusion, the court looked to many of the factors listed earlier, including strength of the mark, similarity of the marks, and actual confusion and found that the NBA's later use of the mark was likely to cause confusion. The court entered summary judgment for DTC.

Counterfeiting

Another form of trademark infringement is counterfeiting, often known as piracy. Section 1127 of the Lanham Act defines a **counterfeit mark** as "a spurious mark that is identical with, or substantially indistinguishable from, a registered mark." Counterfeiting is an intentional effort to produce products that reproduce a genuine trademark without a license or other permission to use the mark. Organizations that attempt to counterfeit the trademarks of a recreation or sport management organization are subject to severe criminal and civil penalties.

Dilution

Dilution law protects the distinctive quality and selling power of a trademark, even if consumers are not actually confused by a non-trademark owner's use of the mark. The Federal Trademark Dilution Act of 1995 defines **dilution** as the lessening of the capacity of a famous mark to identify and distinguish goods or services, regardless of either the presence or absence of competition between the parties, or a likelihood of confusion, mistake, or deception. Dilution can occur in two forms: (1) blurring—when a party uses or modifies a mark and creates the possibility that it will lose its ability to serve as a unique identifier, or (2) tarnishment—where the mark is used in association with unwholesome or shoddy goods and services (Mermin, 2000, pp. 220–221).

In 1999, record company Untertainment was about to release a rap album titled *SDE Sports, Drugs, & Entertainment*. Along with the album, the company constructed a banner in New York City bearing the NBA trademark, while submitting the same advertisement to *Blaze* magazine. In the ad, the NBA player in the mark was holding a gun. After several residents complained to the NBA about their sponsorship of the ads, NBA Properties sued Untertainment claiming trademark infringement and dilution. The court found that the advertisements would create a negative association with the NBA logo, and therefore, under the tarnishment theory of dilution, Untertainment was forced to stop using the advertisement.

Unfair Competition and False Advertising

Unfair competition refers to a broader area of law than normal trademark infringement claims under the Lanham Act. It can involve any activity where one party attempts to deceive or mislead consumers by using the trademarks of another party on its own products to give the consumer the mistaken belief that the products of the infringer are actually the products of the true trademark owner.

When sports organizations seek to protect their trademark rights, they often will bring an unfair competition claim. Section 1125(1)(a) of the Lanham Act provides a cause of action for false designation of origin alleging that an infringer has used the trademark rights of another to deceive consumers as to the affiliation, connection, or association of the infringer with the legitimate trademark owner. Section 1125(1)(b) also provides a cause of action for false advertising alleging that another party has used commercial advertising or promotions to misrepresent the nature, characteristics, quality, or origin of their products.

Defenses

Often a recreation and sport management organization will fight an infringement claim by arguing that either the plaintiff does not have any protectable rights in the trademark, or the defendant's use will not cause consumer confusion. In addition, the organization may claim the trademark has been abandoned, that the doctrine of laches applies, that it is disparaging, that the use was a fair use or parody, or that there has been no infringement due to the presence of certain disclaimers.

Laches

In certain circumstances if trademark owners have neglected to assert their trademark rights in a timely manner, the **doctrine of laches** may limit them from recovery, if such recovery would be prejudicial to the potential infringer. In a case dealing with the University of Pittsburgh, the university was barred from recovery for past infringement when it delayed objecting to the sale of unauthorized clothing and novelty items including its name and mascot for 36 years. However, the university was granted an injunction to stop future unauthorized use of its marks.

Abandonment

Although trademark rights can be renewed continuously through registration, a trademark owner must still actively use the mark for it to remain valid. Section 1127 of the Lanham Act defines **abandonment** as discontinued use of a trademark with the intent not to resume such use, or when any act or omission of the owner of a mark causes it to become the generic name for the goods in connection with which it is used. When a defendant asserts abandonment as a defense, the claim is that the mark has fallen into the public domain because of the plaintiff's lack of use and intent not to resume use. An abandoned mark may be claimed and used by the public at large.

The U.S. Olympic Committee filed a petition to cancel the registration of the Kayser-Roth Corporation for the mark OLYMPIC CHAMPION for "polo shirts, sweat pants, sweat shirts, and athletic shirts and running pants" (*USOC v. Kayser-Roth Corporation*, 2004), claiming that it had abandoned its trademark for these goods. The company initially registered the mark in 1931 and used it on apparel until about 1993. After that time it only used it on socks. The company argued that it intended to continue to use the mark and had attempted to reach agreements with other companies but they were scared off due to the USOC's presumed ownership of the word *OLYMPIC*. Finding that the company had not shown any use of the marks on other apparel since 1993 and that a vague intent to continue to use the mark was not enough, the court cancelled the mark due to abandonment.

Fair Use or Parody

Section 1115(b)(4) of the Lanham Act provides that where a trademark is used fairly and in good faith only to describe the goods or services involved, there is no trademark infringement. For example, a television station's use of the term "Boston Marathon" to describe its unlicensed broadcast of the marathon was not found to be trademark infringement, even though another station was exclusively licensed to broadcast the event. The Court found that this use was merely descriptive of the event being broadcast and did not create viewer confusion.

Courts have also held that parody of a trademark is not infringement. In *Cardtoons, L.C. v. Major League Baseball Players Association* (1996), the court found that parody baseball cards that included caricatures of baseball players along with some commentary did not create confusion regarding the source of the cards.

Disparaging Marks

Trademark protection can also be denied if a mark is shown to be immoral, deceptive, scandalous, or disparaging under Section 1052(a) of the Lanham Act. In *Harjo, et al. v. Pro-Football, Inc.* (1999), Native Americans petitioned to cancel the trademark registrations for the marks "Washington Redskins" and "Redskins," both owned by Pro-Football, Inc., the owners of the NFL's Washington Redskins franchise. The Patent and Trademark Office initially granted the petition to cancel the marks. The team then sued for summary judgment to avoid the cancellation of the marks. The district court reversed, finding that the plaintiff presented insufficient evidence that the marks were disparaging to Native Americans and that the claim was barred by the doctrine of laches because there was a twenty-five-year delay in bringing the suit (2003).

Disclaimers

A potential trademark infringer may also argue that a conspicuously placed **disclaimer** alerting consumers that the product or service does not contain certain attributes or features, and that it is not from a certain source organization, absolves it from liability for infringement. An early case involving disclaimers was *NFL v. Governor of Delaware* (1977). The NFL sued to stop the State of Delaware from conducting a weekly sports lottery tied to the outcome of NFL games. Finding that a disclaimer on the lottery tickets and advertising materials informing consumers that the NFL was not associated with the promotion avoided any possible consumer confusion that the NFL sponsored the lottery, the court denied the NFL's claim.

Licensing

Merchandisers, manufacturers, sponsors, and others often wish to associate themselves with a recreation or sport management trademark owner. One way to do this is through the grant of a license. A **license** is a permit given by the trademark owner that allows another entity to associate their business and/or product with the name, goodwill, logos, symbols, emblems, and designs of the trademark owner. By paying some form of compensation, the company that receives the license (the licensee) can then use the trademark of the licensor to sell its own products. Problems occur when entities other than the licensee attempt to use the licensor's marks or when the licensor becomes unhappy with the licensee's use of the license.

Professional Sports

Most professional sports leagues have developed profitable licensing programs to capitalize on public demand for sports-related items with team and league affiliations. Each of the four major sports leagues (NFL, NBA, NHL, and MLB) have created separate properties divisions (i.e., NBA Properties) that deal with licensing of league and club trademarks to vendors who manufacture and sell products to consumers. The revenue realized from the sale of such licensed products is then divided among the teams within the league, normally on an equal basis.

The players associations also have formed separate entities that handle licensing issues for athletes (i.e., Players, Inc. for the NFL Players Association and the Players Choice Group Licensing Program for the MLB Players Association). These entities provide marketing and licensing services to companies interested in using the names and likenesses of current and past players. Revenues are normally distributed among the players that make up the association on a pro rata basis.

Some players have even gone so far as to seek trademark protection for their own name and likeness. Brett Favre, the current quarterback of the Green Bay Packers, has trademarked his name and image. Only companies given a license from Favre can use his name or likeness to sell their products.

The NCAA

The National Collegiate Athletic Association (NCAA) protects the intellectual property of the approximately 59 trademarks and service marks associated with the NCAA and its championships. In addition, approximately 300 schools license the use of their names and registered trademarks. Through its current licensing and marketing structure, the NCAA has approximately thirty-eight merchandise licensees, eleven nonretail licensees, three corporate champions, and five corporate partners. These licensees may not use the NCAA's marks in advertising to promote their brands. Instead, the marks can only be used to promote the sale of licensed products. On the other hand, the corporate partners may associate their products and services directly with NCAA marks and championships and promote the corporate partner brand in keeping with strict NCAA guidelines (www.ncaa.org).

The Olympics

The International Olympic Committee (IOC) owns the familiar "Olympic Rings" logo and the right to use the mark all over the world. The U.S. Olympic Committee (USOC) owns the exclusive right to use and license the Olympic marks in the United States and vigorously protects the use of its protected marks and terminology. In addition, unauthorized use of the Olympic name or marks may also be held to violate the Ted Stevens Olympic and Amateur Sports Act.

In a recent case, the USOC sued a manufacturer of toy trucks that had applied for a trademark for its trucks bearing the mark "Pan-American." Originally, the Patent and Trademark Office allowed the registration even though the USOC had previously registered such marks as "Pan American Games" and "USA Pan Am Team." The appellate court reversed, noting that the Amateur Sports Act provides the USOC with a higher level of protection for its trademarks than other marks; therefore, the USOC prevailed in its opposition of the "Pan-American" mark.

The Internet

In the mid 1990s, as recreation and sport management organizations began to promote their products and services on the Internet, many found that someone else had already registered their preferred domain name. These "cybersquatters" register famous trademarks as domain names in the hopes of selling them to the famous entity for substantial profit.

In the fall of 1999, two measures were established to combat the now-widespread problem of cybersquatting. The Anti-cybersquatting Consumer Protection Act (ACPA) amended the Lanham Act by creating a specific claim against cybersquatters. The Act outlawed the act of registering, with the bad-faith intent to profit, a domain name that is confusingly similar to a registered or unregistered mark or dilutes a famous mark. The Act allows a court to resolve domain name disputes even when the disputed owner of the name cannot be found or cannot be served in the United States.

A recent case dealing with a claim under the ACPA involved the NCAA, the Illinois High School Association (IHSA), and the domain name "marchmadness.com." The IHSA began using the phrase "March Madness" to refer to its boys' basketball tournaments in the 1940s. The NCAA's first use was in 1982, when CBS broadcaster Brent Musberger used the phrase to describe the NCAA men's basketball tournament. In the early 1990s both the IHSA and the NCAA claimed exclusive trademark rights to the phrase. After going through some initial litigation, the NCAA and IHSA agreed to work together to protect their rights. In 2000, they formed the March Madness Athletic Association (MMAA), and each retained a license to use the phrase in association with their tournaments. After falsely claiming association with the NCAA, Netfire acquired the domain name "marchmadness.com" in 1996. MMAA sued claiming that Netfire was engaging in cybersquatting in violation of the ACPA. Finding that Netfire acted with bad faith to profit from use of the trademarked phrase, and that the domain name was identical or confusingly similar to the actual trademark, the court upheld the district court determination that Netfire violated the ACPA (*March Madness Athletic Association, LLC v. Netfire Inc.*, 2005).

In addition to the ACPA, trademark owners can submit their dispute to a form of alternative dispute resolution. The Uniform Dispute Resolution Process (UDRP) is administered by the Internet Corporation for Assigned Names and Numbers (ICANN). By using the UDRP, a trademark owner must allege that its mark is "identical or confusingly similar" to the mark used by the cybersquatter who has no legitimate rights or interests in the domain name, and that the cybersquatter registered and used the domain name in bad faith. In addition, a UDRP proceeding does not preclude a lawsuit under the ACPA.

In *Canadian Hockey Association v. Mrs Jello LLC* (2005), the Canadian Hockey Association sued a corporation that registered the domain name "hockeycanada.com" and used the domain to sell advertising while also linking to Hockey Canada. The Association secured protection for HOCKEY CANADA as an official mark under the Canadian Trademarks Act. Once the Association filed a complaint to stop the defendant from using the domain name, the defendant replaced the site with links to generic information about Canada. Finding that the domain name was confusingly similar, that the defendant did not have any legitimate interest in the domain name, and that it was registered and used in bad faith, the panel ordered that the domain name be transferred to the plaintiffs.

Ambush Marketing

With rights fees for events such as the Super Bowl and Olympic Games costing several millions of dollars, official sponsors of these events want to ensure they are the only company given the exposure associated with the particular event. Still, companies that are not official sponsors want to create some association with these events to sell their products. **Ambush marketing** refers to the efforts of one company to weaken or attack a competitor's official association with a sports organization or event by using advertising and promotional campaigns designed to confuse consumers and to misrepresent the official sponsorship of the event. However, recreation and sport management organizations are reluctant to challenge ambush marketing campaigns because there is little case law supporting them. Corporations have successfully defended themselves with claims of commercial free speech. In addition, most ambush campaigns are short-lived, and courts support the use of disclaimers allowing ambush companies to make limited use of a registered trademark as long as they avoid creating consumer confusion.

Visa paid $20 million to the IOC for the right to act as the official credit card of the 1992 Olympic Games and $40 million for worldwide marketing rights to the 1994 and 1996 Games. To counter Visa's advertisement of its wide acceptance at the Olympics, American Express bought substantial advertising time on major networks. Although American Express did not use the Olympic five-ring symbol or the word *Olympic*, it referred generically to "winter fun and games," depicted the French Alps, and stated, "In Spain, you won't need a Visa" in its advertisements. The IOC threatened to sue American Express for ambush marketing, asserting that American Express attempted to create the false impression that it was an Olympic sponsor, but no suit was ever filed.

Regardless of the limited success of ambush marketing claims, sport organizations can minimize the negative affects associated with these tactics by developing a comprehensive antiambush marketing plan. As part of this plan, official sponsors should monitor nonsponsor signage and advertisements to ensure that official event names, marks, and logos are not being used (Mitten, Davis, Smith, & Berry, 2005, p. 1010).

Significant Case

◇◇◇

The following case illustrates how a court will examine likelihood of consumer confusion in a trademark infringement case. Of special note is the court's examination of the similarity of the marks and products and overlap in the geographical markets. The court discussed survey evidence used to demonstrate consumer confusion. The court also noted that even though the Colts did not use the contested mark, they did not abandon it over the intervening period of time.

INDIANAPOLIS COLTS, INC. V. METROPOLITAN BALTIMORE FOOTBALL CLUB

United States Court of Appeals for the Seventh Circuit
34 F.3d 410 (7th Cir. 1994)

OPINION:

POSNER, *Chief Judge.* The Indianapolis Colts and the National Football League, to which the Colts belong, brought suit for trademark infringement *(15 U.S.C. §§ 1051 et seq.)* against the Canadian Football League's new team in Baltimore, which wants to call itself the "Baltimore CFL Colts." (Four of the Canadian Football League's teams are American.) The plaintiffs obtained a preliminary injunction against the new team's using the name "Colts," or "Baltimore Colts," or "Baltimore CFL Colts," in connection with the playing of professional football, the broadcast of football games, or the sale of merchandise to football fans and other buyers. The ground for the injunction was that consumers of "Baltimore CFL Colts" merchandise are likely to think, mistakenly, that the new Baltimore team is an NFL team related in some fashion to the Indianapolis Colts, formerly the Baltimore Colts. From the order granting the injunction the new team and its owners appeal to us under *28 U.S.C. § 1292*(a)(1). Since the injunction was granted, the new team has played its first two games—without a name.

A bit of history is necessary to frame the dispute. In 1952, the National Football League permitted one of its teams, the Dallas Texans, which was bankrupt, to move to Baltimore, where it was renamed the "Baltimore Colts." Under that name it became one of the most illustrious teams in the history of professional football. In 1984, the team's owner, with the permission of the NFL, moved the team to Indianapolis, and it was renamed the "Indianapolis Colts." The move, sudden and secretive, outraged the citizens of Baltimore. The city instituted litigation in a futile effort to get the team back—even tried, unsuccessfully, to get the team back by condemnation under the city's power of eminent domain—and the Colts brought a countersuit that also failed. *Indianapolis Colts v. Mayor & City Council of Baltimore, 733 F.2d 484, 741 F.2d 954 (1984), 775 F.2d 177 (7th Cir. 1985).*

Nine years later, the Canadian Football League granted a franchise for a Baltimore team. Baltimoreans clamored for naming the new team the "Baltimore Colts." And so it was named—until the NFL got wind of the name and threatened legal action. The name was then changed to "Baltimore CFL Colts" and publicity launched, merchandise licensed, and other steps taken in preparation for the commencement of play this summer.

* * *

The Baltimore team wanted to call itself the "Baltimore Colts." To improve its litigating posture (we assume), it has consented to insert "CFL" between "Baltimore" and "Colts." A glance at the merchandise in the record explains why this concession to an outraged NFL has been made so readily. On several of the items "CFL" appears in small or blurred letters. And since the Canadian Football League is not well known in the United

States—and "CFL" has none of the instant recognition value of "NFL"—the inclusion of the acronym in the team's name might have little impact on potential buyers even if prominently displayed. Those who know football well know that the new "Baltimore Colts" are a new CFL team wholly unrelated to the old Baltimore Colts; know also that the rules of Canadian football are different from those of American football and that teams don't move from the NFL to the CFL as they might from one conference within the NFL to the other. But those who do *not* know these things—and we shall come shortly to the question whether there are many of these football illiterate—will not be warned off by the letters "CFL." The acronym is a red herring, and the real issue is whether the new Baltimore team can appropriate the name "Baltimore Colts." The entire thrust of the defendants' argument is that it can.

They make a tremendous to-do over the fact that the district judge found that the Indianapolis Colts abandoned the trademark "Baltimore Colts" when they moved to Indianapolis. Well, of course; they were no longer playing football under the name "Baltimore Colts," so could not have used the name as the team's trademark; they could have used it on merchandise but chose not to, until 1991 (another story—and not one we need tell). When a mark is abandoned, it returns to the public domain, and is appropriable anew—in principle. In practice, because "subsequent use of [an] abandoned mark may well evoke a continuing association with the prior use, those who make subsequent use may be required to take reasonable precautions to prevent confusion." 2 McCarthy, *supra,* § 17.01[2], at p. 17-3. This precept is especially important where, as in this case, the former owner of the abandoned mark continues to market the same product or service under a similar name, though we cannot find any previous cases of this kind. No one questions the validity of "Indianapolis Colts" as the trademark of the NFL team that plays out of Indianapolis and was formerly known as the Baltimore Colts. If "Baltimore CFL Colts" is confusingly similar to "Indianapolis Colts" by virtue of the history of the Indianapolis team and the overlapping product and geographical markets served by it and by the new Baltimore team, the latter's use of the abandoned mark would infringe the Indianapolis Colts' new mark. The Colts' abandonment of a mark confusingly similar to their new mark neither broke the continuity of the team in its different locations—it was the same team, merely having a different home base and therefore a different geographical component in its name—nor entitled a third party to pick it up and use it to confuse Colts fans, and other actual or potential consumers of products and services marketed by the Colts or by other National Football League teams, with regard to the identity, sponsorship, or league affiliation of the third party, that is, the new Baltimore team.

* * *

Against this the defendants cite to us with great insistence *Major League Baseball Properties Inc. v. Sed Non Olet Denarius, Ltd., 817 F. Supp. 1103, 1128 (S.D.N.Y. 1993)*, which, over the objection of the Los Angeles Dodgers, allowed a restaurant in Brooklyn to use the name "Brooklyn Dodger" on the ground that "the 'Brooklyn Dodgers' was a non transportable cultural institution separate from the 'Los Angeles Dodgers.' " The defendants in our case argue that the sudden and greatly resented departure of the Baltimore Colts for Indianapolis made the name "Baltimore Colts" available to anyone who would continue the "nontransportable cultural institution" constituted by a football team located in the City of Baltimore. We think this argument very weak, and need not even try to distinguish *Sed Non Olet Denarius* since district court decisions are not authoritative in this or any court of appeals. *Colby v. J.C. Penney Co., 811 F.2d 1119, 1124 (7th Cir. 1987)*. If it were a Supreme Court decision it still would not help the defendants. The "Brooklyn Dodger" was not a baseball team, and there was no risk of confusion. The case might be relevant if the Indianapolis Colts were arguing not confusion but misappropriation: that they own the goodwill associated with the name "Baltimore Colts" and the new Baltimore team is trying to take it from them. Cf. *Quaker Oats Co. v. Mills Co., 134 F.2d 429, 432 (7th Cir. 1943)*. They did make a claim of misappropriation in the district court, but that court rejected the claim and it has not been renewed on appeal. The only claim in our court is that a significant number of consumers will think the new Baltimore team the successor to, or alter ego of, or even the same team as the Baltimore Colts and therefore the Indianapolis Colts, which is the real successor. No one would think the Brooklyn Dodgers baseball team reincarnated in a restaurant.

* * *

. . .for if everyone *knows* there is no contractual or institutional continuity, no pedigree or line of descent, linking the Baltimore-Indianapolis Colts and the new CFL team that wants to call itself the "Baltimore Colts" (or, grudgingly, the "Baltimore CFL Colts"), then there is no harm, at least no harm for which the Lanham Act provides a remedy, in the new Baltimore team's appropriating the name "Baltimore Colts" to play under and sell merchandise under. If not everyone knows, there is harm. Some people who might otherwise watch the Indianapolis Colts (or some other NFL team, for remember that the NFL, representing all the teams, is a coplaintiff) on television may watch the Baltimore CFL Colts instead, thinking they are the "real" Baltimore Colts, and the NFL will lose revenue. A few (doubtless very few) people who might otherwise buy tickets to an NFL game may buy tickets to a Baltimore CFL Colts game instead. Some people who might otherwise buy merchandise stamped with the name "Indianapolis Colts" or the name of some other NFL team may buy

merchandise stamped "Baltimore CFL Colts," thinking it a kin of the NFL's Baltimore Colts in the glory days of Johnny Unitas rather than a newly formed team that plays Canadian football in a Canadian football league. It would be naive to suppose that no consideration of such possibilities occurred to the owners of the new Baltimore team when they were choosing a name, though there is no evidence that it was the dominant or even a major consideration.

Confusion thus is possible, and may even have been desired; but is it likely? There is great variance in consumer competence, and it would be undesirable to impoverish the lexicon of trade names merely to protect the most gullible fringe of the consuming public. The Lanham Act does not cast the net of protection so wide. * * * The legal standard under the Act has been formulated variously, but the various formulations come down to whether it is likely that the challenged mark if permitted to be used by the defendant would cause the plaintiff to lose a substantial number of consumers. Pertinent to this determination is the similarity of the marks and of the parties' products, the knowledge of the average consumer of the product, the overlap in the parties' geographical markets, and the other factors that the cases consider. The aim is to strike a balance between, on the one hand, the interest of the seller of the new product, and of the consuming public, in an arresting, attractive, and informative name that will enable the new product to compete effectively against existing ones, and, on the other hand, the interest of existing sellers, and again of the consuming public, in consumers' being able to know exactly what they are buying without having to incur substantial costs of investigation or inquiry.

To help judges strike the balance, the parties to trademark disputes frequently as here hire professionals in marketing or applied statistics to conduct surveys of consumers. * * *

Both parties presented studies. The defendants' was prepared by Michael Rappeport and is summarized in a perfunctory affidavit by Dr. Rappeport to which the district judge gave little weight. That was a kindness. The heart of Rappeport's study was a survey that consisted of three loaded questions asked in one Baltimore mall.

* * *

The plaintiffs' study, conducted by Jacob Jacoby, was far more substantial and the district judge found it on the whole credible. The 28-page report with its numerous appendices has all the trappings of social scientific rigor. Interviewers showed several hundred consumers in 24 malls scattered around the country shirts and hats licensed by the defendants for sale to consumers. The shirts and hats have "Baltimore CFL Colts" stamped on them. The consumers were asked whether they were football fans, whether they watched football games on television, and whether they ever bought merchandise with a team name on it. Then they were asked, with reference to the "Baltimore CFL Colts" merchandise that they were shown, such questions as whether they knew what sport the team played, what teams it played against, what league the team was in, and whether the team or league needed someone's permission to use this name, and if so whose. If, for example, the respondent answered that the team had to get permission from the Canadian Football League, the interviewer was directed to ask the respondent whether the Canadian Football League had in turn to get permission from someone. There were other questions, none however obviously loaded, and a whole other survey, the purpose of which was to control for "noise," in which another group of mallgoers was asked the identical questions about a hypothetical team unappetizingly named the "Baltimore Horses." The idea was by comparing the answers of the two groups to see whether the source of confusion was the name "Baltimore Colts" or just the name "Baltimore," in which event the injunction would do no good since no one suggests that the new Baltimore team should be forbidden to use "Baltimore" in its name, provided the following word is not "Colts."

* * *

Jacoby's survey of consumers reactions to the "Baltimore CFL Colts" merchandise found rather astonishing levels of confusion not plausibly attributable to the presence of the name "Baltimore" alone, since "Baltimore Horses" engendered much less. * * * Among self-identified football fans, 64 percent thought that the "Baltimore CFL Colts" was either the old (NFL) Baltimore Colts or the Indianapolis Colts. But perhaps this result is not so astonishing. Although most American football fans have heard of Canadian football, many probably are unfamiliar with the acronym "CFL," and as we remarked earlier it is not a very conspicuous part of the team logo stamped on the merchandise. Among fans who watch football on television, 59 percent displayed the same confusion; and even among those who watch football on cable television, which attracts a more educated audience on average and actually carries CFL games, 58 percent were confused when shown the merchandise. Among the minority not confused about who the "Baltimore CFL Colts" are, a substantial minority, ranging from 21 to 34 percent depending on the precise sub-sample, thought the team somehow sponsored or authorized by the Indianapolis Colts or the National Football League.

* * *

But with all this granted, we cannot say that the district judge committed a clear error (the standard, *Scandia Down Corp. v. Euroquilt, Inc., supra, 772 F.2d at 1427-28*) in crediting the major findings of the Jacoby study and inferring from it and the other evidence in the record that the defendants' use of the name "Baltimore CFL Colts" whether for the team or on merchandise was likely to confuse a substantial number of consumers. This mean[s]—given the defendants' failure to raise any issue concerning the respective irreparable harms from granting or denying the preliminary injunction—that the judge's finding concerning likelihood of confusion required that the injunction issue.

* * *

The defendants make some other arguments but they do not have sufficient merit to warrant discussion. The judgment of the district court granting the preliminary injunction is AFFIRMED.

Recent Trends

Collegiate Mascots

Several colleges, including the University of Wisconsin and the University of Iowa, will not schedule competitions against schools that use Native American nicknames or mascots. Under a new policy effective in 2006, the NCAA prohibits colleges from displaying hostile and abusive racial/ethnic/national origin mascots, nicknames, or imagery at any of its championships. Institutions that currently use Native American nicknames must take reasonable steps to cover them up or may be prohibited from wearing them altogether. In 2004 the NCAA asked thirty-three schools to review their use of Native American mascots, and fifteen removed all offending references. Eighteen colleges still use such mascots and nicknames. After an appeal Florida State University was allowed to continue to use its "Seminole" nickname due to its close relationship with the Seminole Tribe of Florida. However, the University of North Dakota lost a similar appeal over their nickname, "Fighting Sioux," because it did not have the support of the three recognized Sioux tribes of North Dakota. Since the NCAA adopted the rule other recreation and sport management organizations, such as state high school athletic associations, have also begun to review the use of Native American trademarks and nicknames in their athletic programs.

Disputes Over Trademarked Apparel

In 2004 and 2005, sports apparel companies brought almost a dozen trademark infringement cases. Disputes involving sports apparel companies included claims against competitors who manufactured confusingly similar products, used confusingly similar logo designs on their apparel, attempted to register confusingly similar marks, used another manufacturer's trademarked terms as designations on their apparel, engaged in illegal cybersquatting by using a domain name that violated another company's trademarks, and sold counterfeit products including another's trademarks. Although the apparel companies did not succeed on all their trademark infringement claims, this proliferation of litigation continues to demonstrate that they will be some of the most vigorous litigants in seeking to protect their products from infringement.

References

Cases

Canadian Hockey Association v. Mrs Jello, LLC, Case No. D2005-1050 (WIPO Arbitration and Mediation Center, December 20, 2005).

Cardtoons, L.C. v. Major League Baseball Players Association, 95 F.3d 959 (10th Cir. 1996).

Dream Team Collectibles, Inc. v. NBA Properties, Inc., 958 F.Supp. 1401 (E.D. Mo. 1997).

Harjo, et al. v. Pro-Football, Inc., 50 U.S.P.Q. 1705 (1999), *rev'd, summary judgment granted in part, summary judgment denied in part*, 68 U.S.P.Q.2d 1225 (2003).

Indianapolis Colts, Inc. v. Metropolitan Baltimore Football Club, Ltd. Partnership, 34 F.3d 410 (7th Cir. 1994).

March Madness Athletic Association, LLC v. Netfire Inc., 120 Fed. Appx. 540 (5th Cir. 2005).

NBA Properties, Inc. v. Untertainment Records LLC, 1999 U.S. Dist. LEXIS 7780 (S.D. NY 1999).

NFL v. Governor of Delaware, 435 F.Supp. 1372 (D. Del. 1977).

United States Olympic Committee v. Kayser-Roth Corporation, 2004 TTAB LEXIS 28 (2004).

United States Olympic Committee v. Toy Truck Lines, 237 F.3d 1331 (Fed. Cir. 2001).

University of Pittsburgh v. Champion Products, Inc., 686 F.2d 1040 (3rd Cir. 1982), *cert. denied* 495 U.S. 1087 (1982).

WCVB-TV v. Boston Athletic Association, 92 F.2d 42 (1st Cir. 1991).

Publications

Anderson, P. M. (1999). *Sports law: A desktop handbook*. Milwaukee, WI: National Sports Law Institute of Marquette University Law School.

McCarthy, J. T. (1991). *McCarthy's desk encyclopedia of intellectual property*. Washington, DC: BNA Books.

McCarthy, J. T. (2005). *McCarthy on trademarks and unfair competition* (Vols. 1 & 4). Eagan, MN: West Group.

Mermin, J. (2000). Interpreting the Federal Trademark Dilution Act of 1995: The logic of the actual dilution requirement. *Boston College Law Review, 42*(1), 207–237.

Mitten, M., Davis, T., Smith, R., & Berry, R. (2005). *Sports law and regulation: Cases, materials, and problems*. New York: Aspen Publishers.

Legislation

The Anti-cybersquatting Consumer Protection Act, 15 U.S.C. § 1125(d) (1999).

The Federal Trademark Act, 15 U.S.C. §§ 1051–1127 (2002).

The Federal Trademark Dilution Act, 15 U.S.C. § 1125(c) (1995).

Ted Stevens Olympic and Amateur Sports Act, 36 U.S.C. §§ 220501–220529 (1998).

8.23 Image Rights

John T. Wolohan
Ithaca College

The term *image rights* relates to a person's name or likeness, such as photograph or other visual representation of the person. When examining the image rights of athletes and other celebrities, historically, the courts found that by seeking fame in their sport or other endeavor, the athletes or celebrities had forfeited their right of privacy. Courts in the past have ruled that the right of privacy was only available to private persons, and once someone, as result of their activities, became a public figure they lost their right of privacy (*O'Brien v. Pabst Sales Co*, 1941).

The courts began to move from this position in the 1950s, when in order to protect athletes and other celebrities against commercial misappropriation and prevent the unjust enrichment of others off a celebrity's reputation, the courts extended the right of privacy to include a **Right of Publicity**. In recognizing such a right, the Second Circuit Court of Appeals held that "in addition to and independent of that right of privacy (which in New York derives from statute), a man has a right in the publicity value of his photograph, . . . and that many prominent persons (especially actors and ball-players), far from having their feelings bruised through public exposure of their likenesses, would feel sorely deprived if they no longer received money for authorizing advertisements popularizing their countenances displayed in newspapers, magazines, busses, trains and subways. This right of publicity would usually yield them no money unless it could be made the subject of an exclusive grant which barred any other advertiser from using their pictures" (*Haelan Laboratories, Inc. v. Topps Chewing Gum, Inc.*, 1953).

Since the Second Circuit Court's decision in *Haelan Laboratories v. Topps*, approximately eleven states have recognized the right of publicity by way of common law, and eighteen states have adopted some form of the right of publicity by statute (McCarthy, 2003). In addition to protecting a person's name or likeness, some states have even begun to broaden the right of publicity by expanding the "traditional meaning of 'name and likeness' to include such things as nicknames, drawings, celebrity look-alikes or by including characteristics such as vocal idiosyncrasies within a more general formulation of identity" (Clay, 1994).

For example, in *Motschenbacher v. R.J. Reynolds Tobacco Co.*, R.J. Reynolds produced some television ads "utilizing a stock color photograph depicting several racing cars on a race track" (*Motschenbacher v. R.J. Reynolds Tobacco Co.*). The drivers in the cars were not visible in the photo, and the cars had been altered, the numbers were changed, and a spoiler was added on which the company placed their product's name. In finding the ads violated Motschenbacher's, a well-known race car driver, right of publicity, the Ninth Circuit Court of Appeals held that even though a professional race car driver's personal likeness was unrecognizable, his identity could still be inferred by the distinctive decorations on his car (*Motschenbacher v. R.J. Reynolds Tobacco Co.*, 1974).

Fundamental Concepts

Right of Publicity

In 1960, William Prosser identified four distinct kinds of invasion of privacy. Although tied together by a common name, Prosser argued that the four different actions have almost nothing in common except that each represents an interference with an individual's right to privacy. "The four different types of interests are:

1. Intrusion upon an individual's seclusion or solitude, or into his or her private affairs;
2. Public disclosure of embarrassing private facts about an individual;
3. Publicity which places an individual in a false light in the public eye; and
4. Appropriation of an individual's name or likeness" (Prosser, 1960). (See also Chapter 4.14, *Other Intentional Torts*).

It is the fourth type of privacy interest identified by Prosser, "appropriation of an individual's name or likeness" (Prosser, 1960), for the benefit of another, usually of a commercial nature, that the courts cite as the right of publicity.

Common Law Misappropriation

The courts have generally found that there are two forms of appropriation. The difference between the two is found not in the activity of the defendant, but in "the nature of the plaintiff's right and the nature of the resulting injury" (McCarthy, 2003). The first type of appropriation is the right of publicity, which is "in essence that the reaction of the public to name and likeness, which may be fortuitous or which may be managed or planned, endows the name and likeness of the person involved with commercially exploitable opportunities" (*Lugosi v. Universal Pictures*, 1979).

The other type of appropriation brings injury to the feelings, that concerns one's own peace of mind, and that is mental and subjective (*Stilson v. Reader's Digest Assn., Inc.*, 1972). The most common form of appropriation involves the use of a person's name or identity in the advertisement of another's products or services. To establish a cause of action for common law misappropriation in these situations, the courts have generally held that an individual must demonstrate the following four elements:

1. the defendant used the plaintiff's identity;
2. the appropriation of plaintiff's name or likeness provided the defendant some advantage, commercially or otherwise;
3. lack of consent; and
4. resulting injury (*Eastwood v. Superior Court*, 1983).

In determining whether there is a cause of action for common law misappropriation, one of the hardest questions for the court to answer is whether an individual's identity or likeness was even used. For example, in *Newcombe v. Adolf Coors Co.*, the Ninth Circuit Court of Appeal was asked to determine whether a beer ad featuring an old-time baseball game, showing a pitcher in a windup position, misappropriated Don Newcombe's image. Even though the player's uniforms did not depict an actual team, and the background did not depict an actual stadium, the Ninth Circuit Court ruled that the player's windup was so distinctive that it made the identity of the player readily identifiable (*Newcombe v. Adolf Coors Co.*, 1998).

Finally, it is important to note that although some states recognize a common law cause of action for the misappropriation of a person's name or likeness, it is not the law in every state. In fact, a number of states still do not recognize an individual's right of privacy or the common law misappropriation of an individual's name or likeness.

Statutory Protection

In addition to the common law, eighteen states have enacted legislation to protect individuals against misappropriation of their image or protect an individual's right of publicity. The eighteen states are California, Florida, Illinois, Indiana, Kentucky, Massachusetts, Nebraska, Nevada, New York, Ohio, Oklahoma, Rhode Island, Tennessee, Texas, Utah, Virginia, Washington, and Wisconsin. The statutory cause of action of misappropriation complements rather than codifies common law and occurs when the plaintiff can show that another "knowingly" used his or her "name, . . . photograph, or likeness, in any manner, on or in products, merchandise, or goods, or for purposes of advertising or selling, or soliciting purchases of, products, merchandise, goods or services, without prior consent" (*Montana v. San Jose Mercury News*, 1995).

A good example of the rights available under statutory law is *Ali v. Playgirl, Inc.* In their February 1978 issue, *Playgirl* printed a portrait of a nude black man in the corner of a boxing ring. The man is unmistakably recognizable as Muhammad Ali, former heavyweight boxing champion, and is accompanied by the phrase "the Greatest." In defense of their use, *Playgirl* argued that because Ali was a public figure, he waived his right of privacy and therefore they did not need his consent.

In examining Ali's rights under section 51 of the New York Civil Rights Law, the federal District Court held that it was clear that *Playgirl* used Ali's portrait or picture for the purpose of trade within the meaning of § 51 without his consent. Such use, the court held, amounted to a wrongful appropriation of the market value of Ali's likeness. As for *Playgirl*'s argument that the use was privileged, the court ruled that "the privilege of using a public figure's picture in connection with an item of news does not extend to commercialization of his personality" (*Ali v. Playgirl, Inc.*, 1978).

Intellectual Property Provisions

In addition to state law, federal law can also be an effective tool in defending a person's right of publicity. Federal law is especially important because the right of privacy is only available to individuals, and corporations and partnerships must rely on theories such as trademark law to prevent the unauthorized commercial use of their identity.

Federal Trademark Law (The Lanham Act)

Although mainly thought of as a means for manufacturers to identify their goods and distinguish them from those manufactured or sold by others, the Lanham Act also protects consumers and competitors from a wide variety of misrepresentations of products and services in commerce, including the unauthorized use of an individual's image rights. Therefore, although narrower in scope than the right of publicity or misappropriation, the federal Trademark Act can be a powerful tool in protecting an athlete's image rights. (See also *Principles of Trademark Law*, Chapter 8.22).

False Endorsement Claims

Commonly referred to as "false endorsement claims," the Lanham Act bars the unauthorized commercial use of a celebrity's identity to help sell a defendant's goods or services when that use is likely to cause confusion among consumers as to the association, sponsorship, or approval of goods or services by another person (15 U.S.C. § 1125(a)).

In deciding whether the unauthorized use of a celebrity's identity is likely to cause confusion in the mind of the consumers, the Ninth Circuit court has developed the following eight factor test. The factors are

1. strength of the plaintiff's mark;
2. relatedness of the goods;
3. similarity of the marks;
4. evidence of actual confusion;
5. marketing channels used;
6. likely degree of purchaser care;
7. defendant's intent in selecting the mark;
8. likelihood of expansion of the product lines (*AMF, Inc. v. Sleekcraft Boats*, 1979).

One example of an athlete using trademark law to prohibit the use of his name is *Abdul-Jabar v. General Motors Corp.* Kareem Abdul-Jabar, a professional basketball player, sued General Motors after they used the name Lew Alcindor in a television commercial without his consent. Abdul-Jabar was born Lew Alcindor and used that name throughout his college and early professional career. He began using the name Abdul-Jabar in 1971, after he converted to the Muslim religion.

In overturning the lower court, the Ninth Circuit Court of Appeals held that the Lanham Act clearly prohibited "false endorsement" claims based on the unauthorized use of a celebrity's identity. As for General Motors' claims that Abdul-Jabar had abandoned the name Lew Alcindor, the Court refused to extend the abandonment defense under federal trademark law to cover a person's name. "One's birth name is integral part of one's identity; it is not bestowed for commercial purposes, nor is it 'kept alive' through commercial use" (*Abdul-Jabar v. General Motors Corp.*, 1996). As for General Motors' defense that its use of the name Lew Alcindor was protected under the "fair use" doctrine, which protects the unauthorized use of a trademark when "the mark is used only to describe the goods or services of a party or their geographic origin," the Court found that there was a genuine issue as to whether the use of Abdul-Jabar's old name implied his endorsement or sponsorship. In support of its decision, the Court noted that because the "use of celebrity endorsements in television commercials is so well established . . . a jury might find an implied endorsement in General Motors' use of the celebrity's name in a commercial" (*Abdul-Jabar v. General Motors Corp.*, 1996).

However, it should be noted that under trademark law most personal names are not inherently distinctive terms and can only receive trademark protection after they obtain secondary meaning (McCarthy, 2003). To obtain secondary meaning, the name or mark must have widespread use and public recognition so that the mark primarily indicates the source of the good or service instead of the good or service itself. For example, *Hirsch v. S.C. Johnson & Son* involved the use of Hirsch's nickname, "Crazylegs," on a shaving gel. The Supreme Court of Wisconsin not only found that Hirsch had a common law right of publicity under Wisconsin law, but that the trial court also "failed to consider the common law of tradename infringement and that, [for there to be an infringement] under tradename law, there need be no evidence of the prior marketing of a product or service under the nickname 'Crazylegs' " (*Hirsch v. S.C. Johnson & Son*, 1979). All that was necessary, the court ruled, was that Hirsch "show that Crazylegs designated the plaintiff's vocation or occupation as a sports figure and that the use of the name on a shaving gel for women created a likelihood of confusion as a sponsorship" (*Hirsch v. S.C. Johnson & Son*).

Defenses under the First Amendment of the United States Constitution

The First Amendment states, "Congress shall make no law respecting establishment of religion, or prohibiting the free exercise thereof; or abridging the freedom of speech, or of the press . . ." (U.S. CONST. Amendment I).

Because the intent of the First Amendment is to protect the dual freedoms of speech and the press, the courts will allow the "unauthorized use of an individual's name or likeness" when it is used for the "dissemination of ideas and information" or for other cultural purposes (McCarthy, 2003). If however, an individual's name or likeness is used for commercial purposes, the courts will not protect it.

The four main First Amendment defenses involving image rights are the newsworthiness doctrine, the incidental use exception, parody defense, and artist expression.

Newsworthiness Doctrine

The newsworthiness doctrine permits the media to use the unauthorized likeness of celebrities or anyone of interest in connection with a news item about the person. The definition of "news" has been given a broad reading and includes matters of public concern and interest. One example of how the doctrine relates to athletes and their image rights is *Montana v. San Jose Mercury News*. Joe Montana sued the *San Jose Mercury News* newspaper for reproducing his name, photograph, and likeness in poster form and selling it to the general public without his consent. In ruling that the newspaper had the right to use Montana's image, the California Court of Appeal held that the newspaper accounts of Montana's performance in two Super Bowls and four championships constituted publication of matters in the public interest and was entitled to protection by the First Amendment of the United States Constitution. In particular, the Court of Appeal held that Montana's name and likeness appeared in the posters for the same reason they appeared on the original newspaper pages: because he was a major player in contemporaneous newsworthy sports events and therefore may be republished in another medium, without the person's written consent. (See also *Other Intentional Torts*, Chapter 4.14).

The Incidental Use Exception

The courts have recognized an incidental use exception in cases where a newspaper or magazine has used, for advertising purposes, the image or photo of an athlete or other celebrity previously printed in a story, for advertisement. The advertisements, the courts have held, are simply "incidental" to the original, newsworthy publication. A good example is *Joe Namath v. Sports Illustrated*. Joe Namath sued *Sports Illustrated* after the magazine used his photograph in advertisements promoting subscriptions without his consent. The photograph used was originally used in the magazine in conjunction with an article published by *Sports Illustrated* concerning the 1969 Super Bowl game.

In holding that the publication and use of Namath's photo in the advertisements did not violate the law, the court held that the use of the photograph, originally used in conjunction with a news article, was merely incidental advertising of the magazine. In particular, the court noted that the reproduction was used to illustrate the quality and content of the magazine in which Namath had earlier been properly and fairly depicted and in no way indicated Namath's endorsement of the magazine.

Parody Defense

The First Amendment also allows for the use of parodies under certain circumstances. For example, parodies that use another person's image, when used in a traditionally noncommercial medium such as a newspaper, magazine, television program, book, or movie will likely be granted First Amendment protection. Parodies used in a commercial context, however, will generally not receive First Amendment protection. An example of the parody defense is *Cardtoons, L.C. v. Major League Baseball Players Association*. Cardtoons, a trading card company, designed "parody" trading cards of active major league baseball players. Cardtoons did not obtain either a license or consent from Major League Baseball Players Association (MLBPA). In ruling for MLBPA, the court stated that although parodies used in a traditionally noncommercial medium such as a newspaper, magazine, television program, book, or movie will likely be granted First Amendment protection, the primary purpose behind Cardtoons' parody is commercial. Commercial speech, the Court held, does not receive the same type of Constitutional protection. First Amendment rights end when Cardtoons preys on the MLBPA's names and likenesses for purely commercial purposes. Indeed, the court found that the only reason for using the players' likenesses and names was to entice the consumer to purchase the product.

Artistic Expression

Another area where the courts will allow the unauthorized use of another's trademark is when the mark is used in an artistic expression. For example, in *New York Racing Association v. Perlmutter Publishing*, the owner of a registered trademark asked the Court to consider whether Perlmutter Publishing's use of their trademark in paintings and other merchandise infringed on the New York Racing Authority's ("NYRA") trademarks. The court, in ruling against NYRA ruled that the inclusion of NYRA's trademarks on T-shirts and other merchandise, would not cause confusion among the average consumers, who would realize that the shirts displayed reproductions. The court found that the evidence showed that defendants use the images to describe Saratoga horse racing and not as an indication of source. Finally, in finding that the paintings were permitted under the First Amendment, the court ruled that the paintings serve the artistically relevant purpose of accurately depicting that scene. The Lanham Act, therefore, does not apply because the interest in free expression outweighs the need to avoid consumer confusion (*New York Racing Association v. Perlmutter Publishing*, 1997).

Significant Case

◇◇◇

Although not a sport case, the Ninth Circuit Court's decision in Vanna White v. Samsung Electronics is important nonetheless because of its expansion of the traditional meaning of "name or likeness" under the Right of Publicity.

VANNA WHITE V. SAMSUNG ELECTRONICS AMERICA

United States Court of Appeals for the Ninth Circuit
971 F.2d 1395 (1992)

Plaintiff Vanna White is the hostess of "Wheel of Fortune," one of the most popular game shows in television history. An estimated forty million people watch the program daily. Capitalizing on the fame which her participation in the show has bestowed on her, White markets her identity to various advertisers.

The dispute in this case arose out of a series of advertisements prepared for Samsung by Deutsch. The series ran in at least half a dozen publications with widespread, and in some cases national, circulation. Each of the advertisements in the series followed the same theme. Each depicted a current item from popular culture and a Samsung electronic product. Each was set in the twenty-first century and conveyed the message that the Samsung product would still be in use by that time. By hypothesizing outrageous future outcomes for the cultural items, the ads created humorous effects. For example, one lampooned current popular notions of an unhealthy diet by depicting a raw steak with the caption: "Revealed to be health food. 2010 A.D." Another depicted irreverent "news"-show host Morton Downey Jr. in front of an American flag with the caption: "Presidential candidate. 2008 A.D."

The advertisement which prompted the current dispute was for Samsung video-cassette recorders (VCRs). The ad depicted a robot, dressed in a wig, gown, and jewelry which Deutsch consciously selected to resemble White's hair and dress. The robot was posed next to a game board which is instantly recognizable as the Wheel of Fortune game show set, in a stance for which White is famous. The caption of the ad read: "Longest-running game show. 2012 A.D." Defendants referred to the ad as the "Vanna White" ad. Unlike the other celebrities used in the campaign, White neither consented to the ads nor was she paid.

Following the circulation of the robot ad, White sued Samsung and Deutsch in federal district court under: (1) California Civil Code § 3344; (2) the California common law right of publicity; and (3) § 43(a) of the Lanham Act, 15 U.S.C. § 1125(a). The district court granted summary judgment against White on each of her claims. White now appeals.

I. Section 3344

White first argues that the district court erred in rejecting her claim under section 3344. Section 3344(a)

provides, in pertinent part, that "any person who knowingly uses another's name, voice, signature, photograph, or likeness, in any manner, . . . for purposes of advertising or selling, . . . without such person's prior consent . . . shall be liable for any damages sustained by the person or persons injured as a result thereof."

White argues that the Samsung advertisement used her "likeness" in contravention of section 3344. In Midler v. Ford Motor Co., 849 F.2d 460 (9th Cir. 1988), this court rejected Bette Midler's section 3344 claim concerning a Ford television commercial in which a Midler "sound-alike" sang a song which Midler had made famous. In rejecting Midler's claim, this court noted that "the defendants did not use Midler's name or anything else whose use is prohibited by the statute. The voice they used was [another person's], not hers. The term 'likeness' refers to a visual image not a vocal imitation." Id. at 463.

In this case, Samsung and Deutsch used a robot with mechanical features, and not, for example, a manikin molded to White's precise features. Without deciding for all purposes when a caricature or impressionistic resemblance might become a "likeness," we agree with the district court that the robot at issue here was not White's "likeness" within the meaning of section 3344. Accordingly, we affirm the court's dismissal of White's section 3344 claim.

II. Right of Publicity

White next argues that the district court erred in granting summary judgment to defendants on White's common law right of publicity claim. In Eastwood v. Superior Court, 149 Cal. App. 3d 409 , 198 Cal. Rptr. 342 (1983), the California court of appeal stated that the common law right of publicity cause of action "may be pleaded by alleging (1) the defendant's use of the plaintiff's identity; (2) the appropriation of plaintiff's name or likeness to defendant's advantage, commercially or otherwise; (3) lack of consent; and (4) resulting injury." Id. at 417 (citing Prosser, Law of Torts (4th ed. 1971) § 117, pp. 804-807). The district court dismissed White's claim for failure to satisfy Eastwood's second prong, reasoning that defendants had not appropriated White's "name or likeness" with their robot ad. We agree that the robot ad did not make use of White's name or likeness. However, the common law right of publicity is not so confined.

The Eastwood court did not hold that the right of publicity cause of action could be pleaded only by alleging an appropriation of name or likeness. Eastwood involved an unauthorized use of photographs of Clint Eastwood and of his name. Accordingly, the Eastwood court had no occasion to consider the extent beyond the use of name or likeness to which the right of publicity reaches. That court held only that the right of publicity cause of action "may be" pleaded by alleging appropriation of name or likeness, not that the action may be pleaded only in those terms.

The "name or likeness" formulation referred to in Eastwood originated not as an element of the right of publicity cause of action, but as a description of the types of cases in which the cause of action had been recognized. The source of this formulation is Prosser, Privacy, 48 Cal.L.Rev. 383, 401-07 (1960), one of the earliest and most enduring articulations of the common law right of publicity cause of action. In looking at the case law to that point, Prosser recognized that right of publicity cases involved one of two basic factual scenarios: name appropriation, and picture or other likeness appropriation. Id. at 401-02, nn.156-57.

Even though Prosser focused on appropriations of name or likeness in discussing the right of publicity, he noted that "it is not impossible that there might be appropriation of the plaintiff's identity, as by impersonation, without the use of either his name or his likeness, and that this would be an invasion of his right of privacy." Id. At 401, n.155. n1 At the time Prosser wrote, he noted however, that "no such case appears to have arisen." Id.

Since Prosser's early formulation, the case law has borne out his insight that the right of publicity is not limited to the appropriation of name or likeness. In Motschenbacher v. R.J. Reynolds Tobacco Co., 498 F.2d 821 (9th Cir. 1974), the defendant had used a photograph of the plaintiff's race car in a television commercial. Although the plaintiff appeared driving the car in the photograph, his features were not visible. Even though the defendant had not appropriated the plaintiff's name or likeness, this court held that plaintiff's California right of publicity claim should reach the jury.

In Midler, this court held that, even though the defendants had not used Midler's name or likeness, Midler had stated a claim for violation of her California common law right of publicity because "the defendants . . . for their own profit in selling their product did appropriate part of her identity" by using a Midler sound-alike. Id. at 463-64.

In Carson v. Here's Johnny Portable Toilets, Inc., 698 F.2d 831 (6th Cir. 1983), the defendant had marketed portable toilets under the brand name "Here's Johnny"—Johnny Carson's signature "Tonight Show" introduction—without Carson's permission. The district court had dismissed Carson's Michigan common law right of publicity claim because the defendants had not used Carson's "name or likeness." Id. at 835. In reversing the district court, the sixth circuit found "the district court's conception of the right of publicity . . . too narrow" and held that the right was implicated because the defendant had appropriated Carson's identity by using, inter alia, the phrase "Here's Johnny." Id. at 835-37.

These cases teach not only that the common law right of publicity reaches means of appropriation other than name or likeness, but that the specific means of appropriation are relevant only for determining whether the defendant has in fact appropriated the plaintiff's identity. The right of publicity does not require that appropriations of identity be accomplished through particular means to be actionable. It is noteworthy that the Midler and Carson defendants not only avoided using the plaintiff's name or likeness, but they also avoided appropriating the celebrity's voice, signature, and photograph. The photograph in Motschenbacher did include the plaintiff, but because the plaintiff was not visible the driver could have been an actor or dummy and the analysis in the case would have been the same.

Although the defendants in these cases avoided the most obvious means of appropriating the plaintiffs' identities, each of their actions directly implicated the commercial interests which the right of publicity is designed to protect. As the Carson court explained:

the right of publicity has developed to protect the commercial interest of celebrities in their identities. The theory of the right is that a celebrity's identity can be valuable in the promotion of products, and the celebrity has an interest that may be protected from the unauthorized commercial exploitation of that identity. . . . If the celebrity's identity is commercially exploited, there has been an invasion of his right whether or not his "name or likeness" is used.

Carson, 698 F.2d at 835. It is not important how the defendant has appropriated the plaintiff's identity, but whether the defendant has done so. Motschenbacher, Midler, and Carson teach the impossibility of treating the right of publicity as guarding only against a laundry list of specific means of appropriating identity. A rule which says that the right of publicity can be infringed only through the use of nine different methods of appropriating identity merely challenges the clever advertising strategist to come up with the tenth.

Indeed, if we treated the means of appropriation as dispositive in our analysis of the right of publicity, we would not only weaken the right but effectively eviscerate it. The right would fail to protect those plaintiffs most in need of its protection. Advertisers use celebrities to promote their products. The more popular the celebrity, the greater the number of people who recognize her, and the greater the visibility for the product. The identities of the most popular celebrities are not only the most attractive for advertisers, but also the easiest to evoke without resorting to obvious means such as name, likeness, or voice.

Consider a hypothetical advertisement which depicts a mechanical robot with male features, an African-American complexion, and a bald head. The robot is wearing black hightop Air Jordan basketball sneakers, and a red basketball uniform with black trim, baggy shorts, and the number 23 (though not revealing "Bulls" or "Jordan" lettering). The ad depicts the robot dunking a basketball one-handed, stiff-armed, legs extended like open scissors, and tongue hanging out. Now envision that this ad is run on television during professional basketball games. Considered individually, the robot's physical attributes, its dress, and its stance tell us little. Taken together, they lead to the only conclusion that any sports viewer who has registered a discernible pulse in the past five years would reach: the ad is about Michael Jordan.

Viewed separately, the individual aspects of the advertisement in the present case say little. Viewed together, they leave little doubt about the celebrity the ad is meant to depict. The female-shaped robot is wearing a long gown, blond wig, and large jewelry. Vanna White dresses exactly like this at times, but so do many other women. The robot is in the process of turning a block letter on a game-board. Vanna White dresses like this while turning letters on a game-board but perhaps similarly attired Scrabble-playing women do this as well. The robot is standing on what looks to be the Wheel of Fortune game show set. Vanna White dresses like this, turns letters, and does this on the Wheel of Fortune game show. She is the only one. Indeed, defendants themselves referred to their ad as the "Vanna White" ad. We are not surprised.

Television and other media create marketable celebrity identity value. Considerable energy and ingenuity are expended by those who have achieved celebrity value to exploit it for profit. The law protects the celebrity's sole right to exploit this value whether the celebrity has achieved her fame out of rare ability, dumb luck, or a combination thereof. We decline Samsung and Deutch's invitation to permit the evisceration of the common law right of publicity through means as facile as those in this case. Because White has alleged facts showing that Samsung and Deutsch had appropriated her identity, the district court erred by rejecting, on summary judgment, White's common law right of publicity claim.

III. The Lanham Act

White's final argument is that the district court erred in denying her claim under § 43(a) of the Lanham Act, 15 U.S.C. § 1125(a). The version of section 43(a) applicable to this case provides, in pertinent part, that "any person who shall . . . use, in connection with any goods or services . . . any false description or representation . . . shall be liable to a civil action . . . by any person who believes that he is or is likely to be damaged by the use of any such false description or designation." 15 U.S.C. § 1125(a).

To prevail on her Lanham Act claim, White is required to show that in running the robot ad, Samsung and Deutsch created a likelihood of confusion over whether White was endorsing Samsung's VCRs.

This circuit recognizes several different multi-factor tests for determining whether a likelihood of confusion exists. None of these tests is correct to the exclusion of the others. Normally, in reviewing the district court's decision, this court will look to the particular test that the district court used. However, because the district court in this case apparently did not use any of the multi-factor tests in making its likelihood of confusion determination, and because this case involves an appeal from summary judgment and we review de novo the district court's determination, we will look for guidance to the 8-factor test enunciated in AMF, Inc. v. Sleekcraft Boats, 599 F.2d 341 (9th Cir. 1979). According to AMF, factors relevant to a likelihood of confusion include:
(1) strength of the plaintiff's mark;
(2) relatedness of the goods;
(3) similarity of the marks;
(4) evidence of actual confusion;
(5) marketing channels used;
(6) likely degree of purchaser care;
(7) defendant's intent in selecting the mark;
(8) likelihood of expansion of the product lines.

We turn now to consider White's claim in light of each factor.

In cases involving confusion over endorsement by a celebrity plaintiff, "mark" means the celebrity's persona. The "strength" of the mark refers to the level of recognition the celebrity enjoys among members of society. If Vanna White is unknown to the segment of the public at whom Samsung's robot ad was directed, then that segment could not be confused as to whether she was endorsing Samsung VCRs. Conversely, if White is well-known, this would allow the possibility of a likelihood of confusion. For the purposes of the Sleekcraft test, White's "mark," or celebrity identity, is strong.

In cases concerning confusion over celebrity endorsement, the plaintiff's "goods" concern the reasons for or source of the plaintiff's fame. Because White's fame is based on her televised performances, her "goods" are closely related to Samsung's VCRs. Indeed, the ad itself reinforced the relationship by informing its readers that they would be taping the "longest-running game show" on Samsung's VCRs well into the future.

The third factor, "similarity of the marks," both supports and contradicts a finding of likelihood of confusion. On the one hand, all of the aspects of the robot ad identify White; on the other, the figure is quite clearly a robot, not a human. This ambiguity means that we must look to the other factors for resolution.

The fourth factor does not favor White's claim because she has presented no evidence of actual confusion.

Fifth, however, White has appeared in the same stance as the robot from the ad in numerous magazines, including the covers of some. Magazines were used as the marketing channels for the robot ad. This factor cuts toward a likelihood of confusion.

Sixth, consumers are not likely to be particularly careful in determining who endorses VCRs, making confusion as to their endorsement more likely.

Concerning the seventh factor, "defendant's intent," the district court found that, in running the robot ad, the defendants had intended a spoof of the "Wheel of Fortune." The relevant question is whether the defendants "intended to profit by confusing consumers" concerning the endorsement of Samsung VCRs. Toho, 645 F.2d 788 (9th Cir. 1981). We do not disagree that defendants intended to spoof Vanna White and "Wheel of Fortune." That does not preclude, however, the possibility that defendants also intended to confuse consumers regarding endorsement. The robot ad was one of a series of ads run by defendants which followed the same theme. Another ad in the series depicted Morton Downey Jr. as a presidential candidate in the year 2008. Doubtless, defendants intended to spoof presidential elections and Mr. Downey through this ad. Consumers, however, would likely believe, and would be correct in so believing, that Mr. Downey was paid for his permission and was endorsing Samsung products. Looking at the series of advertisements as a whole, a jury could reasonably conclude that beneath the surface humor of the series lay an intent to persuade consumers that celebrity Vanna White, like celebrity Downey, was endorsing Samsung products.

Finally, the eighth factor, "likelihood of expansion of the product lines," does not appear apposite to a celebrity endorsement case such as this.

Application of the Sleekcraft factors to this case indicates that the district court erred in rejecting White's Lanham Act claim at the summary judgment stage. In so concluding, we emphasize two facts, however. First, construing the motion papers in White's favor, as we must, we hold only that White has raised a genuine issue of material fact concerning a likelihood of confusion as to her endorsement. Cohen v. Paramount Pictures Corp., 845 F.2d 851, 852-53 (9th Cir. 1989). Whether White's Lanham Act claim should succeed is a matter for the jury. Second, we stress that we reach this conclusion in light of the peculiar facts of this case. In particular, we note that the robot ad identifies White and was part of a series of ads in which other celebrities participated and were paid for their endorsement of Samsung's products.

IV. The Parody Defense

In defense, defendants cite a number of cases for the proposition that their robot ad constituted protected speech. The only cases they cite which are even remotely relevant to this case are Hustler Magazine v. Falwell, 485 U.S. 46, 99 L. Ed. 2d 41 , 108 S. Ct. 876 (1988) and L.L. Bean, Inc. v. Drake Publishers, Inc., 811 F.2d 26 (1st Cir. 1987). Those cases involved parodies of advertisements run for the purpose of poking fun at Jerry Falwell and L.L. Bean, respectively. This case involves a true advertisement run for the purpose of selling Samsung VCRs. The ad's spoof of Vanna White and Wheel of Fortune is subservient and only tangentially related to the ad's primary message: "buy Samsung VCRs." Defendants' parody arguments are better addressed to non-commercial parodies. The difference between a "parody" and a "knock-off" is the difference between fun and profit.

V. Conclusion

In remanding this case, we hold only that White has pleaded claims which can go to the jury for its decision.

Recent Trends

Postmortem Rights

Because of technological advances, an area of growing importance involves the image rights of the dead. In the last twenty years, states have begun to recognize that the right of publicity in addition to being assignable and licensed could also be descendible. Probably the most cited case dealing with the postmortem right of publicity is *Lugosi v. Universal Pictures*. The widow and children of Bela Lugosi, a movie actor famous for his role as Dracula, brought suit against Universal to recover profits made by Universal in licensing of merchandise associated with the film. The family claimed that Universal had misappropriated property, Lugosi's image, they had inherited from Lugosi. In ruling for Universal, the California Supreme Court held that "the right to exploit name and likeness is personal to the artist and must be exercised, if at all, by him during his lifetime" (*Lugosi v. Universal Pictures*, 1979).

As a result of the court's decision in *Lugosi*, California passed Civil Code § 990, which prohibits the use of "a deceased personality's name, voice, signature, photograph, or likeness, in any manner, on or in products, merchandise, or goods, or for purposes of advertising or selling, . . . without prior consent . . . shall be liable for any damages sustained." Some states have followed California's lead in recognizing a right of publicity as a fully transferable and descendible property right. Other states such as New York, however, still do not recognize a postmortem right of publicity.

Sex and the City

In 2005, New York Yankee legend Yogi Berra filed a $10 million lawsuit against Turner Broadcasting Systems for using his name in an advertisement for its *Sex and the City* reruns. The ad, which appeared on buses and billboards and in magazines around the world, features what the suit calls a "rather provocative" photo of Kim Cattrall's promiscuous "Samantha" character and reads, "Yogasm: a) a type of yo-yo trick, b) sex with Yogi Berra, c) what Samantha has with a guy from yoga class."

The suit claimed that TBS never asked Berra for permission to use his name and that the ad "created a false image of Berra that is both contrary to his personality, lifestyle and character as well as abhorrent to him personally." Yogi Berra and TBS eventually agreed to mediation over the dispute and reached a settlement that paid Berra an undisclosed, but reportedly substantial, amount ("Two-Minute Drill," 2005).

References

Cases

Abdul-Jabar v. General Motors Corp., 85 F.3d 407 (9th Cir. 1996).
Ali v. Playgirl, Inc., 447 F.Supp. 723 (1978).
AMF, Inc. v. Sleekcraft Boats, 599 F.2d 341 (9th Cir. 1979).
Cardtoons, L.C. v. Major League Baseball Players Association, 838 F. Supp 1501 (N.D. Okla. 1993).
Eastwood v. Superior Court, 149 Cal. App. 3d 409, 198 Cal. Rptr. 342 (1983).
ETW Corp. v. Jireh Publishing, Inc., 99 F. Supp. 2d 829 (2000).
ETW Corp. v. Jireh Publishing, Inc., 332 F.3d 915 (6th Cir., 2003).
Haelan Laboratories, Inc. v. Topps Chewing Gum, Inc., 202 F.2d 866 (2nd. Cir. 1953).
Hirsch v. S.C. Johnson & Son, 280 N.W. 129 (Wis. 1979).
Joe Namath v. Sports Illustrated, 48 A.D.2d 487; 371 N.Y.S.2d 10 (1975).
Lugosi v. Universal Pictures, 603 P.2d 425 (1979).
Montana v. San Jose Mercury News, 40 Cal. Rptr. 2d 639 (1995).
Motschenbacher v. R.J. Reynolds Tobacco Co., 498 F.2d 821 (1974).
Newcombe v. Adolf Coors Co., 157 F.3d 686 (9th Cir. 1998).
New York Racing Association v. Perlmutter Publishing, 959 F.Supp. 578 (1997).
O'Brien v. Pabst Sales Co., 124 F.2d 167 (1941).
Stilson v. Reader's Digest Assn., Inc., 28 Cal.App.3d 270, 273 (1972).

Publications

Clay, S. (1994). Starstruck: The overextension of celebrity publicity rights in state and federal courts. *Minnesota Law Review, 79*, 485–517.
McCarthy, J. T. (2004). *The rights of publicity and privacy* (3rd ed.). Deerfield IL: Clark Boardman Callaghan.
Prosser, W. (1960) Privacy. *California Law Review, 48*, 383–423.
Two-Minute Drill. (2005, Feb. 2). *Tampa Tribune*, p. 2.

Warren, S., & Brandeis, L. (1890). The right of privacy. *Harvard Law Review, 4,* 193–220.

Wolohan, J. T. (2005). Sports image rights in the United States. In I. S. Blackshaw & R. C. Siekmann (Eds.), *Sports image rights in Europe*. The Hague: T.M.C. Asser Press.

Legislation

California Civil Code § 990.

Lanham Act § 45, 15 U.S.C. § 1125(a).

8.31 Antitrust Law:
PROFESSIONAL SPORT APPLICATIONS

Lisa Pike Masteralexis
University of Massachusetts-Amherst

Professional sport leagues' structure and labor management relations have been imprinted by antitrust cases. Professional sport leagues operate efficiently due to many restrictive practices. No other industry employs such restrictive rules and policies, and thus, the professional sport industry may be more likely to face antitrust challenges. Restraints on free agency and salary spending and restrictions on franchise ownership have opened leagues up to antitrust challenges by players, owners, prospective owners, competitor leagues, cities possessing franchises, cities seeking franchises, and media entities. Antitrust cases have also slipped into the realm of individual professional sport, with an occasional player challenge to rules or a monopoly claim toward their business, tours, or events.

Fundamental Concepts

Antitrust Law

In 1890 Congress passed the Sherman Antitrust Act (Sherman Act) to break up business trusts and monopolies. Section 1 of the act prohibits "every contract, combination, . . . or conspiracy in restraint of trade or commerce among the several states [interstate commerce]" (15 U.S.C. § 1), and section 2 makes it illegal, "to monopolize, attempt to monopolize, or combine or conspire . . . to monopolize" (15 U.S.C. § 2). Violators of the Sherman Act must pay treble damages.

The Sherman Act is dependent on judicial interpretation as its vague language lends itself to different opinions as to the intent and the meaning of crucial terms (Roberts, 1990). As a result, the Supreme Court has adopted three approaches to determine if there has been a violation of Section 1 of the Sherman Act. First, the "rule of reason" is founded on the notion that some restraints are necessary business practices. In other words, where the defendant can prove the conduct that restrains trade is a legitimate business practice and is the least restrictive means for the defendant to achieve that business objective, the rule of reason is a defense. The defense requires an inquiry as to the necessary business practices of the industry, and it must overcome the plaintiff's convictions that the defendant's conduct is unreasonable. This theory has been advanced in sport on many occasions due to the numerous and arguably necessary anticompetitive rules and restrictions generally required for competitive balance among the teams in the league. Such restrictions include player drafts; restrictions on free agency; restraints on salary; restrictions on franchise sale, ownership, and movement; franchise territorial restraints; and revenue sharing, among others, all of which can be justified as necessary for the proper operation of the leagues. Courts will, however, judge such restrictions on their reasonableness or fairness, balancing the business necessity against the degree of anticompetitive behavior encouraged by the practice.

The second approach is where the anticompetitive conduct is deemed *illegal per se*. *Illegal per se* activities are presumed to have no benefit to competition in the industry. Use of the *illegal per se* approach is limited and is applied in two situations: where the Court is examining agreements between traditional business competitions and where the Court is seeking to avoid a lengthy inquiry into an industry's business operations (Greenberg, 1993).

A third approach in which the Court focuses solely on the effect a challenged practice has on consumer welfare has emerged (Roberts, 1990). This approach, however, has yet to be applied in cases in the professional sport industry. Roberts (1990) has argued that this consumer welfare standard will be very important for sport-related antitrust cases and, if applied, would likely limit a plaintiff's success, for the plaintiff would be forced to demonstrate that the league conduct injures consumer welfare. With restrictions on player movement, this would be hard to prove, but with restrictions on franchise movement it might be less so.

Antitrust Law Applied to Baseball

Baseball possesses a unique status in professional sport, as well as American business, by virtue of its *exemption from the antitrust laws*. The exemption results from the 1922 Supreme Court decision, *Federal Baseball Club of Baltimore, Inc. v. National League of Professional Baseball Clubs, et al.* (1922), in which the Court concluded that baseball was neither interstate nor commerce; two elements necessary for federal antitrust laws to apply. The Supreme Court viewed baseball as a professional service business presenting local exhibitions and thus, not commerce. Further, it found the travel of players across state lines was purely incidental and not an essential element of the business of baseball. Over time the exemption has faced attack and been amended by the Curt Flood Act, but *Federal Baseball* is still viewed as controlling.

In *Toolson v. New York Yankees* (1953) and in *Flood v. Kuhn* (1972), baseball players contended that the player reserve system was in violation of federal antitrust law. Major League Baseball's reserve system was made up of two parts. First, every uniform player's contract contained a clause in which they agreed to play for the team the following year at the club's option. Second, each team possessed a reserve list in which the team could protect its players. There was a gentlemen's agreement among the clubs that no team would sign a player on another team's reserve list. Under this system teams could perpetually renew players, and without a free market, the players were forced to stay with those teams. In both decisions the Supreme Court reaffirmed baseball's exemption by shifting the burden to Congress to create legislation to abolish the exemption. *Flood* also encouraged baseball players to use labor relations rather than antitrust law to resolve their disputes over the reserve clause. Incidentally, the Major League Baseball Players Association used labor arbitration to successfully challenge the player reserve system ultimately limiting the reserve clause to a one-year renewal favoring the club (*In Re Twelve Clubs Comprising the National League and Twelve Clubs Comprising the American League and Major League Baseball Players Association*, 1975).

In 1998, Congress finally addressed baseball's exemption with the passage of the Curt Flood Act (15 U.S.C. § 27). Although it does not eliminate baseball's antitrust exemption, it subjects the business of baseball directly relating to or affecting the employment of major leaguers to antitrust laws. In fact, it states that "[o]nly a major league baseball player has standing to sue. . .". The Act also clarifies that the following aspects of the baseball business are still exempt: baseball's business relationship with the minor leagues; the minor league player reserve clause; the amateur draft; franchise expansion, location, or relocation; franchise ownership issues; marketing and sales of the entertainment product of baseball; and licensed properties. This language appears to respond to and reverse the recent court decisions that subject certain business practices to antitrust laws: *Butterworth v. National League of Professional Baseball Clubs*, 1994 (franchise relocation); *Fleer v. Topps Chewing Gum and Major League Baseball Ass'n*, 1981 (baseball card licensing); *Henderson Broadcasting Corp. v. Houston Sports*, 1982 (broadcasting); *Piazza v. Major League Baseball*, 1993 (court concludes baseball's exemption limited to reserve clause); *Postema v. National League of Professional Baseball Clubs*, 1992 (umpiring); and *Twin City Sportservice, Inc. v. Finley*, 1972 (concessions).

Antitrust Law Applied to Other Sports

Players, owners and prospective owners, and other competitors have challenged antitrust laws in the other professional sports. *United States v. International Boxing Club* (1955) was the first case in which antitrust laws were applied to a professional sport. Soon after, the Supreme Court applied the antitrust laws to football in *Radovich v. National Football League* (1957). In *Radovich*, a football player challenged a rule that restricted his signing a contract with a team other than the one that held his rights and that blacklisted him from signing as a player–coach with a team affiliated with the NFL. Radovich contended that the blacklist was a group boycott in restraint of trade. The trial and appellate courts dismissed Radovich's claims on the ground that football, like baseball, was exempt from antitrust due to the *Federal Baseball* precedent. The Supreme Court reversed and held that because of the NFL's radio and television contracts, the NFL was engaged in interstate commerce and subject to the Sherman Act.

Single-Entity Status

Radovich clarified that all other professional leagues are subject to the antitrust laws. In an attempt to gain Section 1 immunity, a number of new leagues have structured themselves as single entities with owners investing in the league, not teams, and the adoption of central operations for business and personnel decisions. The thinking is that if the leagues are organized centrally administered single entities with owner–investors, they cannot contract, combine, or conspire in restraint of trade in the manner that leagues made up of numerous individually owned teams might. Single-entity status for traditionally organized sports leagues has been rejected in numerous cases (*Sullivan v. NFL*, 1994; *Los Angeles Mem'l Coliseum Comm'n v. NFL*, 1984; *NASL v. NFL*, 1982; *Smith v. Pro Football, Inc.*, 1978; *Mackey v. NFL*, 1976). Two cases, however, *Chicago Professional Sports Limited Partnership v. National Basketball Association* (1996) and *Fraser v. Major League Soccer* (2002) have been open to the use of the single entity defense. Although the NBA is organized as a traditional league, the Seventh Circuit Court of Appeals in the *Chicago Bulls* case determined that no case set forth a characterization on how a single entity is structured so it instructed that an analysis be done on a case-by-case or practice-by-practice basis. Thus, the court found it possible that the NBA could act as a single entity when imposing leaguewide limitations on broadcasting through superstations, yet act as a joint venture when imposing restrictions on player mobility. The Seventh Circuit expressly withheld judgment as to whether the NBA was a single entity and remanded the case to district court for such a finding. The case, however, settled out of court in 1996.

Most recently, in *Fraser*, the First Circuit Court of Appeals determined that Major League Soccer (MLS) was a single entity organized as a limited liability company made up of operator–investors who sacrificed local autonomy for centralized operations. Specifically, MLS owns all the teams as well as intellectual property rights, tickets, and broadcast rights. It also sets team schedules, negotiates stadium leases and assumes related liabilities, pays the salaries of referees and other league personnel, and supplies certain equipment. *Fraser* makes it clear that a sports league can be organized uniquely and avoid antitrust liability as long as it is organized as a single entity from its inception, not as a result of revising or restructuring itself to avoid antitrust liability. Keep in mind that although the single-entity defense will not affect the ability to sue leagues under § 2 *Monopolies*, it will serve as an exemption of § 1, the clause generally used to challenge restrictive sport league practices.

Antitrust Challenges by Competitor Leagues

Three Section 2 cases emerged to challenge competitor leagues over the practices of established leagues as monopolistic. Only one of these cases, *Philadelphia World Hockey, Inc. v. Philadelphia Hockey Club, Inc.* (1972), was substantially successful for the plaintiff. In this case, the World Hockey League successfully argued that the NHL monopolized the labor pool of talented players through the use of their reserve system. The NHL's reserve system, like that in baseball, perpetually bound players to a team. The World Hockey Association successfully argued that the system restrained their ability to acquire marquee NHL players.

Two other cases brought by upstart competitors were not as successful. In *American Football League v. National Football League* (1963), the plaintiff was unable to prove that the NFL, by expanding into Dallas and Minneapolis, two cities the AFL was also considering for expansion, was monopolizing the market for professional football. In *United States Football League v. National Football League* (S.D.N.Y., 1986), a jury found that the NFL had monopolized the market for football in the United States, but only awarded nominal damages.

Antitrust Challenges by Prospective Team Owners and Team Owners

Individual franchise owners have challenged league rules on the theory that rules diminish competition. Many league rules restrict opportunities of the individual in favor of the good of the league. Prospective team owners have brought antitrust cases challenging league ownership restrictions that have kept them from becoming owners. The courts in *Levin v. National Basketball Association* (1974) and *Mid-South Grizzlies v. National Football League* (1983) upheld rules requiring three-fourths approval of league owners for transfer of ownership (*Levin*) and admission to the league (*Mid-South Grizzlies*). The most recent of these prospective owner challenges, *Piazza v. Major League Baseball* (1993), involved potential owners who were prevented from purchasing and relocating the San Francisco Giants. The case settled out of court just after the *Piazza* court entered a declaratory judgment that the claim should not be dismissed on the authority of baseball's antitrust exemption.

The most celebrated case of an owner challenging a restrictive franchise policy involved Raiders owner Al Davis in *Los Angeles Memorial Coliseum and the Los Angeles Raiders v. National Football League* (1984). This case involved the Raiders' successful antitrust challenge to league restraints on franchise relocation in which the club convinced the court that the three-fourths vote needed for relocation into the Los Angeles market was unreasonable. At the time it was highly unusual for an owner to sue coowners. However, a new breed of owners, those who have made large investments to purchase and operate teams, have been more willing to challenge league rules or policies on antitrust grounds. Many recent owners view team ownership as an investment opportunity and believe they should be able to maximize the profits of their teams. Some owners such as Jerry Jones of the Cowboys or Bob Kraft of the Patriots do not believe they should share their stadium, marketing, and licensing revenues with others in the league. This represents a major shift from the "league think" philosophy championed by former NFL Commissioner Pete Rozelle. The challenges vary from rules restricting the number of games telecast nationally on a superstation (*Chicago Bulls and WGN v. National Basketball Association*, 1996); ownership policies, such as restrictions against public ownership relocation (*Sullivan v. National Football League*, 1994, *VKK v. National Football League*, 1999); and marketing and revenue sharing (*Dallas Cowboys v. NFL Trust*, 1995 [settled out of court]).

Antitrust Challenges by Individual Athletes

Disciplined athletes have relied on antitrust to challenge the league actions. In *Molinas v. National Basketball Association* (1961), the plaintiff NBA player was suspended for wagering on games in which he was participating. Molinas's application for reinstatement with the league was rejected, and Molinas argued that the expulsion from the league restrained trade because he had no economic alternative to playing basketball in the NBA. The court upheld the suspension, finding that the restraint was a reasonable one, as the NBA had a legitimate interest in banning gambling.

Antitrust Exemption for Sport Broadcasting Contracts

In 1961 Congress passed a law exempting sports leagues' national television deals from antitrust liability (15 U.S.C. §§ 1291–1294). The statute grants professional leagues an exemption from antitrust laws to pool their television rights to increase bargaining power when negotiating leaguewide television packages.

Convergence of Labor and Antitrust Laws

Early on in its history, employers used the Sherman Act against labor movements, claiming workers organizing boycotts or work slowdowns/stoppages were committing conspiracies in restraint of trade. Employers used injunctions to thwart labor activities and the threat of treble damages to chill the labor movement. In 1914 Congress enacted the Clayton Act to exempt organized labor acting in its own self-interest from antitrust liability. However, as organized labor soon discovered, the federal courts willingly continued to grant injunctions against labor activity. In response Congress passed the Norris–La Guardia Act in 1932; often called the Anti-injunction Act because it restricted the federal judiciary's power to grant injunctions against labor unions in labor disputes (see Chapter 8.33, *Labor Law: Professional Sports Applications*)

During the Term of the Collective Bargaining Agreement

Together the Clayton and Norris–La Guardia Acts created an antitrust exemption for unions acting in their own self-interest, but did not protect union-management actions, such as entering into collective bargaining agreements. Collective bargaining agreements are contracts that contain restrictive provisions and as such could be deemed "contracts, combinations or conspiracies in restraint of trade." The U.S. Supreme Court addressed this issue in a number of nonsports cases involving multiemployer bargaining units and established the nonstatutory labor exemption to antitrust law (*Allen Bradley Co. v. Local Union No. 3, International Brotherhood of Electrical Workers*, 1945; *Local Union No. 189, Amalgamated Meat Cutters, and Butcher Workmen of North America, AFL-CIO v. Jewel Tea*, 1965; *United Mineworkers of America v. Pennington*, 1965; and *Connell Construction v. Plumbers*, 1975). The Court balanced the interests of antitrust law against labor law and implied the exemption from the labor statutes that set forth a national labor policy favoring free and private collective bargaining (*Brown v. Pro-Football*, 1996). A goal of federal labor policy is to bring labor and management together to negotiate an arrangement that best suits their needs. The Court found that Congress did not intend for antitrust laws to subvert the goal of achieving labor peace through labor–management relations. The objective of the labor exemption is to protect those mandatory subjects agreed to through good-faith bargaining from antitrust scrutiny by a party to the collective agreement, for it would not be fair to agree to a restrictive practice, receive concessions in exchange for the agreement, and then turn around and sue a counterpart for antitrust violations caused by that restrictive practice. Through these cases, the Supreme Court has established that terms negotiated between labor and management in their collective agreement, which outside a collective agreement would be subject to antitrust law, are in fact exempt from antitrust scrutiny, provided the defendant meets this three-part test:

1. The injured party is a party to the collective bargaining agreement.
2. The subject contested on antitrust grounds is a mandatory subject for bargaining (hours, wages, and other terms and conditions of employment).
3. The collective bargaining agreement was reached through bona fide arms' length bargaining.

Scope of the Labor Exemption

A number of cases have addressed the scope of the labor exemption in the professional sport industry. Injured parties may include past, present, and future players. The league and union are protected from antitrust suits by the labor exemption for suits brought by players not in the league when a collective bargaining agreement with restrictive policies is negotiated (*Wood v. National Basketball Association*, 1987; *Clarett v. National Football League*, 2003). At the time restrictive provisions limit a players' earning capacity, a player is then in the league and must take the burdens of collective bargaining to receive the benefits. The same holds true for suits by former players who may disagree with a union's negotiating decisions and challenge restrictive practices agreed to in negotiation (*Reynolds v. National Football League*, 1978).

Courts have examined practices such as restrictions on free agency, the draft, and salary caps as mandatory subjects. As long as the restriction affects hours, wages, or terms and conditions of employment, courts have found the provisions to be mandatory subjects. For instance, in *Mackey v. National Football League* (1976) the court found that although the Rozelle Rule did not directly deal with hours, wages, and terms and conditions of employment, its effect was to depress player salaries (wages), and thus it was deemed a mandatory subject.

Two cases, *Mackey v. National Football League* (1976) and *McCourt v. California Sports, Inc.* (1979), are useful in examining the concept of arms'-length bargaining. In *Mackey*, a number of former and current football players challenged the Rozelle Rule, a restriction on free agency that required teams signing free agents to pay compensation to the athlete's former team. The owners argued that the labor exemption applied. The Court disagreed, finding that there was no bona fide arms'-length bargaining because the Rozelle Rule remained unchanged from the time it was unilaterally implemented in 1963. Further there was no evidence that the players agreed to the Rozelle Rule as a quid pro quo for better pension benefits and the right to individually negotiate their salaries (as was argued by the NFL in its defense). In fact, the *Mackey* Court found that there was no direct bargaining on the Rozelle Rule. Contrast *Mackey* with *McCourt*, where the NHL's By-Law 9A, a similar free agent compensation structure, was subject to antitrust attack by Dale McCourt, a player named as compensation. The court found that the labor exemption protected the NHL because the players' association had bargained vigorously against By-Law 9A. The Court stated that player benefits were bargained for in connection with the reserve system remaining unchanged, and the inclusion of the free agent compensation clause was not the result of collusion, but of good-faith bargaining.

Duration of the Labor Exemption

The labor exemption continues to protect parties from antitrust scrutiny after a collective bargaining agreement has expired. The subjects of a collective bargaining agreement will survive its expiration because labor law requires the parties to maintain the status quo and continue bargaining for a new agreement until reaching impasse. Impasse occurs when there is a total breakdown in negotiations between union and management and often leads to a strike or a lockout. Like the subjects of the collective bargaining agreement, the labor exemption survives the agreement's expiration provided the parties maintain the status quo. If this were not the case, the players' association may have no incentive to bargain and opt to drag its feet in negotiations until the expiration of the agreement to seek treble damages through an antitrust suit, thereby increasing its leverage in labor negotiations. The duty to maintain the status quo only extends to impasse, and once an employer has bargained in good faith to impasse, the employer may unilaterally impose changes to the mandatory bargaining subjects without incurring antitrust liability, provided those changes are consistent with the latest proposals made to the union prior to impasse.

Significant Case

In this case the National Football League appeals a trial court decision ordering Maurice Clarett eligible to enter the NFL draft on the ground that the NFL's eligibility rules requiring Clarett to wait at least three full football seasons after his high school graduation before entering the draft violate antitrust laws. In reaching its conclusion, the district court held, inter alia, that the eligibility rules are not immune from antitrust scrutiny under the nonstatutory labor exemption

CLARETT V. NATIONAL FOOTBALL LEAGUE

U.S. Court of Appeals for the Second Circuit
369 F.3d 124 (2003)

* * *

Maurice Clarett, former running back for Ohio State University ("OSU") and Big Ten Freshman of the Year, is an accomplished and talented amateur football player. After gaining national attention as a high school player, Clarett became the first college freshman since 1943 to open as a starter at the position of running back for OSU. He led that team through an undefeated season, even scoring the winning touchdown in a double-overtime victory in the 2003 Fiesta Bowl to claim the national championship. Prior to the start of his second college season, however, Clarett was suspended from college play by OSU for reasons widely reported but not relevant here. Forced to sit out his entire sophomore season, Clarett is now interested in turning professional by entering the NFL draft. Clarett is precluded from so doing, however, under the NFL's current rules governing draft eligibility.

* * *

For much of the League's history, therefore, a player, irrespective of whether he actually attended college or not, was barred from entering the draft until he was at least four football seasons removed from high school. The eligibility rules were relaxed in 1990, however, to permit a player to enter the draft three full seasons after that player's high school gracuation. Clarett "graduated high school on December 11, 2001, two-thirds of the way through the 2001 NFL season" and is a season shy of the three necessary to qualify under the draft's eligibility rules. Unwilling to forego the prospect of a year of lucrative professional play or run the risk of a career-compromising injury were his entry into the draft delayed until next year, Clarett filed this suit alleging that the NFL's draft eligibility rules are an unreasonable restraint of trade in violation of Section 1 of the Sherman Act, 15 U.S.C. § 1, and Section 4 of the Clayton Act, 15 U.S.C. § 15.

* * * The current collective bargaining agreement between the NFL and its players union was negotiated between the NFL Management Council ("NFLMC"), which is the NFL member clubs' multi-employer bargaining unit, and the NFL Players Association ("NFLPA"), the NFL players' exclusive bargaining representative. This agreement became effective in 1993 and governs through 2007. Despite the collective bargaining agreement's comprehensiveness with respect to, *inter alia*, the manner in which the NFL clubs select rookies through the draft and the scheme by which rookie compensation is determined, the eligibility rules for the draft do not appear in the agreement.

At the time the collective bargaining agreement became effective, the eligibility rules appeared in the NFL Constitution and Bylaws, which had last been amended in 1992. Specifically, Article XII of the Bylaws ("Article XII"), entitled "Eligibility of Players," prohibited member clubs from selecting any college football player through the draft process who had not first exhausted all college football eligibility, graduated from college, or been out of high school for five football seasons. Clubs were further barred from drafting any person who either did not attend college, or attended college but did not play football, unless that person had been out of high school for four football seasons. Article XII, however, also included an exception that permitted clubs to draft players who had received "Special Eligibility" from the NFL Commissioner. In order to qualify for such special eligibility, a player was required to submit an application before January 6 of the year that he wished to enter the draft and "at least three NFL seasons must have elapsed since the player was graduated from high school." The Commissioner's practice apparently was, and still is, to grant such an application so long as three full football seasons have passed since a player's high school graduation.

Although the eligibility rules do not appear in the text of the collective bargaining agreement, the NFL Constitution and Bylaws that at the time of the agreement's adoption contained the eligibility rules are mentioned in three separate provisions relevant to our discussion. First, in Article III, Section 1 (Scope of Agreement), the collective bargaining agreement states: This Agreement represents the complete understanding of the parties as to all subjects covered herein, and there will be no change in the terms and conditions of this Agreement without mutual consent . . . . The NFLPA and the Management Council waive any rights to bargain with one another concerning any subject covered or not covered in this Agreement for the duration of this Agreement, *including the provisions of the NFL Constitution and Bylaws*; provided, however, that if any proposed change in the NFL Constitution and Bylaws during the term of this Agreement could significantly affect the terms and conditions of employment of NFL players, then the [NFLMC] will give the NFLPA notice of and negotiate the proposed change in good faith. (emphasis added). Second, Article IV, Section 2 (No Suit) provides generally that "neither [the NFLPA] nor any of its members" will sue or support a suit "relating to the presently existing provisions of the Constitution and Bylaws of the NFL as they are currently operative and administered." Third, Article IX, Section 1 (Non-Injury Grievance) makes "any dispute . . . involving the interpretation of, application of, or compliance with, . . . any applicable provision of the NFL Constitution and Bylaws pertaining to terms and conditions of employment of NFL players" subject to the grievance procedures afforded under the collective bargaining agreement.

Before the collective bargaining agreement became effective, a copy of the Constitution and Bylaws, as amended in 1992, was provided by the NFL to the NFLPA along with a letter, dated May 6, 1993, that "confirm[ed] that the attached documents are the presently existing provisions of the Constitution and Bylaws of the NFL referenced in Article IV, Section 2, of the Collective Bargaining Agreement." The May 6 letter was signed by representatives of the NFL and the NFLPA. The only other evidence presented to the district court by the NFL concerning the negotiation of the collective bargaining agreement were the two declarations of Peter Ruocco, Senior Vice President of Labor Relations at the NFLMC. * * *

In 2003, ten years into the life of the collective bargaining agreement, Article XII was amended. Although the substance of most of the eligibility rules was retained, the "Special Eligibility" provision was removed and substituted with the following: If four seasons have not elapsed since the player discontinued high school, he is ineligible for selection, but may apply to the Commissioner for special eligibility.

The Bylaws then refer to a separate memorandum issued by the Commissioner on February 16, 1990—three years before the current collective bargaining agreement became effective—pursuant to his authority under the Bylaws to establish necessary policies and procedures. That memorandum states that "applications for special eligibility for the 1990 draft will be accepted only from college players as to whom three full *college* seasons have elapsed since their high school graduation." (emphasis added). It is this version of the eligibility rules that the NFL relies upon in refusing Clarett special eligibility for this year's draft, and it is this version of the eligibility rules that Clarett seeks to invalidate.

* * * On February 5, 2004, the district court granted summary judgment in favor of Clarett and ordered him eligible to enter this year's draft. First, relying on the test articulated by the Eighth Circuit in *Mackey v. National Football League*, 543 F.2d 606 (8th Cir. 1976), the district court rejected the NFL's argument that the antitrust laws are inapplicable to the eligibility rules because they fall within the non-statutory

labor exemption to the antitrust laws. Specifically, the district court held that the exemption does not apply because the eligibility rules: 1) are not mandatory subjects of collective bargaining, 2) affect only "complete strangers to the bargaining relationship," and 3) were not shown to be the product of arm's-length negotiations between the NFL and its players union.

Second, the district court ruled against the NFL on its contention that Clarett lacked standing because he had not demonstrated a sufficient "antitrust injury" to maintain this suit, holding that the "inability to compete in the market" for NFL players' services is sufficient injury for antitrust purposes.

Third, on the merits of Clarett's antitrust claim, the district court found that the eligibility rules were so "blatantly anticompetitive" that only a "quick look" at the NFL's procompetitive justifications was necessary to reach the conclusion that the eligibility rules were unlawful under the antitrust laws. The NFL had argued that because the eligibility rules prevent less physically and emotionally mature players from entering the league, they justify any incidental anticompetitive effect on the market for NFL players. In so doing, according to the NFL, the eligibility rules guard against less-prepared and younger players entering the League and risking injury to themselves, prevent the sport from being devalued by the higher number of injuries to those young players, protect its member clubs from having to bear the costs of such injuries, and discourage aspiring amateur football players from enhancing their physical condition through unhealthy methods. The district court held that all of these justifications were inadequate as a matter of law, concluding that the NFL's purported concerns could be addressed through less restrictive but equally effective means. * * *

The NFL subsequently moved for a stay pending appeal, which the district court denied. After filing a notice of appeal, the NFL petitioned to have the appeal heard on an expedited basis and again moved to stay the district court's order pending appeal. On March 30, 2004, we agreed to hear the appeal on an expedited basis and set a substantially compressed briefing schedule. Following oral argument on April 19, we granted the NFL's motion to stay the district court's order, citing the NFL's "likelihood of success on the merits" and noting that the resulting harm to Clarett was mitigated by the NFL's promise to "hold a supplemental draft for [Clarett] and all others similarly situated" were the district court's judgment affirmed. Clarett thereafter made successive applications to two Justices of the Supreme Court to lift this Court's stay order. Both applications were denied. Clarett did not participate in the NFL draft.

DISCUSSION

Clarett argues that the NFL clubs are horizontal competitors for the labor of professional football players and thus may not agree that a player will be hired only after three full football seasons have elapsed following that player's high school graduation. That characterization, however, neglects that the labor market for NFL players is organized around a collective bargaining relationship that is provided for and promoted by federal labor law, and that the NFL clubs, as a multi-employer bargaining unit, can act jointly in setting the terms and conditions of players' employment and the rules of the sport without risking antitrust liability. For those reasons, the NFL argues that federal labor law favoring and governing the collective bargaining process precludes the application of the antitrust laws to its eligibility rules. We agree.

* * *

Although "the interaction of the [antitrust laws] and federal labor legislation is an area of law marked more by controversy than by clarity," Wood v. Nat'l Basketball Ass'n, 809 F.2d 954, 959 (2d Cir. 1987) (citing R. Gorman, Labor Law, Unionization and Collective Bargaining 631-35 (1976)), it has long been recognized that in order to accommodate the collective bargaining process, certain concerted activity among and between labor and employers must be held to be beyond the reach of the antitrust laws. See United States v. Hutcheson, 312 U.S. 219, 85 L. Ed. 788, 61 S. Ct. 463 (1941); Apex Hosiery Co. v. Leader, 310 U.S. 469, 84 L. Ed. 1311, 60 S. Ct. 982 (1940). Courts, therefore, have carved out two categories of labor exemptions to the antitrust laws. We deal here only with the non-statutory exemption.

* * *

The Supreme Court has never delineated the precise boundaries of the exemption, and what guidance it has given as to its application has come mostly in cases in which agreements between an employer and a labor union were alleged to have injured or eliminated a competitor in the employer's business or product market. In the face of such allegations, the Court has largely permitted antitrust scrutiny in spite of any resulting detriment to the labor policies favoring collective bargaining.

* * *

Clarett, furthermore, maintains that the boundaries of the exemption were properly identified in, and thus we should follow, the Eighth Circuit's decision in *Mackey v. National Football League*, 543 F.2d 606 (8th Cir. 1976). Mackey involved a challenge brought by NFL players to the League's so-called "Rozelle Rule," which required NFL clubs to compensate any club from which they hired away a player whose contract had expired. Presenting arguments not dissimilar from those made in the present case, the players in Mackey alleged that the Rozelle Rule constituted an unlawful conspiracy amongst the NFL clubs to restrain players' abilities freely to contract their services. The NFL, for its part, asserted that the Rozelle Rule was exempt from the antitrust laws by virtue of its inclusion in the League's collective bargaining agreement with the players union. Noting that the Supreme Court had to that point applied the non-statutory exemption only in *Jewel Tea*, the Eighth Circuit gleaned from the Court's decisions, and Justice White's opinion in *Jewel Tea* in particular, that in order to fall within the non-statutory exemption, a restraint must: 1) primarily affect only the parties to the collective bargaining relationship, 2) concern a mandatory subject of collective bargaining, and 3) be the product of bona fide arm's-length bargaining. Although the Eighth Circuit found that the Rozelle Rule satisfied the first two prongs, it nonetheless refused to apply the exemption after finding that the Rozelle Rule was not the product of arm's-length negotiations. Noting that the Rozelle Rule predated the advent of the collective bargaining relationship between the NFL and its players union, the Eighth Circuit found that the record lacked sufficient evidence to conclude that the players union had received some *quid pro quo* in exchange for including the Rule in the collective bargaining agreement. For that reason, the Eighth Circuit held that the Rozelle Rule did not fall within the non-statutory exemption, and the Rule was invalidated on antitrust grounds.

Relying on *Mackey*, the district court below held that the non-statutory exemption provides no protection to the NFL's draft eligibility rules, because the eligibility rules fail to satisfy any of the three *Mackey* factors. Specifically, the district court found that the rules exclude strangers to the bargaining relationship from entering the draft, do not concern wages, hours or working conditions of current NFL players, and were not the product of bona fide arm's-length negotiations during the process that culminated in the current collective bargaining agreement.

We, however, have never regarded the Eighth Circuit's test in *Mackey* as defining the appropriate limits of the non-statutory exemption. * * * Moreover, we disagree with the Eighth Circuit's assumption in *Mackey* that the Supreme Court's decisions in *Connell*, *Jewel Tea*, *Pennington*, and *Allen Bradley* dictate the appropriate boundaries of the non-statutory exemption for cases in which the only alleged anticompetitive effect of the challenged restraint is on a labor market organized around a collective bargaining relationship. Indeed, we have previously recognized that these decisions are of limited assistance in determining whether an athlete can challenge restraints on the market for professional sports players imposed through a collective bargaining process, because all "involved injuries to *employers* who asserted that they were being excluded from competition in the product market." *Wood v. Nat'l Basketball Ass'n*, 809 F.2d 954, 963 (2d Cir. 1987) (emphasis in original)

Clarett does not contend that the NFL's draft eligibility rules work to the disadvantage of the NFL's competitors in the market for professional football or in some manner protect the NFL's dominance in that mar-

ket. challenges the eligibility rules only on the ground that they are an unreasonable restraint upon the market for players' services. Thus, we need not decide here whether the *Mackey* factors aptly characterize the limits of the exemption in cases in which employers use agreements with their unions to disadvantage their competitors in the product or business market, because our cases have counseled a decidedly different approach where, as here, the plaintiff complains of a restraint upon a unionized labor market characterized by a collective bargaining relationship with a multi-employer bargaining unit. See *Caldwell v. Am. Basketball Ass'n*, 66 F.3d 523 (2d Cir. 1995); *Nat'l Basketball Ass'n v. Williams*, 45 F.3d 684 (2d Cir. 1995); *Wood v. Nat'l Basketball Ass'n*, 809 F.2d 954 (2d Cir. 1987). Moreover, as the discussion below makes clear, the suggestion that the *Mackey* factors provide the proper guideposts in this case simply does not comport with the Supreme Court's most recent treatment of the non-statutory labor exemption in *Brown v. Pro Football, Inc.*, 518 U.S. 231 (1996).

II

Our decisions in Caldwell, *Williams*, and *Wood* all involved players' claims that concerted action of a professional sports league imposed a restraint upon the labor market for players' services and thus violated the antitrust laws. In each case, however, we held that the non-statutory labor exemption defeated the players' claims. Our analysis in each case was rooted in the observation that the relationships among the defendant sports leagues and their players were governed by collective bargaining agreements and thus were subject to the carefully structured regime established by federal labor laws. We reasoned that to permit antitrust suits against sports leagues on the ground that their concerted action imposed a restraint upon the labor market would seriously undermine many of the policies embodied by these labor laws, including the congressional policy favoring collective bargaining, the bargaining parties' freedom of contract, and the widespread use of multi-employer bargaining units. Subsequent to our decisions in this area, similar reasoning led the Supreme Court in *Brown v. Pro Football, Inc.*, 518 U.S. 231 (1996), to hold that the non-statutory exemption protected the NFL's unilateral implementation of new salary caps for developmental squad players after its collective bargaining agreement with the NFL players union had expired and negotiations with the union over that proposal reached an impasse. We need only retrace the path laid down by these prior cases to reach the conclusion that Clarett's antitrust claims must fail.

* * *

A.

The plaintiff in *Wood*, O. Leon Wood, was a star college basketball player who, after being drafted by the Philadelphia 76ers, sued the NBA alleging that its policies regarding, *inter alia*, the entry draft process and team salary caps constituted unlawful agreements among horizontal competitors to eliminate competition for college players. All of the challenged policies, however, were included in a collective bargaining agreement and memorandum of understanding between the NBA and its players union. Because these agreements were the result of the federally mandated bargaining process through which the union and the NBA, in light of the unique economic imperatives of professional basketball, negotiated a host of creative solutions to settle their differences, we held that to permit Wood to challenge particular aspects of their agreement on antitrust grounds would "subvert fundamental principles of our federal labor policy."

Specifically, we found that Wood's claim that the NBA's agreements prevented him from becoming a free agent and negotiating directly with the teams for the best salary contravened the principle of federal labor law that once a majority of employees votes to unionize and elects a representative, individual employees—whether in the bargaining unit or not—no longer possess the right to negotiate with the employer for the best deal possible.)). Rather, the union representative is charged with the responsibility of seeking the best overall deal for employees, which often means that some employees or prospective employees may fare worse than they would in a competitive market free from restraints. We further rejected Wood's contention that the non-statutory exemption did not preclude his challenge because he was not a member of the union when the collective bargaining agreement became effective, observing that new union members often find themselves disadvantaged vis-a-vis more senior union members and that collective bargaining units commonly disadvantage employees outside of, or about to enter, the union.

We also reasoned that to allow Wood to cherry-pick the particular policies with which he took issue would run counter to the "freedom of contract" that labor law intends unions and employers to have during the collective bargaining process, because Wood could negate aspects of the "unique bundle of compromises" struck between the NBA and its players on their way to a peaceful and efficient resolution of their differences. Particularly because Wood challenged agreements concerning mandatory subjects of bargaining, to which labor law attaches a host of rights and obligations, we saw no place for the application of the antitrust laws and found the non-statutory exemption applicable.

Eight years later, in *Williams*, a class of professional basketball players again brought an antitrust suit challenging, *inter alia*, the NBA's draft process and salary caps. This time, however, the restraints challenged by the players were not encompassed in any effective agreement between the NBA and its players union, because the collective bargaining agreement had expired. The challenged policies were implemented unilaterally by the NBA after negotiations with the players union on these subjects reached an impasse. We nevertheless held that the NBA's conduct fell within the non-statutory exemption. Foremost, we found that the players' antitrust claims were inconsistent with federal labor law because they imperiled the legitimacy of multi-employer bargaining, "a process by which employers band together to act as a single entity in bargaining with a common union." From the standpoint of our labor and antitrust laws, we explained that such multi-employer bargaining units are a long-accepted and commonplace means of giving employers the tactical and practical advantages of collective action. Moreover, in the context of sports leagues, we observed that multi-employer bargaining units serve the additional, important purpose of allowing the teams to establish and demand uniformity in the rules necessary for the proper functioning of the sport. Second, we found that legality of conduct undertaken in the course of negotiations over a collective bargaining agreement is an issue committed to the specialized knowledge of the National Labor Relations Board, for which federal labor law provides a "soup-to-nuts array of rules and remedies." * * *

That same year, in *Caldwell*, we heard the appeal of Joe L. Caldwell, a former professional basketball player who after four successful seasons of play was suspended from his team in 1974 and never returned to the game. While a basketball player, Caldwell represented the players in labor negotiations with the league and claimed to have incurred the scorn of his league, the American Basketball Association ("ABA"), as a result. He alleged that the teams consequently agreed among themselves, in violation of the antitrust laws, that he should be fired and then blacklisted from professional play. Despite the district court's finding that the case could "be entirely resolved without any reference whatsoever to the" collective bargaining agreement between the ABA and its players union, we held that the non-statutory exemption defeated Caldwell's claims. * * * Drawing upon our discussion of multi-employer bargaining units in *Williams*, we then observed that the legality *vel non* of his treatment did not become a question of antitrust law simply because the "employers acted jointly in refusing employment." Because such issues are remediable under labor law, we concluded that the non-statutory exemption applied.

The following year, in *Brown*, the Supreme Court was presented with facts similar to *Williams*, and eight Justices agreed that the non-statutory exemption precludes antitrust claims against a professional sports league for unilaterally setting policy with respect to mandatory bargaining subjects after negotiations with the players union over those subjects reach impasse. There, a class of professional football players challenged the NFL's unilateral institution of a policy that permitted each team to establish a new squad of developmental players and capped those players' weekly salaries after negotiations with the players union over that proposal became deadlocked. Approaching the issue largely as a "matter of logic," the Court found that to permit antitrust liability in such a case would call into question a great deal of conduct, such as multi-employer bargaining, that federal labor policy promotes and for which labor law provides an array of rules and remedies. The Court held that the non-statutory labor exemption necessarily applied not only to protect such labor policies but also to prevent "antitrust courts" from usurping the NLRB's responsibility for policing the collective bargaining process.

The Court also rejected a number of potential limits on the exemption that were raised by the players and their supporters. First, the Court held that the exemption was not so narrow as to protect only agreements between the parties that are embodied in an existing collective bargaining agreement. Second, in finding that the League's post-impasse action was protected by the exemption, the Court dismissed the suggestion that the exemption should insulate the concerted action of employers only up to the point at which negotiations reach impasse or a "reasonable time" thereafter. Third, the Court rejected the notion that courts in applying the exemption could distinguish between bargaining "tactics," which the players argued should be exempt, and unilaterally imposed "terms." Finally, the Court refused the players' contention that the labor of professional sports players was unique and that the market for players' services therefore should be treated differently than other organized labor markets for purposes of the non-statutory exemption.

* * *

Clarett argues that his case differs in material respects from *Brown*, but he does not argue, nor do we find, that the Supreme Court's treatment of the non-statutory exemption in that case gives reason to doubt the authority of our prior decisions in *Caldwell, Williams*, and *Wood*. Because we find that our prior decisions in this area fully comport— in approach and result—with the Supreme Court's decision in *Brown*, we regard them as controlling authority. In light of the foregoing jurisprudence, we therefore proceed to the merits of this appeal.

B.

Clarett argues that he is physically qualified to play professional football and that the antitrust laws preclude the NFL teams from agreeing amongst themselves that they will refuse to deal with him simply because he is less than three full football seasons out of high school. Such an arbitrary condition, he argues, imposes an unreasonable restraint upon the competitive market for professional football players' services, and, because it excludes him from entering that market altogether, constitutes a

per se antitrust violation. The issue we must decide is whether subjecting the NFL's eligibility rules to antitrust scrutiny would "subvert fundamental principles of our federal labor policy." For the reasons that follow, we hold that it would and that the non-statutory exemption therefore applies.

Although the NFL has maintained draft eligibility rules in one form or another for much of its history, the "inception of a collective bargaining relationship" between the NFL and its players union some thirty years ago "irrevocably alter[ed] the governing legal regime." Our prior cases highlight a number of consequences resulting from the advent of this collective bargaining relationship that are relevant to Clarett's litigation. For one, prospective players no longer have the right to negotiate directly with the NFL teams over the terms and conditions of their employment. That responsibility is instead committed to the NFL and the players union to accomplish through the collective bargaining process, and throughout that process the NFL and the players union are to have the freedom to craft creative solutions to their differences in light of the economic imperatives of their industry. Furthermore, the NFL teams are permitted to engage in joint conduct with respect to the terms and conditions of players' employment as a multi-employer bargaining unit without risking antitrust liability. The arguments Clarett advances in support of his antitrust claim, however, run counter to each of these basic principles of federal labor law.

Because the NFL players have unionized and have selected the NFLPA as its exclusive bargaining representative, labor law prohibits Clarett from negotiating directly the terms and conditions of his employment with any NFL club, see *NLRB v. Allis-Chalmers Mfg. Co.*, 388 U.S. 175, 180 (1967), and an NFL club would commit an unfair labor practice were it to bargain with Clarett individually without the union's consent, *see Medo Photo Supply Corp. v. NLRB*, 321 U.S. 678 (1944). The terms and conditions of Clarett's employment are instead committed to the collective bargaining table and are reserved to the NFL and the players union's selected representative to negotiate. *Allis-Chalmers Mfg. Co.*, 388 U.S. at 180.

* * *

Clarett's argument that antitrust law should permit him to circumvent this scheme established by federal labor law starts with the contention that the eligibility rules do not constitute a mandatory subject of collective bargaining and thus cannot fall within the protection of the non-statutory exemption. Contrary to the district court, however, we find that the eligibility rules are mandatory bargaining subjects. Though tailored to the unique circumstance of a professional sports league, the eligibility rules for the draft represent a quite literal condition for initial employment and for that reason alone might constitute a mandatory bargaining subject. * * *

But moreover, the eligibility rules constitute a mandatory bargaining subject because they have tangible effects on the wages and working conditions of current NFL players. * * * Furthermore, by reducing competition in the market for entering players, the eligibility rules also affect the job security of veteran players. Because the size of NFL teams is capped, the eligibility rules diminish a veteran player's risk of being replaced by either a drafted rookie or a player who enters the draft and, though not drafted, is then hired as a rookie free agent. * * *

Clarett, however, argues that the eligibility rules are an impermissible bargaining subject because they affect players outside of the union. But simply because the eligibility rules work a hardship on prospective rather than current employees does not render them impermissible. ***Nevertheless, such an arrangement constitutes a permissible, mandatory subject of bargaining despite the fact that it concerns prospective rather than current employees. *** Clarett, however, stresses that the eligibility rules are arbitrary and that requiring him to wait another football season has nothing to do with whether he is in fact qualified for professional play. But Clarett is in this respect no different from the typical worker who is confident that he or she has the skills to fill a job vacancy but does not possess the qualifications or meet the requisite criteria that have been set. In the context of this collective bargaining relationship, the NFL and its players union can agree that an employee will not be hired or considered for employment for nearly any reason whatsoever so long as they do not violate federal laws such as those prohibiting unfair labor practices, 29 U.S.C. § 201 *et seq.*, or discrimination, 42 U.S.C. § 2000e *et seq.*

Even accepting that an individual club could refuse to consider him for employment because he is less than three full seasons out of high school, Clarett contends that the NFL clubs invited antitrust liability when they agreed amongst themselves to impose that same criteria on every prospective player. As a consequence of the NFL's unique position in the professional football market, of course, such joint action deprives Clarett of the opportunity to pursue, at least for the time being, the kind of high-paying, high-profile career he desires. In the context of collective bargaining, however, federal labor policy permits the NFL teams to act collectively as a multi-employer bargaining unit in structuring the rules of play and setting the criteria for player employment. Such concerted action is encouraged as a matter of labor policy and tolerated as a matter of antitrust law, *see Williams*, 45 F.3d at 693, despite the fact that it "plainly involve[s] horizontal competitors for labor acting in concert to set and to implement terms of employment," *Caldwell*, 66 F.3d at 529. * * *

The threat to the operation of federal labor law posed by Clarett's antitrust claims is in no way diminished by Clarett's contention that the rules were not bargained over during the negotiations that preceded the current collective bargaining agreement. The eligibility rules, along with the host of other NFL rules and policies affecting the terms and conditions of NFL players included in the NFL's Constitution and Bylaws, were well known to the union, and a copy of the Constitution and Bylaws was presented to the union during negotiations. Given that the eligibility rules are a mandatory bargaining subject for the reasons set out above, the union or the NFL could have forced the other to the bargaining table if either felt that a change was warranted. Indeed, according to the declaration from the NFLMC's Vice President for Labor Relations, Peter Ruocco, this is exactly what the NFL did.

Although this declaration was the only evidence on this point and went uncontradicted by Clarett below, the district court found that this evidence was insufficient to entitle the NFL to a non-statutory exemption defense as a matter of law. But even disregarding this evidence entirely, the collective bargaining agreement itself makes clear that the union and the NFL reached an agreement with respect to how the eligibility rules would be handled. In the collective bargaining agreement, the union agreed to waive any challenge to the Constitution and Bylaws and thereby acquiesced in the continuing operation of the eligibility rules contained therein—at least for the duration of the agreement. The terms of that waiver not only keep the eligibility rules in effect for the length of the agreement but also leave the NFL in control of any changes to the eligibility rules on the condition that any significant change potentially affecting the terms and conditions of players' employment would be preceded by notice to the union and an opportunity to bargain. The value of such a clause to the NFL is obvious, as control over any changes to the eligibility rules is left in the hands of management at least until the expiration of the collective bargaining agreement. Although it is entirely possible that the players union might not have agreed entirely with the eligibility rules, the union representative might not have regarded any difference of opinion with respect to the eligibility rules as sufficient to warrant the expenditure of precious time at the bargaining table in light of other important issues.

Clarett would have us hold that by reaching this arrangement rather than fixing the eligibility rules in the text of the collective bargaining agreement or in failing to wrangle over the eligibility rules at the bargaining table, the NFL left itself open to antitrust liability. Such a holding, however, would completely contradict prior decisions recognizing that the labor law policies that warrant withholding antitrust scrutiny are not limited to protecting only terms contained in collective bargaining agreements. The reach of those policies, rather, extends as far as is necessary to ensure the successful operation of the collective bargaining *process* and to safeguard the "unique bundle of compromises" reached by the NFL and the players union as a means of settling their differences. It would disregard those policies completely to hold that some "particular *quid pro quo* must be proven to avoid antitrust liability," or to allow Clarett to undo what we assume the NFL and its players union regarded as the most appropriate or expedient means of settling their differences. We have cautioned before that "to the extent that courts prohibit particular solutions for particular problems, they reduce the number and quality of compromises available to unions and employers for resolving their differences." Clarett would have us disregard our own good advice.

The disruptions to federal labor policy that would be occasioned by Clarett's antitrust suit, moreover, would not vindicate any of the antitrust policies that the Supreme Court has said may warrant the withholding of the non-statutory exemption. This is simply not a case in which the NFL is alleged to have conspired with its players union to drive its competitors out of the market for professional football. Nor does Clarett contend that the NFL uses the eligibility rules as an unlawful means of maintaining its dominant position in that market. This lawsuit reflects simply a prospective employee's disagreement with the criteria, established by the employer and the labor union, that he must meet in order to be considered for employment. Any remedies for such a claim are the province of labor law. Allowing Clarett to proceed with his antitrust suit would subvert "principles that have been familiar to, and accepted by, the nation's workers for all of the NLRA's [sixty years] in every industry except professional sports." *Caldwell*, 66 F.3d at 530. We, however, follow the Supreme Court's lead in declining to "fashion an antitrust exemption [so as to give] additional advantages to professional football players . . . that transport workers, coal miners, or meat packers would not enjoy." *Brown*, 518 U.S. at 249.

CONCLUSION

For the foregoing reasons, the judgment of the district court is REVERSED and the case REMANDED with instructions to enter judgment in favor of the NFL. The order of the district court designating Clarett eligible to enter this year's NFL draft is VACATED.

References

Cases

Allen Bradley Co. v. Local Union No. 3, International Brotherhood of Electrical Workers, 325 U.S. 797 (1945).

American Football League v. National Football League, 323 F.2d 124 (4th Cir. 1963).

Brown v. Pro-Football, Inc., 518 U.S. 231 (1996).

Butterworth v. National League of Professional Baseball Clubs, 644 So.2d 1021 (Fla. 1994).

Chicago Bulls and WGN v. National Basketball Association, 95 F.3d 593 (7th Cir. 1996).

Chicago Professional Sports Limited Partnership v. National Basketball Association, 95 F.3d 593 (7th Cir. 1996).

Clarett v. National Football League, 2003.

Connell Construction v. Plumbers, 421 U.S. 616 (1975).

Dallas Cowboys v. NFL Trust, 94-C-9426 (N.D. Cal. 1995).

Federal Baseball Club of Baltimore, Inc. v. National League of Professional Baseball Clubs, et al., 259 U.S. 200 (1922).

Fleer v. Topps Chewing Gum and Major League Baseball Ass'n, 658 F.2d 139 (3rd Cir. 1981).

Flood v. Kuhn, 407 U.S. 258 (1972).

Fraser v. Major League Soccer, 97 F. Supp. 2d 130 (D. Mass. 2000).

Henderson Broadcasting Corp. v. Houston Sports, 541 F. Supp. 263 (S.D. Tex. 1982).

Levin v. National Basketball League, 385 F. Supp. 149 (S.D. N.Y. 1974).

Local Union No. 189, Amalgamated Meat Cutters, and Butcher Workmen of North America, AFL-CIO v. Jewel Tea, 381 U.S. 676 (1965).

Los Angeles Memorial Coliseum and the Los Angeles Raiders v. National Football League, 726 F.2d 1381 (9th Cir. 1984).

Mackey v. National Football League, 543 F.2d 606 (8th Cir. 1976).

McCourt v. California Sports, Inc., 600 F.2d 1193 (6th Cir. 1979).

McNeil v. National Football League, 790 F. Supp. 871 (D. Minn. 1992).

Mid-South Grizzlies v. National Football League, 550 F. Supp. 558 (E.D. Pa. 1982), *aff'd* 720 F.2d 772 (3rd Cir. 1983), *cert. denied*, 467 U.S. 1215 (1984).

Molinas v. National Basketball Association, 190 F. Supp. 241 (S.D. N.Y. 1961).

National Basketball Association v. Williams, 43 F.3d 684 (2nd Cir. 1995).

National Football League v. North American Soccer League, 459 U.S. 1074 (1982).

North American Soccer League v. NFL, 670 F.2d 1249 (2d Cir. 1982).

Philadelphia World Hockey, Inc. v. Philadelphia Hockey Club, Inc., 351 F. Supp. 462 (E.D. Pa. 1972).
Piazza v. Major League Baseball, 831 F. Supp 420 (E.D. Pa. 1993).
Postema v. National League of Professional Baseball Clubs, 799 F. Supp 1475 (S.D. N.Y. 1992).
Powell v. National Football League, 930 F.2d 1293 (8th Cir. 1989).
Radovich v. National Football League, 352 U.S. 445 (1957).
Reynolds v. National Football League, 584 F.2d 280 (8th Cir. 1978).
Smith v. Pro Football, Inc., 593 F.2d 1173 (D.C. Cir. 1978)
State v. Milwaukee, 144 N.W.2d 1 (Wisc. S. Ct. 1966).
Sullivan v. National Football League, 34 F.3d 1091 (1st Cir. 1994).
Toolson v. New York Yankees, 346 U.S. 356 (1953).
Twin City Sportservice, Inc. v. Finley, 365 F. Supp 235 (N.D. Cal. 1972), *rev'd on other grounds*, 512 F.2d 1264 (9th Cir. 1975).
United Mineworkers of America v. Pennington, 381 U.S. 657 (1965).
United States v. International Boxing Club, 348 U.S. 236 (1955).
United States Football League v. National Football League, 644 F. Supp. 1040 (S.D. N.Y. 1986).
VKK v. National Football League, 55 F. Supp. 196 (S.D.N.Y. 1999).
Wood v. National Basketball Association, 809 F.2d 954 (2nd Cir. 1987).

Publications

Greenberg, M. J. (1993). *Sports law practice*. Charlottesville, VA: Michie Co.
Roberts, G. (1990). Antitrust issues in professional sports. In G. Uberstine (Ed.), *Law of professional and amateur sports* (pp. 19-1–19-54. Deerfield, IL: Clark Boardman Callaghan.

Legislation

The Clayton Act of 1914, 15 U.S.C. §§ 12–27 (1989).
The Curt Flood Act of 1998, 15 U.S.C. § 27 (1998).
National Labor Relations Act, 29 U.S.C. § 151-69 (1988).
The Sherman Antitrust Act of 1890, 15 U.S.C. § 1, et seq. (1989).

8.32 Antitrust Law:
AMATEUR SPORT APPLICATIONS

John T. Wolohan
Ithaca College

Unlike professional sports organizations, the courts have afforded the NCAA and other amateur athletic organizations plenty of room under the antitrust laws to preserve the amateur character of athletics. Yet, even though it may be rare to see the courts apply the antitrust laws against the eligibility requirements of an amateur athletic organization, amateur athletic organizations have faced a number of antitrust lawsuits ranging from the unlawful restraint of trade in the television market and the college basketball coaches' market to the unlawful use of their monopoly power to destroy another amateur athletic organization.

Fundamental Concepts

There are two key questions in any effective application of the Sherman Act. The first question is which of the two major sections of the act is best suited to challenge the anticompetitive activities of the defendant. The two major sections of the Sherman Act are Section 1 and Section 2. Once you determine what section of the Sherman Act applies, the second key question in any effective Sherman Act challenge is to identify the markets adversely affected by the anticompetitive actions.

Sherman Antitrust Act

Section 1 of the Sherman Act

Section 1 of the Sherman Act states "[E]very contract, combination in the form of trust or otherwise, or conspiracy, in restraint of trade or commerce among the several States, or with foreign nations, is hereby declared to be illegal." (15 U.S.C. 1)

Not every restraint of trade, however, violates the antitrust law. Because nearly every contract that binds the parties to an agreed course of conduct "is a restraint of trade" of some sort, the Supreme Court has limited the restrictions contained in Section 1 to bar only *unreasonable restraints of trade*" (*NCAA v. Board of Regents of University of Oklahoma*, 1984).

Section 2 of the Sherman Act

Section 2 of the Sherman Act states that "[E]very person who shall monopolize, attempt to monopolize, or combine or conspire with any other person or persons, to monopolize any part of the trade or commerce among the several States, or with foreign nations, shall be deemed guilty of a felony . . ." (15 U.S.C. 2).

Tests Used to Establish a Sherman Antitrust Violation

To prevail on a Section 1 claim under the Sherman Act, the plaintiff must show that the defendant (1) participated in an agreement that (2) unreasonably restrained trade in the relevant market. In determining whether a defendant's conduct unreasonably restrains trade, the courts have developed three tests: the per se rule, the rule of reason, and the "quick look" rule of reason.

Per Se Rule. The *per se rule* condemns practices that are entirely void of redeeming competitive rationales and creates a presumption of a Sherman Antitrust Act violation for certain types of behavior. The reasoning behind the per se rule is that certain types of combinations or agreements will so often amount to an antitrust violation, regardless of the intent of the participants or the justifications offered, that a conclusive rule condemning the conduct is justified. Following this logic, courts have refused to engage in a detailed (and costly) market and effects analysis of conduct that fits into a per se category because such a close look would almost never save the prohibited conduct from Section 1 condemnation. Because the courts are slow to create such strong presumptions, only a handful of categories trigger the per se rule. Examples of conduct that subject a case to the per se rule are price fixing, resale price maintenance, and market allocations. Once a practice is identified as illegal per se, the court need not examine the practice's impact on the market or the procompetitive justifications for the practice advanced by a defendant before finding a violation of antitrust law.

In the 1970s, the Supreme Court sharply altered its antitrust stance by either expressly overruling or limiting the application of the per se rule for most categories, therefore it is only applied in clear-cut cases (Weiler & Roberts, 1998).

Rule of Reason. The *rule of reason* analysis, on the other hand, requires an analysis of the restraint's effect on competition. The rule of reason analysis requires the court to take a careful look at the markets and parties affected and whether the challenged restraint has a substantially adverse effect on competition in the relevant product market.

The focus of the rule of reason inquiry is not so much the legal category in which the conduct falls, but rather the actual purpose and effects of the restraints, and how they affect competition. Therefore, using a case-by-case economic and legal analysis, the court not only evaluates the restraint, but also the actual purpose and effects of the practice and whether the restraint "unreasonably" affects competition under the circumstances. Examples of contracts, combinations, or conspiracies that *"unreasonably"* restrain trade under Section 1 include price fixing, market allocation, group boycotts, and vertical territorial restrictions.

Under a rule of reason analysis, an agreement to restrain trade may still survive scrutiny under Section 1 if the procompetitive benefits of the restraint justify the anticompetitive effects. Justifications offered under the rule of reason may be considered only to the extent that they tend to show that, on balance, "the challenged restraint enhances competition" (*NCAA v. Board of Regents of University of Oklahoma*, 1984).

Finally, even if the defendant can show procompetitive elements, the plaintiff may still show that the restraint is not reasonably necessary to achieve the stated objective. To prove this, the plaintiff may argue that the restraint does not further the stated objective or that there are less restrictive alternatives.

"Quick Look" Rule of Reason. When a practice has obvious anticompetitive effects, such as price fixing, there is no need to prove that the defendant possesses market power. In such a case, the courts have developed a "quick look" rule of reason analysis, and the courts proceed directly to the question of whether the procompetitive justifications advanced for the restraint outweigh the anticompetitive effects.

For example, in *Law v. National Collegiate Athletic Association* (1998), the court, using a quick look rule of reason analysis, found that the undisputed evidence supported a finding of anticompetitive effect. The NCAA adopted the REC Rule to reduce the high cost of part-time coaches' salaries by limiting compensation to entry-level coaches to $16,000 per year. The NCAA does not dispute that the cost reduction has effectively reduced restricted-earnings coaches' salaries. Because the REC Rule was successful in artificially lowering the price of coaching services, no further evidence or analysis is required to find market power to set prices. Thus, the district court did not need to resolve issues of fact pertaining to the definition of the relevant market to support its decision on summary judgment that the REC Rule is a naked price restraint.

Various Athletic Markets

As stated earlier, the second key question in any antitrust challenge is to identify the markets adversely affected by the anticompetitive actions. Following are some of the competitive markets in which the anticompetitive actions of athletic organizations have been challenged.

Student–Athletes

In *Banks v. NCAA*, Braxston Banks, while still a college football player, entered his name into the professional draft. Banks, who was not chosen, brought suit against the NCAA seeking to have his eligibility to play intercollegiate football restored. Banks alleged that the NCAA's rules withdrawing an athlete's eligibility to participate in collegiate sports when the athlete chooses to enter a professional draft or engages an agent to help him secure a position with a professional team are an illegal restraint on trade or commerce in violation of the Sherman Antitrust Act.

The Seventh Circuit Court of Appeals held that Banks failed to allege an anticompetitive effect on a relevant market; at best, the court found that Banks had merely attempted to frame his complaint in antitrust language. Although Banks alleged a restraint on the market of college football players, college institutions who are members of the NCAA, and perhaps an NFL player recruitment market, the complaint failed to explain how these alleged restraints diminish competition in or among the markets. In other words, Banks merely claimed that there was an anticompetitive effect, but he failed to explain what it was.

In *Hairston v. Pacific 10 Conference and NCAA*, the Pac-10 after conducting an eight-month investigation into the allegations of recruiting improprieties, placed the University of Washington football team on probation for recruiting violations. The levied sanctions included, among other things, a two-year bowl ban, a one-year television revenue ban, and a two-year probationary period.

A group of former and current football players at the university sued the conference alleging that the sanctions violated the Sherman Antitrust Act. The Court of Appeals held that the players failed to show that the penalties imposed by the Pac-10 constituted an unreasonable restraint of trade.

In *Smith v. NCAA*, Renee Smith sued the NCAA, alleging that the NCAA's enforcement of a bylaw prohibiting her from participating in athletics while enrolled in a graduate program at an institution other than her undergraduate institution violated the Sherman Antitrust Act. The Court of Appeals held that as matter of first impression, the Sherman Act's restraint of trade provision did not apply to NCAA's promulgation of eligibility rules. Even if the Sherman Act was applicable, the court held, the challenged rule was not unlawful restraint of trade.

Television

In *NCAA v. Board of Regents of the University of Oklahoma*, the U.S. Supreme Court ruled that the NCAA's plan for televising college football games of member institutions violated the Sherman Antitrust Act. The Supreme Court held that the plan on its face constituted a restraint on operation of a free market; that the relevant market was college football; and that the restraints were not justified on the basis of procompetitive effect, protecting live attendance, or maintaining competitive balance among amateur athletic teams.

Women's Athletics

From 1906 to 1980, the NCAA only sponsored men's intercollegiate athletic programs. In 1971, the AIAW was organized to govern women's sports. In 1971–72, AIAW sponsored seven national championships for its 278 members. By 1980–81, AIAW's membership had grown to 961 colleges and universities. In 1981, the NCAA introduced twenty-nine women's championships in twelve sports. During the same season, the AIAW suffered a significant drop in membership and participation in its events. The AIAW's loss in membership dues totaled $124,000, which represented approximately 22 percent of the dues collected the previous year. Forty-nine percent of those institutions leaving AIAW elected to place their women's sports programs under NCAA's governance. The AIAW also suffered promotional losses. The National Broadcasting Company (NBC) decided not to exercise its exclusive television rights to telecast AIAW championships. The Eastman Kodak Company and the Broderick Company also sought to withdraw sponsorship of AIAW achievement awards. Because the AIAW's leadership expected these financial hardships only to worsen, it decided to close for business on June 30, 1982.

The AIAW sued the NCAA alleging that the NCAA unlawfully used its monopoly power in men's college sports to facilitate its entry into women's college sports and to force AIAW out of existence. In *Association for Intercollegiate Athletics for Women v. NCAA*, the Court held that the AIAW failed to prove an illegal agreement between the NCAA and the television network to "tie" television rights to the newly instituted women's basketball championship to the contract with the network for purchase of rights to televise the association's men's basketball championships. The court also held that the AIAW failed to prove specific intent necessary to sustain a claim of attempted monopoly. Even if the conduct of the NCAA was avowedly anticompetitive in purpose, the court found that the record did not support a finding that its effect on the AIAW was the result of anything but direct competition.

College Coaches

In *Law v. National Collegiate Athletic Association*, the Tenth Circuit Court of Appeals upheld the decision of the Kansas District Court that the NCAA bylaws limiting Division I basketball coaching staffs to four members—one head coach, two assistant coaches, and one entry-level coach called a "restricted-earnings" coach and restricting the compensation of restricted-earnings coaches in all Division I sports other than football to a total of $12,000 for the academic year and $4,000 for the summer months had a clear anticompetitive effect in restricting salaries. The Court then looked to the NCAA's justifications for the bylaw (retention of entry-level positions, cost reduction, and maintaining competitiveness) and found that they had no procompetitive value. The NCAA was ordered to pay nearly $22.3 million in damages as a result of the lawsuit. As a result of the treble damages set for violations of the Sherman Act under § 4 of the Clayton Act, the NCAA is potentially liable for approximately $67 million. The case was eventually settled for $54.5 million (Dauner, 2000).

The case began when the NCAA established a Cost Reduction Committee to consider means and strategies for reducing the costs of intercollegiate athletics "without disturbing the competitive balance" among NCAA member institutions. It became the consensus of the committee that reducing the total number of coaching positions would reduce the cost of intercollegiate athletic programs.

The NCAA Bylaws were challenged by a group of restricted-earnings coaches under Section 1 of the Sherman Antitrust Act as an unlawful "contract, combination . . . or conspiracy, in restraint of trade." In upholding the district court's decision, the Tenth Circuit Court of Appeals, using a "quick look" rule of reason analysis, found that the REC Rule was anticompetitive and had no procompetitive rationales and therefore was an unlawful restraint of trade.

In *Hennessey v. NCAA*, assistant football and basketball coaches challenged an NCAA bylaw limiting the number of assistant coaches member institutions could employ at any one time. The Fifth Circuit upheld the rule, concluding that the plaintiff failed to show that the rule was an unreasonable restraint of trade after weighing the anticompetitive effects with the procompetitive benefits of the restriction.

When trying to distinguish the precedents established in *Law v. NCAA* and *Hennessey*, there are two aspects the reader must keep in mind. First, it is important to note that *Hennessey* predates the Supreme Court's opinion in *NCAA v. Board of Regents of University of Oklahoma* (1984). Second, the *Hennessey* court placed the burden of showing the unreasonableness of the coaching restriction on the plaintiff and then found that the plaintiff could not make such a showing because the rule had only recently been implemented. In *Law*, the plaintiff only had the burden of establishing the anticompetitive effect of the restraint at issue. Once the plaintiff met that burden, which the coaches did by showing the naked and effective price fixing character of the agreement, the burden shifted to the defendant to justify the restraint as a "reasonable" one. It is on this step that the defendant NCAA stumbled.

Significant Case

—————◇◇◇—————

The following antitrust case establishes the precedent that even though the NCAA plays a vital role in protecting and preserving the nature of amateur athletics, when its regulations are purely commercial in nature, it will be held to same antitrust standards as other commercial businesses.

NCAA V. BOARD OF REGENTS OF THE UNIVERSITY OF OKLAHOMA

United States Supreme Court
468 U.S. 85 (1984)

Justice STEVENS delivered the opinion of the Court.

The University of Oklahoma and the University of Georgia contend that the National Collegiate Athletic Association has unreasonably restrained trade in the televising of college football games. After an extended trial, the District Court found that the NCAA had violated section 1 of the Sherman Act and granted injunctive relief. The Court of Appeals agreed that the statute had been violated but modified the remedy in some respects. We granted certiorari, and now affirm.

I

The NCAA

Since its inception in 1905, the NCAA has played an important role in the regulation of amateur collegiate sports. It has adopted and promulgated playing rules, standards of amateurism, standards for academic eligibility, regulations concerning recruitment of athletes, and rules governing the size of athletic squads and coaching staffs. In some sports, such as baseball, swimming, basketball, wrestling, and track, it has sponsored and conducted national tournaments. It has not done so in the sport of football, however. With the exception of football, the NCAA has not undertaken any regulation of the televising of athletic events.

The NCAA has approximately 850 voting members. The regular members are classified into separate divisions to reflect differences in size and scope of their athletic programs. Division I includes 276 colleges with major athletic programs; in this group only 187 play intercollegiate football. Divisions II and III include approximately 500 colleges with less extensive athletic programs. Division I has been subdivided into Divisions I-A and I-AA for football.

Some years ago, five major conferences together with major football-playing independent institutions organized the College Football Association (CFA). The original purpose of the CFA was to promote the interests of major football-playing schools within the NCAA structure. The Universities of Oklahoma and Georgia, respondents in this Court, are members of the CFA.

* * *

The Current Plan

The plan adopted in 1981 for the 1982-1985 seasons is at issue in this case. This plan, like each of its predecessors, recites that it is intended to reduce, insofar as possible, the adverse effects of live television upon football game attendance. It provides that "all forms of television of the football games of NCAA member institutions during the Plan control periods shall be in accordance with this Plan." The plan recites that the television committee has awarded rights to negotiate and contract for the telecasting of college football games of members of the NCAA to two "carrying networks."

* * *

In separate agreements with each of the carrying networks, ABC and the Columbia Broadcasting System (CBS), the NCAA granted each the right to telecast the 14 live "exposures" described in the plan, in accordance with the "ground rules" set forth therein. Each of the networks agreed to pay a specified "minimum aggregate compensation to the participating NCAA member institutions" during the 4-year period in an amount that totaled $ 131,750,000. In essence the agreement authorized each network to negotiate directly with member schools for the right to televise their games. The agreement itself does not describe the method of computing the compensation for each game, but the practice that has developed over the years and that the District Court found would be followed under the current agreement involved the setting of a recommended fee by a representative of the NCAA for different types of telecasts, with national telecasts being the most valuable, regional telecasts being less valuable, and Division II or Division III games commanding a still lower price. The aggregate of all these payments presumably equals the total minimum aggregate compensation set forth in the basic agreement. Except for differences in payment between national and regional telecasts, and with respect to Division II and Division III games, the amount that any team receives does not change with the size of the viewing audience, the number of markets in which the game is telecast, or the particular characteristic of the game or the participating teams. Instead, the "ground rules" provide that the carrying networks make alternate selections of those games they wish to televise, and thereby obtain the exclusive right to submit a bid at an essentially fixed price to the institutions involved. See 546 F.Supp., at 1289-1293.

The plan also contains "appearance requirements" and "appearance limitations" which pertain to each of the 2-year periods that the plan is in effect. The basic requirement imposed on each of the two networks is that it must schedule appearances for at least 82 different member institutions during each 2-year period. Under the appearance limitations no member institution is eligible to appear on television more than a total of six times and more than four times nationally, with the appearances to be divided equally between the two carrying networks. See id., at 1293. The number of exposures specified in the contracts also sets an absolute maximum on the number of games that can be broadcast.

Thus, although the current plan is more elaborate than any of its predecessors, it retains the essential features of each of them. It limits the total amount of televised intercollegiate football and the number of games that any one team may televise. No member is permitted to make any sale of television rights except in accordance with the basic plan.

Background of this Controversy

Beginning in 1979 CFA members began to advocate that colleges with major football programs should have a greater voice in the formulation of football television policy than they had in the NCAA. CFA therefore investigated the possibility of negotiating a television agreement of its own, developed an independent plan, and obtained a contract offer from the National Broadcasting Co. (NBC). This contract, which it signed in August 1981, would have allowed a more liberal number of appearances for each institution, and would have increased the overall revenues realized by CFA members.

In response the NCAA publicly announced that it would take disciplinary action against any CFA member that complied with the CFA-NBC contract. The NCAA made it clear that sanctions would not be limited to the football programs of CFA members, but would apply to other sports as well. On September 8, 1981, respondents commenced this action in the United States District Court for the Western District of Oklahoma and obtained a preliminary injunction preventing the NCAA from initiating disciplinary proceedings or otherwise interfering with CFA's efforts to perform its agreement with NBC. Notwithstanding the entry of the injunction, most CFA members were unwilling to commit themselves to the new contractual arrangement with NBC in the face of the threatened sanctions and therefore the agreement was never consummated. See id., at 1286-1287.

* * *

II

There can be no doubt that the challenged practices of the NCAA constitute a "restraint of trade" in the sense that they limit members' freedom to negotiate and enter into their own television contracts. In that sense, however, every contract is a restraint of trade, and as we have repeatedly recognized, the Sherman Act was intended to prohibit only unreasonable restraints of trade.

It is also undeniable that these practices share characteristics of restraints we have previously held unreasonable. The NCAA is an association of schools which compete against each other to attract television revenues, not to mention fans an athletes. As the District Court found, the policies of the NCAA with respect to television rights are ultimately controlled by the vote of member institutions. By participating in an association which prevents member institutions from competing against each other on the basis of price or kind of television rights that can be offered to broadcasters, the NCAA member institutions have created a horizontal restraint—an agreement among competitors on the way in which they will compete with one another. A restraint of this type has often been held to be unreasonable as a matter of law. Because it places a ceiling on the number of games member institutions may televise, the horizontal agreement places an artificial limit on the quantity of televised football that is available to broadcasters and consumers. By restraining the quantity of television rights available for sale, the challenged practices create a limitation on output; our cases have held that such limitations are unreasonable restraints of trade. Moreover, the District Court found that the minimum aggregate price in fact operates to preclude any price negotiation between broadcasters and institutions, thereby constituting horizontal price fixing, perhaps the paradigm of an unreasonable restraint of trade.

Horizontal price fixing and output limitation are ordinarily condemned as a matter of law under an "illegal per se" approach because the probability that these practices are anticompetitive is so high; a per se rule is applied when "the practice facially appears to be one that would always or almost always tend to restrict competition and decrease output." Broadcast Music, Inc. v. Columbia Broadcasting System, Inc., 441 U.S. 1, 19-20 (1979). In such circumstances a restraint is presumed unreasonable without inquiry into the particular market context in which it is found. Nevertheless, we have decided that it would be inappropriate to apply a per se rule to this case. This decision is not based on a lack of judicial experience with this type of arrangement, on the fact that the NCAA is organized as a nonprofit entity, or on our respect for the NCAA's historic role in the preservation and encouragement of intercollegiate amateur athletics. Rather, what is critical is that this case involves an industry in which horizontal restraints on competition are essential if the product is to be available at all.

As Judge Bork has noted: "[Some] activities can only be carried out jointly. Perhaps the leading example is league sports. When a league of professional lacrosse teams is formed, it would be pointless to declare their cooperation illegal on the ground that there are no other professional lacrosse teams." R. Bork, The Antitrust Paradox 278 (1978). What the NCAA and its member institutions market in this case is competition itself—contests between competing institutions. Of course, this would be completely ineffective if there were no rules on which the competitors agreed to create and define the competition to be marketed. A myriad of rules affecting such matters as the size of the field, the number of players on a team, and the extent to which physical violence is to be encouraged or proscribed, all must be agreed upon, and all restrain the manner in which institutions compete. Moreover, the NCAA seeks to market a particular brand of football—college football. The identification of this "product" with an academic tradition differentiates college football from and makes it more popular than professional sports to which it might otherwise be comparable, such as, for example, minor league baseball. In order to preserve the character and quality of the "product," athletes must not be paid, must be required to attend class, and the like. And the integrity of the "product" cannot be preserved except by mutual agreement; if an institution adopted such restrictions unilaterally, its effectiveness as a competitor on the playing field might soon be destroyed. Thus, the NCAA plays a vital role in enabling college football to preserve its character, and as a result enables a product to be marketed which might otherwise be unavailable. In performing this role, its actions widen consumer choice—not only the choices available to sports fans but also those available to athletes—and hence can be viewed as procompetitive.

* * *

Respondents concede that the great majority of the NCAA's regulations enhance competition among member institutions. Thus, despite the fact that this case involves restraints on the ability of member institutions to compete in terms of price and output, a fair evaluation of their competitive character requires consideration of the NCAA's justifications for the restraints.

Our analysis of this case under the Rule of Reason, of course, does not change the ultimate focus of our inquiry. Both per se rules and the Rule of Reason are employed "to form a judgment about the competitive significance of the restraint." National Society of Professional Engineers v. United States, 435 U.S. 679, 692 (1978). A conclusion that a restraint of trade is unreasonable may be "based either (1) on the nature or character of the contracts, or (2) on surrounding circumstances giving rise to the inference or presumption that they were intended to restrain trade and enhance prices. Under either branch of the test, the inquiry is confined to a consideration of impact on competitive conditions."

Per se rules are invoked when surrounding circumstances make the likelihood of anticompetitive conduct so great as to render unjustified further examination of the challenged conduct. But whether the ultimate finding is the product of a presumption or actual market analysis, the essential inquiry remains the same—whether or not the challenged restraint enhances competition. Under the Sherman Act the criterion to be used in judging the validity of a restraint on trade is its impact on competition.

III

Because it restrains price and output, the NCAA's television plan has a significant potential for anticompetitive effects. The findings of the District Court indicate that this potential has been realized. The District Court found that if member institutions were free to sell television rights, many more games would be shown on television, and that the NCAA's output restriction has the effect of raising the price the networks pay for television rights. Moreover, the court found that by fixing a price for television rights to all games, the NCAA creates a price structure that is unresponsive to viewer demand and unrelated to the prices that would prevail in a competitive market. And, of course, since as a practical matter all member institutions need NCAA approval, members have no real choice but to adhere to the NCAA's television controls.

The anticompetitive consequences of this arrangement are apparent. Individual competitors lose their freedom to compete. Price is higher and output lower than they would otherwise be, and both are unresponsive to consumer preference. This latter point is perhaps the most significant, since "Congress designed the Sherman Act as a 'consumer welfare prescription.'" Reiter v. Sonotone Corp., 442 U.S. 330, 343 (1979). A restraint that has the effect of reducing the importance of consumer preference in setting price and output is not consistent with this fundamental goal of anti-trust law. Restrictions on price and output are the paradigmatic examples of restraints of trade that the Sherman Act was intended to prohibit. See Standard Oil Co. v. United States, 221 U.S. 1, 52-60 (1911). At the same time, the television plan eliminates competitors from the market, since only those broadcasters able to bid on television rights covering the entire NCAA can compete. Thus, as the District Court found, many telecasts that would occur in a competitive market are foreclosed by the NCAA's plan.

Petitioner argues, however, that its television plan can have no significant anticompetitive effect since the record indicates that it has no market power—no ability to alter the interaction of supply and demand in the market. We must reject this argument for two reasons, one legal, one factual.

As a matter of law, the absence of proof of market power does not justify a naked restriction on price or output. To the contrary, when there is an agreement not to compete in terms of price or output, "no elaborate industry analysis is required to demonstrate the anticompetitive character of such an agreement." Professional Engineers, 435 U.S., at 692. Petitioner does not quarrel with the District Court's finding that price and output are not responsive to demand. Thus the plan is inconsistent with the Sherman Act's command that price and supply be responsive to consumer preference. We have never required proof of market power in such a case. This naked restraint on price and output requires some competitive justification even in the absence of a detailed market analysis.

As a factual matter, it is evident that petitioner does possess market power. The District Court employed the correct test for determining whether college football broadcasts constitute a separate market—whether there are other products that are reasonably substitutable for televised NCAA football games. Petitioner's argument that it cannot obtain competitive prices from broadcasters since advertisers, and hence broadcasters, can switch from college football to other types of programming simply ignores the findings of the District Court. It found that intercollegiate football telecasts generate an audience uniquely attractive to advertisers and that competitors are unable to offer programming that can attract a similar audience. These findings amply support its conclusion that the NCAA possesses market power. Indeed, the District Court's subsidiary finding that advertisers will pay a premium price per viewer to reach audiences watching college football because of their demographic characteristics is vivid evidence of the uniqueness of this product. Moreover, the District Court's market analysis is firmly supported by our decision in International Boxing Club of New York, Inc. v. United States, 358 U.S. 242 (1959), that championship boxing events are uniquely attractive to fans and hence constitute a market separate from that for nonchampionship events. See id., at 249-252. Thus, respondents have demonstrated that there is a separate market for telecasts of college football which "[rests] on generic qualities differentiating" viewers. Times-Picayune Publishing Co. v. United States, 345 U.S. 594, 613 (1953). It inexorably follows that if college football broadcasts be defined as a separate market—and we are convinced they are—then the NCAA's complete control over those broadcasts provides a solid basis for the District Court's conclusion that the NCAA possesses market power with respect to those broadcasts. "When a product is controlled by one interest, without substitutes available in the market, there is monopoly power."

Thus, the NCAA television plan on its face constitutes a restraint upon the operation of a free market, and the findings of the District Court establish that it has oper-

ated to raise prices and reduce output. Under the Rule of Reason, these hallmarks of anticompetitive behavior place upon petitioner a heavy burden of establishing an affirmative defense which competitively justifies this apparent deviation from the operations of a free market. See Professional Engineers, 435 U.S., at 692-696. We turn now to the NCAA's proffered justifications.

IV

Relying on Broadcast Music, petitioner argues that its television plan constitutes a cooperative "joint venture" which assists in the marketing of broadcast rights and hence is procompetitive. . . . The essential contribution made by the NCAA's arrangement is to define the number of games that may be televised, to establish the price for each exposure, and to define the basic terms of each contract between the network and a home team. The NCAA does not, however, act as a selling agent for any school or for any conference of schools. The selection of individual games, and the negotiation of particular agreements, are matters left to the networks and the individual schools. Thus, the effect of the network plan is not to eliminate individual sales of broadcasts, since these still occur, albeit subject to fixed prices and output limitations. Unlike Broadcast Music's blanket license covering broadcast rights to a large number of individual compositions, here the same rights are still sold on an individual basis, only in a noncompetitive market.

The District Court did not find that the NCAA's television plan produced any procompetitive efficiencies which enhanced the competitiveness of college football television rights; to the contrary it concluded that NCAA football could be marketed just as effectively without the television plan. There is therefore no predicate in the findings for petitioner's efficiency justification. Indeed, petitioner's argument is refuted by the District Court's finding concerning price and output. If the NCAA's television plan produced procompetitive efficiencies, the plan would increase output and reduce the price of televised games. The District Court's contrary findings accordingly undermine petitioner's position. In light of these findings, it cannot be said that "the agreement on price is necessary to market the product at all." Broadcast Music, 441 U.S., at 23. In Broadcast Music, the availability of a package product that no individual could offer enhanced the total volume of music that was sold. Unlike this case, there was no limit of any kind placed on the volume that might be sold in the entire market and each individual remained free to sell his own music without restraint. Here production has been limited, not enhanced. No individual school is free to televise its own games without restraint. The NCAA's efficiency justification is not supported by the record.

Neither is the NCAA's television plan necessary to enable the NCAA to penetrate the market through an attractive package sale. Since broadcasting rights to college football constitute a unique product for which there is no ready substitute, there is no need for collective action in order to enable the product to compete against its nonexistent competitors. This is borne out by the District Court's finding that the NCAA's television plan reduces the volume of television rights sold.

V

Throughout the history of its regulation of intercollegiate football telecasts, the NCAA has indicated its concern with protecting live attendance. This concern, it should be noted, is not with protecting live attendance at games which are shown on television; that type of interest is not at issue in this case. Rather, the concern is that fan interest in a televised game may adversely affect ticket sales for games that will not appear on television.

Although the NORC studies in the 1950's provided some support for the thesis that live attendance would suffer if unlimited television were permitted, the District Court found that there was no evidence to support that theory in today's market. Moreover, as the District Court found, the television plan has evolved in a manner inconsistent with its original design to protect gate attendance. Under the current plan, games are shown on television during all hours that college football games are played. The plan simply does not protect live attendance by ensuring that games will not be shown on television at the same time as live events.

There is, however, a more fundamental reason for rejecting this defense. The NCAA's argument that its television plan is necessary to protect live attendance is not based on a desire to maintain the integrity of college football as a distinct and attractive product, but rather on a fear that the product will not prove sufficiently attractive to draw live attendance when faced with competition from televised games. At bottom the NCAA's position is that ticket sales for most college games are unable to compete in a free market. The television plan protects ticket sales by limiting output—just as any monopolist increases revenues by reducing output. By seeking to insulate live ticket sales from the full spectrum of competition because of its assumption that the product itself is insufficiently attractive to consumers, petitioner forwards a justification that is inconsistent with the basic policy of the Sherman Act. "[The] Rule of Reason does not support a defense based on the assumption that competition itself is unreasonable."

VI

Petitioner argues that the interest in maintaining a competitive balance among amateur athletic teams is legitimate and important and that it justifies the regulations challenged in this case. We agree with the first part of the argument but not the second.

Our decision not to apply a per se rule to this case rests in large part on our recognition that a certain degree of cooperation is necessary if the type of competition that petitioner and its member institutions seek to market is to be preserved. It is reasonable to assume that most of the regulatory controls of the NCAA are justifiable means of fostering competition among amateur athletic teams and therefore procompetitive because they enhance public interest in intercollegiate athletics. The specific restraints on football telecasts that are challenged in this case do not, however, fit into the same mold as do rules defining the conditions of the contest, the eligibility of participants, or the manner in which members of a joint enterprise shall share the responsibilities and the benefits of the total venture.

The NCAA does not claim that its television plan has equalized or is intended to equalize competition within any one league. The plan is nationwide in scope and there is no single league or tournament in which all college football teams compete. There is no evidence of any intent to equalize the strength of teams in Division I-A with those in Division II or Division III, and not even a colorable basis for giving colleges that have no football program at all a voice in the management of the revenues generated by the football programs at other schools. The interest in maintaining a competitive balance that is asserted by the NCAA as a justification for regulating all television of intercollegiate football is not related to any neutral standard or to any readily identifiable group of competitors.

The television plan is not even arguably tailored to serve such an interest. It does not regulate the amount of money that any college may spend on its football program, nor the way in which the colleges may use the revenues that are generated by their football programs, whether derived from the sale of television rights, the sale of tickets, or the sale of concessions or program advertising. The plan simply imposes a restriction on one source of revenue that is more important to some colleges than to others. There is no evidence that this restriction produces any greater measure of equality throughout the NCAA than would a restriction on alumni donations, tuition rates, or any other revenue-producing activity. At the same time, as the District Court found, the NCAA imposes a variety of other restrictions designed to preserve amateurism which are much better tailored to the goal of competitive balance than is the television plan, and which are "clearly sufficient" to preserve competitive balance to the extent it is within the NCAA's power to do so. And much more than speculation supported the District Court's findings on this score. No other NCAA sport employs a similar plan, and in particular the court found that in the most closely analogous sport, college basketball, competitive balance has been maintained without resort to a restrictive television plan.

Perhaps the most important reason for rejecting the argument that the interest in competitive balance is served by the television plan is the District Court's unambiguous and well-supported finding that many more games would be televised in a free market than under the NCAA plan. The hypothesis that legitimates the maintenance of competitive balance as a procompetitive justification under the Rule of Reason is that equal competition will maximize consumer demand for the product. The finding that consumption will materially increase if the controls are removed is a compelling demonstration that they do not in fact serve any such legitimate purpose.

VII

The NCAA plays a critical role in the maintenance of a revered tradition of amateurism in college sports.

There can be no question but that it needs ample latitude to play that role, or that the preservation of the student-athlete in higher education adds richness and diversity to intercollegiate athletics and is entirely consistent with the goals of the Sherman Act. But consistent with the Sherman Act, the role of the NCAA must be to preserve a tradition that might otherwise die; rules that restrict output are hardly consistent with this role. Today we hold only that the record supports the District Court's conclusion that by curtailing output and blunting the ability of member institutions to respond to consumer preference, the NCAA has restricted rather than enhanced the place of intercollegiate athletics in the Nation's life. Accordingly, the judgment of the Court of Appeals is Affirmed.

◇◇◇ **OTHER RELEVANT SIGNIFICANT CASES**

Chapter 8.31 *Antitrust Law: Professional Sport Applications*
Chapter 8.33 *Labor Law: Professional Sport Applications*

Recent Trends

Coaches Union

In 2002, the 320 coaches at the 14 institutions in Pennsylvania's State System of Higher Education joined the Association of Pennsylvania State and College and University Faculties union and entered into a collective-bargaining agreement with the state (Wolohan, 2002). In 2005, a strike by the coaches, which would have cancelled all fall sports, was narrowly averted when the coaches agreed to a new collective bargaining agreement.

Limit on the Number of NCAA Athletic Scholarships

In September 2005, the Federal District Court for the Western District of Washington was asked to determine whether the NCAA and Division I-A schools, in the name of "cost-containment," have entered into an "agreement" or "rule," codified in Bylaw 15.5.5, which artificially and illegally restrains the number of scholarships that a school may award to football team roster members. A group of walk-on players argued that the practice of only allowing 85 scholarships per school for football was an unlawful horizontal restraint of trade in violation of Section 1 of the Sherman Act, 15 U.S.C. § 1, and is a monopolization of the "big-time college football market" in violation of Section 2 of the Sherman Act, 15 U.S.C. § 2. But for the anticompetitive agreement between the Division I-A members of the NCAA to save money by artificially restricting the number of football scholarships awarded by each school, the players argued that they would have received full grant-in-aid scholarships.

By rejecting the NCAA's motion for Summary Judgment, the Court found that the players had alleged sufficient facts to require a trial on the issues. The case should go to trial sometime in 2006 (*In Re NCAA I-A Walk-on Football Players Litigation*).

NCAA vs. NIT Basketball Tournament

In August 2005, nine days into an antitrust trial in New York Federal District Court, the NCAA agreed to pay the Metropolitan Intercollegiate Basketball Association (MIBA) $56.5 million to buy the preseason and postseason National Invitation Tournaments (NIT). The settlement, which pays the five New York City colleges making up the Metropolitan Intercollegiate Basketball Association, ends years of legal fighting over the NCAA's control of college basketball (Moran, 2005).

References

Cases

Association for Intercollegiate Athletics for Women v. NCAA, 735 F.2d 577 (1984).
Banks v. NCAA, 977 F.2d 1081 (7th Cir. 1992).
Hairston v. Pacific 10 Conference, 101 F.3d 1315 (9th Cir. 1996).
Hennessey v. NCAA, 564 F.2d 1136 (5th Cir. 1977).
In Re NCAA I-A Walk-on Football Players Litigation, 398 F. Supp. 2d 1144 (2005).
Law v. NCAA, 134 F.3d 1010 (10th Cir. 1998).
NCAA v. Board of Regents of the University of Oklahoma, 468 U.S. 85 (1984).
Smith v. NCAA, 139 F.3d 180 (3rd Cir. 1998).

Publications

Dauner, J. T. (2000, June 14). Court hears payout arguments from restricted earnings coaches. *The Kansas City Star*, p. D4.
Moran, M. (2005, August 18). NCAA buys NIT for $56.5 million; event will continue. *USA TODAY*, Sec. C, p. 1.
Schemo, D. J. (2003, January 30). Women's athletics; Title IX panel favors lifting antitrust laws. *The New York Times*, Sec. D; P. 2.
Weiler, P.C., & Roberts, G. R. (1998). *Sports and the law*. St. Paul, MN: West Group.
Wolohan, J. T. (2002, December) Union made: Pennsylvania's coaches take a step toward better pay and job security. *Athletic Business, 26*, 18–21.

Legislation

The Sherman Antitrust Act of 1890, 15 U.S.C.A. § 1-7.
The Clayton Act of 1914, 15 U.S.C.A. § 12-27.

Labor Law:
PROFESSIONAL SPORT APPLICATIONS

Lisa Pike Masteralexis
University of Massachusetts-Amherst

Labor laws exist on both state and federal levels. State labor laws apply to public entities, such as a city or state's sports authority or a state university athletic or recreation department. Federal labor laws apply to private employers engaged in a business involving interstate commerce, such as a professional sports league or a sports arena operated by a private facility management company.

Fundamental Concepts

Fair Labor Standards Act

The Fair Labor Standards Act (FLSA) sets forth minimum hourly wages, overtime wages for work exceeding 40 hours, and child labor protections. It also requires record keeping on those aspects by employers. The FLSA contains numerous exemptions from the overtime pay and/or the minimum wage provisions and some from the child labor provisions. Exemptions are narrowly construed against the employer asserting them. Consequently, employers and employees should always closely check the exact terms and conditions of an exemption in light of the employee's actual duties before assuming that the exemption might apply to an employee. The burden of proving the exemption applies rests with the employer. Exemptions that are likely to apply in the sport industry include those for individuals working in executive or administrative positions and those engaged in commissioned sales for the retail or service industry, of which sports and recreation are a part. Further, "an establishment which is an amusement or recreational establishment, if (A) it does not operate for more than seven months in any calendar year, or (B) during the preceding calendar year, its average receipts for any six months of such year were not more than 33-1/3 per centum of its average receipts for the other six months of such year" (FLSA, 29 USC § 213 (a)(3) (2005)) is also exempt from FLSA wage and overtime provisions.

National Labor Relations Act

Enacted in 1935, the National Labor Relations Act (NLRA) applies to private employers. It was drafted to "eliminate . . . or mitigate the causes of certain substantial obstructions to the free flow of commerce . . . by encouraging collective bargaining and by protecting the exercise by workers of full freedom of association, self-organization, and designation of representatives of their own choosing, for the purpose of negotiating the terms and conditions of their employment or other mutual aid or protection" (NLRA, § 151, 2005). In other words, the NLRA set forth employee rights to join or assist unions, engage in concerted activity for economic benefits and work protections, and the right to engage in collective bargaining. It applies to employees and employers in the private sector, drawing distinctions between employees for assignment to bargaining units, such that employees who are in the same bargaining unit need not do the exact same job, but must have common bargaining interests

Through the NLRA Congress created the National Labor Relations Board (NLRB), because it believed a specialized agency charged with regulating labor relations was necessary. Congress also established the NLRB because it mistrusted the manner in which the federal courts, often aligned with employers, handled labor cases. The two primary activities of the NLRB are to conduct secret ballot union elections for certification and decertification and to prevent and remedy unfair labor practices.

Taft-Hartley Act of 1947

There is no doubt that the NLRA was pro-labor. A dozen years later the Taft-Hartley Act amended the NLRA to give balance to labor relations by focusing on rights of employers and non-union members. Among other things, Taft-Hartley amended the NLRA by granting the right of employees to choose to *not* join or assist unions and also a provision that prohibits the union from discriminating against non-union members. Section 9 of the NLRA was amended to include among NLRB responsibilities the decertification of unions as well as certification of unions.

Employee Rights

NLRA §7 established three significant employee rights:

1. the right to join or assist unions and the right not to join or assist unions;
2. the right to engage in collective bargaining through representative of own choosing; and
3. the right to engage in concerted activity for one's own mutual aid and protection (29 USCS §157, 2005).

When employees want to join a union, they must petition the NLRB to conduct a secret ballot election under §9 of the act to determine whether at least one-third of all employees are interested in conducting an election and whether the group is an appropriate unit to collectively bargain with the employer. The NLRB examines the community of interests of the group to determine if there is enough in common to make bargaining successful. **Community of interests** include: commonality of supervision, work rules, and personnel policies; shared work areas, similarity of job duties and working conditions; similarity of methods for evaluation; similarity in pay and benefits; integration and interdependence of operations; and history, if any, of collective bargaining between the parties (Feldacker, 2000; Gold, 1998).

In a case involving the North American Soccer League (NASL), the league challenged the NLRB's certification of all players into a national bargaining unit for purposes of collective bargaining (*North American Soccer League v. NLRB*, 1980). The NASL argued that employee units at the local team level were the appropriate form. The NLRB disagreed, finding that where an employer has assumed sufficient control over the working conditions of employees of its franchisees, the NLRB may require employers to bargain jointly. The court agreed that labor relations were in fact conducted at a leaguewide level and not delegated to individual teams, and thus, the NLRB's designation was appropriate. From the union's perspective, if the NASL successfully limited bargaining to the local level, employers could easily undermine solidarity by trading union supporters. It could also undermine the union's strike threat. For instance, if a team in Boston went on strike, the league could continue to play and just give any team playing Boston a bye. If the league could continue without a franchise, the power of the strike would be severely limited. With the shared revenue structures in place in most leagues, under such a circumstance, the Boston franchise could also still receive a cut of revenues from the other games, severely disabling the leverage of the player's union.

Once a union is designated as an appropriate bargaining unit, elections are held, and a union is certified as the exclusive bargaining representative for employees, two important changes occur for employees. First, management is put on notice that it has a duty to bargain in good faith with the union and second, the union has a duty of fair representation for its employee members.

Duty to Engage in Collective Bargaining

Once a union is in existence, management *must* engage in collective bargaining over mandatory subjects of bargaining or risk being charged with an unfair labor practice under §8 (a)(5) of the NLRA for failing to bargain in good faith (*NLRB v. Katz*, 1962). Mandatory subjects are hours, wages, and terms and conditions of employment. They are those things "plainly germane to the 'working environment' and not those 'managerial decisions which lie at the core of entrepreneurial control' " (*Ford Motor Co. v. NLRB* at 498,

1979). The result of good faith negotiations is to create to a collective bargaining agreement (CBA). Provisions in the CBA for wages are basically anything else that has monetary value including salaries, bonuses, severance and termination pay, and fringe benefits, such as health care, life or disability insurance. The hours provisions cover anything related to time spent at work. Terms and conditions of employment cover the majority of remaining provisions in one's work life, including job security, seniority, grievance and arbitration provisions, drug-testing provisions, safety concerns, and the like.

Beyond mandatory subjects, there are also permissive subjects for bargaining over which management is not obligated to negotiate and the union cannot bargain to impasse. An example of a permissive subject might be if the National Basketball Players Association wanted its logo to appear in all NBA advertisements. An impasse is a stalemate in negotiations that often leads to a strike or a lockout. In collective bargaining relationships, unions often give up the right to strike in return for management giving up the right to lock employees out. Although there is a protected right for employees to engage in concerted activity, unions are allowed to bargain away this right, if the union members so choose. Another word on concerted activity is that it is a protected §7 right, provided the behavior does not become violent.

Duty to bargain in good faith cases often arise in professional sports when the commissioner attempts to make a new rule that impacts mandatory subjects. For instance, in *National Football League Players Association v. National Labor Relations Board*, the NFLPA argued that the NFL commissioner's imposition of a rule and corresponding fines for players leaving the bench during fights without negotiating with the union was a refusal to bargain in good faith (1974).

Duty of Fair Representation

After an election decision and certification by the NLRB, a union becomes the exclusive bargaining representative for *all* employees. The duty of fair representation requires that a union represent *all* employees fairly, even those employees who are in the bargaining unit, but are not union members (*Steele v. Louisville & Nashville Railroad*, 1944). If the union does not represent employees fairly, it qualifies as an unfair labor practice under §8(b) (1) (A) the section that prohibits interference with §7 rights (*Miranda Fuel Co.*, 1962). Fair representation requires that unions must not discriminate or act in an arbitrary or bad faith manner (*Vaca v. Sipes*, 1967). Most duty of fair representation cases challenge decisions to pursue grievances on behalf of employees. In *Peterson v. Kennedy and the NFLPA*, the plaintiff NFL player sued his union for failing to fairly represent him when it erred in not filing his grievance in a timely manner (1985). The court held that because the union's conduct amounted to no more than negligence, it did not meet the standard required for a duty of fair representation case. The court emphasized that unions are not liable for good faith, nondiscriminatory errors of judgment made in interpreting CBAs, in processing grievances or representing them in the process, (*Id.*).

Unfair Labor Practices

Section 8 of the National Labor Relations Act provides the enforcement mechanism by establishing employer and union unfair labor practices.

Employer Discrimination or Retaliation for Union Activity

It is an unfair labor practice for the employer to interfere with, restrain or coerce employees who are engaged in union activity (NLRA, §8(a)(1)). It is also an unfair labor practice to discriminate against employees for such activity and for showing support of the union (NLRA, §8(a)(3)). In theory, this is straightforward, but in practice, like all discrimination cases, its application is difficult. Often workplace discipline, demotion, or termination decisions arise from mixed motives—union animus by the employer combined with an employee's poor work performance or misconduct.

Duty to Bargain in Good Faith

Once a union is certified by the NLRB, management and union have a duty to bargain in good faith over hours, wages, and terms and conditions of employment. Either party can negotiate to impasse and decide whether to use their economic weapons of imposing a strike or a lockout. In practice, management may unilaterally implement its last best offer and still fulfill the duty to bargain in good faith (*Brown v. Pro Football*, 1996). Because there is no duty to bargain over permissive subjects, employers can unilaterally impose permissive and "management rights" subjects. Management rights subjects generally encompass managerial decisions that "lie at the core of entrepreneurial control" (Rabuano, 2002). Management need not negotiate management rights, but it may have to negotiate their effect if they impact mandatory subjects for bargaining. For example, management need not negotiate with the union to relocate a sports franchise to a new city, but will have to negotiate with the players' union over such effects of the decision as how players will cover relocation costs from one city to the next.

Collective Bargaining Relationship

The CBA is a contract that expresses the final negotiations between management and union over the mandatory subjects of their business, and the collective bargaining relationship is an ongoing one. There may be a need for additional negotiations after that document is formed, that require union and management to continue to discuss or negotiate for other issues that affect mandatory subjects. Either side has the right to convince the other side to come back to the bargaining table to discuss or negotiate over a new or current term of employment.

Over the term of the collective bargaining relationship there is also considerable time spent by union and management in the administration of the collective bargaining agreement. An important component of the administration is the reliance on an arbitration process to resolve disputes. Arbitration is a less costly, more efficient alternative to the court system or to union striking or management locking employees out as a means of resolving disagreements. Arbitration clauses are common in labor agreements and create a mechanism for employees and employers to resolve disputes as to interpretations of the CBA or to resolve grievances challenging disciplinary action. There are two forms of arbitration: rights and interest. Rights arbitration is for disputes over the interpretation or application of the contract. Interest arbitration deals with disputes over the actual terms of contract, such as salary arbitration (*Silverman v. MLBPRC*, 1995). In salary arbitration for example, the contract provision delegates to the arbitrator(s) the power to determine the compensation term for a given player based on a salary dispute between the player and the team.

Despite the quality of negotiating or the clarity of the language in the CBA, disputes are bound to arise during the course of the agreement. Disputes can be lodged through a grievance process negotiated into the CBA. The road to an arbitration case starts with one party filing a grievance against the other. Unions will generally file these on behalf of their employees. The contract will set forth a process for resolving the disputes that leads up to the final, binding arbitration hearing. The Steelworkers Trilogy cases established federal policy that an arbitrator's decision should not be the subject of judicial intervention provided that the arbitrator's award is based on the essence of the collective bargaining agreement (*U.S. Steelworkers v. American Mfg. Co.*, 1960; *U.S. Steelworkers v. Warrior Gulf Co.*, 1960; *U.S. Steelworkers v. Enterprise Corp.*, 1960). Thus, a court cannot substitute its decision for an arbitrator's if it does not agree with it. A court can only overturn a decision if the plaintiff can prove the arbitrator has exceeded the scope of the authority granted in the CBA or by the parties.

Professional Sport Labor Relations

Despite the NLRA's enactment in 1935, it took another thirty to forty years before the labor movement took hold in the sport industry. The first decision to enforce union certification in professional sports involved baseball umpires. In the *American League of Professional Baseball Clubs and the Association of National Baseball League Umpires* (1969), Major League Baseball challenged the NLRB's jurisdiction. MLB argued that because it was exempt from antitrust laws under the 1922 U.S. Supreme Court decision in *Federal Baseball*, then it should likewise be exempt from labor laws. Next MLB argued that it had an internal system of self-regulation creating no need for NLRB involvement. The NLRB disagreed, arguing that MLB's internal system would put the umpire before the Commissioner for a final resolution of disputes. The NLRB recognized that the system was designed by the employers who also hire and manage the Commissioner. Without evidence of a neutral third party as the final arbiter, the NLRB noted that this case might just be the beginning of a whole host of employees who might seek NLRB assistance in the future including professional athletes, clubhouse attendants, front office staff, scouts, groundskeepers, and maintenance staff.

Today virtually all major league teams are unionized workplaces for professional athletes, but not for the other employees envisioned by that umpires case in 1969. The reasons for this are varied, and among them might be (1) the far fewer white-collar workers in unions, (2) the high turnover in front office and coaching positions, (3) the competition for jobs might deter people from working together in a union organizing movement, and (4) organizing front office staff or coaches on a national, multiemployer level like the professional athletes is challenging.

Unionized workplaces for professional athlete-employees have been years in the making and are unique because the dynamics of the collective bargaining relationship make every negotiation a battle. The turnover rate for union membership among athletes is high because of their short careers. Most athletes have little job security, causing players to want to achieve the best deal possible in collective bargaining negotiations. With an average career length in professional sports hovering around three years and most collective bargaining agreements having three- to six-year terms, unions are motivated to negotiate for the best contract possible. There is a great disparity between players' talent and thus, their need for the union. A superstar will have far different bargaining goals than a bench player. When negotiating for the collective interests of all players, players' unions must struggle to keep the superstars and average players equally satisfied. Without the solidarity of all players, a players' association loses its strength.

Players' associations are transnational employee bargaining units that negotiate with a transnational multiemployer bargaining unit. The turnover rate for sport union members is far higher than for union members in other industries because athletes' careers are far shorter. Players associations must constantly spread their message to new members. In spreading the message, the players' associations face logistical challenges of being in a large, diverse, geographically expansive bargaining unit. In the high-pressure world of professional team sports, the multiemployer bargaining team also faces challenges by having disparate bargaining priorities, such as large versus small market clubs; corporate versus family ownership; ownership stake in one club versus ownership stakes in a more diverse set of sport/entertainment business venture, such as those ownership groups that have cross-ownership in teams, media ventures, and/or facilities. Despite the very contentious labor struggles between owners and players, leagues do favor unionized workforces in professional sport for the labor exemption protection from antitrust liability that unions provide. The topic is discussed in greater detail in Chapter 8.31, *Antitrust Law.*

Significant Case

———————◇◇◇———————

Palace Sports & Entertainment v. NLRB explores the concept of an employee's right to organize a union in the workplace versus the employer's actions in attempting to undermine the process. It also examines when an employer may terminate a union leader's employment in the workplace when the firing is allegedly made through mixed motives—alleged anti-union animus toward the employee and alleged employee misconduct.

PALACE SPORTS & ENTERTAINMENT, INC., D/B/A ST. PETE FORUM V. NATIONAL LABOR RELATIONS NLRB

United States Court of Appeals for the District of Columbia Circuit
411 F.3d 212 (2005)

EDWARDS, *Circuit Judge*:

I. BACKGROUND

A. *Factual Background*

Palace owns and operates various sports and entertainment arenas. In July 1999, the Company purchased the Ice Palace in Tampa, Florida, an arena which has since become known as the St. Pete Times Forum. Palace assumed various contractual obligations made by the previous owner, including a contract with SMG, a company whose employees maintained the facility and performed the work necessary to effectuate conversions of the arena floor. SMG had a labor contract with the Union.

When Palace purchased the Forum, it decided that it would take control over the maintenance and conversion operations itself instead of employing subcontractors like SMG. On June 30, 2001, when SMG's contracts with the Forum and the Union expired, Palace assumed the maintenance and conversion operations for the arena. The Company hired some of SMG's former employees, including Peter Mullins, a mechanical engineer who had been on the Union's negotiating committee while he was employed by SMG. After he was hired, Mullins and other pro-union employees began soliciting union authorization cards. The presence of this union activity at the Forum resulted in a number of incidents involving the management of the Company, which ultimately resulted in the filing of unfair labor practice charges in this case.

On June 27, 2001, the Company posted a policy prohibiting solicitation by one employee to another "while either is working." In response to some complaints from employees regarding solicitation on behalf of the Union, Palace vice president Sean Henry reviewed this no-solicitation policy with employees at a meeting on July 18. He informed the employees that solicitation in violation of the Company's policy could result in termination. During the course of the meeting, Henry effectively promulgated a rule prohibiting any conversation about the Union. Specifically, Henry told employees that they could "talk about virtually anything" so long as they did not solicit. But by "virtually anything" Henry excluded conversations about the union, because he viewed any discussion regarding the Union as Solicitation.

In mid-July, operations manager Carson Williams asked employee Thomas Roberts whether anyone had approached him "about the union organization process." After Roberts responded that nobody had, Williams said, "I know if anyone comes to you, you will let me know." Also in mid-July, employee George Freire spoke with a new employee and gave him a union authorization card. The next day, Williams told Freire "not to be discussing union issues on the clock or in the building."

Around November 20, 2001, Williams approached Roberts and told him that he "didn't like rumors" and wanted to clear one up. He said that he had heard that Roberts had gone to the NLRB to complain about him, and asked Roberts to explain his action. Roberts answered that he did not know what Williams was talking about, that he had not gone to the NLRB. Williams then conceded that it might have been another employee with the same name as Roberts who had complained to the NLRB, but that "it would all come out and once it did" Williams "would take care of it."

On June 18, 2002, Williams called Mullins to his office to fix a problem with the building's automation system. After the problem was corrected, Williams commented that he would be "lost" without Mullins, to which Mullins replied that he was not planning on going anywhere. Williams then told Mullins that if he "and the rest of the union supporters file for a new election, then you are going to be terminated." When Mullins responded that he could not be fired for "doing something legal," Williams stated that the Company would terminate the leader "and then the rest of you will get in line." Mullins asked Williams who had told him that, and Williams replied, "Sean Henry."

On July 11, 2002, less than a month after this conversation, employee James Carpenter arranged to speak with Henry to complain about Peter Mullins. According to Henry, Carpenter reported that Mullins would not leave him alone, that he "is always . . . talking to me and telling me the merits of the Union." Carpenter told Henry that initially this happened "three, four, five times a week," but that it was now "every time" he saw Mullins. Carpenter further noted that he had told Mullins to leave him alone "dozens of times."

Henry referred the matter to the Company's human resources director, Beth Fields, and, the next day, Henry, Fields, and Williams met with Carpenter. According to a memorandum summarizing this meeting, Carpenter reported being "harassed and solicited" by Mullins. He specifically reported the most recent incident, which had taken place in the employee break room at 7:30 a.m. on July 11, before Carpenter had clocked in but after Mullins began work at 7:00 a.m. Carpenter related that he and another employee went to the break room, where Mullins asked him why he would not join the Union. Carpenter explained that he liked working for Palace and that the Company had been good to him. Mullins told Carpenter that the Union could negotiate a better raise for him, but Carpenter responded that he was not interested and then left. Carpenter reported that Mullins was always "'antagonizing'" him about joining the Union and confronts him "at least 3-5 times per week," and that it was interfering with his work. Following this meeting, Carpenter prepared a written statement, dated July 17, 2002, in which he stated that, "for the past couple of weeks," he had been "stopped in the hallways" and "inside the breakroom" by Mullins "about having the union back into this building," and that he was "getting tired" of it. Carpenter's statement recounted the July 11 break room incident, adding that he told Mullins before walking away, "I don't want to hear about it anymore."

There is no evidence that Carpenter again complained about Mullins after July 11. On July 18, Fields, Henry, and Williams interviewed Mullins regarding Carpenter's complaints. Henry testified that, at that meeting, Mullins stated that he had no idea what Carpenter was talking about. Mullins asserted that Carpenter was already a member of the Union and that he talked to Carpenter about the Union only to answer

Carpenter's questions. Henry also recalls that when he confronted Mullins with Carpenter's claim that he asked Mullins to stop "countless times," Mullins replied, "I don't recall him ever asking me to stop."

In his own testimony, Mullins claimed that he never initiated any conversations about the Union with Carpenter, but rather that Carpenter would bring up the subject and was "confused," "afraid that . . . he was going to lose his job if he supported the Union." Mullins maintained that he never intimidated or harassed Carpenter during these conversations. Regarding the specific incident on July 11, Mullins recalled that Carpenter "brought up the subject about how his father-in-law had told him that he didn't need a union." Mullins responded, "Well, James, you know, in a perfect world you don't need a union . . . [but we are] already making a lot less money since Palace . . . eliminated the contract and, you know, we're not getting overtime after eight."

For his part, Carpenter testified that Mullins had spoken to him about bringing the Union back, and that he replied that he wanted to give the Company a chance. Mullins replied, "Okay." A couple of weeks later, Mullins spoke with him again, and he replied, "No. I don't want it yet." Carpenter testified that Mullins continued to approach him "on several occasions." He explained that when he was in the break room before clocking in and "when I'm going from one job to another job . . . he approaches me and stops and asks me about the Union." On those occasions, Carpenter told Mullins, "I don't want to discuss it right at this moment." Carpenter denied initiating the conversations as Mullins has claimed.

On July 25, 2002, Mullins was issued two disciplinary warnings. The first was a written warning for violating the Company's solicitation policy on July 11, 2002. The warning states that, while on work time, Mullins "asked an employee why he would not join a labor union." The second warning, a final written warning, was for violation of the Company's policy against harassment. It explains that "during the months of June and July 2002," Mullins harassed an employee "in various work areas at least 3 to 5 times a week even after the employee being harassed asked [Mullins] to stop. The employee states that [Mullins] has stopped him in his work area and in his words, 'intimidated' him about joining a labor union while he was on work time. The employee repeatedly asked [Mullins] to stop talking to him about joining a labor union, but [Mullins] continued."

On October 2, 2002, Carpenter signed a union authorization card. Mullins testified that Carpenter requested the card. Carpenter admitted signing the card, but denied requesting it. There is no evidence that Carpenter made any complaint on this occasion. About three weeks later, the Union filed a petition for a representation election.

On October 23, Mullins initiated a conversation with Alice Castillo, an employee of a vendor located in the Forum. The two were discussing a newspaper article regarding wages in Florida when the conversation turned to whether wages in Florida were lower than those paid in northern states. According to Castillo, she asked Mullins what wages were in other southern states like Alabama and Mississippi, in response to which Mullins loudly called her a "Yankee bitch." Mullins denies making the remark. Castillo prepared a statement for her supervisor recounting the incident that was ultimately forwarded to Palace officials.

Upon learning of the incident, Fields spoke with Castillo, who repeated her allegation regarding the incident and stated that "it had been going on for a long time and that she had just had enough." Mullins heard from a fellow employee that Castillo was upset with him over something, and went to her to apologize for anything he may have said that offended her.

On October 31, Henry, Fields, and Williams met with Mullins. Mullins stated that he did not recall calling Castillo a "Yankee bitch"; he also explained that he had apologized to her for anything he may have said. Fields testified that she believed Castillo, because Mullins had only stated that he "did not recall" making the offensive statement. On November 3, Mullins was discharged. Fields testified that the Company fired Mullins because he "made inappropriate comments and his conduct was inappropriate."

B. *The NLRB's Decision*

On the basis of the above evidence, a NLRB Administrative Law Judge ("ALJ") concluded that Palace violated § 8(a)(1) by: (1) prohibiting conversations about the Union while permitting conversations relating to other matters; (2) interrogating employees about their knowledge of employee interest in the Union and directing them to report the union activities of their coworkers; (3) interrogating employees about their communications with the NLRB and threatening reprisals if employees cooperated with the NLRB; and (4) threatening employees with discharge because of their support for the Union.

Considering next the disciplinary warnings issued to Mullins, the ALJ credited Mullins' version of the events on July 11 and, accordingly, found that he did not solicit Carpenter. The ALJ alternatively found that, even if Mullins did solicit Carpenter, Mullins did not violate the Company's solicitation policy, because Mullins talked with Carpenter while engaged in nonwork activity. With respect to the harassment warning, the ALJ credited Mullins' assertion that he never approached Carpenter and found that, even if he had, the encounters to which Carpenter testified did not constitute harassment. Finding that Mullins was disciplined while engaging in protected activity for misconduct he did not commit, the ALJ concluded that Palace violated § 8(a)(1). Without any further explanation, the ALJ found that Mullins was warned for engaging in union activity, and thus concluded that the warning also violated § 8(a) (3).

Turning to Mullins' conversation with Castillo, the ALJ credited Mullins' testimony that he did not make any offensive statement, finding that Castillo either misheard or misunderstood his remark. The ALJ noted, however, that because Mullins was not engaged in protected activity when he committed the alleged misconduct, * * * the Company was entitled to rely on its good-faith belief in Castillo's version of the incident.

Applying the *Wright Line* test for determining the relationship, if any, between employer action and protected employee conduct, the ALJ concluded that the General Counsel had carried his burden of showing that Mullins' union activity was a substantial and motivating factor in Palace's decision to discharge Mullins. The ALJ next considered whether the Company had carried its burden of showing that it would have taken the same disciplinary action even in the absence of Mullins' protected activity. Evaluating the Company's written policies regarding "indecent conduct or language," as well as the only other documented incident in the record regarding such behavior, the ALJ found that Palace had not satisfied its burden. The ALJ accordingly concluded that Mullins' discharge violated § 8(a) (3).

* * * [T]he NLRB affirmed the ALJ's findings and conclusions. The NLRB, however, specifically addressed Mullins' discharge. The NLRB ostensibly applied the *Wright Line* framework, agreeing first with the ALJ that the General Counsel "made the required initial showing that Mullins' union activity was a substantial or motivating factor in his discharge." Proceeding to the question of whether Palace had established that it would have discharged Mullins even in the absence of his protected activity, the NLRB noted that the Company had argued that "Mullins' angry outburst at Castillo created sufficient concern for Title VII liability that it discharged him." The NLRB then concluded that Palace had "failed to show that it would have discharged Mullins even in the absence of his union activity in order to avoid the imposition of Title VII liability." * * *

In reaching this judgment, the NLRB suggested that it would have been "unreasonable" for Palace to discharge Mullins in order to avoid Title VII liability. The NLRB reasoned as follows:

The Supreme Court has held that a single, isolated comment generally is not sufficient to justify the imposition of Title VII liability. *Clark County Such. Dist. v. Breeden*, 532 U.S. 268, 271 (2001). Moreover, even where an employee has been shown to have sexually harassed a co-worker, Title VII does not necessarily require the employee's discharge, so long as the employer takes reasonable action to protect the complainant from further harassment.

Baskerville v. Mulligan International Co., 50 F.3d 428, 432 (7th Cir. 1995).

Based on this understanding of Title VII law, the NLRB concluded:

We recognize that employers have a legitimate interest in preventing workplace sexual harassment and a correlative obligation to respond when such incidents occur. In this case, however, we find that the [Company] has not established that it had reasonable grounds for determining that it had to remove or discipline Mullins in order to avoid liability under Title VII.

On this basis, the NLRB found that Palace's "asserted Title VII concerns" were perpetual. In light of these conclusions, the NLRB ordered Palace to cease and desist from engaging in the unlawful conduct it was found to have committed or, in any like manner, interfering with, restraining, or coercing employees in the exercise of their rights under the Act. The NLRB also ordered Palace to offer Mullins full reinstatement to his former job or a substantially equivalent position, make him whole for any loss of earnings or other benefits, and expunge any records of his disciplinary warnings and discharge.

II. ANALYSIS

* * *

B. *The NLRB's Conclusion That the Warnings Were Unlawful*

Palace challenges the NLRB's conclusion that it committed unfair labor practices in violation of § 8(a) (1) and (3) by issuing the disciplinary warnings to Mullins on July 25, 2002. Because we conclude that the NLRB's § 8(a) (1) finding is supported by substantial evidence, and because Palace offers no persuasive reason to believe that the additional finding under § 8(a) (3) had any material effect on the order, we have no occasion to address the latter finding. * * *

Section 8(a) (1) of the Act makes it an unfair labor practice for an employer "to interfere with, restrain, or coerce employees in the exercise of" their rights to organize, bargain collectively, and engage in concerted activities. 29 U.S.C. § 158(a) (1). * * * In this case, the NLRB found that the warnings violated § 8(a) (1) because Mullins did not in fact engage in the misconduct for which he was disciplined.

* * *

The NLRB, adopting the ALJ's credibility determinations, credited Mullins' testimony regarding his encounters with Carpenter in general, and their July 11 conversation in particular. Accordingly, the NLRB found that, on July 11, Mullins did not ask Carpenter "why he would not join a labor union." Rather, the NLRB accepted Mullins' account that Carpenter approached Mullins, mentioning that his father-in-law had told him that employees did not need a union, and that Mullins merely responded by giving reasons why the employees did need a union, referring to reductions in wages and benefits since the Company became their employer. The NLRB also accepted Mullins' claim that he never approached Carpenter to talk about the Union, but only discussed the subject when Carpenter brought it up.

In crediting Mullins, the NLRB observed that there was "no evidence contradicting" Mullins' assertion that Carpenter was already a union member, and also noted that Carpenter, though called as a witness by the Company, did not testify about the July 11 conversation, and thus failed to contradict Mullins' account of it. The NLRB further cited numerous inconsistencies in Carpenter's statements and concluded that the fact that Carpenter eventually signed a union authorization card in October 2002 "casts serious doubt upon [Carpenter's] assertion that he informed Mullins that he was not interested in the Union and supports Mullins' testimony that Carpenter was 'confused.'"

* * *

Moreover, the NLRB alternatively found that *even if* it were not to credit Mullins' testimony, Mullins' conduct nevertheless would not have constituted violations of Palace's solicitation and harassment policies. Regarding the warning for soliciting Carpenter on July 11, the NLRB concluded that even if Mullins had solicited Carpenter during their conversation, this would not have violated the solicitation policy because "he was engaged in a nonwork activity." * * *

With respect to the second warning, for harassment of Carpenter during June and July of 2002, the NLRB found that, even if Mullins did initiate conversations with Carpenter to the extent alleged by Carpenter, Carpenter's testimony before the NLRB did not establish that he was "harassed," "intimidated," or approached after telling Mullins to stop the conduct cited by the warning. This alternative finding is also supported by substantial evidence.

As the NLRB noted, Carpenter made it clear that he did not fear that Mullins would hurt him. Carpenter also testified that when Mullins approached him, Mullins never physically restrained him; Carpenter would simply tell Mullins that he did not want to discuss the matter and would walk away. Indeed, neither Carpenter nor any other witness cited any conduct by Mullins that could reasonably be thought to constitute "intimidation." Regarding the warning's only specific example of "harassment"—the continued solicitation of Carpenter after he asked Mullins to stop—the NLRB found that Carpenter made no such unequivocal request until July 11. * * * Accordingly, the NLRB reasonably found that Carpenter did not tell Mullins until July 11 not to talk to him about the Union. Thus, in light of

Mullins' undisputed testimony that, after July 11, he did not speak to Carpenter again until October 2002 (when Carpenter signed the authorization card), substantial evidence supports the NLRB's finding that the harassment asserted as the ground for the second warning never occurred.

* * *

On this record, the NLRB reasonably concluded that Palace violated § 8(a)(1) of the Act by issuing the disciplinary warnings to Mullins.

C. *The NLRB's Conclusion That the Discharge Was Unlawful*

* * *

In addressing the § 8(a)(3) charge, the NLRB treated this case as one involving a question of "dual motivation," *i.e.*, a case in which the employer defends against a § 8(a)(3) charge by arguing that, even if an invalid reason might have played some part in the employer's motivation, the employer would have taken the same action against the employee for a permissible reason. The NLRB analyzes such claims under the framework set forth in *Wright Line*, 251 N.L.R.B. at 1089. * * * Under the *Wright Line* test, the general counsel must first show that the protected activity was a motivating factor in the adverse employment decision. If this prima facie showing is made, the burden shifts to the employer to demonstrate that it would have made the adverse decision even had the employee not engaged in protected activity.* * *

The ALJ clearly applied this framework in evaluating Mullins' discharge. After finding that the General Counsel had made out a prima facie showing, the ALJ proceeded to evaluate whether Palace had established that it would have discharged Mullins even in the absence of his protected activity. The ALJ noted that, although Palace characterized Mullins' remark as "sexual harassment," "there is no evidence of any sexual advance by Mullins." The ALJ then discussed the Company's written policies prohibiting "indecent conduct or language," noting that the policies include a progressive disciplinary system whereby "'termination is the *last step*'" in the disciplinary progression. Finally, the ALJ found that, in the only other comparable disciplinary incident in the record, another employee who used "vulgar and profane language towards customers" was only warned after his first offense. This employee was not fired until after a repeat offense. On this record, the ALJ held that the Company had not met its burden under *Wright Line*. *Id.*

The NLRB, at the outset of its decision, announced that it had "decided to affirm the judge's rulings, findings, and conclusions." The NLRB then went on to render its own opinion, employing a rationale to support the finding of a § 8(a)(3) violation that is entirely different from the rationale offered by the ALJ. It is therefore unclear whether the NLRB opinion is intended to supplement or displace the ALJ's rationale in sustaining the § 8(a)(3) charge. The NLRB agreed with the ALJ that the General Counsel had made out a prima facie case. That conclusion was justified: the ALJ found that Mullins' supervisors had threatened to fire him if the Union filed for a new election, and Mullins was indeed fired shortly after the Union filed. The NLRB also agreed that Palace had failed to establish that it would have discharged Mullins even in the absence of his union activity. However, in considering whether the Company had met its burden under *Wright Line*, the NLRB focused almost exclusively on Palace's claim that it would face potential liability under Title VII if it did not dismiss Mullins for his alleged offensive statement to Castillo.

In following this approach, the NLRB stated that the ALJ's decision rested on a finding that Palace "failed to show that it would have discharged Mullins even in the absence of his union activity *in order to avoid the imposition of Title VII liability.*" *Id.* (emphasis added). The NLRB's characterization of the ALJ's decision is perplexing, because, although the ALJ did conclude that there was "no evidence of any sexual advance by Mullins," the ALJ's holding that Palace had violated § 8(a)(3) rested on findings that neither the Company's "progressive disciplinary system" nor the Company's handling of "other documented incidents regarding indecent conduct or language" could explain Palace's decision to fire Mullins. The ALJ's analysis and concluding findings say nothing about Title VII. Indeed, there is *nothing* in the ALJ's opinion even to suggest that Palace argued that the employer fired Mullins in order to avoid the imposition of Title VII liability. And Palace does not contend here that this affirmative defense was specifically raised in the hearing before the ALJ.

Ignoring the ALJ's stated grounds for finding a § 8(a)(3) violation, the NLRB concluded that Palace had "not established that it had reasonable grounds for determining that it had to remove or discipline Mullins in order to avoid liability under Title VII." The basis for this conclusion was the NLRB's view that Title VII liability would not arise from Mullins' single, isolated remark.

The problem here is that, in focusing on Title VII, the NLRB misapplied *Wright Line*. The question under *Wright Line* is whether the Company has established in fact that it would have taken the same action in the absence of any anti-union animus. It is not whether the Company has established that its actions were "reasonable." * * *

As noted above, the NLRB stated that it meant to affirm the ALJ's rulings, findings, and conclusions. But the NLRB's *Wright Line* analysis focuses solely on the Title VII issue and never addresses the ALJ's evaluation of the Company's written policies and disciplinary practices. Therefore, we cannot be sure to what extent the NLRB meant to incorporate the ALJ's analysis in those respects while merely rejecting any implication in the ALJ's decision that sexual harassment arises only in connection with comments containing sexual advances.

* * * On remand, the NLRB should explain the precise reasoning on which it means to rest its conclusion that Mullins' discharge violated the Act. The NLRB should specifically state which portions of the ALJ's analysis it adopts and which parts it rejects. We also note that, although the ALJ appeared to evaluate Mullins' discharge solely under § 8(a)(3), using the *Wright Line* framework, *see Palace Sports & Entm't Inc.*, 342 N.L.R.B. No. 53, 2004 WL 1701333, at *23, the NLRB, without explanation, stated that it "agreed with the judge that [Palace] violated Section 8(a)(1) *and* (3) when it discharged employee Peter Mullins," *342 N.L.R.B. No. 53*, [WL] at *1 (emphasis added). It is unclear whether the NLRB really meant to find that Palace violated § 8(a)(1) when it fired Mullins and, if so, on what grounds. The NLRB can address this issue on remand.

III. CONCLUSION

For the foregoing reasons, we grant in part the NLRB's application for enforcement. We remand the case to the NLRB, however, for clarification of its conclusion that Palace violated the Act by discharging Mullins.

Recent Trends

Drug Testing and Collective Bargaining

In union workplaces, drug testing for substances of abuse (recreational and performance enhancing drugs) is a term or condition of employment addressed at the collective bargaining table. Recently Congress has begun to press all sports for uniform drug-testing policies. Those achieved through collective bargaining are more likely to effectively protect the rights and obligations of employees and employers, especially employee rights. Through a bargaining process an employee's privacy rights, confidentiality of tests, medical concerns, the determination of what drugs to test for and what amounts of those drugs must be in one's system to be subject to suspension, concerns over "what else" the organization might discover in testing, the role of results and international competition, and the like will be negotiated to develop fair provisions. The bargaining table also provides a forum for the two sides to include educational and rehabilitative components to the CBA. Further, union and management may negotiate testing policies and procedures in the context of other aspects of their employment relationship, such as disciplinary actions and arbitration provisions.

Conclusion

Labor law has been a critical component to the U.S. workforce as it has created structures for employees to bargain for safe and productive work environments. Labor laws, along with employment laws, delineate the conduct that is acceptable in the work environment. The NLRA in particular sets forth the parameters of conduct by employers and employees in private-sector unionized workplaces. It sets forth a process of collective bargaining that allows employees and employers to determine what issues must be resolved in their particular workplace and address them through the negotiation process to develop a contract for their workplace. We find the good majority of unionized workforces in the sport industry among professional athletes and in the facility management world. As a manager in the sport industry, it is critical that management decisions are made with an eye toward the collective bargaining agreement and its rules, policies, and procedures, lest you find yourself facing a grievance and arbitration process.

References

Cases

Brown v. Pro Football, Inc., 518 U.S. 231 (1996).
Ford Motor Co. v. NLRB, 441 U.S. 488, 498 (1979).
Miranda Fuel Co., 140 NLRB 181 (1962).
National Football League Players Association v. National Labor Relations Board, 503 F.2d 12 (1974).
NLRB v. Katz, 369 U.S. 736 (1962).
North American Soccer League v. NLRB, 613 F. 2d. 1379 (5th Cir. 1980).
Palace Sports & Entertainment, 2005.
Peterson v. Kennedy and the NFLPA, 771 F.2d 1244 (1985).
Silverman v. Major League Baseball Player Relations Committee, 880 F. Supp. 246 (1995).
Steele v. Louisville & Nashville Railroad Co., 323 U.S. 192 (1944).
The American League of Professional Baseball Clubs and the Association of National Baseball League Umpires, 180 N.L.R.B. 190 (1969).
U.S. Steelworkers v. American Mfg. Co., 363 US 564 (1960).
U.S. Steelworkers v. Warrior Gulf Co., 363 U.S. 574 (1960).
U.S. Steelworkers v. Enterprise Corp., 363 U.S. 593 (1960).
Vaca v. Sipes, 386 U.S. 171 (1967).

Publications

Feldacker, B. (2000). *Labor guide to labor law* (4th ed.). Upper Saddle River, NJ: Prentice Hall.
Gold, M. E. (1998). *An introduction to labor law* (2nd ed.). Ithaca, NY: ILR Press/Cornell University Press.
Rabuano, M. M. (2002). "Comment: An examination of drug testing as a mandatory subject of collective bargaining in major league baseball. *U. Pa. J. Lab. & Emp. L.,4,* 439.

Legislation

Fair Labor Standards Act, 29 USCS § 201, et seq. (2005).
Labor Management Relations Act, 29 USCS § 141, et. seq. (2005).
National Labor Relations Act, 29 USCS § 151, et. seq. (2005).

John T. Wolohan
Ithaca College

Although the creation of the modern sports agent is usually credited to Boston attorney Bob Woolf in the mid-1960s, individuals have been representing athletes as far back as the 1920s. One of the first sports agents was Charles "Cash & Carry" Pyle, who in 1925 reportedly negotiated the contract between Red Grange and the Chicago Bears (Greenberg & Gray, 1998). In truth, however, it was only the rare and special athlete that needed an agent before the 1970s. Before, 1976, most professional athletes were bound to their team through a reserve system and were left with few alternatives and little negotiating power. Contract negotiation in these circumstances was a matter of taking what was offered or refusing to play.

If the athlete was bold enough to actually use an agent, most teams either refused to deal with the agent or dealt the player to another team. For example, in 1967, Jim Ringo, who at the time was a seven-time all-pro, hired an agent to negotiate his contract with the Green Bay Packers. During the negotiations, Vince Lombardi, the general manager of the team, excused himself for five minutes and went into another room to use the phone. When he came back he told the agent that he was in the wrong city if he wanted to negotiate Ringo's contract. The Packers had just traded him to Philadelphia (Greenberg & Gray, 1998).

Beginning in the mid-1970s, due to litigation, arbitration, collective bargaining, and in some instances, the emergence of competing professional leagues, players gained greater freedom and bargaining leverage to market themselves to the highest bidder. As a result, the price for a relatively scarce supply of talent began to rise (Rypma, 1990). At this same time, television and radio rights for sporting events also began to rise. Expanded media coverage and escalating rights fees paid by networks to leagues made professional sports even more popular and profitable. The increased revenues enjoyed by franchise owners allowed them to meet, albeit grudgingly, the increasing player salary demands (Dow, 1990). As professional sports evolved into a multibillion-dollar industry the need for professional representation became more and more essential for many athletes seeking to maximize their individual worth.

Fundamental Concepts

Although few would argue that the services of a competent agent can be extremely valuable for a professional athlete, the emergence of the sport agent in professional sports has not, however, been without problems. For example, the intense competition for a limited supply of quality athletes has encouraged corruption (Shropshire, 1989). The following section outlines some of the attempts by the state and federal governments and other various organizations to protect college and professional athletes, as well as colleges and universities, from actions of unscrupulous agents.

Sport Agent Legislation

Beginning in 1981, there have been numerous attempts to regulate sport agents. Unfortunately, due to a variety of reasons, these attempts have failed to stop the unethical, unscrupulous, and illegal conduct of sport agents.

State Legislative Efforts

In 1981, California became the first state to pass legislation regulating sport agents when it enacted the California Athlete Agents Act. Twenty-five years later, the number of states regulating the activities of sport agents has grown to 39. The problem with trying to regulate sports agents with state-by-state agent legislation, however, is that the majority of the statutes are vague and vary considerably from state to state. This lack of uniformity, in turn, has had an impact on the number of agents registering with the states. For example, because of the inconsistencies among current state statutes and the lack of provisions for reciprocal registration and reasonable fee structures, an agent intending to do business in a large number of states may be forced to comply with a number of different sets of registration requirements and be aware of an equal number of different regulatory schemes and pay the registration fees for each state.

In addition, although states have made an attempt to control the corruption of agents, they have made little attempt to stop incompetent sport agents. The only jurisdiction that currently requires agents to pass a competency examination as a prerequisite to licensure is Florida. The exam tests an agent's knowledge of Florida law and NCAA bylaws.

The Current Trend

From the late 1980s to the present, the focus of state sport agent statutes shifted away from protecting the athlete, to addressing the economic damage an unscrupulous agent could cause for a college or university. This current legislative trend is characterized by provisions requiring notice to school and state before and/ or after the signing of a representation contract, waiting periods for valid contracts, the creation of causes of action in favor of colleges and universities for agent misconduct resulting in damages, and an abandonment or modification of the onerous registration requirements common in earlier legislative schemes (Rodgers, 1988–89).

Agent-specific legislation has not been the panacea many anticipated. States have appeared less than enthusiastic in devoting their limited resources to policing legislative requirements. Not surprisingly, agents prone to abuse have ignored these statutory provisions and continued to conduct business as usual. In addition, differing state requirements have created an administrative nightmare for many honest agents doing business in several states. This, coupled with a perceived lack of enforcement, often encourages the breach of these provisions. State legislation is also criticized as being primarily designed to keep student–athletes eligible and playing for state universities, rather than protecting the athletes and their future professional careers because many classes of athletes are left unprotected by most legislative schemes.

Uniform Athlete Agent Act

The most recent attempt to regulate the sport agent profession began in 1997, when the National Conference of Commissioners on Uniform State Laws (NCCUSL), at the request of several major universities and the NCAA, appointed a drafting committee to develop a uniform statute for regulating sport agents. The NCCUSL is a national association, which endeavors to promote the uniformity of state laws. For example, the NCCUSL is responsible for the drafting and development of the Uniform Commercial Code (UCC).

As a result of their work, the NCCUSL developed the Uniform Athlete Agents Act (UAAA) in the fall of 2000. The stated goal of the UAAA is the protection of student–athletes from unscrupulous agents. To achieve this goal, the UAAA contains a number of important provisions regulating the conduct between athletes and agents. For example, the UAAA requires an agent to provide important information, both professional and criminal in nature. This information enables student–athletes, their parents and family, and university personnel to better evaluate the prospective agent. The UAAA also requires that written notice be provided to institutions when a student–athlete signs an agency contract before their eligibility expires. In addition, the UAAA gives authority to the secretary of state to issue subpoenas that would enable the state to obtain relevant material that ensures compliance with the act. Finally, the UAAA provides for criminal, civil, and administrative penalties with enforcement at the state level (www.ncaa.org/membership/enforcement/agents/uaaa/index.htm).

In addition, the UAAA also covers such key areas as agent registration requirement; liability insurance; notice to educational institution; student–athlete's right to cancel, and penalties. Perhaps the most important part of the UAAA is the section allowing an agent's valid certificate of registration from one state to be honored in all other states that have adopted the act. The success of the reciprocal registration process is contingent on states establishing a reasonable fee schedule, including lower registration fees for reciprocal applications and renewals. Thus, more agents are likely to register due to the efficiency of this process, its practical cost-saving implications for the agent, and the benefits of complying with a single set of regulations.

As of January 2006, the UAAA had been passed in thirty-three states and two territories. In addition, five states have laws dealing with agent behavior on the books that do not conform to the UAAA (see Table 1). However, some critics argued that the UAAA is more interested in protecting NCAA member institutions, than athletes. For example, the UAAA requires agents and student–athlete to notify the institution within seventy-two hours of the signing of a contract, or before the student–athlete's next scheduled athletics event, whichever occurs first. If a prospective student–athlete has signed a contract, the agent must notify the institution where the agent has reasonable grounds to believe the prospect will enroll. Finally, the act provides institutions with a right of action against the agent or former student–athlete for any damages caused by a violation of this act.

table ⟨**1**⟩ States that have passed the UAAA, as of January 2006:

Alabama	Indiana	Montana	Rhode Island
Arizona	Kansas	Nevada	South Carolina
Arkansas	Kentucky	New York	Tennessee
Connecticut	Louisiana	North Carolina	Texas
Delaware	Maryland	North Dakota	Utah
Florida	Minnesota	Oklahoma	Washington
Georgia	Mississippi	Oregon	West Virginia
Idaho	Missouri	Pennsylvania	Wisconsin
			Wyoming

States that have passed non-UAAA laws designed to regulate athlete agents:

California	Michigan
Colorado	Ohio
Iowa	

States that currently have no existing law regulating athlete agents:

Alaska	Maine	New Hampshire*	South Dakota
Hawaii*	Massachusetts	New Jersey*	Vermont
Illinois	Nebraska	New Mexico	Virginia

* States with UAAA legislation in their legislative chambers

National Legislative Efforts

To meet some of the shortcomings of the state's efforts, some people have argued that federal sport agent legislation is needed. Federal legislation would address the jurisdictional ambiguities and substantive inconsistencies of existing state regulation, erase multiple application and fee requirements, and eliminate forum shopping by agents who attempt to avoid states that have legislation.

Federal Legislation

Although there had been earlier attempts to formally introduce legislation in Congress, it was not until September 2004 that Congress passed national legislation regulating the conduct of sports agents. Titled the Sports Agent Responsibility and Trust Act, the Act was sponsored by Tom Osborne, a Republican from Nebraska and the former football coach at the University of Nebraska. Signed into law in October 2004, the new law prohibits agents from making false or misleading promises or providing gifts, cash, and anything else of monetary value to student–athletes or anyone associated with them. In addition, the act also requires agents to give students a written disclosure that they could lose their eligibility to play college sports by signing an agency contract and predating or postdating contracts. Finally, the act requires agents and athletes to notify their college athletic director within seventy-two hours of entering into a contract or before the student's next athletic event, whichever is earlier. Agents who fail to report the contract can be fined as much as $11,000 per day (Pub. L. No. 108 – 304, 2004).

Violations of the act are punishable by the Federal Trade Commission as an unfair or deceptive act or practice. Individual states can also bring a civil action if the attorney general of a state has reason to believe that an interest of the residents of that state has been or is threatened or adversely affected by the engagement of any athlete agent.

It should be noted that like the Uniform Athlete Agents Act of 2000, which this act encourages every state to enact, the Sports Agency Responsibility and Trust Act was signed to protect student–athletes and universities from unscrupulous sports agents. The act does nothing to protect professional athletes from those same unscrupulous sports agents.

Other Regulatory Efforts

Agent-specific legislation is not the only legal means used to regulate the conduct of athlete agents. Other common law or statutory remedies, although not specifically directed at agents, have been used to attempt to control their abusive conduct. For example, the common law civil remedies of breach of contract, misrepresentation, fraud, deceit, and negligence have been applied in cases of agent misconduct (Shropshire, 1989). In addition, various federal and state criminal statutes have been used, albeit with limited success, to attempt to criminally sanction agent misconduct. Sport agent Jim Abernethy, for example, who had signed and provided illegal payments to an athlete before his eligibility had expired, was indicted and convicted at trial on a charge of tampering with a sports contest in the state of Alabama. Abernethy's conviction was overturned on appeal when the Alabama Court of Criminal Appeals construed the Alabama tampering statute in a manner favorable to Abernethy and sport agents in general (Narayanan, 1990).

In addition, such organizations as the NCAA, professional team sports players' associations, the Association of Representatives of Professional Athletes, and the American Bar Association have also become involved in regulating this relationship between athletes and agents.

The National Collegiate Athletic Association (NCAA)

By the mid-1970s, repeated instances of agent abuse prompted the NCAA to promulgate regulations in an attempt to limit the likelihood of an unscrupulous agent preying on a talented, young, and financially naive athlete (Wilde, 1992). NCAA rules provide that "an individual shall be ineligible for participation in an intercollegiate sport if he or she ever has agreed (orally or in writing) to be represented by an agent for the purpose of marketing his or her athletic ability or reputation in that sport," or if the student–athlete receives any type of payment or promise of payment (*NCAA Manual*, 1999–2000, art. 12.3.1).

In a further attempt to prevent agents from "preying" on student–athletes, the NCAA established a voluntary player–agent registration program in 1984 (Rypma, 1990). The program required disclosure of an agent's education and background and imposed notification requirements on the agent prior to contact with a student–athlete (Rypma, 1990). The program's primary flaw, however, was its voluntariness. In addition, the NCAA has no jurisdiction over a sport agent. Therefore, the NCAA is powerless to monitor, regulate, or sanction the activities of agents. Further, as with most regulatory efforts aimed at sport agents, the program also failed to require agents to meet any particular competency qualifications prior to registration. Citing these limitations, the NCAA discontinued its program in 1989 (Rypma, 1990).

The NCAA has not, however, ceased all efforts to control the unscrupulous activities of agents. In 1988 the NCAA began requiring student–athletes participating in the Division I men's basketball tournament and in sanctioned college football bowl games to sign an affidavit certifying that the athlete has not signed with an agent (Cosgrove, 1990). Further, the NCAA authorizes and encourages its member institutions to establish professional sports counseling panels for student–athletes. Under NCAA rules these panels are given authority to assist student–athletes with career choices and in securing competent agent representation. Such panels may review a professional sports contract, assist an athlete in deciding whether to stay in college or to seek a professional career by ascertaining the athlete's professional market value, and provide advice and guidance in the selection of a reputable agent.

As stated earlier, the problem with NCAA regulations is that they do not directly apply to sport agents. NCAA rules and regulations are only applicable to student–athletes and the academic institutions in which the athletes are enrolled. Therefore, an agent can violate NCAA regulations without fear of NCAA sanctions, whereas the student–athlete with whom the agent dealt will likely lose his or her remaining eligibility, and the academic institution will be subject to sanctions (Fluhr, 1999).

Professional Team Sports Players' Associations

The power of the players' associations of the four major sports leagues to regulate sport agents derives from the National Labor Relations Act and other federal labor law. Essentially, the players' associations regulate agents by "requiring their members to hire regulated agents only, and by obtaining the agreement of teams to negotiate with regulated agents only" (Fluhr, 1999). The first professional team sport players' union to initiate a player–agent certification program was the National Football League Players' Association (NFLPA) in 1983 (Rypma, 1990). The 1982 collective bargaining agreement between the NFL and NFLPA had reserved the exclusive right for the NFLPA or "its agent" to negotiate individual NFL player contracts. The 1983 program was established to certify agents as "NFLPA Contract Advisors," who, under the program, are required to use a standard representation agreement, comply with certain limits on compensation for contractual negotiations, and attend periodic training seminars (Ring, 1987). Fines, suspensions, and/or revocations of licenses are among the penalties imposed for noncompliance.

Despite the program's intent to protect athletes from agent incompetence and corruption, several problems still persisted. First, the program, in its original form, did not address the corruption occurring in intercollegiate athletics. Until recently, the NFLPA certification program did not regulate agents negotiating a player's first contract with the league (Dunn, 1988). Only agents representing current NFL players were covered. Alerted to the potential for agent abuse of athletes who had yet to sign their first NFL contract, the program was amended in 1989 to include agents negotiating on behalf of these prospective players (Shropshire, 1989). Second, the plan was limited in scope. The plan regulated only "contract advisors" of NFL players, and its rules prohibit the charging of excessive fees for only contract negotiation and money-handling services. Agents providing other services could charge excessive fees and effectively evade the plan's restrictions (Dunn, 1988). Third, the plan was devoid of any specific criteria for granting or denying agent certification.

Since 1998, however, the NFLPA, by trying to enforce higher standards, has taken a more active role in policing agents. The union has rolled back the maximum percentage that agents can charge players to negotiate a contract from 4 percent to 3 percent, the lowest cut in sports (Freeman, 1998). In 1999, concerned about the quality of the agents representing its players, the NFLPA started testing anyone who registers to become a NFL player's agent. The test covered such areas as the collective bargaining agreement, salary cap issues, and free agency. Any agent who fails the test will not be certified (Freeman, 1998). The NFLPA also requires current agents to take that same test every year, and if they fail, those agents will be suspended and possibly decertified. Any NFL team that negotiates with an agent not sanctioned by the union is subject to a $10,000 fine from the commissioner (Freeman, 1998).

The NFLPA's program, not unlike the plans implemented by other players' unions, also expects applicants to disclose their educational, professional, and employment background, yet it does not require any minimum levels of training, education, skill, or knowledge as a condition for representing professional athletes (Rypma, 1990).

In 1985, the Major League Baseball Players' Association (MLBPA) became the next union to adopt an agent certification plan. The National Basketball Players' Association (NBPA) followed the MLBPA in 1986, when it adopted its agent certification plan. The National Hockey League (NHL), which was the last union to start regulating agents, joined the other major sports leagues in 1996 when it drafted its agent certification program (Couch, 2000). In November 2004, Major League Soccer (MLS) and the players union included language in their collective bargaining agreement that allows the union to develop and implement an agent certification program. However, at the present time, no such program exists.

The general scheme in professional sports leagues is that only those agents registered with the unions can negotiate on behalf of the players (Fluhr, 1999). The unions also require annual registration and fees, annual attendance at seminars, a disciplinary system including an arbitration provision, and the ban on specific conflict of interest situations. Unfortunately, sanctions are rarely levied when the preceding policies are violated either due to lack of knowledge or improper enforcement techniques (Couch, 2000).

The Association of Representatives of Professional Athletes (ARPA)

Created with the intent of cleaning up negative public image sports agents have, a group of agents decided to develop an organization that would enforce a uniform code of conduct or standards. As a result, the Association of Representatives of Professional Athletes (ARPA) was founded in 1978 to provide competent and honest representation to professional athletes. The ARPA's Code of Ethics attempted to ensure integrity, competence, dignity, management responsibility, and confidentiality from agents in the representation of their clients (Dunn, 1988). Unfortunately, notwithstanding its laudable intentions, the ARPA's inability to address the problems of agent incompetence and corruption doomed the organization to failure.

The American Bar Association (ABA)

The ABA's Code of Professional Responsibility has some relevance here. The ABA Code proposes standards of integrity and conduct for all attorneys and has been adopted in some form or another by many state bar associations. The obvious deficiency here is that although many sport agents are attorneys, the code has no effect on agents who are not lawyers (Shropshire, 1989).

Significant Case

────────◇◇◇────────

The following case is perhaps the most famous case of agent abuse. In 1989, Norby Walters was sentenced to five years in prison; his conviction, however, was overturned and remanded for a new trial by the Seventh Circuit (913 F.2d 388). Walters subsequently pleaded guilty to federal mail fraud charges to avoid more serious racketeering and conspiracy charges. Walters' conviction, based on his plea, was also overturned by the Seventh Circuit (997 F.2d 1219). Although their unscrupulous conduct went unpunished by the courts, no case has been as responsible for focusing public awareness on the problems associated with the unscrupulous sport agents, and prompting the development of agent-specific legislation.

UNITED STATES V. WALTERS

United States Court of Appeals for the Seventh Circuit
997 F.2d 1219 (1993)

Opinion: Easterbrook, Circuit Judge.

Norby Walters, who represents entertainers, tried to move into the sports business. He signed 58 college football players to contracts while they were still playing. Walters offered cars and money to those who would agree to use him as their representative in dealing with professional teams. Sports agents receive a percentage of the players' income, so Walters would profit only to the extent he could negotiate contracts for his clients. The athletes' pro prospects depended on successful completion of their collegiate careers. To the NCAA, however, a student who signs a contract with an agent is a professional, ineligible to play on collegiate teams. To avoid jeopardizing his clients' careers, Walters dated the contracts after the end of their eligibility and locked them in a safe. He promised to lie to the universities in re-

sponse to any inquiries. Walters inquired of sports lawyers at Shea & Gould whether this plan of operation would be lawful. The firm rendered an opinion that it would violate the NCAA's rules but not any statute.

Having recruited players willing to fool their universities and the NCAA, Walters discovered that they were equally willing to play false with him. Only 2 of the 58 players fulfilled their end of the bargain; the other 56 kept the cars and money, then signed with other agents. They relied on the fact that the contracts were locked away and dated in the future, and that Walters' business depended on continued secrecy, so he could not very well sue to enforce their promises. When the 56 would neither accept him as their representative nor return the payments, Walters resorted to threats. One player, Maurice Douglass, was told that his legs would be broken before the pro draft unless he repaid Walters' firm. A 75-page indictment charged Walters and his partner Lloyd Bloom with conspiracy, RICO violations (the predicate felony was extortion), and mail fraud. The fraud: causing the universities to pay scholarship funds to athletes who had become ineligible as a result of the agency contracts. The mail: each university required its athletes to verify their eligibility to play, then sent copies by mail to conferences such as the Big Ten.

After a month-long trial and a week of deliberations, the jury convicted Walters and Bloom. We reversed, holding that the district judge had erred in declining to instruct the jury that reliance on Shea & Gould's advice could prevent the formation of intent to defraud the universities. 913 F.2d 388, 391-92 (1990). Any dispute about the adequacy of Walters' disclosure to his lawyers and the bona fides of his reliance was for the jury, we concluded. Because Bloom declined to waive his own attorney-client privilege, we held that the defendants must be retried separately. Id. at 392-93. On remand, Walters asked the district court to dismiss the indictment, arguing that the evidence presented at trial is insufficient to support the convictions. After the judge denied this motion, . . . Walters agreed to enter a conditional Alford plea: he would plead guilty to mail fraud, conceding that the record of the first trial supplies a factual basis for a conviction while reserving his right to contest the sufficiency of that evidence. In return, the prosecutor agreed to dismiss the RICO and conspiracy charges and to return to Walters all property that had been forfeited as a result of his RICO conviction. Thus a case that began with a focus on extortion has become a straight mail fraud prosecution and may undergo yet another transformation. The prosecutor believes that Walters hampered the investigation preceding his indictment. . . . The plea agreement reserves the prosecutor's right to charge Walters with perjury and obstruction of justice if we should reverse the conviction for mail fraud.

"Whoever, having devised . . . any scheme or artifice to defraud, or for obtaining money or property by means of false or fraudulent pretenses, representations, or promises . . . places in any post office or authorized depository for mail matter, any matter or thing whatever to be sent or delivered by the Postal Service . . . or knowingly causes [such matter or thing] to be delivered by mail" commits the crime of mail fraud. 18 U.S.C. § 1341. Norby Walters did not mail anything or cause anyone else to do so (the universities were going to collect and mail the forms no matter what Walters did), but the Supreme Court has expanded the statute beyond its literal terms, holding that a mailing by a third party suffices if it is "incident to an essential part of the scheme." . . . While stating that such mailings can turn ordinary fraud into mail fraud, the Court has cautioned that the statute "does not purport to reach all frauds, but only those limited instances in which the use of the mails is a

part of the execution of the fraud." . . . Everything thus turns on matters of degree. Did the schemers foresee that the mails would be used? Did the mailing advance the success of the scheme? Which parts of a scheme are "essential?" Such questions lack obviously right answers, so it is no surprise that each side to this case can cite several of our decisions in support. . . .

"The relevant question . . . is whether the mailing is part of the execution of the scheme as conceived by the perpetrator at the time." . . . Did the evidence establish that Walters conceived a scheme in which mailings played a role? We think not— indeed, that no reasonable juror could give an affirmative answer to this question. Walters hatched a scheme to make money by taking a percentage of athletes' pro contracts. To get clients he signed students while college eligibility remained, thus avoiding competition from ethical agents. To obtain big pro contracts for these clients he needed to keep the deals secret, so the athletes could finish their collegiate careers. Thus deceit was an ingredient of the plan. We may assume that Walters knew that the universities would ask athletes to verify that they were eligible to compete as amateurs. But what role do the mails play? The plan succeeds so long as the athletes conceal their contracts from their schools (and remain loyal to Walters). Forms verifying eligibility do not help the plan succeed; instead they create a risk that it will be discovered if a student should tell the truth. . . . And it is the forms, not their mailing to the Big Ten, that pose the risk. For all Walters cared, the forms could sit forever in cartons. Movement to someplace else was irrelevant. In Schmuck, where the fraud was selling cars with rolled-back odometers, the mailing was essential to obtain a new and apparently "clean" certificate of title; no certificates of title, no marketable cars, no hope for success. Even so, the Court divided five to four on the question whether the mailing was sufficiently integral to the scheme. A college's mailing to its conference has less to do with the plot's success than the mailings that transferred title in Schmuck.

To this the United States responds that the mailings were essential because, if a college had neglected to send the athletes' forms to the conference, the NCAA would have barred that college's team from competing. Lack of competition would spoil the athletes' pro prospects. Thus the use of the mails was integral to the profits Walters hoped to reap, even though Walters would have been delighted had the colleges neither asked any questions of the athletes nor put the answers in the mail. Let us take this as sufficient under Schmuck (although we have our doubts). The question remains whether Walters caused the universities to use the mails. A person "knowingly causes" the use of the mails when he "acts with the knowledge that the use of the mails will follow in the ordinary course of business, or where such use can reasonably be foreseen." . . . The paradigm is insurance fraud. Perkins tells his auto insurer that his car has been stolen, when in fact it has been sold. The local employee mails the claim to the home office, which mails a check to Perkins. Such mailings in the ordinary course of business are foreseeable. Similarly, a judge who takes a bribe derived from the litigant's bail money causes the use of the mails when the ordinary course is to refund the bond by mail. . . . The prosecutor contends that the same approach covers Walters.

No evidence demonstrates that Walters actually knew that the colleges would mail the athletes' forms. The record is barely sufficient to establish that Walters knew of the forms' existence; it is silent about Walters' knowledge of the forms' disposition. . . . In the end, the prosecutor insists that the large size and interstate nature of the NCAA demonstrate that something would be dropped into the mails. To put this only slightly differently, the prosecutor submits that all frauds involving big organizations necessarily are mail frauds, because big organizations habitually mail things. No evidence put before the jury supports such a claim, and it is hardly appropriate for judicial notice in a criminal case.

There is a deeper problem with the theory of this prosecution. The United States tells us that the universities lost their scholarship money. Money is property; this aspect of the prosecution does not encounter a problem under McNally v. United States, 483 U.S. 350 (1987). Walters emphasizes that the universities put his 58 athletes on scholarship long before he met them and did not pay a penny more than they planned to do. But a jury could conclude that had Walters' clients told the truth, the colleges would have stopped their scholarships, thus saving money. So we must assume that the universities lost property by reason of Walters' deeds. Still, they were not out of pocket to Walters; he planned to profit by taking a percentage of the players' professional incomes, not of their scholarships. Section 1341 condemns "any scheme or artifice to defraud, or for obtaining money or property" (emphasis added). If the universities were the victims, how did he "obtain" their property?, Walters asks.

According to the United States, neither an actual nor a potential transfer of property from the victim to the defendant is essential. It is enough that the victim lose; what (if anything) the schemer hopes to gain plays no role in the definition of the offense. We asked the prosecutor at oral argument whether on this rationale practical jokes violate § 1341. A mails B an invitation to a surprise party for their mutual friend C. B drives his car to the place named in the invitation. But there is no party; the address is a vacant lot; B is the butt of a joke. The invitation came by post; the cost of gasoline means that B is out of pocket. The prosecutor said that this indeed violates § 1341, but that his office pledges to use prosecutorial discretion wisely. Many people will find this position unnerving (what if the prosecutor's policy

changes, or A is politically unpopular and the prosecutor is looking for a way to nail him?). Others, who obey the law out of a sense of civic obligation rather than the fear of sanctions, will alter their conduct no matter what policy the prosecutor follows. Either way, the idea that practical jokes are federal felonies would make a joke of the Supreme Court's assurance that § 1341 does not cover the waterfront of deceit.

Practical jokes rarely come to the attention of federal prosecutors, but large organizations are more successful in gaining the attention of public officials. In this case the mail fraud statute has been invoked to shore up the rules of an influential private association. . . . The NCAA depresses athletes' income—restricting payments to the value of tuition, room, and board, while receiving services of substantially greater worth. The NCAA treats this as desirable preservation of amateur sports; a more jaundiced eye would see it as the use of monopsony power to obtain athletes' services for less than the competitive market price. Walters then is cast in the role of a cheater, increasing the payments to the student athletes. Like other cheaters, Walters found it convenient to hide his activities. If, as the prosecutor believes, his repertory included extortion, he has used methods that the law denies to persons fighting cartels, but for the moment we are concerned only with the deceit that caused the universities to pay stipends to "professional" athletes. For current purposes it matters not whether the NCAA actually monopsonizes the market for players; the point of this discussion is that the prosecutor's theory makes criminals of those who consciously cheat on the rules of a private organization, even if that organization is a cartel. We pursue this point because any theory that makes criminals of cheaters raises a red flag.

Cheaters are not self-conscious champions of the public weal. They are in it for profit, as rapacious and mendacious as those who hope to collect monopoly rents. Maybe more; often members of cartels believe that monopoly serves the public interest, and they take their stand on the platform of business ethics, . . . while cheaters' glasses have been washed with cynical acid. Only Adam Smith's invisible hand turns their self-seeking activities to public benefit. It is cause for regret if prosecutors, assuming that persons with low regard for honesty must be villains, use the criminal laws to suppress the competitive process that undermines cartels. Of course federal laws have been used to enforce cartels before; the Federal Maritime Commission is a cartel-enforcement device. Inconsistent federal laws also occur; the United States both subsidizes tobacco growers and discourages people from smoking. So if the United States simultaneously forbids cartels and forbids undermining cartels by cheating, we shall shrug our shoulders and enforce both laws, condemning practical jokes along the way. But what is it about § 1341 that labels as a crime all deceit that inflicts any loss on anyone? Firms often try to fool their competitors, surprising them with new products that enrich their treasuries at their rivals' expense. Is this mail fraud because large organizations inevitably use the mail? "Any scheme or artifice to defraud, or for obtaining money or property by means of false or fraudulent pretenses, representations, or promises" reads like a description of schemes to get money or property by fraud rather than methods of doing business that incidentally cause losses.

None of the Supreme Court's mail fraud cases deals with a scheme in which the defendant neither obtained nor tried to obtain the victim's property. . . . We have been unable to find any appellate cases squarely resolving the question whether the victim's loss must be an objective of the scheme rather than a byproduct of it, perhaps because prosecutions of the kind this case represents are so rare. According to the prosecutor, however, there have been such cases, and in this circuit. The United States contends that we have already held that a scheme producing an incidental loss violates § 1341. A representative sample of the cases the prosecutor cites shows that we have held no such thing.

Many of our cases ask whether a particular scheme deprived a victim of property. ... They do so not with an emphasis on "deprive" but with an emphasis on "property"—which, until the enactment of 18 U.S.C. § 1346 after Walters' conduct, was essential to avoid the "intangible rights" doctrine that McNally jettisoned. No one doubted that the schemes were designed to enrich the perpetrators at the victims' expense; the only difficulty was the proper characterization of the deprivation. Not until today have we dealt with a scheme in which the defendants' profits were to come from legitimate trans-

actions in the market, rather than at the expense of the victims. Both the "scheme or artifice to defraud" clause and the "obtaining money or property" clause of § 1343 contemplate a transfer of some kind. Accordingly, following both the language of § 1341 and the implication of Tanner, we hold that only a scheme to obtain money or other property from the victim by fraud violates § 1341. A deprivation is a necessary but not a sufficient condition of mail fraud. Losses that occur as byproducts of a deceitful scheme do not satisfy the statutory requirement.

Anticipating that we might come to this conclusion, the prosecutor contends that Walters is nonetheless guilty as an aider and abettor. If Walters did not defraud the universities, the argument goes, then the athletes did. Walters put them up to it and so is guilty under 18 U.S.C. § 2, the argument concludes. But the indictment charged a scheme by Walters to defraud; it did not depict Walters as an aide de camp in the students' scheme. The jury received a boilerplate § 2 instruction; this theory was not argued to the jury, or for that matter to the district court either before or after the remand. Independent problems dog this recasting of the scheme—not least the difficulty of believing that the students hatched a plot to employ fraud to receive scholarships that the universities had awarded them long before Walters arrived on the scene, and the lack of evidence that the students knew about or could foresee any mailings. Walters is by all accounts a nasty and untrustworthy fellow, but the prosecutor did not prove that his efforts to circumvent the NCAA's rules amounted to mail fraud.

REVERSED

 OTHER RELEVANT SIGNIFICANT CASE

Chapter 6.22 *Letters of Intent and Scholarships*

Recent Trends

Criminal and Civil Sanctions

In what was the largest civil award ever involving sport agent misconduct, a Los Angeles jury in November 2002 awarded Leigh Steinberg and his firm Steinberg, Moorad & Dunn $44.6 million in damages ($22.6 million in punitive damages and another $22 million in compensatory damages). Steinberg sued his former partner, David Dunn, and Dunn's new company, Athletes First, after Dunn resigned from Steinberg, Moorad & Dunn and took about six employees and more than 50 of the firm's NFL clients with him.

In March 2005, the Ninth Circuit Court of Appeals overturned the entire $44.6 million judgment when it ruled that the trial court judge failed to tell jurors that the noncompetition clause in David Dunn's contract was invalid under California law. The decision of the Ninth Circuit Court was especially important when you consider that Assante, a Canadian financial services company, paid $120 million for Steinberg, Moorad & Dunn.

Financial Advisors

The National Football League Players Association has established a new program designed to regulate anyone wishing to be a financial advisor to NFL players. To be eligible for the NFLPA's Financial Advisors Program, the first of its kind in professional sports, financial advisors must apply to the NFLPA, which will conduct a background check to ensure that the financial advisors have the appropriate qualifications. By joining the program, all financial advisors agree to abide by a certain set of rules designed to both protect and inform our players.

References

Cases

Steinberg, Moorad & Dunn Inc., v. David Dunn, 136 Fed. Appx. 6; 2005 U.S. App. LEXIS 5162.

U.S. v. Walters, 997 F.2d 1219 (7th Cir. 1993).

U.S. v. Walters and Bloom, 711 F. Supp. 1435 (N.D. Ill. 1989), *reversed and remanded*, 913 F.2d 388 (7th Cir. 1990).

Publications

Cosgrove, D. (1990). A survey of state sport agent legislation: Origins and effects. *Journal of College and University Law, 16,* 433–448.

Couch, B. (2000). How agent competition and corruption affects sports and the athlete-agent relationship and what can be done to control it. *Seton Hall Journal of Sport Law, 10,* 111–137.

Dow, T. (1990). Out of bounds: Time to revamp Texas sports agent legislation. *Southwestern Law Journal, 43,* 1091–1118.

Dunn, D. (1988). Regulation of sports agents: Since at first it hasn't succeeded, try federal legislation. *The Hastings Law Journal, 39,* 1031–1078.

Fluhr, P. (1999). The regulation of sports agents and the quest for uniformity. *Sports Lawyers Journal, 6,* 1–25.

Freeman, M. (1998, July 26). Protecting players from their agents; Misconduct leaves N.F.L. Union fearful of incompetence and greed. *The New York Times,* sec. 8, p. 1, col. 1.

Greenberg, M., & Gray, J. (1998). *Sports law practice* (2nd ed.). Charlottesville, VA: Lexis Law Publishing.

Narayanan, A. (1990). Criminal liability of sports agents: It is time to reline the playing field? *Loyola of Los Angeles Law Review, 24,* 273–316.

NCAA. (1999–2000). *NCAA manual.*

Ring, B. (1987). An analysis of athlete agent certification and regulation: New incentives with old problems. *Loyola Entertainment Law Journal, 7,* 321–335.

Rodgers, J. (1988–89). States revamp defense against agents. *The Sports Lawyer, 6,* 1–7.

Rypma, C. (1990). Sports agents representing athletes: The need for comprehensive state legislation. *Valparaiso University Law Review, 24,* 481–519.

Shropshire, K. (1989). Athlete agent regulation: Proposed legislative revisions and the need for reforms beyond legislation. *Cardozo Arts & Entertainment Law Journal, 8,* 85–112.

Shropshire, K., & Davis, T. (2003). *The business of sport agents.* Philadelphia: University of Pennsylvania Press.

Wilde, T. J. (1992). The regulation of sport agents. *Journal of Legal Aspects of Sport, 2,* 18–29.

Legislation

Sports Agent Responsibility and Trust Act, Pub. L. No. 108–304, 118 Stat. 1125 (2004).

Index

Negligent failure to warn, 147
Negligent hire, 162
Negligent manufacture, 147
Negligent processing, 157
Negligent referral, 163
Negligent retention, 163
Negligent supervision, 162–163
Negotiation, 410
Neutral mediator, 410
News media, 325, 351
    contact person, guidelines for, 328
    dealing with, 327–329
Newsworthiness doctrine, 622–623
Nexus/entanglement theory, 429–430
Noise pollution, 211–212
Nonemployee vehicles, 137
Nonowned automobile, 351
Nonprofit corporations, 28
Notice of appeal, 8
Nuisance law, 187
Number of supervisors, 122

O
Objections, 7
Obligations of landowner, 186
Off-duty law enforcement, 335
Off-road vehicles, 211
Offer, in contract, 365
Officials, violence involving, 224–225
Older high school senior athletes, 125
Older Workers Benefit Protection Act, 581
Omnibus legislation, 83
Open/obvious rule, 198–199
    exception to, 199
Opening statement, 7
Operational procedures, changes in, 336–337
Option to extend, 400
Option to renew, 400
Oral contracts, 366
Ordinary negligence, 38, 59
Organization of information, 19–20
Organization-owned vehicles, 135–136
Orientation program, 339
Outside/supplemental income, 377
Outsourcing, 335
    security, 335
Overbooking, 170
OWBPA. *See* Older Workers Benefit Protection Act
"Owner" of natural environment, 205–206
Owners, antitrust challenges by, 633

P
Padding, 199
Pain and suffering, 8
Parental arbitration agreement, 87
Parental indemnity agreement, 87

Parental permission form, 95, 102–103
Parental waivers, 87
Parking lots, 199
Parody, 623
    trademark law, 611–612
Parol evidence rule, 367
Participant, duties of, 80
Participant agreement, 88–90
    content of, 88–91
Parties protected by waiver, 87
Parties relinquishing rights, waiver, 86–87
Parties to contract, 86–87
Partnerships, 26
Patent law, 601–602
Peer-group, 339
Peer sexual harassment, 571
Per se rule, 645
Performance appraisals, 160
Performance-based appraisal, 160
Periodic inspection, 318
Personal trainers, 98–99
Physical educators, standards of practice, 304
Physical security measures, 337
Places of public accommodation, 519
Plaintiff, 6
Plan for crisis management, 110, 323–326
    communication issues, 325
    developing plan, 324–325
    documentation of, 325
    emergency equipment issues, 325
    facility issues, 325
    follow-up procedures, 325
    news media, 325
    personnel issues, 324–325
Player violence incidents, 223–224
Playgrounds, 199
Playing surfaces, 199
Pocket part, 13
Pollution liability, 349
Prayer, 507
Precedent, 2
Preliminary injunction, 422
Premises liability, 193–204
    bleachers, 199
    constructive notice, 196
    duty of inspection, 196
    duty of landowners, 193–195
    duty to control third persons, 197–198
    duty to make facility reasonably safe, 197–199
    duty to provide for emergency response, 198
    duty to remove/repair dangerous conditions, 196–197
    duty to warn of hidden dangers, 198
    foreseeability, 197
    holes, 199
    legal obligations, 195–200